Robert Oppenheimer

Robert Oppenheimer

A LIFE INSIDE THE CENTER

RAY MONK

DOUBLEDAY *New York London Toronto Sydney Auckland*

www.doubleday.com

Originally published in Great Britain as *Inside the Centre: The Life of
J. Robert Oppenheimer* by Jonathan Cape, a division of The Random
House Group Limited, London, in 2012.

DOUBLEDAY and the portrayal of an anchor with a dolphin are registered
trademarks of Random House, Inc.

Jacket design by Emily Mahon
Front jacket photograph © Corbis
Spine photograph © The Granger Collection, NYC

Library of Congress Cataloging-in-Publication Data
Monk, Ray.
    Robert Oppenheimer : a life inside the center / Ray Monk. — First
U.S. edition.
        pages   cm
    Includes bibliographical references and index.
1. Oppenheimer, J. Robert, 1904–1967. 2. Physicists—United States—
Biography. 3. Atomic bomb—United States—History—20th century.
4. Physicists—United States—Intellectual life—20th century. I. Title.
QC16.O62M66 2013
530.092—dc23
[B]   2012046045

ISBN 978-0-385-50407-2

MANUFACTURED IN THE UNITED STATES OF AMERICA

10 9 8 7 6 5 4 3 2 1

First American Edition

Contents

PART FOUR: 1945–1967

List of Illustrations

First Insert

Oppenheimer with his mother (© Historical/CORBIS); Oppenheimer in the arms of his father (© Historical/CORBIS); Oppenheimer building with blocks (© Historical/CORBIS); 155 Riverside Drive (© Milstein Division of United States History, Local History and Genealogy, The New York Public Library, Astor, Lenox and Tilden Foundations); Oppenheimer at Harvard (© Harvard University Archives); William Boyd (© The National Library of Medicine); Paul Horgan (© J. R. Eyerman/Time & Life Pictures/Getty Images); Frederick Bernheim (image provided by the Duke Medical Center Archives); The Upper Pecos Valley (courtesy of the Palace of the Governors Photo Archives, New Mexico History Museum, Santa Fe/053755); Inside the Cavendish Laboratory, Cambridge (© Omikron/Science Photo Library); Paul Dirac (© Bettmann/CORBIS); Patrick Blackett (© Science Photo Library); Niels Bohr (© Lawrence Berkeley Laboratory/Science Photo Library); Max Born (© Bettmann/CORBIS); Charlotte Riefenstahl (© Göttingen Museum of Chemistry); Werner Heisenberg (© Bettmann/CORBIS); Paul Ehrenfest; Oppenheimer on Lake Zurich with I. I. Rabi, H. M. Mott-Smith and Wolfgang Pauli (© AIP Emilio Segrè Visual Archives); Oppenheimer at Berkeley (courtesy of the Department of Physics, Physics and Astronomy Library); Oppenheimer with Robert Serber (© New York Times/Redux/eyevine); Ernest Lawrence (© AIP Emilio Segrè Visual Archives); Kitty (© Historical/CORBIS); Perro Caliente (© Peter Goodchild); Haakon Chevalier (courtesy of The Bancroft Library, University of California, Berkeley); Frank Oppenheimer; Jean Tatlock (© Dr. Hugh Tatlock); Steve Nelson (© United Press International Photos); Joe Weinberg, Rossi Lomanitz, David Bohm, and Max Friedman; The staff of the Radiation Laboratory in Berkeley (© Science Source/Science Photo Library)

Second Insert

Julian Schwinger (© Estate of Francis Bello/Science Photo Library); Richard Feynman (© Tom Harvey); The Los Alamos Ranch School (© Digital Photo Archive, Department of Energy [DOE], courtesy AIP Emilio Segrè Visual Archives); General Groves (© Los Alamos National Laboratory/Science Photo Library); Enrico Fermi (© Argonne National Laboratory/Science Photo Library); The graphite pile at Stagg Field (© Historical/CORBIS); Hans Bethe (© Science Source/Science Photo Library); Klaus Fuchs (© Keystone/Time & Life Pictures/Getty Images); Edward Teller (© University of California Radiation Laboratory/Science Photo Library); Seth Neddermeyer's early attempts at implosion (courtesy of the Los Alamos National Laboratory Archives); The Nagasaki and Hiroshima bombs (Claus Lunau/Science Photo Library); The "Little Boy" design, as reverse engineered by John Coster-Mullen; Workers at Oak Ridge (© Oak Ridge National Laboratory and Digital Photo Archive, Department of Energy [DOE], courtesy AIP Emilio Segrè Visual Archives); Preparing the Trinity Test (courtesy of the Los Alamos National Laboratory Archives); The Trinity explosion (© Historical/CORBIS); Oppenheimer and Groves at the Trinity Test site (Emilio Segrè Visual Archives/American Institute of Physics/Science Photo Library); The effects of the atomic bombs in Japan (courtesy of the Los Alamos National Laboratory Archives); Oppenheimer and Kitty in Japan, 1960 (© Historical/CORBIS); The cover of the first issue of *Physics Today* (courtesy of Berkeley Laboratory); Albert Einstein and Leo Szilard (© Time & Life Pictures/Getty Images); The Ulam-Teller design (© Carey Sublette and the NuclearWeaponArchive.org); The "Mike" Test; Oppenheimer lectures Ed Murrow (© Bettmann/CORBIS); Oppenheimer with Paul Dirac and Abraham Pais at the Institute for Advanced Study (© Alfred Eisenstaedt/Getty Images); Oppenheimer, Toni, and Peter at Olden Manor, Princeton (© Alfred Eisenstaedt/Time & Life Pictures/Getty Images); Lewis Strauss (© Bettmann/CORBIS); Edward Teller congratulates Oppenheimer on his Fermi Prize (© Ralph Morse/Time & Life Pictures/ Getty Images); Oppenheimer speaking at last visit to Los Alamos (© Oppenheimer Archives/CORBIS); Oppenheimer photographed for *Life* magazine (© Time & Life Pictures/Getty Images)

Preface and Acknowledgments

The origins of this book lie in a review I wrote about fifteen years ago of a reissued edition of *Robert Oppenheimer: Letters and Recollections*, edited by Alice Kimball Smith and Charles Weiner. Until then, I knew about Oppenheimer only what everybody knows: that he was an important physicist, that he led the project to design and build the world's first atomic bomb, and that he had his security clearance taken away from him during the McCarthy era because of suspicions that he was a communist, or even possibly a Soviet agent.

What I did not know until I read this collection of his letters was what a fascinatingly diverse man he was. I did not know that he wrote poetry and short stories, that he had a deep love and wide knowledge of French literature, that he found the Hindu scriptures so inspiring that he learned Sanskrit in order to read them in their original language. Nor did I know how complicated and fragile his personality was, nor how intense his personal relations were with his father, his mother, his girlfriends, his friends and his students.

Learning all this, I was surprised to discover that no full and complete biography of him had, at that point, been written. There was, I said in my review, a really great biography waiting to be written about Oppenheimer, a biography that would attempt to do justice both to his important role in the history and politics of the twentieth century and to the singularity of his mind, to the depth and diversity of his intellectual interests. Such a book would need to describe and explain his contributions to physics and to place them in their historical context. It would need to do the same with regard to his other intellectual interests and to his participation in public life. It would not be an easy book to write. In fact, it seemed perfectly possible that it would never be written.

Since I wrote that review, several books about Oppenheimer have been written and published, which attempt to rise to at least some of the challenges I described. Chief among these is *American Prometheus: The Triumph and Tragedy of J. Robert Oppenheimer* by Kai Bird and Martin J. Sherwin, a book that was a long time in the making and the result of a staggering amount of research. *American Prometheus* is a very fine book indeed, a monumental piece of scholarship that I have had at my side ever since it was published. However (partly to my relief, since I was, by the time this book appeared, engaged on my own book), it is not the book I envisaged when I reviewed Smith and Weiner. Though Bird and Sherwin describe in exhaustive detail Oppenheimer's personal life and his political activities, they either ignore altogether or summarize very briefly his contributions to physics.

To take an example that might seem unimportant, but in fact is not, one would never know from reading Bird and Sherwin's book how much of Oppenheimer's time and intellectual energy was taken up with thinking about mesons. Mesons are subatomic particles, the existence of which was predicted in 1934 and discovered in 1936. For much of Oppenheimer's scientific career they were a puzzle, resisting all attempts to make sense of the apparently contradictory evidence about their nature and their behavior that was gathered from laboratory experiments and observations of cosmic rays. Oppenheimer's student, Edward Gerjuoy, in illustration of his point that "Oppie did his physics, talked about his physics, lived his physics, with an unusual passion," gave as his prime example Oppenheimer's frustrated determination to make sense of mesons: "it bothered him, it tore at him." If one wants to understand Oppenheimer, one might think this passionate, decades-long search for an understanding of mesons is something one should look at. And yet almost nothing is said about it in Bird and Sherwin's book. The word "meson" is not even in the index.

The relationship between a biographical subject and his or her work has often been discussed. Many people, rightly in my opinion, insist that *of course* it is possible to understand a person's work without knowing anything about their lives, Shakespeare being the obvious and most telling example. This does not make biography useless or superfluous, since the understanding of individual people is a worthwhile and interesting pursuit *in itself*. We want to understand Oppenheimer, not *in order* to understand his work, but just because he was an interesting man. However, though it is possible to understand Oppenheimer's work in isolation from his life, the reverse, it seems to me, is not possible: we cannot claim to understand Oppenheimer unless we have at least some understanding of his work, especially when, as Gerjuoy's comments make clear, that work was pursued with such passion and intensity and was such an important part of what made him the person he was.

So, much as I admire Bird and Sherwin's achievement, and much as I have learned from their work, theirs is not the book I imagined after I had read Oppenheimer's letters. Nor, for basically similar reasons, is Charles Thorpe's *Oppenheimer: The Tragic Intellect*, which came out the year after Bird and Sherwin's and which has much of interest to say about Oppenheimer's life as it was affected by, and as it affected, the society and politics of the time, but almost nothing to say about Oppenheimer's life as it was shaped and driven by his desire to understand physics.

Many people, including me, thought that a biography of Oppenheimer that put his contributions to physics at the center of the narrative would be written by the late Abraham Pais, who, it was widely known, had been working on a biography of Oppenheimer for many years before his death in 2000. A renowned particle physicist himself, Pais had known Oppenheimer well at Princeton, and had previously written excellent lives of Bohr and Einstein. Alas, when he died, Pais was a long way from finishing the book. What he *had* written, together with "supplementary material" added by Robert P. Crease, was published in 2006 as *J. Robert Oppenheimer: A Life*. It turned out that what Pais had been concentrating on was not Oppenheimer's contributions to physics (to which he devotes only a short and highly derivative chapter), but rather his directorship of Princeton's Institute for Advanced Study. Those looking for a scientific biography of Oppenheimer were thus forced to look elsewhere.

David C. Cassidy, who had previously written an outstandingly good, scientifically literate biography of Heisenberg, published a biography of Oppenheimer in 2005 that many thought would fill the gap left open by Pais. Cassidy's book, *J. Robert Oppenheimer and the American Century*, certainly gives more prominence to Oppenheimer's scientific work than any previous biography. However, as indicated by his title, Cassidy has, like Thorpe, chosen to approach Oppenheimer's life from a broadly historical and sociological perspective. Though there is much new biographical information in the book, its focus, for much of the time, is on Cassidy's theme of "the American century"—that is, the growth of American political power and the preeminence of American science during the twentieth century.

There is nothing wrong with such an approach, and much to be gained by pursuing it, but it cannot possibly produce the kind of biography that I envisaged and that I have tried to write. Oppenheimer's place in history, his impact on American society and that society's impact on him are all interesting topics, and ones that a biography of him cannot ignore. However, what *most* interests me is Oppenheimer *himself*, his extraordinary intellectual powers, his emotional and psychological complexity and his curious mixture of strengths and weaknesses in dealing with other people. Of the books that have come out in the last few years on Oppenheimer, the one that most closely approximates the one I wanted to write, in terms of balance and focus, is Jeremy Bernstein's wonderful memoir, *Oppenheimer: Portrait of an Enigma*. If Bernstein had chosen to write a full biography rather than a brief memoir, he might well have made my book entirely superfluous.

I have entitled my book [the British edition] "Inside the Centre" for many reasons, the first of which is to indicate my intention of writing an internal rather than an external biography—one that aims, first and foremost, to understand Oppenheimer himself. Of course this does not mean that I am not interested in the social and political background to Oppenheimer's life. On the contrary, I am deeply interested in that background and, indeed, devote my first chapter to the German Jewish community in New York in which he was born and brought up. The legacy of that community, in fact, forms another reason for my title, as it seems to me that Oppenheimer cannot be understood without taking into account the importance of his deeply felt desire to overcome the sense of being an outsider that he inherited from his German Jewish background and his desire to get inside the center of American political and social life. This desire lies at the root of the ambivalence toward his Jewish ancestry that was noted by many of his closest friends, and at the root of what Einstein perceptively described as his unrequited love for the U.S. government. It also, I think, figures largely in his willingness to undertake the enormous task of leading the effort to build the world's first atomic bomb, and his determination after the war to play a leading part in shaping U.S. atomic policy. It must be taken into account too in understanding why he felt compelled to defend himself against charges of disloyalty when it would have been so much easier simply to walk away from the battle.

Moreover, as I have said above, it seems to me that, if one wants to understand Oppenheimer, one must attempt to understand his contributions to science, and the phrase "inside the center" captures some of the themes that dominate that work. Oppenheimer's striving to understand mesons, for example, was driven, at least in part, by a desire to know what forces are acting inside the center of an atom, the pi-meson being the carrier of the strong nuclear force that binds nucleons (neutrons and protons) together. And, of course, the atomic bomb and the hydrogen bomb are possible only because of an understanding—which Oppenheimer helped to create—of the fission and fusion processes undergone by atomic nuclei. What many people consider to be Oppenheimer's greatest contribution to physics—his work in the late 1930s on neutron stars and black holes—sheds light on what happens at the center of a massive star when it has burned up all its hydrogen and gravitational collapse takes over.

Finally, there is Oppenheimer's determination to be at the center of scientific discovery, an ambition that took him first to Cambridge to work at Rutherford's Cavendish Laboratory, and then to Göttingen to work with Max Born at precisely the time when Born was playing a leading part in the creation of quantum mechanics. Eventually, combined with his fervent patriotism, this drove Oppenheimer to make America the world center of advances in physics. At every stage in this development the problems that he and his students chose to tackle were strongly influenced by his insistence on being at the center of theoretical physics, always wanting to be dealing with the fundamental questions, not the peripheral ones.

I am not myself a physicist, but during the ten years that it has taken me to write this book I have made a concerted effort to understand those parts of physics to which Oppenheimer contributed. I have been helped in this by some wonderful historical and expository work that has been published in the last decade or so, most notably those books listed in the Bibliography by Jeremy Bernstein, Helge Kragh, Manjit Kumar, Jagdish Mehra and Helmut Rechenberg, and Silvan Schweber. I have also benefited considerably from the expertise of my friend James Dodd, whose work *The Ideas of Particle Physics: An Introduction for Scientists*, jointly authored with C. D. Coughlan and B. M. Gripaios, is one of the clearest textbooks I have ever read, and whose comments on an early draft of this book were invaluable. At an early stage in the research for this book I also received help from Brian Ridley, who kindly explained some notions in theoretical physics that were confusing me, and, at a much later stage, I received help via email from the physicists Jeremy Bernstein, Silvan Schweber and Kip Thorne.

I would like to extend special thanks to my friend David Pugmire, who has provided me with unstinting encouragement and support throughout the writing of this book and who, when it was finished, read it through with meticulous care, making many astute and helpful comments. In this connection I would also like to thank Mike Cleeter, Sophia Efstathiou, Peter Middleton, Frederic Raphael, Danika Stow-Monk and Alan Thomas, who also read and made helpful comments upon an early draft.

Research on this book necessitated several trips to Washington, D.C., to use the Library of Congress, the staff at which could not possibly have been more helpful and obliging. The same is true of the staff at the Nils Bohr Library in Copenhagen. I also need to thank the staff at my own institution, the University of Southampton, for providing such an excellent service. The university gave me research leave in order to concentrate on the book, for which I am immensely grateful.

In Kristine Puopolo and Dan Franklin I have had the best publishers an author could wish for, giving me great support when I needed it most, showing encouraging faith in me and my project and exercising patience to the point of saintliness. I would also like to thank my editor, Alex Bowler, for his interest in the project, for his indispensable editorial skills and for the many ways in which he helped me to avoid errors and improve my text. The text has been improved in many ways too by the superb copyediting it received from Mandy Greenfield. I could not have written this book without the help of my agent, Gill Coleridge, who has become a good friend as well as an inexhaustible supply of good sense and cheering encouragement. My greatest debt, as always, is to my wonderful partner, Jenny, and our lovely children, Zala, Danika, Zeno and Myron, who are not children anymore, but whose loveliness has kept me going during the sometimes difficult years in which this book was written.

RAY MONK
Southampton
May 2012

Robert Oppenheimer

Part One

1904–1926

1

"Amerika, du hast es besser":
Oppenheimer's German Jewish Background

J. Robert Oppenheimer, his friend
Isidor Rabi once remarked, was
"a man who was put together of many bright shining splinters," who
"never got to be an integrated personality." What prevented Oppenheimer from being fully integrated, Rabi thought, was his denial of a
centrally important part of himself: his Jewishness. As the physicist Felix
Bloch, echoing Rabi, once put it, Oppenheimer "tried to act as if he
were not a Jew and succeeded well because he was a good actor." And,
because he was always acting ("you carried on a charade with him. He
lived a charade," Rabi once remarked), he lost sight of who he really was.
Oppenheimer had an impressive and wide-ranging collection of talents,
abilities and personal characteristics, but where the central, united core
of his personality ought to have been, Rabi thought, there was a gap and
so there was nothing to hold those "bright shining splinters" together. "I
understood his problem," Rabi said, and, when asked what that problem
was, replied simply: "Identity."

Rabi spoke as someone who, by virtue of his background, intelligence and education, was well placed to understand Oppenheimer's
"problem." He and Oppenheimer had a great deal in common: they
were roughly the same age (Rabi was six years older), they were both
theoretical physicists, were both brought up in New York City and were
both descended from European Jewish families. Behind this last similarity, however, lay a fundamental difference. Rabi was proud of his Jewish
inheritance and happy to define himself in terms of it. Though he had no
religious beliefs, and never prayed, he once said that when he saw Orthodox Jews at prayer, the thought that came into his mind was: "These are
my people."

No such thought could have entered Oppenheimer's mind, no matter who he was looking at. There was *no* group to whom he could point and say, "These are my people," and not just because of his ambivalence about his Jewish background. It was also because that background itself, regardless of Oppenheimer's feelings about it, could not have provided him with the sense of belonging and, therefore, the sense of identity that Rabi thought was missing in him. Rabi, despite his lack of religious beliefs, was Jewish in a fairly straightforward and unambiguous way; the Jews simply *were* "his people." Theirs was the community to which he belonged. One cannot say the same about Oppenheimer. The sense in which *he* was Jewish, the sense in which he did—and did not—come from, and belong to, a Jewish community, is far more complicated and, as Rabi has perceptively noted, crucial in understanding the fragility of his sense of identity.

For an understanding of the elusive nature of Oppenheimer's Jewishness, the contrast between his family background and Rabi's is instructive. Despite their many and important similarities, and despite the fact that they grew up within a few miles of each other, Rabi and Oppenheimer were born into and brought up in families that were culturally worlds apart. Rabi was a "Polish Jew." Born in Galicia to a poor, Yiddish-speaking family of Orthodox Jews, he came to New York as an infant and was raised, first in the crowded slums of the Lower East Side and then in a tiny apartment in Brooklyn. Oppenheimer was born not in Europe, but in New York City, to a wealthy family that had abandoned its Jewish faith and traditions a generation earlier. The bustling and crowded "Jewish Ghetto" of the Lower East Side would have seemed utterly alien to the young Oppenheimer, who was brought up in an enormous luxury apartment in the genteel Upper West Side. The family had never spoken Yiddish, and, though German was his father's first language, it was never spoken at home.

And yet, despite regarding himself as neither German nor Jewish, Oppenheimer was seen, by Jews and non-Jews alike, as a "German Jew." In New York in the early twentieth century the central division among the Jewish community was between, on the one hand, the German Jews and, on the other, the Polish and Russian Jews—the differences between the two groups accurately mirrored by the differences between Oppenheimer and Rabi. The German Jews, sometimes called "Uptown Jews," were on the whole wealthier, more assimilated and less religious than their Polish and Russian counterparts, to whom they were notoriously condescending. At the time of Oppenheimer's birth in 1904 there were more Polish and Russian Jews in New York than German Jews, but the Germans assumed leadership of the Jewish community and took it upon themselves to help "Americanize" the Russians and Poles, who reacted with resentment at what they saw as a dismissal of their religion and their customs.

What Rabi called Oppenheimer's problem—the problem of identity—was, in fact, a problem for the entire American Jewish community, perhaps its central problem. Certainly it was the issue at the heart of the tension between the two groups of Jews in New York City. For the Russian and Polish Jews, their sense of identity was bound up with their Jewishness: their Orthodox religious beliefs, their Yiddish language and their Jewish culture and traditions. *That* sense of identity, that culture, however, had been abandoned by the German Jews before they even came to America.

The mass migration of German Jews to America that occurred in the mid-nineteenth century was intimately bound up with their earlier abandonment of the traditional trappings of Jewish identity. *Haskalah*, the Jewish Enlightenment of the late eighteenth century, was an essentially German movement, its prophet being the great Prussian Jewish thinker Moses Mendelssohn. *Haskalah*, which led in turn to that other essentially German movement, Reform Judaism, encouraged Jews to, literally and metaphorically, leave the ghettos in which they had been confined and embrace the modernizing ideas of the wider Western European Enlightenment. This meant using German rather than Hebrew as the language of worship, abandoning traditions and customs that served to isolate Jews from the rest of society, and reforming Jewish education so that it prepared people for the world at large rather than schooling them in a separate culture. The hope that inspired these changes was that, in return for abandoning those aspects of their culture that identified them as radically different from others, the Jews would receive from the gentile world a lifting of the discriminatory laws that affected almost every aspect of their lives, and a full acceptance as members of society with the same legal, financial and political rights as other citizens. Thus fully assimilated, Jews would no longer think of themselves as a separate race or nation, but rather as adherents of a religion. Their nationality would be *German*, and they would be not a bit less German for worshipping in a synagogue rather than a church.

It was the dashing of this hope that persuaded hundreds of thousands of German Jews in the middle decades of the nineteenth century to turn their backs on their home country and look to America—a country founded upon the proposition that the equality of all men and the inalienability of the right to life, liberty and the pursuit of happiness were self-evident truths—to find the freedom and equality they had failed to achieve in Germany. Thus, in the eyes of German Jews, America became not only a refuge from discrimination and prejudice, but also the national embodiment of Enlightenment ideals, the ideals of *Haskalah*. Many of them therefore ceased trying to become accepted as *Germans* and sought instead to become accepted as *Americans*.

"Amerika, du hast es besser." These famous words of Goethe are contained in the poem "Den Vereinigten Staaten" ("To the United States"), written in 1827, when, as an old man, he reflected upon the advantages that youthful America had over the "Old Continent" in having no tradition, no "decaying castles," and being therefore free from the continuous strife that comes from long memories. The image of America that Goethe's poem conjures up is one of a *tabula rasa*, waiting, so to speak, to have its history written upon it. This was an image perfectly suited to arouse the interest and expectations of the German Jews, a group who longed to start afresh, free from the tensions and prejudices of the past.

And so, beginning in the 1820s, the rallying cry "On to America" echoed throughout the Jewish community in Germany. A whole movement grew up dedicated to the encouragement of migration to the United States, publicizing the financial, social and political advantages of the New World, and providing hope and support to those prepared to make what must have been an alarming as well as an exciting fresh start. In books by Europeans who had been to America, in letters to relatives from those who had migrated, and in village meetings where people gathered to hear firsthand accounts of American life from migrants who had returned to visit families, the image of America as "the common man's utopia" was spread, inspiring more and more Jews to set sail for the United States.

A typical example of such inspirational firsthand accounts is a letter written in November 1846 by the journalist and academic Max Lilienthal, which was published in the German Jewish weekly newspaper *Allgemeine Zeitung des Judenthums*. Extolling "the beautiful ground of civil equality" that he had discovered in America, Lilienthal announced: "The old Europe with its restrictions lies behind me like a bad dream . . . At last I breathe in liberty . . . Jew or Christian, Christian or Jew—this old strife is forgotten, and only the man as such is respected and loved." Encouraging others to follow his example, he urged: "Shake off the centuries-old dust of Jew-pressure . . . become a human being like everybody else." And, he promised, in America: "Jewish hearts are open in welcome. Jewish organisations ready to help anyone. Why should you go on carrying the burden of legal exclusion?"

The number of German Jews willing and eager to "shake off the centuries-old dust of Jew-pressure" was so large that it completely transformed the American Jewish community. In 1840, there were just 15,000 Jews in the United States; by 1880, there were 280,000, most of whom were of German origin. This influx of German Jews is known to Jewish historians as the "Second Migration"—the "First Migration" being the arrival in the seventeenth century of a small community of Sephardic Jews. These were descendants of the Jews expelled from Spain and Portugal in the fifteenth century, who, by the nineteenth century, were a well-established part of American life.

These self-styled "old American Sephardic families" took pride in the fact that they had been in America for as many generations as the descendants of the Pilgrim Fathers, and tended to treat the new German arrivals with the kind of lofty disdain with which the German Jews would later treat the Russians and Poles. The first German Jews to arrive in America accepted the leadership of the old Sephardic community and even adopted the Sephardic form of worship. When the number of German Jewish migrants began to increase dramatically, however, the balance of power shifted and the German, Ashkenazi Jews replaced the Sephardim as the leaders of the American Jewish community.

The mass influx into America of Russian and Polish Jews, which took place from 1880 to 1920, formed the "Third Migration," and was on an entirely different scale from the previous two, being measured not in tens of thousands, or in hundreds of thousands, but in millions. Roughly two and a half million Jews from Eastern Europe arrived in the United States during the Third Migration, bringing with them a very different kind of Jewish culture from that of either the Sephardim or the Germans.

The arrival of these Russian and Polish Jews was such an embarrassment to the established German Jewish community that their first reaction to it was to argue, through editorials in their newspaper, *American Hebrew*, and direct lobbying from their organization, the United Hebrew Charities of New York, for the introduction of tougher immigration laws. When this came to nothing and the number of Eastern European Jewish immigrants kept rising, the German Jews set up the Education Alliance, which organized Americanization programs in which the new immigrants were instructed in "the privileges and duties of American citizenship." What drove these measures was not only the German Jews' love of America, but also a dread of the anti-Semitism which they feared the Eastern European Jews would arouse. The Jewish historian Gerald Sorin points out: "These uptowners were very taken with Israel Zangwill's play 'The Melting Pot.' They saw in it a reinforcement of their own proposed solution for the problems of downtown: the sooner immigrants from eastern Europe gave up their cultural distinctiveness and melted into the homogenized mass, the sooner anti-Semitism would also melt."

It was a strategy that German Jews had tried unsuccessfully in Germany, but which seemed to be working in the United States. It required, however, constant vigilance with respect to "cultural distinctiveness," a vigilance that could easily slip into the kind of self-denial of which Rabi accused Oppenheimer. One form this vigilance took was an acute sensitivity among German Jews about their names. Sometimes this led to the abandonment of German-sounding surnames, a notable example being August Schönberg, the son of an impoverished Jewish family from the Rhineland, who would become famous as the millionaire New York banker August Belmont. More often, though, it took the form of changing one's first name and giving to one's children names that sounded reassuringly "American." Joseph Seligman, another millionaire New York banker, brought his brothers, Wolfgang, Jacob and Isaias, over from Germany, but on arrival they became William, James and Jesse. The names of Joseph Seligman's children look like a roll call of American heroes: George Washington Seligman, Edwin Robert Anderson Seligman and Alfred Lincoln Seligman (evidently "Abraham" was considered too Judaic).

Of the American heroes commemorated in these names, the least well known today is undoubtedly Robert Anderson. He was a major in the U.S. army at the time of the outbreak of the Civil War in April 1861 and was involved in the opening hostilities, when Fort Sumter in South Carolina, which was then under his command, came under fire from the Confederates. For holding his ground and defending the fort for thirty-four hours Major Anderson was promoted by Abraham Lincoln to Brigadier General and became a national hero, not just for the duration of the war, but also for many decades afterward. Because of him, the name "Robert" became immensely popular. For anyone wanting to affirm the American identity of their offspring, it was the natural choice. Indeed J. Robert Oppenheimer was to like it so much that he ignored the "J" in his name and was known, by family and friends, simply as "Robert" or "Bob." When he was asked what the "J" stood for, he would reply that it stood for nothing. In fact, as his birth certificate shows, it stands for "Julius," his father's name. For anyone striving to avoid "cultural distinctiveness," the name "Robert Oppenheimer," or even "J. Robert Oppenheimer," had obvious advantages over "Julius Oppenheimer."

Even so, the surname remained, and it was as "culturally distinctive" as a name can be, identifying its bearers' ancestors both geographically and ethnically. "As appears from his name," one of Oppenheimer's professors once wrote in an academic reference, "Oppenheimer is a Jew." If, ignoring *Haskalah*, one clung to the notion of Judaism as defining a race, a nation or a tribe, rather than simply a religion, then the professor was correct. After the Napoleonic decree of 1808, which required Jews to take a surname, "Oppenheimer" was the name adopted by those Jews who lived in the area around the small and fairly obscure town of Oppenheim, which lies in the Hesse area of Germany, between Mainz and Worms, not far from Frankfurt. With regard to J. Robert Oppenheimer, what "appears from his name" is that his ancestors were among those Hessian Jews. Could he look upon *them* and say, "These are my people"? Well, after his political awakening in the 1930s, when his relatives—like all Jews in Germany—were facing the horrors of the Nazis, his determination to play a part in defeating Hitler's regime *did* suggest some feeling of kinship with the victims of the Third Reich. But, until then, his reaction to his German Jewish relatives was to look upon them as if they came from a very distant time and place. When, as a child, he went to Germany on a family visit and met his grandfather, Benjamin Oppenheimer, who still lived just a few miles away from Oppenheim, his impression (or so he later recalled) was of "an unsuccessful small businessman, born himself in a hovel, really, in an almost medieval German village." This, one feels, is the impression of a child used to the wealth of the Upper West Side and the modernity of twentieth-century Manhattan; whether Benjamin would be regarded as "unsuccessful," his birthplace a "hovel" and his home town "medieval" by people with less exalted standards is, I think, doubtful.

The "almost medieval village" was presumably Hanau, a town northeast of Oppenheim, where Benjamin Oppenheimer lived and where his son, Julius, was born in 1871. Julius spent just seventeen years in Hanau before, in 1888, leaving for America. Whatever the truth about Benjamin Oppenheimer's circumstances, the family clearly had aspirations for a better life than was possible in Hanau and, like many other German Jews, thought they could fulfill those aspirations in America. Julius's younger brother and sister, Emil and Hedwig, joined him a few years after he had set sail, and Julius himself was following the example of his two uncles, Solomon and Sigmund Rothfeld ("Sol and Sig" as they were known in the family), who had migrated to the United States a generation earlier.

The ambition may have come from Benjamin's wife, Babette Rothfeld, since the two uncles in question were her brothers. "Sol and Sig" left for America in 1869, nearly twenty years before Julius Oppenheimer came to join them, but more than thirty years after the "Second Migration" had begun. In those thirty years or so, a great deal had happened to the German Jewish community in America. Or, rather, one should say that in those years the American German Jewish community had been created, its development demonstrating both that the United States could indeed realize many of the hopes expressed in Max Lilienthal's letter, and that it could not entirely live up to the promise of being a land in which the "old strife" between Jew and Christian had been forgotten.

By 1869, the German Jewish migrants who had landed in America thirty or so years earlier had formed a successful social group, among whom were a surprisingly large number of families that had become extremely wealthy. Within a single generation, the Seligmans, the Lehmans, the Guggenheims, the Schiffs, the Goldmans and the Sachses had all amassed vast fortunes and become founders of some of the best-known, most successful and most powerful financial and commercial institutions in America. They had also created a fairly tight-knit community, known to its members as "Our Crowd," a Jewish version of the more conspicuously wealthy group of families—the Astors, Vanderbilts, Morgans, Roosevelts, and so on—that constituted New York's gentile high society during this period. "Our Crowd" was a self-consciously cohesive community, whose members worshipped together at the Temple Emanu-El (the Reform Jewish synagogue, whose imposing building on Fifth Avenue, opened in 1868, was a symbol of the success and aspirations of the German Jewish community), socialized together, took holidays together and chose their wives and husbands from each other's families. The conformity of this community was satirized by one of its members, Emanie Sachs, in her novel *Red Damask*:

> Our crowd here. They cover their walls with the same silks. Why there isn't a house we go to, including Sherry's, that hasn't a damask wall. They go to the same dentist and the same grocer and the same concerts. They think alike and act alike and they're scared to death not to talk alike. The men go to jobs their fathers or grandfathers created, and all they do is sit at their desk & let the organizations work.

Behind the conventionality satirized by Sachs was an earnest desire among the wealthy German Jewish community in New York to "fit in," both with each other and with the wider society. As the names given to the Seligman offspring illustrate, what these prosperous German Jews wanted, perhaps above all, was to be accepted as Americans.

The loyalty this generation of German Jewish migrants felt toward the United States had its origin in the contrast between the restrictions they had experienced in Germany and the freedom and opportunities they had found in America. Until the Civil War, America had been for these migrants almost everything that they had been promised it would be. Of course, every Jew in America would, at some time or other, have come across anti-Semitic prejudice, but the state itself was not Hebrews anti-Semitic; there was no institutionalized anti-Semitism enshrined in law, decree or officially sanctioned customs. In the years during and after the Civil War, however, this began to change, partly because of the conspicuous success of the German Jews, and partly because life in the United States for everyone during these years became darker and more troubled.

Most notoriously, in December 1862, eighteen months into the war, General Ulysses Grant issued an order calling for the expulsion of Jews from the military district under his command, which included the states of Mississippi, Kentucky and Tennessee. The justification for this extraordinary order was the suspicion that Jews were engaged in illegal cotton trading. A month before he ordered the expulsion, Grant had issued an order banning Jews from traveling south into the cotton states. When this did not stop the black-market trading, he resorted to expulsion.

Grant's expulsion order came as a great shock to Jews throughout the United States. Writing in 1912, the Zionist Max Nordau remarked that Grant's order showed "how thin the floor between Jews and Hell was (and most probably still is) even in enlightened free America . . . What an object lesson to Jewish optimists." It was the first time that Jews in America had faced anti-Semitism in an institutionalized, officially sanctioned form, and they reacted to it not with resignation and disappointment, but with an angry refusal to accept it. A campaign against the order was organized, including petitions and delegations to the President (at least one of which was led by the aforementioned Max Lilienthal), and, although the episode was a blow to those who believed in America as a land free from Jew-hatred, perhaps the most remarkable thing about it was how quickly the President gave in to the protests. On January 3, 1863, just a few weeks after the order had been issued, President Lincoln instructed Grant to revoke the order. It was therefore, after all, still possible to believe in the United States as a nation without anti-Semitic prejudice, although its image in that respect had been badly tarnished.

In 1869, the year Solomon and Sigmund Rothfeld arrived in New York, Ulysses Grant, having recently been elected President, began what would become, after reelection in 1872, an eight-year period in office. Despite his ill-judged expulsion order in 1862, he was not regarded as an enemy of the Jews. Rather, the opposite. Perhaps the reaction to his notorious order and the humiliation of having to rescind it had made him wary of upsetting Jewish opinion, for among his friends and political allies were many prominent Jews, including Joseph Seligman, whose family company by 1869 had a working capital of more than $6 million and who was at that time acknowledged as the leader of the New York German Jewish community.

In a remarkable move, Grant offered to make Seligman Secretary of the Treasury, an offer which the flattered but surprised Seligman turned down. Grant nevertheless kept up friendly relations with Seligman, and, throughout Grant's tenure in office, Seligman was a regular invitee for lunch at the White House. Partly because of his contacts with high office, Seligman was at this time, one of his biographers records, "becoming more Americanized, more gentilized, losing some of his feeling of Jewishness." He began to spend less and less time at the Harmonie Club, the leading German Jewish gentlemen's club, and more time at the predominantly gentile Union League Club.

What Joseph Seligman seemed determined to prove was that it was possible for a Jew to be accepted by—and, indeed, into—the very highest tier of American society. Unfortunately for him, and for the Jewish (particularly the German Jewish) community as a whole, events in the 1870s appeared to show that there were quite definite and insuperable limits to such acceptance. Seligman's first harsh lesson in this respect came in 1873, when he attempted to establish the first Jewish *commercial* bank (Seligman & Co. had previously been, as all Jewish bankers in the U.S. at that time were, *merchant* bankers only). Despite having a name chosen to sound as English, as non-German and as non-Jewish as possible (the "Anglo-California National Bank") and despite having at its head Richard G. Sneath, "the first gentile and first non family member to be given a place of importance in a Seligman enterprise," the bank was, as Seligman had to concede after just a few years, a failure. "The Bank would have more friends among the Americans," Sneath advised Seligman, "but for their foolish *prejudices* against the *religion of the bank.*"

Further indications that, among wealthy Americans, these "foolish prejudices" were on the increase were to follow. In 1877, in an incident that became famous as the "Seligman Affair," it was brought painfully and unambiguously home to Joseph Seligman and to the country at large that Jews—even immensely wealthy Uptown German Jews, who loved America with more passion than they loved their Jewish heritage and who had friends in the very highest places—were not accepted in polite American society. The incident that forced the issue occurred when Seligman and his family tried to book into the Grand Union Hotel, the grandest hotel in Saratoga, and quite possibly the grandest in the whole United States. It had been owned by Alexander Stewart, the owner of A.T. Stewart & Company, the largest retail store in New York, who had a jealous dislike of Seligman, especially of his friendship with Grant. When Stewart died in 1876, his estate was managed by his friend, Judge Henry

Hilton. For some years the Grand Union Hotel had been losing busi-ness, and Hilton decided that this was because its upper-class guests did not want to mix with Jews. When the Seligman family appeared at the hotel, therefore, they were told that it no longer accepted "Israelites."

Seligman's response was to write a public letter to Hilton, which was published in all the main newspapers throughout the United States. In the furor that followed, most newspapers and the bulk of public opinion took Seligman's side. The comic weekly *Puck* probably captured the pre-vailing view of the affair when it accompanied a two-page cartoon with an editorial that declared: "But in this country the Jew is not ostracized. He stands equal before the law and before society with all his fellow-citizens, of whatever creed or nationality." The clergyman Henry Ward Beecher devoted to the incident one of his famous sermons, "Gentile and Jew," in which he declared his "love and respect" for Seligman.

Despite these public declarations of support, the incident inspired other upper-class hotels and clubs to follow Hilton's lead, and the sen-tence "Hebrews need not apply" became a common sight in advertise-ments for such places. In 1879, the *New York Herald* newspaper ran a story on "The Jews and Coney Island," in which they interviewed Austin Corbin, the president of the Manhattan Beach Company, which had just taken the decision to ban Jews from its hotel and its beach. "We cannot bring the highest social element to Manhattan Beach if the Jews persist in coming," Corbin said. "They won't associate with Jews and that's all there is about it." The whole Seligman Affair, judges Stephen Birming-ham, the author of *"Our Crowd": The Great Jewish Families of New York*, "was to have a profound psychological effect on German Jewish life in New York, making it more defensive and insular, more proud and aloof and self-contained, more cautious."

Joseph Seligman himself was a broken man after the Saratoga inci-dent and lived for just three more years after it. Very few people had tried harder than he to lose whatever "cultural distinctiveness" came from being German and Jewish. In his final years he took a further step in this direction when he gave public support to a movement that might be seen as an attempt by German Jews to lose their Jewishness without either becoming Christian or abandoning the ethical principles central to Judaism. It was called the Ethical Culture Society and it came to pro-vide the spiritual milieu within which J. Robert Oppenheimer was raised.

The leader of the Ethical Culture Society was Felix Adler, a German Jew whose father, Samuel Adler, was, from 1856 to his death in 1873, the rabbi of Temple Emanu-El, the spiritual center of "Our Crowd." When Samuel Adler died, Felix, then just twenty-two years old, was invited to deliver a sermon at the Temple Emanu-El, presumably as a prelude to being invited to take his father's place as rabbi. However, the sermon he gave, "The Judaism of the Future," effectively put paid to any possibility there might have been of him succeeding his father. At the same time, however, it inspired in the minds of many who heard it a vision of what Reform Judaism might evolve into.

In the sermon Adler spoke of the "ruins" of religion, among which he explicitly included Judaism, and asked the question: what remains when the ruins are removed? His answer, which would form the basis both for the Ethical Culture Society and for the *Weltanschauung* in which Oppenheimer was brought up, was: morality. Judaism, Adler proclaimed, was well placed to provide leadership to the religion of the future, since it always had been, essentially, a religion of *deed* rather than creed. In this sense, Adler claimed, Judaism as a moral force "was not given to the Jews alone," but rather had a destiny "to embrace in one great moral state the whole family of men."

Adler's talk of the "ruins" of Judaism did not go down well among the majority of the congregation of Temple Emanu-El, and he was never asked to address the synagogue again. However, for a small but influential minority his view of the "Judaism of the Future" seemed to be the perfect solution to two pressing problems: 1. how to be a Jew if one did not actually believe any elements of the Jewish creed; and 2. how to combine being a good Jew with being a good American.

After a career as a rabbi was denied to him, Adler was offered, and accepted, a professorship in Hebrew at Cornell University. While there, he ran into trouble when he was accused of being an atheist, but, back in New York City, moves were afoot to attract him back as the head of the Judaism of the future—the vision of which he had outlined in his divisive sermon. And so, in 1876, Adler gave a talk in New York in which he announced the establishment of a new organization, the Ethical Culture Society. This was to be a religion without religious belief, a "practical religion." "We propose," Adler announced:

> to entirely exclude prayer and every form of ritual . . . freely do I own to this purpose of reconciliation and candidly do I confess that it is my dearest object to exalt the present movement above the strife of contending sects and parties, and at once to occupy that common ground where we may all meet, believers and unbelievers, for purposes in themselves, lofty and unquestioned by any . . . freedom of thought is a sacred right of every individual man . . . Diversity in the creed, unanimity in the deed. This is that practical religion from which none dissents. This is that Platform broad enough to receive the worshipper and the infidel. This is that common ground where

we may all grasp hands as brothers united in mankind's common cause.

"Adler's proposal for a new movement," Howard B. Radest, a historian of the movement has written, "had the virtue of completing an Americanization without betraying what his listeners regarded as the core of their Jewish faith—its prophetic tradition . . . It was, we suggest, no accident that Adler's address echoed the First Amendment to the American Constitution and the Declaration of Independence, for at Cornell Adler had traced the connection between prophetic and democratic values."

The Ethical Culture Society received its certificate of incorporation in February 1877. It was not then, nor was it ever, a mass movement. In some ways it was more like an exclusive club: to become a member one needed the sponsorship of another member. "The Sunday Meeting," Radest writes, "was a social occasion, too. Here one greeted old friends, came to see and be seen, came to be entertained." It was not a religion at all, still less a proselytizing one. "Ethical Culture seemed to make it difficult for people to discover it or, having discovered it, to find their way into its ranks. In some circles the impression still exists of a rather select group."

Among that select group, right from its inception, were Solomon and Sigmund Rothfeld. With regard to the Rothfeld brothers' time in New York, the historical record is somewhat sketchy. Little is known of their first five years in America, except that they set up some kind of business in the tailoring trade, which must have done fairly well. In 1874–5 they are listed in the New York City *Directory* as "importers of dry goods," with offices in Worth Street, Lower Manhattan. More significant as a measure of their social and financial success, however, is the fact that in the following year they appear as founder charter members of the Ethical Culture Society, along with Joseph Seligman, Jacob Schiff and Henry Morgenthau. Within seven years of being in America, then, the Rothfeld brothers had joined "Our Crowd," the elite of Manhattan German Jewish society.

In 1880, that society (including, no doubt, the Rothfeld brothers) was united in mourning the death of Joseph Seligman, known since the Saratoga incident as "America's leading Jew." Shortly before his death, Seligman had asked that his funeral service should be directed by the Ethical Culture Society. Despite this request, the Seligman family and Gustav Gottheil, the rabbi at Temple Emanu-El, conspired to give him a "proper Jewish funeral" at the synagogue. In addition, a funeral service conducted by Felix Adler was held in Seligman's house, an event that served to cement and increase the acceptance of Adler's society among New York's German Jewish elite.

It was, however, increasingly becoming a *separate* elite. In 1887, the nature of New York's high society was spelled out when the first volume of the *Social Register* for New York appeared, listing the 2,000 or so families that were considered the crème de la crème of Manhattan. Not one of them was Jewish. Its author, Ward McAllister, suggested: "our good Jews might wish to put out a little book of their own." In the face of such painful reminders that they were not accepted by New York high society, many prominent members of the German Jewish community migrated from the Upper East Side of Manhattan (where, along Fifth Avenue, the likes of the Astors had their grand "brownstones") to form what has been described as "the first recognizably German Jewish upper-class neighborhood" on the Upper West Side. It was to this neighborhood that Solomon and Sigmund Rothfeld moved in 1887, after they had joined with their cousin, J. H. Stern, to form Rothfeld, Stern & Co., a company that specialized in importing tailoring materials. Their names would never appear in the *Social Register*, but among their immediate neighbors now were various Goldmans, Sachses and Guggenheims.

Meanwhile the "Third Migration" of Jews to America was gaining momentum and, as the German Jewish community had feared, arousing a new and intensified form of anti-Semitism. In the same year that the *Social Register* was published and the Rothfeld brothers moved to the Upper West Side, an article appeared in *Forum* magazine entitled "Race Prejudice at Summer Resorts," which identified anti-Semitism as "a new feature in the New World." "Only within the present decade," the article stated, "has there been an anti-Jewish sentiment openly displayed in the United States." The blame for this was laid by Alice Rhine, the author of the article, firmly on Judge Hilton, whose exclusion of Jews from his hotel in Saratoga had set an example that other hotel and boardinghouse proprietors had followed. "In seeking reasons for this sweeping ostracism," she wrote, "it is found that the Gentiles charge the Hebrews with being 'too numerous'; 'they swarm everywhere.'" It was also said, she recorded, that Jews lacked refinement; they dressed badly, had bad manners and showed disrespect for the Christian Sabbath.

The kind of anti-Semitism discussed by Rhine was extremely mild, however, compared to the sort that was unleashed at around the same time in *The American Jew*, described as "the book that inaugurated racial anti-Semitism in America." Its author was Telemachus Timayenis, a Greek immigrant. Whereas Rhine described a prejudice against Jews as identified by their culture, their language and their perceived lack of social graces, Timayenis's target was the Jew as a *racial* type, identified by "their hooked noses, restless eyes, elongated ears, square nails, flat feet, round knees, and soft hands." The Jews that he describes with venomous hatred wear "long coats dripping with filth, while their faces and beards looked suety with sluttishness"; they arrive in the United States penniless, and soon—suspiciously soon, according to Timayenis—become prominent bankers, and leaders of American industry. But despite his unease at the wealth of the German Jews, it is the wretched poverty of the eastern European Jews on the Lower East Side that most exercises Timayenis, who is also inclined to despise the Jews *because* they are refugees from prejudice. "Let the Jews of this country understand," he writes, "that the American people do not want, and will not receive, the dregs of a race which has won only scorn and contempt from the people of Europe." The message of *The American Jew*, repeated several times throughout the book, is: "The Jew must go!'

Timayenis, of course, did not speak for the whole American population, the majority of whom would have identified far more readily with the famous sentiments expressed by Emma Lazarus in the poem inscribed on the Statue of Liberty, which was dedicated by President Cleveland in 1886, sentiments that indeed were inspired by the piteous sight of the arrival to New York of the very Jews that had aroused the venom of *The American Jew*:

> *Give me your tired, your poor,*
> *Your huddled masses yearning to breathe free,*
> *The wretched refuse of your teeming shore.*

The Statue of Liberty would have been the first thing that Julius Oppenheimer saw when he came to the United States in 1888 to join his prosperous and well-connected uncles and take his place among "Our Crowd." He was at that time a slim, good-looking, but shy seventeen-year-old who spoke little English. However, he clearly lost no time in joining the cultural, spiritual and (perhaps most importantly) social world of his uncles. In the year of his arrival in New York, he is listed as a member of Adler's Ethical Culture Society. Though he was, of course, immediately given a position in Rothfeld, Stern & Co., he could not yet afford to live on the Upper West Side and, for the first few years before his inexorable rise through the company's hierarchy, lived in rented accommodation in Lower Manhattan, the same part of town in which the company had its office.

In many ways Julius Oppenheimer was arriving in America at a bad time. The so-called "Gilded Age," when unimaginably large fortunes were amassed by the "Robber Barons" (Carnegie in steel, Rockefeller in oil, Vanderbilt in railroads and Astor in real estate), and smaller but still significant fortunes were made by Jewish bankers and traders, was coming to an end, as the country headed toward recession. No doubt related to the darkening economic scene was the growth of racial anti-Semitism, which, while rarely as virulent as that expressed in *The American Jew*, could still shock many of those German Jewish migrants who had believed in America as a land free from the "old strife."

Among these was Jesse Seligman, who had inherited from his brother Joseph the title "New York's leading Jewish banker," and who in 1893 was given a particularly hurtful introduction to the new, more brutal form of anti-Semitism to which parts of American society had succumbed. Together with his brothers Joseph and William, Jesse Seligman had for many years been a member of, and fully accepted by, the predominantly gentile Union League Club. At the time of his death, Joseph Seligman had been a vice president of the club, and in 1893 Jesse—following in his older brother's footsteps once again—was elected a vice president. He therefore did not anticipate any problems when he put up his son, Theodore, a young lawyer recently out of Harvard, for membership. Theodore's application, however, was rejected, the club committee explaining to Jesse that it was "not a personal matter in any way, either as to father or son. The objection is purely racial." Jesse immediately resigned and never set foot inside the Union League Club again. "His bitterness over the episode probably shortened his life, just as the affair with Judge Hilton shortened his brother's," writes Stephen Birmingham. He died just a year after the affair.

The economic recession of 1893–5 hit the clothing industry harder than any other and resulted in mass unemployment, although Rothfeld, Stern & Co. seemed to ride out the recession better than most clothing firms in New York. It moved its office to cheaper accommodation on Bleecker Street, but other than that there was no sign that it suffered very much. In 1895, Julius's younger brother Emil came to New York, by which time Julius, now twenty-four years old, was beginning to make his mark in the firm. In 1900, the company took the decision to specialize in the importation of cloak linings, something on which Julius Oppenheimer quickly became an expert, and from that point he seems to have become the company's leading figure. In 1903, this was recognized when he was made a partner, a move that seems to have persuaded him that the time was right to marry and settle down.

His chosen bride was Ella Friedman, who, though a member of the same German Jewish, Upper West Side community as the Rothfelds and Oppenheimers, was seen as significantly less German, less Jewish and more "American" than Julius. For one thing, Ella was not a migrant; she had been born in America, and English was her first language. According to her son, she did not speak German very well—something that seemed, if anything, to be a source of pride rather than of embarrassment. Her father, Louis Friedman, was indisputably a German Jew, but, having migrated (to Baltimore rather than to New York) in the 1840s, he had been in the U.S. a good deal longer than the Rothfelds or the Oppenheimers. Ella's mother, Cecilia Eger, had herself been born in America and, though from a Germanic background (her father was German, her mother Austrian), was, so it was said in the family anyway, not a German Jew, since she was non-Jewish. The claim is precarious to say the least. Cecilia's mother, Clara Binswanger, was—as her family tree in the American Jewish Archives reveals—about as Jewish as it is possible to be: both her maternal and paternal grandfathers were rabbis. Cecilia's father, David Eger, was a prominent member of the Philadelphia Jewish community, mentioned several times in the 1894 publication *The Jews of Philadelphia*. If J. Robert Oppenheimer inherited his striking blue eyes from his grandmother Cecilia, as was widely believed in the family, it was not because she was, from a genetic point of view, any less Jewish than his paternal grandparents.

Not only was Ella seen as more "American" than the family she was marrying into, but she was also seen as more "refined." During the years that Julius spent working his way up the family textile business, Ella was studying art, first in her native Baltimore and then in Paris, where she made a particular study of the Impressionists. On her return to America she taught art at Barnard College, a liberal arts college for women in New York, which had opened in 1889 as an "annex" of Columbia University and from 1897 was housed in a building next to Columbia in Morningside Heights on the Upper West Side of Manhattan. By the time she met Julius, Ella was an established and accomplished painter, with private students and her own rooftop studio. Her father had died in the early 1890s and she lived with her mother, Cecilia, in an apartment at 148 West 94th Street. Two years older than Julius, she would have been in her mid-thirties when they met, described by a family friend as "a gentle, exquisite, slim, tallish, blue-eyed woman, terribly sensitive, [and] extremely polite." She was born with an unformed right hand. To hide this—and the artificial thumb and finger that she used to compensate for it—she always wore gloves, and her deformity was never once mentioned or even alluded to by the family. When a girlfriend of Robert's once asked him about it, she was met with stony silence.

It is not entirely clear how Julius and Ella met. It may have been that Ella's father was in the textile trade and knew the Rothfeld brothers, or it may have been that they had mutual friends in the Ethical Culture

Society. Both suggestions have been made, although neither seems very likely. Her father had been dead for many years before she and Julius met, and it is not likely that her mother moved in the same circles as the Rothfelds. Nor is there any indication that Ella or anybody else in her family was a member of, or in any way interested in, Adler's society.

It seems more likely that it was their common interest in art that brought them together. By 1903, Julius, as a partner in a thriving company, was a wealthy man and could afford to indulge his growing passion for the visual arts. It is reported that he "spent his free hours on weekends roaming New York's numerous art galleries." If so, given the way that wealth and enthusiasm attract invitations and introductions, it is not difficult to imagine that someone in the New York art world—an artist, an agent, a gallery owner—brought Julius and Ella together.

The cultural refinement that Ella represented was by this time something Julius craved. Though he had left school as a teenager, and had arrived in America speaking little English, he was determined to develop into the "proper gentleman" that his employees later described him as being. He dressed impeccably, acquired the social graces of the upper middle class and read widely, particularly in American and European history. Discovering that a German accent was a barrier to acceptance as a gentleman in the New York of the early twentieth century, Julius took drastic steps to remove all traces of his mother tongue, taking English lessons from an Oxford tutor, from whom he acquired the gentlemanly tones of the British educated elite.

Ella and Julius were married on March 23, 1903, their wedding being the occasion of a very public statement that they did not consider themselves Jewish. The service was performed not by a rabbi, but by Felix Adler himself, and not in accordance with any Jewish tradition, but rather as an illustration of the "New Ideal" preached by the Ethical Culture Society. In his series of discourses, *Creed and Deed*, published in 1886, Adler had written, in connection with his notion of what the "Priests of the New Ideal" might be like: "there are special occasions in these passing years of ours, when the ideal bearings of life come home to us with peculiar force and when we require the priest to be their proper interpreter. Marriage is one of them." And so Ella and Julius were, in a way, married by a priest, but not in a way that implied commitment to any religious creed.

That Felix Adler officiated at Julius's wedding was extremely apt, since in the years that followed Julius was to become one of Adler's leading and most devoted disciples, his rise to prominence in his uncles' company running parallel with his rise within the Ethical Culture movement. At the time of his wedding, as the Rothfeld brothers were entering their sixties and approaching retirement age, Julius Oppenheimer was preparing to take over the running of the company. It was an opportune time to seize the reins. The advent of ready-to-wear suits, which cut overheads, lowered prices and increased demand dramatically, had given the entire tailoring industry an enormous boost, and business was extremely good. The Rothfeld brothers, however, did not live to see the best years of their company. Longevity was never a family trait and both brothers died before they reached seventy, Solomon in 1904 and Sigmund three years later. Upon Sigmund's death, in December 1907, Julius became president of Rothfeld, Stern & Co., which now had offices in that most prestigious of all New York addresses: Fifth Avenue. At thirty-six years old, Julius Oppenheimer was a man of means and substance.

In the same year that he became president of Rothfeld, Stern & Co., Julius was elected onto the Board of Trustees of the Society. The following year he was appointed a member of the Society's Finance Committee. These appointments put him in a position where he was rubbing shoulders with members of some of the most prominent "Our Crowd" families. By the first decade of the twentieth century, the nature of "Our Crowd" was changing somewhat. It was no longer dominated by people like Joseph Seligman, who had come over from Germany and made huge fortunes in business, but rather by their offspring, who typically were not businessmen, but something more refined (if less lucrative). They were men who, having inherited wealth—in some cases vast amounts of it—cared less about commerce than about matters of the intellect, of culture, of the spirit and of politics and society. Among them were the men who succeeded Felix Adler as president of the New York Ethical Culture Society:[1] Edwin Seligman, Joseph's son, who was a professor of economics at Columbia University, then Robert D. Kohn, a famous architect, and Herbert Wolff, a leading civil-rights lawyer.

In Howard B. Radest's history of the Ethical Societies, Julius Oppenheimer's role in the New York Ethical Culture Society is mentioned in passing by Herbert Wolff in an interesting and revealing anecdote:

> In the old days, if there was a deficit . . . Felix Adler would be advised of the amount . . . I remember one year . . . $25,000 was needed. Professor Adler phoned to people like Joseph Plaut, B. Edmund David, Mr. Berolzheimer [the head of the Eagle Pencil Company, who bought St. Simons Island in Georgia], Mr. Oppenheimer, maybe

---

[1] Adler resigned as president of the New York Society in 1882, though of course he remained—as he is described on Julius and Ella's marriage certificate—"Leader of the Society for Ethical Culture."

one or two others. There was a command to appear at his office on a certain specified day at 5 o'clock in the afternoon. He then told these gentlemen that the deficit was $25,000 . . . Each one—there were five present—said that he would undertake ⅕ or $5,000 . . . The other members of the Society were not involved . . . Some of them didn't even know that there was a deficit.

Though he and his society were almost entirely dependent on the money thus received from wealthy businessmen, Adler urged his disciples to accord little respect to making money. Being wealthy might *seem* to be "supremely enviable," he wrote, but "the business of wealth-getting, and of wealth-enjoyment, when viewed at close range, turns out to be a very different matter. Its effect is almost inevitably unfortunate, not only on society at large, but on the mind and character of the wealthy themselves." Indeed, he added: "I would urge the principle of self-limitation in regard to wealth," and he made this "plea to the wealthy":

The first step to take, if they would set themselves right, is to live in the midst of superfluous wealth as if they were not the possessors of it; that is, to take for their own use only what they require for the essentials of a civilized life, and to regard the rest as a deposit for the general good, of which they themselves are not to be the beneficiaries.

By donating $5,000 to the Ethical Culture Society whenever Adler asked him to, Oppenheimer was not only helping the Society, but also enabling himself to live a more ethically cultured life by shedding some potentially harmful superfluous wealth. "The habit of luxurious living is eating into the vitals of society, is defiling the family, and corrupting the state," Adler preached. But, of course, opinions will vary as to what exactly the "essentials of a civilized life" are, and therefore how much wealth is required in order to provide them. Where is one to draw the line between the things that are an essential part of being civilized and the things that are mere luxuries?

Julius and Ella Oppenheimer, though never ostentatious, certainly led what many would consider a luxurious life. Soon after they were married they moved into an apartment at 250 West 94th Street, just down the road from Ella's mother. It was a fairly large apartment in a fairly smart neighborhood, but nothing very out of the ordinary. Where, however, they went way beyond what most people would regard as being *essential* to a civilized life was in the furnishing and decorating of the apartment, particularly with regard to the paintings that adorned its walls. It was in those days customary among wealthy German Jewish New York families to have a private art collection. In this respect, as in so many others, the members of "Our Crowd" tended to veer on the side of conservatism, caution and conformity. Abby, the central character in Emanie Sachs's *Red Damask*, sneers that they "haven't enough physical courage to go in for sports like the rich Gentiles, and a little too much brains. So they go in for art collection with an expert to help. They wouldn't risk a penny on their own tastes."

Left to his own devices, Julius might have fallen into the kind of conservatism mocked by Sachs, but in Ella he had his own expert, one who, having studied Impressionism in Paris, was certainly *not* afraid to risk money on her own taste. The result was an extraordinary private art collection that was to be the pride of the family for generations. It included a Rembrandt etching, paintings by Vuillard, Derain and Renoir, no fewer than three Van Goghs—*Enclosed Field with Rising Sun*, *First Steps (After Millet)* and *Portrait of Adeline Ravoux*—and a "blue period" Picasso, *Mother and Child*.

The private contemplation of fine works of art might be seen as the very opposite of the way of life promoted by the Ethical Culture Society, a society that emphasized social responsibility and the importance of the *deed*, of doing something practical to help those less well off than one-self. This was a society that set up educational programs for the working class; that put forward practical suggestions for improving the health, the working conditions and the housing of the people of New York; that involved itself in trade-union disputes; and that helped set up a number of nationally important campaigning groups—the National Child Labor Committee, the Civil Liberties Union, the Ladies' Garment Workers' Union, the Society for the Advancement of Colored People, and so on. Spending large sums of money (for even though Julius and Ella were "early buyers" of Van Gogh and Picasso, the cost of these paintings was still considerable) on works that would be seen only by one's immediate family and one's closest friends scarcely looks consistent with the ethics that inspired the movement and its many social and political initiatives.

And yet, when looked at in another way, it was not only consistent with Adler's vision, but a fulfillment of it. Despite the practical nature of much of the work of the Ethical Culture Society, and despite its repu-diation of theology, Adler's vision was first and foremost a *spiritual* one. His central motivation was to find a way of preserving the spiritual guid-ance that religions had provided, even after all faith in religious beliefs had been abandoned. He thought he had found what he was looking for in the philosophy of Immanuel Kant, with its emphasis on what Kant called the "Moral Law," which Kant thought *all* of us would find in our hearts. In a famous passage that Adler quotes in his discourses, *Creed and Deed*, Kant writes: "Two things fill the soul with ever new and increasing admiration and reverence: the star-lit heavens above me, and the moral law within me." According to Kant, the moral law is the same for all people at all times and at all places, and according to Adler: "The moral law is the common ground upon which all religious and in fact all true men may meet. It is the one basis of union that remains to us amid the clashing antagonisms of the sects . . . all that is best and grandest in [religious] dogma is due to the inspiration of the moral law in man."

What, then, is the moral law? In Kant's formulation, it is this: "act only in accordance with that maxim through which you can at the same time will that it become a universal law." This means something like: do as you will be done by; or: do to others what you would be happy to have done to you. Adler's formulation, however, is rather different: "The rule reads, 'Act so as to bring out the spiritual personality, the unique nature of the other.'"

One brings out the "spiritual personality" by awakening in other people the sense of the sublime, of the infinite. Art is able to do this, Adler emphasizes, since it is a "high endeavor" and "Truly disinterestedness is the distinguishing mark of every high endeavor." Thus: "The pursuit of the artist is unselfish, the beauty he creates is his reward." The goal of life is to pursue "the Ideal," which "is void of form and its name unutterable." We can find the Ideal within ourselves—in fact, we can *only* find it within ourselves—through the discovery and appreciation of the moral law; and the "high endeavors," of art, science and public service, can help us find it. So the acquisition of fine works of art does not, after all, constitute "luxurious living," but rather a means of fulfilling the "Moral Law."

It was in an environment governed by this idiosyncratic version of the moral law that a concerted effort would be made to "bring out the spiritual personality" of J. Robert Oppenheimer.

2

Childhood

t was in the extraordinarily tasteful
and expensively furnished apart-
ment in West 94th Street that, on April 22, 1904, J. Robert Oppenheimer
was born. To help look after the baby, the Oppenheimers employed a
nursemaid and, later, a governess. They also employed a cook, a chauffeur and three live-in maids to help Ella look after the apartment. There
was no hint of decadence or overindulgence, but it was a luxurious life
and a very sheltered one, too. "My life as a child did not prepare me
in any way for the fact that there are cruel and bitter things," Oppenheimer later recalled. His parents, particularly his mother, saw to it that
everything and everyone with whom he came into contact was refined,
tasteful and pleasant. From everything discordant, ugly or unpleasant he
was shielded and protected. Above all, there was an atmosphere of moral
rectitude. He was, he later considered, "an unctuous, repulsively good
little boy," his upbringing having offered him "no normal, healthy way
to be a bastard."

Oppenheimer grew up surrounded by people trying to be and, as
far as it is possible to tell, succeeding in being *good*. "Not religion as a
duty," ran one of Adler's more austere maxims, "but duty as a religion."
There was *some* levity. Julius is remembered by one of Robert's friends
as "a hearty and laughing kind of person." But the general tone was one
of earnestness and propriety, Julius's attempts at joviality at the dinner
table—sometimes he would even burst into song—being met with acute
embarrassment by his wife and son. A friend later recalled that Robert
Oppenheimer would often be very critical of his father, particularly of
what he perceived to be his vulgarity. On the other hand, he was never
known to utter a word of criticism of his mother. Ella Oppenheimer was,
as far as her son was concerned, beyond any kind of reproach. She, for

her part, seemed determined to ensure that her family lived in a world from which all coarseness, vulgarity and discord had been expunged. She was, a family friend recalled, "a woman who would never allow anything unpleasant to be mentioned at the table." She saw to it that Robert, and later his younger brother Frank, had as little as possible to do with the outside world. When their hair needed cutting, a barber came to the apartment; when they needed medical attention, a doctor was called for; when they needed to go anywhere, the chauffeur would take them in the family limousine. There was, Frank later said, "a general distrust of the pollution of the outside world."

Frank was not born until 1912, when Robert was eight—too late to be a childhood companion. When Robert was not yet four, however, in March 1908, Ella gave birth to her second son, Lewis Frank Oppenheimer, who lived for just forty-five days. His death was one of those unpleasant things that was never mentioned, and a main cause of the air of melancholy that seemed to pervade the Oppenheimer household. One of Robert's friends described Ella as "a mournful person," and one has the feeling that she never stopped mourning the death of her second son. Robert, naturally, had no memories of Lewis, but the ghost of his younger brother haunted the family, and therefore the apartment in which he grew up, in a way that was all the more pervasive because it was unacknowledged. After Lewis's death, Ella, who was always an anxious mother, fretted terribly about any little illness that Robert caught. As Robert, who was never robust, either as a child or as a man, caught a large number of colds and other childhood illnesses, she fretted a great deal. She would only rarely allow him to play with other children, for fear of exposure to disease and infection. As a result, Robert grew up alone, his intellectual interests and abilities developing well beyond his years, but his social skills remaining stunted, thereby creating a sense of separation between himself and other people that, he said, he managed to overcome only in the spring of 1926 at the age of twenty-two.[2]

His parents did everything they could to stimulate Robert's intellectual and artistic interests. "I think my father was one of the most tolerant and human of men," Oppenheimer later said. "His idea of what to do for people was to let them find out what they wanted." In the case of Robert, whose precocious intelligence was manifest from a very early age, this meant providing him with everything in which he showed any interest. When, at about the age of five, he declared an interest in ancient and modern buildings and expressed a desire to become an architect, his father gave him photographs and prints of the great buildings of the

[2] See pages 113–16.

world, together with books on architecture. Responding to his mother's expectations of him, Oppenheimer next declared that he wanted to be first a poet and then a painter, and received in turn volumes of poetry, his own easel and an abundance of brushes and paint. In deference to his mother's wishes, he took piano lessons but they were a great torture for him. The lessons stopped when Robert came down with some childhood illness or other and his mother asked him how he felt. "Just as I do when I have to take piano lessons," he replied, no doubt realizing that the lessons would henceforth be canceled.

The young Oppenheimer had everything a child could wish for—except the thing that most children wish for above all: the company of other children. So, though he acquired impeccable adult manners from an early age and was extremely (perhaps even unnaturally) well behaved, he never experienced the simple childhood pleasures of rambunctiousness and mischief that arise from playing with childhood companions. There was very little fun to be had in the ethically cultured, artistically refined and intellectually advanced Oppenheimer household. In place of fun there was a great deal of achievement, fueled by expectations that were absurdly high and felt by Oppenheimer to be even higher than they actually were. He always felt as if he were letting his parents down, if not intellectually, then morally. "I repaid my parents' confidence in me," he once remarked, "by developing an unpleasant ego which I am sure must have affronted both children and adults who were unfortunate enough to come into contact with me."

In 1909, Ella's mother, now elderly and ailing, moved into the Oppenheimer apartment. In the summer of that year, Robert, then aged five, was introduced to his father's side of the family during a visit to Germany. It was then that he met Benjamin Oppenheimer, who, after watching Robert playing with some building blocks, presented him with an encyclopedia of architecture—a strange gift for a five-year-old, and one that is hard to square with Robert's recollection of Benjamin as an illiterate peasant. Benjamin's other gift was to have a deep influence on the young Robert: a box of rocks, each labeled with its Latin and German names, obviously designed to be the starting point for a collection of minerals. Robert took the bait. Collecting and studying minerals became, and remained throughout his childhood, his main hobby.

What little contact Robert had with other children was restricted to those he met through the Ethical Culture Society. Every Sunday the Society held a meeting that had something of the character of a weekly religious service, except that there were no prayers. At these meetings organ music was played and Felix Adler or a guest speaker would give a lecture, usually of a sermon-like nature. Julius and Ella, naturally, were regular attenders and, while they were at the meeting, Robert would attend the Sunday School, one of the rare occasions at which he was able to mix with other children. Until 1910, these meetings (attendance at which would sometimes reach a thousand) were held in Carnegie Hall, but in October 1910 the Society proudly opened its new, specially commissioned building at 2 West 64th Street, at the corner of Central Park West. At the dedication of the new building, with his parents in the audience, Robert, then aged six, joined the other children from the Society's Sunday School in a presentation on ethical behavior, which was followed by communal singing led by the children.

When Robert started school in September 1911, at the relatively late age of seven (he entered in the second grade), he would already have known many of the children with whom he would be taught, since the school chosen by his parents was, inevitably, the Ethical Culture School, located at 33 Central Park West (just around the corner from the new Society hall). Since the very beginning of the Ethical Culture Society, Adler had seen education as one of its principal activities, and in 1878 he set up a free kindergarten for working-class children. This proved to be very successful and three years later it was expanded into a tuition-free elementary school called the Workingman's School, which, Adler announced in his opening address, aimed to provide working-class children with "a broad and generous education, such as the children of the richest might be glad in some respect to share with them."

As it turned out, the rich were glad to share the excellent education offered by the school, and, indeed, were prepared to pay for the privilege. So in 1890 the school (which had run into grave financial difficulties) started admitting fee-paying students, drawn mainly from the affluent families of the Ethical Culture Society who, because of anti-Semitic prejudice, were finding it impossible to place their children in the best private schools. Within a few years of the introduction of fee-paying students the school changed its character completely, replacing its original mission of providing a model education for the poor with the rather different aim of educating and training future leaders of society in the ideals of the Ethical Culture movement. By the time it moved into its Central Park West building in 1902, only 10 percent of its students were working-class children on scholarships. Most of the other 90 percent were the children of Ethical Culture Society members, attracted not only by an education informed by the ideals of the Ethical Culture movement, but also by the quality of education on offer at the school, which by then was widely recognized as one of the best private schools in the country. Having by this time added a high school to the original elementary school, the Ethical Culture School was seen—by an increasing number of middle-class gentiles as well as by the German Jewish community—as an ideal preparation for admission to the top universities in the country.

Despite the growing number of gentiles among its students, the school in Oppenheimer's day was still widely viewed as a place for the education of Jewish children. The children themselves, however, came largely from families who, like the Oppenheimers, were assimilated to such an extent that their identity as Jewish was no longer entirely clear. One of Oppenheimer's classmates, asked years later for her recollections of him, agreed that Oppenheimer felt uneasy about his Jewishness, but added: "We all did." In its publicity material, the school emphasized its role in *American* culture, particularly in American democracy. "The school is to be a nursery of 're-formers,'" its catalog announced, with the aim of training people who would provide the leadership required to reform society so that it answered to the needs of, and expressed "the ideal aspirations of," American democracy.

The school, then, saw itself as shaping the minds of those who would in later life lead America, whether in politics, business, science or the arts. One might regard this as the application to the entire country of Adler's version of the moral law: "Act so as to bring out the spiritual personality, the unique nature of the other." The school would help America to realize its potential and become itself. Then, with its leaders trained in the ideals of Ethical Culture, America would at last fulfill the hopes of the German Jews who had gone there in the 1840s, expecting to find the embodiment of Enlightenment ideals. Even before he founded the Ethical Culture Society, when he was still a professor at Cornell, Adler had developed an exalted view of American democracy, which, in tracing a direct line between the Jewish prophetic tradition and the American democratic ideal, attributed to the latter a religious significance. In his first set of Sunday-morning lectures, he declared: "To larger truths America is dedicated." America could, he argued, provide both political and spiritual liberty and so break the "spiritual fetters that load thy sons and daughters!" "All over this land," he announced, "thousands are searching and struggling for the better, they know not what." It was his role, the role of the Ethical Culture Society and of the students trained in its school, to teach those thousands what, exactly, they were searching for and thereby to define and exemplify what Adler was fond of calling the "American ideal."

Adler's role as the spokesman for the spiritual importance of Americanization received recognition and support at the highest level when, in 1908, he was appointed by President Roosevelt himself as Theodore Roosevelt Professor at the University of Berlin, where he gave a series of lectures on "The Foundation for Friendly Relations Between Germany and America." In a book that was published some years later, he argued that America represented a "New Ideal." "The American ideal," he declared, "is that of the uncommon quality latent in the common man."

This was something that was to become a central part of Oppenheimer's worldview. If Oppenheimer seemed to later observers strangely untouched, for the most part, by the values of the Ethical Culture Society, with respect to America and what it represented, he was at one with Adler. His greatest love was possibly that which he felt for his country. In his mind at least, the answer to the question about the nature of his identity was simple: he was not German and he was not Jewish, but he was, and was proud to be, American.

In this respect, Oppenheimer was a typical product of the Ethical Culture movement. Besides the patriotic focus in its publicity material, the Ethical Culture School did its best, on every available occasion, to present itself to parents and pupils as first and foremost an *American* school. Four times a year it held festivals in which the pupils would perform plays in front of the parents. These festivals did not include Hanukkah, Yom Kippur, Rosh Hashanah or Passover, but rather Thanksgiving, Christmas, Patriots' Day and a May festival. The first of these that Oppenheimer took part in was the Christmas Festival of 1911, in which the pupils of his year (the second grade) presented a play that drew on elements of Viking mythology—Fire Spirits, Frost Giants, Ice Spirits, and so on—to present the triumph of life over death. It ended with a rousing chorus of "Noël, Noël."

During Oppenheimer's first year at school he and his family moved into a new home. The apartment at West 94th Street was sold, and the family relocated to a much grander apartment that took up the whole eleventh floor at 155 Riverside Drive, a prestigious redbrick block on the Upper West Side right next to Riverside Park, with views of the Hudson River. In recent years 155 Riverside Drive has become famous as the home of the characters in the popular television situation comedy *Will & Grace*, who live on the ninth floor. The scriptwriters no doubt chose Riverside Drive for the same reasons as the Oppenheimer family: it is an impressive address, signaling elegance, wealth and membership of Manhattan's educational and artistic elite. In 1912, it was where some prominent members of the fabulously wealthy Guggenheim family lived, including Benjamin Guggenheim, who, in April of that year, as a first-class passenger on board the fateful maiden voyage of the *Titanic*, famously insisted on facing death "like a gentleman." Also living at Riverside Drive when the Oppenheimers moved there was Benjamin Guggenheim's brother, William, notable for publishing an autobiography in the guise of a biography in which he said of himself that anyone who saw his "light complexion" and the cast of his features "would not have surmised his Semitic ancestry."

When they moved into this large and prestigious apartment the Oppenheimers took with them their impressive collection of paintings, as well as Ella's mother and Robert's governess. Ella was pregnant at the time and, on August 14, 1912, Francis Oppenheimer was born. Frank (as he was always known) was too young to be a a playmate for Robert, but as they grew up they would become close, and Robert's correspondence with his younger brother reveals an intimacy that Oppenheimer was to share with very few people.

Certainly, Oppenheimer had few (if any) close friends at school. He once remarked in later life that it was characteristic that he could not remember any of his classmates. They remembered him, of course. Particularly vivid are the memories of Jane Didisheim (later Jane Kayser), who, fifty years after knowing Robert at school, could recall him in telling detail:

> He was still a little boy; he was very frail, very pink-cheeked, very shy, and very brilliant of course. Very quickly everybody admitted that he was different from all the others and very superior. As far as studies were concerned he was good at everything . . . Aside from that he was physically—you can't say clumsy exactly—he was rather undeveloped, not in the way he behaved but the way he went about, the way he walked, the way he sat. There was something strangely childish about him . . . He was abrupt when he came out of his shyness, but with all that a very polite sort of voice. He never seemed to want to come to the front of anything . . . If he did it was because he couldn't do otherwise . . . because he was so extraordinarily gifted and brilliant—that just pushed him.

Another classmate remembers him as "rather gauche," adding "he didn't really know how to get along with other children." Perhaps thinking that he was playing to his strengths, Oppenheimer—who could not become popular through playing sport or by being mature or streetwise—struck many of his fellow pupils as a little too anxious to demonstrate his intellectual precocity. As one of them put it, he had "a great need to declare his preeminence." "Ask me a question in Latin and I will answer you in Greek," he once remarked to a girl in his class. His math teacher recalled that he was difficult to teach because he was "so far ahead of everybody and very restless," a view echoed by his other teachers. His grades, however, particularly in his early school years, do not confirm this impression of unreachable genius. They certainly were not bad, but they were mostly A– and B+, rather than the consistent A+ that one might have expected.

Outside of school, his interests were scholarly, solitary and characteristic of a much older boy. "When I was ten or twelve years old," he recalled as an adult, "minerals, writing poems and reading, and building with blocks still—architecture—were the three themes that I did."[3] What he meant by the single word "minerals" was the deep interest he had developed in mineralogy following his grandfather's gift of a collection of rocks. On walks around New York's Central Park, on summer holidays on Long Island and on family visits to Germany, Oppenheimer would collect rock samples, which he would then identify and display on Riverside Drive. In pursuit of this hobby, he joined the New York Mineralogical Club, its other members only realizing how young he was after they had invited him to present a paper and found themselves listening to a twelve-year-old boy.

At the end of Oppenheimer's third year of school, when he was ten years old, the First World War broke out. It would be another three years before the United States entered the war, but its effects were felt in America, in New York and among the Oppenheimer family long before that. For Rothfeld, Stern & Co. the war presented an opportunity to make a fortune supplying cloak linings for military uniforms, and, as a result, the Oppenheimers were able to buy a holiday home on Long Island. This was not a small summer house, but a mansion of some twenty-five rooms located in Bay Shore (which Oppenheimer always wrote as "Bayshore"), then fashionable and upmarket. To explore the Great South Bay during their holiday in this house Julius bought a forty-foot sailing yacht, the *Lorelei*, and, a few years later, a twenty-seven-foot sloop for Robert.

Where the war had a less welcome impact on the Oppenheimers, as on the entire German Jewish community in New York, including the Ethical Culture Society, was in widening the publicly perceived gap between being German and being American—providing Julius and others with yet more reasons to lose all traces of their accents and all vestiges of their ethnic origins. For Felix Adler, the war was something of a disaster. His first response to it was to deliver, in October 1914, an address called "The World Crisis and Its Meaning," an expanded version of which was published the following year. "Many of our fellow-citizens

---

[3] It is customary to remark on the elegance of Oppenheimer's spoken and written language, but the curious awkwardness of the unidiomatic "themes that I did" is a feature that recurs surprisingly often in his writing, particularly in his letters.

of German birth," Adler declared, "aside from the profound anxiety descendants of all the nationalities now at war naturally feel for friends at the front, are troubled with a new misgiving as to their own place in the American nation." The reason for this anxiety was plain: "Public opinion in the United States is decisively on the side of the Allies and this practically means on the side of England." But, Adler insisted, America is *not* English; it represents, as he had been saying for thirty years, a New Ideal. "The German ideal," he wrote, "roughly speaking, is that of efficiency." "The national ideal of the English," on the other hand, "may be described as that of *noblesse oblige*." In contrast to both of these was the American ideal, which "is that of the uncommon quality latent in the common man." The task facing adherents of Ethical Culture, Adler told his audience, was to keep alive during the strife the *American* ideal, which, properly understood, was not allied to *either* side in the conflict.

As for the *cause* of the war, Adler offered a surprising analysis. Militarism—identified by many at the time as the cause—was, Adler said, "only a symptom": "If we wish to put the blame rightly, or, setting aside the question of blame, if we wish to place the proximate cause rightly, let us place it on the shoulders of science." "The time will come," Adler announced, "when that scientist [that is, one who puts his work to use for war] will be considered and will consider himself a disgrace to the human race who prostitutes his knowledge of Nature's forces for the destruction of his fellow men."

Adler's address was widely perceived to be a plea for neutrality, and, in the atmosphere of the time, being neutral was regarded as being almost as bad as—indeed, barely distinguishable from—being pro-German. The year after Adler's speech, the *New York Times* hit out at Adler for his "high opinion of the morality of the German people." In the increasingly fervent anti-German atmosphere that was spreading throughout the United States ("Anything German, from symphony to sauerkraut, was suspect," as Howard B. Radest puts it), it took courage to express any opinion other than full-blooded support for the Allies. Certainly no one in the Ethical Culture movement, despite their German heritage, was prepared to be openly in support of the Germans during the war. Some prominent members, however, including John Elliott and David Muzzey, the associate leader of the New York Society, were prepared to publicly support the pacifist case, which put them at odds with Adler himself, whose pro-American position compelled him, after the U.S. entered the war in April 1917, to declare his support for the war. From November 1917 onward, the Ethical Culture meetinghouse followed most other public buildings in flying the U.S. flag. Most of the Ethical Culture leaders who had previously been pacifist followed

Adler in his support for the war, but John Elliott continued to pursue a pacifist line, devoting himself (even at the risk of being thrown out of the Society) to defending the rights of conscientious objectors. In this, Elliott was radically, and increasingly, out of step with Adler, who, in his Easter Sunday sermon of 1917, went so far as to argue that resistance to the war was *treason*.

In the midst of this potentially ruinous split in the Ethical Culture movement, Oppenheimer, now thirteen years old, entered the high-school part of the Ethical Culture School. The school journal, *Inklings*, had by this time nailed its mast firmly to Adler's colors and become belligerently pro-war. Encouraging students to do whatever they could for the war effort—joining the Auxiliary Red Cross, sewing bandages, and so on—*Inklings* declared it to be "the duty of every high school chap to put his shoulder down and buck up for his country": "All of our brave plans and hopes for the future have to be cast aside to give place to the one predominant purpose of the entire nation . . . We are in the fight and we have got to win!'

In its issue of March 1918, the journal expressed its solidarity with those who regarded political dissent as treachery. "In discussing the war," its editors declared, "we must think of rights which are greater than the individual's right to expression of personal views . . . one thing we do not want is opposition to the government." Three months later, this attack on government critics was renewed: "There is no room for dissenters and joy-killers. There is no room for those who complain of the government, of the suffering of the soldiers, of no results, of hard times, etc."

It is doubtful that Oppenheimer shared these sentiments. His father was such an admirer of Adler that it is difficult to imagine him doing anything but following Adler's position at every stage; but there are signs that, during his high-school years, Oppenheimer began to distance himself, both from his father and from the Ethical Culture movement. In a satirical poem that he wrote for his father's birthday he included the slightly mocking line, "he swallowed Adler whole like morality compressed," and in his last year at the Ethical Culture School (1920–1) he wrote a poem for his English teacher which might naturally be read as an indictment of the line taken by Adler and *Inklings* during the war.

The poem is untitled, but an apt name for it might be "The Damning Lie." In its entirety, it reads:

> *In Flanders' fields the sun sinks low*
> *And clouds flamed crimson with its glow*
> *Unnumbered crosses—here we lie*
> *While life & love go swirling by*

Ours—had God decreed it so.
He can not guide you where to go,
He can not prompt with "yes" or "no"
The stage of life; ours was to die
In Flanders' fields—

Yet now we see: We have no foe.
Nurtured by hatreds that must grow
It was, we see, the damning lie
And, in a quaking voice we cry
"Let us have Peace"; the sun sinks low
On Flanders' fields.

RO

The "damning lie" of which the poem speaks is the insistence that it was the duty of those soldiers whose "unnumbered crosses" lie on Flanders' fields to regard the soldiers on the other side as their "foe," to hate them and kill them, even at the expense of their own lives. Once this is seen to be not just untrue, but a lie, the poem seems to suggest, then the faith that had previously compelled its acceptance has to be rejected. The most obvious interpretation of the image of the sinking sun that occurs both at the beginning and at the end of the poem is that it is a metaphor for death—not only the deaths of the buried soldiers, but also of the faith that had guided them to their graves. This would include their faith in God, but also their faith in all those people and institutions that had perpetuated the "damning lie": the priests, the governments—and the leaders of the Ethical Culture Society, together with the teachers and pupils at the Ethical Culture School.

The poem perhaps provides a clue as to what lies behind Rabi's remark about Oppenheimer's relationship with his school and the Ethical Culture movement: "From conversations with him I have the impression that his own regard for the school was not affectionate. Too great a dose of Ethical Culture can often sour the budding intellectual who would prefer a more profound approach to human relations and man's place in the universe." As Julius was so closely associated with the Ethical Culture movement, Oppenheimer, in distancing himself from Ethical Culture, was also distancing himself from his father—a process that, perhaps inevitably, was accompanied by feelings of guilt.

If his first year at high school, 1917–18, was the year in which he broke free, to some extent, of the influence of Ethical Culture and his father, it was also the year in which Oppenheimer acquired a new father-

figure, and possibly someone who could help him find the "more profound approach to human relations" that Rabi mentions him needing.
That man was Herbert Winslow Smith, a Harvard graduate who came
to the Ethical Culture School in 1917 to teach English. He was at that
time still intending to finish a Ph.D. at Harvard, but enjoyed teaching
at the Ethical Culture School so much that he stayed there, his Ph.D.
unfinished and forgotten, for the rest of his life.

Clearly in his element at the Ethical Culture School, Smith became
known as a teacher willing and able to form close relationships with his
pupils. He formed an especially deep interest in Oppenheimer, his later
recollections of whom reveal a predilection for psychoanalysis and an
assumption that he understood the young Oppenheimer as well as, if
not better than, Oppenheimer's own family. One of Smith's repeated
themes is the uneasiness of Oppenheimer's relationship with his father.
Julius Oppenheimer, Smith said, had a touch of "business vulgarity
which acutely embarrassed Robert, although he would never mention
it." Many of Robert's problems, according to Smith, were due to a "pronounced oedipal attitude" toward his father.

It was in the summer after Smith's first year at the school—the summer of 1918, as the First World War was coming to an end—that Oppenheimer, then fourteen years old, underwent an experience that Smith was
convinced was one of the most important of his life, and which was for
Smith the paradigm example of the ways in which Oppenheimer blamed
his father for his suffering.

The incident took place during Oppenheimer's stay at Camp Koenig,
a boys' summer camp on Grindstone Island in Lake Ontario. The camp
was run by Dr. Otto Koenig, the principal of the Sachs Collegiate Institute, a Jewish boys' school on the Upper West Side of New York City.
Koenig's son, Fred, later professor of chemistry at Stanford University,
became Oppenheimer's only friend at the camp. "I often felt," Fred Koenig said years later, "that what happened to Robert in camp that summer
could easily account for much of his behavior—his actions—that people
found so baffling."

At the camp Oppenheimer became the victim of increasingly vicious
bullying. The other boys called him "Cutie" and mocked him for writing to his parents every day and for reading poetry. In one of his letters
home Oppenheimer, perhaps trying to give the entirely false impression
that he was mixing well with the other boys, told his parents that he was
glad to be at the camp because he was learning a great deal from his
fellow campers, especially about sex. This brought his enraged parents
hurriedly to the camp, where his father demanded that the camp director do something about the spread of smut among the boys. When the

camp director duly announced that disciplinary measures would be taken against those caught telling dirty stories, the boys sought their revenge on the telltale who had betrayed them. One evening, while taking a walk, Oppenheimer was captured and dragged to the icehouse, where he was stripped, his buttocks and genitals were painted green and he was tied up and left alone. As Fred Koenig later put it: "They, as it were, crucified him."

Despite this attack, Oppenheimer remained at the camp for the rest of the summer. "I don't know how Robert stuck out those remaining weeks," Koenig said. "Not many boys would have—or could have—but Robert did. It must have been hell for him." Afterward, Oppenheimer mentioned the incident just once, when, at the age of twenty, he confided in Herbert Smith, who had by then become his closest friend. Both Smith and Fred Koenig (the only two friends of Oppenheimer's who knew what he had endured on Grindstone Island) were convinced that it was a—perhaps the—defining moment of his life.

One very interesting detail that Koenig mentioned in his recollections of Oppenheimer at summer camp in 1918 concerns their many walks together:

> We talked as we walked. I remember Robert quoting passage after passage of George Eliot. He found her conviction that there is a cause and effect relationship in human behavior, as well as in nature—her awareness of fate—to be fascinating. We discussed this at length.

What particular passages Oppenheimer knew by heart is not known, though it is known that he was reading *Middlemarch* that summer and was greatly impressed by it. The theme of causal relations in human behavior is highlighted in that book through its central character, Tertius Lydgate, who is himself fascinated by the application of causal explanations to nature (as Eliot puts it, he "longed to demonstrate the more intimate relations of living structure and help to define men's thoughts more accurately after the true order"), but who, ironically, is undone precisely because of his failure to understand human nature, particularly his own and that of his wife.

The character of Lydgate parallels Oppenheimer to an extraordinarily close extent. First and foremost, Lydgate is an outsider, the only character in the book who does not actually come from Middlemarch. We first see him as a young, newly qualified doctor, who, full of optimism and idealism, arrives in the town to establish himself as a family physician. As a boy, Eliot tells us, Lydgate had been a quick learner, who loved books and to whom acquiring knowledge was exceptionally easy: "It was said of him that Lydgate could do anything he liked." However, though he read widely and amassed at least a superficial knowledge and understanding of a vast range of subjects, "no spark had yet kindled in him an intellectual passion." This changed one rainy day when, out of boredom, he took down a volume of an old encyclopedia and began reading the entry on "Anatomy." "From that hour," Eliot writes, "Lydgate felt the growth of an intellectual passion."

Inspired by this passion, Lydgate studies medicine, fired not only by an enthusiasm for achieving a scientific understanding of the human body, but also by an idealistic desire to reform the medical profession and to do some social good. He wants both to be an outstanding practitioner of medicine and to make a significant and lasting theoretical contribution to medical science. He has the natural ability, the training and the circumstances to achieve this demanding dual ambition, but one thing stands in his way: his character. "Lydgate's conceit," Eliot tells us, is "of the arrogant sort, never simpering, never impertinent, but massive in its claims and benevolently contemptuous." Because of this character flaw, Lydgate, despite his good intentions, is not trusted by the people of Middlemarch, who are quick to think the worst of him when he becomes involved with a crooked financier. He ends up as an outwardly successful (that is, wealthy) medical practitioner, who is however inwardly unsuccessful, trapped as he is in a loveless marriage, surrounded by people with whom he feels no sense of companionship and having abandoned all hope of making any serious contribution to the theory of medical science.

In many ways, Lydgate's story parallels and anticipates Oppenheimer's. Though Fred Koenig was sympathetic to Oppenheimer with respect to the treatment he received at the hands of the other boys at camp, he also acknowledged that "to some extent, he asked for it." As Koenig remembers Oppenheimer that summer, he did not just stand out from the other boys, he did so *deliberately*. "Robert enjoyed being different," Koenig recalled. "He was an intellectual snob, a mental exhibitionist." He was "bright and sensitive, but very much in conflict with himself," and, of course, at odds with the people around him.

The inner conflict noted by Koenig was matched by a conflict between Oppenheimer and his father and perhaps, in Oppenheimer's mind at least, between what was expected of him and what, in reality, he was. His later remarks that his childhood "did not prepare me in any way for the fact that there are cruel and bitter things" and that it had offered him "no normal healthy way to be a bastard" are symptomatic, perhaps, of a resentful feeling that his inability to fit in with people was to some extent his parents', and particularly his father's, fault. Smith remembers that, though he "never heard a murmur of criticism on Robert's part of [his] mother," Oppenheimer "was certainly critical enough of [his] father." Indeed, said Smith, "the most important element I think in Robert's life was his feeling that his own parents', particularly his father's, maladroitness had resulted in all sorts of humiliation to him"—chief among which was his "crucifixion" at Camp Koenig.

After the summer of 1918, Oppenheimer returned to school to resume the second of his four high-school grades. The way his schooling was organized was that he progressed from one grade to the next every February, which was the beginning of the school's second term. Each high-school grade was named after a Greek letter, so that he began "alpha grade" in February 1917 and "beta grade" the following year. In February 1919, upon entry into "gamma grade," he took part in a patriotic festival held at school, the centerpiece of which was an allegorical play called *The Light*, which recounted the battle against Brute Force by the combined forces of Peace, Justice and Civilization, culminating in the uniting of nations into the "true brotherhood of man." On the night of the play the school mounted an "Americanization exhibit," which contained, among other things, German helmets brought back from the Western Front by "some of our dough boys." The exhibition might seem somewhat at odds with the theme of the play, but a link between the two might be seen in the Adlerian idea that, in defeating the Germans, the "dough boys" had helped to bring about the realization of the "American Ideal" and thus the triumph of "true brotherhood" over "brute force."

The years 1919–20 and 1920–1, his junior and senior years of high school, were extremely important ones for Oppenheimer's intellectual development. They were the years in which he, like Lydgate in *Middlemarch*, "felt the growth of an intellectual passion." In his case, it was not anatomy that aroused this passion, but chemistry, and what inspired it was not a textbook, but a particularly gifted teacher called Augustus Klock. Known to his students as "Gus," Klock was an extremely popular teacher, remembered affectionately for his fund of jokes, his infectious enthusiasm for his subject and the Herbert Hoover collars he wore. He was to stay at the Ethical Culture school until 1960 and was mentioned by several generations of students as an inspiring teacher, including some who, in various ways, followed in Oppenheimer's footsteps. They include the brothers Hans and Ernest Courant, whose father was a friend of Oppenheimer's and who both became professional physicists, and Robert Lazarus, a renowned theoretical physicist who founded the computing division at the Los Alamos laboratory in New Mexico. In the memories of all of them the inspirational influence of Klock is emphasized, just as it was by Oppenheimer himself. When Klock died in 1963, Oppenheimer wrote:

> It is almost forty-five years since Augustus Klock taught me physics and chemistry . . . He loved these sciences both as craft and knowledge. He loved the devices of the laboratory, and the great discoveries that had been made before, and the view of nature—part order, part puzzle, that is the condition of science. But above all, he loved young people, to whom he hoped to give some touch, some taste, some love of life, and in whose awakening he saw his destiny.

Klock was equally complimentary about Oppenheimer. When, in 1948, he was interviewed for a profile of Oppenheimer in *Time* magazine, Klock remarked: "He was so brilliant that no teacher would have been skillful enough to prevent him from getting an education."

The way the science curriculum at the school was arranged was that physics was taught in the junior year, followed by chemistry in the senior year. In physics, Oppenheimer was introduced to atomic theory, which he described to the *Time* journalist as "A very exciting experience . . . beautiful, wonderful regularities!" Seeing his son so inspired prompted Julius to arrange for Klock to give Robert a special individual intensive course during the summer of 1920. This summer was later recalled by Oppenheimer as an important turning point in his life, arousing in him a life-changing devotion to science:

> We must have spent five days a week together; once in a while we would even go off on a mineral hunting junket as a reward for this. I got interested then in electrolytes and conduction; I didn't know anything about it but I did fiddle with a few experiments [although] I don't remember what they were. I loved chemistry so deeply that I automatically now respond when people want to know how to interest people in science by saying, "Teach them elementary chemistry." Compared to physics, it starts right at the heart of things and very soon you have that connection between what you see and a really very sweeping set of ideas which could exist in physics but is very much less likely to be accessible. I don't know what would have happened if Augustus Klock hadn't been the teacher in this school, but I know that I had a great sense of indebtedness to him. He loved it, and he loved it in three ways: he loved the subject, he loved the bumpy contingent nature of the way in which you actually find out about something, and he loved the excitement that he could stir in young people. In all three ways he was a remarkably good teacher.

For Robert's sixteenth birthday, Julius had given him the twenty-seven-foot sloop mentioned earlier to sail around the Great South Bay during the family's holidays at their home in Bay Shore. Oppenheimer chose for the boat the rather clever name *Trimethy*, after the chemical compound trimethylamine, a colorless liquid that is responsible for the characteristic smell of decomposing fish—a name that at one and the same time announces his love for chemistry and suggests one of the most evocative aspects of the seashore: its smell.

Until he acquired a boat, Oppenheimer had had neither aptitude nor interest in any physical activity. His PE scores at school were uniformly bad, he played as little sport as he could, and he even avoided using stairs whenever he could take a lift instead (his headmaster once wrote to his parents begging them to teach him how to use stairs, because his insistence on waiting for the lift was holding up classes). Once he got his own boat, however, he became adventurous to the point of recklessness. To the astonishment and dismay of Julius and, especially, Ella, Oppenheimer would sail his boat in all weathers, exploring every part of the Great South Bay and the Long Island Sound. Several times Julius had to come and rescue him and escort him home in a motor launch. Once, Oppenheimer and his younger brother Frank had to be rescued by the "Revenuers," the coast-guard officers, because they had run aground on a mud bank. Another time, when trying to dock the boat at Cherry Grove on Fire Island, Robert misjudged the wind and slammed into the dock with such force that he knocked into the water a small girl who had come to watch him moor.

A description of what it was like to accompany the teenage Oppenheimer on his sailing adventures has been left by Francis Fergusson, who has recalled a visit to the Oppenheimers' Bay Shore home in 1921:

> It was a blowy day in spring—very chilly—and the wind made little waves all over the bay and there was rain in the air. It was a little bit scary to me, because I didn't know whether he could do it or not. But he did: he was already a pretty skilled sailor. His mother was watching from the upstairs window and probably having palpitations of all kinds. But he had induced her to let him go. She worried, but she put up with it. We got thoroughly soaked, of course, with the wind and the waves. But I was very impressed.

Fergusson was at this time Oppenheimer's best friend. In fact, he was the only close friend Oppenheimer ever made while he was at the Ethical Culture School.

Oppenheimer's friendship with Fergusson of course suggests that his claim to have been unable to remember the names of any of his class-mates was almost certainly not true. Indeed, among his classmates were a few whose names it seems hard to believe he could not recall. There was Jane Didisheim, for example, who, in the early 1920s came often to the Oppenheimers' flat on Riverside Drive, usually at the invitation of Mrs. Oppenheimer, who evidently hoped to kindle a romance between Jane and her son. Exactly what Oppenheimer's feelings for Jane were it is not possible to tell, but, whatever they were, they were sufficiently strong and sufficiently important to inspire him, when he was at Harvard, to write a story about her. (This story, like all Oppenheimer's fiction, no longer exists.) Then there was Fred Bernheim, who was not strictly a classmate, being a year behind Oppenheimer at school, but was to become one of Oppenheimer's closest friends at Harvard. Finally, there was Inez Pollak, who, together with her sister Kitty, visited Oppenheimer at Harvard, where her uncle, Paul Sachs (the son of Samuel Sachs, the cofounder of Goldman Sachs and an archetypal member of "Our Crowd"), was assis-tant director of the university's Fogg Art Museum, to which he had made significant donations.

It is simply not possible that Oppenheimer could, at any time in his life after meeting him in 1920, have forgotten Francis Fergusson's name. Toward the end of his life, he said of Fergusson: "He is to this day one of my closest friends and our paths have crossed often." What does seem likely, however, is that Oppenheimer might not have regarded this as an exception to his claim not to remember the names of any of his classmates, for the reason that he did not *really* regard Francis as having been one of them. Indeed, the fact that Fergusson was the single person at school with whom Oppenheimer became friends might be seen as a measure of his distance from his classmates, rather than an exception to it. For, as opposed to Jane Didisheim, Fred Bernheim and Inez Pollak, Fergusson was not a product either of the Ethical Culture School or of the cultural milieu from which it had grown. He was only at the school for one year—his (and Oppenheimer's) senior year, 1920–1—and he was, as Oppenheimer evidently felt himself to be, an outsider, among both the Ethical Culture movement and the New York German Jewish com-munity.

Fergusson was, as it were, the very opposite of a New York Jew: he was a gentile from the Southwest, the product of pioneering frontier people who were the very epitome of Theodore Roosevelt's conception of true "Anglo-Saxon" Americans. Fergusson's family (on his mother's side German and on his father's side Irish) had been in the United States for several generations and was, at the time Oppenheimer met him, one of the most established and prominent families in New Mexico. Francis's father, H. B. Fergusson, had been a congressman for New Mexico, first in the 1890s when it was a mere territory and then, after it became a state in 1912, as its first representative in the House of Representatives. When Francis Fergusson came to the Ethical Culture School in 1920, his father had been dead for five years, but was still widely remembered, especially in the Southwest, as the author of the Fergusson Act of 1898, which allocated four million acres of land in New Mexico for educational and other public purposes.

The Fergusson family was not as wealthy as many of the families who sent their children to the Ethical Culture School. They did not have the kind of money that the Goldmans, the Sachs or the Seligmans had. But they had things that Oppenheimer's father, his mother and, above all, Oppenheimer himself, craved: they had literary culture, they had the kind of "class" that comes from membership in America's cultural, intellectual and political elite, and they had a place in the very creation of America. They lived in a grand, adobe-style house in Albuquerque called La Glorieta, which itself has a significant place in the history of the Southwest. Widely regarded as the oldest house in Albuquerque, its origins lie in the seventeenth century, when it was built for, and inhabited by, members of the region's ruling Spanish American elite. During the period (1821–48) when New Mexico was a province of Mexico rather than a territory of the United States, La Glorieta was the home of Manuel Armijo, the governor of the province. Fergusson's family acquired the house in 1864, when his maternal grandfather, Franz Huning, bought it as a home for himself, his wife and their growing family.

As one of the most prominent characters of the old frontier days, Franz Huning is something of a legendary figure in New Mexico. The story of his life was told by him in his memoir, *Trader on the Sante Fe Trail*, and has been retold many times since, in histories of the Southwest, in biographies and in fiction. Arriving in the United States as a teenager in 1848, Huning went west and lived the adventurous and perilous life of a frontier trader, driving oxen along the Sante Fe Trail. When he settled in Albuquerque he opened a general store, which was extremely successful, allowing him to invest in a variety of other ventures, including a flour mill, a sawmill and various ranches and farms. In addition to La Glorieta, he had a very grand house built for himself and his family in a distinctly European style, which became famous locally as "Castle Huning." Toward the end of his life Huning was losing rather than amassing wealth, and it was an important part of the Fergusson family mythology to regard him as a pioneer and a merchant-adventurer, rather than a businessman. He belonged, they insisted, to the "Old West" and, as such, was uncomfortable and out of place with modern commercialism.

When his daughter, Francis Fergusson's mother, was interviewed in the 1930s about her famous father, she emphasized his cultural and scholarly achievements rather than his moneymaking skills, remarking: "I believe he always liked languages better than business." She was especially concerned to tell the interviewer about her father's fluency in Spanish and his role as an interpreter during the American occupation of New Mexico.

On his father's side, too, Francis's family had a quintessentially *American* kind of glamour, again derived from their membership in an elite that had helped to define America and Americans, though in their case the elite in question was part of the "Old South" rather than the "Old West." Francis's grandfather, Sampson Noland Ferguson (the second *s* in the surname was added by Francis's father for a reason that is lost to history), was a Southern gentleman, an aristocratic plantation owner from Alabama, who served as a captain in the Confederate army under his friend, General Lee, and, owing to his commitment to the Confederate cause, lost everything in the Civil War (he, patriotically but unwisely, sold his land for Confederate money). After the family's land and wealth were thus dissipated, his son, Harvey Butler Fergusson (Francis Fergusson's father), came to New Mexico to work as a lawyer. After a few years in the gold-rush town of White Oaks (chiefly remembered now for its associations with Billy the Kid), H. B. Fergusson moved to Albuquerque, where he became a successful lawyer, married Franz Huning's daughter (thus acquiring both La Glorieta and Castle Huning) and then embarked on his political career.

Growing up in Albuquerque and living in its oldest, most historically interesting house, Francis would repeatedly have been told the stories of the Old West, many of which would have involved members of his own family. Like Oppenheimer, he was born in 1904. Unlike Oppenheimer, he was the youngest of four siblings, two of whom—his elder sister, Erna, and his older brother, Harvey—became popular writers, famous most of all for writing about the history, the legends, the people and (in Erna's case) the food of the Southwest. Particularly well known are Erna's *Dancing Gods: Indian Ceremonials of New Mexico and Arizona*, *Our South West* and *Mexican Cookbook* and Harvey's novel, *Wolf Song*, based on the life of Kit Carson, *Rio Grande*, his history of the Southwest, and his memoir, *Home in the West*. By the time Fergusson met Oppenheimer, the literary careers of his soon-to-be-famous siblings had already been launched. Harvey had just published his first novel, *The Blood of the Conquerors*, set among the Spanish American community in New Mexico, and Erna had started writing articles on the history of New Mexico for the *Albuquerque Herald*. Just as Francis's ancestors had played an important part in the making of the West, so his siblings were to become instrumental in shaping the perception of it. To be introduced, as Oppenheimer was soon after getting to know Francis, to the Fergusson family was thus to be introduced to the history and mythology of the Southwest. Both introductions were to have large implications for the course of Oppenheimer's life.

Like his siblings, Francis had aspirations of becoming a writer. Unlike them, he was not content to study either at the University of New Mexico, where Erna had been a student, or at Washington and Lee University, the alma mater of both his father and his brother. He wanted to go to Harvard and, to that end, had come east to attend a high school in the Bronx that would prepare him for Harvard entrance. For his senior year he transferred to the Ethical Culture School, having, presumably, learned of its excellent record of getting students into Harvard. Soon after joining the school he and Oppenheimer had become close friends. Characteristically, Oppenheimer, when he recalled meeting Fergusson, never mentioned the things that most obviously marked him out from his other classmates—that he was a gentile, that he came from a distinguished and prominent family from the Southwest, that his father had been a congressman and that his siblings were famous writers—but rather remembered him as someone "who at that time had some interest in biology," but whose "main interests were really a young man's philosophic interests; he was preoccupied with the old difficulty that if everything is natural how can something be good, in the form [in] which the 19th century writers had sharpened this."

Fergusson, like Oppenheimer, formed a close relationship with Herbert Smith at the Ethical Culture School, and the three of them were to establish an extremely important bond. Smith, Fergusson remembers, was "very, very kind to his students"; he "took on Robert and me and various other people . . . saw them through their troubles and advised them what to do next." Smith's contact with his students, at least his favorite ones, extended well beyond school hours. Oppenheimer, Fergusson and others would be invited to Smith's home in New Jersey, where they would write and discuss literature; and, after they left school, Smith continued to act as their confidant and advisor through correspondence.

Oppenheimer and Fergusson graduated from the Ethical Culture School in 1921, Oppenheimer in February and Fergusson in June. They had both been accepted by Harvard and both expected to go there in October that year, Oppenheimer to study chemistry and Fergusson to study biology. Immediately after his graduation, Oppenheimer spent the spring of 1921 working on a special, advanced-science project at school with Augustus Klock. He then set off for a summer holiday in Europe with his parents and his younger brother, Frank. They went to Germany, from where Oppenheimer set off on his own on what he later called "a long prospecting trip into Bohemia." More specifically, he went to the old mineral mines near what was then called Joachimsthal (now Jáchymov), on the Czech border, an area renowned in the nineteenth century for its silver, and a century later for its uranium. It was an ideal place for a rock collector, and Oppenheimer returned with a suitcase full of interesting specimens. Of more lasting importance to him, however, was that he also returned from the mines with a serious, almost fatal, case of dysentery. He arrived back in New York on a stretcher.

On his parents' insistence, he postponed his admission to Harvard for a year and spent the autumn and winter of 1921–2 at home, recuperating from the dysentery and from colitis, which was to remain a recurring problem for the rest of his life. Seventeen years old and impatient to leave home and take up his place at Harvard, where Fergusson, as planned, started in the autumn of 1921, he was a bad patient. Indeed, these months of convalescence seem to have brought out a hitherto-unseen obnoxious side to his character; he was frequently irritable, and would sometimes lock himself in his room, ignoring his parents' pleas to come out and to be reasonable.

By the spring of 1922, his beleaguered parents had formed a plan to occupy his time and thoughts more profitably, one that would have the additional advantage of getting him off their hands for a while. They approached Herbert Smith to ask him whether he would consider taking a term off work (during which the Oppenheimers would take over the payment of his salary from the school) in order to accompany their son on a trip to the Southwest. The Southwest was chosen partly in order for Oppenheimer to spend some time with Fergusson's family before joining him at Harvard after the summer, and partly because the climate, the fresh air and the spectacular countryside would provide an obvious and beneficial change from New York. The idea that Smith should take an entire term off work, however, was too much for the school, which vetoed the plan, whereupon it was proposed instead that Smith and Oppenheimer should travel to the Southwest during the summer holiday, a proposal that Smith (who had, it seems, performed a similar service earlier for Felix Adler's nephew) was happy to accept.

It was a trip that was to have a deep and lasting influence on Oppenheimer's life. In later life he was fond of saying that he had two loves: physics and the New Mexican desert. Of those, the first was New Mexico.

3

First Love: New Mexico

One reason that Oppenheimer's holiday in the Southwest in the summer of 1922 was to have such deep and lasting effects on the course of his life was that it introduced him to people and places that would remain for him ideals by which others were measured. The Southwest, as Emanie Sachs emphasizes in *Red Damask*, was held in roughly equal measures of awe and contempt by members of the New York Jewish community, who regarded it, whether for good or ill, as the polar opposite of New York City. When her central character, Abby, discovers that her husband, Gilbert, has been offered a job in Texas, she urges him to accept it, on the grounds that, in the Southwest, they could escape from the sense of being outsiders. After all, she reasons, "you can't be an outsider when you're a pioneer." Gilbert, however, prefers to stay in New York, where life is more civilized. "Gilbert," Sachs writes, "had been brought up to value orderly living and art and music and philanthropy and friends who valued them." In drawing the contrast in this way, Sachs has, I think, provided important clues as to what Oppenheimer and Fergusson hoped to find in each other: where Oppenheimer looked to Fergusson and his family for the inspiration of the pioneer spirit and freedom from the sense of being an outsider, Fergusson, it seems likely, regarded Oppenheimer and his family as the very epitome of a life that valued "orderly living and art and music and philanthropy."

In any case, Fergusson's family home in Albuquerque, La Glorieta, was, naturally, the first port of call for Oppenheimer and Smith. There, Fergusson, back from Harvard for the summer, introduced Oppenheimer to his friend Paul Horgan. Horgan would later find fame as a novelist and a historian, especially renowned—like Fergusson's siblings—for writing about the history, characters, landscape and mythology of the Southwest. Born in Buffalo, New York, Horgan had lived in New Mexico since he was twelve, when his family moved to Albuquerque after his father, a vice president of a printing firm, contracted tuberculosis. At the time of meeting Oppenheimer, Horgan was a student at the New Mexico Military Institute in Roswell, where he was to remain for another year before moving to Rochester, New York, in order to study stage production at the Eastman School of Music. His writing career took off a few years after he returned to Roswell in 1926 to take up a post as librarian at the Military Institute.

From their first meeting, Oppenheimer and Horgan took to each other warmly. Despite their differences in background and the fact that Horgan had little interest in science, they seemed to see in each other a kindred spirit. Indeed, among Oppenheimer, Fergusson and Horgan there quickly developed a shared sense of mutual admiration and liking, and, for the first time in his life, Oppenheimer found himself a member of a group of friends who shared interests, thoughts, confidences and experiences. They quickly began to think of themselves as a unit, a set of self-styled "polymaths" that Horgan would later describe as "this pygmy triumvirate" or "this great troika." At the age of eighteen, it seems, Oppenheimer had finally found a group of people his own age to which he felt he *belonged*, and to whom he did not seem strange and alien.

That Oppenheimer could find this sense of belonging only among gentiles in the Southwest is indicative not only of his sense of *not* belonging to the community within which he had been brought up, but also of his desire to actively distance himself from that community and to become a different person with a different social milieu. Before they set out for the Southwest, Oppenheimer startled Herbert Smith by asking him if they could both travel under the name "Smith," passing Oppenheimer off as Smith's younger brother. Smith would have nothing to do with this plan, which he saw as one among many signs of discomfort on Oppenheimer's part with his Jewishness. This discomfort, Smith believed, also lay at the heart of Oppenheimer's illnesses, both his dysentery and his colitis, which, he thought, had more likely psychological than biological origins. After all, Smith wondered, how could Oppenheimer have contracted dysentery when his family were so scrupulous in avoiding all contact with the outside world and drank nothing but bottled water? As for Oppenheimer's colitis, Smith noted that it disappeared very suddenly as soon as they arrived in the Southwest, but reappeared whenever "someone disparaged the Jews." One telling recollection of Smith's concerns an occasion when, in a hurry to get his clothes packed, he asked Oppenheimer for help in folding a jacket. "He looked at me sharply," Smith remembered, "and said, 'Oh yes, the tailor's son would know how to do that, wouldn't he?'"

In New Mexico, among the "great troika" of himself, Fergusson and Horgan,[4] Oppenheimer could, at least temporarily, escape from being the Jewish "tailor's son" from New York City and be part of a culture that defined itself in opposition to trade and business, that saw itself rooted in the mountains, rivers and valleys of the Southwestern countryside and the noble and courageous adventurousness of the pioneers that had tamed it. As Erna Fergusson puts it in her book, *Our South West*:

> The Southwest can never be made into a land that produces bread and butter. But it is infinitely productive of the imponderables so much needed by a world weary of getting and spending. It is a wilderness where a man may get back to the essentials of being a man. It is magnificence forever rewarding to a man courageous enough to seek to renew his soul.

This emphasis on the role of the Southwest in "renewing" the soul pervades much of the work of Horgan and the Fergussons. In the same book, for example, Erna writes:

> Such a country, inscrutable, unconquerable and like nothing his kind had ever seen, naturally affected the man who dared to face it. It made, in fact, a new type of man who may renew himself in other challenging conditions or who may prove to be only a passing phase due to submerge in the babbittry that has come with the trains.

The conquering of the West as a metaphor for conquering the self was one that Horgan was very fond of. For example, in an essay he wrote in the 1940s, he suggested: "Maybe everyone has a kind of early West within himself that has to be discovered, and pioneered, and settled. We did it as a country once. I think plenty of people have done it for themselves as individuals."

That Oppenheimer had, to some extent, "found himself" during his trip to the Southwest, that it enabled him to blossom in ways that had been impossible in New York, is attested to by the way his new friends remembered him during this summer. "He was the most intelligent man I've ever known," Paul Horgan said. "And with this, in that period of his

---

[4] It is possible, I think, that Oppenheimer gave the name "Trinity" to the first atomic-bomb test site in Alamogordo—not far from Albuquerque and Roswell—in memory of the New Mexican "troika" that he had joined in the summer of 1922.

life, he combined incredibly good wit and gaiety and high spirits . . . He had a great superiority but great charm with it, and great simplicity at that time." He also noted Oppenheimer's "exquisite manners," adding: "I've always been puzzled by later reports of his arrogance and his self-centeredness . . . I can't identify that in him at all." The man he describes seems barely recognizable as the awkward, arrogant, socially maladroit teenager remembered by Oppenheimer's schoolmates during his time at the Ethical Culture School, to whom the words "charm," "gaiety" and "high spirits" certainly would not have suggested themselves when attempting to describe his personality.

One of the many ways in which the summer of 1922 brought forward a newly invigorated Oppenheimer was with respect to his interest in, and attraction to, girls. He later confided to his brother Frank that he had become strongly attracted to Horgan's sister, Rosemary, and, later on in the trip, he met a woman with whom it would probably not be too much to say he fell in love. Her name was Katherine Chaves Page and she was then twenty-eight years old and just married to a man twice her age, an "Anglo"[5] businessman called Winthrop Page who lived in Chicago.

Katherine herself was a member of an aristocratic Spanish hidalgo family, who had lived in the Southwest for many generations and had been in their day still more prominent than the Hunings and Fergussons. Their history was even more romantic and evocative of the "Old West." Her grandfather, Manuel Chaves, had been a famous soldier, nicknamed "El Leoncito" ("the little lion") because of his bravery. He was a cousin of the aforementioned governor of New Mexico, Manuel Armijo, and boasted that his lineage could be traced back to one of the original Spanish conquistadores. Having fought the Navajos and the Americans on behalf of the Mexicans, he swore an oath to the United States in 1848 after the American victory in the Mexican-American War and proceeded to fight Apaches and Mexicans on behalf of his newly adopted nation. In the Civil War he fought on the Union side and helped them to defeat an attempt to take New Mexico for the Confederacy. After his famous last battle as an Indian-fighter in 1863, in which he led fifteen men against 100 Navajos, he established a home for himself in the San Mateo Mountains, west of Albuquerque, where he made a living ranching and where he built a family chapel, in which he, his wife and his children were buried.

Katherine's father was Amado Chaves, the second son of Manuel

---

[5] In the Southwest the word was used to describe anyone who was not either of Spanish or of Native American ancestry, so Germans, Norwegians, Danes, and so on were as much "Anglos" as English people were.

Chaves, whose life story could hardly have been in sharper contrast to that of his Indian-, American- and Mexican-fighting father. After studying law and business in Washington, D.C., Amado Chaves returned to New Mexico and pursued a career as a lawyer and politician, becoming mayor of Santa Fe, and then speaker of the legislative assembly of New Mexico and superintendent of the state's public education system. In both capacities he would no doubt have had much contact with H. B. Fergusson, which is presumably how the links between the two families—later cemented by the close friendship of Katherine and Erna Fergusson—began. In 1893, Amado Chaves married the "Anglo" Kate Nichols Foster, the daughter of an English-born architect, and the following year Katherine was born.

As well as the ranch that Amado had inherited from his father in San Mateo, the Chaves family also had a house in Albuquerque that Kate Nichols Foster had designed. In addition they acquired some land in the Upper Pecos Valley, near the town of Cowles, some twenty miles or so north of Santa Fe, where they built a guest ranch (or "dude ranch") called "Los Pinos," high up on the hills with splendid views of the Pecos Valley and the Sangre de Cristo mountains. It was here that Oppenheimer spent the most memorable part of his summer trip to the Southwest, developing not only an attachment to Katherine, but also a deep affection for this part of New Mexico.

To Oppenheimer, the Chaveses, their history, the countryside of northern New Mexico and, especially, Katherine herself were all excitingly and wonderfully grand and he became infatuated. According to Fergusson, Oppenheimer would bring flowers to Katherine "all the time" and would "flatter her to death whenever he saw her." Katherine seems to have enjoyed the attention and to have returned it. "For the first time in his life," Smith later recalled of the time they spent in Los Pinos, Oppenheimer "found himself loved, admired, sought after." Inspired by Katherine's example, Oppenheimer developed a love of horse riding and, together with the rest of the group, explored the slopes and valleys of the area around Cowles; this included—most momentously from a historical point of view—the Pajarito Plateau, upon which stands what is now the town of Los Alamos, but which in the summer of 1922 contained nothing but the Los Alamos Ranch School. A lasting memento of the horse rides Oppenheimer and Katherine took together is what to this day is still called "Lake Katherine," one of the highest lakes in New Mexico, which is contained in a cirque (what in England would be called a coombe) just below Santa Fe Baldy, one of the tallest summits of the Sangre de Cristo mountains. On one of their rides together, Oppenheimer and Katherine, or so the story goes, discovered this hitherto unknown lake.

By the time he and Smith left New Mexico, Oppenheimer was a skilled and proud horseman and was, it seems, determined to prove himself to be as adventurous and as brave as the ancestors of the Fergussons and the Chaveses. On their way back to New York, Oppenheimer and Smith decided to ride on horseback through Colorado. The question thus arose as to which route they should take. Oppenheimer's suggestion was that they should take a trail that led through the highest pass of the snow-capped mountains, a route Smith felt sure would lead to their death by freezing. Eventually they settled the matter by tossing a coin, and, as Smith later commented: "Thank God I won."

On his return to New York, Oppenheimer seemed to everyone who knew him a changed person. His old classmate Jane Didisheim remarked: "He had become less shy. I think he had become gayer also." But his mother's hopes that a romance might develop between Jane and Robert were forlorn. Not only was Robert infatuated with a *very* different kind of woman back west; but he had, emotionally at least, severed himself completely from "Our Crowd" and become a different person—one who, he hoped, would be fit for Harvard.

4

Harvard

The summer hotel that is ruined by admitting Jews meets its fate not because the Jews it admits are of bad character, but because they drive away the Gentiles, and then after the Gentiles have left, they leave also."

These words were written not, as one might think, by an anti-Semitic commentator on the "Seligman Affair," but by Abbot Lawrence Lowell, the president of Harvard. And they were written not in the 1870s, but in the early summer of 1922, just a few months before Oppenheimer was due to take up his place at Harvard to study chemistry. During that summer, Lowell sparked an acrimonious nationwide controversy by announcing publicly that he was seeking measures to restrict the number of Jews that his university admitted. In the previous decade, the proportion of Jews at Harvard had risen sharply from 10 to 20 percent. This was much larger than at most of the other Ivy League universities—at Yale the figure was 7 percent and at Princeton a mere 3 percent—and among both staff and students there was growing talk about the "Jewish problem." Harvard, it was said, was going the same way as Columbia University in New York City, where, by 1920, 40 percent of the students were Jewish. For Lowell, the vice president of the Immigrant Restriction League and a firm believer in the superiority of both the Christian religion and the "Anglo-Saxon race," this was an intolerable prospect.

Unlike his famous predecessor, Charles Eliot, who had used his presidency to establish and build upon Harvard's international reputation as a leading center of academic research, Lowell's first priority was to maintain and, if possible to increase, Harvard's reputation for undergraduate teaching, and, in particular, its reputation for educating students who would go on to be leaders in their chosen field, not just in academic life, but also in commerce, law and politics. His models were Oxford and Cambridge, universities that recruited students of good "breeding" and equipped them with the learning, the manners, the contacts and the confidence to take their place at the very head of society.

The growth in the proportion of Jews at Harvard threatened this vision of what the college ought to be by raising the possibility of "WASP flight," the desertion of the college by the families of the Protestant elite, something that had already occurred at Columbia. To prevent this, Lowell believed that it was necessary, openly and frankly, to restrict the numbers of Jews—that is, to introduce a quota system. It was no good, he thought, trying to limit the number of Jews by adopting criteria, whether of academic ability or of behavior, which gentiles would pass but Jews would fail, since there simply were no such criteria. The problem was not that Jews were not good students, or that they were bad people; it was that, just by being Jews and for no other reason, they were unacceptable, except in small enough numbers, to the "Anglo-Saxon" elite that Lowell's Harvard sought to attract.

Lowell's initial move to restrict the number of Jews was an attempt to persuade Harvard's admissions committee to adopt discriminatory procedures, imposing higher standards on members of the "Hebrew race" than on other applicants, so that only those "Hebrews . . . possessed of extraordinary intellectual capacity together with character above criticism" would be allowed in. When the chairman of the admissions committee refused to adopt such a fundamental change without the explicit assent of Harvard's faculty, Lowell was forced to debate the issue, first with his academic colleagues and then with the public at large. At a faculty meeting on May 23, 1922, Lowell managed to pass a motion calling upon the admissions committee to "take into account the . . . proportionate size of racial and national groups in the membership of Harvard College," but, within a week, he received four separate petitions asking him to call a special meeting to allow the faculty to reconsider a move that one petition described as "a radical departure from the spirit and practice of the College."

The subsequent special faculty meeting, held on June 2, agreed to rescind the motion passed on May 23, but left in place a decision to appoint a special committee "to consider principles and methods for more effectively sifting candidates for admission." Lest anyone was in any doubt about what this meant, Lowell added a statement to the minutes of the meeting making it explicit that "the primary object in appointing a special Committee was to consider the question of Jews." By now, the admissions policies of Harvard were national news, reported in all the main newspapers and the subject of much comment, a good deal of which was vehemently critical of Lowell's methods, aims and motives.

A few weeks after the announcement that the special committee was to be appointed, the *American Hebrew* printed an illuminating exchange of letters between Lowell and the lawyer and Harvard graduate A. A. Benesch. Reminding Lowell that Jacob H. Schiff, Felix Warburg "and other eminent Jews of New York City" (including Benesch himself) had been important contributors to Harvard's endowment fund, the lawyer told Lowell:

> Students of the Jewish faith[6] neither demand nor expect any favors at the hands of the university; but they do expect, and have a right to demand, that they be admitted upon equal terms with students of other faiths and that scholarship and character be the only standards for admission.

In reply, Lowell pointed out the existence of "a rapidly growing anti-Semitic feeling in this country" and claimed that the strength of anti-Semitism among students increased as the number of Jews increased, and that therefore it was best tackled by keeping the proportion of Jews small. Benesch's riposte to this was devastating: "Carrying your suggestion to its logical conclusion would inevitably mean that a complete prohibition against Jewish students in the colleges would solve the problem of anti-Semitism."

Lowell's official response to the controversy he had unleashed was to try to present himself as someone tolerant of minorities, whose chief concern was to establish and maintain racial harmony. "We want," he insisted, "to have both Gentiles and Jews in all colleges and universities and strive to bring the two races together." Unfortunately for Lowell, a rather franker version of his views was made public in December 1922, when details of a private conversation that he had had on the matter with Victor Kramer, a Harvard alumnus, were published in the *New York Times*. The real answer to the problem, Lowell told Kramer, was for Jews to abandon their religion, recognizing that it had been superseded by Christianity. "To be an American," he insisted, "is to be nothing else." If the proportion of Jews at Harvard could be kept down to about 15 percent, Lowell reasoned, then Harvard could "absorb" them—that is, turn them into good Americans.

Throughout Oppenheimer's first academic year at Harvard, while the special committee appointed in June continued to deliberate, Lowell did his best behind the scenes to keep the numbers of Jews down

---

[6] Strikingly, in this exchange, while Benesch speaks of the Jewish "faith," Lowell speaks of the Jewish "race."

by whatever means he could. As Benesch had noted, the proportion of scholarships won by Jewish candidates was, at 50 percent, much greater than the overall proportion of Jews at college, suggesting a disproportionate degree of success when they were allowed to compete on equal terms. Though he had failed to persuade the admissions committee to impose quotas, Lowell had more luck with the dean's office, which was responsible for the allocation of scholarships, persuading it to ensure that the percentage of scholarships allotted to Jews did not exceed the total percentage of Jewish students, and thus, in effect, imposing a quota of about 20 percent.

Another measure was designed specifically to identify Jews among applicants, in order to ensure that Harvard did not unknowingly admit Jews. Starting in the autumn of 1922, all applicants were required to state their "race and color," their religion, the maiden name of their mother, the birthplace of their father and to answer the question: "What change, if any, has been made since birth in your own name or that of your father? (Explain fully.)" As a double check, the school from which the applicant was applying was also asked to indicate the applicant's "religious preference so far as known."

On April 7, 1923, the Committee on Methods of Sifting Candidates for Admissions finally delivered its report. The committee had thirteen members, three of whom were Jews, including Paul Sachs, the uncle of Oppenheimer's Ethical Culture classmate, Inez Pollak. The members had been carefully chosen, not least the Jewish members, to be as sympathetic as possible to Lowell's position. Sachs, for example, was seen as an upper-class German Jew and thus "far removed from the element" (primarily the Russian and Polish Jews) that Lowell was targeting. Despite this, the committee's final report provided little support for Lowell. Its principal recommendation was that "no departure be made from . . . the policy of equal opportunity for all regardless of race and religion."

In the short term, therefore, Lowell's plans were thwarted and the rise in the proportion of Jewish students was allowed to continue for another couple of years. By 1924 it was 25 percent and the following year 27.6 percent. In 1926, after years of persistent fighting, Lowell decided to achieve through stealth what he had failed to achieve openly. When Dean Mendell of Yale visited Harvard that year, he reported: "They are . . . going to reduce their 25 percent Hebrew total to 15 percent or less by simply rejecting without detailed explanation. They are giving no details to any candidate any longer."

The Harvard that eighteen-year-old Oppenheimer entered in the autumn of 1922, then, was a college in the midst of one of the most rancorous controversies in its history, whose president had revealed himself to be fully prepared to pander to the anti-Semitism of some parts of American society in order to pursue his vision of Harvard as an institution for the education of the "Anglo-Saxon" elite. And yet, in the letters that Oppenheimer wrote from Harvard, at least those that survive, he never once mentions, or even so much as alludes to, the controversy. Neither does he give any indication of how the anti-Semitism at college affected him personally, even though his later friend David Hawkins once remarked (presumably on the basis of conversations with Oppenheimer) that it was "not a negligible fact in Robert's background that he had been a victim of considerable anti-Semitism at Harvard and elsewhere."

In the surviving correspondence of the time,[7] there is not only no hint of this, but there are even, here and there, mildly anti-Semitic phrases used by Oppenheimer himself, such as when he addresses Herbert Smith as "Shylock" and when, in a letter to Francis Fergusson, he attributes Smith's "misanthropy" to his having to kowtow to "skinflint Jews." The only time in his letters that Oppenheimer mentions President Lowell is a passing reference in a letter to Smith to "the benign Lowell," which one might imagine must have been meant sarcastically, although the letter provides no indication whatever that this is so. It is as if Oppenheimer were determined to present himself not as a victim of Lowell's prejudices, but as a beneficiary of them.

In his letters to Herbert Smith particularly (and, in his first year at Harvard, the only letters that survive are those to Smith), Oppenheimer strove hard to create the impression that he was fitting in very well with the other students. "Harvard has so far been most delightful," he wrote soon after arriving. "It has crushed none of my romantic illusions of what it ought to have been." "I have," he insisted, "not suffered from loneliness," adding unconvincingly: "There are plenty of amusing fellows with whom to read, talk, play tennis and make expeditions into the hills and toward the water." In fact, throughout his three years at Harvard he had a remarkably small circle of friends, and the few people who knew him well during those years all report that he did not mix easily with the other students.

It is perhaps indicative of how hard it was in Harvard during the 1920s for a Jew—even a Jew as wealthy, as American and as un-Jewish as Oppenheimer—to mix with gentiles that his closest friend at the college was someone whose background was practically identical to his own. Frederick Bernheim was a German Jew from New York who had been

---

[7] It must be stressed that most of Oppenheimer's correspondence from this period has not survived. There are no letters, for example, to or from his parents, though it is certain that he wrote frequently to them throughout his three years at Harvard.

at the Ethical Culture School and had come to Harvard, like Oppenheimer, to study chemistry. In later life he was a very renowned professor
of pharmacology, nominated for the Nobel Prize for his research into
effective treatments for tuberculosis. Bernheim had not known Oppenheimer at school, as he was a year younger, but, as a result of Oppenheimer's enforced "gap year," the two were now freshmen together. As
it happened, as well as studying the same subject, they were living in the
same hall, having both been allocated rooms at Standish Hall, a freshman dormitory facing the Charles River.[8] Standish was not a Jewish
dorm, but it was notable for being one of the few freshman halls that
admitted both Catholics and Jews alongside its predominantly Protestant students.

Both Oppenheimer and Bernheim had arrived at Harvard determined not to allow their ethnic background to restrict their social mobil-
ity. "I wanted not to be involved in a sort of Jewish enclave," Bernheim
later said; "at that time there was a good deal of anti-Semitism, and . . .
[I wanted to] be able to go around with the non-Jewish students, which
I proceeded to do for the first year." Oppenheimer had exactly the same
attitude. Nevertheless the two were thrown together, not just for their
freshman year, but for the whole of their time at Harvard, living in
their second and third years as roommates in a shared house on Mount
Auburn Street.

Largely because of their relative isolation from other students, the
friendship between Bernheim and Oppenheimer became intense—from
Bernheim's point of view, rather *too* intense. Oppenheimer was, Bernheim recalls, "a little bit possessive." Oppenheimer resented it if Bernheim went out with a girl, and would object if Bernheim invited someone
to dinner too often. As Bernheim put it, Oppenheimer had "a sort of
feeling that we should make a unit."

That Oppenheimer had so few friends at college was not entirely
due to the anti-Semitic climate of 1920s Harvard. It was also, to some
extent at least, a matter of his own choosing. He was presented with at
least one golden opportunity to enlarge his circle of friends, but chose
not to take it. Soon after he arrived at Harvard, another ex-student from
the Ethical Culture School, Algernon Black, tried to help him make
friends. Black, who was a couple of years older than Oppenheimer and in
his final year at Harvard, was from a relatively poor, originally Russian,
New York Jewish family. In later life he was to find fame as a broadcaster,
a social reformer and a spokesman for the Ethical Culture Society. At
Harvard he was a leading member of the Liberal Club, one of the few

---

[8] In 1931, Standish and its neighbor Gore Hall combined to form Winthrop House.

student clubs (apart from those that were specifically for them) open to Jewish students. One day, noticing Oppenheimer eating on his own in the club dining room, Black introduced him to John Edsall, a third-year chemistry student who was also an enthusiastic and prominent member of the Liberal Club. An established Bostonian, a gentile and the son of the Harvard Dean of Medicine, Edsall was potentially an invaluable link between Oppenheimer and mainstream Harvard society. He was, moreover, greatly impressed by Oppenheimer's obvious intellectual gifts.

At the time that he and Oppenheimer were introduced by Black, Edsall had just been chosen by the Liberal Club to be the editor of its new journal, which did not yet have a name. It is an indication of the impact Oppenheimer made on Edsall that the title he chose was one suggested to him by Oppenheimer: *The Gad-Fly*. This was an allusion to Socrates's description of himself in Plato's *Apology* as a gadfly whose role in society was "to sting people, and whip them into a fury, all in the service of truth." Eagerly embracing this image, Edsall, in his editorial for the first issue, published in December 1922, announced: "Among the collegiate herd of sacred cows and their worshippers now buzzes the Gad-Fly."

Oppenheimer was persuaded by Edsall to serve as assistant editor and to write for the journal for the first issue and for the second, which came out in March 1923. In truth, however, Oppenheimer had no appetite for this, or, it seems, for any other role in Harvard student politics, and after that left the Liberal Club and wrote no more for its journal. His decision to leave the club at that particular time confirms the impression that he was determined to have nothing at all to do with the controversy at Harvard over the issue of Jewish students. For it was precisely at that time, with Lowell's Committee on Methods of Sifting Candidates for Admissions about to submit its report, that the issue was coming to a head and that the Liberal Club got involved in it, taking a public stand against discriminatory admissions policies. Even while he was a member, Oppenheimer's attitude to the Liberal Club was one of lofty alienation. "I don't know what that was all about," he later said of his brief participation in it. "I felt like a fish out of water." In only his second letter to Smith from Harvard, written in November 1922, he seemed determined to distance himself from the club, referring disparagingly to its "asinine pomposity."

Whether he was aware of it or not (and it is hard to see how he could not be aware of it), Oppenheimer, by quitting the Liberal Club, was cutting off his most promising means of making new friends. He had, as far as one can tell, little more to do with Algernon Black and, it would appear, not much to do with Edsall either, until the two of them renewed their friendship at Cambridge, in England, in 1925. This left him with the "unit" that he had formed with Fred Bernheim. The only other person Oppenheimer would allow to join this "unit"—and, apart from Bernheim, the only close friend Oppenheimer had at Harvard—was another chemistry student, William Clouser Boyd. Boyd was a gentile from Missouri. He has recalled how he and Oppenheimer were classmates in Chemistry 3, which was a course in qualitative analysis.[9] Recognizing Boyd as the most advanced student in the class, Oppenheimer used to show him his work to check that it was right, much to the irritation of some of the other classmates. "Who is this guy Oppenheimer who keeps coming to you?" Boyd remembers one of them saying. "I think he's a pest." "I didn't think he was a pest," Boyd insisted; it was obvious to him that Oppenheimer was "a very talented person, very able and very sensitive, and we had lots of interests in common aside from science. We both tried to write and we wrote poetry, sometimes in French, and we wrote stories in imitation of Chekhov." Here, Boyd and Bernheim differed. While Oppenheimer's literary interests were part of what drew him and Boyd together, they threatened to drive him and Bernheim apart—Bernheim remarking that he found Oppenheimer "a little bit precious in the way he quoted French poetry, Verlaine, Baudelaire and so on. And I tended to resent it."

To Boyd's surprise, the one art Oppenheimer had very little interest in, or understanding of, was music. "I was very fond of music," he remembers, "but once a year he would go to an opera, with me and Bernheim usually, and he'd leave after the first act. He just couldn't take any more. Totally amusical, I thought then." It was a trait that others have commented on as well. Herbert Smith, for example, once said to Oppenheimer: "You're the only physicist I've ever known who wasn't also musical, and I never heard you refer to music."

Like Bernheim, Boyd in later life became an eminent scientist; in his case a professor of immunology at Boston. In the 1950s he was famous for his work on the genetics of race, and, under the name Boyd Ellanby, also for his science-fiction writing, two of his best-known stories being "Category Phoenix" and "Chain Reaction." In a popular science book he wrote with Isaac Asimov called *Races and People*, Boyd used his research to undermine ideas about "races" that were then prevalent, including the very ideas that had had such a baleful influence on Oppenheimer's time at Harvard. There is, Boyd and Asimov argued, no such thing as the

---

[9] "Qualitative analysis" in chemistry contrasts with "quantitative analysis"; whereas the former is concerned with the identification of chemical compounds in a given sample, the latter is concerned with measuring the amount of each compound in the sample.

"Anglo-Saxon" race, nor, they insisted, is "Jew" a racial category. Wide-spread adoption of these views in the 1920s would have utterly trans-formed Oppenheimer's life.

Boyd, Bernheim and Oppenheimer were, Boyd has said, "the clos-est friends any of us had." The three of them formed a "troika" that was a kind of counterpart to the troika that Oppenheimer had formed in the summer of 1922 with Paul Horgan and Francis Fergusson. Between the two "troikas" there was remarkably little contact. With regard to Horgan, this is hardly surprising. During Oppenheimer's first year at Harvard, Horgan was still in New Mexico, completing his final year as a "cadet" at the Military Institute in Roswell. Then, in Oppenheimer's remaining two years, Horgan was in Rochester. The two kept in touch with each other by letter, and, in the summer of 1923, Horgan spent some time at the Oppenheimer family summer house on Long Island, where he evidently met Bernheim. In his later letters to Horgan, Oppen-heimer occasionally mentions Boyd and Bernheim, but there was never any real opportunity for Horgan to get to know Oppenheimer's Harvard friends very well.

On the other hand, as a fellow student at Harvard, Fergusson could very easily have become acquainted with Bernheim and Boyd. Fergusson, of course, had already been at Harvard for a year when Oppenheimer arrived, and during Oppenheimer's freshman year was a sophomore majoring in biology and living in private accommodation on Prescott Street, a short walk from Standish Hall. Oppenheimer saw a good deal of Fergusson at Harvard, and yet Bernheim, when asked years later, was doubtful that he ever met Fergusson. Even more strangely, after Fergusson left, Oppenheimer's letters to him from Harvard never once mention Bernheim.[10] They mention Boyd occasionally, though not very often, and at least once in a tone that reveals Fergusson took a rather condescending attitude toward him, an attitude with which Oppen-heimer seems willing to acquiesce ("Boyd, as you charitably predicted, has improved," he wrote to Fergusson during the Christmas vacation of his second year). Still, between Bernheim and Fergusson there seems to have been absolutely no contact whatever.

One might have thought that Oppenheimer's insistence on compart-mentalizing his friends was based on a desire to separate them into liter-ary and scientific groups, with no contact between the two, and that this is why Fergusson, while at Harvard, had little to do with Boyd and nothing at all to do with Bernheim. The problem with this is that Oppenheimer's

---

[10] After Oppenheimer moved to Cambridge, England, in 1925, his letters to Fergusson, then at Oxford, *do* mention Bernheim, referring to him as "Fred."

friends do not lend themselves to such rigid compartmentalization. One might, roughly speaking, regard Bernheim, Boyd and Oppenheimer as a scientific group and Fergusson, Horgan and Oppenheimer as a literary one, and it is true that Bernheim had little interest in literature and Horgan no interest in science. But Fergusson and Boyd *combined* literary and scientific interests, and in both cases that intellectual breadth was one of the most important things that drew them to Oppenheimer, and him to them. For Oppenheimer, and for at least two of his closest friends, it was crucial that science and literature were *not* kept in strictly separate compartments.

It is more likely, I think, that Oppenheimer kept Boyd and (especially) Bernheim away from Fergusson simply because he did not think they were good enough for Fergusson. Oppenheimer liked and respected Bernheim and Boyd, but he did not *venerate* them as he did Fergusson. From the available correspondence and the reminiscences of the people involved, one gets a strong sense of a "pecking order" among Oppenheimer's friends, with Bernheim and Boyd looking up to Oppenheimer, while Oppenheimer in turn looked up to Fergusson and (to a slightly lesser extent) to Horgan. Fergusson, one feels, was not accustomed to looking up at people, preferring to look down on them. He could even, on occasion, sound condescending toward Oppenheimer himself, well aware of being an ideal to which Oppenheimer aspired. Soon after Oppenheimer arrived at Harvard, Fergusson wrote to Smith, saying that he had "seen something of Robert lately" and reporting: "his conversation this year is a caricature of yours, ornamented with some of Paul's and my more elaborate affectations."

In the same letter Fergusson told Smith about a club he had set up, which was, apart from the Liberal Club, the only club at Harvard that Oppenheimer joined. Its purpose was to discuss science and the philosophy of science at a deeper level than was possible in undergraduate courses. Oppenheimer later referred to it as "a little science club which was partly faculty but mostly graduate." As Fergusson described it to Smith, the motivation in setting the club up was to "get professors to say interesting things": "We meet Mondays in one of the members' rooms—a big room, with a fireplace and deep chairs. We invite a professor to come and address us on anything he wants. When he has finished we discuss. Such at least is the plan." Among its members, Fergusson told Smith, were "an aberrant Cambridge Puritan, a boy from Atlanta, a New York German, learned in chemistry, a Minnesota exquisite, a Greek assistant in philosophy, a mathematics genius, and many other diverse and highly flavored fishes." Despite being both scientists and friends of Oppenheimer, Bernheim and Boyd were not, it seems, invited to join this club (the "New York German, learned in chemistry" could not have been Bernheim, for surely then he would have remembered meeting Fergusson). Indeed, it seems very likely that Oppenheimer was the only freshman invited to join what was clearly intended to be a club primarily for graduate students and staff members.

The diversity of academic disciplines from which the club's members were drawn—philosophy, mathematics and chemistry, as well as, no doubt, others not mentioned by Fergusson—reflects what was for Oppenheimer one of the best things about his time at Harvard. Lowell's emphasis on equipping his students with a broad education rather than encouraging them, or even allowing them, to become narrow specialists may have been inspired by a snobbish reverence for Oxford and Cambridge, but it produced a kind of higher education that was ideally suited to Oppenheimer's abilities and tastes. For many science students at Harvard, the requirement to take freshman courses in humanities was regarded as an unwelcome distraction from "real work," a barrier that had to be overcome as quickly and painlessly as possible. For Oppenheimer, on the other hand, it was an opportunity that he eagerly embraced. In his first year, in addition to two courses in chemistry (one on elementary organic chemistry and the other on qualitative analysis), he took two courses in mathematics (analytic geometry and an introduction to calculus), and three courses in the humanities: one on rhetoric and English composition, one on French prose and poetry and another on the history of philosophy. This last course, taught by the notable Harvard philosopher Ralph Eaton, was remembered by Oppenheimer with particular fondness in later life. Eaton, he said, was "a wonderful man" and the course was "really very good . . . [I] had a nice time with it."

In a letter to Smith, Oppenheimer speaks with satisfaction and pride of the "quiet futility of most of the courses" that he was taking at Harvard, which, he says, are "as amusing as *Crome Yellow* and are at least as delightful in a somewhat Pecosian way." The joint allusion here to the worlds of Ottoline Morrell's Garsington (as satirized by Aldous Huxley) and Katherine Page's Pecos perhaps reveals what Oppenheimer really wanted from Harvard: membership of a cultural, literary and intellectual elite. And perhaps in this there is a further clue as to why he kept Bernheim and Fergusson apart. In his ignorance of, and disdain for, literary culture, in his concentration on chemistry and his readiness to become exactly the kind of narrow specialist looked down upon at Lowell's Harvard (and perhaps also in his German Jewish New York background), Bernheim personified the kind of person who would *not* become—or even aspire to become—a member of the elites, whether based in Oxford, Pecos or Harvard.

Fergusson, however, was already a member of two of those elites (Pecos and Harvard) and was about to become a member of the third. When Oppenheimer arrived at Harvard, he discovered that Fergusson did not expect to stay there very long. He had applied for, and (as it turned out, rightly) expected to receive, a Rhodes Scholarship to go to Oxford, which he planned to use to study not biology, but English literature. Fergusson, in fact, had decided that the milieu of *Crome Yellow* was precisely where he belonged. When, the previous year, during Oppenheimer's enforced convalescence, Fergusson began his studies at Harvard, he had been somewhat disenchanted. Writing to Smith, he said that Harvard "is not an educational institution":

> Instead of five thousand keen, intellectually alive, well-read young men who have come here to think out ideas and to learn the ideas of others, I find five thousand tawdry yokels, yanked from fat farms and snoring small towns, to bellow at ball games.

Fergusson had, it seems, been teased by his fellow students for choosing to visit an art museum rather than watching the annual football game between Harvard and Yale, which made him feel that there was something of a gulf between his sensibilities and those of the typical Harvard student. "I did not come here to be made a 100 percent American; I am not going to be a 'bizzness' man," he told Smith. "I came here to acquire an education, and I hope to be a person of intelligence some day." Unlike Oppenheimer, Fergusson could make these kinds of criticisms, secure in the knowledge that he *was* regarded by the Harvard community as "100 percent American." In fact, in many ways he was the very embodiment of Lowell's ideal student: he was "Anglo-Saxon," a Protestant, an academic all-rounder and a member of America's ruling class. And, despite his preference for art over football, he must have had at least some athletic or sporting prowess, for otherwise he would not have been even a candidate for a Rhodes Scholarship.[11]

Established in 1902 under the terms of the will of the British imperialist Cecil Rhodes, these scholarships were expressly designed to create an Anglo-Saxon elite to govern the world. "I contend," Rhodes once said, "that we are the finest race in the world and that the more of the world we inhabit the better it is for the human race," and it was

---

[11] In connection with Fergusson's disdain for the ritual of the annual Harvard-Yale football match and his (justifiably) confident expectation of a Rhodes Scholarship, it is interesting to compare him with Oppenheimer's freshman friends: Bernheim, who was so keen to get tickets for the match that he applied *twice*, and Boyd, who applied for a Rhodes Scholarship, but was rejected.

in pursuit of such a vision that he founded the scholarships that bear his name. The recipients of these scholarships, drawn from the British Empire, Germany and America, would spend two years at Oxford, after which, it was hoped, they would return to their part of the world, able and motivated to maintain and increase the global dominance of Anglo-Saxon civilization and culture. The selection criteria for these scholarships were widely admired by the presidents of America's Ivy League universities, especially Lowell, who saw in them a model for Harvard to adopt in its admissions procedures. Rhodes had said that he did not want mere "bookworms" to benefit from his scholarship; rather, he was looking for competent scholars who demonstrated "fondness of and success in mainly outdoor sports" and who also possessed "brutality," "moral force of character and of instincts to lead" and "manhood, truth, courage [and] devotion to duty." Rhodes even came up with a formula that gave weights to these considerations: 40 percent scholarship, 20 percent athletics, 20 percent leadership and 20 percent "manhood . . ." To be awarded a Rhodes Scholarship was a mark of academic distinction, but it was not only, or even primarily, that. It was primarily an indication that one was accepted as the sort of person Rhodes thought should rule the world and (therefore) the sort of person Lowell thought Harvard ought to be producing.

Thus, while Oppenheimer at Harvard was reminded at every turn that, no matter what he did, he would never gain admittance to the highest strata of American society, Fergusson, in gaining a Rhodes Scholarship, was confirmed as being exactly the sort of person that particular elite wanted as a member. Though Oppenheimer was to move to England to pursue postgraduate studies, it never occurred to him to apply for a Rhodes Scholarship. Fergusson not only got the Rhodes Scholarship, but he got it to study literature, thus establishing himself in yet another way as a model to which Oppenheimer aspired, but could never reach. Though he had gone to Harvard to study chemistry, what dominates the letters Oppenheimer wrote during his first year and a half at Harvard is his determination to be seen—by Smith, Fergusson and Horgan—as a *literary* man. Again and again in his letters to those three, Oppenheimer mentions stories that he is writing and seeks from them critical reactions to drafts that he has sent them.

For example, in January 1923, he tells Smith: "I am again in the toils of a short story. It is not to be as pretentious or subtle as the last, and so there is some chance of its not being as vile." As summarized by Oppenheimer for Smith, the plot of the story is as follows: a young mining engineer (Oppenheimer, at this time, thought he himself would become a mining engineer after graduating from Harvard), a sophisticated and introspective person, starts his career full of contempt for the miners he encounters, whose filth, poverty and baseness make him laugh. Soon, however, he is brought to realize his own vulnerabilities and to understand that he himself is likely to disintegrate, thus collapsing the gap between himself and the miners. Upon this realization, his complacency vanishes and the story ends with the engineer listening, with respect and even reverence, to a person Oppenheimer describes as "a disgusting and doddering syphilitic, with whom, earlier in the day, he would have nothing to do."

A week or so later, Oppenheimer wrote to Smith with news of another effort: "I shall send you my story, which, at present, is complete but illegible . . . it is taken with scarcely any colitic revisions from an incident of my cousin with my uncle and my aunt." In March, he told Smith that on an expedition to Cape Ann (a rocky peninsula on the northernmost tip of Massachusetts Bay, about thirty miles north of Boston), he had "received another inspiration to write a story," which he described as "very short, exceedingly bad, and only barely justified by the difficulty of the thing." Two months later, he sent Smith some more stories: "Here are the masterpieces . . . Please don't read *Conquest* until the last; I am certain you will dislike it." He assured Smith that Fergusson had liked three of the stories and begged him not to say that *Conquest* was "sentimental drivel," for then: "I shall seek death."

None of these stories survives in any form. Oppenheimer was thorough—and thoroughly effective—in his determination to deny posterity the chance to judge his merits as a novelist and short-story writer. The reason for this is no doubt that he became convinced he had no particular talent in these areas. In his letters during his first year at Harvard, one can see his faith in himself as a writer draining away in the face of the criticisms that his work received from his correspondents. Smith seems to have been comparatively encouraging, while tempering his enthusiasm with what he no doubt thought was gentle and constructive criticism. The criticisms that survive in Oppenheimer's side of the correspondence are that the writing suffered from being an "imitation of Katherine Mansfield" and from an "artificiality of emotional situation." Oppenheimer seemed initially undaunted by these criticisms, defending himself against the first by claiming that his imitation was not "conscious" and against the second by remarking: "I should not have the hardihood to write a story that was not based upon a very real emotional experience."

In the face of Fergusson's criticisms, however, Oppenheimer's short-lived faith in his literary gifts collapsed altogether. One can see this collapse take place in a long letter Oppenheimer wrote to Fergusson during the Christmas vacation of 1923, which he was spending at Bay Shore, while Fergusson was in Oxford, having just finished his first term as a Rhodes scholar. The main purpose of the letter was ostensibly to respond to the opening chapters of a novel that Fergusson was working on, a copy of which he had sent to Oppenheimer. To Smith, Oppenheimer had commented pithily on these chapters, comparing them to the work of Fergusson's by now famous brother, Harvey. He had, he remarked, "nothing but admiration for the Harveyesque slickness and totally unHarveyesque perspicacity" of the opening of the novel. He was, however, "dismayed and rendered hysterical by the notes for its continuation."

To Fergusson himself, Oppenheimer was a good deal less pithy. "I am overwhelmed," he told him, "at the ease and directness and literary slickness of the thing":

> Your style is as simple and unstilted as your brother's, but it is supple enough to keep it from seeming grotesque when you want to say something unusually neat, or when you are concerned with a little modest lyricism.

What he singled out for praise was Fergusson's "skill with people," with the notable exception of the central character of the story, who, Oppenheimer assumed, was based on Fergusson himself. "I find it hard to swallow," Oppenheimer told Fergusson, "in the same person, such naiveté and such sophistication." This led Oppenheimer into a revealing comparison between himself and Fergusson, both as people and as writers:

> I suppose it is never quite possible for us to understand each other's layers of naiveté. And it is that which keeps [me] from agreeing entirely with what you say about the junk I sent you. I think all the snarkiest things you say—and, by the way, thank you for troubling—are perfectly true. Even to me it is obvious that my women are gargoyles and my lyricism either absent or buried. But what I can't understand, for instance, is that you should think the *Rain* thing sophisticated, or the hero, in *Litany*, unnatural . . . What I meant, you see, was that the hero was prevented, being not very intelligent in the first place, from detecting his trouble, or doing anything but maunder about it, by his utterly frivolous and vain and complacent preconceptions which he had so diligently constructed in times of other stress. It may be perfectly true that no rational man would act that way, and that, to you, a knowledge of thermodynamics and a

dilettante dawdling in literature implies a divine intelligence in all things. That's not so. Always you used to insist that a person was either intelligent or not, and—perhaps I misunderstood—not that he might be intelligent here or there, and blind as a fool in everything else.

Having by now left the evaluation of Fergusson's novel far behind, Oppenheimer is compelled to explain why he persists in his "dilettante dawdling in literature" even though, by his own judgment, what he produces is "junk":

> I find these awful people in me from time to time, and their expulsion is the sole excuse for my writing. I have none of that mere glee in narration, the conteur's delight, which you and Chekhov and your brother seem to have. I write to get rid of an ideal and impossible system, and it is, as you so cleverly remark, not writing at all; and it is that which makes the things of so exclusively masturbatic character. I am sorry to have bored you.

It was the last time Oppenheimer wrote to Fergusson for eighteen months and the very last time he mentioned his own attempts at writing fiction in correspondence with anyone. At the age of nineteen, he seems, after spending much of the preceding year and a half making a sustained attempt to prove otherwise to himself and to his friends, to have decided that, whatever he was or might become, he was *not*, and could never be, a writer. That particular "charade" was over.

The truth of Isidor Rabi's observation that Oppenheimer "lived a charade" is especially evident in his letters from Harvard, in which he seems to be trying on personalities, attitudes and manners of speech, much in the way that adolescents characteristically experiment with different signatures. The physicist Jeremy Bernstein, who knew Oppenheimer well toward the end of his life, has said of one of these letters (a typical example) that "the whole tone makes one's flesh creep." And one can see what he means: the letters are written in a horribly self-consciously "literary" style and are often painfully artificial. The tone is that of a young man trying desperately to be someone that he is not. That "someone" might be identified as Francis Fergusson, or the kind of person that Fergusson represented, the type prized at Lowell's Harvard. Oppenheimer's father had acquired the voice and the manners of this type, and Oppenheimer himself had developed some of the literary, intellectual and cultural interests characteristic of its members, but, despite this, Oppenheimer—as his experiences at Harvard would have made clear to him—would never have been accepted as, or mistaken for, this type of student.

Another thing Oppenheimer was not—and Fergusson would again be a constant reminder of this—is the rather different but related type of person that one finds exalted in the literature of the Southwest, the literature that formed the cultural backdrop to the "troika" into which Oppenheimer had been accepted in the summer of 1922. In the novels and essays of Paul Horgan, Erna and Harvey Fergusson and the writers they emulated and admired, one finds a kind of ideology, at the center of which is a particular type of man. One might define this man positively in terms of his courage, his honesty, his horsemanship, his preference for the country over the city, his indifference to making money, and so on, but one might equally define him negatively as *not* a New York Jewish businessman. Horgan and the Fergussons were too liberal, too sophisticated and too "civilized" to be openly and publicly anti-Semitic, but the novelist Willa Cather, whom both Horgan and Harvey Fergusson admired deeply, had no such inhibitions in spelling out the kind of person who might embody the *opposite* of their collective ideal.

In Cather's 1919 short story, "Scandal," the villain was given a name and a history that would have struck a deep and uncomfortable chord with Oppenheimer: he is a rich, Jewish garment manufacturer named Sigmund Stein (the name and occupation are so close to those of Oppenheimer's uncle Sigmund that one can't help wondering if Cather had him in mind), who arrives penniless in the United States, but gets a job at "Rosenthal's garment factory" (again, the surname seems designed to echo the "Rothfeld" of Oppenheimer's uncles) and works his way up the firm. At this point, "Stein" becomes less like Sigmund Rothfeld, but still more uncomfortably like Julius Oppenheimer:

> While he was still at the machine, a hideous, underfed little whipper-snapper, he was already a youth of many-colored ambitions, deeply concerned about his dress, his associates, his recreations. He haunted the old Astor Library and the Metropolitan Museum, learned something about pictures and porcelains, took singing lessons, though he had a voice like a crow's. When he sat down to his baked apple and doughnut in a basement lunch-room, he would prop a book up before him and address his food with as much leisure and ceremony as if he were dining at his club. He held himself at a distance from his fellow-workmen and somehow always managed to impress them with his superiority.

In his endeavor to be accepted into the best society, Stein acquires a fine art collection, learns Spanish and cultivates the company of poets and writers: "His business associates thought him a man of taste and culture, a patron of the arts, a credit to the garment trade." Determined to present an impressive figure in New York society, Stein appears in public arm-in-arm with a famous concert singer called Connie Ayrshire. Or so New York society is led to believe. In fact the woman is an employee of Stein's, a factory girl called Ruby, chosen for her physical similarity to Connie Ayrshire and dressed in clothes identical to those habitually worn by the singer. When Stein marries an heiress from California, the married couple move into a grand house on Fifth Avenue "that used to belong to people of a very different sort," and Stein has no further use for Ruby, whom he abandons to her fate as an impoverished drunk. The final irony is that the real Connie Ayrshire is hired to perform at the Steins' housewarming party, prompting her, at the end of the story, to liken her fate to that of Ruby: "She and I are in the same boat. We are both the victims of circumstance, and in New York so many of the circumstances are Steins."

In her portrayal of Sigmund Stein, Cather has provided an instructive example of the kind of anti-Semitism that formed a backdrop to Oppenheimer's years at Harvard, if not to his entire life. It is an example that is especially unsettling, not only in the strikingly exact parallels between Stein and the Rothfeld/Oppenheimers, but also in the close associations between Cather and the group of writers Oppenheimer had befriended. Paul Horgan had an especially deep admiration for Cather. He had been taught at school by Cather's sister, and had met Cather herself briefly in Santa Fe, when she was researching her novel about the city's famous Archbishop Lamy, *Death Comes for the Archbishop*. Horgan himself was to write a huge biography of Lamy and an essay about Cather called "Willa Cather's Incalculable Distance," in which he celebrated her as "a true artist of prose."

Oppenheimer was evidently influenced by his friends' admiration of Willa Cather, at least to the extent of reading her 1923 novel, *A Lost Lady*, almost as soon as it came out. Whether he shared Horgan's high opinion of Cather's prose, Oppenheimer never said. What seems to have struck him most forcibly was that the world described by her was the world into which he had been accepted in the summer of 1922. "Doesn't A Lost Lady remind you," he wrote to Smith in November 1923, "vaguely and sentimentally, of Mrs. Page?"

At the heart of *A Lost Lady* is an elegiac sense of loss for the Old West, represented by its heroine, Marian Forrester, a woman whose enormous charm seems tied to a society that is passing away—that is, the society the virtues of which are extolled in the works of Harvey Fergusson and Paul Horgan: the pioneering Southwest. In the words of one commentator, Mrs. Forrester "represents civilization in the West, for all the amenities of gracious living which can make life the agreeable and charming thing which at best it can be." Her husband is a railroad-builder who "embodies all the virtues which Willa Cather has led us to expect in a pioneer: the imagination to see, the strength to achieve, and an absolutely incorruptible moral integrity." Like Franz Huning, as portrayed by the Fergussons, Mr. Forrester, though he has made a good deal of money, is represented not as a businessman, but as a "natural aristocrat," a type Cather explicitly contrasts with bankers and businessmen. In *A Lost Lady* the story of Marian Forrester is told largely through the eyes of a young man called Niel Herbert, who, as a teenager, develops an infatuation for her, which over the years is threatened by the changes in her brought about by the death of her husband and the collapse of the values she represents and the culture to which she belongs. What Cather portrays as destroying and then replacing that culture is the world of commerce and moneymaking, the world she had previously personified in the figure of Sigmund Stein, but which here is represented by a young lawyer named Ivy Peters. When, late in the story, Niel Herbert returns to his hometown to discover that, as the Forresters have declined, Ivy Peters has flourished, he reflects:

> The Old West had been settled by dreamers, great-hearted adventurers, who were unpractical to the point of magnificence; a courteous brotherhood, strong in attack but weak in defense, who could conquer but could not hold. Now all the vast territory they had won was to be at the mercy of men like Ivy Peters, who had never dared anything, never risked anything. They would drink up the mirage, dispel the morning freshness, root out the great brooding spirit of the space, the color, the princely carelessness of the pioneer.

What Marian Forrester was to Niel Herbert, Katherine Chaves Page was to Oppenheimer: the embodiment of a noble ideal, the representative of a way of life that was superior to, but threatened by, the culture within which Oppenheimer himself had grown up.

As it happened, during Oppenheimer's first year at Harvard, Mrs. Page was living in New York City, having accepted a one-year position teaching Spanish at Finch Junior College. When he returned home for a few days in February 1923, Oppenheimer invited her, along with Herbert Smith and Jane Didisheim, to dinner on Riverside Drive with his parents. It was an uncomfortable evening. The contrast, as Oppenheimer felt it, between the "princely" romance of the Old West, represented by Katherine, and the world of commerce, represented by his father and his Ethical Culture circle, was almost unbearable for him. After the dinner he wrote to Smith reassuring him that he, at least, had "scintillated more than any of that dismal gathering," adding: "Mrs. Page started bravely enough, but soon grew silent under the weight of paternal banalities and Ethical gossip and Jane's sighs of happiness came disastrously near, I thought, to groans of despair, when someone asked her if she had ever been out west."

That evening was to be the last time Oppenheimer saw Katherine until he returned to New Mexico in the summer of 1925. In the meantime, whenever Smith, Fergusson or Horgan mentioned the Southwest, Oppenheimer responded with effusive yearning for both the society of the Chaveses and the landscape of New Mexico. In January 1923, shortly before Katherine came to Riverside Drive for dinner, he wrote to Smith: "Are you again, O fortunate wretch, to spend a summer in New Mexico?" When he heard from Fergusson that Smith was indeed planning to visit New Mexico that summer, and that Fergusson was planning to take him and his two companions to Hopi country, he declared himself to be "insanely jealous":

> I see you riding down from the mountains to the desert at that hour when thunderstorms and sunsets caparison the sky; I see you in the Pecos "in September, when I'll want my friends to comfort me, you know," spending the moonlight on Grass Mountain; I see you vending the marvels of the upper Loch, of the upper amphitheater at Ouray, of the waterfall at Telluride, the Punch Bowl at San Ysidro—even the prairies round Antonito—to philistine eyes. Do you remember that first evening in Denver when we scrambled our luggage?

And when, in the summer of 1923, Fergusson was back in New Mexico, prior to leaving for Oxford, Oppenheimer wrote:

> But oh, beloved, how I envy you! Three hours sleep: witty, charming; the soul and supporter of Los Pinos; the all but gastronomic consoler to the Pecos' host—successful; doing a little intellectual work on the side; blessed with enormous activity—Mon Dieu—Francis, you choke me with anguish and despair.

And he ended: "Please, I almost whimper it, please write again."

After the following summer, when Smith had again been in New

Mexico, Oppenheimer told him that he wanted to "hear about your adventures":

> . . . and Los Pinos, and the desert, and Mrs. Page, about all those things that gripe and make me notice how blue and sunny the sky is and what an exquisite filigree the chrome and coral leaves make, against it. And if, personatim, you should be able to come up for a day or two, and would, out of that, grant me an hour at tea, I should be so happy that I should smile slobber on your photographs, and talk about Grass Mountain and Ouray.

In the same letter Oppenheimer mentioned "the classic confectionery bearing the Chaves coat of arms." This was a reference to a magnificent cake that Oppenheimer had sent to New Mexico for the seventieth birthday of Katherine's father, Don Amado Chaves, having specially ordered it, at great expense, from a bakery in Manhattan. Smith, who went with him to the bakery to order it, remarked many years later that the gesture was characteristic of Oppenheimer's thoughtfulness and an expression of how pleased he was to be accepted by the Chaves circle. But, however much he may have wished or aspired to have been from a non-Jewish, Southwestern family, preferably with ancestors that could be traced back to the conquistadores, or at least to the pioneers, the reality was that when the vacations came, Oppenheimer returned, not to Pecos, but to the Upper West Side of Manhattan, and not to a family whose history in the United States spanned many generations, but to a nouveau-riche family who only a generation earlier had been (in Oppenheimer's eyes) German "peasants."

In that summer of 1923, Oppenheimer took a holiday job in a laboratory in New Jersey, in the hope, so he told Francis Fergusson in July, of finding an adventure "similarly satisfying" to that he had experienced in New Mexico. Thus he had "searched the plant and the hotel for possible persons"—that is, people who would interest him in something like the way Fergusson, Horgan and Page had interested him. But, he reported:

> Only one wretch have I found, and he penniless and dissipated; but he is six foot seven, has fine black moustachios, is a Bostonian via Oxford, is properly pessimistic and boasts cleverly about the right sort of thing, has read, and well, writes, and is a bit of a scientist. He works at a different plant and lives in a different city, but has come over for an evening a couple of times. But he has lost his job, and is going to South America. He is not a Jew.

Once this non-Jewish, educated Bostonian left, there was nothing keeping Oppenheimer at the laboratory. "The job and people are bourgeois," he told Fergusson, "and lazy and dead; there is little work and nothing to puzzle at; and the establishment has among it less than one sixteenth of a sense of humour. So I am going home."

By the time he wrote to Fergusson again, in the middle of August, Oppenheimer was in Bay Shore, where, he was delighted to report, "Paul [Horgan] has been with me for the past three weeks. Of course I have been happy." The two of them, he wrote, had been "spending a most civilized and unexciting time down here, writing, reading enormously, traveling to town from time to time for books and exhibits and plays, and sallying every evening in tuxedoes, pathetically to ransack Bayshore or Islip for a vestige of adventure." Horgan has recorded that he found the Oppenheimers' house in Bay Shore comfortable, spacious and impressive: "It was my first taste as a resident of rather excessive luxury and grandeur and comfort on that scale. I enjoyed it enormously." He recalls that some days they would go on *Trimethy*, some days they would go riding and other days they would go to the theater in New York.

Horgan had by this time graduated from the Military Institute in New Mexico and, after the summer, was starting his course at the Eastman School of Music in Rochester, in upstate New York. The Oppenheimers had planned to travel to Quebec for the last part of the summer and so agreed to give Paul a lift to Buffalo on the way—Buffalo being not far from Rochester. As Oppenheimer recounted the journey to Fergusson, it was the occasion for the tension between the Old West, as represented by Horgan, and the new money, as represented by his parents, to come to the fore once again:

And toward the end there developed such an intricate panorama of complications that I was regaled with a daily scene. Toward the end, you see, mother and father grew a little jealous of Paul, and a little irritated at the ease with which he disregarded obstacles whose conquests formed the central jewels in the Oppenheimer crown. The matter was further embellished by two luscious complexes, oozing ichor: mother's and father's, which tried to apologize for being Jews; the Horgan's, which whinnied and shied clumsily about richesse and poverty.

Horgan himself was unaware of this "panorama of complications" and remembers only that Oppenheimer's parents were charming and welcoming. About his own "complex" over money, and Mr. and Mrs. Oppenheimer's complex about being Jewish, he remembers nothing.

During the weeks that Oppenheimer spent in Bay Shore that summer he had for company not only Paul Horgan, but also Bernheim and Boyd, both of whom were invited, but probably not at the same time as each other. Boyd was impressed with the elegance of the house and with Oppenheimer's sailing skills; Bernheim, on the other hand, had doubts about Oppenheimer's seamanship and considered the holiday home "just an ordinary kind of house."

What everyone who spent time with Oppenheimer remembers about that summer was that he seemed always, whatever else he was doing, to be reading physics. Paul Horgan recalls:

> ... we would go out on the boat—he was a very good sailor, good navigator—and anchor out in the shallow part of Great South Bay, off Bay Shore, and I would be up on the forward deck, working at a typewriter, writing desperately bad imitations of Chekhov and other short story writers, and Robert would be in the cockpit, sprawled over a book on thermodynamics and chuckling with great connoisseurship over it. It always impressed me very much.

It seems likely that the book Horgan saw Oppenheimer reading while sailing was not "a book on thermodynamics," but rather *The Mathematical Theory of Electricity and Magnetism* by James Jeans. Toward the end of his life Oppenheimer still had the book and mentioned in an interview how "salt-encrusted" his copy of it was, remarking: "it's clear that I studied that when I went sailing in the summer." The importance the book had for him is alluded to in his letter to Fergusson of August 16, written from Bay Shore. Responding to the news that Fergusson had written stories set in both Harvard and Pecos, Oppenheimer writes: "But really, maestro, I am terribly—yes, terribly, eager to see your things, and would even burn my new Jean's Electromagnetics for a glimpse of the Pecos one."

First published in 1908, *The Mathematical Theory of Electricity and Magnetism* was, the author states in the preface, intended to cover the same ground as James Clerk Maxwell's classic 1873 text, *A Treatise on Electricity and Magnetism*, but in a "more elementary" way: "The present book is written more especially for the student, and for the physicist of limited mathematical attainments." Jeans, in fact, had a gift for explaining difficult ideas simply, a gift that he was to put to influential and lucrative use later on in life in his best-selling books *The Universe Around Us* (1929) and *The Mysterious Universe* (1930), as well as in his 1942 book, *Physics and Philosophy*. He was thus the ideal author to guide Oppenheimer through the arcane world of twentieth-century theoretical physics, as Oppenheimer had, up until the summer of 1923, no formal training in physics whatsoever, and rather less training in mathematics than one would expect a physicist to have had at that point in his education.

This had not prevented Oppenheimer, in his first year (as a *chemistry* student) from trying to master, in his spare time as it were, and without any formal guidance, some of the most difficult ideas of modern physics. During that year his scientific interests shifted from chemistry to physics as it gradually dawned on him that, as he later put it, "what I liked in chemistry was very close to physics." After all, he reflected, "if you were reading physical chemistry and you began to run into thermodynamical and statistical ideas you'd want to find out about them." In the same interview, he added: "I can't emphasize strongly enough how *much* I read and more really just in exploration."

> You see, it's a very odd picture; I never had an elementary course in physics except for a very elementary school course and to this day I get panicky when I think about a smoke ring or elastic vibrations. There's nothing there—just a little skin over a hole. In the same way my mathematical formation was, even for those days, very primitive, and this was more than evident in the way I went about some of the things I did later.

His education in physics, he acknowledged, was best characterized as "a very quick, superficial, eager familiarization with some parts of physics, with tremendous lacunae and often with a tremendous lack of practice and discipline."

Characteristically, these lacunae did not prevent Oppenheimer from beginning his career as a physicist by jumping straight into the deep end. In May 1923, toward the end of his first year at Harvard, he wrote to Edwin C. Kemble. Though still a junior member of the physics department, Kemble was notable for being the only *theoretical* physicist at Harvard and for being the only one abreast of developments in the then rapidly developing and unnervingly novel field of quantum theory. In his letter, Oppenheimer asked Kemble for permission to take his course on thermodynamics, Physics 6a, which ran during the autumn semester of the following year. This was, on the face of it, an extraordinary request. Physics 6a was a graduate course, normally taken only by those students who had completed their undergraduate studies and had excelled in advanced-level physics courses. A requirement for taking Physics 6a was that students had successfully completed Physics C, a final-year undergraduate course. Oppenheimer was asking Kemble to waive this requirement.

Besides having not completed Physics C, at this point in his education Oppenheimer had not taken *any* degree-level physics courses. Nor had he audited any. Realizing that, under these circumstances, he would have to present a fairly exceptional case for being regarded as a graduate-level physics student, Oppenheimer provided Kemble with a list (a "partial list," he insisted) of "several works on Thermodynamics and related subjects" that he had read during his first few months at Harvard. The list goes far beyond what one would have expected from an undergraduate majoring in physics, let alone one majoring in chemistry, and demonstrates an impressive linguistic breadth, in that two of the books on the list were in French and another two in German.

Included on the list were some impressively up-to-date textbooks, two of which—*Thermodynamics* by Gilbert Newton Lewis and Merle Randall (which was to go into several editions and become a widely used, usually graduate-level textbook) and James Crowther's *Molecular Physics*—had only just been published that year.[12] Another book on the list, the massive three-volume work *A System of Physical Chemistry* by William C. McC. Lewis, devoted its third volume, first published in 1920,[13] to quantum physics.

As well as being up to date, the list also revealed a much deeper interest in the history and philosophy of science than one would expect from an undergraduate science student. It included, for example, the work usually credited as the very foundation of thermodynamics, "On the Equilibrium of Heterogeneous Substances" by Josiah Willard Gibbs, which was first published as a pair of articles in the journal *Transactions of the Connecticut Academy of Arts and Sciences* between 1874 and 1878. Oppenheimer also included a number of works by scientists known for their contributions to the philosophy of their subject, including Henri Poincaré and Wilhelm Ostwald. The aforementioned William C. McC. Lewis, though much less well known than either Poincaré or Ostwald, was also someone with a deep interest in philosophy. He had, on his appointment to the chair in physical chemistry at Liverpool University in 1914, devoted his inaugural lecture to a philosophical discussion of

---

[12] The first edition of Crowther's *Molecular Physics* was published in 1914, but, given the nature of Oppenheimer's list, it seems likely that he had in mind the third edition, published in 1923.

[13] It is not clear whether Oppenheimer was using the second or third edition of this work. It was, in any case, not the first—published in 1916—since that had only two volumes. For publishing details of the second and third editions, see the Bibliography.

"Physical Chemistry and Scientific Thought," in which he expressed many thoughts that chime with the brief remarks Oppenheimer made on the subject. Urging his listeners not to adhere to an overly rigid demarcation between philosophy and science, Lewis remarked that "any man who has followed a line of directed thought is necessarily a philosopher and science is really only a particular form of philosophy."

At its meeting of June 6, Harvard's physics department considered Oppenheimer's letter to Kemble and, noting that "Mr. Oppenheimer, according to his own statement, had read rather widely in Physics for one of his age," voted to allow him to take Physics 6a without taking Physics C. Surprisingly, no one from the department seems to have done anything to ascertain whether Oppenheimer was telling the truth about having read these books, or to check whether, if he had read them, he had learned anything from them. According to Oppenheimer's recollection: "Years later I was told that when the faculty met to consider this request, George Washington Pierce [a member of the physics department] . . . said, 'Obviously if he says he's read these books, he's a liar, but he should get a Ph.D. for knowing their titles.'"

It would be astonishing if there were not some exaggeration, at the very least, in Oppenheimer's claims to have read all the books that he lists, and there are, indeed, a few indications that he was not *entirely* familiar with them all. For example, the bibliographic information he provides is scanty and occasionally inaccurate. For none of the books does he offer such standard citation details as the first names or the initials of the author, the name of the publisher, the date or place of publication. "On the Equilibrium of Heterogeneous Substances" is listed as "On the Equilibria of Heterogeneous Systems"; the German word *Spektrallinien* in the title of one of the books he lists[14] is given as "Spectrallinien"; and the details of the three-volume work by William C. McC. Lewis mentioned above are given in such a mangled way that a good deal of detective work is needed to identify the books being referred to.[15] If one could get a Ph.D. for knowing these titles, Oppenheimer would, it seems, only just have scraped through the viva.

Nevertheless, when he returned to Harvard for his second year in

[14] Arnold Sommerfeld's *Atombau und Spektrallinien*, which had originally been published in 1919 and by 1923 was available in English as *Atomic Structure and Spectral Lines*, was generally regarded as, in the words of one historian of science, "the textbook bible of the subject for physicists the world over."

[15] *A System of Physical Chemistry* was published in a series called *Textbooks of Physical Chemistry* edited by Sir William Ramsay. Oppenheimer does not give either the title of the series or of Lewis's three-volume work; he only gives the titles of the individual volumes, listing their author as "Ramsay; Lewis."

the autumn of 1923, he did so as someone who, though lacking any kind of formal training in physics, was eager to begin graduate-level courses in the subject. His passion for physics, which became more intense as his undergraduate career progressed, eclipsed and eventually extinguished his earlier preoccupation with short-story writing, a process no doubt helped by the fact that Francis Fergusson was no longer at Harvard, having left for Oxford to pursue his studies in English literature. On the day Fergusson left, Oppenheimer sent him a telegram, delivered to his ship, the SS *Albania*, offering "one last wave of ululation applause" and telling him that "it would delight me to hear from time to time of your achievements." During the following months, he continued to write to Fergusson and also to Horgan in Rochester and to Smith in New York, but his letters grew less frequent and dwelled less and less on literature and more and more on physics—his earlier talk of the stories he had written or planned to write now replaced with talk about equations and theoretical ideas.

Some of the courses he took in his second year provided him with genuine and lasting stimulation. As in his first year, he took a great variety of courses, including a year-long course in French literature, a philosophy course in the theory of knowledge, two mathematics courses and three in chemistry, but it was the graduate physics courses—especially Heat and Elementary Thermodynamics, taught by Edwin Kemble, and Advanced Thermodynamics, taught by the distinguished experimental physicist Percy Bridgman—that really made him come alive intellectually. Astonishingly, his lack of foundational training in physics proved no hindrance to him in mastering the very difficult material these courses contained, and Oppenheimer was not only able to hold his own with the graduate students taking them, many of whom were three or four years older, but quickly established himself as one of the very best students in the classes.

It is customary to describe physics at Harvard at this time as being something of a backwater, with the important theoretical advances being made in Copenhagen and the German universities and the decisive experimental work being done at Cambridge, England. And it is true that neither Kemble nor Bridgman was the equal of such towering figures in physics as Rutherford at Cambridge, Bohr at Copenhagen or Born at Göttingen. However, neither were they entirely negligible figures. Kemble was at the forefront of the development of American theoretical physics and Bridgman was justifiably pleased to have brought him to Harvard, where he provided the foundation for one of the most rapidly growing centers of theoretical physics in the United States. Bridgman himself was an experimenter rather than a theorist, and had little knowledge or understanding of the quantum theory that was then being developed in Europe. He was nevertheless one of the leading American physicists of his generation, a position acknowledged in 1946, when he was awarded the Nobel Prize in Physics for his work on high pressures.

Though Bridgman had fought hard to attract Kemble to Harvard, there is little sign that they became particularly good friends. In many ways they were opposites; Kemble, the theorist, was a devout Christian, while Bridgman, the experimentalist, was a strident atheist. Both of them became enormously impressed with Oppenheimer, though neither of them seemed to grow especially close to him. The only anecdote Bridgman told about Oppenheimer in later life was designed to illustrate his rather off-putting intellectual showiness. Once, he said, he invited Oppenheimer to his house for dinner. Seeing Oppenheimer admiring a picture of the Greek temple at Segesta, Sicily, Bridgman mentioned that it had been built around 400 BC. "I'm sorry to contradict you about the date," responded Oppenheimer, "but I judge from the capitals on the columns that it was built about 50 years earlier."

Oppenheimer was at this time still just nineteen years old. As always, he seemed intellectually much older, and socially and personally much younger. This meant that, on an intellectual level, he was able to mix with people who, on a social and personal level, remained distant from him. One such person was Jeffries Wyman, whom Oppenheimer had probably met during his first year, but who became a friend during this second year, when they were both enrolled in the same graduate physics courses. A few years older than Oppenheimer, Wyman had majored in philosophy before switching to biology. In Oppenheimer's first year at Harvard, Wyman had been in his final year of undergraduate study, planning to enter Harvard Graduate School the following year to take courses in chemistry as well as physics, prior to leaving for England, where he would pursue postgraduate research in biochemistry at Cambridge.

Wyman was as secure and as confident a member of Harvard's intellectual and social elites as it was possible to be. He came from an old, established Bostonian family, many of whom were extremely distinguished. His grandfather, also called Jeffries Wyman, was one of the most celebrated naturalists of his generation and had been professor of anatomy at Harvard in the mid-nineteenth century, as well as the first curator of the Peabody Museum of Archaeology and Ethnology and one of the founders of the National Academy of Sciences. Wyman's best friend, both as an undergraduate at Harvard and throughout much of his life, was John Edsall, whom Oppenheimer had met through the Liberal Club, and who was from a similarly established background.

Wyman had been encouraged to befriend Oppenheimer by Francis Fergusson ("Francis was full of talk about Bob Oppenheimer," Wyman later remembered). In his last-minute telegram to Fergusson, Oppenheimer had been careful to add "Jeffries too sends greetings," in order, perhaps, to let Fergusson know that he and Wyman had indeed become friends. In fact, Wyman's attitude to Oppenheimer was a little circumspect. His initial impressions, he said later, were that Oppenheimer "was a little precious, and perhaps a little arrogant, but very interesting, full of ideas." He noted, as Boyd had, that Oppenheimer was "completely blind to music. In fact he told me that music was positively painful to him." He also remembers that Oppenheimer "found social adjustment very difficult, and I think he was often very unhappy. I suppose he was lonely and he didn't fit in well with the human environment." "We were good friends," Wyman added, "and he had some other friends, but there was something that he lacked, perhaps some more personal and deep emotional contact with people than we were having, because our contacts were largely, I should say wholly, on an intellectual basis. We were young people falling in love with ideas right and left and interested in people who gave us ideas, but there wasn't the warmth of human companionship perhaps."

The nearest Oppenheimer got to "the warmth of human companionship" was with Bernheim and Boyd. For their second and third years, Oppenheimer and Bernheim occupied large adjoining rooms in a house on Mount Auburn Street, known in Harvard as the "Gold Coast" because of its reputation as the place where only the wealthiest students lived. Oppenheimer brought to these rooms oil paintings, etchings and a tea urn in which he brewed only Russian tea. "He wasn't a comfortable person to be around, in a way," Bernheim later commented, "because he always gave the impression that he was thinking very deeply about things. When we roomed together he would spend the evenings locked in his room, trying to do something with Planck's constant or something like that.[16] I had visions of him suddenly bursting forth as a great physicist and here I was just trying to get through Harvard." Boyd was a regular visitor to the house on Mount Auburn Street, and remembers that Oppenheimer seemed never to study, or in any case that "he was pretty careful not to let you catch him at it."

In fact, Oppenheimer did little else *but* study. He was determined to

[16] Referred to by the letter *h*, Planck's constant is a fixed numerical value (6.5×10^{-27}), which is the constant of proportionality between the energy of light and its frequency. It is central to quantum physics, and has been since its inception, being used by Planck and subsequent physicists to describe the very notion of a "quantum" of energy. It is discussed at length in the third volume of Lewis's *A System of Physical Chemistry*.

get through his degree in three years, rather than the customary four (as, indeed, were Bernheim and Boyd), which meant that he had to take six courses at a time, rather than the usual four, but he also audited a number of courses and, in addition, spent vast amounts of time in the library (he later said he "ransacked" the library in something like the way the Goths ransacked Rome), reading an extraordinary number of books on a vast range of subjects. He seemed determined, if not to know everything, then at least to give the impression that he knew everything.

"I am working very hard now," Oppenheimer wrote to Smith in November 1923, "so hard that I fear your epithet of grind." In a subsequent letter, he outlined to Smith the kinds of things that filled his day-to-day existence:

> Generously, you ask what I do . . . I labor, and write innumerable theses, notes, poems, stories, and junk; I go to the math lib and read and to the Phil lib and divide my time between Meinherr Russell and the contemplation of a most beautiful and lovely lady who is writing a thesis on Spinoza—charmingly ironic at that, don't you think? I make stenches in three different labs, listen to Allard gossip about Racine, serve tea and talk learnedly to a few lost souls, go off for the weekend to distill the low grade energy into laughter and exhaustion, read Greek, commit faux pas, search my desk for letters and wish I were dead. Voila.

It is this particular letter of which Jeremy Bernstein has remarked: "The whole tone makes one's flesh creep." And yet it is one of Oppenheimer's most honest and forthright letters. The tone is affected, to be sure, but the picture it draws of his time at Harvard, full of intense and varied intellectual activities, mixed with frustrated glances at apparently unattainable women and the constant battle to keep suicidal depression at bay, rings entirely true.

Jeffries Wyman says about himself and his circle of friends at Harvard: "We were all too much in love with the problems of philosophy and science and the arts and general intellectual life to be thinking about girls." But Oppenheimer's letters to Smith reveal that this was not *entirely* true. As well as the contemplation of the "lovely lady" studying Spinoza described above, there was also, in a letter written in January 1924, mention of a "ravishing creature" who served food to the people who attended a literary salon on Beacon Hill, and "whose charm is pretty largely responsible for my frequent ascents of the hill." For the most part, though, Oppenheimer's company at Harvard was restricted to men. None of his friends remembers him ever taking a girl out.

It was not all hard work, however. Oppenheimer, Bernheim and Boyd would often have dinner at Locke-Ober's, the famously elegant and famously expensive French restaurant in Boston, after which they would walk the six miles back to Cambridge, along the Charles River. Boyd also remembers an occasion on which, during a winter walk along the shore with Oppenheimer and Bernheim, one dared the others to go swimming, upon which they all stripped and plunged into the freezing water. And Bernheim recalls that sometimes they would take a train out of Cambridge, get off at a randomly chosen point and spend the night walking back. There were also weekend trips to Cape Ann. Here, Oppenheimer and Bernheim, sometimes joined by Boyd, would stay overnight at an inn they had discovered at Folly Cove, where the food was extremely good. In a letter to Smith, Oppenheimer claimed that he and Bernheim were thinking of buying, or possibly renting, a "ramshackle cottage way out on Cape Ann," which "lies way above the water, amid huge cliffs of yellow granite, and looks across a miraculously blue ocean to the shore line of Maine." But these plans never came to anything and Bernheim later remarked that, as far as he was concerned, those cliffs of yellow granite existed only in a "mythological landscape" of Oppenheimer's imagining.

Still, these walks and weekend trips aside, Oppenheimer's time was mostly spent in intense study. "Even in the last stages of senile aphasia," as he put it to Smith, "I will not say that education, in an academic sense, was only secondary when I was at college. I plow through about five or ten big scientific books a week." In the New Year of 1924, Smith learned that he had been appointed the new principal of the Ethical Culture high school. Congratulating him, Oppenheimer begged him not to overwork and was also prompted to reflect: "For me, and, I suspect, for you, it was never the opinion merely of the multitude that counted so much; it was the opinion and the conduct of the great."

At the end of the year, Oppenheimer discovered that he had been awarded an A in every course he took, except his second-semester math course in probability, for which he got a B. His A in the notoriously difficult graduate course on thermodynamics, taught by Kemble, was especially noteworthy. For a second-year student of chemistry, who had never taken any undergraduate course in physics, to get an A on this course was completely unheard of. After spending part of the summer with his family in Europe, Oppenheimer returned to Harvard in October 1924 for his final year. Soon after the start of term, he wrote to Smith to tell him that his plans for the following year were not quite decided. One possibility was to follow Edsall and Wyman to Cambridge, England, for, as he told Smith, he had been offered a place at Christ's College. Another was to stay at Harvard ("I cannot decide to leave this Puritanical hole, even for all the vacuity of my life here") and pursue research with Bridgman.

In his final year, Oppenheimer took more courses than ever, and, as always, they were extremely diverse. With a discernible note of excitement, he told Smith: "I am taking a course with Whitehead of Russell & Whitehead, Cambridge, on the Metaphysical presuppositions of science." Whitehead, who had been Bertrand Russell's tutor in mathematics at Cambridge, had become famous as Russell's coauthor of the monumental three-volume *Principia Mathematica*, published in 1910–13, which sought to show that the theorems of arithmetic could be derived from axioms of logic. In 1924, Whitehead, who since the First World War had concentrated on writing philosophy rather than mathematics, accepted an offer from Harvard to join their philosophy department. He was by then already sixty-three years old and was to stay in the United States for the rest of his life (he died in 1947, having retired from teaching ten years earlier).Whitehead's course consisted of seminars rather than lectures and attracted very few students. In this first year it attracted just Oppenheimer and one other brave student. Many years later, writing to Bertrand Russell to congratulate him on his ninetieth birthday, Oppenheimer recalled:

> It is almost forty years ago that we worked through the Principia Mathematica with Whitehead at Harvard. He had largely forgotten, so that he was the perfect teacher, both master and student. I remember how often he would pause with a smile before a sequence of theorems and say to us: "That was a point Bertie always liked." For all the years of my life I have thought of this phrase whenever some high example of intelligence, some humanity, or some rare courage and nobility has come our way.

In addition to Whitehead's course, Oppenheimer took two courses each in chemistry, physics and mathematics and a history course called "History of England from 1688 to the Present Time." He also audited many courses, including a graduate seminar given by the distinguished mathematician George Birkhoff on Sturm-Liouville equations (a type of differential equation), a subject chosen, Oppenheimer later remembered, "because he'd been working on it and wanted to talk about it." Birkhoff, Oppenheimer recalled, "was a remarkable fellow. He would begin: 'Well, you know, walking across the yard this morning it occurred to me...'" Birkhoff's course was, Oppenheimer said, the only mathematics course at Harvard that he remembered with any happiness.

Birkhoff, as well as being Harvard's most eminent mathematician, was also one of its most controversial and eccentric professors, whose interests extended far beyond mathematics. In 1933, after spending a year traveling around the world studying the art, music and poetry of various cultures, he published a book called *Aesthetic Measure*, which put forward a mathematical theory of aesthetics, the center of which was a formula for measuring aesthetic value. He was also passionate about promoting *American* mathematicians, and, in this capacity, famously aroused the ire of Einstein, who in the 1930s was once heard to denounce him as "one of the world's greatest academic anti-Semites," after Birkhoff had urged the appointment of American mathematicians in favor of European Jewish refugees, whose cause Einstein was supporting. In the 1920s, Birkhoff wrote a recommendation for Oppenheimer that included a sentence that one could regard as evidence either of his anti-Semitism or of his willingness to overcome it: "He is Jewish but I should consider him a very fine type of man."

Though it was *theoretical* physics that had excited Oppenheimer's enthusiasm, it is interesting that it never occurred to him to pursue postgraduate research with Kemble, rather than with Bridgman, who was resolutely *experimental* in his approach to the subject. When he looked back on his time at Harvard, it was his relationship with Bridgman that Oppenheimer singled out as most important for his intellectual development. "I found Bridgman a wonderful teacher," he recalled, "because he never really was quite reconciled to things being the way they were and he always thought them out." Bridgman, he said, "was a man to whom one wanted to be an apprentice."

Why Oppenheimer decided against becoming Bridgman's "apprentice," and why he opted instead to pursue research at Cambridge, is not entirely clear. He must have made the decision by the New Year of 1925, since he then wrote to Smith telling him that Christ's College had written to him asking for fees and for "a certificate from my 'head-master' at school, which is you." In April, he wrote to Francis Fergusson, telling him that he would be in England at the end of August or the beginning of September, which would give him time before the start of term to see Fergusson. He proposed that they should go to Wales together, where they could "ruminate conjointly on our sins" and Fergusson could pass on to Oppenheimer the benefit of his experience of English society, in particular "how to treat the tutors & the dukes."

In the meantime, Oppenheimer completed his degree at Harvard. Despite describing his work to Smith as "frantic, bad and graded A," in his final year he, for the first and only time in his undergraduate career, got two Bs: one for Whitehead's course and the other for dynamics. Nevertheless, in June 1925 (though the record notes that it was "as of 1926"),

Oppenheimer was awarded the A.B. summa cum laude (the equivalent of a first-class degree in the UK) in chemistry. Boyd and Bernheim also completed their degrees that summer and the three of them celebrated in Bernheim's room with (this being the period of Prohibition) some laboratory alcohol. As Bernheim remembers it, he and Boyd "got plastered," while Oppenheimer "took one drink and retired."

5

Cambridge

You will tell me how to treat the tutors & the dukes & I shall tremble." Oppenheimer's plea to Fergusson for help in preparing for Cambridge was partly in jest, but it also expressed a very real and deep anxiety. He was indeed trembling at the prospect of trying, and possibly failing, to achieve what Fergusson, with apparently very little effort, had already achieved: namely, acceptance into the highest level of English literary and intellectual society. Herbert Smith understood this all too well and tried to alert Fergusson to it in a letter written shortly before Oppenheimer's arrival in England, in which he advised him that "your ability to show him [Oppenheimer] about should be exercised with great tact, rather than in royal profusion. And instead of flying at your throat—as I remember your being ready to do for George What's-his-name . . . when you were similarly awed by him—I'm afraid he'd merely cease to think his own life worth living."

Oppenheimer's original plan, outlined in the letter quoted in the previous chapter, was to sail to England at the end of August or the beginning of September 1925, leaving him a few weeks before the start of term, which he hoped to spend in Wales together with Fergusson, "sailing and recuperating from America." In a subsequent letter, written in July, this plan had changed somewhat. Giving an exact date on which he expected to arrive in England—September 16—Oppenheimer told Fergusson that he intended to see him in Cambridge soon after this date, and then, after a couple of weeks in Cambridge ("to see about laboratory facilities and such matters"), he planned to go with Fergusson not sailing in Wales, but walking in Cornwall.

In the meantime, Oppenheimer spent much of August in New Mexico, which he had not visited since his trip there in the summer of 1922, but which remained the place he most cherished and in which he felt most appreciated and accepted. This time he was accompanied by his parents and Frank, who was now thirteen. "The Parents are really quite pleased with the place," Oppenheimer wrote to Smith from Los Pinos, "and are starting to ride a little. Curiously enough they enjoy the frivolous courtesy of the place, and all is well." In fact, Julius and Ella spent most of the trip staying in luxury at the exclusive and expensive Bishop's Lodge hotel, on the outskirts of Santa Fe, joining their son at the Pages' ranch for just a few days. Most of Oppenheimer's time was spent with Katherine Page and Paul Horgan, who was back in New Mexico after finishing his course at Rochester. Horgan remembers one ride in particular, in which he and Oppenheimer, crossing the Sangre de Cristo mountain range, got caught in a thunderstorm, "immense, huge, pounding rain," to shelter from which they sat under their horses while they ate their lunch. "I was looking at Robert," Horgan recalls, "and all of a sudden I noticed his hair was standing straight up . . . responding to the static. Marvelous."

After this restorative time among the camaraderie of his New Mexican friends, Oppenheimer returned to New York to find rejection and his first taste of academic failure. Waiting for him on his return was a letter from Cambridge telling him that his application to study with Sir Ernest Rutherford as a research student had been rejected (though the offer of a place at Christ's College still stood). This was a powerful blow. The reason Oppenheimer had chosen to go to Cambridge, rather than staying at Harvard and continuing to work with Bridgman, was that he hoped to work with Rutherford, so as, he later said, to get "near the center" of the world of physics.

In fact, Rutherford had, for many years, been right *at* the center. A New Zealander by birth, he had arrived in Cambridge in 1895 to pursue postgraduate work and had been in England ever since, apart from a nine-year spell at McGill University in Montreal from 1898 to 1907, where he conducted the research into radioactivity that won him the Nobel Prize in Chemistry. In 1907 he was appointed professor of physics at the University of Manchester, where he stayed until 1919, when— now Sir Ernest Rutherford (having been knighted in 1914)—he returned to Cambridge as director of the Cavendish Laboratory. Since its creation in 1874, under its first director, James Clerk Maxwell, the Cavendish had been recognized as the world's foremost center of experimental physics. In 1925, Rutherford's list of honors and titles was completed when he was admitted into the Order of Merit, generally regarded as the most prestigious award it is possible to receive in the British honors system.

What Oppenheimer would have known Rutherford for, and what

most people today still know him for, is his development, in 1911, of the planetary model of the atom, which pictures an atom as consisting of a positively charged nucleus around which orbit negatively charged electrons. This was a revolutionary way of picturing the atom, which it took imagination, intuition and a willingness to be led by experimental evidence to conceive. Rutherford's predecessor at the Cavendish, J. J. Thomson, had paved the way by being the first person to demonstrate that an atom was not the indivisible, hard ball previously imagined, when in 1897 he discovered the existence of particles, later called electrons, that were *part of* an atom. These tiny "subatomic" particles, Thomson showed, were negatively charged, which, given that atoms themselves were neutral, meant that the other part of the atom had to be positively charged. As Thomson pictured it, an atom was made up of a positively charged mass into which electrons were embedded. On this "plum pud- ding" model, the positive charge was understood to be evenly spread throughout the atom. In a series of ingenious experiments conducted at Manchester, Rutherford demonstrated that this could not be so and that the positive charge of an atom was, rather, concentrated in a tiny "nucleus." To appreciate *how* tiny this nucleus is, if an atom were the size of a golf course, then the nucleus would be the size of just one of its holes. According to Rutherford's model, the electrons orbit this nucleus like planets around the sun. An atom is less like a plum pudding and more like a solar system.

Rutherford's theory was significantly refined in 1913 by the man whom Oppenheimer would come to admire more than anyone else in the world: the Danish physicist Niels Bohr. Bohr had arrived in Cam- bridge in 1911 to work with J. J. Thomson, but was disappointed to discover that Thomson, then in his fifties and past his best as a scientist, was uninterested in him or his work. After meeting Rutherford when he came to give a paper at Cambridge, Bohr decided he would rather work with him than with Thomson and so transferred from Cambridge to Manchester. At Manchester, under Rutherford's benign and sympathetic guidance, Bohr devoted himself to the theoretical problems raised by Rutherford's model of the atom. At the heart of these problems was the fact that, according to the laws of physics as they were then understood, the atom as pictured by Rutherford would be inherently unstable. New- ton's laws of motion tell us that an object moving in a circle undergoes acceleration, and Maxwell's theory of electromagnetism tells us that a charged particle, like an electron, will lose energy in the form of electro- magnetic radiation as it accelerates (it will, in other words, emit light). Very quickly, the electron's energy would be completely dissipated and, unable to continue its orbital motion, it would collapse into the atomic nucleus. As this did not, in fact, happen, something had to be wrong, either with Rutherford's model or with classical physics—or, as it turned out, with both.

Bohr's daring solution, outlined in a series of three papers published in 1913, was to jettison classical physical laws and replace them with what is now called "old quantum theory," but which Oppenheimer, as a student, would have known simply as "quantum theory." On the "Rutherford-Bohr model," as it was henceforth known, the electrons in an atom are held in their orbits by the electromagnetic attraction between the negatively charged electrons and the positively charged atomic nucleus. In order to understand the behavior of electrons in their "static orbits," Bohr maintained, we need to appeal, not to the laws of classical physics, but rather to the quantum theory developed by Planck and Einstein in their attempts to understand the behavior of the "photons" of light. Electrons do not, as classical theory would suggest, lose energy as they orbit the nucleus, so long as they stay in the same orbits. They absorb or emit energy only when they move from one orbit (or, as Bohr would now have it, "stationary state") to another, and when they do that, they move, not in a continuous motion, but in jumps or "quanta," the mathematics of which is centered on h, Planck's famous constant, which Oppenheimer had spent so much time pondering at Harvard. Furthermore, according to Bohr, electrons are only "permitted" certain states; namely those allowed for in the mathematics of quantum theory. The properties of chemicals are determined by the number of electrons they have, which gets larger and larger as one goes through the periodic table, from the lightest element, hydrogen, which has just one electron, to the heaviest, uranium, which has ninety-two. As more electrons are added, they are allotted places in the "stationary states" around the nucleus. If an electron jumps from one state to another, then (and only then) does it emit light. Otherwise, it stays in its state, suffering no energy loss. Why electrons are only permitted certain states Bohr could not explain, but the hypothesis that they were so restricted turned out to be too powerful to ignore; it allowed an extraordinarily neat account of the molecular structure of chemicals to be given that provided a physical explanation of the entire periodic table.

A detailed account of the Rutherford-Bohr model of the atom, and of the "old quantum theory" of which it forms a fundamental part, is given in William C. McC. Lewis's *Quantum Theory*, the third volume of *A System of Physical Chemistry*, one of those works that Oppenheimer claimed to have read in his first year at Harvard. Another one of those works, Arnold Sommerfeld's *Atombau und Spektrallinien*, was entirely devoted to that model, Sommerfeld's account of which became accepted not only as the definitive statement of Bohr's theory, but also as a significant improvement upon it, so that the model came to be called the "Bohr-Sommerfeld model."

Having, at least purportedly, read Lewis and Sommerfeld, and having heard Rutherford's name mentioned in all the physics courses he took at Harvard, as well as in his conversations with Bridgman and Kemble, it is not surprising that Oppenheimer would regard the Cavendish Laboratory as being at, or at least near, the "center" of new developments in physics. What *is* a little curious, however, is that Oppenheimer should have wanted to pursue research in *experimental* rather than theoretical physics. After all, in his letter to Fergusson from Harvard in the spring of 1925 he had remarked, in relation to some work he had been doing with Bridgman: "that brief excursion convinces me that my genre, whatever it is, is not experimental science." Given this realization, and the fact that it had been *theoretical* physics that had fascinated him since his first year at Harvard, why did he apply to work in a laboratory with a man known throughout the world as an experimentalist? In an effort to explain this later in life, Oppenheimer said that he did not know that one could make a living as a theoretical physicist. This is difficult to believe. After all, he was taught by Edwin Kemble, whom he surely knew to be a theoretical physicist, even if he had not realized that many, perhaps most, of the physicists he had read or read about—Bohr, Einstein, Sommerfeld, and so on—were also theoretical physicists. It seems that he decided he wanted to be at Cambridge because that is where many of his Harvard friends had gone, and, having decided that, he was led by the reputation of Rutherford and the Cavendish, and by Cambridge's preeminence in experimental physics and its comparative neglect of theoretical physics, to attempt to overcome his ineptitude for experimental work.

It would turn out to be a grievous error of judgment. For one thing, it put Bridgman in a difficult position when it came to writing Oppenheimer a reference recommending him to Rutherford. While Bridgman could say in all honesty that Oppenheimer had a "perfectly prodigious power of assimilation," "a high degree of originality" and "much mathematical power," he felt obliged to point out that "his weakness is on the experimental side":

> His type of mind is analytical, rather than physical, and he is not at home in the manipulation of the laboratory . . . [in his laboratory work, Oppenheimer] was evidently much handicapped by his lack of familiarity with ordinary physical manipulations.

Bridgman also felt obliged to add: "As appears from his name, Oppenheimer is a Jew, but entirely without the usual qualifications of his race. He is a tall, well set-up young man, with a rather engaging diffidence of manner, and I think you need have no hesitation whatever for any reason of this sort in considering his application."

In the context of the anti-Semitism that plagued American academic life in the 1920s, and in particular the ongoing controversy at Harvard about Lowell's desire to impose quotas on Jewish students, Bridgman's remarks are entirely understandable and clearly well intentioned. However, they were, as far as Rutherford was concerned, entirely unnecessary and possibly offensive in their assumption of a background prejudice against Jews who were *not* tall, "well set-up" and diffident. It is certainly not true that there was no anti-Semitism in British academic life, but Rutherford himself was, as far as one can tell, entirely free from it. Raised on a farm in New Zealand, he was emphatically not a typical Cambridge professor; his outlook was robustly and resolutely egalitarian, without snobbery or racism. In the 1930s, he became the first president of the Council for Assisting Refugee Academics, which was formed to help Jewish academics forced to flee Nazi Germany. That Oppenheimer's name betrayed a Jewish ancestry would have been of no concern whatsoever to him.

However, that Oppenheimer's weakness as a physicist was "on the experimental side" would surely have persuaded Rutherford that he was not an ideal candidate for a postgraduate research position at the Cavendish. Accordingly, in the letter that Oppenheimer received on his return to New York from New Mexico, Rutherford wrote that, as he already had so many "excellent applicants," he could not take Oppenheimer on as a research student, at least for a time. While his place at Christ's College was still open, then, Oppenheimer would have to suffer the indignity of being, for a while at least, an undergraduate student. Later in the academic year, Oppenheimer was told, he could be accepted as a graduate student, so long as the Cambridge authorities were, in the meantime, convinced that he had some aptitude for original work, whether experimental or practical.

The registrar at Christ's College, responsible for graduate admissions, was the famous explorer Raymond Priestley, who had been a member of first Shackleton's and then Scott's expeditions to the Antarctic, the latter of which was the subject of Priestley's best-selling book, *Antarctic Adventure*. In the First World War, Priestley was decorated with the Military Cross for his part in the celebrated capture by the Allies of the Riqueval Bridge, which he wrote about in another popular book, *Breaking the Hindenburg Line*. After the war he was elected a Fellow of

Christ's and devoted himself to academic administration. After receiving Rutherford's rejection, Oppenheimer wrote to Priestley, telling him that he would be taking up his offered place, but that he "should like to be admitted to the University as a research student as soon as possible." "If admission cannot be granted at once," Oppenheimer added, "I should be quite willing to wait a term."

As soon as he arrived in Cambridge on September 16, 1925, before setting off on his walking holiday with Fergusson, Oppenheimer wrote again to Priestley, formally applying to be considered as a graduate student, reading in physics, analysis and physical chemistry, in preparation for undertaking "as soon as it seems advisable" a research problem in physics. He was particularly interested, he told Priestley, in the theory of electronic conduction, especially those aspects of it "which can give an indication of the laws of force to which the motion of electrons is subject." He would, he said, "be very glad of an opportunity for further experimental work, and, if possible, for critical advice in the corresponding theoretical problems." In support of his application for graduate status, Oppenheimer wrote out a list of all the relevant courses he had taken at Harvard and submitted his degree, his grade cards and his references. "If any more definite information is required," his letter to Priestley ends, "I shall be glad to try to give it. I am twenty-one years old."

Having thus made his case to be admitted as a doctoral student, rather than the undergraduate he officially still was, Oppenheimer set off on his walking holiday in Cornwall with Fergusson. For the reasons anticipated by Smith, this tour with Fergusson, instead of easing Oppenheimer gently into English social life, seems to have left him feeling intimidated, awed and firmly persuaded that he would never be accepted by "the tutors & the dukes." Fergusson, during his two years in England, had become associated with the very set of artists, writers and intellectuals that Oppenheimer had read about in Aldous Huxley's *Crome Yellow*, and who met at Ottoline Morrell's Oxford home, Garsington. This included, but was not restricted to, the Bloomsbury Group of Virginia Woolf and John Maynard Keynes. As Oppenheimer put it in a letter to Smith, Fergusson "knows everyone at Oxford; he goes to tea with Lady Ottoline Morrell, the high priestess of civilized society & the patroness of Eliot & Berty;[17] & he is a member of a congress of litterateurs who meet every summer at Pontigny to talk about 'Mysticism & Literature' & other such modest things."

The meetings at Pontigny that Oppenheimer mentions here were a series of annual colloquia that took place every year between 1910 and

---

[17] T. S. Eliot and Bertrand Russell.

1939 at the former Cistercian abbey at Pontigny in Burgundy. They were organized by the philosopher and literary critic Paul Desjardins, who owned the abbey. "To be invited to Pontigny," writes a biographer of one of the regular attendees, Prince Mirsky, "was to be recognised as a member of European intellectual aristocracy." Though the leading figures at Pontigny were French intellectuals, such as André Gide and Charles Du Bos, there were also many connections between the Pontigny colloquia and the Bloomsbury/Morrell Group. Roger Fry and Lytton Strachey (both members of the Bloomsbury Group and regular invitees to Garsington), for example, were habitual attendees at Pontigny.

That Fergusson moved in such grand literary and intellectual circles was daunting enough, but even more dispiriting was what Fergusson later described as the "rather Russian account" he gave Oppenheimer of what it was like to be an American student in Europe—an account that seems to have left Oppenheimer with the conviction that he would forever be shut out from whatever was best in Cambridge life. After their walking tour, Oppenheimer wrote to Fergusson, telling him: "I do not think that Cambridge can be quite so bad as Oxford. But its excellencies are just as fantastically inaccessible, and there are vast, sloppy strata where there is nothing, absolutely nothing, to be found." He had not entirely given up hope, however. "By next term," he told Fergusson, "I think I may have some people to show you."

Whether Oppenheimer ever did find any people at Cambridge he thought impressive enough to introduce to Fergusson is doubtful. As it had been at Harvard, his social circle was small. In fact, to begin with, it consisted of some of the very same people he had mixed with at Harvard, many of whom were now at Cambridge. Jeffries Wyman and John Edsall had arrived there the previous year, although, after a month or so, Wyman decided to transfer to University College London in order to work with the physiologist Archibald Vivian Hill, famous (as Wyman himself would later be) for his research on hemoglobin. Edsall decided to stay at Cambridge, living in St. John's College and working at the Cambridge Biochemistry Laboratory under the supervision of the eminent biochemist F. Gowland Hopkins. Though Wyman was in London, he and Edsall saw much of each other and both thrived in England, socially and intellectually.

Oppenheimer might have expected his closest companion to have been Fred Bernheim, who arrived in Cambridge at the same time as him, in order, like Edsall and Wyman, to study biochemistry. Bernheim, however, was determined to liberate himself from what he had often felt was the overbearing and suffocating atmosphere of his friendship with Oppenheimer. Having settled into King's College, Bernheim made the

Biochemistry Laboratory the center of his personal as well as his scholarly life. It was there that he met his future wife, Mary L. C. Hare, who would herself become a biochemist of some eminence. In a letter to Fergusson of November 15, 1925, Oppenheimer mentions "some terrible complications with Fred, and an awful evening, two weeks ago, in the moon." The Moon was presumably a pub in Cambridge, and the complications were no doubt connected with the fact that Bernheim seemed content to accept that the friendship he and Oppenheimer had shared at Harvard had not survived the move to Cambridge. "I have not seen him since," Oppenheimer told Fergusson, "and blush when I think of him."

So, with Bernheim keeping him at arm's length, Edsall and Wyman sharing a bond that did not include him, and Fergusson established in a milieu that was not open to him (and into which Fergusson showed no sign of wanting to introduce him), Oppenheimer's initial few months at Cambridge were isolated. Nor was he making any new friends. Christ's was a smaller and less well-endowed college than either King's (where Bernheim was) or St. John's (where Edsall was), but equally ancient, having been founded in 1505 by Lady Margaret Beaufort, Henry VIII's grandmother. It was distinguished by a tradition of academic excellence in both science and poetry, being the college of England's most famous scientist, Charles Darwin, and arguably her greatest poet, John Milton. Of the students who studied there who belonged to Oppenheimer's generation, one of the most notable was C. P. Snow, the physicist and novelist, who, in his 1959 lecture "The Two Cultures," famously lamented the gulf between scientists and literary intellectuals. Christ's, evidently, was a college in which scientific and literary gifts could be nurtured side by side. Moreover, it was a college unusually friendly to students from America. The master of the college at the time Oppenheimer arrived was the zoologist Sir Arthur Shipley, who combined his academic work with writing popular and literary books and had spent some time in the United States as part of the British University Mission, one of whose aims was to promote postgraduate study by Americans at British universities. Such a college, one might have thought, would have been Oppenheimer's natural home. And yet his time at Christ's was brief, difficult and the most emotionally turbulent few months of his life.

Surely one reason that Oppenheimer seems to have made no new friends at Christ's is that, instead of living in college, he lodged in what he described as a "miserable hole" somewhere in the city. He took all his meals in college, but, even so, seems not to have befriended—or been befriended by—any of his fellow students. Nor, to begin with, did he make any friends among his fellow physicists. This was no doubt partly because of his status. Not being a research postgraduate, he would not, initially at least, have mixed much with the famously brilliant young men who worked with Rutherford at this time. He would, rather, have been expected to attend undergraduate lectures and spend his time at the Cavendish, learning basic laboratory skills instead of pursuing original research. After just a month of this lonely and humiliating existence, Oppenheimer wrote to Fergusson, spelling out his situation in uncharacteristically direct language: "I am having a pretty bad time. The lab work is a terrible bore, and I am so bad at it that it is impossible to feel that I am learning anything . . . The lectures are vile. And you know the rest."

The most detailed record of Oppenheimer's misery during his first term at Cambridge is contained in a curious document written by Fergusson dated "February 1926" and entitled "Account of the Adventures of Robert Oppenheimer in Europe." In chronicling (and, in later interviews, recollecting) Oppenheimer's emotional upheavals during this period, Fergusson takes a resolutely psychoanalytical approach, emphasizing Oppenheimer's relations with his parents and his sexual frustration, the combination of which he evidently sees as the cause of the trouble. Oppenheimer, Fergusson records, "was completely at a loss about his sex life." His initial impression on seeing Oppenheimer again, Fergusson remembered, was that he "seemed more self-confident, strong and upstanding," which he attributed to Oppenheimer's having "nearly managed to fall in love with an attractive gentile in New Mexico." Within a few months of Oppenheimer's time at Cambridge, however, Fergusson describes him as having a "first class case of depression"—a depression that was "further increased and made specific by the struggle he was carrying on with his mother."

In the autumn of 1925, Oppenheimer's parents, alarmed by the state of their son's mind, insisted on traveling to Cambridge in order to be with him. Fergusson's journal contains an extraordinary description, presumably based on what he had been told by Oppenheimer, of their arrival in England. Oppenheimer, having arranged to meet them from their ship, caught a train to Southampton and, according to Fergusson:

> He found himself in a third-class carriage with a man and a woman who were making love, and though he tried to read thermodynamics he could not concentrate. When the man left, he [Oppenheimer] kissed the woman. She did not seem unduly surprised. But he was at once overcome with remorse, fell on his knees, his feet sprawling, and with many tears, begged her pardon.

After this, Oppenheimer fled the compartment. At Southampton, on his way out of the station, he saw the woman below him when he was on the stairs, and tried to drop his suitcase on her head. "Fortunately," writes Fergusson, "he missed."[18]

From Southampton train station, Oppenheimer proceeded to the port. Before he saw either his mother or father, however, he caught sight of Inez Pollak, his old classmate from Ethical Culture. Apparently, Inez had been invited by Oppenheimer's mother, who, as Fergusson put it, "tried to put them together" as a cure for Oppenheimer's depression. One of the many complications concerning this arrangement was that, according to Fergusson, Ella Oppenheimer considered Inez to be "ridiculously unworthy" of her son.

So Oppenheimer returned to Cambridge with his mother, his father and the hapless Inez Pollak, whom he did his best to "court." Fergusson writes that Oppenheimer "did a very good and chiefly rhetorical imitation of being in love with her" and that she "responded in kind." This led to them sharing a bed together, although this did not go according to plan: "There they lay, tremulous with cold, afraid to do anything. And Inez began to sob. Then Robert began to sob." At that moment they heard Ella Oppenheimer knocking on the door and shouting, "Let me in, Inez, why won't you let me in? I know Robert is in there." Shortly after this Inez left for Italy, her parting gift from Oppenheimer being a copy of *The Possessed* by Dostoyevsky.

At this point, with his parents still in Cambridge, Oppenheimer's mental state was at its very worst. Fergusson's emphasis on the importance of Oppenheimer's sexual frustration as a cause of his emotional problems is entirely understandable, but there were other important causes, not least the fact that he felt, for the first time in his life, unequal to the academic demands made on him. "The academic standard here would depeople Harvard over night," he told Fergusson. All the scientists at Cambridge were "uncommonly skillful at blowing glass and solving differential equations."

To help him acquire some of the skills required of an experimental physicist, Oppenheimer had been assigned a tutor at the Cavendish. This was Patrick Blackett, who in later life would win the Nobel Prize in Physics, become ennobled as Baron Blackett and be awarded the Order of Merit. In the mid-1920s, Blackett was a dashing and glamorous figure, described by the literary critic I. A. Richards as "a young Oedipus. Tall, slim, beautifully balanced and always looking better dressed than anyone." Before coming to Cambridge he had served in the navy, seeing

---

[18] It is impossible to tell how much of this story is true. Can one believe that Oppenheimer deliberately dropped his suitcase, intending it to hit the woman? Did he really kiss her? And, perhaps most improbably of all: can one really imagine him traveling third-class?

action during the First World War at the Battle of Jutland and winning promotion from midshipman to lieutenant. After the war he was sent by the admiralty to Magdalene College, where he studied mathematics and physics. His great ability was quickly recognized and, by the time Oppenheimer arrived at the Cavendish, Blackett (by then a Fellow of King's) was regarded by Rutherford and his colleagues as one of the most valued members of their team. In March 1924, Blackett married Constanza Bayon, a beautiful and brilliant language student at Newnham, who, for some reason, was always known as "Pat."

In the summer of 1924, Blackett had made one of his most important contributions to physics when he managed to photograph a nuclear transformation process taking place. This was the culmination of a research project that he had been asked to undertake by Rutherford, exploring what happens when a nitrogen nucleus is hit by an alpha particle.[19] Rutherford knew that a proton (a positively charged subatomic particle that forms part of the nucleus) would be emitted by the particle, but did not know whether, after the collision, the alpha particle would be deflected away from the nitrogen nucleus or absorbed by it. Rutherford thought the former more likely, but Blackett's photographs proved the latter. What Rutherford had imagined was a "disintegration process" was actually an "integration" process; the nitrogen nucleus absorbed the alpha particle (minus the emitted proton), thereby transmuting into an isotope of oxygen.[20] Blackett's remarkable photographs, reproduced many times since, showed this transmutation of one element into another, this "modern alchemy," taking place.

When the great German experimental physicist James Franck came to Cambridge in 1924 to give a paper, Blackett got to know him and arranged to spend the following academic year, 1924–5, at Franck's own university, Göttingen, which was acquiring a reputation of being at the center of the exciting developments then taking place in physics. Franck himself won the Nobel Prize in 1925 for the experiments he and his

---

[19] An alpha particle, as Rutherford was the first to establish, is a helium nucleus. It is (we now know, though this was not known before the discovery of neutrons in 1932) made up of two protons and two neutrons. What Rutherford and the physicists of the 1920s knew about alpha particles/helium nuclei was that they had an atomic weight of 4 and that they, like all nuclei, were positively charged. Chiefly, however, alpha particles were associated in the minds of the scientists of this period with what Rutherford had christened "alpha radiation," which occurs when a radioactive element such as radium decays. The radioactive decay simply is the emission of alpha particles. As these particles include two protons, the decayed radium (atomic number 88) turns into radon (atomic number 86), and then, successively, into polonium (84) and lead (82).

[20] Nitrogen has atomic number 7, so that when it absorbs a proton it becomes element number 8—i.e., oxygen.

fellow Nobel laureate, Gustav Hertz, had performed, which provided experimental confirmation of the Bohr-Rutherford model of the atom. At Göttingen, Franck worked closely with the leading theoretical physicist at the university, Max Born, and together they built up an internationally renowned center for research in physics that was to rival and even surpass Cambridge, attracting to Göttingen some of the best students and researchers in physics throughout the world. Blackett thrived at Göttingen and returned to Cambridge brimming with excitement over the latest developments in quantum theory. He and his wife gained a reputation for being the "handsomest, gayest, happiest pair in Cambridge" and their home in Bateman Street became "a favourite haunt of left-wing and Bohemian academics."

To Oppenheimer, Blackett was, like Francis Fergusson, a model of unattainable excellence and a reminder of his own failures and inadequacies. As a physicist, Blackett was especially proficient in the very aspects of research that Oppenheimer found difficult: namely, those involving laboratory skills. A glimpse of Blackett's views on the importance of laboratory skills is provided in his contribution to a collection of essays that was published in the 1930s. The aim of the collection was to provide prospective Cambridge applicants with information about the various subjects studied at the university, each subject being introduced by a distinguished Cambridge practitioner of it (Richard Braithwaite on philosophy, C. P. Snow on chemistry, C. H. Waddington on biology, and so on). Blackett's contribution was an essay on "The Craft of Experimental Physics" that has since become one of his most-quoted pieces of writing and is revealing as an indication of the demands made upon Oppenheimer during his time as Blackett's tutee.

The experimental physicist, Blackett writes, "is a Jack-of-All-Trades, a versatile but amateur craftsman":

> He must blow glass and turn metal, though he could not earn his living as a glass-blower nor ever be considered as a skilled mechanic; he must carpenter, photograph, wire electric circuits and be a master of gadgets of all kinds; he may find invaluable a training as an engineer and can profit always by utilising his gifts as a mathematician. In such activities will he be engaged for three-quarters of his working day.

"The combination of these abilities in one individual with the right temperament to use them is rare," Blackett adds. "Many a theoretically gifted student may fail, while learning to be an experimenter, through clumsy fingers."

His confidence already severely dented by Rutherford's rejection of him as a research student, Oppenheimer's self-esteem took a further battering when he failed abjectly to live up to the demanding criteria spelled out by Blackett for being a successful experimental physicist. He simply did not have the practical abilities emphasized by Blackett, and his unsuccessful attempts to acquire such abilities brought him deep unhappiness. This, together with his other emotional problems, led him, within a few months of being at Cambridge, to the brink of mental, emotional and physical collapse.

At Harvard, Oppenheimer might have behaved in ways that struck people as odd, affected or intense, but at Cambridge his behavior was not just strange—it was indicative of severe mental instability. Sometimes, he later recalled, he would stand alone in front of a blackboard for hours, chalk in hand, waiting for inspiration to strike. On other occasions the silence would be broken by his own voice, repeating over and over again, "The point is, the point is . . . the point is." Once Rutherford himself was alarmed to see Oppenheimer fall fainting to the floor of the laboratory. In an interview he gave late in life, Jeffries Wyman recalled that Oppenheimer told him he "felt so miserable in Cambridge, so unhappy, that he used to get down on the floor and roll from side to side."

Most bizarre, though, was an event that occurred toward the end of Oppenheimer's first term at Cambridge. In what looks like an attempt to murder his tutor, or at the very least to make him seriously ill, Oppenheimer left on Blackett's desk an apple poisoned with toxic chemicals. The act seems charged with symbolism: Oppenheimer as the jealous queen leaving a poisoned apple for Snow White, the "fairest of them all," whose beauty and goodness are admired by everybody. The incident was hushed up at the time, and none of his friends knew about it until they were told of it by Oppenheimer himself, usually in some more or less misleading version. That his feelings toward Blackett mixed fervent admiration with fierce jealousy, however, was obvious to those who knew him well. John Edsall, for example, noticed the jealousy and speculated plausibly about what had aroused it. It was, he suggested, due to Oppenheimer's feeling that:

> Blackett was brilliant and handsome and a man of great social charm, and combining all this with great brilliance as a scientist—and I think he had a sense of his own comparative awkwardness and perhaps a personal sense of being physically unattractive compared to Blackett and so on.

There has been some confusion (most of it created by Oppenheimer himself) as to whether he really did leave an apple on Blackett's desk or whether his claim to have done so should be regarded as metaphorical. In his interview with Martin Sherwin, conducted in 1979, Francis Fergusson says that Openheimer told him that "he had actually used cyanide or something somewhere," suggesting that the attempted poisoning had been very real indeed. Fergusson adds: "Fortunately the tutor discovered it. Of course there was hell to pay with Cambridge."

In fact, Cambridge seems to have reacted with extraordinary equanimity. They did not press criminal charges, nor did they expel Oppenheimer or even suspend him. The reason for this seems to be that his parents were still in Cambridge. His father negotiated an agreement with the university authorities, according to which Oppenheimer would be allowed to continue his studies and merely be put on probation, on condition that he agreed to undergo frequent treatment by a Harley Street psychiatrist.

Fergusson describes meeting Oppenheimer in London after one of his psychiatric sessions. "I saw him standing on the corner," he recalls, "waiting for me, with his hat on one side of his head, looking absolutely weird." And he went on, "He looked crazy at that time . . . He was sort of standing around, looking like he might run or do something drastic." When he asked Oppenheimer how the session had gone, Oppenheimer "said that the guy was too stupid to follow him and that he knew more about his troubles than the doctor did."

As soon as this dreadful first term at Cambridge was over, Oppenheimer was taken by his parents to France for a recuperative holiday. He later remembered that on a cold, rainy day he was walking along the Brittany coast when, just as Smith had foreseen: "I was on the point of bumping myself off." A few days after Christmas 1925, Oppenheimer had arranged to meet Fergusson in Paris, where he told him about the poisoned-apple incident and confessed that there was some doubt as to whether he would be allowed to continue as a student at Cambridge. "My reaction was dismay," Fergusson later told Sherwin, adding, somewhat oddly: "But then, when he talked about it, I thought he had sort of gone beyond it, and that he was having trouble with his father."

In Paris, Fergusson said, Oppenheimer "began to get very queer." Considering that, up to this point in his narrative Fergusson had described Oppenheimer as: (a) forcing himself upon a woman in a train carriage, (b) attempting to injure that woman by dropping a suitcase on her, (c) sobbing at the prospect of sex with an old school friend, and (d) attempting to murder his university tutor by presenting him with a poisoned apple, the word "began" seems a little out of place. But Oppenheimer's behavior in Paris, as described by Fergusson, was very odd indeed. After finding that her son had locked her into her hotel room, Ella insisted that he see a Parisian psychiatrist. The diagnosis was sexual frustration and the prescription, accordingly, sex with a prostitute.

Soon after this, Fergusson went to see Oppenheimer in his Parisian hotel room and discovered him to be in "one of his ambiguous moods." He showed Oppenheimer some poetry written by his girlfriend, Frances Keeley, and told him that she was now his fiancée. Then, Fergusson describes:

> I leaned over to pick up a book, and he jumped on me from behind with a trunk strap and wound it around my neck. I was quite scared for a little while. We must have made some noise. And then I managed to pull aside and he fell to the ground weeping.

Having failed to kill one paragon of excellence, it seems, Oppenheimer was moved to attempt to kill the other.

When Oppenheimer returned to Cambridge, he wrote to Fergusson:

> You should have, not a letter, but a pilgrimage to Oxford, made in a hair shirt, with much fasting and snow and prayer. But I will keep my remorse and gratitude, and the shame I feel for my inadequacy to you, until I can do something rather less useless for you. I do not understand your forbearance nor your charity, but you must know that I will not forget them.

The nearest Oppenheimer came to explaining his odd behavior was to highlight the importance of what he described in this letter to Fergusson as "the awful fact of excellence": "As you know, it is that fact now, combined with my inability to solder two copper wires together, which is probably succeeding in getting me crazy."

Oppenheimer was by this time a graduate research student, though not, as he had earlier hoped, supervised by Rutherford, but rather by Rutherford's predecessor, the aged and semiretired J. J. Thomson. When Rutherford took over as director of the Cavendish in 1919, he insisted on having complete control and got Thomson to put in writing that he would not in any way interfere with Rutherford's running of the place. In return for this assurance, Thomson was granted space in the laboratory for his own research and was allowed to supervise some research students. These tended to be the ones, like Oppenheimer, that Rutherford did not want to supervise.

Thomson was nearly seventy years old and had been for many years somewhat off the pace in the rapidly changing world of theoretical physics. The monumental developments in the subject that had occurred in the early twentieth century were things that he either ignored or resisted. He never accepted either Einstein's theory of relativity or Rutherford's planetary model of the atom, and quantum theory had passed him by altogether. In his old age, he remained deeply devoted to Trinity College and developed an absorbing interest in gardening. He is remembered fondly by those who knew him as genial and kind, but he was not the man to guide an emotionally turbulent, brilliant young man—suffering agonies of sexual frustration, social isolation and a crippling ineptitude for practical laboratory work—through the intricacies of modern physics.

The details of Oppenheimer's research under Thomson's supervision are now lost. In a letter to Fergusson of November 1925, he says that Thomson "thought my experiments quite good, but didn't help much otherwise," but he does not say what those experiments were. Later in life he described his research as a study of "what happened with beams of electrons and thin films of metal," a description that could perfectly well apply to a good deal of the research conducted at the Cavendish during this period, but which also ties in with Oppenheimer's description to Priestley that September of his intended research topic: the theory of electronic conduction, especially those aspects of it "which can give an indication of the laws of force to which the motion of electrons is subject." To make the "thin films of metal" he needed for this research, Oppenheimer had to undergo what he later recalled as "the miseries of evaporating beryllium on to collodion, and then getting rid of the collodion, and so on." The resulting beryllium films were used not only by Oppenheimer, but also by James Chadwick, Rutherford's second-in-command at the Cavendish, famous for the discovery of neutrons in 1932.

"The business in the laboratory was really quite a sham," Oppenheimer later remarked, "but it got me into the laboratory, where I heard talk and found out a good deal of what people were interested in." In other words, the only value he later saw in his experience of experimental physics at Cambridge was that it stimulated his interest in contemporary developments in *theoretical* physics. As it turns out, that stimulus was enough to help him eventually overcome the acute psychological problems he had suffered in the autumn of 1925. John Edsall remembers that in the New Year of 1926, though it was obvious that Oppenheimer was undergoing some sort of crisis ("there was a tremendous inner turmoil"), he nevertheless "kept on doing a tremendous amount of work, thinking, reading, discussing things."

What brought about this burst of activity was Oppenheimer's discovery that theoretical physics was undergoing what the Nobel laureate Steven Weinberg has described as "the most profound revolution in
physical theory since the birth of modern physics in the seventeenth century." Most of the important contributions to this "profound revolution"
were made by young physicists just a few years older than Oppenheimer
himself. It was, it was commonly remarked, the period of *Knabenphysik*
(boy physics).

The "boys" in question fully realized that they were living in exciting times. Oppenheimer, soon after arriving at Cambridge, found himself caught up in that excitement. In November 1925, he had written to
Fergusson saying that there were "certainly some good physicists" at
Cambridge, emphasizing "the young ones I mean." He had, he told Fergusson, "been taken to all sorts of meetings," including "several rather
pallid science clubs." Pallid or not, it was at these science clubs that
Oppenheimer was introduced to the epoch-making work in theoretical physics that was then going on, and where he got to meet and get to
know some of the *Knaben* who were ushering in the new epoch.

The best known of these clubs is the Kapitza Club, which had been
formed by the Russian physicist Peter Kapitza upon his arrival at the
Cavendish in 1921, to provide an informal atmosphere within which
ideas in physics could be discussed and debated. Kapitza, the son of a
tsarist general, but a fervent supporter of the Bolshevik revolution, was
one of the most colorful characters at the Cavendish and a favorite of
Rutherford's. He and Blackett vied with each other to be regarded as
Rutherford's chief assistant. The club Kapitza established in his own
name became an important forum for the exploration of new ideas in
physics, providing both a means by which experimentalists and theorists
at Cambridge could learn from each other and an opportunity for Cambridge physicists to hear papers from distinguished physicists from other
countries. Blackett was a member of this club and it was no doubt he
who introduced Oppenheimer to it. The club met at the young experimentalist John Cockcroft's room in the Cavendish, where, in addition
to Kapitza himself, Oppenheimer would have encountered not only all
the leading experimental physicists at Cambridge, but also the man who
would very soon become recognized as one of the world's leading theorists: Paul Dirac.

Just two years older than Oppenheimer, Dirac had been a research
graduate student in physics at St. John's College since 1923, having previously completed degrees in both electrical engineering and applied
mathematics at the University of Bristol. He was tall and thin and had a
reputation for saying as little as possible. He would now almost certainly

be diagnosed as "autistic"; the many stories that circulated about him describe the kind of behavior characteristic of Asperger's syndrome. He combined an extraordinarily intense, obsessive interest in mathematics and physics with an almost complete lack of interest in anything else, including politics, literature and everyday conversation. Oppenheimer, remembering Dirac later in life, remarked that he was "not easily understood [and] not concerned to be understood. I thought he was absolutely grand."

Coming from a relatively impoverished, lower-middle-class family in Bristol, Dirac was certainly not "grand" in the social sense, but there was, undeniably, a certain grandeur in his exceptional intellectual ability. That he was socially awkward may have been, for Oppenheimer, an advantage; there is no sign that Dirac, for all his extraordinary brilliance, induced in Oppenheimer the murderous envy that Fergusson and Blackett had provoked. Dirac may have been the cleverest graduate physicist at Cambridge, and possibly even the greatest scientist the university had produced since Newton, but he did not, like Fergusson, mix with Europe's literary, artistic and philosophical elite; nor was he, like Blackett, widely regarded as the most handsome, best-dressed and most charismatic figure on the Cambridge social scene. Oppenheimer was thus able to admire him without feeling awed or envious.

Though still a graduate student, Dirac was invited to give a course of lectures on quantum theory in the academic year 1925–6. Entitled "Quantum Theory (Recent Developments)," it was the first course on quantum mechanics ever given at a British university. Among the few students who attended it was Oppenheimer, who, like the other attendees, was no doubt conscious of the privilege of being given access to Dirac's latest thoughts on the subject before they were announced and published to the outside world. "Dirac gave us what he himself had recently done," remembers one member of this privileged group, adding: "We did not, it is true, form a very sociable group, but for anyone there it was impossible to forget the sense of excitement at the new work."

Possibly through Dirac, or possibly through Blackett, Oppenheimer was introduced to the $\nabla^2 V$ Club, usually referred to as the "Del Squared V Club," ∇ being a mathematical symbol and ∇^2 being an operator (the "Laplacian operator") frequently used in theoretical physics. Where the Kapitza Club consisted mainly of experimental physicists, the $\nabla^2 V$ Club was for theorists. There Oppenheimer would have met all the leading theoretical physicists at Cambridge, including most notably Ralph Fowler, Dirac's supervisor and Rutherford's son-in-law. Fowler, who has been described as "a generous-spirited man with the build of Henry VIII and the voice of a drill sergeant," was, until Dirac's fame overshadowed him, the foremost theoretical physicist at Cambridge and, crucially for both Dirac and Oppenheimer, the one most fully abreast of developments on the continent.[21]

It was Fowler, for instance, who was first aware of the importance of the work of the French physicist Louis de Broglie, the man who took the initial steps toward the quantum-mechanics revolution. De Broglie, a member of one of the most ancient and distinguished French aristocratic families, had studied medieval history at the University of Paris before, under the influence of his elder brother, switching to physics. In the autumn of 1923, two years before Oppenheimer's arrival at Cambridge, de Broglie had published a series of three short papers in the French journal *Comptes rendus*, putting forward the outlandish suggestion that electrons should be regarded as being *both* particles and waves.

The inspiration for this was Einstein's Nobel Prize–winning suggestion in 1905 that light, previously thought of as consisting of waves, should be thought of as being made up of discrete "quanta," or "photons" as they are now called. Einstein had used this idea to account for the "photoelectric effect"—that is, the fact that, when light is shone onto a metal surface, electrons are emitted, the energy of the electrons depending not on the intensity of the light, but on its frequency. This quantum theory of light (or, more generally, of electromagnetic radiation) was confirmed in 1922 in a series of experiments conducted by the American physicist Arthur Compton. De Broglie, in a flash of inspiration, saw that, if Einstein's suggestion regarding light were extended to electrons, some of the difficulties faced by the Rutherford-Bohr-Sommerfeld model of the atom might be overcome. In particular, it would be possible to answer the question that Rutherford, with his unerring instinct for the heart of a problem, had raised about Bohr's model of the atom: how do electrons "know" which orbits to travel on? Or, to put it another way, why are electrons only "allowed" certain orbits? De Broglie's hypothesis of the wave-particle duality of electrons provided a brilliant answer to this: as electrons are waves, they can only circle the nucleus in certain orbits, namely those that correspond to multiple whole units of their wavelengths.

To begin with, de Broglie's brilliant idea aroused remarkably little interest among physicists. Fowler was one of the first to see any value in it, and it was he who in October 1923 submitted to the *Philosophical Magazine* an English version of de Broglie's articles. Entitled "A Tentative Theory of Light Quanta," this appeared in print in February

---

[21] It is indicative of the attitude toward theoretical physics at Cambridge during this period that Fowler's official position was college lecturer in mathematics.

1924, and, though it made de Broglie's revolutionary idea accessible to English-speaking physicists, it failed to attract very much attention. In fact, it required the advocacy of Einstein himself to make theorists take de Broglie seriously. In the spring of 1924, de Broglie wrote up his ideas and presented them as a Ph.D. thesis, which was examined the following November. One of the examiners was Paul Langevin, who sent de Broglie's thesis to Einstein, asking him what he thought. The reply was unequivocal: "He has lifted a corner of the great veil," wrote Einstein. De Broglie was duly awarded his doctorate and, five years later, after his hypothesis had been confirmed experimentally, was awarded the Nobel Prize.

Once it had been applauded by Einstein, de Broglie's audacious idea of wave-particle duality caught the imagination of physicists everywhere. Patrick Blackett was reported to have returned from his year in Göttingen "brimful of talk and enthusiasm about de Broglie and wave mechanics." In August 1925, a month before Oppenheimer arrived at Cambridge, Paul Dirac gave a paper to the Kapitza Club on de Broglie's ideas.

By then, however, the attention of the few physicists keeping abreast of these developments had shifted to the work of the young German physicist Werner Heisenberg. Having received his doctorate (supervised by Arnold Sommerfeld) from the University of Munich in 1923, when he was still only twenty-one, Heisenberg moved to Göttingen to take up a position as Max Born's assistant. During the first half of the academic year 1924–5, as Born was due to be in the United States on a lecture tour (which, in the event, he postponed until the following year), Heisenberg arranged to spend some months at Bohr's institute in Copenhagen. There at the same time, taking sabbatical leave from Cambridge, was Ralph Fowler, who was thus able to add Heisenberg to his already impressive list of personal contacts among the leading and up-and-coming physicists in Europe. Meanwhile, Patrick Blackett was at Göttingen, discussing with Franck and Born (and then, when he returned to Göttingen in April 1925, with Heisenberg) the wave-particle duality of the electron posited by de Broglie.

Though de Broglie's theory gave a convincing explanation of why electrons were confined to the orbits, or energy states, specified in Bohr's model of the atom, it introduced an enormous problem of its own: how *could* an electron possibly be *both* a particle and a wave? We can picture electrons as waves vibrating around the nucleus, or we can picture them as material objects orbiting the nucleus, but we cannot, surely, picture them as both at the same time. De Broglie's initial attempt to solve this conundrum was to imagine electrons as particles moving along a wavelike path, but this stripped the theory of its power to explain Bohr's orbits, since no good explanation could be given as to *why* electrons were tied to those wavelike paths. The beauty of de Broglie's theory lay precisely in the thought that an electron *was* a wave, the wavelength of which explained the "static orbits" of Bohr's theory. And yet there were very good reasons for believing, and abundant experimental evidence to suggest, that electrons were particles.

Heisenberg's novel response to this problem was to jettison all talk of orbits, particles and waves and refrain from picturing the electron *at all*. We must, he declared, confine ourselves to what can be observed. We cannot observe the orbiting of the nucleus by the electron; all we can observe is the energy given off by an electron when it "jumps" from one state to another. The reason we can observe *this* is that the energy in question takes the form of visible light, thus enabling the technique of investigation known as spectroscopy: the study of the spectra of light emitted by electrons of various elements, which allows physicists to associate each element with its characteristic and unique spectrum of colored light. It is upon the data provided by spectroscopy that Bohr's theory of atomic structure was built (hence the title of Sommerfeld's classic book on the subject: *Atombau und Spektrallinien* [Atomic Structure and Spectral Lines]), and when Heisenberg announced his intention of confining himself to what can be observed, he meant primarily: observed using the techniques of spectroscopy.

In June 1925, shortly after he returned to Göttingen from Copenhagen, Heisenberg, ill with hay fever, decided to recuperate on the North Sea island of Helgoland. There, thinking alone about the strictly observable properties of electrons, inspiration struck him and he formulated the basic ideas of the branch of physics that was to claim the attention of Oppenheimer and most of his contemporaries: quantum mechanics. The fundamental aim of this branch of physics is to provide quantum theory with a mechanics—that is, a mathematical model that would explain the apparently bizarre movements of electrons and of subatomic particles generally. What occurred to Heisenberg in Helgoland was (to him) a brand-new kind of mathematics, which one could use to model the behavior of electrons.

At the heart of this mathematics was a numbering system that assigned to electrons a pair of numbers, p (representing the electron's *momentum*—that is, its mass multiplied by its velocity) and q (representing the electron's *position*), and a technique of multiplying these pairs of numbers. The troubling aspect of this new mathematical model was that the multiplication rules for it were not commutative—that is, $p \times q$ was not, in general, equal to $q \times p$. Heisenberg had no explanation for this departure from the basic rules of arithmetic, nor could he offer a picture of the physical processes that obeyed such odd rules. What he did have was a mathematical modeling of the behavior of electrons, and this itself was exciting enough to ensure that he did not sleep very much in Helgoland; and enough, too, to ensure that, six years later, he won the Nobel Prize.

Returning to Göttingen in a state of excitement and optimism about his new work, Heisenberg hurriedly wrote up his new theory as a paper entitled "Quantum Theoretical Reinterpretation of Kinematic and Mechanical Relations," which he gave to Born to submit for publication, while he himself left for Cambridge to fulfill a prior arrangement to deliver a talk to the Kapitza Club. The talk, delivered on July 28, 1925, was not on his revolutionary new ideas, but Heisenberg did mention his recently written paper to his host, Fowler, who asked to see it when Heisenberg had proof copies available. When, at the beginning of September, Fowler duly received a proof copy, he sent it to Dirac with a scribbled message on the front page: "What do you think of this? I shall be glad to hear."

Dirac was at this time in Bristol for the summer vacation. After an initial glance at Heisenberg's paper, he put it to one side, seeing little interest in it. When he returned to Cambridge in October, he took up the paper again and this time became fascinated with it and quickly convinced of its fundamental importance. He realized that the key to it was the noncommutative multiplications that had puzzled Heisenberg, and, unlike Heisenberg, he recognized these as being akin to a mathematical construction called a "Poisson bracket," which had been introduced into mathematics in the nineteenth century. Using the method of Poisson brackets, Dirac provided Heisenberg's theory with a new mathematical foundation, the center of which was the equation $(p \times q) - (q \times p)$ $= ih/2\pi$, which not only says that the multiplication of p and q is noncommutative (if it were commutative, of course, $(p \times q) - (q \times p)$ would be equal to zero), but also provides an exact quantity by which $p \times q$ differs from $q \times p$, a quantity that uses the magical ingredient h, Planck's constant, together with that equally mysterious "imaginary" number, i, which is the square root of -1.

By the time Heisenberg's paper was published in November 1925, Dirac had sent his own paper—immodestly entitled "The Fundamental Equations of Quantum Mechanics"—to the *Proceedings of the Royal Society* for publication in December. Astonishingly, the very same fundamental equation that Dirac had discovered had, at the same time, been discovered independently by Born and his new assistant, Pascual Jordan, who included it in a paper that they wrote together in September. Like

Dirac, Born and Jordan realized that the noncommutativity in Heisenberg's mathematics was not unprecedented, though they saw affinities not with Poisson brackets, but with the matrix mathematics developed in the nineteenth century by the British mathematician Arthur Cayley. In October, Born, Jordan and Heisenberg worked together to produce a long and detailed paper called "On Quantum Mechanics II" (often referred to as the *Drei-Männer-Arbeit*, the "Three-Man Paper"), which provided a rigorous mathematical foundation for Heisenberg's new quantum mechanics, but which, because it was received by the *Zeitschrift für Physik* nine days after the *Proceedings of the Royal Society* received Dirac's paper, cannot claim to have been the first to do so.

By the New Year of 1926, then, a revolution in physics had taken place; the basic theory of quantum mechanics had been formulated and had received two different, but essentially similar, mathematical foundations. And Oppenheimer, merely by being at Cambridge during the academic year of 1925–6 and getting to know Fowler and Dirac, was right at the center of events. The effect on him was galvanizing and he began to immerse himself in the rapid developments that followed the birth of this new subject.

Among these developments was Dirac's second paper on the new theory, "Quantum Mechanics and a Preliminary Investigation of the Hydrogen Atom," sent off for publication at the end of January 1926, which introduced a now-famous distinction between classical numbers, or "c-numbers," which commute, and quantum numbers, or "q-numbers," which do not. Before this article appeared in print, Dirac presented it on March 2 as a paper to the Del Squared V Club, with Oppenheimer among those present. The club minutes record that after Dirac's paper there followed a "lengthy discussion," in which, no doubt, Oppenheimer took a full part.

On March 7, Oppenheimer wrote a letter to Fergusson, the tone of which is markedly different from his previous letter of January 23, written shortly after, and mainly to apologize for, the bizarre attempted strangling in Paris. Whereas then he had struck a remorseful and confessional tone, now he sounds brisk, businesslike and jocular. "My regret at not having strangled you is now intellectual rather than emotional," he told Fergusson, assuring him that, if he chose to visit Oppenheimer in Cambridge before he went to Italy "it will be perfectly safe & I shall be very glad to see you." Rather warily, Fergusson responded positively to this invitation and came to Cambridge sometime in March. Oppenheimer, he recalls, put him up in a room next door to his own, "and I remember thinking that I'd better make sure that he didn't turn up in the night, so I put a chair up against the door. But nothing happened."

When Fergusson alluded to Oppenheimer's behavior during the Christmas vacation, Oppenheimer told him not to worry; he was, he insisted, "over that."

Oppenheimer told Fergusson that he would probably have to spend the Easter vacation at Cambridge because he had so much work to do. Almost certainly, the work in question consisted not of his laboratory experiments, but rather of a paper in theoretical physics that was to become his first publication. If he could take a break from this work, he told Fergusson, he would go for a short walking holiday in Corsica with Wyman and Edsall, in which case, he wrote, he hoped that he would be able to meet Fergusson in Italy. In the event, Oppenheimer did manage to tear himself away from his theoretical studies for the projected holiday in Corsica, though he did not, as it turned out, succeed in joining Fergusson in Italy.

Shortly before he left for Corsica, Oppenheimer, along with the rest of the theoretical physics community, received a bolt out of the blue. On March 13, the German academic journal *Annalen der Physik* published an article by the Austrian physicist Erwin Schrödinger called "Quantization as a Problem of Proper Values" which seemed to put the recent quantum-mechanics revolution in a completely new light. Or rather, it seemed to show how it would look in the *old* light, before the advent of *Knabenphysik*. In particular, what Schrödinger—who, at thirty-eight years old, was himself certainly no *Knabe*—appeared to demonstrate was that quantum mechanics could quite readily be absorbed into old, familiar physics using old familiar mathematics. All the results that had been derived by Heisenberg, Born, Jordan and Dirac using esoteric and obscure methods of mathematics could, Schrödinger demonstrated, equally be derived from a theory that used only that most well-understood and widely used of mathematical tools: the differential equation. Moreover (and this was either a great advantage or a step backward, depending on one's understanding of the physics of electrons), unlike the theories of Heisenberg, Born, Jordan and Dirac, Schrödinger's theory allowed one to *visualize* what was happening inside an atom. Building on de Broglie's work, Schrödinger's theory called on one to imagine that an electron simply *is* a wave. In place of the term "quantum mechanics," therefore, Schrödinger called his theory "wave mechanics."

The reaction among physicists, particularly the older ones, to Schrödinger's theory (which would be developed over three further landmark papers published in 1926) was almost universally and unrestrainedly enthusiastic. Max Planck wrote to Schrödinger, telling him that he had read his first paper "like an eager child hearing the solution to a riddle that had plagued him for a long time." Einstein told him "the idea of your work springs from true genius." Even Max Born became quickly convinced that wave mechanics provided the "deepest form of the quantum laws." Heisenberg, however, hated Schrödinger's theory, seeing in it a desperate attempt to cling to an outdated and unsupportable visualization of the "orbits" of electrons. Dirac, too, disliked Schrödinger's theory, at least initially. When, however, it was proved—by Dirac, Schrödinger and many others—that, mathematically, Schrödinger's theory was equivalent to both the matrix mechanics of Born, Jordan and Heisenberg and the "fundamental equations" of Dirac himself, Dirac overcame his objections and treated Schrödinger's version of the theory as an interesting, and sometimes useful, alternative formulation of quantum mathematics.

Once the mathematical equivalence of the three versions of quantum mechanics was realized, there remained the question—which Dirac was inclined to dismiss as "philosophical," but which Born, Heisenberg, Bohr and others regarded as fundamental—namely: how does one understand the physical reality that can be modeled equally by each of these three different theories? What, exactly, is being modeled by the mathematics? What, really, *is* an electron? A particle? A wave? Could it possibly be both? Might it possibly be neither? How should one, if indeed one should at all, *picture* an electron and its movements?

With these questions hanging in the air over the entire community of theoretical physicists, Oppenheimer embarked on his holiday with Wyman and Edsall, his mind more or less completely preoccupied with the exciting developments in quantum theory. In a short autobiographical article that Edsall wrote at the end of his life, he remembers Oppenheimer during this holiday as "passionately eager to solve the problems of quantum physics." Oppenheimer, Edsall writes, was, unlike their mutual friend Dirac (whom Edsall knew as a fellow graduate student at St. John's College), "intensely articulate"; he "conveyed to me the deep excitement and promise of what was going on in quantum mechanics . . . The feeling that he gave me for the central importance of the subject stayed with me."

There was a great deal of talk during this holiday. For ten days, Edsall, Wyman and Oppenheimer walked through the mountainous Corsican countryside, covering the entire length of the island, beginning in the north and ending in the impressive medieval citadel of Bonifacio, on the southernmost tip of the island, overlooking the strait that separates Corsica from Sardinia. They spent their nights in small inns, peasant huts or even occasionally out in the open. They had, it seems, very little to do with the locals, and so, spending all day and all night together, there was plenty of time and opportunity for discussion. As well as physics, Oppenheimer talked of French and Russian literature, especially Dostoyevsky. When Edsall expressed a preference for Tolstoy, Oppenheimer insisted: "No, no. Dostoevsky is superior. He gets to the soul and torment of man." Once, in a conversation about people who had achieved great things, whether in science or literature, Oppenheimer remarked: "The kind of person that I admire most would be one who becomes extraordinarily good at doing a lot of things but maintains a tear-stained countenance."

Despite this remark, the Oppenheimer remembered by Edsall and Wyman during this holiday was far removed indeed from the Oppenheimer that Fergusson had encountered in France just three months previously. They even, on one occasion, saw him convulsed with mirth. What prompted this unprecedented event was a misunderstanding between Edsall and the Corsican police over some photographs that Edsall was taking of the famous fortifications at Bonifacio. Convinced that he was some kind of spy, the police took Edsall to the station for questioning. Wyman and Oppenheimer accompanied him, and, while they sat waiting in a corridor, they could hear Edsall trying to explain that he was not a spy, but a tourist. Though he himself could not stop laughing at the absurdity of the situation, Wyman was astonished when he looked up at Oppenheimer to see him slapping his thighs and chuckling.

This incident at Bonifacio, coming at the end of the trio's ten-day hike, suggests that, from Oppenheimer's point of view, the holiday achieved its purpose of helping him to unwind and fully regain his sanity. In fact, it seems to have done much more than that. Several times throughout his life Oppenheimer emphasized the enormous importance that these ten spring days in Corsica had for him. They had an impact similar to, but even greater than, his first trip to New Mexico in 1922. Indeed, Oppenheimer suggested on a number of occasions, this holiday was the turning point in his life.

To one of his earliest biographers, Nuel Pharr Davis, whose *Lawrence & Oppenheimer* was published the year after Oppenheimer's death, he spoke of "what began for me in Corsica" and drew attention to the significance of an undocumented episode that occurred during his time there, an episode that he described as "a great and lasting part" of his life. The reason he was telling him about this, Oppenheimer told Pharr Davis, was to counteract the impression that the turning point in his life had been the security trial in 1954: "You see, don't you, that I'm proving this point to you now. With something important to me not in those records." As for what that "something" was, Oppenheimer was teasingly evasive. "You ask whether I will tell you the full story or whether you must dig it out," he wrote to Pharr Davis. "But it is known to few and they won't tell. You can't dig it out. What you need to know is that it was not a mere love affair, not a love affair at all, but love." "Geography," he added, "was henceforth the only separation I recognized, but for me it was not a real separation."

Pharr Davis guessed that what Oppenheimer was alluding to here was a love for "a European girl who could not marry him." This is perhaps true, but, even if it is, there is clearly more to understand about why Oppenheimer's spring break in Corsica was such an important event in his life. His later friend Haakon Chevalier recalled Oppenheimer once telling him, many years after the event, that "one of the great experiences in his life" occurred in Corsica in 1926. The experience in question, however, had nothing to do with a "European girl," or anyway not a real one. It was, rather, his reading of Proust's *À la recherche du temps perdu*.

Once, when the topic of cruelty came into the conversation, Chevalier recalled, Oppenheimer surprised him by quoting from memory, word for word, a passage from Proust's novel. The passage comes in the first volume of *Du côté de chez Swann*, when Mademoiselle Vinteuil goads her lesbian lover to spit on a photograph of her recently departed father. In describing this scene, Proust emphasizes to his readers that there is something theatrical about Mlle. Vinteuil's "sadism." She is not *really* evil; rather, she finds it erotic to pretend to be so. In fact, Proust writes, it is precisely *because* she is not really evil that she *can* derive orgasmic pleasure from the grotesque performance of her lover. In the passage Oppenheimer memorized and recited to Chevalier, Proust writes:

> Perhaps she would not have considered evil to be so rare, so extraordinary, so estranging a state, to which it was so restful to emigrate, had she been able to discern in herself, as in everyone, that indifference to the sufferings one causes, an indifference which, whatever names one may give it, is the terrible and permanent form of cruelty.

Why did this passage mean so much to Oppenheimer that he learned it by heart? And why was reading it one of the great experiences of his life?

A clue to this might be contained in some remarks Oppenheimer made toward the end of his life, when he took part in a series of conferences partially sponsored by the Congress for Cultural Freedom—a group of politically liberal intellectuals united by their opposition to communism—on the relationship between science and culture. "We most of all should try to be experts on the worst among ourselves," he said at one such meeting, and, as if to confirm that he had always been acutely aware of the worst in himself, he made the following confession:

> Up to now and even more in the days of my almost infinitely pro-longed adolescence, I hardly took any action, hardly did anything, or failed to do anything, whether it was a paper on physics, or a lecture, or how I read a book, how I talked to a friend, how I loved, that did not arouse in me a very great sense of revulsion and of wrong.
>
> It turned out to be impossible . . . for me to live with anybody else, without understanding that what I saw was only one part of the truth . . . and in an attempt to break out and be a reasonable man, I had to realize that my own worries about what I did were valid and were important, but that they were not the whole story, that there must be a complementary way of looking at them, because other people did not see them as I did. And I needed what they saw, needed them.

In other words, Oppenheimer was able to live with other people only when he came to see that they did not necessarily see him as he saw himself, and therefore that his words and deeds did not arouse in others the sense of revulsion they aroused in him. This realization, brought about perhaps by a combination of Proust, conversations with good friends and the pleasures of the Corsican countryside, had an enormous effect on him. When he returned from Corsica, he said, he "felt much kinder and more tolerant" and "could now relate to others."

Oddly, Oppenheimer chose to leave Corsica in a way that persuaded Wyman and Edsall that he was still, after all, a little mad—or at least, as Wyman later put it, "passing through a great emotional crisis." Having reached Bonifacio, the plan was to proceed to Sardinia, but, while the three of them were having dinner at their inn, a waiter approached Oppenheimer to tell him when the next boat left for France. Naturally, Edsall and Wyman immediately asked him why he was leaving so abruptly and unexpectedly. "I can't bear to speak of it," said Oppenheimer, "but I've got to go." As Wyman later remembered it, the three of them drank a little more wine and then Oppenheimer said: "Well, perhaps I can tell you why I have to go. I've done a terrible thing. I've put a poisoned apple on Blackett's desk and I've got to go back and see what happened." Why Oppenheimer should, in an effort to explain his decision to return to Cambridge in the spring of 1926, confess to something he had done seven months earlier, suggesting that he had only just done it, takes some understanding. Indeed, it might well be inexplicable, though it seems reasonable to suppose that, having spent ten days and nights living so closely with Edsall and Wyman, Oppenheimer felt obliged to confess to them the secret of his bizarre behavior the previous autumn.

However, the reason he wanted to get back to Cambridge, it seems safe to suppose, is that he wanted to finish writing his paper on quantum physics, and, with this in mind, it is possible to arrive at the following speculative explanation of his "confession" to Wyman and Edsall: before he set off for Corsica, Oppenheimer had left on Blackett's desk an early draft of his first paper on quantum mechanics, which he now, ten days into his holiday in Corsica, realized contained serious errors (that is, it was "poisoned"). Desperate to get back to Cambridge to continue work on his paper and to correct the mistakes it contained, and feeling obliged to confess his previous sins to Edsall and Wyman, he exploited the analogy to tell them a story that contained, at one and the same time, a literal confession about what he had done the previous autumn and a metaphorical explanation of why he had to break short his holiday and return to Cambridge. Whether there is any truth at all in this speculative suggestion, what is not in doubt is that, after his holiday in Corsica, Oppenheimer was a different person. Whereas just a few months earlier he had felt paralyzed, depressed and unequal to the demands made upon him, now he was confident, productive and energetic.

When he returned to England in the spring of 1926 the country was in political turmoil, heading toward the general strike, which lasted from May 3 to May 12. The country was engulfed in class war, with the middle classes doing everything they could to negate the effects of the strike. At Cambridge, this involved undergraduates temporarily abandoning their studies in order to drive buses or trains or lorries—anything to keep deliveries going and prevent the economy and society from grinding to a halt. So many Cambridge students took part in these strike-breaking activities that the university decided to postpone the summer exams. A minority of students and academics, including Patrick Blackett, were on the side of the workers and voiced their support for the strike. Paul Dirac, meanwhile, ignored it and spent this time finishing his Ph.D. thesis. Entitled simply "Quantum Mechanics," it was the first doctoral thesis ever to be submitted on the subject and contained work that had already been recognized as being of fundamental importance.

Oppenheimer, who had not yet even begun work on his Ph.D. thesis, managed, within a few weeks of returning from Corsica, to complete the paper that was to become his first publication. Its title was "On the Quantum Theory of Vibration-Rotation Bands." On May 24, 1926, it was received by the Cambridge Philosophical Society, the venerable scientific society (established in 1819 "for the purpose of promoting scientific inquiry") to which Oppenheimer had been elected as an "associate" in January 1926, and was published in their *Proceedings* in July. Though he was later disparaging about it ("That was a mess, that first paper"), the very fact that he was able, so soon after his severe problems during the winter, to write a publishable paper on a subject right at the cutting edge of advanced physical theory was a notable achievement.

The paper might be seen as one of the earliest contributions to the subject of "quantum chemistry," in that it attempts to apply the new quantum mechanics of Heisenberg, Born, Jordan, Dirac and Schrödinger (all of whose papers are cited in it) to the understanding not of atoms, but of molecules. In particular, Oppenheimer seeks to show the applicability of Dirac's version of the mathematics of quantum mechanics to the understanding of diatomic molecules; that is, molecules, like those of oxygen (O_2) and hydrogen (H_2), that consist of two atoms. The vibration and rotation of these molecules produce characteristic spectra of electromagnetic radiation, the frequencies of which Oppenheimer attempts in this paper to derive from within Dirac's theory.

Compared with what Dirac was producing at this time, Oppenheimer's first paper was a minor piece of work. It addresses a problem that is of secondary, rather than fundamental, importance, and, moreover, it has a weakness that would have been unthinkable in anything by Dirac: it contains mathematical errors. Nevertheless, its publication was enough to transform Oppenheimer from a failing experimental physicist to an up-and-coming theorist. When distinguished visitors came to Cambridge, Oppenheimer was now introduced to them as one of the *Knaben* leading the revolution in theoretical physics. When Paul Ehrenfest, the professor of physics at Leiden, came to Cambridge, for example, Oppenheimer remembers that "we went out on the river and talked about collision problems, Coulomb's law . . . and so on." A short while after Ehrenfest's visit to Cambridge, Oppenheimer met him again, when he and other American physicists at Cambridge spent a week at the University of Leiden. There he met Ehrenfest's young, but already famous, assistants, Samuel Goudsmit and George Uhlenbeck, who together had been the first to put forward the idea that electrons possess the property of spin. Oppenheimer's reception among the theoretical physicists at Leiden recalls his acceptance by the literary "troika" in New Mexico in 1922. Uhlenbeck remembers Oppenheimer as being a "very warm person" who was "so involved in physics" that it "was as if we were old friends because [we] had so many things in common." Oppenheimer, for his part, recalls that it was "wonderful" at Leiden and that he "realized then that some of the troubles of the winter had been exacerbated by the English customs."

Back in Cambridge, Oppenheimer resumed his theoretical studies and began work on a second paper on quantum mechanics, this time on what is known as the "two-body problem." This is, in general, the problem of providing a mathematical model of two bodies orbiting one another. Newton had provided a solution of this problem for classical physics, and Dirac and Schrödinger had investigated it from the point of view of quantum mechanics. Oppenheimer's aim was to provide a more complete quantum-mechanical solution to this problem than had so far been achieved.

At the beginning of June 1926, while hard at work on this problem, Oppenheimer had one of the most memorable moments of his time at Cambridge—indeed, of his entire life—when he was introduced to Niels Bohr. Bohr, who was in England to receive the honor of being made a foreign member of the Royal Society, happened to be in Rutherford's room at the Cavendish when Oppenheimer walked in. Rutherford, who by then looked upon Oppenheimer as a promising theorist rather than a distinctly unpromising experimentalist, immediately introduced him to Bohr. As custom and politeness demanded in such a situation, Bohr asked Oppenheimer what he was working on and, on being told that it was the two-body problem, asked him how it was going. "I'm in difficulties," Oppenheimer replied. "Are the difficulties mathematical or physical?" Bohr asked. "I don't know," Oppenheimer answered, prompting Bohr to remark: "That's bad." The encounter made a deep and lasting impression on Oppenheimer. After meeting Bohr, he once said, "I forgot about beryllium and films and decided to try to learn the trade of becoming a theoretical physicist." Bohr's question to him, he thought, was a very good one, a question that went right to the heart of his difficulties. "I thought it put a rather useful glare on the extent to which I became embroiled in formal questions without stepping back to see what they really had to do with the physics of the problem."

Perhaps because of the arithmetical mistakes in his first paper, Oppenheimer took immense care to ensure that the mathematics in this second paper was free from error. Edsall remembers how, at Oppenheimer's request, he spent hours one Sunday checking the figures in this paper, even though he himself had little idea what they meant. His reward was a footnote acknowledging his help while misspelling his name ("I am indebted to Mr J.T. Edsahl for checking these calculations"). By the middle of July the paper was finished and it appeared that month in the *Proceedings of the Cambridge Philosophical Society* under the title "On the Quantum Theory of the Problem of the Two Bodies."

By a fortuitous coincidence, this second paper brought Oppenheimer to the attention of one of the leading figures in quantum mechanics at the very point when he was making his greatest contribution to the subject. That figure was Max Born, who had already played a key role in the development of the matrix version of quantum mechanics and was on the brink of providing the definitive interpretation of the theory. A summary of that interpretation had been given in a short paper that Born published on July 10, 1926, called "Zur Quantenmechanik der Stossvorgänge" ("On the Quantum Mechanics of Collision Processes"). Ten days later, Born sent off a longer, more polished and refined paper with the same title to the journal *Zeitschrift für Physik*, and on July 29—three days after the publication of Oppenheimer's second paper—Born came to Cambridge to deliver this paper as a talk to the Kapitza Club with the English title "On the Quantum Mechanics of Collisions of Atoms and Electrons." This paper was to have a profound impact on the way quantum mechanics was understood, addressing head-on exactly the question raised by Bohr's brief discussion with Oppenheimer, the question about how one was to understand the physical reality that lay behind the mathematics of quantum mechanics.

The immediate aim of Born's paper was to bring quantum mechanics to bear on the subject of how particles behave when they collide with each other; his more general intention was to provide an interpretation of the mathematical formulae of quantum mechanics. In both respects, his conclusions were startling, from both a physical and a philosophical point of view; so startling that many people, including Einstein, refused to accept them. Still more remarkable, especially in the light of Einstein's resistance, is the fact that those conclusions became widely accepted and remain today the generally held view among scientists.

Regarding collisions, Born showed that quantum mechanics, unlike classical Newtonian mechanics, is nondeterministic. In Newtonian mechanics, what happens to one body after it collides with another (for example, a billiard ball hitting another billiard ball) is entirely determined by the laws of motion. So, if you repeat a collision (hit a billiard ball into another in exactly the same way), exactly the same thing will happen. If the ball deflected to the left the first time, it would deflect to the left every time you repeated the shot. In quantum mechanics, however, the situation is very different. According to Born, quantum mechanics allows identical experiments to have different outcomes: one time, the particle might be deflected to the left; another time, to the right. Any outcome is *possible*; some outcomes, however, are more *probable* than others. It is this feature of quantum mechanics that persuaded Einstein that the theory could not possibly be right and prompted him to make his famous remark (in a letter to Born): "God does not play dice."

The nondeterministic, probabilistic nature of quantum mechanics provided Born with an intriguing answer to the general question regarding the physical reality described by its equations, allowing him to decide between the particle-like "quanta" described by the mathematics of Heisenberg and Dirac and the waves described by Schrödinger's differential equations. Basically, he came down on the side of regarding electrons as particles, while providing an ingenious explanation for why Schrödinger's wave mechanics "worked." Schrödinger believed that the success of his wave functions showed that de Broglie was right—electrons *are* waves—and his problem was to explain why, in countless experiments (including the original experiments of J. J. Thomson back in the 1890s), electrons seemed to behave like particles. For Born, it was the other way around; electrons *were* particles (or at least discrete "quanta") and what required explanation was why they *seemed* to behave like waves. His answer to this last question invoked the probabilistic nature of quantum theory that he had demonstrated in his analysis of collisions. The waves of de Broglie and Schrödinger, Born argued, had no physical reality. Rather, they were probability waves. What they described was the probability of an electron being in a particular place at a particular time. Quantum mechanics, according to Born, is unable to say definitely whether an electron is or is not at a particular place at a particular time; it can only say what the odds are that it is here or there. And this is not because of the limitations of our knowledge; it is an inherent feature of physical reality, linked to its nondeterministic nature. This "statistical interpretation of quantum mechanics," as it became known, was quickly adopted by other leading physicists, most notably Heisenberg and Bohr (who famously defended it against Einstein on numerous occasions), and it was for discovering it that Born was awarded the Nobel Prize, though oddly not until 1954, more than twenty years after the same honor had been awarded to de Broglie, Heisenberg, Schrödinger and Dirac.[22]

Though Born had already sent his paper to the *Zeitschrift*, it had not yet been published when he came to Cambridge to deliver his talk to the Kapitza Club on July 29, 1926. When it was published, in September 1926, a footnote had been added, acknowledging the importance of Oppenheimer's paper on the two-body problem. For a twenty-two-year-old research student who had not yet completed a Ph.D. thesis, this was a significant feather in his cap. Born was evidently very impressed with

---

[22] As far as I know, no authoritative answer has been given as to why it took so long to award Born the Nobel Prize. Jeremy Bernstein has speculated that it is because, in 1933, when Heisenberg, Dirac and Schrödinger were honored, it would have been natural to have included Born and Jordan, but Jordan was a member of the Nazi Party and unacceptable. Therefore the committee had to wait until they had a reason for giving it to Born alone. This might explain why Born did not receive the prize in 1933, but it hardly explains why he had to wait a further twenty-one years.

Oppenheimer. In the second week of August, Born returned to England to read a paper at the annual meeting of the British Association for the Advancement of Science, which that year was held in Oxford. The paper, entitled "Physical Aspects of Quantum Mechanics," was Born's most direct statement yet on the question of how, in the light of quantum mechanics, we are to understand physical reality, and was responsible for spreading his idea of probability waves to theoretical physicists in Britain. When the paper was published in *Nature* the following year, it carried the following acknowledgment: "Translated by Mr Robert Oppenheimer. The author is very much obliged to Mr Oppenheimer for his careful translation."

By the summer of 1926, then, Oppenheimer had not only established himself as a promising young theorist; he had become a collaborator with the person who at that time was leading the effort of the international community of physicists to understand the extraordinary world of quantum mechanics. He had, in fact, positioned himself where he had wanted to be: at the "center" of theoretical physics. His year at Cambridge had allowed him to achieve this, partly because it had enabled him to see that, in 1926, the center of theoretical physics was not Cambridge, but Göttingen. The person to work with was not Ernest Rutherford, or even Niels Bohr, but rather Max Born. Accordingly, on August 18, 1926, a week after the meeting at Oxford, Oppenheimer wrote to Raymond Priestley, asking for permission to spend the following year at Göttingen, under the supervision of Born, who, Oppenheimer informed Priestley, was "particularly interested in the problems at which I hoped to work." Reflecting on his decision to leave Cambridge for Göttingen, Oppenheimer later said that, though he "had very great misgivings about myself on all fronts," he still felt determined to pursue his inclination to become a theoretical physicist: "Here was something I felt just driven to try."

He may have had misgivings, but he must also have known that, in pursuing this inclination, he had every chance of meeting with success. He had never stood any chance of impressing the "tutors & the dukes" of British high society, he would never have been invited to Garsington or to Pontigny, and he would never be described (as Blackett had been by I. A. Richards) as "a young Oedipus," but he *had* succeeded in impressing one of the foremost quantum physicists in the world—an achievement that brought him not just near the center of theoretical physics, but right inside it.

Part Two

1926—1941

6

Göttingen

In the starkest contrast to his arrival in Cambridge just a year earlier, Oppenheimer arrived in Göttingen in the summer of 1926 in a state of almost unrestrained self-confidence. As Max Born put it, Oppenheimer seemed "conscious of his superiority." In his autobiography Born complains several times about Oppenheimer's arrogance, without appearing to recognize the central role he himself had played in nurturing it. Whereas at Cambridge, Oppenheimer arrived having been rejected by the leading physicist there, at Göttingen he arrived having been *invited* by the leading physicist there, who made no secret of the fact that he was extremely impressed with, and indeed a little intimidated by, Oppenheimer's intelligence.

Though apparently unaware of what it revealed, Born tells a story that perfectly conveys the role he played in allowing, even encouraging, Oppenheimer to be "conscious of his superiority." The story concerns Born's most famous paper, "The Quantum Mechanics of Collision Processes," the one that he read to the Kapitza Club in July 1926, when he first met Oppenheimer. Born says that when he finished writing the paper, he showed it to Oppenheimer in order for him to check the difficult and involved calculations it contained. This must have been, I think, in August 1926, when Born returned to England to read the paper that Oppenheimer translated to the British Association for the Advancement of Science at Oxford. Born had by then received the proofs of "The Quantum Mechanics of Collision Processes" from the *Zeitschrift für Physik*, and it is presumably these proofs that he showed to Oppenheimer. What would immediately have struck Oppenheimer, and boosted his confidence enormously, was the footnote Born added to the paper at the proof stage drawing attention to the importance of Oppenheimer's work on the two-body problem. Born, who was self-critical to a fault, says that he asked Oppenheimer to check the calculations because "I was never very good at long calculations and always made silly mistakes." All his students knew this, he says, but Oppenheimer "was the only one frank and rude enough to say it without joking." For, after he had checked the paper, Oppenheimer returned it to Born, saying, with an astonished expression: "I couldn't find any mistake—did you really do this alone?" "I was not offended," Born insists. "It actually increased my esteem for his remarkable personality."

Born was at that time a forty-three-year-old professor at one of the most distinguished universities in the world, at the height of his career, having, in the preceding few years, published work of fundamental, Nobel Prize–winning importance—work that persuaded brilliant young physicists from all over the world to come to Göttingen to study with him. Oppenheimer, meanwhile, was a twenty-two-year-old student, recently recovered from a severe mental illness, who was entirely unknown to the world at large and whose publications to date numbered just two articles. From the point of view of mathematical competence, Born had taken a Ph.D. in mathematics, examined by David Hilbert, widely recognized as the greatest mathematician of his day, who regarded Born as a student of exceptional mathematical ability. Born was also regarded by his peers in theoretical physics as a scientist whose *greatest strength* was his facility with difficult and esoteric mathematics. Oppenheimer, on the other hand, had not yet taken a Ph.D. in either mathematics or physics, and, though regarded as an undergraduate as someone who, in Percy Bridgman's words, had "much mathematical power," acknowledged himself that there were significant gaps in his mathematical education. His first published paper had been marred by mathematical errors and throughout his life he would have a reputation among physicists as someone prone to mistakes in mathematical calculations. Objectively, there was no reason whatsoever for Born to look up to Oppenheimer, particularly with regard to his mathematical acumen, nor was there any excuse for Oppenheimer to look down on Born. That, within a month of knowing each other, their relationship developed in a way that made it possible for Oppenheimer to be condescending toward Born about his mathematical competence says a great deal about the personalities of both men; about Born's insecurities and about Oppenheimer's ability to, as it were, cast a spell.

Another key to understanding Oppenheimer's self-assurance at Göttingen, compared to the self-doubts and anxieties he had felt at Cambridge, may lie in the contrast between the two universities themselves. The University of Göttingen, though not the oldest in Germany (Heidelberg, Leipzig and several others predate it by hundreds of years), is certainly one of the most prestigious and is commonly held to be Germany's equivalent to Cambridge (with Heidelberg its equivalent to Oxford). What would have struck Oppenheimer when he arrived in Göttingen in the summer of 1926, however, are the many ways in which it is very *unlike* Cambridge. These differences are immediately apparent: the University of Göttingen's oldest and grandest buildings are elegant and graceful, rather than Gothic and ecclesiastical, betraying its origins in the eighteenth-century Enlightenment, rather than in thirteenth-century monastic scholarship. Not being a collegiate university, it has no dons, fellows or high table. It has its own famous and celebrated esoteric rituals (the most famous of which is that Ph.D. students should, on passing their oral examination, be carried by cart to the market square in the center of town, where they have to kiss the statue of the *Gänseliesel*, the goose girl), but it does not have the weight of 700 years of tradition bearing down upon it.

Moreover, the postwar atmosphere of a defeated nation is very different from that of the victors. At Göttingen in the 1920s one would not have been aware of living in a carefree "Jazz Age" or the "Roaring Twenties"; neither was there any parallel to the calculatedly unconventional, self-consciously effete aestheticism that characterized British university life in the postwar period: the world depicted, for example, in Evelyn Waugh's *Brideshead Revisited*. The atmosphere at Göttingen in the 1920s was emphatically not "gay." Rather, as Oppenheimer later put it, it was "bitter, sullen . . . discontent and angry and loaded with all those ingredients which were later to produce a major disaster." Göttingen was, as this description hints, fertile ground for the then-burgeoning Nazi movement. In 1922, one of the very first branches of the Nazi Party was set up there and three years later, just a year before Oppenheimer arrived, a chemistry student named Achim Gercke, later a key figure in the Nazi movement, began to compile a list of Jewish professors at the university, so that, when the Nazis came to power, they would immediately know whom to expel in the name of racial purity.

The portentous sullenness created by such racial hatred was felt deeply by Oppenheimer, who, after less than a year, was glad to leave Göttingen. And yet, despite all this, for the nine months or so that he was there, Oppenheimer thrived at Göttingen as conspicuously as he had foundered at Cambridge. The anger, the resentment, the increasingly vehement and vicious anti-Semitism, though of course extremely unpleasant, were not, as it turned out, as debilitating or oppressive as the "excellence" at Cambridge had been. At Göttingen, no matter what else he had to endure, he did not have to deal with people who mixed

with dukes, who felt comfortable at high table, and who discussed literature and philosophy with internationally renowned French intellectuals.
Rather, at Göttingen, *he* was the one who intimidated people with his
social, intellectual and cultural preeminence, as exhibited by his ostentatious wealth, his mastery of the French language and French poetry,
his astonishingly wide-ranging knowledge and his refined taste in everything from literature to clothes, architecture to hand luggage.

If anyone at Göttingen seemed aristocratic, it was Oppenheimer
himself, who was elaborately well mannered in an almost courtly fashion and seemed to take toward his fellow students an attitude of *noblesse
oblige*. Word got out among the other graduate students that, if you
admired any of Oppenheimer's possessions, he would feel obliged to
present it to you as a gift. Soon after he arrived at Göttingen he and some
other students traveled by train to Hamburg to attend a seminar. Among
the group was a doctoral student named Charlotte Riefenstahl (no relation to the filmmaker Leni Riefenstahl), who, when the group's luggage
was collected together at the platform, could not help noticing a very
fine, and obviously extremely expensive, pigskin bag, which looked out
of place among the cheap and battered suitcases surrounding it. When
she asked whose it was, she received the answer: "Who else but Oppenheimer's." Intrigued, she sought out Oppenheimer, sat next to him on
the train home and, somewhat to his bafflement, complimented him on
his beautiful luggage. Thus began a friendship that Oppenheimer, in
his courtly way, tried unsuccessfully to turn into a romance, and, sure
enough, when he left Göttingen, he insisted on giving his pigskin bag to
Fräulein Riefenstahl.

Postwar Göttingen provided Oppenheimer with plenty of opportunities for condescension, full as it was with people who had fallen on hard
times. Among those was the family with whom Oppenheimer lodged. At
Cambridge he had complained of the "miserable hole" he lodged in; at
Göttingen, his lodgings were in a large and comfortable house on Gies-
marlandstrasse owned by a recently impoverished family. The family
were the Carios, who, Oppenheimer later remembered, "had the typical
bitterness on which the Nazi movement rested." Dr. Cario was a physician who, having lost his savings as a result of postwar inflation, also lost
his job when he was disqualified for malpractice. To make a living and to
keep their spacious home, the family was forced to take lodgers, which
was clearly a source of resentment and humiliation for them.

Among those lodgers were two other physicists, Karl T. Compton
and Edward Condon (the connection between the Cario family and
the physics department may have been made through Dr. Cario's son,
who was a physics student). Condon was a couple of years older than

Oppenheimer, and, on the face of it at least, further advanced academically, having completed his Ph.D. at Berkeley that summer. Like many other postdoctoral American physicists, he decided to come to Germany to study with the pioneers of quantum mechanics. He came quickly to regret his choice of Göttingen, finding that Max Born, with whom he had wanted to study, was unwilling to spare him much time or attention. As Born remembers it: "The Americans were too numerous for me to have much time for all of them."

> Some of them, such as Condon, were therefore disgruntled. He complained about everything in Göttingen: the primitive digs without a proper bath, the food in the restaurants, the bad bus services, etc., and last but not least the overworked professor who had so little time for him.

It was not an easy time for Condon. His only income was a small postdoctoral fellowship, and, though just twenty-four, he had a wife and baby to support. Such pressures were entirely alien to Oppenheimer, who did nothing to disguise his own great wealth and took an uncomprehendingly lofty view of Condon's domestic commitments. An incident that stayed in Condon's mind, and that he relayed many years later, concerns an occasion when Oppenheimer invited him and his wife, Emilie, for a walk. Emilie explained that she had to refuse the invitation because she had to look after their infant child. "All right," replied Oppenheimer, "we'll leave you to your peasant tasks."

Though clearly intended as a joke, such displays of faux-aristocratic hauteur were, from Condon's point of view, irritating rather than amusing, but what Condon found even worse was Oppenheimer's determination to impress upon everybody at Göttingen just how very *clever* he was. "Trouble is," Condon once remarked, "that Oppie is so quick on the trigger intellectually that he puts the other guy at a disadvantage. And, dammit, he is always right, or at least right enough." Oppenheimer did not, like Condon, arrive at Göttingen with a doctorate. However, what Oppenheimer did have—and what Condon was never to have, but what he most craved at Göttingen—was Max Born's admiration and respect. "He and Born became very close friends," Condon later remembered, "and saw a great deal of each other, so much so, that Born did not see much of the other theoretical physics students who had come there to work with him."

Born's respect for Oppenheimer was clear to everyone at Göttingen and seemed to elevate him above his fellow students. But, having got away with taking a condescending attitude toward Born himself, it was not only his fellow postgraduates and postdoctoral students like Condon that Oppenheimer felt able to look down upon, but also established physicists such as his other co-lodger, Karl T. Compton. Compton was not an easy target for superciliousness. He came from an extremely distinguished family; his father, Elias Compton, was dean of the University of Wooster, and his brother, William, would later become president of the State College of Washington. His other brother, Arthur, was a world-renowned experimental physicist, with whose work Oppenheimer would certainly have been familiar. Arthur Compton's most famous work was his discovery in 1922 of the "scattering" of X-rays, a discovery for which he received the Nobel Prize in Physics in 1927 and, since 1923, he had been professor of physics at the University of Chicago. Though Arthur did not lodge with the Cario family, he, like his brother Karl, was spending the year 1926–7 in Göttingen. In his memoir, *Atomic Quest*, he recalls how he met Oppenheimer "when he was a member of the colony of American students of James Franck and Max Born at Göttingen," and describes him as "one of the very best interpreters of the mathematical theories to those of us who were working more directly with the experiments." Coming from the man about to win the Nobel Prize, this is an extraordinary compliment to pay a twenty-two-year-old who had not yet completed his Ph.D. thesis.

Though not a Nobel laureate, Karl Compton himself was, when Oppenheimer met him, an established physicist and a man of some eminence. Thirty-nine years old, he was a full professor at Princeton and a key figure in the American scientific establishment. He was already vice president of the American Physical Society and, during Oppenheimer's year at Göttingen, was to become its president. Compton was also that year made chairman of the physics section of the National Academy of Sciences. His career culminated just a few years later, in 1930, when he was appointed president of the Massachusetts Institute of Technology.

Extraordinarily, despite his many distinctions, honors and positions, Compton felt intimidated by Oppenheimer. He is reported as feeling that, though he could hold his own with the younger man in science, when Oppenheimer talked about literature, philosophy or politics, he felt at a loss. For his part, Oppenheimer felt able to be as condescending toward Compton as he was toward Condon. In a letter to Francis Fergusson, of November 1926, he wrote:

> There are about 20 American physicists & such here. Most of them are over thirty. Professors at Princeton or California [where Condon had taken his Ph.D.] or some such place, married, respectable.

They are mostly pretty good at physics, but completely uneducated & unspoiled. They envy the Germans their intellectual adroitness, & want physics to come to America.

Of course, as usual in Oppenheimer's letters to Fergusson, one has to make allowance for his apparent need to impress and his consequent compulsion to show off. Thus, telling Fergusson in uncharacteristically direct terms that "the science is much better than at Cambridge, & on the whole, probably the best to be found," he could not resist adding:

They are working very hard here & combining a fantastically impregnable metaphysical disingenuousness with the gogetting habits of a wall-paper manufacturer. The result is that the work done here has an almost demoniac lack of plausibility to it & is highly successful.

The description this offers of Born's statistical interpretation of quantum mechanics, alluding to both its success in making sense of the results obtained from experiment and the high philosophical (metaphysical) cost it exacts (the abandonment of causal determinism), is very apt, but it could be seen to be so, surely, *only* by someone who already knew something about it.

Even allowing for a certain theatrical tendency to exaggerate, there is an extraordinarily self-confident tone in this letter, and in the few others from this period that survive. Oppenheimer tells Fergusson that he is not sure whether he will go back to Cambridge before he returns to the States, and adds, almost as a casual aside: "I'll probably get a degree here in March." At the root of the extreme confidence manifested in his relations with others, and in his prediction that he could complete his Ph.D. within six months of arriving at Göttingen, was his close relationship with Born, with whom—in striking contrast to Condon—he spent an immense amount of time, not only in lectures and seminars, but also at Born's home. Within a very short time he became regarded, and came to regard himself, not as Born's student, but as his collaborator. For example, in a letter to Edwin Kemble, written about two weeks after his letter to Fergusson, Oppenheimer uses the phrase "another problem on which Prof. Born and I are working," as if he and the head of the most prestigious center of theoretical physics in the world at that point were now essentially partners.

Nor did he seem to regard himself as the junior partner in this collaboration. In Born's seminar on quantum mechanics, Oppenheimer would unapologetically interrupt whoever was speaking—whether another student or Born himself—walk up to the blackboard, take the chalk from the speaker's hand and say something like "No, that is wrong," "That is not how it is done" or "This can be done much better in the following manner." This lordly manner impressed his fellow students, one of whom later remarked, "I felt as if he were an inhabitant of Olympus who had strayed among humans and was doing his best to appear human." But it also irritated them. Some of them complained to Born and asked him to do something about it. "But," Born writes in his autobiography, "I was a little afraid of Oppenheimer, and my half-hearted attempts to stop him were unsuccessful."

Still, however brilliant Oppenheimer was, and however certain he himself was of the value of what he had to say, the students had come to Göttingen to learn from Born, not him. And so, one day, Born arrived at his seminar to find on his desk a sheet of paper disguised as a piece of medieval parchment, upon which was written, in archaic ornamental script, a threat to boycott the seminars unless Oppenheimer's disruptions ceased. The driving force behind the document, Born later came to believe, was the future Nobel laureate Maria Göppert, then a precocious twenty-year-old undergraduate physics student. Realizing that he had to take the boycott threat seriously, but still afraid to confront Oppenheimer directly, Born devised an elaborate plan to make Oppenheimer aware of the trouble he was causing. The next time Oppenheimer came around to Born's house, Born left the "parchment" document on his desk, then exited the room to take a prearranged call from his wife, Heidi. "This plot worked," Born writes in his autobiography. "When I returned I found him rather pale and not so voluble as usual. And the interruptions in the seminar ceased altogether." Born worried for the rest of his life whether he had offended Oppenheimer in this way and was inclined to believe that Oppenheimer's lingering resentment over the incident was the reason why, in later life, Born never received any invitations from universities in the U.S.

Born's intense interest in, and admiration of, Oppenheimer naturally aroused the interest of other physicists and, by the end of 1926, Oppenheimer—though he had not by then published anything remotely comparable to the path-breaking work of Dirac, Heisenberg, Jordan and Born himself—was beginning to be spoken of in the same breath. At that time the U.S. National Research Council was, in partnership with the Rockefeller Foundation, looking to fund promising young American physicists who could bring to the U.S. a knowledge and understanding of cutting-edge European physics. (This is what Oppenheimer was alluding to in his letter to Fergusson when he wrote that "They [the

American physicists at Göttingen] envy the Germans their intellectual adroitness, & want physics to come to America.") In his role as a member of the NRC's fellowship selection committee, Karl Compton reported to the Rockefeller Foundation on December 6, 1926: "As far as I can learn, Condon and a very young chap named Oppenheimer are the star performers in physics." Two weeks later, this view was echoed by Born himself, who, when asked by the Rockefeller Foundation for his opinion on the young American physicists he had encountered, wrote: "I would like to point out here only one who rises above the average. He is Mr Robert Oppenheimer, a young American who is extraordinarily good in mathematics, has good physical understanding and promises to become an exceptional scholar."

Oppenheimer's growing reputation at Göttingen—one is tempted to call it "mystique"—was not, however, *entirely* based on Born's high opinion of him. By the end of 1926, he was producing written work that was at least beginning to justify the things said about him by Compton and others. Most significant was an article he sent to *Zeitschrift für Physik* on Christmas Eve entitled "Zur Quantentheorie kontinuierlicher Spektren" ("On the Quantum Theory of Continuous Spectra"), which formed his Ph.D. thesis and was, at twenty-five pages, one of the longest articles he ever published. The distinguished physicist Abraham Pais has described this article as "quite important," since it introduced various mathematical techniques that are still in use. In particular, Oppenheimer devised for this article a method of calculating, in a quantum-mechanical way, the absorption of light by hydrogen, a method that is used even now for understanding the physical processes that occur in the interiors of stars. This, Pais emphasizes, was "unexplored territory at the time," and, as such, must be regarded as some kind of breakthrough, although, compared to the work of Dirac, Heisenberg, Jordan and Born, it was a fairly minor breakthrough, an *application* of the theory of quantum mechanics, rather than a fundamental step in the creation and development of that theory.

Paul Dirac, whom Oppenheimer venerated as a physicist perhaps more than any other except Niels Bohr, took a notoriously austere view of work that was not of the first importance. At St. John's College, he once crushed a fellow doctoral student, Robert Schlapp—who was then researching the reflection of X-rays from crystals—with the remark, "You ought to tackle fundamental problems, not peripheral ones." Later in life, when he gave a public lecture on "The Development of Quantum Mechanics," Dirac conveyed the same attitude. Talking about the time just after the initial formulation of quantum mechanics, he remarked: "It was very easy in those days for any second-rate physicist to do first-rate work." What he meant, he explained, was that, once the mathematical techniques of quantum mechanics had been developed:

> It was then an interesting game people could play to take the various models of dynamical systems, which we were used to in the Newtonian theory, and transform them into the new mechanics of Heisenberg . . . Whenever one solved one of the little problems, one could write a paper about it.

It is not entirely clear that Dirac would have regarded the topic of Oppenheimer's Ph.D. thesis as "one of the little problems," but it seems entirely possible.

Oppenheimer was to get to know Dirac very well in the second half of his stay at Göttingen, since in February 1927 Dirac arrived in Göttingen and moved into the Cario family house, replacing the disgruntled Condon, who had left for Munich, hoping to receive from Arnold Sommerfeld the attention he had failed to receive from Born. "The most exciting time I had in Göttingen," Oppenheimer once said, "and perhaps the most exciting time in my life was when Dirac arrived and gave me the proofs of his paper on the quantum theory of radiation."

It is unlikely that the excitement was reciprocated. Dirac was a notoriously solitary man. An interviewer once said to Dirac: "Oppenheimer indicates that, when he was in Göttingen, he thinks you saw as much or more of him than anyone else there." "That is so," Dirac replied. "We sometimes went for long walks together, although I had many walks alone." Though Oppenheimer often expressed his admiration for Dirac, there is, as far as I am aware, just one occasion on which Dirac is on record as expressing admiration for Oppenheimer, and that is a rather special case, since the occasion was Dirac's acceptance of the J. Robert Oppenheimer Memorial Prize, an annual prize awarded by the University of Miami. "I am especially happy to be awarded the Oppenheimer Prize," Dirac said in his speech, "because I was a great friend and admirer of Oppenheimer." Strikingly, however, when he specifies the "admirable qualities" that he saw in Oppenheimer, his emphasis is on expository gifts rather than on scientific achievement. His admiration for Oppenheimer, he makes clear, centers on his expertise "as a chairman for a discussion or a colloquium."

Unlike Karl Compton, Dirac was not impressed by Oppenheimer's knowledge of and interest in literature. On the contrary, he rather disapproved of it. Once he remarked to Oppenheimer: "I don't see how you can work on physics and write poetry at the same time. In science, you want to say something nobody knew before, in words everyone can understand. In poetry, you are bound to say something that everybody knows already in words that nobody can understand."

Dirac came to Göttingen from Bohr's institute in Copenhagen, where he had been since September 1926, and where he had produced two pieces of fundamentally important work. The first laid the foundation for what is now known as "transformation theory," showing how one can transform any statement of quantum physics written in Schrödinger's wave theory into one written either in Heisenberg's matrices or Dirac's brackets. The second (the one Oppenheimer alludes to in the quotation above) established a new and important field of study: quantum electrodynamics, bringing quantum mechanics to bear on the understanding of electromagnetic radiation.

Though Oppenheimer's work did not approach the importance of Dirac's, at Göttingen the two were often associated with each other as young, brilliant theorists at the cutting edge of the new physics. In a letter to S. W. Stratton, president of the Massachusetts Institute of Technology, written on February 13, 1927, Born repeated the view he had earlier reported to the Rockefeller Foundation, that, among the Americans working at Göttingen, Oppenheimer stood out as being "quite excellent." A few weeks later, the American physicist Earle Kennard wrote to a friend: "There are three young geniuses in theory here, each less intelligible to me than the others." The three were Oppenheimer, Jordan and Dirac.

American physicists were very keen to be kept abreast of theoretical developments in Europe because, as they were all aware, important things were happening so quickly that it was a constant battle to stay with the pace. As Edward Condon once put it: "Great ideas were coming out so fast during that period that one got an altogether wrong impression of the normal rate of progress in theoretical physics."

In March 1927, Heisenberg published an article called "On the Intuitive Content of Quantum-theoretical Kinematics and Mechanics," which contained the first expression of the idea that everyone now associates with quantum theory: the uncertainty principle. This states that there must always be some degree of uncertainty in our knowledge of quantum-mechanical systems, such as the interiors of atoms. Heisenberg showed that if quantum mechanics is correct (and, for the purpose of the article, Heisenberg used Dirac's formulation of the theory, because that was the most general), then the more precise our determination of the *position* of a subatomic particle, the less precise will be our determination of its *momentum*, and vice versa. The reason for this is that subatomic particles, such as electrons, are so small that ordinary visible light will not be sufficient to fix their positions, because the wavelength of the light is much bigger than the particle. To fix the position of the particle more precisely, one would have to use electromagnetic radiation with much shorter waves (and therefore greater frequencies), such as gamma radiation. But these high-frequency waves carry great energy, enough to deflect, and thereby alter the momentum of, the electron. So, we can be precise about the position of an electron only by affecting (and thereby introducing some imprecision in the measurement of) its momentum, and we can only gain a precise measurement of its momentum if we use low-energy, low-frequency radiation, the wavelengths of which are too great for a precise determination of position.

A few months before Heisenberg's uncertainty paper was published, Oppenheimer wrote a letter to George Uhlenbeck in Leiden, showing that he himself was giving at least some thought to fundamental questions about the interpretation of quantum mechanics. "My own feeling," he told Uhlenbeck, "is that, whereas it is often correct to regard ψ [the wave function] as a probability amplitude, this interpretation is not the most fundamental one. It seems to me that the problem has entered a new stage now, & essentially because of Dirac's last paper." He was right, of course, that the problem had entered—or was about to enter, after the publication of Heisenberg's paper—a new stage. But, despite being shared by, among others, Einstein, Oppenheimer's feeling that Born's probabilistic interpretation of the wave function is not the most fundamental has not, so far, been justified; the search for a yet more fundamental interpretation still goes on.

Oppenheimer's own research, as he outlined to Uhlenbeck, did not center on this fundamental question of interpretation, but consisted rather in the kind of problem disparaged by Dirac: showing that quantum mechanics could be successfully applied to, as Oppenheimer put it, "such effects as polarization & depolarization of mercury resonance lines & impact radiation." This work led to two papers, both of which were published in *Zeitschrift für Physik*, the journal most associated with the leading work in quantum mechanics.

Oppenheimer had been prompted to write to Uhlenbeck after meeting one of his colleagues, the experimental physicist E. C. Wiersma, who came to Göttingen to give a paper. Wiersma had evidently told Oppenheimer that Uhlenbeck had accepted a position at the University of Michigan, starting the following academic year. "I am very glad," Oppenheimer told Uhlenbeck. "I shall be going to America (Pasadena) next July & if you think of going at the same time & have no better plans, perhaps we might arrange to go together."

Oppenheimer had, shortly before this, received a letter offering him one of the National Research Council postdoctoral fellowships. Given that he had not actually applied for such a fellowship and that he had not yet received his doctorate, this is a measure both of how far Oppenheimer's reputation had spread by the spring of 1927 and of how keen American universities were at this time to attract physicists with expertise in quantum mechanics. His decision to use the fellowship to go to the California Institute of Technology (Caltech) in Pasadena shows how powerful the pull of the American Southwest remained for him, as other prestigious universities were only too eager to attract him, not the least of which was Harvard.

On April 3, 1927, Oppenheimer's old mentor at Harvard, Percy Bridgman—apparently unaware that Oppenheimer had already been offered an NRC fellowship—wrote to him, hoping to lure him back to Harvard. "From what I hear," Bridgman wrote, "I judge that you have your doctor's degree already. I saw Fowler in Oxford last August, and he gave the most glowing account of the work you had been doing with him."

> Had you thought of applying for a National Research Fellowship for next year in case you are getting your degree? If this appeals to you at all I am sure that we would all be very glad indeed to have you at Harvard again and together with Kemble and Slater[23] you ought to make a team that would get some significant theoretical work done.

Perhaps in response to this approach, Oppenheimer changed his plans somewhat and arranged to spend his time as an NRC postdoctoral fellow first at Harvard and then at Caltech.

For now, though, he had to actually get his Ph.D., which, as everyone assumed, was purely a formality. The paper he had already published the previous December was accepted as a Ph.D. dissertation, and a viva (an oral examination) was scheduled for May 11, the examiners being Born and James Franck. Neither examiner had any doubt that Oppenheimer should pass and the examination was kept fairly short. Franck spent about twenty minutes asking Oppenheimer questions and, on leaving the examination room, was heard to say: "I'm glad that is over. He was on the point of questioning me." The dissertation was passed "with distinction." One problem remained: officially, Oppenheimer was not even a student at Göttingen. He had, it seems, neglected to register. Remarkably, Born persuaded the authorities to overlook this argu-

[23] John C. Slater, then a young physics professor at Harvard. Later he became chairman of the physics department at MIT.

ably fundamental problem, on the extraordinarily implausible grounds of Oppenheimer's poverty. "Economic circumstances," he wrote to the Prussian Ministry of Education, "render it impossible for Herr Oppenheimer to remain in Göttingen after the end of the summer term."

Actually, by this time Born had a vested interest in ensuring that Oppenheimer did not spend more time than was necessary in Göttingen. The two had begun to collaborate and the partnership was proving to be, from Born's point of view, extremely stressful. Working with Oppenheimer seemed to strip him of his self-belief and render him incapable of scientific work. "My soul was nearly destroyed by that man," he wrote to Paul Ehrenfest soon after Oppenheimer left; and, returning to the subject in another letter to Ehrenfest about a year later, he claimed that Oppenheimer's "presence destroyed the last remnants of my scientific capabilities." The nearest he came to explaining the destructive effect Oppenheimer had was his remark to Ehrenfest: "Through his manner to know everything better and to continue any idea you give him, he has paralyzed all of us for three-quarters of a year." In other words, the problem with Oppenheimer was that he always wanted to be *better* than the people around him.

The most lasting fruit of the collaboration between Born and Oppenheimer was a published paper, "Zur Quantentheorie der Molekeln" ("On the Quantum Theory of Molecules"), which, though one of the least well known of Born's works, is to this day the most frequently cited of all Oppenheimer's publications. In the field of quantum chemistry it is considered a classic paper, and every undergraduate textbook in that field has a section on the paper's central idea, which has become known as the "Born-Oppenheimer approximation."

As Oppenheimer once put it, the purpose of the paper is to use quantum mechanics to explain "why molecules were molecules." It was chemistry that had first attracted Oppenheimer to science, and one of his hopes for quantum mechanics was that it could be used to shed light on the fundamental nature of chemical compounds. His first paper, written while he was still in Cambridge, had sought to take an initial step in that direction; now, together with Born, he was determined to show how quantum mechanics could be extended from the understanding of atomic structures to the understanding of molecular structures. This was an extremely ambitious undertaking.

The calculation of the energy states of molecules is *far* more complicated than that of atoms, which is, in any case, immensely complicated—so complicated that it has only ever been done completely for the very simplest atoms, such as that of hydrogen, which consists of a single proton and a single electron. The complications arise from, among other things, the fact that the wave function at the heart of quantum mechanics describes a *three-dimensional* wave. The possible positions of an electron are envisaged in three dimensions, x, y, z, and so the associated wave of the electron—which, according to Born's statistical interpretation of the theory, provides the probabilities of the electron being in any of the positions describable for possible values of x, y and z—is three-dimensional.

The electrons, these three-dimensional waves, are pictured as orbiting the nucleus, which is itself in motion, vibrating and rotating. The total energy of an atom is given by the energies of the electrons, together with the rotational and vibrational energies of the nucleus. With just one electron—as in the case of hydrogen—this is complicated enough, but with two or more electrons, it becomes dizzyingly complicated, since, with the introduction of each new electron, one has to take into account the forces operating between one electron and another and between the electrons and the nucleus. Now, consider a molecule, which is made up of two or more atoms, and one can see how the complications increase exponentially. Think, for example, of a molecule of water, which is made of two hydrogen atoms and an oxygen atom. Each hydrogen atom has a single electron, while each oxygen atom has eight electrons. So, there are three nuclei and ten electrons in the molecule. To calculate the total energy of the molecule, one has to calculate the energy of each electron, the energy of each of the three nuclei *and* the energy of the molecule itself, which, of course, will also be in motion.

What Born and Oppenheimer presented in their joint paper was a mathematical technique—which has since become a cornerstone of the entire discipline of quantum chemistry—for calculating the energy of a molecule through a series of approximations. First, the energies of the electrons are calculated on the assumption that the nuclei are stationary. This is an approximation, but not a wild one, since the mass of the nucleus is so much greater than that of the electrons that, from the point of view of the electron, so to speak, the nucleus *is* stationary. Then, the vibrations of the nucleus are calculated, and finally the rotational energy of the molecule. Though each of these calculations is an approximation, the result is to turn what had previously been a completely impossible calculation into one that, though difficult, is at least possible, thereby enabling one to bring the insights of quantum mechanics to bear on the questions that had attracted Oppenheimer to science in the first place— questions about the fundamental nature of chemical substances.

The paper had a difficult gestation. Its first draft, produced by Oppenheimer during the Easter vacation of 1927, was only five pages long. "I thought this was about right," Oppenheimer later said. "It was very light of touch and it seemed to me all that was necessary." Born thought otherwise. He was, he later recalled, "horrified" by Oppenheimer's first draft and used his position as the senior partner to insist upon a more expansive rewrite. "I didn't like it," Oppenheimer later said, "but it was obviously not possible for me to protest to a senior author."

Because of the wrangling over presentation, and the rewriting it necessitated, the paper was not sent off for publication until the end of August 1927. In the meantime, in June, Edwin Kemble visited Göttingen and reported to a Harvard colleague:

> Oppenheimer is turning out to be even more brilliant than we thought when we had him at Harvard. He is turning out new work very rapidly and is able to hold his own with any of the galaxy of young mathematical physicists here. Unfortunately Born tells me that he has the same difficulty about expressing himself clearly in writing which we observed at Harvard.

About two weeks later, much to Born's relief, Oppenheimer left Göttingen.

He left with a doctorate, a growing international reputation as one of the most brilliant young physicists of his generation, and a small but important circle of friends united by their brilliant intelligence, their eminence and their shared passion for understanding the strange world of quantum mechanics. It was this last aspect that dominated his own memories of Göttingen. "In the sense which had not been true in Cambridge and certainly not at Harvard," Oppenheimer remembered, "I was part of a little community of people who had some common interests and tastes and many common interests in physics."

One should not, however, be misled by these memories to think of Oppenheimer being part of a community of people at Göttingen itself. As Born told Ehrenfest, the paralyzing effect that Oppenheimer had exerted on Born himself was felt also by his students (as Born rather melodramatically put it, Oppenheimer "ruined my young people"). No, the "community" that Oppenheimer had in mind consisted of people who came to Göttingen as visiting scholars from other institutions. Of the people he mentioned by name as members of that community, not one of them was a physicist based at Göttingen. Indeed, with regard to two of them—Gregor Wentzel, who was at the University of Leipzig, and Wolfgang Pauli, from the University of Hamburg—he was not even sure whether he met them in Göttingen or in Hamburg (the latter seems more likely). The one person he mentioned by name who was actually based at Göttingen was Richard Courant, who was a mathematician rather than a physicist and had very little to do with the development of quantum mechanics. The final person named by Oppenheimer in connection with the "little community" was Werner Heisenberg, who continued to be based at Copenhagen until the autumn of 1927, when he was made a professor at Leipzig.

If there is a single person at Göttingen with whom Oppenheimer might conceivably have formed some sort of community during his time there, it is Paul Dirac, who in June 1927 left Göttingen for Leiden, where he stayed as a guest of Paul Ehrenfest for a month before returning to Cambridge. When it was time for Oppenheimer to leave Göttingen, he followed Dirac to Leiden, joining him as Ehrenfest's guest. This is what prompted Born, in the letter quoted previously, to write to Ehrenfest about Oppenheimer. Most of the letter, dated July 16, 1927, is typewritten and concerned with matters of a professional interest. Then, in a handwritten postscript, Born wrote:

> Oppenheimer, who was with me for a long time, is now with you. I should like to know what you think of him. Your judgment will not be influenced by the fact that I openly admit that I have never suffered as much with anybody as with him. He is doubtless very gifted but without mental discipline. He's outwardly very modest but inwardly very arrogant. Through his manner to know everything better and to continue any idea you give to him, he has paralyzed all of us for three-quarters of a year. I can breathe again since he's gone and start to find the courage to work. My young people have the same experience. Do not let yourself keep him for any length of time.

Ehrenfest evidently replied in a way that indicated that he did not share Born's view of Oppenheimer. "Your information about Oppenheimer was very valuable to me," Born told him in a letter of August 7, 1927. "I know that he is a very fine and decent man but one can't help it if someone gets on your nerves." By the time Born wrote this, Oppenheimer himself was back in the U.S., having set sail to New York from Liverpool in mid-July. His plan was to spend the rest of the summer with his family before taking up his postdoctoral fellowship at Harvard in October.

It was, in some ways, an unfortunate time for a quantum physicist to be leaving Europe, since two of the most significant events in the history of quantum mechanics were about to happen, the first in Italy and the second in Belgium. The first was the announcement by Niels Bohr of the principle of complementarity, the importance of which Oppenheimer himself in later life was to emphasize at every opportunity and which, together with Heisenberg's uncertainty principle, forms the so-called

Copenhagen Interpretation of quantum mechanics. The principle of complementarity says that waves and particles are inconsistent, but complementary, features of the reality of photons and electrons. Light really is made up of particle-like quanta (photons) *and* it really does consist of waves. Depending on how we measure it, we see it as waves or as particles, but never both. Nevertheless, for a complete understanding of photons and electrons, both are necessary. We must not attempt to reduce waves to particles or particles to waves, Bohr thought; we must rather accept each as complementing the other.

Bohr announced the principle of complementarity in a paper called "The Quantum Postulate and the Recent Development of Atomic Theory," which he delivered at the International Physics Congress, held in Como, Italy, in September 1927. In the paper, he argued that complementarity was the bedrock upon which quantum theory was based. The uncertainty principle, for example, Bohr claimed, was simply a consequence of complementarity; that we cannot measure *both* position and momentum precisely at the same time is a special case of the more general truth that we cannot see an electron or a photon both as a particle and a wave at the same time. To complementarity and the uncertainty principle, Bohr added Born's statistical interpretation of Schrödinger's wave function, to form what he now regarded as a complete and finished theory—that is, quantum mechanics—but which others regard as the three essential elements merely of the Copenhagen Interpretation of quantum mechanics. Either way, it is the most influential and most important set of ideas in twentieth-century physics, with consequences that go way beyond physical science to the most basic and general philosophical ideas. If Born's statistical interpretation of the wave function requires one to abandon determinism, the uncertainty principle forces one to abandon the age-old conception of causality, which held that, given a complete description of the position and momentum of an object, one could causally predict its future. Meanwhile, the principle of complementarity seems to force one to rethink the very idea of an "outside world," the idea that we can observe the things and events around us without interfering with them. On Bohr's understanding, to observe is to measure, and to measure is to influence which side of the wave-particle duality we are dealing with (since it is the method of measurement that determines whether we see waves or particles). Virginia Woolf, in emphasizing the importance of the art exhibition "Manet and the Post-Impressionists," once famously remarked: "On or about December 1910, human character changed." In the same spirit, one might say: "On or about September 1927, the physical world changed."

Attending the Como conference were more than seventy physicists from all over the world. Born was there to give a paper on the statistical interpretation of the wave function. Heisenberg was there and, though he did not give a paper, he spoke in support of Bohr's paper, giving, in the process, his own outline of uncertainty. Also there were Rutherford, de Broglie, Wolfgang Pauli, Arnold Sommerfeld and Arthur Compton. If Oppenheimer had been in Europe at the time, he would surely have attended.

The second momentous event in the autumn of 1927 was the fifth Solvay Congress, held in Brussels during the last week in October. The Solvay Congresses (named after their sponsor, the Belgian industrialist Ernest Solvay) had begun in 1911, the first in the series having the theme "Radiation and the Quanta." The idea was to gather together the twenty or so most distinguished physicists in the world to hammer out an ongoing, open question. The star of the first conference had been the young Albert Einstein. After the second conference in 1913, the series was interrupted by the First World War and then deeply affected by the postwar exclusion of German physicists, which condemned the third and fourth conferences, held respectively in 1921 and 1924, to a discussion of the most fundamental questions in the absence of many of the leading physicists.

No such problems beset the fifth Solvay Congress, which was anticipated with great excitement within the international community of theoretical physicists for a number of reasons. First, its theme of "Electrons and Photons" was the hot topic of the day, and the wording of the invitation (the Solvay Congresses were strictly invitation-only) made it clear that the "conference will be devoted to the new quantum mechanics and to questions connected with it." Second, since the admission of Germany into the League of Nations in 1926, German scientists could no longer be treated as members of an enemy country, which meant that the conference could invite not only quantum pioneers like Max Planck, but also the leading members of the younger generation of German physicists, such as Heisenberg and Born, who had founded, developed and shaped the new quantum theory. Finally, the readmittance of German physicists into the international community meant that Albert Einstein, the leading opponent of the new theory, could engage publicly with its chief proponents.

And so the stage was set for what has gone down in history as *the* great debate about the science and philosophy of quantum mechanics, in which almost all the most notable defenders and opponents of the new theory—the radical consequences of which had been spelled out and emphasized by Born, Heisenberg and Bohr—were gathered in one place. The defenders included, as well as Bohr, Born and Heisenberg, Paul Dirac and Wolfgang Pauli. Representing the opposition were Einstein, Planck, Schrödinger and de Broglie. Also present were Marie Curie, Arthur Compton and Ralph Fowler. It was an extraordinarily prestigious group; of the twenty-nine people who attended, seventeen were or would become Nobel Prize winners. At stake in their discussions was not only a new physical theory, but a proposed fundamental change in the way we think about determinism, causality and the nature of scientific theory. One way of crystallizing the issue that lay at the center of the debates, using a phrase that recurred again and again during the conference, is to ask the question that Einstein had raised in his letter to Born: Does God play dice or not?

The congress ran from Monday, October 24 to Friday, October 28. The format chosen was for reports to be delivered on various aspects of quantum mechanics, with each of them followed by a lengthy discussion. Only five reports were delivered during the entire conference, such was the determination of the organizers to give plenty of time for discussion. On the first day, reports were given by William L. Bragg from Manchester on X-ray reflection and Arthur Compton on the photoelectric effect. The following day, Louis de Broglie reported on "The New Dynamics of Quanta," outlining and defending his own view—which received almost no support from the delegates—that both wave and particle existed, although not as envisaged by Bohr and Born, but rather in a way that visualized particles being guided or "piloted" by waves.

Throughout these early papers, Einstein remained silent. He even stayed silent when, on Wednesday, October 26, Born and Heisenberg presented a joint report on quantum mechanics that seemed calculated to provoke him into discussion. After outlining matrix mechanics, transformation theory, the probability interpretation, uncertainty and complementarity, Born and Heisenberg ended with the uncompromising statement: "We consider quantum mechanics to be a closed theory, whose fundamental physical and mathematical assumptions are no longer susceptible of any modification."

Einstein finally broke his silence on the last day of the conference, when, in place of reports, the organizers had arranged for the entire day to be taken up with a wide-ranging general discussion that was to be the climax of the whole event. As it turned out, the discussion was dominated by a series of exchanges between Bohr and Einstein. First Einstein would propose what he took to be a fatal flaw in quantum mechanics, then Bohr would respond, invariably identifying a flaw in Einstein's own arguments. In a letter to his students at Leiden, Ehrenfest described Bohr as "towering over everybody . . . step by step defeating everybody." This reflected the general view. As the conference closed, Heisenberg wrote:

"I am satisfied in every respect with the scientific results. Bohr's and my views have been generally accepted; at least serious objections are no longer being made, not even by Einstein and Schrödinger."

At the Como conference quantum mechanics had received its definitive and final statement; at the fifth Solvay Congress, in the form it had been given at Como, it triumphed over its most influential skeptics. One imagines that Oppenheimer would have longed to be in Europe at this moment when the movement to which he had pinned his colors came of age and emerged victorious. However, competing—and winning—against his desire to be at the forefront of modern physics was his love of America. In the summer of 1927, with quantum mechanics poised to make its greatest triumph, his deepest desire was to be back home; he had by then been away for almost two years and was extremely homesick.

Oppenheimer wanted to spend time revisiting familiar places and being with his family, especially his brother. To his dismay, his parents had sold the Bay Shore house the previous winter, but his boat, the *Trimethy*, was still moored there and so he and Frank were still able to go sailing along the Long Island coast. After a while the two of them took the boat up to Nantucket Island, Massachussetts, where they joined their parents for a holiday. There, Frank remembers: "My brother and I spent most of the days painting with oils on canvas the dunes and grassy hills."

Oppenheimer no doubt enjoyed creating a permanent reminder of the countryside he loved, and had missed during his two years in Europe. At Leiden, in his anxiety to return home, he had evidently overdone his praise of his homeland. "He's too much," a fellow student remarked. "According to Oppenheimer, even the flowers smell better in America." It wasn't just the landscape he loved, either. Along with other American physicists studying in Europe, Oppenheimer had been upset by how little respect there was for American science among Europeans. As Isidor Rabi put it: "We were not highly regarded, I must say, nor was there any thought that America would amount to anything as far as physics was concerned. There were a few people, certainly, but one looked down their noses on Americans . . . We felt very bad about this." A sense of what American physicists had to put up with can be gained from Paul Dirac's response when he was asked in 1927 by Edward Condon if he would like to visit America: "There are no physicists in America."

The NRC fellowship scheme was one way of stimulating American physics; another was attracting European physicists to work in American universities. Max Born, during his visit to the U.S. in 1925–6, had received several job offers. He declined, but many others accepted, including Oppenheimer's Dutch friends George Uhlenbeck and Samuel Goudsmit, who both accepted positions at the University of Michigan, starting in the autumn of 1927. Charlotte Riefenstahl, meanwhile, was offered and accepted a job at Vassar College.

So it was that in the late summer of 1927, Uhlenbeck, Goudsmit and Riefenstahl, along with Uhlenbeck's new wife, Else, traveled together to New York aboard the SS *Baltic*. There at the dockside to welcome them to America was Oppenheimer, together with his father's car, complete with uniformed chauffeur. "We all got the real Oppenheimer treatment," Goudsmit later said, "but it was for Charlotte's benefit really. He met us in this great chauffeur-driven limousine, and took us downtown to a hotel he had selected in Greenwich Village." The hotel was the Brevoort, one of New York City's oldest and most famous hotels, known for its French cuisine and fine wines, and chosen by Oppenheimer for his guests because of its European atmosphere. In the evening, Oppenheimer treated the party to dinner at a Brooklyn hotel from which they could see the lighted Manhattan skyline. Having persuaded the Uhlenbecks to delay their journey to Ann Arbor, the next day he took them, together with Charlotte, to meet his parents at their apartment on Riverside Drive. Else Uhlenbeck later recalled the beautifully furnished living room, the Van Gogh and other paintings, Mrs. Oppenheimer's graciousness and Frank, just turned fifteen, standing at the door looking shy and awkward.

After the Uhlenbecks and Goudsmit left for Ann Arbor, Charlotte stayed in New York for a few weeks, where, as Oppenheimer's guest, she ate at the very finest restaurants in the city. As she was well aware, she was being courted, but the courtship was short-lived. This was not only because she had to leave for Vassar, and he for Harvard, but also because she came to think that Oppenheimer was not emotionally ready for a romantic attachment. She found the atmosphere at Riverside Drive stifling, and Oppenheimer evasive and detached whenever she asked him anything personal, for example about his past. She was particularly put off when she asked him about his mother's gloved hand and was met with a stony silence. If, when she arrived in New York, she was tempted to consider Oppenheimer a possible future husband, by the time she left such temptations had been overcome.

7

Postdoctoral Fellow

In the summer of 1927, when Oppenheimer started his period as a postdoctoral fellow, he must have arrived at Harvard with a scientific paper already written, or at least nearly finished. For his first published article as "J. R. Oppenheimer. National Research Fellow" is dated "August 1927" and is reported as having been sent from the Jefferson Physical Laboratory at Harvard. The article, published in the *Physical Review*, is entitled "Three Notes on the Quantum Theory of Aperiodic Effects," and is today one of his better-known and most-cited publications, containing as it does one of the earliest discussions by a physicist of the strange phenomenon of "tunneling," whereby a particle, such as an electron or an alpha particle, can "tunnel" its way through a barrier, even though it lacks the energy that classical physics would require it to have to perform such a feat.

Oppenheimer was at Harvard for a mere five months (he left for Caltech at the end of 1927), but he published two more articles during his time there: one on the polarization of impact radiation in the *Proceedings of the National Academy of Sciences* and another on the capture of electrons by alpha particles in the *Physical Review*. In a letter to Paul Dirac, written on November 28, Oppenheimer—after sending his "very best felicitations" on the news that Dirac had been made a Fellow of St. John's College—gave Dirac a fairly detailed summary of all three papers, perhaps revealing that, despite describing them as "a lot of little things, but nothing at all important," he was actually quite proud of his productivity.

Oppenheimer also mentioned to Dirac that he had sent a paper on what is known as the "Ramsauer effect" to Ehrenfest. The Ramsauer effect is a phenomenon discovered by the German physicist Carl

Ramsauer that defies explanation by Newtonian physics, but is explicable using quantum mechanics. What Ramsauer discovered was that when electrons move through certain gases, the probability of a collision between an individual electron and an individual atom of the gas does not, as Newtonian physics would predict, decrease with the energy of the electron; rather, at a certain low energy, the probability of collision reaches a minimum below which it will not sink. The explanation for this relies upon taking into account the wavelike properties of the electron in a quantum-mechanical way.

Oppenheimer thought he had an alternative explanation of the Ramsauer effect, one that could be generalized for all atoms and molecules. Unfortunately, Ehrenfest noticed several errors in Oppenheimer's calculations, forcing Oppenheimer to delay publication of the paper. While he reworked his figures, he published a short note in the *Proceedings of the National Academy of Sciences*, announcing his conclusions and promising: "Details of the theory will be published elsewhere." In fact, the paper was abandoned and contributed only to Oppenheimer's reputation as a physicist who, while undeniably brilliant, was prone to making mathematical mistakes.

Not that such errors affected his ability to intimidate. Philip Morse, who would later enjoy an illustrious career as a physicist and an administrator, was in 1927 a Ph.D. student at Princeton, and has recalled in his autobiography how, when he came to Harvard to attend a seminar that autumn, he met "a thin high-strung postdoctoral fellow by the name of Oppenheimer, who gave me a bad case of inferiority by talking mysteriously about Dirac electrons and quaternions. I didn't know what he was talking about and his talk didn't enlighten me." "Oppie always affected me that way," Morse adds. "I never could figure out whether his sibylline declarations were just a form of one-upmanship or whether he really did see a lot more in a theory than I did. Some of both, I finally decided."

Oppenheimer seems to have made few new friends during this second period at Harvard, but he did reestablish contact with two old friends: John Edsall, who was then at Harvard Medical School, and William Boyd, who was studying for a Ph.D. in biochemistry at Boston University Medical School. With Boyd in particular, Oppenheimer shared an unusual intimacy. He told Boyd about his psychological problems at Cambridge and also showed him a poem he had written, which Boyd encouraged him to send to Harvard's avant-garde literary magazine, *Hound & Horn*, which had just been founded by a group of English undergraduates inspired by T. S. Eliot's *The Criterion*. The poem, in full, is as follows:

CROSSING

It was evening when we came to the river
with a low moon over the desert
that we had lost in the mountains, forgotten,
what with the cold and the sweating
and the ranges barring the sky.
And when we found it again,
in the dry hills down by the river,
half withered, we had
the hot winds against us.

There were two palms by the landing:
the yuccas were flowering; there was
a light on the far shore, and tamarisks.
We waited a long time, in silence.
Then we heard the oars creaking
and, afterwards, I remember,
the boatman called to us.
We did not look back at the mountains.

One of Oppenheimer's earliest biographers, Denise Royal, has interpreted the poem as an expression of Oppenheimer's "own dry, sterile intellectuality," but it seems more obviously a nostalgic evocation of his beloved New Mexico. Far from being sterile, the desert in the poem—with its yuccas, palms and tamarisks—is fertile, warm and welcoming, its "forgotten" new moon appearing to call Oppenheimer from the "cold" mountains that he is leaving behind without so much as a backward glance. These mountains might, it seems to me, represent the peaks of academia—Cambridge, Göttingen and Harvard—that he is anxious to leave in favor of a return to the New Mexico desert.

In any case, as soon as the Christmas holiday season was over, Oppenheimer left Harvard and headed for the Southwest, to spend the rest of his NRC fellowship at the California Institute of Technology (Caltech) in Pasadena. Ten miles northeast of Los Angeles in the South California desert, Pasadena was then a fairly small town (with about 50,000 inhabitants), notable mainly for two things: first, hosting the Rose Bowl, an annual college football game that has been played in Pasadena on the first day of each new year since 1902; and second, the California Institute of Technology itself, which though only six years old in 1927, was already recognized as one of the leading centers of scientific research in the U.S. At the head of Caltech (his official title was "Chairman of the

Executive Council") was the Nobel Prize–winning physicist Robert A. Millikan, who, while often derided as a pompous anti-Semite, was an extraordinarily successful fund-raiser and administrator.

From its beginnings in 1921, Caltech had a special relationship with the National Research Council. Its founder, the astronomer George Ellery Hale, had been the chairman of the NRC, and, through the influence of first Hale and then Millikan (who got to know Hale when he served as vice chairman of the NRC), a substantial proportion of NRC fellows conducted their research at Caltech. Through his connections with the NRC, Millikan would have received reports about Oppenheimer from Göttingen and Harvard, and was clearly already considering him as a potential permanent member of the staff.

At this time appropriately trained physicists—that is, those who had studied under the leading quantum physicists in Europe—were scarce and the competition to hire them was intense. This is reflected in the first surviving letter that Oppenheimer wrote from Pasadena, which was to Kemble at Harvard, advising him about potential appointments. William Houston, who was then assistant professor of physics at Caltech, was, Oppenheimer told Kemble, "very much the man you want," though "You may have a little trouble getting him, as they are very fond of him here." (Oppenheimer, it is a little easy to forget, was still only twenty-three.)

Oppenheimer also mentioned to Kemble the work of one of Caltech's most promising young chemists, Linus Pauling. For a short while, Pauling and Oppenheimer got on very well. Pauling's interests coincided with Oppenheimer's and, in time, he was to produce the definitive textbook on a subject very close to Oppenheimer's heart, the theory of chemical bonding (as Oppenheimer had put it: what makes a molecule a molecule). Pauling's graduate work had been on the use of X-ray diffraction to determine the structure of crystals, and he had, before he met Oppenheimer, published several papers on the crystal structure of minerals. In an act of extraordinary kindness that shows how much regard he must have had for Pauling, Oppenheimer gave him his entire collection of minerals—the collection he had built up since the age of five, when his grandfather presented him with the box of rocks that had first inspired his interest in science. Pauling, Oppenheimer later recalled, "was then still stuck on crystals—inorganic crystals—so that he not only used them but he was very pleased [with] these enormous calcites."

Oppenheimer and Pauling formed a plan of working together on what is now known as quantum chemistry. In particular, they intended to produce jointly authored work on the nature of the chemical bond.

However, before this work had got very far, Pauling cut off his relations with Oppenheimer. The reason was that Oppenheimer was taking far too much interest in Pauling's pretty wife, Ava. Conforming to what one would later recognize as Oppenheimer's "type," Ava Helen Pauling was not only very attractive, she was also socially aware and politically active. She is credited with inspiring and encouraging her husband's later concern with the issues of nuclear proliferation and world peace.[24] Oppenheimer made a bizarre approach to Ava one day; while her husband was at work, he went to their house and invited her to join him—without her husband—on a "tryst to Mexico." She refused and told her husband about it, whereupon he decided to have nothing more to do with Oppenheimer. After Linus Pauling's death, there was discovered among his papers a Caltech envelope marked "Poems by J. Robert Oppenheimer 1928." It contained eleven poems: six on nature, three on love, and two on aging and death. It is possible that Oppenheimer presented this collection to Pauling, but more likely, I think, that he gave it to Ava, as part of his clumsy attempt to seduce her.

In a letter he wrote to Frank at about the time he was wooing Ava Pauling, Oppenheimer offered his teenage brother some advice on how to treat women—advice that, he wrote, "may possibly be of use to you, as the fruit and outcome of my erotic labors." The woman's profession, he told Frank, was "to make you waste your time with her," while "it is your profession to keep clear." "The whole thing," he added, "is only important for people who have time to waste. For you and me, it isn't."

> And for the last rule: Don't worry about girls, and don't make love to girls, unless you have to: DON'T DO IT AS A DUTY. Try to find out, by watching yourself, what you really want; if you approve of it, try to get it; if you disapprove of it, try to get over it.

Another woman in whom Oppenheimer showed special interest during his time at Caltech was as unavailable to him as Ava Pauling had been. This was Helen Campbell, who was a friend and Vassar classmate of Inez Pollak, and, when Oppenheimer first met her, was engaged to a physicist at Berkeley called Samuel K. Allison. She and Allison married in May 1928. This, however, did not deter Oppenheimer from spending as much time alone with her as he could. He took her out to dinner, read

[24] Pauling was awarded the Nobel Peace Prize in 1962 for his campaigns against nuclear-weapon testing. As he had already, in 1954, been awarded the Nobel Prize for Chemistry, he thereby became, along with Marie Curie, one of only two people to have received two Nobel Prizes in different fields.

Baudelaire to her and talked with her about psychoanalysis and New Mexico. It did not lead to romance, but neither did it lead to Samuel Allison breaking off contact with Oppenheimer.

While Oppenheimer was having his amorous advances rebuffed, he himself was fending off professional advances from universities. He later recalled that he had "many invitations to university positions, one or two in Europe, and perhaps ten in the United States." In his letter to Frank he says: "I am trying to decide whether to take a professorship at the University of California next year or go abroad." He had visited Berkeley and was attracted to it partly because it was *not* an important center of theoretical research, thus offering him, as it were, a blank sheet upon which to write his own script. Or, as he put it:

> I thought I'd like to go to Berkeley because it was a desert. There was no theoretical physics and I thought it would be nice to try to start something. I also thought it would be dangerous because I'd be too far out of touch, so I kept the connection with Caltech.

What he wanted was a joint appointment, working half the time at Berkeley and the other half at Caltech.

Meanwhile, he was being assiduously courted by Harvard. On April 10, 1928, Professor Theodore Lyman, director of the department of physics at Harvard, wrote to Oppenheimer offering him a lectureship. Oppenheimer replied on April 21, saying that he would "like to be able to accept" the offer, but he "planned to spend next year in Europe." About two weeks later, Oppenheimer wrote again to Lyman, finally refusing the offer at Harvard and telling him that he had accepted instead precisely the arrangement he had wanted: first he would spend the following year abroad, then he would take up a joint appointment, dividing himself between Berkeley and Caltech.

Oppenheimer's plan to spend a year abroad conducting postdoctoral research under the guidance of the great European physicists was perhaps a result of what he described in his letter to Edwin Kemble as "the Ramsauer fiasco," feeling that he still needed to improve his technical competence if he was to make important contributions to theoretical physics. Explaining the decision to the head of the Berkeley physics department, Elmer Hall, Oppenheimer said it was based on his intention to "try to learn a little physics there." Abraham Pais thought, more specifically, that Oppenheimer's experiences at Caltech "revealed to him his deficiencies in mathematics," which made him want to return to Europe. Because he wanted to pursue postdoctoral work in Europe rather than the U.S., Oppenheimer's application to renew his NRC fellowship came under the auspices of the Rockefeller Foundation's International Education Board, which on April 26, 1928, considered and approved Oppenheimer's application to work on "problems of quantum mechanics" first with Ralph Fowler in Cambridge and then with either Ehrenfest in Leiden or Bohr in Copenhagen.

Having thus secured both his fellowship for the year 1928–9 and his two teaching positions, starting the year after that, Oppenheimer left Caltech in July 1928, intending to spend the first part of the summer at Ann Arbor and the second part in New Mexico with his family. The attraction of Ann Arbor was not only the chance it offered of reuniting with Goudsmit and Uhlenbeck, but also the opportunity of attending the famous summer school in theoretical physics, which had become (and would remain until the Second World War) an annual event, attracting distinguished theoretical physicists from all over the world.

From Ann Arbor, Oppenheimer on August 2 wrote to the International Education Board to tell them that he would have to postpone his fellowship because he had tuberculosis and "several doctors have told me that it would not be very wise to go abroad until I am better." For a few years Oppenheimer had suffered from a nasty, persistent cough, caused no doubt by his heavy smoking, but it is unlikely that he had tuberculosis. Frank, asked many years later, thought there never had been a secure and confirmed diagnosis of tuberculosis, leading some to wonder—just as Herbert Smith had wondered about Oppenheimer's "dysentery" before starting at Harvard—whether Oppenheimer, ill with worry about whether he could meet the expectations he and others had of himself, had invented a medical cause for his feeling unwell, one that would allow him to delay the challenge that he faced.

After the summer school finished, Oppenheimer headed for New Mexico, as planned. In his letter to Frank the previous spring, Oppenheimer had asked him what his plans were for the summer. "If you are out here [that is, in the Southwest]," he suggested, "we might knock around for a fortnight on the desert." During Oppenheimer's time at Caltech, his family's situation had changed somewhat. Having already sold the Bay Shore house, in 1928 they sold the Riverside Drive apartment too and moved into a smaller apartment on Park Avenue, between 47th and 48th Streets in midtown Manhattan—then, as now, one of the most expensive areas in the world. Frank, who would turn sixteen on August 14, 1928, was, like his older brother, tall, slim and good-looking, but without his brother's intensity and instability.

While Oppenheimer had been attending the summer school at Ann Arbor, Frank had been at a summer camp in Colorado. They arranged to meet at Katherine Page's house in Los Pinos. Oppenheimer arrived a few days before Frank and was taken by Katherine to a cabin a mile or so from her ranch at Cowles. It was built of half-trunks and adobe mortar and commanded a magnificent view of the Sangre de Cristo mountains and the Pecos River. "Like it?" Katherine asked, and when Oppenheimer nodded, she told him that it was available for rent. "Hot dog!" said Oppenheimer. "That's what you should call it," Katherine told him. "Hot Dog. *Perro Caliente.*"

When Frank arrived, he and Oppenheimer moved into Perro Caliente, which they persuaded their father that winter to lease. When the lease ran out in 1947, Oppenheimer bought it outright. For the rest of his life Perro Caliente was to be his refuge. For two weeks, Oppenheimer and his brother stayed at the cabin and cemented a mutual admiration for, and bond with, each other. Almost every day they rode in the mountains, acquiring a reputation among the locals for expert horsemanship. While they rode, they talked about physics, poetry, literature, philosophy and religion. Francis Fergusson visited them and would later tell how, after a hot and tiring day on the range, he headed for the icebox in the cabin, to find only half a bottle of vodka, a jar of pickled artichokes, some caviar and a can of chicken livers.

Despite this inadequate nutrition, Oppenheimer's health improved enormously during his time in New Mexico, and on August 25 he wrote from there to the NRC's Fellowship Board, thanking them for their letter of August 16 (in which, in response to Oppenheimer's statement that he had tuberculosis, they had told him that his fellowship had been withdrawn) and telling them: "It now seems certain that I shall be able to take the fellowship of the International Education Board . . . I therefore very much hope that the withdrawal of the fellowship will not prove permanent."

Understandably perplexed, the IEB asked Oppenheimer to undergo a complete medical examination. The Oppenheimer brothers had arranged, after their two-week sojourn in New Mexico, to meet their parents at the Broadmoor Hotel in Colorado Springs. Thus it was in Colorado Springs that Oppenheimer underwent the medical examination insisted upon by the IEB. It took place on September 18, 1928, and was conducted by a Dr. Gerald B. Webb, who found no trace of tuberculosis and reported that, apart from having some ten months previously a "slight sinus infection and slight tonsillitis since," Oppenheimer was in "first class" medical condition. After receiving this report, the NRC approved the IEB stipend, although, unusually, it was not for twelve months but for nine, starting on November 1.

In the meantime, after taking a few driving lessons, the Oppenheimer brothers bought a car, a Chrysler Roadster, and set off for Pasadena. Before they were even out of Colorado, they had an accident. With Frank at the wheel, the car skidded on some loose gravel and rolled over into a ditch. The windscreen was shattered, the cloth top ruined and Oppenheimer's right arm broken. Remarkably, they got the car running again the next day, but Frank drove it onto a slab of rock from which they were unable to move. They spent that night on the desert floor, as Frank remembered it, "sipping from a bottle of spirits . . . and sucking on some lemons." Oppenheimer arrived in Pasadena disheveled, unshaven, one arm in a sling and with little time to pack and prepare to leave for Europe. However, during what had been an eventful and memorable summer, his little brother had been transformed into his closest friend.

In his original submission to the NRC for a postdoctoral fellowship, Oppenheimer had stated his intention of starting on September 16, working first with Fowler in Cambridge and then with either Ehrenfest in Leiden or Bohr in Copenhagen. In the event, with the fellowship starting in November, he went straight to Leiden. Of all the great physicists he had met during his previous two years in Europe, it was Ehrenfest with whom he formed the closest attachment. They all admired Oppenheimer's manifest intellect, but Ehrenfest really *liked* him.

And for Ehrenfest, more than perhaps any other great scientist, liking people and being liked by them was important. A working-class Jew from Vienna who became the successor to the great H. A. Lorentz at Leiden, Ehrenfest was a man of passionate intensity, who inspired admiration as a physicist and devotion as a teacher and friend. His biographer Martin Klein has written of him:

> His way of being alive involved thinking about physics, talking and arguing about physics, working to his utmost to understand physics, and teaching it to anyone who showed an interest in it—students, colleagues, laymen, casual acquaintances, children. Others have been as intensely committed to science, but Ehrenfest was unique in his need to have close human contacts as an essential part of doing physics, in the breadth of human experience and the range of emotions that went into his scientific activity.

His close friend Einstein said:

> He was not merely the best teacher in our profession whom I have ever known; he was also passionately preoccupied with the development and destiny of men, especially his students. To understand

others, to gain their friendship and trust, to aid anyone embroiled in outer or inner struggles, to encourage youthful talent—all this was his real element, almost more than his immersion in scientific problems.

Though perfectly capable of following highly abstract mathematics, Ehrenfest was famous among physicists for distrusting overly complicated formalistic treatments of physical problems. In this, he was often contrasted with Max Born. The great physicist Victor Weisskopf, who studied at Göttingen, remarked that Ehrenfest taught him "to distrust the complicated mathematics and formalisms that were then very popular at Göttingen" and thereby "showed me how to get at the real physics."

When, in the early summer of 1928, Oppenheimer expressed a desire to spend some of his time as a postdoctoral student working with Ehrenfest at Leiden, he naturally wrote to Ehrenfest asking for his support and received in reply the following characteristically forthright and warm response:

> If you intend to mount heavy mathematical artillery again during your coming year in Europe, I would ask you not only not to come to Leiden, but if possible not even to Holland, and just because I am really so fond of you and want to keep it that way. But if, on the contrary, you want to spend at least your first few months patiently, comfortably and joyfully in discussions that keep coming back to the same few points, chatting about a few basic questions with me and our young people—and without thinking much about publishing (!!!)—why then I welcome you with open arms!!

Though it had been Ehrenfest who had spotted the mathematical mistakes in Oppenheimer's Ramsauer paper, it is typical of him that his concern was not that Oppenheimer was incompetent in mathematics, but that he would attach too much importance to it. Ehrenfest's greatest concern in physics was always with attaining *clarity*, genuine understanding.

Oppenheimer in later life emphasized how much he admired Ehrenfest. "I thought of him," he once said, "in semi-Socratic terms, and I thought I would learn something from him and indeed certainly did." The intention of both Oppenheimer and Ehrenfest was that Oppenheimer would, during his time at Leiden, not only pursue his own research, but also act as Ehrenfest's assistant. To everybody's astonishment, Oppenheimer, in this latter capacity, gave a few seminars at Leiden *in Dutch*, a language he seemed to have learned in a matter of months. "I don't think it was very good Dutch," he later recalled, but it was, nevertheless, greatly appreciated.

However, Oppenheimer's principal interest was his own research, and, despite his great admiration of Ehrenfest, he could not be persuaded to abandon altogether his tendency to look for mathematical techniques to solve the questions of physics. "I think that his [Ehrenfest's] interest in simplicity and clarity was really a great thing," Oppenheimer once said, "but I probably still had a fascination with formalism and complication, so that the large part of what had me stuck or engaged was not his dish." Very quickly after arriving at Leiden, therefore, Oppenheimer came to think that—his affection for, and admiration of, Ehrenfest notwithstanding—he would be better off somewhere else. "There was not a great deal of life in the physics in Leiden at the time," he recalled. "I think Ehrenfest was depressed: I don't think that I was of great interest to him then. I don't think he told me what was on his mind and I have a recollection of quiet and gloom."

Indeed, Ehrenfest *was* depressed, far more so than anybody realized at the time. Two things drove him to depression. The first was the state of physics, which seemed to move further and further away from the kind of clarity he himself sought to achieve, in favor of mathematical techniques, the physical interpretation of which remained clouded in mystery and controversy. The second was his youngest son, Vassily ("Wassik"), who was born with Down syndrome. Within a few years these two pressures would weigh more and more heavily on Ehrenfest. Finally, he could stand no more, as he tried to explain in a letter that he wrote (but never sent) to a number of his closest friends, including Bohr and Einstein. "I absolutely do not know any more how to carry further during the next few months the burden of my life, which has become unbearable," he began, adding:

> In recent years it has become ever more difficult for me to follow the developments in physics with understanding. After trying, ever more enervated and torn, I have finally given up in desperation. This made me completely weary of life . . . I did feel condemned to live on mainly because of the economic cares for the children. I tried other things, but that helps only briefly. Therefore I concentrate more and more on the precise details of suicide. I have no other practical possibility than suicide, and that after having first killed Wassik. Forgive me . . .

On September 25, 1933, having made arrangements for his other children, Ehrenfest accompanied Wassik to the Professor Watering Institute in Amsterdam, where he was being treated. While they sat in the waiting room, Ehrenfest shot Wassik and then himself. "None of us," Oppenheimer wrote to Ehrenfest's former assistant Uhlenbeck, "who were his students, shall be quite free of guilt in this his desperation."

Of course, in November 1928, Oppenheimer had no way of knowing just how deep Ehrenfest's depression was and to what it would drive him. He knew only that he wanted to get away from Leiden, which, he said later, "spoiled this period from the point of view of physics." After his disappointing time with Ehrenfest, Oppenheimer intended to go to Copenhagen to work with Bohr, but, as an interim measure, he spent a few weeks at the University of Utrecht with Bohr's old student and disciple Hendrik Kramers. "Bohr is Allah," Wolfgang Pauli once said, "and Kramers is his Prophet." Another frequently made comparison was with Michael Faraday and James Clerk Maxwell, with Bohr being the intuitive Faraday and Kramers the mathematically minded Maxwell. Kramers was in many ways ideally suited to being Oppenheimer's mentor, not only because of his inclination toward formal ways of approaching physics, but because of the many other things they had in common, including a veneration of Bohr and a wide range of intellectual and cultural interests. Kramers, for example, combined being a professor of physics with playing the cello to a very high standard, writing poetry and editing a literary magazine. Indeed, though they did not become especially close, Oppenheimer and Kramers got on very well, and Oppenheimer enjoyed his time at Utrecht, the most lasting legacy of which was the nickname he acquired there: Opje. Though the anglicized version, Oppie, became more widely known and used, among Oppenheimer's closest friends Opje was the preferred form.

From Utrecht, on December 30, 1928, Oppenheimer wrote a long letter to Frank, who had written an essay on aesthetics and had sent it to his brother. Consequently, most of the letter is taken up with an interesting extended discussion of the subject, which shows not only how close the two brothers had become, but also how much deep thought Oppenheimer had given to the subject. Frank's central point in the essay had evidently been that an expression of personal, individual taste ("I like it," and so on) is not an artistic judgment. With this, Oppenheimer agreed. In a rather schoolmasterly way, however, he ticked Frank off for showing "a lamentable ignorance of history in the matter," but added that that was "almost irrelevant." More problematic, Oppenheimer maintained, was a difficulty that faced anybody who wanted to insist on the universality and objectivity of artistic standards, namely that "appreciation of art is in fact neither universal nor objective, that it depends on education, experience, taste; that, in its critical aspects, it is defined only by the 'I like its' of the sensitive and the initiated." The solution to this difficulty, Oppenheimer suggested, was to accept that "the value of a picture is best defined as relative, not to the person, but to what one may vaguely call the civilization: the public, traditional culture and experience of the civilization for which it was painted." He recommended that Frank read Roger Fry's *Transformations: Critical and Speculative Essays on Art*, which had been published the previous year. The letter ended with some entirely general advice: "discipline, work, honesty, and, toward other people, a solicitude for their welfare and as complete an indifference as possible to their good opinion."

A few days later, on January 3, 1929, Oppenheimer was back in Leiden, from where he wrote to the IEB's Paris office, saying that, "at the suggestion of Ehrenfest and of Kramers," he had changed his plans: instead of going from Leiden to Copenhagen to work with Bohr, he now intended to go to Zurich to work with Wolfgang Pauli. He had, he said, written to Pauli asking for his consent and still intended to go to Copenhagen after he had worked with Pauli. "I hope," he concluded, "that it will be possible for you to grant this permission without waiting for the discretion of the American Board; for I should like to leave Leiden in the next weeks." The following week, Ehrenfest wrote to the IEB, saying that Oppenheimer ("a very ingenious physicist") would be better off going to Zurich, not only for educational reasons, but also because of his health, in particular "that obstinate cough which had not been in order since his arrival in Holland." "Please," pleaded Ehrenfest, "put this charming, fine—but whose health is questionable—young man under medical control, but without letting him know that I wrote you about it."

Ehrenfest, it seems, had very strong views about where Oppenheimer should go in order to develop to its fullest his potential as a physicist. Part of Ehrenfest being, as Einstein put it, "passionately preoccupied with the development and destiny of men" was that he took an intense interest in where and with whom his students should study. In the case of Oppenheimer, he felt strongly, as Oppenheimer later told an interviewer, "that Bohr with his largeness and vagueness was not the medicine I needed." Rather, Ehrenfest felt that Oppenheimer needed "someone who was a professional calculating physicist," who could give him "more discipline and more schooling," and the man he chose for this task was Wolfgang Pauli.

As Abraham Pais has said, Ehrenfest's view that Pauli rather than Bohr could offer Oppenheimer what he most needed was "a wise judgement with far-reaching consequences for Robert's career." Ehrenfest had evidently come to this conclusion soon after Oppenheimer's arrival in Leiden. In a letter to Pauli of November 26, 1928, he urged him to accept Oppenheimer, and showed, in the process, how perceptive he was about Oppenheimer's strengths and weaknesses, how much he liked him and how much he cared about making sure that Oppenheimer worked with the *right* person. He was writing, he told Pauli, "about a physicist (a good one though), namely Oppenheimer."

> The poor devil is with us in Leiden . . . under pressure of my school-masterly character. He has always very witty ideas . . . But then the great misery starts that I cannot grasp anything that cannot be "visu-alised." And, although he then with imperturbable calm and kindness tries to meet my wishes, the result is that I bother more than help him. He does not think of complaining . . . I am really convinced that, for the full development of his (great) scientific talent, Oppen-heimer still needs "RECHTZEITIG a bisserl (!) LIEBEVOLL zurechtge-prügelt worden sollte" [timely and a bit lovingly to be beaten into shape]. He thoroughly deserves this kindness since he is a rare and decent fellow . . . Therefore I would like it very much if he can come to you after Leiden. This idea appeals very much to him.

The man at the IEB's Paris office charged to deal with Oppenheimer was Dr. W. J. Robbins, to whom Oppenheimer wrote on January 23, 1929, enclosing a note from Pauli approving his plan of working with him, and saying that he was now already in Zurich, having made the trip at his own expense, which came to $15 for his fare and $29 for his luggage. In a subsequent letter of February 4, he explained: "The lug-gage was frightfully expensive, because of the weight of the books and offprints. I can see no reason, a priori, why the Board should pay for this." He also told Robbins, perhaps confusingly: "I did not, of course, leave Holland until I had assurance from Professor Pauli that I might work with him; but I had no letter which I could submit to the Board to indicate his consent."

A possible explanation for this last statement is that Pauli gave his consent not in a letter, but face-to-face. In the middle of January 1929, both Oppenheimer and Pauli were in Leipzig, attending a regional meeting of the German Physical Society. Both had been drawn by the presence there of Heisenberg: Oppenheimer to hear him lecture on his recent work on ferromagnetism, and Pauli to discuss a piece of work that he and Heisenberg had planned to write jointly.

Heisenberg had been at Leipzig since 1927, when, at the astonish-ingly young age of twenty-five, he had been appointed to the chair of physics there. At about the same time, his interests and Pauli's began to converge, both stimulated by the work of Dirac's that had so excited Oppenheimer at Göttingen. What Dirac had achieved in that work was to take the first step in the direction of a theory that would unite quantum mechanics and electrodynamics into what is now known as QED, or quantum electrodynamics. Oppenheimer had been disappointed that Dirac had not developed that theory at Göttingen; now, Heisenberg and Pauli were about to combine their formidable energies and talents in the pursuit of such a development, and, fortunately for Oppenheimer, they were about to do this just at the moment when he was going to start work with Pauli.

In its classical form, electrodynamics—the understanding of electromagnetic forces—received its definitive formulation in the differential equations of James Clerk Maxwell, who, in the 1860s, was the first to realize that light was a form of electromagnetic radiation. In Clerk Maxwell's theory, developed and refined by later physicists, such as Heinrich Hertz, electromagnetic radiation was understood to consist of waves in the "ether," which, after the discovery of the electron by Thomson in 1896, was considered to be an electromagnetic "field" that mediated between individual electrons. All this changed with Einstein's work in 1905: first, the ether was abolished; second, electromagnetic radiation was seen as consisting of discrete "quanta"; third, energy and matter were now regarded as equivalent to each other (this is the importance of the famous equation $E = mc^2$); and finally, in accordance with the theory of relativity, the speed of light (as of all electromagnetic radiation) was held to be the same for all observers, faster than which nothing was allowed to travel, which necessitated fundamental changes in the equations used to calculate the energies of waves of radiation or particles of matter.

The problem was that no consistent theory of electrodynamics had yet emerged that took into account these revolutions in physics brought by Einstein and then later by quantum theory. Einstein had shown how the basic equations of electrodynamics could be made relativistic, but they still described the continuous waves of classical electrodynamics, not the discontinuous "quantized" light envisaged by Einstein and in quantum theory. What was needed, and what Dirac had shown might be possible, was a relativistic quantum-field theory.

As soon as he read Dirac's 1927 paper, Pauli wrote to Heisenberg proposing a project to construct a complete quantum electrodynamics analogous to the Clerk Maxwell formulation of the classical theory. That year, both had too much else to do to make much progress on this, but the following year the project received fresh stimulus, again provided by Dirac, who published a paper with the Royal Society that introduced what is now known as the "Dirac equation." This is an equation for calculating the energy of electrons that, unlike the famous Schrödinger wave function, takes relativity into account, a factor that becomes increasingly important as the speed of the electrons approaches the speed of light.

Furthermore, the Dirac equation could deal more naturally and more easily than the Schrödinger function with the "spin" of electrons and therefore with Pauli's great contribution to physics: the exclusion principle. Formulated by Pauli in 1924, the exclusion principle was hailed by Einstein as a "new law of nature," and its importance was recognized and appreciated more and more as theoretical physics developed in the 1920s and '30s. In Heisenberg's lecture on ferromagnetism that Oppenheimer attended at Leipzig, for example, much use was made of the exclusion principle. Eventually, prompted by Einstein, its importance was recognized by the Nobel Prize committee, who in 1945 awarded Pauli the Nobel Prize in Physics on the basis of the exclusion principle (Heisenberg's contribution was recognized much earlier—he received *his* Nobel Prize in 1932).

What the principle states is that no two electrons in the same atom can exist in the same quantum state, where the quantum state of an electron is characterized by four "quantum numbers." One of these numbers, postulated by Pauli, is a two-valued "degree of freedom," which Oppenheimer's friends Goudsmit and Uhlenbeck identified in 1925 as the "spin" of an electron. Because the spin of the electron is measured to be one half that of Planck's constant, and the spin of the photon is an integral unit, the equations describing the behaviors of the two particles are different. Dirac's equation provides the relativistically correct treatment of spin $\frac{1}{2}$ particles such as the electron.[25]

What Pauli and Heisenberg hoped to do was use the conceptual tools and the mathematical techniques that Dirac had provided to forge their proposed quantum-field theory. It was a huge challenge and they had very little time to rise to it, since Heisenberg was committed to a lecture tour of the United States, beginning on March 1, 1929, that would keep him away from Europe for most of the rest of the year. Nevertheless, rise to it they did, and the paper, "On the Quantum Dynamics of Wave Fields," was duly delivered for publication before Heisenberg's departure for the United States.

From the very beginning of his association with Pauli, therefore, Oppenheimer was present at the birth of important new ideas, and Pauli's joint paper with Heisenberg was to set the agenda for Oppen-

---

[25] I am grateful to my friend James Dodd for explaining this to me.

heimer's own research during his time at Zurich and for many years after that. This contributed to something that Oppenheimer's later student and friend Robert Serber noted, namely that during his time with Pauli, Oppenheimer's "interests changed and thereafter were devoted to the more fundamental questions of physics."

Apart from allowing him to introduce himself to Pauli and gain his consent for coming to Zurich, Oppenheimer's brief time at Leipzig in January of 1929 was important for another reason. For it was there that he met for the first time the man who would come to know and understand him perhaps better than any other: Isidor Rabi. "I first met him in Leipzig," Rabi later recalled. "He had just got his degree a year or so before, and there were a lot of stories about him—as a personality: his good wit, his sarcasm and so on." The two got on so well not only because of the similarities in their New York Jewish background mentioned earlier, but also because of their shared sense of affronted pride when faced by the attitude toward American scientists that prevailed in Europe. After working at Hamburg under the great experimental physicist Otto Stern, Rabi had come to think that German students were no better than American students. In fact, he came to think the American system of university education was on the whole better: "What we needed were the leaders." He and Oppenheimer were united in their determination to be two of those leaders.

Like Oppenheimer, Rabi was being funded by an IEB fellowship. After spending the first few months of his fellowship in Hamburg, with Stern, Rabi had gone to Leipzig in the New Year of 1929 hoping to study under Heisenberg. When he arrived there, however, he learned of Heisenberg's plan to leave for the U.S. at the beginning of March and so decided, on Heisenberg's advice, to go to Zurich to work with Pauli. It was at Zurich, from February to July 1929, that the friendship between Rabi and Oppenheimer blossomed. "I got to know him quite well," Rabi recalled, "because our intellectual interests about various things—science, philosophy, religion, painting—were similar and different from the interests of most young physicists at that time. We saw a good deal of one another."

As Ehrenfest foresaw, Zurich was just the right place for Oppenheimer, and Pauli just the right man. Summing up his experiences in Europe as an IEB fellow, Oppenheimer later said:

The time with Ehrenfest had seemed terribly inadequate to what was really in Ehrenfest and the time with Kramers had seemed good but not very substantial—very good personally, very close, but not very substantial. The time with Pauli seemed just very, very good indeed.

"I got," he said, "to be not only extremely respectful but also extremely fond of Pauli and I learned a lot from him."

In his younger days, Pauli had been Max Born's assistant at Göttingen, but Oppenheimer's relationship with Pauli could not have been more different from that with Born, nor could there be a character whose personality differed more sharply from Born's than Pauli's. Where Born was fragile and introverted, Pauli was blunt and unafraid to give offense. He was known as "the Wrath of God" because of the ferocity of his criticisms of shoddy thinking. He was, from a young age, impossible to intimidate. As a young graduate student in Munich, Pauli had attended a talk given by Einstein and contributed to the discussion by saying: "You know, what Mr. Einstein said is not so stupid!" Once, in discussion with a colleague who asked him to slow down because he could not think as fast as Pauli, Pauli replied: "I do not mind if you think slowly, but I do object when you publish more quickly than you can think." Most famously, he once said of an unclear paper: "Das ist nicht nur nicht richtig, es ist nicht einmal falsch!" ("Not only is it not right, it's not even wrong.") His own reputation was based as much on his contributions to public discussion and on his voluminous correspondence with the top physicists of the day as it was on his publications, and he was entirely indifferent to the concern for priority that worried many scientists.

Oppenheimer did not altogether escape Pauli's biting wit. "His ideas are always very interesting," Pauli is reported to have said about Oppenheimer, "but his calculations are always wrong." Pauli would also impersonate Oppenheimer's habit of murmuring "nim-nim-nim" while he was thinking what to say and groping for words, and took to calling him "the nim-nim-nim man." Rabi recalls: "Pauli once remarked to me that Oppenheimer seemed to treat physics as an avocation and psychoanalysis as a vocation." On the whole, however, Pauli had, from the beginning, a good impression of Oppenheimer, as he reported in a letter to Ehrenfest of February 15, 1929: "I believe that Oppenheimer is quite comfortable in Zurich, that he can work well here, and that scientifically it will still be possible to pull many good things out of him."

His strength is that he has many and good ideas, and has much imagination. His weakness is that he is much too quickly satisfied with poorly based statements, that he does not answer his own often quite interesting questions for lack of perseverance and thoroughness, and that he leaves his problems in a half-digested stage of conjecture, belief or disbelief.

This acute analysis contains few surprises, but Pauli then goes on to criticize Oppenheimer for something that nobody had noticed before: his respect for authority. Oppenheimer, Pauli told Ehrenfest, "considers all I say as final and definitive truth. I do not know the origins of this need for others' authority." That Oppenheimer had such a need would certainly have been news to Born.

At Zurich, Oppenheimer seems to have come close to finding what he had claimed to (but alas failed to) find at Göttingen, namely, a community of like-minded scholars. Rudolf Peierls, who had been a student of Heisenberg's at Leipzig, but who had received and taken the same advice as Rabi to transfer to Zurich, has described the spring and early summer of 1929 as "rather short for all that seems to have happened." As well as writing a great deal, he recalls, there was "plenty of time for concerts and cinema, and for sailing."

> It was then easy to rent a sailboat for a few hours, and I liked to take friends out on the lake. I even persuaded Pauli to come sailing—I cherish a photo showing him, Robert Oppenheimer, and I. I. Rabi on the boat.

The photograph survives and shows a dapper-looking Oppenheimer, cigarette in hand and hat on head, talking to Rabi and another young American physicist called H. M. Mott-Smith. All three look lost in thought and deep in conversation. Meanwhile, on the right of the picture, Pauli, smiling mischievously, stares at the camera.

In a description that recalls his fellow students' impressions of his undergraduate days at Harvard, Rabi remembers that Oppenheimer "worked very hard that spring but had a gift of concealing his assiduous application with an air of easy nonchalance."

> Actually, he was engaged in a very difficult calculation of the opacity of surfaces of stars to their internal radiation, an important constant in the theoretical construction of stellar models. He spoke little of these problems and seemed to be much more interested in literature, especially the Hindu classics and the more esoteric Western writers.

Though it was an intellectually fruitful period for him, Oppenheimer published only one paper during his time at Zurich, a paper called "Über

die Strahlung der freien Elektronen im Coulombfeld" ("On the Radiation of Electrons in a Coulomb Field"), which he sent to the *Zeitschrift
für Physik* on May 6, 1929. Pauli was extremely impressed with this piece
of work. "Using flawless methods," he wrote to Sommerfeld in Munich,
Oppenheimer "has calculated everything one can desire."

In a letter to Bohr of July, Pauli described Oppenheimer's paper as
"a continuation of the work of Heisenberg and myself on QED" and
for a while there was talk of a three-way collaboration. As it turned
out, Heisenberg and Pauli published the second (and final) part of their
jointly authored attempt to formulate new rules for quantum electrodynamics as a two-man paper (with an acknowledgment to Oppenheimer)
in September 1929, while Oppenheimer waited until November, when
he was back in the U.S., to deliver his own contribution to the subject: a
paper for the *Physical Review* entitled "Note on the Theory of the Interaction of Field and Matter."

A possible explanation for the abandonment of the plan to work
together with Heisenberg and Pauli lies in Oppenheimer's continued
bad health. The persistent cough that had so alarmed Ehrenfest did not
go away, and Dr. Robbins of the Rockefeller Foundation kept (as he was
asked to by Ehrenfest) a close eye on the situation. On April 30, 1929,
Robbins wrote to Oppenheimer: "First and foremost is the question of
your health." It would, Robbins said (apparently in response to a request
from Oppenheimer), be quite appropriate to terminate his IEB fellowship a month early in order for him to prepare his teaching in Berkeley
for the coming academic year. The fellowship was due to finish at the
end of July, so, presumably, Robbins was now expecting it to finish at the
end of June.

In a letter written on May 14, in reply to Robbins's letter of April,
Oppenheimer said that he was "fairly certain that I shall be able to continue with the work until July" and he still hoped, as he had originally
stated was his intention, to visit Bohr in Copenhagen for two weeks at the
end of June. Oppenheimer devoted the rest of this letter to an attempt
to answer Robbins's request for some suggestions as to how the difficulties experienced by American students in Europe might be overcome.
Oppenheimer's analysis of those difficulties, perhaps inevitably, strikes
an autobiographical note. They are, he began, "most acute in men who
combine a certain weakness, timidity, hesitancy of character with a quite
robust vanity—or, perhaps, more accurately—with an urgent desire for
excellence." These students, he went on, are away from their friends,
and also "from the pampering of an American university, and from a
language which they can control," and are "introduced to the more criti-

cal, more disciplined, more professional science of Europe." This state of affairs:

> induces in the victim a state of surrender, and a false metaphysical melancholy which replaces, and makes impossible, an active participation in the European scheme, and an honest attempt to learn from it. The melancholy is presumably unpleasant; it is usually dissipated by return to America, and the consequent renewal of the pampering. But it acts as a protective coating for the American against that which he was sent to Europe to learn; almost always it is a sterile melancholy. It is the melancholy of the little boy who will not play because he has been snubbed.

Oppenheimer's suggested solution was a lot less interesting than his description of the problem. "I think," he told Robbins, "that the most useful preventative would be to let the men know a little better what their situation will be, and to warn them of the collapse, so that they may be on their guard against it, and may make a conscious and specific effort to avert it."

Oppenheimer never did go to Copenhagen, nor did he stay in Zurich till his fellowship finished at the end of July. Instead he terminated his fellowship a month early and returned to the U.S. in July. This may have been because of his cough, or it may have been, as he had earlier explained to Robbins, because he was anxious to leave himself enough time to prepare for his teaching duties in California. But the letter to Robbins suggests another reason: he simply wanted to get back home. He himself wrote in later life: "In the spring of 1929 I returned to the United States. I was homesick for this country, and in fact I did not leave it again for nineteen years."

Oppenheimer's homesickness at the end of his time in Zurich is illustrated by an episode recounted by Felix Bloch, who was then a young physicist working with Pauli. Bloch remembers visiting Oppenheimer's apartment in Zurich and being struck by the many things he had brought with him from New Mexico: "I was particularly impressed by the beautiful Navajo rug he had on his sofa." Bloch had never been to the U.S. and asked Oppenheimer to tell him about his country. Had he not had a genuine interest in knowing more about the U.S., he later told Oppenheimer's first biographer, Denise Royal, he might easily have regretted his request, such was "the intensity of Oppenheimer's affection for his country."

On May 6, 1929, Oppenheimer wrote to Frank, thanking him for the birthday present Frank had sent of a book on Degas (Oppenheimer turned twenty-five on April 22), and suggesting arrangements for the coming summer in New Mexico. First, he told Frank, Perro Caliente— "house and six acres and stream"—was theirs for the next four years and there was an allowance of $300 for restoration. Second, Katherine Page would go out to the Pecos in May, Julius and Ella would be ready to leave New York by the middle of June, and he himself would be back in the U.S. "about the middle of July" and "determined not to spend more than a week or so in the East." So, he concluded, Frank should take their parents out west in the middle of June, and he "and a suitable friend" should "try to open up the place, get horses, learn to cook, make the hacienda as nearly habitable as you can, and see the country." Meanwhile, he assured Frank, he himself planned to "come straight out to the Pecos, and have about three weeks there."

So it was that in June 1929 Frank arrived at Los Pinos with two school friends, Ian Martin and Roger Lewis. From a Sears, Roebuck catalog Frank ordered furniture, rugs and kitchen equipment, and he and his friends stayed with Katherine Page while they waited for it to arrive. Shortly after the arrival of the mail-order goods, Oppenheimer himself arrived with a wagon loaded with bootleg whisky, mineral oil, peanut butter and Viennese sausages. For the next three weeks the four of them spent the days riding the mountains and the nights reading and drinking. "We'd get sort of drunk," Frank remembered, "when we were high up, and we'd act all kind of silly." Oppenheimer had to leave sooner than Frank. He went first to Pasadena and then to Berkeley, from where he wrote to his brother, thanking him for a letter in which he provided an account of what he and his friends had been up to since Oppenheimer's departure. "It made me a little envious," Oppenheimer confessed, "and pleased me awfully to hear of gay times at Perro Caliente. And I can think how let down you will feel now that it is so nearly time to close up." As Oppenheimer prepared to begin his career as a teacher of physics, it was the New Mexican desert that restored his physical and spiritual health sufficiently for him to feel able to meet the challenges ahead.

8

An *American* School
of Theoretical Physics

didn't start to make a school," Oppenheimer said toward the end of his life, recalling his early days at Berkeley, "I didn't start to look for students. I started really as a propagator of the theory which I loved, about which I continued to learn more." The latter part of this statement is clearly true, but the first part seems contradicted by remarks he made elsewhere in the same interview that have already been quoted: "I thought I'd like to go to Berkeley because it was a desert. There was no theoretical physics and I thought it would be nice to try to start something."

In fact, he *did* build a school at Berkeley, one that the eminent physicist Hans Bethe has described as "the greatest school of theoretical physics that the United States has ever known." And, despite his statement to the contrary, Oppenheimer went to Berkeley precisely in order to build a school. It had become important to him, as it had to Rabi, and to many American physicists who had experienced the condescension directed at them by their European counterparts, to establish a world center for theoretical physics *in the U.S.* In some of his remarks about Berkeley, however, he indulges in a bit of condescension of his own. For example, his description of Berkeley as a "desert" and his statement that there was no theoretical physics there are both a little overstated. After all, Edward Condon, whom Oppenheimer had met at Göttingen, had studied at Berkeley, both as an undergraduate and as a graduate, and had learned enough theoretical physics to get a Ph.D. in the subject and to be accepted as a postdoctoral student by both Max Born and Arnold Sommerfeld.

What is true, however, and what Condon's career illustrates, is that if, as a Berkeley graduate, one wanted to pursue research on quantum mechanics under the supervision of leading experts in that field, it was essential to leave Berkeley and, preferably, go to Europe. Condon has given vivid accounts of some of the people who taught him at Berkeley in the early 1920s, and, while he clearly admired many of them, he would have been the first to admit that most of them were not top-flight research scientists. In fact, the professor who had the greatest influence on him, William Howell Williams, conducted no original research, published not a single paper and remained almost entirely unknown to the wider scientific community. After a brief career as a soldier, Williams had become a high-school teacher of physics—an "extraordinarily good" one, according to Condon—and then a lecturer in physics at Berkeley. In time, he was promoted to full professor, but, because he never completed his Ph.D., his promotion was slow, and, in his subsequent bitterness and insecurity Williams turned to drink. "In other words," Condon concludes, "[Williams] never fitted into the normal academic pattern, but he was a very sympathetic and understanding person . . . and he also was an extremely able interpreter of modern theoretical physics."

The chairman of the Berkeley physics department in the days when Condon was a student there was E. P. Lewis, an experimental physicist who, Condon recalls, "had a certain amount of spectroscopic work going on with very crude and home-made apparatus. He belonged really to that school of love and string and sealing wax, the junkiest kind of home-made apparatus." Lewis was not a physicist of the first rank, but he did publish more than seventy papers during his lifetime. When he died in 1926, he was replaced by a man called Elmer Hall, who, like Williams, does not seem to have published anything during his entire career. Hall was, however, still chair of the department when Oppenheimer joined in 1929, and remained in that post until his death in 1932.

One of the people at Berkeley most dedicated to improving and expanding its physics department was a professor of chemistry. Gilbert N. Lewis, one of America's most distinguished physical chemists, had been at Berkeley since 1912, and was to stay there until his death in 1946. Though he was in the chemistry department, Lewis often worked with physicists, including, most notably, Richard Tolman at Caltech. Together with Merle Randall, his colleague at Berkeley, Lewis cowrote the book on thermodynamics that became the standard teaching text for graduate-level courses on the subject (it was one of the books Oppenheimer claimed to have read at the end of his first year at Harvard), and was well known and well regarded by both chemists and physicists.

Helped and encouraged by Gilbert Lewis, the transformation of the physics department at Berkeley into one of the world's leading centers of physical research did not begin in 1929 with the appointment of

Oppenheimer, but rather in 1918, with the appointment of Raymond T. Birge. Birge, like E. P. Lewis, was a spectroscopist, and, like Gilbert N. Lewis, was interested in the area of scientific research where physics and chemistry meet. During the early part of his career at Berkeley he published a number of papers that made significant contributions to the "old quantum theory" (the theory that centered on the Rutherford-Bohr-Sommerfeld model of the atom), including one that was cited by Sommerfeld himself in his "bible," *Atombau und Spektrallinien*. For an American scientist in the early 1920s even to be noticed by the leading European scientists was unusual; to be cited by an acknowledged authority like Sommerfeld was a rare honor indeed. In recognition of his role in thus putting Berkeley physics on the map, Birge was made a full professor in 1926. Though he would not take over as chairman of the department until after E. P. Lewis's death in 1932, Birge was, when Oppenheimer joined in 1929 (and had been for some time before that), recognized as its leading figure.

Condon seems not to have liked Birge, labeling him one of the "pedants" who held back the promotion of William Howell Williams, thereby driving him to drink. Nevertheless, it was Birge who was responsible for most of the major steps that enabled Berkeley's physics department to compete with the best in the world. Though Birge shared Gilbert Lewis's enthusiasm for bridging the gap between chemistry and physics, ironically the close cooperation between the two departments at Berkeley was, to begin with, hampered by a clash between these two major figures. The clash was caused by Birge's insistence on teaching the Rutherford-Bohr-Sommerfeld model of the atom, which contradicted Lewis's own "cubical" theory. In a short time, of course, the Rutherford-Bohr-Sommerfeld model prevailed, and many chemists at Berkeley, including at least two who went on to win the Nobel Prize—William Giauque and Harold Urey—acquired their understanding of that model from Birge's lectures.

Because Birge, unlike his predecessors at Berkeley, published work that was read and cited by the leading European physicists, those physicists became more inclined to visit Berkeley. It was after a visit from Max Born that Condon was inspired to go to Göttingen; other great physicists to visit the department during the 1920s were Heisenberg, Sommerfeld and Ehrenfest. Birge also attracted to Berkeley home-grown American physicists who were active research scientists and conversant with modern theoretical work, most notably Leonard Loeb, who joined the department in 1923 and was promoted to full professor in 1929, the year Oppenheimer joined. Though Condon singled out William Howell Williams for special praise as a teacher, it was principally from Birge and Loeb that he acquired his knowledge and understanding of modern theoretical physics.

Birge and Loeb made it their joint business to expand the physics department and made sure every promising young American scientist knew that if they came to Berkeley they would be well paid, enjoy a perfect atmosphere for research and have excellent opportunities for rapid promotion. Before the appointment of Oppenheimer, their greatest success in this recruitment drive was with the young experimental physicist Ernest Lawrence, originally from South Dakota. Since 1927, Lawrence had been an assistant professor of physics at Yale, where he had completed his Ph.D. under the English physicist William Swann. Swann left Yale the same year, after which Lawrence grew dissatisfied. He did not get on well with the chairman of the physics department, John Zeleny, who refused to allow him to supervise graduate students, reserving them for more senior members of faculty. Lawrence was also impatient for promotion to associate professor, which Zeleny again refused. Hearing that Birge and Loeb were keen to build up the Berkeley department, Lawrence wrote to them and received an offer of an associate professorship, which he immediately accepted. Zeleny's parting words to Lawrence's family were: "Ernest is making a mistake."

Lawrence arrived at Berkeley in the summer of 1928, and discovered to his delight that, far from having to fight to concentrate on graduate teaching and research, such concentration was exactly what Birge, Loeb and Hall wanted from him. Encouraged by this, Lawrence threw himself without restraint into his work. He slept on campus at the faculty club, gave classes on electromagnetic theory and devoted himself to physics all day and every day, including weekends. At the center of his work was a preoccupation with solving a problem that had been articulated by none other than Ernest Rutherford. Rutherford, noting that all progress so far made in understanding atomic structure had come about through the bombardment of atoms by various particles such as alpha particles, drew attention to the dangers of relying on nature, in the form of naturally radioactive substances like radium, to provide these bombarding particles. In a lecture to the Royal Society in 1927, Rutherford urged his colleagues throughout the world to put their minds to devising a means of producing high-energy particles artificially. This would not only free researchers from their dependence on relatively rare radioactive substances, but might also mean that particles could be produced that had even more energy, and therefore more potential for atomic disintegration, than those released by naturally occurring radioactivity.

It was Lawrence's chief ambition to rise to that challenge. By the time

Oppenheimer arrived at Berkeley, a year after him, Lawrence had not yet built his first cyclotron (as his particle accelerator came to be called), but he had already achieved the conceptual breakthrough that subsequently allowed him to design and build it. The breakthrough came one afternoon in the university library. Lawrence was casually flicking through a German electrical-engineering journal when he saw a diagram of a device for producing high voltages using positively charged particles. Essentially, the device increased the energy of the particles by alternately pulling them toward a negative charge and then pushing them away by switching to a positive charge. Immediately, Lawrence realized that this basic principle, if applied to a device with circular trajectories, might allow one to keep increasing the energy of the ions almost without limit. The next day, he was seen hurrying across campus looking extremely elated and called out to a colleague's wife: "I'm going to be famous."

During Oppenheimer's first year at Berkeley, Lawrence began to build his cyclotron, which in January 1931 successfully accelerated hydrogen ions up to energies of 80,000 volts.[26] The following year, a considerably bigger machine achieved one million volts. Inspired by this success, the university set up the Radiation Laboratory, specifically for the purpose of conducting research using the cyclotron, and in 1936 it became an official department of the University of California, with Lawrence as its director. Three years later, Lawrence became the first person employed at an American state university to receive the Nobel Prize, by which time, no doubt, even John Zeleny would have admitted that neither Berkeley's decision to hire Lawrence nor Lawrence's decision to leave Yale had been a mistake.

From the moment he arrived at Berkeley and moved into the faculty club, Oppenheimer took to Lawrence warmly. He admired what he described as Lawrence's "unbelievable vitality and love of life," which allowed him to "work all day, run off for tennis, and work half the night." For the first few years of Oppenheimer's work at Berkeley, he and Lawrence spent a good deal of time together. They were not only united by their shared devotion to physics; there was also between them the attraction of opposites. Lawrence had an open, confident and untroubled manner. He made friends easily and had none of Oppenheimer's enigmatic elusiveness. Harold F. Cherniss, who was a doctoral student in classics at Berkeley when he met Oppenheimer in 1929, remarked: "The

---

[26] One electron volt is the energy of an electron when it has experienced the potential of one volt. In the context of discussing the energies of particles, physicists frequently abbreviate "electron volts" to simply "volts."

more intimately I was acquainted with him, the less I knew about him." Oppenheimer, Cherniss thought, "wanted friends very much," but "he didn't know how to make friends."

Oppenheimer may not have been very good at developing close friendships, but he knew how to charm people, and partly through Lawrence and partly through the magnetism exerted by his own exotic appeal, he quickly became integrated into the social life at Berkeley. "His mere physical appearance," Cherniss remembers, "his voice and his manners made people fall in love with him—male, female. Almost everybody." A story often told later of his first few days at Berkeley concerns a picnic that the Berkeley physicists and their wives had arranged in order for him to get to know everybody. Seizing the opportunity to impress, Oppenheimer said he would take care of the food, promising to cook for them an Indonesian dish called *nasi goreng*, which he had been taught by George Uhlenbeck's wife, Else. After they had driven across the Bay and Oppenheimer produced the dish, however, it was met with universal repugnance ("It tasted like sweepings from a Bombay gutter," one person there remembered) and was ever after referred to as "nasty gory." Not only was it foul, but there was not enough of it, Oppenheimer assuming that everyone else would be content, as he was, with just a mouthful. After waiting unsuccessfully for Oppenheimer to realize that they were all still hungry, the members of the group were relieved when Lawrence announced: "We passed a hot-dog stand about two miles back." To Oppenheimer's evident bewilderment, everyone immediately got in the car and went looking for the hot-dog stand.

"I have been pretty busy," Oppenheimer wrote to Frank on September 7, 1929, shortly before the start of term, "preparing lectures and giving miscellaneous counsel and working and getting to know people." In his next letter he offered Frank himself some counsel when he returned to the question of how to treat women, or "the refractory problem of the *jeunes filles newyorkaises*," as Oppenheimer put it. Frank had evidently mentioned being ill at ease with women, in response to which Oppenheimer's counsel was to associate only with those women who took responsibility for putting him at ease. "The obligation," he told Frank, "is always on the girl for making a go of conversation: if she does not accept the obligation, nothing that you can do will make the negotiations pleasant."

Perhaps this advice offers some clue as to why Oppenheimer's relations with women during this time seem to have been restricted to those who were already married. To meet a woman who was the wife of a colleague did not impose on him the obligation to initiate contact, with all the potential for embarrassment and risk of rejection that is involved in, say, asking a woman out for a date. Helen Allison, with whom Oppenheimer had flirted during his time as an NRC fellow at Caltech in 1928, remembers at Berkeley "young wives falling for Robert, charmed by his conversation, gifts of flowers, etc." Oppenheimer, she thought, "had an eye for women," but his attentions "should not be taken too seriously."

"I can't think that it would be terrible of me to say—" Oppenheimer wrote to Frank, "and it is occasionally true—that I need physics more than friends." At Berkeley, Oppenheimer was eventually able to combine his need for friends with his need for, and love of, physics, and to combine both with his desire to build an *American* school of theoretical physics by finding his friends from among his students. This, however, was a long process. In the first year or two, most of the students who took his courses found them incomprehensible and him intimidating.

The lectures Oppenheimer mentions preparing in his letter to Frank were part of a graduate course on quantum mechanics that he gave in the first semester of the 1929–30 academic year. His teaching at Berkeley was entirely confined to graduates. It was, he said later, "very rarely and only in quite different contexts that I ever worked with undergraduates. I think they didn't think I'd be any good for them and it didn't occur to me to ask to teach freshman physics or anything like that." As well as the course on quantum mechanics, he gave a graduate seminar concentrating on some aspect of theoretical physics, the title of which rotated between "Introduction to Theoretical Physics" and "Methods of Theoretical Physics." Oppenheimer did not approach this teaching in the spirit of someone preparing students for an exam (in fact, as some of his students complained, he never set them any tests and so had no formal means of assessing how much they had understood). Rather, as he says in the quotation given at the beginning of this chapter, he approached it from the point of view of "a propagator of the theory which I loved." As far as he was concerned, he was there not to teach—and certainly not to assess—students, but to bring quantum mechanics to Berkeley.

"I think from all I hear I was a very difficult lecturer," he admitted. "I started as a lecturer who made things very difficult." Oppenheimer's notes for his lectures on quantum mechanics survive and show that he did indeed make great demands upon his students. The way he remembered it was that "I found myself . . . the only one who understood what this was all about, and the gift which my high-school teacher of English had noted for explaining technical things came into action." Presumably by "this" he meant quantum mechanics, though in fact he was not the only one at Berkeley with any understanding of quantum mechanics: Birge, Loeb, Williams and Lawrence were all familiar with the Schrödinger wave-function version of the theory. All of them, however, were unfamiliar with, and baffled by, Heisenberg's matrix mechanics and Dirac's transformation theory, and these are what, just two weeks into the course, Oppenheimer asked his students to understand. Naturally many of them struggled, and when they asked for further elucidation, they were referred to books, most of which were written in German.

"Almost immediately," Birge later said, "students came to complain that he was going too fast." Birge asked to see Oppenheimer's notes and, after reading them, urged his students to persevere. Oppenheimer, meanwhile, complained to Birge: "I'm going so slowly that I'm not getting anywhere." "This," Birge recalled, "was my first intimation of the speed at which Oppenheimer's mind worked." Oppenheimer delivered his lectures in a low, quiet voice, while smoking incessantly; as soon as he finished a cigarette, he stubbed it out and lit a new one, almost in a single action. "Since we couldn't understand what he was saying," one of his students remembered, "we watched the cigarette. We were always expecting him to write on the board with it and smoke the chalk, but I don't think he ever did."

For the first two years of his joint post Oppenheimer would lecture at Berkeley from August until Christmas and then journey 350 miles south to Pasadena, teaching at Caltech from January until June, before spending as much of the summer as he could in New Mexico. After two years of this, Berkeley (the administrators of which were never entirely happy with having to share Oppenheimer with another university) changed the dates of their semesters, so that the first semester extended into January, making this arrangement impossible. Oppenheimer was determined to maintain the connection with Caltech, so he negotiated with Berkeley an agreement to teach at Caltech for the last six weeks of the academic year, just before the summer break. In this way, the fifty-fifty split that he had originally envisaged was transformed into an arrangement whereby he was basically employed by Berkeley, but released by them to spend a few weeks each year in Pasadena.

"In Pasadena," Oppenheimer later said, "I taught all right, but it was never an important part of the Caltech curriculum except conceivably that first year in the spring of '30 when I was there a long time and where I probably gave a pretty good 'course of sprouts' in quantum theory." The title of this "course of sprouts" was "Topics in Theoretical Physics." Again, it was restricted to graduates, and, perhaps because Oppenheimer had higher expectations of Caltech students than he had of Berkeley students, it was pitched at an even higher level, consisting of dense and concentrated discussions of subjects dealt with in recent research papers.

His first lecture in this course attracted about forty students, among whom was Carl D. Anderson, then a Ph.D. student and later a very eminent physicist. "I didn't know what Oppenheimer was talking about," Anderson has recalled. "He, in those days, was not a good lecturer. He paced back and forth, and wherever he happened to be at that instant, he would write some squiggles on the blackboard—part of an equation— and they were scattered all over at random." Within a few weeks Anderson was the only student still registered for the course. When he, too, went to see Oppenheimer to ask him for permission to drop the course, Oppenheimer pleaded with him to stay—without Anderson, he would have no course, and without a course, he would have no official position at Caltech. As an inducement, Oppenheimer promised Anderson that, if he remained on the course, he would be guaranteed to get an A, on which basis Anderson remained.

In addition to his "course of sprouts," Oppenheimer was persuaded by Richard Tolman to give some extra evening lectures on Dirac's quantum electrodynamics. These were open to anyone who wanted to come, but were intended chiefly for academic members of staff. In the event, the first of the proposed series was attended by about a dozen people. Again, Carl Anderson was present and remembers that, after Oppenheimer had talked for about two hours, Richard Tolman got up and said: "Robert, I didn't understand a damn word you said tonight, except . . ." And then he went up to the blackboard and wrote an equation. "That's all I understood." In reply, Oppenheimer told him that he had got that equation wrong. "And," says Anderson, "there was never a second meeting of this attempt on Oppenheimer's part to tell various people, mostly faculty, what Dirac's theory was all about."

During this first spring at Pasadena, Oppenheimer was visited by his parents. The previous year Julius had sold his share of the family business. Whether by luck or judgment, it is impossible to say, but Julius had thus protected the family fortune from the effects of the Wall Street Crash of October 1929. So little impact did the crash have on his family, and so little interest did he show in politics at this time, that Oppenheimer later recalled that he did not even know the crash had happened until long after the event, when he was told about it by Ernest Lawrence. In March 1930, Julius and Ella, their fabulous wealth still intact, came out west to visit their son. "We had a delightful evening at the Tolmans," Julius wrote to Frank from Pasadena. "Tomorrow afternoon we are going there for tea and shall meet a number of the professors and some other of Robert's friends, and on Friday we are going with Mrs. Tolman to Los Angeles to hear the Tchaikovsky concert." Robert, Julius wrote, was "very busy with conferences, lectures, and his own work, but we manage to see him a short time daily."

Julius was unhappy about the state of Oppenheimer's car, an old

Chrysler, and so, "against severe protest," insisted on buying him a new one, which "he is most delighted with . . . he has reduced his speed about 50% from what he used to drive, so we hope no further accidents will occur." The recklessness of Oppenheimer's driving was legendary. In a previous letter to Frank, he himself had written: "From time to time I take out the Chrysler, and scare one of my friends out of all sanity by wheeling corners at seventy. The car will do seventy-five without a tremor. I am and shall be a vile driver." The accident Julius mentions is possibly the occasion on which Oppenheimer crashed his car while trying to impress and scare his passenger, the writer Natalie Raymond ("Nat" as she was known to her friends, one of whom described her as "a dare-devil, an adventurer"), by racing a train. She was knocked unconscious and, at first, Oppenheimer thought she was dead. Her compensation was to be presented by Julius with a Cézanne drawing and a small painting by the French artist Maurice de Vlaminck.

The day after Julius wrote to Frank, Oppenheimer also wrote to him. Oppenheimer's letter is one of the most interesting he ever sent his brother, containing as it does a series of reflections on what Rabi recognized as Oppenheimer's central problem: identity. Frank had written to him expressing a fear characteristic of his age (he was then seventeen), namely that the Frank his older brother had known had disappeared. Oppenheimer responded with warmth and reassurance. "It is not easy," he told Frank, "to believe that the Frank I know is completely vanished; and I should be very very sorry if that were so." Nevertheless, he paid Frank the compliment of treating the issue he had raised—the question of personal identity—with complete seriousness. "I think," he wrote, "that you do overestimate the inconstancy and incoherence of personal life":

> for I believe that throughout the variations—and they are wild enough, God knows—there is, there should be, and in mature people there comes more and more to be a certain unity, which makes it possible to recognize a man in his most diverse operations, a kind of specific personal stamp.

Oppenheimer was, evidently, inclined to take philosophical questions very seriously indeed, for a reason he spelled out to Frank: "The reason why a bad philosophy leads to such hell is that it is what you think and want and treasure and foster in the times of preparation that determines what you do in the pinch, and that it takes an error to father a sin." The letter ended with the affectionate plea: "Don't you go and change too much, now; because I think you were pretty damn nice before."

As he did at Berkeley, Oppenheimer lived, while he lectured at

Caltech, in the faculty club. His friends in Pasadena included Richard Tolman, whom he already knew, and the Danish physicist Charles C. Lauritsen. Tolman and his wife, Ruth, became especially close friends (it was they who introduced Oppenheimer to Natalie Raymond), and he often dined at the Tolmans' home, as did his parents when they were in Pasadena. Contact with people like Tolman and Lauritsen, people who were closely in touch with recent developments in physics, was one of the main reasons Oppenheimer was reluctant to give up his position at Caltech.

However, although it was at Caltech that Oppenheimer thus stayed in touch with current research, it was at Berkeley that he hoped to build his peculiarly American school of theoretical physics. To accomplish this, he knew that he would have to attract to Berkeley more able students than the ones he had inherited, and so, at the many conferences and meetings he attended, he kept an eye out for possible recruits. One of the most promising recruiting grounds in this respect was the summer school at Ann Arbor, which, together with a restorative few weeks at Perro Caliente, became one of the annual fixtures of his summers. The very first graduate student to begin a Ph.D. thesis under Oppenheimer's supervision had gone to Berkeley as a result of having attended the summer school at Ann Arbor. This was Melba Phillips, originally from Indiana, who, while a master's student at Battle Creek College in Michigan, had attended the summer school and been inspired by a course given by Edward Condon on quantum mechanics. On Condon's recommendation, she applied to Berkeley and found herself in the autumn of 1930 being assigned Oppenheimer as her Ph.D. supervisor.

By that time, Oppenheimer already had three Ph.D. students, but they had begun their research work under another supervisor. They were Harvey Hall and J. Franklin Carlson, both of whom had started under William Howell Williams, and Leo Nedelsky, who had been working with Samuel Allison. All three flourished under Oppenheimer and went on to have successful careers in physics. Oppenheimer devoted considerable energy to his Ph.D. students, working closely with them and making sure that when they left Berkeley they had significant publications to their name. To achieve this, he developed a practice of publishing joint papers with his Ph.D. students, and during the 1930s a good proportion of his work consisted of such joint publications.

The first to benefit from this was Harvey Hall, with whom Oppenheimer published a major two-part article called "Relativistic Theory of the Photoelectric Effect," which was received by the *Physical Review* on May 7, 1931. The photoelectric effect is the name given to the emission of electrons when metal is exposed to light of a certain frequency. The phenomenon has enormous importance in the development of physics because it was in an attempt to explain it that Einstein put forward the proposal that light is made up of particle-like "quanta," upon which quantum physics was built. The specific subject of the Hall-Oppenheimer article was the application to the observations of this phenomenon of Dirac's theory of the electron. This was also the subject of Hall's Ph.D. thesis, which was submitted and passed in the summer of 1931, making Hall Oppenheimer's first Ph.D. student to complete his doctorate.

In the late 1940s, the San Francisco office of the FBI, looking for dirt on Oppenheimer, found an employee of the University of California, a "very reliable individual" (in fact, it was Oppenheimer's colleague Leonard Loeb, who formed an intense dislike of Oppenheimer), who claimed that it was "common knowledge" at Berkeley that Oppenheimer had "homosexual tendencies" and that he was "having an affair with Hall." Rumors get repeated and thus persist, but in this case there is very little substantiation. Hall was not, as far as anyone knows, homosexual. He married in 1934, had two sons and a daughter, and was to remain with his wife, Mary, for sixty-nine years (he died in 2003, at the age of ninety-nine). Evidence that Oppenheimer was homosexual, or even that he was believed to be so, is also scarce. David Cassidy, in his biography of Oppenheimer, quotes a letter from Robert Millikan to Richard Tolman from 1945, in which Millikan claims that at various times both Pauling and Lawrence had expressed doubts over "the character of [Oppenheimer's] influence on younger associates," but, apart from being thirdhand hearsay, it is not at all clear what exactly (other than a vague sense of moral impropriety) is being suggested here.

Most physicists, when considering the collaboration between Hall and Oppenheimer, have been more concerned about the sloppiness of their mathematics than the supposed looseness of their morals. Quoting with approval a remark made by one of Oppenheimer's later students, Robert Serber, that Oppenheimer's "physics was good, but his arithmetic awful," Abraham Pais has drawn attention to the serious "carelessness" in the work on the photoelectric effect that Oppenheimer published with Hall. A central claim in their paper was that experimental results showed that something was wrong with the theory of quantum electrodynamics as so far developed. In particular, they claimed that observations of photoelectric phenomena had revealed energies of electrons far greater—twenty-five times greater—than were predicted by the Dirac equation, and that therefore there must be some error in the theory based on this equation. In fact, as Pais points out: "The error was his." Oppenheimer and Hall had simply miscalculated.

At the root of the problem was not only Oppenheimer's legendarily erratic mathematics, but also his almost obsessive conviction, and determination to prove, that there was something wrong with the Dirac equation and the theory of quantum electrodynamics built upon it. Serber has remarked that this determination created a "fundamental barrier to Oppenheimer's success in making progress with the difficulties of quantum electrodynamics"—a good illustration of which is Oppenheimer's short paper "On the Theory of Electrons and Protons," which he published in the *Physical Review* as a "letter to the editor" in the spring of 1930.[27] The paper deals with an acknowledged problem in Dirac's theory of electrons, which is that the Dirac equation allows for solutions that attribute negative energy to electrons. Dirac referred to these negative-energy states as "holes" and suggested that they might represent the place of *positively* charged particles. As the only positively charged particle then known was the proton, Dirac suggested that the negative-energy states are actually occupied by protons.

Oppenheimer, however, showed that these positive charges in Dirac's theory could not have the mass of a proton (which is much bigger—about 2,000 times bigger—than that of an electron), but must rather have the same mass as an electron. In other words, the theory demands the existence of a hitherto unknown particle: a positively charged electron, or what is now known as a "positron." But because he was convinced that the theory was wrong, Oppenheimer did not draw from his arguments the obvious conclusion, namely that positrons must exist. He thought he had found not evidence for the existence of positrons, but rather another reason for thinking something was amiss with the Dirac equation.

Dirac accepted Oppenheimer's argument about the mass of the "anti-electron," but, having faith in his famous equation, drew the conclusion that Oppenheimer's skepticism prevented him from drawing, and announced in a paper written in the spring of 1931 "a new kind of particle, unknown to experimental physics, having the same mass and opposite charge to an electron." Later in the year, during a lecture at Princeton, Dirac insisted that these anti-electrons "are not to be considered as a mathematical fiction; it should be possible to detect them by experimental means." When, shortly later, experimental evidence for the existence of positrons was announced, it was Dirac, not Oppenheimer, who got the credit for having correctly predicted it.

During his attendance at the Ann Arbor summer school in 1931, Oppenheimer was able to renew personal contact with the European

[27] The advantage of publishing a short paper as a letter to the editor is that it can appear in print within a very brief time—Oppenheimer's letter was dated February 14, 1930, and appeared in the March 1 issue of the journal. The disadvantage is that it has less authority than if it has gone through the normal peer-review procedure.

physicists, including Wolfgang Pauli, who arrived full of talk about yet another "new kind of particle, unknown to experimental physics," which he called the "neutron." It was an unfortunate choice of word, since "neutron" had already been used by Rutherford for something very different from what Pauli had in mind. In 1920, Rutherford had suggested that the nuclei of atoms heavier than hydrogen contained not only protons, but also neutral particles of a similar mass, to which he gave the name "neutrons." He proposed this as a way of making sense of observational data concerning the mass and electrical charge of various nuclei. For example, a helium nucleus (an alpha particle) has four times the mass of a proton, but only twice the charge, which would make sense if, instead of being made up of four protons, the helium nucleus consisted of two protons and two neutrons. Attempts to discover this neutral particle, however, proved unsuccessful, although at the very time that Pauli was talking about *his* neutron at Ann Arbor, moves were afoot at the Cavendish that would shortly result in experimental confirmation of Rutherford's.

Pauli's "neutron" was put forward to solve a very different problem. This "neutron" was much smaller than Rutherford's and was something that Pauli thought must exist in order to explain beta radiation. The distinction between alpha and beta radiation had been made by Rutherford in 1897, and subsequently it was discovered that alpha radiation consists of alpha particles—that is, helium nuclei—while the much more penetrative beta radiation consists of streams of electrons, which are emitted from a decaying nucleus.[28]

The problem that Pauli sought to solve arose out of experimental observations that showed that beta radiation did not always have the same energy; rather, there was a continuous energy spectrum in beta decay, with electrons being emitted with a range of energies from near-zero upward. If we are to understand beta radiation as the decay of a nucleus with a given and fixed mass, then the electrons that are emitted ought to be emitted with the *same* energy in every case, otherwise energy is not conserved—the energy of the decayed nucleus plus the electron is *not* equal to the energy of the original nucleus. Some mass or energy has gone missing. So, in the face of the observed fact of the continuous

[28] A full understanding of beta decay was not arrived at until a few years after Pauli's postulation of the neutrino, and therefore many years after Rutherford's original identification and naming of it. What Rutherford knew was that there was a form of radioactive decay different from alpha decay, in which the radiation consisted not of positively charged helium nuclei, but of much smaller, negatively charged particles, which he correctly identified as electrons. What was subsequently discovered is that these electrons are being emitted from neutrons that are decaying into protons.

spectra of beta emissions, either what was usually considered a fundamental physical principle—the law of the conservation of energy—had
to be abandoned or beta radiation could not be understood as simply the
emission of electrons; something else had to be going on.[29]

In response to this problem, Bohr, among others, was prepared to
abandon conservation of energy, but for Pauli this was too great a step,
and, in order to preserve conservation of energy, he suggested what he
called a "desperate way out": "To wit, the possibility that there could
exist in the nucleus electrically neutral particles, which I shall call neutrons . . . The mass of the neutrons should be of the same order of magnitude as the electron mass . . . The continuous beta-spectrum would
then become understandable from the assumption that in beta-decay a
neutron is emitted along with the electron, in such a way that the sum of
the energies of the neutron and the electron is constant." In other words,
Pauli's "neutron" would supply the missing energy: the energies of the
electron, the decayed nucleus *and* the "neutron" would equal the energy
of the nucleus before decay.

Pauli's remarks quoted above were made in December 1930 in a letter to colleagues attending a conference on radioactivity, where the main
topic of discussion was the problem of the continuous beta spectrum.
He was evidently tentative about the proposed new particle (which he
later called "that foolish child of the crisis of my life"),[30] since he did not
publish anything about it in the period between writing the above letter
and his attendance at the Ann Arbor summer school in 1931. Nor did he
present a paper about it at Ann Arbor. He did, however, talk a great deal
about it, both in private conversations and in seminars. Among those
listening intently to him were Oppenheimer and J. Franklin Carlson
("Frank Carlson" to everyone who knew him), who, since Hall's graduation the previous year, was now the student with whom Oppenheimer
worked most closely. As a result of listening to Pauli's discussions, Carlson and Oppenheimer left Ann Arbor with an idea of how Pauli's hypothetical new particle could furnish the topic for both future joint research
and for Carlson's Ph.D. thesis.

After Ann Arbor, Oppenheimer spent some time at Perro Cali-

---

[29] To understand the problem, it might help to give an example. A nucleus of cobalt (with
atomic number 27) undergoes beta decay and so gains a proton, thus transforming into
nickel (atomic number 28). In this process, an electron is emitted. What puzzled Pauli and
other physicists at this time was that, when this happens, the figures often do not add up:
the total energy of (in this case) the nickel nucleus plus the electron sometimes does, and
sometimes does not, equal the energy of the original cobalt nucleus, depending on the
energy of the electron, which varies along a continuous spectrum.

[30] Pauli was at the time going through an emotionally draining divorce from his first wife.

ente with Frank, and then went to New York to visit his parents, before returning on August 10 to Berkeley. From there he wrote to Frank, who was still in New Mexico. In Michigan, Oppenheimer had bought Frank a secondhand car, a Packard Roadster that he called Ichabod, possibly after the Old Testament character, or possibly with reference to Robert Browning's poem "Waring," about a departed friend, of which verse six begins:

> Ichabod, Ichabod,
> The glory is departed!
> Travels Waring East away?
> Who, of knowledge, by hearsay,
> Reports a man upstarted
> Somewhere as a god.

Frank, Oppenheimer wrote, could collect Ichabod from the Packard dealership in Ann Arbor, where he had left it to be repaired. What state the car was in when Oppenheimer bought it is not known, but after he had used it to drive to Ann Arbor, it was in urgent need of repair. Summer-school participants remember Oppenheimer's arrival in Ichabod: everybody heard a loud crunch as the rim of one of its wheels hit the gravel, and graduate students rushed out to change the flat tire.

Frank was then about to start his second year as a physics student at Johns Hopkins University, and it seems that the plan was for him, once he had collected the car, to drive to New York to see their parents, before heading off for Baltimore. Ella Oppenheimer had recently been diagnosed with leukemia. "I am afraid you will find mother pretty weak and miserable," Oppenheimer warned Frank. "The reports have not been very encouraging." He added that he intended to go to New York at Christmas: "I have a long vacation, and shall plan to spend most of it with her."

In the event, Ella's condition worsened rather more quickly than had been anticipated and Oppenheimer was forced to fly to New York midway through the semester. On October 6, 1931, Oppenheimer received a telegram from his father: "Mother critically ill. Not expected to live." Denise Royal, in her 1969 biography of Oppenheimer, quotes "a friend" who saw Oppenheimer shortly after he received the telegram and remembers the agony on his face: "He had a terribly desolate look. 'My mother's dying. My mother's dying,' he repeated over and again."

Before this, Oppenheimer, together with Frank Carlson, had written a short notice, another "letter to the editor" of the *Physical Review*, announcing a new line of research that would, they promised, be developed in a subsequent article. The aim of the research was to investigate whether the "neutron" discussed by Pauli at Ann Arbor might hold the key to an ongoing scientific mystery: the nature of cosmic rays.

The suggestive name "cosmic ray" had been coined by Robert Millikan at Caltech in the 1920s, but the phenomenon of very penetrative radiation occurring high in the earth's atmosphere had been identified and studied in the first few years of the twentieth century. Millikan became fascinated by these "rays" and was the first to prove that they entered the earth's atmosphere from outer space (hence "cosmic"). In the 1920s and '30s, Millikan was involved in several controversies regarding the composition of cosmic rays, most notably with Arthur Compton, who held that they consisted primarily of protons. Millikan, on the other hand, thought they consisted of photons—that is, they were not particles at all, but pure electromagnetic radiation. At stake in this dispute, at least from Millikan's point of view, was something deeper and more general than a mere scientific disagreement. For Millikan, indeed, the issue had *religious* significance.

For both Compton and Millikan, and for everybody else interested in cosmic rays, the intriguing thing about them is their extraordinary energy, which in the 1920s and '30s was measured at up to 100 million electron volts (since then, energies far higher than that have been detected). There were two ways such energy could be released: either heavy atoms were decaying and releasing protons and electrons as they transformed into lighter elements, or light atoms were fusing with other light atoms to form heavier elements, releasing gamma radiation as they did so. In other words, only two things would produce such energetic rays: the decay of matter or the creation of it. Millikan was religiously committed to the latter view: cosmic rays, he believed, were the "birth cries" of new atoms created by God to counter the effects of decay, and, as such, it was important for him to believe—and to convince others to believe—that they were made up of photons.

In their "letter to the editor," Oppenheimer and Carlson dismissed both Millikan's view that cosmic rays were photons and also Compton's view that they were made up of protons. Perhaps, they suggested, cosmic rays might consist of the "neutrons" posited by Pauli. At the end of their note, Oppenheimer and Carlson promised that the results of their calculations of the collisions between electrons and Pauli's neutrons would be "published very shortly."

Oppenheimer and Carlson's letter was dated October 9, 1931. Three days after that, Oppenheimer was in New York to be at his mother's bedside as she lay dying. "I found my mother terribly low," he wrote to Lawrence, "almost beyond hope."

Every day since I have been here she has seemed a little stronger, a little more herself. She is in very great pain and piteously terribly weak; but there is a bare chance that she may have still a little period of remission. I have been able to talk with her a little; she is tired and sad, but without desperation; she is unbelievably sweet.

Four days later, Oppenheimer wrote again to Lawrence, thanking him for his "sweet message" and "lovely roses." "Things are pretty bad here," he told him. "Mother, after a short reprise, has been growing rapidly very much worse; she is comatose, now; and death is very near."

We cannot help feeling now a little grateful that she should not have to suffer more, that she should not know the despair and misery of a long hopeless illness. She has been always hopeful and serene; and the last thing she said to me was, "Yes—California."

Ella died the following day. Oppenheimer's old friend and teacher Herbert Smith spent that afternoon with him, and remembers him saying immediately after his mother's death: "I am the loneliest man in the world."

Oppenheimer's letters to Lawrence from New York show how much he disliked being away from Berkeley, from physics and from the school of young theorists that he was developing. "I feel pretty awful to be away so long," he told Lawrence. "You will do what you can for the fatherless theoretical children, won't you?" In the following letter he insisted: "You must let me know if there is anything that I can do for you here; and if a word from me can be of any help to my deserted students, do not, please, hesitate to ask for it."

As soon as he decently could, Oppenheimer returned to his "deserted students" in Berkeley. Before he did so, he arranged to meet his father, together with Frank, in New Orleans in December. The plan was for the three of them to spend ten days together there over the Christmas period, before Oppenheimer, Frank and, no doubt, a number of Oppenheimer's students, including Frank Carlson, attended the meeting of the American Physical Society, which was held in New Orleans on December 29 and 30.

Coming so soon after Ella's death, it is hard to imagine the family holiday being anything other than mournful, and, as it happened, the American Physical Society meeting was also quite an ordeal. Robert Millikan—who as president of Caltech was, in some sense, Oppenheimer's boss—chose these meetings to publicly, vociferously and belligerently defend his theological understanding of cosmic rays against non-believers, including Oppenheimer and Carlson, whose letter to the editor of the *Physical Review* dismissing Millikan's views had appeared in print in November. Millikan evidently felt that he had much to lose if his views on cosmic rays were publicly discredited, since he had devoted a good deal of time and energy to trying to persuade not only his fellow physicists, but also the general public, of those views. He had been interviewed by the *New York Times* on the subject, and had given many public presentations of his claim that cosmic rays were evidence of God's existence and His beneficence. In the New Year of 1932, *Time* magazine carried an interview with him in which he made the same claim. It was evidently not a view that he was willing to give up lightly.

Clearly shaken by the vehemence of Millikan's attack in New Orleans, Oppenheimer, in a letter to Lawrence written on the way back to California, thanked him for the "comforting words" he had whispered to him during Millikan's onslaught. "I was pretty much in need of them," he told Lawrence, "feeling ashamed of my report, and distressed rather by Millikan's hostility and his lack of scruple." He also told Lawrence that he had received a call from a news reporter, saying that he had been sent by Lawrence and asking him his views on the controversy, but "I did not give him anything; I hope that in that I did not offend your wishes."

If Oppenheimer was hoping that, by not parading his dispute with Millikan before the general public, he could soften Millikan's attitude, he was mistaken. For the rest of his life Millikan treated Oppenheimer with unremitting hostility. "Millikan loathed Oppenheimer," Birge recalls, "wouldn't match the promotions we gave him here, and harassed him maliciously." At Berkeley, Oppenheimer had been promoted to an associate professorship at the start of the 1931–2 academic year, but it would be another three years before Caltech followed suit. "Millikan just left his name in the faculty register," Birge remarked, "and made him miserable when the chance came."

Instead of giving his response to Millikan's attack to a news reporter, Oppenheimer no doubt wanted to return to the issues involved in a dignified and properly academic fashion, by fulfilling the promise he and Carlson had made in their note to the *Physical Review* to publish "very shortly" their calculations concerning the collisions between electrons and Pauli's "neutrons." However, almost as soon as he returned to Berkeley from New Orleans, the work he and Carlson were planning to undertake was overtaken by a series of momentous experimental discoveries that has led to the year of 1932 being described as a miraculous year in physics.

The first of these was announced in a paper published in the January 1, 1932, issue of the *Physical Review* entitled "A Hydrogen Isotope of Mass 2." The paper had three authors: Ferdinand Brickwedde, G. N. Murphy and Harold Urey, the last of whom, after gaining his Ph.D. at Berkeley under Gilbert Lewis, was an associate professor at Columbia University. What Urey and his colleagues had to report was the discovery of deuterium, an isotope of hydrogen that is twice as heavy, having an atomic mass of 2, rather than 1.[31] Physicists had long wanted to find a chemical with an atomic mass of two because of the potential such a thing would offer for the investigation of the structure of nuclei. The nucleus of hydrogen, with an atomic mass of just one, has no structure, while all other known chemicals, prior to the discovery of deuterium, had three or more particles in their nuclei and so had a structure too complicated to investigate in detail. Deuterium, however—the "hydrogen atom of nuclear physics," as the physicist Victor Weisskopf once called it—allowed physicists to bring to the study of nuclei everything they knew about two-body systems, thus making extremely detailed calculations possible.

The nucleus of deuterium is a perfect example of the kind of thing that had persuaded Rutherford back in 1920 that there must be such a thing as a neutral particle with the same mass as a proton. In fact, with remarkable prescience, Rutherford had explicitly predicted "the possible existence of an atom of mass nearly 2 carrying one charge, which is to be regarded as an isotope of hydrogen." The fact that, as Rutherford had predicted, deuterium has twice the mass, but the same charge as normal hydrogen, would seem to indicate that the additional mass has no charge, which in turn would be perfectly explained if one were to imagine the deuterium nucleus to consist, as Rutherford had imagined, of one proton and one neutron. The only thing blocking this way of picturing it was that neutrons had not yet been discovered. However, this barrier was removed little more than a month after Urey's announcement of the discovery of deuterium, when, on February 27, 1932, there appeared in *Nature* a letter to the editor by James Chadwick of the Cavendish Laboratory, which, with undue but characteristic restraint, Chadwick entitled "Possible Existence of a Neutron."

What Chadwick presented in this short communication was what almost every physicist who read it agreed to be conclusive evidence of the existence of neutrons. Chadwick had collected this evidence from a

---

[31] The notion of an isotope originated in 1912, when the chemist Frederick Soddy coined the word to describe two or more atoms that occupy the same place in the periodic table, but have different radioactive properties. After the discovery of the neutron in 1932, it was realized that two isotopes of the same element differ with respect to the number of neutrons in their nuclei.

series of experiments that he performed, working day and night,[32] over a period of three weeks in the first two months of 1932. His inspiration came from a piece published in the journal *Comptes rendus* on January 18, 1932, in which the French physicists Frédéric Joliot and his wife, Irène Curie, described a puzzling phenomenon they had witnessed in an experiment in which they bombarded beryllium with very energetic alpha particles emitted from polonium. What they recorded was that this produced extremely powerful radiation from the beryllium, which they assumed to be gamma radiation—that is, photons. So powerful was this "gamma radiation" that when they placed paraffin wax in front of it, it knocked protons out of the wax with an energy of 4.5 million volts. In order to achieve this, the supposed gamma radiation would have required an energy of about fifty-five million volts, an energy previously encountered only by those studying cosmic rays.

When Chadwick read this report, he realized immediately that a more likely explanation of the phenomenon recorded by Joliot and Curie was that the protons were being knocked out of the paraffin wax by *neutrons*, which, being roughly the same size as protons, would need a kinetic energy only slightly larger than that of the protons they set in motion. Using what, by today's standards, looks like a makeshift and unimpressive piece of equipment, Chadwick was able to repeat the experiment conducted by Joliot and Curie, and to extend it by showing that the radiation from beryllium ejects particles from hydrogen, helium, lithium, carbon, oxygen and argon. His results, he stated in his letter to *Nature*, were difficult to explain if one assumed, as Joliot and Curie had done, that the emissions from beryllium were gamma radiation, adding: "The difficulties disappear, however, if it be assumed that the radiation consists of particles of mass 1 and charge 0, or neutrons."

By the time he wrote up his results in full for the June 1932 issue of *Proceedings of the Royal Society*, Chadwick had overcome any doubts and his paper was published under the less tentative title "The Existence of a Neutron." Oppenheimer and Carlson seem to have waited for this full version of Chadwick's report to appear before returning to the subject of neutrons, since it was not until July 18, 1932, that they fulfilled the promise they had made the previous October and sent their own detailed paper on "The Impacts of Fast Electrons and Magnetic Neutrons" to the *Physical Review*. Perhaps somewhat oddly, Oppenheimer and Carlson do not mention Chadwick or cite his work (though they are surely alluding to it when they mention experimental evidence for the existence of neu-

---

[32] C. P. Snow reports that, during this period, a "dialogue passed into Cavendish tradition: 'Tired, Chadwick?' 'Not too tired to work.'"

trons). One might suppose that this is because they were concerned with *Pauli's* neutron, which has a mass thousands of times smaller than that of Chadwick's, but this is not borne out by the paper, which shows, rather, a confusion between the two.

On the one hand, Oppenheimer and Carlson speak of the neutron as "a hypothetical elementary neutral particle" whose existence was "tentatively proposed by Pauli." On the other hand, though they point out that Pauli had supposed this hypothetical particle would have a mass "not much greater than the electron," they say: "One may, however, assume that the neutron has a mass close to that of the proton"—an assumption surely based on Chadwick's calculations. The notion of a "magnetic neutron" employed by Oppenheimer and Carlson is, then, an uneasy mixture of the very different notions of Pauli and Chadwick. It is therefore perhaps not surprising that their paper should end with the conclusion that it is unlikely that cosmic rays consist of such "magnetic neutrons," since "there is no experimental evidence for the existence of a particle like the magnetic neutron."

That Oppenheimer and Carlson were not the only ones confused about the relation between Pauli's hypothetical particle and the discoveries of Chadwick is suggested by a witty pastiche of Goethe's play *Faust* that was performed at Bohr's institute in Copenhagen in April 1932. In this version of the Faustian legend, the role of Mephistopheles is played by Pauli, who is trying to tempt "Faust"—Ehrenfest—into believing in a particle that has no mass and no charge (and is therefore practically undetectable). Oppenheimer is given a very brief part in the play, in a scene that takes place at "Mrs. Ann Arbor's Speakeasy" (the Ann Arbor summer school). There, Mephisto/Pauli tempts the drunken "American physicists sitting sadly at the Bar," including Oppenheimer, into accepting the existence of the neutron. In the finale of the play, Chadwick appears "and says, with pride":

> *The* Neutron *has come to be.*
> *Loaded with mass is he.*
> *Of Charge, forever free.*
> *Pauli, do you agree?*

To which Mephisto/Pauli replies:

> *That which experiment has found—*
> *Though theory had no part in—*
> *Is always reckoned more than sound*
> *To put your mind and heart in.*

Good luck, you heavyweight Ersatz—
We welcome you with pleasure.

In 1934, the Italian physicist Enrico Fermi proposed the name "neu-trino" (little neutron) to distinguish Pauli's hypothetical particle from Chadwick's "heavyweight," and it would not be until 1955 that experimental confirmation of the existence of neutrinos would be produced. Oppenheimer and Carlson's idea that Pauli's neutrino might hold the key to understanding the nature of cosmic rays was sunk by the confusion between the two neutral particles, and, in any case, turned out to be wrong—*whichever* "neutron" it concerned.

Having his ideas overtaken by experimental developments seems to have had a salutary effect on Oppenheimer, who henceforth made it his business to know *everything* going on in experimental physics. Raymond Birge has recalled: "In our seminars Oppenheimer knew more experimental physics than even the experimental physicists did. He could reel off figures and equations relating to experiments better than any experimental physicist in the room." Among the seminars in question were the weekly Wednesday-afternoon colloquia, where experimentalists and theorists met for discussion, and the Journal Club, which met every Tuesday evening to go through recent work, both experimental and theoretical. Lawrence's assistant, Milton Stanley Livingston, remembers that at these meetings the experimentalists "sat afraid to ask Oppenheimer anything," with the exception of Lawrence himself, who won their admiration for his willingness to "pop up and ask something silly."

This close collaboration between theorists and experimentalists at Berkeley was to be mutually beneficial in the mid- to late 1930s, but in the crucial year of 1932 there are signs that communication was not all it should have been: not only was Oppenheimer wrong-footed by experimental developments, but Lawrence seemed to be held back by a lack of appreciation of certain crucial theoretical points.

Most of Lawrence's efforts were directed at building bigger and bigger cyclotrons and accelerating protons to greater and greater energies. A key moment in this development came in February 1932, when his latest cyclotron succeeded in accelerating protons to an energy of one million volts. "I wrote the figure on the blackboard," Livingston later remembered. "Lawrence came in late one evening. He saw the board, looked at the microammeter to check the resonance current and literally danced around the room." Ever the publicist, Lawrence lost no time in spreading the news, and the next day Livingston recalls: "We were busy all that day demonstrating million-volt protons to eager viewers." The *San Francisco Examiner* sent a reporter to Berkeley to see what was going on, and announced excitedly that Lawrence and Livingston "are setting about trying to break up the atom and release its terrific energy." Reporting on plans to build an even bigger cyclotron, the *Examiner* went on: "With the greater magnet, they hope to shatter the atom completely with an ultimate 25,000,000-volt impact."

But, as quantum theorists had known for many years before this, and as Oppenheimer must surely have been aware, there was a very good chance of splitting the atom with much lower energies than these. Indeed, the key theoretical point in understanding this centers on a phenomenon that Oppenheimer himself had been among the first to consider: the mysterious process known as "quantum tunneling." Due to the fact that, according to quantum theory, protons, along with electrons, and so on, are *both* particles and waves, there is a significant possibility that the particles that make up a nucleus can suddenly appear *outside* the electrical barrier (the "Coulomb barrier") that surrounds the nucleus. Rutherford had known about the phenomenon, but had pictured it as electrons pulling protons out of their shell, like tugboats pulling liners out to sea. It was the Russian physicist George Gamow who first realized that it was a direct consequence of the wavelike nature of subatomic particles, and that quantum mechanics offered the means to quantify and predict the probability of such "tunneling" occurring.

Gamow's analysis appeared in print twice in quick succession in the autumn of 1928: in German in the *Zeitschrift für Physik* on October 12, and in English in *Nature* on November 24. Actually, in terms of being the first to publish such an analysis, Gamow had narrowly been beaten to it by an article by Edward Condon and Ronald Gurney that appeared in *Nature* in September, but, from the point of view of the history of splitting the atom, Gamow's account is more important for two reasons: first, unlike Condon and Gurney, Gamow was less concerned with how protons might get out of the nucleus than how they might get *in*; and second, it was Gamow's account that stimulated the work that led to the world's first splitting of the atom.

Shortly before it was published, an advance copy of Gamow's *Zeitschrift* article was sent to John Cockcroft at the Cavendish Laboratory, who saw immediately its implication that atoms might be split with relatively low-voltage protons. Rutherford, when he made a public appeal for progress in artificial acceleration of particles, had thought that one needed eight million volts or more. However, in a series of calculations that Cockcroft wrote out, showed to Rutherford, but did not publish, he demonstrated that, if Gamow's analysis was correct, a "mere" 300,000 volts would probably be enough.

Encouraged by Rutherford, Cockcroft worked together with his Cavendish colleague Ernest Walton to design and build a machine capable of accelerating protons to the required 300,000 volts. By May 1930, they had a machine capable of 280,000 volts and felt able the following August to publish an account of their work in the *Proceedings of the Royal Society*, in which they took the possibly risky step of making public Cockcroft's calculation that 300,000 volts would be enough to penetrate the nucleus and so split the atom. Around the same time, however, Rutherford gave a speech in which he claimed: "What we require is an apparatus to give us a potential of the order of ten million volts." Whether Rutherford believed this, or whether these words were a smokescreen, is difficult to say, but, knowing perfectly well that Lawrence and his team were constructing machines capable of more than one million volts, Rutherford continued to encourage Cockcroft and Walton in their endeavors using more modest machinery.

In January 1932, Cockcroft received a letter from his old friend Joseph Boyce, who told him: "I have just been on a very brief visit in California and thought you might be interested in a brief report on high-voltage work there." The "place on the coast where things are really going on," reported Boyce, "is Berkeley":

> Lawrence is just moving into an old wooden building back of the physics building, where he hopes to have six different high-speed particle outfits. One is to move over the present device by which he whirls protons in a magnetic field and in a very high frequency tuned electric field and so is able to give them velocities a little in excess of a million volts.

> Lawrence, Boyce added, "is a very able director, has many graduate students, adequate financial backing, and his work so far . . . has achieved sufficient success to justify great confidence in his future."

In the light of such reports, Rutherford's encouragement became more urgent. On April 14, 1932, after they had been told by Rutherford to "stop messing about and wasting their time," Cockcroft and Walton, without any great hopes of success, fired some accelerated protons at a sample of lithium, a very light metal with an atomic mass of 7. The result was so astonishing that Rutherford and Chadwick were called to the laboratory to verify that there was no mistake in their observations. What they all saw were the familiar scintillations that told of the emission of alpha particles.[33] There was only one conclusion to draw: the

---

[33] When an alpha particle hits a screen made of a suitable substance (zinc sulfide was the most commonly used), it emits a tiny flash of light known as a "scintillation." The experi-

protons had caused the lithium nucleus to break up, forming two alpha particles (that is, helium nuclei, which have an atomic mass of 4, which makes perfect mathematical sense, since the combined atomic masses of the lithium nucleus plus the proton is 8, equivalent to two helium nuclei). In other words, what Cockcroft and Walton had achieved was the world's first splitting of the atom by artificial means. What is more, they had done it with protons accelerated to a voltage significantly below the 300,000 that Cockcroft had calculated. In subsequent tests, they discovered that lithium nuclei could be disintegrated at 125,000 volts, which was far below what anybody had thought possible.

When Cockcroft and Walton measured the energy of the alpha particles emitted from the reaction, the results provided both dramatic confirmation of the most famous equation in science—$E = mc^2$—and a startling illustration of the kind of energy that can be released by an atomic reaction. For the answer was eight million volts. Since from each lithium nucleus there emerged two alpha particles, this means that, from the collision of a single proton, traveling with an energy of 125,000 volts, with a single lithium nucleus, sixteen million volts of energy had been released (two alpha particles, each with an energy of eight million volts). Little wonder, then, that people immediately started to wonder how such tremendous energy releases might be used in explosives.

Partly because he was acutely conscious that this kind of speculation would inevitably follow the announcement of their achievement, Rutherford—after helping Cockcroft and Walton write up their experiment for *Nature*—urged upon them the importance of keeping quiet about it until a sober account had appeared in print. But, as Walton spelled out in a letter written to his girlfriend, Freda, this was not Rutherford's only reason for not letting the news leak out. "We know," Walton wrote, "that people in the States are working along similar lines and Rutherford would like to see any credit going to the Cavendish. He is not fond of American physicists in general on account of their tendency to do a great deal of boasting about very little."

And yet Rutherford was evidently itching to announce the news. On April 28, 1932, two days before the report for *Nature* appeared, he chaired a meeting at the Royal Society in London on "The Structure of Atomic Nuclei," which had been organized primarily to allow discussion of Chadwick's discovery of the neutron. Rutherford arranged for

---

ments of Rutherford and his team at the Cavendish—and, indeed, the work pursued at most advanced physics laboratories—made use of this fact to detect the presence of alpha particles.

Cockcroft and Walton to be present at this occasion, and then, before introducing Chadwick, announced their achievement in disintegrating the lithium nucleus.

Two days later the *Nature* piece appeared, but, meanwhile, Rutherford's announcement at the Royal Society had attracted the attention of the press, and on Sunday May 1, 1932, the *Reynold's Illustrated News*, under the heading "SCIENCE'S GREATEST DISCOVERY," reported:

> A dream of scientists has been realised. The atom has been split, and the limitless energy thus released may transform civilisation . . . This is the greatest scientific discovery of the age.

The same day the *Sunday Express* went with: "The Atom Split. But World Still Safe," while the *Daily Mirror* pleaded: "Let it be split, so long as it does not explode." The idea that atom-splitting would lead to extremely powerful bombs had been around since the 1920s. Bertrand Russell mentioned it in his 1923 best-seller *The ABC of Atoms*, and it formed the central idea in a play called *Wings over Europe*, in which scientists threaten world leaders that they will use atom bombs to destroy the major cities of the world unless an international policy is agreed to use the tremendous energy released by nuclear reactions. The play had premiered in New York in 1928, but, by a strange coincidence, was showing in London at the very time that news broke about the splitting of the atom by Cockcroft and Walton.

As it turned out, of course, the fear of the energy that might be released from within a nucleus was, in general, well founded. However, for the moment it was premature; the kind of energy release observed in the disintegration of lithium, though extremely impressive, could not be used to make explosives. This is for two reasons. First, though there is a dramatic difference between the energy of the penetrating protons and the energy of the released alpha particles, one has to bear in mind that, at 125,000 volts, only one proton in about ten million will penetrate the nucleus. Thus, the total energy needed to release the sixteen million volts of the two alpha particles is about 1.25 billion volts. Second, an explosive requires a chain reaction, which had not yet been witnessed and which could not possibly occur with the disintegration of a light element like lithium. Rutherford's famous dismissal as "moonshine" of the idea that atomic-splitting might be a source of energy in the future was, therefore, perfectly reasonable in the light of what was then known. However, it was while pondering a report of that remark in *The Times* that it suddenly occurred to the Hungarian scientist Leo Szilard, that, if one could find an element that disintegrated when bombarded with neutrons, and if that element emitted two neutrons for every one it absorbed, then a chain reaction could occur that *would* be a source of enormous energy.

It would take a few years for the rest of the world to catch up with Szilard. Meanwhile, the story of Cockcroft and Walton's achievement was picked up by newspapers all over the world, including the *New York Times*, which in its Sunday edition on May 8, under the heading "The Atom Is Giving Up Its Mighty Secrets," described the experiment and commented: "Never was a result more unexpected obtained." This was no doubt read by Ernest Lawrence, who was at that time preparing to get married to Mary Blumer in New Haven, Connecticut. The wedding took place on May 14, by which time, it is certain, Lawrence knew that he had been preempted as the first person to smash the atom. It is therefore not true, as legend has it, that he heard the news while on honeymoon. It is possible, however, that the telegram his assistant James Brady remembers receiving—"Cockcroft and Walton have disintegrated the lithium atom. Get lithium from chemistry department and start preparations to repeat with cyclotron"—was sent by him while still on honeymoon.

The news from the Cavendish did not stop Lawrence from building bigger and bigger machines, nor did it damage his ability to attract huge funds for these projects—indeed, if anything, it helped by stirring up interest—but it must have made him aware of the importance of being well informed about theory, just as Chadwick's discovery of the neutron had made Oppenheimer aware of the importance of keeping up with experimental developments.

The fourth and final major development in experimental physics during the *annus mirabilis* of 1932—the discovery of the positron by Carl Anderson of Caltech—exhibited a lack of communication between theorists and experimentalists that seems nothing short of bizarre. As Graham Farmelo, Paul Dirac's biographer, has said: "Many of the characters in this strange denouement, including Dirac, behaved in ways that are now barely comprehensible."

Among those characters whose behavior seems inexplicable was Oppenheimer himself. There are several reasons why one might have expected Oppenheimer to have been in close contact with Anderson while he conducted the research that led to the discovery of the positron. In the first place, Anderson, as we have seen, had been a student of his. Indeed, during his first lecture course at Caltech in 1930, Anderson had been his *only* student. Second, though Anderson's postdoctoral research was conducted with Millikan rather than with Oppenheimer, it was on a subject in which Oppenheimer had a deep interest: the nature of cosmic rays. Third, the hypothetical existence of the positron, a particle with the same mass as an electron but with a positive rather than negative charge, had been discussed by Oppenheimer in print, when he showed that Dirac's theory of quantum electrodynamics—the very theory he had tried to explain in a lecture attended by Anderson—demanded it. And yet, despite all this, when Anderson discovered the positron, he did so apparently unaware that the existence of such a particle had been predicted by Dirac, or indeed that the possibility of its existence had been discussed at all by anybody.

Anderson had started his research on cosmic rays in the autumn of 1930, after he had completed his Ph.D. Though he worked with Millikan, he regarded Millikan's theological view of cosmic rays as mere wishful thinking, and certainly did not feel himself obliged to provide evidence for it. Rather, he wanted to gather hard evidence about the nature of cosmic rays, and so developed a method of photographing their activity inside a cloud chamber, which allowed him to make visual records of the paths of charged particles emitted from cosmic-ray collisions. By the autumn of 1931, Anderson had about 1,000 such photographs and, in November, he wrote to Millikan, who was then in Cambridge in order to give a paper at the Cavendish, sending him some photographs that puzzled him. What the photographs appeared to show were collisions that resulted in the simultaneous emission of a negatively charged particle, which was surely an electron, and a positively charged particle, which Anderson assumed to be a proton.

Millikan could shed little light on these photographs, but exhibited them at the Cavendish anyway, presenting them merely as evidence of the tremendous energies of cosmic rays, which he thought explicable only by adopting his own theological interpretation of them. Among Millikan's audience at the Cavendish, however, was Patrick Blackett, who was deeply intrigued by Anderson's photographs and resolved to find an explanation for them. In fact, the explanation for the phenomenon Anderson had photographed had already been given by Dirac in his lecture at Princeton in October, in which he had said that it should be possible to detect positrons—or, as he was calling them at this time, "anti-electrons"—experimentally. In collisions between pairs of ultra-energy photons, Dirac explained, sometimes the photons should disappear and in their place should appear a pair of particles: an electron and an "anti-electron," a process subsequently named "pair production."

Clearly, this is what had happened inside Anderson's cloud chamber, but when Millikan addressed the Cavendish in November, Dirac was still in Princeton, and nobody else seems to have made the connection between Dirac's prediction and Anderson's photographs. Why did the connection not occur to Oppenheimer? Or, if it did, why did he not mention it to Anderson? Late in life, Anderson recalled that around this time he "talked to Oppenheimer quite a bit," but also that "I found it hard to talk to Oppenheimer because his answers were usually, at least to me, encased in some sort of mysticism. I couldn't understand what he was saying, but the idea of pair production, if he had said that, I would have understood." As Farmelo remarks: "It beggars belief that Oppenheimer never pointed out the connection between Dirac's theory and Anderson's experiment to Dirac, to Anderson or to anyone else. Yet that appears to be what happened."

Several possibilities suggest themselves. One is that the idea of pair production simply did not occur to Oppenheimer. After all, he was not at Dirac's Princeton lecture and the lecture had not been published, so he might well have remained ignorant of Dirac's latest thoughts on the question. But even if the specific notion of pair production did not occur to him, it still seems odd that he did not mention what he had already said in print—namely that Dirac's theory demanded the existence of a positively charged particle with the same mass as the electron. Another thought is that he was reluctant to help someone working on cosmic rays with Millikan, because he assumed that the point of his research was to lend support to an analysis of cosmic rays that he thought was mistaken. Most likely, though, is that he was still so convinced that Dirac's theory was wrong that the last thing he thought Anderson could possibly have photographed was evidence that it was right. This does not entirely resolve the puzzle, since it raises the question: if Oppenheimer did not think Anderson had photographed the positron, what did he think he had photographed? A proton?

In any case, after he had shown his photographs to Millikan, it was to be another nine months before Anderson's further experiments allowed him to summon up the confidence to go into print with the claim that he had discovered a new particle. In that time, Urey discovered deuterium, Chadwick discovered the neutron, and Cockcroft and Walton split the atom. Meanwhile, Dirac himself was losing faith in his own theory. In April 1932, shortly before the dramatic announcement of Cockcroft and Walton's achievement, Dirac was in Copenhagen, attending the meeting at which the pastiche of Goethe's *Faust* mentioned above was performed. Dirac, of course, appears as a character in the play, which pokes fun at his "hole" theory of quantum electrodynamics. Throughout the meeting, in fact, Dirac had to put up with a great deal of skepticism about his theory. Nobody, it seems, believed it, least of all Bohr, who is recorded as saying: "Tell us, Dirac, do you really believe in that stuff?" Dirac did not say so publicly, but a couple of years later he told Heisenberg that he had, privately, ceased to believe in his theory in the months before the discovery of the positron was made public. In July 1932, a month before Dirac's thirtieth birthday, it was announced that he was to succeed Sir Joseph Larmor as the Lucasian Professor of Mathematics at Cambridge, the chair that had previously been held by Isaac Newton and was subsequently to be held by Stephen Hawking. The appointment made Dirac financially secure, but it also came with expectations. It was thus a bad time to be associated with a discredited theory.

Of course, Dirac's theory was soon to be confirmed, but it took an extraordinarily long time for anyone to realize or admit that it *had* been confirmed. On August 2, 1932, Anderson obtained a photograph of a track that seemed to have been left by an electron except that, from the direction of its curvature, he could see that it was *positively* charged. Still knowing nothing of Dirac's "anti-electron," Anderson thought he had discovered a previously unknown and unsuspected particle. The discovery of a new particle, however, was such a rare and unexpected event that he took his time to consider all other possibilities before he committed himself in print to the claim that that was what had happened. Not until the beginning of September did he send a short report of his discovery, with the tentative title "The Apparent Existence of Easily Deflectable Positives," to the journal *Science*. The two-page article ended with the statement: "It seems necessary to call upon a positively charged particle having a mass comparable with that of an electron."

Unlike the previous major breakthroughs of 1932, the discovery of the positron was not immediately heralded as an important achievement. Very few people seem to have even read Anderson's report and, of those who did, most seem not to have believed it. Anderson did not publish his fully worked-out follow-up article in the *Physical Review* until March 1933. Astonishingly, in the intervening period, even now that the discovery of the positron had been announced in print, Oppenheimer still did not mention to Anderson that his discovery confirmed Dirac's prediction, nor did he tell him the explanation of how positrons appear that Dirac's theory provides. "It is surprising to me," Anderson later said, with admirable restraint, "that Oppenheimer during the six months after I first published the paper on the positron—I had no idea, even though I'd searched my mind and gone nuts trying to figure out how these things could be—it's very surprising to me that Oppie didn't think of that idea. It's the sort of thing you would have expected him to think of." It is all the more surprising because in a letter to Frank, undated but almost certainly written in the autumn of 1932, Oppenheimer mentions "Anderson's positively charged electrons" as one of the things he and his students were thinking about.

On February 17, 1933, before Anderson had sent off his detailed paper to the *Physical Review*, he was shocked to read in the newspapers that the discovery of the "positive electron" had been announced in London *by someone else*. The person in question was Patrick Blackett, Oppenheimer's old laboratory supervisor, who, since Millikan's presentation of Anderson's photographs at the Cavendish in November 1931, had been conducting his own researches into cosmic rays and taking his own, even more impressive photographs. In this he had been helped by an Italian visitor to the Cavendish, Giuseppe Occhialini, whom everyone knew as "Beppo." Occhialini had arrived at the Cavendish already having had some experience in investigating cosmic rays using Geiger counters. Together, Blackett and Occhialini devised an ingenious method of getting cosmic rays to, as it were, take photographs of themselves. They did this by placing Geiger counters above and below a cloud chamber, in such a way that when a cosmic ray was detected, a photograph was taken.

Blackett and Occhialini did not read Anderson's report in *Science* until January 1933, by which time they had amassed an impressive collection of photographs that showed, even more clearly than Anderson's pictures, the paths of positively charged particles. Where they had a huge advantage over Anderson was in having the time, the goodwill and the active interest of Paul Dirac, who realized that their photographs confirmed his prediction of the "anti-electron" and was thus able to overcome his previous doubts about his own theory. "I was quite intimate with Blackett at the time," Dirac later remembered, "and told him about my relativistic theory of the electron."

Thus, with Dirac's help, when Blackett and Occhialini presented their results in public, which they did on February 16, 1933, at the Royal Society in London, they were able, unlike Anderson, not only to announce a new particle, but also to *explain* how that particle was produced. And it was the explanation that made the new particle so interesting. For this was an even more astonishing illustration of the Einsteinian formula $E = mc^2$ than the splitting of the atom had been. The formula asserts the equivalence of mass and energy, and what Cockcroft and Walton had demonstrated was an example of mass being converted into energy and, in the process, they had shown just *how much* energy could be released from a small amount of mass—as Einstein's formula asserts. But what Patrick Blackett was able to show—using dramatic photographs of rays from outer space, no less—was the equivalence going in the other direction: energy becoming mass! Whereas Anderson had "gone nuts" trying to work out how positrons could possibly exist, Blackett knew perfectly well from his discussions with Dirac how they could be: they had been created by the conversion of energy into mass, in accordance with the "pair production" that was predicted by Dirac's theory. In presenting his photographs of the "positive electron" (as he called it at this time), Blackett was scrupulous in spelling out its connections with Dirac's theory, showing on the one hand how it provided evidence for that theory, and on the other hand how the theory helped to explain things about the particle that might be puzzling. For not only could Dirac's theory explain how the particle came into being, but it could also explain why the positron had remained undetected for so long. The answer is that, as an "anti-particle," it has a very short life because, as soon as it comes into contact with its opposite number—in this case, an electron—it is annihilated.

In the starkest contrast to Anderson's announcement the previous September, Blackett and Occhialini's results were immediately hailed as an important, indeed sensational, breakthrough. The morning after Blackett's presentation at the Royal Society, their achievement was reported in the *New York Times*, the *Manchester Guardian* and the London *Daily Herald*, which described it as the "Greatest Atom Discovery of the Century." Whenever he was interviewed by reporters, however, Blackett was careful to stress that he had been anticipated, and that the real discoverer of this new positive particle was Anderson. When Anderson's own detailed treatment of the particle appeared in the *Physical Review*, however, it was already old news, except for one thing. In place of Dirac's "anti-electron" and Blackett's "positive electron," Anderson introduced the name that subsequently stuck: the positron.

The astonishing series of breakthroughs in 1932 occupied Nobel Prize committees for many years to come: Harold Urey won the Nobel Prize in Chemistry in 1934 for his discovery of deuterium, while the Nobel Prize in Physics went to Paul Dirac in 1933, partly, at least, for his prediction of the positron; James Chadwick in 1935, for discovering the neutron; Carl Anderson in 1936, for his discovery of the positron; Ernest Lawrence in 1939, for inventing the cyclotron; Patrick Blackett in 1948, for his work on nuclear physics and cosmic rays (chief among which was his identification of the positron as Dirac's "anti-electron"); and Cockcroft and Walton in 1951, for splitting the atomic nucleus.

These breakthroughs also provided the topics for research pursued by Oppenheimer and his students for the following few years, concentrating as they did on the investigation of deuterium, cosmic rays, the positron and the phenomenon of pair production. From the point of view of American physics, the encouraging thing about the list of Nobel laureates created by the breakthroughs of 1932 was that three of them (Urey, Anderson and Lawrence) were American. All three of them, however, were experimentalists. In theory, the Americans still lagged behind the Europeans, though they were catching up. Oppenheimer's contributions to the theoretical issues of that day may have been a step or two behind the leading Europeans, and he may have made some glaring errors here and there, and, in the case of Anderson, shown an inexplicable reticence, but he had at least *made* contributions, some of which were discussed at the forefront of physical theory. Moreover, he had done this without once, since the start of his appointments in California, setting foot in Europe.

By this time, Oppenheimer was settled in California. At Berkeley, he had moved out of the faculty club at the start of the 1931–2 academic year, and into what he described to Frank as "a little house up on the hill with a view of the cities and of the most beautiful harbor in the world . . . There is a sleeping porch; and I sleep under the Yaqui[34] and the stars and imagine I am on the porch at Perro Caliente." After the family holiday in New Orleans following Ella's death, Oppenheimer brought his father with him when he returned to California. For a few weeks in the New Year of 1932 they lived together; not, however, in Berkeley, but in Pasadena, which Julius preferred. Julius, Oppenheimer told Frank, "is very much pleased with this place, liking the cottage—which is in fact excruciatingly ugly—and not I think sorry to have me under the same roof."

He reassured Frank that their father, who was by now sixty years old, "looks well, better than in months." Julius, in fact, was enjoying himself in Pasadena, learning French, attending concerts, taking driving lessons and even joining in some academic seminars. Every morning, Oppenheimer reported, Julius and he were served breakfast by the Tolmans' maid, Moline, who "after I am gone listens with enchanting patience to F[ather]'s reports on high finance." On January 18, 1932, Julius himself wrote to Frank, telling him: "I am meeting lots of Robert's friends and yet I believe that I have not interfered with his activities." Julius, impressed both with his son and with Caltech for having such distinguished connections, reported to Frank that Robert "has had a couple of short talks with Einstein."

These talks would probably have taken place during the second of Einstein's three visits to Caltech. During the first, in the New Year of 1930, he came to love Pasadena so much that he took to calling it "paradise." In between discussing cosmic rays with Millikan and relativity with Tolman, Einstein had toured the movie studios of Hollywood, had dinner at Charlie Chaplin's Beverly Hills home and attended a banquet in his honor, at which there had been 200 guests. So much in demand was

[34] I am rather puzzled as to what Oppenheimer might mean by this. The Yaqui are a Native American tribe, whose original lands were in what is now Mexico, California and Arizona. Presumably, further up the hill on which Oppenheimer's house stood, there lived a group of Yaqui people.

he that a millionairess gave Caltech $10,000 for the privilege of meeting him. Evidently hoping to recruit him permanently, Millikan invited him back for the New Year of 1932—a visit that, at Einstein's request, was rather more low-key. Though he loved California, Einstein was less impressed with Millikan, whose political conservatism clashed with his own determination to speak out on behalf of the poor, the dispossessed and the persecuted.

More to Einstein's taste was the educator Abraham Flexner, who, having secured funding of $5 million, was in the process of establishing an Institute for Advanced Study. During Einstein's second visit to California, Flexner took the opportunity to sound him out about the possibility of joining his proposed new institute. The reply was encouraging enough for Flexner to visit Einstein in Germany during the summer of 1932, where he told Einstein that the new institute would be based in Princeton and asked him to name his own price and conditions. Einstein initially declined, but the rapid growth in the power and influence of the Nazis in Germany forced him to reconsider. When he left Germany for his third visit to Caltech in December 1932, his ostensible plan was to return to Germany two months later before taking up his position at Flexner's new institute, but in reality he probably knew that he would not be returning.

While Einstein was in Pasadena in January 1933, the news came that Hitler had been made Chancellor. He was still there on March 5 when he heard that the Nazi Party had received the most votes (44 percent) of any party in Germany's general election. Einstein returned to Europe at the end of March, but sensibly did not step foot in Germany, where his home had been seized, his books burned and his theories officially repudiated as "Jewish science." Throughout the new "Reich" scientists who were not, like the physicist Philipp Lenard, active Nazis or, like Max Planck or Werner Heisenberg, prepared to work under the Nazis, were making plans to leave Germany. The many Jewish scientists, of course, had no choice. Max Born, having been thrown out of Göttingen because he was Jewish, prepared to move to England, where Cambridge had offered to take him. Leo Szilard, meanwhile, left Germany with his life savings hidden in his shoes. After a few months in England, Einstein returned to the United States and, with much fanfare, took up his appointment at the Institute for Advanced Study. He never once returned to Europe.

Of all this turmoil in Germany—the home of his ancestors and some of his not-very-distant relations, as well as of many of the scientists for whom he had the greatest regard—there is not a single word in Oppenheimer's letters, even when he touches on subjects that relate to it. For example, in a letter to Frank written on March 12, 1932, he tells him that their father, his health having been restored by his time in California, is now returning to New York. "I have urged him very strongly not to go to Europe alone this summer," Oppenheimer writes. One might think this advice was prompted by Oppenheimer's concern at his father placing himself at the mercy of the violent anti-Semitism that had erupted in Germany. The rest of the letter suggests, however, that his concern was not about the conditions in Germany, but merely about his father's physical condition. "Only if things should break unexpectedly well," he writes, "e.g. should he find a very good person to travel with, ought he, or will he, go abroad." He adds: "I have said that next summer I should consider going myself, that in that case we could at least cross both ways together."

Again, in October 1933, he wrote to his brother about Frank's plans to study at Cambridge. "The theoretical physics should be awfully good in Cambridge," he told him, "with Dirac there, and Born." But nowhere does he reflect on, or even mention, *why* Born was in Cambridge. In March 1934, he responded to an appeal for financial support for dismissed German physicists by pledging 3 percent of his salary for two years. Apart from that, he remained silent until his interest in political and social questions was finally aroused in 1936. Until then, his attitude is summed up by a remark he once made to Leo Nedelsky: "Tell me, what has politics to do with truth, goodness and beauty?"

Oppenheimer's concern with truth, goodness and beauty led him in the early 1930s to a serious study of ancient Hindu literature; so serious, indeed, that he took lessons in Sanskrit so that he could read the Hindu texts in their original language. The first mention of this comes in his letter to Frank of August 10, 1931, in which he writes: "I am learning Sanskrit, enjoying it very much, and enjoying again the sweet luxury of being taught."

His teacher was Arthur Ryder, who was professor of Sanskrit at Berkeley. Harold Cherniss has described Ryder as "a friend half divine in his great humanity." In his views on education, he was a curious mixture of the ultra-traditionalist and the iconoclast. He believed on the one hand that a university education ought to consist primarily of Latin, Greek and mathematics (with the other sciences and humanities given as a reward to good students and the social sciences ignored altogether). On the other hand, his approach to the teaching of Sanskrit was refreshingly free from the deadening hand of dry scholarship. He regarded the learning of Sanskrit as the opening of a door onto great literature, not as an academic discipline. Perhaps for that reason he was the ideal teacher for Oppenheimer, who held him in enormously high regard. "Ryder felt and thought and talked as a stoic," Oppenheimer once told a journalist, extolling him as "a special subclass of the people who have a tragic sense of life, in that they attribute to human actions the completely decisive role in the difference between salvation and damnation. Ryder knew that a man could commit irretrievable error, and that in the face of this fact, all others were secondary."

Oppenheimer gave few details of his learning of Sanskrit or of his reading of the Hindu classics. In a letter to Frank of January 1932, he alludes very briefly to the Hindu god Shiva; the following autumn he mentions that he is reading "the Cakuntala" (more usually spelled Shakuntala, a verse play written by the great Sanskrit poet and dramatist Kalidasa) and promises Frank that at their next meeting he will afflict him "with clumsy translations of the superb poems"; and a year later that he is reading the Bhagavad Gita, which "is very easy and quite marvelous." Then, in June 1934, he writes to Frank, thanking him for "the precious Meghaduta and rather too learned *Veda*," which were presumably birthday presents. "The Meghaduta I read with Ryder, with delight, some ease, and great enchantment," Oppenheimer told his brother. "The Veda lies on my shelf, a reproach to my indolence." Otherwise known as "The Cloud Messenger," the Meghaduta is a poem by Kalidasa that tells how a cloud is used to take a message from an exiled subject of Kubera, the god of wealth, to his wife in the Himalayan Mountains. The *Vedas* are the most ancient of Hindu scriptures, consisting of hymns, poems and mantras.

Apart from these very brief mentions of Sanskrit literature, Oppenheimer's only other allusion to Hinduism in his correspondence comes in yet another letter to Frank, in which he tells him that he has called his third and latest car "Garuda," after, he says, "the mechanical bird which the carpenter made for his friend the weaver who loved a princess"—a description that shows a knowledge of the collection of fables known as the *Panchatantra*, rather than of the *Upanishads* scriptures, or the epic poem the *Mahabharata*, in both of which Garuda is depicted quite differently as a minor deity who carries the supreme god, Vishnu.

Though detailed discussion of his reading is absent, one can see the influence of Hinduism in much of what Oppenheimer writes to his brother. For example, in a letter to Frank, undated but probably written in January 1932, he speaks of "that *delectatio contemplationis* which is the reward and reason of our way of life" and says that, though such things are not to be expected, nevertheless "we try to do everything to invite them, cultivate a little leisure, and a certain detached solitariness, and a quiet discipline which uses but transcends the discipline of our duties."

In some ways, these remarks carry echoes of some of Felix Adler's maxims, but, in their emphasis on detachment, separateness and transcendence they seem closer to the Bhagavad Gita than to the Ethical Culture movement, with its encouragement to *engage* politically and socially so as to improve the lives of others. Even more clearly indebted to Hindu ideas is the extended disquisition on the notion of discipline that Oppenheimer included in a letter to Frank two months later. The view Oppenheimer puts forward there is that discipline is to be valued independently from, and more than, "its earthly fruit." "Discipline is good for the soul," as Oppenheimer puts it, and it is not good because it leads to good results, or because it enables us to *do* things. That discipline is good for the soul "is more fundamental than any of the grounds given for its goodness." It is, as it were, good *in itself*. What Oppenheimer writes about discipline to Frank is worth quoting at length, because it offers, I think, some valuable clues about the way he looked at life, and how that enabled him to do the things he did.

> I believe that through discipline, though not through discipline alone, we can achieve serenity, and a certain small but precious measure of freedom from the accidents of incarnation, and charity, and that detachment which preserves the world which it renounces. I believe that through discipline we learn to preserve what is essential to our happiness in more and more adverse circumstances, and to abandon with simplicity what would else have seemed to us indispensable; that we come a little to see the world without the gross distortion of personal desire, and in seeing it so, accept more easily our earthly privation and its earthly horror—But because I believe that the reward of discipline is greater than its immediate objective, I would not have you think that discipline without objective is possible: in its nature discipline involves the subjection of the soul to some perhaps minor end; and that end must be real, if the discipline is not to be factitious. Therefore I think that all things which evoke discipline: study, and our duties to men and to the commonwealth, war, and personal hardship, and even the need for subsistence, ought to be greeted by us with profound gratitude; for only through them can we attain the least detachment, and only so can we know peace.

These thoughts carry direct echoes of the Bhagavad Gita, which begins on the battlefield with the great warrior Prince Arjuna despairing at the suffering of war and coming to doubt that there is any glory in killing the "teachers, fathers and sons" who face him. He therefore wants no more part in the "evil of destruction." The god Krishna, however, tells him that his concern for the deaths of his kinsmen and enemies is misplaced, since the spirit does not perish with the body and it is the spirit

The infant Oppenheimer with his mother, Ella.

Oppenheimer in the arms of his father, Julius, whom he later described as "one of the most tolerant and human of men."

Oppenheimer (right) at about ten, with a friend, pursuing one of his childhood passions: building with blocks.

(Below) 155 Riverside Drive, Oppenheimer's childhood home (the picture was taken in 1910, just a year before the Oppenheimer family moved there).

NO. 155 RIVERSIDE DRIVE.

South Corner Eighty-eighth Street.

The building located at the South corner of 88th St. and Riverside Drive, known as No. 155 Riverside Drive, is a twelve-story fireproof apartment house. It has two apartments on a floor, one of nine rooms, three baths and thirteen closets, and the other containing ten rooms, three baths and sixteen closets.

There are two elevators, one for service, and the other for passengers. The house is particularly well laid out, as shown by the plans below. The section in which the house is situated is one of the finest on the Drive.

№ 155 Riverside Drive

Court 25 Feet Wide

TYPICAL FLOOR PLAN OF No. 155 RIVERSIDE DRIVE.

"A little precious, and perhaps a little arrogant, but very interesting, full of ideas." Oppenheimer at Harvard.

(*Left*) William Boyd, one of the few close friends Oppenheimer had at Harvard.

(*Right*) One of Oppenheimer's best friends from New Mexico, the writer Paul Horgan.

(*Left*) Frederick Bernheim, Oppenheimer's friend and Harvard roommate.

The Upper Pecos Valley, Oppenheimer's favorite landscape, where "for the first time in his life," according to Herbert Smith, who accompanied him on his first visit there in 1922, Oppenheimer "found himself loved, admired, sought after."

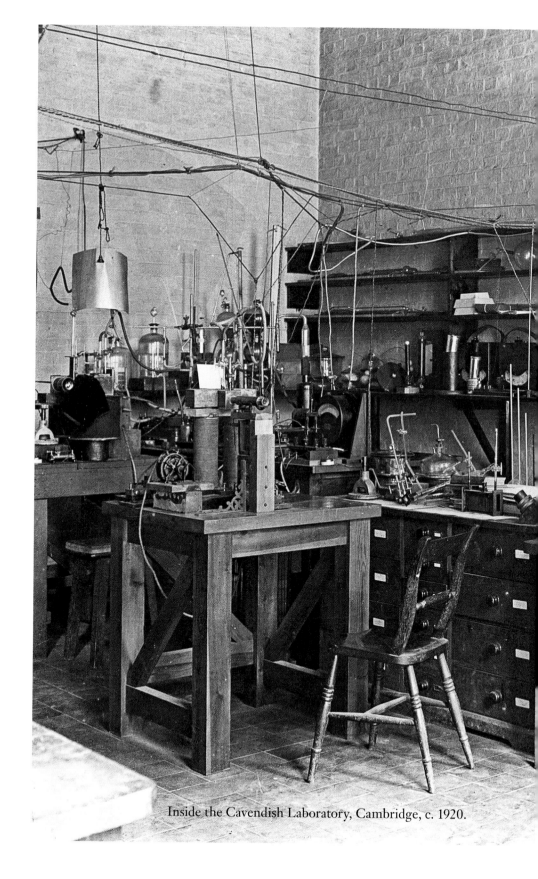
Inside the Cavendish Laboratory, Cambridge, c. 1920.

(Above left) The great Cambridge physicist Paul Dirac. *(Above right)* Patrick Blackett, "a young Oedipus. Tall, slim, beautifully balanced and always looking better dressed than anyone."

Niels Bohr, the man whom Oppenheimer admired over all others, in 1922.

Max Born (seated),
Oppenheimer's Ph.D.
supervisor at Göttingen,
in 1922. Behind him
(left to right) are: William
Osler, Niels Bohr, James
Franck, and Oscar Klein.

Charlotte Riefenstahl (center).

Werner Heisenberg in 1933, the year after he was awarded the Nobel Prize.

Paul Ehrenfest in 1927.

Oppenheimer on Lake Zurich with I. I. Rabi, H. M. Mott-Smith, and (smiling rather sinisterly at the camera) Wolfgang Pauli, 1929.

(Left) Oppenheimer in 1930 during his first year at Berkeley.

(Below) Oppenheimer with his close friend and scientific collaborator, Robert Serber.

(Above) Ernest Lawrence at Berkeley in the 1930s with one of the early cyclotrons.

(Left) Oppenheimer's wife, Kitty, who was almost universally disliked among his colleagues at Los Alamos and later at Princeton.

Perro Caliente—
"hot dog!"

Haakon Chevalier, whose very brief,
halfhearted, and unsuccessful attempt
to contribute to Soviet espionage had
deep and lasting consequences for
Oppenheimer and himself.

Frank Oppenheimer.

Jean Tatlock, Oppenheimer's fiancée and fellow traveler in 1930s radical politics.

(Left) Steve Nelson, a leading figure in the U.S. Communist Party and in the attempts to provide the Soviet Union with the allies' atomic secrets.

Joe Weinberg, Rossi Lomanitz, David Bohm, and Max Friedman pose for a street photographer, a picture that would arouse the FBI's interest in all four for many years after it was taken.

The staff of the Radiation Laboratory in Berkeley sitting on the 60-inch cyclotron in 1939. Lawrence is in the front row, fourth from the left; Oppenheimer is in the top row at the back with a pipe in his mouth.

alone that is of value. Arjuna must fight, Krishna urges, not because of what fighting will accomplish, but rather because it is his duty to fight. "Set thy heart upon thy work," Krishna says, "but never on its reward. Work not for a reward; but never cease to do thy work." Toward the end of the book Krishna preaches "freedom from the chains of attachment, even from a selfish attachment to one's children, wife or home," a freedom achievable by "retiring to solitary places, and avoiding the noisy multitude," Krishna continues: "A constant yearning to know the inner Spirit, and a vision of Truth which gives liberation: this is true wisdom leading to vision." He then speaks of Sattva, Rajas and Tamas—light, fire and darkness—and says: "Any work when it is well done bears the pure harmony of Sattva" and "From Sattva arises wisdom."

According to Isidor Rabi, Oppenheimer "would have been a much better physicist if he had studied the Talmud rather than Sanskrit . . . it would have given him a greater sense of himself." Rabi was inclined to link Oppenheimer's interest in Sanskrit texts with his expertise in French literature; both, he thought, were part of Oppenheimer's attempt to persuade himself and others that he was not Jewish. If he had mastered the literature of his own tradition, rather than those of others, Rabi thought, Oppenheimer would not have had the problems that come with denying one's own background. "The Jewish tradition," Rabi thought, "even if you don't know it in detail, is so strong that you renounce it at your own peril. Doesn't mean you have to be orthodox, or even practise it, but if you turn your back on it, having been born into it, you're in trouble."

As we have seen, the sense in which Oppenheimer was "born into" the Jewish tradition is elusive, perhaps *too* elusive for Rabi's point to be persuasive, because there is no clear way in which we can see Oppenheimer turning his back on his own tradition. In his family, as in many of the German Jewish families that made up Oppenheimer's cultural background, the back-turning had been done a generation or two earlier. In the introduction he wrote to the published collection of speeches given at Oppenheimer's memorial, Rabi offered another reason for thinking that the influence of Hinduism on Oppenheimer's physics had been for the worse, this time in an effort to explain "why men of Oppenheimer's gifts do not discover everything worth discovering." The answer, he suggests, is that "in some respects Oppenheimer was over-educated in those fields which lie outside the scientific tradition, such as his interest in religion, in the Hindu religion in particular, which resulted in a feeling for the mystery of the universe that surrounded him almost like a fog. He saw physics clearly, looking toward what had already been done, but at the border he tended to feel that there was much more of the mysterious and novel than there actually was."

He was insufficiently confident of the power of the intellectual tools
he already possessed and did not drive his thought to the very end
because he felt instinctively that new ideas and new methods were
necessary to go further than he and his students had already gone.
Some may call it a lack of faith, but in my opinion it was more a turning away from the hard, crude methods of theoretical physics into a
mystical realm of broad intuition.

It is difficult to know whether the work that Oppenheimer did in
the period after 1932 exemplifies or refutes Rabi's remarks. On the one
hand, this was one of Oppenheimer's most impressively concentrated
periods of work, during which he worked on the most fundamental,
and difficult, problems that theoretical physics had to face at that time.
Addressing these problems took all of the very considerable talents and
energy at Oppenheimer's disposal. Or, anyway, most of them; it is true
that he combined his work in physics with, for example, learning Sanskrit and reading ancient Greek—things that most of us would regard as
significant achievements in their own right—but, for the most part, he
approached physics at this time with something of the attitude recommended by Krishna in the Bhagavad Gita: freedom from attachments,
seclusion from the "noisy multitude" and, above all perhaps, a "constant
yearning to know." If he showed some interest in things of beauty, such
as the literature he read, he showed almost none in the social and political upheavals that were happening at that time. Whether one thinks of
this as a good or a bad thing, it is certainly hard to see that it hindered his
progress in physics, and hard too to regard it as anything but an application of the outlook he had acquired from Hinduism.

On the other hand, despite his extremely hard work and his utter
absorption in physics at this time, it is true that he did not accomplish
anything remotely comparable to the achievements of Bohr, Heisenberg, Dirac et al. And the reason for that may have something to do with
his Hindu-influenced attitudes. Regarding work as being valuable for its
own sake, regardless of its results, may have inspired in him a devotion
to work that others lacked, but it may also, as Rabi suspected, have made
him less single-minded than the very best physicists with regard to *solving* problems, and more accepting of the idea that some problems were
simply insoluble. Someone like James Chadwick or Ernest Lawrence, or
even Paul Dirac, worked at a problem *in order to solve it*; Oppenheimer
took pleasure *in the work itself.*

And yet, if Oppenheimer approached physics from the point of view
of someone who saw in it "truth, goodness and beauty," he also had at
least *one* practical result in mind—namely, the development and growth

of the peculiarly American school of theoretical physics that he had set out to create. In contrast to Paul Dirac, say, who had very few graduate students and spent very little time with those he had, Oppenheimer did almost everything, including his own research, with his students.

For both Oppenheimer and his students, the research agenda was set by the remarkable discoveries of 1932, as Oppenheimer spelled out in his letter to Frank in the autumn of that year. He begins his report with the very distinction that forms the heart of the Bhagavad Gita view of work: "The work is fine: not in the fruits but the doing." He goes on:

> There are lots of eager students, and we are busy studying nuclei and neutrons and disintegrations; trying to make some peace between the inadequate theory and the absurd revolutionary experiments . . . We have been running a nuclear seminar, in addition to the usual ones, trying to make some order out of the great chaos, not getting very far with that. We are supplementing the paper I wrote last summer [the one he published with Frank Carlson on "magnetic neutrons"] with a study of the radiation in electron–electron impacts, and worrying about the neutron and Anderson's positively charged electrons, and cleaning up a few residual problems in atomic physics. I take it that there will be a lull in the theory for a time; and that when the theory advances, it will be very wild and very wonderful indeed.

During the year 1932–3, Frank Carlson, having received his Ph.D. in April 1932, was Oppenheimer's research associate, Melba Phillips was in the final year of her Ph.D. studies, and Leo Nedelsky, who, like Carlson, had completed his Ph.D. in 1932, was still in Berkeley, having had no success in finding an appointment. Harvey Hall, meanwhile, had found a job at Columbia as an instructor in physics. Oppenheimer, perhaps thinking he was helping out, asked Nedelsky to lecture for him during the weeks he left Berkeley to go to Caltech. "It won't be any trouble," Oppenheimer told him, "it's all in a book." The book, however, turned out to be in Dutch. When Nedelsky reported that this would be a problem, Oppenheimer airily replied: "But it's such easy Dutch."

In 1932, these graduate students were joined by some postdoctoral students, holders of the coveted National Research Fellowship, who, now that Oppenheimer was there, regarded Berkeley as a serious rival to Cambridge, Copenhagen and Göttingen as a place in which to pursue postdoctoral research. In 1932–3, Oppenheimer worked with two of these NRF postdoctoral students. The first was Wendell Furry, a Methodist minister's son from Indiana, who had taken his Ph.D. at the University of Illinois. Furry had attended the Ann Arbor summer school in 1931 and had been deeply impressed at seeing Oppenheimer, the only American invited to share the platform with the galaxy of European stars on display, standing up to none other than Wolfgang Pauli. When he went to Berkeley, however (to begin with at any rate), Furry felt hopelessly out of his depth, finding that when he attended Oppenheimer's lectures he did not understand a word of them. It took him a year to regain his confidence.

In the meantime, Oppenheimer began to work closely with Milton Plesset, his second National Research Fellow, though he had arrived not at Berkeley but at Caltech, initially hoping to work with Paul Epstein, the Russian physicist who had been there since 1921. Plesset had done his Ph.D. at Yale on a subject close to Oppenheimer's heart, Dirac's theory of the electron, and so it was natural that Oppenheimer would take some interest in his work and that they should start working together. After all, people who understood Dirac's quantum electrodynamics were few and far between. As Plesset later recalled: "The state of theoretical physics in this country at that time was not very advanced, except for Oppenheimer." When Oppenheimer arrived in Pasadena, Plesset remembers, "things really started to move." He and Oppenheimer got interested in what Plesset describes as "a problem with the Dirac electron" and together they wrote a short paper that "put a new light on the Dirac theory."

That paper, entitled "On the Production of the Positive Electron," was published as a letter to the editor in the *Physical Review* in the summer of 1933 and is the first of a series of papers in which Oppenheimer, usually together with one of his students, attempted to address what he saw as the problems in Dirac's theory of the electron. This had been an ongoing preoccupation of his since Dirac had first shown him the theory in 1928, but, after the discovery of the positron in 1932, this preoccupation took on a rather different form. He could no longer, as he had before, point to the negative energy states in the theory as evidence of a problem; these states were filled, as Dirac had predicted, with positively charged particles. Indeed, the paper jointly written by Oppenheimer and Plesset begins with the following acknowledgment: "The experimental discovery of the positive electron gives us a striking confirmation of Dirac's theory of the electron." It had quickly been confirmed that positrons could be created not only by the impact of cosmic rays, but also in the laboratory. In their paper, Oppenheimer and Plesset discuss, in particular, the experiments at Caltech conducted by Carl Anderson and his colleague Seth Neddermeyer, in which they showed that pairs of electrons and positrons are created when the very energetic gamma radiation from thorium C" passes through lead. From Dirac's theory, they point out, one can make predictions about the frequency of pair production that are confirmed by the experimental evidence, but only—and this is where Oppenheimer thought major changes in the theory were needed and where his interest really lay—up to energies of a certain limit. Beyond that limit, Oppenheimer and Plesset claim, the theory fails.

In the penultimate paragraph of their short paper, Oppenheimer and Plesset make what Abraham Pais has described as a "fundamental observation," namely that "fast electrons and positives [positrons] . . . will themselves tend to produce further pairs"—a prescient anticipation of the phenomenon of *showering* that would later be studied intensely by physicists, including Oppenheimer himself. Pais is less complimentary about the mathematics in the paper, pointing out: "Their final formula was wrong, as usual, as others rapidly noted."

These two aspects of Oppenheimer's work—his originality and his mathematical carelessness—are neatly captured in a recommendation that Ralph Fowler wrote to Edwin Kemble of Harvard, when Harvard expressed an interest in trying to lure Oppenheimer away from California. Kemble knew Oppenheimer himself, of course, but he also knew that Fowler had seen him on many occasions during his rise to prominence, the latest of which was a visit Fowler made to Berkeley in the autumn of 1932. Dated November 30, 1933, Fowler's report reads:

> I fancy he is not a very good lecturer and his work is still apt to be full of mistakes due to lack of care, but it is work of the highest originality and he has an extremely stimulating influence in a theoretical school as I had ample opportunities of learning last fall.

Nevertheless, despite his unreliable mathematics, Oppenheimer was successfully putting both Berkeley and Caltech on the international map. When distinguished physicists came to California, the man who made the most impression on them was usually Oppenheimer. This was certainly the case when God himself, Niels Bohr, came to Pasadena in the summer of 1933. This was the only opportunity Oppenheimer had had to discuss physics with his greatest scientific idol since their initial meeting at Cambridge in 1926, and it seems to have been remembered by both as a pleasant and instructive occasion. At the very end of their 1933 paper, Oppenheimer and Plesset extend their "profound thanks" to Niels Bohr, "who has helped us to understand the essential consistency of the theory which we have here applied." For his part, Bohr was very pleased to be able to discuss physics with Oppenheimer, his meeting with whom seems to have been the highlight of his visit. He was much less enchanted with Millikan, but nevertheless agreed to meet the trustees of Caltech to tell them how well the school of physics was doing. On June 14, 1933, Oppenheimer wrote to Bohr to thank him for his visit, and to send him a copy of the paper he had written with Plesset, who was about to leave Pasadena to spend a year at Bohr's institute.

Plesset remembers that Bohr's institute that summer was "swarming" with refugees from Nazi Germany, mostly Jewish scientists. Shortly after Plesset's arrival, the institute held its annual seminar, which for a number of reasons is remembered as a melancholy occasion. Dirac, Heisenberg and Ehrenfest were among the attendees, and Plesset recalls "a lot of discussion over the validity of Dirac's theory. People were groping still."

In especially poor spirits at Bohr's seminar was Paul Ehrenfest, who was described as looking "pudgy-faced and overweight" and "losing his grip on physics." When the time came to leave, Dirac, who had grown close to Ehrenfest, saw him waiting for a taxi, looking flustered and unhappy, and thanked him for his contributions to the discussions. This elicited from Ehrenfest an extreme and, for Dirac, extremely worrying, reaction: "What you have said, coming from a young man like you, means very much to me because, maybe, a man such as I feels he has no force to live." A few days later, the dreadful news came that Ehrenfest had shot himself, prompting Dirac to write a four-page letter to Bohr describing in detail his last moments with Ehrenfest and telling him that he could not help blaming himself for what had happened.

News of Ehrenfest's death seems to have reached Oppenheimer rather slowly. On October 7, 1933, nearly two weeks after the suicide, he wrote to Frank, apparently still unaware of it. What was more on his mind was what he described as the "work with pairs," which he told Frank "has gone along nicely." He was now more certain than ever that Dirac's "theory gives the wrong answer for the production of very high energy pairs" and seemed confident that he and his students were making progress in "cleaning up the formalism."

Oppenheimer's close attention to experimental work in this period is illustrated in the letter to Frank, as are some of the problems that it caused him. Lawrence, he writes, "has definitely established the instability of the H_2 [deuterium] nucleus. It decomposes upon collision into neutron and proton, to the tune of about six million volts." This, he adds, with a discernible note of triumph, makes a "hopeless obstacle" to Heisenberg's theory of the nucleus. As it turned out, Heisenberg's theory was a good deal more trustworthy than Lawrence's observations.

Lawrence that autumn was given the honor of being invited to the seventh Solvay Congress in Brussels, which was held in the week of

October 22–29, 1933. The theme originally chosen was the application of quantum mechanics to chemistry, but, in the light of the momentous discoveries of 1932, this was changed to the nucleus. Lawrence's invitation was the source of great pride at Berkeley. It was, his Ph.D. student Robert Thornton has said, "Lawrence's first European recognition." When the time came for Lawrence to leave for Belgium: "The whole staff went down to the train to see him off. Next morning they got together in the lab and then took off for a kind of two-day picnic climbing Mount Lassen. They were so happy you'd have thought they were all going to talk at the Solvay Congress."

Unfortunately for Lawrence, his appearance at the Solvay Congress turned out to be something of a humiliation. Heisenberg, Bohr, Chadwick and Irène Curie all used the occasion to express skepticism about his results, unimpressed by his claim that they had been obtained (and could only be obtained) with a machine capable of 800,000 volts. No matter how many volts he had at his command, they insisted, from a theoretical point of view, his interpretation of his results did not make sense. According to Nuel Pharr Davis: "Lawrence left the conference feeling bad." A colleague at Berkeley described it as "one of Lawrence's saddest experiences." About a month later, it was shown by scientists at the Carnegie Institution in Washington that Lawrence's results had been skewed by impurities.

From Oppenheimer's point of view, Lawrence's trip to Brussels had a benefit quite independent of Lawrence's own work and reputation; namely, that it would allow Lawrence to hear, and report back to Oppenheimer on, Paul Dirac's latest thoughts. Dirac's paper, entitled "Theory of the Positron," was on *precisely* the topic that consumed Oppenheimer's thoughts and energies during this period, and he was pleased to see that, in some respects, Dirac's thoughts were moving in his direction. However, just as Oppenheimer was immersing himself in quantum electrodynamics, Dirac was becoming disillusioned with it. In particular, he despaired of ever solving the problem that Oppenheimer had been among the first to point out and discuss: the problem that the theory gave infinite answers to questions that seemed to demand a finite answer. These infinities plagued the whole subject of quantum electrodynamics until its reformulation in the late 1940s by Richard Feynman, Freeman Dyson, Julian Schwinger and Sin-Itiro Tomonaga.

For the next two years, however, quantum electrodynamics was almost the sole topic of Oppenheimer's thoughts, his correspondence and the papers he wrote with his students. His ambition was nothing less than a reformulation of the kind that was finally achieved in the late 1940s. As he put it in a letter to George Uhlenbeck, he and his students were hoping to develop a general formalism together with its physical interpretation. "The formalism," he told Uhlenbeck, "has some resemblance to Schrödinger's earlier attempts . . . The theory seems very pretty to me, and is in every way consistent with the possibilities of measurement."

His work continued, however, to be dogged by mathematical error. In November 1933, he and Leo Nedelsky sent a letter to the editor of the *Physical Review* entitled "The Production of Positives by Nuclear Gamma Rays," in which they presented a method of calculating the probability that an electron-positron pair would be produced by the gamma rays emitted by a nucleus. Three months later, they were forced to publish an erratum confessing that in their final formula they had missed a factor of one third.

Oppenheimer nevertheless continued to publish important work, the most ambitious of which was a paper entitled "On the Theory of the Electron and the Positive,"[35] which was received by the *Physical Review* on December 1, 1933. This, his largest and most important paper during this period, was written jointly with Wendell Furry, who, now in his second year as an NRF, had recovered his confidence and his productivity. He was even able, on occasion at least, to stand up to Oppenheimer. During this period, it is reported, "it was a common sight to see them pacing the streets of Berkeley, engaged in constant harangue. Colleagues would hoist a thumb in their direction and observe that 'The Fuzzy and the Furry are in conference.'"

> Once they paused on a corner while Oppenheimer threw up his arms and said, "Wendell, you *have* to rationalize everything. You seem to be completely incapable of understanding anything that cannot be put into words." Furry smiled, gratified by the remark. Oppenheimer rocked back and roared at him, "I didn't mean that as a compliment."

Their paper aimed at nothing less than a completely new formulation of Dirac's theory of the electron, one that sought to avoid the inconsistencies and the infinities of Dirac's theory and to capture at a more fundamental level the physical realities of electrons and positrons.

The theory as formulated by Furry and Oppenheimer was widely recognized as a formal improvement on Dirac's version, and Oppenheimer

---

[35] It would not be until the summer of the following year that Oppenheimer became resigned to the word "positron," which he regarded as a barbaric mixture of Latin (*posi-*) and Greek (*-tron*).

was very proud of it. He sent it to, among others, Bohr, Uhlenbeck, Pauli and Dirac. He also presented a version of it to the Boston meeting of the American Physical Society in December 1933. Few people, however, were persuaded that it represented a major, fundamental advance on Dirac's work. Pauli was especially dismissive, writing to Heisenberg on January 21, 1934: "A short while ago, Oppenheimer sent me a manuscript . . . that completely ignored the problems treated by Dirac and ourselves." From Dirac himself there was no response at all. In order to elicit at least some response, Oppenheimer tried taking advantage of the fact that Frank was in Cambridge, writing to him on January 7, 1934, and telling him that he had sent the paper to Dirac. "I do not know how Dirac liked what we wrote," Oppenheimer told Frank, "but if you see him you might warn him that we shall send more presently."

In a letter to the editor of the *Physical Review*, dated February 12, 1934, Oppenheimer and Furry pointed out some serious problems with their own theory, and then, four months later, sent another letter pointing out problems with Dirac's new version of the theory. And still, as Oppenheimer complained in a letter to Uhlenbeck, "from Dirac we have not had a murmur." The following year, Oppenheimer persuaded Dirac to come to Pasadena and further persuaded him to listen to a fifteen-minute presentation by two graduate students who worked on quantum electrodynamics, seeking to build on Dirac's work. After the presentation was over, the students braced themselves for Dirac's comments. The only question Dirac asked, however, was: "Where is the nearest post office?"

Almost as if it were cause and effect, what Dirac's biographer calls his "golden creative streak" came to an end just at the time he received the highest honor that a scientist can receive: the Nobel Prize. The telephone call telling him that he was to share the 1933 prize in physics with Erwin Schrödinger came on November 9. Almost pathologically wary of publicity, Dirac's first impulse was to turn it down, but Rutherford warned him: "A refusal will get you more publicity." And so the following month, accompanied by his mother, Dirac traveled to Stockholm to receive the prize. His mother did not share either Dirac's taciturn nature or his dislike of publicity, so, while he avoided the press, she was only too happy to give interviews. Asked by one journalist about her son's interest in the opposite sex, she replied: "He is not interested in young women." And so, inevitably, the next day, the newspaper headline was: "Thirty-One-Year-Old Professor Dirac Never Looks at Girls."

Just two months later, Oppenheimer was himself the subject of a somewhat similar headline. "Forgetful Prof Parks Girl, Takes Self Home" announced the *San Francisco Chronicle* on February 14, 1934, underneath which it told the story of how, at four o'clock in the morning, a policeman on patrol in the hills overlooking Berkeley had found Melba Phillips in a panic, sitting alone in a parked car that belonged to Oppenheimer. She and Oppenheimer had been sitting in the car together, she told police, when he had excused himself to go for a walk. Now, two hours later, he had still not returned. The police searched the area for him and then phoned the Berkeley faculty club, where he was staying at the time. The staff of the faculty club found him in bed, asleep. The newspaper report says that Oppenheimer told police that, after leaving the car, he had forgotten about Melba and gone home. Raymond Birge, in telling this story, comments: "Like all geniuses, Oppenheimer was very absent-minded." But, in fact, he wasn't. "I never saw the slightest evidence of any absentmindedness in Oppie," one of his students recalls, "quite the contrary in fact."

If one resists the temptation to think that this "absentmindedness" was merely an affectation, then one seems forced to conclude two things: first, that the problems of quantum electrodynamics had a really extraordinary hold on Oppenheimer's thoughts at this time; and second, that his interest in Melba Phillips was, by comparison, slight. In any case, though Melba stayed at Berkeley for another year, and would join in with the intellectual and social life centered on Oppenheimer's graduate students, she never again agreed to go on a date with her erstwhile Ph.D. supervisor (she had received her Ph.D. in May 1933).

On June 4, 1934, Oppenheimer wrote to Frank, who was still in Cambridge, telling him that, though he was continuing to work on "disentangling the still existing miseries of positron theory," he hoped his latest "manifesto," written jointly with Furry, would be his last word on the subject. Theoretical physics, he told Frank, "is in hell of a way," largely due to "the utter impossibility of making a rigorous calculation of anything at all." He mentioned that he had been asked to go to Princeton for a year and permanently to Harvard: "But I turned down these seductions, thinking more highly of my present jobs, where it is a little less difficult for me to believe in my usefulness, and where the good Californian wine consoles for the hardness of physics and the poor powers of the human mind." That summer he would be at Perro Caliente without Frank, but with the Uhlenbecks: "We are going to miss you terribly, and it is with very mixed feelings that I shall return to the mountains without you."

Oppenheimer drove to New Mexico from Ann Arbor, where he attended the summer school, with the Uhlenbecks as his passengers. He had boasted to Frank that "Garuda does ninety-five with an unopened throttle," but in demonstrating his car's speed to the Uhlenbecks by racing trains across the open prairie, he got something in his eye that scratched his eyeball so badly that, for a while, he had to wear an eye-patch and George Uhlenbeck had to take over the driving. After a six-week holiday in Perro Caliente, the Uhlenbecks returned to Berkeley with Oppenheimer. When they finally got back to Ann Arbor, George Uhlenbeck learned that Hendrik Kramers had been invited to succeed Ehrenfest at Leiden and that he, George, had been invited in turn to succeed Kramers at Utrecht. Much as he loved America and Ann Arbor, there was never any doubt that he would accept. Oppenheimer wrote to him acknowledging the inevitability that he would accept, but express-ing his sadness "that the American part of you, which has grown so big, will gradually disappear." "I have such a feeling about America," Oppen-heimer wrote. "And let us think, if you must leave us now, that you will come back some time to America; that by accepting in full the responsi-bilities of being a Dutchman, you will have earned for yourself the right to be a little of an American too."

That summer, Oppenheimer's burgeoning school of theoretical physics—what Wolfgang Pauli described as the "nim-nim-nim boys"—was strengthened by the arrival of no fewer than three new NRC fellows: Robert Serber, Edwin Uehling and Frederick W. Brown. This repre-sented nearly half the total number of awards for theoretical physics in the whole United States (three out of seven), showing that, by now, after just five years, Oppenheimer had succeeded in his aim of transforming Berkeley into the leading school of theoretical physics in the country.

Robert Serber, who had taken his Ph.D. at the University of Wis-consin, had originally planned to spend his National Research Fel-lowship at Princeton working with the Hungarian-American physicist Eugene Wigner, but, just like Wendell Furry before him, he decided after attending the Ann Arbor summer school and seeing Oppenheimer in action that Berkeley was the place to be. "When I arrived," he remem-bers, "I discovered that most of the National Research Fellows in theo-retical physics were already there." "The word had gotten around," he said in an interview many years later; "Oppenheimer had the most lively school in theoretical physics in the country then."

One of the Ph.D. students to arrive that year was Willis E. Lamb, the future Nobel laureate and Oxford professor, who, after graduating in chemistry from Berkeley, had decided to pursue doctorate work in physics, and, as he later put it, "naturally I wanted to work with Oppen-heimer." "Oppenheimer's office," Lamb remembers, "was room 219 LeConte Hall."

As were many of his students, I was given a small table in the room. Oppenheimer had no desk, but only a table in the middle of the room, heavily strewn with papers. One wall was entirely covered by a blackboard and hardly ever erased. One set of open shelves had reprints of Oppenheimer's publications. I was allowed to have a copy of most of these.

More details of the way Oppenheimer worked with his students have been given by Serber:

His group would consist of eight or ten graduate students and about a half dozen postdoctoral fellows. He would meet the group once a day in his office. A little before the appointed time its members would straggle in and dispose themselves on the tables and about the walls. Oppie would come in and discuss with one after another the status of the student's research problem, while the others listened and offered comments. All were exposed to a broad range of topics. Oppenheimer was interested in everything, and one subject after another was introduced and coexisted with all the others. In an afternoon we might discuss electrodynamics, cosmic rays, astrophysics and nuclear physics.

Undeterred by the criticisms of colleagues—one of whom likened him to a mother hen fussing over her chickens—Oppenheimer quite deliberately set out to mold his group of graduate students (Ph.D. students as well as NRC fellows) into a *social* as well as an intellectual unit.

The first evening that Edwin Uehling spent with this group very nearly gave him a criminal record. It started at Oppenheimer's apartment, where Uehling and his wife were invited to meet Oppenheimer's other graduate students, including Melba Phillips. Then they had dinner at a Mexican restaurant, where they drank wine and listened to music until after midnight, after which, on the way back to Berkeley, they were chased by the police because they—Oppenheimer in "Garuda" and Uehling in his Buick—were speeding. After a police car collided with Uehling's Buick, Uehling was charged with dangerous driving (later reduced to not observing due caution) and Oppenheimer with speeding, but, much to everyone's relief, the incident was not reported in the press.

Oppenheimer (at that time thirty years old), Serber emphasizes, "was a bachelor then, and a part of his social life intertwined with ours."

Often we worked late and continued the discussion through dinner and then later at his apartment on Shasta Road. When we tired of our problems, or cleaned up the point at issue, the talk would turn to art, music, literature and politics. If the work was going badly we might give up and go to a movie. Sometimes we took a night off and had a Mexican dinner in Oakland or went to a good restaurant in San Francisco. In the early days this meant taking the Berkeley ferry and a ride across the bay. The ferries back to Berkeley didn't run very often late at night, and this required passing the time waiting for them at the bars and night clubs near the ferry dock. Frequently we missed several ferries.

After the Berkeley spring semester ended in April, and it was time for Oppenheimer to leave for Pasadena, Serber recalls: "Many of his students made the annual trek with him."

Some things were easier in those days. We thought nothing of giving up our houses or apartments in Berkeley, confident that we could find a garden cottage in Pasadena for twenty-five dollars a month. We didn't own more than could be packed in the back of a car. In Pasadena, in addition to being exposed to the new information on physics, we led an active social life. The Tolmans were good friends, and we had very warm relations with Charlie Lauritsen and his group . . . We spent many evenings at the Mexican restaurants on Olivera Street and many nights partying in Charlie Lauritsen's garden.

Danish by birth, Lauritsen had been in the United States since 1916, when he emigrated with his wife and small baby, and in Pasadena since 1926. Before he came to Caltech and started an academic career, he had been a radio engineer—a background he put to good use in his work in experimental physics. At Caltech's high-voltage laboratory Lauritsen worked on developing "super-voltage" X-rays for use in medicine. Then, after Cockcroft and Walton succeeded in splitting the atom, Lauritsen, now working at the new Kellogg Radiation Laboratory, converted one of the X-ray tubes into a particle accelerator, and began work on the artificial production of neutrons and the bombardment of deuterium.

In the early summer of 1934, Oppenheimer and Lauritsen wrote a short paper together about the scattering of gamma rays produced by thorium C". It was the only paper they ever wrote together, but they continued to have a great influence on each other's work. Lauritsen, like Lawrence in Berkeley, would look to Oppenheimer to keep him informed about the latest developments in theory, while Oppenheimer kept a close eye on Lauritsen's laboratory work, looking for things that needed explaining and that might provide the subject matter for papers written by himself and his students.

Another avenue for collaborative work opened up in the summer of 1934 with the arrival at Stanford University of Felix Bloch. Bloch was a Jewish physicist from Switzerland, whom Oppenheimer had known and liked in Zurich. After leaving Zurich, Bloch had worked with Bohr in Copenhagen and with Enrico Fermi in Rome before accepting a post as a lecturer at Leipzig. He was driven out of his job by the Nazi regime and, like many others, came to the United States. Along with (to mention only the most prominent) Einstein at Princeton, Hans Bethe at Cornell and James Franck at Johns Hopkins, Bloch thus became part of the extraordinary enrichment of American physics that was brought about through the absorption of Jewish émigrés. Indeed, within a few years the United States had replaced Germany as the world's leading center for the study of physics, partly because many of the people who had made Germany preeminent in the field were now working in American universities. As the relentlessly patriotic Oppenheimer was quick to point out, these refugees would not have had the impact they did had there not been "a rather sturdy indigenous effort in physics," but Oppenheimer, of all people, knew the influence that world-leading physicists could have.

For this reason, no doubt, as well as for the reason that he happened to like and respect him, Oppenheimer helped to find Bloch a position at Stanford, which is about thirty miles south of Berkeley, on the other side of the San Francisco Bay. Every week, after Bloch's arrival in California, there would be a joint seminar open to both his students and Oppenheimer's: one week at Stanford, the next at Berkeley. As Bloch later remembered them: "One of us would go up and tell about something he had thought about and read about, and then there would be discussions. It was very stimulating for me. I did not feel quite as isolated as I would have felt otherwise."

After the seminar, Oppenheimer would treat the entire group (which would vary in size between twelve and twenty people) to dinner at Jack's, his favorite restaurant in San Francisco, "a fish place down in the harbour," as Bloch remembered it. "These were post-depression days," Serber recalls, "and students were poor. The world of good food and good wines and gracious living was far from the experience of many of them, and Oppie was introducing them to an unfamiliar way of life." On one occasion, Serber says, "Bloch grew expansive, and leaned over and picked up the check. He looked at it, blinked, leaned over again and put it back down."

Wendell Furry was no longer at Berkeley, as Oppenheimer had succeeded in finding him a job at Harvard, starting in the autumn of 1934. The series of Oppenheimer-Furry papers therefore came to an end, and Oppenheimer worked instead on a joint paper with Melba Phillips, who since completing her thesis in 1933 had been unable to find a full-time academic post and so had stayed at Berkeley. "There were no jobs," she remembered, "but one could get enough part-time work, part-time teaching, to live; and we stayed and did work, grading papers and so forth. There were several of us who did that. I stayed there for two more years, and it was during that period that I taught practically everything that was thrown my way, filling in for everybody, it felt like."

In the spring of 1935, a promising topic for Oppenheimer and Phillips to work on together was provided by Lawrence's cyclotron experiments. After the debacle of the Solvay Congress at the end of October 1933, Lawrence's work had received fresh impetus in January 1934, with the startling discovery that it was possible to create radioactive materials artificially. The discovery had been made in Paris by Frédéric and Irène Joliot-Curie (the pair combined surnames after their marriage in 1926), who showed that, by bombarding boron with alpha particles, it was possible to create a radioactive isotope of nitrogen, and by bombarding aluminum, radioactive phosphorus was produced. As the medical applications for radioactive materials were by then being explored and the demand for them was therefore increasing, the discovery attracted a great deal of excitement because it promised a cheap and plentiful supply. Laboratories all over Europe and America began to turn their attention to the possibilities opened up by this discovery. In Rome, most notably, Enrico Fermi decided to see what happens when one bombards elements with neutrons rather than alpha particles, and discovered that it was possible to create radioactive materials in that way too.

In the Radiation Laboratory at Berkeley, work was dramatically interrupted by Lawrence on the day he saw the Joliot-Curies' article in *Comptes rendus*. Running through the door waving a copy of the article, Lawrence translated for the benefit of his staff some key sentences, including one that made direct reference to the power of the cyclotron. Noting that their own apparatus was puny by comparison, the Joliot-Curies speculated what might be achievable with something like the cyclotron. For example, they said, nitrogen-13, which should be radioactive, might be produced by bombarding carbon with deuterons—that is, deuterium nuclei, which, because they have only half the atomic mass of alpha particles, should be roughly twice as penetrative. Immediately the cyclotron was set up to fire a beam of deuterons at a sample of carbon and a Geiger counter wired up to record any radioactivity produced. "*Click . . . click . . . click . . .* went the Geiger counter," recalled Milton Livingston. "It was a sound that no one who was there would ever forget."

Throughout 1934, Lawrence's cyclotron was put to use making radioactive materials, many of which had never been seen before. "It was a wonderful time," one of Lawrence's assistants later said. "Radioactive elements fell in our laps as though we were shaking apples off a tree." The *New York Times* ran an editorial on Lawrence, in which it said: "Transmutation [and] the release of atomic energy are no longer mere romantic possibilities." In the wake of this excitement, Lawrence was courted by rival universities even more assiduously than Oppenheimer had been, and to keep him the University of California increased his salary so that he became by far the best-paid scientist there. The Radiation Laboratory was made independent from the physics department, given its own budget and its own director: Lawrence.

Meanwhile, relations between the theoretical physicists and the "Rad Lab" grew ever closer. One of the new generation of physicists appointed to positions in the lab, Ed McMillan, became an accepted member of the Oppenheimer group and often joined them on their trips to San Francisco. Likewise, Oppenheimer and his students became familiar faces in the laboratory. The topic of Oppenheimer's joint paper with Melba Phillips was provided by experiments conducted by Ed McMillan, Lawrence and a postdoctoral student at the Rad Lab called Robert Thornton. What Lawrence, McMillan and Thornton had discovered was that radioactive isotopes could be created by the bombardment of various elements with deuterons with less energy than the prevailing theory predicted.

In their paper, "Note on the Transmutation Function for Deuterons," Oppenheimer and Phillips gave an explanation for this that was quickly accepted—the "Oppenheimer-Phillips process" becoming an accepted part of nuclear physics and finding its way into the textbooks. Together with the Born–Oppenheimer approximation, the Oppenheimer-Phillips process became Oppenheimer's best-known piece of work among students and experimental physicists. The process in question is this: when an element, for example carbon, is bombarded with deuterons, the neutron in the deuteron binds with the carbon atom to form an isotope, in this case carbon-13, while the proton is emitted. The reason this process happens at lower energies than one would expect, Oppenheimer and Phillips explain, is that the deuteron is less stable than the target nucleus and, as it moves toward the target, it does so, so to speak, "neutron-first," so that the neutron is able to overcome the electrostatic barrier that then repels the proton.

In the spring of 1935, Oppenheimer wrote to Lawrence from Pasadena to say that he was sending Melba Phillips "an outline of the calculations & plots I have made for the deuteron transmutation functions." The analysis, he reported, "turned out pretty complicated, & I have spent most of the nights of this week with slide rule & graph paper." The results, he stressed, needed to be checked by Melba very carefully: "You must give M time to work it over." As this suggests, Melba Phillips was a more competent and more careful mathematician than Oppenheimer, and was often turned to when difficult calculations needed to be made. In fact, many of his students were better mathematicians than he was. Willis Lamb remembers: "Oppenheimer's lectures were a revelation. The equations he wrote on the board were not always reliable. We learned to apply correction-factor operators to allow for incorrect signs and numerical coefficients." However, if Oppenheimer benefited from Melba Phillips's mathematical skills, she benefited from his intuitions into the nature of physical phenomena and his reputation. After their joint paper was published in the summer of 1935, she suddenly found jobs coming her way: first a teaching post at Bryn Mawr and then, more prestigiously, a research fellowship at the Institute for Advanced Study in Princeton.

Because of the nature of the experimental work going on at both Berkeley and Pasadena, involving as it did much bombardment of nuclei and many transmutations and disintegrations to explain, Oppenheimer was drawn into the area of nuclear physics, where his contributions, such as his joint paper with Melba Phillips, were accepted readily and warmly applauded. However, it was not where his heart was. "I never found nuclear physics so beautiful," he was once quoted as saying. He much preferred to think about electrodynamics and field theory. He never spelled out why this was, but his interest in Hinduism and the remarks by Rabi quoted earlier perhaps provide a clue: he preferred to think about what *connected* things than what disintegrated them. Dirac's relativistic quantum electrodynamics excited him because it promised to bring together relativity theory and quantum theory. His disappointment with it, I suspect, was not fundamentally to do with the troublesome infinities, but rather had to do with the fact that, in its talk of particles, anti-particles and "holes," it presented a vision of discrete and separate things, rather than one of the interconnectedness of everything.

Oppenheimer wrote little on quantum electrodynamics after 1935, but he kept up with the literature on it and his students continued to work on it and, in some cases, make important contributions to it. One suspects that his disengagement from it—as well as having to do with his interest in other rapidly developing areas, such as cosmic-ray research and nuclear physics—had something to do, like his initial engagement with it, with his relations with Paul Dirac.

Dirac spent the year 1934–5 at the Institute for Advanced Study in Princeton, where he worked on the second edition of his classic text, *The Principles of Quantum Mechanics*. Remarkably, Dirac, then thirty-two years old, found love in Princeton, when he met Eugene Wigner's sister, Margit, whom he married in 1937. Even after their marriage, according to the many Dirac stories that circulate among physicists, he was in the habit of introducing her as "Wigner's sister" rather than as "my wife, Margit." Oppenheimer visited Princeton in the new year of 1935, but Dirac was away. He did, however, see Einstein and visit the Institute for Advanced Study, but, as he wrote to Frank, his impressions were not favorable: "Princeton is a madhouse: its solipsistic luminaries shining in separate & helpless desolation. Einstein is completely cuckoo; Dirac was still in Georgia. I could be of absolutely no use at such a place, but it took a lot of conversation & arm waving to get Weyl[36] to take a *no*."

It would evidently take something more connected to the real world than the Institute for Advanced Study to tempt Oppenheimer away from the school of physics that he had so successfully built up.

---

[36] The great German mathematician Hermann Weyl had been at the institute in Princeton since 1933.

9

Unstable Cores

Until the summer of 1935, the longest, most intimate, most revealing letters that Oppenheimer wrote were to his brother, Frank. In that summer, however, the series of letters came to a temporary end when Frank moved to California. He did so to begin a Ph.D. at Caltech with Charles Lauritsen ("Charlie" to both Oppenheimers and to most people who knew him). Frank was then twenty-three years old. Since graduating from Johns Hopkins two years earlier, he had spent about eighteen months at the Cavendish in Cambridge and another six months at the University of Florence. He had also spent some time in Germany. Though he always felt himself to be under the shadow of his accomplished older brother, there was one respect in which, by the time he returned to the U.S., he had succeeded where Robert had failed: he had mastered the skills needed for laboratory work and to become an experimental physicist.

Another way in which Frank differed from his brother was that, throughout his school and university education, he had taken an active interest in politics. From the first, his political sympathies were with the downtrodden. "I remember once," he laughingly said in an interview, recalling an incident during his school days, "I went with some friends to hear a concert at Carnegie Hall that didn't have a conductor. It was a kind of 'down with the bosses' movement." In the 1928 presidential election, Frank, while still at school, had taken part in the campaign to elect the Democratic Party candidate, Al Smith, who famously aroused the fierce and frightening antagonism of the Ku Klux Klan, both for his liberal politics and for being a Roman Catholic. The campaign was unsuccessful—Smith was beaten by Herbert Hoover—but it provided a focus for liberal politics in the U.S. that paved the way for Franklin D. Roosevelt's victory in 1932 and the "New Deal" that followed.

In the light of what was to occur in the 1950s, one interesting aspect of the 1928 Smith campaign was the candidate's use of the word "un-American" to characterize not those on the left of American politics, but those on the right. When he arrived in Oklahoma City to be greeted by the Ku Klux Klan burning crosses, Smith said: "To inject bigotry, hatred, intolerance and un-American sectarian division into a campaign. Nothing could be so out of line with the spirit of America. Nothing could be so foreign to the teachings of Jefferson. Nothing could be so contradictory of our whole history." He went on: "The best way to kill anything un-American is to drag it out into the open, because anything un-American cannot live in the sunlight."

Frank Oppenheimer's approach to politics is perfectly captured in these quotations. As he drifted further and further to the left, he did so quite openly, feeling that he had nothing to hide, and feeling also that not only was there nothing unpatriotic about left-wing politics, but indeed such politics were perfectly in keeping with the spirit and the history of America. If you were brought up, as Frank and Robert Oppenheimer were, to believe that America was the embodiment of the tolerance, freedom and egalitarianism that the German Jews of the nineteenth century had left their homeland to find, then it would have been—and was—utterly alien to think of its spirit as being represented and defended by such people as the Ku Klux Klan or, later, the paranoid anti-communists of the McCarthy period. It was, as Al Smith had said, the bigotry of those people, not the targets of their bigotry, that was "un-American."

"When I went to Hopkins," Frank continued in the interview quoted above, "I knew quite a few people . . . I didn't know whether they were party members or not, but they were interested in left-wing politics, and I learned about it." In England, he was "a little more on the fringe" of radical politics, but in Italy "there were people there of varying degrees of leftness," including Patrick Blackett's coworker on the discovery of the positron, Giuseppe Occhialini, who by then had returned to the University of Florence and was, according to Frank, "quite left." Mussolini's Italy, which had been a Fascist state for many years, had, during Frank's time there, just embarked on its aggressive foreign policy: "It was the year before the Abyssinian War. There was a brigade of soldiers just below the lab there, who were always singing and cheering."

The singing and cheering of the Italian soldiers, though a constant reminder of the nature of the military dictatorship that ruled the country, was not felt by Frank to be especially menacing. "In Italy," Frank remembers, "the soldiers didn't seem especially aggressive. I never saw any of them marching. The policemen weren't any different, and were probably gentler, than New York policemen. The towns seemed very relaxed to me." In Germany the previous year, however: "I had seen people marching down the streets, and really sort of lots of this behavior in the bars, and the whole society seemed corrupt. And then I had some relatives there who could tell me some of the terrible things." Having mixed with left-wing people at Johns Hopkins, the Cavendish and the University of Florence, and having seen for himself the viciousness of the Nazi regime in Germany, it was only natural that, when he went to California, Frank should choose as his friends people concerned about the threat of fascism and interested in improving the lot of the poor and the dispossessed.

In fact, Frank already knew a number of such people, namely some of his brother's students, among whom were a few who would later achieve fame because their politics offended the American right. One of these was the unassuming Wendell Furry, who had left for Harvard in 1934. At Harvard, Furry joined the Communist Party and therefore became a target for McCarthyites in the 1950s. Furry won the admiration of many by refusing either to take cover behind the Fifth Amendment or to name any of his comrades in the Party. Likewise, Harvard won admiration for refusing to sack Furry. The case left deep scars, however. In a book called *Moscow Stories*, published in 2006, the writer and expert in Russian affairs Loren R. Graham describes how, coming himself from Farmersburg, the same small town in Indiana in which Furry had grown up, he became fascinated by Furry's story. As a small child, he had been told by his schoolteacher that he was the cleverest boy she had ever taught, with one exception: Wendell Furry. And yet, she said, she was ashamed of Furry and hoped that Graham did not end up like him. "How *did* he end up?" Graham asked. "He is a communist," came the reply. That was in 1941. Many years later, in 1974, Graham met Furry and they swapped stories about Farmersburg. A short while after that meeting Furry retired and a few years later he died. "In the last months of his life," according to Graham:

> after the death of his wife Betty from cancer, the old physicist was confined to a nursing home near Fresh Pond in Cambridge, where he had nightmares about the persecution he and his family endured years earlier. In the night, to the stupefaction of the attendants, he would cry out, "The FBI, the FBI, they are after me! Call the American Civil Liberties Union and Gerald Berlin [Furry's lawyer]!"

Melba Phillips came from a remarkably similar background to Wendell Furry. She, too, was raised by a Methodist family in a small town in a farming community in Indiana, in a place called Hazleton, just fifty or sixty miles south of Farmersburg. And she, too, became politically radical, though it is not clear whether she ever became a member of the Communist Party. When, in the McCarthy period, she was summoned to answer questions about her political activities in the 1930s, she refused to say whether or not she had ever been a member of the Party, pleading the Fifth Amendment. For this, she was sacked from her position at Brooklyn College.

There is no documentary record of Frank Oppenheimer ever meeting Wendell Furry, but, given how much time Furry spent with Robert Oppenheimer between 1932 and 1934, it would be surprising if they had never come across each other. Certainly, Frank knew Melba Phillips very well indeed, and the two of them became close friends and remained so until Frank's death. Her memories of Frank are particularly warm. She met him first, she remembers, at Perro Caliente in the summer of 1932, "when I stopped for a few days on the way back to school from a visit to my family in Indiana."

> As I got off the train at Glorietta Pass there they were—Robert, whom I knew from Berkeley, Frank, and Roger Lewis, who was the Damon to Frank's Pythias or vice versa. Frank was turning 20 that summer; I was five years older and working on a Ph.D. The back of the car was already loaded with supplies for the ranch, but we crowded in, drove up to Cowles in relative comfort, thence up the dirt road to the cabin . . .
>
> Perro Caliente, our destination, had many visitors over the years . . . We ate, and later slept, on the porch, looking toward the mountains across the valley, but the evenings were cold even in August. After dinner there was a roaring fire in the big living room, good talk, and Frank playing the flute. I have a vivid memory of Frank playing . . . He usually played in the evening, at least during my first visit there.

"We were not political in any overt way," Melba said of herself, Oppenheimer and her fellow students, but, her biographer writes, "the grim news from Germany in 1933–4, and the labor unrest that hit California during the Great Depression, motivated them to take an active interest in world affairs."

As we have seen, in the year 1933–4 there is little in Oppenheimer's correspondence or anywhere else to indicate the "active interest" in politics described here, but, coinciding with the arrival of Robert Serber and his wife, Charlotte, in the summer of 1934, there is at least *some* indication of such interest. In Serber's autobiography there is an intriguing account of a rally in support of the longshoremen's strike in 1934, which Oppenheimer was invited to attend. He, in turn, invited Serber, Charlotte and Melba Phillips to come along. As Serber remembers it: "We were sitting up high in a balcony, and by the end we were caught up in the enthusiasm of the strikers, shouting with them, 'Strike! Strike! Strike!'"

This makes it sound as if the rally they attended was being held to decide upon strike action, but this cannot be right, since the strike (which was a major event in the history of both unionization and the Communist Party in America) had begun in May 1934, before Serber met Oppenheimer. More likely, it was one of the meetings held in July 1934, when the longshoremen's strike escalated into a general strike, after two strikers had been killed by police firing into a crowd of pickets. The general strike ended soon afterward, but the result was an increase in the power of the longshoremen's union and an improvement in their terms of employment—victories that the Communist Party would claim for itself.

At the time of Frank's arrival at Caltech, Robert Serber had been a National Research Fellow at Berkeley for a year and had become the person closest to Oppenheimer, both personally and scientifically, and would remain so until his departure in 1938. Though Serber was, like Oppenheimer himself, more interested in physics than politics, he had grown up in an environment of which political engagement was an accepted and expected part. He and his wife both came from fairly well-off Jewish families in Philadelphia. His father was a lawyer active in the local Democratic Party, while Charlotte's father, a doctor, was a well-known leftist radical. In the 1940s, both Robert and Charlotte Serber would receive close attention from the FBI, though their agents could never gather enough incriminating evidence against Robert to justify taking any action against him. This almost certainly means that Robert Serber never joined the Communist Party. When the question was put directly to him in the 1940s, however, Oppenheimer expressed the belief that Charlotte probably was a member.

Almost certainly, the first contact that either of the Oppenheimer brothers had with someone happy to call themselves a communist was when, in the spring of 1936, halfway through Frank's first year at Caltech, they met a twenty-four-year-old graduate student of economics at Berkeley called Jacquenette Quann. "Jackie" (as everyone called her) was a working-class French-Canadian woman, who worked as a waitress and babysitter to pay her way through university. While an undergraduate, she had joined the Young Communist League, attracted to it not through any intellectual commitment to Marxism-Leninism, but rather through its involvement with practical issues, such as the rights of workers and the threat of fascism, about which she was concerned. She came into the Oppenheimers' lives quite by accident one evening when she was babysitting for Wenonah Nedelsky, the estranged wife of Oppenheimer's student Leo Nedelsky. Robert, accompanied by Frank, went to visit Wenonah and the two of them met Jackie, whose plain-speaking exuberance quickly won Frank over. Within a short time he and Jackie were lovers, and that summer he invited her to Perro Caliente. On September 15, 1936, they were married.

Oppenheimer did not approve of his younger brother's rush into matrimony. "He tried to put us off from getting married," Jackie later said. "He was always saying things like 'Of course, you're much older than Frank'—I'm eight months older actually—and saying that Frank wasn't ready for it. Later he used to refer to me as 'the waitress my brother has married.'" In a formal statement he wrote at the time of his security hearing in 1954, Oppenheimer wrote tersely: "My brother Frank married in 1936. Our relations thereafter were inevitably less intimate than before." Under cross-examination, he elaborated on this a little, adding that not only were relations between him and Frank less intimate after Frank's marriage, but they were also "occasionally perhaps somewhat more strained." More expansive is a statement quoted by Peter Michelmore in his 1969 book, *The Swift Years: The Robert Oppenheimer Story*, the source of which Michelmore does not give. Frank's "defection," Michelmore writes, "hurt Robert deeply, for he wrote petulantly of his brother's marriage, 'It was an act of emancipation and rebellion on his part against his dependence on me. Our early intimacy was never again established.'"

Apart from his evident anxiety at losing the most intimate, most important relationship he had, another worry Robert had about Jackie's influence on Frank was that it was bad for his physics. Frank, Robert later said, "worked fairly well at physics but he was slow. It took him a long time to get his doctor's degree. He was very much distracted by his other interests." It is sometimes assumed that something similar happened to Robert Oppenheimer—that after he began to take an interest in politics his work in physics lost some of its earlier intensity. In fact, the opposite is true: the very best physics he ever wrote was produced precisely during the period of his political awakening.

During the period 1935–8—while he was in his early thirties—the focus of that work was provided by Oppenheimer's continued interest in cosmic rays. During the 1930s, there were two reasons for a physicist to be interested in cosmic rays: first, they were an interesting and puzzling phenomenon in their own right, presenting physicists with the challenge of saying what they were made of and how they originated; and second, their tremendous energy allowed physicists their only opportunity (until the advent of particle accelerators many times more powerful than Lawrence's early cyclotrons) of seeing whether physical theories, such as quantum electrodynamics, successfully held up when used to measure and predict the behavior of particles traveling at something approaching the speed of light, which is when relativistic effects become relevant.

For these reasons, the study of cosmic rays became the focus in the 1930s for some of the most interesting experimental physics and some of the leading theoretical work; the experimentalists would take off on adventurous expeditions to far-flung corners of the world to measure radiations at high altitudes, and the theorists would use the information thus obtained to test the validity of theories and to inspire new insights into the makeup of the physical world, which with every step forward seemed to be more complicated and stranger than anybody had imagined.

Oppenheimer was well placed to contribute to this work, since some of the most important observations of cosmic rays were being undertaken by two experimentalists at Caltech: Carl Anderson, the discoverer of the positron, and his colleague Seth Neddermeyer. In a paper he published at the end of 1934 entitled "Are the Formulae for the Absorption of High Energy Radiations Valid?," Oppenheimer paid tribute to the work of these two in a footnote that read: "Such clarity as there is in this account of the experimental situation I owe entirely to Dr. Anderson and Mr. Neddermeyer, who have with great patience explained to me just what the evidence is, what it indicates, and how little it proves."

At the beginning of that paper Oppenheimer notes that the observations of cosmic rays made by Anderson and Neddermeyer have "made it possible to extend our knowledge of the specific ionization and energy loss of electrons from particles of a few million volts on up to a few billion." Despite the progress made at Berkeley by Lawrence's Radiation Laboratory, it would be some time before that kind of energy could be created artificially. With regard to what those observations of such extraordinary energies reveal about the accepted formulae for calculating high-energy radiation, Oppenheimer remarks that it is "possible to do justice to the great penetration of the cosmic rays only by admitting that the formulae are wrong, or by postulating some other and less absorbable component of the rays to account for their penetration." It is a dichotomy reminiscent of that which Oppenheimer had earlier posed in relation to positively charged electrons: either Dirac's theory of the electron was wrong, or such particles had to exist. And just as in this earlier case, Oppenheimer missed out on an important advance in physical theory by choosing the wrong side of the dichotomy, saying that the theory was wrong, rather than insisting that this "less absorbable component" of cosmic rays had to exist. For, as would be revealed in the ensuing years, this "less absorbable component" was yet another new particle.

During 1935, Oppenheimer's intellectual energies, as we have seen, were directed toward the questions that arose from the artificial creation of radioactive isotopes, questions that gave rise to the paper he and Melba Phillips wrote in the summer of 1935, which introduced the "Oppenheimer-Phillips process." In turning from the analysis of what happens when a deuteron splits into a proton and a neutron to the consideration of cosmic rays, Oppenheimer may have thought that he was, temporarily at least, leaving nuclear physics behind. However, nuclear physics and cosmic-ray physics were about to come together in an unexpected way. In the early part of 1935, an article appeared in an obscure journal that remained completely unknown to people researching cosmic rays and would not have seemed relevant to their research even if they had known of it. Nevertheless, that article was to play a major role in the subsequent development of cosmic-ray physics, to provide a theory that is still accepted today in fundamental nuclear physics, and to change the subsequent course of particle physics.

The article in question was entitled "On the Interaction of Elementary Particles I" and appeared in the *Proceedings of the Physical and Mathematical Society of Japan*, which had received it at the end of November 1934. Its author was a Japanese theoretical physicist called Hideki Yukawa, who had come up with a novel theory to answer a fundamental question in nuclear physics: what holds the particles in a nucleus—the protons and the neutrons—together? Clearly, protons and neutrons are not held together by electrostatic forces, since neutrons do not have any charge. Nor can they be held together by gravity, as the gravitational force is very many orders of magnitude too weak to account for the binding energies observed. Yukawa put forward the bold suggestion that there is a hitherto-unknown basic physical force—now known as the "strong nuclear force"—that exerts a pull between the protons and the neutrons in the nucleus. He further hypothesized that there must be a hitherto-unknown particle, which would have a mass somewhere between an electron and a proton, that would carry the force, in much the same way that, in quantum electrodynamics, electromagnetism is carried by the photon. Yukawa even speculated that this new particle "may also have some bearing on the shower produced by cosmic rays." American university libraries did not, as a rule, subscribe to *Proceedings of the Physical and Mathematical Society of Japan*, but Yukawa sent Oppenheimer a copy of it. For about eighteen months after its publication Oppenheimer might well have been the only English-speaking scientist to have read it.

As it turned out, cosmic-ray research would indeed confirm Yukawa's hypothesis of a particle bigger than an electron but smaller than a proton, and, thus confirmed, that hypothesis would in turn provide the solution to the puzzle about the penetrative power of cosmic rays that had prompted Oppenheimer to talk about their having a "less absorbable component." However, as would become gradually clear (it took about twelve years, beginning in 1935) amid much confusion and controversy, the penetrative particle in cosmic rays is *not* the carrier of the "strong nuclear force"—*that* is another particle somewhat like it. How confused the initial picture of these particles was can be gleaned from their changing nomenclature: to begin with, before it was realized they were different, they were called "mesotrons," which was changed to "mesons" for reasons of linguistic probity (the Greek word for "middle" being "*mesos*" rather than "*mesotros*"); then, to distinguish them from each other, the one that is a component of cosmic rays was called a "μ-meson" (mu-meson), and the one that is the carrier of the strong nuclear force was called the "π-meson" (pi-meson). Then it was decided that mesons are by definition carriers of the strong nuclear force and therefore that the mu-meson is not a meson at all. It was accordingly renamed the "muon," while the other was renamed the "pion." Playing a leading role in both the creation and the clearing up of these confusions, and thus being there at the birth of what has grown into the (for most people) utterly bewildering new discipline of particle physics, were Oppenheimer and his students.

Much of the key observational evidence of cosmic rays that led to the discovery of the "mesotron" was collected by Anderson and Neddermeyer at the summit of Pikes Peak in the Rocky Mountains, where they went in the summer of 1935. There, at an altitude of about 14,000 feet, they set up the equipment they had brought with them and took thousands of photographs of extremely high-energy cosmic-ray collisions. Without knowing anything about Yukawa's article, Anderson wrote to Millikan at Caltech from the top of Pikes Peak to say he thought he had evidence of a particle intermediate in mass between electrons and protons. He was a cautious man, however, and did not want to publish this result until he was completely sure of it. It was therefore not until the summer of 1936 that Anderson and Neddermeyer published a scholarly account of their trip to Pikes Peak in the *Physical Review*. Entitled "Cloud Chamber Observations of Cosmic Rays at 4,300 Meters and Near Sea Level," their article reproduced some of their more dramatic photographs, taken both at Pikes Peak and in Pasadena, and in a very modest and hesitant way tried to make sense of them. Without actually declaring that they had found a new particle, they gave good reasons why the penetrative particle they had photographed could not be either a proton or an electron. They also made the important announcement that their observations refuted something that had been widely believed by physicists, namely that the theory of quantum electrodynamics broke down when applied to particles of extremely high energy. They had observed particles at more than one billion volts, they recorded, and the theory had stood up very well.

It was this last aspect of the article that most interested Oppenheimer. He had been saying for years that the theory broke down at high energies, but he did not seem to mind being proved wrong on that account. On the contrary, he seemed delighted with the findings reported by Anderson and Neddermeyer, not least because they allowed him to pick a theoretical fight with Heisenberg, a fight he felt confident of winning. Heisenberg had recently been drawn into the analysis of cosmic rays, thinking that he had a new insight that would shed light on their nature. The insight in question was one derived from recent work published by Enrico Fermi on the subject of beta decay. Taking up the issue that had prompted Pauli to suggest the neutrino (a name conferred on the as-yet-undiscovered particle by Fermi), Fermi had proposed a completely new analysis of beta radiation that bore a striking analogy to Yukawa's new analysis of nuclear forces. The analogy was no accident; Fermi's theory was published at the beginning of 1934, about ten months before Yukawa's, and was one of the main inspirations for Yukawa's theory. Like Yukawa, what Fermi proposed was the introduction of a new basic force into physics—what is now called the "weak nuclear force"—to explain beta emissions. This new force would act upon electrons, neutrinos and nucleons (protons and neutrons) and would explain the process whereby a neutron decays into a proton, emitting as it does so beta radiation (electrons) and neutrinos.

In a paper that he published in June 1936, Heisenberg suggested that this new force field postulated by Fermi held the key to understanding cosmic rays. In particular, he believed that the phenomenon that had earlier attracted the attention of Oppenheimer—the "showers" of electron/positron production—might be explained by Fermi's new field. At the root of Heisenberg's analysis was the belief that the accepted theory of quantum electrodynamics broke down at the extremely high energies observed in cosmic radiation. As Anderson and Neddermeyer had shown this belief to be false, the motivation for Heisenberg's theory had disappeared. This was pointed out in a confrontational manner by Oppenheimer in a paper called "On Multiplicative Showers," which he cowrote with Frank Carlson (for whom he had not yet managed to find an academic position and who therefore remained at Berkeley and Caltech), and sent to the *Physical Review* at the end of 1936. "It would seem," declared Oppenheimer and Carlson, that Heisenberg's theory "is without cogent experimental foundation; and we believe that in fact it rests on an abusive extension of the formalism of the theory of the electron neutrino field."

Oppenheimer and Carlson ended their paper with the suggestion that the observations of Anderson and Neddermeyer pointed to "another cosmic ray component" that would explain the showers that seem unlikely to have been made by electrons or protons. In this, of course, they were simply echoing what Anderson and Neddermeyer had said. The latter pair had been convinced that they had evidence of a new particle ever since they went to Pikes Peak in the summer of 1935, and in May 1937 they finally committed themselves in print to the claim that their observations showed "the presence of some particles less massive than protons but more penetrating than electrons." Their caution, however, proved costly, in that, in the same volume of the *Physical Review* that their article was published, there appeared a short report of experiments conducted by two physicists at Harvard, J. C. Street and E. C. Stevenson, which seemed to establish the existence of exactly the same new particle. It is therefore not uncommon, much to Anderson's later chagrin, for it to be said and written that the particle was discovered by Street and Stevenson.

In a letter to the editor of the *Physical Review*, dated June 1, 1937, and published under the heading "Note on the Nature of Cosmic-Ray Particles," Oppenheimer and Serber drew attention to the fact that Yukawa had seemingly predicted this new particle. Many years later, Serber noted proudly that this was the first time anyone had referred to Yukawa's paper and that "a very conscious purpose of our paper was to call attention to Yukawa's idea." This was not their only purpose, however. Their paper was also, though it did not mention Heisenberg by name, part of Oppenheimer's ongoing campaign against Heisenberg, drawing attention as it did to Yukawa's suggestion that "the possibility of exchanging such particles of intermediate mass would offer a more natural explanation of the range and magnitude of the exchange forces between proton and neutron than the Fermi theory of the electron-neutrino field."

In the same issue of the *Physical Review* appeared an article that Oppenheimer and Serber had written a little earlier, in March 1937, together with Lothar Nordheim and his wife, Gertrude. Lothar Nordheim was a German physicist, who, because he was Jewish, had had to leave his position in Göttingen. Through the Emergency Committee for Displaced Scholars, he had been given a visiting professorship at Purdue University in Indiana. Nordheim was considered an expert on Fermi's theory of beta decay, so his appearance in the United States provided Oppenheimer with a good opportunity to publish an authoritative refutation of Heisenberg's use of that theory, which is what their joint paper, called "The Disintegration of High-Energy Protons," amounts to. The argument the four authors outline is that, when Fermi's theory is brought to bear on observations of the disintegration of protons (by this time it was known that protons were the main component of cosmic rays), it completely fails to explain the phenomenon of cosmic-ray showers. "The point of view adopted by Heisenberg in his theory of showers," Oppenheimer and his fellow authors write, is to regard as valid "just those implications of present theory which would at first seem most subject to suspicion." In the light of their analysis, they conclude bluntly, Heisenberg's theory "no longer affords any explanation of showers."

Immediately before the publication of these new discoveries and these attacks on his theory, Heisenberg was, as he wrote to Pauli on April 26, 1937, "optimistic concerning the discovery of Fermi processes in cosmic radiation." Three days later, Heisenberg, still professor of physics at Leipzig, got married. After his honeymoon he was due to take up a new, more prestigious appointment in Munich, as Arnold Sommerfeld's successor. His appointment to this coveted position, however, was delayed by the maneuvering of hard-line Nazis, distrustful of the "white Jew" that they accused Heisenberg of being. Heisenberg wanted to travel, but it was not until the spring of 1938 that he was allowed to leave Germany to visit Britain, from where, he wrote to his wife that "it is important to me now to lose myself entirely in physics." At both Cambridge and Manchester he spent many hours discussing cosmic rays and the new Yukawa particle with people who knew what they were talking about, such as Patrick Blackett. From what he learned from these discussions, Heisenberg was able to marshal new arguments for his view on cosmic radiation. Or at least part of that view. He gave up (because it had been effectively destroyed) the claim that Fermi's theory could explain cosmic-ray showers, but retained the view that had motivated that claim, namely that quantum-electrodynamic theory ceased to be valid above a certain energy, and that the showers associated with the newly discovered particle were proof of that fact.

In May 1938, Heisenberg wrote a paper called "The Limits of Applicability of the Present Quantum Theory," which he sent to Bohr in Copenhagen and delivered as a lecture to several audiences made up of those German physicists who had chosen to stay in Hitler's Germany. In the early summer of 1939, Heisenberg was again allowed to leave Germany and this time went to the United States, where he spent a month visiting old colleagues and friends at various American universities. The highlight of his visit was a symposium on cosmic rays at Chicago, where a dispirited Heisenberg listened as one paper after another poured scorn on his latest theory. Most scornful of all was Oppenheimer. "According to Heisenberg's recollection of the meeting," writes David Cassidy in his biography of Heisenberg, "the animated discussion following his session soon degenerated into a shouting match between himself and J. Robert Oppenheimer." At the beginning of August, Heisenberg set off to return to Germany. Scarcely more than a month later, his country would be at war with Britain.

It was clearly very important to Oppenheimer to win his argument with Heisenberg and one senses that, for him at least, there was more at stake than the cogency or otherwise of certain views about the nature of cosmic-ray showers. It was important to him not only to win that argument, but also to *defeat* Heisenberg. Winning the argument would be a triumph of American science over German science, striking a blow against the Nazi regime, whose ridiculous views about the dangers of "Jewish science" and the superiority of "*deutsche Physik*" Heisenberg now represented, not because those were his views but because, as a patriotic German, he had decided to work for the Nazis rather than leave the country.

What Oppenheimer later called his "smouldering fury about the treatment of Jews in Germany" had served to awaken in him a sense of comradeship with the German Jews in general and, in particular, with his own family. After his father died on September 20, 1937, Oppenheimer arranged for Julius's youngest sister, Hedwig Stern, together with her son, Alfred, and his family to emigrate to the United States. Hedwig had originally planned to live in New York, but Oppenheimer persuaded her and her family to settle instead in Berkeley. She lived there for the rest of her life and remained very fond of her nephew. When she died in 1966, Alfred wrote to Oppenheimer to say that she had led a full and active life and that: "Your closeness has made it richer still."

Alfred has recalled a significant and revealing conversation he had with Oppenheimer soon after he and his mother arrived in the United States. When, he remembered, he asked Oppenheimer how they would fare in America and what America was really like, Oppenheimer replied:

It is big here, not just geographically, but in thinking and spirit. You can move with ease from place to place and among people of all social rank and economic standing. And all people have the possibility to a high degree of influencing their destiny because they have the democratic means. There is a direction for the people and for the country, but this is re-evaluated all the time. You have seen atrocities in Europe and you wonder, can it happen here? I would reply that there is a lack of coercion here, a depressurizing safety valve built into the very nature of a democracy like America's. Totalitarianism is far less likely here than in Europe.

These comments were made at the very time, toward the end of 1937, that Oppenheimer was undergoing a political awakening, which would later lead him to face charges of being "un-American."

Anger at the Nazi persecution of the Jews and a feeling of identity with that Jewish community were important factors in Oppenheimer's shift in the 1930s from someone who demanded to know "what has politics to do with truth, goodness and beauty?" to someone deeply and actively committed to radical politics. But there were other factors compelling him in that direction. He himself mentioned the importance of seeing "what the depression was doing to my students." That is, they could not get jobs, or the jobs they could get were inadequate, which made Oppenheimer, who had taken such a conspicuous lack of interest in the stock-market crash of 1929, begin, as he put it, "to understand how deeply political and economic events could affect men's lives." When, after his father's death, he came into his inheritance, he made a will leaving his money to Berkeley to provide fellowships for graduate students.

Another important factor in his involvement with left-wing groups, again emphasized by Oppenheimer himself, was his need for *comradeship*. "I began," he said, "to feel the need to participate more fully in the life of the community." When he started to join with others to pursue political goals, he felt something he often longed for, but very rarely achieved: a sense of *belonging*: "I liked the new sense of companionship, and at the time felt that I was coming to be part of the life of my time and country." Robert Serber's account of what seems to have been Oppenheimer's very first act of engagement with the political tumult of the 1930s—his participation in the rally in support of the longshoremen's strike in 1934, which ended with the improbable image of Oppenheimer shouting "Strike! Strike! Strike!" along with the crowd—seems to bear this out.

"The matter which most engaged my sympathies and interests," Oppenheimer wrote, "was the war in Spain."

This was not a matter of understanding and informed convictions. I had never been to Spain: I knew a little of its literature; I knew nothing of its history or politics or contemporary problems. But like a great many other Americans I was emotionally committed to the Loyalist cause. I contributed to various organizations for Spanish relief. I went to, and helped with, many parties, bazaars, and the like. Even when the war in Spain was manifestly lost, these activities continued. The end of the war and the defeat of the Loyalists caused me great sorrow.

The Spanish Civil War began on July 17, 1936, when a group of generals led by the fascist General Franco, and supported by various conservative and nationalist groups, attempted to remove by force the elected leftist government. It ended in April 1939 with a victory for the fascists. As soon as the war broke out, it became a cause célèbre among left-leaning people, especially those in Britain and the United States, who saw it as the front line in the battle between fascism and democracy. The governments of the democratic countries, however, were prepared to do little to help the Loyalist cause, leaving the Soviet Union as the one country prepared to help.

This state of affairs meant that the international effort to support the Loyalist government and oppose the spread of fascism was led by the international Communist Party, which thus seized the opportunity to increase its influence. So dominant was the Communist Party in the various campaigns and projects designed to provide help to the Loyalists that it was more or less impossible to contribute to those campaigns and projects without coming into contact with, and working alongside, communists. More than 3,000 U.S. citizens went to Spain to serve the Loyalist cause, some as soldiers (two entire battalions, with the patriotic names Abraham Lincoln and George Washington, were made up of volunteers from America), others as doctors, nurses, ambulance drivers, and so on. Not all of them were communists by any means, but simply to get to Spain they would all have had to work with communists, since it was the Communist Party that was organizing the operation: arranging boats to Spain, trains across the country and helping to place the volunteers where they might be of most help to the cause.

There is some question about whether—and, if so, in what sense— Oppenheimer ever became a member of the Communist Party, but there is no question that he became what is known as a "fellow traveler." The first sign of his being interested in communism (rather than merely supportive of left-wing causes such as the longshoremen's strike in 1934) occurred in the summer of 1936, when he astonished a friend by claiming to have read all three volumes of Marx's *Das Kapital* on the train from Berkeley to New York. At around the same time he claimed to have bought and read the complete works of Lenin. There is little in his recorded conversations, his writings or his correspondence to suggest a detailed familiarity with Marx's *Kapital* and the complete works of Lenin, so perhaps one should treat these claims with some skepticism, but the mere fact that he made them suggests a fairly radical break with the past.

It also provides some justification for his often quoted remark "Beginning in late 1936, my interests began to change," a remark that has frequently misled people into thinking that there was a shift in his interests *away* from physics. As we have seen, this was very far from the case. Another mistake that is often made is to think that Oppenheimer was referring here to one particular event that happened in 1936, namely his meeting and falling in love with Jean Tatlock.

In 1936, Jean Tatlock was twenty-two years old and a medical student at Stanford, hoping to become a psychiatrist. She is remembered by those who knew her at this time as slim, beautiful and intense. Her father was John Tatlock, a professor of English literature at Berkeley and widely recognized as one of the world's leading experts on the work of Geoffrey Chaucer. Jean had grown up in Cambridge, Massachusetts, because her father was at Harvard before switching to Berkeley. While studying English literature at Vassar, she took a year off to take pre-med courses at Berkeley, and then in 1935 began her medical studies at Stanford. During her year at Berkeley (1933–4), she had joined the Communist Party and wrote regularly for its newspaper, the *Western Worker*. She was not, however, ideologically committed to communism. Indeed, ideologically she was, from a communist point of view, hopelessly bourgeois, being far more interested in—and, one suspects, knowledgeable about—the works of Freud and Jung than those of Marx.

Oppenheimer met Jean Tatlock at a fund-raising party for the Spanish Loyalist cause hosted by his landlady, Mary Ellen Washburn, who was later described by the FBI as an "active member of the Communist Party." This meeting, according to Oppenheimer, took place in "the spring of 1936," but, as the Spanish Civil War did not break out until July of that year, it seems more plausible to assume it occurred some time soon after that. In any case, by the autumn of 1936 he and Jean were dating. Though there was a considerable age gap (he had turned thirty-two in 1936, and so was ten years older than her), he was, by all accounts, completely in love with her.

Her role in "radicalizing" him, however, seems to have been overplayed. It is true that she was a member of the Communist Party and, as such, deeper into radical activism than he was. But on the other hand, her membership of the Party, probably because of her commitment to

Freudian psychoanalysis, was, as Oppenheimer put it, an "on again, off again" affair. Communism, Oppenheimer wrote, "never seemed to provide for her what she was seeking. I do not believe that her interests were really political." Though he and Jean were both drawn into, and sympathetic toward, the leftist political currents that converged on the efforts to support the Loyalists in Spain, it was, one suspects, far more important to them and their intimacy that they had in common both a deep love of literature and a fervent interest in psychiatry.

It was primarily with others that Oppenheimer would develop his interest in left-wing politics. With Jean, he shared a love of, for example, the poetry of John Donne (a particular favorite of hers) and an exploration of the depths of the human soul, which the theories of Freud and Jung promised to shed light upon. When Oppenheimer said that he did not believe Jean's interests were really political, and that communism could not provide what she was seeking, what he seemed to have in mind was the evident fact that Jean's problems were fundamentally psychological.

As the daughter of a Harvard and later a Berkeley professor, Jean knew how to behave in the company of sophisticated and intellectual people. She was, as Robert Serber noted, "quite composed in any social gathering." In this respect she differed from, for example, Frank's wife, Jackie, who neither knew nor cared how one should behave in the "social gatherings" that the Oppenheimers were accustomed to attend. And yet, whereas Jackie was robustly defiant about the way she was, Jean was plagued by self-doubts. Serber remembers that she had "these terrible depressions," which would affect Oppenheimer: "He'd be depressed some days, because he was having trouble with Jean."

At the root of Oppenheimer's "trouble with Jean," it seemed, was the fact that she did not love him as much as he loved her. Their love affair lasted from the autumn of 1936 to the spring of 1939, during which time he twice proposed to her. She turned him down on both occasions and the end, when it came, was brought about by her. As he had many years earlier with Charlotte Riefenstahl, Oppenheimer turned Jean away from him by courting her a little too insistently. He overdid it. "No more flowers, please Robert," she would tell him. Refusing to listen, Oppenheimer would appear with more flowers. One time she threw his gardenias to the floor, shouting to her friend: "Tell him to go away, tell him I am not here." Serber remembers that Jean "disappeared for weeks, months sometimes, and then would taunt Robert mercilessly. She would taunt him about whom she had been with and what they had been doing. She seemed determined to hurt him, perhaps because she knew Robert loved her so much." By 1939, this—the greatest love Oppenheimer had yet known and, in the opinion of some of his friends, the greatest love he would ever know—was over.

In the three years of his relationship with Jean Tatlock, Oppenheimer's world changed completely. Though he always denied that he had ever been a member of the Communist Party, he did once admit that he "had probably belonged to every Communist-front organization on the west coast." When the remark was quoted back at him, he said it was not true and that it was a "half-jocular overstatement," but it does, it seems to me, capture the spirit of his involvement with communism pretty accurately.

Always more open and less complicated than his older brother, Frank Oppenheimer made no secret of the fact that he had become a member of the Communist Party. He and Jackie joined the Party together early in 1937, after they had seen a membership application form in *People's World*, the West Coast Communist Party magazine. "We clipped it out and sent it in," Frank said later. "We were really quite overt about it—completely overt about it." It was Party policy at that time for members to have an alias. Frank's was "Frank Folsom," after the famous California prison. Soon after he joined, he drove to Berkeley to tell Robert the news. According to Oppenheimer himself, he was "quite upset" about Frank joining the Party, though he does not say why. One imagines that it was because he was very aware that Communist Party members found it hard to get jobs, and, as Oppenheimer knew only too well from the experiences of his students, academic jobs were hard enough to find anyway.

Despite his reaction to this news, Oppenheimer accepted an invitation from Frank and Jackie to attend a Communist Party meeting at their house in Pasadena, "the only thing," he later claimed, "recognizable to me as a Communist Party meeting that I have ever attended." With something of the tone with which he is said to have referred to Jackie as "the waitress my brother married," Oppenheimer described the event in the following terms:

> The meeting made no detailed impression on me, but I do remember there was a lot of fuss about getting the literature distributed, and I do remember that the principal item under discussion was segregation in the municipal pool in Pasadena. The unit was concerned about that and they talked about it. It made a rather pathetic impression on me. It was a mixed unit of some colored people and some who were not colored.

I remember vividly walking away from the meeting with Bridges

[Calvin Bridges, a geneticist at Caltech] and his saying "What a sad spectacle" or "What a pathetic sight" or something like that.

The meeting was of what was known as a "street unit" of the Communist Party, consisting of local people, most of whom, because Frank and Jackie lived in a predominantly black neighborhood, were black. The campaign to desegregate the local swimming pool was remembered very differently by Frank, who was clearly shocked at the treatment then meted out to black people: "It's really hard to imagine; they just allowed blacks in Wednesday afternoon and evening, and then they drained the pool Thursday morning." The campaign to end this segregation was not successful, but it illustrates the kind of practical issue that moved Jackie and Frank to join the Communist Party.

Shortly afterward Frank was asked by the Party to make use of his Caltech connections to organize a communist group at the university, leaving Jackie to continue leading the "street unit." Much against Frank's own inclinations, the university group was secret. It consisted of about six members, including the chemist Sidney Weinbaum and the rocketeers Frank Malina and Hsue-Shen Tsien, all of whom preserved strict secrecy because, as Frank put it, "they were scared of losing their jobs."

Oppenheimer had nothing to do with Frank's secret Caltech group and quite possibly did not know of its existence. He was, however, drawn into Communist Party activities in a number of different ways. Through his participation in the Spanish Civil War campaigns, he made contact with the prominent left-winger Thomas Addis. Addis was professor of medicine at Stanford and, as such, knew Jean well. One day, Oppenheimer recalled, Addis asked Oppenheimer to come to his laboratory in Stanford to discuss how he could best serve the Loyalist cause in Spain. He said, "You are giving all this money through these relief organizations. If you want to do good, let it go through Communist channels, and it will really help." "He made it clear," Oppenheimer wrote, "that this money, unlike that which went to the relief organizations, would go straight to the fighting effort." He went on: "I did so contribute; usually when he communicated with me, explaining the nature of the need, I gave him sums in cash, probably never much less than a hundred dollars, and occasionally perhaps somewhat more than that, several times during the winter."

Between 1937 and 1942 Oppenheimer would meet Addis—or Isaac Folkoff, the treasurer of the local Communist Party—several times a year and hand over between $100 and $300 in cash to be used by the Communist Party as they saw fit. His income at that time was about $15,000, made up of a university salary of around $5,000 and $10,000 from his inheritance (this was at a time when one of Oppenheimer's students considered himself to be comfortably well off when he received a grant of $650 a year). As he later estimated that, through Addis and Folkoff, he was giving the Communist Party about $1,000 a year, this means that he was supporting the party to the tune of about 7 percent of his (extremely large) income. In the light of these statistics, the question of whether he was actually a card-carrying member of the Party becomes somewhat academic. He was, in a very practical and real sense, a supporter of the Communist Party. Moreover, in terms of the time, effort and money spent on Party activities, he was a very committed supporter, far more so than many people who *did* pay their membership dues and carry a membership card.

When Oppenheimer was later accused (simply by throwing his own words back at him) of having joined Communist Party front organizations, one of the more unlikely and puzzling examples given was the Western Consumers Union. This was an organization led by the Berkeley economist Robert A. Brady, dedicated to testing various consumer products and providing people with information that would enable them to make informed choices about which products to buy. It still exists and is not now, nor has it ever been, a communist organization. Brady was well known as an anti-fascist, but not as a communist. The Western Consumers Union was listed by the House Committee on Un-American Activities as a subversive organization, a communist front, from 1944 to 1954. This perhaps indicates that there was some evidence of an (apparently unsuccessful) attempt to infiltrate the organization by the Communist Party, but it may equally signify nothing more than the notorious paranoia of that particular committee.

What is odd, and what Oppenheimer himself clearly found hard to explain, was how and why he found himself a member of the council that ran the Western Consumers Union. When questioned about it later, he said that he had been asked to join by Brady and his wife, Mildred Edie, who both "had enthusiasm" for it. "It was a very inappropriate thing for me to do," he conceded: "I know nothing about the business." Of his involvement with the Western Consumers Union, the documentary record consists of three letters written by Oppenheimer: one to Mildred Edie giving a halfhearted report on his attempts to find buyers and testers for various products, and two to Brady saying that he was too busy to attend meetings of the council. Though the Western Consumers Union would be mentioned repeatedly in future attempts to paint Oppenheimer as a dangerous subversive, there was in truth very little there from which to create such a picture.

Of far greater significance was Oppenheimer's involvement in the

Teachers' Union, which was affiliated to the American Federation of Labor, and which represented the interests not just of schoolteachers, but also of university lecturers and professors. It was through the Teachers' Union that Oppenheimer got to know Haakon Chevalier, who came from a mixed French and Norwegian background and taught French literature at Berkeley. Tall, blond and handsome, Chevalier cut an impressive figure. He was three years older than Oppenheimer and far more worldly. He had married his first wife, Ruth, in 1922, and, after divorcing her in 1930, married his second wife, Barbara, in 1931. Barbara was an heiress, and the Chevaliers lived in great comfort in a large home that became the center of radical, left-wing Berkeley society. When he and Oppenheimer met in 1937, Chevalier was probably already a member of the Communist Party.

Certainly, according to his later account, Chevalier was already a member of the Teachers' Union when he met Oppenheimer, and the two of them set up a Berkeley campus branch, "Local 349," with Chevalier as president and Oppenheimer as "recording secretary." "For four years," Chevalier has recalled, "we worked, with some success, to increase union membership both in the schools and in the university, to promote action to improve teaching conditions and standards and to encourage a more active participation on the part of teachers in political and community life." The focus, however, was not as sharply on issues relating to teachers as one might have assumed:

> In bursts of what I suppose can only be described as immature fervor we felt ourselves called upon, in our union meetings, to make pronouncements and to pass resolutions on all sorts of political, civil rights and even international issues extraneous to the business of the Teachers Union and thereby caused, I am afraid, a certain amount of disaffection and pangs of conscience among some of our more timid members.

As part of this wider remit, the Teachers' Union organized fundraising parties on behalf of the Spanish Loyalists, which, according to Chevalier, were "invariably lively and successful affairs" that raised "thousands of dollars for the alleviation of human suffering." Though Oppenheimer later dismissed the Teachers' Union as a "miserable thing" that "fell apart because it grew into a debating society," he also specifically listed his participation in it as an example of the comradeship that had drawn him into radical politics.

Another form that this comradeship possibly took, a far more controversial form, was Oppenheimer's involvement in what Chevalier has described privately as a Communist Party "unit." Publicly, in his memoir of Oppenheimer, Chevalier describes the formation of this unit as follows:

> We had decided, Oppenheimer and I, at our first meeting—this I do remember—to ask a small number of our friends, all colleagues, whom both of us knew, respected and trusted, and who shared our views, to join us and to form a discussion group that would meet from time to time, as occasion might dictate. This group—the number, in the course of time, varied from six to ten—was promptly formed, and we met, more or less regularly, every week or two during college sessions, not at all during the long summers, for the next five years. Our last reunion, as far as I remember, must have been in the late fall of 1942.

This is not how Chevalier had originally wanted to describe the group. What he had wanted to write, he told Oppenheimer in a letter written in 1964, was the "story . . . of your and my membership in the same unit of the CP from 1938 to 1942." As Oppenheimer had always denied Party membership, Chevalier's letter naturally horrified him. "I have never been a member of the Communist Party," he replied, "and thus have never been a member of a Communist Party unit. I, of course, have always known this. I thought you did too. I have said so officially time and time again." In the light of this, Chevalier spoke in his book of the "discussion group" mentioned above. To another member of this unit/discussion group, the union organizer, Lou Goldblatt, Chevalier wrote: "I had originally planned to reveal the fact that O. had been, from 1937 to 1943, a CP member,[37] which I knew directly. On thinking it over, I decided that I shouldn't, even though the fact is of considerable historical importance."

That Chevalier was not alone in regarding this group as a secret Communist Party unit has become apparent in two documents that have recently been made public on the website associated with Gregg Herken's book, *Brotherhood of the Bomb*. The first of these is an unpublished manuscript by Chevalier's wife entitled "Robert Oppenheimer and Haakon Chevalier: From the Memoirs of Barbara Chevalier." After telling the story of how Oppenheimer read Marx on a train, Barbara Chevalier adds: "Shortly thereafter he and Haakon joined a secret unit of the Communist Party. There must have been 6 or 8 members—a doc-

---

[37] Chevalier was evidently a little hazy on the exact years, as these do not match the dates he gave in his letter to Oppenheimer.

tor, a wealthy businessman (maybe)." Later in the memoir she writes: "Oppie's membership in a closed unit was very secret indeed."

The gist of Barbara Chevalier's account is confirmed in another unpublished document made available on the same website, "Venturing Outside the Ivory Tower: The Political Autobiography of a College Professor" by the Berkeley history professor Gordon Griffiths. Griffiths describes how, in 1939, when he returned to Berkeley after studying at Oxford, he wanted to resume membership of the U.S. Communist Party, but his new wife, Mary, was worried about the idea. A compromise, suggested by the graduate mathematician and Communist Party member Kenneth May, was adopted whereby Griffiths "could perform a useful function for the Party that involved little or no risk of exposure." That function was to liaise between the Party and what Griffiths describes as "the faculty Communist group," the Berkeley members of which were Chevalier, Oppenheimer and the Icelandic scholar Arthur Brodeur. To those three names, Chevalier, in private correspondence, has added names from outside the Berkeley faculty: Thomas Addis of Stanford, Robert Muir of the California Labor Bureau, Lou Goldblatt and the anthropologist Paul Radin.[38]

This group, Griffiths writes, "met regularly, to the best of my recollection, twice a month, in the evening at Chevalier's or Oppenheimer's house." Griffiths's job was to deliver party literature to the group and collect membership dues from Chevalier and Brodeur. Presumably alluding to Oppenheimer's arrangements with Addis, Griffiths writes: "I was given to understand that Oppenheimer, as a man of independent wealth, made his contribution through some special channel." "Nobody carried a party card," Griffiths remembers. "If payment of dues was the only test of membership, I could not testify that Oppenheimer was a member, but I can say, without any qualification, that all three men considered themselves to be Communists."

In the light of this evidence, it is hard to resist the conclusion that Oppenheimer was a member of a secret communist unit at Berkeley, very like the one that his brother had helped to set up in Pasadena. It is perfectly possible, however, to square that with Oppenheimer's repeated denials that he was a member of the Communist Party, if one uses as the criteria of membership the payment of dues and the possession of a

---

[38] It has worried some people that Griffiths mentions three members of the unit, while Chevalier mentions seven. However, Griffiths does not say it only had three members. He says rather: "Of the several hundred members of the faculty at Berkeley three were members of the communist group." As neither Addis nor Radin was at Berkeley during the period in question and the other two were not university people at all, this is perfectly consistent with Chevalier's description of the group having seven members.

membership card. The question of whether Oppenheimer was a communist or not is thus rather like the question of whether he was or was not a German Jew. He did not consider himself to be German, Jewish or communist, and yet, as those words are commonly used, he was ethnically a German Jew and politically a communist. One does not have to accuse either Oppenheimer or common usage of being *wrong* here; one just has to be careful in distinguishing the *sense* in which he was and was not German or Jewish or a communist.

And to say that Oppenheimer was indeed a member of a secret communist unit is not to lend any support to the notion that Oppenheimer was engaged in anything subversive. Not everything secret is subversive. According to Griffiths, this secret group did not do very much "that could not have been done as a group of liberals or Democrats." They encouraged each other to support the Teachers' Union and the Loyalist cause in the Spanish Civil War and they discussed current events from a broadly Marxist point of view. "In short," Griffiths concludes, "there was nothing subversive or treasonable about our activity." It should not be imagined, for example, that this "secret unit" of the Communist Party took its orders from the Soviet Union, or even from the American Communist Party. True, Griffiths collected dues and delivered party literature, but there was no acknowledgment on anybody's part that the Party could tell these people what to do or what to think. When Chevalier was asked what made this unit a Communist Party group rather than "just a group of people who were Left," he replied: "We paid dues." Asked whether they received any orders, he answered: "No. In a sense we weren't [regular party members]."

Oppenheimer's silence about the "secret unit" to which he belonged is impressively resolute and unyielding. Never once, in all his subsequent interviews, interrogations and cross-examinations—some of which were conducted by people trained at the highest level in the skills required to prise secrets out of people—did he even hint at its existence. But then, as he himself said: "Look, I have had a lot of secrets in my head a long time. It does not matter who I associate with. I don't talk about those secrets." Not revealing things about himself was something he was extraordinarily good at.

Leaving Oppenheimer's impressive silence about the "secret unit" aside, there is nothing in what has been revealed about it that does not square with his own statements about his attitudes toward the Communist Party. He himself acknowledged that, because of the groups he joined, the people he was friends with and the financial contributions he made to the Party, he "might well have appeared at the time as quite close to the Communist Party—perhaps even to some people as belonging to it." However, one has to remember, he emphasized, that it was quite common in the 1930s for communists and noncommunists to work together: "This was the era of what the Communists then called the United Front, in which they joined with many non-Communist groups in support of humanitarian objectives. Many of these objectives engaged my interest." But: "I never was a member of the Communist Party. I never accepted Communist dogma or theory; in fact, it never made sense to me."

When pressed to confirm that he knew "that Communists stood for certain doctrines, and certain philosophies and took certain positions," Oppenheimer replied:

> . . . it seems clear to me that there were tactical positions on current issues, which might be very sensible-looking or popular or might coincide with the views of a lot of people who were not Communists. There was also the conviction as to the nature of history, the role of the classes and the changing society, the nature of the Soviet Union, which I would assume was the core of Communist doctrine.

Clearly, it was important to Oppenheimer to distinguish these two kinds of convictions. He might share with the Communist Party views on the Spanish Civil War or the rise of fascism or the unionizing rights of workers, but this did not mean that he shared, or even found comprehensible, the general, philosophical views that communists were supposed to hold, such as "dialectical materialism . . . the more or less determinate course of history and the importance of the class war" (which were the three that Oppenheimer named in addition to the ones mentioned above).

Of course, this still leaves undecided Oppenheimer's views on a range of issues associated with communism. Did he believe in the inevitable collapse of capitalism? Did he look forward to a revolution that would result in the dictatorship of the proletariat? I think the implied answer to these two questions—implied by the above quotations—is "no." And neither, as far as I know, is there anything in Oppenheimer's recorded utterances to suggest otherwise. What he did believe in, and is on record as arguing for, is *socialism*, which he thought was the natural outcome of Roosevelt's New Deal. In a political tract, published under the auspices of the Communist Party of California, which Oppenheimer is reliably said (by Chevalier and Griffiths) to have written, he quotes with approval a statement about the New Deal: "once start such things and you are on the road to socialism; once worry about the food and work and life of your poor, and you can't stop." "We agreed with that," Oppenheimer writes, "we regarded it as an argument for the New Deal, not against it." "We tend to believe," he goes on, "that any consistent effort to raise the standard of living, to promote the culture and freedom and political responsibility of the people as a whole will lead to socialism."

In regarding the Communist Party as an ally of the New Deal, Oppenheimer was very far from being alone. Indeed, this was *precisely* how the American Communist Party presented itself in the 1930s, as primarily an *American* party, rather than as an agent of the Comintern. In 1937, its internal structure was reorganized so that it looked more like traditional American political parties. Its leader, Earl Browder, in the words of Maurice Isserman, a historian of the Party, "wanted to be a leader of a national movement with power and influence of its own." Under Browder:

> The Communists began to identify themselves as part of the political coalition that supported the New Deal's domestic programs, while enthusiastically welcoming every move by the Roosevelt Adminis- tration that could be interpreted as favoring collective international security. The Communists argued that their own political program corresponded to Roosevelt's true intentions.

The slogan that Browder adopted for his party in the period 1936–9 could hardly have been more suited to a man of Oppenheimer's political outlook: "Communism Is Twentieth Century Americanism."

Isserman's analysis of the effectiveness of this slogan on its target audience during the late 1930s rings very loud bells for anyone familiar with Oppenheimer's background:

> A significant proportion of those who joined then and stuck with the movement were the children of Jewish immigrants (the percentage of Jewish membership in the CP, about 15 percent in the mid-1920s, grew to around half the party's strength in the 1930s and 1940s).
>
> Like every second generation in the history of American immigra- tion, they hungered for the full assimilation that had eluded their parents' grasp. Had they come of age in less unsettled times they might have chosen another route, but in the early 1930s it seemed for a moment as if an American version of the October Revolution offered the quickest and surest path from marginality to influence and integration.

In his 1936 essay "What Is Communism?" Earl Browder responded to the question asked of communists by the editorials in the newspapers of William Randolph Hearst—"If you don't like this country, why don't you go back where you came from?"—with the following exuberantly patriotic rhetoric:

> The truth is . . . we Communists like this country very much. We cannot think of any other spot on the globe where we would rather be than exactly this one. We love our country.
>
> . . . We are determined to save our country from the hell of capitalism. And most of us were born here, so Hearst's gag is not addressed to us anyway.
>
> . . . The revolutionary tradition is the heart of Americanism. That is incontestable, unless we are ready to agree that Americanism means what Hearst says, slavery to outlived institutions, preservation of privilege, the degradation of the masses.
>
> We Communists claim the revolutionary traditions of Americanism. We are the only ones who consciously continue those traditions and apply them to the problems of today.
>
> *We are the Americans and Communism is the Americanism of the twentieth century* . . .
>
> Americanism, in this revolutionary sense, means to stand in the forefront of human progress. It means never to submit to the forces of decay and death. It means constantly to free ourselves of the old, the outworn, the decaying, and to press forward to the young, the vital, the living, the expanding.

This, one feels, is an outlook with considerable appeal to the man who grew up with the sermons of Adler on the meaning of America and the importance of the "Americanization" of Jewish immigrants, and who lectured, among others, Felix Bloch, George Uhlenbeck and Alfred Stern on the virtues of his home country.

With regard to the Soviet Union, Oppenheimer later said, "the talk that I heard at that time had predisposed me to make much of the economic progress and general level of welfare in Russia, and little of its political tyranny." But his views on that changed, first by reading about the show trials, and then, more decisively, in the summer of 1938, when three physicists whose opinions he respected—George Placzek, Victor Weisskopf and Marcel Schein—talked to him about their own experiences of Russia. Placzek, Weisskopf and Schein were all from Central European Jewish backgrounds; Placzek from Moravia, Weisskopf from Vienna and Schein from Bohemia. They were also all first-rate physicists. As life for Jews became unbearable under Nazi-controlled areas of Europe, the United States was not the only country to realize that some of those Jews could make extremely valuable contributions to its universities. The Soviet Union also extended a helping hand to Jewish scientists, and succeeded in attracting Schein and Guido Beck to the University of Odessa, and then, through Beck, persuaded Placzek and Weisskopf to work with the Russian physicist Lev Landau at his new institute in Kharkov, near Kiev.

By 1938, it had all gone horribly wrong for everyone concerned. Landau was investigated during the Great Purge, arrested and imprisoned; and Beck, Schein, Placzek and Weisskopf were forced to flee, horrified at what they had witnessed. As Oppenheimer put it, the description of the Soviet Union he received from these three very well-respected scientists was of "a land of purge and terror, of ludicrously bad management and of a long-suffering people." "It's worse than you can imagine," Weisskopf told him. "It's a morass." As Weisskopf later remarked: "These conversations had a very deep influence on Robert. This was a decisive week in his life." This is confirmed by a letter written a few months later by Felix Bloch to Isidor Rabi. Oppenheimer, Bloch wrote, "is fine and sends you his greetings; honestly, I don't think you wore him out but at least he does not praise Russia too loudly any more which is good progress."

Oppenheimer might also have received a fairly clear-eyed picture of what was happening in the Soviet Union from one of his students. George Volkoff, who came to Berkeley to work with Oppenheimer in 1936, was born in Moscow, but brought up in Manchuria, where his father worked as a schoolteacher. Volkoff left Manchuria to study physics at the University of British Columbia in Canada, and never saw his parents again. His mother died in Manchuria, and in 1936 his father returned to Russia, where he was caught up in the purges and sent to Siberia, dying there in 1943. "Alone in North America," an obituary of Volkoff stated, "it did not help George emotionally that many of his associates continued to have rosy views of the Soviet Union."

With Volkoff, Oppenheimer wrote one of his most interesting papers, one of a series of three, each written with a different coauthor, on a subject with which Oppenheimer had not previously been associated: astrophysics. Though these papers received little attention at the time, they are now generally considered to be his greatest work, free of the mathematical errors that dogged his work on quantum electrodynamics and containing original and prescient insights that have been the basis of much subsequent important work. Many people think that, if he had lived a little longer, Oppenheimer would have received the Nobel Prize for these papers.

The particular subject of the paper Oppenheimer wrote with Volkoff at the end of 1938 was the physics of neutron stars. The concept of a neutron star had been introduced into physics just five years earlier at a meeting of the American Physical Society in 1933, only a year after the discovery of the neutron, by the Swiss physicist Fritz Zwicky and the German astronomer Walter Baade. Both were based in Pasadena, Zwicky at Caltech and Baade at the Mount Wilson Observatory. Zwicky, like many people at Caltech, was interested in cosmic rays, and, via Millikan's view that these rays were the "birth cries" of matter coming to us from outer space, this led him to a subject that Baade was already interested in: supernovae.

Supernovae are extraordinarily bright explosions in outer space, which have been observed and recorded at irregular intervals since the second century AD. One of the most famous appeared in AD 1054, when it was recorded by court astronomers in China, who described it as a "guest star" and noted that it was brighter than Venus or any other star. It stayed visible, even in daylight, for twenty-three days, and at night could be seen for two years. In 1572 another supernova was observed by the Danish astronomer Tycho Brahe, who wrote a book about it, *De Nova Stella*, in which he showed that this "new star" had to be further away from us than the moon and that therefore the view that the "starry heavens" were immutable was wrong.

The word "supernova" was introduced in the early 1930s by Baade and Zwicky. Even though their term incorporated from ancient descriptions the word "nova," with its suggestions that these temporary bright stars were "new," they were the first to develop a theory that explained supernovae as the *death*-throes of a star. A supernova, in their account, is a stellar explosion that marks the "cessation of its existence as an ordinary star." They also "tentatively" suggested what is now the accepted theory, that "the super-nova process represents the transition of an ordinary star into a neutron star."

To understand what a neutron star is, it is helpful to consider the kind of dying star known as a "white dwarf." In the nineteenth century, a mysterious star named Sirius B was discovered, which was much fainter than its partner, Sirius A. It was assumed that this was because it was cooler, but it was found to be, in fact, much hotter. This could only mean that it was, by comparison, extremely small. It was a star with the mass of our sun, but the volume of a mere planet; in other words, its density was extraordinary—much higher than anything encountered on earth. In the 1920s, these small, dense stars were given the name "white dwarfs" and a theory was developed to explain them. The theory was that ordinary stars, such as our sun, are huge furnaces of hydrogen—the pressure and the heat at their core being sufficient to fuse hydrogen nuclei into helium (though how, exactly, that nuclear fusion worked was not clear until

Hans Bethe's work on the question was published in 1939). After a time, which will be several billions of years, the star runs out of hydrogen, and is no longer able to keep itself stable through thermonuclear reactions. At that stage, gravity takes over, and pulls all the particles that make up the star toward the center. The star thus gets smaller and smaller and denser and denser. Eventually it gets so dense that there is no longer any room for the atomic electrons[39] to move about as they do in normal conditions. At this point, the "white dwarf" cannot get any smaller or denser and so achieves stability, the stability being attributable to what is called the "degeneracy pressure" of the atomic electrons—namely, the fact that they are now all pressed together, unable to move.

In 1931 the Indian physicist Subrahmanyan Chandrasekhar showed that the process described above meant that white dwarfs had a maximum mass, which he calculated to be 1.4 solar masses (where a "solar mass" is a mass equivalent to that of our sun). Anything with a mass greater than that, Chandrasekhar demonstrated, would exert a gravitational force too great for even degeneracy pressure to withstand. Most stars (something over 90 percent) are estimated to fall below the "Chandrasekhar limit," but that still means that a significant number of stars will not end up as white dwarfs. What happens to *them* is the problem solved by Baade and Zwicky and the notion of a "neutron star."

A star with a core of more than 1.4 solar masses will exert enough gravitational pressure to overcome degeneracy pressure with really spectacular consequences. A massive star, in its dying phases, will consist of layers of matter, each layer getting more and more dense as one approaches the core. If the core is over the Chandrasekhar limit, the moment will arrive when it suddenly collapses under gravitational pressure. In one-tenth of a second, the material that makes up the core will explode and disintegrate into its basic constituent particles—protons, neutrons, electrons. At the fantastically high temperatures that are generated by this process, the velocities of the electrons approach that of light. But, being in such a dense, degenerate state, they have nowhere to go. And so, at terrifically high energies, they are pushed into the protons themselves, forming neutrons. This process, called "neutronization," results in an enormous increase in density; the core of the star is no longer made up of chemicals of any sort; it is rather one big nucleus. As this happens, the outer layers of the star, the non-neutronized sections, fall toward the center, but are repelled by a shock wave of enormous energy that blows the star to smithereens. If the star originally had a

[39] "Atomic electrons" are those outside the nucleus, as opposed to those that are emitted from the nucleus in beta decay.

mass twenty-five times the size of our sun, then what would be left is a neutron core with a mass equal to our sun and a volume the size not of a planet or even of a country, but of a city. The rest of the mass would be blown away. That explosion is a supernova, and the remaining core is a neutron star.

Ever since he arrived in California, Oppenheimer had taken an interest in the work being done at the Mount Wilson Observatory. In 1933, he gave a talk on "Stars and Nuclei" to the Mount Wilson–Caltech Astronomy and Physics Club. His interest in astrophysics was evidently reawakened by Volkoff, who gave a talk at Berkeley in 1937 on "The Source of Stellar Energy." This, as we have seen, is where astrophysics and nuclear physics meet, since the source of stellar energy is to be found in nuclear reactions. In 1938, Oppenheimer organized a symposium on "nuclear transformations and their astrophysical significance" for that year's meeting of the American Physical Society, which was held in San Diego. Oppenheimer was to give a paper on stellar energy, but before the meeting he learned that whatever he had to say on that subject was about to be trumped by Hans Bethe's Nobel Prize–winning work on the subject.

Soon after the meeting Oppenheimer published the first of his three papers on astrophysics, a letter to the editor of the *Physical Review* written jointly with Serber, called "On the Stability of Stellar Neutron Cores." Acknowledging their debt to Bethe for "an interesting discussion of these questions," Oppenheimer and Serber took up the question that had recently been discussed by Lev Landau: was there, for neutron stars, an equivalent to the "Chandrasekhar limit"? That is to say, does a neutron core have to be of some certain mass in order to remain stable? Like Landau, Oppenheimer and Serber considered a possible minimum limit, rather than a maximum, and came to the conclusion that Landau's estimate of 0.001 solar masses was too low. The minimum limit was, they reckoned, more like 0.1 solar masses.

The second paper in the series, the one written with Volkoff and entitled "On Massive Neutron Cores," was received by the *Physical Review* on January 3, 1939. An altogether more substantial piece of work than the Oppenheimer-Serber paper, it is often credited now with presenting the first serious theory of neutron stars. From it comes what has become known as the "Oppenheimer-Volkoff limit," an upper limit for a stable neutron core, which they calculated to be 0.7 solar masses. The present estimate is between 3 and 5 solar masses. It was notoriously difficult to do the calculation for the reasons that Oppenheimer and Volkoff spelled out. First, the nuclear forces that operate between neutrons were not as well understood as the electromagnetic forces that operate between the electrons in a white dwarf. Second, when considering white dwarfs it is not necessary to take relativistic effects into account; the gravitational forces are weak enough for Newtonian theory to be sufficient. With the enormous gravitational forces at work in a neutron star, however, one needs to use general relativity, which introduces extremely complex and difficult equations.

Despite these difficulties, Oppenheimer and Volkoff laid out the basic theory of neutron stars—nearly thirty years before there were any empirical grounds for believing that such things really exist. The abstruse mathematics in the article, versions of which now appear in astrophysics textbooks under the name "Oppenheimer-Volkoff (O-V) equation of hydrostatic equilibrium," was apparently the work of Volkoff alone. "I remember being greatly overawed by having to explain to Oppenheimer and Tolman what I had done," he later remembered. "We were sitting out on the lawn of the old faculty club at Berkeley. Amidst the nice green grass and tall trees, here were these two venerated gentlemen and here I was, a graduate student just completing my Ph.D., explaining my calculations." What those calculations showed was extremely interesting: first, that neutron stars *could* indeed exist, so long as their mass was greater than 0.1 solar masses and less than 0.7 solar masses; second, that "the question of what happens, after energy sources are exhausted, to stars of mass greater than 1.5 solar masses still remains unanswered";[40] and most intriguingly of all: "There would seem to be only two answers possible to the question of the 'final' behavior of very massive stars: either the equation of state we have used so far fails to describe the behavior of highly condensed matter . . . or the star will continue to contract indefinitely, never reaching equilibrium." According to their calculations, in other words, there is nothing, in stars with sufficient mass, to prevent the gravitational collapse from carrying on indefinitely, but how can something collapse, as it were, infinitely? The alternatives presented by their work, they concluded, "require serious consideration."

Even to have raised the question of indefinite gravitational collapse required impressive boldness and imagination, but in his next paper Oppenheimer went one better: he answered it. The third and final paper

---

[40] The figures here are perhaps confusing. The Chandrasekhar limit of 1.4 solar masses given previously is a calculation of how much mass a white dwarf can have without collapsing into a neutron star. The Oppenheimer-Volkoff limit of 0.7 solar masses is a calculation of how much mass a neutron star can have and still be stable—that is, without collapsing further. What happens to a neutron star that continues to collapse is an unanswered question, which is why Oppenheimer says the question of what happens to large stars (those more massive than 1.5 suns) still remains unsolved. The full story about the gravitational collapse of large stars, he is indicating, has yet to be told.

in this series on astrophysics, though more or less completely ignored for nearly thirty years after its publication, has now become the most respected of them all. Jeremy Bernstein has called it "one of the great papers in twentieth-century physics." Cowritten with Hartland Snyder, who is remembered by Robert Serber as "the best mathematician of our Berkeley group," it is entitled "On Continued Gravitational Contraction" and was published in the September 1939 issue of the *Physical Review*.

The paper is celebrated for predicting the existence of what are now, and have been since the 1960s, called "black holes," the next stage of a dying star of sufficient mass after it has passed through the white dwarf, supernova and neutron-star phases. "When all thermonuclear sources of energy are exhausted," runs the very first line of the paper, "a sufficiently heavy star will collapse." Furthermore, unless its mass is reduced in various ways (for example, by radiation) to that of our sun, "this contraction will continue indefinitely."

The genius and the novelty of the paper lie in giving an account of what "indefinite contraction" might mean. In the death of a massive star, we have imagined it going from many times bigger than our sun (its initial state as a glowing furnace of hydrogen) to something about the size of a planet (a white dwarf), then something about the size of, say, San Francisco (a neutron star). At each stage, its density gets greater and greater. Now we must imagine it contracting toward what is called a "singularity," namely *zero* volume and *infinite* density. As Oppenheimer put it in a letter to George Uhlenbeck while he was working on this paper: "The results have been very odd." To describe this "oddness," Oppenheimer and Snyder use the field equations of Einstein's theory of relativity, the physical realities of which they illustrate from the points of view of two observers: one far away from the collapsing mass and the other inside it. It is a feature of relativity that, from the point of view of someone outside a gravitational field, time inside the field will run more and more slowly as the strength of the gravitation increases. Therefore, to an outside observer, the collapse of the mass will take an infinite amount of time; to the unfortunate observer inside the gravitational field, on the other hand, it is all over in an instant. Moreover, *nothing* can escape from the indefinitely collapsing mass, not even radiation; the blackness of a black star is absolute. "The star thus tends to close itself off from any communication with a distant observer," Oppenheimer and Snyder write; "only its gravitational field persists."

In four pages, mostly filled with the imposing equations of relativistic gravitational theory, Oppenheimer and Snyder provided a way of understanding the collapse of a neutron star into a black hole, the implications of which are still being explored today. Pick up a popular book on black holes now and the chances are that what you will see is a description extending over several pages, even several chapters, of the physical realities that correspond to the equations of Oppenheimer and Snyder. Almost certainly, the book will also attempt to convey the nature of black holes using the device adopted by Oppenheimer and Snyder of imagining two observers.

And yet, during Oppenheimer's lifetime, this remarkable paper—and the ones preceding it written with Serber and Volkoff—were greeted with silence from both astronomers and physicists. This silence ended with the discovery in 1967 of "pulsars," which, it was realized, are rotating neutron stars; the following year it was discovered that what had been known for a long time as the Crab Nebula was in fact the remnant of the 1064 supernova and that in the middle of it was a neutron star. Since then, neutron stars have even been photographed. As for black holes, though they have not been (and could not be) photographed, there is now abundant evidence that they exist and they are the subject of intensive theorizing and observational work.

One of the leading figures in the study of black holes, John Archibald Wheeler, was also one of the first people to revive interest in Oppenheimer's work on the subject, and is credited with having introduced the term "black hole." In the 1960s, shortly before Oppenheimer's death, Wheeler tried to talk to him about his work on gravitational collapse, but Oppenheimer was not interested. Had he lived just a few years longer, Oppenheimer would have seen the empirical evidence which confirmed that the theory developed by him and his students in the late 1930s was not just a piece of mathematics, but was a description of physical reality.

One reason for the initial lack of interest in these great papers of Oppenheimer and his students has to do with the timing of two very different events. Oppenheimer's paper with Volkoff was written in the very month that it was announced that scientists in Germany had discovered nuclear fission; his paper with Snyder, meanwhile, was published on the very day that the Second World War began. For the time being, the question of what happened inside a massive stellar core was of far less interest, and far less import, than the questions of what might be made to happen inside a uranium nucleus and what might become of Europe.

10

Fission

The response of scientists to the news of nuclear fission in the New Year of 1939 was in itself a remarkable chain reaction, with Oppenheimer and his colleagues on the West Coast of America somewhat at the end of the chain.

It began with two chemists in Berlin, the eminent Otto Hahn and his young assistant Fritz Strassmann. They had been bombarding uranium with fairly slow, low-energy neutrons, trying to repeat the experiments conducted in Paris by Irène Curie and her assistant, which had produced some puzzling results. On December 19, 1938, Hahn wrote to his friend and former colleague Lise Meitner, who, because she was Jewish, had recently fled Germany and was now in Sweden. Meitner was a very able physicist to whom Hahn had often appealed in the past to explain his results. Now he asked her to explain something that had utterly perplexed him and Strassmann: when their slow neutrons hit uranium, the result seemed to be the emission of *barium*.

To understand why this was so puzzling, one has to take a step back and survey what had been achieved up to that point in the way of changing one element into another. Rutherford, back in 1919, had been the first modern alchemist, changing nitrogen into oxygen by bombarding it with alpha particles. What, exactly, was happening in this process was made clear by the photographs Blackett took in 1924: nitrogen, with atomic mass 14, was absorbing the alpha particle (mass 4), producing oxygen (mass 17) and emitting a proton (mass 1), or, in symbols: $N^{14} + \alpha^4 \rightarrow O^{17} + p^1$. Then, in 1932, Cockcroft and Walton had split a lithium atom by bombarding it with protons, and again there was no mystery about what was happening: lithium (mass 7) was absorbing a proton (mass 1) and then splitting into two helium nuclei, each with a mass of 4: $\text{Li}^7 + \text{p}^1 \rightarrow \alpha^4 + \alpha^4$.

At the heart of these processes is not only some fairly basic arithmetic ($14 + 4 = 17 + 1$ and $7 + 1 = 4 + 4$), but also some fairly basic chipping away at atomic nuclei, with nothing more dramatic than the absorption and emission here and there of an alpha particle and/or a proton. But it is impossible to understand how barium could be emitted from uranium by such means. Uranium is a very heavy element. In fact, it is the heaviest naturally occurring element. It has ninety-two protons and, in its most common and stable form, 146 neutrons, giving it an atomic mass of 238. Barium has fifty-six protons and, in its most common and stable form, eighty-two neutrons, giving it a mass of 138. You cannot, therefore, get barium from uranium by either adding or subtracting a proton or an alpha particle; you need to lose about 100 nucleons (protons and/or neutrons)! Whatever that is, it is not "chipping."

Hahn and Strassmann had already strained credulity by suggesting earlier that what they had witnessed was the emission of an isotope of radium (atomic number 88, atomic mass 223–8), but it was just about conceivable how this might happen by, as they said, "the emission of two successive alpha particles" (together with a couple of neutrons or protons). But no amount of juggling with the figures could explain how barium could be emitted from uranium on the assumption that transmutation was due to the emission or absorption of protons, neutrons or alpha particles. Something else was going on, something not previously encountered.

In Sweden, Meitner was joined by her nephew Otto Frisch, a young physicist who had lately been working in Copenhagen with Niels Bohr. On Christmas Eve 1938, Frisch and Meitner discussed the results obtained by Hahn and Strassmann. "But it's impossible," Frisch remembers them thinking. "You couldn't chip a hundred particles off a nucleus in one blow."

Following a suggestion by George Gamow, Bohr had recently put forward the idea that an atomic nucleus is more like a liquid drop than a billiard ball; not a hard, stable object, but something continually moving, wobbling, with the forces acting not only on it but in it, pulling it in different directions. Among those forces in an atomic nucleus is the electrostatic repulsion that protons exert on one another. Seen like this, the heavier the nucleus is, the *less* stable it should be, because it will have more protons, all trying to pull away from the others. That is, in fact, why no elements heavier than uranium exist in nature; as soon as they are created, they pull themselves apart.

This fact was not well understood in 1938. Up to then, scientists thought that by bombarding uranium with neutrons they would create heavier, "transuranic" elements. They thought that the uranium would absorb a neutron, which would then, through beta decay, transform into a proton, thus creating a new, heavier element. Thinking about the results Hahn and Strassmann had obtained in terms of Bohr's image of the nucleus as a drop of water, Frisch and Meitner realized that the opposite had happened: instead of the uranium absorbing a neutron, the neutron had hit a wobbling nucleus (which they pictured like a balloon full of water, pinched at the middle), making it wobble a bit more until it split in half. Frisch and Meitner also realized that this splitting—to which Frisch gave the name "fission"—would release enormous amounts of energy, namely the binding energy holding the nucleons of the uranium nuclei together. They were able to be fairly precise about how much energy would be released, since they knew that the separated pieces of the split uranium nucleus—one of barium, the other (therefore) of krypton[41]— would have a slightly smaller combined mass than that of the original nucleus, and were able to calculate what that difference would be. The answer is: a mass equal to one-fifth of a proton. Then, using the famous formula $E = mc^2$, they could convert that mass into energy and thus work out that the amount of energy released by the fission of uranium is 200 million electron volts, which, not coincidently, is exactly the amount of energy Frisch and Meitner had calculated would be needed to pull the protons apart.

All this was understood by Frisch and Meitner on Christmas Eve 1938. For about a week they were the sole possessors of this (potentially, at least, literally) earth-shattering knowledge. Then, on January 1, 1939, Meitner wrote to Hahn, telling him that she and Frisch "consider it *perhaps* possible energetically after all that such a heavy nucleus bursts." Two days later Frisch was back in Copenhagen, where he told Bohr the news. "I hadn't spoken for half a minute," Frisch remembers, "when he struck his head with his fist and said, 'Oh, what idiots we have been that we haven't seen that before.'"

By January 6, Frisch and Meitner, working together on the phone, had drafted a paper on fission that they intended to send to *Nature*. Bohr was leaving for the United States the next day, and before he left Frisch told him about the paper and handed him two pages of it, which was all he had been able to type out in the time available. He also told Bohr about an experiment he proposed to conduct in Copenhagen to confirm Hahn and Strassmann's result. Bohr promised not to mention fission in

---

[41] Take the fifty-six protons of barium from the ninety-two of uranium, and you are left with thirty-six, the atomic number of krypton.

America, until he had heard from Frisch that his paper had been received by *Nature*. Frisch decided not to send the theoretical paper he had written with his aunt until he had conducted his experiments. These were done quickly and did indeed confirm the remarkable fact that uranium can be split apart by slow neutrons, thus releasing enormous amounts of nuclear energy. Frisch dashed off a paper reporting on his experiments and on January 16 sent both papers to *Nature*.

On the same day, Bohr, accompanied by his colleague Léon Rosenfeld, arrived in New York. On the way over the two of them had read the pages that Frisch had given Bohr, and had spent almost the entire time discussing fission. Bohr, however, forgot to mention to Rosenfeld his promise to Frisch not to discuss it with the Americans. When they arrived in New York they were met by Enrico Fermi, who had, after receiving the 1938 Nobel Prize, fled Italy and was now working at Columbia University. With Fermi was the Princeton physicist John Archibald Wheeler. While Bohr went off with Fermi to spend the day and night as his guest in New York, Wheeler accompanied Rosenfeld to Princeton. Thus it was that, on the train from New York to Princeton, Wheeler became the first person in America to hear that nuclear fission had been achieved.

It so happened that that day, a Monday, was when the physics department at Princeton held its Journal Club, where they discussed new results in physics. Naturally, therefore, Wheeler asked Rosenfeld to give a short report of fission to the assembled faculty members and graduate students, and, of course, the news caused quite a stir. Isidor Rabi and Willis Lamb, who were both then working at Columbia University, happened to be at Princeton that week, so they returned to New York bearing the news to, among others, Fermi (to whom Bohr, of course, had said nothing). Fermi at once devised an experiment similar to Frisch's to confirm the result, and meanwhile Bohr continued on his journey across the United States, now (having written a letter to *Nature* giving appropriate credit to Frisch and Meitner) feeling free to discuss fission with anyone who wanted to discuss it, which was almost everyone he met.

His next stop was Washington, to attend the annual Theoretical Physics Conference, cosponsored by the Carnegie Institution and George Washington University. There, in front of fifty-one of America's best physicists, including Harold Urey, George Gamow, Edward Teller, Hans Bethe and George Uhlenbeck (who was now back at the University of Michigan, having just returned from Holland), Bohr announced the news. Immediately two experimentalists at the Carnegie Institution returned to their labs to set up an experiment.

By now, before Frisch and Meitner's paper had even appeared in print, it seemed as if every physicist on the East Coast knew about fission, and at least two laboratories had conducted experiments that confirmed the results. The news had still not hit the West Coast (as one physicist remarked: "We didn't make long-distance calls in those days"), but this was about to change. Attending the Washington conference was a science writer from the *Washington Evening Star*, whose report on the sensational discovery was published on January 28. The next day, the *San Francisco Chronicle* picked up the story.

Luis W. Alvarez, a colleague of Lawrence's at the Radiation Laboratory, seems to have been the first physicist at Berkeley to receive the news. He later recalled:

> I remember exactly how I heard about it. I was sitting in the barber chair in Stevens Union having my hair cut, reading the *Chronicle*. I didn't subscribe to the *Chronicle*, I just happened to be reading it, and in the second section, buried away some place, was an announcement that some German chemists had found that the uranium atom split into two pieces when it was bombarded with neutrons—that's all there was to it. So I remember telling the barber to stop cutting my hair and I got right out of that barber chair and ran as fast as I could to the Radiation Laboratory where my student Phil Abelson, who is now editor of *Science*, had been working very hard to try and find out what transuranium elements were produced when neutrons hit uranium; he was so close to discovering fission that it was almost pitiful. He would have been there, guaranteed, in another few weeks.

When Alvarez arrived at the laboratory, panting, with his news about fission, Abelson was there, making observations on what he thought were traces of transuranic elements. Alvarez recalls:

> I played it kind of dramatically when I saw Phil. I said: "Phil, I've got something to tell you but want you to lie down first." So being a good graduate student he lay down on the table right alongside the control room of the cyclotron. "Phil, what you are looking at are not transuranium elements, they are elements in the middle of the periodic table." . . . I showed him what was in the *Chronicle*, and of course he was terribly depressed.

Like many other American experimental physicists, Alvarez, on hearing about fission, immediately set up an experiment to confirm it.

Only after he had the experiment up and running did Oppenheimer hear the news. His first reaction was "That's impossible" and, according to Alvarez, he "gave a lot of theoretical reasons why fission couldn't really happen."

> When I invited him over to look at the oscilloscope later, when we saw the big pulses, I would say that in less than fifteen minutes Robert had decided that this was indeed a real effect and, more importantly, he had decided that some neutrons would probably boil off in the reaction, and that you could make bombs and generate power, all inside of a few minutes. He just had a block on the thing because he was so sure that Coulomb barriers wouldn't permit the nucleus to undergo fission. But it was amazing to see how rapidly his mind worked, and he came to the right conclusions.

That day, Oppenheimer called Felix Bloch at Stanford. "You must come to Berkeley immediately," he told him. "There is something of the utmost importance I must show you." "There was a note of urgency in his voice," Bloch later said, "one I don't recall ever hearing in Oppenheimer before." As soon as Bloch arrived in Berkeley, Oppenheimer's first words to him were: "They have discovered fission." Glenn T. Seaborg, a chemist at Berkeley, remembers that, very soon after the news hit the West Coast, a seminar was held to discuss uranium fission. "I do not recall ever seeing Oppie so stimulated and so full of ideas."

Oppenheimer's almost feverish excitement is clear from the letter he wrote to Willie Fowler, a day or two after hearing about fission, both in its content and in its breathless style. It reads as if it were written in an enormous hurry:

> The U business is unbelievable. We first saw it in the papers, wired for more dope and have had a lot of reports since. You know it started with Hahn's finding that what he had taken for Ra in one of the U activities fractionally crystallized with Ba. And then the recognition that the ekauranium [transuranic] series was chemically compatible with a series starting with Ma, running on through Rhe and Os and Pd. And then understanding suddenly why there were such long chains of beta decay, to get rid of the neutron excess with which half a U nucleus would start . . . Many points are still unclear: where are the short lived high energy betas one would expect? Are there strong gammas as one would think from the big dipole moments of the pieces? In how many ways does the U come apart? At random,

as one might guess, or only in certain ways? And most of all, are there many neutrons that come off during the splitting, or from the excited pieces? If there are then a 10 cm cube of U would be quite something.

"What do you think?" he asked Fowler. "It is, I think, exciting, not in the rare way of positrons and mesotrons, but in a good honest practical way."

As it turned out, Fowler was not very interested. When he was later asked about when and how he had first heard of fission, he replied airily: "I remember very vaguely about fission. I guess we got the word from Oppenheimer. I would be hard put to say for sure."

> At that time, we weren't doing very much with neutrons and didn't have any strong neutron sources, so I frankly can't remember wanting to do anything in that area, and I don't believe Charlie [Lauritsen] did. We were so busy with the things we were doing ourselves at that time that we did not respond to the fission discovery in the way that many other labs did. There was always the joke, "Well, that's heavy element physics, we're in the business of bombarding light elements, nothing heavier than neon around here." So I never did any experiments in fission and I'm pretty sure that Charlie didn't.

Oppenheimer's excitement about the discovery seems, from the very beginning, to have had its roots not in pure science, but in the possibility that it would lead to extremely powerful explosives. That, presumably, is what he meant when he said to Fowler that it was interesting "in a good honest practical way." It is certainly what he meant when he mentioned how "interesting" a 10-cm cube of uranium would be, as is made clear in a letter he wrote to Uhlenbeck on February 5. If it turned out, Oppenheimer said, that a significant number of neutrons were released with the fission reaction, then a chain reaction could occur, in which case: "I think it really not too improbable that a ten cm cube of uranium deuteride (one should have something to slow the neutrons without capturing them) might very well blow itself to hell."

Robert Serber had in the summer of 1938 left Berkeley to take up an assistant professorship at the University of Illinois in Urbana, but, Serber says in his autobiography, "Oppie would write me every Sunday."

> From one of those Sunday letters, which I received in January 1939, I learned of the discovery of fission. In that first letter Oppie men-

tioned the possibility of nuclear power and of an explosive. My immediate reaction, and I'm sure that of most other nuclear theorists, was that I should have thought of fission myself.

Oppenheimer no doubt missed Serber badly during those frenetic opening months of 1939. There is nobody with whom he would rather have discussed the implications of fission than Serber, nobody whose help he would rather have had in thinking through all the questions that he had listed in his letter to Willie Fowler. However, with Serber miles away in the Midwest, and Fowler (like, it seems, the rest of Caltech) uninterested, Oppenheimer turned to his students.

As students completed their Ph.D. theses and moved on—the lucky ones to academic appointments—the group of graduates that surrounded Oppenheimer and followed him between Berkeley and Pasadena was continually changing, their adoration and unconscious imitation of him the only thing that stayed constant. In the summer of 1938, Willis Lamb graduated and moved to New York, where, as mentioned earlier, he worked at Columbia University. George Volkoff and Hartland Snyder, however, were still at Berkeley, and so were two other students, Philip Morrison and Sidney Dancoff. Following in Volkoff's footsteps, two other University of British Columbia graduates had joined Oppenheimer: Robert Christy in 1936 and the Japanese-born Shuichi Kusaka in 1937. Two new students in the academic year 1938–9 were Bernard Peters and Joseph Weinberg.

In Berkeley, even among other students, Oppenheimer's graduates were considered a bohemian crowd. Morrison has been described as "a scrappy little man on fire with his science," who "hitch-hiked from Pittsburgh and lunched on cat meat to stay near Oppenheimer." Joe Weinberg, meanwhile, "had originally started from the Lower East Side of New York and eventually found his way to the mecca with the clothes he wore and a spare pair of shoes in a paper sack." Raymond Birge became concerned about the class of people Oppenheimer was attracting. "New York Jews flocked out here to him and some were not as nice as he was," Birge said. "Lawrence and I were very concerned to have people here who were nice people as well as good students."

Indeed, it had been Birge's concern to have "nice people" at Berkeley that had prevented Oppenheimer from securing a job for Robert Serber there. When he urged Birge to appoint Serber, Birge is reputed to have said (not to Oppenheimer, but in a letter to someone else): "One Jew in the department is enough." Birge and Lawrence laid down two rules governing appointments: 1. no one with a Ph.D. from Berkeley; and

2. no bohemians. The first ruled out Oppenheimer's graduate students, the second his NRC fellowship students like Serber.

To Lawrence's great displeasure, almost all of Oppenheimer's students were left-wing and many of them already were (or later became) members of the Communist Party. Of them all, Bernard Peters had the most colorful past. He was a German Jew who had escaped Dachau and arrived in the U.S. with his wife, Hannah, in 1934. They settled in New York, where, while Hannah trained as a doctor, Peters worked in an import business. In 1937, when Hannah finished her medical degree, they bought a car and drove out west, where Hannah became a research fellow at Stanford and Peters worked as a longshoreman. Through Jean Tatlock they met Oppenheimer, who encouraged Peters to come to Berkeley as a graduate student in physics.

For some reason, Joe Weinberg did not start in September 1938, but arrived rather in February 1939. He had, it seems, been sent there mid-term by his physics professor at Wisconsin, Gregory Breit, who told him that Berkeley was one of the few places in the world where "a person as crazy as you could be acceptable." As soon as he arrived, Weinberg went to Oppenheimer's room, to find a meeting in full flow. After being introduced to, among others, Lawrence, Snyder, Morrison and Dancoff, he joined Morrison and Dancoff for lunch at the student-union restaurant. The conversation was dominated by fission and a telegram that had recently arrived from Bohr. "On the basis of the data," Weinberg remembered, "we designed a bomb." Morrison, however, was convinced that it would not work, that the chain reaction would peter out before leading to an explosion. Nevertheless, Morrison recalls that, within a week of them all learning about fission, "there was on the blackboard in Robert Oppenheimer's office a drawing—a very bad, an execrable drawing—of a bomb."

Remarkably, despite all this excitement, there is no evidence that, in the months that followed, Oppenheimer did any serious scientific work on the theory of nuclear fission; no evidence, for example, of any sustained attempt to answer the questions that he told Fowler urgently needed addressing. There is instead a rather conspicuous silence on the subject. Although in February 1939 his students were apparently designing bombs in the student-union canteen and he was leaving drawings of explosives on his blackboard for all to see, after that, until the autumn of 1941 when he was invited to contribute to the U.S. bomb project, one searches in vain for the word "bomb," or indeed the word "fission," in his letters and in the recollections of conversations with friends. The only recorded exception to this silence that I know of is Fowler's recollection that at Caltech "Oppie gave some lectures on what was essentially the Bohr-Wheeler theory of fission."

Assuming this was in the summer of 1939, then Oppenheimer, characteristically, was lecturing on a brand-new theory, one that had yet to appear in print. It was, moreover, one that was directly applicable to the questions Oppenheimer had raised upon hearing the news of fission, and therefore to the question of whether fission could lead to the construction of an atomic bomb. The theory was worked out by Bohr and Wheeler in Princeton in the spring of 1939, written out by Wheeler in June and appeared in the *Physical Review* on September 1, in the same issue that contained Oppenheimer and Snyder's seminal article on black holes.

The origins of the Bohr-Wheeler theory lie in conversations the two had in Princeton in the first week of February 1939, after they returned from the Washington conference. With the entire community of American physicists still buzzing with the news of fission, Bohr asked Wheeler if he would like to work on a more detailed theory of the phenomenon. "It was an exciting time," says Wheeler in his autobiography, though he emphasizes that, for them at least, the excitement was to do with pure science, not explosives: "Bombs and reactors were only in the backs of our minds as we worked together. We were trying to understand a new nuclear phenomenon, not design anything."

To inform their theoretical deliberations, Bohr and Wheeler asked the experimental physicists at Princeton to conduct some experiments to determine how the probability of fission in uranium varies with the energy of the incoming neutrons. The results were puzzling: the probability is high for high-energy neutrons and diminishes as the energy diminishes, until, at very low energies, it becomes high again. Why should this be? Taking a walk to ponder this question, Bohr, accompanied by Rosenfeld, went from the faculty club to Einstein's office (which he was borrowing at the time), where he rushed to the blackboard, saying: "Now listen: I have it all."

What Bohr had realized was that the high probability of fission at low energies was due to a rare isotope of uranium, U-235, present only in 0.7 percent of natural uranium. The more common form of uranium, U-238, being more stable, requires higher-energy neutrons to split it. Low-energy neutrons stand a higher chance of hitting the nucleus, because their wavelengths are longer, but upon impact they will only split the more unstable U-235 nuclei. So, high-energy neutrons stand a good chance of splitting any uranium nuclei they happen to hit, including those of U-238, while low-energy neutrons stand a good chance of hitting all nuclei, and of splitting those of U-235, but the neutrons in between are not traveling fast enough to split U-238, or slow enough to stand a good chance of hitting anything.

On February 7, Bohr sent the *Physical Review* an initial paper that did not go into all the theoretical details that he and Wheeler had discussed, but did announce the important conclusion they had reached: that fission by slow neutrons was possible only in less than 1 percent of naturally occurring uranium. Oppenheimer must have read this, and must have made use of it in his lectures on fission at Caltech, but there is no mention of it in his correspondence.

The next important question to answer was: are neutrons—so-called "secondary" neutrons—emitted during the fission process ("If there are then a 10 cm cube of U would be quite something")? The answer to this was provided by Leo Szilard early in March 1939, after some experiments he conducted at Columbia seemed to establish that "the number of neutrons emitted per fission [is] about two"—a result quickly confirmed by experiments in other laboratories, including Fermi's. This meant that the chain reaction imagined by Szilard when he pondered Rutherford's lecture on the splitting of the atom some years earlier was indeed a possibility. "That night," Szilard said later, "there was little doubt in my mind that the world was headed for grief."

In the light of these results, Szilard, accompanied by Fermi and Eugene Wigner, tried to warn the U.S. government about the danger. Through George Pegram, dean of physics at Columbia, they managed to secure a meeting between Fermi and Admiral Stanford C. Hooper, technical assistant to the Chief of Naval Operations. At the meeting, however, Fermi made the mistake of lecturing the admiral on neutron physics rather than talking about bombs. His lecture therefore failed to inspire the required sense of urgency. "Couldn't you arouse the admiral's interest in the atomic bomb?" Fermi's wife asked him many years later. "You are using big words," Fermi replied. "You forget that in March 1939, there was little likelihood of an atomic bomb."

Szilard and Fermi had both written papers reporting on the neutron-emission experiments, but Szilard persuaded Fermi that, for the moment at least, they should not be published. At Princeton, Szilard and Wigner met Bohr in order to persuade him not to publish any further research on fission. At this meeting they were joined by yet another Hungarian, and a man who would subsequently play a major role in Oppenheimer's life: Edward Teller. Four years younger than Oppenheimer, Teller had left Hungary for Germany when he was just eighteen. He took his Ph.D. at Leipzig, with Heisenberg as his supervisor, and then worked with Bohr in Copenhagen, before taking up a position at George Washington University, in Washington, D.C., in 1935. By 1939, he was an established part of the American scientific world, known equally for his scientific brilliance and his personal pugnaciousness.

On this occasion the three Hungarians failed to persuade Bohr of the necessity to keep fission research under wraps. Bohr hated secrecy, believing openness to be essential to the progress of science. He was also not convinced that the secondary emission of neutrons alone guaranteed the possibility of an atomic bomb. It would make the bomb possible *if* one could get hold of a sufficiently large lump of pure (or fairly pure) U-235, but such are the difficulties of isotope separation that Bohr was convinced it would never happen. "It can never be done," he insisted, "unless you turn the United States into one huge factory."

In March and April, the Paris group led by Frédéric Joliot-Curie published two papers (in English) reporting their own experiments on secondary neutrons and giving their own conclusion that, in a sufficiently large amount of uranium, a chain reaction was indeed possible. After this, Szilard has recalled, "Fermi was adamant that withholding publication made no sense." He might equally have drawn the opposite conclusion. As soon as these papers came to the attention of the Reich Ministry of Education, the German government imposed a ban on the export of uranium and set up a conference that initiated a research program on nuclear fission.

On July 12, 1939, Szilard and Wigner made their now-famous trip to Peconic, Long Island, to meet Einstein. Their initial reason for wanting to talk to Einstein was that they knew he was on good terms with the King and Queen of the Belgians. The Congo, then a Belgian colony, owned the world's largest supply of uranium, and Szilard and Wigner wanted, through Einstein, to alert the Belgians to the global importance of their uranium supplies. First they had to explain to Einstein what had been discovered about fission and secondary neutrons, all of which (despite the fact that some of the key ideas had been discovered in his room at Princeton and written on his blackboard) was new to him. Then the three of them drafted a letter to the Belgian ambassador in Washington, a copy of which they sent to the U.S. State Department. Back in New York, Szilard, worrying about whether they had done the right thing, sought the counsel of a prominent banker, Alexander Sachs, who had served as advisor to the Roosevelt government. Sachs's advice was that the letter should not have gone to a government department; rather, it should go directly to the President.

So on August 2, this time accompanied by Teller, Szilard returned to Long Island to see Einstein again, and the three of them worked on a letter to Roosevelt, which, after going through several drafts, ended up warning the President that, in light of the experiments on secondary neutrons conducted by Joliot, Fermi and Szilard, "it may become possible to set up a nuclear chain reaction in a large mass of uranium, by which vast amounts of power and large quantities of new radium-like elements would be generated." This, they went on, "would also lead to the construction of bombs. A single bomb of this type, carried by boat and exploded in a port, might very well destroy the whole port together with some of the surrounding territory." They recommended that the President set up a permanent contact between the government and the physicists working on chain reactions. The letter was signed "Yours very truly, Albert Einstein." After several delays, on October 11, 1939, it was delivered in person to the President by Sachs. "What you are after," Roosevelt is reported to have said to Sachs, "is to see that the Nazis don't blow us up." "Precisely," replied Sachs. Ten days later, the U.S. bomb project, in its initial form as the Advisory Committee on Uranium, was born.

Despite his evident excitement about fission and its possible application to weaponry when the news first broke, there is nothing to indicate that, throughout the months that led up to Sachs's crucial meeting with Roosevelt, Oppenheimer was in any way concerned with or involved in—or even particularly interested in—the scientific breakthroughs and political maneuvers that culminated in the establishment of the U.S. research program. Other than his lectures on the Bohr-Wheeler theory of fission in the spring and summer of 1939, he seems to have concentrated on other things, principally his paper with Snyder on black holes. It is thus a curious fact that while Szilard, Fermi, Wheeler, Bohr and many other physicists (both theoretical and experimental) were establishing the relevant facts about the fission of uranium and laying down the fundamental principles upon which the physics of the atom bomb was built, Oppenheimer—the "father of the atom bomb"—was contemplating the gravitational collapse of stars in outer space, and in the process making his greatest ever contribution to science.

Why Oppenheimer seemed so uninterested in fission during these crucial months is something of a mystery. It is possible, of course, that he remained intensely interested in fission from February 1939 until his involvement in the U.S. bomb project two and a half years later, but that the conversations in which this interest was discussed went unrecorded and unrecalled, and the writings that expressed it have not survived. However, given how thoroughly this period has been researched, how many interviews with the relevant people have been conducted, and what an intense spotlight has been shone by historians on these months, this seems unlikely. Nor is this apparent lack of interest in fission confined to Oppenheimer; it extends also to his friends and students. At both Berkeley and Caltech his friends and colleagues seemed reluctant to pursue the science of nuclear fission, while his students, though they had seemed to share his initial enthusiasm, were writing their Ph.D. theses on other things: Volkoff and Snyder on astrophysics, Christy on cosmic rays, Kusaka on the mesotron, and Dancoff, Morrison and Weinberg on quantum electrodynamics.

In January 1940, a very thorough review of the literature on fission by the Princeton physicist Louis Turner was published in *Reviews of Modern Physics*. In his introductory paragraph Turner notes that "Although less than a year had passed since the discovery by Hahn and Strassmann that the capture of neutrons by uranium nuclei may lead to their disruption to form lighter nuclei, nearly one hundred papers on this subject have already appeared." Turner then summarizes the findings of those papers under such headings as "Neutrons Produced in Fission," "Theory of Fission," "Secondary Neutrons," and so on. At the end of his review article Turner lists all the papers that he had discussed, among which are strikingly few by scientists at Berkeley and Caltech. There is nothing by Oppenheimer or any of his students, nothing by Lawrence or any of his students, and only three by people working at the Rad Lab: one by Abelson, one by Ed McMillan and one by a new arrival, the Jewish Italian physicist Emilio Segrè.

Segrè, who had worked with Fermi in Italy, joined the Rad Lab in the autumn of 1938. He was drawn there by the possibilities of the cyclotron, but, as he describes in his autobiography, soon after he arrived he began to understand why those possibilities had so far failed to result in important discoveries and fundamental scientific breakthroughs. "The more familiar I became with the Rad Lab," Segrè writes, "the more surprised I was; it operated very differently from any other laboratory I had been in. There were many students, but they seemed to me to be left to themselves, without scientific guidance."

> The truth was that Lawrence's interest centered on the cyclotron and on building the Rad Lab's diverse activities; his knowledge of and interest in nuclear physics were limited. Students, in practice, served as cheap labor for the building and tending of the cyclotron and any move that might divert them from this task was frowned upon. It was difficult for me to understand the scientific policy of the Rad Lab. The cyclotron was a unique device, with seemingly infinite potential, but the main concern of those who controlled it was apparently to make the machine bigger and put it to work in areas

outside of physics; there was little thought given to making proper use of what was on hand for nuclear studies.

The "areas outside of physics" that Segrè mentions here are primarily areas of medical research. Though Lawrence always stressed in public how important the cyclotron was to fundamental physics, to others, particularly to those with money to donate, he emphasized the value of the cyclotron for producing radioactive isotopes that had applications in both medical research and practical medicine. There was no doubt that the machine had proved its worth for that purpose; Segrè's concern was evidently that students attracted to the Rad Lab with the intention of pursuing fundamental physical research were instead used to keep the cyclotron going as a kind of factory for producing isotopes.

Segrè's view that Lawrence's knowledge of, and interest in, nuclear physics was limited was held by many other scientists, but many too would have agreed with the following summary of Lawrence's strengths and weaknesses given by Hans Bethe:

> Lawrence was a tremendous influence on the development of physics, good in that he made people conscious of big accelerators. His enthusiasm for this one instrument of research was marvellous. So was the way he could make big foundations and government agencies give him money. He was not so much interested in the results of research—he left that to others—and in this sense he was not even a good physicist.

Bethe seems right on all counts. Despite being wrong-footed time and time again by new discoveries in physics, despite, as Heilbron and Seidel put it in their history of the Rad Lab, "the disagreeable fact that no major discovery had yet been made in any cyclotron laboratory," Lawrence somehow managed to turn each lost opportunity into a successful case for pouring more and more money into his ambitions of building bigger and bigger machines.

Though he had at his disposal the world's most powerful accelerator, and a budget that other laboratories could only dream of, Lawrence had missed every major discovery in physics since 1932: deuterium and the neutron, the splitting of the lithium nucleus, the positron, the artificial creation of radioactive isotopes, the mesotron and, finally, nuclear fission—all of them had been discovered either by using much less powerful equipment than the Berkeley cyclotrons or by analyzing cosmic rays, the high energies of which are provided by nature free of charge.

And yet, despite his conspicuous lack of scientific achievement, in the 1930s Lawrence was by far America's most famous scientist. In 1937 *Time* magazine put him on their cover, calling him "the cyclotron man, foremost U.S. destroyer and creator of atoms." His lecture tours were a great success, he had honorary degrees conferred on him by South Dakota, Princeton and Yale, and he was showered with grants, prizes and donations. He was an extremely successful promoter of his own product, and, in the face of much evidence to the contrary, was remarkably good at persuading people, especially those with funds, that what was needed for scientific breakthroughs in nuclear physics were bigger and bigger cyclotrons. Measured by the diameter of their magnets, the inexorable progress was this: the 11-inch was followed by the 27-inch, and then a 37-inch.

When news of fission broke, Lawrence's mind was concentrated on getting his newest and biggest cyclotron to date—a 60-inch—up and running. In the wake of the announcement of fission, and with a brass neck that had got him where he was, Lawrence sent letters to physicists around the world, detailing the "successes" of the Rad Lab, and claiming that curiosity about fission among his colleagues was so overwhelming that many of them were committing the "heresy" of suspending work on the planned new cyclotron in order to study fission. "For obvious reasons," Lawrence pointed out, "we want to find out whether neutrons are given off in the splitting process." On that point, too, the Rad Lab was scooped; while Alvarez gained inconclusive results from the cyclotron, Fermi, Szilard and Joliot provided the affirmative answer that set the U.S. bomb project in motion. Meanwhile, Lawrence went back to the task of setting up the 60-inch cyclotron, and when, in the summer of 1939, it was up and running, he started thinking about his next machine, which he said would have a 120-inch magnet, weigh 2,000 tons and be capable of energies of 100 million volts.

Although it is easy to sneer at Lawrence's obsession with bigger and bigger machines and at the fact that, as Bethe put it, he was "not even a good physicist," one should also remember the other half of Bethe's assessment, his statement that: "Lawrence was a tremendous influence on the development of physics, good in that he made people conscious of big accelerators." The American public were not entirely wrong to regard him as their greatest scientist. The 60-inch cyclotron that distracted Lawrence from the news of fission, for example, was used to make significant scientific discoveries in 1940 and thereafter. In this way, Lawrence, despite his limitations as a scientist, did indeed make an important contribution to science. Segrè reports that Lawrence had expected to receive the Nobel Prize in 1938 and was disappointed when it went instead to Fermi. Lawrence may not have been completely surprised, then, to learn, as he did on November 9, 1939, that his time had come. He was to receive the 1939 Nobel Prize "for the invention and development of the cyclotron and for the results obtained by its aid, especially with regard to artificially radioactive elements."

When the award was presented to him on February 29, 1940 (in Berkeley rather than in Sweden, because of the dangers of traveling in Europe), Lawrence used his acceptance speech to plead for funding for his new dream machine, which had now swollen to a 184-inch model, weighing 3,000 tons, the cost of which would be about $2 million. Two months later, he heard that the Rockefeller Foundation had agreed to give him $1.15 million to develop the new cyclotron, which, together with other contributions, guaranteed that it would be built. In acknowledging his thanks, Lawrence said that he expected it to be complete by the summer of 1944, barring any "unforeseen difficulties." Of course, there were any number of unforeseen difficulties, but the 184-inch cyclotron *was* built and, after being pressed into service as the first "Calutron" during the war, underwent a fundamental redesign as a "synchrocyclotron," which produced beams of deuterons with energies of nearly 200 million volts and was used to make important scientific breakthroughs. What in 1939 looked like a distraction from real science, in favor of a misguided obsession with mere size, looked after the war like a prescient anticipation of the age of "big science." Lawrence's instinct that larger and larger machines capable of greater and greater voltages would be essential to the scientific research of the future turned out to be entirely correct.

It was not just in relation to science that Segrè found his new colleagues at Berkeley unsophisticated. "Talking politics with American colleagues," he says, "I found an incomprehension of things European that was appalling to me." Illustrative of what he meant were Lawrence's sometimes extraordinarily naïve and ill-informed reactions to, and views about, European affairs. Shortly after the Munich Agreement in October 1938, for example, Lawrence wrote to the British scientist Wilfrid Mann, who had recently returned to London after working at the Rad Lab: "You have been having a very anxious time recently, but let us hope the war clouds have passed and that we have ahead of us *at least a decade* of peace. I don't think it absurd to believe it is possible that we have seen a turning point in history, that henceforth international disputes of great powers will be settled by peaceful negotiations and not by war." On August 29, 1939, just three days before Germany invaded Poland, Lawrence wrote to his parents: "I still think war is going to be avoided. All this discussion must mean that Hitler is backing down."

But what of Oppenheimer? Segrè has some equally tart observations about him. Oppenheimer, he says:

. . . was considered a demigod by himself and others at Berkeley, and as such he spake in learned and obscure fashions. Besides, he knew quantum mechanics well, and in this he was unique at Berkeley. He taught it in none too easy a fashion, which showed off his prowess and attracted a number of gifted students. Oppenheimer's loyal disciples hung on his words and put on corresponding airs. Just as we in Rome had acquired Fermi's intonation, in Berkeley Oppenheimer's students walked as if they had flat feet, an infirmity of their master's.

With regard to the celebrated cultural sophistication of Oppenheimer and his students, Segrè was not impressed:

Oppenheimer and his group did not inspire in me the awe that they perhaps expected. I had the impression that their celebrated general culture was not superior to that expected in a boy who had attended a good European high school. I was already acquainted with most of their cultural discoveries, and I found Oppenheimer's ostentation slightly ridiculous. In physics I was used to Fermi, who had a quite different solidity, coupled with a simplicity that contrasted with Oppenheimer's erudite complexities.

It is with regard to politics, however, that Segrè is especially damning. "Oppenheimer and most of his acolytes," he says, "followed the political line of the Communist Party of the United States, which was highly uncritical and simple-minded." He had the impression that Oppenheimer regarded him as a "great Fascist" ("I was a Fascist Party member, as every Italian state employee was required to be by law, but it did not take much acumen to figure out that I could not be a Fascist at heart"), while, according to him, Oppenheimer—in following the Communist Party line—"deemed that the European quarrels were caused by capitalist imperialists, and that Holy Communism would avoid them."

In the light of the reports quoted earlier—that Oppenheimer's faith in the Soviet Union was strongly undermined in the summer of 1938— one might think Segrè misunderstood the degree to which Oppenheimer was prepared to follow slavishly the Communist Party line, or that at the very least he was exaggerating. What evidence there is, however, supports Segrè. A key event here is the Treaty of Non-Aggression, signed by Germany and the Soviet Union on August 23, 1939, which shocked most liberals and a good number of Communist Party members, and effectively put an end to the strategy Earl Browder had pursued throughout the 1930s of presenting the Communist Party as the upholder of, and natural heir to, the tradition of American liberalism. Indeed, the pact put Browder and the American Communist Party in an extraordinarily difficult position and ended any hope they might have had of continuing to be part of a broad "popular front." After years of upholding communism as the one force that had the strength and determination to halt the spread of fascism in Europe, how could Browder and the Communist Party possibly justify an agreement—something close to an alliance— between the world's most repugnant fascist state and its only communist state? Against his own inclinations, Browder was forced to insist in public that the pact was "a wonderful contribution to peace" and to deny that it made Poland's position more insecure. He, however, was obliged by his position to follow the party line; Oppenheimer was not.

In 1954 Oppenheimer mentioned the Nazi-Soviet pact as one of the things that influenced his "changing opinion of Russia," but also insisted that this "did not mean a sharp break for me with those who hold to different views." Those who held to different views, of course, included all who, despite everything, maintained the Party line, for instance all of Oppenheimer's friends and students—and there were many—who remained members of the Communist Party after the signing of the pact. One of those was Haakon Chevalier, who in his book *Oppenheimer: The Story of a Friendship* raises the question of the pact and then, ostensibly in order to illustrate the quality of Oppenheimer's analyses of political events, offers the following account of Oppenheimer's reaction to the anti-communist feeling that followed:

> It was in the fall of 1939, too, that Opje[42] proved himself to be such an impressive and effective political analyst. The Soviet-German pact, and later the invasion of Poland by the USSR and the Soviet war with Finland, had confused and upset many people, even among the most open-minded and liberal. Opje had such a simple, lucid way of presenting facts and arguments that one felt in him a kind of passionate commitment which was contagious. He communicated with extraordinary effectiveness his own conviction that political events were motivated by human events that could be made to yield their significance if examined objectively, in the light of the factors that had conditioned them.

After reading this account, what Oppenheimer actually thought of the pact, or of the war, remains utterly opaque. The documentary record is a little clearer. In a letter to Willie Fowler at Caltech that seems to

[42] While most people in California anglicised it to "Oppie," Chevalier insisted on keeping to the Dutch original of the nickname.

have been written on or about September 9, 1939, Oppenheimer writes: "I know Charlie [Lauritsen] will say a melancholy I told you so over the Nazisoviet [*sic*] pact, but I am not paying any bets yet on any aspect of the hocus-pocus except maybe that the Germans are pretty well into Poland. *Ça stink.*"

In the ensuing months of what is commonly called the "phoney war," while no hostilities were exchanged between Germany and France or Britain, Poland was divided up between Germany and the Soviet Union and the latter invaded Finland. The belief that the Nazi-Soviet pact was nothing more than a cynical temporary agreement between two dictatorships, allowing each to expand without fear of the other, seemed to be amply confirmed. Moreover, because the Soviet Union seemed so indifferent to the plight of the European democracies—indeed, its propaganda seemed to hold the British Empire in greater contempt than Nazi Germany—and its foreign policy so out of keeping with anything with which American liberal opinion could sympathize, it seemed no longer possible, so long as the American Communist Party took its "line" from Moscow, to believe that the views of the Party were those that a loyal American, concerned only with local, American issues, would have arrived at independently.

And yet, in his February 1940 pamphlet *Report to Our Colleagues* mentioned previously,[43] that is exactly the belief for which Oppenheimer tried to argue. Published under the auspices of the "College Faculties Committee, Communist Party of California," this pamphlet had as its purpose presenting to academic colleagues at Berkeley, Stanford and Caltech the political views of the discussion group/Communist Party unit to which Oppenheimer, Chevalier and others belonged. According to Gordon Griffiths, Oppenheimer was not the sole author of this pamphlet, but he "took special pride in it."

How Oppenheimer could have been proud of the document is something of a puzzle, since it contains almost no original thought, being simply a presentation of the official Communist Party line, nor does it contain any fine writing or telling phrase; its style is that of a Party tract. What it seeks to persuade "colleagues" of is that the attacks on the Communist Party made in the wake of the Nazi-Soviet pact and the invasions of Poland and Finland should be seen not in relation to global politics, but rather in relation to *American* politics and in particular the plight of the poor and the unemployed in the U.S. Instead of focusing on the pact made between Hitler and Stalin, the report urges, colleagues should look at the "strange things" that were happening to the New Deal, and,

---

[43] See p. 249.

in particular, to the cuts in relief funding that had been announced at both a federal level by Roosevelt and a local level by the California legislature. In this context, the report argues, it can be seen that the purpose of the attacks on communists is "to disrupt the democratic forces, to destroy unions in general and CIO [Congress of Industrial Organizations] unions in particular, to make possible the cutting of relief, to force the abandonment of the great program of peace, security and work that is the basis of the movement toward a democratic front."

Despite its attempt to focus on issues such as poor relief and unemployment, what comes through most strongly in the *Report* is its echoing of the slogan of the Communist Party manifesto: "Keep America Out of the Imperialist War!" The communists, the *Report* claims, possess "some of the clearest voices that oppose a war between the United States and Russia," the silencing of which, it alleges, is the hidden motive behind the attacks being made on the Communist Party. It would, the report emphasizes and reiterates, "be an evil thing for this country to go to war, or to join a war, against Russia." Warming to its theme, it goes on: "In a war against Russia almost anything could be illegal except the rich making money and the poor dying."

This fear of a war with Russia is evident too in the second and last *Report to Our Colleagues*, published in April 1940, which states unequivocally: "There has never been a clearer issue than that of keeping this country out of the war in Europe." When the report tries to make this clarity apparent, however, it slips into communist rhetoric that makes uncomfortable reading for anyone inclined to think Segrè was being misleading about Oppenheimer's political views:

> Europe is in the throes of a war. It is a common thought, and a likely one, that when the war is over Europe will be socialist, and the British Empire gone. We think that Roosevelt is assuming the role of preserving the old order in Europe and that he plans, if need be, to use the wealth and the lives of this country to carry it out. We think, that is, that Roosevelt is not only a "war monger" but a counter-revolutionary war-monger. We think it is this that has turned him from something of a progressive to very much of a reactionary.

So, *why* is it so clear that the U.S. should stay out of the war? Because, it seems, if it stays out, the British Empire will collapse, which will be a good thing. But won't that signal the victory of Nazism rather than of socialism? How does one get from the collapse of the British Empire to the "likely" outcome of a socialist Europe? The most natural interpretation of this seems to be that Oppenheimer (and the "College Faculties

Committee, Communist Party of California") foresees the defeat of Britain being followed by the defeat of a weakened Germany at the hands of the Soviet Union. If this is right (and it is hard to find an alternative that would make sense of the above passage), then, if anything, Segrè was being kind in his characterization of Oppenheimer's views ("that the European quarrels were caused by capitalist imperialists, and that Holy Communism would avoid them"). Oppenheimer's view seems rather to be: the war is actually a good thing, precisely because it is caused by capitalist imperialists, who, in defeating and weakening each other, will allow "socialism," in the form of the Soviet Union, to triumph over Europe—but *only* if the U.S. stays out of the struggle, thereby allowing the defeat of Britain to take place.

It is possible, I think, that these *Reports to Our Colleagues* help to explain the curious avoidance of research into fission and its possible use in explosives by Oppenheimer and his students, despite their evident excitement at, and absorption in, the issue when it was first announced. Given the emphasis manifest in these reports on the need for the United States to stay out of the war, together with the repeatedly expressed fear that America would *not* stay out of the war, but rather go into it with the intention of fighting Russia, it seems at least possible that Oppenheimer and his students avoided work on the physics of fission because they did not want to contribute to a war they passionately believed the United States should not be involved in. One is reminded here of Felix Adler's argument for American neutrality in the First World War, and of his denunciation of any scientist willing to put his or her services at the disposal of the war effort: "The time will come when that scientist will be considered and will consider himself a disgrace to the human race who prostitutes his knowledge of Nature's forces for the destruction of his fellow men."

Report to Our Colleagues had originally been intended as an ongoing series of publications. The fact that there were only ever two of them, Chevalier says, is "for some reason which I have forgotten—possibly because of the rapidly changing perspectives in the world situation." Certainly Oppenheimer's own political perspective seems to have changed rapidly and fundamentally within just a few months of the publication of the second *Report*, the change prompted by sudden, drastic and shocking developments in the world. After the Nazi invasion of Denmark and Norway in April 1940, the collapse of Holland and Belgium in May and the fall of France in June, was it possible for a liberal intellectual to continue to believe that it was of the utmost importance for the U.S. to remain neutral? With most of Western Europe under the control of Hitler's Germany, Spain under Franco and Italy under Mussolini, was it still possible to think that a socialist Europe was the "likely" outcome of the war? And, finally, could Oppenheimer still believe, as he appears to have done up until April 1940, that the Soviet Union had acted wisely and in the interests of the "democratic front" in signing a nonaggression pact with Germany, thereby standing by while this rapid expansion of the Reich took place?

If Hans Bethe's recollections are accurate, the answer to all those questions is "no." In the summer of 1940, Bethe met Oppenheimer at a conference held by the American Physical Society in Seattle from June 18 to 21. On June 20, Bethe and Oppenheimer (together with Volkoff and Snyder) took part in a seminar on "The Present Crisis in the Quantum Theory of Fields." This was about a fortnight after the British evacuation from Dunkirk, two days after the German army marched into Paris and two days before the French surrender, when, at Hitler's insistence, the armistice was signed in the very railway coach that had been used in November 1918 for the armistice that ended the First World War.

In these dark times, Bethe remembers a party of about ten people at the home of Edwin Uehling, previously a student of Oppenheimer's and now a professor at the University of Washington in Seattle. During his time at the conference Oppenheimer was a guest at the Uehlings' house. At this party, Bethe recalls a conversation about the European situation in which there were expressed some deep anxieties about the future. Oppenheimer, Bethe remembers, addressed the group in the following words:

> This is a time when the whole of western civilization is at stake. France, one of the great exponents of western civilization, has fallen, and we must see to it that Britain and the United States don't fall as well. We have to defend western values against the Nazis. And because of the Molotov–von Ribbentrop pact [i.e. the Nazi-Soviet pact] we can have no truck with the Communists.

Bethe thinks this may have been "the first occasion in which Oppenheimer talked about political matters not from the standpoint of the left, but from the standpoint of the West." If Bethe's recollections are accurate, then a mere two months after the publication of the second *Report to Our Colleagues*, Oppenheimer had adopted *exactly* the view that he was, in that report, concerned to refute: namely, that it was important to take sides in the war in order to protect democracy against fascism.

However, apart from the remark "we can have no truck with the Communists," Oppenheimer's views, as reported by Bethe, are not quite as far from those of the American Communist Party as they might at first appear. As Maurice Isserman writes in his history of the American Communist Party:

> The Communists, for all their hostility to the Allied cause, were unprepared for and dismayed by the swift collapse of French resistance in May 1940. They assumed, as Stalin had when he signed the non-aggression pact, that the German and French armies were relatively well matched. When and if the "phoney war" ever came to an end, the Communists expected the conflict to turn into a stalemate similar to the one on the western front in the First World War.

Isserman provides telling quotations from the communist press during the sequence of Nazi victories. After the fall of Norway, the *People's World* attacked Britain as "the greatest danger to Europe and all mankind"; after Beligum and Holland were overrun, the *Daily Worker* could still maintain: "This is not our war"; but, writes Isserman: "The fall of France eventually provoked some anxious second thoughts among Communists." Communists who had previously excused the Nazi-Soviet pact "now had to face up to the possibility that Hitler got the better bargain." In June, the *Daily Worker* even printed a letter from one of its readers, asking the question that was surely on the minds of many communists in the summer of 1940: "Will not Hitler, in the event of a crushing victory over Great Britain and France, turn his armies against the USSR?"

It may be, as Bethe believed, that Oppenheimer's speech to his fellow physicists in Seattle represented a shift in his allegiance away from the Communist Party and toward the West, as represented by Britain, France and the U.S., but, after the fall of Norway, Denmark, Belgium, Holland and France, and the apparent imminent fall of Britain, it is also clear that many American communists had begun to wonder whether their previous analysis of world events had been correct, whether the interests of the Soviet Union and socialism were *really* best served by the collapse of Great Britain and the nonintervention of the U.S. It was rather looking as though the Soviet Union, Great Britain and the U.S. had a shared interest in defeating the (now massively extended) Third Reich.

Most Americans, of course, neither knew nor cared how American communists were reacting to the new, deeply alarming situation in Europe. What struck them was that the Communist Party was closely connected with the Soviet Union, which had signed a deal with Nazi Germany that had allowed—indeed, seemed designed to allow—that deeply alarming situation to occur. Thus was generated a "Red Scare" that prefigured the anti-communism of the 1950s and made life extremely uncomfortable for communists in America. In June 1940, soon after the collapse of France, Congress passed the Alien Registration Act, better known as the Smith Act, which required all resident noncitizens to be registered and fingerprinted. It also authorized the deportation of foreigners belonging to revolutionary groups, and, most damagingly for the Communist Party, made it a crime to conspire to advocate or teach the necessity or desirability of overthrowing the government. After this Act came into force, it was no longer necessary to prove that an individual had, in fact, acted to overthrow the government, nor that he or she had advocated the overthrow of the government; all that was necessary was to show that the individual in question had joined an organization that favored such advocacy. The Smith Act was hotly followed by the Voorhis Act, which required all organizations "subject to foreign control" to register with the Justice Department.

These two Acts signaled the start of a state-sponsored harassment of the Communist Party. Local party offices were raided by police, files were confiscated, suspected Communist Party members were purged from public office, and an official view was adopted that "the very acceptance of Communist Party membership is, in and of itself, an overt act incompatible with the public service." It was widely believed that the rapid fall of France was attributable to "fifth columnists," and that America urgently needed to identify and weed out those people in public life whose loyalties lay with foreign powers. By the autumn of 1940, the American Communist Party was an unpopular and beleaguered organization, deeply distrusted by the government and the people and only barely legal. In the wake of the Voorhis Act, the party felt forced to end its formal affiliation with the Comintern. This helped preserve its legality, though it was not enough to guarantee its acceptance. In the presidential elections of November 1940, the Communist Party succeeded in getting Earl Browder onto only twenty-two state ballots; in the other states, its participation in the ballot was either refused outright or made impossible by the intimidation of sponsors and supporters.

Oppenheimer himself was a passionate supporter of Roosevelt during this election, urging upon his friends, colleagues and students the importance of returning the author of the New Deal for a third term. This does suggest a fairly complete volte-face from the view of Roosevelt as a "war monger" that he had advocated in his April *Report*, though evidence as to why he changed his mind about the President is extremely scarce. From the point of view of his career, however, as he knew only too well, it would have been suicidal to have openly supported the communists.

In the summer of 1940, then, Oppenheimer had many good reasons for distancing himself from the Communist Party, one of which may indeed have been, as Bethe thought, that his own views had changed, that he had been shocked by the collapse of France into seeing things from the perspective of defending the West rather than that of supporting "socialism" as represented by the Soviet Union. That *something* important to him took place at the Uehlings' Seattle home is confirmed by a letter that Oppenheimer wrote to them on July 4, thanking them for their hospitality, the tone of which goes far beyond that of a normal "bread-and-butter" thank-you letter. Oppenheimer, writing from the Tolmans' house in Pasadena, told "Ruth & Ed": "It is time now that I wrote a word to you of the sweet days together in your home . . . I hope you will still have warm memories of a visit which was to your visitor so sweet." Oppenheimer told the Uehlings that in about a week's time he would be going to Perro Caliente with Frank, Jackie and their baby daughter, Judith. Oppenheimer does not mention this to the Uehlings, but he had also invited some other people to New Mexico that summer: Robert and Charlotte Serber and Katherine and Richard Harrison.

Oppenheimer had met Katherine ("Kitty") Harrison at a party at Charles Lauritsen's house the previous summer, and the two had become strongly attracted to each other. She later said that she "fell in love with Robert that day, but hoped to conceal it." At the time she was twenty-nine years old, six years younger than Oppenheimer. Richard Harrison was her third husband. The wedding had taken place in November 1938, less than a year before she met Oppenheimer, and already it was clear that the marriage was not a success. For most of those nine months Kitty had lived apart from her husband. He was a British doctor whom she had known as a teenager and then met again in Philadelphia in the spring of 1938, when she was studying biology at the University of Pennsylvania. Shortly after their wedding, Harrison moved to Pasadena to take up a residency, while she stayed in Philadelphia to finish her degree. She had, by this time, decided that it was "an impossible marriage" and that she was ready to leave him.

Kitty's life up until her move to Pasadena had been eventful and emotionally tumultuous. She had been born Katherine Puening, in Germany, her family emigrating to the U.S. when she was just two years old. Her father, Franz Puening, was an engineer; her mother, Kaethe Vissering, was from a prominent European aristocratic family, the main branches of which were Dutch and German. Through her mother, Kitty was related to (among many other members of Europe's aristocracy) King Albert I of Belgium and Queen Victoria of Great Britain. Wilhelm Keitel, Hitler's field marshal and de facto war minister, was her mother's cousin. She liked to describe herself as a "German princess," though it is not entirely clear what her claim to that title was. She told friends that her father was a "prince of a small principality in Westphalia"; if so, it is something of a mystery why he chose to work as an engineer in a Pittsburgh steel company. He begged her to keep quiet about her aristocratic background, but somehow everybody who knew her knew all about it.

Throughout her life Kitty combined an aristocratic hauteur with a leaning toward bohemianism. At the age of twenty-two she married her first husband, a musician she met in Paris called Frank Ramseyer. After a few months, however, she discovered that he was both homosexual and a drug addict. The marriage was annulled and she returned to America. At a New Year's Eve party in 1933 she was introduced to Joe Dallett, the son of a wealthy German Jewish businessman and a member of the Communist Party. "I fell in love with him at this party," Kitty later said, "and I never stopped loving him." Less than two months later she and Dallett were married and living in Youngstown, Ohio, where he worked as a union organizer.

Very quickly Kitty discovered that life as the wife of a Communist Party union organizer was not as glamorous as she had perhaps imagined it to be. "These were days of poverty such as I had never before experienced," she recalled with horror.

> We lived in a house, part of which we rented for $5 per month. Our only income was a relief payment of $12.40 every two weeks. The house had a kitchen, but the stove leaked and it was impossible to cook. Our food consisted of two meals a day which we got at a grimy restaurant. The price was 15¢ each and the meal consisted of soup, meat, potato, cabbage, a doughnut and coffee.

"Because of Joe's insistence," Kitty remembers, "I was finally permitted to join the Party, but not until I had done a number of tasks which were extremely painful to me, such as selling the *Daily Worker* on the street and passing out leaflets at the steel mill."

Clearly, this was no life for a princess. "As time went on," she later said, "although Joe and I continued to be very much in love, the poverty became more and more depressing to me." Finally, in June 1936, after less than three years of marriage, "I told Joe that I could no longer live under such conditions and that I was separating from him."

She moved to England, where her parents were then living, and became a student at a school of dress design. For some months she heard nothing from Dallett, but then discovered that her mother had been intercepting his letters. After writing to him asking him to take her back, she found out that he was coming to Europe, having volunteered to fight in the Spanish Civil War. In March 1937, she was briefly reunited with Dallett, when she met him, together with his Communist Party colleague Steve Nelson, in Paris. After a few days there, Dallett and Nelson continued to Spain, while Kitty returned to London. Seven months later, leading a battalion in an offensive against the fascist-held town of Fuentes del Ebro, Dallett was shot and killed by machine-gun fire. At that time Nelson was in Paris, where he was joined by Kitty, who had hoped to go from there to Spain to reunite with her husband. It was Nelson who told her the news about Dallett's death. "She literally collapsed and hung on to me," Nelson later recalled. "I became a substitute for Joe, in a sense. She hugged me and cried, and I couldn't maintain my composure."

When she returned to the States, Kitty agreed to the publication of Joe's letters to her under the title *Letters from Spain*. After living with Nelson and his wife in New York City for a few months, Kitty moved to Philadelphia, where she met and married Richard Harrison. By coincidence, while she was living and studying there, she met Robert and Charlotte Serber. In his autobiography Robert Serber describes how, after leaving Berkeley in September 1938 for the job at the University of Illinois, he and Charlotte went back to Philadelphia to spend some time with their respective parents before he started at Urbana. At the home of Charlotte's parents, Robert remembers, "we met a very attractive girl, Kitty Puening, a biology student." She and Charlotte's father, it seemed, moved in the same social and political circles. The next time Serber met Kitty was at that fateful garden party held by the Lauritsens in Pasadena in the summer of 1939.

Even after their move to Urbana, the Serbers continued to spend their summers in the west, dividing their time between Berkeley, Pasadena and Perro Caliente. In the summer of 1940, when they arrived at Berkeley, Oppenheimer was just about to leave for New Mexico, where they, together with Frank and Jackie, were due to join him later. Oppenheimer told Serber that he had invited Richard and Kitty Harrison, but that Richard could not make it. "Kitty might come alone," Oppenheimer said. "You could bring her with you. I'll leave it up to you. But if you do it might have serious consequences." As Oppenheimer had clearly hoped they would, the Serbers brought Kitty along with them. A day or two after they arrived, Serber recalls, Oppenheimer and Kitty rode out to Los Pinos to stay overnight as guests of Katherine Page. The next day, after they had returned, Katherine, "looking very aristocratic on her bay horse, came trotting up to the ranch house and presented Kitty with her nightgown, which had been found under Oppie's pillow. The rest of us made no comment."

That afternoon Kitty and Jackie went riding, "and when they returned, Jackie, who was on the lead horse, had a stiff neck from conversing over her shoulder." Jackie formed a deep and lasting dislike of Kitty, whom in her forthright way she described as "a bitch." "Kitty was a schemer," Jackie said. "She was a phoney. All her political convictions were phoney, all her ideas were borrowed. Honestly, she's one of the few really evil people I've known in my life." It is a view that is echoed by Abraham Pais, who knew both Oppenheimers well in their later years. Kitty, Pais once said, is "the most despicable female I have ever known." Serber, on the other hand, was devoted to her.

As Oppenheimer had predicted to Serber, bringing Kitty to Perro Caliente had "serious consequences." By the end of the summer, Kitty was pregnant with Oppenheimer's child. Richard Harrison, who presumably knew that his wife was having an affair with Oppenheimer and that his marriage to Kitty stood no chance of working, agreed that a quick divorce was in the interests of everyone concerned. After Kitty had spent the required six weeks living in Reno, she was able to obtain a divorce, and the day the divorce came through—November 1, 1940—she and Oppenheimer were married. Soon after the wedding, Oppenheimer and Kitty moved into a large rented house at 10 Kenilworth Court, Berkeley, which became the social center not only of Oppenheimer's group of graduate students, but also of left-wing Berkeley political life.

Oppenheimer's remark to Bethe that "we can have no truck with the Communists"—whatever it *did* mean—certainly did not mean that he was prepared to turn his back on the people whose solidarity in political sympathies and activities he had so cherished since 1936. As he himself made clear, and as was perhaps inevitable, his personal and social life was intertwined with his political campaigning in a way that made it difficult, if not impossible, to extricate himself from that political life, even had he wanted to. His colleagues who were Communist Party members were also his family, his friends and his students. A party given by him and Kitty at Kenilworth Court, therefore, would have been, to the FBI and to every other observer, indistinguishable from a social gathering of communists.

Oppenheimer's marriage to Kitty extended his social circle to include not only the "parlour pinks" with whom he had previously mixed—the communist professors, lecturers and students who formed the "units" that he and his brother had joined—but also high-level communist officials and organizers, the kind of people whom, especially during the "Red Scare" of 1940 onward, the American security services kept closely within their sights. This is not because Kitty's commitment to anything one might call communist ideology was any stronger than his—if anything, it was a good deal weaker—but rather because she was the widow of Joe Dallett, a martyr to the Loyalist cause in Spain and a Communist Party hero.

One of these high-level communists was Steve Nelson. Since Kitty had lived with him and his wife in 1938, she and Nelson had had no contact with each other. In the meantime, Nelson had risen within the ranks of the Communist Party, having been identified as an up-and-coming leader.

Nelson's real name was Stefan Mesarosh. He was born in Croatia and spoke English with a heavy Croatian accent. He came to the U.S. in 1920, aged seventeen, and became a U.S. citizen five years later. In the intervening period he had joined the Communist Party. In 1929, he became a full-time functionary of the Party and was sent to the International Lenin School in Moscow to be trained in espionage techniques. During his two-year training period he was sent on clandestine missions to Germany, Switzerland, France, India and China. After serving in Spain and rising to the rank of lieutenant colonel, he was sent to southern California, where his job was to ferret out party infiltrators and to steal the files of organizations hostile to the American Communist Party.

In 1939, Nelson was transferred to San Francisco to become chairman of the local branch of the Party. The following year, after the passing of the Smith and Voorhis Acts, he went "underground," ready to lead the local Party in secret in the event that (as then looked likely) the organization became illegal. He spent much of this time living under an assumed name in a cabin in Redwood City, California.

It was while he was living thus, in the autumn of 1940, that Nelson met Oppenheimer, of whom he had previously never heard. They met at a fund-raising party in Berkeley, in aid of refugees from the Spanish Civil War (which had ended in defeat for the Loyalists in April 1939). Oppenheimer was the featured speaker at this party and in his speech he said that the fascist victory in Spain had led directly to the outbreak of war in Europe. After he had given his speech, Oppenheimer approached Nelson and said: "I'm going to marry a friend of yours, Steve." When he explained what he meant, Nelson exclaimed "Kitty Dallett!," whereupon Kitty appeared and the two old comrades hugged. Subsequently, Nelson and his wife visited the Oppenheimers at their home in Kenilworth Court.

Another person whom the FBI was extremely interested in was William Schneiderman, district organizer of the California branch of the Party and a man whose political activities were a cause for concern at the very highest level of American government. On May 18, 1940, J. Edgar Hoover had written to the Secretary of the Treasury, Henry Morgenthau, to tell him that a "confidential source" (that is, a wiretap) had heard Schneiderman tell a party meeting in San Francisco that the Communist Party intended to use its influence in the relevant workers' unions to delay production in aircraft factories, chemical plants and shipyards. This was enough to ensure that wherever Schneiderman went, an FBI agent followed. On December 1, 1940, this led the FBI to Chevalier's house, where Schneiderman addressed a meeting of communists and communist sympathizers, explaining to them the latest changes in the party line. The FBI agents keeping surveillance outside the house made a record of the registration plates of all the cars parked outside, one of which they later discovered belonged to Oppenheimer.

Chevalier did not know Schneiderman well and neither did Oppenheimer. Asked about this meeting in 1946 by the FBI, Oppenheimer denied all knowledge of it; asked again in 1950, he said he now remembered it since his wife had refreshed his memory. In his security hearing in 1954 he remembered it in some detail, recalling that about twenty people were present, including Thomas Addis and Isaac Folkoff, the Communist Party treasurer to whom he continued to give regular payments of between $100 and $150 a month. He also remembered that the purpose of the meeting was "to acquaint the interested gentry with the present line or the then line of the Communist Party."

By the same means with which they heard Schneiderman's plans for delaying factory production, the FBI heard Folkoff refer to Oppenheimer as "the big shot." This, together with Oppenheimer's presence at a meeting at which Schneiderman presented the Communist Party line, was sufficient cause for the FBI to start treating Oppenheimer as a potentially dangerous subversive and, on March 28, 1941, it opened what was to become over the years a massive file on Oppenheimer. On the same day, Oppenheimer's name was added to a list drawn up by the FBI of "persons to be considered for custodial detention pending investigation in the event of a national emergency." A short while later, Oppenheimer wrote to Willie Fowler in Pasadena, saying that he might not be able to make it to Washington for the forthcoming April conference on elementary particles. "I may be out of a job by then," he wrote, "because UC is going to be investigated next week for radicalism and the story is that the committee members are no gentlemen and that they don't like me. We'll do the best we can."

As it happened, the investigation into radicalism at Berkeley presented Oppenheimer with few problems. The fact remained, however, that in maintaining contact with and lending financial support to the

Communist Party, Oppenheimer was, as he well knew, playing with fire. In case he needed reminding of this fact, a demonstration of it close to home was given in the summer of 1941 with respect to his brother. Frank had finished his Ph.D. at Caltech in the summer of 1939 and had then, no doubt through Robert's help, got a job at Stanford, working with Felix Bloch. After just two years, however, Stanford let Frank know that they would not be renewing his contract; he was out of work. One contributing factor here was that Frank and Bloch did not get on with one another, but it was also made clear to Frank that his Communist Party membership and his political activities were barriers to keeping his job. At about this time Frank and Jackie left the Party, but the damage his membership had done to his career was by no means over.

On May 12, 1941, just seven months into her marriage to Oppenheimer, Kitty gave birth to a baby boy, whom they named Peter. By this time of the year they were in Pasadena, from where they wrote to the Chevaliers inviting them to meet the new arrival. Thus it was that Chevalier was with Oppenheimer in Pasadena on June 22, 1941, when they heard the news that Nazi Germany had broken its pact with the Soviet Union and had begun an invasion of Russia. "It was on our way to the beach that we heard over the radio of the Nazi invasion of the Soviet Union," Chevalier remembered, "and as we drove, both shocked and terribly excited by the news, we heard the whole of Churchill's speech denouncing Hitler and welcoming the Soviet Union as an ally, pledging Great Britain's full cooperation in a united war effort."

That night, Chevalier recalls, "we sat up with Opje and Kitty till the small hours, listening to the news broadcasts and trying to analyze the significance of this latest Nazi move." Apparently blind to the irony of what he is describing, Chevalier remarks: "Hitler had destroyed at one stroke the dangerous fiction, so prevalent in liberal and political circles, that fascism and communism were but two different versions of the same totalitarian philosophy. The communist and democratic forces were now allies committed to fighting their common fascist enemy."

The entry of the Soviet Union into the war came as something of a relief to many American communists, since it brought them back onto the same side as their countrymen. The U.S. had not yet actually entered the conflict, but preparations for war were going on everywhere. In a letter to the Uehlings written just a few days after Peter was born and about a month before the Nazi attack on Russia, Oppenheimer, again warmly thanking the Uehlings for their hospitality the previous summer ("even now a year later I want to thank you for it again"), wrote disconsolately: "I think we'll go to war." At this time the imminence of war was something from which he felt detached and which he saw as inimical to the development of his subject. "I expect," he told the Uehlings, "unless there is a drastic change in policy on the part of the research boards, that physics in our sense will just about stop by next year."

As he conceded, though, the war preparations had been good for physics in at least one sense: for the first time since he started teaching, students graduating with higher degrees in physics were almost guaranteed employment. With regard to a position that the Uehlings' own university had advertised for a spectroscopist, Oppenheimer wrote: "You are going to find it pretty hard to get *any* decent physicist these days, with the demand suddenly exceeding the supply." If they were wanting to employ any theoretical physicists at Seattle, Oppenheimer added, "there will be some first rate ones coming up next year."

> This year's crop is pretty well spoken for already. The situation in Berkeley & here in Pasadena is in some ways very gloomy: here especially almost all the men active in physics have been taken away for war work. Those left are swamped in administrative & teaching duties & their own defense problems. The number of graduates too is way down: the losses heaviest among the men about to finish in nuclear physics, but noticeable all along the line. In Berkeley we've lost Alvarez, McMillan, 2/3 Lawrence, [Bernice] Brode, Loeb. Only the last is not missed.

Oppenheimer always liked to be "at the center," and it is clear from this letter that he felt that he and his diminishing band of graduates working on, as he put it, "theories of mesotron field & the light they throw on 'Heisenberg' showers, proton isobars, scattering & other such recondite matters" were being confined to the periphery—the center being the secret work on nuclear physics from which, for the moment at least, he was excluded.

Actually, just as Oppenheimer's work on neutron stars and black holes, which had looked so exotic in 1938–9, now looks like his greatest achievement in physics, so the "recondite" work that he and his students pursued in the period 1939–41, which looked peripheral at a time when nuclear physics held sway with physicists and research funding bodies, now looks more central. This is particularly true in the area of quantum electrodynamics, in which the work done under Oppenheimer at Berkeley is now being recognized as a precursor to the work done by the people—Julian Schwinger, Richard Feynman, Freeman Dyson and Sin-Itiro Tomonaga—who finalized that theory in the late 1940s. In fact, one of Oppenheimer's students, Sidney Dancoff, came extremely close to arriving at something similar to that later version of quantum electrodynamics, and, according to the historian of science, Silvan Schweber, would have got there before Schwinger et al., had he not made a mistake in his calculations.

Oppenheimer thought very highly of Dancoff, as can be seen by a letter he wrote to F. Wheeler Loomis, the chairman of the physics department at the University of Illinois, in May 1940, urging him to offer Dancoff the one-year instructorship that, through Serber, Oppenheimer knew Loomis had going vacant. Lawrence, Oppenheimer told Loomis, had wanted to employ Dancoff in the Radiation Laboratory, "but we are all agreed that that is not the ideal place for him." Dancoff was, Oppenheimer wrote, "a good physicist, well trained and with good ideas and great technical facility in calculation." The only reason he did not already have an academic position was that "jobs for theorists are not too common, and he has had the competition of older men of greater reputation: Schiff, Schwinger, Snyder for instance in Berkeley." In response, Loomis offered the one-year post to Dancoff, who then remained at Illinois for the rest of his short life (he died in 1951, shortly before his thirty-eighth birthday).

Of the "older men of greater reputation" that Oppenheimer mentions, the odd one out would seem to be Hartland Snyder, who was not, in fact, any older than Dancoff (they were the same age) and who was, academically, slightly behind, finishing his Ph.D. six months after Dancoff. Snyder, though, had the enormous advantage of being Oppenheimer's coauthor on their classic paper on black holes, while, for some reason, Oppenheimer never published anything with Dancoff.

The other two were indeed more senior. Leonard Schiff, a New York Jew of Lithuanian background, had come to Berkeley as an NRC fellow, and in the summer of 1938 was given the challenging task of replacing Robert Serber as Oppenheimer's research associate. Schiff would later become known as a brilliant teacher and the author of a commonly used textbook on quantum mechanics that was based on Oppenheimer's lectures at Berkeley. However, possibly because he was dissatisfied with him as a replacement for Serber, Oppenheimer is recorded as being rather cruel to Schiff. Edward Gerjuoy, who started work as a graduate student of Oppenheimer's at Berkeley in 1938, the same time that Schiff began his two-year stint as Oppenheimer's research associate, reports that when Schiff gave a seminar discussion of a book with some rather difficult mathematics in it, Oppenheimer "asked Schiff searching questions about each and every equation Schiff wrote down." "On more than a few occasions," Gerjuoy remembers, "Oppie had Schiff, who was a gentle soul, visibly on the verge of tears."

Julian Schwinger, who replaced Schiff as Oppenheimer's research associate in the summer of 1940, though no less gentle than Schiff, was too brilliant a physicist and too confident in his abilities to be browbeaten in the same way. Schwinger, who would go on to win the Nobel Prize in 1965 for his part in the development of the modern formulation of quantum electrodynamics, could hold his own with *any* physicist. At Schwinger's first seminar as Oppenheimer's research assistant, Gerjuoy recalls, Oppenheimer's students "were wondering how long it would take Julian to shrivel under Oppie's questioning." They were in for a shock:

> Julian started talking and very soon Oppie, in accordance with his usual practice, asked Julian a question, which Julian answered. More questions came; more questions were answered. After about a dozen questions, answered by Julian with no visible sign of distress whatsoever, Oppie stopped firing questions and let him finish his seminar essentially without further interruption. Nor did he ever again unduly interrupt during any succeeding seminar of Julian's.

By the time he gave this seminar Schwinger had already been at Berkeley for more than a year, having arrived as an NRC postdoctoral student in the summer of 1939. He was from a remarkably similar background to Oppenheimer. His father, a German-speaking Jew from Central Europe, arrived in the U.S. as a teenager in 1880, made a fortune in the clothing trade and bought a large apartment on the Upper West Side of Manhattan. In fact, the apartment in which Schwinger grew up was on the very same street, Riverside Drive, that Oppenheimer had grown up on. As a child, Schwinger was precocious even by Oppenheimer's standards. At the age of thirteen he read, and understood, Dirac's *The Principles of Quantum Mechanics*, which he later described as "my bible." At the age of sixteen Schwinger wrote his first paper on quantum-field theory, which remained unpublished, but the following year he published two letters to the editor of the *Physical Review*. He was then a student at City College, New York, where, bored by lectures that just told him what he already knew, he developed what would become a lifelong habit of sleeping during the day and beginning work in the evening. After a year, he transferred to Columbia to work with Isidor Rabi, who held him in such high regard that he asked Schwinger—while still an undergraduate—to lecture to his graduate students when he was out of town. In the summer of 1936, still only eighteen, Schwinger received his undergraduate degree.

Less than a year later, Schwinger was ready to submit his Ph.D. thesis, but Columbia's rules would not allow him to graduate with a Ph.D. without spending at least two years in residence, so he published the work as a collection of articles, which, when the time came, he bound together and presented as his Ph.D. work. To stop him getting bored, Rabi arranged for Schwinger to spend the first part of the academic year 1937–8 at the University of Wisconsin, working with Gregory Breit and Eugene Wigner. By the time he returned to Columbia in the spring of 1938, Schwinger was a young physicist with an international reputation and was being offered academic positions at several universities, both in Europe and in the U.S. Despite the many alternatives offered to him, Schwinger chose to apply for an NRC fellowship in order to spend some time at Berkeley working with Oppenheimer. Rabi recalls that he tried to persuade Schwinger to go to Zurich to work with Wolfgang Pauli, but Schwinger "thought Oppenheimer was a more interesting physicist." When he was asked later in life about this decision, Schwinger replied: "Oppenheimer was *the* name in American theoretical physics. Where else could I have gone?" That the most intellectually precocious, sought-after young theoretical physicist in the country should choose to stay in America rather than sit at the feet of one of the founders of quantum theory in Europe, and that, in particular, he would rather work with Oppenheimer than with Pauli, was the fulfillment of Oppenheimer's ambitions for himself and for the department he had built up. One might, without too much hyperbole, regard Schwinger's decision to go to Berkeley as a symbolic moment, marking the point at which the center of gravity in theoretical physics shifted from Europe to the United States.

Of course it is possible that, in the summer of 1939, Schwinger had other reasons for not wanting to travel to Europe. In fact, as it happened, the day he arrived in Berkeley was September 1, the very day the German army invaded Poland. Nevertheless, it is clear from the things he read, the things he cites in his published papers and the problems that he chose to work on, that Schwinger regarded the work being done by Oppenheimer and those influenced by him as more interesting and more important than anything going on in Europe at that time.

Though he was still only twenty-one when he came to Berkeley as an NRC fellow, Schwinger's reputation among theoretical physicists as a rare talent preceded him and Oppenheimer had heard much about him before they met. In turn, Schwinger knew about Oppenheimer's reputation as a teacher and he arrived determined to resist any attempt at domination. It would, he knew, be a struggle. Oppenheimer, Schwinger recalls, "was overwhelming. [He] was not only impressive, he *liked* to impress. He was a showman. I was impressed, no question about it. But I also resisted him." At first, this resistance led to some friction between the two. Rabi remembered:

I spoke to Oppenheimer later and he was terribly disappointed. He came to the point of writing a letter to the National Research Council suggesting that Julian go somewhere else, because it took a man like Oppenheimer quite a bit to get used to Julian. Pauli once referred to Oppenheimer's students as being *Zunicker*. Somebody who knows enough German knows what this means—people who nod heads—and Julian was not that way—that, and his hours.

One source of tension was Schwinger's refusal to cooperate with Oppenheimer's way of working with his graduate students. As Schwinger recalls:

At the early stage perhaps I didn't measure up in the sense of ritual, in which everybody would come into Oppenheimer's office at some early hour of the morning and they would sit around and talk. I presume I was still a late riser and so never came to these get-togethers. Maybe he didn't like my dissident ways at first. I never heard a direct statement, but it's very plausible that I was a strange fish to begin with until he appreciated that I could produce nevertheless. So perhaps in the first month he didn't quite like the "cut of my jib."

Oppenheimer and Schwinger soon overcame their initial difficulties with each other—Oppenheimer learned to accept Schwinger's refusal to come to his office in the morning, and Schwinger reminded himself that "After all, I was there to learn from him"—and, within two months of Schwinger's arrival, they were collaborating on a joint letter to the editor of the *Physical Review*. The subject was a problem arising out of some results of experiments performed by Lauritsen and Fowler at Caltech, the explanation of which Oppenheimer thought might require the postulation of new physical forces. Oppenheimer had given the problem to Schiff, who had made no headway with it. In an interview much later in life, Schwinger remembered: "Schiff was then Oppenheimer's assistant in Berkeley, and the problem got handed down from one to the next. Oppenheimer was interested in this, so Schiff said, 'Hey, Schwinger, why don't you look into this?' So I did. And obviously it got done in a day or so." The key to solving the puzzle, as it had been several times in the past when Oppenheimer had thought that experimental results showed the breakdown of quantum electrodynamics, was the realization that the existing theory was perfectly adequate to explain the laboratory observations.

The solution to the problem was Schwinger's, but the wording of the letter was Oppenheimer's, and Schwinger was not entirely happy with the result. In particular, he was irritated that, having presented Schwinger's solution, Oppenheimer then, characteristically, went on to speculate about cases where the theory might *not* hold. Schwinger later said:

> He wrote that letter to the *Physical Review* incorporating whatever calculations and ideas I had but at the same time mentioning other possibilities. To me it was a purely electrodynamic process and exactly what was to be expected. On the other hand he, in the spirit of the time, was convinced that electrodynamics had broken down and so in the letter there is still a reference to the possibility of some new short-range force between electrons and protons, which I had no great stock in, but there it was.

One of the most important things demonstrated by Oppenheimer and Schwinger in their jointly written letter was the physical reality of what is called "vacuum polarization," which, in Schwinger's words "means no more than the fact that an electron-positron combination is coupled to the electromagnetic field and it may show itself as real or virtual." Ironically, it was Sidney Dancoff's neglect of this very phenomenon that lay at the heart of his error mentioned earlier, the error that prevented him from anticipating Schwinger's greatest contribution to physics: the "renormalization" of quantum electrodynamics. As Schwinger's biographers remark, though he and Dancoff got to know each other well at Berkeley, "history might have developed differently if the two of them had had more time to discuss their respective research interests in greater detail."

After Schwinger's year as an NRC fellow expired in the summer of 1940, Oppenheimer immediately appointed him as Schiff's replacement as research associate. In that role Schwinger stayed for just a year, during which the focus of his and Oppenheimer's research interests was the attempt to understand the particle that Oppenheimer in those days still called the "mesotron" (it was not until after the war that he began calling it the "meson"). As we now know, and as mentioned in the previous chapter, what Oppenheimer called the "mesotron" was, in fact, two very different particles: the mu-meson (or muon), which is a component part of cosmic rays, and the pi-meson (or pion), which is the carrier of the strong nuclear force. In the period from 1939 to 1942 almost all of Oppenheimer's published work, and a good deal of the work undertaken by his graduate and postdoctoral students, was devoted to solving the puzzles of the "mesotron," most of which arose from the mistaken assumption that the mu-meson and pi-meson were the same thing.

In trying to explain how Oppenheimer exerted such an inspirational influence on his students, Edward Gerjuoy writes: "I feel Oppie did his physics, talked about his physics, lived his physics, with an unusual passion, which had to inspire students; in any event it sure inspired me." As an example of this passion, Gerjuoy describes Oppenheimer's absorption in the problem of the "mesotron":

> To give you just one of many possible illustrations, it bothered him, it tore at him, that he didn't understand how the pi mesons, which in nuclei were so strongly interacting, penetrated the earth's atmosphere so readily. Maybe he should have hit upon the idea that the mesons reaching the earth's surface really weren't pi mesons, but instead were other weakly interacting mesons—those we now term mu mesons; but since he hadn't conceived of mu mesons he couldn't stop talking about the anomaly that atmospheric penetration by pi mesons represented, in seminar after seminar and in less formal conversations with groups of his students.

At about the same time that he cowrote his letter to the editor with Schwinger, Oppenheimer put his name to a long article, cowritten with Robert Serber and Hartland Snyder, called "The Production of Soft Secondaries by Mesotrons," in which they analyzed the "soft component" of cosmic rays as being made up of electrons and gamma rays that were released in mesotron "showers." Their conclusion was the familiar one: that the standard quantum theory is sufficient to explain the emissions of electrons and gamma rays up to a certain energy, but that "the problem of extending the formulae above these critical energies probably goes beyond the framework of the present theory." That "probably," together with the speculative suggestion of the breakdown of the theory, was exactly the kind of thing to which Schwinger had so strongly objected.

Schwinger himself spent much of his time at Berkeley puzzling over the "mesotron"—as his biographers correctly note, "everybody at Berkeley was talking about mesons"—and, in addition to his joint work with Oppenheimer, wrote papers on the subject with William Rarita, a physicist from Brooklyn College who was then on a sabbatical visit to Berkeley, and with Herbert Corben, an Australian, who after studying at Cambridge had come to Berkeley on a postdoctoral fellowship. In a letter to the editor of the *Physical Review* published in March 1941, called "On the Spin of the Mesotron," Oppenheimer referred to this work of Schwinger, Rarita and Corben, and to a paper by Robert Christy and Shuichi Kusaka, and to yet another on the subject by Eldred Nelson, also a graduate student of his. All three of these students—Christy,

Kusaka and Nelson—wrote their Ph.D. theses on mesotrons. The general impression of these publications is that almost all the finest minds at America's greatest center of theoretical physics were engaged in trying to understand the huge discrepancy between the observed properties of the particles that make up cosmic rays with the theoretical calculations based on standard quantum electrodynamics. Here is the clearest instance yet of Serber's remark that Oppenheimer's progress was hindered by his almost obsessive conviction that the standard theory was wrong; if he had trusted that theory a little more, it would surely have occurred to him that the discrepancies were due to the misidentification of the cosmic-ray particle (the muon) with the Yukawa particle (the pion).

In June 1941, Oppenheimer and Schwinger sent another jointly written paper, "On the Interaction of Mesotrons and Nuclei," to the *Physical Review*, this time concentrating on the "mesotron" as the carrier of the strong nuclear force—that is, the pion. The paper was, according to Schwinger's later recollection, essentially written by him, Oppenheimer simply adding his name to it after it had been written. Indeed, he implied, it could not have been written by Oppenheimer, involving as it did quantum-mechanical treatments of meson fields, the mathematics of which was beyond Oppenheimer's competence. Oppenheimer, Schwinger said, was "adequate technically to deal with the semi-classical treatment of spin," but "He was not adequate, or at least he never attempted to follow or join in, with the quantum treatment, which was more elaborate." "Well," he added, with more than a hint of condescension, "he was trying to keep his hands in lots of different topics and it is very difficult to work intensively on all these subjects."

A few days after that paper was sent off, Schwinger and Oppenheimer both presented several papers at an American Physical Society meeting in Pasadena, although not with each other. One of Schwinger's papers was with Edward Gerjuoy, and two of Oppenheimer's papers (both on mesotrons) were jointly written, one with Christy and the other with Nelson. After that, Schwinger left California to take up a place at Purdue University. Despite the fact that, as Schwinger later put it, "I still did not quite know how to act in the face of His Majesty," he and Oppenheimer parted on good terms. Neither, however, seemed particularly sorry to part; Schwinger was not offered, nor did he apply for, another year as Oppenheimer's research associate. He left with his admiration for Oppenheimer still intact, but tempered somewhat by what he saw as Oppenheimer's loss of creativity due to his acceptance of the role of organizer and manager, rather than that of a single-minded research physicist. Oppenheimer, Schwinger later said, "very much insisted on displaying that he was on top of everything, which he very often was," but, inevitably, in striving to be on top of *everything*, Oppenheimer skirted over the details of particular subjects, and, for Schwinger, the details were everything. Oppenheimer's grasp of specific topics, Schwinger recalled, "became more and more superficial, which I regretted very much. It was a lesson to me, never to lose completely your touch with the subject, otherwise it's all over." Oppenheimer, he thought, "could pull it off better than most people":

> He did have a quick brain. There was no question about that, but I think the brain must be supplemented by long hours of practice that go into the fluidity and ease. Without the technical practice, sooner or later you get lost.

Schwinger's comments on Oppenheimer are perceptive. As he was possibly the first person to realize, the summer of 1941 marked the end of Oppenheimer's time as a creative scientist and the beginning of an entirely different phase in his life.

Schwinger's recollections of Oppenheimer having lost touch with his subject chime with Oppenheimer's letter to the Uehlings in May, in which he struck a melancholy note about the future of "physics in our sense." As we have seen, however, that letter conveys a sense of Oppenheimer feeling out of touch not so much with theoretical physics as with "all the men active in physics [who] have been taken away for war work." And, after all, he was right to feel that important work was being done from which he was excluded. By the summer of 1941, much progress had been made on the physics of fission and its possible application to explosives, which Oppenheimer would have known nothing about. Most crucially, an unexpected answer had been provided to one of the questions Oppenheimer had first raised when the discovery of fission had been announced: what is the critical mass of uranium? The question of critical mass could be put like this: given that neutrons are released in fission and that a chain reaction is therefore possible, how large would a lump of uranium have to be in order to sustain a chain reaction long enough to produce a massive explosion? In a small amount of uranium, the neutrons released by fission would escape from the surface before they had initiated another fissure. The question that arises, then, is: how large would a piece of uranium have to be in order for the neutrons to set up a fission chain reaction rather than escape from the surface?

One answer to that question with which Oppenheimer *would* have been familiar was published by Rudolf Peierls in October 1939. Peierls was a German Jewish physicist whom Oppenheimer had met in Zurich and who had been in England since 1933. Since 1937 Peierls had been professor of physics at the University of Birmingham. In the *Proceedings of the Cambridge Philosophical Society* for October 1939 he published a formula for calculating critical mass and applied it to a simplified case of natural uranium fissioned by unmoderated fast neutrons. The answer he obtained was that the critical mass was several tons—too much for a practical weapon—a result that confirmed what Bohr had already said: an atomic bomb was not a realistic proposition.

By the time Peierls's paper was published, he had been joined in Birmingham by another German Jewish refugee physicist, the codiscoverer of fission, Otto Frisch. Frisch had also been thinking about critical mass and had asked himself a question that, remarkably, no other physicist had yet asked. "One day in February or March 1940," Peierls later recalled, "Frisch said, 'Suppose someone gave you a quantity of pure 235 isotope—what would happen?'" In order to calculate accurately the critical mass of pure uranium-235, Frisch and Peierls needed what theoretical physicists call "the numbers"—namely, the basic facts established by experiment and observation. In this case, one of "the numbers" was already well known—the number of neutrons released per fission—but for much of the rest they had to guess. They did not know, for example, the fission cross-section for uranium-235 (that is, how likely it was that a neutron hitting a uranium-235 nucleus would cause it to fission), but from Bohr and Wheeler's work they felt able to assume that *every* neutron that hits a nucleus would produce fission (this turned out not to be quite right, but it was close enough). Further informed guesses allowed them to calculate how quickly the chain reaction would go through the uranium, how many "generations" of fission would take place before the uranium expanded too much for further fission to take place, and how much energy would be released.

The result staggered them. Far from being measured in tons, as Bohr and every other physicist had previously calculated the critical mass of natural uranium fissioned by slow neutrons to be, Frisch and Peierls calculated the critical mass of pure uranium-235 fissioned by fast neutrons to be about one kilogram. In fact, as we now know, because all the relevant "numbers" have been determined by laboratory experiment, it is rather more than that, being about fifteen kilograms. Nevertheless, as Frisch and Peierls were the first to realize, it is a matter of kilograms, not tons. And the energy release from that relatively small lump of uranium would be enormous. Frisch and Peierls calculated it to be equivalent to several thousand tons of TNT. The problem, of course, is that the separation of U-235 from natural uranium is difficult—so difficult that most people who had considered it did not regard it as a practical means of making a bomb. In the light of the calculations made by Frisch and Peierls, however, it looked considerably more practical. To be sure, an expensive industrial plant would have to be built, but, as Peierls remembers himself and Frisch saying to each other: "Even if this plant costs as much as a battleship, it would be worth having."

For the second time in just under two years Frisch found himself one of only two people in possession of a shattering piece of information. Realizing that what had occurred to them might also occur to scientists working for the Nazis (Heisenberg, for one, was more than capable of doing the same calculations), Frisch and Peierls quickly wrote up their analysis as a two-part report—the first part, "Memorandum on the Properties of a Radioactive 'Super-bomb,'" stating their conclusions in nontechnical terms, and the second, "On the Construction of a 'Super-bomb'; Based on a Nuclear Chain Reaction in Uranium," providing the technical details. As Jeremy Bernstein has said: "What is impressive about these papers is their absolute clarity." No one who read them could fail to be convinced that, if a fairly small lump of the 235 isotope could be separated from natural uranium, a bomb of awesome power could be constructed. Frisch and Peierls even explained how such a bomb could function: two subcritical lumps of uranium-235 could be brought together, thus forming a critical mass. "Once assembled," they remarked, "the bomb would explode within a second or less, since one neutron is sufficient to start the reaction and there are several neutrons passing through the bomb every second, from the cosmic radiation." This was, essentially, the design of the bomb that exploded over Hiroshima some five years after it was conceived by Frisch and Peierls (though, in the Hiroshima bomb, a neutron initiator—a mixture of polonium and beryllium—was used, rather than relying on passing cosmic rays).

Frisch was at this time still classed as an enemy alien, and Peierls had only just received British citizenship; neither would be a candidate for active participation in the British war effort. So they gave their memorandum to Mark Oliphant, the head of the physics department at Birmingham, who had been responsible for recruiting both of them, and who, after adding a covering note declaring "I am convinced that the whole thing must be taken rather seriously," sent it to Henry Tizard, an Oxford-trained chemist who served as the civilian chairman of the British government's Committee on the Scientific Survey of Air Defence. Tizard then set up a separate committee, consisting entirely of people who had learned their physics at the Cavendish: Oliphant, Chadwick,

Cockcroft and, as chairman, G. P. Thomson. The committee met for the first time on April 10, 1940, and, according to Oliphant, was immediately "electrified by the possibility" of an atomic bomb.

"Electrified" was hardly a word that one could have used at this time to describe the Advisory Committee on Uranium, which President Roosevelt had set up in October 1939 under the chairmanship of the government scientist Lyman Briggs, a man more noted for caution than for dynamism. After its first meeting a report had been sent to the President, recommending that Fermi and Szilard be provided with the pure graphite and uranium they needed to investigate the possibility of a controlled chain reaction, and advising the President such a chain reaction might be useful as a "source of power in submarines." After reading the report, Roosevelt said he wanted to keep it on file. In the summer of 1940, the uranium committee was absorbed into the newly formed National Defense Research Council (NDRC), headed by James Conant of Harvard and Vannevar Bush of the Carnegie Institution. Briggs was kept on as head of the fission project, but he now reported to Conant.

Meanwhile, the war effort in Britain was revitalized in May by the election of Winston Churchill. The following month, with the fall of France, Britain saw itself as standing alone in resisting the menace of Nazi Germany, and a renewed determination to succeed in that resistance was felt across the entire country. G. P. Thomson's committee was not immune to that sense of determination. In June it renamed itself the "MAUD Committee" after an apparently enigmatic telegram from Lise Meitner to an English friend, which read: "MET NIELS AND MARGRETHE RECENTLY BOTH WELL BUT UNHAPPY ABOUT EVENTS PLEASE INFORM COCK-CROFT AND MAUD RAY KENT." The message was sent to Cockcroft, who thought "Maud Ray Kent" must be an anagram for "Radium Taken," confirming suspicions that the Germans were taking radium from laboratories in occupied countries. Later, they discovered that Maud Ray was the name of a woman who lived in Kent.

In December 1940, the MAUD Committee received a report from Franz Simon, another émigré German physicist working in Britain, concerning the estimated cost of a plant capable of separating one kilogram of uranium-235 from natural uranium. The cost of such a plant, Simon said, would be about £5 million. The following February, Conant flew to London to establish communication between his committee and the British government. He was impressed by what he saw; it was, he said, "the most extraordinary experience of my life."

> I saw a stout-hearted population under bombardment. I saw an unflinching government with its back against the wall. Almost every

hour I saw or heard something that made me proud to be a member of the human race.

Remarkably, it was in London that Conant, the man to whom the head of the U.S. fission research project now reported, first heard about the possibility of using fission to create an atomic bomb. The subject came up in conversation with Frederick Lindemann, Winston Churchill's scientific advisor, with whom Conant had lunch at a London club. According to Conant's later recollection, Lindemann "introduced the subject of the study of fission of uranium atoms."

> I reacted by repeating the doubts I had expressed and heard expressed at NDRC meetings . . . "You have left out of consideration," said [Lindemann], "the possibility of the construction of a bomb of enormous power." "How would that be possible?" I asked. "By first separating uranium 235," he said, "and then arranging for the two portions of the element to be brought together suddenly so that the resulting mass would spontaneously undergo a self-sustaining reaction."

Conant did not press the subject, since "this was entirely an unofficial and private communication and represented a highly speculative scheme," but the fact remained that, when he returned to the U.S., there was now at least one person involved in the American uranium research project who understood that a fission bomb was not a remote possibility.

Meanwhile, Ernest Lawrence was becoming increasingly exasperated by the lack of urgency shown by Briggs's uranium committee and took every opportunity to let his feelings be known to anyone with any influence in Washington. When Conant, soon after his trip to Britain, went to Berkeley to give a paper, Lawrence took the chance to urge him to "light a fire under the Briggs committee." Briggs came under further pressure when Kenneth Bainbridge, a nuclear physicist from Harvard, followed Conant to Britain and was invited to attend a meeting of the MAUD Committee. There Bainbridge discovered in detail what Conant had heard in passing: that the British had "a very good idea of the critical mass and assembly" and that they thought an atomic weapon could be made in three years.

Bainbridge's report led Vannevar Bush to appoint a new committee to take "an energetic but dispassionate review of the entire situation." Lawrence was asked to serve on this committee and Arthur Compton was chosen as its head. The review was completed quickly and the committee's report delivered on May 17, 1941. Unlike the Frisch-Peierls memorandum, Compton's report did not emphasize the importance of fast-neutron fission, and played down the possibility of an atomic bomb. Its central focus was the importance of Fermi's experiment to produce a chain reaction in natural uranium.

The report led to further agonizingly slow progress and the establishment of yet another bureaucratic organization: the Office of Scientific Research and Development, with Bush as its director, answerable only to the President. The key word here is "development." This committee had authority not only to initiate research, but also to employ engineers and technicians to actually *produce* things. Bush's move upward left Conant in sole charge of the NDRC.

In yet another effort to get things moving in the U.S., the British MAUD Committee invited Charles Lauritsen, then in England working for the NDRC, to attend its meeting of July 2, 1941, to hear the committee's draft final report, drawn up by G. P. Thomson. Lauritsen listened, took notes and a week later reported the MAUD findings to Bush. The report concluded that it would be possible to make a uranium bomb with twenty-five pounds of uranium-235, which would cost about £5 million to produce. In spite of this very large cost, the report considered "that the destructive effect, both material and moral, is so great that every effort should be made to produce bombs of this kind." With this report in hand, Conant later said, it became clear to both him and to Bush that "a major push along the lines outlined was in order."

In order, perhaps, but—to the increasing dismay of the British— still not in effect. At the end of August, Mark Oliphant flew to the U.S. to see what was happening. "If Congress knew the true history of the atomic-energy project," Leo Szilard once said, "I have no doubt but that it would create a special medal to be given to meddling foreigners for distinguished services, and Dr. Oliphant would be the first to receive one." In Washington, Oliphant called on Briggs and was "amazed and distressed" to find that "this inarticulate and unimpressive man" had put the MAUD Committee's reports in a safe, without showing them to the other members of the uranium committee. As soon as he could, he met with the uranium committee and, to the shock of some of them, spelled out the possibilities of using fission to make an explosive. It was the first time some of the committee had heard the word "bomb" used in this context. One of its members, Samuel Allison, later recalled: "I thought we were making a power source for submarines."

From Washington, Oliphant flew to California to meet Lawrence, who, he had reason to believe, had a greater sense of urgency about the project than prevailed among the government scientists. On September 21, 1941, Lawrence drove Oliphant up "Cyclotron Hill" to see the site of the still-to-be-built 184-inch cyclotron. When they returned to Lawrence's office, they were joined by Oppenheimer. Assuming that Oppenheimer was privy to the official secrets that he and Lawrence had been discussing, Oliphant continued to talk about the MAUD report, about the optimism that the British scientists had expressed concerning the possibility of building an atomic bomb, and about the cooperation between Britain and the States on the research and development of the bomb. Noting that Lawrence had begun to look extremely uncomfortable, and registering the shocked expression on Oppenheimer's face, Oliphant realized that he had just revealed to Oppenheimer for the first time the existence of a project to build an atomic bomb. Clearing his throat, Oppenheimer suggested to Oliphant that it might be advisable not to continue this conversation, since he was not involved with the project. "But that's terrible," replied Oliphant. "We need you."

By thus passing this information on to him, Oliphant may possibly have guaranteed that Oppenheimer *would* become involved in the project. For, even if it had not been decided that Oppenheimer's theoretical skills would be invaluable to the project, he now knew too much to be left out.

Part Three

1941–1945

11

In on the Secret

After he had let slip to Oppenheimer the Allies' most important and most closely guarded military secret, Oliphant returned to Washington, leaving a written summary of the MAUD report's findings with Lawrence. In Washington, Lawrence had arranged for Oliphant to meet Bush and Conant, but from both Oliphant received a rather frosty reception. Adopting a somewhat stricter approach to official secrets than had prevailed in California, neither Bush nor Conant would admit to knowing anything about the MAUD report and both gave Oliphant the cold shoulder. To Bush, Conant dismissed Oliphant's information as "gossip among nuclear physicists on forbidden subjects," and remarked testily: "Oliphant's behavior does not help the cause of secrecy."

The encounter between Oliphant and Bush and Conant reveals a fundamental difference between the priorities of Britain and the United States at this time. For the British, maintaining strict secrecy was of secondary importance to the crucial task of building an atomic bomb before the Germans, who, they had reason to believe, were pressing ahead with their own atomic-weapons program.

From the perspective of the U.S., things looked rather different. America was not yet at war with Germany, nor was the Soviet Union yet its ally. Indeed, insofar as the Americans regarded themselves as being at war in the autumn of 1941, it was a war of espionage *against* the Soviet Union. The truly breathtaking extent of Soviet espionage—industrial, scientific and military—during this period would not become fully apparent until many years after the war, but the U.S. authorities already knew enough to be certain that the Russian embassy in Washington and the consulates in New York and San Francisco were operating as centers of a major spying operation. Using an elaborate system of "legals" and "illegals"—the former operating under their own names, the latter working under cover of false names and disguises—and employing a mixture of people working through the American Communist Party and others working directly for the Soviet Union, a vast amount of information was being collected from manufacturing companies, universities, military bases and government offices and sent via official cables to Moscow.

In Britain, the Soviet espionage operation had been, and continued to be throughout the war, extraordinarily effective. The "Cambridge Five"—Anthony Blunt, Guy Burgess, Donald Maclean, Kim Philby and John Cairncross—alone were responsible for the handing over to Moscow of a substantial number of top British military secrets. Partly, no doubt, because of their status as accepted members of the British social and educational elite, they were, with only minimal security checks, appointed to the kind of positions that gave them access to the Allies' most closely guarded documents (Blunt, Cairncross and Philby worked for British intelligence, while Maclean and, intermittently, Burgess were employed by the Foreign Office). Through Cairncross, for example, the Soviets received, just a week or so after the final meeting of the MAUD Committee, a full account of that meeting and a copy of its final report.

Neither Britain nor the U.S. knew about the activities of these five until after the war. They were exposed by an operation that the U.S. had put into place precisely because of their suspicions of the Soviets. This was the so-called "Venona" project, in accordance with which the U.S. telegraph companies were instructed to keep a copy of every cable sent from the U.S. to Moscow. These messages, hundreds of thousands of them, were preserved and studied and, after many of them had been decoded, provided the U.S. authorities with a detailed picture of the astonishing extent and success of Soviet espionage.

The decoding, however, could not be done in time to prevent most of the espionage that occurred during the war, and the U.S. had to rely chiefly on the counterintelligence efforts of the FBI. While the British lacked the manpower, and to some extent the will, to do very much about Soviet espionage, the U.S. could afford to invest the vast sums it took to employ several thousand FBI agents to try to prevent *their* secrets from being handed over to Moscow.

Because the FBI knew that the American Communist Party played a key role in the information-gathering efforts of the Soviets, they naturally centered their counterintelligence effort on Communist Party members and people close to them. Thus it was that, while Oliphant was eagerly revealing to Oppenheimer the secret of the British and the American atomic-bomb projects, the FBI was keeping a file on him.

At this time, though the FBI regarded Oppenheimer as suspicious, they did not treat the surveillance of him as a particularly high priority. They may have kept a file on him, but they did not—as they did with people identified as senior figures in the Soviet espionage network—have him followed, bug his phone or install microphones in his house. And, in fact, the file they opened on him in March 1941 contained, six months later, very little. It recorded: 1. his attendance at Chevalier's home at a meeting in December 1940, at which Isaac Folkoff and William Schneiderman were also present; 2. Folkoff's reference to him as "the big shot"; 3. his subscription to the Communist Party newspaper, *People's World*; and 4. his membership of several Communist front organizations. And that was about it. It was more than enough to persuade J. Edgar Hoover that Oppenheimer needed to be watched, but it fell a long way short of suggesting that he was engaged in any kind of espionage. Of course, before his meeting with Oliphant, Oppenheimer, even if he had wanted to hand over secret information to the Soviets, would have been unable to do so, since he did not have access to any secrets. In the months after that meeting and, indirectly at least, as a result of that meeting, that was to change drastically.

With Ernest Lawrence (if not with Bush and Conant), Oliphant had succeeded in his aim of using the MAUD Committee's findings to instill a sense of urgency with regard to the development of an atomic bomb, and, in his desire to hurry the project along, Lawrence had an influential ally in Arthur Compton. On September 25, 1941, somewhat to his annoyance, Conant was subjected to what he described to Bush as an "involuntary conference" on the atomic bomb with Lawrence and Compton. This took place at Compton's home in Chicago, where Conant was staying as a guest while attending the celebrations commemorating the fiftieth anniversary of Chicago University. Unknown to Conant, Compton had invited Lawrence, who was also in Chicago for the celebrations, to come to his home to present to Conant his case for pressing urgently ahead with the development of the bomb. After taking the opportunity to reprimand Lawrence for allowing the secret of the bomb to be given away to Oppenheimer, Conant listened to Lawrence's arguments for adopting the MAUD Committee's findings and working with the British on building the bomb. Then, turning to Lawrence, Conant said: "Ernest, you say you are convinced of the importance of these fission bombs. Are you ready to devote the next several years of your life to getting them made?" After a moment's hesitation, Lawrence replied: "If you tell me this is my job, I'll do it."

Though it had been discussed unofficially by American scientists for months, and Lauritsen had supplied officials with a précis, the MAUD report was not officially delivered to Conant until October 3, 1941. Six days later, Bush presented its findings to President Roosevelt, whose response was to set up a high-level policy group—consisting of Bush and Conant, together with the Vice President, the Secretary of War and the Army Chief of Staff—who would henceforth be responsible for the management of the atomic-bomb project, acting on advice from Arthur Compton's committee. In response to this development, Compton called a meeting of his committee for October 21 in Schenectady, in upstate New York. A week before the meeting, Lawrence cabled Compton to say: "Oppenheimer has important new ideas. Think it desirable he meet with us Tuesday. Can you arrange invitation?" After a second request, in which Lawrence emphasized that he had "a great deal of confidence in Oppenheimer," Compton capitulated and agreed to allow Lawrence to bring him.

Within a month of his impromptu meeting with Oliphant, therefore, Oppenheimer had gone from being completely ignorant of, and excluded from, the U.S. atomic-bomb program to being right at the heart of it. This seems to have resulted in a flurry of what the FBI, at least, regarded as extremely suspicious Communist Party activity on Oppenheimer's part. On October 3, 1941, the agency learned from a "reliable confidential informant" (a wiretap on Folkoff's phone) that Folkoff had been in touch with Oppenheimer to advise him that he would not be able to meet him at the weekend and had instead arranged for him to meet Steve Nelson. Three days later, from the same "informant" the FBI learned that Nelson had contacted Folkoff to say that he had received $100 from "him." Then, on October 14, a mere week before the Schenectady meeting, the wiretap revealed that Oppenheimer had contacted Folkoff to ask him to arrange for Rudy Lambert (the head of the California Communist Party labor commission) to contact him and to tell him that "Steve" had contacted him and given him a message for Folkoff.

There is no record of Oppenheimer's meeting with Lambert—nor even any confirmation that it took place—nor is there any way of knowing what message Steve Nelson wished to pass on to Folkoff via Oppenheimer. Coming at precisely the moment when Lawrence was pressing for Oppenheimer to be invited to a secret meeting to discuss progress on the atomic bomb, it is natural to wonder whether Oppenheimer might have been passing on information about this meeting to people who would then be able to inform Moscow. On the basis of the available evidence, however, it seems more likely that Oppenheimer's purpose was to let Folkoff know that henceforth his contacts with the Party would be severely reduced.

Oppenheimer knew (from Frank's experience, for example) how

damaging it could be to one's career to be perceived as a communist, and there are many signs that, by the autumn of 1941, what he wanted more than anything was to be involved in government work related to the war—work which, he well knew, was wholly incompatible with close associations with the Communist Party. In his letter to Willie Fowler in the spring of 1941 mentioned earlier, Oppenheimer had written: "I think surely if I were asked to do a job I could do really well and that needed doing I'd not refuse." The sense one has from Oppenheimer's letters of the spring and summer of 1941 is that he felt excluded from what was important, an impression supported by the Berkeley chemist Martin Kamen, who recalls that, though Oppenheimer had previously been the person everybody spoke to about their research, in 1941 this began to change:

> All of a sudden, nobody's talking to him. He's out of it. There's something big going on over there [at the Rad Lab], but he doesn't know what it is. And so he was getting more and more frustrated and Lawrence is very worried because he feels that, after all, Oppenheimer can certainly figure out what's going on, so the security is nonsense to keep him out of it. Better to have him in. And I imagine that's what finally happened; they said it's easier to monitor him if he's inside the project than outside.

Oppenheimer himself said that he was "not without envy" of the men he knew who had gone off to work on radar or other aspects of military research, "but it was not until my first connection with the rudimentary atomic-energy enterprise that I began to see any way in which I could be of direct use."

As usual, Oppenheimer's behavior was ambiguous and difficult to interpret. If he had wanted to avoid political controversy in order to "be of direct use," it was rather odd of him, on October 13, 1941, to write a strongly worded letter of protest to Senator F. R. Coudert, who was cochairman of the committee appointed by the State of New York to investigate communist infiltration of the New York City college system. After making the perfectly reasonable point that the Bill of Rights "guarantees not the right to a belief, but the right to express that belief, in speech or in writing," and that therefore the teachers accused of communism were engaged in "practices specifically protected by the Bill of Rights," Oppenheimer could not help himself ending his letter with some straightforward and, in the context, surely superfluous, abuse: "It took your own statement, with its sanctimonious equivocations and its red baiting, to get me to believe that the stories of mixed cajolery, intimidation and arrogance on the part of the committee of which you are the chairman, are in fact true." This is not the tone of a man determined to keep a low profile and avoid offending the political establishment. The vitriol in the letter, however, might be seen as further evidence of Oppenheimer's frustration and anxiety over the possibility that he might be excluded from war-related work because of his connections with the Communist Party, and his anger at the implied suggestion that he was not entirely loyal to the U.S.

A week after thus registering his disapproval of those who would deny communists their constitutional rights, Oppenheimer was traveling with Lawrence across the U.S., from Berkeley to Schenectady, to take part in a meeting that would turn out to be an important milestone in the Allied project to build an atomic bomb. The meeting opened with Lawrence reading Oliphant's summary of the MAUD report. Compton then reported on various meetings that he had had with leading scientists, at which he received the latest information on key scientific questions relating to the bomb from those most qualified to give it. One assumes that much of this information would have been new to Oppenheimer.

Compton reported that in his meetings with Fermi he had received an estimate of the critical mass of U-235 that put it at about 100 pounds. This was considerably more than the Frisch-Peierls estimate, but still low enough to make the bomb a practical proposition. But, whether one needed two pounds or 100 pounds, the extraction of U-235 from natural uranium remained an extraordinarily difficult task. Compton's advice on how best to tackle this problem came from the Nobel Prize–winning chemist Harold Urey, who told Compton about the various methods of separating the fissionable isotope, all of which would require a massive investment in time and manpower if they were to produce enough U-235 to make a bomb.

The most promising methods of separation, Urey told Compton (and Compton reported to the Schenectady meeting), were gaseous diffusion and centrifugal separation. The former requires the uranium to be converted from a metal into a gas and then forced through the microscopic holes of a filter, or "barrier." Because the U-235 isotope is slightly lighter than U-238, it will pass through the barrier more readily, so that the barrier will act as a way of "enriching" the uranium—that is, increasing the proportion of U-235. Among the many problems with this method are that the gas is extraordinarily corrosive and the process has to be repeated many times, making it laboriously slow. At the time of Compton's meeting with Urey, only microscopic amounts of enriched uranium had been produced by this method. The idea that it might furnish the basis for production of the isotope on an industrial scale looked fanciful.

Similar problems attended the centrifuge method, which is today the main method used to enrich uranium, but which in 1941 was a new and relatively untested technique. The basic idea is to place the uranium, again in a gaseous form, in a cylinder, which is then rotated very quickly, forcing the heavier U-238 to the outer edge and concentrating the lighter U-235 near the center. Considering both methods fairly promising, Urey gave it as his view that the assembly of a critical mass of U-235 was, though extremely difficult, quite achievable with sufficient resources.

An alternative to the arduous business of collecting together an appreciable amount of U-235 was to make a bomb from the newly discovered element of plutonium, or "element 94," as it was then still known (it did not receive its name or its symbol, Pu, until March 1942). Plutonium does not exist in nature. It is one of the elusive "transuranics"—elements heavier than uranium—that Fermi and others had been looking for, and which they thought would be the result of bombarding uranium with neutrons. That transuranic elements could be created had been believed by physicists for a long time, and that element 94 would be fissionable had been predicted by Bohr and Wheeler in their classic papers on fission in 1939.

In his January 1940 summary paper on the literature of fission Louis Turner had drawn attention to the possibility that there might be alternatives to U-235 as a fissionable material. If, instead of fissioning, an atom of U-238 *captures* the neutron fired at it, then it becomes U-239, which, Turner suggested, might fission. But, even if it did not, it would almost certainly be unstable and thus, by beta decay, transmute into the hitherto-unknown element 93 (that is, an element with 93 protons—one more than uranium). And this element would, in turn, decay into element 94, which, Turner predicted, would be even more fissionable than U-235.

Turner was right on all counts, as would eventually be shown by a series of experiments in 1940 and 1941. In the spring of 1940, using the 60-inch cyclotron, Ed McMillan and Phil Abelson produced element 93—later named neptunium (Neptune being the planet beyond Uranus)—by bombarding uranium with neutrons. Astonishingly, they *published* their results. Their paper announcing the discovery of element 93 appeared in the *Physical Review* of June 1940, much to the disgust of James Chadwick, who persuaded the British embassy to make a formal protest to Berkeley. Though the British were, compared to the U.S., not particularly vigilant about the protection of their war secrets from

Soviet espionage, the open publication of work directly helpful to the Nazi bomb project was something about which they were emphatically not prepared to take a relaxed view.

On February 23, 1941, Glenn Seaborg and his research team at Berkeley, again using the 60-inch cyclotron, made a conclusive identification of element 94 from the decay of element 93, and a month later showed that this element would, indeed, fission like U-235. This time they did not publish. Instead, Seaborg, together with Eugene Wigner at Princeton, joined Compton's team of advisors, whom they told that element 94 was indeed more fissionable than U-235 and that it was realistic to believe that a critical mass of it could be produced in a uranium nuclear reactor.

So Compton's report to the Schenactady meeting concluded that, according to the best scientific advice he had received, an atomic bomb *was* a possibility. The next person to speak was Oppenheimer, who gave his own estimate of the critical mass of U-235, which he put at about 220 pounds—more conservative than Fermi's estimate, but more or less in the same ballpark (hundreds, rather than thousands, of pounds).

Compton's biggest disappointment at this meeting was with the engineers who were present (at the express insistence of Bush) in order to provide practical estimates of how long the bomb would take to build and how much it would cost. The reason the meeting was held at Schenectady was that this was the site of the laboratories of General Electric, who provided the engineers. And yet, to Compton's exasperation, the engineers refused to offer any opinion regarding the likely timescale and/or cost of the project. There was, in their opinion, simply too little data even to hazard a guess. As some kind of answer was needed, Compton himself suggested a time of three and a half years and a cost of "some hundreds of millions of dollars"—an estimate that, at Bush's suggestion, he played down in his final report, "lest the government should be frightened off."

In his autobiography Compton reported that he had "always been rather proud of these forecasts, considering the limited data." His estimate of the time required to build a bomb was indeed remarkably accurate. Once the project was formally under way, it did indeed take three and a half years to complete. The cost, however, would turn out to be $2 *billion*, largely because of the difficulties of isotope separation.

On the basis of the Schenectady meeting, Compton prepared a report which stated unequivocally that "a fission bomb of superlatively destructive power will result from bringing quickly together a sufficient mass of element U-235" and recommended: "Full effort toward making atomic bombs is essential to the safety of the nation and the free world." After Compton presented this report to Bush on November 6, Bush in turn presented it to the President on November 27.

On December 6, Bush gathered together a small group consisting of himself, Conant, Briggs, Lawrence and Compton to hear the President's response to Compton's report. This was that a new committee should be constituted. It was to be called S-1 (that is, "Section One," the first section of the Office of Scientific Research and Development), and its membership should consist of Conant, Briggs, Lawrence and Compton, together with Eger V. Murphree, the director of research at Standard Oil, Columbia's George Pegram and Harold Urey, both of whom were at that time in England learning about the creation of the parallel British project, called, with a deliberate attempt to be misleading, the "Tube Alloys" project. The S-1 committee, with a budget of several million dollars, was to spend six months investigating further the possibility of making atomic bombs, and, if after that time it looked likely that such bombs were feasible, then practically unlimited funds would be made available to see the project through to completion.

Conant was made chairman of this new committee, with Briggs as vice chairman. Urey was to take charge of investigating the diffusion method, Murphree was to assume responsibility for researching the centrifuge method, and Lawrence was to investigate a new method that he had devised, using converted cyclotrons to separate the uranium isotopes electromagnetically. Compton had the dual responsibilities of the design of the bomb and research into the possible use of plutonium, which meant overseeing the construction of the world's first nuclear reactor.

Oppenheimer was not included in the S-1 committee, which perhaps indicates that, though his contributions to the Schenectady meeting were valued, he was considered too unreliable from a political point of view to be included in such sensitive work. Lawrence was determined to involve Oppenheimer, but in this he was not helped by Oppenheimer's apparent determination to remain involved in left-wing political activity. When Oppenheimer invited Lawrence to a meeting at his home of the American Association of Scientific Workers (a union organization), Lawrence refused to attend and banned his staff from attending. "I don't think it's a good idea," he told Oppenheimer. "I don't want you to join it. I know nothing wrong with it, but we're planning big things in connection with the war effort, and it wouldn't be right. I want no occasion for somebody in Washington to find fault with us." In reply, on the day that Lawrence left for Washington to receive the President's response to Compton's report, Oppenheimer wrote to him:

I had hoped to see you before you left, but will write this to assure you that there will be no further difficulties at any time with the A.A.S.W. I think that your own feeling about the men working directly with you will have a good deal of weight also with those scientists whose defense efforts are not in the Radiation Laboratory, and I doubt very much whether anyone will want to start at this time an organization which could in any way embarrass, divide or interfere with the work we have in hand.

In the light of this letter, it is surprising, to say the least, that on December 6—the very day that Lawrence was in Washington receiving President Roosevelt's response—Oppenheimer chose to attend a fundraising event for veterans of the Spanish Civil War, which, he surely knew, would be attended by almost every high-ranking Communist Party official in California and, as such, was almost certain to bring him to the renewed attention of the FBI.

The party was held at the home of Louise Bransten, known to the FBI as an intimate friend of Gregory Kheifetz, an agent for the NKVD (the forerunner of the KGB) working undercover at the Soviet consulate in San Francisco. Kheifetz had been instructed to find out about U.S. uranium research and so had been cultivating scientists. He was no doubt delighted to be introduced to Oppenheimer, and, according to Jerold and Leona Schecter in their controversial book *Sacred Secrets*, the two had lunch the next day, at which Oppenheimer expressed concern that the Germans would build an atomic bomb before the Allies. The Schecters also claim that at this lunch Oppenheimer told Kheifetz about Einstein's famous letter to Roosevelt and about a secret project involving outstanding physicists, including Nobel Prize winners.

If what the Schecters say is true, it would explain the reference to Oppenheimer in a letter written by a Soviet intelligence officer in 1944, which claims that Oppenheimer—"one of the leaders of scientific work on uranium in the USA"—while "an unlisted member of the apparatus of Comrade Browder, informed us about the beginning of the work." It is possible to be skeptical both about this letter and about the account offered by the Schecters of Oppenheimer's lunch with Kheifetz, but, even if one takes both at face value, one still does not get a picture of Oppenheimer as engaged in Soviet espionage. He knew a *lot* more than he is reported as telling Kheifetz, and, though it would have been indiscreet of him to mention Einstein's letter and the existence of the secret project, such revelations do not begin to compare with the actions of real spies like the "Cambridge Five," or even with Oliphant's behavior in Berkeley. In any case, by the time of Oppenheimer's alleged lunch with

Kheifetz, the U.S. and the Soviet Union were allies, since, if it took place the day after the fund-raising party for Spanish war veterans, then it occurred on December 7, 1941, the day that the Japanese attack on Pearl Harbor brought the U.S. into the Second World War.

When the S-1 committee met on December 18, 1941, the new political and military situation had made the project in which they were engaged far more urgent. At this meeting, Pegram and Urey reported back from England on the optimism that prevailed there regarding the diffusion method of isotope separation, and Lawrence presented a convincing case for the practicality of the electromagnetic method. Urey also reported on research undertaken by Jesse W. Beams at Virginia, which suggested that the centrifugal method was entirely feasible. It says much about the state of play regarding all these methods, however, that Compton regarded the production of plutonium to be in some ways easier and more practical than any of them; after all, in order for that to work, one had to: 1. produce a nuclear chain reaction, which had never before been achieved; 2. operate this reaction at a level to produce the quantities of plutonium needed, a feat that no one at the time knew was even possible; and 3., in Compton's words, "learn the chemistry and metallurgy of the new chemical element plutonium, so that when the plutonium was made within the uranium it could be extracted, reduced to metal and fashioned into the shapes required for the bomb." Faced with the newly urgent imperative to make a success of their project and with the seemingly equal claims of each of the four methods of producing fissionable material, the S-1 committee made the momentous decision to pursue them all.

As Compton points out in his autobiography: "The period from December 1941, when authority was given to push the atomic project, until June 1942, when the Army assumed responsibility, was critical." It was during this period that those, like Lawrence and Compton, who believed an atomic bomb could be built had to produce convincing evidence that it was possible, and produce a workable plan for making the bomb in three or four years.

At the next meeting of the S-1 committee, held at Compton's house on January 24, 1942, the decision was made to base the work on the uranium chain reaction and the production of plutonium in one place, rather than keep it dispersed throughout various American universities. Pegram, naturally, wanted that place to be Columbia, where Fermi and Szilard had been working together on a nuclear reactor throughout the previous year. Lawrence argued vigorously for the project to be based at Berkeley. Princeton was also considered a possibility. In the end, Compton settled on his own university, Chicago. "You'll never get a chain reaction going here," Lawrence scoffed. "The whole tempo of the University of Chicago is too slow." Compton countered by promising to have the chain reaction going by the end of the year. "I'll bet you a thousand dollars you won't," said Lawrence, but when Compton took the bet, immediately lowered the stakes to "a 5 cent cigar." "I won the bet," Compton remarks in his autobiography, "but I haven't yet received the cigar."

During the spring of 1942, Fermi, Szilard and others prepared to relocate to Chicago to join what Compton had decided to call the "Metallurgical Laboratory." At the same time Oppenheimer was moving, step by step, from the periphery of the project into its very center. At every stage in this development his progress was threatened by the suspicions aroused by his radical politics and the circles of friends and associates into which those politics had placed him. During this period many of the people whose job it was to protect the U.S. from Soviet espionage grew increasingly suspicious of Oppenheimer and there were several requests to place him under tighter surveillance. On January 26, 1942, Special Agent N. J. L. Pieper of the San Francisco office of the FBI wrote to J. Edgar Hoover, listing Oppenheimer as one of four people (the others were Addis, Chevalier and a man called Alexander Kaun) who "represent, in the opinion of this office, a group which is inimical to the welfare of this country." Pieper recommended that "the highly confidential source of information and surveillance mentioned in Bureau teletype of recent date should be utilized"—that is, their telephones should be bugged and microphones should be installed in their homes. "This group of individuals," Pieper went on, "is on such a plane that it is unlikely that any confidential Party informant now available to this office will be able to reach them and determine their actual position in the Party."

In his reply, dated February 10, Hoover granted permission to maintain "technical surveillance" of Chevalier and Kaun, but not of Addis and Oppenheimer. Pieper tried again in March and was again refused, Hoover reminding him that in future he should "follow proper procedure" and ask for such permission by phone rather than by letter. Evidently, if and when the day came for him to grant permission to tap Oppenheimer's phone, Hoover was reluctant to have a written record of that decision.

At this time Hoover knew nothing about the U.S. bomb project or the S-1 committee. The worries that he and his agents had about Oppenheimer were quite general ones, based on the understandable (if not infallible) assumption that anyone who regularly met the likes of Nelson, Folkoff, Schneiderman and Kheifetz was up to no good. If Hoover had known that Oppenheimer was in possession of detailed top-secret information regarding the development of a weapon that the U.S.

government was beginning to believe would win the war for them, there is surely no doubt that he would have placed him under the closest possible surveillance.

James Conant *was* aware of how much Oppenheimer knew, and he also, after Oliphant's visit, had good reason for thinking that the security standards at Berkeley were not all they should have been. He was therefore a worried man. In February 1942, he summoned First Lieutenant John Lansdale of the U.S. Army Military Intelligence Service to his office and explained to him that the U.S. was in a race with the Germans to build an atomic weapon. "Whoever gets this first will win the war," Conant told him, adding that it was therefore important to find out if the physicists at Berkeley could be trusted to keep a secret. As instructed by Conant, Lansdale traveled to Berkeley and, under the cover of being a law student, spent two weeks assessing the situation. What he discovered horrified Conant. Lansdale found that he was able to wander freely around the site of the unfinished 184-inch cyclotron (soon to be converted into a uranium-enriching machine), and that Lawrence's work on a government project to build an explosive was common knowledge at Berkeley and the subject of open and casual conversations in the cafeteria. "Oh! . . . Oh! . . . Oh my goodness!" Conant is reported to have uttered at the news. In response, he sent Lansdale back to Berkeley, this time in uniform, to give the physicists a dressing-down and to warn them that breaches in security could undermine the project.

By March 9, 1942, when Bush wrote a progress report to President Roosevelt, Lawrence's electromagnetic method of enriching uranium seemed to be emerging as the front-runner among the various methods of producing U-235. Bush recommended to the President that a centrifuge plant should be built, which, he suggested, could be up and running by the end of 1943. A gaseous-diffusion plant, Bush advised, could start to deliver weapon-grade uranium by the end of 1944. An electromagnetic plant, however, could be completed by the summer of 1943.

Though Oppenheimer was not yet officially part of the U.S. bomb project, he was, in practice, devoting all his energies to it, having been brought into it "through the back door," as it were, by Lawrence. For most of his time at Berkeley, Lawrence had been in the habit of bringing to Oppenheimer theoretical problems raised by his experimental work, and he saw no reason to stop doing that now. Indeed, for Lawrence it was more important than ever to make use of Oppenheimer's acute mind, since so much now depended on understanding the enrichment and possible fission of uranium before their German rivals.

So immersed was Oppenheimer in his collaborative work with Lawrence on bomb-related questions that, even though he was not officially employed on war work, he wrote to Robert Millikan on March 20, 1942, resigning his part-time post at Caltech in order to give his full attention to war-related research. "New and compelling reasons," wrote Oppenheimer, "have arisen for my leaving Berkeley as little as possible." Six days later, Lawrence wrote to Conant, suggesting that Oppenheimer's involvement in the work of the S-1 committee be made official, or, as Lawrence put it, urging "the desirability of asking Oppenheimer to serve as a member of S-1":

> I think he would be a tremendous asset in every way. He combines a penetrating insight into the theoretical aspects of the whole program with solid common sense, which sometimes in certain directions seems to be lacking, and I am sure that you and Dr. Bush would find him a useful adviser.

With Lansdale's report from Berkeley still fresh in his mind, Conant was in no hurry to bring a suspected security risk on board. Conant was, however, unable to tell Lawrence who he should and should not appoint to the Rad Lab and thus was unable to prevent Lawrence from inadvertently creating one of the biggest security nightmares of the entire U.S. bomb project. For, in involving Oppenheimer in his work, Lawrence was also opening the door to Oppenheimer's students and, in this way—despite Lawrence's own political conservatism and hostility to left-wing political activity—the Rad Lab acquired a reputation as a hotbed of radicalism. Lawrence had already taken on Frank Oppenheimer, who, after Pearl Harbor, was put in charge of building the 184-inch cyclotron. According to the historian Gregg Herken, Lawrence's "boys"—the other Rad Lab scientists—remembered Frank "nervously chain-smoking, pacing back and forth on the wooden latticework that rose above the big magnet."

Lawrence's plan was to persuade the government, via the S-1 committee, to invest hundreds of millions of dollars in a large-scale industrial plant of "Calutrons" (as he was calling the modified cyclotrons) in order to produce the U-235 required for the bomb. It was a plan beset with all kinds of problems, some of which required a better understanding than they had at this time of the physics behind the electromagnetic separation of isotopes, which is where Oppenheimer and his students came in.

Thus it was that in the early summer of 1942 two of Oppenheimer's students, Stanley Frankel and Eldred Nelson, were working on the "theoretical" problem of how to improve the focusing of the Calutron beam. Their paper on the subject was shown by Oppenheimer to another of his students, Rossi Lomanitz. "Uranium was never mentioned," Lomanitz

later said. "It didn't need to be." Lomanitz was one of a group of Oppenheimer's students who were active in radical politics and, quite probably,
members of the Communist Party. Among the other members of this
group were Lomanitz's roommate, David Bohm, and their close friend
Max Friedman, both of whom were recruited by Oppenheimer into the
Rad Lab over the spring and summer of 1942. A fourth member, Joe
Weinberg, was considered *too* radical to be employed on such security-
sensitive work.

The 184-inch Calutron was switched on for the first time on May
26, 1942, by which time Oppenheimer, though he had not yet received
security clearance, was playing a pivotal role in the work of the S-1
committee. Without actually becoming a member of the committee, as
Lawrence had proposed, Oppenheimer was appointed as a consultant,
with special responsibility for investigating the physics of fast-neutron
collisions. His predecessor in this position was Gregory Breit, a physicist at the University of Wisconsin (it had been Breit who suggested
that Joe Weinberg transfer from Wisconsin to Berkeley to work with
Oppenheimer), who had been involved in the uranium project from the
beginning. Breit had a reputation for being a difficult man to work with,
partly because of his almost obsessive concern with secrecy. As one of the
editors of the *Physical Review*, Breit had used his influence to persuade
physicists to impose upon themselves a voluntary ban on publishing anything that might have military value for the duration of the war. When
the S-1 committee was formed, Breit was asked by Compton to act in a
consultancy role as the head of a small group advising the committee on
the physics of fast neutrons and the related question of the design of the
bomb. Breit's official title, which Oppenheimer took delight in inherit-
ing, was "Co-ordinator of Rapid Rupture."

It is not entirely clear *when* Oppenheimer was asked to take over
from Breit. In his autobiography Robert Serber recalls that "a few weeks
after Pearl Harbor"—so, around Christmastime 1941—he received a
phone call from Oppenheimer, who told him that he was in Chicago and
wanted to come to Urbana to talk to Serber about something. When
he arrived, the two went for a walk in the countryside: "There, alone in
that rural setting, he told me that he was going to be appointed to head
the weapons end of the atomic-bomb project, to replace Gregory Breit
in that position." Oppenheimer wanted Serber to come to Berkeley as
his assistant on the project. Serber agreed to come, but, he says, could
not leave Urbana until the end of that semester and so did not arrive in
Berkeley until the end of April 1942.

Clearly, however, Oppenheimer could not replace Breit until Breit
left, which he did not do until May. It seems possible that, from Decem-

ber 1941 until May 1942, Oppenheimer and Breit were working alongside one another. One of Breit's tasks in his role as "Co-ordinator of
Rapid Rupture" was to hold a series of seminars in order to allow the
exchange of ideas among members of his small group. For a while, at
least, these seminars were held at Chicago, with both Oppenheimer and
Breit taking part. Samuel Allison, a member of Breit's group, recalls:

> Breit was always frightened something would be revealed in the
> seminars. Oppenheimer was frightened something would not. I
> backed Oppenheimer and challenged Breit to cut the censorship.
> He accused me of being reckless and hostile to him. I failed. The
> seminars became uninformative.

"Breit was a terrible choice," another member of the Met Lab stated.
"He was actually capable of turning a technical problem into a fist fight."
Nuel Pharr Davis, in his book on Oppenheimer and Lawrence, records
a power struggle between Oppenheimer and Breit over leadership of
Breit's group:

> Compton, who had become impressed with something firm and bold
> in Oppenheimer's manner, gave Breit no backing. Breit realized that
> Oppenheimer stood for the new climate of opinion. He tentatively
> suggested Oppenheimer visit him on his home grounds at Wiscon-
> sin to thresh their difficulties out, and he hinted that Oppenheimer
> might like to make Wisconsin his base so that they could work closely
> together. But when the time came to give a definite invitation, Breit
> simply could not do it. He turned in his resignation to Compton and
> got completely out of the fission project on June 1, 1942.

One of the few pieces of documentary evidence relating to Breit's
replacement by Oppenheimer is a letter Breit wrote to Briggs on May
18, 1942. "I do not believe that secrecy conditions are satisfactory in Dr.
Compton's project," Breit wrote:

> Within the Chicago project there are several individuals strongly
> opposed to secrecy. One of the men, for example, coaxed my sec-
> retary there to give him some official reports out of my safe while I
> was away on a trip . . . The same individual talks quite freely within
> the group . . . I have heard him advocate the principle that all parts
> of the work are so closely interrelated that it is desirable to discuss
> them as a whole.

That individual was Enrico Fermi, who, it will be remembered, took a great deal of persuading back in 1939 that secrecy should be imposed. There was evidently no way that Fermi and Breit could continue to work together on the same project, and, as Fermi was entirely indispensable, it was Breit who left, providing Oppenheimer with his first official position as part of the U.S. atomic-bomb project.

Strictly speaking, Oppenheimer was still not officially allowed to know anything about the project, not even the fact of its existence, since he did not yet have security clearance. On April 28, 1942, he filled out a government security questionnaire, but his application for clearance took more than a year to be approved. Meanwhile he not only continued to have access to the deliberations of the people charged with providing the U.S. with its first atomic bomb, but also to play an increasingly central role in shaping those deliberations.

At about the same time that Oppenheimer filled out his security form, Robert and Charlotte Serber arrived in Berkeley. As Serber recalls, the day after they arrived:

> I went down to Oppie's office in Le Conte Hall where he had accumulated a number of British documents concerning bomb design. I remember there was a paper on critical mass and something on efficiency, I don't remember. The papers were rudimentary but were really quite helpful in getting us started.

Seven months after Oliphant's visit, it seems, the MAUD report was still serving a role as inspiration.

Compton, it will be remembered, had been given six months from December 1941 in which to make the case for investing hundreds of millions of dollars in the atomic-bomb project, and that time was coming to an end. At a meeting of the S-1 committee on May 23, 1942, it was decided to recommend going ahead with what were now five methods of providing fissionable material for a bomb—centrifuge, gaseous diffusion, electromagnetic separation and two different methods of producing plutonium—at an estimated cost of $500 million. On June 17, Compton's suggestions were approved by President Roosevelt, who also recommended transferring the project from civilian to military control.

From that moment on, the U.S. no longer had a research project led by scientists with the aim of investigating the possibility of building an atomic bomb; it had an engineering project run by the U.S. Army with the aim of actually building an atomic bomb. And security now was no longer a matter of voluntary agreements; it was something imposed on the project by a team of 300 members of the U.S. Army's Counter Intelligence Corps, under the able leadership of (the newly promoted) Captain John Lansdale. Three days after the President had given his approval to Compton's recommendations, the project was discussed at the highest possible political level, when, at the second Washington conference, Roosevelt and Churchill agreed that America and Great Britain should cooperate with each other in their joint effort to beat the Nazis in the race to produce the world's first atomic bomb.

At this point, Oppenheimer's part in the joint project was still the fairly minor one that he had inherited from Breit. However, the discussion group he led had two main tasks—to investigate fast-neutron collisions and to think about bomb design—and the second of these was hardly a peripheral concern. In effect, Oppenheimer, though his application for security clearance had not yet been approved and he was not yet a member of the S-1 committee, was now in charge of designing the bomb.

His main accomplice in this crucial task was Serber, who within a month or so of arriving at Berkeley achieved more in getting the bomb designed than Breit's team had managed in the previous five months. He was helped by having at his disposal the combined talents of Stanley Frankel and Eldred Nelson, the two graduate students of Oppenheimer's who had helped to improve the beam of the Calutron. They were still employed by Lawrence at the Rad Lab, but, so long as, in Serber's words, "I didn't take up so much time that Ernest's requirements suffered," Serber had them as his assistants. He assigned them the task of improving the calculation of critical mass and was surprised when they came back to him with a formula that allowed an exact solution to the problem, "provided, of course, one knew all the physical constants, such as the value of the cross sections and the number of neutrons per fission." As far as those difficulties were concerned, no more theory was necessary; all that was required were the results of further experiments.

While Nelson and Frankel were calculating critical mass, Serber looked into the problem of efficiency. When a lump of uranium goes critical, not *all* the material will fission, because the uranium will expand with the heat and be blown apart by the explosion before most of it fissions. So the problem of efficiency is: how much of the uranium in a bomb will actually fission and therefore be converted into explosive energy? Given the extreme difficulty of separating U-235 from natural uranium, the question of efficiency was very important, since the more efficient the bomb, the less enriched uranium would be required.

The basic design of the uranium bomb had already been laid out by Frisch and Peierls in their memorandum of 1940: two subcritical pieces of uranium would be brought together to form one supercritical piece. The problem with this design was that, for it to work, the two pieces would have to be brought together *very* quickly, otherwise a stray neutron would most likely set off a chain reaction before the two pieces were in place, causing the bomb to "fizzle." To avoid this, the fissionable materials had to be extremely pure, and the "gun" firing the two pieces together had to be extremely fast. This meant that Oppenheimer's team had to investigate and solve two sets of questions, one involving the chemistry of uranium and plutonium and the other involving firearms and explosives.

Faced with these kinds of problems, Oppenheimer's instinct was the exact opposite of Breit's; whereas Breit had wanted above all to protect the secrecy of the discussions among his group, even if that meant inhibiting those discussions, Oppenheimer wanted above all to encourage those discussions, even if that meant compromising a little on security. In July 1942, therefore, he and Serber decided to host a meeting at Berkeley of, as Oppenheimer put it, "luminaries"—top-level physicists whose expertise might be brought to bear on the problems facing them.

The man Oppenheimer wanted most urgently involved in this meeting was someone who, up to this point, had not been involved in the bomb project at all, and who had, in fact, remained deeply skeptical that an atomic bomb could possibly be built. That man was Hans Bethe, widely regarded at this time as the leading nuclear physicist in the world. Bethe's review articles of the late 1930s were seen as being so authoritative they had become known as "Bethe's Bible." His work on stellar energy, which was eventually (in 1967) to win him the Nobel Prize, was well known to Oppenheimer, as it was to most physicists, providing as it does a profound and fundamentally important analysis of how nuclear fusion lies at the heart of the energy produced by stars.

Having been removed from his post at Tübingen because he was partly Jewish, Bethe had, since 1935, been at Cornell, where he was to remain for the rest of his career. Though he badly wanted to contribute to the Allied war effort, he had refused to have anything to do with the atomic-bomb project because he thought it extremely unlikely to succeed. "Separating isotopes of such a heavy element [as uranium] was clearly a very difficult thing to do," he later said, "and I thought we would never succeed in any practical way." To help enlist Bethe, Oppenheimer approached John H. van Vleck, a professor of physics at Harvard, and asked him to convince Bethe that his participation was necessary.

Though not yet fully convinced that the project would be successful, Bethe agreed to come to the meeting at Berkeley organized by Oppenheimer and Serber. On the way, he stopped at Chicago to pick up his old friend Edward Teller, who had also been invited. At Chicago, Teller explained to Bethe the progress that had been made at the Met Lab and, in particular, the progress made with the project led by Fermi and Szilard to create plutonium in a nuclear reactor. At what was to become the famous rackets court at Stagg Field, Bethe saw the "tremendous stacks of graphite" that Fermi and Szilard had amassed as part of what would be the world's first nuclear reactor.[44] "I then," he remembered, "became convinced that the atom-bomb project was real and that it would probably work."

For his part, Teller was *so* convinced the fission bomb would work that he had lost interest in it as a theoretical problem. Much more interesting to him was the possibility, first mentioned speculatively to him by Fermi one day over lunch, of a *fusion* bomb. Just as the fission of heavy elements releases great amounts of energy, so does the fusion of lighter elements. In fact, fusion—if it could be achieved—offers much greater yields of energy than fission.

The individual nucleons that make up a nucleus have a greater total mass than the nucleus itself. In combining to make up a nucleus, they lose some of their mass. This is called "mass defect." The missing mass is converted into the energy required to hold the nucleons together—that is, it becomes what is called "binding energy." In both fission and fusion, nuclei with comparatively low binding energies are converted into nuclei with high binding energies—that is, elements with comparatively high mass per nucleon are converted into elements with comparatively low mass per nucleon. As Frisch and Meitner were the first to realize, this missing mass is released as energy, potentially as a massive explosion.

It sounds contradictory that *both* the fusion of lighter elements and the fission of heavier elements release energy. One might expect that, if energy is released by the process of fission, it would be absorbed by the process of fusion. The explanation for this lies in what is known as the "curve of binding energy." Not all elements have the same binding energy. Neither does the difference go up or down in continuous proportion to the mass of the element. Rather, the binding energy starts off small for the lightest elements, such as hydrogen, helium and lithium,

[44] The reactor Fermi was building was one that would use uranium-238 to generate nuclear energy through fission. Being a reactor rather than a bomb, it needed slow neutrons rather then fast ones, the aim being to produce a *controlled* fission chain reaction, not an explosion. The piles of graphite were to serve as what is called a "moderator," the purpose of which is to slow the neutrons down. A by-product of this kind of reactor is plutonium. If it worked, Fermi's experiment would show two crucial facts: first, that it is possible to initiate a chain reaction in uranium-238; and second, that it is possible to produce plutonium on a more or less industrial scale.

and then increases until one gets to iron (atomic number 26, with a mass of 56), then it decreases again.

Thus, while it is true that the collected mass of the individual nucleons that make up a uranium nucleus will be greater than the mass of the nucleus itself—just as the collected mass of the individual nucleons that make up a helium nucleus will be greater than the nucleus itself—it is also true, as noted in the previous chapter, that the collected mass of the separated pieces of the split uranium nucleus (say, barium, krypton, plus two neutrons) will have a slightly *smaller* combined mass than that of the original nucleus. The reason for this is to be found in the curve of binding energy, which shows that the mass defect (binding energy) for barium and krypton is greater than that for uranium, so those nuclei have a correspondingly lower mass per nucleon *either* than the nucleons considered individually *or* than the nucleons combined into a uranium nucleus.

Thus, if you fuse together nuclei of elements lighter than iron, *or* fission nuclei heavier than iron, the result will be the creation of nuclei that have a greater mass defect than the ones you started with, and thus a tremendous release of energy in accordance with the equation $E = mc^2$. The amount of energy released per fusion of, say, hydrogen is less (by about one-tenth) than the amount of energy released per fission of uranium, but, because the nuclei are so much lighter (by about one-fiftieth) and therefore there are more of them in any given quantity of material, the energy release *per kilogram* will be far greater in fusion than in fission.

It had been assumed that a fusion bomb was an impossibility because of the tremendous heat that would be required to get the nuclei moving energetically enough to fuse together. To get a fusion reaction going, one would have to reproduce something similar to the conditions that prevail inside the sun. What Fermi mentioned casually to Teller over lunch was the possibility that such heat might, after all, be created: by fission. At Chicago, Teller, together with the young physicist Emil Konopinski, set to work on a report on the possibility of a fusion bomb and concluded that, as Teller later put it, "heavy hydrogen [deuterium or tritium] actually could be ignited by an atomic bomb to produce an explosion of tremendous magnitude."

When he was invited to the meeting organized by Oppenheimer and Serber, Teller asked that Konopinski should also be included, and, when Bethe arrived in Chicago to accompany him to Berkeley, he found that Teller's mind was racing far ahead of the issue they were being collected together to think about. "We had a compartment on the train to California, so we could talk freely," Bethe remembered. "Teller told me that the fission bomb was all well and good and, essentially, was now a sure thing. In reality, the work had hardly begun. Teller likes to jump to conclusions. He said that what we really should think about was the possibility of igniting deuterium by a fission weapon—the hydrogen bomb."

Apart from Bethe, Konopinski, Teller and van Vleck, Oppenheimer had also invited Felix Bloch from Stanford and Richard Tolman from Caltech. So, with Serber, Nelson, Frankel and himself, that made ten. According to one account, the meeting began with an attempt by Oppenheimer to bring the contributors face-to-face with the fact that what they were doing was planning to build a bomb of hitherto unimaginable power. To help them to visualize what this might entail (and presumably to overcome any lingering squeamishness there might be about the fact that they were engaged in the design of an explosive), Oppenheimer drew their attention to some details of a large explosion that had occurred in 1917 in the harbor of Halifax, Nova Scotia. The explosion was caused by a collision between two ships, one of which was carrying 5,000 tons of TNT, and resulted in the deaths of up to 2,000 people and the destruction of an area of almost one square mile. No one knew how powerful the atomic bomb would be, but the best guess was that it would be several times more powerful than the Halifax explosion (in fact, the Hiroshima bomb was three times and the Nagasaki bomb four times more powerful, though the number of people killed in each case was more than twenty times the number killed in Halifax).

With everybody's mind thus focused, Serber explained what had been done so far, both by Breit's team and, in the preceding few months, by Oppenheimer's. Nelson and Frankel then gave their critical-mass calculations and, remembers Serber; "Everybody agreed that it looked under good control from a theorist's point of view." Bethe's recollections confirm Serber's impression. "The theory of the fission bomb was well taken care of by Serber and two of his young people," he remarked later. They "seemed to have it well under control so we felt we didn't need to do much."

With all the "luminaries" apparently agreeing with his view that the fission bomb was essentially "now a sure thing," Teller turned the discussion away from fission and toward fusion. As Serber remembers it, what Teller was proposing was "a detonation wave in liquid deuterium set off by being heated by the explosion of an atomic bomb." In his autobiography Serber describes how, when Teller mentioned this idea, "everybody forgot about the A-bomb, as if it were old hat, something settled, no problem, and turned with enthusiasm to something new."

Everyone present realized that if the "Super" (as they began calling it) could be made to work, it would be many times more powerful than an atomic bomb. In an atomic bomb, one kilogram of uranium would explode with the force of (roughly) 15,000–20,000 tons of TNT; in a thermonuclear, hydrogen bomb, one kilogram of deuterium would explode with the force of 80,000–100,000 tons. Moreover, deuterium is relatively cheap and plentiful. Twenty-six pounds of it would not be difficult to acquire, and that, potentially, could make a bomb equivalent to about one million tons of TNT.

That was startling enough, but, recalls Serber:

> At one point Edward [Teller] asked if the fission bomb could ignite the earth's atmosphere. In view of the difficulties encountered in considering the Super this seemed extremely unlikely, but in view of the importance of the consequences, Hans [Bethe] took a look at it and put numbers to the improbability.

While Bethe was looking at the numbers, Oppenheimer—who took the apocalyptic scenario presented by Teller more seriously than either Serber or Bethe—made a long-distance call to Compton to tell him that his group had "found something very disturbing." Compton asked how soon Oppenheimer could come to Chicago to see him and talk about it. The following day came Oppenheimer's reply. And so, early the next morning, Oppenheimer took the train to Chicago, where Compton met him in his car. As they drove back to Compton's house, Oppenheimer recounted the discussion that his group had been having about fission, fusion and the possibility of global catastrophe, which, as Compton writes, "could not be passed over lightly."

> Was there really any chance that an atomic bomb would trigger the explosion of the nitrogen in the atmosphere or of the hydrogen in the ocean? This would be the ultimate catastrophe. Better to accept the slavery of the Nazis than to run a chance of drawing the final curtain on mankind!

With Compton, Oppenheimer agreed there could be only one answer to the crisis, which was, in Compton's words: "Oppenheimer's team must go ahead with their calculations. Unless they came up with a firm and reliable conclusion that our atomic bombs could not explode the air or the sea, these bombs must never be made."

By the time Oppenheimer got back, Bethe had done the figures and discovered, as he put it, "some unjustified assumptions in Teller's calculations." Bethe, in fact, never took seriously the idea that they could destroy the earth's atmosphere and was surprised that Oppenheimer had thought it worth troubling Compton with, "but then Oppie was a more

enthusiastic character than I was. I would have waited until we knew
more."

With the apocalyptic worry disposed of, the group got back to discussing bomb physics, again concentrating on the "Super." What came
as a pleasant surprise to the members of the group, even to those who
knew Oppenheimer well, was what an extraordinarily capable chairman
he showed himself to be. Oppenheimer had never previously organized
anything—he had never, for example, served as chairman of his department at Berkeley—and yet, here he was, in charge of nine of the country's most distinguished physicists, revealing himself to be an able leader
who commanded the respect of everyone present.

"The conference didn't exactly end," remembers Serber, "it sort of
fizzled out. After a week people began to leave, some stayed on a couple
of weeks longer." For everyone involved, it had been a memorable series
of discussions, Oppenheimer's handling of which had been a revelation.
"As Chairman, Oppenheimer showed a refined, sure, informal touch,"
Teller later said. "I don't know how he had acquired this facility for handling people. Those who knew him well were really surprised. I suppose
it was the kind of knowledge a politician or administrator has to pick
up somewhere." It was crucial to the success of the meetings, however,
that these political and administrative gifts went hand-in-hand with the
kind of deep insight into both science and scientists that was required to
get the best out of the participants. "A spirit of spontaneity, adventure
and surprise prevailed during those weeks in Berkeley," Teller remarked,
"and each member of the group helped move the discussion toward
a positive conclusion." These sentiments were echoed by Bethe, who
recalled: "The intellectual experience was unforgettable."

> We were forever inventing new tricks, finding ways to calculate, and
> rejecting most of the tricks on the basis of the calculations. Now I
> could see at first-hand the tremendous intellectual power of Oppen-
> heimer, who was the unquestioned leader of our group.

By the time the conference had "fizzled" to an end, Oppenheimer's
own reputation and position within the U.S. bomb project had been
transformed from that of a useful, but not essential advisor to that of an
indispensable leader and facilitator.

His report from the meeting of the "luminaries" was received and
approved by the S-1 committee toward the end of August 1942. Its central message was that an atomic (fission) bomb could indeed be built,
but that it "would require a major scientific and technical effort." Such
a bomb would need more U-235 than some previous estimates had

suggested—about 66 pounds—but its power would be something like 150 times greater than had previously been thought—that is, equivalent to about 100,000 tons of TNT. The report also touched on the possibility of the "Super," saying that a 66-pound fission bomb could, in principle, be used to initiate a fusion explosion in liquid deuterium, two or three tons of which would explode with the force of 100 million tons of TNT, completely destroying an area of 360 square miles.

In the light of the conclusions drawn by Oppenheimer, the S-1 committee submitted a report to Bush, summarizing the findings of the "luminaries" and claiming that enough fissionable material for an atomic-bomb test could be obtained by March 1944. "We have become convinced," the report stated, "that success in this program before the enemy can succeed is necessary for victory. We also believe that success of this program will win the war if it has not previously been terminated."

By the end of August 1942, Bush was giving it as his opinion that "nothing should stand in the way of putting this whole affair through to a conclusion." To him, it was clear that what was now required was strong leadership. The same thought had occurred to General Brehon B. Somervell, who was in charge of the section of the army that included the Engineering Corps, and Somervell knew just the man to provide that strong leadership.

That man was Colonel Leslie Groves, a large and indomitable figure, who stood six feet tall and weighed about 250 pounds. Lieutenant Colonel Kenneth D. Nichols, who served under him for many years, called him "the biggest sonovabitch I've ever met in my life, but also one of the most capable individuals." Groves had recently undertaken successfully the demanding task of supervising the construction of the Pentagon, which, impressively, he completed well within the budget he had been allocated. For this, and other reasons, he had a reputation for being a man who got things done. On September 17, 1942, he was in Washington, testifying to the Military Affairs Committee, when he met General Somervell, who told him: "The Secretary of War has selected you for a very important assignment."

Groves was not particularly happy about this appointment, even though Somervell told him that if he did it correctly, "it will win the war." Groves wanted to get out of Washington and into battle, commanding soldiers, not directing civilian scientists. The silver lining offered to him was that, as reward for taking on the job, he would be promoted to brigadier general. The project of which General Groves (as everybody henceforth called him) was now in overall charge had already been christened the "Manhattan Project" by his predecessor, Colonel Marshall, who worked out of an office in Manhattan. Even though Groves had his office in Washington rather than Manhattan, he kept this previous name for the project, its misleading connotations considered by him to be an asset.

From the very beginning, Groves ran the project with a characteristic determination to get the job done and let nothing and nobody stand in his way. With a confidence and speed that inspired both admiration and fear, he took several decisive steps in the first few days of his appointment. On his first day in command, he sent Nichols to buy 1,250 tons of uranium ore from the Belgians, who had been trying to interest the U.S. government in it for the previous six months. The next day, he persuaded ("bullied" is probably the word) the civilian head of the War Production Board to give the Manhattan Project a top-priority AAA rating, which meant that he would not have to compete with any other war project for funds and resources. The same day, he acquired for the project a plot of land in Tennessee that extended over 50,000 acres. It was called Oak Ridge and would serve as the site for the industrial plants that would be required to produce the enriched uranium needed for the bomb.

As yet, however, it had not been decided exactly what plants would be built at Oak Ridge. Having been briefed by Bush on the work of the S-1 committee, Groves decided to visit every major site involved in the project. He began with the Westinghouse Research Laboratory in Pittsburgh and the University of Virginia, which were responsible for the development of the centrifuge method of isotope separation. At both places, Groves was horrified to learn how little had been achieved and in what a leisurely manner the work was being conducted. Though it would become in modern times the main method of enriching uranium, the centrifuge method was, on Groves's orders, abandoned by the Manhattan Project.

Groves next went to New York to visit Columbia, where Harold Urey and his colleague John Dunning were working on the gaseous-diffusion method. There, Groves discovered that the *theory* of gaseous diffusion was developing nicely, but it had not been used to produce even a speck of U-235, nor did it look at all likely that it could be used on an industrial scale for a long time.

On October 5, Groves went to Chicago, where he was shown the pile of graphite that was being amassed for the nuclear reactor, and where he attended a meeting of the scientists working at the Met Lab. It was an impressive group that included no fewer than three Nobel laureates (Compton, Fermi and Franck), as well as Szilard, Wigner and about a dozen others. However, the meeting was tense; the scientists, especially Szilard, were suspicious of the military, and Groves was contemptuous of what he regarded as the arrogance and impracticality of the theorists. At the end of the meeting, Groves told the scientists that, though he did not have a Ph.D., he had ten years of formal education after he left college, so "That would be the equivalent of about two PhDs, wouldn't it?" There was an embarrassed silence, and then Groves left. "You see what I told you?" Szilard exclaimed after Groves had gone. "How can you work with people like that?"

After Chicago, Groves traveled to Berkeley to meet Lawrence and see the Calutron, which Lawrence demonstrated with all the winning, boyish enthusiasm that had served him so well and landed him so many prizes and so much research funding in the past. Groves, however, was not especially impressed with the machinery or especially charmed by Lawrence's breezy optimism. Rather, he saw in Lawrence the same frustrating failure to see the project in industrial, rather than academic, terms that he had seen everywhere else. Groves wanted someone to start talking about getting *pounds*, not micrograms, of enriched uranium. Instead of which, Lawrence, having shown Groves the magnificence of the 184-inch Calutron, was forced to admit, when asked how much uranium he had separated so far: "Well, actually, we don't get any sizeable separation at all. I mean, not yet. This is still experimental, you see . . ."

Oppenheimer's first meeting with Groves took place on October 8, 1942, at a lunch hosted by Robert Sproul, president of Berkeley. In some ways, the meeting is reminiscent of the moment in 1926 when, as an unknown, twenty-two-year-old graduate student at Cambridge, Oppenheimer had been introduced to Max Born, then the leading theorist in the emerging field of quantum mechanics. At that meeting Oppenheimer had seemed to cast a spell over Born, a spell that resulted in an invitation to come to Göttingen, the very center of research into quantum mechanics, where he was treated as if he in some way had superiority over Born. Similarly, when he met Groves, Oppenheimer was, compared to the people Groves had already met, a relatively junior member of the project. He was not, like Compton, Fermi, Franck and Lawrence, a Nobel Prize winner; nor was he, like Szilard, Teller and Wigner, an originator of the atomic-bomb project. Moreover, he seemed, in his love of French poetry, his absorption in the literature of Hinduism and his resolutely *theoretical* approach to physics, the very personification of the remote academic whom Groves had come to despise.

And yet, on meeting the thirty-eight-year-old Oppenheimer, Groves was immediately won over, feeling that here, at last, was someone who could see and understand the *real* problems that the project faced. A clue to Oppenheimer's success with both Born and Groves perhaps lies in a remark Haakon Chevalier once made about him: "He was always, without seeming effort, aware of, and responsive to, everyone in the room, and was constantly anticipating unspoken wishes."

Certainly, Oppenheimer seems to have had an unerring sense of what Groves wished to hear. In his own account of the history of the Manhattan Project, *Now It Can Be Told*, Groves says remarkably little about his first meeting with Oppenheimer, and nothing at all about his own first impressions. He says only that at this first meeting they "discussed at some length the results of his study and the methods by which he had reached his conclusions." From this, it is impossible to say why Groves took such a liking to Oppenheimer, but in the autobiographical statement that Oppenheimer prepared for his security case in 1954, one begins to realize what Groves might have seen in him. Remembering the period immediately after the meeting of "luminaries" at Berkeley in July 1942, Oppenheimer writes:

> In later summer, after a review of the experimental work, I became convinced, as did others, that a major change was called for in the work on the bomb itself. We needed a central laboratory devoted wholly to this purpose, where people could talk freely with each other, where theoretical ideas and experimental findings could affect each other, where the waste and frustration and error of the many compartmentalized experimental studies could be eliminated, where we could begin to come to grips with chemical, metallurgical, engineering, and ordnance problems that had so far received no consideration. We therefore sought to establish this laboratory for a direct attack on all the problems inherent in the most rapid possible development and production of atomic bombs.

He also says that, when Groves assumed control of the project, "I discussed with him the need for an atomic bomb laboratory," and reveals that he, at least, was happy with the idea of "making it a Military Establishment in which key personnel would be commissioned as officers," even to the extent of taking the first steps toward joining the army himself.

If *this* is what Groves meant by "the results of his study and the methods by which he had reached his conclusions," then one can see why he liked what he heard so much. From the other scientists he had been met with either condescension and hostility or a resolute determination to impress and appear upbeat. Now here was a scientist talking Groves's language and echoing his own thoughts and frustrations, expressing the dissatisfaction that he himself had felt about the pace of the work being carried out, and emphasizing the need for a major change in the organization, for more central control, in order to get the project moving more quickly. All this, one imagines, was music to Groves's ears.

So impressed was Groves that a week later, while he was again visiting Chicago, he asked Oppenheimer to join him in order to discuss his idea of a central laboratory. Then, when the time came for Groves to leave for New York, he asked Oppenheimer to accompany him on the journey. So it was that Oppenheimer and Groves, together with Kenneth Nichols and Colonel Marshall—all four of them squeezed into a tiny compartment on a train—discussed how and where the bomb laboratory might be created. From this conversation the idea of a single laboratory was developed, now envisaged as a place, preferably in a remote location away from prying eyes and ears, where all the scientists working on the design and production of the bomb—rather than on chain reactions, methods of isotope separation, and the like—could be gathered together. There, under the watchful control and guidance of the military, the scientists could pursue their work, while sharing with each other (but not with anybody else) their ideas and information.

Before he set off for Chicago, Oppenheimer wrote to John Manley, the experimental physicist who had been appointed as his assistant, telling him that Groves had seemed "convinced of the necessity for proceeding immediately with the construction of the laboratory and the reorganization of our work." He also advised him that "some far reaching geographical change in plans seems to be on the cards," since Groves had apparently gone off his original idea of placing the laboratory at Oak Ridge (in fact, Oppenheimer had talked him out of it, on the grounds that the laboratory should not be envisaged as a mere appendage of the isotope-separation plant).

Manley, who was a specialist in neutron physics, had worked with Fermi and Szilard at Columbia before taking up a position at the University of Illinois in 1937. Since January 1942 he had been a member of the Met Lab at Chicago, where he remained after his appointment as Oppenheimer's assistant in fast-neutron research. "I let myself be persuaded to join Oppenheimer with some misgivings," he later recalled. "I had only briefly met him. I had given a colloquium in Berkeley a year or two before and I was somewhat frightened of his evident erudition and his lack of interest in mundane affairs."

To Manley's surprise, he and Oppenheimer got on well. While Oppenheimer and his team at Berkeley made calculations, Manley's task was to supply them with measurements taken from experiments using the particle accelerators at no fewer than nine universities. "I can't tell you how *difficult* those experiments were," Manley wrote. "The amounts of material to work with were infinitesimal . . . just practically invisible quantities." Particularly frustrating was the problem of liaising with the various centers of research, which was the main factor in persuading Oppenheimer and Manley of the need for a single laboratory.

In a subsequent letter written after his train ride to New York with Groves, Oppenheimer told Manley that Groves had been out west and that "the question of site is well along toward settlement." Evidently, by this time (the first week of November 1942), Oppenheimer had managed to steer Groves's thoughts about the location of the laboratory toward the countryside that Oppenheimer knew and loved best: the mountains of northern New Mexico. "It is a lovely spot," Oppenheimer told Manley, "and in every way satisfactory, and the only points which now have to be settled are whether the human and legal aspects of the necessary evacuations make insuperable difficulties." The delicate nature of one of these difficulties is perhaps indicated at the end of the letter, where he reveals that he is not sending a copy of it to Compton. He would, he wrote, be happy if Manley told Compton "anything about the developments in physics that you think he would like to hear." But, he implored: "Don't tell him about the laboratory." As he grew closer to Groves, as the theoretical subgroup of S-1 that he headed acquired a greater and greater role, and as the plans for a central laboratory seemed more and more likely to succeed, Oppenheimer surely guessed that Compton's position as the head of the scientific aspect of the Manhattan Project was likely to be short-lived. If the plan for a central laboratory went ahead and Oppenheimer were placed in charge of that laboratory, then, instead of Oppenheimer working as a consultant for a project headed by Compton, Compton would, in effect, be working for a project led by Oppenheimer.

On November 16, Oppenheimer, together with Ed McMillan and Colonel Dudley, visited Jemez Springs, New Mexico. In the afternoon they were joined by Groves, who, confirming the view that Oppenheimer and McMillan had already come to, pronounced abruptly as soon as he arrived: "This will never do." The canyon was too deep, its walls too steep to consider as a suitable spot for a major program of building. Oppenheimer then suggested as an alternative a boys' school on the east side of the Jemez range that was built on a flat mesa: the Los Alamos Ranch School. "As soon as Groves saw it," McMillan later recalled, "he said, in effect, 'This is the place.'" On December 7, 1942, the school was issued with a formal notice of eviction, and it closed the following February. A month after that, the first scientists arrived at what was, by then, a bomb laboratory. Officially, it was now called "Project Y."[45]

From the time that Oppenheimer and Groves first discussed the possibility of a single laboratory in October 1942 until the time that scientists began arriving at Los Alamos in March 1943, there seems to have been an assumption, particularly on Oppenheimer's part, that he himself would be appointed as its director. However, it is far from clear when the decision was made to appoint Oppenheimer as the head of this laboratory.[46] He did not receive his formal letter of invitation to take up the post, signed by Conant and Groves, until February 1943, but the decision must have been taken at least a month or two before that. In *Now It Can Be Told*, Groves discusses the decision at some length, emphasizing that, although Oppenheimer had headed the Berkeley study group, "neither Bush, Conant nor I felt that we were in any way committed to his appointment as director of Project Y." Moreover, "no one with whom I talked showed any great enthusiasm about Oppenheimer as a possible director of the project."

There were, as Groves makes clear, some very powerful reasons for that lack of enthusiasm. Not only had Oppenheimer never directed a laboratory of any kind before, but he had never directed *anything*. He "had had almost no administrative experience of any kind," as Groves puts it. Also (and this point seems to have weighed particularly heavily on Groves's mind), Oppenheimer, unlike the heads of the major laboratories associated with the Manhattan Project—Compton at Chicago, Urey at Columbia and Lawrence at Berkeley—did not have a Nobel Prize. He thus, says Groves, lacked "the prestige among his fellow scientists that I would have liked the project leader to possess." Finally there was the problem that, as Groves puts it, Oppenheimer's "background included much that was not to our liking by any means." This last problem was to rumble on for some months *after* Oppenheimer's appointment, with the security organization ("which was not yet under my complete control," Groves writes) unwilling to grant clearance to someone with so many links to important communists.

In his book, Groves seems to suggest that he appointed Oppenheimer, despite the many reasons not to, simply because "it became

[45] Just as Oak Ridge was "Site X," so Hanford was "Site W," the electromagnetic plant at Oak Ridge was "Y-12," the gaseous-diffusion plant was "K-25," the uranium reactor at Oak Ridge "X-10" and the thermal diffusion plant "S-50."

[46] Gregg Herken, in *Brotherhood of the Bomb*, says it was on the train between Chicago and New York on October 15, 1942, but offers no evidence for this.

apparent that we were not going to find a better man." Of the "bet-ter men" he considered, Lawrence could not be spared from the elec-tromagnetic project, Compton could not be spared from Chicago, and Urey, as a chemist rather than a physicist, was not qualified. There were, of course, other possibilities—Lawrence pushed hard for Groves to appoint Ed McMillan—but it is fairly clear that Groves *liked* Oppen-heimer and believed strongly that he was the man for the job. When Oppenheimer was asked many years later to explain why Groves chose him, his reply illustrated why throughout his life he had struck people as arrogant. Groves, he said, "had a fatal weakness for good men."

By November 30, 1942, when he wrote to Conant summarizing the results of recent scientific work, Oppenheimer seemed already to regard himself as the de facto head of the new laboratory. He speaks of "the men we are after," and warns Conant:

> The job we have to do will not be possible without personnel sub-stantially greater than that which we now have available, and I shall only be misleading you and all others concerned with the S-1 project if I were to promise to get the work done without this help.

As it turned out, the men Oppenheimer was after included many of the top scientists in the country. To get them, as he was advised by both Isidor Rabi and the Cornell physicist Robert Bacher, he would have to drop the idea of the laboratory being a military establishment. The sci-entists he wanted and needed, they told him, would hardly be willing to join the army and conduct their research in uniform.

Having shelved that idea, Oppenheimer—clearly in as great a hurry as Groves to get the project moving—was able to recruit many of the people he wanted by the end of the year. In this he was helped enor-mously by Manley, who knew personally almost every physicist in the U.S. working on fast-neutron research. As Manley remembers: "I was supposed to talk to people in the fast neutron groups at Princeton and Wisconsin and try to persuade them to come to Los Alamos." One prob-lem with this was that Manley himself had never been to New Mexico and knew nothing about Los Alamos:

> So I dug out some maps of New Mexico and I looked all over those maps trying to find where it might be. He'd said it was near the "Hamos" Mountains, and I looked for HAMOS and I couldn't find it on the map, on *any* map of New Mexico. I hadn't any Spanish and, of course, I didn't know that those doggone mountains are spelled JEMEZ.

Despite his inability to find Los Alamos on the map, Manley did succeed in persuading most of the physicists he spoke to to join the project.

Equally important was his success in appropriating the machines that the experimentalists would need. From Wisconsin he obtained two Van de Graaff generators, from Harvard a cyclotron, and from Illinois his own Cockcroft-Walton accelerator. To make tracking these things more difficult, they were sent first to a medical officer in St. Louis, Missouri, and from there to Los Alamos. The difficulty of getting the necessary equipment to the remote spot in the New Mexico mountains made Manley wonder "whether, if Oppenheimer had been an experimental physicist and known that experimental physics is really 90 percent plumbing and you've *got* to have all that equipment and tools and so on, he would ever have agreed to start a laboratory in this isolated place."

Much as he respected and grew to admire and like Oppenheimer, Manley was, especially to begin with, acutely conscious of Oppenheimer's lack of experience of both laboratories and administration, and took a good deal of persuading that Oppenheimer was actually capable of administering a large laboratory. His doubts were increased by the fact that Oppenheimer seemed to take so little interest in how the laboratory might be organized. "I bugged Oppie for I don't know how many months about an organization chart—who was going to be responsible for this and who was going to be responsible for that. But each time he would seem to be as unresponsive as an experimental physicist would think a theorist would be." Finally, in January 1943, Manley flew out to California and went to Oppenheimer's office. As he pushed open the door he noticed that Edward Condon was there: "Oppie practically threw a piece of paper at me as I came in the door and said, 'Here's your damned organization chart.'"

The organization described by the chart, which remained in place for the first year of the laboratory's existence, divided the lab into four main sections: 1. Theoretical, which initially was to be led by Oppenheimer himself; 2. Experimental, headed by Robert Bacher; 3. Chemistry and Metallurgy, led by the Berkeley chemist Joseph Kennedy and the British-born metallurgist Cyril S. Smith; and 4. Ordnance, which would, in time (it took some months to find the right man for this job), be headed by William "Deak" Parsons of the U.S. Navy. Each of these divisions (except the Theoretical Division, which was by far the smallest) was split into groups, so that, for example, the Experimental Division contained a "Cyclotron Group," led by Robert Wilson, which was charged with (among other things) the crucial task of measuring the time it takes for neutrons to be emitted after fission. Manley himself was put in charge of the "D-D Group," which had responsibility for determining by experiment which material (candidates included tungsten, carbon and beryllium) could best be used as a "tamper" to bounce escaping neutrons back into the fissioning uranium, thereby improving the bomb's efficiency.

The reason Condon was in Oppenheimer's office was that Oppenheimer had decided to appoint him as associate director of the laboratory. Oppenheimer's first choice for that role was another old friend from his student days in Europe, Isidor Rabi, but Rabi could not be persuaded to accept the job. He had several reasons for not wanting to move to Los Alamos. First, his wife, Helen, was vehemently opposed to going there. Second, Rabi thought the project to build a fission bomb had only a fifty-fifty chance of success. And third, he considered the work he was then doing on radar to be a crucial contribution to the war effort. Fourth, and perhaps most importantly, he was, as he later wrote, "*strongly* opposed to bombing," on the grounds that "You drop a bomb and it falls on the just and the unjust." Nevertheless, he was prepared to act as a consultant on the project, and came often to oversee developments and offer advice.

The first piece of advice Rabi offered was to make an important change to the organization chart that Oppenheimer had drawn up. There was simply no way, Rabi urged (and Bacher seconded), that Oppenheimer could combine being director with being head of a division. Oppenheimer thus changed his mind and put Hans Bethe in charge of the Theoretical Division, a choice that was as obvious as it was excellent, but which offended Edward Teller, who felt that he should have got the job.

While Oppenheimer and Manley were arranging the Los Alamos laboratory, the Met Lab in Chicago achieved the first fundamentally important milestone in the pursuit of a fission bomb by creating the world's first chain reaction. It happened on December 2, 1942, a very cold Chicago winter's day. Fermi, knowing the time was right for the pile he had constructed to go critical, had gathered about twenty people in the rackets court at Stagg Field, and was conducting affairs with complete confidence that everything would go as planned. One of the people present was the physicist Herb Anderson, who remembers: "the sound of the neutron counter, clickety-clack, clickety-clack. Then the clicks came more and more rapidly, and after a while they began to merge into a roar . . . Suddenly Fermi raised his hand. 'The pile has gone critical,' he announced." Compton, who had watched the momentous event, returned to his office and phoned Conant. "The Italian navigator has just landed in the New World," he told him.

Within a few weeks of this dramatic demonstration that a controlled nuclear reaction was possible—and the consequent realization that plutonium could indeed be manufactured on an industrial scale—work started on two sites that together would constitute an almost unimaginably huge engineering project. In addition to the site in Oak Ridge, Tennessee, the Manhattan Project acquired a site at Hanford in the state of Washington, which would be used for a series of plutonium-producing reactors, the prototype of which was quickly constructed at Oak Ridge. Immediately, the Army Engineering Corps began to supervise the building of houses, the construction of roads and the recruitment of workers. Each site would require tens of thousands of people. Within a few months, both Hanford and Oak Ridge would be fairly sizeable towns. In areas where the depression of the 1930s had led to large-scale unemployment, the prospect of well-paid work was extremely welcome and neither site had trouble finding the requisite workforce, even though the people thus hired were told nothing about the purpose of the work they were doing. It is one of the most extraordinary aspects of the Manhattan Project that the existence of an atomic-bomb building program was successfully kept secret from the very people who worked on the plants that supplied the necessary fissionable material.

At its peak, the Manhattan Project employed more than 150,000 workers, the majority of whom worked at Oak Ridge or Hanford. They included more than 80,000 construction workers and about 68,000 operations and research personnel. Most of the latter were employed on dull, repetitive tasks that were necessary to keep the isotope separation plants and the reactors going. An excellent social history of the Manhattan Project, *Atomic Spaces* by Peter Bacon Hales, has attempted to convey what it was like to work at these sites. "New workers entering these factories," Hales writes, "found them to be confusing and sometimes terrifying warrens of piping, walls of analog dials, valves and knobs, marked with Bakelite labels in the arcane language of the engineer. The electromagnetic plant alone used close to 250,000 valves to control the materials coursing through 1,175 miles of piping."

Most of the people employed to watch the dials and turn the valves and knobs were women. They were trained only in the skills required to do their specific job, which might be, for example, turning a knob when a dial they were watching moved too far to the left or to the right. What the dial was measuring and what the knob was controlling were kept secret from them and, while at work, they were not allowed to talk to their fellow employees, but only with their immediate superiors. Faced with almost any alternative, few people would have chosen to work under such conditions, but Groves did everything he could to ensure that, for many people, there was no alternative. He persuaded the Secretary of War, Robert Patterson, for example, to issue a directive to the U.S. Employment Service, instructing it to ensure that in its offices near Oak

Ridge and Hanford "workers must not be offered any other employment until after they have been rejected for employment on these projects."

Most of the workers at these plants lived in rapidly built basic flats and houses that were constructed especially for them close to their places of work. Shops, schools, post offices and even town halls were built to ensure that the workers had as few reasons as possible to venture outside the perimeters of the site in which they lived, and over time these sites became home to something close to the kind of communities one might find in any other American small town.

Meanwhile, by the end of December 1942, Oppenheimer was playing a leading role himself in the creation of a new town and a new community at Los Alamos. In a letter he wrote to Hans and Rose Bethe on December 28, he discussed not physics or bombs, but such things as the salaries on offer to scientists willing to come to Los Alamos (20 percent on top of what they were already earning), the arrangements under way for the management of the town, what kind of school education would be provided and by whom, how many hospitals there would be, what laundry facilities would exist, what kind of restaurants would be available, what recreation would be on offer, how mail would be collected and delivered and what the housing would be like. The man in charge of the construction and management of the town was Colonel J. M. Harmon, and, Oppenheimer told the Bethes, the best guarantee that the arrangements would be satisfactory "is in the great effort and generosity that Harmon and Groves have both brought to setting up this odd community and in their evident desire to make a real success of it."

In his attempts to lure the scientists he wanted, it was perhaps inevitable that Oppenheimer would become involved in all aspects of planning for life in this "odd community." After all, in urging them to come to Los Alamos, he was asking them not only to join a laboratory, but to take part in a new, hitherto untried and somewhat bizarre way of life: an isolated, self-contained community dedicated to a single task and committed to the utmost secrecy. And yet, for all that, his primary responsibility was for the *scientific* aspects of the work, as Conant and Groves made plain in a long letter of February 25, 1943, laying out Oppenheimer's new job description.

"We are addressing this letter to you," they began, "as the Scientific Director of the special laboratory in New Mexico in order to confirm our many conversations on the matters of organization and responsibility." The laboratory, they went on, "will be concerned with the development and final manufacture of an instrument of war." Its work was to be divided into two periods: the first would be devoted to "experimental studies in science, engineering and ordnance," while the second would

involve "large-scale experiments involving difficult ordnance procedures and the handling of highly dangerous material." During the first
period, the laboratory "will be on a strictly civilian basis," but when the
work enters the second period ("which will not be earlier than January
1, 1944"), "the scientific and engineering staff will be composed of commissioned officers." The militarization of the scientific staff thus outlined never took place, but the letter shows just how reluctant the leaders
of the Manhattan Project were to abandon it.

The laboratory, the letter further spelled out, was part of a larger
project run by the Military Policy Committee, chaired by Bush and, in
his absence, Conant. Groves "has been given over-all executive responsibility for this project." The responsibilities of the Scientific Director—
Oppenheimer—were given in this letter as:

a. The conduct of the scientific work so that the desired goals as
outlined by the Military Policy Committee are achieved at the earliest possible dates.
b. The maintenance of secrecy by the civilian personnel under his
control as well as their families.

As the Los Alamos Ranch School was being transformed by a massive and hurried construction program into a town fit to serve as home
to some of the greatest scientists in the world and their families, Oppenheimer spent the first few months of 1943 preparing to achieve the goals
he had been set by Conant and Groves. His plan was to begin the scientific work of the laboratory in the spring of 1943 with a series of introductory lectures given by Serber, which would summarize the current
state of knowledge (most of which had not been published because of the
voluntary self-censorship adopted by scientists in this area), followed by
a large conference at which the work still remaining to be done would
be outlined. In preparing for this conference, which was scheduled to
take place in April 1943, Oppenheimer was helped enormously by Isidor
Rabi, who became, as Hans Bethe put it, "the fatherly advisor to Oppie."

Oppenheimer himself moved to New Mexico on March 16, 1943,
about three weeks before most of the other scientists and about a month
before the conference was due to start. Shortly before he left Berkeley, an incident, later widely known as the "Chevalier Affair," took place
that would come to haunt him for the rest of his life. It happened at
the Oppenheimers' home during a dinner party they gave for the Chevaliers, knowing that they would not be seeing them again for a long
time. Shortly before, Chevalier had been approached by George Eltenton, a British chemist and member of the Communist Party who lived

in Berkeley and worked for Shell. Toward the end of 1942, Eltenton himself had been approached by people from the Soviet consulate in San Francisco, asking him if he knew anything about the work being done at the Rad Lab at Berkeley—work which, the Soviets believed, was of great military importance.

One reason they had for this belief was that Steve Nelson had been tipped off about it by a member of the Young Communist League called Lloyd Lehmann, who, on October 10, 1942, was caught on the FBI microphones installed in Nelson's house telling Nelson that "an important weapon was being developed." Unfortunately for Oppenheimer, Nelson and Lehmann then went on to talk about someone working on the project who was "considered a 'Red,'" who had been involved in the Teachers' Committee and the Spanish Committee, but whom the government allowed to remain because he was such a good scientist. As the FBI would have been quick to realize, the man meant here was most likely Oppenheimer. Much more damaging were the remarks caught by the microphone about Rossi Lomanitz, who, it was said, was working on the project, but was "considering quitting it."[47] To this, Nelson was heard to say that it was important that Lomanitz stay on the project in order to provide the Party with information about it. Naturally, it was agreed, Lomanitz would have to function as an undercover Party member. This recorded conversation in Nelson's house would have extremely far-reaching consequences for Lomanitz. For the rest of the war he would be kept under tight surveillance, and strict measures would be taken to separate him from any military and government secrets.

In response to this request for information about the projected new weapon, Eltenton told Peter Ivanov from the Soviet consulate that he would ask Chevalier to approach Oppenheimer. Chevalier agreed to do what he could, with the result that, when he arrived at the Oppenheimers' home for the dinner party, he was, essentially, on a spying mission. Chevalier's side of the story—given in his memoir, *The Story of a Friendship*— is that he was not approaching Oppenheimer for information, but rather alerting him to the fact that Eltenton had proposed sharing whatever information he had with Soviet scientists. It is, however, rather difficult to believe that, not least because Chevalier's wife, Barbara, has dismissed it as a fabrication. According to her: "Haakon was one hundred percent in favor of finding out what Oppie was doing and reporting it back to

---

[47] That Lomanitz was at this time considering leaving his work at the Rad Lab was confirmed in an interview with Martin Sherwin in 1979, in which he discussed his moral qualms about creating such a powerful weapon and said that when he mentioned those qualms to Oppenheimer, Oppenheimer's response was: "Look, what if the Nazis get it first?"

Eltenton. I believe Haakon also believed that Oppie would be in favor of cooperating with the Russians. I know because we had a big fight over it beforehand."

Oppenheimer, at his security hearing in 1954, said that, at this dinner party, Chevalier followed him into the kitchen and, when the two of them were alone, told him that he had seen George Eltenton recently and that Eltenton had a "means of getting technical information to Soviet scientists." Oppenheimer says he reacted to this by saying something like "But that is treason" or "That is a terrible thing to do," with which Chevalier agreed and no more was said: "It was a brief conversation."

Eltenton later told the FBI that, after this dinner, Chevalier told him there was "no chance whatsoever of obtaining any data" and that "Oppenheimer did not approve." He also said that the next time Ivanov came to his house, he told Ivanov that Oppenheimer had refused to cooperate. By this time FBI microphones had picked up several remarks indicating that Oppenheimer was distancing himself from his former friends in the Communist Party. In the conversation between Nelson, Lehmann and a third man mentioned earlier it was said of the scientist who had been considered a "Red" that, though he had in the past been active in Communist Party activities, he was now "jittery." Then, in December, they heard Nelson saying that Bernard Peters had told him that Oppenheimer could not be active in the Party, because of his involvement in a special project.

Shortly after Chevalier's ham-fisted and unsuccessful attempt to recruit him as a spy, Oppenheimer arranged to meet Nelson for lunch. "I just want to say goodbye to you," Oppenheimer told him. From a security point of view, Oppenheimer's behavior during this lunch was unimpeachable. He told Nelson that he was leaving to take part in work that was related to the war effort, but did not tell Nelson what that work was about or where he was going. The impression Nelson formed from this meeting was that Oppenheimer, influenced by his wife, was determined to make a name for himself, and that that determination was turning him away from the Communist Party. "I think now he's gone a little further away from whatever association he had with us," Nelson remarked to a fellow communist a few weeks after this lunch with Oppenheimer: "Now he's got the one thing in the world, and that's this project and that project is going to wean him from his friends." Nelson was right; this lunchtime meeting in March 1943 was the last time he ever saw Oppenheimer.

Nelson's impression that Oppenheimer's all-consuming interest in "this project" was driven by ambition, and that this ambition was fueled by Kitty, was surely right. Missing, however, from Nelson's assessment was the importance of Oppenheimer's deeply felt and lifelong patriotism. In the 1930s he had set out to build an *American* school of theoretical physics that would enable the U.S. to replace Germany as the leading center for research in that area; now he had a chance to lead a project that would not only demonstrate the superiority of American physics, but would also, in so doing, equip the U.S. with a weapon that would enable it to win the war against Germany.

The idea that he would endanger this position for the sake of doing a favor to old friends, or for the sake of enabling the Soviet Union to build a bomb of its own, is risible, as Chevalier had discovered. In arranging his farewell dinner with Chevalier and his farewell lunch with Nelson, there is a sense that Oppenheimer was not only saying goodbye to them, but was also marking the transition in his life from one phase to another. As he prepared to leave for New Mexico, he evidently saw himself as leaving behind not only his old comrades, but also his politically radical past. As he was to discover, however, the security services saw it rather differently.

12

Los Alamos 1: Security

Bulldozers moved in, and other weird machines roared up and down digging ditches for the foundations of future buildings. Everything was conducted in an element of extreme haste and mystery."

This is how Peggy Pond Church, daughter of Ashley Pond, the founder of the Los Alamos Ranch School, remembered the noisy and bewildering chaos that engulfed her previously tranquil home in the first few months of 1943. The task of making real Oppenheimer's vision of an atomic-bomb laboratory in his beloved New Mexico mountains was enormous and hugely difficult, the more so because it had to be done extremely quickly and, as far as possible, in secret. Several thousand workmen, none of whom knew the purpose of the facility they were helping to construct, labored hard to build roads, homes, offices and laboratories, under great pressure to get everything done as soon as was humanly possible.

Despite these intense efforts, when Oppenheimer arrived on March 16, 1943, nothing was yet finished. He and his family were due to move into the building that had been the headmaster's house, but, like all the other early arrivals, Oppenheimer spent the first few weeks living, not at Los Alamos, but at a hotel in Santa Fe, thirty-five miles southeast of Los Alamos. The nearest city of any size, Santa Fe became the first port of call for anybody going up to the new laboratory. There, the Manhattan Project acquired an office at 109 East Palace, an adobe building in the oldest part of the city that had once belonged to a Spanish conquistador. This office was where all new recruits initially reported for work. To run it, Oppenheimer employed a local woman called Dorothy McKibbin, whose job it was to welcome new arrivals, issue them with security passes and arrange transport for them to Los Alamos. Until its task was finished, Mrs. McKibbin never knew, and never asked, what the purpose of the laboratory was. Her devotion to both Oppenheimer and her task was, however, unerring, and her enthusiasm for greeting the scientists, engineers and others who descended on her adopted hometown unflagging.

Among the first scientists to arrive after Oppenheimer were John Manley, Robert Serber and Hans Bethe, whose wife, Rose, came a week before him in order to help Oppenheimer arrange the living spaces. The first to be housed in Los Alamos were Oppenheimer and Kitty, who, together with the infant Peter (his second birthday still more than a month away), were finally able to move into their new home by the end of March. Though not at all grand by normal standards, the Oppenheimers' house, a one-story log-and-stone cottage, was to become the envy of the entire Los Alamos community. Though it lacked a kitchen, it was one of only six houses on the Hill that had its own bathtub. Very soon, those six became known collectively as "Bathtub Row," the most elite housing Los Alamos could offer.

Most people who knew them well thought that Kitty was very pleased that her husband had been appointed to direct such an important enterprise as the United States atomic bomb laboratory, and many considered her to be proud to the point of being haughty in her dealings with her husband's employees, but it should not be assumed that she *liked* being at Los Alamos. On the contrary, her life there seemed to be one of almost unrelieved torment. She had no interest in doing what might have been expected of the director's wife: holding parties and being at the center of the laboratory's social life. She took herself too seriously as a scientist and an intellectual for that. To begin with, she was given a part-time job as a laboratory technician, working with a team studying the medical effects of radiation, but she soon abandoned that, and sank into a listless, depressed and lonely existence, enlivened only by bouts of drinking, sometimes with others, but often alone. Peter, meanwhile, received little attention from *either* of his parents.

Soon after the Oppenheimers came the Serbers, who, to begin with, lived in what was known as the "Big House." This had previously been the boys' dormitory and, with just one big bathroom in the entire building, was intended for single men. As those single men began to arrive, the unsuitability of the Big House for married couples became increasingly manifest ("two or three fellows were embarrassed by walking in on Charlotte while she was taking a shower," Serber remembers), and, after a little while, the Serbers moved into one of the specially built duplexes. These consisted of two apartments next to each other, each apartment having its own bathroom, which, by the standards of the housing at Los Alamos, was luxurious to an enviable extent.

The Serbers' immediate neighbors in this duplex were Robert and Jane Wilson, who had recently arrived from Princeton. Wilson was there as head of the Cyclotron Group, part of the Experimental Physics Division led by Robert Bacher. His participation was crucial, not only because he was one of the leading experimental physicists in the field of neutron research, but also because he brought with him Princeton's cyclotron, one of the very few accelerators that the new laboratory had at its disposal. The others were two Van de Graaff generators from Wisconsin, which were put at the disposal of the Electrostatic Generator Group led by J. H. Williams from the University of Minnesota, and Manley's own Cockroft-Walton accelerator, which accompanied him from Illinois and provided the data that Manley's "D-D Source Group" used to work out what material would form the best "tamper."

None of these machines was up and running until June 1943, which is when experimental physics at Los Alamos really started. Getting the machines to Los Alamos and then setting them up in an as-yet-uncompleted laboratory at the top of a mountain in a remote part of New Mexico was so difficult that it seemed to some of those charged with accomplishing it an almost insane plan. To get to Los Alamos from Santa Fe required crossing the Rio Grande at a place called Otowi, where there was what Serber has described as "a toy one-lane suspension bridge that looked as if it might be safe for two horses." "It was hard to believe," writes Serber, "that all the construction trucks for Los Alamos had to cross that bridge and then climb 1,500 feet up a perilous switch-backed dirt road to the top of Los Alamos Mesa."

Among those who had their doubts about the wisdom of building the laboratory in such a place was John Manley, whose job it was to work with the army engineers on the design and construction of the laboratories that would house the accelerators. Manley recalls that he was particularly concerned with the long, narrow building that would house the two Van de Graaff generators and the Cockroft-Walton machine. As he told the engineers, the Van de Graaffs were extremely heavy machines that would need a good, strong foundation underneath them, while the Cockroft-Walton was a tall vertical machine that required a basement. Given these requirements, Manley writes: "Cost and construction time could obviously be saved if they selected the terrain properly"—that is, the building should be built over a slope, with the Cockroft-Walton machine in the lower, deeper part of the building. When he went to inspect the buildings, however, Manley discovered that, instead of making use of the sloping terrain, the engineers had needlessly created their own slope by actually digging a basement for the Cockcroft-Walton machine and then using the resulting debris to make the foundation for the Van de Graaffs. "That was my introduction to army engineering," Manley remarked.

Part of the point of building the new laboratory in a remote part of New Mexico was to keep it from prying eyes, but, of course, in some ways it was far more conspicuous there than it would have been in a large center of population. In a small town like Santa Fe, the arrival of dozens of strangers could not possibly go unnoticed. In fact, as locals were quick to see and remark upon, there were two distinct kinds of strangers descending on their town: first, there were the young bohemian-looking characters with open-necked shirts, who seemed polite, if a little unworldly; and then there were the besuited, slightly threatening men in fedora hats who invariably went around in twos and had a watchful, furtive demeanor. That the first group were scientists was rather less obvious than that the second group were security agents.

Most of those agents would have been working for the army, rather than the FBI. In March 1943, the FBI was explicitly ordered by Major General Strong, the head of G-2 (the branch of the U.S. Army concerned with counterintelligence), to close its file on Oppenheimer. Security issues relating to anyone—even civilians—working on a military project, Strong insisted, were the responsibility of the army. Astonishingly, the FBI was not officially informed about the Manhattan Project until April 1943, after it had learned of its existence through their surveillance of Communist Party leaders. Though under orders to confine themselves to civilians, FBI agents would inevitably often find themselves covering the same ground, even following some of the same people, as G-2 agents, and, despite the reluctance of military intelligence to confide in them, the FBI was generally quick to inform G-2 of anything that might concern them. Complementing these two security agencies, and sometimes causing further complications, was the Manhattan Project's own security organization, which, though officially part of G-2, was under the direct command of General Groves, and thus to some extent separate from it. To start with, this organization consisted of just a few men, whose main job was to liaise with G-2 and the FBI, but by the autumn of 1943 it was large enough for Groves to insist that it took over all security responsibilities relating to the project. As Los Alamos, Oak Ridge and Hanford continued to expand, so did the Manhattan Project's own security force, so that by the end of the war it had working for it nearly 500 "creeps," as the agents came to be called.

The man whom Groves chose to head the Manhattan Project's own security force was John Lansdale, who, after a series of rapid promotions, was by this time a Lieutenant Colonel. Lansdale worked closely with Groves, who evidently shared Conant's high opinion of him. Like Groves, he was based in Washington, but most of the people working for him were based on the West Coast. At Berkeley, for example, Lansdale set up a secret, disguised office, run by Lieutenant Lyall Johnson, which became the center of a covert surveillance operation, keeping a watchful eye on the research scientists working at the Rad Lab.

Before the Manhattan Project took complete responsibility for its own security, there was something of a turf war between John Lansdale and G-2's head of counterintelligence for the West Coast, Lieutenant Colonel Boris Pash. Pash was a formidable figure. Even by the standards of military security officers, he was passionately and belligerently anticommunist, his antagonism fueled partly by his family history and his personal experience of fighting the Bolsheviks in Russia. He had been born in the U.S., but was from a Russian family (his father was a Russian Orthodox bishop, based in San Francisco) and had gone to Russia during the civil war that followed the revolution in order to fight alongside the White Army. Since America's entry into the Second World War, Pash had been an enthusiastic and dedicated member of the U.S. Army's counterintelligence division, welcoming the opportunity to hunt down Soviet spies, among whom, he was convinced, was Oppenheimer himself—a conviction that remained with him throughout the war and beyond. When, after the war, newspapers reported the spying activities of the Soviet spy Klaus Fuchs, Pash was reported as remarking that he "would next be reading about Dr. Oppenheimer's involvement in such activities." When he was asked at Oppenheimer's security hearings in 1954 whether in 1943 he considered Oppenheimer a security risk, he replied straightforwardly: "Yes I did."

From his office in San Francisco, Pash orchestrated an intense security effort to keep Oppenheimer under surveillance: his phone was tapped, microphones were installed in his home, agents were employed to act as his chauffeur, and wherever Oppenheimer went, G-2 men followed. At Los Alamos, the G-2 man in charge of security was Captain Peer de Silva, who was as convinced as Pash that Oppenheimer was a security risk, and who was under orders from Pash to keep Oppenheimer under the closest possible scrutiny.

It is unclear how aware Oppenheimer was of the intensity with which he was being scrutinized by security agents. It is said that the agents who served as his drivers were thwarted in their efforts to hear what he was saying to his fellow passengers because of his habit of winding the window down in order to create a wind noise that would drown out his conversation. This may have been a clever ploy to prevent his conversations from being heard by men he knew to be security agents, but it seems equally possible that, on the assumption that he thought his drivers were civilians, it was a perfectly sensible precaution.

When he arrived at Los Alamos, Oppenheimer was in the extremely odd and vulnerable position of having been appointed director of the most secret laboratory in the country while still not having the security clearance that would normally be a prerequisite for taking up even the most junior appointment in that laboratory. He and Groves seemed to take the view that he could start work before receiving his clearance, on the assumption that it would eventually be granted. Pash and de Silva were rather of the opinion that Oppenheimer's request for clearance should be refused and that he should be removed from the bomb project as soon as possible.

Two weeks after Oppenheimer moved to New Mexico, at a time when he and his colleagues were still making hurried preparations for the opening of the new laboratory, Pash received news from the FBI that would, he thought, finally convince the authorities that his suspicions of Oppenheimer were well founded. It concerned a conversation picked up by the "technical surveillance" of Steve Nelson's home between Nelson and a man known to the FBI at this time only as "Joe" (which is how Nelson addressed him in the conversation). As the FBI would discover two months later, "Joe" was Oppenheimer's friend and ex-student Joe Weinberg.

The conversation took place in the early hours of the morning on March 30, 1943. Weinberg had arrived at Nelson's house the previous evening, telling Nelson's wife, Margaret, that he had some important information to pass on—so important that he was prepared to wait several hours for Nelson to return home in order to discuss it with him. As Nelson discovered when he got home, the information Weinberg had was indeed of great importance and was bound to be of enormous interest to the Soviet Union: people engaged in the new weapon project (which, Weinberg thought at this time, would include himself) were about to be relocated to a remote spot where experiments on explosives could be conducted in secret. Clearly feeling nervous and (as he freely admitted to Nelson) "a little bit scared," Weinberg spoke in a whisper when giving Nelson some technical details of the project. The classified information that he passed on to Nelson centered on developments at Oak Ridge, which Weinberg must have heard about from friends who worked at the Rad Lab. The FBI notes on the conversation at this point become a little sketchy—it was evidently difficult to hear what Weinberg was saying—but the gist is clear enough. A separation plant, Weinberg told Nelson, was already being built in Tennessee that was expected to employ thousands of people, the separation method being "preferably that of the magnetic spectrograph with electrical and magnetic focusing." Toward the end of the conversation Weinberg discussed with Nelson how he might be able to provide information in the future via his sister, who lived in New York, and Nelson emphasized how important it was not to put anything in writing.

The conversation left no doubt at all that Weinberg was willing, indeed eager, to play an important role in Soviet espionage. And though the FBI did not yet know who "Joe" was, they did know that he was an ex-student of Oppenheimer's. That much was clear from the conversation, in which Oppenheimer was mentioned several times, usually referred to as "the professor." Pash clearly thought the mere fact that Oppenheimer was associated with two people plotting espionage would be enough to establish him as a security risk, but in fact the FBI notes of the conversation provide pretty good grounds for thinking that Oppenheimer was *not* a risk. Whenever "the professor" came up in the conversation, either Nelson or Weinberg (or both) made some comment to the effect that he had cut his links to the Party and that he was emphatically not prepared to pass on secrets to the Soviet Union.

At one point, Nelson remarked that Oppenheimer was "very much worried now and we make him feel uncomfortable," to which Weinberg responded by saying that Oppenheimer kept him off the project because he was worried that he would "attract more attention" and also because "he fears that I will propagandize." Oppenheimer, Weinberg told Nelson, had "changed a bit . . . You won't believe the change that has taken place." Nelson agreed, saying: "To my sorrow, his wife is influencing him in the wrong direction." Evidently on the basis of his recent farewell lunch with Oppenheimer, Nelson told Weinberg that Oppenheimer, encouraged by his wife, was keen to dissociate himself from his former colleagues in the Communist Party, because he did not want to threaten his central role in the important project to which he had been recruited.

Even if it did not implicate Oppenheimer, this conversation between Weinberg and Nelson provided irrefutable evidence of a threat to the security of a top-secret military project, and, as such, it was taken very seriously indeed by the FBI, to whom "Joe's" information was as much a revelation as it was to Nelson. The FBI immediately delivered a transcript of the conversation to Colonel Pash, whose response was to fly to Washington to tell Groves and Lansdale that he had evidence of Oppenheimer's involvement in espionage.

Of course, what Pash had was fairly conclusive evidence that Oppenheimer—much to the disappointment of his former friends in the Communist Party—was *not* involved in espionage. Indeed, from the point of view of incriminating Oppenheimer, the conversation between Nelson and "Joe" did not tell Groves and Lansdale anything new; it simply confirmed what they already knew about him, and what they had discussed with each other many times, namely that he had a history of close associations with communists. Lansdale later recalled that when he and Groves first looked through Oppenheimer's FBI file (he could not remember exactly when this was, but thought it was while Los Alamos was still being built, so probably sometime in the first two months of 1943), Oppenheimer's political history caused them "a great deal of concern" and they discussed it at length. "General Groves's view, as I recall," Lansdale said, "was (a) that Dr. Oppenheimer was essential; (b) that in his judgment—and he had gotten to know Dr. Oppenheimer very well by that time—he was loyal; and (c) we would clear him for this work whatever the reports said." So, on the question of Oppenheimer's loyalty, General Groves had already firmly made up his mind, and he was a man who trusted his own judgment. Nothing short of incontrovertible evidence that Oppenheimer was a security risk would make him drop his conviction that Oppenheimer was the man to get the job done.

However, it was now clear that the Soviets already knew much about the American atomic-bomb project (more, for example, than the FBI knew at the time) and that, unless the flow of information was stopped immediately, there was a strong possibility they would very soon know a good deal more. It thus became a matter of urgent importance to discover the identity of "Joe" and prevent him having any further access to sensitive information. So seriously did G-2 take this that they immediately established a closer working relationship with the FBI. Thus, on April 5, 1943, General Strong met J. Edgar Hoover's assistant, E. A. Tamm, to inform him officially of the existence of the Manhattan Project. The following day, Groves and Lansdale met with two representatives of the FBI to discuss ways in which the two security organizations might cooperate in order to establish "Joe's" identity and protect the project from Soviet espionage.

A few days before those meetings the FBI had already gathered some counterintelligence that was, they now realized, of immediate interest to G-2's attempt to maintain the security of the Manhattan Project. In response to the conversation between Nelson and "Joe," they had decided to keep Nelson under constant, twenty-four-hour surveillance, and on April 1 their agents had seen him walk to a corner shop, from where he phoned the Soviet consulate in San Francisco to arrange a meeting with Ivanov. When the meeting subsequently took place, on April 6, FBI agents were there to observe it. Then, on April 10, FBI agents watching

Nelson's house noted the arrival there of none other than Vasily Zubilin, the head of the NKVD espionage operation, who was based at the Soviet embassy in Washington. The microphones inside the house picked up a long conversation between the two about the structure of the Soviet espionage operation and the respective roles played within it by the American Communist Party and the NKVD (Nelson was worried that the former was being bypassed by the latter). Agents also heard Zubilin counting out large amounts of money to give to Nelson, who exclaimed: "Jesus, you count money like a banker." Presumably Nelson and Zubilin soon realized that U.S. counterintelligence was onto them, because this was the last time that either was recorded as having anything to do with espionage.

While the security forces were trying to discover his identity, Weinberg managed to insinuate himself into a position in which he would have access to secret information. Sometime in April 1943, Oppenheimer, despite his earlier reservations about hiring Weinberg, employed him at the Rad Lab to work on some calculations that were part of the effort to improve the focusing of the beam of the Calutron. Of course, Oppenheimer knew nothing of the recorded conversation between Weinberg and Nelson. However, Pash and de Silva later cited Oppenheimer's willingness to employ Weinberg as evidence of his complicity with Soviet espionage. Lansdale, on the other hand, when asked years later about this period, not only did not see anything suspicious in Oppenheimer's behavior, but went out of his way to praise Oppenheimer for being "very helpful" in the attempt to impress upon his fellow scientists at Los Alamos the importance of maintaining strict security.

"The scientists en masse presented an extremely difficult problem," Lansdale said, adding: "I hope my scientist friends will forgive me, but the very nature of them made things difficult." Scientists, by their very nature, like to *share* information, which put them somewhat at odds with the people whose job it was to ensure that information was not shared. From both sides there was, from the very beginning, mutual incomprehension. In the many reminiscences of Los Alamos written by scientists, the security arrangements are almost invariably regarded with a mixture of contempt and amusement. Robert Serber, for example, describes the initial attempts to secure the Los Alamos site as comically lax and amateurish. "Oppie," he writes, "wrote passes for us on University of California stationery which didn't well survive being carried in hip pockets."

As Serber remembers it, the first guards at the site were Spanish American construction workers who were "dragooned to man the gate." After that, the army took over "and brought in MPs who were mostly ex–New York cops and put the New York cops on the horses—probably none of them had ever seen a horse before—and set them to patrolling the fences." Unsurprisingly, "they called that off after a couple of weeks."

Serber also remembers taking part in a plan, devised by Oppenheimer and army security, to spread false rumors about what was happening at the Mesa. The rationale behind this is given in a letter from Oppenheimer to Groves, dated April 30, 1943. "We propose," Oppenheimer wrote:

> that it be let known that the Los Alamos Project is working on a new type of rocket and that the detail should be added that this is a largely electrical device. We feel that the story will have a certain credibility; that the loud noises which we will soon be making here will fit in with the subject and that the fact, unfortunately not kept completely secret, that we are installing a good deal of electrical equipment, and the further fact that we have a large group of civilian specialists would fit in quite well.

What struck Oppenheimer as a credible plan, however, turned out, in practice, to be a laughable failure. Together with others from the laboratory, Serber was instructed to go to a bar in Santa Fe and start talking in a loud voice about the electric rocket they were working on. The problem they encountered was that, no matter how loudly they discussed it, no one seemed very interested. Eventually Serber approached a drunk at the bar and said to him: "Do you know what we're doing at Los Alamos? We're building an electric rocket!" It was, Serber admits, mission unaccomplished: "the FBI and Army Intelligence never reported picking up any rumors about electric rockets."

Equally unsuccessful was another idea Oppenheimer came up with to mislead potential snoops, this time involving Wolfgang Pauli, who since 1940 had been a physics professor at Princeton. Oppenheimer's idea, he told Pauli in a letter written in May 1943, was one "that I think deserves to be taken seriously, although I know that you will laugh at it." It was that Pauli could use his "great talents for physics and burlesque" by writing phoney articles on aspects of theoretical physics and publishing them under the names of, for example, Bethe, Teller, Serber and Oppenheimer, thus forestalling questions the enemy might have about why these top physicists had apparently stopped publishing any work and preventing them from drawing the obvious conclusion that, as Oppenheimer put it, "we are finding good uses for our physicists."

In his reply, Pauli reported that he was having problems getting funding for his research from the Rockefeller Foundation and the director of the Institute for Advanced Study, and so, though he "would be glad to be helpful in the suggested way," he felt compelled to publish what he was writing under his own name in order "to prove to the quoted money-givers that after all I am working on something for their money," fearing, he added, "their sense for burlesque to be rather undeveloped." In any case, Pauli wrote, he doubted the scheme would work, since why would the enemy not believe that "the persons whose names figure as authors are not occupied beside some scientific work also with war problems?" And then "the whole Don-Quichotery would be in vain."

Despite the suspicions of him entertained by Pash, de Silva and other security officers, then, Oppenheimer seemed, on the face of it, wholeheartedly—if sometimes quixotically—in support of the security efforts of army intelligence. In this, as Lansdale pointed out, he stood out among his fellow scientists, some of whom, like Serber, adopted an attitude of amused disdain toward the security restrictions, while others were openly contemptuous and provocative. As he has recounted in his famous public lecture, "Los Alamos from Below," chief among the latter was Richard Feynman.

Feynman was among the first to arrive at Los Alamos, being part of what Oppenheimer described as a "job lot" of scientists from Princeton who came with Robert Wilson. He would later win the Nobel Prize and become one of the best-known physicists in the world, but in 1943 Feynman was a young man of twenty-four who had only just completed his Ph.D. thesis. Though young, he had already impressed many of the most eminent scientists in America with the sharpness of his intellect and the originality of his mind—Wilson at Princeton and Teller at Chicago among them—and was very shortly to make a deep impression on Hans Bethe at Los Alamos. To the security staff at Los Alamos, however, Feynman was a mischievous and vexatious nuisance.

From the very beginning, Feynman was determined to thumb his nose at the precautions he was asked to adopt. All the physicists at Princeton had been told not to buy their train tickets to Albuquerque, New Mexico, from Princeton, since it was a small station and, if everyone bought tickets to Albuquerque from there, suspicions would be aroused. "And so," Feynman later said, "everybody bought their tickets somewhere else." Everyone, that is, except Feynman, "because I figured if everybody bought their tickets somewhere else . . ."

Once at Los Alamos, Feynman discovered to his horror that his letters to his wife, and hers to him, were being examined and, at times, censored. His wife, on learning this, repeatedly mentioned in her letters to him that she felt uncomfortable knowing that the censor was looking over her shoulder as she wrote. This led to Feynman receiving a note: "Please inform your wife not to mention censorship in her letters."

But, of course, as Feynman gleefully pointed out, he himself was under instructions not to mention censorship, so he wrote back: "I have been instructed to inform my wife not to mention censorship. How in the heck am I going to do it?" Feynman was presented with another opportunity to be a thorn in the side of the security effort when he discovered that the workmen on the site had cut themselves a hole in the fence, so as to enable them to leave for home without having to go through the official gate. So Feynman went out through the gate, walked around to the hole, came back in and then went out again through the gate, "until the sergeant at the gate began to wonder what was happening. How come this guy is always going out and never coming in?"

In the memoirs of the scientists who worked at Los Alamos, the pervasive presence of the army and the security measures they imposed are almost universally prominent. Apart from the extraordinary location, the fact that the laboratory was a military establishment was, in the eyes of the civilian scientists—most of whom would have had little or no prior experience of being with soldiers and working under army regulations—its most novel and noteworthy aspect. For many of these scientists, Groves was the very embodiment of everything they found strange, irksome and idiotic about the army. As such, he often appears in scientists' recollections of Los Alamos as a figure of fun, a man whose limited understanding of physics and brutish manner made him a legitimate target of derision. Edward Teller, for example, though claiming to have "neutral" feelings about Groves (and therefore, he emphasizes, better feelings about him than most of the scientists at Los Alamos), remarks that Groves's opening speech to the scientists "seemed about what would be expected from a person who knew nothing about the project he was supervising." Teller says that he was puzzled to hear that Groves had complained about Hungarian being spoken on the site, since he and his wife were at the time the only Hungarians there and had spoken Hungarian only in their own apartment. Then he discovered that Groves had heard Felix Bloch's sons speaking in their Swiss German dialect and "had confused that strange language with one even more peculiar."

The task of maintaining good relations between the scientists and the military officers fell to the associate director of the laboratory, Edward Condon. In his autobiography, Groves goes so far as to say that maintaining good relations was Condon's "major responsibility." Whether or not it was his principal task, it was certainly a difficult and thankless one, made much worse by the fact that Condon and Groves very quickly developed extremely poor opinions of each other ("Condon was not a happy choice," Groves remarks dismissively). The biggest issue on which they failed to see eye-to-eye was "compartmentalization,"

the policy—which Groves regarded as "the very heart of security"—
according to which workers on the Manhattan Project knew only what
they needed to know in order to do their jobs and no more. The workers
at Oak Ridge and Hanford, for example, did not know that they were
helping to produce uranium and plutonium, nor did the workers at one
site even know of the existence of the other. It was this policy that had
resulted in the strange situation mentioned earlier, of the FBI investigating breaches to the security of a project the existence of which they
were officially unaware. Groves felt strongly that this policy should apply
also to scientists, so that those working at the Met Lab at Chicago, for
example, should know nothing about what was going on at Los Alamos.

Condon thought this was ridiculous and fundamentally incompatible with the successful pursuit of science. The issue came to a head
toward the end of April, just six weeks after Oppenheimer and Condon had moved to Los Alamos, when Oppenheimer flew to Chicago
to discuss the schedule for plutonium production with Arthur Compton. Groves was furious and, on Oppenheimer's return, stormed into
Oppenheimer's office to make his feelings known to both Oppenheimer
and Condon. Condon stood up to Groves and defended this breach of
compartmentalization, but was puzzled to see that Oppenheimer was not
supporting him. A few days later, Condon resigned, giving his reasons in
a long letter to Oppenheimer. "The thing that upsets me most," he told
Oppenheimer, "is the extraordinary close security policy."

> I do not feel qualified to question the wisdom of this since I am
> totally unaware of the extent of enemy espionage and sabotage activ-
> ities. I only want to say that in my case I found that the extreme
> concern with security was morbidly depressing—especially the dis-
> cussion about censoring mail and telephone calls, the possible mili-
> tarization and complete isolation of the personnel from the outside
> world. I know that before long all such concerns would make me so
> depressed as to be of little if any value.

He was, he said, "so shocked that I could hardly believe my ears"
when Groves reproached them for discussing technical questions with
Compton: "I feel so strongly that this policy puts you in the position of
trying to do an extremely difficult job with three hands tied behind your
back that I cannot accept the view that such internal compartmentalization of the larger project is proper."

So alien did this way of thinking strike Groves that he was convinced
Condon had kept the real reason for his resignation quiet. "The considerations he cited in his letter of resignation," Groves said of Condon,

"did not seem to justify his departure." His own impression, he went on, was that Condon was "motivated primarily by a feeling that the work in which we were engaged would not be successful, that the Manhattan Project was going to fail, and that he did not want to be connected with it." As far as I am aware, there is no evidence in anything Condon wrote or said to support Groves's interpretation of his reasons for leaving the project.

During his brief time at Los Alamos, Condon made at least one important and lasting contribution, not only to the work of the laboratory, but also to the physics of atomic-bomb manufacture, and that was his writing up and editing of Robert Serber's introductory lectures, which formed *The Los Alamos Primer* (the title was Condon's), a copy of which was given to every scientist on their arrival. There are several references among the memoirs and histories of Los Alamos to the fact that Serber was not a particularly good lecturer, but in print the lectures present a masterfully lucid account of bomb physics, some of the credit for which must go to Condon.

There were five lectures, the first of which was given on April 5, 1943, and the last on April 14. The first lecture begins with the admirably clear and forthright statement: "The object of the project is to produce a *practical military weapon* in the form of a bomb in which the energy is released by a fast-neutron chain reaction in one or more of the materials known to show nuclear fission." Actually, from a security point of view, in its use of the word "bomb," this statement was a little *too* clear. "After a couple of minutes," Serber later recalled, "Oppie sent John Manley up to tell me not to use that word. Too many workmen around, Manley said. They were worried about security. I should use 'gadget' instead." The word "gadget" stuck and became the one everyone at Los Alamos used to refer to the thing they were designing and manufacturing.

After spelling out the purpose of the project, Serber's lectures go on to summarize the current state of knowledge regarding all aspects of bomb physics, much of which had remained unpublished and was therefore news to anyone not previously involved in the atomic-bomb project. He begins with a discussion of the fission process itself, emphasizing that the energy release in fission is, per atom, more than *ten million times* that of an ordinary combustion process, such as that of a fire or a chemical explosion. Serber then explains the phenomenon of a chain reaction and says that it would take eighty generations of reactions to fission one kilogram of U-235. Those eighty generations would take place in 0.8 microseconds (a microsecond being one-millionth of a second), producing an explosion equivalent to 20,000 tons of TNT.

The lectures next provide a summary of what was then known about the physics and chemistry of the relevant materials, U-238, U-235 and Pu-239, and explain how plutonium is produced from uranium by a series of nuclear reactions. The calculations required to estimate critical mass are given and explained, and are used to provide a basic figure of 200 kilograms for U-235, which, Serber explains, "more exact diffusion theory" developed at Berkeley in the summer of 1942 brought down to 60 kilograms. When a tamper is used to reflect back neutrons that would otherwise escape, Serber goes on, the critical mass for U-235 would possibly be as low as 15 kilograms, and for Pu-239 lower still. But, he was at pains to emphasize, all this was, in the spring of 1943, theoretical and uncertain. A large part of the task facing the laboratory was to provide experimental data upon which more reliable and accurate calculations could be made:

> To improve our estimates requires a better knowledge of the proper-ties of bomb materials and tamper: neutron multiplication number, elastic and inelastic cross sections, overall experiments on tamper materials. Finally, however, when materials are available, the critical masses will have to be determined by actual test.

In a section headed "Damage," Serber demonstrated just how much scientists already knew about the devastation that an atomic bomb would cause. "Several kinds of damage will be caused by the bomb," he stated. First, there would be the damage from neutron radiation, which he estimated to be effective within 1,000 yards of the explosion. In notes that Serber added in 1992[48] to the published version of *The Los Alamos Primer*, he says that in 1943 he had "overlooked a more serious source of lethal radiation," namely the release of extremely energetic gamma radiation, the range of which, for the Hiroshima bomb, was 4,000 feet. Second, there is the damage caused by the blast or shock wave. Serber estimates that a bomb equivalent to 100,000 tons of TNT would have a destructive radius of about two miles. Other topics covered by his intro-ductory lectures included the efficiency of the explosion (the proportion of the material that is actually fissioned before it all expands and blows apart), the possible methods of detonation and the various techniques of assembly.

The very last thing Serber dealt with in these lectures, under the heading "Shooting," was the question of how the bomb was to be

---

[48] Despite being a heavy smoker and working for much of his life with powerfully radioac-tive materials, Serber lived to an impressive old age, dying in 1997 (some thirty years after Oppenheimer) at the age of eighty-eight.

"fired"—how, that is, the subcritical pieces of fissionable material (uranium or plutonium) were to be brought together to form a supercritical mass. The first method he considered was the simple mechanism envisaged by Frisch and Peierls in their memorandum, in which a small "bullet" of the material is fired into a subcritical mass, thus making it supercritical. This had the advantage of being very straightforward, but the disadvantage of posing enormous ordnance problems, namely those of designing and manufacturing a "gun" capable of firing the "bullet" sufficiently quickly to prevent the bomb fizzling before it exploded. Another method discussed by Serber was the "implosion" method, which was eventually used in the world's first atomic-bomb explosion in July 1945. In this method pieces of the material are arranged in a circle and then brought together very quickly.

Though it has long been associated with Seth Neddermeyer, implosion was not invented by him, but rather by Richard Tolman, who suggested it at the Berkeley conference in 1942. Tolman and Serber collaborated on a memorandum on the subject at that time and, when urged by Conant and Bush to pursue the method in March 1943, Oppenheimer replied: "Serber is looking into it." In Oppenheimer's original organizational chart of Los Alamos, the investigation of implosion was one of the things that was earmarked as Serber's responsibility. Neddermeyer, however, became an enthusiastic advocate of the idea after hearing Serber's lecture, and immediately dedicated himself to its development.

Neddermeyer's development of the implosion concept was presented to the other scientists at Los Alamos at a major ten-day conference that began the day after Serber's lectures finished. From April 15 to 24, while the laboratories were still being built and the infrastructure of the growing town of Los Alamos was still being developed, an extraordinary collection of the best scientists in America—both native Americans and émigrés, those now working on the program and those still working at their own universities—met to discuss the scientific questions that needed to be answered if an atomic bomb was ever going to be built.

On the first day of the conference, Oppenheimer, covering some of the same ground as Serber, summarized the present state of knowledge. With regard to the production of fissionable material by the enormous plants being constructed at Oak Ridge and Hanford, he told his audience that he estimated that from early 1944 100 grams of uranium-235 and, a year later, 300 grams of plutonium could be shipped every day. Oppenheimer also discussed the "Super" that had so captured Teller's imagination the previous summer, but insisted that it was at a much earlier stage of development than the "gadget" and, as such, of decidedly secondary importance. On the two subsequent days Manley laid out the details of

the forthcoming experimental program, and Bethe discussed the physical constants that needed to be discovered, such as the critical mass,
the number of neutrons emitted per fission, the various cross-sections
and the efficiency of the explosion. On day four Serber led a discussion
on the tamper. The issues covered in subsequent discussions included:
experimental methods, the properties of natural uranium, detonation by
gun method, the chain reaction produced by "the pile" at Chicago, and,
finally, the ways in which the critical mass, timescale and damage of the
bomb might be discovered experimentally.

It was, of course, soon after this conference that Condon left the
project, which made some reorganization necessary. Back in November 1942, Conant had convened a committee to review progress in the
various research projects then under way relating to the production of
an atomic bomb. Chaired by Warren K. Lewis, a professor of chemical engineering at MIT, this review committee produced a report on
December 4, recommending the continuation of a concerted program of
plutonium production via the pile process then being pursued by Fermi
at Chicago. In May 1943, a second Lewis committee was given the task
of reviewing the Los Alamos program. Up until then, the running of the
laboratory had been the responsibility of a planning board, the membership of which had grown steadily. At its first meeting of March 6, 1943,
the planning board had consisted of Oppenheimer, Condon, Wilson,
McMillan, Manley and Serber. A few weeks later, this board had grown
in two directions: Oppenheimer and Condon heading a subgroup concerned with the administration of the laboratory, while Wilson, Serber
and others took responsibility for planning the scientific program. At two
subsequent meetings in early April, several more scientists were added to
the board, including Feynman, Teller, Bethe and Neddermeyer. Now, in
addition to planning the first three months of the experimental program,
due to start in June, the board also discussed the problems that arose
from the rapid expansion of the laboratory. Already it had 150 members
of staff, and the available housing was almost filled. The board decided
to delay any further hiring and recommended that the laboratory should
"be more far-sighted about expansion" in the future.

Members of the Lewis committee attended these planning board
meetings, after which they produced a report that judged progress to be
satisfactory, but recommended that the laboratory should be considerably expanded so as to include within its remit not only the design and
manufacture of the bomb, but also, for example, the investigation of the
metallurgy and purification of plutonium (previously chiefly the responsibility of the Met Lab in Chicago) and all issues relating to the ordnance
of the bomb—that is, the design and manufacture of the specific mecha-

nisms for firing and using the bomb. As the official history puts it, this report destroyed altogether "the original concept of Los Alamos as a small physical laboratory."

Prior to the Lewis committee's report, ordnance had been the responsibility of Richard Tolman and was treated as a scientific set of problems. The report, however, reflected Groves's view that ordnance needed to be dealt with by someone with a practical rather than a purely scientific frame of mind, "so that," as Groves put it, "we will have service equipment instead of some dream child." The kind of person Groves wanted "would have to set up ballistic tests of experimental bombs, plan for the combat use of the weapon and quite possibly be the one to use the bomb in actual battle." In other words, it had to be a military man.

After trying and failing to find someone he thought could do the job among the list of army ordnance officers, Groves turned to Bush in Washington, who recommended a naval officer: Commander William "Deak" Parsons, a man with several years' experience of ordnance and gunnery research. On May 5, 1943, Parsons was ordered to report without delay to Admiral Ernest King, and, he later recalled, "I was plunged into the Manhattan District with a set of verbal orders and a discussion with Admiral King lasting less than ten minutes." Groves, in his autobiography, says that, on meeting Parsons, he was immediately impressed with his "understanding of the interplay between military forces and advanced scientific theory" and claims that "within a few minutes I was sure that he was the man for the job."

The following day, Parsons was introduced to Oppenheimer and the two of them took the train together to Los Alamos. During the journey, Parsons has recalled, they agreed that, while the scientists would "produce the nuclear guts of the gadget," Parsons's division would be responsible for engineering those guts into "a totally reliable service weapon." Parsons had no background in nuclear physics, but what he, with his background in ordnance, could see that the scientists had not, even now, appreciated was the scale of the task facing them. When Parsons first arrived at Los Alamos in May 1943, Oppenheimer's plan of the laboratory had swollen from his original conception of about a dozen scientists and staff to a workforce of about 300 people. A few days later, as a result of Parsons's reappraisal of the situation, the anticipated workforce had more than doubled, most of the increase going into the ordnance-engineering division. After sizing up the situation at Los Alamos, Parsons returned to Washington for a few weeks. When he reported for work at Los Alamos in June, he had been promoted to captain, and made it clear to everyone that he regarded himself as firmly in charge of his part of the operation. Working under him, as group heads, were Ed McMillan, Charles Critchfield and Seth Neddermeyer, the last of whom had by this time become head of the Implosion Experimentation Group. Within two months, Parsons had added five more groups to his division and, in the words of his biographer, "pulled together a top-notch ordnance-development team, [begun] the design of the nuclear gun, brought new support to the implosion method of nuclear assembly, readied the test range at Anchor Ranch, [begun] the planning for the tactical delivery of the bomb, and started testing scale models." Considering there was at this time almost no uranium, and absolutely no plutonium available for experiments, this was pretty remarkable progress.

Notwithstanding Oppenheimer's somewhat optimistic estimates of the daily production of uranium and plutonium to be expected in the coming years, the scientists and engineers at Los Alamos knew that it would be two years or so until enough fissionable material would be available to actually build a bomb. Their job, the urgency of which was felt by everyone concerned, was to have the theory, design and manufacture problems solved in time for the arrival of sufficient quantities of the fissionable materials. As one history of the Manhattan Project puts it, once the material was ready to use, "every month's delay had to be counted as a loss to the war." The fact that fissionable material was in such short supply at the start of the new laboratory's work meant that, to a much larger extent than would otherwise have been the case, the enterprise was reliant upon *theory*. Thus the theoretical physicists that Oppenheimer had recruited—which included, of course, a good proportion of the best in the country—were absolutely central to the project, *even though* it was, in essence, an engineering project. As Feynman once put it: "All science stopped during the war except the little bit that was done at Los Alamos. And that was not much science; it was mostly engineering."

Unlike the experimentalists, who required the equipment to be up and running before they could begin their work, the theoreticians could start right away. So, during the months of May and June, while the builders continued to construct houses and laboratories, and the leaders of the project continued to construct ever more elaborate organizational charts and to revise upward their estimates of how many people the project would need, the theoreticians—needing only their slide rules, their minds and, occasionally, a blackboard—could get on with their calculations. As Teller had emphasized the previous summer in Berkeley, the basic science of the atomic bomb had already been done. There was no doubt, from a theoretical perspective, that the fission of uranium or plutonium could potentially produce an explosive of enormous power. There was no fundamental theoretical science left to do regarding the fission process. On the other hand, in the spring of 1943, the idea of a bomb based upon the science of fission was *only* theoretical. The Met Lab in Chicago had succeeded in producing a chain reaction, but nobody had even come close to building an atomic bomb. In order to make that a reality, the theoreticians needed to work with the experimentalists and the engineers, not only in the formulation of fundamentally new physics, but also in the performing of certain mathematical calculations that only they could do because only they understood.

"Every day," Feynman remembers, "I would study and read, study and read. It was a very hectic time." Though still young and as yet relatively undistinguished, Feynman quickly established a lively rapport with Bethe. As Feynman remembers it, Bethe would come into their office, explaining his ideas, and Feynman would say: "No, no, you're crazy. It'll go like this."

> And he says, "Just a moment" and explains how *he's* not crazy, *I'm* crazy. And we keep on going like this. You see, when I hear about physics, I just think about physics, and I don't know who I'm talking to, so I say dopey thinks like "no, no, you're wrong," or "you're crazy." But it turned out that's exactly what he needed.

Despite the fact that it fundamentally contradicted the idea of compartmentalization, Oppenheimer insisted on having a weekly colloquium, in which scientists could exchange information and criticize each other's ideas. Having failed to recruit Rabi and to keep Condon, he became more and more accommodating to the anti-military sensibilities of many top scientists. For example, after the April conference, he decided that the perfect man to lead the Experimental Physics Division was Robert Bacher. Bacher accepted the position, but only after he made it clear to Oppenheimer that his letter of acceptance should be regarded also as a letter of resignation if the laboratory ever became, as was officially still the intention, fully militarized. Partly because of the trenchant opposition to militarization shown by Bacher and his fellow scientists, the intention to bring the laboratory under full military control was never realized. As Bacher rather diplomatically recalled:

> It had been planned that Los Alamos would turn to be a military laboratory, but I think Groves, who was a very sagacious man about such things, even though he first thought that compartmentalization

was the most important thing that you could have in a laboratory, began to realize that that would defeat him, he'd defeat himself in this, and that the very openness that a civilian laboratory had was a big advantage, and it provided very much greater flexibility.

It seems possible that in insisting on making his views on militarization clear from the start, Bacher was responding to what had happened to Condon, who had left Los Alamos bewildered by Oppenheimer's willingness to conform to the dictates of military authority, even when they conflicted with the requirements of science. As Condon suspected, Oppenheimer shared his views on compartmentalization—as, surely, did all the scientists at Los Alamos—but what Condon did not know was that Oppenheimer was not in a position to openly support Condon's objections to the security arrangements at Los Alamos. As he himself did not yet have security clearance, Oppenheimer could ill afford to alienate those responsible for providing security. Indeed, as a result of Joe Weinberg's late-night conversation with Steve Nelson, things were far worse than Oppenheimer himself could possibly have known.

In the spring of 1943, at the time that Condon left the project and the organization of the laboratory was being put into place, the chances of Oppenheimer being granted security clearance did not look good. Though Weinberg had not yet been identified as "Joe," the authorities knew perfectly well who "the professor" was, and Pash and de Silva were not alone in their view that a man who numbered among his friends and students at least three people who were either actively engaged in Soviet espionage or closely associated with those who were (Nelson, Lomanitz and the as-yet-unidentified "Joe") was not the man to appoint as the head of the U.S.'s most important and most secret military research project. And that was before they knew anything about Haakon Chevalier's attempt to persuade Oppenheimer to aid Eltenton's espionage efforts— the disclosure of which, Oppenheimer knew, would almost certainly bring an end to his directorship of the Los Alamos laboratory before it had really begun.

And so Oppenheimer kept that particular secret to himself for several months, during which he was followed everywhere by Pash's agents, who continued to hunt for irrefutable confirmation that he was not to be trusted. Meanwhile, the FBI stepped up its investigation of those civilians not employed by the Manhattan Project who yet seemed to be taking an unhealthy interest in it, particularly those people who had a history of involvement with the Communist Party. This, of course, included some of the radical young scientists connected with Berkeley's

Radiation Laboratory, the best known of whom, to both the FBI and to army intelligence, was Lomanitz, whose every movement was now closely watched by both agencies.

In June 1943, the constant surveillance of Lomanitz resulted in the identification of Weinberg as "Joe." A G-2 agent following Lomanitz saw him pose with three friends for a picture taken by a commercial photographer at one of the entrances to the Berkeley campus. As soon as the four men were out of sight, the agent approached the photographer and bought the negative of the picture he had taken. The other three men in the photograph were identified as David Bohm, Max Friedman and Joseph Weinberg, and in a short while the agency was able to identify Weinberg as "Joe." All four of the people in the photograph were physicists at Berkeley, all of them politically radical and all of them associated with Oppenheimer (Bohm, Lomanitz and Weinberg had been students of his, and Friedman was regarded socially as a member of the same group).

For the rest of the war each of these four friends was watched closely by the security services, who saw to it that none of them had any access whatsoever to sensitive information. When Oppenheimer asked for Bohm to be transferred to Los Alamos, his request was refused on the grounds that Bohm could not possibly be granted security clearance. Lomanitz, meanwhile, was offered a job liaising between the Rad Lab and Oak Ridge, but before he could take up the position he was drafted into the army. Friedman was hired first by the Rad Lab and then by the Met Lab in Chicago, but was quickly fired from both. Weinberg, like Lomanitz, was drafted into the army. As a direct result of the monitoring of Weinberg's conversation with Nelson in March 1943, then, the Soviets would have received no further information about the U.S. bomb project from Weinberg, Lomanitz, Bohm, Friedman or Nelson. That particular "spy ring" was effectively shut down.

The idea that those four, together with Nelson, constituted a spy ring is not altogether fanciful; Weinberg, for one, had shown himself perfectly prepared to pass secret information to the Soviets via Nelson. And, given their connections with Oppenheimer, and the fact that Oppenheimer had recruited (or at least tried to recruit) at least three of them to positions that would give them access to secret information, it was perfectly natural to suspect Oppenheimer of being in some sense a member of that "spy ring."

In June 1943, at about the same time that Weinberg was being identified as "Joe," Oppenheimer himself provided further reason for suspicion when, followed, as ever, by army intelligence agents, he left Los Alamos for Berkeley. His ostensible reason for the trip was to recruit a personal assistant, his chosen candidate for the job being his friend, the Berkeley philosopher David Hawkins—a man with many connections to radical, left-wing politics, suspected by the FBI of being a communist. Such a choice added a little more credibility to Pash's suspicions of him, but much more serious grounds for questioning his judgment, if not his loyalty, were provided by Oppenheimer's decision to use this trip to California to pay a visit to his ex-lover, Jean Tatlock, who was at this time living in San Francisco.

By the summer of 1943 Jean was far more interested in psychology than politics—she was working as a child psychiatrist at Mount Zion Hospital, and was herself receiving psychoanalysis from the Freudian doctor Siegfried Bernfeld—but, nevertheless, she was well known to the security services as a woman with a history of communist sympathies, activities and connections. Before Oppenheimer left for Los Alamos in March, Jean had asked him to visit her, but he had refused. When he was asked later why, on this occasion, he did see her, he replied:

> She had indicated a great desire to see me before we left. At that time I couldn't go. For one thing, I wasn't supposed to say where we were going or anything. I felt that she had to see me. She was undergoing psychiatric treatment. She was extremely unhappy.

Asked *why* she "had to" see him, Oppenheimer replied: "Because she was still in love with me."

What transpired when the two met is recorded in some detail by the report that Pash's agents sent to the FBI. On June 14, 1943, those agents reported, Oppenheimer went from Berkeley to San Francisco, where he was met by Jean Tatlock, "who kissed him." The two then drove in her car to a local bar, where they ate and had a few drinks, after which Jean drove them back to her apartment on Montgomery Street, San Francisco. The agents, sitting in a car outside the apartment, noted that at half past eleven the lights went off, and the following morning. Oppenheimer and Jean left the building together. That evening the two met again in downtown San Francisco, where they "greeted each other affectionately" and then went to have dinner together at a place called Kit Carson's Grill. After dinner Jean drove him to the airport, where he caught a plane back to New Mexico.

At this time, of course, Oppenheimer did not know that Joe Weinberg had incriminated both himself and, potentially, everybody close to him. But he did know that he himself was regarded with some suspicion by those whose job it was to provide the Manhattan Project with security from espionage, and he presumably also knew, or might well have surmised, that the success or failure of his application for security clearance was therefore still in the balance. Given this, and given that he was in daily contact with members of U.S. Army intelligence, it is surprising that he did not assume, or at the very least suspect, that his every movement was being watched. Or, even more surprising, that he chose to spend a night with Jean even though he was most likely being kept under surveillance. At his security hearing in 1954, he squirmed uncomfortably when asked about the occasion:

> Q. You have no reason to believe she wasn't a Communist, do you?
> A. No.
> Q. You spent the night with her, didn't you?
> A. Yes.
> Q. That is when you were working on a secret war project?
> A. Yes.
> Q. Did you think that consistent with good security?
> A. It was, as a matter of fact. Not a word—it was not good practice.[49]

"Not good practice" hardly does justice to the scale of Oppenheimer's lapse in judgment at this point. Taking everything we know about Oppenheimer and Jean Tatlock at this time, it seems extremely unlikely that what they talked about that night was the work being conducted at Los Alamos, but, to a mind full of suspicion (of both communists in general and of Oppenheimer in particular), it was natural to imagine that Oppenheimer might be using Tatlock as a go-between, in order to pass on to the Soviet Union details of the Manhattan Project.

Certainly such thoughts occurred to Pash, who, on June 29, 1943, two weeks after Oppenheimer's trip to Berkeley and San Francisco, made a formal recommendation to the Pentagon to refuse security clearance to Oppenheimer on the grounds that he "may be connected with the Communist Party," citing in evidence Oppenheimer's visit to Jean and his decision to appoint Hawkins as his assistant. Pash recommended not only that Oppenheimer be replaced as scientific director of Los Alamos, but also that he be thoroughly investigated and interviewed.

Fortunately for Oppenheimer, Groves trusted Pash's judgment less than that of John Lansdale. At about the same time as he wrote to the Pentagon recommending Oppenheimer's dismissal, Pash wrote a memo to Lansdale suggesting that, if Oppenheimer was not fired, then he should be summoned to Washington to be told that the security ser-

---

[49] This is how it appears in the transcript. Presumably what Oppenheimer actually said was: "No, in a word, it was not good practice."

vices knew all about his communist connections and warned that the authorities would not tolerate any attempt by Oppenheimer to pass classified information to members of the Communist Party. Pash considered Oppenheimer to be potentially disloyal to his country, but, like Steve Nelson, he also saw how important it was to Oppenheimer to be heading an important government project and thought that the threat of losing his high-profile job, his reputation and his honor would be enough to keep him in check. "Consequently," Pash concluded, "it is felt that he would lend every effort to cooperating with the Government in any plan which would leave him in charge."

Lansdale's view of Oppenheimer differed sharply from Pash's. He had by this time met Oppenheimer and Kitty at Los Alamos several times and had come to the conclusion that Oppenheimer was neither a communist nor a threat to security. When he was asked at Oppenheimer's security case in 1954 why, in 1943, he had formed the judgment that Oppenheimer was not a communist, Lansdale gave the following interesting reply:

> My working definition of a Communist is a person who is more loyal to Russia than to the United States. That is the definition I formed very early during my work on the Communist problem in the War Department, and which I still think is a sound definition. You will note that has nothing to do with political ideas.
>
> Unquestionably Dr. Oppenheimer was what we would characterize and as hide-bound a Republican as myself characterizes as extremely liberal, not to say radical. Unfortunately, in this problem of determining who is and who is not a Communist, determining who is loyal and who is not, the signs which point the way to persons to be investigated or to check on are very frequently political liberalism of an extreme kind. The difficult judgment is to distinguish between the person whose views are political and the person who is a Communist, because communism is not a political thing at all.

Lansdale, as he later emphasized in the same testimony, considered Oppenheimer to be a loyal American citizen who would put the interests of his own country first, and was therefore, according to the above definition, *not* a communist. Asked whether he had formed the same impression about Kitty, he replied:

> Mrs. Oppenheimer impressed me as a strong woman with strong convictions.
>
> She impressed me as the type of person who could have been, and

I could see she certainly was, a Communist. It requires a very strong person to be a real Communist.

However, Kitty's strength of personality was, Lansdale came to think, a force acting in favor of Oppenheimer's trustworthiness:

> I formed the conviction over many interviews with her and many discussions with her that she had formed the conviction that Dr. Oppenheimer was the most important thing in her life and that his future required that he stay away from Communist associations and associations with people of that ilk.
>
> It was my belief that her strength of character—I think strength of character is the wrong word—her strength of will was a powerful influence in keeping Dr. Oppenheimer away from what we would regard as dangerous associations.

In other words, Lansdale had come to exactly the same conclusion as Steve Nelson: influenced by Kitty, Oppenheimer was quite prepared to separate himself from his old communist friends and comrades in order to maintain the trust of the U.S. government and therefore hold on to his position as head of an important military project.

In a memo to Groves written in July 1943, Lansdale outlined this view of Oppenheimer and his wife. While listing all the "derogatory information" that the FBI and G-2 had gathered about Oppenheimer— his connections with communist front organizations, his friendship with leading Communist Party members, his personal connections with Jean Tatlock and Haakon Chevalier ("believed to be a Communist Party member"), and reliable reports from within the Communist Party that he was considered a member—and conceding that this information was troubling, Lansdale opposed Pash's recommendation that Oppenheimer should be denied clearance and fired. As an alternative he recommended Pash's fall-back position, but instead of placing the emphasis where Pash had placed it—on the use of the derogatory information to intimidate Oppenheimer into refusing to have anything to do with espionage— Lansdale emphasized the possibility that their information, and the possibly dire consequences it might have for Oppenheimer, could be used to persuade him to turn informant. Oppenheimer, Lansdale suggested, should be told that there were doubts about his loyalty "because of his known interest in the Communist Party and his association with and friendship for certain members of the Communist Party" and invited to prove his loyalty by providing Groves and Lansdale with information about any threats to security that he might have heard about. In other words, Oppenheimer should be made to feel that, in order to demonstrate his loyalty to his country, he would have to betray his old friends in the Communist Party.

In the light of Lansdale's assessment, Groves took a characteristically decisive step. On July 20, 1943, he issued the following instructions to the U.S. District Engineer:

> In accordance with my verbal instructions of July 15, it is desired that clearance be issued for the employment of Julius Robert Oppenheimer without delay, irrespective of the information which you have concerning Mr. Oppenheimer. He is absolutely essential to the project.

Oppenheimer was thus granted his clearance, though this, of course, did not put an end to the matter. Pash and de Silva were still convinced that he was aiding and abetting Soviet espionage, while Groves and Lansdale, convinced that he was not, were determined to use him to reveal further information about people who were. At precisely the time when experimental work at Los Alamos could begin, therefore, Oppenheimer spent much of his time involved in various ways with issues of security. This no doubt contributed to his feeling, which he conveyed at this time to Robert Bacher, that he was not equal to the task with which he had been charged. In response, Bacher told him what Groves also clearly believed: he had no alternative but to continue, since there was no one else capable of doing the job.

Oppenheimer's resolve to carry on was surely fortified by a letter he received at the beginning of July 1943 from President Roosevelt himself, asking him to assure the scientists working at Los Alamos that their efforts were appreciated: "I am sure we can rely on their continued wholehearted and unselfish labors. Whatever the enemy may be planning, American science will be equal to the challenge." In his reply, Oppenheimer took the opportunity to emphasize to the President how importantly he took the security of the project:

> You would be glad to know how greatly your words of reassurance were appreciated by us. There will be many times in the months ahead when we shall remember them.
>
> It is perhaps appropriate that I should in turn transmit to you the assurance that we as a group and as individual Americans are profoundly aware of our responsibility, for the security of our project

as well as for its rapid and effective completion. It is a great source of encouragement to us that we have in this your support and understanding.

That Oppenheimer was not entirely trusted by those for whom he worked was made clear in a letter that he received from General Groves written on July 29, 1943, telling him that henceforth he was requested: (a) to "refrain from flying in airplanes of any description"; (b) that he should be accompanied by "a competent, able bodied, armed guard" acting as chauffeur during any road trip "above a few miles"; and (c) that, in driving about Los Alamos, "a guard of some kind should be used, particularly during hours of darkness."

This letter was evidently part of a tightening of security that was soon to have the drastic and lasting consequences mentioned earlier for those ex-students of Oppenheimer's who were identified as actual or possible communist spies. The first affected was Lomanitz, who on July 27 was told by Ernest Lawrence that he had been promoted to group leader at the Rad Lab, having responsibility for overseeing the building of Calutrons at Oak Ridge. Three days later, before he could take up his new position, Lomanitz received a letter telling him that he had been drafted into the army. "It was really a sort of a strange thing," Lomanitz later explained, "because Dr. Lawrence had just had a talk with me about some new work that he wanted me to undertake which was supposedly more important, which was to go out to Oakridge and be a liaison man between Berkeley and Oakridge while Oakridge was building a couple of hundred of these machines."

Neither Lomanitz nor Lawrence, of course, knew that the FBI had been listening to Lehmann's indiscreet conversation with Steve Nelson back in October 1942, or that Lomanitz's comradely photograph with Weinberg, Friedman and Bohm had led to all four of them being identified as members of an espionage ring. Both were puzzled. According to Lomanitz, Lawrence's initial reaction was: "Oh, there has to be a mistake. I'll take care of it." But, Lomanitz discovered: "It turned out that it was not a mistake and he was not able to take care of it." Not that he didn't try. Lansdale remembers: "Ernest Lawrence yelled and screamed louder than anybody else about us taking Lomanitz away from him." In his desperation, Lomanitz phoned Oppenheimer at Los Alamos, who immediately sent off a telegram to the Pentagon saying that a "very serious mistake is being made. Lomanitz now only man at Berkeley who can take this responsibility." On July 31, 1943, Oppenheimer cabled Lomanitz, saying: "Have requested in proper places reconsideration of support for your deferment. Cannot guarantee outcome but have made strong request."

As Oppenheimer, Lomanitz and Lawrence all discovered, however, the army was implacable in its decision not to allow Lomanitz to work on the atomic-bomb project and to enlist him. Toward the end of his life, in 2001, Lomanitz gave an interview in which he revealed that, nearly sixty years after the event, he still believed that the purpose in getting him out of Berkeley was not to prevent a security leak, but rather to weaken and then to close down the Rad Lab branch of the Federation of Architects, Engineers, Chemists and Technicians (FAECT), which he and Oppenheimer had helped to establish and to run.

In fact, it was the other way around: the authorities were indeed keen to close down the Rad Lab branch of FAECT, but this was because they saw it as a communist front organization and a threat to the security of the bomb project. Removing Lomanitz was part of an attack not on trade unionism, but specifically on the Communist Party and, more specifically, on the use made of communist members of FAECT by Soviet intelligence to gain information on U.S. military programs. It was Lansdale's hope that Oppenheimer's vulnerability with regard to his past associations with the Communist Party would allow him to be exploited by the security services to aid them in that attack.

Some confirmation that Lansdale's hopes might be well founded in this respect came from a meeting he had with Oppenheimer at Los Alamos on August 10, 1943, a full report of which is contained in a memo he sent Groves two days later. Lansdale told Groves he had made it clear to Oppenheimer that it was no use asking the authorities to defer Lomanitz's draft, since "he had been guilty of indiscretions which could not be overlooked or condoned." Oppenheimer—perhaps assuming, like Lomanitz, that what the authorities had against his ex-student was his involvement in political (rather than espionage) activities—told Lansdale that he had insisted very strongly to Lomanitz that, if he joined the atomic-bomb project, "he must forego all political activity." He also told Lansdale "he knew that Lomanitz had been very much of a Red as a boy when he first came to the University of California," but professed to have no knowledge of his political activities since then. When told by Lansdale that the investigation of Lomanitz had revealed that he had certainly not forgone any political activity, Oppenheimer, according to Lansdale, replied: "That makes me mad." Lansdale goes on:

There then ensued a general discussion of the Communist Party. Oppenheimer was told that from a military intelligence standpoint we were quite unconcerned with a man's political or social beliefs, and we were only concerned with preventing the transmission of classified information to unauthorized persons, wherever that person's loyalties might lie, or whatever his social, political, or religious beliefs might be.

At this point in the conversation, Oppenheimer endeavored to give Lansdale the impression that he himself took a rather tougher line against Communist Party members than that taken by the army:

[He] stated that he did not agree with us with respect to the Communist Party. He stated that he did not want anybody working for him on the project that was a member of the Communist Party. He stated that the reason for that was that "one always had a question of divided loyalty." He stated that the discipline of the Communist Party was very severe and was not compatible with complete loyalty to the project. He made it clear he was not referring to people who had been members of the Communist Party, stating that he knew several now at Los Alamos who had been members. He was referring only to present membership in the Communist Party.

"Oppenheimer gave every appearance of sincerity in this discussion," Lansdale concluded, telling Groves that his own view was that "what Dr. Oppenheimer was trying to convey was, in the case of Lomanitz, that Lomanitz had been worried about his obligations to the party, and that Oppenheimer had told him that he must give up the party if he came on the project." He also "had the definite impression that Oppenheimer was trying to indicate that he had been a member of the party, and had definitely severed his connections upon engaging in this work." "On the whole," Lansdale's memo ends, "it seemed that Oppenheimer, in a rather subtle way, was anxious to indicate to this officer his position in that regard."

On August 12, the day that Lansdale wrote his memo about Oppenheimer to Groves, FBI agents watched as Bohm, Friedman and Lomanitz arrived at a meeting at Weinberg's apartment that was also attended by Steve Nelson and his Communist Party assistant, Bernadette Doyle. The surveillance of Lomanitz and his friends was part of an extensive FBI operation entitled "CINRAD"—"Communist Infiltration of the Radiation Laboratory"—which was eventually to build up files on more than 300 Communist Party members in Berkeley. So seriously was the threat to security posed by the group of communists at the Rad Lab taken that it was discussed at the highest possible level. On August 17, Groves, after presenting a progress report on the atomic-bomb project to the U.S. government's Top Policy Group, went on to summarize the army's investigation of what he called the "California trouble." On the same day he had delivered to Henry Stimson, the Secretary of War, a draft memo for the President advising that FAECT should be ordered to stop all activity regarding the Radiation Laboratory. Within a few months the memo achieved its end when FAECT's Rad Lab branch was forced to close.

Lansdale's conversation with Oppenheimer of August 10 evidently persuaded Oppenheimer that it was not enough for him to distance himself from his old communist friends and comrades; he also had to be seen to be active in combating the threat to security that they represented. The clumsy attempt by Chevalier to enlist his aid in George Eltenton's espionage activities, about which he had previously been entirely quiet, now seemed to him to offer a relatively harmless way of giving the security forces what they wanted: information on communist espionage attempts. Not that Oppenheimer wanted to inform on Chevalier, but Eltenton seemed a promising target. After all, Eltenton was no friend of his and he had, much to Oppenheimer's annoyance, actively sought to involve both him and Chevalier in espionage. A few days after his conversation with Lansdale, therefore, Oppenheimer went to see Groves and gave him Eltenton's name as someone who needed to be watched.

About a week later, on August 25, 1943, Oppenheimer went to Berkeley with, it seems, the intention of addressing the problems that Lansdale had discussed regarding security at the Rad Lab. He first went to the secret office of Lieutenant Lyall Johnson and asked him whether it would be all right to speak to Lomanitz, who at that time was still on campus, continuing to hope that his draft into the army could be deferred. Johnson granted Oppenheimer permission to speak to Lomanitz, though he stressed that in his opinion Lomanitz was dangerous. As he was leaving Johnson's office, Oppenheimer told him (as he had previously told Groves) that there was a man called George Eltenton of whom the security officers in Berkeley should be aware. Eltenton, Oppenheimer told Johnson, worked for Shell and was an active member of FAECT.

Oppenheimer then went to Lawrence's office in the Rad Lab, where he had arranged to meet Lomanitz. It is not entirely clear exactly why Oppenheimer wanted to meet Lomanitz. Was he still trying to help Lomanitz keep his job at the Rad Lab? Was he trying to find out what truth there was in what Lansdale had said about Lomanitz—that he had, despite his promise to Oppenheimer, kept up his political activities, including taking an active part in FAECT business, and that he had been guilty of "indiscretion"? Or was his purpose to pass on to Lomanitz the fact that he had aroused the suspicions of counterintelligence officers?

The evidence is scanty and restricted to what Oppenheimer himself told Pash, Lansdale and the security hearing of 1954. At his hearing, Oppenheimer said: "With the approval or the suggestion, I don't remember, of the security officer, I endeavored to persuade Lomanitz to get the thing straight with the security people." To Lansdale, Oppenheimer revealed that Lomanitz had told him that he was being "framed." "I said I think that's nonsense, why would you be framed, and he said, 'Well, part of the general scheme . . . maybe they're after bigger game than the party.'"

In other words, Lomanitz thought, as he continued to think for the rest of his life, that the aim of the authorities in drafting him into the army was to destroy FAECT. Oppenheimer claims that by this time he had come to the view that it was a lost cause to keep Lomanitz at the Rad Lab. "I persuaded him, I think," Oppenheimer told Lansdale, "that he should not try to stay on the project there."

Worried about being overheard by Lawrence's secretarial staff, and also perhaps suspecting that Lawrence's office was being bugged,[50] Oppenheimer and Lomanitz went outside to continue their discussion on the street, after which Oppenheimer returned to Lawrence's office to find Weinberg and Bohm waiting to see him. Oppenheimer told Lansdale:

> These two fellows were concerned with only one thing. They said they had worked closely with Rossi [Lomanitz], they thought he was a good guy and that they thought he was being framed for his activities in the union and his political sympathies, and they thought that because of this they were also in danger of such a nature that they should get out of the project into some other useful work or they were likely to be treated the same way.

In response, Oppenheimer claimed, he told them "if they were violating any of the three rules which meant active in union, maintaining any contacts with Reds, not maintaining discretion, they were useless to the project." When Lawrence briefly appeared, Oppenheimer asked him to witness the promises of Weinberg and Bohm to stay away from politics. That night, Oppenheimer had dinner in Berkeley with Robert Bacher, and was overheard by "creeps" telling Bacher that he had given Lawrence "hell" over the lax security at the Rad Lab.

---

[50] In his interview of 2001 Lomanitz said: "I remember that it was his [Oppenheimer's] habit that if one talked about something, 'Let's just walk outside and talk about it out there.' In other words, he assumed that the phones were tapped."

The indications are that Oppenheimer, when he went to bed on the night of August 25, 1943, probably considered that he had done much that day to improve both the security position at Berkeley and his own reputation among the security officers. He had volunteered information about possible communist spies, had told Lomanitz to forget his promised group leadership, had elicited promises from Weinberg and Bohm to stay away from politics, and had given Lawrence a dressing-down about the weak security in the Rad Lab. Not a bad day's work, he might have felt. However, what he had done was to sow the seeds for his own downfall and that of many of his friends, students and colleagues.

For what he had succeeded in conveying to Lyall Johnson was very different from what he had meant to convey. What interested Johnson about the "information" Oppenheimer had provided was not that George Eltenton was a communist, active in FAECT and keen to supply the Soviets with information about U.S. military projects. The security services already knew *that*. What interested Johnson was that *Oppenheimer* knew that. As soon as Oppenheimer left his office, therefore, Johnson phoned Boris Pash to tell him about his meeting with Oppenheimer. To Pash, this looked like the opportunity he had been waiting for to prove Oppenheimer's involvement in Soviet espionage. Pash immediately arranged to see Oppenheimer the following morning and also arranged for their conversation to be recorded. The result was a recording that would be played, replayed, transcribed and minutely analyzed for the rest of Oppenheimer's life and beyond.

In responding to questions from Pash and Johnson about Eltenton, Oppenheimer seems in this recorded interview to be extraordinarily inept, which some commentators have attributed to his arrogance in not taking seriously the possibility that he might be intellectually outmaneuvered by people of inferior intelligence. What seems most apparent, however, is that Oppenheimer was simply not prepared for the questions he received. He went to Johnson's office on the morning of August 26, expecting to discuss Lomanitz with Johnson alone. He did not expect Pash to be there, did not expect the conversation to be recorded and did not expect to be questioned about Eltenton. He thought, it appears, that the security officers would simply be grateful that he had provided them with a possible lead, not that they would grill him about it. After all, when he told Groves about Eltenton, he did not have to face lots of searching questions about *how* he knew Eltenton to be involved in espionage. For this reason it seems not to have occurred to him that, if he was to keep Chevalier's name out of it, he had better have a convincing explanation of how he came to know about Eltenton. When called upon to provide such an explanation, therefore, he responded in the worst possible way by making up a story on the spot, one that could not possibly withstand the intense scrutiny it received—a "cock and bull story," as he was later compelled to confess.

Pash began by telling Oppenheimer what a pleasure it was to be able to speak to him face-to-face, since, in maintaining the security of the atomic-bomb project, he felt as if General Groves had "placed a certain responsibility in me and it's like having a child, that you can't see, by remote control." Then, getting straight to the point, he continued: "Mr. Johnson told me about the little incident, or conversation, taking place yesterday in which I am very much interested and it had me worried all day yesterday since he called me."

How far Oppenheimer was understanding the mentality of security officers is revealed in his reply to this, in which he assumed that what Pash was worried about was his conversation with Lomanitz. He also showed himself willing to be far more critical of Lomanitz than was strictly necessary in the circumstances:

> I was rather uncertain as to whether I should or should not talk to him [Lomanitz] when I was here. I was unwilling to do it without authorization. What I wanted to tell this fellow was that he had been indiscreet. I know that that's right that he had revealed information. I know that saying that much might in some cases embarrass him. It doesn't seem to have been capable of embarrassing him to put it bluntly.

"That is not the particular interest I have," Pash told him. "It is something a little more, in my opinion, more serious. Mr. Johnson said there was a possibility that there may be some other groups interested."

Clearly wrong-footed by this, and entirely unprepared for it, Oppenheimer started to babble, ending up by appearing to endorse the idea of sharing information about the atomic bomb with the Russians:

> I think that is true, but I have no first-hand knowledge that would be, for that reason, useful, but I think it is true that a man, whose name I never heard, who was attached to the Soviet consul, has indicated indirectly through intermediary people concerned in this project that he was in a position to transmit, without any danger of a leak, or scandal, or anything of that kind, information, which they might supply . . . I will take it to be assumed that a man attached to the Soviet consulate might be doing this. But since I know it to be

a fact, I have been particularly concerned about any indiscretions which took place in circles close to the consul or which might come in contact with it. To put it quite frankly, I would feel friendly to the idea of the Commander-in-Chief informing the Russians that we were working on this problem. At least, I can see that there might be some arguments for doing that, but I do not feel friendly to the idea of having it moved out the back door. I think that it might not hurt to be on the lookout for it.

Refusing to be deflected from his main purpose, Pash then pressed Oppenheimer: "Could you give me a little more specific information as to exactly what information you have?" At this point, having not thought through an adequate story, Oppenheimer fell back on equivocation, vagueness and straightforward dishonesty. The approaches for information, he claimed, "were always to other people, who were troubled by them and discussed them with me." Furthermore, he told Pash, "the approaches were always quite indirect, so I feel that to give more, perhaps, than one name, would be to implicate people whose attitude was one of bewilderment rather than one of cooperation." The one name he was prepared to give was the one he had already given: Eltenton.

He has probably been asked to do what he can to provide information. Whether he is successful or not, I couldn't know. But he talked to a friend of his who is also an acquaintance of one of the men on the project, and that was one of the channels by which this thing went. Now I think that to go beyond that would be to put a lot of names down, of people who are not only innocent but whose attitude was 100 percent effective.

At this point Oppenheimer probably realized he was in trouble. He had said that Eltenton had approached, possibly through intermediaries, people working on the atomic-bomb project for information to pass on to the Soviet Union, and, as he by this point in the conversation no doubt realized, Pash was not going to rest until he had secured the names of the intermediaries, the people who had been approached and (though Pash and his colleagues probably already knew this part) Eltenton's contact at the Soviet consulate. With regard to the last of these, Oppenheimer responded:

I mean I don't know the name of the man attached to the consulate. I think I may have been told or I may not have been told and I have, at least not purposely, but actually forgotten. He is—and he may not be here now. These incidents occurred of the order of about five, six, seven, months ago.

Again, this response gave away more information than was necessary. He did not need to inform Pash that he was possibly told the name of Eltenton's contact at the Soviet consulate, nor did he need to reveal that he knew, at least roughly, *when* these incidents took place.

With regard to the names of the people who had been approached, Oppenheimer at first tried to evade the question, and then, perhaps realizing he had to say *something*, began to concoct his "cock and bull story": "I have known two or three cases, and I think two of the men were with me at Los Alamos. They are men who are very closely associated with me." Now he had committed himself to saying *far more* than he needed to. He knew, of course, of one person who had been approached, through an intermediary, by Eltenton: namely himself. Did he really know of one or two others who had been similarly approached? He later claimed that he did not, that these other cases simply did not exist. So why on earth did he tell Pash and Johnson that he knew two or three people "closely associated" with himself who had been approached indirectly by Eltenton for information on the bomb project? The only explanation he gave for this at his security hearing was: "I was an idiot." Indeed, under the circumstances, it is hard to think of anything more idiotic, which shows, I think, how little prepared Oppenheimer was for the questions Pash and Johnson put to him.

When asked to name the intermediary, Oppenheimer's initial response was: "I think it would be a mistake . . . I think I have told you where the initiative came from and that the other things were almost purely accident and it would involve people who ought not be involved in this." When pressed, he gave a few hints, some of them entirely unhelpful ("He is a man whose sympathies are certainly very far left, whatever his affiliations, and he may or may not have regular contacts with a political group"), and some that might indeed lead his inquisitors to Chevalier ("It's a member of the faculty, but not on the project").

When Pash and Johnson returned to the question of who this nameless intermediary had approached, Oppenheimer again provided a curious detail. Asked if the people who had been approached had been contacted at the same time, he replied: "They were contacted within a week of each other . . . but not in each other's presence." "And then," said Pash, "from what you first heard, there is someone else who probably still remains here who was contacted as well." "I think that is true," replied Oppenheimer. Driving home the importance of this point, Pash emphasized that, according to Oppenheimer's story, there had been a plan to leak information to the Soviet consulate from contacts who worked on the atomic-bomb project, "and we may not have known all the contacts." "That is certainly true," replied Oppenheimer. "That is why I mentioned it." After a bit more prevarication he let slip further details about the people who had been approached: first, that they "have a feeling toward this country and have signed the Espionage Act"; second, that one of the men "has gone, or is scheduled to go, to Site X [Oak Ridge]." Putting all these hints together, it would have been natural to come to the conclusion that General Groves was to reach: that two of the people Oppenheimer had described as being approached by Eltenton were himself and his brother Frank, and that his evasions had to do with his desire—his duty—to protect Frank.

Several times toward the end of the discussion, Pash let Oppenheimer know in no uncertain terms that he had not heard the last of this. He repeatedly asked Oppenheimer if it would be all right to interview him again at Los Alamos, to which Oppenheimer gave his evidently unenthusiastic assent. Pash also referred repeatedly to the fact that he would not drop his attempts to discover the name of the intermediary. "We certainly would give a lot of thanks and appreciation for the name of that intermediary," he told Oppenheimer, since "we are going to have to spend a lot of time and effort which we ordinarily would not in trying to . . . trying to run him down before we even can get on to these others." The clear implication was that, in withholding his name, Oppenheimer was not protecting the intermediary; rather, he was just wasting the time of military-intelligence officers. "We will be hot under the collar until we find out what is going on," Pash promised.

Before he left, Oppenheimer tried two further tactics to rescue the situation. The first was to make grandiose declarations of his loyalty to his country and of his own concern for security ("I think that I would be perfectly willing to be shot if I had done anything wrong"). The second was, rather ignobly, to insist that security at his Los Alamos was a good deal better than it was at Lawrence's Rad Lab ("I feel responsible for every detail of this sort of thing down at our place and I will be willing to go quite far in saying that everything is 100 percent in order. That doesn't go for this place up here"). Neither tactic made any impression on Pash; he was, he told Oppenheimer, like a bloodhound on a trail and, whatever Oppenheimer might say or do, that trail was going to lead him to the identities of (a) Oppenheimer's intermediary, and (b) the three members of the bomb project who had been approached to leak information to the Soviets.

The conversation left Pash more convinced than ever that Oppenheimer was involved in espionage, and, though he had been unable to convince either Groves or Lansdale of this, his view was shared by other important members of the security services, who shared also his fervent desire to protect the bomb project from Oppenheimer's complicity. The FBI had always regarded Oppenheimer with suspicion and were only too pleased to ally themselves with Pash's campaign against him. On August 27, the day after Oppenheimer's disastrous meeting with Pash and Johnson, an FBI agent recommended placing a wiretap on Jean Tatlock's phone, on the grounds that Oppenheimer might use either her or her telephone in order to contact "the Comintern Apparatus." Five days later, J. Edgar Hoover took up the suggestion in a memo to the Attorney General, saying that tapping her phone would help in "determining the identities of espionage agents within the Comintern Apparatus," because she was "the paramour of an individual possessed of vital secret information regarding this nation's war effort" and "a contact of members of the Comintern Apparatus." Jean's phone was duly tapped, but no information relevant to the protection of the U.S. was ever gathered by such means.

On September 2, 1943, the day after Hoover's memo to the Attorney General, the case against Oppenheimer was summarized in a memo to Pash written by Pash's man at Los Alamos, Captain Peer de Silva. With regard to the recent developments in the espionage case relating to the Manhattan Project, de Silva began, "the part played by J.R. Oppenheimer is believed to take on a more vital significance than has heretofore been apparent." After summarizing Oppenheimer's discussion with Pash and Johnson, de Silva states: "The writer wishes to go on record as saying that J.R. Oppenheimer is playing a key part in the attempts of the Soviet Union to secure, by espionage, highly secret information which is vital to the security of the United States." In support of this view, de Silva writes that Oppenheimer, despite having gone on record as believing that Communist Party membership is incompatible with access to military secrets, "has allowed a tight clique of known Communists or Communist sympathizers to grow up about him within the project, until they comprise a large proportion of the key personnel in whose hands the success and security of the project is entrusted." "In the opinion of this officer," de Silva goes on, "Oppenheimer either must be incredibly naïve and almost childlike in his sense of reality, or he himself is extremely clever and disloyal. The former possibility is not borne out in the opinion of the officers who have spoken with him at length." What struck de Silva about Oppenheimer's recent disclosure of information regarding Eltenton and his unnamed intermediary was its timing: immediately after Oppenheimer had been alerted to the fact that his ex-students were being investigated for leaking information. "Until alerted to the fact that an investigation was in progress," de Silva wrote, Oppenheimer "made absolutely no attempt to inform any responsible authority of the incidents which he definitely knew to have occurred and which, he claims, he did not approve."

De Silva concluded that "Oppenheimer is deeply concerned with gaining a worldwide reputation as a scientist, and a place in history" through his leadership of the Los Alamos laboratory. The army, he maintained, "is in the position of being able to allow him to do so or to destroy his name, reputation, and career, if it should choose to do so." He ended up suggesting that, if "strongly presented to him," the fact that the army could destroy his reputation, "would possibly give him a different view of his position with respect to the Army, which has been, heretofore, one in which he has been dominant because of his supposed essentiality."

Four days later, this uncompromising assessment was sent to Lansdale by Pash, who added to it the statement: "This Office is still of the opinion that Oppenheimer is not to be fully trusted and that his loyalty to a Nation is divided. It is believed that the only undivided loyalty that he can give is to science and it is strongly felt that if in his position the Soviet Government could offer more for the advancement of his scientific cause he would select that Government as the one to which he would express his loyalty."

Meanwhile, the close surveillance of Weinberg and his friends continued. On September 3, the day after de Silva wrote his memo to Pash, agents following Weinberg saw him post a thick, large envelope addressed to Al Flanigan, a graduate student at Berkeley and a friend of Steve Nelson's. When the agents opened the envelope they found that it contained a manuscript article entitled "The Communist Party and the Professions," together with a brief, unsigned covering note, which said: "Please do not communicate with me during this period, nor discuss with others my reasons for this request." The note also asked Flanigan to pass this message on to "S. or B."—presumably Steve Nelson and Bernadette Doyle—"without mentioning my name." Copies of the manuscript and the note were sent to Pash, who regarded them as evidence that the purpose of Oppenheimer's meeting with Weinberg and Bohm was to tip them off that they were being watched.

On September 12, Lansdale conducted an interview with Oppenheimer, this time in Groves's office in Washington. Like Pash's interview a couple of weeks earlier, it was recorded and transcribed. The tone of the interview, however, was very different. As Lansdale made clear to Oppenheimer, he liked, admired and trusted him. He began the interview by telling Oppenheimer, "without intent of flattery or compliment-ing or anything else," that "you're probably the most intelligent man I ever met," and ended it by emphasizing: "I want you to know that I like you personally, and believe me it's so. I have no suspicions whatsoever, and I don't want you to feel that I have." Everything he later did and said suggests that Lansdale was being quite sincere in these remarks.

Lansdale's purpose, too, was quite different from Pash's. He did not want to trip Oppenheimer into revealing his complicity with espionage; he wanted, rather, to extract from him information that might be helpful in identifying those who were involved in espionage. And, in particular, he wanted the name of the intermediary whom Eltenton had used to try to obtain secret information regarding the Manhattan Project. The way Oppenheimer began the conversation shows that he still had not understood that the security forces regarded the Eltenton espionage attempt as a much bigger concern than the "indiscretions" committed by Lomanitz and his friends. For, when Lansdale mentioned his interview with Pash, Oppenheimer immediately launched into an explanation of why he wanted to talk to Lomanitz, as if *that* was what Lansdale would be most concerned about:

> I thought I might be able to talk him out of some of this foolishness so I asked Johnson for permission to do that. I had a rather long discussion with Lomanitz which I should describe as pretty unsuc-cessful, or at least only partially successful. And, of course, Johnson had expressed the opinion that he was dangerous and why, and that Pash ought to be brought in on it. So I told Pash some of the reasons why I thought it was dangerous and I suppose that is probably what you mean.

Straightaway, Lansdale let him know that his main concern was the intelligence and counterintelligence surrounding the attempts by the Soviet Union to penetrate the secrets of the Manhattan Project. Sum-ming up the situation, he told Oppenheimer, "They know, we know they know, about Tennessee, about Los Alamos, and Chicago," given which: "It is essential that we know the channels of communication." Appearing to recognize and sympathize with the feeling of many of the scientists that security concerns were actually an obstacle to getting the job done, Lansdale told Oppenheimer that he had a delicate line to tread. "We don't want to protect the thing to death," he remarked, but, on the other hand, it was clear that *some* degree of protection was needed. And, there-fore, Lansdale needed the name of that intermediary. Oppenheimer, however, refused to provide the name: "I've thought about it a good deal because Pash and Groves both asked me for the name, and I feel that I should not give it." "I don't see how," Lansdale told him, "you can have any hesitancy in disclosing the name of the man who has actually been engaged in an attempt at espionage to a foreign power in time of war." But Oppenheimer was implacable in his refusal to land Chevalier in what he knew would be a lot of trouble.

Changing tack, Lansdale tried to use Oppenheimer's communist past to glean information about Communist Party members. "Who do you know," he asked, "on the project in Berkeley who are . . . or have been members of the Communist Party?" Unhelpfully, Oppenheimer replied: "I know for a fact, I know, I learned on my last visit to Berkeley, that both Lomanitz and Weinberg were members." Pressed to tell Lansdale something he did not already know, Oppenheimer—seemingly at random—chose to identify Charlotte Serber as having been in the past a member of the Communist Party. When asked whether Robert Serber had been a member, Oppenheimer replied: "I think it possible, but I don't know."

> LANSDALE. Now, have you yourself ever been a member of the Communist Party?
> OPPENHEIMER. No.
> LANSDALE. You've probably belonged to every front organization on the coast.
> OPPENHEIMER. Just about.

In Lansdale's search for names of Communist Party members, an awkward moment for Oppenheimer came when his inquisitor asked: "How about Haakon Chevalier?" On this occasion, however, Oppenheimer remained cool and unflustered. "Is he a member of the Party?" he responded, adding: "He is a member of the faculty and I know him well. I wouldn't be surprised if he were a member, he is quite a Red." Frustrated by such suave evasions, Lansdale laid his cards on the table:

> we've got the case of Dr. J. R. Oppenheimer, whose wife was at one time a member of the party anyway, who himself knows many prominent Communists, associates with them, who belongs to a large number of so-called front organizations and may perhaps have contributed financially to the party himself, who becomes aware of an espionage attempt by the party six months ago and doesn't mention

it, and who still won't make a complete disclosure. I may say that I've made up my mind that you yourself are OK or otherwise I wouldn't be talking to you like this, see?

"I'd better be. That's all I've got to say," Oppenheimer replied.

At the end of what had been, from his point of view, a frustrating and fruitless interview Lansdale warned Oppenheimer, with respect to the name of the intermediary: "Don't think it's the last time I'm going to ask you, 'cause it isn't." Before he left, Oppenheimer—rather needlessly, but in an evident determination to appear to be cooperative—volunteered the suspicion that Bernard Peters was involved in the Communist Party: "I know that he was in Germany, and that he was actually in prison there, and I also know that he has always expressed a very great interest in the Communists, and I think whether he is a member or not would perhaps partly depend on whether he was a citizen or whether he was working on a war job."

While Lansdale was expressing his liking for and admiration of Oppenheimer, Pash was doing his best to expose him as a spy. Ten days before Lansdale's interview with Oppenheimer, Pash had sent Groves an insistent, slightly nagging memo, telling him: "It is essential that name of professor [that is, the intermediary between Eltenton and Oppenheimer] be made available in order that investigation can continue properly." He went on to "request names of individuals contacted by professor in order to eliminate unnecessary investigation and following of leads which may come to the attention of this office." "Has anyone," he demanded to know, "approached JRO at any time while he was connected with the project? If so, was it the professor, Eltenton, or some other party?"

One imagines that Groves was not used to being addressed in this manner by someone of lower rank and that he did not much care for Pash's tone or for Pash himself, who was, in his obsessive pursuit of Oppenheimer, in danger of becoming a nuisance. Nevertheless when he, Oppenheimer and Lansdale traveled together on a train to Chicago a day or two after Oppenheimer's interview with Lansdale, Groves took the opportunity to put to Oppenheimer the questions Pash had raised with him. The topics discussed were summarized in a memo by Lansdale dated September 14. According to this memo, Oppenheimer's attitude to Lomanitz had hardened somewhat since his discussion with Lansdale a day or two earlier. Whereas then he had described his discussion with Lomanitz as "pretty unsuccessful, or at least only partially successful," now he described it as "very unsatisfactory" and Lomanitz himself as "defiant." The memo goes on: "Oppenheimer was sorry that he had

ever had anything to do with him [Lomanitz], and he did not desire any
further connection with him." With regard to the name of the Berkeley
professor who had acted as Eltenton's intermediary, Lansdale's memo
states:

> Oppenheimer's attitude was that he would give the name of the
> intermediate contact at the University of California if pressed to do
> so, and told by General Groves that we had to have it, but that he
> did not want to do so because he did not believe that any further
> contacts had been made and was confident that the contacts that
> had been with the project had not produced any information. He
> intimated further that it was a question of getting friends of his into
> difficulties and causing unnecessary troubles when no useful purpose
> could be served.

Groves then put several names to Oppenheimer that Pash had suggested as possibilities for the people this intermediary had contacted.
Among them was Al Flanigan, "who now appears," wrote Lansdale,
"from subsequent developments to be the contact." Oppenheimer told
Groves and Lansdale that he did not know Flanigan except casually, "but
that he had the reputation of being a real 'Red.'" This, presumably, ruled
Flanigan out, since Oppenheimer had previously said he knew the three
contacts rather well. As far as one can tell from the memo, the rest of
the conversation was taken up with Oppenheimer telling Groves and
Lansdale what they already knew: that Kitty, Frank and Charlotte Serber
had been Communist Party members and that he himself, though not a
member of the party, had been a member of several Communist Party
front organizations.

Possibly the most significant thing to emerge from this train of
conversation was the weakness of Oppenheimer's loyalty to Lomanitz,
Weinberg, Bohm and Friedman, all of whom were henceforth to face
whatever difficulties their loyalty to the Communist Party brought them
without much in the way of support from Oppenheimer. Lomanitz had
tried extremely hard to find jobs on the West Coast that would entitle
him to defer his draft, but every time he was offered such a post, the offer
would be withdrawn before he could be issued with such a deferment.
On one occasion Friedman, who had just bought a new Pontiac, drove
Lomanitz around the Bay Area looking for work, and they found a new
company that made radar tubes and was interested in hiring Lomanitz.
As Lomanitz later remembered it, when the man in charge started hag-
gling about wages, he said to him: "Look. I'm making $300 a month

right now. I'll go to work for you for half that if you'll just send in immediately a request for my deferment." He was offered the job, and the man duly applied for deferment. The next day, however, Lomanitz was told by his local draft board that the application had been withdrawn. Friedman, meanwhile, was advised by his former employers at Berkeley that he would do better if he moved out of the area.

So it was that Lomanitz and Friedman left Berkeley on the same day, September 23, Friedman dropping Lomanitz off at the army induction center before setting off for Denver, Colorado, looking for a new job. Before they left, the two of them drafted a letter to Oppenheimer, explaining the problems they had been experiencing ("Promised jobs kept disappearing at the last moment") and stating as their "firm conviction" that "union discrimination is the cause of all that has happened." The night before they left, Weinberg hosted a farewell party for them at his apartment, where he was heard by counterintelligence agents, listening to the conversation via the microphones they had installed, telling them that, in the words of an agent's report, "he didn't believe Max [Friedman] was in his present predicament because of his Union affiliations but because of something else." A few days later, Lomanitz tried calling Oppenheimer at Los Alamos, but Oppenheimer refused to take the call.

Throughout the following months, Groves and Lansdale continued to insist to suspicious colleagues in the security services that, as Groves put it to a G-2 officer, Oppenheimer "will continue to be loyal to the United States." Groves, especially, did not want Oppenheimer to be distracted from his work at the laboratory by insistent and incessant questioning about his communist past and associates. He wanted Oppenheimer to get on with the job of building a bomb. Pash, meanwhile, devoted a great deal of time to trying to identify Eltenton's intermediary and contacts, making lists of suspects—invariably drawn from the physics and chemistry departments at Berkeley—which he distributed to G-2 and the FBI offices. At Oppenheimer's security hearing, Pash recalled how Oppenheimer's mention of, but refusal to name, a contact of Eltenton's who had gone, or was about to go, to Oak Ridge involved him in a "tedious project": "We had to go through files, try to find out who was going to go to site X." By this means he identified just one suspect, "and I took measures to stop—at least I asked General Groves to stop the man's movement to that area." Another time, according to Philip Stern, the author of a book on the Oppenheimer security case, one of the people identified by Pash as a candidate for one of Eltenton's contacts "suddenly, and without prior indication, boarded the *Daylight*, the crack San Francisco–Los Angeles train":

In order to gain time to get his agent to Los Angeles, Pash ordered the train stopped en route. Unhappily, his order was carried out in a most peremptory and undiplomatic way. Railroad officials were outraged. They complained to the commanding general, but since Pash's project was ultrasecret, Pash had not informed his superiors of his actions; nor could they pry any information out of the Colonel even after the rude train-stopping was traced to him. The ironic footnote is that the object of Pash's pursuit turned out to have nothing whatever to do with the case.

In November 1943, Groves seized upon a perfect opportunity to get Pash off the case and to make more constructive use of his bloodhound instincts. The opportunity arose as a result of the turning fortunes of the Allies. The past year had seen a series of decisive Allied victories that left no doubt that the question was not *whether* but *when* the Nazis would be defeated. In November 1942, the British under General Montgomery had routed Rommel's army at the Battle of El Alamein in Egypt, while the Americans landed a huge force in Morocco and Algeria, ready to link up with the British. In January 1943, the Russians won the hard-fought and extremely bloody Battle of Stalingrad, forcing the Germans to begin their long retreat from Russia and Eastern Europe. Six months later, in July 1943, the Russians beat the Germans in the massive tank battle at Kursk, and an Allied force of British, Canadian and American soldiers landed in Sicily, preparing to move through Italy. In September, the Italians surrendered and the following month declared war on Germany, whose forces still occupied much of Italy. Plans were afoot for two major Allied landings: the first in Anzio, in preparation for retaking Rome and driving the Germans out of Italy, and the second in Normandy, in preparation for retaking Paris and driving the Germans out of France. Meanwhile, the Russians were making steady progress pushing the Germans out of Poland.

In his Thanksgiving Day proclamation of November 25, 1943, President Roosevelt was able to find much for which to give thanks:

> God's help to us has been great in this year of the march towards world-wide liberty. In brotherhood with warriors of other United Nations our gallant men have won victories, have freed our homes from fear, have made tyranny tremble, and have laid the foundation for freedom of life in a world which will be free.

It is a proclamation that captures the tone of that time. Very few people doubted that the Allies would win the war. One very important question, however, remained unanswered and, for many who understood its importance, the optimism they felt about the seemingly inevitable defeat of the Nazis was tempered by anxiety. That question was: how far had the Germans got in building an atomic bomb? After all, everyone knew that, in Heisenberg, the Germans had someone who was, from a scientific point of view, every bit as able as Oppenheimer to exploit the tremendous energy released by nuclear fission in the manufacture of a deadly weapon. And, in persuading scientists to come to Los Alamos, Oppenheimer would almost invariably make use of this anxiety, arguing that it was important for everyone who could be useful to the project to join it, because not only was it of the utmost importance that the Allies beat the Germans in this deadly race, but the Germans had got a head start.

And so a mission was formed to accompany what was confidently assumed would be the successful Allied landings in Europe. Its aim was to determine what progress the Italians and the Nazis had made on the bomb. Heading the scientific side of the mission was Oppenheimer's old friend from Holland, Sam Goudsmit; heading the military side, so he was informed on the day Roosevelt made his Thanksgiving proclamation, was Lieutenant Colonel Boris Pash. The mission was called Alsos, the Greek for "Groves." On December 7, 1943, it left for North Africa, and within a week was in Naples, where it was based for the next few months, during which Pash, Goudsmit and their subordinates tried to find out as much as they could glean from Italian scientists.

On November 27, shortly before he left for North Africa, Pash forwarded to Lansdale a memo entitled "Possible identity of unnamed professor referred to by Dr. J. R. Oppenheimer," which had been written by Lieutenant James S. Murray, one of Pash's agents. "Efforts of this office during the past month," Murray wrote, "have been directed in an attempt to ascertain the identity of the professor contact." He went on:

> A record check of all professors and associates in both the physics and chemistry departments at the University of California was made with the Federal Bureau of Investigation and the results thereof contained in a progress report from this office dated October 20, 1943. A continued survey and check has been made and it is believed that it is entirely possible that the professor might be one of the following.

Murray then listed nine Berkeley scientists, one of whom was Joe Weinberg, whom he thought were candidates for being the unnamed professor. Of course, Chevalier was not one of those listed, since he was not a physicist or a chemist. With the implication that he had narrowed down the search to those nine people, Pash left Washington for North Africa.

A week or so after Pash left the U.S., those nine names were put aside after the true identity of Eltenton's intermediary was at last revealed. On December 12, during a visit to Los Alamos, Groves called Oppenheimer to his office and ordered him to reveal the intermediary. Oppenheimer duly named Chevalier, but did not admit that he himself was the person whom Chevalier had contacted for information on Eltenton's behalf. The following day, Lansdale wrote to the FBI, telling them what they surely ought to have known already: that Oppenheimer had told army security that three members of the atomic-bomb project had, as Lansdale put it, "advised him that they were approached by an unnamed professor at the University of California to commit espionage."

Lansdale went on to provide the fresh information that, having been ordered to name the professor, Oppenheimer had named Chevalier. The same day, Colonel Nichols, Groves's second-in-command, sent telegrams to Lieutenant Johnson in Berkeley, de Silva in Santa Fe and the security officer at Oak Ridge, telling them that Oppenheimer had named Chevalier as Eltenton's intermediary. The telegrams differed slightly (the one to de Silva, for example, mistakenly referred to Chevalier as a professor at the Rad Lab), but all three stated that Oppenheimer had expressed the belief that Chevalier had not approached anyone "other than [the] three original attempts."

When Lansdale was asked at Oppenheimer's security hearing to recall the first time he heard that Haakon Chevalier was the man he and (more strenuously) Pash had been trying to identify since the previous August, he was puzzled that his memory of the event did not match the written record. What he remembered, he said, was that Oppenheimer, at the time he named Chevalier, also revised his previous account about the three contacts, saying that there had actually been just one contact and that was his brother, Frank. Having read the contemporaneous documents, Lansdale testified, he could see that "the information was that the contact was with three persons . . . I have no explanation as to how I translate it from three into one." And he went on: "I called General Groves last night and discussed it with him in an attempt to fathom that and I can't figure it out. But the record shows clearly that there were three."

Groves was also puzzled. Asked whether he recalled the conversation in which Oppenheimer revealed Chevalier's name to him, he replied:

"Yes, but I have seen so many versions of it. I don't think I was confused before, but I am certainly starting to become confused today." "It was always my impression that he wanted to protect his brother," Groves added.

So the contemporaneous telegrams tell one story, Lansdale's memory tells another, and Groves's somewhat confused recollection seems, rather shakily, to support Lansdale. To add to the confusion, Oppenheimer told a third version of his conversation with Groves. According to Oppenheimer: "When I did identify Chevalier, which was to General Groves, I told him of course that there were not three people, that this had occurred in our house, that this was me."

Oppenheimer's claim that he told Groves the only person Chevalier had contacted was himself is not supported by any record or any recollection and can, I think, be discounted, since it is contradicted by every other account. The question that remains, then, is: did he, as the telegrams sent out on December 13, 1943, suggest, stick with his story that Chevalier had contacted three people, or did he, as Lansdale's memory and Groves's less clear impression indicate, tell Groves that the story of the three contacts had been a "cock and bull story," and that there had been only one contact and that contact was Frank?

The answer seems to be the latter. In FBI interviews with Groves, Lansdale and the U.S. Army lawyer Major William Consodine, the following story emerges: when ordered to name Eltenton's intermediary, Oppenheimer named Chevalier. When asked to name Chevalier's three contacts, however, Oppenheimer agreed to do so only on condition that Groves kept the names to himself, and, in particular, that he did not pass the names on to the FBI. Assuming that the three were Lomanitz, Weinberg and Bohm or Friedman—and therefore already under surveillance—Groves agreed. Oppenheimer then told him that there had been only one contact, namely Frank. When Groves returned to Washington, he discussed Oppenheimer's response with Lansdale and Consodine, and asked them whether he should be bound by his promise to Oppenheimer not to reveal Frank's name to the FBI. Consodine argued that he was not bound, because the demands of national security overrode those of a personal promise. Groves, however, was worried that, if he revealed Frank's name to the FBI, Oppenheimer would leave the project and—as Groves had long believed that Oppenheimer was essential to the project—that was, to him, more or less unthinkable.

So Groves honored his promise not to reveal Frank's name to the FBI, and the telegrams that were sent out to the various army-security offices duly maintained Oppenheimer's original "cock and bull story" about there being three contacts. Meanwhile, Lansdale, uncharacteristically and quite possibly uniquely, disobeyed Groves.[51] "I remember distinctly," Lansdale was to tell the security hearing of 1954, "going over to the FBI and visiting Mr. [E. A.] Tamm, who was then, I believe, assistant to J. Edgar Hoover, and Mr. [Lish] Whitson, who was the FBI Communist expert, [and telling them] that it was Frank Oppenheimer and that we had got that information, or that General Groves had obtained that information, on the express term that it would not be passed on." He added:

> Nothing could be clearer in my memory than that incident of going over at night and talking to Tamm and Whitson. Nothing could be clearer in my memory than General Groves's direction that I was not to pass it on to anybody, which I promptly violated in a very unmilitary manner . . . General Groves told me that, but I found it necessary to violate General Groves's direction in that regard and to give to the Bureau the identity of Frank Oppenheimer.

Just as Groves seems not to have let Nichols in on the secret, so Hoover and Tamm seem to have kept their own subordinates in the dark—at least for a while. By March 5, 1944, however, the story about Frank must have become known to FBI agents investigating the communist infiltration of the Rad Lab, since it is mentioned in a memo of that date entitled "Cinrad." The memo was written by FBI agent William Harvey and says that, after conferring with Groves, Oppenheimer "finally stated that only one person had been approached by Chevalier, that one person being his brother, Frank Oppenheimer."

What seems to have bothered Groves (and almost everybody who subsequently investigated the matter—including the FBI, army security, lawyers, journalists, historians and biographers) amazingly little about this story is that it stands no chance whatsoever of being true. If Chevalier approached Frank (and there is no evidence at all that he did, and prima facie evidence, in the form of denials by both Chevalier and Frank, that he did not), then it is *not* true that he approached only one person, since by Oppenheimer's and Chevalier's own admissions, Chevalier *did* approach Oppenheimer. So either Frank and Chevalier were lying, and

---

[51] The idea that Lansdale would disobey an order given to him by his commanding officer is so unlikely that one is forced to speculate that he informed the FBI of Frank's name with Groves's full permission—the pretense that this was against Groves's wishes allowing him to maintain that he *had* kept his promise to Oppenheimer, and the fact that Lansdale informed the FBI orally rather than in writing preventing anyone from proving otherwise. That he and Lansdale had connived to deceive Oppenheimer might also, I think, explain Groves's uncharacteristically foggy recollection of the event.

Chevalier approached both Frank and Robert Oppenheimer—in which case, Oppenheimer was lying to Groves about there being only one contact—or Chevalier did not approach Frank, in which case the story Oppenheimer told Groves in December 1943 is every bit as much (and quite possibly more) of a "cock and bull story" as the one he had told Pash in October. Either way, if his aim had been to protect Chevalier, that had gone horribly wrong. If his aim had been to protect Frank, then he had achieved partial and temporary success. If, on the other hand, his aim had been to protect himself, at least for as long as it took to build the bomb, then he had achieved complete success, but only because, given Groves's determination to keep him as director of Los Alamos, almost nothing he could have done would have resulted in failure in that regard.

Shortly before he named Chevalier to Groves, Oppenheimer had exchanged some very warm and sympathetic letters with him. In November 1943, Chevalier, not knowing where Oppenheimer was or what he was working on, wrote him what he later described as an "SOS call." "Are you still in this world?" he wrote to his old friend. "Yes, I know you are, but I am less sure about myself. I am in deep trouble. All my foundations seem to have been knocked out from under me, and I am alone dangling in space, with no ties, no hope, no future, only a past—such as it is." "I am close to despair," he went on, "and in such a moment, I think of you and I wish you were about to talk to."

> I don't know if this will reach you, which is the reason why I do not write you more. I should like to hear from you if you can spare time for the personally human, in these days when the human seems to become depersonalized.

On December 3—having in the meantime, to his astonishment and delight, received a reply—Chevalier wrote again: "I can't tell you how much it meant to me to receive your warm and unmistakably Oppjesque letter. I was startled, too, for when I wrote my SOS call I had no hope of receiving an answer." His despair, he explained, was partly to do with the breakup of his marriage, but also to do with his unwillingness, after a year's sabbatical, to return to teaching at Berkeley when he felt that, in the middle of the war, there were so many more important jobs to be done:

> I am, I suppose, in a sense a symbol of our time—perhaps an unimportant and negative one. I have certain talents, strong feelings and convictions and a definite capacity for work—and I have no place in this world. I feel very close to people and to the important problems

of our time, and yet I seem to be unable to get into a position where I can fulfill an important function.

Chevalier was writing from New York. He told Oppenheimer:

The specific reason I came here was to get a war-job. I came here with very good sponsorship—in fact I was asked to come here to work in the OWI [Office of War Information] and eventually be sent overseas in the Outpost Division. I have been here since the first of September and the job is still hanging fire, so to speak, for reasons that you know. I am investigating all possibilities, but it is likely that I will find the same obstacles elsewhere. Meanwhile my money ran out . . . I nearly got a job on Time at $150 a week a few weeks ago, but again was blocked in the last round on the same grounds.

In January 1944, Chevalier learned that his application for clearance for his proposed job at the Office of War Information had been rejected. In his memoir of his friendship with Oppenheimer, Chevalier recalls how, after four months of waiting to hear about his application for security clearance, he was called into the office of Joe Barnes from the Office of War Information:

His face was somber. He had just come back from Washington and there, exceptionally, he had been shown my FBI file. He said it contained allegations that were so fantastic as to be utterly unbelievable. "Someone obviously has it in for you," he said.

Chevalier did not learn until many years later exactly what these allegations were that had cost him his job at the OWI. "The last thing I could have imagined was that they had anything to do with Opje."

For the rest of the war, and for some time after that, Chevalier was put under close surveillance by the FBI, whose agents monitored his every move. He himself seems to have remained entirely unaware that he was being trailed, watched and listened to. For the first six months of 1944 he stayed in New York, earning a living as a journalist, translator and interpreter, before returning to California and eventually to teaching at Berkeley. Not until after the war was he interviewed by the FBI. Until then they were evidently hoping that their surveillance of him would lead to more information about Soviet espionage, which it did not.

The surveillance of Jean Tatlock, meanwhile, had been in operation since the end of August 1943 and had continued even after Pash's departure in November, the FBI evidently sharing Pash's view that she might be a go-between for Oppenheimer and the Soviet Union. By the time the Los Alamos laboratory was up and running, however, Jean Tatlock had little interest in politics, consumed as she was by more personal anxieties. On January 5, 1944, Charlotte Serber received a telegram from a friend of Jean's in Berkeley, Mary Ellen Washburn, telling her that Jean had committed suicide the previous day and asking her to break the news to Oppenheimer. She took the telegram to her husband, who in turn went to see Oppenheimer. "When I got to his office," Robert Serber writes in his autobiography, "I saw by his face that he had already heard. He was deeply grieved."

Jean's body had been discovered by her father the morning after she died. Worried that she had not been answering her phone, he had gone to her apartment, where, after getting no reply by ringing the doorbell, he climbed in through a window. He found her in the bath, her head submerged in water. On her dining-room table he found a suicide note, saying that she had become "disgusted with everything," that she thought she "would have been a liability all my life," and that, in killing herself, she felt that "at least I could take away the burden of a paralyzed soul from a fighting world."

How had Oppenheimer heard the news of Jean's suicide before Serber could tell him? The answer seems to be through the security services' surveillance of her apartment. According to Bird and Sherwin's biography of Oppenheimer, Captain Peer de Silva—a man committed to Pash's view that Oppenheimer and Tatlock were engaged in espionage—claims in an unpublished manuscript to have been the person who first informed Oppenheimer that Jean had killed herself. When told, de Silva writes, Oppenheimer "went on at considerable length about the depth of his emotion for Jean, saying that there was really no one else to whom he could speak." Bird and Sherwin, citing several instances of de Silva getting his facts wrong (for instance, de Silva asserts wrongly that Jean had cut her throat), insist: "De Silva is not a reliable observer, and it is not credible that Oppenheimer would confide in him." That de Silva is not a reliable witness is demonstrably true, and that Oppenheimer would not treat him as a confidant is almost certainly also correct. However, I find it entirely plausible to suppose that, apart from Jean's distraught father, the first people to learn of her suicide were the FBI and G-2, and, though Oppenheimer had no reason to regard de Silva as someone in whom to confide, I also find it perfectly believable that he responded to the news in the way that de Silva reports. After all, Oppenheimer obviously at this stage did not realize quite how deeply de Silva held him in contempt or how suspicious he was of him.

On January 6, the day after Oppenheimer learned of Jean's suicide, de Silva wrote a memo to the army security agent Captain Calvert at Oak Ridge, headed "Conversation with J.R. Oppenheimer," in which he reported the substance of a talk that he had had with Oppenheimer en route to Santa Fe. "During the course of the conversation," de Silva wrote, "Oppenheimer touched on the subject of what persons at Berkeley were in his opinion truly dangerous."

> He named David Joseph Bohm and Bernard Peters as being so. Oppenheimer stated, however, that somehow he did not believe that Bohm's temperament and personality were those of a dangerous person and implied that his dangerousness lay in the possibility of his being influenced by others. Peters, on the other hand, he described as a "crazy person" and one whose actions would be unpredictable. He described Peters as being "quite a Red" and stated that his background was filled with incidents which indicated his tendency toward direct action.

When presented later with de Silva's description of this conversation, Oppenheimer doubted its accuracy. The tone was wrong, he thought, and he also doubted that he had ever said Bohm was dangerous, since he was certain that he had never believed he was. He also rejected the implication in de Silva's memo that he himself had initiated the conversation and volunteered the opinion that Bohm and Peters were dangerous. "I think," Oppenheimer said, "what I was asked by de Silva [was] 'Here are four names, Bohm, Weinberg, and somebody else and Peters; which of these would you regard as the most likely to be dangerous?' and I think I answered Peters."

Even if we accept Oppenheimer's version of the conversation, it is impossible to avoid the impression that he betrayed someone who had been his student and his political comrade, if not his friend, and whose wife had been for a time his doctor. And, as he was repeatedly asked at his security case, if he considered Peters to be unpredictable, crazy and potentially dangerous, why, in the autumn of 1942, had he asked Peters and his wife to come to Los Alamos? His unconvincing answer was that he believed that, though Peters had been a member of the Communist Party in Germany, he had ceased to be so during the time of his friendship with Oppenheimer, and that Peters was not dangerous in October 1942, but became so after he had turned down Oppenheimer's invitation to come to work at Los Alamos.

Quite why Oppenheimer wanted to, or at the very least was willing to, blacken Peters's reputation is unclear. Like many of the things he said to security officers during these years, his remarks about Peters would come back to haunt him and severely damage his own reputation. There are some indications that Oppenheimer came to dislike Peters personally (when Sam Goudsmit once asked him about Peters, Oppenheimer replied: "Just look at him. Can't you see he can't be trusted?"), which might explain his cavalier attitude toward Peters's reputation. In the case of David Bohm, though, there is not even that possible explanation.

Just as he had with Peters, Oppenheimer had tried to recruit Bohm for Los Alamos. In March 1943, however, he was told that Bohm had been refused clearance, supposedly on the grounds that he still had relatives in Germany. Oppenheimer was understandably skeptical that those were the *real* grounds, and, despite his supposed remarks to de Silva about Bohm being potentially dangerous if led the wrong way, he was still, a year later, prepared to consider bringing Bohm to Los Alamos. On March 12, 1944, just two months after his conversation with de Silva, Oppenheimer was in Berkeley on business and, of course, being watched closely by army counterintelligence agents. What they learned was that Oppenheimer, during this trip, stayed at a hotel with Frank. Agents saw the Oppenheimer brothers leave the hotel and walk up and down the road outside, "engaged in earnest conversation with each other." Then David Bohm appeared, and "J.R. Oppenheimer and Bohm engaged in conversation for five minutes but Frank stood about 10 feet away from them and did not participate in the conversation."

When he returned to Los Alamos, Oppenheimer—presumably realizing that his conversation with Bohm had been observed, reported and filed—went to see de Silva to volunteer information about it. According to a memo written by de Silva on March 22, 1944, Oppenheimer told him that:

> ...just as he was preparing to leave his hotel at Berkeley on his return trip, David Joseph Bohm came to see him. Bohm inquired about the possibilities of his being transferred to project Y on a permanent basis, stating that he had a "strange feeling of insecurity" in his present surroundings. Oppenheimer stated he did not commit himself to Bohm but told him that he would let Bohm know if an opportunity were open at this project, and that if Bohm did not hear from Oppenheimer he should assume that such an arrangement was not workable and to forget the matter. Oppenheimer asked the undersigned if he would have objections to Bohm coming to project Y. The undersigned answered yes. Oppenheimer agreed and said the matter was therefore closed.

Bohm, like Weinberg, would spend the rest of the war at Berkeley, with agents monitoring his every movement, listening to his every phone call and making sure he had no access whatsoever to classified information. Oppenheimer, meanwhile, was able to forget, at least for a time, the suspicions leveled against his loyalty to the United States, and get on with the task of designing and building an atomic bomb.

13

Los Alamos 2: Implosion

A key moment in the development of the Allied atomic bomb was the signing by Churchill and Roosevelt on August 19, 1943, of the Quebec Agreement, which, in effect, subsumed the British "Tube Alloys" program under the Manhattan Project. "It is vital to our common safety in the present war," the agreement stated, "to bring the Tube Alloys project to fruition at the earliest moment," and "this may be more speedily achieved if all available British and American brains and resources are pooled." One of the terms of this agreement was that "In the field of scientific research and development there shall be full and effective interchange of information and ideas between those in the two countries engaged in the same sections of the field." Another was that "we will not either of us communicate any information about Tube Alloys to third parties except by mutual consent." As it turned out, these two terms were not consistent with each other. As the Venona transcripts were later to reveal, so effective was the Soviet penetration of the British atomic-bomb project and so ineffective was British counterintelligence that it was not possible to share information with the British without at the same time inadvertently communicating it to the Soviet Union.

Since the very beginning of the Tube Alloys project the Soviet Union had gained information on many of its secrets, primarily through the efforts of the Cambridge Five. Those five did not, however, have access to the detailed, technical information that the Soviets would need to build their own bomb. For that, they needed a scientist working on the project, and, from the summer of 1941, they had just such a person: a quiet, unobtrusive German, whom Hans Bethe once described as the only physicist he had ever met who had truly changed the course of history. His name was Klaus Fuchs.

Fuchs was a committed socialist and fervent anti-Nazi who had fled Germany in 1933, at the age of twenty-two. He studied at Bristol under Nevill Mott and at Edinburgh under Max Born, before, in May 1941, being invited by Rudolf Peierls to join the Tube Alloys project. By that time he had become a British citizen. Taking the view for which Oppenheimer had expressed sympathy in his discussions with Pash and Lansdale—namely that the Soviets had a right to know what their allies had discovered about the feasibility of making an atomic bomb—Fuchs considered it his duty to pass on to the Soviet Union any information that might be useful to them.

In August 1941, Fuchs established contact with an NKVD agent and from then on was, to the later dismay and astonishment of Peierls and his wife (with whom Fuchs lived in Birmingham), a regular informant on the progress of the Allied bomb project. That Fuchs was able to act so easily as a Soviet informant is an illustration of the differences between the British and the American attitudes to security, the British being more interested in the fact that Fuchs was an outstanding physicist with something to contribute to the Tube Alloys project than they were in the fact that he was a potential security risk—something they might well have discovered for themselves, had they shown a little more interest. As early as 1934, the German authorities had informed the British that Fuchs was a communist, but this tip-off was dismissed because it came from the Gestapo. In January 1943, the question of Fuchs's political activities was again raised, this time by British security, but an MI5 officer declared herself unconcerned. Fuchs, she said, "bears a good personal reputation and is considered a decent fellow." Later that year, the same officer observed: "As he [Fuchs] has been in his present job for some years without apparently causing any trouble, I think we can safely let him continue in it." In November 1943, as a result of the Quebec Agreement, the British scientists working on Tube Alloys were told they were transferring to the United States. Unfortunately for the U.S. project, clearance for these scientists was in the hands of MI5, who, concerning Fuchs, reported: "He is rather safer in America. It would not be easy for Fuchs to make contacts with communists there." Before he left the UK, Fuchs was given instructions via the Soviet intelligence service on how to do just that.

The first group of scientists to leave the UK to join the Manhattan Project included James Chadwick and Otto Frisch from Liverpool, William Penney from London, James Tuck from Oxford and Peierls and Fuchs from Birmingham. While the others went to Los Alamos, Peierls and Fuchs went to New York to work at Columbia on the development of the gaseous-diffusion method of isotope separation. Much of this work was written up by Fuchs himself, who managed to send copies of all his papers to the Soviets. Fuchs's contact in New York was Harry Gold, a chemist who had been acting as a Soviet courier since 1940. On February 5, 1944, Gold received from Fuchs a detailed report on gaseous diffusion and other aspects of the atomic-bomb project, which he then delivered to Soviet intelligence officers. Throughout his time in New York, which lasted until he was transferred to Los Alamos in August 1944, Fuchs met regularly with Gold, and, after a break of a few months, managed to resume contact with the Soviets while at Los Alamos.

Most of the scientists working on the Manhattan Project were shocked and disapproving when they learned after the war what Fuchs had done. They felt betrayed. On the other hand, the view that the Soviets, as allies, ought to be treated like the British and given access to information about the bomb was fairly widespread. What worried the scientists far more was the thought that the Germans might get the bomb. "We were desperately afraid that the Germans would beat us in our objective," Rudolf Peierls wrote. "Of course, everybody was anxious to know what progress, if any, the Germans were making with atomic energy." When Peierls was asked by British intelligence for suggestions on ways of finding out how far the German project had developed, he provided a list of names of people whose movements should, if possible, be watched. At the head of the list, of course, was Heisenberg. In reply, Peierls received a message from British intelligence that said Heisenberg had been in the UK shortly before the war, "and we have no record that he ever left the country." "I was shocked by this reaction," Peierls writes, "and reflected that if this was a fair sample of British intelligence, the outlook seemed grim."

His faith in the reliability of British security thus diminished, Peierls did a little intelligence-gathering of his own. He looked through recent editions of German academic journals in physics, copies of which were obtained by his university through neutral countries. In particular, he looked at the *Physikalische Zeitschrift*, which published a list of the lecture courses in physics in all German universities. With a few notable exceptions, such as Heisenberg, Peierls was reassured to find that most German physicists "were in their normal places and teaching their normal subjects." He concluded that, though there "did seem to be some atomic research going on, and Heisenberg and a few others were probably connected with it . . . the picture emerged that Germany had no crash program, no large-scale project that required a major participation by scientists."

As the Alsos mission was soon to discover, Peierls was quite correct. Others, however, particularly those working for the Manhattan Project, were less sanguine. On August 21, 1943, Bethe and Teller wrote to Oppenheimer, expressing their concern about recent newspaper reports that the Germans might be in possession of a powerful new weapon, which was expected to be ready sometime between November 1943 and January 1944. Their guess was that this new weapon was an atomic bomb: "It is not necessary to describe the probable consequences which would result if this proves to be the case."

Until 1944, Allied information about the progress of the Nazi bomb project remained scarce. Outside Germany, one of the few people to have had any kind of contact with Heisenberg since the war started was Niels Bohr. The nature and purpose of that contact, however, have been the subject of controversy ever since an account of it was published in 1956 in the German edition of the book *Brighter Than a Thousand Suns*, by the German journalist and writer Robert Jungk. The basis of that account was a letter written by Heisenberg to Jungk, in which he describes how, in September 1941, he took the opportunity of a visit to Copenhagen to attend a scientific meeting to call upon his old friend Bohr. At the outbreak of war Denmark had been a neutral country, but since April 1940 it had been under German occupation. As Bohr was half-Jewish and openly anti-Nazi, his position in Denmark was perilous, but, because of the semi-autonomy that the Nazis granted Denmark, he was not in any immediate danger.

He was, though—as both he and Heisenberg were fully aware— under close surveillance, and so, Heisenberg told Jungk, when he visited Bohr at his office, the two decided to take a walk through town while they talked. During this walk, Heisenberg claimed, he asked Bohr "whether it was right for physicists to devote themselves in wartime to the uranium problem—as there was the possibility that progress in that sphere could lead to grave consequences in the technique of war." Heisenberg remembers that Bohr reacted to this question with frightened alarm. The last time Bohr had thought deeply about fission—in Princeton in 1939 together with John Wheeler—he had concluded that there was no danger of anyone actually making an atomic bomb because of the difficulties of isotope separation. "Do you really think that uranium fission could be utilised for the construction of weapons?" Heisenberg recalls Bohr asking him, to which Heisenberg replied: "I know that this is in principle possible, but it would require a terrific technical effort, which, one can only hope, cannot be realised in this war." He went on:

> Bohr was shocked by my reply, obviously assuming that I had intended to convey to him that Germany had made great progress in the direction of manufacturing atomic weapons. Although I tried

subsequently to correct this false impression, I probably did not succeed in winning Bohr's complete trust.

When Bohr read this account, he was appalled at how little it accorded with his own memory of that meeting, and so he wrote, but did not send, a letter to Heisenberg, repudiating it. "Personally," he wrote, "I remember every word of our conversations, which took place on a background of extreme sorrow and tension for us here in Denmark." What made a particularly strong impression on him, he told Heisenberg, was "that you and [Heisenberg's colleague, Carl von] Weizsäcker expressed your definite conviction that Germany would win and that it was therefore quite foolish for us to maintain the hope of a different outcome of the war." He also remembered Heisenberg giving him the "firm impression that, under your leadership, everything was being done in Germany to develop atomic weapons":

> I listened to this without speaking since [a] great matter for mankind was at issue in which, despite our personal friendship, we had to be regarded as representatives of two sides engaged in mortal combat. That my silence and gravity, as you write in the letter, could be taken as an expression of shock at your reports that it was possible to make an atomic bomb is a quite peculiar misunderstanding, which must be due to the great tension in your own mind. From the day three years earlier when I realized that slow neutrons could only cause fission in Uranium 235 and not 238, it was of course obvious to me that a bomb with certain effect could be produced by separating the uraniums. In June 1939 I had even given a public lecture in Birmingham about uranium fission, where I talked about the effects of such a bomb but of course added that the technical preparations would be so large that one did not know how soon they could be overcome. If anything in my behaviour could be interpreted as shock, it did not derive from such reports but rather from the news, as I had to understand it, that Germany was participating vigorously in a race to be the first with atomic weapons.

Years later Oppenheimer, evidently basing his account on what he had heard from Bohr, said that Bohr had thought that Heisenberg and Weizsäcker came to Copenhagen "less to tell what they knew than to see if Bohr knew anything that they did not."

After his visit from Heisenberg, Bohr stayed in Denmark for another two years, during which time the situation for Danes hostile to the Nazis became ever worse. In the summer of 1943, the semi-autonomy enjoyed by Denmark throughout its occupation by Germany came to an abrupt end when, enraged by the Danes' refusal to obey an order to declare martial law, the Nazis reoccupied Copenhagen. Soon afterward it became very clear that Danish Jews—even those who were internationally renowned, Nobel Prize–winning physicists—were no longer safe. In the autumn of 1943, Bohr received a warning that he was about to be arrested by the Gestapo, whereupon he made plans to escape to Britain with his family.

Earlier that year, in January, Bohr had received, through clandestine means, a letter from James Chadwick, urging him to leave Denmark and promising him a warm welcome in Britain "and an opportunity of service in the common cause." Realizing that this was an effort to enlist him for the Allied attempt to build an atom bomb, Bohr replied turning the offer down. Not only, he told Chadwick, did he feel it his duty "to help resist the threat against the freedom of our institutions and to assist in the protection of the exiled scientists who have sought refuge here," but also "I have to the best of my judgment convinced myself that, in spite of all future prospects, any immediate use of the latest marvellous discoveries of atomic physics is impracticable." However, he did not rule out a change of prospects, circumstances or mind in the future, and then, he promised Chadwick, "I shall make an effort to join my friends and I shall be most thankful for any support they might be able to give me for this purpose."

A few months later, in August 1943, Bohr wrote again to Chadwick announcing a change of mind. "In view," he told Chadwick, "of the rumours going around the world, that large scale preparations are being made for the production of metallic Uranium, and heavy water to be used in atomic bombs, I wish to modify my statement as regards the impracticability of an immediate use of the discoveries in nuclear physics."

What had changed his mind? Jeremy Bernstein has suggested (persuasively, I think) that the cause of Bohr's volte-face was a visit he received in Copenhagen from the German physicist J. Hans D. Jensen in the summer of 1943. Jensen had been urged to speak to Bohr by Heisenberg, who, realizing that his own visit to Copenhagen had been something of a disaster, thought Jensen—well known among physicists to be politically left-wing—might soften Bohr's attitude toward the German atomic program. Much had happened in the two years that separated the two visits. In September 1941, when Heisenberg had visited Bohr, there was every reason to think that the Germans might win the war, and some reason, among the German physicists associated with what was officially known as the "Uranium Research Program," to think that the Nazis might be ahead of the Allies in the race to build an atomic bomb.

At an early stage, the Nazi bomb project had abandoned any attempt to build a bomb from uranium-235. The effort involved in separating uranium isotopes on an industrial scale was more than the wartime economy of Nazi Germany could cope with, especially as nobody on the Nazi side had realized what Frisch and Peierls realized—namely that the critical mass of U-235, using fast rather than slow neutrons, was surprisingly small. As was revealed after the war, Heisenberg's thinking about critical mass was fundamentally flawed. On his calculations, a bomb would require about one ton of pure U-235, and obtaining such a quantity was clearly out of the question. What Heisenberg and the other German physicists had realized at a fairly early stage, however, was that plutonium would be just as good as U-235 in a fission bomb and that it could be produced relatively easily in a nuclear reactor using unenriched uranium and slow neutrons.

For most of the war, therefore, the Nazi atomic project concentrated on building a reactor. The design of this reactor underwent several changes, but at an early stage it was decided not to use graphite as a moderator, as Fermi had done in Chicago, but rather to use heavy water. Heavy water differs from ordinary water in that its molecules consist not of two atoms of ordinary hydrogen and an atom of oxygen (H_2O), but rather of two atoms of deuterium and an atom of oxygen (D_2O or ^2H_2O), deuterium being the isotope of hydrogen the nucleus of which has a neutron as well as a proton. It is indeed possible to build a reactor using heavy water as a moderator, and several such reactors have in fact been constructed; the first to go critical was built by the Allies in Argonne, Illinois, in 1944. The problem, however, is that such reactors need many tons of heavy water (the one at Argonne used 6½ tons), which, though nothing like as difficult to obtain as uranium-235, is not easy to produce.

With the occupation of Norway in 1940, the Germans acquired the first and largest heavy-water production plant in the world, the Vemork plant at Lake Tinn, about eighty miles west of Oslo, which produced about twelve tons a year. The supply of heavy water from Vemork to the German atomic-bomb project, however, was successfully interrupted by a series of Allied attacks on the plant, most notably a commando raid in February 1943, a bombing raid in November 1943 and, finally, the sinking, in February 1944, of a ship loaded with heavy water that the Nazis were attempting to transfer to Germany. Heisenberg had estimated that a reactor built with the purpose of producing plutonium would need about five tons of heavy water. Thanks to the Allied operations in Norway, the German bomb project received in total during the war no more than three tons. Meanwhile, as part of the Canadian contribution to the Manhattan Project, a plant in Trail, British Columbia, was, from 1943 onward, producing six tons a year.

In the face of the huge technical and theoretical problems that stood in the way of designing and building an atomic bomb, and in the light of the deteriorating economic and military situation of Nazi Germany as the war went on, the German bomb project was scaled down at exactly the time when the Allied project gained its irresistible momentum, namely in the first half of 1943. When Heisenberg came to Copenhagen in September 1941, Nazi Germany had an atomic-bomb program based on the plan of building a heavy-water nuclear reactor that would produce enough plutonium to build a bomb; by the time Jensen visited Copenhagen in the summer of 1943, it had been conceded by the Nazis that there was little chance of nuclear energy having any direct military use for them and the sole purpose of what was left of their atomic program was to build a reactor for industrial purposes. In May 1943, Heisenberg gave a lecture to engineers and military officers in which he outlined a possible design for such a reactor. His design used plates of uranium, three tons of it, immersed in one and a half tons of heavy water. When Jensen visited Bohr he explained this design and emphasized that the intention was to use it for civil rather than military purposes.

Bohr evidently took from his conversation with Jensen only the information that the Germans were pressing ahead with the utilization of fission energy, without taking seriously, or perhaps without believing, the assurances that the intention was to build only a reactor, not a bomb—hence his remark to Chadwick that "large-scale preparations are being made for the production of metallic Uranium, and heavy water to be used in atomic bombs." As is shown by the rest of his letter to Chadwick, Bohr's knowledge and understanding of atomic-bomb physics at this time were fairly rudimentary and indeed, in some important respects, flawed and confused. He clearly knew nothing at all about plutonium and evidently believed that bombs could be made using slow neutrons and heavy water. The differences between an atomic reactor and an atomic bomb were obviously still not clear in his mind.

When he left Denmark to go to Britain, Bohr took with him a drawing of the reactor Jensen had described to him, apparently believing it to show the design of the Nazi atomic bomb and therefore thinking it had great military significance.[52] Bohr and his wife escaped Denmark by boat

---

[52] Thomas Powers (see *Heisenberg's War*) believes that this drawing was given to Bohr by Heisenberg, but this was emphatically denied by Bohr's son, which is why Bernstein

to Sweden and then by plane to Britain, arriving in Croydon, near London, on October 5, 1943. He was met from the plane by Chadwick, who took him to the Savoy Hotel in London, where he brought Bohr up to date on the developments in the Tube Alloys project: the Frisch-Peierls memorandum, the MAUD report and the Manhattan Project. That evening, Bohr officially became a member of the Tube Alloys project, and therefore part of the British "brains and resources" that the Quebec Agreement had stipulated should be shared with the U.S.

So it was that Bohr and his son, Aage, who was by this time a notable physicist in his own right and who had followed his parents to London, sailed to America at the end of November 1943 as part of the British mission to join the Manhattan Project. They arrived in New York on December 6, and then went to Washington to meet General Groves, after which they traveled with Groves by train to New Mexico, where Oppenheimer, with great and evident delight, welcomed them. After giving "Nicholas Baker" and his son "James" (as Niels and Aage Bohr were code-named) time to settle in, Oppenheimer convened a meeting of some of his most senior scientists, including Bacher, Bethe, Serber and Teller, to discuss the drawing that Bohr had brought with him and which he had already discussed with Groves. "It was clearly a drawing of a reactor," Hans Bethe later recalled, "but when we saw it our conclusion was that these Germans were totally crazy—did they want to throw a reactor down on London?" The following day, Oppenheimer was able to write to Groves telling him that what was depicted in the drawing Bohr had brought with him from Denmark "would be a quite useless military weapon."

Though Bohr had much to learn and very little to teach about the physics of the atomic bomb, he was so revered and so inspirational that having him at Los Alamos seemed to lift the spirits of all the scientists there. On January 17, 1944, after Bohr had left Los Alamos for Washington, Oppenheimer wrote to Groves to say that he hoped Bohr's collaboration with the project would continue, "since it has been of great help to us and is likely to be so throughout the year":

> By word and deed Dr. Baker has done everything he could to support this project and to indicate that he is sympathetic not only with its purposes and general method of procedure, but with the policies and achievements of the project's overall direction. I should like to make it quite clear that the effect of his presence on the morale of

---

developed the account that I have followed, which traces the origin of the drawing to Jensen's visit to Bohr in 1943.

those with whom he came in contact was always positive and always helpful, and that I see every reason to anticipate that this will be true in the future.

"Bohr at Los Alamos was marvelous," Oppenheimer said years later. He "took a lively technical interest" in what was going on and talked to many people, but his real function there, Oppenheimer said, was that:

> he made the enterprise which looked so macabre seem hopeful and he spoke with contempt of Hitler, who with a few hundred tanks and planes had hoped to enslave Europe; he said nothing like that would happen again and his own high hope [was] that the outcome would be good and that in this the role of objectivity, friendliness, cooperation that science had established would play a helpful part—all this was something that . . . we wished very much to believe.

By giving the project his blessing, Bohr, in the minds of many of the scientists at Los Alamos, gave it a legitimacy and a prestige that it did not have before, and this renewed their enthusiasm for the task and their willingness to put up with the otherwise uncongenial military situation in which they found themselves. That, presumably, is what the official history of Los Alamos means when it states that Bohr's influence "was to bring about stronger and more consistent cooperation with the army in the pursuit of the common goal." Regarding the technicalities of building a bomb, Bohr, despite his interest in the work being done at Los Alamos, realized that he had little to contribute. "They didn't need my help in making the atom bomb," he is reported to have told a friend after the war. What he *did* have to contribute—and in this respect he exerted an enormous influence on Oppenheimer's own thinking—were some wide-ranging thoughts on the politics of the bomb, which, had they been adopted, might have had a profound impact on the subsequent history of the world during the second half of the twentieth century.

When, almost as soon as he arrived in England, he was brought up to speed by Chadwick on the progress that had been made in designing and building a bomb, Bohr was disconcerted to discover how little thought had been devoted, either in England or in the United States, to the political implications the bomb would have for the postwar world. On his second night in England Bohr dined with Sir John Anderson (later Lord Waverley), who was then Chancellor of the Exchequer and the Cabinet minister responsible for Tube Alloys. Anderson was unusual among politicians in having a reasonably good grasp of the science behind the bomb, having studied science at the University of Leipzig, where he wrote his dissertation on the chemistry of uranium. Oppenheimer had a great deal of respect for Anderson, whom he described as "a conservative, dour and remarkably sweet man, who was very congenial in his spirit to Bohr and was a good friend to him." It was Anderson who invited Bohr to join the Tube Alloys project and then to go to Los Alamos as a member of the British mission.

Because of the universal esteem in which he was held, Bohr, though in many ways a simple and unassuming man, was given access to people at the very top of the social and political order. While he was in Washington, before he went to Los Alamos, a reception in his honor was held at the Danish embassy, at which he was able to renew his acquaintance with Felix Frankfurter, a Supreme Court associate and a close personal friend of the President. Though there was little opportunity on this occasion for extended discussion, Frankfurter invited Bohr to have lunch with him the next time he was in Washington.

When he left Los Alamos at the end of January 1944, Bohr went to Washington to take up this invitation. By this time he had thought very seriously about the postwar situation and had had what he regarded as a revelation about the "complementarity" of atomic bombs—a revelation as important, he believed, as his earlier epiphany regarding the complementarity of subatomic particles. Just as electrons are at one and the same time waves and particles, so, Bohr now believed, atomic bombs were at one and the same time the greatest danger to mankind and the greatest boon. Atomic bombs could put an end to civilization and human life itself, or, precisely because of that, they could bring an end to war. What was needed, Bohr felt, was a spirit of cooperation and, above all, *openness*. If the power of atomic bombs was made clear to everybody, Bohr reasoned, there would be at least the possibility of cooperation and therefore the possibility that this terrible weapon could turn out, because of its very terribleness, to be the best thing mankind had ever invented.

Bohr's view was therefore the exact opposite of the policy that the U.S. had adopted ever since the discovery of fission. Where that policy had been based on the attempt to prevent the Soviets from acquiring the "secret" of the bomb, Bohr believed that the best thing would be to consult the Soviet Union about the dangers to humanity posed by the development of such powerful weapons, and to treat the problem of controlling such weapons as one that demanded international cooperation rather than competition. In this way, he believed, those weapons would force upon the countries of the world a fundamental change in international relations, one that would make war itself obsolete.

Astonishingly, Frankfurter was sympathetic to Bohr's ideas and, even more astonishingly, thought President Roosevelt would be responsive to them. He thus offered to arrange a meeting between Bohr and Roosevelt. In a private memorandum he wrote about a year later, Frankfurter says that, when he mentioned Bohr's ideas to Roosevelt, the President "shared the hope that the project might bring about a turning point in history." The atomic bomb, Roosevelt told Frankfurter, "worried him to death," and he "was very eager for all the help he could have in dealing with the problem." He was therefore keen to meet Bohr, but, he said, he would not discuss this crucially important issue behind the back of his ally Winston Churchill, and so, before he met Bohr, he wanted Bohr to meet Churchill.

At the beginning of April 1944, therefore, Bohr, accompanied by Aage, flew to London for a meeting with Churchill. Shortly before, Anderson had written a memorandum for Churchill outlining Bohr's ideas and recommending that the Soviet Union be informed about "this devastating weapon." He went on to propose that it be invited "to collaborate with us in preparing a scheme for international control." On his copy of the memorandum Churchill had written beside the word "collaborate" the uncompromising reaction: "On no account."

Churchill kept Bohr waiting for over a month and did not see him until May 16. In the meantime, Bohr received via the Soviet embassy an invitation to go to the Soviet Union, "where everything will be done to give you and your family a shelter and where we now have all the necessary conditions for carrying on scientific work." He was also told by a Soviet official that they knew he had been in America and was asked directly what information he had received about the war work of American scientists, a question to which Bohr responded with bland generalities.

After his warm reception by Anderson and Frankfurter, Bohr's meeting with Churchill was a bitter disappointment. The meeting lasted a bare thirty minutes, most of which was taken up with Churchill's vehement dismissal of the idea of sharing information about the bomb with the Soviet Union. Bohr left the meeting under no doubt that his "revelation" would, if Churchill had anything to do with it, have no influence whatsoever on shaping Allied policy in the postwar period. This rebuff was something about which he remained angry for the rest of his life. "It was perfectly absurd to believe that the Russians cannot do what others can," he later said. "There never was any secret about nuclear energy." Churchill, for his part, dismissed Bohr from his mind—remarking to Frederick Lindemann (now Lord Cherwell), who had accompanied Bohr to Downing Street: "I did not like the man when you showed him to me, with his hair all over his head"—and turned his attention back to the preparations for D-Day.

These landings took place on June 6, 1944, and by the time Bohr left England an Allied force of several hundred thousand men was advancing through France. Back in Washington, he was urged by Frankfurter to put his ideas down in writing in the form of a memorandum for the President. This led to a meeting with Roosevelt in August, in which Roosevelt expressed sympathy for Bohr's ideas and suggested that Churchill could be won around. After Roosevelt and Churchill met in September, however, the opposite happened: Roosevelt came around to Churchill's view on the matter, the two of them agreeing not only that "the suggestion that the world should be informed regarding tube alloys, with a view to international agreement regarding its control and use, is not accepted," but also that "Enquiries should be made regarding the activities of Professor Bohr and steps taken to ensure that he is responsible for no leakage of information particularly to the Russians."

"The President and I are much worried about Professor Bohr," Churchill wrote to Cherwell on September 20, citing as grounds for concern Bohr's unauthorized discussions with Frankfurter and his contacts with the Soviet Union. "It seems to me," Churchill declared, "Bohr ought to be confined or at any rate made to see that he is very near the edge of mortal crimes." In the event, Churchill was dissuaded from actually locking Bohr up, but that was the end of Bohr's personal contacts with the leaders of the Western world. After recounting this story in his lectures on Bohr, Oppenheimer remarks: "This was not funny, it was terrible and it shows how very wise men, dealing with very great men, can be very wrong."

By the autumn of 1944, when Churchill and Roosevelt were agreeing to dismiss any notion of sharing the "secret" of the atomic bomb, it was becoming increasingly clear to the Allies that the Nazis, though fully aware of the potential military use of nuclear fission, had achieved only very limited progress toward building a bomb. In February 1944, the Alsos mission had returned to Washington from Italy, where they had been able to do little but wait for the Allies to break through the German lines. After the landings at Anzio in January, the Allied forces had met with determined resistance at Monte Cassino, preventing them from advancing into Rome. When the Germans were finally defeated at Monte Cassino in May, however, the Alsos mission returned to Italy, and Colonel Pash was able to enter Rome with the victorious Allied forces on June 5.

After questioning the leading physicists left in Italy and finding that they knew next to nothing about the German atomic-bomb program, Pash and his team switched to France, where they followed the advance of the massive force that had landed on D-Day. In August 1944, following the liberation of Paris, Alsos was able to interrogate Frédéric Joliot-Curie, who told them at least *something* they did not already know, namely that the German program was probably led by Kurt Diebner. Then, finally, in November 1944, after Strasbourg was taken by the Allies, Pash and Goudsmit, after reading through files taken from Weizsäcker's office, had pretty conclusive proof that the Germans had not so far managed to construct a working nuclear reactor, and that they had no serious program to build an atomic bomb.

The knowledge that there was no danger at all of the Nazis building an atomic bomb before the Allies did not have the effect that one might have expected. Most of the scientists who had been recruited to Los Alamos had been persuaded to work on the project because of the awful possibility of losing the race against the Nazis. Now that it was clear there was no such possibility, did that not call into question the whole rationale of the Allied bomb project? In fact, only one person left the project after the discovery of the rudimentary state of the Nazi bomb effort. That man was Joseph Rotblat, a Polish Jew who had done pioneering work on nuclear fission at the University of Warsaw, after which he was offered a fellowship at Liverpool to work with Chadwick. He arrived in Liverpool in the summer of 1939, having left his wife in Poland because she was too ill to travel. The intention was that she would follow him to England, but after the Nazi invasion of Poland she was unable to leave the country and he was unable to return. He never saw her again.

Feeling deeply the anxiety aroused by the prospect of the Nazis being first to develop the atomic bomb, Rotblat was an enthusiastic participant in the British Tube Alloys project and was happy to go with the British mission to Los Alamos. In March 1944, however, when he had been at Los Alamos for just two months, he received what he later described as a "disagreeable shock," when, at a dinner party given by the Chadwicks, he heard Groves say: "You realise of course that the main purpose of this project is to subdue the Russkies." "Until then," Rotblat said, "I had thought that our work was to prevent a Nazi victory, and now I was told that the weapon we were preparing was intended for use against the people who were making extreme sacrifices for that very aim." On December 8, 1944, very soon after it had been established beyond all reasonable doubt that there was no danger either of the Nazis winning the war or of them developing the bomb, Rotblat left the Manhattan Project. Despite efforts by the FBI to show that he had been a Soviet spy, he went on to have an outstanding career as a physicist. Feeling betrayed by the use of the atomic bomb against the Japanese, Rotblat devoted himself for the rest of his life to the cause of nuclear disarmament, his contribution to which was recognized by the award of the Nobel Peace Prize in 1995.

Astonishingly, Rotblat was the only person ever to leave the Manhattan Project on grounds of conscience. Why? A clue, perhaps, is contained in Fermi's remark, when, during a visit to Los Alamos, he exclaimed to Oppenheimer: "I believe your people actually *want* to make a bomb." Though most of them had originally been motivated by the thought of the Nazis getting there first, after a while at Los Alamos they simply wanted to see the project through to a successful conclusion. This, I think, cannot be understood without taking into account just *how* successful Oppenheimer was as the director of the Los Alamos laboratory.

When scientists were asked to recall their time at Los Alamos, one thing that is repeated over and over again is how inspirational Oppenheimer was. His influence went beyond that of a laboratory director; he was seen as the leader of an entire community—a community that was somehow purer, more noble, *better* than the world from which it was so conspicuously and effectively cut off. For his book on Oppenheimer and Lawrence, Nuel Pharr Davis collected a series of eulogies of Oppenheimer from those who had worked with him on the bomb. Among them was the British scientist James Tuck, who captured the prevailing mood of the place when he described Los Alamos as "the most exclusive club in the world," where "I found a spirit of Athens, of Plato, of an ideal republic":

> By the grace of God the American government got the right man. His function here was not to do penetrating original research but to inspire it. It required a surpassing knowledge of science and of scientists to sit above warring groups and unify them. A lesser man could not have done it. Scientists are not necessarily cultured, especially in America. Oppenheimer had to be. The people who had been gathered here from so many parts of the world needed a great gentleman to serve under. I think that's why they remember that golden time with enormous emotion.

True, Oppenheimer had never managed a laboratory (or anything) before, and as a physicist he was as purely theoretical as it is possible to be. And yet, in a way that amazed and impressed everybody who knew him, his entire life up to that point—his early interest in minerals, his determinedly wide-ranging education at Harvard, his absorption in the literature and art of America, France, England, Germany, Italy and Holland, his mastery of several European languages, his omnivorous devouring of all aspects of theoretical physics and his close following of major developments in experimental physics—turned out to be the perfect preparation for the task he had been set. He was the ideal man to lead

Los Alamos, considered not just as a laboratory, but also as a new kind of city, one with far more than the normal proportion of extremely clever people and one, moreover, devoted to the accomplishing of a single, extraordinarily demanding task.

Hans Bethe memorably remarked to Pharr Davis that Oppenheimer "worked at physics mainly because he found physics the best way to do philosophy," adding: "This undoubtedly had something to do with the magnificent way he led Los Alamos." Bethe is surely right. Oppenheimer could bring to the task the intellectual detachment of a man who could see the bigger picture and therefore not get bogged down in detail. However, though this is true and important, what sticks in many people's minds is the remarkable way in which he could grasp the details in every aspect of the laboratory's work. Norris Bradbury, who was to replace Oppenheimer as the director of Los Alamos, recalls: "Oppenheimer could understand everything, and there were some hard physics problems here to understand."

> I've seen him deal incredibly well with what looked like dead-end situations technically speaking. It was not that his decisions were always correct. But they always opened up a course of action where none had been apparent. They were made with a sense of dedication that moved the whole laboratory. Don't forget what an extravagant collection of prima donnas we had here. By his own knowledge and personality he kept them inspired and going forward.

"He could understand anything," echoed Robert Serber. "One thing I noticed: he would show up at innumerable different meetings at Los Alamos, listen and summarize in such a way as to make amazing sense. Nobody else I ever knew could comprehend so quickly."

> And along with this, he developed tremendous tact. There was a big advisory council that gave Los Alamos the appearance of a democracy just because he handled it so well. Everybody was convinced that his problems were the urgent and important ones, because Oppenheimer thought so.

Oppenheimer had arrived on "the Hill" (as people who lived there called Los Alamos) determined to use all his persuasiveness, all the power of his many and varied intellectual gifts and the best physicists in the country (and beyond) to solve the very difficult problem he had been set: to design and build a type of bomb that no one had ever seen, which could be manufactured with either of two metals, one of which was a rare isotope of uranium that was *extremely* difficult to separate and the other a metal that did not exist in nature, and which, up to that point, existed only in microscopic amounts. The design of this bomb was dependent upon a number of facts about these metals that so far remained unknown: what were the critical masses of U-235 and plutonium? What were their densities? When they fissioned, how many neutrons were released per fission? How fast did the emitted neutrons travel? And, given the time restraints placed upon the completion of this project—the target set was two bombs, usable for military purposes, to be produced by the summer of 1945—the design of these bombs had to proceed *alongside* (not after) the scientific discovery of these facts. In other words, the bomb had to be engineered in the dark, with the expectation that it would be *re*-engineered when light dawned. This was extremely wasteful, but the U.S. government was apparently prepared to give Groves an unlimited budget to see this project through.

From the very beginning it had been decided that *both* uranium and plutonium bombs would be built. Each had its advantages and disadvantages. The advantage of uranium was that, thanks to the early theoretical work done by Bohr and Wheeler in 1939 and the intensive experimental work subsequently carried out in both Britain and America, the basic science of the fission process for U-235 was pretty well known and understood. It is true, as David Hawkins points out in his official history of Los Alamos, that in April 1943, when the scientists started to gather on the Hill, there were still two possible reasons for doubting that an atomic bomb using U-235 could be made. The first was that "the neutron number had not been measured for fission induced by fast neutrons, but only for 'slow' fission." The second was that "the time between fissions in a fast chain might be longer than had been assumed." However, even Hawkins concedes it was "extremely unlikely" that either of these questions, once settled, would turn out to provide a serious barrier in the way of building a uranium bomb. And so, rather quickly, it was proved. By the end of 1943, both these questions had been answered: the neutron number for fast fission was greater than two, and therefore an explosive chain reaction using fast neutrons could be produced just as surely as Fermi in Chicago had produced a controlled, nonexplosive chain reaction using slow neutrons. And, as Robert Wilson established, the time between fissions in U-235 was *not* long enough to prevent an explosion from occurring.

After the first nine months of the laboratory's work, then, the science of a uranium bomb was, as Teller had announced it as being a year earlier, a solved problem. The problem was, as Bohr had seen in 1939 and as the Germans had discovered for themselves, that the effort involved in separating enough U-235 to make a bomb was almost unimaginably huge. When Bohr arrived in Los Alamos, having been brought up to date on the Manhattan Project by Chadwick, Groves and Oppenheimer, he said to Teller: "You see, I told you it couldn't be done without turning the whole country into a factory. You have done just that."

In fact, at the end of 1943, it was beginning to look as if even turning the whole country into a factory might not be enough; the construction of the enormous electromagnetic and gaseous-diffusion plants at Oak Ridge, occupying several square miles and employing tens of thousands of people, did not look likely to produce what was required to make one bomb, let alone two. The Y-12 (electromagnetic) site, in the words of the historian of the atomic bomb, Richard Rhodes, was by that time "dead in the water with hardly a gram of U-235 to show for all its enormous expense." Neither had gaseous diffusion—though it was looking like a more promising method than electromagnetic separation—yet produced any significant amounts of enriched uranium. In January 1944, the navy began work on a plant in Philadelphia that used a different method of isotope separation: thermal diffusion. As this looked promising, a thermal-diffusion plant, S-50, was added to the existing plants at Oak Ridge. In the meantime, Lawrence and the Rad Lab team at Berkeley worked around the clock to get the Calutrons at Y-12 working, while the physicists at Columbia, supported by Fuchs and Peierls, worked equally hard trying to perfect the gaseous-diffusion plants at K-25; but it was clear to Groves and Oppenheimer that, even with this truly colossal effort, there was no possibility whatsoever of having enough U-235 to make two bombs by the summer of 1945. If they were going to achieve this target, they would have to produce at least one plutonium bomb.

But, of course, plutonium too had its problems. Just as the severe difficulties in separating uranium-235 had convinced the Germans that the *only* practical route to the atomic bomb lay in producing plutonium, so the British Tube Alloys project had considered only the uranium bomb, for reasons equally compelling: plutonium does not exist in nature and nobody knew very much about it. The idea that one could build a bomb using a metal, the basic science of which had yet to be done, seemed fanciful. At Los Alamos, Oppenheimer set about coordinating that basic science, while *at the same time*, designing a bomb that would make use of its results. Inevitably, therefore, there was a lot of guesswork and many false starts.

Given that the physics of uranium fission was relatively well advanced and the task of making a bomb out of uranium (assuming enough U-235 could eventually be produced) relatively straightforward, the Los Alamos laboratory concentrated its considerable financial and intellectual resources on the plutonium bomb. When the scientists at Los Alamos talked of the "gadget," what they were referring to more often than not was the plutonium bomb. And, in particular, during the first year of the laboratory's work, they were referring to a plutonium bomb using what Serber in his introductory lectures had called the "gun assembly method." This is the basic bomb design originally envisaged by Frisch and Peierls in their memorandum, in which the fissionable material—uranium-235 or plutonium—is split into two subcritical parts, one larger than the other. The smaller part is then fired into the larger part, thus assembling a supercritical mass of the fissionable substance.

Though much about the chemistry and metallurgy of plutonium remained to be discovered, two extremely important things about it were already known. The first was that its critical mass is smaller than that of U-235, though exactly how much smaller had yet to be determined. The second was something brought to Oppenheimer's attention by Glenn Seaborg, the discoverer of plutonium, just before work at Los Alamos began, the full significance of which would not be appreciated until the summer of 1944, when the realization dawned that, in fact, it threatened to undermine the entire bomb project.

What Seaborg pointed out was that plutonium, despite its many advantages as a fissionable bomb material, had a potential disadvantage, which has to do with what is called "spontaneous fission." Unlike ordinary nuclear fission, spontaneous fission does not require the nucleus of an atom to be hit by a neutron; it is, rather, a kind of radioactive decay, like the alpha emissions of substances such as radium (or, indeed, uranium and plutonium)—something that occurs without anything being done to the material. When spontaneous fission takes place, the result is the same as ordinary nuclear fission: the nucleus splits, neutrons are emitted and energy is released. Spontaneous fission created a problem for gun-assembly atomic bombs because the neutrons emitted by it might set off a chain reaction before the two pieces of the fissionable material could be brought together. This chain reaction, though it would produce a great deal of heat and energy, would not be explosive, and therefore the bomb would "fizzle."

Just as it was known that heavy nuclei with odd mass numbers—U-235 and Pu-239—are more liable to undergo ordinary nuclear fission, so it was known that those with even mass numbers, such as U-238, are more likely to undergo spontaneous fission. This meant, Seaborg explained to Oppenheimer, that Pu-240, an isotope of plutonium, would be likely to have a high rate of spontaneous fission. In the spring of 1943, this was a merely theoretical worry, since no Pu-240 had yet been created, but, Seaborg warned, it was likely that the plutonium produced in a nuclear reactor would not be pure Pu-239, but rather a mixture of Pu-239 and Pu-240. This is because in a reactor there are far more free neutrons flying around than in a laboratory accelerator such as a cyclotron (until the nuclear reactors at Oak Ridge and Hanford started to go critical, the only plutonium anyone had ever seen had been produced by cyclotrons), and it is therefore more likely that some Pu-239 nuclei would absorb a neutron and become Pu-240.

To begin with, this warning of spontaneous fission, though taken seriously, was not treated as potentially fatal to the entire project, largely because it was assumed that the differences between accelerator-produced plutonium and reactor-produced plutonium would not be so very great. Soon after work got under way at Los Alamos, Emilio Segrè was put in charge of experiments designed to measure the rate of spontaneous fission in both uranium and plutonium, using material obtained from cyclotrons, and his initial results were very encouraging. The rate was, he discovered, not large enough to make the gun method impossible. True, the gun in the plutonium bomb would have to fire its "bullet" pretty fast, and the gun barrel would have to be pretty long, but there seemed to be no reason, in principle, why such a gun could not be designed and built. One thing making it easier, ballistics experts were quick to point out, was that, unlike almost every other gun ever made, it would be fired just once, so durability was not an issue.

When the figures were established, Deak Parsons and his rapidly growing ordnance team were set the task of designing a gun capable of firing a piece of plutonium a distance of seventeen feet into another larger piece of plutonium at a speed of 3,000 feet per second. Making this task much more demanding was the fact that they were to do so in advance of any hard information about the relevant chemical and metallurgical properties of plutonium. Dealing with such uncertainties might be what theoretical—and, to a lesser extent, experimental—physicists did for a living, but it was not what engineers were used to. The first three men chosen to head the Engineering Group in Parsons's division left after a short time in the job, because, as Parsons put it, of the "frustrations which these people experienced when one week they thought they had a problem in mind, and had evolved a solution, only to find, when they proposed it, that the concept of the problem had changed in the meantime and their solution was irrelevant."

Despite the many difficulties and uncertainties, by January 1944 the "gadget" had been designed and a suitable name, the "Thin Man," had been chosen for it. All that remained, so it was believed, was for Parsons and his Ordnance Division to test the dropping of it and work out the details of its internal ballistics. A few months later, however, in April

1944, Segrè finally received some samples of reactor-produced plutonium and, to everybody's horror, discovered that the rate of spontaneous fission was *five times* that of the cyclotron-produced samples he had measured earlier. Just as Seaborg had warned, the plutonium had far more Pu-240 in it than that produced by a cyclotron. The alarming but inescapable conclusion was that the "Thin Man" was a nonstarter. The whole idea of a gun-assembly plutonium bomb—the idea that up until then had formed the central focus for almost all the work done at Los Alamos—would have to be abandoned.

This was devastating news, but in Segrè's earlier measurements of spontaneous fission in uranium there was a silver lining: a gun-assembly bomb made with uranium *would* work and, in fact, was even more straightforward than they had thought. The uranium bullet could be fired at a mere 1,000 feet per second and the length of the gun could be reduced from seventeen feet to six. Thus, in place of the plutonium "Thin Man" bomb, there emerged the uranium "Little Boy," the bomb that would be dropped on Hiroshima. So confident were Oppenheimer and his colleagues that "Little Boy" would work that they did not see any need to test it. The bomb was designed and built and then left to one side, waiting for the U-235 that would form both the bullet and its target.

Until recently, every book about the history of the atomic bomb has contained a false description of Little Boy's design. Perhaps misled by the Frisch-Peierls memorandum and by *The Los Alamos Primer*, the published accounts of the bomb invariably state that the gun assembly worked by firing a small uranium bullet into a slightly subcritical mass of U-235, thus forcing it to go supercritical. In fact, the material was split almost in half: at one end of the gun was a group of rings of U-235 that formed 40 percent of the supercritical mass, and at the other end another group of slightly larger rings that formed 60 percent. And it was this latter, larger group that was fired onto the smaller group. At the same time, neutrons were emitted from a polonium-beryllium "initiator," thus causing the supercritical mass to explode.

For more than fifty years this was an official secret, known only to those who worked on the bomb. Then, in 2004, a truck driver from Illinois called John Coster-Mullen published a book that contained the first-ever publicly available accurate description of the Little Boy bomb. Coster-Mullen's hobby was model-making and he had set himself the task of producing an accurate model of the Hiroshima bomb, to accomplish which he made a close study of every photograph and every document available. His research convinced him that the accounts published up to that time were wrong, and he set about correcting them. That he, a man without a university degree in physics (or, indeed, anything else), was able to reverse-engineer the bomb and produce an accurate and detailed account of its design shows, perhaps, the wisdom of Bohr's remark that there never was any secret about how to make a fission bomb. Or, as Coster-Mullen himself has put it, what his research has shown is that the real secret of the atomic bomb is how easy it is to build one.

At the beginning of July 1944, Oppenheimer broke the news to the scientists gathered for the Los Alamos weekly meeting that the plutonium "gadget," as it had been conceived up until that point, would have to be abandoned; there was absolutely no prospect of producing a gun-assembly plutonium bomb. The reason it took three months to make this announcement is that Segrè, Oppenheimer and Groves, so appalled were they at the consequences of Segrè's results, kept hoping that further experiments, further measurements, would show those results to be incorrect. Alas, no matter how many times Segrè and his team counted the spontaneous fissions produced by reactor-produced plutonium, the result was always the same: too high for gun assembly to be workable. Groves had even been reluctant to inform the scientists at the Met Lab in Chicago of the results. When, at the beginning of June 1944, Robert Bacher told him of his intention to report Segrè's findings to the scientists there, Groves replied: "Do you think that needs to be reported to them?" "Of course," Bacher replied, "it's a fundamental fact of the material they're working on." When he did tell them, Bacher recalls that Compton "went just as white as that sheet of paper."

In the late spring of 1944, then, it looked extremely doubtful that the Manhattan Project would succeed in achieving the goals set for it. For, if there was no prospect of a gun-assembly plutonium bomb, neither, given the agonizingly slow progress at Oak Ridge, was there any hope of producing two gun-assembly uranium bombs by the following summer. If they were to meet the target set for them, therefore, they would have to start from scratch and design a plutonium bomb fundamentally different from the "gadget" they had had in mind during the previous year.

That the laboratory was able to do just that is astonishing and demonstrates, as well as the resolute determination of everyone involved, the foresight and adaptability that Oppenheimer brought to his task as director. Thanks to his foresight, an alternative to the gun-assembly plutonium bomb lay ready to hand: the implosion method of detonation, first suggested by Richard Tolman, elaborated upon by Robert Serber and pursued with tenacious dedication at Los Alamos by Seth Neddermeyer. Oppenheimer's adaptability is shown in the way that, in the summer of 1944, he reorganized the whole laboratory, turning it away from the "Thin Man" and toward what became known as the "Fat Man," the plutonium implosion bomb that would—thanks to an almost unimaginably intense effort—be ready for military use just a year later.

For the first six months of work at Los Alamos, implosion was very much a side issue, comparable in that respect to the work Edward Teller was pursuing on the "Super." Like the Super, it was seen as something that was potentially interesting, both scientifically and militarily, but, compared to the gun-assembly gadget, of marginal concern to the project. To pursue implosion, Neddermeyer had a team of just eight people, who spent their time in a remote canyon performing experiments with explosives that most people on the Hill thought were leading nowhere. Among those sceptics was L. T. E. Thompson, a naval ballistics expert whom Parsons consulted and whose judgment he trusted above that of any other advisor. "Dr. Tommy" (as he was known to Parsons and his family) came to Los Alamos in the summer of 1943 and observed a demonstration given by Neddermeyer of the basic idea of implosion. "It seems to me," Thompson announced afterward, "there is a fundamental difficulty with the system that makes it quite certain not to be satisfactory."

The "system" he was commenting upon was, in some important respects, quite different from the implosion device first envisaged by Tolman and described by Serber. What Tolman and Serber had imagined was a way of assembling a critical mass of plutonium (or uranium) that brought together several pieces of the metal arranged in a circle. What Neddermeyer had in mind, rather, was something more subtle, which would exploit the fact that critical mass is affected by density. For a fairly straightforward reason, the critical mass of a dense piece of material is lower than that of a less-dense piece. The reason is that, in a dense piece of matter, the distance—and therefore the time—that a neutron has to travel before it causes fission is smaller, and so, the denser the material is, the smaller it can be while still being able to undergo the eighty generations of fission needed for an explosion.

Neddermeyer's concept of implosion exploited this fact in a novel way. Instead of having a bomb that *assembled* a critical mass by bringing together two or more subcritical masses—which was the idea behind both the gun-assembly design and the Tolman-Serber version of implosion—Neddermeyer proposed turning a subcritical mass of material into a supercritical mass by squeezing it. His design called for a subcritical hollow sphere of uranium or plutonium to be blown inward, imploded, uniformly, so that its density increased to the point at which it would go supercritical. The squeezing would be achieved by explosives arranged around the sphere. The "fundamental difficulty" that Thompson identified was that the design required the external pressure on the sphere to be exactly symmetrical. If it were not, the sphere would not be transformed into a denser sphere, but rather flattened, "in about the manner of a dead tennis ball hit with a hammer," as Thompson put it in a letter to Oppenheimer of June 1943.

Until September 1943, Neddermeyer was almost alone at Los Alamos in thinking that this problem could be overcome and that implosion would turn out to offer a practical method of creating an atomic bomb. In their efforts to solve the problem, Neddermeyer and his team conducted experiments in which they surrounded stove pipes with TNT, which they then detonated, trying to get the pipes to collapse symmetrically. The results were not encouraging. Those who were called upon to witness these experiments, and the nonsymmetrically flattened pipes they invariably produced, were unimpressed. Then, in September 1943, Oppenheimer, Groves and some of the leading theoreticians at Los Alamos suddenly began to take implosion more seriously and to regard it as a centrally important part of the laboratory's work. This was six months before Segrè's devastating news about the spontaneous fission of reactor-produced plutonium, and was completely unrelated to any perceived problems with the gun-assembly design. The renewed interest in implosion was, rather, stimulated at this early stage by the problems in obtaining significant amounts of enriched uranium, in the light of which a method that offered the possibility of building a bomb that required a smaller critical mass of uranium and did not need such pure uranium seemed well worth exploring.

Fresh hope for the implosion program was provided that September by a visit to Los Alamos of John von Neumann. Von Neumann was a Jewish émigré from Budapest who was considered, among some extraordinarily stiff competition (Teller, Szilard, Wigner, to name but three), to be the most brilliant of the Hungarian scientists associated with the Manhattan Project. Having, while still a young man, made fundamentally important contributions to a wide variety of disciplines (including logic, mathematics, quantum theory and economics), von Neumann moved to the United States in 1930, and in 1933, at the age of twenty-nine, was appointed professor of mathematics at Princeton's Institute for Advanced Study. He had the kind of mind that could turn to anything and, as luck would have it, during the war he became interested in the mathematics and physics of explosives. This led to a series of consultancies, mainly for the U.S. Navy, in which he demonstrated time and time again the military usefulness of a powerful intellect. Oppenheimer and Parsons were desperate to get him to Los Alamos, but were unable to tempt him to come on a full-time basis. The best they could do was persuade him to make "an occasional visit to Santa Fe," as Parsons put it in a letter to him of August 1943.

On his first such visit, at the end of September 1943, von Neumann, during the two weeks that he was at Los Alamos, put the implosion program on a completely different footing, replacing the skeptical indifference toward the project that had prevailed up until that point with a lively, intense and optimistic interest. This was largely because of the seriousness with which he himself treated Neddermeyer's research. Such was the awe in which von Neumann was held that the leading scientists at Los Alamos began to think that, if *he* was interested in implosion, there must be something to it. With regard to the technical problem that Neddermeyer was attempting to solve, von Neumann's initial contribution was to suggest two things: 1. increase the amount of explosive used to implode the fissionable material so as to increase the speed of the implosion; and 2. use "shaped" explosive charges, which make better use of the physical properties of shock waves (in the mathematics of which von Neumann was by this time probably the world's leading expert).

Shaped charges (or "hollow charges" as they are known in Britain) had been discovered in the nineteenth century, but were not exploited militarily until the advent of armor-piercing shells in the Second World War. The basic idea is that, instead of having a solid explosive charge— like, say, a stick of dynamite—one hollows the charge out, leaving an empty space. It was found that this concentrates the energy produced by the explosion (because the energy released rushes to fill the empty space), allowing more penetrative weapons to be designed and built. Von Neumann was an expert on this kind of charge and realized that if, instead of simply surrounding his target material with TNT, Neddermeyer arranged a series of shaped charges around it and was then able to ensure the charges all went off at the same time, implosion might just work.

Charles Critchfield, who was a member of Neddermeyer's team, has described how von Neumann's suggestions "woke everybody up." After von Neumann's visit, he remembered, Teller called him, saying: "Why didn't you tell me about this stuff?" At a meeting of the Los Alamos Governing Board of October 28, 1943, Oppenheimer gave reasons for giving high priority to the implosion program—reasons based largely on the interest that von Neumann had shown in it. He mentioned in passing that von Neumann believed that the speed of implosion (if the charge was great enough and arranged well enough) was so great that "there is less danger of pre-detonation," but at this stage what really excited Oppenheimer, Groves and Teller about implosion was the promise it offered of reducing the quantity of enriched uranium needed to make a bomb. In his report to the Governing Board of November 4, 1943, Oppenheimer remarked that "both Groves and Conant seemed very much in favor of pushing the implosion method . . . the only one which offers some hope of justification for the electromagnetic method." In other words, the only remaining hope for the hugely expensive Calutrons at Oak Ridge was not that they could produce enough enriched uranium for a gun-assembly bomb—that clearly looked like a false hope—but rather that they might produce enough, slightly impure, uranium to make an implosion bomb.

If implosion looked more interesting, attractive and promising after von Neumann's visit, it also became more urgent—too urgent to leave in the hands of Neddermeyer and his tiny group. Oppenheimer thus began to enlarge the program and recruit into it people with more experience of explosives. His first target was George Kistiakowsky, the Ukrainian-born professor of chemistry at Harvard, who was director of the National Defense Research Committee's Explosive Research Laboratory at Bruceton, Pennsylvania, and probably the most eminent expert on the chemistry of explosives in the U.S. Kistiakowsky was at first reluctant to come to Los Alamos, "partly," he later said, "because I didn't think the bomb would be ready in time and I was interested in helping to win the war." He nevertheless agreed to visit Los Alamos in October 1943 as a consultant. What he found dismayed him. "The situation is a mess," he wrote to Conant after his visit. "The real difficulty is that there is a serious lack of mutual confidence between Parsons and Neddermeyer." Furthermore, though Parsons "is now committed to a vigorous prosecution" of implosion research, it "is doubtful that he believes in its success."

Kistiakowsky recommended an enlargement and a reorganization of the implosion program, with the appointment of a new leader for it, someone who could work with Parsons. Though he was still reluctant to commit himself to the task, it was clear to everyone that he himself was the right man for it. However, he took some time to see what was staring everybody else in the face and did not join the laboratory on a full-time basis until February 1944. In the meantime, while still acting as a consultant, he set about reorganizing the research program, providing it with a more rigorous scientific method and a detailed list of particular experimental studies to carry out. When he eventually joined Los Alamos, it was as a deputy leader of the Ordnance Division, with responsibility for implosion (with Ed McMillan as the other deputy, with responsibility for gun assembly). Kistiakowsky and McMillan were also made members of the Governing Board, as was Kenneth Bainbridge, who was at the same time appointed leader of a newly created division dedicated to the problems of bomb assembly.

Though much research still needed to be done, certain features of the design of the implosion bomb were fixed in the autumn of 1943. Its maximum size, for example, was determined by the size of the bomb bay in the B-29 bomber that would be used to deliver it: five by twelve feet. Also, it was realized from the beginning that an implosion bomb could not be long and slender, but would have to be round and large, hence the name "Fat Man." Apparently, the hope was that anyone listening covertly to discussions about modifying B-29s to accommodate "Thin Man" and "Fat Man" would interpret them as referring to plans to transport, respectively, President Roosevelt and Prime Minister Churchill.

Directing the program to design and build "Thin Man," which lasted from March 1943 to July 1944, had been a demanding job, but its demands paled before those required to complete "Fat Man" by the deadline of the summer of 1945. This latter was a truly gargantuan task that involved, among other things: mastering, and in some cases, inventing new mathematical techniques to describe and predict the behavior of shock waves; determining, by experiment and observation, the right shape for the explosive charges that would be used to implode the fissionable material; inventing a method of initiating the chain reaction in an implosion device; developing a new branch of physics (the hydrodynamics of implosion);[53] and designing and constructing a kind of bomb that no one before the war had even envisaged.

Moreover, for Oppenheimer, it involved maintaining smooth personal relations with, on the one hand, military and security men, and, on the other, prickly, obsessive scientists with large and easily bruised egos. Seth Neddermeyer was not an easy man, and he had developed an intense obsession with making his version of implosion work. In effectively sidelining him, while keeping him working on the program under the leadership of someone else, Oppenheimer demonstrated rare tact, sensitivity and understanding.

In March 1944, still thinking of implosion as a means of making a uranium bomb with as little uranium as possible, Oppenheimer wrote to Groves that the "prime objective" of the laboratory for the coming year was "to bring to a successful conclusion the development of the implosion unit with U-235." The arrival of the British mission at the

---

[53] The reason the word used in this context is "hydrodynamics" rather than simply "dynamics" is that, under the enormous pressure of implosion, the material used—uranium or plutonium—starts acting like a liquid rather than a solid.

Julian Schwinger, who became Oppenheimer's research assistant in 1940 and went on to develop quantum electrodynamics, win the Nobel Prize, and be recognized as one of America's greatest-ever physicists.

The young, brilliant, and mischievous Richard Feynman, who became Schwinger's main rival for being the greatest physicist the United States has ever produced.

The Los Alamos Ranch School, which became the site of the laboratory that produced the world's first atomic bombs.

The indomitable General Groves, whose fearsome power of will was an important factor in the success of the Manhattan Project.

(*Above*) Enrico Fermi in Chicago in 1942, at a time when he was working on the project that would succeed in producing the world's first fission chain reaction.

The graphite pile at Stagg Field in Chicago, where, on December 2, 1942, Fermi and his team successfully produced a chain reaction, thereby showing that it was indeed possible to produce energy through nuclear fission.

(*Above*) Hans Bethe in the 1940s.

(*Above right*) Klaus Fuchs.

(*Right*) Edward Teller, 1956.

(*Below*) Typically unimpressive results of Seth Neddermeyer's early attempts at implosion.

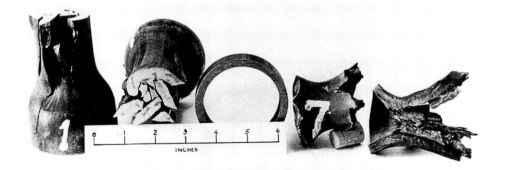

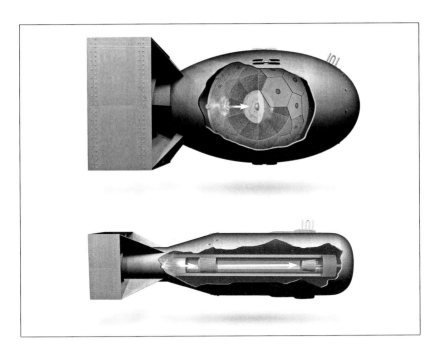

The Nagasaki and Hiroshima bombs.

The "Little Boy" design, as reverse engineered by John Coster-Mullen.

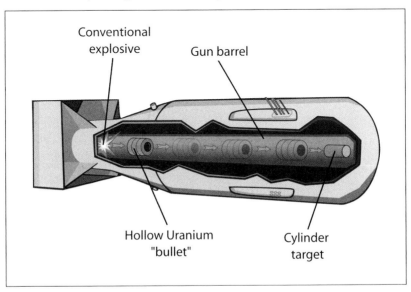

Workers at Oak Ridge, Tennessee. Though they did not know it, what they were doing was controlling the isotope-separation plants that produced the enriched uranium that was used in the bomb that destroyed Hiroshima.

(*Above and left*) Preparing the Trinity test, the world's first experience of an atomic explosion

The Trinity explosion. "A few people laughed, a few people cried. Most people were silent. I remembered the line from the Hindu scripture, the Bhagavad Gita: Vishnu is trying to persuade the prince that he should do his duty and to impress him takes on his multiarmed form and says: 'Now I am become death, the destroyer of worlds.'"

(*Right*) Oppenheimer and Groves at the Trinity test site.

(*Above*) Photograph taken by Robert Serber of the effects of the atomic bombs in Japan.

(*Facing page, top*) Oppenheimer and Kitty in Japan, 1960.

(*Facing page, bottom*) The cover of the first issue of *Physics Today*, May 1948. Oppenheimer was by this time so famous he could be represented just by his hat.

PHYSICS *today*

TRENDS IN AMERICAN SCIENCE by Vannevar Bush . . . . *See Page 5*

VOL 1 NO 1 ● MAY 1948

Albert Einstein and Leo Szilard in 1946, recreating for the film *Atomic Power* the moment in 1939 when they drafted the famous letter to President Roosevelt that led to the creation of the Manhattan Project.

The "technically sweet" Ulam-Teller design of the hydrogen bomb.

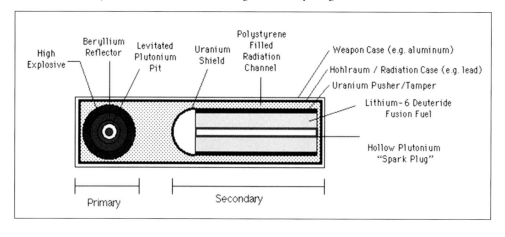

The "Mike" test in 1952, the first successful explosion of a fusion device, the force of which was 800 to 1,000 times more powerful than the Hiroshima bomb.

Oppenheimer lectures Ed Murrow on physics during the making of the television program *See It Now*.

(Above) Oppenheimer with Paul Dirac and Abraham Pais at the Institute for Advanced Study, Princeton.

(Right) Oppenheimer, Toni, and Peter at Olden Manor, Princeton.

Lewis Strauss.

(Right) Edward Teller congratulates Oppenheimer on his Fermi Prize award in 1964, attracting icy looks from Kitty.

(Below) Oppenheimer giving a speech during his last visit to Los Alamos in 1964.

Oppenheimer photographed for *Life* magazine, 1949.

end of 1943 and the beginning of 1944 gave Oppenheimer the opportunity to pick yet more brains for hints on how to solve the problem of squeezing a ball of uranium without deforming it. Chief among these fresh brains was that of Rudolf Peierls, who, when implosion research received its new impetus, was still attached to the Columbia University group in New York, but who in February 1944 came to Los Alamos for a visit. "At that time," Peierls writes in his autobiography, "the laboratory was urgently required to obtain numerical solutions to the equations for the implosion." As it happened, the equation required "was of the same form as that for the blast wave in air, for which I had done my numerical experiments . . . I therefore came just at the right time to explain the step-by-step method by which the equation could be solved and the limits of the size of the steps." Doing it step-by-step was important, because these calculations were to be done on IBM punch-card machines, the ancestors of modern computers. After the February visit Oppenheimer wrote to Groves confirming the usefulness of his discussions with Peierls, with whom, he reported, he had gone "into the technical aspects of the British methods in considerable detail." Oppenheimer was now "planning to attack the implosion problem along these lines with the highest possible urgency."

Developing implosion was both a theoretical and an experimental matter. Indeed, as had been shown during von Neumann's visit in the autumn of 1943, implosion raised theoretical questions interesting enough even for Edward Teller, who had steadfastly refused even to pretend to be stimulated by what he regarded as the merely engineering problems raised by the gun-assembly method. After his visit to Los Alamos, von Neumann kept up a correspondence with Teller, and in January 1944, Teller was appointed head of a small group of the Theoretical Division, devoted to solving the mathematical and theoretical problems raised by implosion. After Peierls's visit in February, the work of this group was centered on using the mathematical techniques developed by the British.

The effort—indeed, the perceived need—to solve the problems of implosion was soon considered sufficiently important for Bethe, in March 1944, to reorganize the entire Theoretical Division to meet "the great and increased urgency of the implosion program." In accordance with this reorganization, Teller was put in charge of group T-1, the responsibilities of which were officially described as "Hydrodynamics of Implosion, Super." Oppenheimer and Bethe both thought it was obvious that the first of these was the more important. Teller, however, whose interest in implosion in January seems to have waned by March, thought otherwise, and from the spring of 1944 onward spent almost all his time working on the Super. The short section of his autobiography that he devotes to his abandonment of work on implosion presents a somewhat unclear picture of why, exactly, he lost interest in it. After describing "Johnny" von Neumann's visit to Los Alamos and his conversations with him about "fast" implosion, Teller seems keen to convey the importance of those discussions and to highlight his own role in them:

> The next morning, Johnny and I presented our findings to Oppenheimer. He immediately grasped their implications. Within a week, magnificent administrator that he was, he had turned the direction of the research around. From then on, our main efforts were no longer devoted to a gun-assembled weapon but rather to the implosion assembly.[54]

But, having stressed his role in providing the guiding ideas of the implosion problem, Teller recounts how, after "Johnny" had left, Bethe called him into his office and told him: "I want you to take charge of solving the equations that will be needed to calculate implosion." This, Teller says, was a task he was reluctant to take on because it "seemed far too difficult": "Not only were other people more capable than I of providing such work, but I also suspected that a job that formidable might not be completed in time to have any influence on a bomb that could be used during this war."

As a reason for concentrating on the Super—which stood no chance whatsoever of being completed in time to influence the outcome of the war—this seems strikingly unconvincing. Besides, if Teller had originated the central ideas that inspired the renewed interest in implosion, who did he think could possibly be more capable of seeing it through to completion?

Interspersed with his account of how he helped to establish and then backed away from the rejuvenated implosion program, Teller provides some personal reflections that, one suspects, are more to the point in explaining why he abandoned it. Though he enjoyed Bethe's company, Teller says, "as physicists we approach problems differently." Whereas Bethe was a brick builder, Teller was a brick layer; he liked to *build*

---

[54] This was a more gradual process than Teller implies. The shift of focus from gun assembly to implosion, as I have tried to describe, was motivated by many different considerations and received many different impetuses, the visit to Los Alamos by John von Neumann being but one of them. The visit of Peierls was another. The really crucial development, however—the one that made it absolutely imperative to solve the problems of implosion—was the discovery in the spring of 1944 that it was impossible to build a gun-assembly bomb using reactor-generated plutonium.

things, rather than provide other people with the tools: "I much prefer (and am better at) exploring the various structures that can be made from brick, and seeing how the bricks stack up." Then, apparently apropos of nothing, Teller confesses that when Oppenheimer told him that he had appointed Bethe as head of the Theoretical Division, "I was a little hurt." "I had worked on the atom bomb project longer than Bethe. I had worked hard and fairly effectively on recruiting, and on helping Oppie organize the lab during the first chaotic weeks."

In other words, it seems to be implied, Teller quit working on implosion because he could not bear the thought of being consigned to working on a mere brick-building task, working under another brick builder. He wanted to be working not on small mathematical tasks in the service of a goal set by someone else, but on large tasks in which he could pursue his own vision. He wanted to be the boss, not the under-laborer—especially if it turned out that the particular under-laboring task he had been set was one that someone else, namely Peierls, was better at than he.

On May 1, 1944, Oppenheimer wrote to Groves, asking if, as a matter of the "greatest urgency," Teller ("who is, in my opinion and Bethe's, quite unsuited for this responsibility") could be relieved of his role in the implosion program and replaced by Peierls. But even now, and despite the tone of his letter to Groves, Oppenheimer did not completely fall out with Teller. On the contrary, he actively encouraged him to devote his energies to the Super and even—at a time when he and the entire laboratory were stretched to the limit—made time to see him for an hour's discussion every week.

Peierls came to Los Alamos to take up leadership of the implosion theory group on June 3, 1944. Soon afterward Oppenheimer gave a party for Lord Cherwell, Churchill's scientific advisor, but somehow forgot to invite Peierls. When he came to Peierls's office the next day to offer abject apologies for this unintended slight, Oppenheimer told him: "There is an element of comfort in this situation: it might have happened with Edward Teller."

Shortly before Peierls's arrival, a major breakthrough in the theory of implosion was made by another member of the British mission, James Tuck, who had worked previously on armor-piercing shells. Drawing on that work, he came up with a means of solving the problem of creating the smooth, symmetrical, inward-moving spherical shock wave that implosion required, which had, in practice, until this point proved impossible to create. The best one could do was simulate such a spherical shock wave by placing jets of explosive energy in a spherical arrangement. This, however, created a series of diverging and converging shock waves, the physics and mathematics of which were at this time only imperfectly understood. What Tuck, building on von Neumann's suggestion of shaped charges, envisaged was a way of arranging the explosive charges so that the waves of energy produced by them converged. The arrangement Tuck had in mind called for a series of "lenses," analogous to optical lenses. Just as an optical lens forces waves of light to converge on a target, so Tuck's lenses would force waves of explosive energy to converge, thus increasing their force and enabling the "fast implosion" envisaged by von Neumann to be realized. Such an arrangement was, however, as David Hawkins puts it in his official history of Los Alamos, "a completely untried and undeveloped method, which no one wished to employ unless it became absolutely necessary to do so." After Segrè's shattering news about spontaneous fission in reactor plutonium, it looked as if it might indeed be necessary to employ this untried method. The laboratory needed to take risks. After all, in the summer of 1944, a mere twelve months before the deadline for producing the bomb, there was, as Hawkins puts it, "not a single experimental result that gave good reason to believe that a plutonium bomb could be made at all."

In August 1944, then, the entire laboratory was reorganized to reflect the central importance of the effort to solve the many problems that stood in the way of making an implosion bomb. Stanislaw ("Stan") Ulam, the Polish mathematician and friend of Teller's who arrived in Los Alamos at the end of 1943, has recalled with amusement the "fascination with organizational charts" that he found at Los Alamos:

> At meetings, theoretical talks were interesting enough, but whenever an organizational chart was displayed, I could feel the whole audience come to life with pleasure at seeing something concrete and definite ("Who is responsible to whom," etc.).

As a result of the August 1944 reorganization, those charts became more complicated as divisions multiplied, new groups were added and hundreds more men were recruited. Oppenheimer calculated that, if the laboratory were to solve the problems of implosion in time to have a plutonium bomb ready for the summer of 1945, he would need an additional 600 men. These, of course, would not all have to be distinguished physicists, chemists or ballistics experts. What was needed was relatively unskilled labor to carry out the experiments and make the observations and measurements that were required to solve the many scientific problems that remained unsolved. Why did Oppenheimer need so many men? The answer lies in the sheer number of questions raised by implosion. For example, in order to understand the nature of implosion itself, and to know what was needed to achieve the smooth symmetrical shock wave it required, literally thousands of experiments—analogous to, but far more sophisticated than, those conducted by Neddermeyer and his team on stove pipes—needed to be carried out.

In September 1944, the theoretician Robert Christy suggested that the metal to be imploded should be a solid ball, rather than the hollow sphere envisaged by Neddermeyer. After this had been accepted, the problem of implosion was tackled by experiment after experiment in which the implosion of a solid sphere of metal, usually cadmium, was attempted and measurements taken to see how close each successive attempt had come to producing that elusive uniform, symmetrical shock wave. The methods used to make these measurements were many and varied, and some were invented at Los Alamos. For example, Robert Serber came up with a novel idea that became the basis of what was called the "RaLa method." The idea was to put a radioactive substance—the one chosen was an isotope of lanthanum (La-140), called Radiolanthanum (hence "RaLa")—at the center of the metal sphere being imploded. The gamma rays emitted by this radioactive source would be absorbed by the metal in proportion to its density, so the density changes in the metal as it was imploded could be measured by recording the intensity of the gamma radiation before, during and after the detonation. In this way, they could see how close they were to achieving a uniform, symmetrical shock wave. Other methods of measuring what happens when a lump of metal is imploded were devised using X-rays and photographs.

In addition to these meticulous experiments and observations concerned with the nature of implosion, much experimental work had to be carried out in order to design and manufacture the shaped explosive charges, providing answers to such questions as: what material should the explosive charge be made of? how, exactly, should it be shaped? and how should the shaped charges, the "lenses," be arranged around the plutonium core? As a result of these experiments, a design was arrived at that was far more complex than the gun-assembly bomb originally planned. The weapon that was now envisaged looked like an enormous football, at the center of which was a 3½-inch solid sphere of plutonium with a hole for the initiator, around which was a uranium tamper with a diameter of nine inches, in turn surrounded by thirty-two explosive charges, all carefully shaped into "lenses," concentrating the shock wave at the center of the sphere. In all, "Fat Man" would be fifty-four inches wide and weigh nearly 5,500 pounds.

This design—which, astonishingly, was arrived at in February 1945, just six months after the major reorganization—was the outcome of observing innumerable detonations, requiring tens of thousands of charges. To supply these, the laboratory had its own workshop, which became in effect a factory, employing dozens of young men. These men, like most of the 600 extra people that Oppenheimer had estimated he needed, were "SEDs," members of the U.S. Army's Special Engineering Detachment. "They were kids mostly," Kistiakowsky said, "with partial college education, but there were even a few Ph.D.s." The SEDs had a difficult time at Los Alamos, where they worked the long hours of the scientists, while keeping up the disciplined and tightly structured life of soldiers. They lived not in the kind of houses or apartments provided for the scientists, but in crowded barracks, within which they had just a tiny space of their own. "We had reveille at six," one of them recalled, "we had drill and exercises at six-thirty and the fatigues until eight a.m.—and sometimes, working on something in the workshops, we had not gotten to bed until two or three in the morning."

Of course, with such a massive influx of personnel, it was inevitable that standards of security would decline. It was clearly impossible to watch the movements of every one of the hundreds of people who came to Los Alamos in the summer of 1944, and in any case it seems not to have occurred to Groves, de Silva or Lansdale that among the young men of the Special Engineering Detachment there might be some who would be willing to spy for the Soviet Union. And yet there was at least one such person, David Greenglass, whose willingness to pass information to the Soviets, though it may not have been very significant in increasing Soviet knowledge of the bomb, would turn out to have drastic consequences for his sister and her husband, Ethel and Julius Rosenberg.

Greenglass had studied mechanical engineering before, at the age of twenty-one, being inducted into the U.S. Army in 1943. He and his wife, Ruth, were at that time both members of the Communist Party. After working for a while at Oak Ridge, Greenglass was sent to Los Alamos in August 1944, as part of the Special Engineering Detachment. During his time at Oak Ridge, and for the first three months of working at Los Alamos, Greenglass did not know that he was working on the atomic-bomb project. At Los Alamos he was employed in the workshop making molds for the shaped explosives that were needed for the implosion experiments. He had no idea what these "lenses" were for, and no understanding of the implosion process of which they were such an essential part.

Greenglass learned that he was working on the atomic-bomb project in November 1944, when he was told by his wife, Ruth, who in turn had been told by the Rosenbergs. At the Rosenbergs' expense, Ruth (who lived in New York) had gone to New Mexico to visit her husband, whom she had not seen since his transfer to Los Alamos. They spent a few days together in Albuquerque, where Ruth relayed the information to Greenglass. The Rosenbergs had been communists since the early 1930s, and

Julius Rosenberg was the hub of a spy network that sought to gather information about secret military and industrial projects. Before she left New York, the Rosenbergs gave Ruth Greenglass a list of questions to ask her husband about the layout and the personnel at Los Alamos.

A few months later, in January 1945, David Greenglass came to New York on leave and provided the Rosenbergs with a description and a drawing of the lens molds he was making. He also, then or later, provided the Rosenbergs with a rough, and presumably not very useful, drawing of the "Fat Man" bomb. After Greenglass's return to Los Alamos, Julius Rosenberg arranged for him to meet a Soviet contact periodically to pass on anything else he had managed to find out. That contact was none other than Harry Gold, the man Fuchs had been meeting to share information about gaseous diffusion. Indeed, it would be via the connections with Fuchs and Gold that Greenglass, and therefore the Rosenbergs, were exposed as spies in 1950. At the Rosenbergs' trial, Greenglass testified against his sister, leading her to be executed alongside her husband on June 19, 1953. Greenglass himself was sentenced to fifteen years in prison. In 1960, after serving ten years, he was released and rejoined his wife in New York. Nearly forty years later, he told a reporter from the *New York Times* that his testimony against his sister had been a lie told in order to protect his wife, who was never charged in connection with the affair.

The Greenglass affair clearly upset John Lansdale. Speaking in 1954, at Oppenheimer's security hearing, he referred twice to "the inexcusable Greenglass case." The word "inexcusable" seems to have been chosen by Lansdale to refer not to Greenglass's behavior (though no doubt he would have thought it applicable to that), but to his own lapse in failing to catch Greenglass. "He is certainly an example of one we missed," he remarked ruefully. When he was asked to confirm that Oppenheimer had no responsibility for Greenglass "in any way, shape or form," Lansdale replied: "I don't believe so. I will take full responsibility for that one. That was the outstanding blunder of the century."

Of course, from a security point of view, the much more serious espionage of Klaus Fuchs was a far bigger blunder, but in that case Lansdale could perhaps take some comfort from the fact that it was a blunder committed by the British security services rather than his own. Unknown to Lansdale, however, there had been at least one other "blunder" committed by his own team, one that led to the Soviets acquiring much more useful information than they ever got from David Greenglass. Again it involved a young man brought to Los Alamos in 1944, though this time a fully fledged scientist rather than a relatively uninformed member of SED.

The man in question was Theodore Hall. Known as "Ted Hall" for most of his life, he was the youngest child of a Russian Jewish family, the Holtzbergs, from New York. The change of name came when he was eleven, when his older brother, Ed, discovered that a Jewish name was a barrier to employment. A precociously brilliant boy, Ted won a place to study at the prestigious Townsend Harris High School. Already he had dreams of being a physicist. When his mother asked what he would like for his twelfth birthday, he told her he wanted *The Mysterious Universe* by James Jeans. In 1942, just before his seventeenth birthday, Hall, who had already spent two years at Queens College, transferred to Harvard. There his imagination was fired by a course on "Kinetic Theory and Statistical Mechanics," given by Oppenheimer's ex-student and collaborator Wendell Furry. The following year, still only eighteen, Hall took a postgraduate class on quantum mechanics and attracted the attention of its convenor, John H. van Vleck, one of the "luminaries" who had taken part in the pre–Los Alamos seminars at Berkeley in the summer of 1942. When Bush told van Vleck and Edwin Kemble, who was still at Harvard, that more bright physicists were needed for Los Alamos, Hall was one of those selected, becoming, in the New Year of 1944, the youngest scientist to work on the bomb project.

At first, Hall was assigned to work under Bruno Benedetto Rossi, measuring fission cross-sections using fast neutrons on the U-235 that was beginning to arrive from Oak Ridge. While he was working on this, in June 1944, Hall graduated *in absentia* from Harvard. Soon afterward he was promoted to a new position as leader of a team making and testing equipment for the RaLa experiments. In particular, Hall and his team were making the ionization chambers that would detect the gamma rays emitted from the radioactive lanthanum. "We were turning out ionization chambers like sausages," Hall later said. "It made me feel funny to blow up all those ionization chambers we had built so carefully. We would just destroy them and build some more."

In October 1944, soon after his nineteenth birthday, Hall was given two weeks' leave, which he spent in New York. While there, he decided to tell the Soviet Union about the work being done at Los Alamos. He was not recruited, nor was he bribed. His decision was made quite unilaterally and independently. When he tried to explain it later in life, he said: "It seemed to me that an American monopoly was dangerous and should be prevented." Hall's method of contacting the Soviets was remarkable for its lack of guile. He simply walked into the offices of Amtorg, the Soviet import-export company, and told the first person he saw there, a man stacking boxes, that he had secret information he would like to share. The man put him in touch with Sergei Kurnakov, a writer and journalist who was also a low-ranking NKVD officer. When Hall met Kurnakov, he handed him a file that he had written containing a report on the activities at Los Alamos, which was subsequently sent to Moscow. By the time he returned to Los Alamos, Hall was officially a Soviet agent, with his own code-name: Mlad, an old Slavic word for "young."

After his return to Los Alamos, Hall took part in several crucial RaLa experiments that culminated in a set of three, conducted in February 1945, which finally produced the smooth shock wave they had been looking for. The crucial step that made this possible was the invention by Luis Alvarez of an electric detonator that enabled all the shaped explosives to be detonated at exactly the same time. After repeating the successful experiment on February 24, the design for "Fat Man" was settled. "Now we have our bomb," Oppenheimer was heard to exclaim.

Almost as soon as the design was complete, Soviet agents received details of it. On February 16, 1945, Klaus Fuchs, who had been out of contact with the Soviets since his move from New York to Los Alamos in August 1944, met Harry Gold in Boston, where Fuchs's sister lived. The information Fuchs was able to hand Gold was wide-ranging, detailed and accurate; it covered the design of the bomb, the metallurgy of plutonium, Segrè's results on spontaneous fission in plutonium and much more. However, because of the convoluted logistics of espionage, Fuchs's report did not reach Moscow until April 1945, by which time the Soviets already had a report on the two types of bomb being developed at Los Alamos, less detailed than Fuchs's, but no less accurate. The source of this information was almost certainly "Mlad," with some additional details from David Greenglass.

When Lansdale spoke in 1954 of the Greenglass case as the "blunder of the century," he would not have known anything about Hall's more serious espionage. The FBI, on the other hand, knew about Hall from the same source that they knew about Fuchs, Gold and Greenglass: the Venona transcripts. Unlike Fuchs, Gold and Greenglass, however, Hall, when he was interviewed by the FBI, made no confession; he simply denied everything. Faced with the choice of attempting to prosecute Hall on the basis of Venona evidence—and therefore revealing to the outside world the existence of that evidence—or of keeping Venona a secret at the expense of letting Hall go free, the FBI chose not to prosecute. Hall was therefore able to pursue a successful career as a scientist, ending up as the director of a biological laboratory in Cambridge, England, where he lived from 1962 until his death from cancer in 1999. Toward the end of his life, when his role in Soviet espionage became widely known through the publication of the Venona transcripts, Hall made an unrepentant statement, declaring that "in essence, from the perspective of my 71 years, I still think that brash youth [his earlier self] had the right end of the stick. I am no longer that person; but I am by no means ashamed of him."

What Fuchs and Hall handed over to the Soviets in the spring of 1945—the design of the plutonium implosion bomb—was arguably Oppenheimer's greatest achievement. Not that he himself had designed it, but it was he who had planned and coordinated the remarkable effort required to produce the design; he who had led weekly meetings of scientists to bring problems out into the open; he who had been able to discuss the mathematics of implosion with Peierls, the merits of various explosive materials with Kistiakowsky, the implications of RaLa experiments with Rossi, the invention of electric detonators with Alvarez, and to oversee dozens of groups of scientists employing hundreds of SEDs on thousands of experiments. It was the birth of what is known today as "Big Science."

The effort involved in leading and coordinating a scientific project on such an unprecedented scale was having a physically observable effect on Oppenheimer. In 1944, he was still only forty, but he looked at least ten years older. He had always been slender, but, by the end of the year, his weight had dropped to 115 pounds and he looked gaunt. He had been a heavy smoker for years, but now he was never without a cigarette or a pipe and his persistent, nasty cough got worse. He also drank too much, though in this respect he was outdone by Kitty, upon whom the strain seemed, if anything, to take an even greater toll.

As the wife of the director, Kitty was in a perfect position to be Los Alamos's leading hostess, at the very center of its social life. This was, however, a role she had absolutely no interest in filling. She and Oppenheimer gave parties, but they were infrequent and rather joyless affairs. While Deak Parsons's wife, Martha, moved to fill the vacant position of social hub, Kitty became an increasingly isolated figure. "She didn't get along very well with women," remarked Priscilla Duffield, Oppenheimer's secretary, and her imperious manner and sharp tongue also alienated many men. Kitty was, Duffield said, "one of the few people I've ever heard men—and very nice men—call a bitch . . . She could be really mean. She could also cause trouble for you, so you had to be very careful."

It is a view echoed by many, including Phil Morrison's wife, Emily, who recalled that, though Kitty could be "very bewitching," she was certainly "someone to be wary of." Kitty would, Emily Morrison later said, adopt and reject people apparently at random, so that even those she treated well felt insecure in her friendship, watching her be mean to others and wondering whether they would be next to feel her spite.

Of the people she suddenly turned on, one of the most difficult for Oppenheimer was Charlotte Serber, who, for some reason, Kitty suddenly stopped having anything to do with. "Everybody was aware of it, and it was very hurtful," remembered Shirley Barnett, the wife of the Oppenheimers' pediatrician. "But Kitty was capable of that." Barnett herself was adopted by Kitty as a companion, because, she thought, "I was young and less threatening than the others." Kitty would take her shopping to Santa Fe or Albuquerque. "She always had a bottle of something with her when she was driving, and you could always tell when she was getting drunk because she would talk more freely." "She was fascinating," Barnett concluded, "but not very nice."

Jackie Oppenheimer, who came to Los Alamos in early 1945, when Frank was transferred there from Oak Ridge, recalled her own unhappy experiences of Kitty and her drinking:

> It was known that we didn't get on well together and she seemed determined that we should be seen together. On one occasion she asked me to cocktails—this was four o'clock in the afternoon. When I arrived, there was Kitty and just four or five other women—drinking companions—and we just sat there with very little conversation—drinking. It was awful and I never went again.

Making Kitty's life more difficult, and driving her deeper into alcoholism, was the birth of her daughter, Katherine. "Toni," as she would be known throughout her life, was born on December 7, 1944, right in the middle of the most intense period of Oppenheimer's time as director. This was when the search for a workable implosion design was at its most feverish, and before it was known that it would end successfully. It was when Oppenheimer was at his busiest and most anxious, and, though the baby was publicly heralded as a source of great delight and an endless stream of visitors came to the hospital especially to see her and to share (what was assumed to be) the Oppenheimers' joy, the truth was, at that point in their lives, the responsibility of looking after a baby was the very last thing either Kitty or Robert Oppenheimer wanted.

Jackie Oppenheimer was shocked when she arrived at Los Alamos to discover that, after Toni's birth, Kitty "would go off on a shopping trip for days to Albuquerque or even to the West Coast and leave the children in the hands of a maid." Even more shocking to some was the fact that in April 1945, when Toni was just four months old, Kitty left Los Alamos for Pittsburgh, taking Peter, now nearly four years old, with her, but leaving baby Toni in the hands of a friend called Pat Sherr, who had recently had a miscarriage. She would not return for three and a half months, during which time Oppenheimer, fantastically busy, showed little inclination to spend much time with his daughter. "It was all very strange," Sherr later said. "He would come and sit and chat with me, but he wouldn't ask to see the baby." Then, one day, shortly before Kitty's return, Oppenheimer asked Sherr if she would like to adopt Toni. "Of course not," Sherr replied. Why would he even ask such a thing? "Because," said Oppenheimer, "I can't love her."

Poor little Toni arrived at a bad time, her first six months coinciding with the preparations for perhaps the most momentous scientific experiment in history: the test of the implosion bomb. The decision to conduct a full-scale test of an implosion bomb had been made back in March 1944, a month or so before it was finally established that implosion was the only hope for a plutonium bomb. Implosion was such a complicated and as yet little-understood process that it was felt such a test would be necessary. Responsibility for organizing the test was given to E-9, a specially created group of the Engineering Division, which after the massive reorganization of the late summer of 1944 became "X-2 Development, Engineering, Tests," part of Kistiakowsky's Explosives Division. The group leader was Kenneth Bainbridge.

In March 1945, X-2 was dissolved and Bainbridge was put in charge of what by then had acquired the name "Trinity Project." When Oppenheimer was asked many years later about the name "Trinity," he gave characteristically evasive answers. In 1962, Groves himself asked Oppenheimer about it, suggesting that perhaps the name was chosen because it would be inconspicuous in an area where a lot of rivers and peaks were called "Trinity." In his reply, Oppenheimer rejected that suggestion. "Why I chose the name," he told Groves, "is not clear, but I know what thoughts were in my mind. There is a poem of John Donne,[55] written just before his death, which I know and love. From it a quotation":

> *As West and East*
> *In all flat Maps—and I am one—are one*
> *So death doth touch the Resurrection.*

"That still does not make a Trinity," Oppenheimer acknowledged, "but in another, better known devotional poem[56] Donne opens, 'Batter my heart, three person'd God'; beyond this, I have no clues whatever."

These allusions to Donne suggest that Oppenheimer chose the name in memory of Jean Tatlock, who loved Donne's poetry, but it also

[55] "Hymne to God, My God, in My Sicknesse."

[56] "Holy Sonnet 14."

seems possible that the name occurred to Oppenheimer in memory of the "pygmy triumvirate," the "great troika" of which he had been a part during his first trip to New Mexico. After all, the site chosen for the Trinity test, the Jornada del Muerto region northwest of Alamogordo, was not very far from areas of New Mexico—Roswell and Albuquerque, in particular—associated with that group, especially with Paul Horgan, the man who had coined those names.

The decision to use the Jornada del Muerto was made in September 1944, after which the U.S. Army took steps to secure an area occupying more than 400 square miles for the use of the test. On this site a base camp was constructed, which was ready by the end of December 1944. This then became home to a detachment of military police led by Lieutenant H. C. Bush.

With the successful conclusion of the implosion research in February 1945, Groves announced that the design of "Fat Man" was frozen. That job was finished. The following month, Oppenheimer created a new division, the Trinity Project Division, made up chiefly of scientists from the Research Division, which would have responsibility for the coming test in Jornada del Muerto. The division leader was Kenneth Bainbridge. Despite all the work that had been done on the metallurgy of plutonium, the energy release of fission using fast neutrons, and so on, there was little consensus on exactly how big the blast would be when the Fat Man bomb went off. Some were still skeptical that it would work at all, while among those who expected some kind of explosion the estimates of the energy yield, in terms of equivalent amounts of TNT, varied from 200 to 10,000 tons.

As Bainbridge was beginning the preparations for the Trinity test, the world outside Los Alamos was changing quickly and drastically. Hitler's Third Reich was collapsing rapidly, under assault from the east by the Russians, from the west by the Allies, and from the air by the most relentless and deadly bombing campaign the world had ever seen. In February 1945 the historic city of Dresden was reduced to a smoking ruin when nearly 4,000 tons of high-explosive bombs and incendiary devices were dropped on it by more than 1,000 British and American heavy bombers. About 25,000 people were killed and more or less the entire city was destroyed. Berlin, too, came under heavy bombardment, and by April Russian tanks were approaching the city.

On April 12, 1945, on the brink of victory over the Germans, President Roosevelt suddenly died of a brain hemorrhage. At Los Alamos, three days later, a memorial service was held in a cinema, at which Oppenheimer, as Philip Morrison later put it, "spoke very quietly for two or three minutes out of his heart and ours." The memorial address that Oppenheimer gave on that occasion has subsequently been published, revealing its eloquence to be tinged with a slightly histrionic note that was perhaps in keeping with the mood of his audience. "We have been living through years of great evil," Oppenheimer said, "and of great terror."

> Roosevelt has been our President, our Commander-in-Chief and, in an old-fashioned and unperverted sense, our leader. All over the world men have looked to him for guidance, and have seen symbolized in him their hope that the evils of this time would not be repeated; that the terrible sacrifices which have been made, and those that are still to be made, would lead to a world more fit for human habitation. It is in such times of evil that men recognize their helplessness and their profound dependence. One is reminded of medieval days, when the death of a good and wise and just king plunged his country into despair and mourning.

He ended with reflections on a quotation from the Bhagavad Gita: "Man is a creature whose substance is faith. What his faith is, he is."

> The faith of Roosevelt is one that is shared by millions of men and women in every country of the world. For this reason it is possible to maintain the hope, for this reason it is right that we should dedicate ourselves to the hope that his good works will not have ended with his death.

Just over two weeks after Roosevelt's death, Hitler too was dead, having shot himself in his bunker under Berlin on finally accepting that the war was lost. A week later, on May 8, 1945, the Germans offered their unconditional surrender.

At Los Alamos, the defeat of Germany did not in any way diminish the sense of urgency with which the newly established Trinity Project Division set about its task of organizing the test of the plutonium bomb. Before attempting the full test, it was decided that a kind of dress rehearsal should be conducted, using 100 tons of TNT. The point of this was to calibrate and test the equipment that would be used for the real thing. This rehearsal took place on the morning of May 7, 1945. The TNT, stacked on a platform on top of a 20-foot tower, was exploded and measurements taken of the blast effect, the shock waves and the damage to equipment.

By this time, it was clear to everybody—as it had long been clear to Groves, if not to Oppenheimer—that, if the bomb was going to be used, it would be used against the Japanese. Already B-29 bombers had inflicted on Japan a bombing campaign even more intense and more deadly than that unleashed upon Germany, with the cities of Tokyo, Nagoya, Osaka and Kobe bearing the brunt of the attacks. The fire-bombing of Tokyo on March 9 and 10, during which nearly 2,000 tons of incendiary bombs were dropped, setting large parts of the city ablaze and killing around 100,000 people, was at the time the most destructive air raid ever witnessed.

Yet, however deadly the attacks, they seemed to produce little dimi-nution in the will to fight among the Japanese people, and it seemed clear that, if Japan were to be defeated, it would have to be, like Ger-many, invaded by an enormous land army. In his autobiography, *Now It Can Be Told*, Groves draws attention to the plans drawn up by the U.S. military during 1945 for an invasion of Japan, and the potentially colossal U.S. casualties those plans predicted. Back in the summer of 1944, the Joint Chiefs of Staff had adopted a strategy for the invasion of Japan that envisaged an assault on Kyushu, Japan's southernmost island, on October 1, 1945, with the final push into Tokyo taking place three months later. This basic plan was confirmed as Allied strategy in April 1945, when it was estimated that thirty-six divisions—more than 1.5 mil-lion men—would be required, and, Groves adds darkly, "it was recog-nized that casualties would be heavy." On May 25, 1945, recalibrated orders were given to the heads of the three armed forces to prepare the invasion of Kyushu, starting that November.

Meanwhile, Groves was hoping that the Manhattan Project would make such an invasion unnecessary, thereby providing an adequate response to the question Groves feared more than any other: what had the American people got from the $2 billion they had spent on the devel-opment of the atomic bomb? For Groves, the question that needed to be addressed was not *whether* to drop the bomb on Japan, but on which Japanese city or cities it should be dropped. On May 10 and 11, Oppen-heimer hosted at Los Alamos meetings of the newly constituted Tar-get Committee, which established criteria for the selection of targets. The minutes of these meetings have now been published and provide a chillingly matter-of-fact record of the way those present contemplated, with apparent calm, the deaths of tens of thousands of people and the destruction of sites of great historic and religious importance. The four targets recommended by the meeting were, in order: 1. Kyoto, 2. Hiro-shima, 3. Yokohama and 4. Kokura Arsenal. The first two of these were rated AA. Of the first, the minutes comment: "From the psychological point of view there is the advantage that Kyoto is an intellectual center for Japan and the people there are more apt to appreciate the significance of such a weapon as the gadget." Hiroshima, it is remarked, "is a good radar target and it is such a size that a large part of the city could be extensively damaged." "There are adjacent hills which are likely to produce a focusing effect which would considerably increase the blast damage." The influence of Bohr is discernible when, under the heading of "Psychological Factors in Target Selection," it is noted that, as well as "obtaining the greatest psychological effect against Japan," they should also aim at "making the initial use sufficiently spectacular for the importance of the weapon to be internationally recognized when publicity on it is released."

Oppenheimer was also appointed, together with Fermi, Lawrence and Arthur Compton, as a member of the Scientific Advisory Panel to the War Department's Interim Committee, which had the task of planning postwar atomic policy. At a meeting of this committee on May 31, 1945, the minutes reveal that the committee's chairman, Secretary of War Henry L. Stimson, "expressed the view, a view shared by General Marshall, that this project should not be considered simply in terms of military weapons, but as a new relationship of man to the universe." What Stimson meant by this, apparently, was that:

> This discovery might be compared to the discoveries of the Copernican theory and of the laws of gravity, but far more important than these in its effect on the lives of men. While the advances in the field to date had been fostered by the needs of war, it was important to realize that the implications of the project went far beyond the needs of the present war. It must be controlled if possible to make it an assurance of peace rather than a menace to civilization.

Later in the meeting this theme was picked up by Oppenheimer, who took the opportunity to present Bohr's vision of openness. He is recorded as arguing:

> It might be wise for the United States to offer to the world free interchange of information with particular emphasis on the development of peace-time uses. The basic goal of all endeavors in the field should be the enlargement of human welfare. If we were to offer to exchange information before the bomb was actually used, our moral position would be greatly strengthened.

The tone of the meeting became markedly less high-minded during the discussion of the "effect of the bombing on the Japanese and their will to fight." Oppenheimer stressed that in this connection "several strikes would be feasible," and that "the visual effect of an atomic bombing would be tremendous. It would be accompanied by a brilliant luminescence which would rise to a height of 10,000 to 20,000 feet. The neutron effect of the explosion would be dangerous to life for a radius of at least two-thirds of a mile." As for the number of deaths that such an explosion might cause, Oppenheimer offered the (extremely conservative, as it turned out) figure of 20,000, based, he reported, on the assumption that the occupants of the bombed city would seek shelter when the air raid began and that most of them would be under shelter by the time the bomb went off.[57]

"After much discussion concerning various types of targets and the effects to be produced," the minutes state, Stimson expressed the view that "we could not give the Japanese any warning; that we could not concentrate on a civilian area; but that we should seek to make a profound psychological impression on as many of the inhabitants as possible." The "most desirable target," in Stimson's view, "would be a vital war plant employing a large number of workers and closely surrounded by workers' houses."

Evidently to Groves's chagrin, Stimson ruled out Kyoto as a target city, on the grounds that, as Groves puts it in his autobiography, it was "the ancient capital of Japan, a historical city and one that was of great religious significance to the Japanese." Stimson, Groves reports, had visited Kyoto when he was Governor General of the Philippines "and had been very much impressed by its ancient culture." "On the other hand," writes Groves, "I particularly wanted Kyoto as a target because . . . it was large enough in area for us to gain complete knowledge of the effects of an atomic bomb. Hiroshima was not nearly so satisfactory in this respect. I also felt quite strongly, as had other members of the Target Committee, that Kyoto was one of the most important military targets in Japan." Groves did not let the matter drop and repeatedly urged the choice of Kyoto as the first target of an atomic bomb right up until the Potsdam Conference in July, at which Stalin, Churchill and the new President, Harry S. Truman, decided the future of Europe. From Potsdam, Stimson sent a telegram saying that he had discussed the matter with President Truman, who agreed with him. "There was," Groves says, "no further talk about Kyoto after that."

---

[57] Given the experience of bombing up to that point, this is perhaps a natural assumption. However, as the "air raid" in question would consist of a single airplane, there was little reason to suppose that the city's occupants would realize they were about to be bombed. In fact, the inhabitants of Hiroshima did not pay much attention to the plane that dropped the bomb that destroyed their city, precisely because they did not—could not—imagine an air raid that did not involve a great number of airplanes.

Though Stimson thus saved Kyoto and urged the case for a military rather than a civilian target, the assumption that the bomb would be used against the Japanese was not challenged by anybody on the committee. Nor was there much dissent from this assumption among the scientists at Los Alamos. There was, of course, some discussion of the political and moral questions surrounding their work, especially after it became clear that Germany did not have a serious atomic-bomb project and then that the war against Germany would end in victory without the bomb. Oppenheimer, however, rather discouraged such discussions. Robert Wilson remembers organizing a public meeting at Los Alamos to discuss "The Impact of the Gadget on Civilization," which about twenty people attended, including Oppenheimer, who, on this and other occasions, put forward the argument he had learned from Bohr: the bomb was such a powerful weapon that it had a chance of being the best thing that had ever happened to mankind by bringing an end to war itself, but it could do this only if its awesome power were made clear to everyone and this could, in turn, only be done if it were actually used.

At Los Alamos there was a general acceptance of this argument, but not so at the Met Lab in Chicago, where the scientists had, throughout the war, been more prepared to be openly at odds with Groves and the military. Indeed, at the Interim Committee meeting of May 31, 1945, one of the topics for discussion was "Handling of Undesirable Scientists," a heading under which Groves, according to the minutes, "stated that the program had been plagued since its inception by the presence of certain scientists of doubtful discretion and uncertain loyalty." Not coincidentally, the next item for discussion was "Chicago Group."

Chief among the "undesirable scientists" at Chicago was Leo Szilard, whom Groves had wanted to intern as an undesirable alien. As the war was coming to an end, as the work of the Manhattan Project was nearing completion, and as preparations for the Trinity test continued their inexorable path toward the demonstration of the power of nuclear fission, Szilard—the man who had first envisaged a chain reaction and who had been instrumental in the famous letter from Einstein to Roosevelt that urged the launching of the atomic-bomb project—began to turn his mind to the political and social implications of the bomb. He quickly became convinced that the use of the atomic bomb against Japan would have extremely grave consequences for postwar politics. Before Roosevelt's death, Szilard had tried to alert him to the dangers of a nuclear arms race and the consequent importance of international control of atomic bombs, putting forward the argument that using the bomb against Japan would accelerate the former and jeopardize the latter. Then, after Truman was sworn in, Szilard tried to arrange a meeting with him to discuss the political issues raised by the bomb. He was told instead to meet James Byrnes, the South Carolinian who would soon be appointed Secretary of State. The meeting was a disaster, with Byrnes dismissing Szilard as someone whose "general demeanor and . . . desire to participate in policy-making made an unfavorable impression on me," while Szilard came away angry, frustrated and depressed at what he saw as Byrnes's inability to understand *anything*.

Szilard, however, was not easily deflected and the day before the Interim Committee's meeting of May 31 he traveled to Washington to try to persuade Oppenheimer that it would be a serious mistake to use the bomb against Japanese cities. "The atomic bomb is shit," Szilard remembers Oppenheimer saying on this occasion, "a weapon with no military significance. It will make a big bang—a very big bang—but it is not a weapon which is useful in war." Oppenheimer restated his view that the bomb should be used against the Japanese, but that the Russians should be told about the bomb and its intended use. "Don't you think," he told Szilard, "that if we tell the Russians what we intend to do and then use the bomb in Japan, the Russians will understand it?" "They'll understand it only too well," Szilard replied.

Prompted by Arthur Compton, who promised to convey the opinions of Chicago scientists to the Scientific Panel ahead of the next meeting of the Interim Committee in June, Szilard organized a committee of like-minded souls, including most notably Glenn Seaborg, the discoverer of plutonium, under the chairmanship of James Franck, the Nobel laureate, who had been in charge of experimental physics at Göttingen during Oppenheimer's time there, to prepare a written account of his views. The result was what has become known as the Franck Report, which was sent to Henry Stimson on June 12, 1945. In place of the Bohr-Oppenheimer vision of an end to war brought about by a demonstration of the unprecedentedly deadly power of atomic bombs, the authors of the Franck Report urged the importance of an "international agreement on total prevention of nuclear war." What they shared with Bohr was the view that the "secret" of the bomb was an illusion: other nations could, of course, they emphasized, work out how an atomic bomb was made. Where they differed from Oppenheimer and his fellow members of the Target and the Interim committees was on the question of whether it was justified to use the bomb to kill huge numbers of Japanese people. What the Franck Report recommended was a demonstration before "the eyes of representatives of all the United Nations" of the power of the atomic bomb. This could be done, they urged, by exploding the bomb "on the desert or a barren island," and then giving Japan an ultimatum to surrender. Only if the Japanese refused to surrender should the bomb be used against them.

The main focus of the report, however, was not Japan, but the postwar international situation. "Nuclear bombs," the report emphatically reiterated, "cannot possibly remain a 'secret weapon' at the exclusive disposal of this country for more than a few years. The scientific facts on which their construction is based are well known to scientists of other countries." Therefore:

> Unless an effective international control of nuclear explosives is instituted, a race for nuclear armaments is certain to ensue following the first revelation of our possession of nuclear weapons to the world. Within ten years other countries may have nuclear bombs, each of which, weighing less than a ton, could destroy an urban area of more than ten miles. In the war to which such an armaments race is likely to lead, the United States, with its agglomeration of population and industry in comparatively few metropolitan districts, will be at a disadvantage compared to nations whose population and industry are scattered over large areas.

Using the bomb against the Japanese, the report argued, could have far-reaching consequences for both the United States and the entire world, for: "If the United States were to be the first to release this new means of indiscriminate destruction upon mankind, she would sacrifice public support throughout the world, precipitate the race for armaments, and prejudice the possibility of reaching an international agreement on the future control of such weapons." The report was an extraordinarily farsighted and persuasive document that demanded to be taken seriously, not only because of the intrinsic merits of its arguments, but also because it was written by scientists who had been central to the development of the atomic bomb from the very beginning and who understood, as well as anyone, its destructive power.

The task of formulating an official response to the report was delegated by Stimson to the Scientific Panel, who reported back to the Interim Committee in a memo dated June 16, 1945. "It is clear," Oppenheimer, Fermi, Lawrence and Compton wrote, "that we, as scientific men, have no proprietary rights [and] . . . no claim to special competence in solving the political, social, and military problems which are presented by the advent of atomic power." Nevertheless, they were prepared to weigh up the competing views that: (a) a demonstration of the bomb should be given in order to induce the surrender of the Japanese; and (b) the bomb provided an "opportunity of saving American lives by immediate military use." "We find ourselves," they reported, "closer to the latter views: we can propose no technical demonstration likely to bring an end to the war; we see no acceptable alternative to direct military use."

At its meeting of June 21, 1945, therefore, the Interim Committee felt able to reaffirm its position that, as a War Department memo put it, "the weapon should be used against Japan at the earliest opportunity, that it be used without warning, and that it be used on a dual target, namely, a military installation or war plant surrounded by or adjacent to homes or other buildings most susceptible to damage." The committee also recommended that, at the forthcoming "Big Three" meeting in Potsdam, "there would be considerable advantage, if the opportunity arises . . . in having the President advise the Russians simply that we are working intensely on this weapon and that, if we succeed as we think we will, we plan to use it against the enemy."

Meanwhile, Szilard, having lost his battle to influence the Interim Committee, was hard at work visiting scientists and trying to persuade them to put on record their opposition to using the bomb against Japanese cities. "I understand that at frequently recurring intervals Dr. Szilard is absent from his assigned place of work at the Metallurgical Laboratory in Chicago," Groves wrote to Compton on June 29, "and further that he travels extensively between Chicago, New York and Washington, DC." Szilard had written a petition to the President, urging him "to rule that the United States shall not resort to the use of atomic bombs in this war unless the terms which will be imposed upon Japan have been made public in detail and Japan knowing these terms has refused to surrender," which he was circulating among the scientists involved with the Manhattan Project, trying to get as many of them as possible to sign it.

The petition went first to the Met Lab, then to the scientists at Oak Ridge and finally to Los Alamos. In a letter to accompany the petition, Szilard wrote:

> However small the chance might be that our petition may influence the course of events, I personally feel that it would be a matter of importance if a large number of scientists who have worked in this field went clearly and unmistakably on record as to their opposition on moral grounds to the use of these bombs in the present phase of the war.

"The fact that the people in the United States are unaware of the choice which faces us," he added, "increases our responsibility in this matter."

One of the people to whom Szilard sent a copy of the petition, together with this letter, was Edward Teller, who recalls that it "made good sense to me, and I could think of no reason that those of us at Los Alamos who agreed shouldn't sign it."

Before signing and circulating the petition, however, Teller discussed it with Oppenheimer, who, he later wrote, began talking about Franck and Szilard "in a way that, until then, he had reserved for General Groves." Then Oppenheimer asked Teller: "What do they know about Japanese psychology? How can they judge the way to end the war?" According to Teller's recollection, Oppenheimer's view was that such decisions were best made by "our political leaders" rather than "individuals who happened to work on the bomb project." As a result of this conversation, Teller, somewhat to his later regret, refused to sign the petition.

Oppenheimer's opposition to Szilard's views carried great weight at Los Alamos, a fact of which Szilard himself was well aware. "Of course," he wrote in a letter addressed to some of the scientists at Los Alamos whom he knew and liked best, "you will find only a few people on your project who are willing to sign such a petition. I am sure you will find many boys confused as to what kind of thing a moral issue is." In fact, the petition did not have even the limited influence that Szilard hoped for it, since it never reached the President. That Szilard's views were shared by many of the scientists working on the project was, however, put on record when Compton was asked by Colonel Nichols about the views of his colleagues at the Met Lab. An opinion poll was conducted, in which about two-thirds of the scientists at the Met Lab took part. The poll asked the respondents to say which of five statements most accurately represented their view. Nearly half—46 percent—chose statement 2, which read: "Give a military demonstration in Japan, to be followed by a renewed opportunity for surrender before full use of the weapons is employed." A further 26 percent chose statement 3: "Give an experimental demonstration in this country, with representatives of Japan present; followed by a new opportunity for surrender before full use of the weapons is employed." Thus, 72 percent of those polled agreed with Franck and Szilard that the bomb should be demonstrated to the Japanese before being used against their cities. Only 15 percent chose statement 1: "Use the weapons in the manner that is from the military point of view most effective in bringing about prompt Japanese surrender at minimum human cost to our armed forces." Nevertheless, by the time this poll was conducted,[58] this last statement was the one that most accurately represented U.S. government policy.

---

[58] The date of the poll is a little uncertain because of a confusion in the record. The memo

According to Richard Rhodes's excellent book *The Making of the Atomic Bomb*, Truman made the decision to drop the bomb on Japan on June 1, the day after the Interim Committee had recommended at its May 31 meeting "that the bomb be used against Japan as soon as possible; that it be used on a war plant surrounded by workers' homes; and that it be used without prior warning." Henry Stimson, as Secretary for War, was ultimately responsible for that advice, but he remained deeply troubled by the thought of using the bomb to obliterate Japanese cities, while preferring that to the drawn-out bloodshed that would result from an attempted invasion. What Stimson wanted, ideally, was to make it possible for Japan to surrender before it was either invaded or bombed into submission.

On July 2, Stimson prepared a memo to Truman entitled "Proposed Program for Japan," in which he reviewed the appalling loss of life that would result from an invasion of Japan and suggested that this prospect might be avoided by "giving them a warning of what is to come and a definite opportunity to capitulate." After all, he argued, "Japan is not a nation composed wholly of mad fanatics of an entirely different mentality from ours" and: "We have a national interest in creating, if possible, a condition wherein the Japanese nation may live as a peaceful and useful member of the future Pacific community." Because he realized it was an extremely important consideration for the Japanese, Stimson added that in his opinion, when giving the Japanese an opportunity to surrender, "we should add that we do not exclude a constitutional monarchy under the present dynasty," which would, he advised the President, "substantially add to the chances of acceptance." By this time, however, Stimson's influence on Truman was much less than that of James Byrnes, who was sworn in as Secretary of State on July 3 and was inclined to take a much less conciliatory line on Japan.

During the first few days of July, preparations were under way for two events that would coincide and would determine the shape of postwar politics: the Trinity test in New Mexico and the Potsdam summit in Germany. In the minds of those shaping the military and foreign policies of the United States, these two events were linked in the sense that, it was hoped, the Trinity test would strengthen Truman's hand in the Potsdam negotiations.

The date fixed for the Trinity test was July 16, which was, not coincidentally, the day that the Potsdam conference began. The dress

---

containing the results of the poll is dated July 13, 1945, but it gives the date of the poll as July 18. Assuming that the memo was not, in fact, written five days before the events it describes, it seems most likely that the first date is an error and that the poll did indeed take place on July 18.

rehearsal conducted two months earlier—the "100-ton test," as it came to be known (though that figure was an approximation)—had provided an invaluable opportunity to go through the complicated set of procedures that such a test would involve. On a wooden platform some 800 yards away from the proposed ground zero of the Trinity test, a huge pile of TNT was detonated, while the instruments developed by Bainbridge's team measured, among other things, how far the radioactive particles were dispersed, the optical and nuclear effects of the blast and, most crucially for the coming test, the yield of the blast. This last measurement confirmed the accuracy of their gauges, which successfully showed that the 108 tons of TNT had exploded with the energy of 108 tons of TNT. Now they could be confident that they would indeed learn from the Trinity test itself exactly what the yield of the Fat Man implosion bomb was.

Preparations for Trinity were, like almost everything associated with the Manhattan Project, conducted on an almost unimaginably vast scale. This was a scientific experiment like no other. Several roads and many houses had to be built especially for it. At the end of 1944, the camp at the Trinity site had housing for 160 military personnel. On June 1, 1945, there were, in addition to the military personnel, 210 scientists and technical aides there. By the middle of July this figure had grown to 250, and on the eve of the test there were 425 people camped there.

The gadget itself was assembled on Friday, July 13, a date chosen with black humor by Kistiakowsky, in order, he said, to bring luck. The time chosen for the test was 4 a.m. on the morning of July 16. "This hour," says Groves, "had been fixed with the thought that an explosion at that time would attract the least attention from casual observers in the surrounding area, since everyone would be asleep." Groves and Oppenheimer agreed to meet at 1 a.m. that morning. Groves urged Oppenheimer to get some sleep beforehand and "set the example by doing so myself." Oppenheimer, however, slept not a wink.

At the appointed hour, Oppenheimer and Groves met and went to the control dugout, "South 10,000," an observation site named after its distance in yards (about five and a half miles) from ground zero. From then on, reports Groves:

Every five or ten minutes, Oppenheimer and I would leave the dugout and go outside and discuss the weather. I was devoting myself during this period to shielding Oppenheimer from the excitement swirling around us, so that he could consider the situation as calmly as possible, for the decisions to be taken had to be governed largely by his appraisal of the technical factors involved.

Because of bad weather, the test was delayed until 5:30 a.m. With twenty minutes to go, Samuel Allison started the countdown over a loudspeaker. At 5:25 a.m., to indicate that there were just five minutes to go, a rocket was fired into the air; another was fired at 5:29 to say that there was just one minute left. To everybody there, it felt like an awfully long minute. "I never realized seconds could be so long," James Conant whispered to Groves. Everyone else was silent.

Then, finally, at precisely 5:29 and 45 seconds, those present witnessed the world's first atomic explosion. "My first impression," Groves recalled, "was one of tremendous light, and then, as I turned, I saw the now familiar fireball." He had planned, after the test, on having discussions with Oppenheimer on some important points regarding the bomb, but:

> These plans proved utterly impracticable, for no one who had witnessed the test was in a frame of mind to discuss anything. The reaction was simply too great. It was not only that we had achieved success with the bomb; but that everyone—scientists, military officers, and engineers—realized that we had been personal participants in, and eyewitnesses to, a major milestone in the world's history and had a sobering appreciation of what the results of our work would be.

Oppenheimer's recollections of Trinity, filmed for a television documentary in 1965, have provided what remains his most famous utterance—indeed, one of the most famous utterances of the twentieth century. "We knew the world would not be the same," he said.

> A few people laughed, a few people cried. Most people were silent. I remembered the line from the Hindu scripture, the Bhagavad Gita: Vishnu is trying to persuade the prince that he should do his duty, and to impress him, takes on his multi-armed form and says: "Now I am become death, the destroyer of worlds." I suppose we all thought that one way or another.

Because of its use in this context by Oppenheimer, "Now I am become death, the destroyer of worlds" has become one of the best-known lines from the Bhagavad Gita. Those who go looking for them, however, often fail to find them, since in most English translations of the text they do not appear. The Sanskrit word that Oppenheimer translates as "death" is more usually rendered as "time," so that, for example, in the Penguin Classics edition, the line is given as: "I am all-powerful Time, which destroys all things." In the famous translation by the nineteenth-century poet Edwin Arnold it appears as: "Thou seest Me as Time, who kills, Time who brings all to doom, The Slayer Time, Ancient of Days, come hither to consume," which conveys an image diametrically opposed to that of a sudden release of deadly power. Oppenheimer, however, was following the example of his Sanskrit teacher, Arthur Ryder, whose translation reads: "Death am I, and my present task destruction."

A vivid description of Oppenheimer at the moment of the explosion has been left by Groves's assistant, Brigadier General Thomas F. Farrell. "Dr. Oppenheimer," Farrell remembers, "on whom had rested a very heavy burden, grew tenser as the last second ticked off. He scarcely breathed."

> He held on to a post to steady himself. For the last few seconds, he stared directly ahead and then when the announcer shouted "Now!" and there came this tremendous burst of light followed shortly thereafter by the deep growling roar of the explosion, his face relaxed into an expression of tremendous relief.

It was that sense of relief that was felt most palpably by the majority of the scientists there. "Some people claim to have wondered at the time about the future of mankind," Norris Bradbury remarked. "I didn't. We were at war and the damned thing worked." Similarly, when Frank Oppenheimer, who was with his brother when the bomb went off, was asked about their initial reaction, he recalled: "I think we just said 'It worked.'"

The *New York Times* journalist William L. Laurence, who had been chosen by Groves to describe the event for posterity, remembers the euphoric emotional release brought on by the realization among the scientists that their huge, complicated—and extremely expensive—task had been completed successfully: "A loud cry filled the air. The little groups that hitherto had stood rooted to the earth like desert plants broke into dance." Scientists took it in turns to howl jubilantly into the PA system.

For some, that sense of euphoric relief was short-lived and tempered by exhaustion and anxiety. As Victor Weisskopf put it: "Our first feeling was one of elation, then we realized we were tired, and then we were worried." When Fermi returned to Los Alamos, his wife Laura remembers: "He seemed shrunken and aged, made of old parchment, so entirely dried out and browned was he by the desert sun and exhausted by the ordeal." Rabi has recalled that, though initially he was "thrilled," after a few minutes, "I had goose flesh all over me when I realized what this meant for the future of humanity." When, back at base camp, Rabi caught sight of Oppenheimer returning from the dugout in a jeep he shared with Farrell, he did not see a man contemplating the Hindu scriptures, but a disconcerting triumphalism: "I'll never forget his walk; I'll never forget the way he stepped out of the car . . . his walk was like *High Noon* . . . this kind of strut. He had done it." Farrell walked over to Groves and said: "The war is over." "Yes," replied Groves, "after we drop two bombs on Japan."

The power of the bomb was estimated to be around 20,000 tons of TNT, which was at the high end of the various predictions made by the Los Alamos scientists. (The scientists had a betting pool to see who could come closest to guessing the exact yield of the bomb; the prize went to Rabi, who had guessed 18,000 tons.) The light from the blast could be seen more than 100 miles away and the heat generated by it could be felt twenty miles away. The U.S. Army did everything they could to keep it out of the newspapers, but there was no hope of keeping something of that magnitude a secret. "My God," one security official remarked, "you might as well try to hide the Mississippi River." Instead, they issued a press release claiming that the blast was due to the accidental explosion of a "remotely located ammunition magazine."

Just a few hours after the blast, at 8 a.m., Groves called George Harrison in Washington, who in turn sent a coded cable to Stimson in Potsdam:

> Operated on this morning. Diagnosis not yet complete but results seem satisfactory and already exceed expectations. Local press release necessary as interest extends great distance. Dr. Groves pleased. He returns tomorrow. I will keep you posted.

The following day, Harrison sent another message, using a more elaborate series of coded remarks to provide some details:

> Doctor Groves has just returned most enthusiastic and confident that the little boy is as husky as his big brother. The light in his eyes discernible from here to Highold and I could hear his screams from here to my farm.

Decoded, this meant: 1. that the uranium "Little Boy" device was likely to be as powerful as the plutonium "Fat Man" bomb tested at Trinity; 2. that the light from the bomb could be seen 200 miles away (200 miles being the distance from Washington to Highold on Long Island);[59] and 3. that the sound of the explosion traveled about forty miles (the distance from Washington to Stimson's farm in Upperville, Virginia).

---

[59] This was probably an exaggeration.

Stimson immediately passed this information on to Truman, who was, Stimson later recalled, "tremendously pepped up by it." A few days later, Stimson received a long memo from Groves, written together with Farrell, which combined statistical details of the test with personal impressions of what it was like to be there. "For the first time in history," Groves wrote, "there was a nuclear explosion. And what an explosion!"

> For a brief period there was a lighting effect within a radius of 20 miles equal to several suns in midday; a huge ball of fire was formed which lasted for several seconds. This ball mushroomed and rose to a height of over ten thousand feet before it dimmed.

The mushroom cloud, Groves wrote, "deposited its dust and radioactive materials over a wide area." Following and monitoring the cloud were several doctors and scientists, who reported finding some radioactive material as much as 120 miles away, but at no place, Groves told Stimson, was the level of radioactivity high enough to necessitate evacuation.

With his memo, Groves enclosed a number of other descriptions of the test, including the one by Farrell quoted earlier, which concluded on an apocalyptic note. The "awesome roar" of the blast, Farrell wrote, "warned of doomsday and made us feel that we puny things were blasphemous to dare tamper with the forces heretofore reserved to the Almighty." "The feeling of the entire assembly," Groves added, "was similar to that described by General Farrell, with even the uninitiated feeling profound awe." An even stronger feeling, he went on, was that the faith of those responsible for this "Herculean project" had been justified:

> I personally thought of Blondin crossing Niagara Falls on his tight rope, only to me this tight rope had lasted for three years and of my repeated confident-appearing assurances that such a thing was possible and that we would do it.

Groves's memo reached Potsdam on July 21. By this time Churchill had already been told about Trinity, but Truman and his advisors were still unsure about how to play it with regard to the Russians. In a diary entry of July 19, Stimson, reflecting on the repressiveness of Stalin's regime and the contrast with "a nation whose system rests upon free speech and all the elements of freedom, as does ours," recorded that he was "beginning to feel that our committee which met in Washington on this subject and was so set upon opening communications with the

Russians on the subject may have been thinking in a vacuum." When, two days later, Groves's memo arrived, Stimson read it out in its entirety to Truman and Byrnes: "They were immensely pleased. Truman said it gave him an entirely new feeling of confidence." The memo was then shown to Churchill. The four of them, Stimson recorded in his diary, were "unanimous in thinking that it was advisable to tell the Russians at least that we were working on that subject, and intended to use it if and when it was successfully finished."

14

Los Alamos 3: Heavy with Misgiving

On July 23, 1945, barely a week after the Trinity test, the U.S. Secretary of War, Henry L. Stimson, recorded in his diary a conversation he had had that day with George Marshall, the Army Chief of Staff, in which the two had agreed that "now with our new weapon we would not need the assistance of the Russians to conquer Japan." The following day, Truman told Stalin about the atomic bomb. Or rather, as Truman later recalled it: "I casually mentioned to Stalin that we had a new weapon of unusual destructive force." To Truman's great surprise, Stalin showed little interest. "All he said was that he was glad to hear it and hoped we would make 'good use of it against the Japanese.'" Stalin, of course, already knew a great deal about the Manhattan Project, and the Soviets had been told by Fuchs in May that a test of the bomb was being planned for July. What Truman and his advisors did not know was that the Soviet Union's own atomic-bomb project was already well under way, accelerated by the information provided by Fuchs, Greenglass et al.

On the same day that Truman had this strangely muted exchange with Stalin, a directive—drafted by Groves and approved by Marshall and Stimson—was issued to General Carl Spaatz, the new commander of the Strategic Air Forces, which would be responsible for delivering the bomb. The air force, the directive stated, "will deliver its first special bomb as soon as weather will permit visual bombing after about August 3, 1945, on one of the targets: Hiroshima, Kokura, Niigata and Nagasaki." Two days later, the Potsdam Declaration was issued, calling for the Japanese to surrender and defining the surrender terms acceptable to the U.S. and the UK, which, on that very day, had a new Prime Minister, Clement Attlee having decisively beaten Churchill in the UK's general election.

"The prodigious land, sea and air forces of the United States, the British Empire and of China," the declaration announced, "are poised to strike the final blows upon Japan." And therefore: "We call upon the government of Japan to proclaim now that unconditional surrender of all Japanese armed forces, and to provide proper and adequate assurances of their good faith in such action. The alternative for Japan is prompt and utter destruction." Truman instructed Stimson that the directive of July 24, ordering General Spaatz to deliver the bomb as soon after August 3 as the weather permitted, "would stand unless I notified him that the Japanese reply to our ultimatum was acceptable." On July 28, Radio Tokyo announced that the Japanese government would continue to fight. The official Japanese response was "Mokusatsu," the meaning of which has been much debated by historians. It was interpreted by the U.S. to mean "ignore," but it can also mean "treat with silent contempt." Neither meaning, of course, would constitute a response that Truman was likely to regard as acceptable, and so Japan had now to face the "prompt and utter destruction" promised by the Potsdam Declaration.

At Los Alamos by this time the euphoria of the Trinity test had given way to a somber mood, as they went about the task of preparing the bomb. In the minds of many was the dreadful realization that, as Sam Allison put it: "They're going to take this thing and fry hundreds of Japanese!" The *High Noon* strut that Rabi had seen in Oppenheimer immediately after Trinity was no longer in evidence. His secretary, Anne Wilson, recalls that he looked depressed rather than triumphant, as if he were thinking: "Oh God, what have we done! All this work, and people are going to die in the thousands." One day, noticing that Oppenheimer seemed particularly distressed, Wilson asked him what was wrong. He replied: "I just keep thinking about all those poor little people."

On the day of the Trinity test, the Little Boy casing was shipped to Tinian, an island in the western Pacific, south of Japan, from where the U.S. Air Force had decided the atomic bombing raids would be launched. Soon afterward the enriched uranium to be placed in the casing was flown out, the final assembly of the bomb to be performed by a team of about sixty people from Los Alamos, including Deak Parsons, Luis Alvarez, Phil Morrison and Robert Serber. For this specific task the scientists were put in uniforms and given ranks: Serber was, to his great pride, made a colonel, Alvarez a lieutenant colonel and all the others captains. Two huts at the air force base served as "laboratories," one for Little Boy, one for Fat Man.

Which of the four Japanese cities mentioned in the directive to General Spaatz would be the first to be bombed was not decided until a few days before the raid. On July 30, Spaatz cabled Washington to say that he had heard that Hiroshima was the only one of the four that did not have Allied prisoner-of-war camps. In reply, he received orders that "Hiroshima should be given first priority." That day, the assembly of Little Boy was completed and General Farrell reported to Groves that the mission could be flown the following day, August 1. This, however, proved to be impossible because of the weather, a typhoon making flying impossible.

The man chosen to pilot the B-29 bomber that would deliver the bomb was Colonel Paul Tibbets, who, on August 4, after three days of anxious weather-watching, called a briefing for the crews of the seven planes that would be used during the mission (one for the bomb, three for a cloud-cover assessment the day before the drop, two to photograph and observe the bombing, and a seventh as a spare in case the first malfunctioned). The crewmen were astonished when they arrived at the meeting to find the briefing hut surrounded by military policemen armed with rifles. They were even more astonished when Tibbets introduced Deak Parsons, who told them that the bomb they were about to drop was the most destructive weapon ever made. When Parsons had finished, Tibbets took over to tell the men how honored he and they were to be taking part in a raid that would "shorten the war by at least six months."

The following day, Tibbets named the plane he had chosen to fly after his mother—*Enola Gay*—and hurriedly found a sign-writer to paint the name in foot-high letters immediately below the pilot's window. A few hours later, at 2:45 a.m. on August 6, the newly named *Enola Gay* set off from Tinian on its way to Hiroshima. Mid-flight, Tibbets announced to the crew that the weapon they were carrying was in fact an atomic bomb. The journey took more than six hours. At 9:14 Tinian time (8:14 a.m. local time), the bomb was dropped over Hiroshima. "Fellows," Tibbets announced on the *Enola Gay's* intercom, "you have just dropped the first atomic bomb in history." What the crewmen experienced was a blinding glare, followed by two shock waves so intense they thought they had been hit by heavy guns. After the second shock wave, Tibbets has recalled: "We turned back to look at Hiroshima. The city was hidden by that awful cloud . . . boiling up, mushrooming, terrible and incredibly tall."

As they looked back, the crewmen were awestruck to see that where, two minutes earlier there had been a city, there was now what one of them likened to "a pot of boiling black oil." The tail gunner, Robert Caron, had the best view:

I was trying to describe the mushroom, this turbulent mass. I saw fires springing up in different places, like flames shooting up on a bed of coals. I was asked to count them. I said, "Count them?" Hell, I gave up when there were about fifteen, they were coming too fast to count. I can still see it—that mushroom and that turbulent mass—it looked like lava or molasses covering the whole city, and it seemed to flow outward up into the foothills where the little valleys would come into the plain, with fires starting up all over, so pretty soon it was hard to see anything because of the smoke.

With a yield of 12,500 tons of TNT, the Hiroshima bomb was a good deal less powerful than the Fat Man tested at Trinity. To the people of Hiroshima, however, it was a destructive force the like of which none of them could previously have imagined. The temperature at the hypercenter of the explosion was an inconceivable 5,400°F, enough to inflict primary burns on everybody within a two-mile radius. But it was not only the heat and power of the blast that terrified and confused the population of the city (estimated to have been about 255,000), but also the instantaneous suddenness of that power. "I just could not understand," one witness later said, "why our surroundings had changed so greatly in one instant." The appalling horror experienced by the inhabitants of Hiroshima was conveyed with searing intensity and vividness by the writer John Hersey in a long article, based on eyewitness accounts, that was published in the *New Yorker* in August 1946. Indeed, the magazine devoted its entire issue to the piece, something it had never done before and has never done since. It did so on this occasion, the editors explained, "in the conviction that few of us have yet comprehended the all but incredible destructive power of this weapon, and that everyone might well take time to consider the terrible implications of its use."

The article was a publishing sensation. The issue sold out within hours of publication, the entire text was broadcast on the radio and a book version was rushed out, which became a best-seller. To some extent, Hersey's account of Hiroshima was a fulfillment of the hope that Bohr had instilled in Oppenheimer and which became, in the absence of a genuine possibility that the Germans would build an atom bomb first, Oppenheimer's rationale for building the bomb and recommending its use on civilians: the hope, that is, that the shock of seeing just how powerful the bomb was would be so great that the people and governments of the world would demand international cooperation to end war.

Certainly few things could be more shocking than the scenes described, with a restraint that makes them even more powerful, in

Hersey's article. Rather than attempting a synoptic overview of the destruction, Hersey concentrates on the stories of particular individuals, such as the Reverend Mr. Kiyoshi Tanimoto, who, at the time of the explosion, was helping a friend to move some belongings to a house two miles out of town, where they would be safe from the bombing raids that they, like everyone in Hiroshima, feared and expected to come soon (Hiroshima being the only important city, other than Kyoto, that had thus far not been heavily bombed). Along the way, the two men heard the air siren that warned of the approach of American planes, and then the all-clear that was sounded when it was realized that only three planes were approaching. Then, just outside the house (so about two miles from the center of the explosion), they saw a tremendous flash of light. Mr. Tanimoto dived to the floor. When he stood up again, he saw that his friend's house had collapsed. He ran into town, thinking he could help people. As he approached the city center, he passed hundreds of badly burned people fleeing in the opposite direction. There were collapsed buildings, fires and desperate, wounded people everywhere he looked. Wanting to rescue people trapped on sandspits in the river, he took a boat, which had been surrounded by a group of five nearly naked and badly burned men, and began to ferry the wounded away from the fires. At one sandspit Tanimoto saw a group of about twenty men and women, and, writes Hersey:

> He drove the boat onto the bank and urged them to get aboard. They did not move and he realized that they were too weak to lift themselves. He reached down and took a woman by the hands, but her skin slipped off in huge glovelike pieces.

Many more eyewitness accounts have subsequently been published, confirming and adding to the details in Hersey's terrifying and horrible account. One man recalls that the streets were full of people whose skin was black and hanging from their bodies. "Many of them died along the road—I can still picture them in my mind—like walking ghosts." Other horrors described include "a woman with her jaw missing and her tongue hanging out of her mouth," "people with their bowels and brains coming out," a "dead child lying there and another who seemed to be crawling over him in order to run away, both of them burned to blackness." To one person who saw many such dreadful sights, however, the most shocking experience was of climbing a hill and looking down and seeing "that Hiroshima had disappeared . . . Hiroshima didn't exist—that was mainly what I saw—Hiroshima just didn't exist." Almost all the buildings in the city (the official estimate was 70,000 out of 76,000) were damaged or destroyed by the bomb. As for casualties, there has been some dispute, but the best estimate seems to be 135,000, of which 66,000 died and 69,000 were injured. In other words, the casualties amounted to more than half of the total population. Of the people who were 3,000 feet or closer to the center of the blast, the bomb killed more than 90 percent.

It would be some weeks before the harrowing details of the suffering inflicted upon the people of Hiroshima were known to the scientists who made it possible. Indeed, it took nearly a day for the bare fact of the bombing to reach most of them. Two notable exceptions were Deak Parsons, who was aboard the *Enola Gay* during its fateful mission, in order to carry out, mid-flight, the very last stages of assembly, and Luis Alvarez, who was aboard one of the two observation planes that accompanied *Enola Gay*. The first person to hear the news who was not actually on one of the planes was General Farrell, who was on Tinian island. At about 9:40 a.m. local time—twenty-five minutes after the explosion—Farrell received a radio message from Parsons, who was on the *Enola Gay*, heading back to Tinian:

> Deak to Farrell: Results in all respects clear-cut and successful. Immediate action to carry out further plans [that is, prepare for the second bomb] is recommended. Greater visible effects than at Alamogordo. Target was Hiroshima. Proceeding to Tinian with normal conditions in airplane.

The remark about the visible effects being greater than at the Trinity test gave Farrell the impression that the yield of the bomb was at least 20,000 tons of TNT.

The time difference between Tinian and Washington is fourteen hours, so when the *Enola Gay* left Tinian at 2:45 a.m. on Monday, August 6, it was 12:45 p.m. on Sunday, August 5 in Washington. That morning Groves had arrived at his office to find a cable telling him that takeoff was scheduled for that day. He therefore waited for the report of the takeoff. By 2 p.m. he had heard nothing, so, to relieve the tension, he went out to play tennis. That evening at 6:45, while having dinner at the Army-Navy Club, he was called to the phone and told that the plane had left on schedule. In fact, this was just half an hour before the bomb would be dropped on Hiroshima, but of course neither Groves nor whoever he spoke to in Tinian would have known that. After dinner, Groves went back to his office to spend the night there, awaiting news from the Pacific. "The hours went by," he writes in his autobiography, "more slowly than I ever imagined hours could go by, and still there was no news." At 11:30 p.m.—nearly four hours after the original message—Groves received a copy of the report of the bombing that Parsons had sent to Farrell from the *Enola Gay*. After he received this message, Groves remembers, "I went to sleep on the cot that had been brought into my office, after telling the Duty Officer to call me when the next message came in."

At about 3 p.m. local time on August 6 (1 a.m. in Washington), the *Enola Gay* returned to Tinian. It arrived in triumph, with 200 or more soldiers, technicians and scientists there to greet it and cheer the crew. General Spaatz was there to pin the Distinguished Service Cross on the breast of Colonel Tibbets's overalls. Afterward, in the briefing room, Parsons was awarded the Silver Star. Four and a half hours later, Groves was awakened to be told that a cable had arrived from General Farrell, reporting "additional information furnished by Parsons, crews, and observers on return to Tinian." Parsons and other observers, Farrell reported, "felt this strike was tremendous and awesome even in comparison with New Mexico test."

President Truman had not yet arrived back in the States from the Potsdam conference. He heard the news midway across the Atlantic Ocean on board the USS *Augusta*. As he tells the story in his *Memoirs*: "I was eating lunch with members of the *Augusta*'s crew when Captain Frank Graham, White House Map Room watch officer, handed me the following message":

To the President
From the Secretary of War

  Big bomb dropped on Hiroshima August 5 at 7:15 p.m. Washington time. First reports indicate complete success which was even more conspicuous than earlier test.

"I was greatly moved," Truman writes. "I telephoned Byrnes aboard ship to give him the news and then said to the group of sailors around me, 'This is the greatest thing in history. It's time for us to get home.'"

In Truman's absence, it fell to Groves, with the assistance of William L. Laurence, the *New York Times* journalist whom he had invited to witness Trinity, to prepare a statement about the bombing. The announcement, read out by the President's press secretary, was made at 11 a.m., Washington time. Containing, as it did, the first public acknowledgment of the atomic-bomb project, it had a sensational impact throughout the world. "Sixteen hours ago," it began:

an American airplane dropped one bomb on Hiroshima, an important Japanese Army base. That bomb had more power than 20,000 tons of TNT . . . It is an atomic bomb. It is a harnessing of the basic power of the universe. The force from which the sun draws its power has been loosed against those who brought war to the Far East.

"We have spent two billion dollars on the greatest scientific gamble in history," the statement continued, "and won." If the Japanese did not now accept the terms of the Potsdam ultimatum, they could "expect a rain of ruin from the air, the like of which has never been seen on this earth."

Much to his chagrin, listening to this statement on the radio—at what, for him in Los Alamos, would have been 9 a.m. on the morning of Monday August 6—was the first confirmation Oppenheimer had that the bomb had gone off successfully. He had expected to be told before it was made public. Indeed, he had sent his assistant John Manley to Washington with the express purpose of phoning him as soon as the news reached Groves's office. Just as Manley was about to phone, however, Groves stopped him, telling him that no one was to tell anybody about it until the President had announced it.

There was, perhaps, some consolation for Oppenheimer in the fact that the statement emphasized the importance of what it called "the achievement of scientific brains in putting together infinitely complex pieces of knowledge held by many men in different fields of science into a workable plan": "The battle of the laboratories held fateful risks for us as well as the battles of the air, land and sea, and we have now won the battle of the laboratories as we have won the other battles."

At Los Alamos, the effect of the announcement was an emotional release every bit as powerful as that which had followed the Trinity test. On that occasion it had been centered on the demonstration that what they had been designing and building actually *worked*. On this occasion it was to do with the fact that, where previously they had worked in furtive secrecy, now the spotlight had been shone upon them. What they had achieved had been recognized—by the President no less—as a crucially important task. They were celebrities.

That evening at Los Alamos there was a big assembly to celebrate their success. Oppenheimer made a dramatic entrance, walking from the back of the room to the stage and, once there, clasping his hands together like a prize-winning boxer. To ecstatic cheering, Oppenheimer told the crowd that it was too early to say what the results of the bombing had been, but that "the Japanese didn't like it." His only regret, he said, was that "we hadn't developed the bomb in time to use it against the

Germans." This, according to the young physicist who later recalled the event, "practically raised the roof."

The following day, August 7, 1945, the front pages of newspapers all over the world were dominated by the extraordinary revelations contained in the statement made on Truman's behalf, about the destruction of Hiroshima, the atomic-bomb project and about Oppenheimer. Overnight, Los Alamos changed from being a secret to being the most talked-about place in the world. Among those talking about it were the German physicists who had worked on the abortive Nazi bomb project, including Heisenberg, Weizsäcker and Otto Hahn, the last of whom had first announced the startling fact about nuclear fission back in January 1939. Those scientists had been captured by the Allies and at the time of the Hiroshima bombing were being held in a country house in Cambridgeshire called Farm Hall. Unknown to the scientists, microphones placed around the house were picking up almost every word they said to each other, so that a complete record exists of how they reacted to the news about Hiroshima.

The officer in charge of Farm Hall, Major T. H. Ritter, reported in a memo that, shortly before dinner on the evening of August 6, he told Hahn that the BBC had announced that an atomic bomb had been dropped.

> Hahn was completely shattered by the news and said he felt personally responsible for the deaths of hundreds of thousands of people, as it was his original discovery which had made the bomb possible. He told me that he had originally contemplated suicide when he realised the terrible potentialities of his discovery and he felt that now these had been realised and he was to blame. With the help of considerable alcoholic stimulant he was calmed down and we went down to dinner where he announced the news to the assembled guests.

The news was greeted with incredulity, particularly by Heisenberg, who declared: "I don't believe a word of the whole thing." The reason he gave for his skepticism reveals how little the German scientists knew about atomic-bomb physics. Such a bomb, Heisenberg declared, would require "ten tons of pure U-235," which, understandably, he did not believe the Allies could possibly have acquired.

Heisenberg's skepticism, however, did not last long. At 9 p.m. that evening, the German scientists gathered around a radio set to listen to the BBC news. It began: "Here is the news: It's dominated by a tremendous achievement of Allied scientists—the production of the atomic bomb." "The greatest destructive power devised by man," the report continued, "went into action this morning—the atomic bomb. British, American and Canadian scientists have succeeded, where Germans failed, in harnessing the basic power of the universe."

Some details in the report that captured the attention of the German scientists included: 1. that the cost of the project was £500 million (equivalent to $2 billion at the time); 2. that up to 125,000 people were employed in the factories that were built for the program, few of whom knew what they were producing; and 3. that the material used to make the bomb was uranium.

The report also included a statement prepared by Churchill before he left office, which emphasized the part played by Britain in the bomb program, especially in its early stages. "By God's mercy," Churchill said, somewhat rubbing it in for those listening at Farm Hall, "British and American science outpaced all German efforts. These were on a considerable scale, but far behind." "The whole burden of execution," he declared, "constitutes one of the greatest triumphs of American—or indeed human—genius of which there is a record."

Listening to the broadcast made the German scientists appreciate the colossal scale of the Manhattan Project. "We were unable to work on that scale," Hahn remarked to his colleagues, later adding: "I am thankful we didn't succeed." Heisenberg recalled that about a year earlier he had been told by someone in the German Foreign Office that the Americans had threatened to drop a uranium bomb on Dresden if the Germans did not surrender soon. "I was asked whether I thought it possible, and with complete conviction, I replied 'No.'"

The next day, August 7, the German scientists at Farm Hall—like millions of people all over the world—spent the entire morning poring over the newspaper reports of the Hiroshima bombing. Among the other impressed readers of the newspapers that day was Haakon Chevalier, who, on learning what his old friend had been up to, wrote him a note of congratulations, telling him: "You are probably the most famous man in the world today . . . I want you to know that we are very proud of you." It was three weeks before he received a reply.

The delay was possibly partly to do with Oppenheimer's difficulties in knowing what to say to a man whom he had named to the security services as the key go-between in what was regarded as one of the most serious attempts at atomic espionage of the entire war. However, even without that problem, Oppenheimer would have had little time for purely personal correspondence in the days immediately after the Hiroshima bombing. The scientific task was done, but much was happening—politically, militarily and socially.

Truman finally returned to Washington from Potsdam on the evening of August 7 and was immediately caught up in a whirlwind of activity generated by Groves, who was determined to proceed as quickly as possible with a second atomic bombing of Japan. He and Admiral William Purnell, Groves writes in his autobiography, "had often discussed the importance of having the second blow follow the first one quickly, so that the Japanese would not have time to recover their balance." This second bomb would have to be of the Fat Man type, there being no chance of assembling another uranium bomb at this stage (in fact, the Little Boy bomb remained one of a kind; the Fat Man design, despite its complicated assembly, being easier to manufacture, safer to transport and more powerful). After the success of the Trinity test, the only thing standing in the way of using a Fat Man bomb in Japan was the availability of plutonium. Groves had originally been advised that a plutonium bomb could be ready to use on August 20. At the end of July, this was revised to August 11. Groves, however, was too impatient to wait that long and, somewhat against the advice he was given by the scientists, saw to it that the bomb was assembled, loaded and ready to use by the evening of August 8.

At Tinian, therefore, there was little time to reflect on the Hiroshima bomb. Bernard O'Keefe, a young navy officer who was part of the assembly team, remembers: "With the success of the Hiroshima weapon, the pressure to be ready with the much more complex implosion device became excruciating."

> Everyone felt that the sooner we could get off another mission, the more likely it was that the Japanese would feel that we had large quantities of the devices and would surrender sooner. We were certain that one day saved would mean that the war would be over one day sooner.

While the bomb that would destroy Nagasaki was being hurriedly assembled, diplomatic maneuvers were being pursued with equal urgency—the bombing of Hiroshima having accelerated both the Soviet Union's plans for joining the war against Japan and the Japanese plans for negotiating peace. On August 8, the Japanese Foreign Minister was hoping to secure Soviet mediation in the search for acceptable surrender terms. When, however, his ambassador in Moscow met the Soviet Foreign Minister, Vyacheslav Molotov, he was told that, far from brokering a peace, the Soviet Union was entering the war against Japan, with effect from the following day. Bearing in mind the time difference between Moscow and Japan, this meant that, within two hours of that meeting, at midnight local time, the 1.6 million Soviet troops that had massed on the Manchurian border received their orders to attack.

Meanwhile, at Tinian the Fat Man bomb assembled by O'Keefe and his team was loaded into the bomb bay of a B-29 called *Bock's Car*, named after its usual pilot, Frederick Bock. On this mission, however, the bomber would be piloted by Major Charles W. Sweeney, who had been told that his primary target was Kokura, one of Japan's most important arsenals. The secondary target was the port of Nagasaki, an important center of shipbuilding. Neither the President nor Oppenheimer and the rest of the Scientific Advisory Panel were involved in the decision to carry out this second atomic bombing. Indeed, no separate decision was made, or deemed necessary. The directive of July 24 had ordered General Spaatz to drop the first bomb "after about August 3" and subsequent bombs "as soon as made ready by the project staff." He would therefore keep dropping whatever bombs were made available to him until he was ordered to stop.

Just before dawn on August 9, *Bock's Car* took off from Tinian. Unlike the first mission, this second one was beset with problems. For one thing, the weather—squally showers and storms—was hardly ideal. Second, they discovered just before takeoff that *Bock's Car* had a defective fuel pump, which meant that 800 gallons of fuel could not be pumped into the engine from the bomb bay. This meant that the plane would have to fly to Japan and back with the extra weight of those gallons of fuel. Despite these problems, so keen were Groves and Purnell to get a second bomb off quickly that there was no question of delaying the flight. Immediately before taking off, Sweeney was approached by Purnell. "Young man," he said, "do you know how much that bomb cost?" "About twenty-five million dollars," Sweeney replied. "See that we get our money's worth," Purnell told him.

Accompanied by just one observation plane (the other got separated in the bad weather), *Bock's Car* arrived at Kokura at 10:44 a.m. local time to find that the target was obscured by cloud. Sweeney therefore decided to switch to Nagasaki. The sky above that city too was covered in cloud, but at about 11 a.m. a hole opened in the cloud cover long enough (twenty seconds) for the bombardier to see the target. The bomb was dropped and exploded with a force significantly greater than that of the Hiroshima Little Boy bomb: 22,000 rather than 12,500 tons of TNT. Because the hills around the city contained the blast, however, the casualties at Nagasaki were not quite so high. The best estimate seems to be that at the moment of impact around 40,000 people died and 60,000 were injured. It is thought that, by 1946, mainly because of the lingering effects of radiation, the number of deaths caused by the bomb had risen to about 70,000.

Robert Serber was supposed to be on one of the observation planes for this second mission, but the pilot ordered him off the plane because he did not have a parachute. As Serber was the only one who knew how to operate the high-speed camera that was to have been used, no photographs of the raid were taken from the air. Even if he had been on board, no photographs would have been taken, since the plane in question was the one that got separated. When the bomb was being dropped on Nagasaki, that observation plane was still flying over Kokura. By the time the pilot realized what had happened and flew to Nagasaki, the bomb had been dropped and the mushroom cloud had already appeared. "The only picture we got," recalls Serber ruefully, "was taken by his tail gunner with a snapshot camera."

Moments before the bomb was dropped, the other observation plane dropped some instruments attached to parachutes that would enable the scientists to measure the force of the blast and some of its effects. Among those instruments was a pressure cylinder to which Serber, Alvarez and Morrison had attached a personal letter to the Japanese physicist Ryokichi Sagane, whom they had known at Berkeley and who was then a professor at the University of Tokyo. The point of the letter was to tell Sagane on good authority about the threat facing Japan:

> You have known for several years that an atomic bomb could be built if a nation were willing to pay the enormous cost of preparing the necessary material. Now that you have seen that we have constructed the production plants, there can be no doubt in your mind that all the output of those factories, working 24 hours a day, will be exploded on your homeland.
>
> . . . We implore you to confirm these facts to your leaders, and to do your utmost to stop the destruction and waste of life which can only result in the total annihilation of all your cities if continued. As scientists we deplore the use to which a beautiful discovery has been put, but we can assure you that unless Japan surrenders at once, this rain of atomic bombs will increase manifold in fury.

To some extent, this threat of more bombs was a bluff. Immediately after the Nagasaki bombing the Allies did not possess any more atomic bombs. It is true that, as Groves puts it, "our entire organization both at Los Alamos and on Tinian was maintained in a state of complete readiness to prepare additional bombs," but, as he himself reported to General Marshall, the earliest date at which the next bomb could be assembled for use was August 17, and almost everybody expected the war to be over by then. Even Groves says that when he received reports indicating that the Nagasaki bomb had inflicted a smaller number of casualties than they had expected, he was relieved, "for by that time I was certain that Japan was through and that the war could not continue for more than a few days."

In fact, the very day after the bombing of Nagasaki, Washington received a message sent via Switzerland that the Japanese were ready to accept the terms of the Potsdam Declaration, except one: they would not accept "any demand which prejudices the prerogatives of His Majesty as a Sovereign Ruler." At the same time the Japanese government issued an urgent plea to the United States to call a halt to the atomic bombing. This bomb, the Japanese declared, had "the most cruel effects humanity has ever known." Its use in "massacring a great number of old people, women, children; destroying and burning down Shinto and Buddhist temples, schools, hospitals, living quarters, etc.," the statement claimed, constituted a "new crime against humanity and civilization."

It was not just the Japanese who had had enough of the terrifying carnage of nuclear warfare. From the diary of Henry Wallace, who was at the time a member of Truman's cabinet, we learn that on August 10 Truman gave the order to stop the atomic bombing. Truman, Wallace records, "said the thought of wiping out another 100,000 people was too horrible. He didn't like the idea of killing, as he said, 'all those kids.'" The following day, James Byrnes, as Secretary of State, responded to the not-quite unconditional Japanese offer of surrender in a way that sought to nullify the one condition they had made, insisting:

> From the moment of surrender the authority of the Emperor and the Japanese Government to rule the state shall be subject to the Supreme Commander of the Allied powers who will take such steps as he deems proper to effectuate the surrender terms.

Despite having people around him who were urging him to continue the fight, Emperor Hirohito realized there was no sane course of action left open to him other than the acceptance of these terms. "I cannot endure the thought of letting my people suffer any longer," he told his ministers and counselors on the morning of August 14. "A continuation of the war would bring death to tens, perhaps even hundreds, of thousands of persons. The whole nation would be reduced to ashes. How then could I carry on the wishes of my imperial ancestors?"

Later that day, Truman announced that Japan had accepted the terms of surrender offered by the Allies. The war was over. The following day, the Emperor took the unprecedented step of broadcasting a message to his subjects, telling them that, partly because "the enemy has begun to employ a new and most cruel bomb, the power of which to do damage is indeed incalculable," he had ordered the acceptance of the Potsdam Declaration.

"Seldom, if ever," commented the journalist and broadcaster Edward Murrow, "has a war ended leaving the victors with such a sense of uncertainty and fear, with such a realization that the future is obscure and that survival is not assured." To be sure, "VJ Day" was celebrated with parties and processions, both in the UK and in the U.S. Especially relieved and thankful that the war was over were the three million U.S. servicemen poised to launch an invasion of Japan in October, few of whom had any doubt that what had saved them was the atomic bomb. "Let me tell you," writes Serber in his autobiography, "we were really heroes out there in the Pacific. There were an awful lot of guys who weren't looking forward to landing on the Japanese beaches." One of those men awaiting orders to invade was Rossi Lomanitz, who wrote to his old teacher: "Hey, Oppie, you're about the best loved man in these parts."

On the day of the surrender Serber wrote to his wife, Charlotte, from Tinian, telling her: "There's surprisingly little excitement or jubilation here. The army seems to be taking the news quite soberly . . . There is no sign at all, so far, of any celebration." At Los Alamos, the celebrations of peace were led by the GIs, who sounded sirens and klaxons and partied all over the laboratory. Among the scientists, there were mixed feelings. George Kistiakowsky remembers:

> A whole damn bunch started wanting to arrange to fire 21 guns. We didn't have any guns so I got hold of one of my young assistants and we drove to the explosive store and got out 21 cases, 50-pound cases of composite TNT, set them up in the field and exploded them. It was quite a show. Then I came back to the party and was told I'd exploded only 20.

However, the sense of triumph among the scientists at Los Alamos had been severely mitigated by the knowledge that their work had resulted in the deaths of tens—perhaps hundreds—of thousands of people. And many of them were struggling to see those deaths as justified, especially in connection with the second bombing. Otto Frisch recalls: "Few of us could see any moral reason for dropping a second bomb . . . Most of us thought the Japanese would have surrendered in a few days anyhow."

Certainly Oppenheimer was not, as he had been after Trinity, swag-

gering like a cowboy, nor was he, as he had been after Hiroshima, raising his hands in the air like a prize-winning boxer. On the contrary, on
August 9, the day of the Nagasaki bombing, he was described in an FBI
report as being a "nervous wreck," and the following day, when Lawrence came to Los Alamos for a meeting of the Scientific Advisory Panel,
he found Oppenheimer unable to keep his mind for long off the distressing news of casualties from Nagasaki. Even before the bomb on Nagasaki, Oppenheimer was brought face-to-face with some of the extremely
unpleasant realities of atomic bombing when he was asked to comment
on reports of long-term damage from radiation. In a newspaper report
published on August 8, he was quoted as saying: "There is every reason
to believe that there was no appreciable radioactivity on the ground at
Hiroshima and what little there was decayed very rapidly." If Oppenheimer did not already know when he made that remark that it was misleading, he soon would know. In the days, weeks, months and years that
followed, more and more information emerged from Hiroshima and
Nagasaki, not only about the utterly horrific scenes in the immediate
aftermath of the bombings, but also about the grisly and deadly long-
term effects of radiation poisoning.

According to Alice Kimball Smith, who was there at the time, there
was at Los Alamos in the days following Nagasaki an increasing "revulsion" toward the bombings, which, even for those who thought they
were justified by the end of war, brought with it "an intensely personal
experience of the reality of evil." Some comfort was felt, says Smith,
when word got round that "Oppie says that the atomic bomb is so terrible a weapon that war is now impossible."

This, of course, is the justification for using the bomb against civilians
that Oppenheimer acquired from Bohr, and which he in turn persuaded
many others to adopt. Though it had some plausibility as a justification
for dropping *one* bomb, it was very hard to see how it justified the bombing of Nagasaki. Shirley Barnett, one of Oppenheimer's secretaries at
Los Alamos, was probably speaking for many when she said: "The reasons for using the first bomb were valid. I didn't have any doubts about
it. But I did feel bad about Nagasaki. The biggest sadness of my life, and
that of many others, was the dropping of the second bomb."

In his remorse and anxiety following the second bomb ("He smoked
constantly, constantly, constantly," Dorothy McKibbin remembers of
those days), Oppenheimer was determined to do everything he could
to fulfill Bohr's vision of the good that might come from the terrible
weapon he had built. The report of the Scientific Advisory Panel that
Lawrence had traveled to Los Alamos to help him write is dominated by
that vision of an end of war—representing it as the only sane response,

not only to the fearsome demonstration of the power of atomic bombs that the world had just witnessed, but also to the even more fearsome weapons that would inevitably be built in the future. Emphasizing that the panel was unable to recommend ways to ensure U.S. hegemony in the field of atomic weapons, the report—in the form of a letter from Oppenheimer to Stimson—stated: "We believe that the safety of this nation . . . can be based only on making future wars impossible." The concluding remarks urged upon the Interim Committee a "unanimous and urgent recommendation" that "all steps be taken, all necessary international arrangements be made, to this end."

On August 17, Oppenheimer traveled to Washington to deliver the letter personally to Stimson's aide, George Harrison (Stimson himself was away), and also to Vannevar Bush. In conversation with these two, Oppenheimer, as he later put it in a letter to Lawrence, "had an opportunity with them to explain in more detail than was appropriate in a letter what our common feelings were in this all important thing." These "common feelings," it seems, arose out of the "revulsion" described by Alice Kimball Smith. What Oppenheimer told Harrison and Bush was that the scientists "felt reluctant to promise that much real good could come of continuing atomic-bomb work" and would be rather inclined to regard such bombs as "just like poison gasses after the last war." This last analogy might suggest—though Oppenheimer does not spell this out in his letter to Lawrence—that they were urging the government to make atom bombs illegal.

Oppenheimer evidently had hopes of winning the politicians in Washington around to his own and Bohr's point of view, and there were some grounds for those hopes. After all, the government had taken what seemed to many at the time the extraordinary step of publishing on August 12, 1945—two days before the Japanese surrender and the end of the war—a fairly full and, on the face of it, fairly open account of the Manhattan Project: *Atomic Energy for Military Purposes*, written by the Princeton physicist Henry Smyth, in collaboration with Richard Tolman. The "Smyth Report," as it came to be known, became at once a best-seller. The openness of the U.S. government was applauded by many and severely criticized by others, including the British scientist James Chadwick.

Phil Morrison recalls reading the manuscript of the report at Los Alamos and marveling: "Could all this be printed out so plainly for all to read, when we had kept it quiet for so long? It was a little shocking." But, he adds: "Our excitement dwindled on publication . . . the most vivid Los Alamos material had largely been excised under the sober blue pencils of Richard Tolman's office." Neither Hiroshima nor Nagasaki is mentioned in the report. "Rather," writes Morrison, "this is the narrative of a Manhattan Project that for the physicists and for this document alike reached its peak at Trinity." And the apparent openness is largely an illusion. What worried Chadwick and others is that some clues are given about the merits of different methods of isotope separation; but nothing is revealed about the biggest secret of the Manhattan Project: implosion. All in all, the purpose of the Smyth Report was not to share information, but to establish the limits of what could and, perhaps more importantly, could not be shared.

If the publication of the Smyth Report on August 12 had aroused in Oppenheimer and his colleagues hopes that the climate of opinion in Washington was, at the end of the war, favorable to a Bohr-like perspective on nuclear weapons, then his meetings with Harrison and Bush on August 17 soon showed those hopes to be ill-founded. With regard to international cooperation, Oppenheimer told Lawrence: "I had the fairly clear impression from the talks that things had gone most badly at Potsdam, and that little or no progress had been made in interesting the Russians in collaboration or control."

"While I was in Washington," he added, "two things happened, both rather gloomy." The first was that President Truman had issued "an absolute Ukase, forbidding any disclosures on the atomic bomb." The second was that Harrison showed Oppenheimer's letter to Secretary Byrnes, "who sent back word just as I was leaving that 'in the present critical international situation there was no alternative to pushing the MED [Manhattan Engineer District] program full steam ahead.' This may have been somewhat garbled in transmission, but I fear not."

A "memo for the record," written on August 18 by George Harrison, shows that Oppenheimer's fears were well founded. "Secretary Byrnes," Harrison writes, "was definitely of the opinion that it would be difficult to do anything on the international level at the present time and that in his opinion we should continue the Manhattan Project with full force."

> Secretary Byrnes felt so strongly about all this that he requested me to tell Dr. Oppenheimer for the time being his proposal about an international agreement was not practical and that he and the rest of the gang should pursue their work full force.

Frustrated and demoralized, Oppenheimer returned to Los Alamos, and then, with Kitty, took a break for a few days at Perro Caliente. From there, he caught up on his personal correspondence, including a belated reply to Chevalier's letter of August 7. Chevalier had written not just to send congratulations, but also to empathize with the ambivalence that he was sure Oppenheimer must be feeling. "I can understand now," Chevalier wrote, "the sombre note in you during our last meetings." "There is a weight in such a venture which few men in history have had to bear. I know that with your love of men, it is no light thing to have had a part, and a great part, in a diabolical contrivance for destroying them."

Oppenheimer's reply, written on August 27, responded to and echoed this solemn tone. "The thing had to be done, Haakon," he told his old friend, while conceding: "Circumstances are heavy with misgiving, and far, far more difficult than they should be, had we power to re-make the world to be as we think it."

The same tone pervades other letters that he wrote during this retreat to the Pecos, several of them to important people from his past whom he had not seen for many years, and who, like Chevalier, had sent their congratulations on his now-famous achievement. To his old teacher Herbert Smith, he wrote: "You will believe that this undertaking has not been without its misgivings; they are heavy on us today, when the future, which has so many elements of high promise, is yet only a stone's throw from despair." In a letter to his old Harvard friend, Frederick Bernheim, he wrote that he and Kitty had come to their ranch "in an earnest but not too sanguine search for sanity." His letter ends ominously: "There would seem to be some great headaches ahead."

While at the ranch, Oppenheimer took the opportunity to think seriously about what he would do after he left Los Alamos, which would be sometime in the autumn. Having replaced Lawrence as the most famous scientist in the country, he was not short of offers. Columbia, Princeton and Harvard had all made it clear to him that they were prepared to offer him a very large salary. He was tempted by these offers, not only because of the pay, but because he had serious doubts about whether he wanted to return to either Berkeley or Caltech. During his time at Los Alamos he had been frustrated and exasperated by the difficulties he had experienced in dealing with the University of California, to whose provost, Monroe Deutsch, he wrote immediately before he set out for the Pecos. "You will understand," he told Deutsch, "that I did not come lightly or irresponsibly to a position of feud with the officers of the University. Nevertheless I wish that you would express to them my profound regret that the project could not be operated in a spirit of greater mutual confidence and cordiality."

Having got that off his chest, Oppenheimer then wrote a long letter to Charles Lauritsen at Caltech expressing several misgivings about returning there and asking various questions, none of which, he emphasized, were *conditions* of his return, "but I think it will be apparent that what we do will be affected by the answers collectively." He wanted to know, for example, what provisions there would be to support graduate students, and whether the department had enough money to buy a big cyclotron. He also urged on Lauritsen the merits of attracting Rabi to Pasadena. "Don't you yourself think," he wrote, "that it would be a good idea to bring a man, not ingrown in the institute, of such rare qualities as scientist and man?" But, more important than all these things, was his last question:

> Would the institute welcome and support, if in conscience we thought it right, my advisory participation in future atomic national policy? I am plenty worried about this, far more of course than about the personal things, and if there were a real chance of helping would want to feel that this was welcome.

After the horrors of Hiroshima and Nagasaki, what Oppenheimer wanted, more than anything, was a chance to turn the atomic bomb into—as he put it in a letter to an old family friend called Marcy Bier— "a real instrument in the establishment of peace." That, he told her, "is almost the only thing right now that seems to matter."

At the beginning of September, Oppenheimer returned to Los Alamos to find that it was facing its first fatality. Henry K. Daghlian was a young physicist who had joined Los Alamos in the autumn of 1944, when, aged just twenty-three, he was recruited to work with Otto Frisch on the notorious "tickling the dragon's tail" experiments. These involved bringing a mass of fissionable material to near-critical levels, a process Richard Feynman remarked was like tickling the tail of a sleeping dragon. Daghlian survived that experience, but on August 21, 1945, suffered an accident when performing similar experiments on plutonium. The point of these experiments was to determine how the critical mass of plutonium could be reduced by a tamper of tungsten carbide, and what Daghlian was doing was surrounding a plutonium core with bricks of the tamper material. As he was moving the final brick over the core, he was alerted by neutron counters to the fact that the addition of that brick would make the plutonium core supercritical. He tried to withdraw the brick quickly, but dropped it onto the plutonium assembly, at which point there was a burst of light and a release of vast amounts of radiation. He quickly disassembled the tamper he had built, but his body had been exposed to about 500 rem of radiation, and his right hand to about 20,000 rem (where 1,000 is regarded as a fatal dose). Immediately after the accident, Daghlian was rushed to the Los Alamos hospital, where he died on September 15. During those last twenty-six days of his life he suffered terribly from nausea, vomiting and, toward the end, an inability to reason.

The haunting thought that could not now be dispelled was that what Henry Daghlian was suffering had been inflicted upon countless Japanese people in Hiroshima and Nagasaki, thereby challenging in the most dramatic way possible the sanguine responses given by Oppenheimer and Groves to the publicly expressed concern about the effects of radiation. The issue was one that especially irked Groves, who was determined to show to the public at large that reports of lingering radiation and the horrors of radiation sickness were exaggerated and that the risk presented by radiation poisoning was very small. Indeed, Groves thought the reports of radiation sickness were a Japanese hoax. To back himself up, he phoned a military doctor at Oak Ridge, Lieutenant Colonel Rea, and read out what the newspapers had reported about the suffering of radiation-sickness victims. "I think it's good propaganda," Rea told him. "That's the feeling I have," Groves replied.

Groves was sufficiently troubled by the issue, however, to send a team of scientists to Japan to investigate the levels of radiation in Hiroshima and Nagasaki and to study its effects. Among the team, which was headed by General Farrell, were Phil Morrison and Robert Serber. "I'll be delayed a couple of weeks in returning," Serber wrote to his wife. "There's a rather unpleasant job still to do." After being in Japan for a couple of days, he told her: "The most striking impression continues to be the complete breakdown, bankruptcy, destitution of everything in Japan." In a subsequent letter he wrote that any sympathy he might have felt for the Japanese people had been dispelled by meeting prisoners of war and hearing their stories of "callousness, starvation, and slave labour." The tone changed again, however, when he got to Nagasaki and saw for himself the damage wrought by the bomb. "The ruins were hard enough to endure," he wrote in his autobiography, "but the really harrowing experience was a visit to a Nagasaki hospital."

> It was a makeshift hospital, a building with the front wall blown out, the patients on cots inside and on stretchers outside on the ground. This was five weeks after the bombing and the patients were mostly suffering from flash burn or radiation sickness.

About three weeks earlier, soon after the survey team had arrived in Japan, General Farrell gave a press conference at the Imperial Hotel in Tokyo, at which he stated unequivocally that there was no radioactivity left on the ground at Hiroshima and Nagasaki and that all those who had died had been killed either by the blast or by the fires. No one, he insisted, had died from radiation sickness. When the Australian journalist Wilfred Burchett challenged this, saying that he had been to Hiroshima and had seen for himself people dying of radiation sickness, Farrell accused him of having succumbed to "Japanese propaganda." Now Serber, Morrison and the other members of the team were seeing for themselves that Farrell had been wrong. It is true that their Geiger counters had been unable to detect radioactivity on the ground, but it was also undeniably true that many people, several weeks after the blasts, were dying horribly, as Henry K. Daghlian had died, because of their exposure to radiation.

Serber and Morrison arrived back at Los Alamos on October 15. In a report that he gave to the people of Los Alamos (published as "Serber Describes Japan" in the *Los Alamos Newsletter*), Serber wrote: "No one that has not actually seen the completeness of the destruction in Hiroshima and Nagasaki can have any idea of what a terrible thing atomic warfare is." In the light of that terror, Serber told his readers (and fellow workers in creating the bomb): "I hoped that there would be an unanimous insistence on the free interchange among all nations of information dealing with atomic power. The alternative seems to me a desperate arms race and one that can only end in terrible catastrophe."

By now this was a view shared by many, probably most, of the scientists at Los Alamos, who, indeed, had formed an organization—the Association of Los Alamos Scientists[60]—with the express purpose of campaigning for such a position. The origins of this organization go back to the spring of 1945, when concerned scientists at Los Alamos got together for informal discussions of the political consequences of their work. This led, after the war, to a meeting of about sixty scientists on August 20, 1945, at which they elected a committee, charged with the task of drawing up a statement of aims and organizing a more general meeting. By this time, those involved were unanimously agreed that, as one of their members put it, "the international control of atomic energy was the vital issue and should be the only issue with which the organization was concerned." At a mass meeting on August 30, attended by no fewer than 500 people, the structure of the organization was decided and an executive committee, chaired by the young physicist William Higinbotham, was elected. Members of the committee included, among others, John Manley, Victor Weisskopf and Robert Wilson, the last of whom felt especially strongly about the issues raised, partly because

---

[60] That the initials of this organization spell out the word "alas" was probably intentional, but I have seen no conclusive confirmation of this.

he had tried—and failed—to generate public discussion about these issues before the bombing of Hiroshima, and partly because he had felt betrayed by the decision to use the bomb, without warning and without discussion among the scientists who had built it, on civilians.

Within a week of this meeting the executive-committee members of ALAS had drafted a document urging upon the Truman administration a policy of international cooperation. "In the event of future wars," the document warned, the use of atomic bombs "would quickly and thoroughly annihilate the important cities in all countries involved." It must be assumed that "bombs will be developed which will be many times more effective" than the Hiroshima and Nagasaki bombs, and, moreover, that those bombs "will be available in large numbers." Echoing the Scientific Advisory Panel report drafted by Oppenheimer soon after the Nagasaki bombing, the ALAS document emphasized that there was very little defense against such bombs, and that there was no "secret" about how to build a bomb: "The development of the atomic bomb has involved no new fundamental principles or concepts; it consisted entirely in the application and extension of information which was known throughout the world before intensive work started." It was therefore "highly probable that with sufficient effort, other countries, who may, in fact, be well underway at this moment, could develop an atomic bomb within a few years." What the scientists therefore presented as the only sane policy—the only policy that would avoid a disastrous arms race—was one of openness and collaboration with other countries in order to achieve the international control of atomic weapons that was a prerequisite for avoiding the horrors of future atomic war.

On September 9, 1945, Oppenheimer sent a copy of the ALAS statement to George Harrison, telling him that it had been circulated to 300 scientists, just three of whom had refused to sign it. "You will probably recognize," he told Harrison, "that the views presented are in closest harmony to those I have discussed with the Interim Committee." A week went by without any response from the Truman administration, and on September 18 Oppenheimer flew to Washington to act as an emissary for the Los Alamos scientists. In a teletype message back to Los Alamos, he reported:

> Mr. Harrison points out that since this document was presented to the President, who has regarded it as an expression of scientists' views, it is not appropriate for anyone other than the President to release it for publication. It is my feeling, and the general feeling of all with whom I have talked, that public discussion of the issues involved is very much to be desired, but that it should follow rather

than precede the President's statement of national policy, which will be conveyed in his message to Congress.

It is a measure of how trusted and revered Oppenheimer was among the scientists at Los Alamos that the executive committee of ALAS was able to convince its members to agree to the suppression of their document—at least until Truman announced his policy.

The policy recommended by Truman was put before Congress on October 3 in the form of the May-Johnson Bill, named after its proposers: Representative Andrew May and Senator Edwin Johnson. To the dismay of many scientists—most notably, and most vocally, Leo Szilard and Harold Urey—the bill seemed to be founded upon the view that the United States had a "secret" that it needed to protect, rather than the philosophy of openness recommended by ALAS. May and Johnson were seen, by both the army and its critics, as politicians friendly to the military—May was the chairman of the House of Representatives Military Affairs Committee and Johnson was a member of the corresponding Senate Military Affairs Committee—and their bill reflected the military concern for security. Scientists guilty of violating security, the bill proposed, should be, at the very least, fined $100,000 and, at worst, imprisoned for up to ten years.

"If this bill passes," Szilard said at a meeting of the Atomic Scientists at Chicago (a group set up in parallel with, and with similar aims to, ALAS), "we have no choice but to get out of this work." It is true, as Groves emphasized publicly at the time and emphasizes again in his autobiography, that the bill did not propose military control of atomic energy. What it proposed instead was the establishment of an Atomic Energy Commission, which would have authority over all aspects, both peaceful and military, of the U.S.'s atomic energy program. There would be nine commissioners, appointed by the President, who would be part-time and would appoint a general manager to conduct the day-to-day business. However, what worried scientists was not only the draconian measures proposed for maintaining secrecy (which, almost all scientists felt, was a lost cause—for the reasons given in the ALAS document), but also that military men would be allowed to serve as commissioners. The Atomic Energy Commission would not be, as most scientists felt it should be, an entirely civilian body.

The May-Johnson Bill was passed quickly by the House, but when it reached the Senate it stalled over a territorial dispute between the Military Affairs Committee and the Foreign Relations Committee about who had jurisdiction over atomic-energy affairs. The consequent delay allowed opponents of the bill to marshal their forces. Led by Szilard, the scientists who had worked for the Manhattan Project—at Chicago, Oak Ridge and Los Alamos—began campaigning for the May-Johnson Bill to be scrapped and for the appointment of a joint congressional committee to reconsider atomic policy.

To many people's surprise, Oppenheimer not only did not join this campaign, but argued publicly against it, declaring his support for the bill and urging his colleagues to support it as well. On October 7, Oppenheimer returned from Washington to Los Alamos with a copy of the bill, which he discussed with the ALAS executive committee, telling them that he, Lawrence, Compton and Fermi were all in favor of passing the bill, on the grounds that it was the best way of getting what they all wanted: international cooperation on controlling atomic bombs. Astonishingly, the result of that discussion was that the committee voted unanimously to support the bill, putting ALAS somewhat at odds with many of the other scientists involved in the Manhattan Project at Chicago and Oak Ridge.

Why was Oppenheimer prepared to side with the military and use his influence among scientists to give the military what they wanted? Frank Oppenheimer, himself active in ALAS, has said that his brother "felt that he had to change things from within." This may be so, but one cannot help thinking that Oppenheimer was spending more effort in ensuring that he stayed "within" than he did attempting to effect any change. It is reminiscent of his willingness, when the Los Alamos laboratory was being established, to wear military uniform and attempt to persuade all the other scientists to follow suit. As on that occasion, Oppenheimer, in supporting the May-Johnson Bill, had underestimated the strength of the opposing feeling.

On October 11, Herbert Anderson, who after working at Los Alamos had moved back to Chicago at the end of the war, wrote to William Higinbotham expressing some of that feeling. "I must confess," he told him, "my confidence in our leaders Oppenheimer, Lawrence, Compton and Fermi, all members of the Scientific Panel advising the Interim Committee and who enjoined us to have faith in them and not influence this legislation, is shaken." Anderson's own view, shared by many at Chicago, was that the security measures proposed by the bill were "frightening." "They place every scientist in jeopardy of a jail sentence or a large fine."

Making sure that the scientists opposing the May-Johnson Bill did not give up without a fight, Ed Condon, Leo Szilard and others traveled to Washington to meet sympathetic Congressmen the day after Anderson's letter to Higinbotham. They found it surprisingly easy to gain a sympathetic hearing. "Mention to a Senator's secretary at the door that you're a 'nuclear physicist' and you come from Los Alamos," Szilard's assistant, Bernard Feld, said, "and you were ushered right in to see the Senator."

Meanwhile, Robert Wilson, who did not share either Oppenheimer's view of the May-Johnson Bill or the ALAS executive committee's faith in Oppenheimer, took it upon himself to rewrite the original ALAS document and issue it as a press release. "It was a declaration of independence from our leaders at Los Alamos," Wilson later said, adding that the lesson he had learned was that those leaders, however admirable they might be, were, if put in a position of power, "not necessarily to be relied upon." The press release, which made the front page of the *New York Times*, again made it very clear that, in contrast to the May-Johnson Bill's emphasis on the importance of tight security, the scientists who had created the atomic bomb did not believe the technology could be kept a secret for very long. "The scientific background necessary to develop an atomic bomb," the statement began, "is generally known throughout the world."

> The technical design and industrial methods of production are at present the secret of this country, Great Britain and Canada. However, it is certain that other countries can achieve these ends by independent research. Before many years they also may be manufacturing bombs, bombs which may be tens, hundreds, or even thousands of times more powerful than those which caused such devastation at Hiroshima and Nagasaki.

Wilson's statement was published on October 14. The next day, Robert Serber returned to Los Alamos from Japan. He thus arrived to find everybody discussing politics, and in particular the issue that he, with his firsthand experiences in Nagasaki and Hiroshima still fresh in his mind, regarded as of crucial importance: the necessity for international cooperation.

As it happened, the following day was Oppenheimer's last as director of Los Alamos and the occasion for a large ceremony at which he, on behalf of the laboratory, accepted from General Groves the Army-Navy Award for Excellence and a Certificate of Appreciation from the Secretary of War. To a crowd of several thousand, practically the entire population of Los Alamos, Oppenheimer delivered what Dorothy McKibbin has described as "one of the best speeches that has ever been done." It was certainly a very skillful piece of work. Somehow it managed to address the controversy that had engulfed the atomic scientists in a way that avoided saying anything particularly controversial and also expressed what many people felt. "It is our hope," he began, "that in years to come we may look at this scroll, and all that it signifies, with pride."

> Today that pride must be tempered with concern. If atomic bombs are to be added as new weapons to the arsenals of the warring world, or to the arsenals of nations preparing for war, then the time will come when mankind will curse the names of Los Alamos and Hiroshima.

"The peoples of this world must unite or they will perish," he went on. The war had "written these words," and the atomic bomb "has spelled them out for all men to understand."

Immediately after the ceremony Oppenheimer went to Washington. He went with the earnest intention of doing whatever he could, wielding whatever political influence his newfound fame had given him, to ensure that the world, in the face of the threat of annihilation brought about by atomic bombs, united rather than perished. As he left for Washington, however, he knew that, despite the warm reception given to his speech at Los Alamos, he had been unable even to unite those scientists who agreed with him about the importance of international cooperation and control of atomic energy. Dealing with top-level politicians and military men who did not share this point of view was, he well knew, going to be the biggest challenge he had yet faced.

Part Four

1945−1967

15

The Insider Scientist

The day after his resignation as director of the Los Alamos laboratory, Oppenheimer was in Washington to give evidence to Congress as it considered the May-Johnson Bill. "He'd better be careful," his secretary, Anne Wilson, said to her predecessor, Priscilla Greene. "He is going to get into terrible trouble." What prompted this sense that he was in danger, she later said, was her awareness of how many enemies Oppenheimer had made. "The woods," she remarked, "were always thick with people who had nasty things to say about Robert." It was, she observed, the downside of being so charismatic: "There were always people who were vying for his attention, and those who felt snubbed by him, or felt hurt because they thought Robert didn't love them anymore."

In Washington, Oppenheimer spoke to a Senate subcommittee on science on October 17, 1945, and to the House Committee on Military Affairs the following day. To the senators, Oppenheimer emphasized that his testimony would be "somewhat academic," corresponding "to my position as professor of physics rather than to my position as maker of bombs." He spoke in general terms about the need scientists felt for freedom, making what he described as "a plea for not over-organizing the work of scientists, and for trusting, as we have in the past, their own judgment of what work is worth doing." The implication was clear: even though it had turned out that the work of scientists had enormous political and military consequences, the planning of scientific research should not be placed in the hands of politicians or the military, but rather handed back to the scientists themselves. In context, this was a somewhat odd point to emphasize, given that he was in Washington to lend support to a bill widely disliked by scientists precisely because they saw it as handing control of their work over to the military.

The tension between Oppenheimer's plea for scientific freedom and his support for a bill that sought to enforce secrecy through the use of extremely harsh punishments was exploited by Howard J. Curtis from the Association of Oak Ridge Scientists, who was there to give evidence against the bill. "If the so-called secret of the atomic bomb is to be kept in this country," Curtis argued, "then American science as we have known it, will cease to exist." Science, as Oppenheimer himself had stressed, required freedom, and that was clearly incompatible with the bill's proposals for trying to keep some scientific facts a secret. Oppenheimer tried to argue that, because technology and science were two different things, there was "no technical difficulty about keeping considerable parts of this secret" without interfering with scientific research, but Curtis rejected this, since: "The two are so closely connected that it would be impossible to pick out any single fact and say 'this is a scientific fact, devoid of industrial applications' and any attempt to do so seems ludicrous." The only solution to the problem of secrecy, Curtis concluded, was international control of atomic energy.

Oppenheimer's problem was that he agreed entirely with this point of view, but had somehow managed to position himself on the other side of the argument. The reason was that he did not much care what domestic policy was adopted, since he was certain the real issue was the international question; whatever domestic policy was adopted would be a stopgap measure, since it would have to be changed in the light of any international agreement that was reached. He backed the May-Johnson Bill, therefore, not because he believed it was a wise policy, but because he wanted to see some bill—any bill—passed so that the real questions, the international questions, could be discussed.

Not that his advocacy of the May-Johnson Bill was particularly full-blooded. Indeed, it seemed almost deliberately feeble. Upon being asked specifically what he thought of the bill, he replied airily: "The Johnson bill, I don't know much about." So lukewarm was his support of the bill that the following day his remarks were reported by one newspaper as an "oblique attack" on it. The apparent revelation (it is very hard to believe that he was telling the truth) that he did not actually know much about the bill was received by the scientists at Los Alamos, whom he had earnestly urged to support it, with understandable misgivings. It is reported that when he met some ALAS members after giving his testimony, he received what one of them described as "the coolest reception I have ever seen Oppie given by a group of scientists." At the next meeting of the ALAS executive committee Victor Weisskopf recommended that in future "Oppie's suggestions be studied more critically."

After his appearance at the Senate, Oppenheimer attended a dinner organized by Watson Davies of the Science Service news agency, with the aim of educating senators about atomic energy. Fermi, who also supported the May-Johnson Bill, had been invited, as had (representing the other side of the debate) Condon, Szilard and Urey. Among the senators present was Brien McMahon, the Democratic senator for Connecticut, who had become the champion in the Senate of those opposed to the May-Johnson Bill. Also present were two members of Truman's government, James Newman and Henry A. Wallace, who were likewise sympathetic to the scientists opposing the bill. If Oppenheimer did not already realize it, the dinner must have made him aware that the May-Johnson Bill—disliked by scientists, opposed by influential senators and even rejected by members of Truman's administration—had very little chance of becoming law. He was on the losing side.

Henry Wallace, who had been Vice President during Roosevelt's third term and was now Truman's Commerce Secretary, recorded in his diary that at the dinner Oppenheimer told him he wanted to speak to him privately. They agreed to meet the following morning to walk together through downtown Washington up to Wallace's office at the Department of Commerce, before Oppenheimer went on to Capitol Hill to give evidence to the House of Representatives. "I never saw a man in such an extremely nervous state as Oppenheimer," Wallace wrote. "He seemed to feel that the destruction of the entire human race was imminent . . . He thinks the mishandling of the situation at Potsdam has prepared the way for the eventual slaughter of tens of millions or perhaps hundreds of millions of innocent people." Seeing that Oppenheimer obviously wanted to have a personal and direct influence on U.S. policy, Wallace advised him to contact the new Secretary of War, Robert Patterson, asking for an appointment with the President.

After leaving Wallace, Oppenheimer went to give evidence to the House Committee on Military Affairs, the meeting chaired by Andrew May himself. A number of other scientists had also been invited, including Ed Condon and Leo Szilard. May opened proceedings at 10 a.m. with a short speech in which he denied that his committee was trying to rush the bill through and promised to give "patient consideration" to the scientists who had come to give evidence. Then he called his first witness, "a Dr. Sighland"—that is, Leo Szilard. In his testimony Szilard outlined his own proposal for the control of atomic energy, which involved dividing the task into three—1. the production of fissile materials; 2. the organization of scientific research; and 3. the design and production of bombs—each to be administered by a government-owned, civilian corporation. Under his plan there would also be a commission, consisting of cabinet members, which would coordinate national and foreign policy relating to atomic energy. In the question period that followed Szilard was asked very few questions about his proposal and a great many about his nationality and his disputes with the army. He was followed by Herbert Anderson, who read out a statement from scientists at Oak Ridge and Chicago that expressed their criticisms of the May-Johnson Bill.

After a break for lunch, Compton and Oppenheimer gave their testimonies. Oppenheimer's, Szilard later said, was a "masterpiece." What he meant, it seems, is that it was a masterly piece of equivocation. "He talked in such a manner that the congressmen present thought he was for the bill but the physicists present all thought that he was against the bill." For example, when asked if he thought it was a good bill, Oppenheimer replied:

> The bill was drafted with the detailed supervision of Dr. Bush and Dr. Conant, with the knowledge and agreement of the former Secretary of War, Mr. Stimson . . . I think if they liked the philosophy of this bill and urged this bill it is a very strong argument.

"To the congressmen," Szilard said, "this might mean that Oppenheimer thinks this is a good bill, but no physicist believes that Oppenheimer will form an opinion on the basis of his good opinion of somebody else's opinion."

It seems possible that Szilard (assuming he was not being sarcastic) was crediting Oppenheimer here with too much subtlety. It may be that, realizing the May-Johnson Bill was a lost cause, Oppenheimer shifted his emphasis away from defending the bill and toward flattering the people who, whatever the fate of the bill, would help to determine the atomic policy of the United States. When he was asked whether he was bothered by the fact that the May-Johnson Bill allowed military men to act as commissioners, he replied: "I think it is a matter not what uniform a man wears but what kind of man he is." He added: "I cannot think of an administrator in whom I would have more confidence than General Marshall."

In connection with the issue at stake in the dispute between himself and Curtis, Oppenheimer endeavored to put some distance between science and bomb-making. Producing the bomb, he said, was "an enormous technological development," but: "It was not science, and its whole spirit was one of frantic exploitation of the known; it was not that of the sober, modest attempt to penetrate the unknown." His chief concern, it seems, both on this occasion and during the previous day's meeting, was to make what he described as "a plea for leaving much of the scientific strength of the country in the universities and technical schools, the small institutions in which scientists have worked in the past and in which they will have the leisure and privacy to think those essential, dangerous thoughts which are the true substance of science."

The plea was well made, and revealing of Oppenheimer's own desire at the time to leave the bomb-making of Los Alamos behind him in favor of a return to the purity of theoretical physics, but, as an argument in favor of the May-Johnson Bill, it was, to say the least, unconvincing. Indeed, the proposers of that bill might well have thought that, with supporters like Oppenheimer, they had little need of enemies. In any case, the bill was rejected and a Senate special committee on atomic energy was set up, with Brien McMahon as its chairman, to consider the issues afresh and propose alternative legislation. The first round in what would be an ongoing battle between the scientists and the military for control of atomic-energy policy had thus been won by the scientists. Oppenheimer, in his efforts to play the part of an "insider scientist," had succeeded—for the time being anyway—only in being pushed a little further away from the center.

A golden opportunity to reverse this and to gain access to the very top of U.S. policy-making came on October 25, just a week after his ineffective testimony to Congress, when, having followed Wallace's advice, Oppenheimer was granted an interview with the President. The meeting, however, went badly, resulting in Truman telling his Undersecretary of State, Dean Acheson: "I don't want to see that son-of-a-bitch in this office ever again." Evidently Oppenheimer's remarkable ability to charm just the right person at just the right time—which had worked so well with Max Born in 1926 and General Groves in 1942—had, on this occasion, deserted him.

No doubt part of the problem was that Oppenheimer's view of Truman was clouded by the conviction he had expressed to Wallace: that Truman had made a terrible mess of things at Potsdam. By not being open with the Russians and gaining their trust in preparation for international collaboration on atomic weapons, Truman, Oppenheimer believed, had missed a chance—perhaps the only chance—to avert a nuclear arms race, thereby exposing humanity to the possibility of a war fought with atomic bombs and the consequent slaughter of hundreds of millions of people. He was therefore not inclined, as he would have been if he had met Roosevelt, to treat the President with deferential respect. So when Truman began the conversation by telling Oppenheimer, in reference to the debates then going on about the May-Johnson Bill and its alternatives, "The first thing is to define the national problem, then the international," Oppenheimer did nothing to disguise or conceal his disagreement. He sat in silence for an uncomfortably long time, and then, when Truman looked at him impatiently for a response, simply contradicted him. "Perhaps," Oppenheimer said, "it would be best first to define the international problem."

The interview went from bad to worse when Truman asked Oppenheimer when he thought the Russians would develop their own atomic bomb. Oppenheimer replied, as he had when asked the same question in Congress, that he did not know. Truman then said that he *did* know. The answer, he said confidently, was "never." Obviously Truman had not understood what Oppenheimer had said in his final Scientific Panel report and what the Los Alamos scientists had tried to tell him in their ALAS document: that the technology of using the energy released from nuclear fission to make a bomb was not something that could be kept a secret; it was something that scientists everywhere, including Russia, would be able to work out for themselves. Two days after this meeting with Oppenheimer, Truman showed his lack of understanding of this point again, this time in public, when in his Navy Day address given in New York he spoke of keeping the destructive power of atomic bombs in the possession of the U.S. as a "sacred trust."

"I saw him [Oppenheimer] pretty often around that time," William Higinbotham has recalled. "From the way he looked, I think I could tell that Truman's statement and the incomprehension it showed just knocked the heart out of him." In the interview with Truman, Oppenheimer's dejection must have been visibly manifest, since Truman—shocked at the gap between Oppenheimer's reputation as a suave, brilliant, articulate high achiever and the hesitant, mumbling figure in front of him—was moved to ask what the matter was. "Mr. President," said Oppenheimer slowly, "I feel I have blood on my hands." The remark infuriated Truman and effectively put an end both to the meeting and to Oppenheimer's chances of being treated by the President as a trusted insider. "I told him," Truman said afterward, "the blood was on my hands—to let me worry about that." Six months after the meeting, Truman was still railing against the "cry-baby scientist" who had come to his office "and spent most of his time wringing his hands and telling me they had blood on them because of his discovery of atomic energy." Truman's final words to Oppenheimer were: "Don't worry, we're going to work something out, and you're going to help us." As he left the Oval Office, however, Oppenheimer would have been only too aware that he was not, and never would be, someone the President would turn to if he wanted help.

Oppenheimer left Washington a chastened man. His attempts to insinuate himself into the top levels of U.S. politics had failed, and in making them he had alienated the politically active scientists whom he had hoped to lead. A chance to win back the trust of some of those scientists came at the beginning of November, when he was invited back to Los Alamos to give a speech to ALAS. It was a chance that he seized. His return to Los Alamos was a triumph. Five hundred people crammed into the largest movie theater on the Hill to hear him, and, according to Alice Kimball Smith: "Years later, when former ALAS members were asked about postwar political activity, the answer invariably began (and sometimes ended) with 'I remember Oppie's speech.'"

In content and tone the speech contrasted sharply with the testimony Oppenheimer had given in Washington. Indeed, in several places, it flatly contradicted what he had said in Washington. For example, whereas he had told the House of Representatives that making the bomb had been "an enormous technological development," but "it was not science," in his speech to ALAS he emphasized that it *was* science and that was precisely the motivation for doing it. There were many motives for being involved in making the bomb, Oppenheimer said in his speech. There was the fear that the enemy would get there first, there was the sense of adventure, there were various political considerations. "But when you come right down to it," Oppenheimer told the members of ALAS, "the reason we did this job is because it was an organic necessity."

> If you are a scientist you cannot stop such a thing. If you are a scientist you believe that it is good to find out how the world works; that it is good to find out what the realities are; that it is good to turn over to mankind at large the greatest possible power to control the world and to deal with it according to its lights and values.

Similarly inconsistent with what he had said in Washington were the remarks in the speech about secrecy. Whereas in his appearance before the Senate he had defended the May-Johnson Bill's concern with secrecy, to the scientists at Los Alamos he declared that "the almost unanimous resistance of scientists to the imposition of control and secrecy is a justified position," since "secrecy strikes at the very root of what science is."

Again whereas in Washington he had been respectful to the point of being deferential to those in power, in this speech he was openly critical of the President, remarking that "the views suggested in the President's Navy Day speech are not entirely encouraging." In particular, he took issue with Truman's U.S.-centric view of the issue: the idea that the world could, and had to, look to the U.S. to keep possession of atomic bombs as a "sacred trust." This "insistent tone of unilateral responsibility for the handling of atomic weapons," Oppenheimer told his audience, "is surely the thing which must have troubled you, and which troubled me, in the official statements."

In place of Truman's insistence on putting America's interests first, and domestic concerns before international ones, Oppenheimer outlined a robustly international perspective. What he proposed was agreement between nations, first to set up an international atomic-energy commission that, without any interference from the heads of any particular state, had control over the development of peaceful uses of atomic energy, and second to "say that no bombs be made." In every respect the speech echoed the views of the scientists at Los Alamos, and they left the theater feeling that Oppenheimer had spoken for them. He may have failed to win the President around to his way of seeing the issues, but he had at least reestablished himself as the voice, the heart and the conscience of the Los Alamos scientists.

Oppenheimer had begun his ALAS speech with a rueful remark about himself. He would like, he said, to speak to them as a fellow scientist, adding: "If some of you have long memories, perhaps you will regard it as justified." It felt like a long time had passed since he was able to concentrate on the kind of pure, disinterested, theoretical physics that he loved, and he was anxious to return to that way of thinking. That is why he had resigned his directorship of Los Alamos so quickly; he wanted to return to academic life. Though he was flattered by the offers from the East—Harvard, Princeton, Columbia—what he wanted most of all was to return to either Berkeley or Caltech, or both. As he explained in a letter to Conant, rejecting the Harvard offer, "I would like to go back to California for the rest of my days" because "I have a sense of belonging there which I will probably not get over."

Nevertheless, as his letters of August to Deutsch, Lawrence and Lauritsen had revealed, he had serious misgivings about both Berkeley and Caltech. In letters to Sproul and Birge written at the end of September, he asked them to say frankly whether, in the light of the quarrels he had had with officials from the University of California during his war work, he would be entirely welcome at Berkeley. Both assured him that he would find an extremely warm welcome there, but he remained unconvinced. His doubts about Caltech were more easily overcome and on October 16, the day he resigned from Los Alamos, he wrote to William Houston, the chair of the physics department at Caltech, formally accepting the offer of a professorship of physics and promising to arrive in Pasadena during the first week of November. For the moment, nothing was decided about Berkeley. He had not actually resigned his position there, so the door remained open for him to return. For the time being, his leave of absence was extended, giving him more time to decide whether he wanted to return.

In the meantime, after giving his ALAS speech, he and Kitty drove to California. Leaving Kitty in Berkeley, Oppenheimer went on to Pasadena, where he stayed as a guest of the Tolmans. For the following term this was to be the pattern: Oppenheimer spending one or two nights a week in Pasadena, while Kitty and the children remained in Berkeley. At Caltech, he later claimed: "I did actually give a course, but it is obscure to me how I gave it now." Indeed, it is difficult to see how he could possibly have given a course. As well as arriving late, he was called back to Washington several times to give evidence to McMahon's Senate special committee. "I was sort of reluctant to do it," he later said, "on the ground that I hoped to stay put. But I came back."

What compelled him to keep going back to Washington, despite the strong urge to "stay put," was the hope that he might have some influence in directing U.S. policy away from the unilateralism of Truman's public utterances and toward the internationalism espoused by most scientists. The gulf between scientists and politicians, and the horror with which scientists contemplated military control over scientific research, were increased at the end of November 1945, when newspapers reported that U.S. forces in Japan had seized and destroyed five cyclotrons that belonged to Japanese universities. The machines were cut to pieces with welding torches and then the fragmented parts were buried deep in the Pacific Ocean. The brutality, the incomprehension and the naked stupidity of this act filled scientists everywhere with revulsion and ended forever any chance of atomic scientists in the States agreeing to allow the U.S. Army any role in directing and organizing their research.

In his efforts to push forward an internationalist perspective on atomic energy, Oppenheimer discovered that he had an extremely welcome ally. Isidor Rabi, it turned out, had been thinking along exactly the same lines. Rabi was then living on Riverside Drive, where Oppenheimer grew up, and, when Rabi was on the East Coast Oppenheimer would often stay with him. "Oppenheimer and I met frequently and discussed these questions thoroughly," Rabi later told Jeremy Bernstein. "I remember one meeting with him, on Christmas Day of 1945, in my apartment. From the window of my study we could watch blocks of ice floating past on the Hudson." By the end of that evening Rabi and Oppenheimer had arrived at a plan for taking control of atomic-energy policy out of the hands of individual governments and giving it to the international community as a whole.

In the New Year of 1946, Oppenheimer was provided with an opportunity of putting his and Rabi's plan into effect when he was appointed to a Board of Consultants advising a special committee drawn up by Secretary Byrnes. The committee was charged with the task of drawing up a proposal for international control of nuclear weapons and was chaired by Undersecretary of State Dean Acheson. He appointed as chair of the Board of Consultants a liberal New Dealer, David Lilienthal. From Oppenheimer's point of view, Lilienthal turned out to be a perfect choice, not least because he developed a respect for Oppenheimer that bordered on hero worship.

Oppenheimer and Lilienthal first met on January 22, 1946, when Oppenheimer came to Washington to attend the first meeting of the Board of Consultants. They met in Oppenheimer's hotel room, where, Lilienthal recorded in his diary, Oppenheimer "walked back and forth, making funny 'high' sounds between sentences or phrases as he paced the room, looking at the floor." "I left liking him," he added, "greatly impressed with his flash of a mind." The next day, when he saw Oppenheimer in action in a meeting of Acheson's committee (the members of which included Conant, Bush and Groves), Lilienthal's admiration was unrestrained. Oppenheimer, he wrote, was "an extraordinary personage" and "a really *great* teacher"—his evidence to the committee being, for Lilienthal, "one of the most memorable intellectual and emotional experiences of my life." He later told the lawyer Herbert Marks that it was "worth living a lifetime just to know that mankind has been able to produce such a being" as Oppenheimer.

Nor was Lilienthal alone in his admiration of Oppenheimer. "All the participants, I think," Dean Acheson later wrote, "agree that the most stimulating and creative mind among us was Robert Oppenheimer's." Not that Oppenheimer's influence was universally welcomed. Groves, in particular, looked on in dismay at the way things were going. He had not wanted to appoint a Board of Consultants, believing that he, Conant and Bush "knew more about the broad aspects of the problem . . . than any panel that could be assembled," and did not like the composition of the board that was, against his advice, appointed. Lilienthal, Groves remarked, "had little or no knowledge of the subject whatever," and he was rather scathing about the reverence for Oppenheimer that prevailed among the members of the board. "Everybody genuflected," he sniffed. "Lilienthal got so bad he would consult Oppie on what tie to wear in the morning."

Not only was Oppenheimer the most respected person on the Board of Consultants, but he was also the only scientist. He therefore had little trouble imposing his views on the other members and turning the whole process of framing a proposed international policy on atomic energy into a vehicle for advancing the views that Bohr had developed during the war and that he and Rabi had discussed on Christmas Day. The first meeting of the Board was on January 23, and from then until the Board submitted its report to the Secretary of State on March 16, the business of drafting the proposal took up all of Oppenheimer's time. He later described the first few weeks like this:

> The way it worked is that we met and in the first few weeks, a week or two, my job was that of teacher. I would get back at the blackboard and say you can make energy this way in a periodic table, and that way and that way. This is the way bombs are made and reactors are made. I gave, in other words, a course. I gave parts of this course also to Mr. Acheson and Mr. McCloy at night informally. Then we listened to parts of it that I didn't know anything about, where the raw materials were, and what kind of headache that was. Then everybody was kind of depressed, the way people are about the atom, and we decided to take a recess.

On February 2, Oppenheimer sent Lilienthal a long memo that became the foundation of the board's report. Its central idea was very radical. What Oppenheimer proposed was that a single international agency, the Atomic Development Authority, should be established with extremely far-reaching powers. It would not only have responsibility for all aspects of the development and control of atomic energy, including the power to inspect the atomic facilities in any nation in the world, but would also actually own all the uranium and every atomic-energy plant in the world. Under the terms of Oppenheimer's proposal, no nation would be allowed to build atomic bombs and no nation would be *able* to build atom bombs, since all the materials necessary for such bombs would be in the hands of the Atomic Development Authority.

On March 7, Acheson's committee, together with its associated Board of Consultants, met to discuss and vote on a plan that was substantially drawn from Oppenheimer's memo. Remarkably, all except one voted in favor of the plan. Predictably the one exception was Groves, who was implacably opposed to the idea of giving up the U.S. monopoly of atomic weapons and handing over to the United Nations America's uranium, its separation plants, its plutonium plants and its advanced knowledge. Despite Groves's opposition, however, the plan was approved, and, after a few revisions and amendments were made, was sent to Secretary of State Byrnes on March 16. To Groves's horror, the State Department authorized publication of the report, which became known as the "Acheson-Lilienthal Plan." Acheson's committee had advised against publication, Groves says in his autobiography, since "we did not feel it wise to disclose to the Russians just how far the United States was willing to go in sharing its knowledge before negotiations had even been arranged for."

In fact, the United States government was *not* willing to go as far as the Acheson-Lilienthal Plan proposed, and quickly took steps to ensure that it would not be required to do so. On March 5, just two days before the Acheson committee met to consider Oppenheimer's plan, the thinking that would dominate the policy of both the U.S. and the UK was expressed with great force by Winston Churchill in a speech he gave in Fulton, Missouri. The speech, which is generally regarded as marking the beginning of the Cold War, famously described the growth of Soviet influence in Eastern Europe as the descent of an "iron curtain," behind which was "the Soviet Sphere." The spread of Soviet influence, he urged, must be contained by—if necessary—military force. The view put forward by Churchill could not have been more antithetical to Oppenheimer's. Indeed, at times he gave the impression of arguing directly against the views that were embodied in the Acheson-Lilienthal Plan:

> It would nevertheless, ladies and gentlemen, be wrong and imprudent to entrust the secret knowledge or experience of the atomic bomb, which the United States, Great Britain and Canada now share, to the world organisation [the UN], while it is still in its infancy. It would be criminal madness to cast it adrift in this still agitated and un-united world. No one in any country has slept less well in their beds because this knowledge and the method and the raw materials to apply it are at present largely retained in American hands.

Having lost the last election to Clement Attlee, Churchill was not at this time Prime Minister and was not, officially at any rate, speaking for the UK or the U.S. government. But any doubts that the views of Truman and Byrnes accorded better with those of Churchill than with those advanced in the Acheson-Lilienthal Plan would soon be removed.

On the very day that he received the plan, Byrnes appointed as his spokesman at the United Nations on the international control of atomic energy a seventy-five-year-old financier called Bernard Baruch, who, he knew, would be opposed to its proposals. "That was the day I gave up hope," Oppenheimer later said. As well as being politically conservative and skeptical about international control of atomic energy, Baruch had a vested interest in *not* surrendering ownership of uranium, having investments in a company that had a stake in uranium mines. As soon as he was appointed, Baruch set to work on "revising" the Acheson-Lilienthal Plan, turning it into, as Byrnes put it to Acheson, "a workable plan." To help him in this aim, Baruch chose a team of politically right-wing advisors that included two bankers, a mining engineer and, as "interpreter of military policy," General Groves.

Three months separated the appointment of Baruch on March 16 and his appearance at the United Nations, where he presented the U.S. proposal for international control of atomic energy on June 14. During those months the proposal underwent fundamental changes that altered completely its character as an expression of the Bohr-Rabi-Oppenheimer philosophy of international cooperation. Also during those months Oppenheimer's personal position as a trusted and prestigious advisor to the U.S. government was fatally compromised by an increasingly vicious campaign against him, led by powerful figures in the U.S. political establishment.

Chief among those figures was J. Edgar Hoover, the head of the FBI, whose opinion that Oppenheimer was a dangerous and subversive communist had been entirely unaffected by the fame and celebrity that Oppenheimer had acquired as "Father of the Atom Bomb." On April 26, 1946, Hoover wrote to the Attorney General, Tom C. Clark, recommending "technical surveillance" (that is, wiretapping) of Oppenheimer "for the purpose of determining the extent of his contacts with Soviet agents, and for the additional purpose of identifying other espionage agents." Permission was granted, and a bug was installed on Oppenheimer's phone on May 8. It did not take the Oppenheimers long to work out that they were being listened to. Every phone call was transcribed and sent by the FBI San Francisco office to Hoover, including a conversation between Oppenheimer and Kitty on May 10 that included the following exchange:

JRO: . . . Are you there, dear?
KO: Yes
JRO: The FBI must just have hung up.
KO: (Giggles)

Two days later, the FBI summary of another conversation between Oppenheimer and Kitty included the following: "At this point there was a clicking sound and Oppenheimer asked, 'Are you still there? I wonder who's listening to us?' Kitty replies lackadaisically, 'The FBI, dear.'"

The transcripts of Oppenheimer's phone calls were forwarded to Byrnes, who would have taken special interest in the disparaging way in which Oppenheimer discussed Baruch—whom he invariably called "the old man"—in these conversations.

Relations between Oppenheimer and Baruch during this time went from bad to worse. They first met early in April, at a time when Baruch was trying to recruit Oppenheimer as a scientific advisor. The meeting, reminiscent of Oppenheimer's encounter with Truman the previous October, was a disaster. Baruch forced Oppenheimer to admit that his proposals, with their emphasis on openness and cooperation, were fundamentally incompatible with the character of Stalin's Soviet regime. Baruch also horrified Oppenheimer by revealing some of the ways in which he wanted to amend the Acheson-Lilienthal Plan. The United Nations, Baruch thought, should authorize the U.S. to keep a stockpile of atomic bombs to serve as a deterrent. He also wanted to restrict the power of the proposed Atomic Development Authority in two crucial ways: first, it should not own and control uranium mines; and second, it should not have power over the development of atomic energy. Oppenheimer left the meeting convinced that he could not possibly work with Baruch, and turned down the invitation to act as his scientific advisor.

In what was possibly a tactical error, Oppenheimer did not confine himself to private expressions of his views on international control of atomic energy; he also gave public lectures on the subject. Wherever he lectured there was sure to be an FBI agent in the audience, who would send Hoover a summary of what he had said. In one such lecture, given at Cornell on May 15, Oppenheimer told his audience grimly: "Mark my words, if there is no international control of atomic energy, the next war will be fought to prevent an atomic war, but it will not be successful." In another, given in Pittsburgh the following day, he talked of his proposed international Atomic Development Authority as a "world government," remarking that what the Acheson-Lilienthal Plan amounted to was the "renunciation of national sovereignty."

In the burgeoning FBI file on Oppenheimer, these views were duly recorded and cited when the Bureau was called upon to justify its continued surveillance of Oppenheimer. That surveillance, an FBI report states, "has from day to day kept this office aware of Dr. Oppenheimer's travels about the country and the subject matter of many of his speeches as well as information as to his opinions on highly controversial matters concerning the atom bomb." The report concludes:

In view of the above recommendation of the San Francisco Field Division and the further fact that through Oppenheimer's telephone conversations with other scientists working on a draft of an international plan for the control of atomic energy, it is helpful in determining Oppenheimer's actual views on this subject, it is recommended that this technical surveillance be continued.

The FBI file also contains a letter to the Secretary of War, Robert Patterson, from a certain Gregory C. Bern, dated June 3, 1946, describing the atomic bomb as "the United States' top military secret" and castigating those atomic scientists who were "engaged in treasonable activity to transfer our military secret to our greatest enemy, the Soviet government." "Of course," Bern goes on, "this plot is concealed in their so-called 'bomb-control' idea via the media of the UNO, of which the Soviet government is a member." "It must be noted that Robert Oppenheimer is a member of two Communist Front organizations and therefore his agitation for the plan which would place us at the mercy of Soviet war criminals is easily explainable."

The view, expressed by almost all competent atomic scientists, that there was no "secret" about how to build an atomic bomb was thus not only rejected by influential people in the U.S. political establishment, but was regarded as a treasonous plot. Whereas the scientists knew that their counterparts in Russia and elsewhere would be able to work out how the energy from fission could be used to make a bomb, many politicians and military leaders—to most of whom the physics of fission was an utter mystery—shared Truman's view that the Russians were incapable of penetrating that mystery. Among them was General Groves, who, on March 14, 1946, just two days before the Acheson-Lilienthal Plan was sent to the State Department, gave a talk at the Waldorf Hotel in New York, in which he was reported by the writer Merle Miller as telling his audience "that the United States didn't need to worry about the Russians ever making a bomb. 'Why,' he said, smiling, 'those people can't even make a jeep.' You should have heard the applause; thunderous is the only way to describe it; a great many people stood and cheered." This was the man on whom Baruch was relying for military advice. On that advice Baruch added to his panel of consultants Edgar Sengier, a Belgian mining magnate who had worked with Groves on supplying the Manhattan Project with uranium ore, and who had an even greater stake than Baruch himself in ensuring that ownership of uranium was not transferred to an international agency.

On May 17, the day after his lecture in Pittsburgh, Oppenheimer was back in Washington to attend a meeting with Baruch that had been arranged by Acheson, who was hoping to bring all sides together. In response to Oppenheimer's lectures and newspaper interviews, Baruch had complained to Acheson about being undercut. Oppenheimer himself remembered: "Mr. Baruch told me that I had scooped his speech that he was going to make at the opening of the UN. That was not true."

At the meeting Baruch made it clear to Oppenheimer just how far his own views diverged from those that had informed the Acheson-Lilienthal Plan. Unsurprisingly, given the vested interests of himself and at least one of his advisors, Baruch was not prepared to advocate the international ownership of uranium. He also insisted on building into the plan some procedures for punishing nations that violated its terms. The punishment he had in mind, it turned out, would be administered by the U.S., using its stockpile of atomic weapons. He also announced at this meeting that he would be proposing that the Soviet Union should give up its right to veto the actions of the new international atomic authority. In short, what Baruch was preparing to propose at the United Nations was exactly what Oppenheimer had wanted to avoid: the continuation of the U.S. monopoly of atomic weapons, the preservation of national ownership of the means of making atomic weapons and the imposition by force of a policy of preventing other nations from acquiring such weapons. This was not a proposal motivated by internationalism, but one that sought to preserve the national interests of the United States.

To nobody's surprise, when the "Baruch Plan" (as it was now known) was presented to the United Nations Energy Commission at its meeting in New York on June 14, it was emphatically rejected by the Soviet Union. On June 19, the Soviets countered with their own proposal that all existing stockpiles of atomic weapons should first be destroyed and then a committee should be established to discuss the exchange of scientific information. This, in turn, was rejected by the United States. For several months afterward negotiations continued, without any real hope of coming to an agreement.

Meanwhile the FBI continued its close surveillance of Oppenheimer, listening to his phone conversations, following him everywhere he went and making a note of everything he did and everyone he spoke to. Almost daily, Hoover would receive reports from the San Francisco office, detailing Oppenheimer's activities. As evidence that Oppenheimer "would place us at the mercy of Soviet war criminals," however, these reports were, to say the least, unconvincing. Whenever called upon to justify their suspicion of Oppenheimer, the FBI invariably resorted to repeating what was already known: that Oppenheimer had belonged to several Communist Party front organizations in the 1930s, that he had several friends who were members of, or sympathetic to, the Communist Party and, most damningly of all, that Oppenheimer, by his own admission, had been approached by his friend Chevalier to leak information about the atomic-bomb project to the Soviet Union.

This last piece of "derogatory information" is repeated over and over again in the FBI file, as if it held the key to a major conspiracy. And when, on June 4, Chevalier himself came to Oppenheimer's house, FBI agents were there, eager to report to Hoover that "the Oppenheimers were friendly with the man believed to be Chevalier." Hoover was also sent a transcript of a phone conversation between Chevalier and Kitty that took place when Oppenheimer himself was away on June 13, and of an unsuccessful attempt by Chevalier to contact Kitty on June 18.

About a week later, on June 26, Chevalier, who had only been back in Berkeley for about a month, received an unexpected and extremely unwelcome visit at his home from two FBI agents, who demanded that he accompany them to their San Francisco office. Once there, Chevalier was subjected to a tough, eight-hour-long interview, focusing on his relationships with George Eltenton and Oppenheimer. Every now and then, Chevalier later recalled, one of the agents would speak "in monosyllables and brief, enigmatic phrases," to someone on the telephone. It turned out that he was speaking to another agent based in the FBI office in Oakland, where George Eltenton was being interviewed. Eventually one of the FBI agents said to Chevalier: "I have here three affidavits from three scientists on the atomic bomb project. Each of them testifies that you approached him on three separate occasions for the purpose of obtaining secret information on the atomic bomb on behalf of Russian agents."

Puzzled by the mention of *three* scientists, but sure now that the FBI must somehow have received information about his conversation with Eltenton and his abortive attempt to approach Oppenheimer on Eltenton's behalf, Chevalier told the agents the story, such as it was, of his extremely brief and unsuccessful experience of acting on behalf of Soviet intelligence. At the same time, in Oakland, Eltenton told roughly the same story: after being approached by Peter Ivanov from the Soviet consulate, he had asked Chevalier to ask Oppenheimer if he would be willing to pass information to the Soviets. A few days later, Eltenton said, Chevalier "dropped by my house and told me that there was no chance whatsoever of obtaining any data and Dr. Oppenheimer did not approve." No matter how many times they were asked, no matter how much pressure was put on them, neither Chevalier nor Eltenton said anything that provided any support to the idea that three scientists had been approached. Indeed, Chevalier put his claim in writing: "I approached no one except Oppenheimer to request information concerning the work of the radiation laboratory."

Despite all their strenuous—indeed, obsessive—attempts to prove Oppenheimer's complicity in a major espionage effort, all the FBI had to show for hours of interviewing and days of surveillance was evidence of a momentary, clumsy exchange between Oppenheimer and Chevalier, in which Oppenheimer refused to provide information. Why, despite the lack of any kind of evidence, was the FBI so convinced that Oppenheimer *must* be in league with the Soviet Union? The answer seems to be that they were unable, otherwise, to account for his postwar political views. On the other hand, Chevalier, on his return to Berkeley in the summer of 1946, was shocked to discover how far Oppenheimer's political views had shifted to the right and how *anti*-Soviet he had become. "I cannot tell you why," Oppenheimer told Chevalier, "but I assure you I have real reason to change my mind about Russia. They are not what you believe them to be."

This is not how it seemed to the FBI. They had no direct evidence that he was pro-Russian (despite looking very hard to find some), but there were two aspects to his postwar political attitudes that they found hard to explain without attributing to him a desire to help the Soviet Union. The first was his, to their minds, otherwise unfathomable advice to the U.S. to give up its monopoly of atomic weapons, share information with the Soviets and cooperate with them on the development and control of atomic energy. The second was his apparently fervent conviction that no more atom bombs should be built and his opposition to any further atomic bomb tests.

When he was asked what should become of Los Alamos after the war, Oppenheimer replied: "Give it back to the Indians." Of course, such a plan was never even considered. Instead, though employing far fewer people, it continued to exist after the war as both a research establishment and as an atomic-bomb production facility, with Norris Bradbury replacing Oppenheimer as director. Its first postwar task was to produce further "Fat Man"–type bombs, some of which would be stockpiled and others set aside for a series of tests that was planned to take place in the summer of 1946.

These tests, code-named "Operation Crossroads," were first devised at the end of 1945 as a means of investigating the effect of an atomic bomb on a naval fleet. The idea was to assemble a fleet of obsolete and captured ships, some German and some Japanese, and then attempt to destroy them in various ways using atomic bombs. Three such tests were planned. In the first, named Able, a B-29 was to drop a bomb over the fleet; in the second, Baker, a bomb was to be exploded just below the surface of the sea, attacking the fleet from below; while in the third, Charlie, a bomb was to be exploded half a mile under the ships. The place chosen for the tests was Bikini Atoll, in the middle of the Pacific Ocean. Unlike the Trinity test, these were not to be secret, but rather extremely public, with the media and observers from all over the world, including Russia, invited to witness what was expected (and no doubt hoped) to be a shocking spectacle.

Adding further to both President Truman's dislike of him and the FBI's suspicion of him, Oppenheimer wanted nothing to do with Operation Crossroads. The tests were originally scheduled for May 1946, but, at the request of Secretary Byrnes (who did not want them to influence the negotiations over international control of atomic energy), were postponed until July. On May 3, responding to a request that he attend the tests and contribute to the analysis of the results gained from them, Oppenheimer wrote to Truman asking to be excluded from the scientific panel associated with the tests. Like many other scientists, Oppenheimer told Truman, he had misgivings about their scientific value and whether they could possibly reveal anything that was not already known. After all, on the basis of what had already been witnessed at Trinity, Hiroshima and Nagasaki, it could safely be predicted that "If an atomic bomb comes close enough to a ship, even a capital one, it will sink it." And if the point was to investigate the effects of radiation, this could be done much more cheaply and more effectively in the laboratory. But, over and above those considerations, Oppenheimer raised doubts about "the appropriateness of a purely military test of atomic weapons" at a time when "our plans for effectively eliminating them from national armaments are in their earliest beginnings." In other words, for Oppenheimer it seemed at best pointless and at worst dangerous for the U.S. to be testing bombs at the very time when it was (or anyway, in Oppenheimer's view, ought to have been) trying to convince the world to adopt a plan designed to ensure that no further bombs were made or used. The point was lost on Truman, who forwarded Oppenheimer's letter to Acheson, adding a short note dismissing Oppenheimer as the "cry-baby scientist," who had come to the White House six months earlier.

Oppenheimer's opposition to the tests became known to the press, by whom he was perfectly prepared to be quoted on the subject. On June 11, the San Francisco office of the FBI sent Hoover a transcript of a phone conversation between Oppenheimer and a journalist for the *New York Herald Tribune* called Steve White. The pair discussed the forthcoming Bikini test, Oppenheimer confirming it as his view that there was no need for a test to determine that any ship within a certain radius of an atomic bomb would be destroyed. The conversation continued:

> WHITE: I also have another quotation here but I haven't got your
>   name on it.
> OPPENHEIMER: What's that?
> WHITE: If the bomb fails entirely, it will likely prove something. It
>   will prove that you can't do these things without good people.
> OPPENHEIMER: OK. That shouldn't have my name on.

Many of the misgivings that Oppenheimer expressed to Truman and to the press were expressed persuasively in an anonymous article published in the February 15, 1946, edition of the *Bulletin of the Atomic Scientists of Chicago*, a journal that had only been in existence for two months, but was already recognized as the voice of the politically concerned scientists of the Manhattan Project. In addition to the points made by Oppenheimer in his conversation with White, the *Bulletin* article also made the telling, and, as it turned out, prescient observation:

> Naval vessels are mechanically stronger than buildings, so that over comparable distances, the effect of a bomb on a warship would be less than on a building. Most of the ships will be several miles away from the explosion, so that they will probably remain afloat. Those who have been led to expect the overwhelming destruction of the fleet will thus be disappointed and public opinion may be lulled into a feeling of false security—along the line of "Oh, the atomic bomb is not so terrible—it's just another big bomb."

In fact, this is just what happened at the first test, Able, which took place on July 1, 1946, in front of an audience of more than a hundred people, including two observers from the Soviet Union. The fleet to be destroyed consisted of twenty-three ships, the central target of which was the battleship USS *Nevada*. Of these, only two were sunk by the initial blast (within twenty-four hours, a further three sank); the *Nevada* remained afloat. "Dressed in all the trappings of an exaggerated and sometimes frivolous publicity," *The Economist* reported, "the first Bikini atom bomb experiment has left rather the impression of a fireworks display which slightly misfired." One of the Soviet observers remarked that the damage inflicted by the bomb was "not so much." In fact, the blast, measured at 23,000 tons of TNT, was as powerful as any bomb that had yet been exploded, and the test *did* provide incontrovertible evidence of the devastating effect of radiation. On board the ships were hundreds of mice, rats, goats and pigs, the death rate of which was enough to suggest that, though the *Nevada* remained afloat, had it been fully manned, it would, within a few days have been, a "ghost ship," a floating coffin for a crew whose every member would have died.

The second test, Baker, took place on July 25 and provided a much more arresting display. A "Fat Man" bomb was suspended beneath a landing craft and detonated just ninety feet underwater. The result was spectacular indeed: the landing craft was vaporized and a huge vertical column of water and steam was created, which destroyed ten ships. By this time, however, there was little public interest in, and much criticism of, the tests. The Soviet reaction was expressed in a *Pravda* editorial that described the tests as "common blackmail," which "fundamentally undermined the belief in the seriousness of American talk about atomic disarmament." The third test, Charlie, was called off.

The day before the Baker test, Lilienthal recorded in his diary a meeting with Oppenheimer in his hotel room in Washington. Oppenheimer, he wrote, "is in deep despair about the way things are going in the negotiations in New York."

> It is difficult to record how profoundly hopeless he thinks it is; indeed, when I said that there are some situations in which one cannot acknowledge despair, he took me to task for this, in a gentle but firm way, saying that it was this sense of a "reservoir of hope" that was quite wrong, for it does not exist.

If the Baruch Plan failed, Oppenheimer told Lilienthal, it:

> will be construed by us as a demonstration of Russia's warlike intentions. And this will fit perfectly into the plans of that growing number who want to put the country on a war footing, first psychologically, then actually. The Army directing the country's research; Red-baiting; treating all labor organizations, CIO first, as Communist and therefore traitorous etc.

Lilienthal recorded that Oppenheimer "paced up and down in the frenetic way," saying all this "in a really heart-breaking tone."

> He is really a tragic figure; with all his great attractiveness, brilliance of mind. As I left him he looked so sad: "I am ready to go anywhere and do anything, but I am bankrupt of further ideas. And I find that physics and the teaching of physics, which is my life, now seems irrelevant." It was this last that really wrung my heart.

Oppenheimer did in fact, during that summer, make some moves toward returning to physics. He finally agreed, for example, to return to his old arrangement of lecturing at Berkeley for half the year and Caltech for the other half, beginning that autumn. After his experiences at Los Alamos and, during the year following the war, his experience of being part of U.S. policy-making at the very top of the political process, he no doubt knew that he could not simply return to his prewar life. Nevertheless, there are signs that at least part of him wanted just that. Even during the war, despite his quip to Pauli that "for the last four years

I have had only classified thoughts," he had managed to publish at least one article on theoretical physics. Admittedly the article in question— "Cosmic Rays: Report of Recent Progress, 1936–1941," published in a collection commemorating the seventy-fifth anniversary of the University of California—was synoptic and introductory, rather than an original contribution to research. Nevertheless, it gives some indication of what Oppenheimer was hoping to return to when the war was over. In a section on "Mesons and Nuclei" Oppenheimer discusses the puzzles that arise from the enigmatic Yukawa particle, to which he had devoted so much of his energy during the 1930s. The existence of this particle— named the "meson" because its mass put it somewhere in the middle between the tiny electron and the comparatively huge proton—was postulated by Yukawa in order to explain nuclear forces, and, it was thought, was observed in cosmic rays. The troubles arose from the fact that the properties of the particle detectable in cosmic rays were not consistent with it being the particle postulated by Yukawa. "The situation in this respect," Oppenheimer writes, "is not only rather complicated; it is also very incompletely understood, and presents at the moment the principal challenge to theoretical physics."

It was this "principal challenge" to which Oppenheimer wanted to devote himself. Astonishingly, even right in the middle of the UN negotiations over international atomic-energy policy, he had managed to pursue original research into an aspect of this challenge. On June 26, 1946, the *Physical Review* received a paper jointly written by Oppenheimer and Hans Bethe entitled "Reaction of Radiation on Electron Scattering and Heitler's Theory of Radiation Damping." This was a response to work published in 1941 and 1942 by the German Jewish physicist Walter Heitler, who, after escaping Hitler's Germany, had worked first at Bristol with Nevill Mott and then at Dublin with Erwin Schrödinger. At Dublin, Heitler collaborated with the Chinese physicist Peng Huanwu on a mathematical theory that, they hoped, would contribute to the understanding of cosmic rays, mesons and quantum electrodynamics. The paper by Oppenheimer and Bethe (which, at eight pages, was by Oppenheimer's standards fairly long) was a reaction to the Heitler-Peng paper, "The Influence of Radiation Damping on the Scattering of Mesons," which had been published in the *Proceedings of the Cambridge Philosophical Society* in 1942. What Oppenheimer and Bethe showed was that the equations devised by Heitler and Peng had only limited success in describing the scattering of electrons by electromagnetic energy. As an attempt to meet the "principal challenge," this paper with Bethe was small beer, but, given what else Oppenheimer was doing in the summer of 1946, its very existence is something of a marvel.

On returning to California that summer after his work on the Baruch Plan, Oppenheimer narrowly missed what might have become an opportunity to build on the extraordinary work on astrophysics that he had done immediately before the war, the work now regarded as his most important contribution to science. Waiting for him on his return to Berkeley was a letter, dated July 15, 1946, from the Harvard astronomer Donald Menzel, whom Oppenheimer had known in the 1920s and '30s, when Menzel was working at the Lick Observatory in California. What Menzel wanted was to arouse Oppenheimer's interest in some speculations he had regarding the structure of the sun. His suggestion, prompted in part by Bethe's seminal work on solar structure, was that the sun should be regarded as an enormous atom, with most of its mass concentrated in an extremely dense "nucleus." "I think that this problem is important from the physical standpoint," Menzel told Oppenheimer, "because it may be tied up with the generation of cosmic rays." Next time Oppenheimer was in the east, he suggested, perhaps the two of them could meet in New York, Philadelphia or Washington to talk about it.

Oppenheimer's reply, written on August 8, was fairly encouraging. "I would like to talk over with you your ideas on stellar interiors," he told Menzel, suggesting that the forthcoming American Physical Society meeting in Princeton might provide an opportunity. "I may have to come East before then," Oppenheimer wrote, "but I devoutly hope not." Menzel, as he told Oppenheimer in a subsequent letter, was unable to attend the Princeton meeting, but was still hoping to lure Oppenheimer into further thinking on the subject. "There are certainly a lot of interesting and important problems in astrophysics," Menzel told Oppenheimer, "relating to atomic structure, nuclear structure, and interpretation of spectra. If only we could get together once in a while, as we used to many years ago, I am sure we could have a lot of fun."

Even while Oppenheimer and Menzel were exchanging these letters, however, moves were afoot in Washington that would guarantee that both Oppenheimer's devout hope not to return to the east and Menzel's hope that he and Oppenheimer could have fun discussing astrophysics were destined to be thwarted. On August 1, President Truman signed the McMahon Bill, bringing into law the Atomic Energy Act.

Brien McMahon had first presented his bill to Congress in December 1945 as an alternative to the defeated May-Johnson Bill. Its fundamental principle was to ensure—as the May-Johnson Bill had so conspicuously failed to—that atomic-energy policy was kept in civilian rather than military hands. Its chief means of ensuring this was through the creation of the entirely civilian Atomic Energy Commission (AEC), which would have responsibility for the development and control of both military and nonmilitary uses of atomic energy. The man Truman chose to be the first chairman of the AEC was David Lilienthal, thus ensuring that Oppenheimer would be called back to Washington to play a key role in the shaping of U.S. atomic-energy policy.

The Atomic Energy Commission was a five-man body, which, according to the terms of the McMahon Act, took over from the Manhattan Project on January 1, 1947. This meant, for example, that Los Alamos was now a civilian rather than a military establishment. Apart from Lilienthal, the commissioners were Sumner T. Pike, a businessman from New England; William T. Waymack, a farmer and newspaper editor from Iowa; Robert F. Bacher, the only scientist on the commission; and Lewis L. Strauss, a politically conservative banker and reserve admiral. Strauss, who insisted that his name be pronounced "straws," was a former shoe salesman who had become extremely wealthy and, through acting as an aide to President Hoover, politically influential. On October 24, 1946, Oppenheimer was recorded by the FBI as remarking about Strauss: "He is not greatly cultivated but will not obstruct things."

By the time he discovered the makeup of the AEC, Oppenheimer himself had already been interviewed by the FBI, in what was both a follow-up to the Bureau's interviews with Chevalier and Eltenton and, presumably, a precautionary move prior to Oppenheimer's involvement in the work of Lilienthal's commission. Given that he knew his phone was being bugged by the FBI, it cannot have come as much of a surprise to Oppenheimer when FBI agents arrived at his Berkeley office to interview him, especially as, by then, he had already heard from Chevalier about his ordeal in June.

In his book, *Oppenheimer: The Story of a Friendship*, Chevalier describes going to a cocktail party at the Oppenheimers' house, at which he told Oppenheimer about his FBI interview. He does not give a date, but as he describes it as "a kind of house-rewarming," it is natural to suppose that it took place sometime in August 1946, soon after Oppenheimer's return to Berkeley from Washington. Chevalier remembers that he and his wife "had been asked to come early, so as to have a private visit before the rest of the guests arrived." The FBI interview was so much on his mind, Chevalier recalls, "that after the first exchange of greetings I almost immediately broached the subject. Opje's face at once darkened. 'Let's go outside,' he said."

Out in the garden, away from the FBI's "technical surveillance," Chevalier gave Oppenheimer a detailed account of the interview. Oppenheimer, he says, "was obviously greatly upset. He asked me endless questions. We paced back and forth on the uneven ground." Oppenheimer told Chevalier that he had been right to tell the FBI about his 1942 conversation with him concerning Eltenton, and, in turn, sought Chevalier's reassurance that he had been right to tell the FBI about the same thing. "I had to report that conversation, you know . . ." he told Chevalier. Chevalier was not altogether convinced of the necessity of that, and when he asked Oppenheimer about the alleged approaches to *three* scientists, Oppenheimer "gave no answer. He was extremely nervous and tense." When Kitty arrived to tell him that the other guests were arriving, he dismissed her and continued asking Chevalier questions. Then, when Kitty appeared a second time, this time more insistent, "Opje let loose with a flood of foul language, called Kitty vile names and told her to mind her goddam business and to get the . . . hell out." It was, Chevalier reports, "the first time I had seen Opje behave immoderately. I could not imagine what could have provoked his intemperate outburst."

It was about a month later, on September 5, that Oppenheimer himself was interviewed by Bureau agents—the same ones who had interviewed Eltenton in June. However much it had unnerved and disturbed him, his conversation with Chevalier had at least given Oppenheimer some idea of what he might say to limit the damage he had done with his careless interview with Pash back in 1943. The story he told was the one that the FBI had heard from Chevalier and Eltenton. With regard to the part of the story that Chevalier and Eltenton repeatedly and consistently denied—the part about the mysterious *three* scientists—Oppenheimer now claimed that this was a concoction on his part, designed to protect Chevalier's identity. How, exactly, it was supposed to do that was something that he failed to explain throughout his life, despite being asked to do so many, many times. Oppenheimer told the agents that he would be reluctant to testify against Chevalier, and that he had not told Chevalier that he had mentioned his name in connection with the alleged espionage incident (which, of course, was not true). He also gave the surely false impression of being surprised that Joe Weinberg was a communist. Meanwhile, in a repetition of the strategy used with Chevalier and Eltenton, Weinberg himself was at the same time being interviewed by the FBI. He too was less than entirely honest, denying ever having met Steve Nelson at Nelson's house. As the FBI now had documented evidence that both Oppenheimer and Weinberg had provided false statements, Hoover evidently thought there was a case for prosecution and sent copies of these interviews to the Attorney General. To Hoover's great disappointment, the Attorney General decided against prosecution. As his agents continued their surveillance of Oppenheimer, Hoover bided his time, confident that another chance to use his "derogatory information" about Oppenheimer would present itself.

As many people noted at the time, the four commissioners chosen to work with Lilienthal on the AEC were an odd selection in that, apart from Bacher, none of them knew very much about atomic energy. How were a banker, a farmer and a businessman supposed to make informed and expert judgments on such things as the development of civilian uses of atomic energy or the nature and size of the USA's arsenal of atomic weapons? How were they expected to oversee the future development of Los Alamos, Oak Ridge and Hanford? The answer was to appoint a panel of experts to advise them. This panel was called the General Advisory Committee, and, unlike the AEC itself, it was packed with experts from the very top of the field. Eight people in total were chosen to sit on the General Advisory Committee, and an extremely impressive collection they were: James Conant, Isidor Rabi, Glenn Seaborg, Cyril Smith, Lee DuBridge (the president of Caltech), Hood Worthington of Du Pont (who had built the nuclear reactors at Hanford), Hartley Rowe of United Fruit and, of course, Oppenheimer.

In December 1946, Lewis Strauss flew to California to meet Oppenheimer. He went not only to discuss AEC business, but also to make Oppenheimer an offer. In his capacity as a trustee of the Institute for Advanced Study in Princeton, Strauss had been authorized by the other trustees to offer Oppenheimer the job of director of the institute, with effect from October 1947. The English-literature scholar Frank Aydelotte, who had been the institute's director since 1939, had earlier in the year announced his intention of retiring, and, after a survey of faculty members, it emerged that the most popular choice to replace him was Oppenheimer.

Rather prematurely, on December 23, the *New York Times* reported that Oppenheimer would be joining the institute as director the following autumn. In fact, Oppenheimer had not yet made up his mind, and, somewhat to Strauss's annoyance, would not do so for another three months. There are strong signs that uppermost in his mind during this long deliberation was the question of whether or not he could attract exciting young physicists to Princeton. When Strauss reported back to the institute's trustees, he told them: "Dr. Oppenheimer has requested that in addition to administrative duties, he be permitted to devote some of his time to teaching in order that he may remain in direct contact with young scholars." As the institute was a research-only establishment and did not actually have any students, this request was met by asking Princeton University to select a handful of graduate students for Oppenheimer to teach.

It was not only bright graduate students that Oppenheimer wanted contact with, however. He also longed to discuss physics with the brightest young research scientists who, having completed their graduate work, were beginning their careers. As Oppenheimer knew from his own experience as a postdoctoral student, these were the people who would be taking the next big steps in the subject. These young people, however, were always in demand, and, at the end of the war, there was extremely tight competition for the rising stars. One of Oppenheimer's frustrations with Berkeley was the failure of its physics department to attract, or even to attempt to attract, Richard Feynman, about whom Oppenheimer had written to Birge as early as November 1943. Feynman was, Oppenheimer told Birge, "in every way so outstanding and clearly recognized as such, that I think it appropriate to call his name to your attention, with the urgent request that you consider him for a position in the department at the earliest time that that is possible." Six months later he wrote again, stressing the urgency of the situation in the light of the fact that Feynman had already been offered a position at Cornell. On October 5, 1944, Oppenheimer wrote rather testily to Birge to tell him that it was too late: Feynman had accepted the position at Cornell. "I shall of course," he told him, "do my best to call to your attention any men who are available and whom we should want to recommend strongly for the department."

Feynman's chief rival as leading young physicist in the United States was Julian Schwinger, who was at this time the subject of an undignified struggle to secure his services between van Vleck at Harvard and Rabi at Columbia. When Schwinger visited Berkeley at the end of 1946, Oppenheimer could not resist trying to recruit him. "Would you like to come to Berkeley?" Oppenheimer asked him directly. As it happened, Schwinger rather liked the idea of living in California, but he very much did not like the idea of working with Oppenheimer, because of the danger of being overwhelmed by him. As Schwinger later remembered the conversation: "And then he said—and this still bothers me—'Would it change your opinion any if you learned that I wasn't staying here?' He did not tell me that he was going off to Princeton."

Schwinger, though tempted (especially after he knew that Oppenheimer would no longer be at Berkeley), turned the offer down and went to Harvard instead. Trying to explain the decision in later life, he said: "I still said no, and now I'm not sure why. But I have the feeling that I was shocked by his duplicity."

Another rising young physicist at this time, though significantly less well established and less revered than Feynman and Schwinger, was Abraham Pais, a Dutch Jewish physicist who had worked with Bohr in Copenhagen and had been invited to spend the year 1946–7 at the Institute for Advanced Study in Princeton. As a young physicist who had earned Bohr's respect, Pais was in great demand and, within a few months of being in the States, had received job offers from the University of Illinois, UCLA, the University of North Carolina and Columbia. Despite these offers, Pais continued to assume that when his year at Princeton was up, he would return to Bohr's institute in Copenhagen.

Oppenheimer, however, had other ideas. Pais had met Oppenheimer within a few days of arriving in the U.S. in September 1946, when he gave a paper at the annual meeting of the American Physical Society, which that year was held in New York. At the meeting, Pais naturally gravitated toward his fellow Dutchmen, Uhlenbeck, Goudsmit and Kramers, the last of whom, during one of the sessions, scribbled a note, saying: "Turn around and pay your respects to Robert Oppenheimer." Pais recalls:

> I turned and there, right behind me, sat the great man, who up to that moment had been known to me only from newspaper articles. He grinned pleasantly at me and stretched out his hand, which I shook. Most remarkably—or so I thought—he sat there in a short-sleeved open shirt.

Pais's second meeting with Oppenheimer came on the last day of January 1947, when he attended that year's meeting of the American Physical Society, again in New York, but this time at Columbia. On that occasion Oppenheimer had been invited to give the annual Richtmyer Memorial Lecture, his subject being "Creation and Destruction of Mesons." Pais remembers:

> Oppenheimer spoke before a packed house. He was a rhetor rather than a speaker. Then, as on numerous occasions, I was struck by his priestly style. It was, one might say, as if he were aiming at initiating his audience into Nature's divine mysteries.

After the lecture, Pais went to say hello to Oppenheimer, who said that he had something urgent he needed to discuss with him. Would Pais wait until he could disengage himself from the crowd? "As I stood waiting," Pais later recalled:

> I tried to play back what he had just said, and I recall my thought: What the Hell do I remember about his talk? I had been intrigued, nay moved, by his words, but now I found myself unable to reconstruct anything of substance. I would now say that this was not just a matter of stupidity on my part.

"Let's walk down Broadway and find a bar," Oppenheimer suggested to Pais when he finally succeeded in shaking off the crowd. Having found a bar, Oppenheimer told Pais that he had been offered the directorship of the Institute for Advanced Study and pleaded with him to keep open the possibility of remaining there. A few months went by, and then in early April 1947, having decided to accept an offer from Harvard, Pais received a call from Oppenheimer. "I have just accepted the directorship of the Institute for Advanced Study," Oppenheimer told him, "and I desperately hope that you will be there next year, so that we can begin building up theoretical physics there." Flattered by the personal attention and the pleading tone, Pais changed his mind about Harvard and accepted.

The job at Princeton held many attractions for Oppenheimer, among which were the small, interdisciplinary nature of the establishment, the chance it gave him—as he had done when he first arrived at Berkeley—to *build* an important center of theoretical physics and, not least, the fact that it would relieve him of the necessity to make so many cross-continental air flights. Flying so often from east to west, spending so much of his life on airplanes and in airports, was wearing him out. Thus, to a certain extent, his appointment as director of the Institute for Advanced Study and his appointment as a member of the Atomic Energy Commission's General Advisory Committee were linked: accepting the first would enable him to fulfill more easily his duties for the second.

On January 8, 1947, Oppenheimer was in Washington for the first meeting of the GAC. He arrived late, only to discover that the others had voted him, in his absence, their chairman. For the next few years the GAC was to be, in effect, Oppenheimer's committee and, given the balance of intellectual power between the two panels, this meant also that his was to be the dominant voice in the AEC. One might have expected him to use that influence to pursue the internationalist perspective that he had inherited from Bohr and that he had worked so hard to push during the previous year. However, the failure of the negotiations at the UN had deeply disillusioned him. True, he had not liked the way that Baruch had modified the proposals or the belligerent way in which he had negotiated for them, but much more disillusioning was the intransigence of the Soviet Union. When Hans Bethe came to Berkeley that January, he was surprised, as Chevalier had been, by the vehemence of Oppenheimer's anti-Soviet views. The two of them, Bethe remembered, had "quite long conversations about the fate of the atomic energy control plan. He told me then that he had given up all hope that the Russians would agree to a plan."

Particularly he pointed out how much the Russian plan was designed to serve the Russian interests and no other interests, namely, to deprive us immediately of the one weapon which would stop the Russians from going into Western Europe, if they so chose, and not give us any guarantee on the other hand that there would really be a control of atomic energy, nor give us any guarantee that we would be safe from Russian atomic attack at some later time.

FBI microphones would have recorded this conversation, as they would have recorded Oppenheimer expressing similar views on very many occasions, none of which dented J. Edgar Hoover's apparently immovable conviction that Oppenheimer was a communist sympathizer and a potential Soviet spy. His appointment to the GAC gave Hoover the opportunity to launch a renewed investigation into Oppenheimer. Indeed, it presented him with the *duty* of doing so, it being one of the measures of the McMahon Act that all AEC employees who had previously been cleared to work on the Manhattan Project had to be investigated by the FBI. So, in February 1947, FBI agents interviewed dozens of Oppenheimer's friends and colleagues and, in the light of the information gathered (none of which gave any new grounds for suspicion), a fresh dossier on Oppenheimer was written. Before sending this to the AEC, Hoover sent it, along with another dossier on Frank Oppenheimer, to General Vaughan, Truman's military aide. "You will note," Hoover wrote in his accompanying letter, "that both these individuals have a good overall knowledge of the Atom Bomb Project, and that both have been strongly alleged to be members of the Communist Party."

About a week later, on Saturday, March 8, Hoover sent the same document to the AEC. The following Monday the commissioners met to discuss what to do about the FBI file. Conant and Bush announced themselves unconcerned; there was nothing in this new dossier, they said, that added to what they had seen, and dismissed, in 1942. When asked for his opinion, the AEC's lawyer, Joseph Volpe, replied:

Well, if anyone were to print this stuff in this file and say it is about the top civilian advisor to the Atomic Energy Commission, there would be terrible trouble. His background is awful. But your responsibility is to determine whether this man is a security risk *now*, and except for the Chevalier incident, I don't see anything in this file to establish that he might be.

The commissioner most shocked by the FBI's revelations was Lewis Strauss, who, Volpe recalls, was "visibly shaken" by them. Oppenheimer had told him the previous December, in connection with the offer of the Princeton job, that there was "derogatory information" about him, but Strauss had not seemed worried. Now he and Lilienthal, as chair of the commissioners, were forced to take this information seriously.

On March 11, the AEC members decided to take the issue straight to the top and went to the White House to tell the President about the FBI suspicions of Oppenheimer. Of course Truman already knew about those suspicions and was not very concerned about them. At that particular moment Truman was much more concerned about the crises in Greece and Turkey, both of which looked in danger of falling under communist rule, becoming part of what Churchill had described as "the Soviet Sphere." In response to this threat, on March 12, 1947, Truman announced to Congress what became known as the Truman Doctrine, the policy of lending support to "free peoples" threatened by communism. As it happened, Oppenheimer was in Washington at this time and received from Acheson a preview of the Truman Doctrine. "He wanted me to be quite clear," Oppenheimer later said, "that we were entering into an adversary relationship with the Soviets, and whatever we did in the atomic talk we should bear that in mind." Soon after this, Baruch's successor as U.S. spokesman on atomic energy at the UN, Frederick Osborn, was surprised to hear Oppenheimer say that the U.S. should simply withdraw from talks with the Soviet Union, which, he said, would never agree to a workable plan.

While Truman was busy formulating the Truman Doctrine, he told the AEC members that he was too busy to meet them and instead they met his aide, Clark Clifford, who, to their relief, did not seem very concerned about Oppenheimer's FBI file either. By the end of March the AEC had testimonials vouching for Oppenheimer's loyalty from an impressive array of people, including Secretary of War Robert Patterson and General Groves. On August 11, the AEC were ready to agree unanimously to approve Oppenheimer for clearance, by which time the FBI, for the time being anyway, had decided to cease their "technical surveillance" of him. He was officially no longer regarded as a security risk. On the contrary, he was now the man most responsible for framing U.S. policy on the development of atomic energy.

What makes the doubts about Oppenheimer's loyalty seem so perverse is that, from this distance anyway, one of his most striking characteristics is his deep, and sometimes fierce, devotion to his country. It is one of the very few things that remained constant throughout his life and is clearly evident in almost everything he did. It was behind both the extraordinary energy and effort that he put into directing Los Alamos and his determination to play a leading role in the formation and execu-

tion of America's atomic policies. It is also evident—and had been from
the very beginning of his academic career—in his concern to establish
the U.S. as the world's center of theoretical physics.

In the postwar period Oppenheimer was to see that dream he had
had in the 1920s—of America replacing Germany as the country where
the most fundamental developments in physics took place—become a
reality. Moreover, he himself was able to play a leading part in making
it a reality, not (as he had done before the war) through his publications
and his teaching, but rather through the influence that he wielded at a
series of important conferences.

The first, and most important, of these was the Shelter Island Conference, which took place in June 1947 and has gone down in history
as one of the most important conferences in the development of physics in the twentieth century. Rabi said it "would be remembered as the
1911 Solvay Congress is remembered, for having been the starting-point
of remarkable new developments," while Richard Feynman has said:
"There have been many conferences in the world since, but I've never
felt any to be as important as this."

Shelter Island was the conference at which Willis Lamb introduced
the discoveries about hydrogen spectra—the so-called Lamb shift—for
which he won the Nobel Prize. It was at Shelter Island, too, that Rabi
reported on experiments conducted in his laboratory at Columbia, which
measured, with an unprecedented degree of accuracy, the magnetic
interactions between the protons and electrons in hydrogen and found
that the measurements obtained disagreed, slightly but significantly (by
about 0.22 percent), with those derived from the then-accepted theory.
The conference was also the occasion at which Robert Marshak first proposed that the puzzles about the meson, to which Oppenheimer himself
had devoted so much thought over the previous decade, could be solved
by what became known as the "two-meson hypothesis." Moreover, it
was at this conference that Richard Feynman gave the first public presentation of what became known as "Feynman diagrams"[61] and, in the
attempt to understand the startling series of experimental observations
that had been made in 1947, the seeds were sown for the major advances
in quantum electrodynamics that Feynman and Schwinger were to make
in the coming years.

Not only were all these young physicists American, but, unlike
Oppenheimer and most of his generation, all of them had been graduate

---

[61] A Feynman diagram is a pictorial representation of the interactions of subatomic particles. A typical diagram might show, for example, an electron and a positron annihilating
each other, emitting waves of electromagnetic energy.

students at American universities: Lamb at Berkeley, Marshak at Cornell, Feynman at Princeton and Schwinger at Columbia. For a long time the U.S. had been the country in which the best physics was being done (much of it by refugees, emigrants and people trained overseas), but now it was also the country producing the best physicists.

In terms of the number of participants, the Shelter Island Conference was not large. Just twenty-three people took part, but every one of them was either a world-renowned scientist (like Bethe, Fermi, Rabi, Teller, Uhlenbeck and Wheeler) or widely identified as an up-and-coming star (for example, Feynman, Pais and Schwinger). Together with Kramers and Weisskopf, Oppenheimer was asked to act as a "discussion leader," each of whom was asked to draw up an outline of what they thought ought to be discussed under the general heading "Foundations of Quantum Mechanics." Weisskopf's outline was divided into three: 1. problems in quantum electrodynamics; 2. problems in understanding nuclear and meson phenomena; and 3. proposed experiments using high-energy particles. Kramers concentrated entirely on issues in quantum electrodynamics, while Oppenheimer's outline was focused solely on the problems of understanding mesons and, in particular, the discrepancy between the currently accepted theory and experimental results.

One such result (mentioned by name in Weisskopf's outline and alluded to in Oppenheimer's) was an experiment carried out in Italy during the war, of which Oppenheimer, in a nontechnical lecture he gave later in the year, gave an excited and colorful account. Now confident of America's unquestioned position at the forefront of physics, he could afford to be generous in his assessment of work in Europe, and told his audience that "of the two or three important experimental discoveries of the last two years, two at least come from Europe":

> One was carried out long before its publication in the cellar of an old house in Rome by three Italians who were under sentence of death from the Germans because they belonged to the Italian Resistance. They were rescued by an uncle of one of the men from a labor squad at Cassino, and smuggled into a cellar in Rome. They got bored there, and they started to do experiments. These experiments were published last spring; and in the field of fundamental physics they created a real revolution in our thinking.

The Italian scientists in question were Marcello Conversi, Ettore Pancini and Oreste Piccioni (when Fermi gave a seminar explaining the importance of their experiment, he remarked jokingly that he "would not dare to pronounce those names"). In February 1947, the *Physical*

Review published a letter of theirs, "On the Disintegration of Negative Mesons," reporting on experiments they had conducted in 1945, which showed conclusively that something was fundamentally wrong with meson theory as it then stood. According to that theory, the mesons found in cosmic rays were also the particles that Yukawa had suggested as carriers for the nuclear force that binds protons and neutrons together in a nucleus. Mesons are found with both negative and positive charges, and, if that theory is correct, then negative mesons should always be absorbed by surrounding nuclei, whereas positive mesons should not. Because every nucleus is positively charged, positively charged mesons should be repelled, and instead of being absorbed will decay very quickly (mesons have a life of only a few microseconds) into electrons and neutrinos. What Conversi, Pancini and Piccioni found was that, contrary to the theory, negatively charged mesons—though absorbed by the nucleus of the relatively heavy element of iron—decayed in carbon, which is a much lighter element. What Weisskopf and Oppenheimer wanted the illustrious scientists gathering at Shelter Island to discuss was: what is going on? Why do the carbon nuclei not absorb the negatively charged mesons?

The conference started on Monday, June 2, at the Ram's Head Inn, Shelter Island, at the tip of Long Island. Reflecting the postwar celebrity of nuclear physicists, the event was reported in gushing terms by the *New York Herald Tribune*:

> Twenty-three of the country's best known theoretical physicists—the men who made the atom bomb—gathered today in a rural inn to begin three days of discussion and study, during which they hope to straighten out a few of the difficulties that beset modern physics.
>
> It is doubtful there has ever been a conference quite like this one. The physicists, backed by the National Academy of Science, have taken over the Ram's Head Inn . . . The conference is taking place with almost complete informality, aided by the fact that the scientists have the inn all to themselves and feel that there is no one to mind if they take off their coats and get to work.

The organizer of the conference, Duncan MacInnes, recorded in his diary that "it was immediately evident that Oppenheimer was the moving spirit of the affair," while the chairman of the conference, Karl Darrow, has recorded:

> As the conference went on the ascendancy of Oppenheimer became more evident—the analysis (often caustic) of nearly every argument,

that magnificent English never marred by hesitation or groping for words (I never heard "catharsis" used in a discourse on [physics], or the clever word "mesoniferous," which is probably O's invention), the dry humour, the perpetually-recurring comment that one idea or another was certainly wrong, and the respect with which he was heard.

Abraham Pais says his recollections confirm these impressions:

I had heard Oppenheimer speak before but had never yet seen him in action directing a group of physicists during their scientific deliberations. At that he was simply masterful, interrupting with leading questions (at physics gatherings interruptions are standard procedure), summarizing the main points just discussed, and suggesting how to proceed from there.

The first day was dominated by the reports of Lamb and Rabi of the startling experimental results mentioned above. Lamb's experiments, conducted like Rabi's at Columbia, and, again like Rabi's experiments, using radar technology developed during the war, measured the energy of electrons far more precisely than had previously been possible and established that electrons in hydrogen atoms do not behave as Paul Dirac's theory would predict. Electrons at one level, Lamb discovered, have a higher energy than those at another, rather than (as Dirac's theory would suggest) all of them having the same energy. An explanation of this "shift" would, as Oppenheimer suggested in the discussion that followed Lamb's presentation, require a new understanding of quantum electrodynamics (QED). The results reported by Rabi of experiments conducted by two students of his, John Nafe and Edward Nelson, also seemed to call for adjustments to QED, since they gave accurate and reliable measures of the "magnetic moments" of the electrons in hydrogen that contradicted what the Dirac theory would predict. During the second day papers by Kramers and Weisskopf addressed the theoretical issues raised by what became known respectively as the Lamb shift and the "anomalous magnetic moment," and Schwinger indicated during the discussion of Kramers' paper what shape might be taken by the new understanding of QED that these observational results seemed to demand.

On the final day of the conference, June 4, Oppenheimer led an extended discussion of the problems physicists faced in understanding mesons. In the ensuing discussion Robert Marshak made his now-famous suggestion that these puzzles might be solved by distinguishing two kinds of meson, one bigger than the other. The bigger of the two would be the Yukawa particle, responsible for the strong nuclear force, which decays into the smaller of the two—that is, the mesons found in cosmic rays—which in turn decay into electrons. In fact, though the participants at the Shelter Island Conference did not yet know this, experimental evidence confirming Marshak's hypothesis had already been published.

In the issue of the British journal *Nature* published on May 24, 1947 (and therefore not available in the States until a few days after the Shelter Island Conference), a group of experimental physicists based at Bristol and led by Cecil Powell reported on some investigations they had conducted, which demonstrated the existence of a process whereby what they called a "primary" meson could decay into a "secondary" meson. The authors of this report pointed out that the existence of this process resolved many of the puzzles about mesons, including those presented by the experiments of the Italian group. These experiments by Powell and his group form the second example that Oppenheimer gave in his lecture, mentioned earlier, of important experimental discoveries coming from Europe.

In a letter he wrote to Frank Jewett, the president of the National Academy of Sciences, Oppenheimer described the Shelter Island Conference as "unexpectedly fruitful." "The three days were a joy to us," he told Jewett, adding that the participants "came away a good deal more certain of the directions in which progress may lie." A few months later, when, in the aftermath of the conference, several fundamentally important papers had been published by those present, Oppenheimer was even more effusive, saying that the conference was, for most of the participants, "the most successful conference we had ever attended." Out of it, he claimed, had come "a new understanding of the probable role of the meson in physical theory, and the beginnings of a resolution of the long outstanding paradoxes of the quantum electrodynamics." By the end of the year, he was circulating plans for a second meeting to be held the following spring.

When the conference finished, Oppenheimer did not return to California, but went on instead to Harvard, where he was to receive an honorary degree. To avoid the usual difficulties of traveling to or from Shelter Island, he arranged for a private seaplane to fly him from Port Jefferson to Bridgeport, Connecticut, where he could catch a train to Boston. As Schwinger, who taught at Harvard, and Rossi and Weisskopf, who were both at MIT, also had to return to Boston, Oppenheimer invited them to join him. On the way they flew into a storm, so the pilot decided to land at the only available place, which happened to be a naval base, which civilian aircraft were not supposed to use. They disembarked to find an angry naval officer waiting to give them a dressing-down. "Don't worry," Oppenheimer said to the pilot. "Let me handle this." As he stepped off the plane he offered his outstretched hand to the officer and said calmly: "My name is Oppenheimer." "*The* Oppenheimer?" gasped the officer. Upon being reassured that he was indeed in the presence of the most famous physicist in the country, the officer changed his attitude completely, welcomed Oppenheimer and his companions to the officers' club where they were served tea and biscuits, and then arranged for them to be driven to the local railway station, from where they were able to take a train to Boston.

Having at last reached Harvard, Oppenheimer was awarded his honorary degree at the graduation ceremony on June 5. The ceremony turned out to be a historic occasion, because, in a speech that he gave to the graduates, General Marshall announced a major new policy initiative: the European Recovery Program, or Marshall Plan as it became known, which offered billions of U.S. dollars to European countries, on the condition of closer cooperation.

Oppenheimer, as his evidence to Congress in support of the May-Johnson Bill had shown, had a deep admiration for General Marshall. Haakon Chevalier tells a revealing story that illustrates not only Oppenheimer's warm regard for Marshall, but also his delight at finding himself moving in the same circles as the esteemed Secretary of State, whom *Time* magazine would that year name as "Man of the Year." Chevalier recalls meeting Phil Morrison in New York during this period and, in the course of catching up and reminiscing, asking him about Oppenheimer. "I hardly see him any more," Morrison replied. "We no longer speak the same language . . . He moves in a different circle." To illustrate what he meant, Morrison told Chevalier that at one of his most recent meetings with him, Oppenheimer kept saying, "George thinks this . . ." and "George says that. . . ." Eventually Morrison felt compelled to ask who this "George" was. "You understand," he told Chevalier, "General Marshall to me is General Marshall, or the Secretary of State—not George." Oppenheimer, he remarked, had changed profoundly: "He thinks he's God."

In the summer of 1947, as he, Kitty and the children prepared to leave California to move into Olden Manor, the splendid residence reserved for the director of Princeton's Institute for Advanced Study, Oppenheimer was at the very height of his reputation, among scientists, politicians and the general public. As the sociologist Philip Rieff has written, during these years "Oppenheimer became a symbol of the new status of science in American society. His thin handsome face and figure replaced Einstein's as the public image of genius." Anne Wilson's concern that he would get into "terrible trouble" in the East seemed, for the moment at least, to have been misplaced.

16

The Booming Years

his is an unreal place," Abraham Pais wrote, after he had been at Princeton's Institute for Advanced Study for a few months. "Bohr comes into my office to talk, I look out at the window and see Einstein walking home with his assistant. Two offices away sits Dirac. Downstairs sits Oppenheimer."

Apart from Einstein, the two other great physicists Pais mentions, Bohr and Dirac, were brought to the institute by Oppenheimer during his very first year there. Both were figures who had for Oppenheimer great symbolic importance: Bohr, the physicist from the previous generation for whom Oppenheimer had the greatest respect and the man whom he revered above all others; and Dirac, the greatest physicist of Oppenheimer's own generation, whose career had been closely watched by Oppenheimer, sometimes with rivalry, but always with enormous admiration. It was no surprise that Oppenheimer wanted to attract Bohr and Dirac to the institute, but Pais himself was, in fact, more representative of Oppenheimer's ambitions for the place. As Oppenheimer well knew, the next big steps in physics would not be taken by men of Bohr and Einstein's generation, or even by those of Oppenheimer and Dirac's generation; they would be taken by people the age of Pais, Schwinger, Feynman and so on. It was those young people, above all, whom he wanted to come to Princeton to be "directed" by him.

Having insisted that his contract permit him to devote some of his time to teaching graduate students, Oppenheimer abandoned the plan of depending on the trustees of the institute to identify suitable students at Princeton, and instead took the precaution of bringing his own. In a move that recalls the annual migration from Berkeley to Pasadena that students like Serber were prepared to take in the 1920s and '30s in order to maximize their time with Oppenheimer, in the summer of 1947 no fewer than five students—Hal Lewis, Robert Finkelstein, Saul Epstein, Leslie Foldy and Sig Wouthuysen—came with Oppenheimer when he left California for the East.

In December 1947, soon after Oppenheimer moved to Princeton, *Life* magazine ran an article about the institute under the heading "The Thinkers: The Institute for Advanced Study Is Their Haven." The atomic bomb, the piece began by saying, was a "devastating projection of this century's most abstruse thinking." In the light of this demonstration of the power of thought, "the thinker has come into his own," and therefore the institute, being "one of the most imposing collections of minds gathered in one place," had become recognized as "one of the most important places on earth."

The photographs accompanying the article, however, picture for the most part a distinctly unimposing collection of elderly men: the economist Walter W. Stewart reclining on his couch and looking as if he is about to fall asleep; the classics scholar Benjamin Merritt peering through a magnifying glass at an ancient Greek inscription; the mathematician Oswald Veblen leaning back in his chair and staring with apparent bewilderment at his desk; and, of course, Einstein, who is pictured twice, once in front of an audience and again sitting with Oppenheimer, telling him, according to the caption, "about his newest attempts to explain matter in terms of space," and looking in both pictures like an ancient Old Testament prophet.

In the starkest contrast to these pictures are two of Oppenheimer. In the first—captioned "talking shop"—he is shown engaged in obviously earnest and intense discussion with Dirac and Pais, all three of them looking quite sure that what they are discussing is of great importance. In the second—captioned "Oppenheimer's students"—Oppenheimer is shown perched on a desk, with five young men evidently hanging on to his every word. By accident or design, the contrast between the two sets of photographs sends a very clear message: under Oppenheimer, the institute would no longer be the resting place for eminent old men whose best work was behind them; it was to be a place where up-and-coming young men who meant business would make new and fundamental contributions to scientific knowledge.

These were exciting years for physics, as Oppenheimer, after the Shelter Island Conference, knew they would be, and he was determined to be, as far as possible, at the center of developments. Indeed, though Oppenheimer was at this time chairman of the Atomic Energy Commission's General Advisory Committee, and as such perhaps the most influential person in the country in the development of America's atomic policies, and though he had moved east partly so that his regular trips to Washington would not be so difficult or time-consuming, it was actually physics, rather than politics, that dominated his first two years at Princeton. As he had done in the 1930s, he published jointly with his students. In October 1947 he submitted the paper he had given at Shelter Island, "The Multiple Production of Mesons," to the *Physical Review* as a joint publication, cowritten with Hal Lewis and Sig Wouthuysen. A few months later he submitted another paper, "Note on the Stimulated Decay of Negative Mesons," this time cowritten with Saul Epstein and Robert Finkelstein. But, more importantly, he directed his students to the area where, in the wake of Shelter Island, the fundamentally important new steps would be taken: that is, to quantum electrodynamics, in which, as Oppenheimer knew, the solution to the puzzles posed by the recent experiments conducted at Columbia would be found.

Oppenheimer encouraged the young physicists at the institute to attend the many important seminars and conferences being given at that time, not just in America, but also in Europe. For example, he encouraged Pais to travel to a small conference in Copenhagen in September 1947, where Cecil Powell reported on his recent experiments at Bristol, which demonstrated the truth of Marshak's "two-meson" hypothesis. It was there that Pais first heard the names that would soon become accepted for the two particles: the pi-meson and the mu-meson. When he returned, Oppenheimer asked Pais to give a seminar reporting on what he had learned at Copenhagen. To Pais's surprise, Einstein turned up to hear his account of Powell's work. "It was," says Pais, "the only occasion in all my institute years that I saw Einstein present at a physics seminar given by someone other than himself."

Oppenheimer was so excited by the developments in physics during this time that he could not resist mentioning them, or at least alluding to them, even in his public, nontechnical lectures. One example of this—his mention of the experiments conducted by the three Italian scientists, Conversi, Pancini and Piccioni, in his lecture "Atomic Energy as a Contemporary Problem," given in September 1947—has already been mentioned. Another example occurred a couple of months later. On November 13–15, 1947, Oppenheimer was in Washington to attend the tenth Washington Conference on Theoretical Physics. Also there was Schwinger, who gave a report on a series of calculations that he had made relating to the quantum-mechanical interactions between electrons and photons, particles and radiation, in a relativistic field. These calculations were so subtle, so intricate and so complicated that Schwinger was possibly the only man then alive who could have performed them, but they also pointed to the fundamental change in QED that was needed to account for the Lamb shift and the anomalous magnetic moment of the electron. Feynman, who was at the conference, reports that he himself "did not have time to understand what exactly Schwinger had done," but he knew that, whatever it was, it had to be interesting, because "it got Oppy so excited." What excited Oppenheimer was the possibility that *both* the energy shift of electrons observed by Lamb *and* the anomalous increase in the magnetic charge of electrons reported by Rabi, Nafe and Nelson could be accounted for by the *same* set of calculations. This strongly suggested that something new and important had been discovered about the way electrons react to their own magnetic fields.

"The importance of Schwinger's calculation cannot be underestimated," writes the physicist and historian of physics Silvan Schweber:

> In the course of theoretical developments there sometimes occur important calculations that alter the way the community thinks about particular approaches. Schwinger's calculation is one such instance. By indicating, as Feynman had noted, that "the discrepancy in the hyperfine structure of the hydrogen atom . . . could be explained *on the same basis* as that of the electromagnetic self-energy, as can the line shift of Lamb," Schwinger had transformed the perception of quantum electrodynamics. He had made it into an effective, coherent, and consistent computational scheme.

Just ten days after the Washington conference, on November 25, Oppenheimer gave a public lecture at MIT entitled "Physics in the Contemporary World." His theme was the "temporarily disastrous effect on the prosecution of pure science" that the Second World War had had, because of the "demands of military technology," and the speed with which the science of physics, especially, had recovered from that disastrous effect. "It has," he told his audience, "been an exciting and an inspiring sight to watch the recovery—a recovery testifying to extraordinary vitality and vigor in this human activity. Today, barely two years after the end of hostilities, physics is booming."

As examples of the booming progress that physics was then making, Oppenheimer mentioned three things: 1. the new discoveries about mesons and the consequent progress in understanding elementary particles ("Almost every month has surprises for us in the findings about these particles. We are meeting new ones for which we are not prepared. We are learning how poorly we had identified the properties even of our old friends among them"); 2. Schwinger's dramatic improvements to Dirac's QED ("A newly vigorous criterion for the adequacy of our knowledge of the interactions of radiation and matter. Thus we are beginning to see in this field at least a partial resolution, and I am myself inclined to think rather more than that, of the paradoxes that have plagued the professional theorists for two decades"); and 3. the identification of the pi-meson as the Yukawa particle ("the increasing understanding of those forces which give to atomic nuclei their great stability, and to their trans-mutations their great violence"). Finally he mentioned the importance of recognizing the connections between these three:

> It is the prevailing view that a true understanding of these forces may well not be separable from the ordering of our experience with regard to elementary particles, and that it may also turn on an exten-sion to new fields of recent advances in electrodynamics.

Unfortunately, Oppenheimer's central message in this lecture—that physics was emerging from its wartime shackles into a new golden era of exciting fundamental progress—has been largely lost to posterity because of a momentary lapse into hyperbole. Referring to the role that scientists played not only in developing the atomic bomb, but also in recommend-ing their development and advising on their use, he remarked: "In some sort of crude sense which no vulgarity, no humor, no overstatement can quite extinguish, the physicists have known sin; and this is a knowledge which they cannot lose." So arresting was this remark, and so widely reported, that it came to overshadow everything else Oppenheimer said in this lecture. The lecture has thus acquired a reputation for being a gloomy and introspective confession of guilt rather than for being what it is—a cheery celebration of the dawn of a golden age of physics.

As is shown by Oppenheimer's mention in his MIT lecture of the possibility of solving "the paradoxes that have plagued the professional theorists for two decades," the reason he was so excited about Schwing-er's calculations was not just that they promised to explain both sets of the experiments conducted at Columbia, but also because, in doing so, they promised to solve the problems in quantum electrodynamics that Oppenheimer himself had worked on before the war. In particu-lar, Schwinger's work offered a way of overcoming the problems that Oppenheimer had long believed pointed to a fundamental flaw in Dirac's theory. These problems centered on the fact that, though the theory seemed in general to work well, at various points when one tried to use it to make very precise or detailed calculations, the answers it gave had to be wrong because they involved infinities, where the answer (for exam-ple, to questions about the energy of an electron at a certain state) *had* to be finite. This was the problem that Sidney Dancoff came so close to solving back in 1939. Now, it seemed, Schwinger was on the brink of providing the definitive solution.

Oppenheimer was not the only physicist excited at the progress promised by Schwinger's calculations. On his way back to Harvard from the Washington conference, Schwinger paid a visit to Columbia, where he gave a progress report on his groundbreaking work. After he had gone, Rabi wrote to Bethe, telling him that, in his view, Schwinger's theory was undoubtedly correct. He concluded: "God is great!" Bethe replied in equally excited terms: "I have heard about Schwinger's theory and find it very wonderful . . . It is certainly wonderful how those experiments of yours have given a completely new slant to a theory and how the theory has blossomed in a relatively short time. It is as exciting as in the early days of quantum mechanics."

In late December 1947, Schwinger sent a report of his treatment of the anomalous magnetic moment to the *Physical Review*, in the course of which he mentioned the work that Dancoff had done with Oppenheimer in 1939 and the "confusion" it had generated. Before this paper appeared in print, physicists had a chance to hear Schwinger report on his new theory at the annual meeting of the American Physical Society, which was held at Columbia from January 29 to 31, 1948. Oppenheimer and Pais attended the meeting, taking the train together from Princeton to New York on January 29. Their main interest, of course, was to hear Schwinger. He, however, was not scheduled to speak until the last day. In the meantime, Pais remembers, he and Oppenheimer were impressed by one of the other speakers, a young British physicist called Freeman Dyson. "As he proceeded to give his talk," Pais recalls, "Robert and I nodded at each other: this kid is smart." Educated at Winchester public school and at Trinity College, Cambridge, Dyson was a member of a very distinguished British family, his father being the well-known composer George Dyson. At the time Oppenheimer and Pais met him, Dyson was six months into a visiting fellowship at Cornell, where he had been working with Bethe and Feynman. After his talk, Oppenheimer approached him and invited him to spend the following academic year at the institute, an invitation Dyson promptly accepted.

When the time came for Schwinger's lecture on the final day of the conference, it was discovered that 1,600 people had registered to hear him speak. The afternoon's session was hurriedly rearranged so that he could give his lecture twice. In a letter that Dyson wrote his parents about the meeting, the excitement generated by Schwinger's paper is vividly captured:

The great event came on Saturday morning, and was an hour's talk by Schwinger, in which he gave a masterly survey of the new theory which he has the greatest share in constructing and at the end made a dramatic announcement of a still newer and more powerful theory, which is still in embryo. This talk was so brilliant that he was asked to repeat it in the afternoon session, various unfortunate lesser lights being displaced in his favour. There were tremendous cheers when he announced that the crucial experiment had supported his theory: the magnetic splitting of two of the spectral lines of gallium (an obscure element hitherto remarkable only for being a liquid metal like mercury) were found to be in the ratio of 2.00114 to 1: the old theory gave for this ratio exactly 2 to 1, while the Schwinger theory gave 2.0016 to 1.

Feynman was at this historic talk and, in the discussion period, said that he had a different method of calculating the magnetic moment of the electron and that his calculations supported Schwinger. "I was not showing off," Feynman later said. "I was just trying to say that there's no problem, for I had done the same thing that he had done and it had come out all right." The problem was, as Feynman later conceded: "People knew Schwinger, but most of them did not know me."

I heard later from several people who were at the APS meeting that I sounded funny to them. "The great Julian Schwinger was talking when this little squirt got up and said, 'I have already done this, Daddy, you're in no trouble at all! Everything will be OK!'"

Feynman's time would come, but, for the moment, all eyes were on Schwinger. Schwinger's opportunity to present in detail the "still newer and more powerful theory" mentioned by Dyson came at the end of March 1948, when the second conference in the series that had begun the previous year at Shelter Island was held. As, by common consent, Oppenheimer was the dominant figure at Shelter Island, it was only natural that he should take a lead in organizing and securing funding for this second conference. Just a few days after the Shelter Island Conference had finished, Oppenheimer was writing to the National Academy of Sciences, urging them to support a second conference.

On December 10, 1947, Oppenheimer had circulated all the participants of the Shelter Island Conference, suggesting that the next one should be held from March 30 to April 2, 1948—days when he knew his distinguished visitors to the institute, Bohr and Dirac, would be free to attend. As the Ram's Head Inn was not available during those days, Oppenheimer and Pais went looking for an alternative and found what they considered to be an ideal place, a hotel in the Pocono Mountains, Pennsylvania, called Pocono Manor.

At Pocono, Schwinger was given as much time as he wanted and delivered a talk that took up almost an entire day. At the end of it, Oppenheimer was heard to remark: "Now it does not matter any more whether things are infinite." John Wheeler took notes of the talk, which covered no fewer than forty pages. Pais has described Schwinger's talk as "a major tour de force in which he unveiled a detailed new calculus." Dyson was not there ("I was not invited because I was not yet an expert"), but he had good firsthand accounts of the talk from Bethe and Feynman. Schwinger, Dyson writes, "had a new theory of quantum electrodynamics which explained all the Columbia experiments. His theory was built on orthodox principles and was a masterpiece of mathematical technique. His calculations were extremely complicated, and few in the audience stayed with him all the way through the eight-hour exposition. But Oppy understood and approved everything."

One thing Oppenheimer did not yet understand, however, was Feynman's own version of quantum electrodynamics, which he presented after Schwinger in a paper called "Alternative Formulation of Quantum Electrodynamics." Dyson, who had got to know Feynman well by this time and liked him a great deal, writes: "Dick tried to tell the exhausted listeners how he could explain the same experiments much more simply using his own unorthodox methods. Nobody understood a word that Dick said. At the end Oppy made some scathing comments and that was that. Dick came home from the meeting very depressed." Pais, who was, of course, actually there, remembers it slightly differently. No one could follow Feynman's methods, he recalled, but "the speed with which Feynman could reproduce results also found by Schwinger convinced us that he was on to something." Certainly Schwinger thought Feynman was on to something. "The Pocono conference," he later said, "was my first opportunity to learn what Feynman was doing," and "as his talk proceeded, I could see points of similarity." Feynman himself remembers that at Pocono he and Schwinger "got together in the hallway and although we'd come from the end of the earth with different ideas, we had climbed the same mountain from different sides and we could check each other's equations."

Actually, Feynman and Schwinger were not the only two climbers of this particular mountain, as Oppenheimer discovered when he returned to Princeton. Waiting for him there was a letter from the Japanese physicist Sin-Itiro Tomonaga, telling him about recent work done in Japan that seemed in some important respects to anticipate Schwinger's work, or, anyway, to have arrived independently at very similar results. Tomonaga and his colleagues had been stimulated by reading Sidney Dancoff's 1939 paper to attempt exactly what Schwinger had achieved: a way of avoiding infinities in QED. Moreover, their method of accomplishing this, though not as fully worked out as Schwinger's, was, from a mathematical point of view, practically identical. With the letter Tomonaga sent Oppenheimer a collection of papers by the Japanese scientists that would appear in the Japanese English-language journal *Progress of Theoretical Physics*.

Upon receiving this package from Tomonaga, Oppenheimer sent him a telegram: "Grateful for your letter and papers. Found most interesting and valuable mostly paralleling much work done here. Strongly suggest you write a summary account of present state and views for prompt publication in *Physical Review*. Glad to arrange." Oppenheimer also sent a copy of Tomonaga's letter to all the participants of the Pocono Manor conference, telling them: "Just because we were able to hear Schwinger's beautiful report, we may better be able to appreciate this independent development."

Tomonaga was only too pleased to take Oppenheimer's advice, and on May 28, 1948, Oppenheimer received his summary of the work done in Japan, which was subsequently published in the July 15 edition of *Physical Review*, under the title "On Infinite Field Reactions in Quantum Field Theory," together with an accompanying note from Oppenheimer, which spoke of the "remarkable work carried out in Japan in recent years." On April 11, after seeing the letter from Tomonaga that Oppenheimer had sent to all the Pocono delegates, Freeman Dyson wrote to his parents, correctly pointing out: "The reason that everyone is so enormously pleased with this work of Tomonaga is partly political."

Long-sighted scientists are worried by the growing danger of nationalism in American science, and even more in the minds of the politicians and industrialists who finance science. In the public mind, experimental science at least is a thing only Americans know how to do, and the fact that some theorists have had to be imported from Europe is rather grudgingly admitted. In this atmosphere the new Schwinger theory tended to be acclaimed as a demonstration that now even in theoretical physics America has nothing to learn, now for the first time she has produced her own Einstein. You can see that if the scientists can say that even in this chosen field of physics America was anticipated and indeed by a member of the much-despised race of Japanese, this will be a strong card to play against nationalistic politics.

Things had come full circle since the days when Rabi, Condon and Oppenheimer had suffered from an acute awareness of the condescension with which European theoretical physicists treated their American counterparts. Now those same scientists had to check themselves and celebrate the achievements of others, so as not to appear to be basking in their own, self-evident superiority. For there is no doubt that there was at this time a sense in America that, as Oppenheimer had said in his MIT lecture, science, and particularly physics, was booming.

One reflection of this was the launch of a new, semi-popular magazine called *Physics Today*, the first issue of which was published in May 1948. The magazine was published by the American Institute of Physics, the "whole idea" of which was, in the words of one of its historians, to bring "mutually unacquainted specialists in all branches of physics together into a kind of operational unity for enhancement of physics as an important field of human endeavour." The aim of the magazine, in the words of the same historian, was "to present the special fields in interesting terms that all physicists and most laymen could understand." There were attempts by the magazine to resist the kind of nationalism that Freeman Dyson mentions in his letter to his parents—it included, for example, reports on what was happening in physics in England and the rest of Europe—but, nevertheless, the leading article of its first issue was a piece by Vannevar Bush on "Trends in American Science." Moreover, its first cover was a piece of triumphalism that would have been understood *only* in America. What the cover showed was a hat, resting on a piece of machinery. What the editor of the magazine assumed (no doubt correctly) their readers would know was that this hat, being a pork-pie hat, was *Oppenheimer*'s hat, and that the machinery was a cyclotron. The editor's intention was to symbolize the triumph of civilian over military control of atomic energy. Whether or not he was successful in that, what is indisputably symbolized by the cover is the pivotal and iconic role played by Oppenheimer during this period—so famous that he did not actually need to be pictured in order to be represented.

In June 1948, Oppenheimer returned to California to take part in a three-day conference at Caltech on cosmic rays that had been organized to celebrate Robert Millikan's eightieth birthday. Among those present were John Wheeler, Bruno Rossi, Carl Anderson, Frank Oppenheimer and two experimental physicists, George Rochester from Manchester and Louis Leprince-Ringuet from Paris, both of whom had collected evidence from cosmic-ray observations of yet another meson, this one (soon to be called the K-meson or kaon) much heavier than the pi-meson and the mu-meson. A brief contemporary report of the conference published in the magazine *Engineering and Science Monthly* states laconically: "Out of it all came general agreement that the symposium was an extremely successful affair; that our knowledge of these mysterious rays that bombard the earth from outer space is still fragmentary but progressing well, and that no one has yet determined from whence they come or how they originated."

A similar impression is given in the concluding remarks to the symposium that Caltech's president, Lee DuBridge, had asked Oppenheimer to give. Indeed, in these remarks Oppenheimer appears far more interested in the recent developments in theoretical physics made by Schwinger than he does in anything that was actually discussed during the symposium. After remarking that he found it "hard to disbelieve Leprince-Ringuet's evidence for a very heavy meson," he quickly turned his summary into an exposition of "the developments in electrodynamics that are so much associated with Schwinger's name," speculating that in those developments may lie a solution to the unsolved problems in cosmic-ray studies and particle physics.

Still more obsessed with the new QED than Oppenheimer was Freeman Dyson, who developed during the summer of 1948 a fervent ambition to understand fully all three versions of the new theory—Schwinger's, Tomonaga's and Feynman's—and demonstrate the equivalence of all three. Dyson was disappointed not to have been invited to the Pocono conference in March, but delighted when Bethe showed him Tomonaga's papers, particularly as one of the things Tomonaga demonstrated was something that Feynman had been saying for a long time: that Schwinger's results could be obtained without the formidably difficult mathematics that Schwinger himself had used to derive them. "To me that was very important," Dyson later said. "It gave me the idea that this was after all simple."

In order to improve his understanding of Schwinger's theory, Dyson signed up for the Ann Arbor summer school in Michigan, where Schwinger would be delivering a series of lectures. Up to that point the main source for Schwinger's ideas were the notes taken of his mammoth Pocono talk. This would change over the next two years, as Schwinger wrote up his ideas in a series of important articles that were published in the *Physical Review*, but, for a young physicist like Dyson, impatient to master the new theory, the Ann Arbor lectures were a golden opportunity to learn it straight from its originator.

The summer school was due to start on July 19, two weeks after the end of term at Cornell. During his year at Cornell, Dyson had seen much of Feynman and had come not only to admire him, but to like him a great deal. To fill those two weeks, then, Dyson accepted an offer he received from Feynman to accompany him on a trip to Albuquerque, "where love had drawn him." Being with Feynman twenty-four hours a day as they traveled across the United States provided Dyson with the perfect chance to understand Feynman's own version of the new theory, which, like Schwinger's, was as yet unpublished. "I knew," Dyson writes in his autobiographical book, *Disturbing the Universe*, "that somewhere hidden in Dick's ideas was the key to a theory of quantum electrody-namics simpler and more physical than Julian Schwinger's elaborate con-struction." By the time he left Feynman to go to Ann Arbor, Dyson had a pretty firm grasp of that key.

From Ann Arbor, Dyson wrote to his parents:

> Yesterday the great Schwinger arrived, and for the first time I spoke to him; with him arrived a lot of new people who came to hear him especially. His talks have been from the first minute excellent; there is no doubt he has taken a lot of trouble to polish up his theory for presentation at this meeting. I think in a few months we shall have forgotten what pre-Schwinger physics was like.

The lectures that Schwinger gave during the five weeks of the sum-mer school were, in fact, identical to the series of articles that would soon start appearing in print. In *Disturbing the Universe* Dyson says he learned less from the lectures—which he describes as "a marvel of polished ele-gance, like a difficult violin sonata played by a virtuoso, more technique than music"—than from personal conversations with Schwinger. In the lectures, Dyson says, Schwinger's theory "was a cut diamond, brilliant and dazzling," but in conversation, "I saw it in the rough, the way he saw it himself before he started the cutting and polishing. In this way I was able to grasp much better his way of thinking." After spending five weeks working through "every step of Schwinger's lectures and every word of our conversations," Dyson felt that he "understood Schwinger's theory as well as anybody could understand it, with the possible exception of Schwinger."

After the summer school, Dyson took a two-week holiday in Califor-nia, during which he did not think about physics, and then, in Septem-ber, on a Greyhound bus heading back east, he experienced some kind of epiphany. "As we were droning across Nebraska," Dyson recalls, ideas "came bursting into my consciousness like an explosion."

Feynman's pictures and Schwinger's equations began sorting themselves out in my head with a clarity they had never had before. For the first time I was able to put them all together. For an hour or two I arranged and rearranged the pieces. Then I knew that they all fitted. I had no pencil or paper, but everything was so clear I did not need to write it down. Feynman and Schwinger were just looking at the same set of ideas from two different sides. Putting their methods together, you would have a theory of quantum electrodynamics that combined the mathematical precision of Schwinger with the practical flexibility of Feynman.

By the time he reached Princeton to take up the one-year fellowship that Oppenheimer had offered him at the institute, Dyson had already mapped out the paper he would write, the title of which would be "The Radiation Theories of Tomonaga, Schwinger and Feynman." Walking to the institute for the first time, he reflected that he—a twenty-four-year-old at the start of his career and with no major publications to his name—felt himself in a position "to teach the great Oppenheimer how to do physics."

According to a letter he wrote his parents, Dyson, after spending "five days stuck in my rooms, writing and thinking with a concentration which nearly killed me," finished writing his article on the seventh day of being in Princeton. As it happened, Oppenheimer was not at that time in Princeton, but in Europe, where he would remain for the next six weeks, attending conferences in France, England, Denmark and Belgium and revisiting old haunts and old friends. Dyson, together with seven other young physicists who had been invited to spend the year at the institute (most of them students of Schwinger's), was using Oppenheimer's office while a new building that would contain their individual offices was hurriedly being completed.

Actually, though Dyson did not know it, Oppenheimer already knew the general outline of the paper, since, before completing it, Dyson had written to Bethe "announcing the triumph." In his letter, he told Bethe: "I have succeeded in re-formulating the Schwinger method, without any changes of substance, so that it gives immediately all the advantages of Feynman theory," adding: "Incidentally, the complete equivalence of Schwinger and Feynman is now demonstrated." Like Oppenheimer, Bethe was then in Europe, and a few days after he received Dyson's letter, he and Oppenheimer were both in Birmingham attending a four-day conference on "Problems of Nuclear Physics," which was held on September 14–18. The organizer of the conference was Rudolf Peierls, who remembers:

In the middle of the conference somebody had a letter from Dyson . . . summarizing the results he had just obtained in linking the Feynman and Schwinger approaches and showing connections and also in proving that the infinities could be thrown out not merely in the first order in which they appeared but to all orders, which was an important formal result.

There had been very few international conferences since the war ended, and at these European meetings the tendency was for the Europeans to learn what was happening in America. Everywhere he went, Oppenheimer wrote home to Frank, "there is the phrase 'you see, we are somewhat out of things.'" His return to Europe had, he told his brother, confirmed him in the knowledge "that it is in America largely that it will be decided what manner of world we are to live in."

At the eighth Solvay Congress, held in Brussels from September 27 to October 2, 1948, Oppenheimer was asked to report on progress in quantum electrodynamics. His report, of course, emphasized the importance of Schwinger's work. After a historical account of the development of the "old" QED by Dirac, Pauli and Heisenberg, Oppenheimer's report stressed the infinity problems that theory gave rise to, citing his own 1930 paper on the subject. To solve these problems, he told his audience, "more powerful methods are required," the development of which "occurred in two steps, the first largely, the second almost wholly, due to Schwinger." Oppenheimer's account of Schwinger's breakthroughs, however, was markedly free of the excitement with which he had discussed them earlier in the year. Indeed, the tone of the report was strikingly downbeat, especially toward the end, where Oppenheimer drew attention to some perceived weaknesses in the theory, such as the fact that it could not deal with the forces acting between mesons inside nucleons. These weaknesses, he concluded, suggested that the new quantum electrodynamics was not a "closed"—that is, a completed—system. Schwinger had made an important step forward, but his was not the last word on the subject.

Back in Princeton, Dyson, having sent his paper on Feynman, Schwinger and Tomonaga off to the *Physical Review* (it was received on October 6, 1948), was awaiting Oppenheimer's return from Europe with some trepidation. On October 10, he wrote to his parents: "The atmosphere at the Institute during these last days has been rather like the first scene in 'Murder in the Cathedral' with the women of Canterbury awaiting the return of their archbishop." A few days later, when Oppenheimer finally arrived back, Dyson was astonished to discover that he seemed not only to have lost his enthusiasm for the new QED, but to have become actively hostile toward it. Oppenheimer was, Dyson wrote home, "unreceptive to new ideas in general, and Feynman in particular."

In *Disturbing the Universe* Dyson writes that he had known that Oppenheimer did not appreciate Feynman:

> but it came as a shock to hear him now violently opposing Schwinger, his own student, whose work he had acclaimed so enthusiastically six months earlier. He had somehow become convinced during his stay in Europe that physics was in need of radically new ideas, that this quantum electrodynamics of Schwinger and Feynman was just another misguided attempt to patch up old ideas with fancy mathematics.

Why Oppenheimer's attitude to the new theory changed so drastically after his trip to Europe in the autumn of 1948 is something of a mystery. He never explained it to Dyson or to anyone else, and no documents or recorded conversations exist that can shed much light on it. It is possible that he was influenced by spending several weeks in an atmosphere very different from the triumphant, optimistic mood that prevailed among American scientists during this time. It seems possible, too, that he was influenced by specific views of individual European scientists, many of whom were much more skeptical toward, and less impressed with, Schwinger's theory than their American counterparts. As the historian of science Jagdish Mehra puts it: "The old guard in Europe was not altogether satisfied with Schwinger's breakthroughs." Particularly resistant was Paul Dirac, who remained unconvinced by the new theory till his dying day. When Dyson once asked Dirac what he thought of the new developments, Dirac replied: "I might have thought the new ideas were correct if they had not been so ugly." It was a view that Dirac was to state in print in many places, including a paper he published in 1951, which provided a new theory of the electron. In it he wrote:

> Recent work by Lamb, Schwinger, Feynman and others has been very successful in setting up rules for handling the infinities and subtracting them away, so as to leave finite residues which can be compared with experiments, but the resulting theory is an ugly and incomplete one and cannot be considered as a satisfactory solution of the problem of the electron.

Dirac's use of the word "incomplete" here echoes so strongly the sentiments expressed by Oppenheimer that one is very tempted to imagine that, more than anything else, it was the influence of discussions with Dirac that prompted Oppenheimer's change of attitude toward Schwinger's theory. Dirac was, after all, at the eighth Solvay Congress and is on record as having responded to Oppenheimer's report with an attack on the new theory.

Whatever its cause, Oppenheimer's change of heart put a great strain on his relations with Dyson. Within a few days of his return to Princeton, Oppenheimer gave Dyson a copy of the report he had delivered at the Solvay Congress. Dyson, already upset at Oppenheimer's attitude toward his paper on Feynman, Schwinger and Tomonaga, was sufficiently horrified by Oppenheimer's report to write a memo on the subject. On October 17, Dyson sent the memo to Oppenheimer, together with a note that explained that he had written it because "I disagree rather strongly with the point of view expressed in your Solvay Report." The memo consisted of six numbered points, almost all of which centered on a defense of Feynman's version of the new theory. "As a result of using both the old-fashioned quantum-electrodynamics (Heisenberg-Pauli) and Feynman electrodynamics," Dyson wrote, "I am convinced that the Feynman theory is considerably easier to use, understand, and teach."

Dyson was naturally apprehensive about Oppenheimer's reaction to this memo, but, in fact, the next time the two met Oppenheimer told him that he was delighted by it and had arranged for Dyson to give a seminar twice a week for the following four weeks, as an opportunity for him to put his views to the other members of the institute. As Dyson discovered at the first seminar in the series, however, Oppenheimer evidently saw these occasions as being an opportunity for *him* to express his views as well. In the next letter home to his parents, Dyson wrote about how difficult Oppenheimer had made it for him to put across his ideas:

> I have been observing rather carefully his behaviour during seminars. If one is saying, for the benefit of the rest of the audience, things that he knows already, he cannot resist hurrying on to something else; then when one says things that he doesn't know or immediately agree with, he breaks in before the point is fully explained with acute and sometimes devastating criticisms, to which it is impossible to reply adequately even when he is wrong. If one watches him one can see that he is moving around nervously all the time, never stops smoking, and I believe that his impatience is largely beyond his control.

During the second seminar, "we had our fiercest public battle so far, when I criticized some unwarrantably pessimistic remarks he had made about the Schwinger theory. He came down on me like a ton of bricks, and conclusively won the argument so far as the public was concerned." The following day, Dyson told his parents, he was rescued by Hans Bethe, who came down to talk to the seminar "about some calculations he was doing with the Feynman theory."

> He was received in the style to which I am accustomed, with incessant interruptions and confused babbling of voices, and had great difficulty in making even his main point clear; while this was going on he stood very calmly and said nothing, only grinned at me as if to say "Now I can see what you are up against." After that he began to make openings for me, saying in answer to a question "Well I have no doubt Dyson will have told you all about that," at which point I was not slow to say in as deliberate a tone as possible, "I am afraid I have not got to that yet." Finally Bethe made a peroration in which he said explicitly that the Feynman theory is much the best theory and that people must learn it if they want to avoid talking nonsense; things which I had begun saying but in vain.

After the seminar Bethe and Oppenheimer dined together, and during dinner Bethe must have said something about Oppenheimer's treatment of Dyson, because after that Oppenheimer listened to Dyson without interrupting, and at the end of the last seminar made a short speech saying how much they had all learned from Dyson's talks. The next morning, Dyson found in his mailbox a short note from Oppenheimer, saying simply "*Nolo Contendere*," a legal term derived from the Latin for "I do not wish to contend."

By the time these seminars had finished, toward the end of November 1948, Dyson had achieved, simply by word of mouth (his paper would not actually appear in print until February 1949), a reputation, in both America and Europe, as an extremely gifted and promising young physicist, and he was consequently bombarded with job offers. The Commonwealth Fellowship that had allowed him to spend two years in the U.S. stipulated that, when those two years were over, he had to return to either Great Britain or one of the Commonwealth countries. He was therefore unable to accept a position that Rabi offered him at Columbia, which he deeply regretted. "It's a grim prospect," he told his parents, "to be cut off without more than rumours and months-old reports of what Feynman or Schwinger or Columbia or Berkeley is doing."

To avoid this "grim prospect" becoming a permanent state of affairs, Oppenheimer made Dyson a generous proposal, based on a very flattering comparison. Both Bohr and Dirac, Oppenheimer told Dyson, had felt compelled to return to their home countries after their visiting fellowships at the institute, but he had made for them an arrangement whereby they could visit the institute every third year so that they could keep in touch with people and developments in the United States. "Certainly," Oppenheimer told Dyson, "we shall be able to do something of the kind for you." A short while later, Dyson went to see Oppenheimer to tell him that, among British universities, he had received offers from Birmingham, Bristol and Cambridge, and to ask for advice on choosing between the three. "Well," said Oppenheimer, "Birmingham has much the best theoretical physicist to work with, Peierls; Bristol has much the best experimental physicist, Powell; Cambridge has some excellent architecture." Perhaps, by this time, Oppenheimer had broken free of the spell exerted by Dirac. In any case, Dyson chose to go to Birmingham.

Intoxicated by his newfound celebrity, Dyson wrote to his parents: "I am really becoming a Big Shot." However, as a celebrity, he was nowhere near being in Oppenheimer's league. On November 8, 1948, in the middle of Dyson's series of seminars, the cover of *Time* magazine was taken up with a painting of Oppenheimer, looking thoughtful and troubled, beneath which was the quotation (which, in the context of the Dyson-Oppenheimer exchanges, acquires a rather ironic flavor): "What we don't understand we explain to each other." The article heralded by the cover was a long, surprisingly intimate profile of Oppenheimer, who seemed to have taken a liking to the interviewer, to whom he revealed many things about himself that he did not often reveal, even to close friends. Many of his remarks about his childhood that seem to appear in every article or book written about him—that he was an "unctuous, repulsively good little boy," that his life as a child "did not prepare me in any way for the fact that there are cruel and bitter things," that his home offered him "no normal, healthy way to be a bastard," and so on—have their origin in this *Time* article. His life is told in some detail, using both his words and those of his friends, schoolmates and teachers, including—and here, in the increasingly hysterical anti-communism that was sweeping through the States at the time, he was taking something of a calculated risk—his active involvement in left-wing politics during the 1930s, when, he is quoted as saying, "I woke up to a recognition that politics was a part of life."

> I became a real left-winger, joined the Teachers Union, had lots of Communist friends. It was what most people do in college or late high school. The Thomas Committee doesn't like this, but I'm not ashamed of it; I'm more ashamed of the lateness. Most of what I

believed then now seems complete nonsense, but it was an essential part of becoming a whole man. If it hadn't been for this late but indispensable education, I couldn't have done the job at Los Alamos at all.

The "Thomas Committee" mentioned by Oppenheimer was the House of Representatives' Committee on Un-American Activities (HUAC), which, under the chairmanship of J. Parnell Thomas, had been holding hearings throughout the spring and summer of 1948, investigating alleged communist subversion. The most sensational outcome of these hearings came in August 1948, when Whittaker Chambers, a senior editor at *Time* magazine, accused Alger Hiss, a lawyer and an official in the State Department, of having been a member of a secret communist cell. At the time that Oppenheimer was being interviewed for *Time*, Hiss was engaged in legal proceedings against Chambers, which, following the revelation by Chambers of fresh evidence against Hiss, were to lead to Hiss's conviction, and subsequent imprisonment, in 1950 for perjury.

In a letter he had written Frank from Europe, Oppenheimer remarked how hard it had been while he was away "to follow in detail what all is up with the Thomas Committee," and describing the Hiss case as "a menacing portent." Oppenheimer was evidently (and rightly) concerned that HUAC would come gunning for Frank, and advised him to get himself a good lawyer, someone like Herb Marks, who, Oppenheimer told his brother, knew his way round Washington, Congress and the press. Coincidentally, when the *Time* profile of Oppenheimer came out, among those who wrote to him about it was Herb Marks, who complimented him particularly on the "pre-trial" touch—presumably a reference to Oppenheimer's open disclosure of his left-wing past. Replying to Marks, Oppenheimer told him that was the only thing he had liked about the article, "where I saw an opportunity, long solicited, but not before available."

The *Time* piece ended with some remarks about the Institute for Advanced Study, which Oppenheimer said he liked to think of as an "intellectual hotel," a "place for transient thinkers to rest, recover and refresh themselves before continuing on their way." He hoped that some people, Oppenheimer told his interviewer, like Dirac and Bohr, would make periodic returns to Princeton, so as not to lose touch with the U.S. His recent experiences in Birmingham and Brussels had shown him how "despairing the life of the intellect had become in postwar Europe," which had given him a renewed sense of the importance of the institute: "Viewed from Princeton, the Institute might have its shortcomings;

viewed from Europe, it had something of the special glow of a monastery in the Dark Ages."

In an earlier interview, this time for the *New York Times*, published in April 1948, Oppenheimer had apparently given a rather different impression of his role as the institute's director. Suppose, the reporter had written (in remarks presumably based on things Oppenheimer had said), you had funds based on a $21 million endowment, and:

> Suppose you could use this fund to invite as your salaried house-guests the world's greatest scholars, scientists and creative artists— your favorite poet, the author of the book that interested you so much, the European scientist with whom you would like to mull over some speculations about the nature of the universe. That's pre-cisely the set-up that Oppenheimer enjoys. He can indulge every interest and curiosity.

The *New York Times* description actually gives a fairly accurate account of how Oppenheimer used the funds placed at his disposal. In almost every appointment he made, one can see a very personal influ-ence at play. This has already been mentioned in connection with Bohr and Dirac, but it is no less evident in those who came the following year. These included, for example, Oppenheimer's old friend Francis Fergus-son, who, in the many years since he and Oppenheimer had last seen each other, had become an eminent critic and writer on theater. Fer-gusson taught at Bennington College, Vermont, where he founded the drama department. During his time at the institute Fergusson wrote *The Idea of a Theatre*, which was to become his best-known work. Another old friend who arrived at the institute in 1948 was Harold Cherniss, the ancient-Greek scholar whom Oppenheimer had known at Berkeley. No less personal, albeit in a different way, was Oppenheimer's invitation to the Japanese physicist Hideki Yukawa, whose work had had such a pro-found influence on Oppenheimer's and who also arrived in 1948.

Finally there was T. S. Eliot, who had long been both Oppenheimer's favorite poet and Fergusson's. Indeed, over the years Fergusson had published many essays about various aspects of Eliot's work. Eliot, too, came in 1948, arriving while Oppenheimer was still in Europe. Dyson remembers him as being "prim and shy." Eliot, he says, "appeared each day in the lounge at teatime, sitting by himself with a newspaper and a teacup." Neither Dyson nor any of his contemporaries could muster the courage to approach him. "None of our gang of young scientists," Dyson recalls, "succeeded in penetrating the barrier of fame and reserve that surrounded Eliot like a glass case around a mummy." Pais says he "was dying to have conversations with Eliot but refrained from approaching him, less out of shyness than from an ingrained sense not to bother him with trivia." He did, however, have one conversation with the great poet, when they happened to share a lift. "This is a nice elevator," Eliot remarked, to which Pais replied: "Yes, this is a nice elevator." "That," Pais writes, "was all the conversation with Eliot I ever had."

Eliot's biographer Peter Ackroyd says that Eliot "felt lonely and homesick" at Princeton, precisely because "he suffered from the fate of many famous men"—that is, "most people were afraid to talk to him." In November 1948, it was announced that Eliot had won the Nobel Prize in Literature. Consequently, according to Dyson: "Newspapermen swarmed around him and he retreated even further into his shell." Years later, Dyson asked Oppenheimer what he thought of Eliot. He replied that, though he loved Eliot's poetry and regarded him as a genius, he was disappointed with his stay at the institute. "I invited Eliot here," Oppenheimer told Dyson, "in the hope that he would produce another masterpiece, and all he did here was to work on *The Cocktail Party*, the worst thing he ever wrote."

Dyson's time at the institute, on the other hand, despite his acrimonious spat with Oppenheimer, was a triumph, and, in fact, Oppenheimer became one of his leading admirers and supporters. Before submitting for publication the report he gave at the Solvay Congress, Oppenheimer rewrote it, adding to it several mentions of Dyson's paper on Feynman, Schwinger and Tomonaga (which he describes as being "in press") and drawing attention to Dyson's own original contributions to the theory that—Oppenheimer's temporary doubts notwithstanding—had so captured the imaginations of physicists during the latter part of 1948. On December 30, Oppenheimer wrote to Peierls in Birmingham:

> One piece of news which you need to know is how very very good Dyson is. He wants to return, and in fact must return, to England for the next years, but we have made a flexible arrangement with him to come back here for as many semesters as he can spare. I think he likes the arrangement and we are all delighted by it.

In January 1949, Dyson went with Oppenheimer to New York to attend the annual meeting of the American Physical Society, of which Oppenheimer had recently been elected president. On the first day of the meeting, Dyson wrote to his parents, he received confirmation of his own celebrity when a young physicist from Columbia gave a talk during which he repeatedly referred to the "beautiful theory of Feynman-Dyson." The next day, Dyson recalls, "Oppenheimer gave a presidential address in the biggest hall":

> and such was the glamour of his name after being on the cover of *Time* that the hall was packed with two thousand people half an hour before he was due to start. He spoke on the title "Fields and Quanta" and gave a very good historical summary of the vicissitudes of our attempts to understand the behaviour of atoms and radiation. At the end he spoke with great enthusiasm of my work and said that it was pointing the way for the immediate future even if it did not seem deep enough to carry us farther than that. I was thinking happily to myself: Last year it was Julian Schwinger, this year it is me. Who will it be next year?

It was not only Oppenheimer whose interests were moving away from Schwinger and toward Feynman and Dyson; the whole physics community was moving in the same direction. Dyson's paper would not appear in print until shortly after the conference, and Feynman's classic papers setting out his version of QED would not appear until September 1949, but word of mouth is a quick, efficient and powerful means of communication and, even before these papers came out, there was much talk among physicists of "Feynman diagrams" or, for a while at least, "Dyson graphs."

This January 1949 meeting has, in fact, gone down in history as the moment when not just the world at large, but Feynman himself, realized the power of his diagrammatic methods of performing the extraordinarily intricate calculations required in quantum electrodynamics. It was this meeting, Feynman later said, "when I really knew I had something. That was the moment that I really knew that I had to publish—that I had gotten ahead of the world." The particular incident that prompted this realization was one that involved Oppenheimer, and, more specifically, it involved Oppenheimer's relish for publicly crushing the views and arguments of others.

Murray Slotnick, a young physicist at Cornell who had worked with Hans Bethe, reported at the meeting on a certain extremely complicated calculation in meson theory that he had done relating to the interaction between a neutron and the electrostatic field of an electron. He had done this calculation for both "pseudoscalar" and "pseudovector" interactions, getting a finite result for the first and an infinite result for the second. In the discussion period after Slotnick's presentation, Oppenheimer flummoxed Slotnick by asking "What about Case's Theorem?" When asked to explain what he meant, Oppenheimer said that Kenneth Case, an ex-student of Schwinger's who was now at the Institute for Advanced Study, had just proven that the two kinds of interactions *had* to be the same—a proof that Case would be presenting to the conference the following day. Since Slotnick's calculations violated Case's Theorem, Oppenheimer insisted, they had to be wrong. As Case's Theorem had not been published, nor was there even a pre-print of it available, Slotnick, naturally, did not know how to respond, and so allowed Oppenheimer's point to stand and accepted that his own work had been summarily refuted.

Feynman was not there during this exchange, but when he arrived at the conference later that day he was asked for his opinion on Slotnick's calculation and "Case's Theorem." Feynman had never studied meson theory, but his methods of calculation using "Feynman diagrams" had been developed precisely to perform calculations relating to interactions between particles and electrostatic fields, so he was pretty sure that he could do this calculation. Sure enough, after a few hours that evening, he had results for both the pseudoscalar and pseudovector cases, results that confirmed his hunch that Slotnick was right. The next day, Feynman sought out Slotnick and showed him his work of the previous evening. Slotnick was absolutely dumbstruck. He had spent two years on this problem, and Feynman had solved it in an evening. Not only that, but Feynman's calculation was more fine-grained than Slotnick's, since he had built in a variable for the momentum transferred by the electron, a complication that Slotnick had ignored. It was Slotnick's flabbergasted reaction that convinced Feynman that he really had something wonderful. "That was the moment I got my Nobel Prize," Feynman said, "when Slotnick told me that he had been working two years . . . That was an exciting moment."

That day, after Case had given his talk, Feynman got up and asked: "But what about Slotnick's calculation? Your theorem must be wrong because a simple calculation shows that it's correct. I checked Slotnick's calculation and I agree with it." "I had fun with that," Feynman later remarked. After the conference he worked out what was wrong with Case's reasoning, a laborious task, since it involved working with Schwinger's formalism. What made it worthwhile was the demonstration that, as Dyson had been saying for a long time, Feynman's methods were easier and quicker to use than Schwinger's and, therefore, likely to give more reliable results. After the meeting Feynman worked hard to write up his version of the new theory and on April 8, 1949, the *Physical Review* received "The Theory of Positrons," the first published account by Feynman of his method of calculating the energies of electrons and positrons—that is, his first statement of the new QED. Three days after delivering this paper, Feynman was in Oldstone-on-the-Hudson, Peek-skill, about forty miles north of New York City, for the third and final conference in the series that had begun at Shelter Island two years earlier.

Like the one at Pocono, this conference was organized by Oppenheimer, who, a month before it began, had sent to the invitees a rather brisk, businesslike letter, informing them that the Oldstone Inn had been reserved for the nights of April 10–14. "We will start work on Monday morning and should have four full days together." Twenty-four scientists attended the conference. Among those who had not been at the other two were Yukawa, now a visiting fellow at the institute, and Freeman Dyson, whose invitation was recognition of his newfound status as a member of the elite group of leading physicists.

"We had lovely weather for the conference," Dyson wrote to his parents soon after it had finished, "and could sit outside whenever we were not conferring. However, since the conference was run by Oppenheimer, that was not often."

> One of the things which simply amazes me about Oppenheimer is his mental and physical indefatigability; this must have a lot to do with his performance during the war. There was no fixed program for the conference, and so we just talked as much or as little as we liked; nevertheless Oppenheimer had us in there every day from ten a.m. till seven p.m. with only short breaks, and on the first day also after supper from eight till ten, this night session being only dropped on the second day after a general rebellion. And all through these sessions Oppenheimer was wide awake, listening to everything that was said and obviously absorbing it.

Everyone agreed that this Oldstone conference was, as Pais puts it, "Feynman's show." Having worked out his methods systematically, Feynman was now able to demonstrate them persuasively, and at Oldstone, Pais writes, Feynman's version of QED "began its rapid and never-waning rise in popularity." At the end of the meeting Oppenheimer wrote to the National Academy of Sciences, the sponsors of all three conferences in the series, expressing, on behalf of the people who had taken part, "a real sense of satisfaction for the fruitfulness and value of the conference." He added:

> The two years since the first conference have marked some changes in the state of fundamental physics, in large part a consequence of our meetings. The problems of electrodynamics which appeared so

insoluble at our first meeting, and which began to yield during the following year, have now reached a certain solution; and it is possible, though in these matters prediction is hazardous, that the subject will remain closed for some time.

Remarkably, he was not exaggerating. During the two years of these conferences, QED went from being a set of unsolved problems to what Feynman insisted was a part of physics that "is *known*, rather than a part that is unknown." "At the present time," Feynman declared in 1983, more than thirty years after the theory was developed, "I can proudly say that there is *no significant difference* between experiment and theory!"

We physicists are always checking to see if there is something the matter with the theory. That's the game, because if there *is* something the matter, it's interesting! But so far, we have found nothing wrong with the theory of quantum electrodynamics. It is, therefore, I would say, the jewel of our physics—our proudest possession.

In 1965, Feynman, Schwinger and Tomonaga were awarded the Nobel Prize in Physics for their respective contributions to constructing this "jewel." Dyson has been called the greatest physicist not to have won the prize, his main rival for that title being Oppenheimer himself.

17

Massive Retaliation

During the two years that American physicists excitedly solved the problems of quantum electrodynamics—or excitedly watched them being solved—the world outside became a much darker place. The Berlin Blockade of 1948–9 and the Communist Party victories in Czechoslovakia (1948) and Hungary (1949) had persuaded public opinion in the West that the Soviet Union was indeed, as Churchill had predicted, attempting to expand its sphere of influence and that democracy therefore had to be defended from the communist threat. The postwar world that many scientists had dreamed of in 1945—a world of international cooperation, based on the mutual recognition of the folly of a nuclear arms race—never looked like materializing. Instead what transpired was exactly what the scientists had warned against: growing tensions between the world's superpowers brought about and fostered by the mutual suspicion, paranoia and fear that inevitably accompanied the forlorn attempt to keep scientific facts secret from scientists.

In December 1948, Oppenheimer gave a lecture in Rochester entitled "The Open Mind," in which, while accepting the failure of past attempts to cooperate with the Soviet Union and agreeing that the blame for that failure lay chiefly with the Soviets, he emphasized, against the prevailing cultural current, the advantages of openness and magnanimity in international relations. "We need to remember that we are a powerful nation," he urged. The United States did not have to conduct its affairs in an atmosphere of fearful suspicion. The policies developed and pursued in such an atmosphere "appear to commit us to a future of secrecy and to an imminent threat of war." As a model of an alternative attitude, Oppenheimer cited the example of Ulysses Grant, who, at the end of the

Civil War, spoke to the defeated Confederate General Lee and allowed Lee's troops to keep their horses, since "they would need them for the spring plowing." Even in recognition of the evils committed by the Soviets in the past, Oppenheimer urged, Americans should keep an open mind about the future and act from a position of magnanimous strength rather than fearful weakness.

When he gave this lecture Oppenheimer possibly imagined himself to be, as he believed the United States to be, in a position of unassailable strength. It was just a month earlier that he had been on the cover of *Time* magazine, which began its long article on him with an impressive list of his achievements and titles:

> More & more physicists are coming to know the Institute as the home of an authentic contemporary hero of their trade: Dr. J. (for nothing) Robert Oppenheimer, who is president of the American Physical Society, chairman of the technical advisers to the Atomic Energy Commission, and one of the world's top theoretical physicists. Laymen know him as the man who bossed the production of the atom bomb. Last week, at 44, Oppenheimer was beginning his second year as director of the Institute for Advanced Study.

In the years that followed, however, it would be shown that none of those titles and achievements could save him from the very fear and suspicion against which he had campaigned. For five years, starting in the summer of 1949, his standing—among his fellow scientists, among politicians and among military men—would be systematically attacked in a concerted and successful attempt to ruin him. What made the attack all the more pitiable to watch was the fact that his enemies were able to use against him his own personal and moral weaknesses, which were often cruelly exposed during these years.

The first serious blow to Oppenheimer's reputation, and the moment when those personal and moral frailties were first held up for all to see, was his appearance before HUAC on June 7, 1949. As Oppenheimer had correctly remarked in his letter to Frank the previous October, the revelations about Alger Hiss that had come out of the HUAC hearings were a "menacing portent" of things to come. Having investigated communist "subversion" among actors in Hollywood and politicians in Washington, in April 1949 the committee, under its new chairman, John Wood, turned its attentions to scientists, and, in particular, to the group of young radicals at Berkeley that had so concerned the FBI and military security during the war.

The four young scientists whose group photograph had been bought by an agent tailing Rossi Lomanitz—David Bohm, who was now teaching physics at Princeton University; Max Friedman, who, having changed his name to Ken Manfred, was at the University of Puerto Rico; Joseph Weinberg, who was now a colleague of Frank's at Minnesota, and Lomanitz himself, who was teaching at Fisk University, Nashville, Tennessee—were all subpoenaed to testify before HUAC. All of them except Weinberg pleaded the Fifth Amendment. Weinberg, who of course did not know the FBI had a transcript of his conversation with Steve Nelson back in March 1943, continued to deny any involvement with espionage.

In contrast, Oppenheimer knew all about his FBI file and what it contained, and was very alarmed to discover that one of the six members of HUAC, Harold Velde, was a former FBI man. When his turn to testify duly arrived, Oppenheimer took with him the AEC's lawyer, Joseph Volpe. As it turned out, the meeting seemed to go quite well. The committee members went out of their way to assure Oppenheimer that *his* loyalty, having been vouched for by General Groves, was not in doubt. In response to their polite and gentle, even deferential, questioning, Oppenheimer repeated what had by now become the standard version of the "Chevalier Affair" (the chief feature of which was that Chevalier had approached just *one* scientist, namely Oppenheimer himself) and was no doubt relieved not to be asked why he had originally claimed that Chevalier had approached *three* scientists. He also gave bland and protective answers to questions about Lomanitz and Weinberg. When asked about Frank, he said: "Mr. Chairman, I will answer the questions you put to me. I ask you not to press these questions about my brother. If they are important to you, you can ask him. I will answer, if asked, but I beg you not to ask me these questions." Remarkably, the response to this was to withdraw the question.

With regard to the unfortunate Bernard Peters, however, Oppenheimer revealed himself to be willing not only to confirm the damaging things he had said to Peer de Silva in January 1944, but also to elaborate on them. He confirmed that he had described Peters as "a dangerous man and quite Red," and added that Peters had been a member of the German Communist Party, but had "violently denounced" the American Communist Party, because it was "too constitutional and conciliatory an organization, not sufficiently dedicated to the overthrow of the Government by force and violence." Perhaps most extraordinary, though, were Oppenheimer's remarks when asked to explain his comment to de Silva that Peters's past had been filled with incident that pointed toward "direct action." As grounds for believing Peters to be prone to such action, Oppenheimer cited:

Incidents in Germany where he [Peters] fought street battles against the National Socialists on account of Communists; being placed in a concentration camp; escaping by guile. It seemed to me those were past incidents not pointing to temperance.

The implied suggestion seemed to be that being placed in a concentration camp and then escaping from it were evidence of some sort of character flaw in Peters. When asked how he knew Peters had been in the German Communist Party, Oppenheimer replied: "It was well known. Among other things, he told me."

These remarks about Peters not only go beyond what Oppenheimer had said to de Silva, but also go way beyond what was required of him on this occasion. When one tries to explain why he was prepared to say so many damaging things about a man who had been his student and friend, the only thing that comes to mind is that he thought that, if he gave the appearance of candor, his bland evasions about his other students, about Chevalier and about Frank would be more likely to be accepted. He must also have believed (though this would have required extraordinary naïvete in the circumstances) that, because this was a closed, executive session with no reporters present, what he said would never be made public. At the hearing there were some signs that, if Oppenheimer's aim had been to charm the committee into trusting him, then he had been successful. The committee members did not probe him about these other people, and yet seemed delighted by his testimony. At the end of the session, all six members of the panel came down to shake his hand, and one of them, the future President Richard Nixon, made a short speech:

> Before we adjourn, I would like to say—and I am sure this is the sense of all who are here—I have noted for some time the work done by Dr. Oppenheimer and I think we all have been tremendously impressed with him and are mighty happy we have him in the position he has in our program.

Bernard Peters, who was at this time an assistant professor at the University of Rochester, was called before the committee the very next day, but was not faced with Oppenheimer's allegations. Instead, in a session that lasted a mere twenty minutes and was presumably an attempt to get him to perjure himself, he was given the opportunity (which he took) to deny that he had been a member of the Communist Party, either in Germany or in the U.S. On his way back to Rochester, Peters visited Oppenheimer at Princeton and asked him what he had told HUAC.

Oppenheimer replied: "God guided their questions so that I did not say anything derogatory."

A week later, however, both Oppenheimer and Peters received a very nasty shock. On June 15, 1949, a Rochester newspaper, the *Times-Union*, had on its front page the headline "Dr. Oppenheimer once termed Peters 'quite Red,'" beneath which was a full account of what Oppenheimer had said about Peters, both to de Silva and to HUAC. Clearly someone (the chief suspect is surely Velde, the FBI man on the committee) had leaked this information to the newspaper.

On the day this newspaper article was published, Peters was in Idaho Springs, Colorado, attending a conference on cosmic rays. Also there were Hans Bethe, Ed Condon and Frank Oppenheimer. Victor Weisskopf had intended to be there, but on the way had stopped to visit David Hawkins, who lived in Boulder, Colorado, and was enjoying himself so much that he decided to skip the conference and stay in Boulder. Weisskopf, however, read the article, and—like Bethe, Condon, Frank and Peters himself—was appalled by it. All five of them wrote to Oppenheimer expressing their anger and disappointment.

In his letter, Weisskopf mentioned that he did not actually like Peters very much, "because of his intransigence and his lack of humour and human understanding," but, he told Oppenheimer: "If Peters loses his job because of the statement about his political leanings made by *you* . . . we are all losing something that is irreparable. Namely confidence in *you*." Here, Weisskopf had put his finger on the central point, and, one suspects, the main purpose of leaking the testimony: not to ruin Peters, but to undermine the respect Oppenheimer enjoyed among his fellow scientists.

Condon's letter also made an excellent point. He had, he said, "lost a good deal of sleep trying to figure out how you could have talked this way about a man whom you have known so long, and of whom you know so well how good a physicist and good a citizen he is":

> One is tempted to feel that you are so foolish as to think that you can buy immunity for yourself by turning informer. I hope this is not true. You know very well that once these people decide to go into your own dossier and make it public that it will make these "revelations" that you have made so far look pretty tame.

Bethe's letter, meanwhile, was concerned with what could be done practically to limit the damage to Peters's career. He urged Oppenheimer to write to the president of Rochester University correcting the impression that Peters was a dangerous subversive.

Peters himself, accompanied by Frank (the pair were working on a joint project analyzing cosmic rays), went to see Oppenheimer personally. It was, he reported to Weisskopf, "rather dismal." Oppenheimer confirmed that he had indeed said the things attributed to him, but that it had been a "terrible mistake" on his part. At first, Oppenheimer had refused to write a public retraction of his testimony, but Weisskopf's letter changed his mind about that, and he wrote a partial retraction, which he sent to a different Rochester newspaper and which Peters, sending Weisskopf a copy of it, called "a not very successful piece of double-talk." Oppenheimer, Peters added, "was obviously scared to tears of the hearings but that is hardly an explanation." His letter concludes: "I found it a rather sad experience to see a man whom I regarded very highly in such a state of moral despair." Similar feelings were expressed by the other young physicists who had so revered Oppenheimer at Berkeley. "I think mostly," Lomanitz said, speaking for them all, "we came to feel sad personally about the man's weaknesses, and also very sorry that he was not able to give any kind of leadership needed during very bad times."

As it happened, the incident did not ruin Peters's career. Displaying a moral steadfastness that was all too rare during these troubled times, Alan Valentine, the president of the University of Rochester, not only refused to fire Peters, but promoted him to full professor. The University of Minnesota showed no such resoluteness, however, and fired Weinberg after he had been charged with perjury, even though (because the evidence obtained from the wiretap in Nelson's house was not produced) he was acquitted. A similar fate befell Bohm and Lomanitz, both of whom lost their academic jobs.

On June 14, 1949, the day before the Rochester *Times-Union* broke the story of Oppenheimer's testimony against Peters, it was Frank's turn to be summoned before HUAC. Frank was at that point in the worst position of all of them, since he had gone on record as denying that he had ever been a member of the Communist Party. Two years earlier, on the basis, obviously, of leaked FBI documents, the Washington *Times-Herald* had published a front-page story with the headline "U.S. Atom Scientist's Brother Exposed as Communist Who Worked on A-Bomb." The newspaper emphasized that "the official report on Frank Oppenheimer in no way reflects on the loyalty or the ability of his brother, Dr. J. Robert Oppenheimer," but claimed (correctly) to have evidence that Frank was "a card-carrying member of the Communist Party."

When, the day after this story was published, Frank was asked to comment on it, he made a fundamental error. Instead of saying "no comment," he rather foolishly said he had never been a Communist Party member, a lie he repeated to the authorities at the University of Minnesota. Now, at his HUAC hearing in June 1949, Frank decided to tell the truth and admitted that he and Jackie had been members of the Communist Party for three and a half years, beginning in 1937. Despite repeated requests to name other members, Frank refused to do so. Prior to testifying before HUAC, he had been to see J. W. Buchta, the head of the physics department at Minnesota, to tell him that he had, indeed, been a member of the Communist Party, and handed him a letter of resignation "just in case"—the assumption being that this was a mere courtesy and that his resignation would not be acted upon. Within hours of giving his testimony, however, while he was still in Washington, Frank heard from newspaper reporters that the University of Minnesota had accepted his resignation. A week later, more than fifty physicists, including Hans Bethe, signed a joint letter, sent from the Idaho Springs conference in Colorado, asking the president of the university, James Morrill, to change his mind and reinstate Frank. Edward Teller wrote a separate letter, saying that, although he had "never agreed with Frank Oppenheimer on politics," he thought he was a very good physicist. "I always liked him," Teller added, and besides, he told Morrill, he strongly believed in "the freedom to make mistakes." One person who was conspicuous in not offering vociferous public support for Frank was his brother. "Jackie was absolutely furious," a friend of Frank has said, "and that was causing a lot of pain in that family."

Despite the pleas of Frank's fellow physicists, Morrill refused to let Frank keep his job. In desperation, Frank turned to his old friend and colleague Ernest Lawrence at Berkeley. The last time he had seen Lawrence, on a trip to Berkeley from Minnesota, Lawrence had put his arm round him and said: "Come back any time you want to." Now, however, Lawrence would have nothing to do with him. "Frank Oppenheimer is no longer welcome in this laboratory," read a telegram from the Rad Lab. "What is going on?" Frank wrote to Lawrence. "Who has changed, you or I? Have I betrayed my country or your lab? Of course not. I have done nothing." Finding it impossible to get a university job, Frank bought a ranch in Colorado and, much to his brother's disdain, would work as a rancher for the next ten years.

By the end of June 1949, then, leaked FBI documents had severely weakened the esteem in which Oppenheimer was held by his fellow scientists, had wrecked the careers of several of his ex-students, and had all but destroyed the closest and most important emotional relationship of his life: that with his brother. In the same month Oppenheimer himself took a major step toward his own ruin when he made an implacable enemy of a man who, on more than one account, was in a position to do him great harm.

That man was Lewis Strauss, who was both a member of the AEC and a trustee of the Institute for Advanced Study. Within a few years he would be chairman of both the AEC and the institute's board of trustees. He was a vain man who craved above all admiration and respect. Oppenheimer felt neither admiration nor respect for Strauss and made no secret of it. Two years earlier, Strauss had felt slighted by Oppenheimer, when Oppenheimer gave evidence to the AEC concerning the possible military uses of radioactive isotopes. Such isotopes were a by-product of the nuclear reactors at, for example, Oak Ridge and Hanford, which fell under the administration of the AEC, and it had been U.S. policy to allow the isotopes to be sent abroad to friendly countries to be used in scientific research. In the spring of 1947, Strauss attempted to reverse that policy on the grounds that the isotopes might be used for military purposes. When asked for his opinion on the matter, Oppenheimer simply dismissed Strauss's concerns as not worthy of serious attention, and, much to his chagrin, Strauss found himself outvoted on the issue by four to one.

Now, in June 1949, Strauss, who had never accepted that he was wrong about the possible military application of isotopes, had another chance to reverse the policy. This time the occasion was not a closed session of a small committee in an out-of-the-way office, but a full Congressional hearing, with cameras and reporters present, held in the huge Caucus Room of the Senate. The hearing was before the Joint Committee on Atomic Energy, which had been set up in 1946 to "oversee" the AEC and had the power, if necessary, to veto AEC decisions. In 1949, the chairman of the Joint Committee was Brien McMahon, who had become an enthusiastic advocate of the policy of building huge stockpiles of atomic bombs. Also on the committee was the right-wing Republican senator Bourke Hickenlooper, who had a fierce distrust of the AEC and of Oppenheimer in particular. The general purpose of the hearings now under way was to investigate Hickenlooper's allegations that the AEC was guilty of "incredible mismanagement." Strauss, whose political views were in general close to Hickenlooper's, had succeeded in enlisting the senator as an ally in his campaign to stop the export of radioactive isotopes, the practice of which was now examined as an example of the alleged mismanagement of the AEC. On June 9, Strauss had testified before the Joint Committee that isotopes might, indeed, have some military value and that therefore he was against their export. Hickenlooper agreed. When the U.S. provided other nations with isotopes, he said, it was embarking on a program "inimical to our national defense."

This was the context in which Oppenheimer gave his very public, and subsequently heavily reported, demolition of Strauss's position. Oppenheimer himself, of course, was not without vanity, especially about his legendary ability to make fools of others. Jeremy Bernstein remembers that at physics seminars at the institute, Oppenheimer "sat in the front row, and if he made what he thought was a witty comment he would look around to make sure that we had all taken it in." He liked an audience, and this hearing provided him with a large and attentive one.

The specific issue at hand was whether the U.S. should, as they had been requested, provide Norway with an isotope of iron, Fe-59, to use in the monitoring of the manufacture of molten steel. Strauss had discovered that one of the members of the Norwegian research team was a communist, which, in his eyes and Hickenlooper's, made all the more pressing the question of whether Fe-59 could have any conceivable military use. When called upon as a witness, Oppenheimer made it clear that his purpose was not only to refute Strauss's view, but to subject it to lacerating ridicule. "No one," he said, "can force me to say that you cannot use these isotopes for atomic energy."

> You can use a shovel for atomic energy; in fact you do. You can use a bottle of beer for atomic energy. In fact, you do. But to get some perspective, the fact is that during the war and after the war these materials have played no significant part, and in my knowledge, no part at all.

As Philip Stern, who was there at the time, has noted: "Even to an observer who had no background on the issues and personalities involved, it was clear that Oppenheimer was making a fool of someone." The AEC lawyer Joe Volpe was sitting next to Oppenheimer and, looking over to where Strauss was sitting, saw Strauss's eyes narrowing, his jaws working and color rising in his face. From that point on, he said, he kept "one eye on Oppenheimer and the committee and one eye on Strauss." Rubbing salt into the wound, Oppenheimer continued: "My own rating of the importance of isotopes in this broad sense is that they are far less important than electronic devices, but far more important than, let us say, vitamins, somewhere in between." The official record of the meeting records at this point: "[laughter]." When Oppenheimer stepped down, he said to Volpe: "Well, Joe, how did I do?" "*Too* well, Robert," Volpe replied. "Much too well." Years later, David Lilienthal, recalling the sight of Strauss at the end of Oppenheimer's testimony, remarked: "There was a look of hatred there that you don't see very often in a man's face."

A few months later the cover of *Life* magazine carried a photograph of Oppenheimer that Abraham Pais has described as "the best picture of

him I know." Looking extraordinarily self-confident and strikingly handsome, he is staring straight at the camera, intense but relaxed, with his
head resting on his right hand, while in his left hand burns a cigarette.
Inside the magazine there is another arresting image of him, standing
in front of a blackboard, upon which are written impressively unintel-
ligible symbols. The caption to the photograph explains: "Equations at
top of the board describe processes of meson production in cosmic ray
explosions. Those below pertain to certain interactions in quantum field
theory."

The *Life* profile covers much the same ground as the previous year's
Time magazine piece, but in both content and tone it is interestingly
and significantly different. The emphasis in *Time* had been on Oppenheimer as a leader—of physicists, of the institute and of humanity. It
delved fairly deeply into his politics, both the radical views of his past
and his later campaigns for international control of atomic energy, and
hardly at all into his achievements in science, not one of which, in fact,
was mentioned. In these respects the *Life* piece could not have been
more different. It does not mention his radical past at all, and talks about
his postwar involvement in politics as if it had been something imposed
upon him against his will ("although he tried to immerse himself again
in academic duties at California and Cal Tech, the demands made on him
by various branches of the government were so numerous that he found
himself spending much of his time in the air between the West Coast and
Washington").

In the *Life* article, the emphasis was instead firmly on Oppenheimer
as a scientist, and not just one who had done good work in the past, but
a practicing physicist at the top of his game, whose work was at the cutting edge of his field: particle physics. Indeed, one would almost get the
impression from this article that Oppenheimer had retired from politics
to concentrate on physics. The article quotes Oppenheimer as saying
that those physicists who, during the war, were "off doing the devil's
work making armaments and whatnot—things that have nothing to do
with physics" were now "back at their real work—the sober, modest,
consecrated task of penetrating the unknown."

The article then goes on to describe in some detail both Oppenheimer's own contributions to physics, concentrating in particular on the
Oppenheimer-Phillips effect and his role in the development of positron
and meson theory, and the present state of physics. Rather oddly, the
author, Lincoln Barnett, does not mention the QED revolution that had
just taken place, or Oppenheimer's midwifery role in that revolution.
The article does, however, give a good idea of what issues were dominat-
ing physics in the summer of 1949, by which time the QED revolution

was complete, and physicists had turned their attention away from quantum electrodynamics and toward the attempt to understand elementary particles.

This was a field in which everything was unclear and, seemingly, getting a little bit more unclear with every discovery, and the article conveys well the confused state of particle physics during this time, emphasizing in particular the alarming growth in the number of elementary particles that were being discovered. Where previously there had been three—the electron, the proton and the neutron—there were now fifteen.[62] These included some that most people had by this time got used to, such as the photon, the neutrino and the positron, and also some recently discovered exotica such as the pi-meson (in positive, negative and neutral forms), the mu-meson (likewise) and the tau-meson (the heavy meson, soon to be renamed the K-meson or kaon). Nearly half a page of this article is devoted to a table, grouping these fifteen particles into five categories: nucleons, electrons, mesons, massless particles and "probable particles."

"Almost every month has surprises for us in the findings about these particles," Oppenheimer is quoted as saying. Indeed, "what we are forced to call elementary particles retain neither permanence nor identity." For example, protons and neutrons might really be composites: "each of these may have some kind of bare substructure in the center and around it, bound closely to it, a cloud of mesons." His hope was that "what is at the moment just a picture of chaos will ultimately reveal again that deep harmony and order which one has always found in the physical world when one has pushed hard, and which is very beautiful indeed."

The impression is given that this revelation of deep harmony would come, if it came at all, from people working at the institute, "the world's foremost center of elementary particle research." In particular, the article suggests, it might come from Oppenheimer himself, who, having before the war "devoted most of his investigative efforts to the study of mesons, their role in the atomic world and their possible relation to nuclear force," was now working "in close partnership with Yukawa whom he recently brought to the Institute," in a renewed attempt to solve those questions—questions that constituted "the deepest and most urgent challenge to physics at the present time."

In fact, almost all of this is a fantasy. It is as if Oppenheimer had bewitched the *Life* writer into accepting as fact what was merely wishful thinking on Oppenheimer's part. Oppenheimer may have *wanted* to work with Yukawa on meson theory—indeed, that was surely the rea-

---

[62] Within the next two decades this would grow to more than 200.

son he invited Yukawa to the institute—but the two of them never collaborated on a single piece of work, and by the time this *Life* article was
published, October 1949, Yukawa had left the institute for a professorship at Columbia. Nor was it true that the Institute for Advanced Study
was "the world's foremost center of elementary particle research." There
were in 1949 just a handful of particle physicists at the institute, only
one of whom was doing important original work in the subject, namely
Abraham Pais, who, curiously, is not mentioned in this article. Oppenheimer does not mention, for example, that less than two years earlier
Pais had made an important and, as it turned out, lasting contribution to
the taxonomy of the rapidly proliferating elementary particles, when he
introduced the term "lepton" to characterize particles like electrons and
positrons (and, it would soon be realized, mu-mesons) that are not subject to the strong nuclear force. However, while there is no sign of Pais
in this article, the influence of Yukawa is apparent in almost everything
Oppenheimer is quoted as saying, much of which strongly echoes things
noted by Yukawa in a survey article that he published in July 1949 called
"Models and Methods in the Meson Theory."

Finally, and most significantly, it is not true that Oppenheimer was
at this time making important contributions to particle physics. Indeed,
this article was published at precisely the time when he effectively
ceased to be an active research scientist altogether. In January 1949 he
had published a short paragraph in *Reviews of Modern Physics* as part of a
discussion on the disintegration and nuclear absorption of mesons, but
this was to be his last-ever publication in physics.[63] He continued to be
an avid follower of cutting-edge research, and could be relied upon to
summarize the important work in more or less any given area of the
subject, but he himself did not make a single original contribution to
particle physics—or indeed to any branch of the subject—from January
1949 till the day he died. Nor did he provide the kind of leadership in
particle physics that he had provided in QED with his running of the
Shelter Island, Pocono and Oldstone conferences. After Oldstone, it was
decided to end that particular series and to put in its place a series that
concentrated solely on particle physics. These were organized not by
Oppenheimer, but by Robert Marshak at the University of Rochester.
It was at places like Rochester, Columbia, Chicago and Berkeley that
most of the leading work in particle physics would be done in the 1950s;

---

[63] In 1950, in an unprecedented and unrepeated foray into biology, he published a short,
cowritten article entitled "Internal Conversion in the Photosynthetic Mechanism of Blue
Green Algae."

places, that is, with large experimental-physics departments and, crucially, large particle accelerators. The institute had neither—as the *Life* article was at pains to stress, it had no laboratory of any sort.

One way of reading this article is to see it as a response by Oppenheimer to the attacks upon him and other left-wing physicists by the FBI and HUAC, as his way of saying that he was happy to withdraw from the fight, to give up politics and return to pure research. But as he did not, in fact, return to pure research or give up politics (he did not, for example, resign his chairmanship of the GAC), perhaps the best way to read the article is as an insight into what Oppenheimer, in the autumn of 1949, *wished* his life was like: dominated by fundamental research ("Of his manifold activities, however, the one that gives him the fullest measure of satisfaction, the one he considers his *real* calling is exploration") at the very center of progress in theoretical physics, and in the company of other people absorbed in the struggle to understand the nature of physical matter.

Actually, what dominated his life at this point, and would (as he well knew) dominate it for the foreseeable future, was the fact that a month earlier irrefutable evidence had been obtained that the Soviet Union had exploded its own atomic bomb. This fact is mentioned in the *Life* article, but in a way that seeks to downplay its importance. From the perspective of the physicists who took part in the "devil's work making armaments," the article says blithely, "the news that Russia has at last produced an atomic bomb comes as no great surprise, nor does it appear in the aftermath of this revelation that their endeavors will now be diverted as they were by the recent war." This, like so much of the article, was wishful thinking. As chairman of the General Advisory Committee, it fell to Oppenheimer to advise the AEC, and therefore the U.S. government, on how to respond to the news that the Soviet Union had its own atomic bombs. This was such a heavy burden that it does not take much imagination to see why Oppenheimer would wish to pretend that it did not exist.

The evidence for the Soviet bomb consisted of tiny samples of fission products, isotopes of cerium and yttrium (Ce-141 and Y-91), which had been detected on September 3, 1949, in rainwater collected and analyzed by the U.S. Navy and in the air by an air-force reconnaissance plane flying over Japan. On September 19, a group of experts that included Oppenheimer concluded that, with very little doubt, the radioactive traces came from a bomb exploded by the Soviet Union on August 29. The following day, President Truman was informed (his first reaction was to refuse to believe it, so convinced was he of the inferiority of Soviet science and technology), and three days later, September 23, Truman publicly announced: "We have evidence that within recent weeks an atomic explosion occurred in the USSR."

That evening Oppenheimer received a phone call from a very worried Edward Teller. "What shall we do? What shall I do?" Teller asked Oppenheimer. Teller was at that point dividing his time between Chicago, where he worked on theoretical physics, and Los Alamos, where he worked on what had been his pet project for many years: the Super, the hydrogen bomb. "Just go back to Los Alamos and keep working," Oppenheimer told him. Then, after a long pause, during which Teller was clearly waiting for some additional response, Oppenheimer added: "Keep your shirt on."

To Teller it seemed obvious that the best—indeed, the only rational— response to the fact that the Soviet Union now had the atomic bomb was an accelerated program to develop the Super. For surely, he reasoned, if the Soviets had worked out how to build a fission bomb, they would also have realized that a much more powerful fusion bomb was at least a theoretical possibility, and therefore it was essential to the protection of the United States that it get a hydrogen bomb before the Soviets. Similar thoughts had occurred to Lewis Strauss in Washington and to Alvarez and Lawrence in Berkeley, and it was not long before the four of them united in a campaign to persuade the President to authorize such an accelerated program. At the very time that Oppenheimer was telling *Life* magazine that the news about the Russian bomb would not mean that the endeavors of physicists "will now be diverted as they were by the recent war," three of the most respected physicists in the country were plotting with the man whose fierce hatred Oppenheimer had just aroused, to ensure that the endeavors of physicists were indeed so diverted.

The plotters moved quickly. On October 5, Lawrence phoned Strauss, as a result of which Strauss wrote a memo to his fellow AEC members calling for a crash program to develop the hydrogen bomb, using words that carried an ironic echo of Oppenheimer's. "We should now," he wrote, "make an intensive effort to get ahead with the Super. By intensive effort, I am thinking of a commitment in talent and money comparable, if necessary, to that which produced the first atomic bomb. That is the way to stay ahead." Lilienthal responded to this memo by asking Oppenheimer to arrange a special meeting of the GAC in order to advise the AEC on what to do about the Soviet bomb. Oppenheimer duly arranged the meeting, but, because of the busy schedules of the various eminent scientists on the committee, the earliest date on which he could get everybody together was October 29.

In the intervening three weeks, intensive lobbying was undertaken on behalf of the idea that a crash program for the Super was the correct response to the Soviet bomb. On October 6, Alvarez and Lawrence flew out to Washington from Berkeley, making an overnight stop at Los Alamos to confer with Teller and others about the current state of research into the feasibility of the Super. Teller's view (not widely shared among physicists at this time) was that "it was highly probable that we could produce a fusion weapon." "In the present situation," Lawrence delighted Teller by responding, "there is no question but that you must go ahead." Lawrence and Alvarez then proceeded to Washington, where they used all of Lawrence's considerable influence to meet as many high-ranking officials as they could. These included members of the Joint Committee on Atomic Energy, advisors to the Defense Department, and anybody else who might have the ear of the President. They also met each of the AEC commissioners, attempting to undermine what they considered the baleful influence of Oppenheimer. One result of their efforts was the appearance of General Hoyt Vandenberg, the Chief of Staff of the fairly recently established U.S. Air Force,[64] before the Joint Committee on October 14, when he stated: "Having the Super weapon would place the United States in the superior position that it had enjoyed up to the end of September by having exclusive possession of the weapon." Satisfied with their work, Alvarez and Lawrence then returned to Berkeley.

At about the same time, Teller set off on his own lobbying trip, stopping first in Chicago, where he hoped to enlist Fermi to be the head of the new crash program. Fermi, however, flatly refused even to consider it. Teller went next to Cornell, where he found Bethe more sympathetic. Bethe promised Teller that he would be willing to return to Los Alamos to work on the Super. While Teller was at Cornell, Bethe got a call from Oppenheimer, asking him to come to Princeton. When Bethe said that Teller happened to be there, Oppenheimer extended the invitation to him. On October 21, then, Bethe and Teller went to Oppenheimer's office at the institute, where Oppenheimer showed them a letter he had just received from Conant, expressing vehement hostility to the Super, which, Conant said, would be built "over my dead body."[65] Oppenheimer did not express his own opinion, but Bethe says: "Probably Oppenheimer wanted to influence us against the development of

---

[64] It is a surprise to many, particularly in the UK (whose Royal Air Force was established in 1918), that the U.S. Air Force only became a separate branch of the U.S. military as late as September 1947. Before that the air service had been part of the army.

[65] That phrase was remembered by Teller. Whatever else was in the letter is lost to history, since, rather oddly, it does not survive among the many boxes of correspondence that Oppenheimer diligently filed and preserved. Conant's biographer, James G. Hershberg, has speculated—plausibly, to my mind—that Conant asked Oppenheimer to destroy it.

the hydrogen bomb and didn't want to do it in his own words, so he used Conant's letter instead."

A letter that Oppenheimer wrote to Conant that day suggests that Bethe might not have been right about that. The view that Oppenheimer expresses to Conant is that the AEC had no alternative but to embark on a crash program to develop the hydrogen bomb, and therefore the GAC had no alternative but to recommend such a program, not because the bomb was a good idea, scientifically or militarily, but because the political climate made any other course of action impossible. It has to be remembered that at this point Teller did not (despite what he told Lawrence) have a workable design of a hydrogen bomb, or any clear idea of how such a workable design might be arrived at. Nobody doubted that fusion was, in principle, possible, or that, if a way could be devised of fusing the nuclei of hydrogen (or, more likely, one of its isotopes, deuterium or tritium), enormous amounts of energy could be released. Neither did anyone doubt that if a fusion bomb could be built, its power would be colossal, measured in megatons, not kilotons, of TNT. The problem that had yet to be solved, however, was how the massively high temperatures required to initiate the fusion process could be created in a device that could, conceivably, be delivered successfully by an airplane or even a boat.

"On the technical side," Oppenheimer told Conant, the Super was "a weapon of unknown design, cost, deliverability, and military value." But, he added, "a very great change has taken place in the climate of opinion," brought about partly by the fact that "two experienced promoters have been at work, i.e., Ernest Lawrence and Edward Teller." As a result, the Joint Congressional Committee, "having tried to find something to chew on ever since September 23rd, has at last found its answer: We must have a Super and we must have it fast." Thus, Oppenheimer concluded: "It would be folly to oppose the exploration of this weapon," even though "I am not sure the miserable thing will work, nor that it can be gotten to a target except by ox cart." Moreover:

> It seems likely to me even further to worsen the unbalance of our present war plans. What does worry me is that this thing appears to have caught the imagination, both of the congressional and military people, as the answer to the problems posed by the Russian advance . . . that we become committed to it as the way to save the country and the peace seems to me full of dangers.

As the date for the fateful meeting approached, Lawrence asked Robert Serber to go to Washington to present his proposal to build heavy-water reactors as part of the program to investigate fusion. Serber had been at Berkeley since 1946, and had taken over Oppenheimer's graduate courses. On the subject of the Super, his sympathies were with Oppenheimer, having earlier studied Teller's design for a fusion bomb and identified its flaws. "I told Ernest that the Super wouldn't work," Serber later wrote, "that Edward didn't know how to build a thermo-nuclear bomb." He nevertheless agreed to go and present Lawrence's proposals for the reactors, which, he thought, might be useful even if a fusion bomb could not be made to work. Serber arrived in Princeton the day before the meeting and stayed overnight with the Oppenheimers. Oppenheimer told Serber that Conant was very much against developing the Super, and showed him Conant's letter, which Serber remembers as saying "that the United States should not build such a weapon. It said that if the Russians did so and used it against us, we could very well retaliate with our stockpile of atomic weapons." "I was astonished," Serber writes. "The East was evidently a completely different world from California. I had no idea that people like Conant and Oppenheimer would harbour any such ideas. At Berkeley they would have been unthinkable."

Actually, as Oppenheimer had indicated in his letter to Conant, the idea that the United States should not go ahead with an accelerated program to build the Super was only very slightly more thinkable in the East than in Berkeley, and yet the GAC, after its meeting on October 28–29, 1949 ("perhaps the most important one in its history," as Pais writes), ended up endorsing just that idea and recommending it to the AEC. It has often (most insistently by Teller) been supposed that, in advising the AEC against a crash program to develop the Super, the GAC was bowing to the will of Oppenheimer. In fact, it would be truer to say that Oppenheimer was bending to the will of Conant, for the view that came out of the meeting was a good deal closer to Conant's pre-meeting view than it was to Oppenheimer's.

Prior to the meeting, Glenn Seaborg had written to excuse himself from it on the grounds that he would be in Sweden that weekend, giving a series of lectures on the transuranic elements, having been invited by the Royal Academy of Sciences. "The clear implication," he said later, "was that they were looking me over for the Nobel Prize, so I wasn't about to miss the trip." On the meeting to discuss the Super, Seaborg recalled: "I expressed my opinion in a letter to Oppie. I said that the idea of another horribly destructive weapon was disheartening, but that we had no choice but to develop the Super because the Soviet Union certainly would." In fact what Seaborg wrote was a good deal more verbose and less clear than his later paraphrasing would suggest:

Although I deplore the prospect of our country putting a tremendous effort into this, I must confess that I have been unable to come to the conclusion that we should not . . . My present feeling would perhaps be best summarized by saying that I would have to hear some good arguments before I could take on sufficient courage to recommend not going towards such a program.

James Conant could not attend the meeting until the second day. The remaining members of the committee—Oliver Buckley, Lee DuBridge, Enrico Fermi, John Manley, Isidor Rabi, Cyril Smith and Oppenheimer himself—were all there on the first morning, which was to be devoted to a series of talks from experts on various aspects of the matter in hand.

The first to give evidence was George Kennan, the political scientist and historian. Having served under both George Marshall and his successor as Secretary of State, Dean Acheson, Kennan was, by this time, one of the most influential advisors on foreign policy, particularly with regard to Soviet affairs. On this occasion, he may have had a decisive effect on the development of the meeting by introducing a thought that had not, it seems, previously occurred to anyone else present. This was that the Soviet Union, given that its economy and industry were still in ruins after the devastation of the war, might not want to embark on an expensive arms race and might be willing to negotiate an agreement that ensured that neither side developed the hydrogen bomb. That thought certainly seems to have shaped much of what followed.

After Kennan came Bethe, who reported on the present state of research on the Super, emphasizing the technical problems that had yet to be solved. Then Serber did what he had been asked to do by Lawrence, which was basically a sales pitch, urging the committee to commission the Berkeley Rad Lab to build reactors that would increase the production of plutonium and tritium. After he had delivered this pitch, Serber did not fly back to Berkeley, but stayed overnight, returning with Oppenheimer the next morning to the AEC's offices. "I met Luis [Alvarez] in the lobby of the AEC building," Serber remembers, "and we watched as the GAC members assembled, and later were impressed by the constellations of stars on the shoulders of the Joint Chiefs and other high-ranking officers going by to testify."

Among those Joint Chiefs were General Omar Bradley of the army and General Lauris Norstad of the air force, neither of whom seems to have given much thought to the military purpose of having a hydrogen bomb. Both said there was no choice but to build the Super, but when asked what advantages it might have over a stockpile of atomic bombs, Norstad was silent and Bradley replied: "mostly psychological."

At the lunch break Oppenheimer went with Alvarez and Serber to a nearby restaurant, where Serber was surprised and Alvarez was appalled to be told that the mood of the meeting was swinging *away* from a recommendation for a crash program. As Alvarez later remembered his lunchtime conversation with Oppenheimer:

> He said that he did not think the United States should build the hydrogen bomb, and the main reason he gave for this, if my memory serves me correctly, and I think it does, was that if we built a hydrogen bomb, the Russians would build a hydrogen bomb, whereas if we did not build a hydrogen bomb, then the Russians would not build a hydrogen bomb.

After lunch, an angry and disappointed Alvarez set off back to Berkeley, convinced, as he later put it, that "the program we were planning to start was not one that the top man in the scientific development of the AEC wanted to have done." In his diary at the time, he noted that he had had an "interesting talk with Oppie," in which he saw, however, some "pretty foggy thinking."

That afternoon the GAC members, together with four of the five AEC commissioners, talked through all the issues involved. Before he arrived at the meeting, Rabi had believed both that (as Lilienthal summarized Rabi's views in his diary) the "decision to go ahead will be made; only question is who will be willing to join in it" and that the crash program was indeed the answer to the Russian atomic bomb. Fermi had been of the opinion that (again, in Lilienthal's words) "one must explore it and do it and that doesn't foreclose the question: should it be made use of?," while Oppenheimer had believed, as he said in his letter to Conant, that it would be folly to resist the crash program. Apart from these two, all the other GAC members present at this meeting had arrived believing, for a mixture of technical, strategic and moral reasons, that it would be wrong to develop the hydrogen bomb, even if some of them believed (as Oppenheimer did) that the decision to build the bomb was, for political reasons, unavoidable. By the end of the afternoon session, however, this political pessimism had been overcome and the GAC members had reached a unanimous decision *not* to recommend a crash program, with Rabi and Fermi—perhaps having Kennan's testimony in mind—believing it was important to stress that this should be conditional on getting an *international* agreement not to pursue research on the Super. At the end of the meeing Oppenheimer suggested that they spend the evening writing reports and reconvene the next morning.

Three reports were written that evening. Manley and Oppenheimer wrote the main report, which was signed by all eight attending committee members. Part One of this report recommended an increase in the production of reactors, isotope-separation plants and atomic bombs, particularly "an intensification of efforts to make atomic weapons available for tactical purposes." This last recommendation shows how far Oppenheimer's thinking had changed since the end of the war, being, as it is, the exact opposite of his earlier Bohr-inspired view. At the center of that earlier view was the thought that atomic bombs were not simply a new, more deadly weapon; they were a radically different *kind* of weapon, so powerful that the (rational) fear of using them might put an end to war itself. Now Oppenheimer was advocating atomic bombs as tactical devices, treating them *precisely* as just another weapon.

This change in attitude seems to have been prompted by two things: 1. the heavy burden of having led a project that resulted in the deaths of tens of thousands of Japanese civilians,[66] and 2. his disillusionment following the breakdown of talks to negotiate international control of atomic weapons. He no longer believed in the notion of a bomb too big to use (if he did, the Super was, surely, just that), and he had no wish to be instrumental in the creation of a bomb that could kill civilians on a scale many times greater than the bomb that had been unleashed on Hiroshima. An atomic bomb designed to be used as a tactical weapon, against soldiers rather than civilians, was, for him, a lesser evil than a hydrogen bomb that was many times too big to be used in such a way and could *only* be used for the mass slaughter of civilians.

Part Two of the main report spells this reasoning out. It takes a fairly optimistic view of the chances of overcoming the technical problems in the way of developing the Super: "We believe that an imaginative and concerted attack on the problem has a better than even chance of producing the weapon within five years." But it then addresses the question of why anyone would *want* to develop such a weapon. Given that "it has generally been estimated that the weapon would have an explosive effect some hundreds of times that of present fission bombs," one had to face the question of what might be involved in actually using this weapon:

> It is clear that the use of this weapon would bring about the destruction of innumerable human lives; it is not a weapon that can be used exclusively for the destruction of material installations of military or semi-military purposes. Its use therefore carries much further

---

[66] This burden seems also to have influenced other members of the GAC. Conant, for example, said at the meeting that he felt he was "seeing the same film, and a punk one, for the second time," while Rowe remarked: "We built one Frankenstein."

than the atomic bomb itself the policy of exterminating civilian populations.

Part Three of the report then provides the committee's response to the question put to it: would it recommend a crash program to develop the Super? Here Oppenheimer and Manley were careful to spell out where there was unanimity and where there was not:

> Although the members of the Advisory Committee are not unanimous in their proposals as to what should be done with regard to the Super bomb, there are certain elements of unanimity among us. We all hope that by one means or another, the development of these weapons can be avoided. We are all reluctant to see the United States take the initiative in precipitating this development. We are all agreed that it would be wrong at the present moment to commit ourselves to an all-out effort towards its development.
>
> We are somewhat divided as to the nature of the commitment not to develop the weapon. The majority feel that this should be an unqualified commitment.
>
> Others feel that it should be made conditional on the response of the Soviet government to a proposal to renounce such development.

Appended to this main report were the two other reports. The first, written by Conant and DuBridge, and signed by those two plus Buckley, Oppenheimer, Rowe and Smith, spoke of the Super as a "weapon of genocide." Moving slightly away from the issue of whether a *crash* program should be initiated, this "majority report" (as it came to be called) committed itself unequivocally to the recommendation that *no* program of any sort to build this weapon should be pursued: "We believe a super bomb should never be produced." That the Russians might build a Super should not frighten the U.S. into building one, the report insisted, since: "Should they use the weapon against us, reprisals by our large stock of atomic bombs would be comparatively effective to the use of a super." Finally, Conant and DuBridge wrote: "In determining not to proceed to develop the super bomb, we see a unique opportunity of providing by example some limitations on the totality of war and thus limiting the fear and arousing the hopes of mankind."

The second appendix, the "minority report," written and signed by Fermi and Rabi, describes the Super as "necessarily an evil thing considered in any light" and argues that it would therefore be wrong for the U.S. to initiate a program of building such a bomb without first inviting "the nations of the world to join us in a solemn pledge not to proceed."

When questioned about this at Oppenheimer's security hearing, Fermi said that his view was that, if it turned out not to be possible to get an international agreement to outlaw research into the Super, then the U.S. "should with considerable regret, go ahead." Of this view, however, there is no trace in the report drawn up by him and Rabi.

The GAC recommendations were not reported in the press and could not be, as they remained classified information. The main report had recommended that "enough be declassified about the super bomb so that a public statement of policy can be made at this time," but, for the moment, public discussion of the Super was illegal. Edward Teller, however, was not a man to be deflected from his purpose by such niceties, and he made it his business to find out what the GAC had advised. First, he spoke to Fermi, who, Teller wrote to his friend Maria Mayer, "did not tell me what the General Advisory Committee proposed," but "He did tell me what his own ideas are. He said: 'You and I and Truman and Stalin would be happy if further great developments were impossible. So, why do we not make an agreement to refrain from such development?'"

Teller added: "I have never been so frightened as I am now when I hear his argument of compromise." Hearing Fermi's views produced in Teller the same despondency that listening to Oppenheimer had produced in Alvarez. "Washington," Teller told Mayer, "will try every substitute rather than decide to make an all-out effort . . . What I saw in Washington makes it quite clear that there are big forces working for compromise and for delay." On the other hand: "There are also forces which work for action."

Teller got a glimpse of how powerful these latter forces were when he was summoned to Brien McMahon's office in Washington. "Before I could say anything," Teller records in his memoirs, "McMahon said, 'Have you heard about the GAC report? It just makes me sick.'" McMahon then introduced Teller to William Borden, his aide. "If you can't reach me, talk to Bill," McMahon told Teller. "He has my complete confidence." As Teller quickly discovered, Borden was a man after his own heart. In fact, he was possibly the only person of influence in Washington who was *more* frightened of the Soviet Union than Teller himself was. In 1946, Borden had published a book called *There Will Be No Time: The Revolution in Strategy*, in which he argued that, unless the U.S. and the Soviet Union united "into a single sovereignty" (which, of course, he considered extremely unlikely), then war between the two was inevitable. Impressed by the German V-2 rockets that had attacked London in 1944 and by the awesome power of the Hiroshima bomb, Borden predicted that future wars would be fought by rockets tipped with nuclear warheads. It followed, he thought, that the U.S. should equip itself with the largest, most powerful nuclear arsenal it possibly could. In January 1949, after McMahon had replaced Hickenlooper as chairman of the Joint Committee on Atomic Energy, he appointed Borden as the committee's executive director. After his meeting with McMahon and Borden, Teller must have realized that, with men like this in positions of power, the "big forces working for compromise and for delay" were not going to have it all their own way.

Throughout November 1949 a great and acrimonious battle took place in Washington over the H-bomb, the two sides seemingly evenly matched and the outcome unpredictable. Oppenheimer and Rabi had both believed it to be inevitable that the views of Teller and the Joint Committee would prevail, but, in adding their signatures to the GAC report, they had made such an outcome rather less certain. Another setback for Teller came when he received a phone call from Hans Bethe saying that he would not, after all, be prepared to join Teller's proposed H-bomb project. Teller, as was his wont, saw in the decision the malignant influence of Oppenheimer, but, just as he was wrong to believe that it had been Oppenheimer who had swung opinion at the GAC meeting, so he was wrong again on this occasion. What had dissuaded Bethe from working on the hydrogen bomb was not Oppenheimer, but a conversation Bethe had had in Princeton with Victor Weisskopf and George Placzek. "Weisskopf vividly described to me a war with hydrogen bombs," Bethe later said, "what it would mean to destroy a whole city like New York with one bomb and how hydrogen bombs would change the military balance by making the attack still more powerful and the defense still less powerful." A few days after this conversation, he told Teller he would not join the project: "He was disappointed. I felt relieved."

Another blow to Teller's position came on November 9, when the AEC met to consider what course of action they should recommend to the President in the light of the GAC report. The result was a three-to-two majority in favor of the GAC view: Pike and Smyth siding with Lilienthal in opposing the accelerated Super program, and Gordon Dean supporting Strauss, who, of course, was strongly in favor of such a program. More hope for the GAC position came later that day, when the AEC recommendations were presented by Lilienthal to the President. According to John Manley, Lilienthal, after seeing the President, "came back feeling happy" because Truman had said "that he was not going to be blitzed into this thing by the military establishment."

On the other hand, the Secretary of State, Dean Acheson, who had in the past seen eye-to-eye with both Oppenheimer and Lilienthal, was unpersuaded by the GAC's arguments, particularly those in the "majority report," which, though they had been written by Conant, Acheson asked

Oppenheimer to defend. "You know," Acheson told Gordon Arneson, "I listened as carefully as I knew how, but I don't understand what 'Oppie' was trying to say. How can you persuade a paranoid adversary to disarm 'by example?'" Acheson had recently been appointed by President Truman onto a three-man special committee to consider the hydrogen-bomb question, the other members of which were David Lilienthal and the Defense Secretary, Louis Johnson, who was firmly convinced of the need for the United States to acquire the Super as quickly as possible. Meanwhile, Borden drafted a long letter to be sent to Truman on McMahon's behalf, outlining in urgent tones the case for an immediate crash program. "If we let Russia get the super first," the letter insisted, "catastrophe becomes all but certain—whereas, if we get it first, there exists a chance of saving ourselves."

On December 2–3, 1949, the GAC reconvened to consider the issue again, but, Oppenheimer reported to the AEC, none of them wished to change the views they had expressed in October. Lewis Strauss, however, was not going to rely on Oppenheimer to convey his opinion. Instead, he wrote directly to the President, telling him: "I believe that the United States must be as completely armed as any possible enemy."

> From this, it follows that I believe it unwise to renounce, unilaterally, any weapon which an enemy can reasonably be expected to possess. I recommend that the President direct the Atomic Energy Commission to proceed with the development of the thermonuclear bomb as the highest priority subject only to the judgment of the Department of Defense as to its value as a weapon, and of the advice of the Department of State as to the diplomatic consequences of its unilateral renunciation of its possession.

As Strauss knew very well, the Secretaries of Defense and State were at one with him on this question.

More decisive than Strauss's letter was a memo sent to Secretary Johnson by the Joint Chiefs of Staff on January 13, 1950, arguing that the Super "would improve our defense in the broadest sense, as a potential offensive weapon, a possible deterrent to war, a potential retaliatory weapon, as well as a defensive weapon against enemy forces." The emphasis of the scientists in their GAC reports on the fearsome power of the Super may have backfired, since it allowed the Joint Chiefs to point out that it would be preferable "that such a possibility be at the will and control of the United States rather than of an enemy."

Without showing it first to the special committee, Johnson forwarded this memo to the President, who remarked that it "made a lot of sense." On January 31, 1950, the special committee met the President to give its advice to go ahead with the Super, but by then Truman had already decided to do just that. When Lilienthal expressed his own opposition to the committee's recommendation, Truman cut him short. "What the Hell are we waiting for?" he said. "Let's get on with it." That day, Truman announced to the world that he had directed the AEC "to continue its work on all forms of atomic weapons, including the so-called hydrogen or super-bomb."

Rabi was furious, not so much that the decision had been taken against GAC advice, or even that it had been taken without any attempt to negotiate with the Soviet Union, as he and Fermi had recommended. What angered him, he later said, was that, in making this announcement, Truman had "alerted the world that we were going to make a hydrogen bomb at a time when we didn't even know how to make one." This, Rabi thought, was one of the worst things the President could have done: "I never forgave Truman."

As it happened, that day was Lewis Strauss's birthday, and to mark what was now, for him, a double celebration, he held a party to which all GAC members were invited. At the party Strauss walked over to Oppenheimer to introduce his son and his son's new wife. To Strauss's mortification, Oppenheimer did not even bother to turn around; he simply extended a hand over his shoulder. Later, at the same party, Oppenheimer was spotted by a *New York Times* reporter, standing alone. "You don't look jubilant," the reporter said, to which, after a long pause, Oppenheimer replied: "This is the plague of Thebes." Abraham Pais has taken this characteristically gnomic remark to refer to a legion of soldiers from Thebes, the "10,000 knights," who, after refusing to fight the Christians they had been ordered by the emperor to attack, were slaughtered. It seems much more likely, however (as the philosopher and science historian Robert Crease points out in a footnote to Pais's account), that Oppenheimer was referring to the plague that, in *Oedipus Rex*, is sent by the gods to punish Thebes for the crime of harboring the killer of Laius. The idea, surely, is that the President's order to develop the hydrogen bomb was a punishment inflicted upon the scientists who developed the atomic bomb, for the "sin" of allowing themselves to be used as weaponeers.

From any point of view, the U.S. program to develop the hydrogen bomb had got off to a very bad start. Of the fourteen people whose job it now was to pursue that program—the five AEC commissioners and the nine members of the GAC—eleven of them had voted against it. Of the other three, one, Seaborg, had abstained, and only one, Strauss, had any real enthusiasm for the project. At the same time the people who had lobbied hard for the program had no direct responsibility for or control over its implementation. None of the scientists strongly in favor of it—Lawrence, Teller and Alvarez—were members of either the AEC or the GAC. Moreover, thanks to the McMahon Act, the control of atomic energy was in civilian hands, and consequently none of the Joint Chiefs of Staff, whose views had been so influential in establishing the program, could play the role that General Groves had played in seeing the Manhattan Project through to a successful conclusion.

The result was a perpetual struggle between those who actually wanted to see a hydrogen bomb produced and those whose job it was to produce it. Perhaps what should have happened is the mass resignation of all those members of the AEC and GAC who had voted against the program, and their replacement with people eager to push the project through. Lilienthal had already announced his imminent retirement, letting it be known that he would leave when the issue of the Super had finally been resolved (he left in April 1950). Many of the others, including Oppenheimer and Rabi, were tempted to resign, but were talked out of it by Lilienthal. The AEC and GAC, after all, had responsibility for all aspects of atomic energy, not just weapons, and their responsibility for nuclear weapons was not confined to, or even concentrated on, the development of the hydrogen bomb. Overseeing the design, production and stockpiling of atomic bombs was at this time as important as, if not more important than, implementing the President's demand for a hydrogen-bomb program. One reason for staying, therefore, was to ensure that the hydrogen program did not dominate all other aspects of atomic-energy development.

Another reason was to ensure that there remained people in influential positions who were able and willing to think about the hydrogen bomb in something other than what Oppenheimer later dismissively referred to as "prudential and game-theoretical terms." Bethe had changed his mind about joining Teller's program after Weisskopf had spelled out to him "what it would mean to destroy a whole city like New York with one bomb," and that imaginative realization of the scale of the horror that such a powerful bomb might cause is present throughout the GAC reports. Most of the scientists who wrote those reports had worked on the Manhattan Project and knew what it felt like to have created a weapon capable of killing tens of thousands of people in an instant. The moral responsibility for creating a weapon a hundred, even a thousand, times more powerful than the Hiroshima bomb was something they wanted about as much as the people of Thebes wanted the plague. This, not disloyalty, was surely the explanation for some of the hyperbole (the talk, for example, of genocide) in those reports, and for their apparent acceptance of the shoddy thinking criticized by, among others, Alvarez and Acheson. The idea that the Soviet Union might follow the moral example of the United States if it chose not to develop the hydrogen bomb was not subversion, but rather wishful thinking.

That the other side in this struggle—Strauss, Borden, Teller, McMahon, and so on—so often saw subversion where there was, in fact, only wishful thinking, or even sometimes well-reasoned and justified moral scruples, is also understandable, for the decision to go ahead with the hydrogen bomb coincided with a series of shocking revelations about the extent of subversion in the Manhattan Project. On the basis of the Venona transcripts, the U.S. authorities had identified Fuchs as a spy back in September 1949. The same transcripts told them that there had been at least one other spy working at Los Alamos with access to highly classified documents relating to the atomic bomb. Within a few months the trail that began with Fuchs led first to Harry Gold, who was arrested in March 1950, and then, in successive months beginning in June, to David Greenglass, Julius Rosenberg and Ethel Rosenberg.

On February 9, 1950, just a few days after Fuchs's confession, Senator Joseph McCarthy launched the era—and the paranoia—named after him, when, in a speech in Wheeling, West Virginia, he claimed to have "here in my hand" a list of 205 people "that were made known to the Secretary of State as being members of the Communist Party and who nevertheless are still working and shaping policy in the State Department." In subsequent speeches by McCarthy the number of people on his list would vary, sometimes to as low as fifty-seven, but the basic idea that the U.S. establishment had been penetrated by a "fifth column" intent on destroying it would be a pervasive force in American politics for years to come.

The President was not told about Fuchs until after he had confessed on January 24, but J. Edgar Hoover had told Strauss both about Fuchs and about the other, as-yet-unidentified spy, in October. Strauss did not inform either his fellow commissioners on the AEC or the members of the GAC about this until after Fuchs's confession. In the meantime he gave much thought to the identity of the other spy, his top suspect being Oppenheimer. To Hoover, Strauss remarked that the furor over Fuchs "will make a good many men who are in the same profession as Fuchs very careful of what they say publicly."

Actually, those in the same profession as Fuchs (assuming that Strauss meant physics rather than espionage) were among the least troubled by the revelation that Fuchs had given information about the atomic bomb to the Soviets, since, as they had been saying for years, they never took seriously the idea that the science and technology behind the bomb could possibly be kept secret. As for the fact that Fuchs had had access at every stage to Teller's work on the hydrogen bomb, this worried Oppenheimer still less. In fact, he told the Joint Committee on Atomic Energy on February 27, 1950, it would be a good thing if Fuchs had passed on to the Soviets Teller's H-bomb design, since that would set them back a few years, as Teller's bomb stood no chance of working.

In March 1950 the editor of the *Bulletin of the Atomic Scientists*, Eugene Rabinowitch, decided to devote almost the entire issue to the H-bomb. The special issue begins with a report of President Truman's announcement of the accelerated program to build the H-bomb, and an account of how the project to build such a bomb, which had supposedly been a state secret, first became public. The first public acknowledgment that such a program existed was made by the senator from Colorado, Edwin Johnson (a member of the Joint Committee), in a television debate broadcast on November 1, 1949. The debate was on the subject "Is there too much secrecy in our atomic program?" and Johnson was there to argue the case that there was not *enough* secrecy. In the course of making his argument, however, Johnson revealed several state secrets. "Our scientists," he said:

> already have created a bomb that has six times the effectiveness of the bomb that was dropped on Nagasaki and they're not satisfied at all; they want one that has a thousand times the effect of that terrible bomb that was dropped on Nagasaki that snuffed out the lives of 50,000 people just like that. And that's the secret, that's the big secret that the scientists in America are so anxious to divulge to the whole scientific world.

This "naïve and monumental indiscretion," Rabinowitch tells his readers, has allowed him to do what he has wanted to do for years, which is to use his magazine to discuss the "grave moral implications" that have to be considered when thinking about the decision to develop the hydrogen bomb.

Inside the issue is an impassioned statement, signed by twelve prominent physicists, including Hans Bethe, Sam Allison, Ken Bainbridge, Charles Lauritsen and Victor Weisskopf, urging the U.S. government to "make a solemn declaration that we shall never use this bomb first." The use of this bomb, the physicists say, "would be a betrayal of all standards of morality." There can only be one justification for developing this bomb, they conclude, "and that is to prevent its use."

A short statement by Oppenheimer is printed in the magazine, taken from his contribution to a television debate hosted by Eleanor Roosevelt broadcast on February 12, 1950, in which he says:

> There is grave danger for us that these decisions have been taken on the basis of facts held secret. This is not because the men who must contribute to the decisions, or must make them, are lacking in wisdom; it is because wisdom itself cannot flourish, nor even truth be determined, without the give and take of debate and criticism. The relevant facts could be of little use to an enemy, yet they are indispensable for an understanding of questions of policy.

Also taking part in the television program was Hans Bethe, who, because he was not a member of either the GAC or the AEC, was free to speak a little more candidly than Oppenheimer and used that freedom to echo the plea that he was to sign in the *Bulletin*. "Hydrogen bombs," he said in the program, "can only mean a wholesale destruction of civilian populations," and so it was important that the U.S. pledged that it would never be the first to use such bombs. Oppenheimer was not in a position to make such a statement or to sign such a plea, but, Bethe wrote to Weisskopf after the television program: "I had a long talk with Oppie, who agreed very much with what we had done and were doing. He emphasized the necessity of keeping the issue alive and I very much agree with him."

In the issue of the *Bulletin* devoted to the hydrogen bomb, space was given to Teller for a rallying cry to physicists to get "Back to the Laboratories!" The tone and the message of Teller's piece were the very opposite of those Oppenheimer had tried to convey in his *Life* profile of October 1949, and it is probably no coincidence that, when choosing a topic in theoretical physics to stand for the self-indulgence of not getting involved in building the H-bomb, Teller chose the area most associated with Oppenheimer. "Our scientific community," Teller writes, "has been out on a honeymoon with mesons. The holiday is over. Hydrogen bombs will not produce themselves." The rest of the special issue of the magazine, filled as it is with scientists reflecting on the horror of the H-bomb, goes some way toward explaining why this rallying cry fell on deaf ears.

One of the few first-rate physicists to respond to Teller's call was John Wheeler. "In my mind," Wheeler says in his autobiography, "I was answering a call to national service." He considered it urgent that the U.S. react to the Soviet bomb with "a priority program to develop a thermonuclear weapon before the Soviets did." Given this attitude, it "was a great disappointment to me that so few of my colleagues shared my view that a national scientific mobilization was called for." Oppenheimer, he had heard, had remarked: "Let Teller and Wheeler go ahead. Let them fall on their faces." Oppenheimer's own attitude at this time Wheeler sums up as:

> . . . the hydrogen bomb can't be done, or if it can be done it will take too long, or if it can be done and doesn't take too long, it will require too large a fraction of the nation's scientific manpower, or if it doesn't require too large a fraction of the nation's labor force, it will be too massive to deliver, or if it is deliverable, we oughtn't to make it.

On February 17, Teller had written to Oppenheimer from Los Alamos, asking him to join the project. "Things have advanced to a desperate urgency here," he told him, "and I should be most anxious indeed if you could come and help us." Oppenheimer was not to be persuaded. He might be chairman of the advisory panel to the U.S. body charged with implementing the policy of pushing ahead with the hydrogen bomb, but, such were the complications of those times, it did not follow that he himself would be prepared to work on the project.

While Teller was having trouble persuading his fellow scientists to work on the H-bomb, the urgency of beating the Soviets to it was deeply felt by politicians. On March 10, Truman issued an order to the AEC for the thermonuclear weapons program to be "regarded as a matter of the highest urgency"; specifically, the production of such weapons was to receive greater priority than the stockpiling of atomic weapons. Truman's order set a goal of producing ten thermonuclear bombs a year.

In April 1950, the *Bulletin of the Atomic Scientists* published an article by Bethe, who was, after all, the world's greatest authority on thermonuclear processes, which contained a timely reminder that certain basic scientific problems needed to be solved before hydrogen bombs could be built, and that it was not at this point at all clear that those problems would be solved:

> Whether the temperatures required to start a thermonuclear reaction between heavy hydrogen nuclei, even under the most favourable conditions, can be achieved on earth is a major problem in the development of the fusion bomb. To find a way of detonating such bombs will require much research and considerable time.

Talking of producing ten H-bombs a year, the subtext went, looked a little premature. It was as if, in 1939, before anyone knew whether an atomic bomb could possibly be built, the U.S. President had publicly announced a crash program to build one, and then in 1944, before any tests had been carried out, the President had ordered Groves to pursue a goal of producing ten implosion bombs a year. The rest of Bethe's article concentrated on the moral questions raised by the H-bomb, as did an article published in the May issue of the *Bulletin* by Robert Bacher. The following month, however, something happened to change Bethe's mind: communist North Korea invaded South Korea.

Back in February, Bethe had written to Norris Bradbury, Oppenheimer's successor as director of Los Alamos, explaining why he would not work on the hydrogen bomb. Even though it was, after Truman's announcement, national policy to develop the H-bomb, Bethe told Bradbury: "I still believe that it is morally wrong and unwise for our national security to develop this weapon." Nevertheless, he concluded this letter by saying: "In case of war, I would obviously reconsider my position." True to his word, after the Korean War broke out, he decided, after all, to join Teller at Los Alamos to work on the H-bomb.

By the time Bethe joined the H-bomb project, Teller had succeeded in recruiting some extremely able people, including John von Neumann, Stanislaw Ulam and John Wheeler, all of whom were delighted by the arrival of Bethe. "With his wonderful virtuosity in mathematical physics," Ulam wrote, "and with his ability to solve analytical problems of nuclear physics, he helped significantly." The Los Alamos team was at that time in need of all the help they could get, since they had still not solved their main problem: how to create the enormously high temperatures needed to initiate the fusion process.

Bethe had not gone to Los Alamos hoping to solve the problem, but rather to prove that it could not be solved. The best possible outcome, he believed, would be that a hydrogen bomb turned out to be against the laws of physics. Indeed, in the summer of 1950 there was some reason to believe that the Super could not be made. For instance, it had been demonstrated mathematically that Teller's design—what became known as the "classical Super"—would not work. In March 1950, Ulam and his friend and colleague Cornelius Everett had presented Teller with the results of a long and tedious set of calculations they had performed, which gave the classical Super very little hope of initiating fusion. Teller, Ulam recalls, "was not easily reconciled to our results. I learned that the bad news drove him once to tears of frustration." Things got worse, from Teller's point of view, when von Neumann reported that he had done the same set of calculations on his new computer in Princeton and the results tallied with those of Ulam and Everett. One day, when Ulam was visiting von Neumann at Princeton, they called on Oppenheimer, who had heard about these mathematical results and, according to Ulam, "seemed rather glad to learn of the difficulties." Despite everything, Teller, von Neumann and Ulam still believed that they could solve the initiation problem and that an H-bomb could be built. They scheduled for the following year a series of important experiments called the Greenhouse Tests. These would not test a bomb—they were still a very long way from having a bomb to test—but would have the more limited goal of trying to achieve the initiation of the fusion process.

Oppenheimer—no doubt because, like Bethe, he *hoped* an H-bomb could not be built—was convinced that the technical problems were insoluble, or, anyway, that it would take a long time to solve them. Much of what he said and did in these years, including the things that struck his opponents as evidence of disloyalty, was based on that conviction. One example is the work that he did, starting in the autumn of 1950, for something called the Long Range Objectives Panel. This was a committee set up by Robert LeBaron, the Deputy Secretary of Defense for atomic-energy matters and chairman of the Military Liaison Committee (whose job it was to liaise between the AEC and the military). Its purpose was to examine and report on the long-term role that nuclear weapons might play in foreign policy and in the formation of military tactics and strategy. Also on the panel were fellow H-bomb skeptics Robert Bacher and Charles Lauritsen, and several enthusiasts for the H-bomb, including Luis Alvarez, General Nichols of the army and General Wilson of the air force.

Both Alvarez and Wilson remember being shocked during the discussions of this panel at Oppenheimer's attitude toward the hydrogen bomb. Alvarez remembers Oppenheimer saying: "We all agree that the hydrogen bomb program should be stopped, but if we were to stop it or to suggest that it be stopped, this would cause so much disruption at Los Alamos and in other laboratories where they are doing instrumentation work that I feel that we should let it go on, and it will die a natural death with the coming tests." When those tests failed, Alvarez remembers Oppenheimer saying, that "will be the natural time to chop the hydrogen-bomb program off." Much less specifically, Wilson remembers:

> The panel contained some conservative statements on the possibility or the feasibility of an early production of a thermonuclear weapon.

These reservations were made on technical grounds. They were simply not challengeable by the military. They did, however, cause some concern in the military.

So concerned was General Wilson about what he saw of Oppenheimer during these panel meetings that "I felt compelled to go to the Director of Intelligence to express my concern over what I felt was a pattern of action that was simply not helpful to national defense."

The panel's report, written by Oppenheimer and delivered in February 1951, emphasized—as Oppenheimer's GAC report of the previous October had emphasized—the importance of tactical atomic weapons, which, it was claimed, were (as opposed to hydrogen bombs) theoretically sound, made efficient use of fissile material and were militarily more effective, both offensively and defensively. The feasibility of hydrogen bombs, the report pointed out, had not yet been demonstrated, and so the H-bomb program had to be seen, despite the President's public announcement of a crash program and his urgent command to the AEC to make that program its top priority, as a long-term project. "In fact," Oppenheimer wrote, "we believe that only a timely recognition of the long range character of the thermonuclear program will tend to make available for the basic studies of the fission weapon program the resources of the Los Alamos Laboratory."

These words may have been written by Oppenheimer, but the report containing them was signed by all members of the panel, leading, some months later, to an enraged Teller demanding of Alvarez: "Luis, how could you have ever signed that report, feeling the way you do about hydrogen bombs?" When Alvarez replied that he thought it was a harmless statement about the importance of small atomic bombs, Teller told him:

> You go back and read that report and you will see that it essentially says that the hydrogen bomb program is interfering with the small weapons program, and it has caused me no end of trouble at Los Alamos. It is being used against our program. It is slowing it down and it could easily kill it.

At about the same time as the Long Range Objectives Panel report was delivered, Oppenheimer published in the *Bulletin of the Atomic Scientists* an article entitled "Comments on the Military Value of the Atom," which, subject to the restraints of official secrecy, made available to the public the thinking that had gone into the report. "To the first impression that the atomic weapon was a decisive, an absolute military power," he begins, "there was a reaction: it is another weapon, it is 'just another weapon.'" Without once mentioning the hydrogen bomb, Oppenheimer then seeks in this article to undermine the entire thinking behind strategic bombing (thereby undermining the only conceivable use the hydrogen bomb might have). When we think of the atomic bomb, Oppenheimer writes, we think "of the specific use that was made of it against Hiroshima and Nagasaki":

> We think of it as an instrument of strategic bombing, for the destruction of lives and of plants, principally in cities. It is the decisive, even if perhaps not the final, step in a development that may have started at Guernica, that was characterized by the blitz against London, by the British raids on Hamburg, by our fire raids on Tokyo, and by Hiroshima.

As against this conception of the military use of atomic bombs, Oppenheimer rather cleverly quotes from a statement given in 1949 by Admiral Ralph Ofstie, in which he expresses the opinion that "strategic air warfare, as practiced in the past and as proposed in the future, is militarily unsound and of limited effect, and is morally wrong, and is decidedly harmful to the stability of the postwar world." These views, Oppenheimer points out, were expressed before the Korean War, and now, because of that war: "Much of what was clear to Admiral Ofstie then has become clear to all of us today." He then goes on to suggest that using atomic bombs against military rather than civilian targets, though certainly not as desirable as the avoidance of war itself, was at least preferable to "the extreme form of the atom bomb as a strategic weapon." The article ends with an account of Oppenheimer's meeting with Nehru, India's Prime Minister, during the latter's visit to the United States in May 1950. When Oppenheimer took the opportunity to ask Nehru whether he had found any appreciation during his time in the States of the Hindu notion of control, or restraint, Nehru replied: "I cannot believe that any great people would be without it." The article ends with Oppenheimer's declaration: "I believe the American people are a great people."

In opposing the very concept of strategic bombing, Oppenheimer was setting his face against the prevailing trend of U.S. military thinking and exposing himself to the wrath of some of the most powerful people in the U.S. A few months after the publication of this article he was given a chance to dig himself deeper into that hole when he was invited to join a research program called "Project Vista." This was a project that had grown out of exactly the kind of thinking that Oppenheimer had recommended in his *Bulletin* article. In September 1950, the much-decorated and very popular U.S. Army general James Gavin was charged with the task of investigating "the possible tactical employment of nuclear weapons." This was three months into the Korean War, and the clear implication was that General Gavin would identify some way of using tactical atomic weapons in the Korean conflict. Gathering together a group of experts, among whom was Charles Lauritsen, Gavin and his group went to Korea to review the situation. On their return to the States, Lauritsen suggested forming a "study group of top scientists and military men" to look into the possibility of using nuclear rockets to provide tactical air support to the troops on the ground.

At the same time Lee DuBridge had been approached by the air force to consider the possibility of using the scientific expertise at Caltech to address both strategic and tactical problems faced by airmen. After discussing this with some of his colleagues, including Lauritsen, the "Caltech group," as DuBridge put it in a letter to Willie Fowler, "expressed the feeling that it was not qualified or greatly interested in the strategic air problem, but that the tactical air problem, particularly the problem of close support of ground troops, was more nearly in line with our interests, and the group agreed to give the matter further thought."

The result was an extraordinarily lucrative contract for Caltech: in return for a fee of $600,000, Caltech would conduct a nine-month research project, lasting from April to December 1951, to look into the problems of tactical warfare, both on the ground and in the air. Though the contract was with the army, all three services would be involved. Willie Fowler was appointed director of the project, and the base of operations was to be the Vista del Arroyo Hotel in Pasadena.

Although it grew out of the Korean conflict, Project Vista concentrated more and more of its attention on Europe, particularly after the beginning of what would turn out to be long and drawn-out armistice negotiations with the North Koreans in July 1951. What the scientists involved in Project Vista hoped to achieve was to divert U.S. military thinking away from strategic bombing and toward the use of atomic weapons to provide tactical support. "All of us," Fowler recalled, "were rather opposed to strategic bombing, that is, to a complete dependence on SAC [Strategic Air Command] and were determined to acquaint the DOD [Department of Defense] with the fact that there were other ways of defending Europe."

Oppenheimer was invited to join Project Vista in July 1951, and from then until its final report was written in the New Year of 1952 he played an increasingly influential role in its thinking. He ended up writing one chapter of the report himself and had a hand in drafting several others, including the introduction. With regard to the defense of Western Europe, the report argued that the annihilation of Russian cities by strategic bombing was something Europeans feared rather than welcomed, because of the danger of provoking retaliatory attacks on *their* cities. "On the other hand," the report insisted, "if we plan also to use our air power (including strategic, tactical, and Naval units) to destroy the march of Russian armies, we can win the confidence of the NATO nations."

Such thinking was, of course, anathema to the Strategic Air Command and also to the air force generally. When a preliminary version of the report was presented at Caltech toward the end of 1951, it produced an "explosion" from the air force, which saw in it not just ill-considered advice, but dangerous subversion—an attempt to undermine the only arm of the military that stood any hope of defeating, or even of containing, the Soviet Union. Air-force generals became seriously alarmed when members of the Vista team—DuBridge, Lauritsen and Oppenheimer—went to Europe to discuss their report with NATO top brass, including General Eisenhower, the Supreme Commander, and General Norstad, who was by this time Eisenhower's Air Deputy and Commander-in-Chief of the Allied Air Forces. Norstad was not as horrified by the report as his air-force colleagues back in the U.S. had been, but he did suggest to DuBridge, Lauritsen and Oppenheimer that they get rid of any suggestion that strategic bombing and the tactical use of atomic weapons were somehow incompatible.

Encouraged by this relatively warm reaction, the authors of the report returned to Caltech to work on the final version, which was finished by February 1952. Because of the horrified reaction of the air force, however, the report was suppressed almost as soon as it was delivered. Thomas Finletter, the Secretary of the air force, ordered all copies to be sent to his office in Washington, where most of them were destroyed and the remaining few hidden under lock and key. Shortly before that, Finletter and General Vandenberg, Chief of Staff of the air force, issued orders that Oppenheimer was no longer to be used as a consultant in any further studies relating to the air force and that classified air-force documents were, despite his security clearance, to be kept away from him. As far as the air force was concerned, what Project Vista showed was that Oppenheimer could not be trusted.

The reason for this was not just the attitude that Oppenheimer, and the report he had helped to write, expressed about strategic bombing. It was also what was said and, perhaps more importantly, what was not said, in the report about the hydrogen bomb. In a report that touched upon (even if it did not concentrate on) the uses of strategic bombing, one might have expected some discussion of the Super. In fact there are only allusions to, and implied rebuffs of, this promised new weapon. "We have found no great new weapons—and we believe we can get along with those we have," the report says (in the chapter written by Oppenheimer). The report also committed itself to the view that, for strategic bombing, a yield of between one and fifty kilotons was ideal, with no use at all envisaged for bombs in the megaton range. The implication was that even if the H-bomb could be built, it would have no role to play in the defense of Europe.

This was all the more troubling to the air-force leaders because, as they well knew, during the time that Project Vista was being conceived and then carried out (from the end of 1950 to the beginning of 1952), the prospects for overcoming the technical problems in the way of developing the hydrogen bomb improved dramatically. The lowest point for the Super program was probably the spring and early summer of 1950, when the calculations of Ulam and Everett, and then von Neumann, showed that Teller's "classical Super" design would not work. Soon after that, however, Bethe and Fermi arrived at Los Alamos and genuine progress started being made.

Crucial to the overall success of the project would be the "Greenhouse" series of tests that had been scheduled for May 1951, and which Oppenheimer and many others assumed would fail. Four tests were planned, but the crucial one, scheduled for May 9, 1951, was the third, code-named "George." What George would test was not a bomb, but a device that Teller had designed called the "Cylinder." The idea, in the words of one of its planners, was to use an atomic explosion "to send material down a tube and cause a thermonuclear reaction of small magnitude in deuterium." The design called for the atomic explosion to take the form of a bomb with a yield of 500 kilotons of TNT (about thirty-five times more powerful than the Hiroshima bomb), which would then ignite a fusion reaction in a tiny amount (less than one ounce) of deuterium and tritium. It was, says the Princeton physicist Robert Jastrow, "like using a blast furnace to light a match." Where the Cylinder differed from the classical Super was that the fusion between the deuterium and the tritium was to be initiated not by a flow of high-energy neutrons, but by radiation, in the form of X-rays, traveling from the atomic explosion through a pipe. As it turned out, though no one knew this when the design for the Cylinder was completed in October 1950, this idea of using X-rays was to prove a turning point for the whole program.

Just after the design of the Cylinder was finalized, Oppenheimer organized a visit of the GAC to Los Alamos to inspect progress. This was mainly for the benefit of new members, the most notable of whom was the chemist Willard Libby, a future Nobel laureate who was an enthusiastic proponent of the H-bomb program. Also taking part in this visit was Gordon Dean, who, after Lilienthal's departure, was now chairman of the AEC. In his report of the visit Oppenheimer announced himself to be impressed by the "new and elaborate instrumentation" developed for the Greenhouse tests, particularly with the new information that might be gained through the investigation of "the flow of radiation from fission weapons into materials of varying density." Such information, he acknowledged, "will be relevant to many thermonuclear models." No one, however, believed that the George test would demonstrate the feasibility of a hydrogen bomb.

Thanks primarily to Stanislaw Ulam, this was very soon to change. In December 1950, Ulam had the idea that has since become known as "super-compression," but which Ulam called "hydrodynamic lensing." This was not, initially, anything to do with hydrogen bombs; it was a new atomic-bomb design, motivated by the desire to make more efficient use of fissionable material such as uranium and plutonium. The central idea was to use the energy from one atomic bomb to compress a small piece of fissionable material, thereby creating a second, more powerful explosion. This sounds less efficient, since two pieces of fissionable material are being used instead of one. However, the energy created by the first explosion is so great that it can be used to implode a much smaller lump of, say, plutonium than would otherwise be needed, making it, in fact, much more efficient.

In the New Year of 1951, it occurred to Ulam how this basic design might be applied to the problem of igniting fusion. His wife, Françoise, has remembered how one day at about noon she found Ulam "staring intensely out of a window in our living room with a very strange expression on his face." "Peering unseeing into the garden, he said, 'I found a way to make it work.' 'What work?' I asked. 'The Super,' he replied. 'It is a totally different scheme, and it will change the course of history.'"

Ulam's new H-bomb design called for an atomic "primary" to set off a fusion "secondary," using very high-energy neutrons. When he described it to Teller, however, Teller—perhaps with the Cylinder design in mind—saw that Ulam's design could be improved by using the *radiation*, rather than the neutron flow, from the primary to compress a piece of fusible material. This is what became known as the "Ulam-Teller" design, which, as both men realized in January 1951, was a very considerable improvement on the "classical Super." "From then on," Ulam says, "pessimism gave way to hope." "Edward is full of enthusiasm about these possibilities," Ulam wrote to von Neumann in February 1951, adding skittishly: "This is perhaps an indication they will not work." Hans

Bethe, meanwhile, was extremely impressed: "The new concept was to me, who had been rather closely associated with the program, about as surprising as the discovery of fission had been to physicists in 1939."

In a series of papers written in February and March 1951, several refinements were added to the Ulam-Teller design, one of which was to place a rod of plutonium—a "spark plug"—inside the fusible material and another of which was to surround the fusible material with a uranium tamper. Together, these two refinements considerably increased the anticipated yield of the bomb, the explosion of which was now a three-stage process: 1. an implosive fission reaction in the "primary" produces radiation of extraordinarily high energy, which compresses the fusible material, causing a fission reaction in the plutonium "spark plug" at its center; 2. this raises the temperature high enough—and, crucially, quickly enough—to bring about a fusion reaction in the fusible material; 3. this, in turn, causes a fission reaction in the surrounding uranium. As Jeremy Bernstein summarizes the process: "The sequence is fission-fusion-fission, with most of the energy from a hydrogen bomb actually coming from fission."

The final report explaining this device, credited to both Teller and Ulam, was entitled "On Heterocatalytic Detonations I: Hydrodynamic Lenses and Radiation Mirrors," and dated March 9, 1951. In the light of this new design, the George test, held on May 9, acquired a new significance, promising as it did to provide experimental data on radiation implosion. The location chosen for the Greenhouse tests was the Eniwetok Atoll, on the northwest end of the Marshall Islands in the Pacific: 8,500 men were flown out there to carry out the extensive and elaborate preparations for the tests. The scientific observers included, apart from Teller, Ernest Lawrence and Gordon Dean.

The explosion of the Cylinder certainly produced an impressive blast. The yield was measured at 225 kilotons—not quite the 500 kilotons originally envisaged, but, even so, at least fifteen times more powerful than the Hiroshima bomb—and the fireball it produced was estimated to be 1,800 feet high. Whether fusion had taken place, however, could not be known until certain measurements had been carried out. While waiting for the results of those measurements, Teller went swimming with Lawrence. "When I came out of the water to stand on the white sands of the beach," Teller later remembered, "I told Lawrence that I thought the experiment had been a failure. He thought otherwise, and bet me five dollars." The next day, the results showed that Lawrence had won the bet. The world's first man-made fusion reaction had taken place. That tiny amount of deuterium and tritium—less than one ounce—had yielded twenty-five kilotons of explosive energy, twice the force that had destroyed Hiroshima.

Oppenheimer's prediction that the test would be a disaster and would mark the point at which the hydrogen-bomb project was abandoned could not have been more wrong. As urged by Gordon Dean, Oppenheimer convened a meeting of the GAC to discuss the improved prospects for the Super at Princeton on June 16–17. Teller, naturally, was invited. The agenda for the meeting envisaged a discussion first of the results obtained from the Greenhouse tests, moving on to theoretical results concerning the classical Super, before finally considering the Ulam-Teller design. Teller, however, had no patience for that, and interrupted the first presentation to talk about the promise of this novel design. As he explained the new concept, all the scientists present, including Oppenheimer, could see its potential and it immediately won the backing of the GAC. "The outcome of the meeting," Oppenheimer later said, "was an agreed program and a fixing of priorities and effort both for Los Alamos and for other aspects of the Commission's work. This program has been an outstanding success."

When asked to explain why his reaction to the Ulam-Teller design differed so markedly from his 1949 reaction to the classical Super, Oppenheimer said:

> It is my judgment in these things that when you see something that is technically sweet, you go ahead and do it and you argue about what to do about it only after you have had your technical success. That is the way it was with the atomic bomb. I do not think anybody opposed making it; there were some debates about what to do with it after it was made. I cannot very well imagine if we had known in late 1949 what we got to know by early 1951 that the tone of our report would have been the same.

This is not entirely convincing. The technical problems of the classical Super certainly played a part in the GAC's recommendation in 1949 not to pursue a crash program, but what seemed more decisive were the moral considerations raised and urged by Conant. The moral issues raised by this new design were exactly the same as those raised by the old design. If anything, the fact that the new design stood a better chance of working would seem to make those moral issues more pressing. Moreover, as Oppenheimer later said, though from a technical point of view he could consider the hydrogen-bomb design "a sweet and lovely and beautiful job," he "still thought it was a dreadful weapon."

As even Teller acknowledged, however, the attitude of Oppenheimer, the GAC and the AEC changed after this meeting of June 1951. Now the AEC got fully behind the program and gave it all the resources it needed. In September 1951, with the AEC's backing, the thermonuclear division at Los Alamos began making preparations for a full test of the Ulam-Teller bomb, and on November 1, 1952, scarcely more than a year later, that test (code-named "Mike") was duly carried out and was a stunning success, the bomb exploding with an awe-inspiring yield of ten megatons (about 700 Hiroshima bombs).

Thus, less than three years after President Truman's announcement of its existence, the AEC had brought the crash program to build a hydrogen bomb to a successful conclusion. Why then had Teller and others complained so bitterly that Oppenheimer was delaying the development of the bomb? There simply was no delay. The bomb was, on the contrary, developed with remarkable speed and the program to construct it managed with exactly the kind of scientific and administrative skill that had been so admired in the Manhattan Project. It all went surprisingly smoothly.

To understand the complaints and the bitterness, one has to understand the role that Edward Teller played in the construction of the world's first hydrogen bomb, and, in particular, how surprisingly small that role was. The bomb that was exploded in the "Mike" test of November 1952 was built to the Ulam-Teller design, but that, more or less, was Teller's only contribution to it. To Teller's great chagrin, in September 1951, when Los Alamos began in earnest its program of building a hydrogen bomb, the man appointed by Norris Bradbury to serve as director of that program was not Teller himself, but Marshall Holloway, a graduate of Cornell, who had been at Los Alamos since 1943. During the Crossroads tests Holloway had been deputy scientific director, and had then been appointed leader of the Los Alamos Weapons Division. Despite filling these senior positions, he was a strangely obscure figure. When he died, a memorial tribute ended with the words: "In spite of the remarkable success of the 'Mike' operation, Marshall remained almost anonymous except to his colleagues."

Teller disliked Holloway even before he was chosen to lead Teller's pet project. In his memoir Teller writes:

> Somewhat negative in his approach to life in general, Holloway had not cooperated on any project pertaining to the Super. Bradbury could not have appointed anyone who would have slowed the work on the program more effectively, nor anyone with whom I would have found it more frustrating to work.

Within a week of Holloway's appointment as director Teller walked out of Los Alamos and left the project altogether. Despite losing his most brilliant physicist, Bradbury was unrepentant. Great scientist though he was, Teller was no manager. He was too impetuous, too fiery and too unpopular. "If I'd given him control of the program," Bradbury later said, "I'd have half my division leaders quit."

So, when Los Alamos was finally doing what Teller had wanted it to do for years—actually building a hydrogen bomb—Teller himself was back in Chicago, nursing his wounded pride. To begin with, he spent his time on some interesting theoretical work, calculating the blast effects of hydrogen bombs. It had been assumed by Oppenheimer, Conant and others on the GAC that there was no limit to the destructiveness of the hydrogen bomb, one thing that, they argued, "makes its very existence and the knowledge of its construction a danger to humanity as a whole." Teller's calculations showed this was not true. As they got more powerful, hydrogen bombs did not, in fact, get more destructive. A 100-megaton bomb, for example, would not have ten times the destructive power of a ten-megaton bomb. Indeed, it would hardly be *any* more destructive. Both would blow, in Teller's words, "a chunk of the atmosphere, weighing perhaps a billion tons," into the air. The bigger bomb, however, would not destroy a bigger "chunk"; it would, rather, blow the same-sized chunk into the air at three times the speed.

Interesting though such calculations were, Teller hankered after laboratory work, and, in particular, weapon-laboratory work. He could, of course, have returned to Los Alamos, where his expertise could have been put to practical use. Bradbury had made it clear that he would be welcome there as a scientist, if not as a director. Another ex-colleague at Los Alamos has said: "A lot of us were really teed-off at Edward, because if he would have sat down and applied himself to the job, it would of course have gone faster." What Teller did instead was to use the considerable amounts of spare time he now had on his hands to campaign for the establishment of a second weapons laboratory that would act as a rival to Los Alamos.

As Los Alamos was at that time making excellent progress toward completing the program it had been asked to undertake, the case for a second, competing laboratory was hard to make. Teller's ostensible reason was that the pace of progress at Los Alamos was too slow and needed competition to speed it up. This might have appeared quite a strong argument in 1950, but, from the autumn of 1951 onward, the speed and efficiency of progress at Los Alamos undermined it completely.

Among the members of the GAC and the AEC there was little enthusiasm for a second laboratory, the general view being that expressed by

Oppenheimer in a letter to Gordon Dean in October 1951: such a thing was "neither necessary nor in any real sense feasible." There were, however, two important dissenters. The first was Thomas Murray, who had been on the AEC since March 1950, when both Lewis Strauss and David Lilienthal resigned from it, and who quickly allied himself with those who believed that progress on the H-bomb program was proceeding too slowly. Murray had been convinced since the June 1951 meeting in Princeton that a new laboratory, dedicated to developing the Super, was necessary. The other exception was Willard Libby, a close friend of Teller's, who tried and failed to convince the GAC of the need for a second laboratory in October 1951.

On December 13, 1951, Teller came to Washington to present his case for a second laboratory to the GAC in person. Teller believes that the argument he presented that day was "among the very best I have ever made." He was, he says, "constrained, logical and polite." He was not, however, convincing. All those present, except Libby and Murray (who, though not a member of the GAC, had been invited to attend), remained unpersuaded.

Also in Washington at that time was Ernest Lawrence, who by this stage was firmly in the pro-Teller and anti-Oppenheimer camp, so much so that Robert Serber—having been told by Rabi, "You have to choose between Ernest and Oppie"—had felt compelled to leave Berkeley out of loyalty to Oppenheimer. From the summer of 1951 onward, Serber was a colleague of Rabi's at Columbia. After the GAC meeting of December 1951, Murray met Lawrence, who made it clear that he supported Teller's campaign for a second laboratory and that he would be happy to work with Teller to establish one. In early February 1952, Teller visited Lawrence at Berkeley and the two of them drove out to Livermore, a site about thirty miles east of Berkeley owned by the University of California, upon which Lawrence had built a large particle accelerator called the MTA. Livermore, Lawrence told Teller, would be the ideal place for the proposed second laboratory.

With such enthusiastic support from one of the most successful scientific promoters of all time, the prospects for the second laboratory were now looking very good, in spite of the fact that the AEC and the GAC continued throughout the winter of 1951–2 to reject the idea. What Teller and Lawrence had shown in 1949, however, was that, with the right kind of political support, it was possible to impose a policy upon the AEC, rather than wait for that policy to be recommended by the GAC. It was a lesson that Teller had learned very well.

What helped Teller enormously was that he was able to exploit the reputation Los Alamos still had as "Oppie's lab," and the considerable reserves of bad feeling that by then existed toward Oppenheimer himself among U.S. policy-makers. The list of people whom Teller successfully recruited to his campaign for a second laboratory during the first half of 1952 reads like a roll call of all those powerful men whose suspicion and hatred Oppenheimer had aroused during the previous two or three years. Moreover, in exploiting that suspicion and hatred, Teller served to raise them to new levels.

Chief among those powerful haters of Oppenheimer, of course, was Lewis Strauss, whom Teller describes in his memoir as "a courteous man with a deep-seated sense of decency," and who was the first person in Washington to whom Teller went for support. Strauss promised to do whatever he could to help, and indeed went much further. "Strauss told me," Teller later revealed, "he loved me like a brother-in-law." Another enthusiastic recruit to Teller's campaign was David Griggs, a geophysicist at UCLA, who had for years acted as a consultant for the air force and who, in September 1951, was appointed the air force's chief scientist. "I think it would be fair to say," Teller later wrote, "that without Dave Griggs, Lawrence Livermore Laboratory [the name given to Teller's second weapons laboratory] would not have come into existence. He introduced me to many influential people and succeeded in developing a lot of friends for the idea."

David Griggs, along with Lewis Strauss, William Borden and Thomas Finletter, was one of the few people who actually believed that Oppenheimer might be working for the Soviet Union. Teller, despite his personal and professional animosities toward Oppenheimer, believed no such thing, but that such beliefs were held by people of influence was certainly a factor in his favor in setting up his proposed second laboratory, and he did nothing to challenge them. On the contrary, he went out of his way to encourage them. In April 1952, an FBI report said that sometime earlier Teller had, in response to questions about Philip Morrison, told an FBI agent that Morrison "has the reputation among physicists of being extremely far to the left." Then, though he had not been asked about Oppenheimer, Teller added: "Oppenheimer, Robert Serber and Morrison are considered the three most extreme leftists among physicists," and that "most of Oppenheimer's students at Berkeley had absorbed Oppenheimer's leftist views."

In May 1952, Teller gave two interviews to the FBI, one on the 10th and another on the 27th, in which Oppenheimer was the main topic. Teller's main charge was that Oppenheimer "delayed or attempted to delay or hinder the development of the H-bomb," which he said could have been completed by 1951 if it had not been for Oppenheimer's opposition. In fact, at the very time this interview was being conducted, the

Los Alamos program—recommended by Oppenheimer and abandoned by Teller—had just succeeded in developing the world's first H-bomb, ready for testing five months later. Teller also told the FBI agent that, though he himself did not believe Oppenheimer to be disloyal, "a lot of people believe Oppenheimer opposed the development of the H-bomb on 'direct orders from Moscow.'" Perhaps Teller's most damaging comment about Oppenheimer, however, was his remark that he "would do most anything" to get Oppenheimer off the GAC. Coming from the man widely regarded as the U.S.'s greatest authority on hydrogen bombs, this was a powerful statement.

As Teller would have known perfectly well, his new friend "Dave" Griggs was one of those people who thought Oppenheimer was acting on orders from Moscow. Griggs was an air-force man through and through, and, like many U.S. Air Force men, had been appalled at the views expressed by Oppenheimer in the Project Vista report, which, he seemed to think, could only be explained by assuming that Oppenheimer was deliberately trying to undermine the military strength of the U.S. At Oppenheimer's security hearing in 1954, Griggs stated unequivocally: "I want to say, and I can't emphasize too strongly, that Dr. Oppenheimer is the only one of my scientific acquaintances about whom I have ever felt there was a serious question as to their loyalty." When asked about his support for Teller's idea of a second weapons laboratory, Griggs said: "We felt at the time we are speaking of, namely, late 1951 and early 1952, the effort on this [hydrogen bomb] program was not as great as the circumstances required under the President's directive." Again it is worth emphasizing that the dates specified by Griggs, "late 1951 and early 1952," coincide *precisely* with the period when the "effort on this program" was at its very greatest.

One of the most important ways in which Griggs helped Teller to realize his ambitions of establishing a second laboratory was by introducing him to Thomas Finletter, the Secretary of the air force. Finletter became so convinced of the need for a second laboratory to rival Los Alamos that he stated that, if the AEC was not prepared to establish one, then the air force would. Step by step, then, Teller's campaign was moving upward through the ranks of the American political hierarchy. What Teller himself regarded as the "crucial interview" came when, on Finletter's recommendation, the Secretary of Defense, Robert Lovett, agreed to meet him. After their meeting Lovett wrote to the AEC recommending a second laboratory. By April 1952, it was clear that the AEC would have to give way to the political tide Teller had created, and after two more months of particularly intensive campaigning—both for the laboratory and against Oppenheimer—on June 9, 1952, Gordon Dean finally wrote to the University of California on behalf of the AEC, asking them to approve the establishment of a new weapons laboratory at Livermore. The Lawrence Livermore Laboratory opened on September 2, 1952. Teller had won.

The price of Teller's victory—a price that he, Lawrence, Strauss, Griggs and Finletter were only too willing, indeed pleased, to pay—was the ruin of Oppenheimer's reputation in Washington. When Teller began his campaign in the autumn of 1951, Oppenheimer was still a respected and influential figure in Washington; by the time that campaign ended a year later, Oppenheimer was, from a political point of view, more or less a spent force.

During that year the private whispering about Oppenheimer that had been going on for years became louder and more insistent and the public attacks on him became more common and more vicious. It is as if the campaign to establish the Livermore Laboratory and the campaign to oust Oppenheimer from the GAC and blacken his political reputation became merged into a single political movement. Those who supported the second laboratory were, to a man, those most vocal in their disapproval of Oppenheimer. When Thomas Murray visited Berkeley, for example, Lawrence told him at some length how disillusioned he had become with Oppenheimer and how opposed he was to Oppenheimer's continued membership of the GAC. Two weeks later, Kenneth Pitzer, who had been director of research for the AEC from 1949 until his resignation in 1952, gave a speech to the American Chemical Society that, in the spirit of Teller and Strauss, blamed the GAC for the slow progress of the H-bomb program. Afterward he told the FBI that he "now is doubtful as to the loyalty of Dr. Oppenheimer."

During May 1952, as the campaign for Livermore reached its climax, so too did the attacks on Oppenheimer. On May 9, Oppenheimer had lunch with Conant and DuBridge, the three of them gloomily aware of which way the political winds were blowing. That night Conant recorded in his diary: "Some of the 'boys' have their axe out for the three of us on the GAC of AEC. Claim we have 'dragged our heels' on H bomb. Dirty words about Oppie!" Ten days later this sense of a concerted attack on Oppenheimer was felt by Gordon Dean, who reported in his diary that at the annual meeting of the American Physical Society, he had heard much "vitriolic talk" about Oppenheimer, "notably from some of the University of California contingent."

It was during this month, May 1952, that Teller gave his interviews to the FBI, telling them that he would do anything to get Oppenheimer off the GAC and handing them gossip that some people believed Oppenheimer to be taking his orders from Moscow. At the end of the month,

Hoover sent transcripts of those interviews, together with transcripts of interviews with Pitzer and Libby, to the Justice Department, the White House and the AEC.

Oppenheimer, of course, knew what was afoot, and a meeting he had with David Griggs on May 23 shows how much the campaign against him was unsettling him. The origin of this meeting lay in a lunch Griggs had attended during the annual meeting of the National Academy of Sciences. Over lunch, Griggs had met DuBridge and Rabi and expressed the view that the GAC was not doing enough to push through the accelerated H-bomb program ordered by the President. Rabi told him that if he could read the minutes of the GAC meetings, he would see that this was not true and suggested that he ask Oppenheimer to show him the minutes.

So the next time he was in Princeton, which was May 23, Griggs called on Oppenheimer. "I didn't really expect that I would be allowed to read the minutes of the General Advisory Committee," Griggs later said, "and it turned out that this was not offered by Dr. Oppenheimer." The two spoke for about an hour, during which Oppenheimer, referring in particular to the Princeton meeting of June 1951, attempted to convince Griggs that the GAC was fully committed to the H-bomb project. The conversation took a somewhat uncomfortable turn when Griggs moved on to the subject of a bit of tittle-tattle about Thomas Finletter. A story was going around that Finletter, at a meeting with the Secretary of Defense, had been heard to remark that if the U.S. had a certain number of hydrogen bombs it could rule the world. Griggs was concerned about this story circulating, because it "suggested that we had irresponsible warmongers at the head of the Air Force at that time." He therefore asked Oppenheimer if he himself had been spreading the story and, if so, what grounds he had for thinking it true. Oppenheimer replied that he had heard this story from an unimpeachable source and dismissed Griggs's vehement insistence that it was false.

The discussion got even more tense when Oppenheimer asked Griggs if he thought he, Oppenheimer, was pro-Russian or just confused. "As near as I can recall," Griggs said, "I responded that I wished I knew." Oppenheimer then asked Griggs whether he had impugned his loyalty to high officials in the Defense Department, "and I believe I responded simply, yes, or something like that." The meeting ended with Oppenheimer calling Griggs a "paranoid."

Four days later, Bethe went to see Griggs in order to lighten the increasingly tense atmosphere between the air force and some of America's leading atomic scientists. Bethe later recalled that the occasion was surprisingly pleasant:

Dr Griggs had been very much an exponent of the view that Los Alamos was not doing its job right and very much an exponent of the view that thermonuclear weapons and only the biggest thermonuclear weapons should be the main part of the weapons arsenal of the United States. I had very much disagreed with this, with both of these points, and so I expected that we would have really a very unpleasant fight on this matter. We didn't.

On all the issues that divided Griggs and Oppenheimer—the alleged need for a second weapons laboratory, the importance of strategic bombing, the hydrogen bomb, the value of openness versus the need for secrecy, and so on—Bethe's sympathies were, in every case, with Oppenheimer, and yet Griggs clearly did not regard Bethe as a dangerous subversive, nor did he appear to dislike him. Why the difference?

The answer seems to be twofold. First, Griggs seems to have thought that Oppenheimer was not just—as, presumably, he believed Bethe to be—expressing a series of misguided opinions; rather, his opinions were part of a "pattern of behavior" (a phrase used often by Oppenheimer's detractors at this time) that identified him as someone working actively against U.S. interests. Second, on a personal level, Oppenheimer seems to have aroused in Griggs something close to hatred. Leona Libby, Willard Libby's wife, describes their friend "Dave" Griggs in glowing terms: "a pillar of honesty, a fine scientist, a strong servant of the military and of the weapons laboratories, very careful to think clearly, and devastatingly outspoken." He was, she says, "strongly built, with blue eyes that could become very cold and fierce when he encountered bad science, hypocrisy, or other unpleasantness." Recounting some of the details of Griggs's testimony against Oppenheimer at the security hearing, Leona Libby writes: "I remember how his blue eyes blazed coldly when he felt strongly on an issue, as he surely did on this one."

Though Oppenheimer, when he felt so inclined and the occasion demanded it, was capable of charming almost anyone, he seemed to go out of his way during this period to antagonize and offend his political opponents. Having twice publicly humiliated Lewis Strauss, and having offended Griggs by calling him "paranoid," Oppenheimer, a few weeks after this latter incident, seemed determined to antagonize one of the most powerful people in the U.S. military establishment: Thomas Finletter. The occasion was a lunch that Finletter's aides, William Burden and Garrison Norton, had arranged in the hope that meeting face-to-face would help Oppenheimer and Finletter overcome some of their disagreements. Griggs was also invited, and a few days before the meeting provided Finletter with an "eyes only" memo, describing in detail his own recent encounter with Oppenheimer. The lunch was, one of its participants later recalled, one of the most uncomfortable events at which he had ever been present. Oppenheimer arrived late and was steadfastly unresponsive to any attempt to engage him in conversation. His manner seemed to suggest contempt for everyone in the room, and, as soon as the meal was over, he turned his back on his fellow diners and walked away. After Oppenheimer had gone, Finletter laughed and said to his aides: "I don't think you fellows have convinced me I should feel any more positively about Dr. Oppenheimer."

Oppenheimer's term as a member of the GAC was coming to an end in the summer of 1952. There is some uncertainty about whether he wanted to renew his position on the committee or whether, like Conant and DuBridge (whose membership in the GAC was also coming to an end), he was looking forward to freeing himself from the pressures and unpleasantness that surrounded U.S. nuclear politics at this time. On June 14, 1952, Conant wrote in his diary with evident delight: "Lee DuBridge and I are through as members of the GAC!! 10½ years of almost continuous official conversations with a bad business now threatening to become really bad!!" Two days earlier Oppenheimer had told Dean that he, too, would not be seeking reappointment after his term came to an end, but in his case there is no indication that he was delighted to leave.

On the contrary, there are signs that Oppenheimer's resignation was forced upon him, or, at the very least, that it was made clear to him that he would not be reappointed even if he wished to be. By the time Oppenheimer told Dean he no longer wished to serve on the GAC there was a formidable campaign against his reappointment. In April 1952, Kenneth Pitzer had told the FBI that one of the reasons he alerted them to his suspicions about Oppenheimer was that, as an FBI memo puts it, "he is very much concerned about the above at the present time inasmuch as it is his opinion that J. Robert Oppenheimer is now 'making a play' to be reappointed." The following month, Willard Libby let it be known to the FBI that he, too, "believed it would be extremely wise not to reappoint Oppenheimer to the General Advisory Committee." In the light of these views, together with those of Teller, Strauss, Griggs, Finletter, Borden and others, Oppenheimer's chances of being reappointed were extremely slim. Indeed, Brien McMahon told the FBI at the end of May that he "is personally going to talk to the President," to tell him that he had "worked out a plan whereby Oppenheimer would take the initiative and decline to serve another term by an exchange of letters and everybody will be happy."

The exchange of letters in question was read out at Oppenheimer's security hearing. It included one from Gordon Dean to Oppenheimer, thanking him for his "magnificent" contribution to "the Commission and the country," and another, ostensibly from President Truman, but in fact drafted by Dean, expressing the President's "deep sense of personal regret" that Oppenheimer had chosen to step down from the GAC and his gratitude for the "lasting and immensely valuable contribution to the national security and to atomic energy progress in this Nation" that Oppenheimer had made.

More surprising than Oppenheimer's decision not to seek reappointment as a member of the GAC was his appointment by Dean on a one-year contract as a consultant to the AEC. Since this made it necessary to extend Oppenheimer's security clearance for another year, it meant that the campaign by his many enemies to separate him from the military secrets of the U.S. would continue. It is natural to assume that this appointment was part of the deal mentioned by McMahon to get Oppenheimer off the GAC. Whether this was so, or whether Oppenheimer was persuaded against his own inclinations to stay as a consultant, the fact that he accepted the position shows on his part a desire, or anyway a willingness, to stay in the line of fire and to keep on fighting a series of battles that, he surely knew by this time, he had no chance of winning.

Griggs, Strauss and others thought that the explanation for this willingness to continue the fight was that Oppenheimer was determined to maintain access to military secrets so that he could betray them to the Soviet Union. However, despite all the efforts of the FBI and Oppenheimer's political enemies, not a shred of evidence for this suspicion emerged, unless, like Griggs and Strauss, one regards Oppenheimer's political views and the advice he gave to government departments as evidence of disloyalty, in which case one has to explain why the many people who shared those views—Bethe, Rabi, Conant, DuBridge, and numerous others—were not also regarded as potential security risks. The explanation offered for this by many of Oppenheimer's enemies is that he exerted some kind of mysterious control over these people in order to get them to accept obviously muddleheaded political opinions. The idea that men with the intellectual power and strength of character of Bethe, Conant and Rabi could possibly be controlled in this way is so ludicrous that one has to regard this "explanation" as a *reductio ad absurdum* of the whole view, and one is forced to offer a different explanation as to why Oppenheimer would subject himself to the constant attacks upon him that accompanied his involvement in political questions.

In the immediate postwar period that explanation might well have been the appeal of the prestige, glamour and intoxicating sense of importance that went with being on close terms with America's political leaders—being able, for example, to call the Secretary of State and the

Secretary of Defense by their first names. But by 1952, when Oppenheimer was disliked, or at the very least held in suspicion by nearly every
person in high office in Washington, this explanation fails. Fortunately,
another explanation is lying to hand, forcing itself upon one as the simple and obvious truth: Oppenheimer continued to act as a consultant to
government projects, thereby exposing himself to all sorts of exhausting
conflicts and crushing unpleasantness, precisely *because* of his love of, and
loyalty to, his country. He did it for the same reason that he underwent
the extreme rigors of leading Los Alamos: because he felt that it was,
using the word that underpins the morality of the Bhagavad Gita, his
duty to do it.

In July 1952, immediately after his decision to leave the GAC and
to accept the one-year consultancy appointment, Oppenheimer was
involved in a project that was regarded by David Griggs—as he emphasized in his 1954 testimony against Oppenheimer—as further evidence
of his disloyalty, but which is much more naturally seen as an expression
of his patriotism and his desire to see America well protected against
the possibility of nuclear attack. That project was a summer school at
the Lincoln Laboratory, organized by Jerrold Zacharias, the laboratory's
associate director.

The Lincoln Laboratory was then a fairly new establishment, having
been set up as the result of a study, to which Oppenheimer had contributed, called "Project Charles." The aim of Project Charles had been to
investigate the feasibility of building an air-defense system to protect
the United States against nuclear attack from the Soviet Union. The
conclusion reached was that such a system *was* feasible, which led to the
launch in 1951 of "Project Lincoln," a huge program, funded by the air
force to the tune of $20 million, charged with the task of making such
a system a reality. The Lincoln Laboratory, which was housed on the
grounds of MIT and then on a purpose-built site about fifteen miles
northwest of Boston, opened in September 1951 with Francis Wheeler
Loomis as its first director. After a year—by which time the laboratory
was employing more than 1,000 people—Loomis handed over to Albert
G. Hill, who, like Loomis, had spent the war working on radar at MIT's
radiation laboratory.

Indeed, the reason the Lincoln Laboratory had originally been based
at MIT was to make use of the considerable expertise on radar that had
been developed there during the war by scientists such as Loomis, Hill
and, most notably, Oppenheimer's friend Isidor Rabi. For radar was at the
very heart of the Lincoln Project, its guiding concept—soon to acquire
the acronym SAGE ("Semi-Automatic Ground Environment")—being
to build a network of radars designed to provide early warning of air

attacks. The data from these radars would be tracked by a series of computers that would then be used to guide weapons to destroy the enemy aircraft before they were able to drop their bombs.

The idea of the summer school at the Lincoln Laboratory emerged from discussions that Jerrold Zacharias had with another friend of Oppenheimer's, Charlie Lauritsen, in the spring of 1952. As Zacharias later recalled, he and Lauritsen were concerned about the "technical, military, and economic questions" that arose from the program of providing America with air defense against nuclear attack, and "decided that we should talk this over with certain others whom we knew very well." First they talked to Albert Hill, who was then the associate director of Lincoln Laboratory, and then: "We decided we would talk it over with Dr. Oppenheimer and Dr. Rabi."

The summer school started on July 1, 1952, and lasted for about two months, with Oppenheimer, Lauritsen and Rabi participating on a part-time basis at the beginning and at the end. One of the tasks of the summer school was to consider how and where the U.S. was vulnerable to Soviet air attack. They decided the greatest vulnerability came from the possibility that Soviet bombers might approach the United States by flying directly over the North Pole, and so they recommended what became known as the "DEW (Distant Early Warning) line." This was a line of thirty-five radar stations, stretching right across the northernmost tip of the North American continent, from Alaska in the west to Greenland in the east, which would give between three and six hours' warning of any attack from the north. This advice was passed on to the air force by Zacharias in September 1952 and was acted upon straightaway, so that by the end of that year work was under way to construct the radar stations.

The air force and the Department of Defense were very pleased with the advice they received from the summer school and with the work done by the Lincoln Project, both of which, it was generally agreed, had considerably strengthened the U.S. air-defense system. And yet, if all you knew about the summer school was the description David Griggs gave of it in his evidence at Oppenheimer's security hearing, you would think it was not a well-received study acting on behalf of the U.S. Air Force, but a subversive communist plot. Lending considerable credence to Oppenheimer's description of him as "paranoid," Griggs talked of a semi-secret group of four with the name "ZORC" (the letters standing for Zacharias, Oppenheimer, Rabi and Charles Lauritsen), dedicated to undermining U.S. Strategic Air Command under the guise of developing an air-defense system. Some of the people involved in the summer school had told him, Griggs said, that "in order to achieve world peace," it was necessary "not only to strengthen the Air Defense of the continental United States, but also to give up something, and the thing that was recommended that we give up was the Strategic Air Command."

The suggestion that the U.S. should give up its Strategic Air Command upset him, Griggs continued, because he did not think the members of the summer school had "the background nor were charged with the responsibility of considering in any detail or considering at all the fact of the activities of the Strategic Air Command." "I felt that for any group to make such recommendations it was necessary that they know as much about the Strategic Air Command and the general strategic picture as they knew about the Air Defense Command."

This anxiety, however, was completely misplaced, since the summer school did *not*, in fact, recommend the abolition of Strategic Air Command, as Griggs would later admit in an exchange with Oppenheimer's lawyers that makes clear how bizarre his earlier statements were:

> GRIGGS. I should say what I don't believe I did say this morning, that I believe that as a result of the Lincoln summer study our air defense is materially improved.
>
> Q. Was that the main object of the Lincoln summer study, to find ways to improve our air defense?
>
> GRIGGS. Yes, sir.
>
> Q. And did the Lincoln study ever recommend the giving-up of any part of our strategic air power?
>
> GRIGGS. No, not to my knowledge.

Griggs's mention of "world peace" possibly indicates a confusion on his part between the discussions that took place during the Lincoln summer school and the meetings of another committee in which Oppenheimer was participating during this period, namely the Department of State's Disarmament Panel. This was a panel of consultants appointed by Dean Acheson to advise the government in connection with the work of the United Nations Disarmament Commission. Besides Oppenheimer, the other members of the panel, announced on April 28, 1952, included Vannevar Bush and Allen W. Dulles, the deputy director of the CIA.

At their inaugural meeting the panel voted Oppenheimer as its chairman. The dominant voice, however, was that of Vannevar Bush, who, while serving on the panel, became convinced of the view that Fermi and Rabi had proposed in their "minority report" in October 1949: namely that the U.S. should attempt to negotiate with the USSR a ban on testing (and, therefore, on successfully developing) thermonuclear bombs. At the second meeting of the Disarmament Panel, held on May 6, 1952,

Bush raised the possibility of a test ban, which he argued, as Fermi and Rabi had argued three years earlier, "would not require inspection and control," since an H-bomb explosion would be so easy to detect. Led by Bush, and encouraged from the chair by Oppenheimer, the Disarmament Panel thus moved in a direction that had been unforeseen by Acheson and, from the point of view of Washington's political and military establishment, was entirely unwelcome.

By the end of the summer of 1952, the panel was convinced not only of the wisdom of a negotiated test ban, but also of the desirability of postponing the Mike test, scheduled for November 1. In a paper submitted to the President in September, the panel urged Truman to cancel the test in order to keep alive the possibility of negotiating a test ban with the Soviet Union. The test was, the panel argued, a "point of no return," since, afterward, the Soviet Union would surely regard any proposal to ban thermonuclear testing as motivated simply by the U.S.'s desire to stay ahead in the race. Also, the panel suggested, the testing of such a powerful bomb would alienate other countries besides the Soviet Union, convincing them that the U.S. "is irrevocably committed to a strategy of destroying its enemies by indiscriminate means and at whatever cost."

As well as arguing for a postponement on the grounds of international relations, the panel stressed its belief that the test was fatally ill timed because it coincided with the presidential election, the polling day for which would be November 4, just three days after the test was scheduled to take place. Indeed, the panel's report was entitled "The Timing of the Thermonuclear Test." It was widely (and, as it turned out, correctly) expected that the Democrats would lose the election, which meant that the test would take place just when the U.S. was exchanging one administration for another—surely not the best time for the country to be crossing a "point of no return."

By the summer of 1952, it was more or less clear that the next U.S. government would be a Republican one, led by General Eisenhower, which was, if anything, *less* likely than Truman's administration to be receptive to the ideas of the Disarmament Panel. For some years a "draft Eisenhower" campaign, with the slogan "I like Ike," had been urging Eisenhower to stand and marshaling the considerable popular support that he enjoyed throughout the country. Meanwhile Truman, who was becoming less and less popular, made it clear that he would not seek reelection. After Eisenhower fought his first primary in March 1952, winning a landslide victory, there was little doubt that he would be the Republican candidate, or that he would beat whoever the Democrats chose as their candidate, which, in July 1952, turned out to be Adlai Stevenson.

In a campaign speech to the American Legion on August 25, 1952, Eisenhower declared that the U.S. had need of security forces "whose destructive and retaliatory power is so great that it causes nightmares in the Kremlin whenever they think of attacking us." This commitment to exactly the kind of policy against which Oppenheimer had been warning for years was made even more explicit in the public statements of John Foster Dulles (the brother of Allen W. Dulles, Oppenheimer's colleague on the Disarmament Panel), who was Eisenhower's Secretary of State–elect. In a speech he gave in November 1951, Dulles asked rhetorically why the Soviet Union had not attacked Germany or Japan, and answered:

> The most reasonable explanation is that the rulers of Russia knew that if they indulged in this open aggression in any area of vital concern to the United States or which by treaty we were bound to defend, their sources and means of power would have been visited with incredible means of destruction. Thus the free world has been getting the security of deterrent striking power.

In an article that he published in *Life* magazine called "A Policy of Boldness," Dulles gave what became regarded as the classic statement of the doctrine of "massive retaliation." How, Dulles asked, was the U.S. to defend the "free world" against Soviet aggression? To attempt to match the Red Army "man for man, gun for gun and tank for tank" would, he urged, "mean real strength nowhere and bankruptcy everywhere":

> There is one solution and only one: that is for the free world to develop the will and organize the means to retaliate instantly against open aggression by Red armies, so that, if it occurred anywhere, we could and would strike back where it hurts, by means of our choosing.

The policy Dulles recommended in this article called upon the creation "of means to hit with shattering effectiveness the sources of power and lines of communication of the Sovietized world." "Today," he wrote, "atomic power, coupled with strategic air and sea power, provides the community of free nations with vast new possibilities of organizing a community power to stop open aggression before it starts and reduce, to vanishing point, the risk of general war."

In 1952, the American general public was extremely receptive to such views for three reasons: 1. the fear of communism and of Soviet expansionism made the American people open to the idea that *something* had to be done to deter the Soviets from further acts of aggression; 2. the prolonged, costly and indecisive Korean War had made Americans wary of engaging with communist armies on the ground; and 3. there was widespread support for reducing government spending. The policy of "massive retaliation" was successfully sold as a way of meeting all three of these objectives: deterring Soviet aggression in a way that did not involve either the deaths of U.S. soldiers or the expense of maintaining an army and a navy that could conceivably match the armies of the Soviet Union and China. In the context of such thinking, the development of thermonuclear bombs—the ultimate deterrence—seemed to make a good deal of sense.

The members of the Disarmament Panel, then, were politically isolated, with few allies among Truman's Democrats and even fewer among Eisenhower's Republicans. This did not deter them from trying as hard as they could to prevent the U.S. from making what they considered to be the potentially catastrophic mistake of going ahead with the Mike test. One very powerful—and, as it turned out, prescient—reason they gave for not going ahead was that the fallout from the test would provide the Soviet Union with valuable clues about the Ulam-Teller design. Despite the strength of this argument, by the autumn of 1952 practically the only person in the whole of the U.S.'s security establishment—comprising the GAC, the AEC, the Joint Chiefs of Staff, the Joint Committee on Atomic Energy, the Departments of State and of Defense—sympathetic to a ban on H-bomb tests was Isidor Rabi, Oppenheimer's successor as chair of the GAC. Most other members of those committees, departments and advisory bodies were not only opposed to the idea of a ban, but deeply suspicious of it.

When on October 9 the National Security Council met to discuss the Disarmament Panel's paper, there was no support at all for its recommendation of a test ban. Indeed, Robert Lovett, the Secretary of Defense, clearly felt uncomfortable about even discussing such a suggestion. It made him feel vulnerable. The minutes of the meeting record that Lovett "felt that any such idea should be immediately put out of mind and that any papers that might exist on the subject should be destroyed." Such was the shadow cast by Joseph McCarthy during this period.

Even the more limited proposal that the Mike test be postponed until after the presidential election failed to gain many adherents, despite being supported by some members of the GAC and AEC. Truman himself, though he would not publicly and officially change the date, let it be known to the AEC that he "would certainly be pleased if technical reasons cause a postponement." One of the commissioners, Eugene Zuckert, was duly sent out to Eniwetok to see if any such technical reasons could be found. None could, and so, on October 30, the National

Security Council gave its approval to the series of "Ivy" tests of which Mike was a part.

A day later, at 7:15 a.m. local time on the morning of November 1 (still October 31 in the U.S.), the first Ulam-Teller hydrogen bomb to be tested exploded on the tiny island of Elugelab (less than a mile long, with an area considerably smaller than a square mile), at the northern-most tip of the Eniwetok Atoll. A few millionths of a second later, the island of Elugelab no longer existed; it had been completely vaporized by a blast that was measured at ten megatons, 800–1,000 times more power-ful than the Hiroshima bomb. The fireball from the blast was three miles wide, producing heat that, even thirty miles away, felt as if someone had opened a hot oven. The blast lifted into the air some eighty million tons of earth and seabed that would be deposited as fallout all over the world. Several thousand people were there, all of them stunned by the enormity of the explosion. "You would swear that the whole world was on fire," wrote one of them to his wife.

One person who was *not* there was Edward Teller, despite the fact that, although he had refused to have anything to do with the Los Alamos team that organized and carried out the Mike test, he was still regarded as the "father of the H-bomb." At the time the bomb went off Teller was in Berkeley, where a seismograph had been set up to monitor the seismic wave that would be produced by the explosion. The sound waves took twenty minutes to travel from Eniwetok to the California coast, but even so Teller was able to estimate the yield of the bomb before anyone at Los Alamos had heard anything. With a not entirely appropriate sense of paternal pride (the Mike test bomb was, after all, as much Marshall Holloway's "baby" as it was his), Teller sent a telegram to his former col-leagues, announcing: "It's a boy."

A week after the Mike test, this sense of triumph was notably absent among the group of scientists, including Oppenheimer, that constituted the Science Advisory Committee to the Office of Defense Mobilization. Among them was Lee DuBridge, who was strongly inclined to resign from the committee on the grounds that, as the decision to go ahead with the Mike test showed, the government had no intention of listen-ing to its scientific advisors. DuBridge was persuaded to stay, but he was hardly reassured when another member of the committee, the president of MIT, James R. Killian, leaned over to him and whispered: "Some peo-ple in the Air Force are going to be after Oppenheimer and we've got to know about it and be ready for it."

The device that obliterated the island of Elugelab was not a deliver-able bomb. This is because it used as its fusion-fuel liquid deuterium, which boils at 23.5 degrees Kelvin (minus-250 degrees Celsius). This meant that heavy and unwieldy cryogenic equipment—twenty tons of it—had to be used to maintain the deuterium at below this extremely low temperature. This, in turn, meant that the "bomb" weighed more than eighty tons, about twenty times more than the "Little Boy" fission bomb and much too heavy to be considered a practical weapon. No one doubted, however, that if the Ulam-Teller design worked with liquid deuterium, it would also work with lithium-6, which is a solid metal, perfectly suited for a practical, deliverable bomb.

The Mike test could indeed, then, be seen as, in William Borden's phrase, the "thermonuclear Trinity." Nevertheless, through its very success, it confirmed something that Oppenheimer and his dwindling (and increasingly isolated) band of political supporters had been saying for the previous four years: with a yield of ten megatons, the H-bomb was, surely, *too* big to be considered as a military weapon. Who could imagine actually using a bomb powerful enough to destroy completely, in a single moment, a large city like London or New York? This thought seems not to have diminished the sense of triumph felt by those responsible for the H-bomb's development. For Teller, particularly, even though he had not been part of the Los Alamos team responsible for the Mike test, this was a moment of celebration. Having received a detailed report of the test results, he decided to go to Princeton to keep his friend John Wheeler up to date and to thank him for the support he had given him at a time when Teller had felt shunned by other scientists with experience of nuclear armaments.

While Teller was at Princeton, Oppenheimer invited him over for a drink at Olden Manor, an occasion remembered by Teller in his memoir in the following extraordinary anecdote:

> As we sat in his living room, Oppenheimer commented that now we knew the test device worked, we should find a way to use it to bring the Korean War to a successful conclusion. I was astounded and asked how that could be done. Oppie explained that we should build a duplicate device somewhere in Korea and force the communist troops to concentrate nearby so that the detonation of the device would wipe them all out.

Then, after he had returned to Chicago, Teller received a phone call from Oppenheimer, who asked if he remembered their conversation in Princeton: "I assured him that I did. He then explained that he just wanted me to know that he had found a way to get his suggestion to President Elect Eisenhower." Teller, who "had not thought of the hydrogen bomb as designed for battlefield use, except possibly in an extreme crisis," naturally recorded that he "could not understand Oppenheimer's behavior."

The most obvious explanation, surely, is that Oppenheimer was pulling Teller's leg, teasing him about the military uselessness of his newborn "boy." Given that it was too big to transport (as Teller himself cheerfully concedes, the Mike device "was so huge and clumsy that a hundred oxcarts would barely get it to a target!"), it would have to be assembled on the spot where it was to be used, and, assuming that its purpose was to attack a *military* target and not to kill millions of civilians in a large city, then the scenario described by Oppenheimer to Teller was the *only* conceivable way in which it could be used. Of course, given the possibility of using lithium-6 as a fuel, an H-bomb *could* be made that was not vulnerable to exactly this kind of ridicule (if that is what it was), but, as we have seen, Oppenheimer did not think a transportable H-bomb was a practical military weapon either.

In the aftermath of the Mike test, Oppenheimer was evidently in a provocative frame of mind. The final report of the Disarmament Panel, which was delivered to Dean Acheson in January 1953, just before Acheson gave way to his Republican counterpart, John Foster Dulles, contained several recommendations that to Acheson would have been seen as misguided, but to Dulles would have been complete anathema. While Dulles had made clear his adherence to the policy of massive retaliation, the report recommended reducing "our commitment to the use of nuclear weapons." The five main proposals of the report were: 1. a policy of greater "candor" about nuclear weapons with regard to the American people; 2. better communication with the U.S.'s allies regarding nuclear matters; 3. greater priority and attention to air-defense systems; 4. withdrawal from the fruitless UN disarmament discussions; 5. better communications with the Soviet Union. Eisenhower was initially surprisingly sympathetic to these proposals, but in the month he received them, his first month in office, he took a step that would more or less ensure that this report had no impact whatsoever on U.S. policy: he appointed Lewis Strauss as his atomic-energy advisor.

Both Strauss and Eisenhower were present when, on February 17, 1953, Oppenheimer gave a lecture in New York to the Council on Foreign Relations that was an abridged, and somewhat censored, version of the Disarmament Panel's report. The talk, entitled "Atomic Weapons and American Policy," is notable for the directness of its style and tone— Oppenheimer, for once, abandoning his usual allusiveness in favor of plain speaking. He later said about himself and his colleagues on the Disarmament Panel that in the course of their work they "became very vividly and painfully aware of what an unregulated arms race would lead to in the course of years," and it is this awareness and a determination to communicate it that, above everything else, pervade this talk.

Oppenheimer begins with the thwarted hope, following "the bright light of the first atomic explosion," that "this might mark, not merely the end of a great and terrible war, but the end of such wars for mankind." Again, as he had done many times previously, he pins the blame for the thwarting of that hope firmly on the Soviet Union: "Openness, friendliness and cooperation did not seem to be what the Soviet government most prized on this earth." Once that hope was dashed, Oppenheimer goes on, the "Free World" took refuge behind the "shield" of nuclear bombs. "The rule for the atom was: 'Let us stay ahead. Let us be sure that we are ahead of the enemy.'" However, according to Oppenheimer, this rule is no longer sufficient, because of the nature of the arms race that it has led to. At this point, Oppenheimer makes clear, his mission to communicate the perils of that arms race runs aground because of the secrecy to which he is opposed, but to which he is nevertheless bound. "It is easy to say 'Let us look at the arms race.' I must tell about it without communicating anything. I must reveal its nature without revealing anything; and this I propose to do."

Oppenheimer could not, for example, mention the hydrogen bomb, nor did he feel able to mention two of the Disarmament Panel's five recommendations (those to do with withdrawing from UN discussions and establishing better communication with the Soviet Union). This left him with the task of putting the case publicly for the other three recommendations, concentrating in particular on the first: the need for greater candor.

"It is my opinion," Oppenheimer told his audience, "that we should all know—not precisely, but quantitatively and, above all, authoritatively—where we stand in these matters." For, he said, his experience was that when the facts of the matter were brought to the attention of "any responsible group," the result was "a great sense of anxiety and somberness." He estimated the Soviet Union to be about four years behind the U.S. in the development and stockpiling of more and more powerful nuclear weapons, but this was "likely to be small comfort" when it was realized that "our twenty-thousandth bomb . . . will not in any deep strategic sense offset their two-thousandth." Such was the terrifying nature of this arms race.

One reason Oppenheimer gave for greater candor was the importance of allowing the public to reflect, in an informed way, on the security policies that were being pursued in their name, but the details of which they were not allowed to know. Rather bravely, in the face of the political winds then blowing, Oppenheimer gave as an example of such a questionable policy the plan to use nuclear weapons and "a rather rigid commitment to their use in a very massive, initial, unremitting strategic assault on the enemy." This fresh attack on the doctrine of massive retaliation, of course, would have been duly noted by Strauss, Griggs, Borden and the rest of the military establishment.

"The prevailing view," Oppenheimer said, "is that we are probably faced with a long period of cold war in which conflict, tension and armaments are to be with us."

> The trouble then is just this: During this period the atomic clock[67] ticks faster and faster; we may anticipate a state of affairs in which two Great Powers will each be in a position to put an end to the civilization and life of the other, though not without risking its own. We may be likened to two scorpions in a bottle, each capable of killing the other, but only at the risk of his own life.

In such a situation, Oppenheimer insisted: "We need strength to be able to ask whether our plans for the use of the atom are, all things considered, right or wrong." And this is where the need for openness and candor makes itself clear, since: "We do not operate well when the important facts, the essential conditions, which limit and determine our choice are unknown. We do not operate well when they are known, in secrecy and fear, only to a few men."

In a startling display of his own candor, Oppenheimer went on to give some examples of the foolishness of trusting these "few men." The first was Truman: "It must be disturbing that an ex-President of the United States, who has been briefed on what we know about the Soviet atomic capability, can publicly call in doubt all conclusions from the evidence." The allusion here is to a statement Truman made to the press on January 26, in which he said: "I am not convinced Russia has the bomb. I am not convinced the Russians have the know-how to put the complicated mechanism together to make an A-bomb work. I am not convinced they have the bomb."

Oppenheimer's next two examples were clearly identifiable as General Groves and Arthur Compton:

---

[67] Though this talk is not generally allusive, this mention of an atomic clock *is* an allusion. It alludes to the "doomsday clock" that appeared on every cover of the *Bulletin of the Atomic Scientists* from June 1947 onward. The closer the clock is to midnight, the closer the threat of global nuclear war. The February 1953 issue of the *Bulletin* showed the clock at two minutes to midnight, the closest it had ever been.

It must be shocking when this doubt, so recently expressed, is compounded by two men, one of them a most distinguished scientist, who headed one of the great projects of the Manhattan District during the war, and one of them a brilliant officer, who was in over-all charge of the Manhattan District.

Compton, when asked about Truman's skepticism about the bomb, had delighted the President by saying that in his view it was "problematical" that the Soviets had the bomb, while Groves had told the press that the fact that there had been a nuclear explosion in Russia "does not prove that they have the bomb in workable form."

Oppenheimer then went on to cite a less readily identifiable "high officer of the Air Defense Command" who had said "only a few months ago, in a most serious discussion of measures for the continental defense of the United States," that it was "not really our policy to attempt to protect this country, for that is so big a job that it would interfere with our retaliatory capabilities." "Such follies," Oppenheimer added caustically, "can occur only when even the men who know the facts can find no one to talk to about them, when the facts are too secret for discussion, and thus for thought."

Having dealt with the need for candor at some length, Oppenheimer covered his next two points—the need for greater cooperation with allies and the importance of improving air-defense systems—much more briefly. He ended on a portentous note: "We need to be clear that there will not be many great atomic wars for us, nor for our institutions. It is important that there not be one."

It was an uncompromising and courageous speech. Somewhat surprisingly there was, initially at least, some sign that Oppenheimer's views might have an impact on the new administration. Eisenhower, impressed by the Disarmament Panel's report, and now by this speech, for the next few months encouraged the development of what became known as "Operation Candor." The fact that Eisenhower seemed sympathetic to Oppenheimer's views, however, seemed to Lewis Strauss and his allies only to make it more urgent and more important to combat, and finally to destroy once and for all, Oppenheimer's influence on American policy.

In the May issue of *Fortune* magazine appeared an article that contained the most sustained and direct assault yet on Oppenheimer's reputation. It was entitled "The Hidden Struggle for the H-bomb: The Story of Dr. Oppenheimer's Persistent Campaign to Reverse U.S. Military Strategy," and began dramatically: "A life and death struggle over national military policy has developed between a highly influential group of American scientists and the military." The "prime mover" among these scientists was identified as Oppenheimer, and the central issue at stake the tenability of the doctrine of massive retaliation. Oppenheimer, the article stated, had "no confidence in the military's assumption that SAC [Strategic Air Command] as a weapon of mass destruction is a real deterrent to Soviet action," and was asking the U.S. "to throw away its strongest weapon for defense."

The article was published anonymously, but was in fact written by Charles Murphy, a reserve officer in the U.S. Air Force and the author of a regular column in *Fortune* called "Defense and Strategy." Just as Murphy's column invariably presented the air-force view and reflected close communication with people at the very top of the air force, so this article on Oppenheimer reflected at every turn the views of Griggs, Finletter and Strauss. The May issue of *Fortune* would have gone on sale sometime in April, which means that the article was most likely written in March, soon after Oppenheimer delivered his confrontational speech in New York, so it seems natural to assume that its publication represented the rising of Strauss and the air force to what they saw as Oppenheimer's public provocation. David Lilienthal described the *Fortune* piece as "another nasty and obviously inspired article attacking Robert Oppenheimer in a snide way."

Lilienthal, surely rightly, saw the hand of Strauss at work in Murphy's attack on Oppenheimer, but at times it was the hand of Griggs that was most evident. Take, for example, this retelling of Griggs's paranoid version of the Lincoln summer school: under the byline "ZORC Takes Up the Fight," Murphy wrote:

A test of Teller's thermonuclear device was scheduled for late 1952 at Eniwetok. Oppenheimer tried to stop the test. In April 1952, Secretary Acheson appointed him to the State Department Disarmament Committee of which he became chairman. Here was generated a proposal that the President should announce that the United States had decided on humanitarian grounds not to bring the weapon to final test and that it would regard the detonation of a similar device by any other power as an act of war.

Mr. Truman was not persuaded. That project cost Oppenheimer his place on the General Advisory Committee. When his term expired that summer he was not reappointed. Neither were DuBridge nor Conant who supported him throughout. Now came a shift in tactics. At a meeting of scientists in Washington that spring there formed around Oppenheimer a group calling themselves ZORC, Z for Jerrold R. Zacharias, an MIT physicist; O for Oppenheimer; R for Rabi; and C for Charles Lauritsen.

The previous slur campaigns against Oppenheimer had been more or less confined to the secluded corridors of power. This *Fortune* article was the first shot in a *public* campaign against him, the beginning of a concerted effort to bring the disputes between Oppenheimer and the U.S. military establishment out into the open. One predictable consequence was that Oppenheimer's case came to the attention of Joseph McCarthy. On May 11, an FBI memo written by assistant director L. B. Nichols records that McCarthy's aide, Roy Cohn, had called him to ask what he thought about the McCarthy committee (the Senate Permanent Subcommittee on Investigations, to give it its official name) "calling in Oppenheimer and launching an investigation." Nichols, the memo records, told Cohn "not to be precipitous." The next day, Cohn and McCarthy visited J. Edgar Hoover to discuss the possibility of investigating Oppenheimer. In an internal FBI memo, Hoover explained how he had put McCarthy off by telling him that "a great deal of preliminary spade work" would need to be undertaken before going public with an investigation of someone as eminent and influential as Oppenheimer. Strauss, with whom Hoover was working closely with regard to Oppenheimer, subsequently wrote to Senator Robert Taft, asking him to block any attempt by McCarthy to investigate Oppenheimer. "The McCarthy committee is not the place for such an investigation," Strauss wrote, "and the present is not the time." Strauss was determined to strip Oppenheimer of his security clearance and did not want his carefully laid plans ruined by the far less meticulous operations of the senator from Wisconsin.

Oppenheimer's one-year contract as a consultant to the AEC was due to expire at the end of June 1953, and Strauss was very concerned to see that it was not renewed. In this he had a powerful ally in the FBI, the surviving files of which record what amounts to a conspiracy to oust Oppenheimer from government. On May 25, another assistant director, D. M. Ladd, wrote to Hoover to tell him that "Admiral Strauss" had been to see him because he is "still concerned about the activities of J. Robert Oppenheimer." In particular, Ladd wrote, Strauss was concerned to see that Oppenheimer had an appointment to see President Eisenhower that week. "The Admiral was wondering whether there was any objection to his briefing President Eisenhower very generally with reference to Oppenheimer's background when he, Strauss, sees the President at 3:30 this afternoon." Ladd had told Strauss that the Bureau "certainly had no objection to his briefing the President," and that, of course, he was welcome to use Oppenheimer's FBI file for that briefing.

That afternoon, at his meeting with the President, Strauss was invited to become the next chairman of the AEC. Having provided Eisenhower with a "briefing" about Oppenheimer's background, Strauss replied that he "could not do the job at the AEC if Oppenheimer was connected in any way with the program." Two days later, when Oppenheimer arrived for *his* appointment at the White House, he, in turn, gave the President a briefing, this time about Operation Candor. In the light of his earlier conversation with Strauss, however, Eisenhower's enthusiasm—both for Operation Candor and for Oppenheimer—was on the wane, and, sometime after Oppenheimer had left, Eisenhower told his aide C. D. Jackson (who happened to be the publisher of *Fortune* magazine) that he "did not completely trust" Oppenheimer.

In his war against Oppenheimer, Strauss was winning. He did not have it all his own way, though. It was still, officially, government policy to pursue (or at least to investigate the viability of pursuing) both Operation Candor and the other recommendations of the Disarmament Panel, which is why on June 5 it was decided, despite Strauss's vigorously and repeatedly expressed objections, to renew Oppenheimer's consultancy contract with the AEC for another year. He would thus have security clearance and, potentially, some influence on U.S. atomic policy until June 30, 1954. The day that decision was taken, say the authors of a long and detailed history of the AEC, "was perhaps the most fateful date in Robert Oppenheimer's life." Their remark is based on an observation of Lewis Strauss, who pointed out: "It was this contract which involved the AEC in the clearance of Dr. Oppenheimer and which required that the Commission, rather than some other agency of the Government, be made responsible to hear and resolve the charges against him."

Despite what he had said to Eisenhower, Strauss *did* accept the chairmanship of the AEC even though Oppenheimer was still connected with it. According to an FBI memo, Strauss "reluctantly agreed to accept the post of chairman of the Atomic Energy Commission effective July 1, 1953," but only after the President had "drafted" him "against his wishes":

> Strauss was advised that the Bureau desired to work closely with him in his new duties with the AEC. He commented that the only bright part in his taking over these new difficult duties was the fact that the FBI had been most cooperative with him and he felt he could rely on the Director and the Bureau in matters of mutual interest.

Within a week of taking up his duties as chairman Strauss ordered the removal from Oppenheimer's office at Princeton of all classified AEC documents, ostensibly to save the expense of hiring a security guard to protect them.

Meanwhile, in an effort to keep the recommendations of the Disarmament Panel alive, Oppenheimer had his New York lecture, "Atomic Weapons and American Policy," published in two separate places in the summer of 1953. It appeared in the July issues of both *Foreign Affairs* and the *Bulletin of the Atomic Scientists*, the journals being chosen, no doubt, in order to maximize the exposure of his views to both politicians and scientists. What the appearance of the *Fortune* article in May signaled, however, was that Strauss was winning his war against Oppenheimer among the media as well as among the politicians, for the owner and editor-in-chief of *Fortune* was Henry Luce, who was also owner and editor-in-chief of both *Time* and *Life*. The days of those two latter magazines carrying long, admiring profiles of Oppenheimer were over.

Indeed, on the occasion of Strauss's appointment as chair of the AEC, *Time* published an admiring, albeit short, profile of *him*. Under the heading "Dissenter's Return," the piece made clear where the magazine's sympathies now lay in the battle between Strauss and Oppenheimer:

> To Dissenter Strauss, more than any other man, the U.S. owes its possession of the hydrogen bomb. In 1950, after a long fight against the combined forces of prestige-heavy atomic scientists such as Dr. Robert Oppenheimer and all other Atomic Energy commissioners save Gordon Dean, Strauss persuaded Harry Truman that the U.S. should proceed with construction of the H-bomb.
>
> Weary of his constant battle with the other commissioners, Strauss resigned from the AEC in 1950, and returned to New York to become financial adviser to the Rockefellers. Last week, as he prepared to move back into the AEC building, Lewis Strauss was hailed by Democrats and Republicans alike as one of the President's best appointments.

Oppenheimer's campaign for openness, disarmament and dialogue with the Soviet Union received a devastating setback in August 1953, when it was announced that the Soviets had tested their first hydrogen bomb. Nicknamed "Joe 4," the Soviet device, having a yield of "only" 400 kilotons, was a puny thing compared to the ten-megaton Mike blast, but, in other respects, it was possible to argue that the Soviets were *ahead* in the arms race. For Joe 4 used lithium-6 deuteride as its fuel, which meant that, unlike Mike, it was a deployable bomb. On the other hand, its basic design was crude compared to the technical "sweetness" of the Ulam-Teller bomb, and some comfort could be taken from the fact that, until the Soviets discovered what Ulam and Teller had discovered—namely that radiation, rather than neutrons, should be used to bring about the fusion reaction—they would not be able to develop a "true" H-bomb—that is, one with a yield in the megaton range. However, whatever comfort this provided was dispelled by the realization that it was only a matter of time before the Soviet scientists discovered the principle of the Ulam-Teller design, and the sheer fear induced by the brute fact that the Soviet Union had the H-bomb. Those who had argued that the U.S. should develop the Super quickly before the Soviets got there, it now seemed, had had their view confirmed.

In the wake of the news of the Soviet H-bomb, the chances of Oppenheimer getting a sympathetic hearing for Operation Candor shrank to almost zero. The September 7 edition of *Life* magazine carried an editorial discussing Oppenheimer's "Atomic Weapons and American Policy," which it characterized as presenting "the opposition to present U.S. policy." What was meant by "present U.S. policy," it seems, was massive retaliation:

> We have supposed the only major deterrent to atomic aggression is our ability to hit back even harder—to apply swift and terrible retribution. But this policy Dr. Oppenheimer implies is a spur or a goad to the Soviet Union. As an alternative, Dr. Oppenheimer calls for a heroic effort to improve our atomic defenses . . .
>
> His argument is an echo of an old line of appeasement for which there is in the world a curious lingering nostalgia . . . no purely defensive effort, however mighty, can ever deter an aggressor bent on atomic attack.
>
> This would seem to leave us no choice at all but steadily to build our air fleets and our atomic stockpiles. Any change in accent or emphasis that detracts from our power to hit back weakens our hand in the world.

A month later, following Eisenhower's statement that, in light of the fact that "the Soviets now have the capability of atomic attack on us," the U.S. did not intend "to disclose the details of our strength in atomic weapons of any sort," the *Life* editorial declared:

> First, it can be inferred, hopefully, that we have heard the end of "Operation Candor." That half-baked phrase, implying that the public have hitherto been deceived, had two versions. One, recommended by J. Robert Oppenheimer, would have disclosed military secrets, such as the size of our atomic stockpile, which Chairman Strauss says would be much more meaningful to Soviet strategists than to American opinion. This Eisenhower has decided against.

Two weeks later the cover of *Time* magazine featured none other than "U.S. Atom Boss Lewis Strauss." The article accompanying the front cover began with a description of the "radioactive air mass from Siberia" that indicated the Russians had exploded a thermonuclear bomb. "To a quiet, courtly Virginian of deep religious faith and independent character," the article went on, "the cloud was a vindication of a rather lonely fight."

> Had it not been for Strauss's personal convictions about Russian intentions, back in late 1949, the U.S. might have had no thermonuclear superbomb of its own. Conceivably, the new Russian bomb could have been hurled on the world as an unchallengeable ultimatum, could by this week have changed the political balance of power around the world.

At the end of October 1953, the commitment of the U.S. government to a policy of massive retaliation was made official when the President gave his approval to the policies outlined in the National Security Council policy document NSC 162/2. The "primary threat to the security, free institutions, and fundamental values of the United States," the document says, is posed by the Soviet Union. Stalin may have died, and there may continue to be in the short term some uncertainty about who will replace him, but: "The Soviet leaders can be expected to continue to base their policy on the conviction of irreconcilable hostility between the bloc and the non-communist world."

In addition: "The capability of the USSR to attack the United States with atomic weapons had been continuously growing and will be materially enhanced by hydrogen weapons." Air defense will be useful, "but will not eliminate the chance of a crippling blow." In the face of the Soviet threat, the policy document declares, the security of the United States requires the development and maintenance of "a strong military posture, with emphasis on the capability of inflicting massive retaliatory damage by offensive striking power." The ideas that Oppenheimer had spent the last four years arguing against were now explicitly embodied in U.S. policy. Meanwhile, those who considered Oppenheimer to be not simply mistaken, but actually treasonous, were moving in for the kill.

18

Falsus in uno[68]

William Borden's time as executive director of the Joint Committee on Atomic Energy finished at the end of May 1953. A week or two before he left, while he still had security clearance, he was given Oppenheimer's AEC security file by Strauss in order to make a close study of it. After he left the committee he no longer had any kind of government job, and should therefore have given the file back. However, quite illegally, Strauss let him keep it for a further three months. Ever since Strauss had been told that Klaus Fuchs had not acted alone, that there had been another Soviet spy at Los Alamos, he had suspected that Oppenheimer was that second spy, and he was hoping that Borden would be able to substantiate that claim sufficiently well for a solid case to be made for stripping Oppenheimer of his security clearance.

As he studied the FBI file, Borden became obsessed with the details of the case, which, he came to believe, pointed to the conclusion that Oppenheimer was indeed a Soviet agent. In the autumn of 1953 Borden prepared his own summary of the evidence, which, at just three and a half pages, was much shorter than the various FBI summaries and, Borden believed, much clearer. On November 7, he sent his summary to J. Edgar Hoover, telling him: "The purpose of this letter is to state my own exhaustively considered opinion, based upon years of study of the available classified evidence, that more probably than not J. Robert Oppenheimer is an agent of the Soviet Union." His summary organizes the evidence into four groups, though it is not entirely clear what

------

[68] The title is an allusion to the Latin phrase *falsus in uno, falsus in omnibus*, which means "false in one, false in all." In law the phrase is used to indicate that, if a witness has been shown to lie once, then his or her entire testimony cannot be trusted.

the organizing principle is. The first group lists all the evidence that Oppenheimer—through his friends, his colleagues, his brother, his wife and his "mistress" (Jean Tatlock)—had close links with the Communist Party. The second group consists mostly of things that have little or no bearing on the question of whether or not he was a Soviet agent (for example, "In April 1942 his name was formally submitted for security clearance"), except the last, which accuses Oppenheimer of having lied to Groves and the FBI. The third group is mostly about the sharp difference between Oppenheimer's attitudes to the atomic and hydrogen bombs before the war (when he was enthusiastic about them) and after the war (when his enthusiasm for them evaporated). And the fourth group concerns Oppenheimer's alleged use of his influence in the postwar period to retard U.S. defense projects, most notably the development of the hydrogen bomb.

None of this, of course, amounted to evidence that Oppenheimer had acted as a Soviet agent, and nor was any of it news to Hoover. Perhaps for that reason Hoover waited nearly three weeks before doing anything with Borden's letter. During that time, suspicions about Oppenheimer were being raised all over Washington and beyond. On November 12, the *Evening Star* newspaper ran a story under the heading "FBI Report on Vast Spy Ring Shocked U.S. Leaders in 1945," which contained the statement: "A top atomic scientist was a Communist and had been approached to furnish atomic bomb secrets from the Manhattan Project to the Soviet Consulate in San Francisco through professors at the University of California." As an FBI memo of November 18 concedes, this information came from a 1945 summary of Soviet espionage in the United States that the FBI had leaked to HUAC. "In addition," the memo says, "it appears members of the press have been informed of the material appearing in the summary."

Around the same time, Borden sent versions of his letter to various members of the Joint Committee on Atomic Energy, who in turn showed it to the Republican senator Bourke B. Hickenlooper, a man known as a fervent anti-communist. Evidently Borden was anxious that his letter be acted upon. The pressure on Hoover to do *something* with Borden's letter mounted when, on November 24, Joseph McCarthy— whose interest in Oppenheimer was by this time well known—delivered a speech, broadcast on both radio and television, in which he accused the Eisenhower administration of "whining, whimpering appeasement" in its dealings with communists. Three days later, Hoover distributed copies of Borden's letter to the President, Attorney General Herbert Brownell, Defense Secretary Charles Wilson and Lewis Strauss. On December 3, Eisenhower ordered that a "blank wall" be constructed separating

Oppenheimer from atomic secrets. From that day on, Oppenheimer's security clearance was suspended.

Oppenheimer himself had been in London since early November and was blithely unaware of Borden's letter to Hoover and the chain of events it had set off. The suspension of Oppenheimer's security clearance was for the moment kept secret, not only from the press, but also from Oppenheimer himself, who, the FBI believed, might flee to the Soviet Union if he knew what was happening in Washington. Oppenheimer had gone to London in order to give the Reith Lectures, a series of six talks sponsored each year by the BBC. To be chosen as a Reith Lecturer was a great honor, and Oppenheimer attracted a good deal of publicity. A photograph in the *Sunday Express* on November 15, 1953, shows the forty-nine-year-old wandering alone through London's Mayfair district, wearing an expensive-looking three-piece suit and his famous pork-pie hat, with a cigarette in his left hand. The accompanying text, ironically, concentrates on his freedom: "He moves about as a free man. Free, that is, from the hordes of G-men who dogged his steps when he went to France and Germany in 1951." In fact, his every step was being watched by the FBI.

The following week, Oppenheimer was the subject of an admiring profile in *The Observer*, which unwittingly contained some phrases that would have struck an ominous note back in Washington:

> He is said to have done more than anyone to make Congressmen understand the implications of nuclear fission. Like most of his colleagues, he was appalled by the destructive power which had been unleashed, and his first reaction was to suppose that the atom bomb made future wars unthinkable and national sovereignty obsolete. He was an early advocate of sharing the secrets with Russia, and of jointly controlling the manufacture of bombs . . . In public and private he has constantly opposed the United States policy of extreme secrecy in atomic matters.

As for the Reith Lectures themselves, they were generally regarded by their British audience as something of a disappointment. As *The Economist* put it: "Something different was expected from the man who had engineered the mightiest scientific experiment in history." The advertised aim of the lectures, the overall title of which was "Science and the Common Understanding," was to examine "what there is new in atomic physics that is relevant, helpful and inspiriting for men to know," but this promised more novelty than Oppenheimer delivered. The disappointment was "at finding that the ideas expressed are, on the whole, familiar ones." What Oppenheimer had to say turned out to be "an oft-told tale." By "new in atomic physics" Oppenheimer seemed to mean "atomic physics as it was thirty years ago," since his focus was on the "heroic period" of quantum physics in the 1920s, and even then he spent a long time getting there. His first lecture was on Newton, his second on Rutherford and his third on Bohr and the "old" quantum theory. Only in the fourth lecture did he get on to the wave-particle duality at the heart of quantum mechanics, together with the notion that was always at the heart of his thinking: complementarity. The fifth lecture attempts to show how the notion of complementarity can be applied outside physics, to an understanding of human nature and society, for example; and the sixth lecture rounds the whole thing off with a series of more or less empty platitudes, such as the following, which is the concluding sentence:

> For us as for all men, change and eternity, specialization and unity, instrument and final purpose, community and individual man alone, complementary each to the other, both require and define our bonds and our freedom.

Rarely have so many words been used to say so little. The contrast, both in style and content, with "Atomic Weapons and American Policy" could not be greater. There, he had something urgent to say that he wanted to communicate as clearly as possible; here, in the Reith Lectures, his wordy and obscure style seems designed to disguise the fact that he really has nothing to say. Robert Crease's damning phrase about Oppenheimer's public lectures—that they are "rhetorically evocative and conceptually stagnant"—is in general somewhat unfair, but about the Reith Lectures it is devastatingly accurate.

Only twice does Oppenheimer's style free itself from the verbose torpor that characterizes the lectures as a whole. The first time is in the second lecture, when he takes a digression from Rutherford to talk about more recent developments, describing how "the story of sub-nuclear matter began to unfold and ramify":

> A whole new family of hitherto unknown, and, for the most part, unrecognised and unexpected objects began to emerge from the nuclear encounters. The first of these were the various mesons, some charged and some uncharged, about ten times lighter than the proton and some hundreds of times heavier than the electron. In the last years there have appeared in increasing variety objects heavier than the mesons, other objects heavier even than protons, whose names are still being changed from month to month, by solemn confer-

ences. Physicists call them vaguely, and rather helplessly, "the new particles." They are without exception unstable, as in the neutron. They disintegrate after a time which varies from one millionth to less than a billionth of a second into other lighter components. Some of these components are in turn unfamiliar to physics and are themselves in turn unstable. We do not know how to give a clear meaning to this question. We do not know why they have the mass and charge they do, or anything much about them. They are the greatest puzzle in today's physics.

If only, one can imagine the British audiences thinking, he had chosen this as his subject.

The second time the lectures come to life is when Oppenheimer touches on the question of whether there will ever be a scientific explanation of consciousness. "It seems rather unlikely," he says, "that we shall be able to describe in physio-chemical terms the physiological phenomena which accompany a conscious thought or sentiment, or will."

Today the outcome is uncertain. Whatever the outcome, we know that, should an understanding of the physical correlate of elements of consciousness indeed be available, it will not be the appropriate description for the thinking man himself, for the clarification of his thoughts, the resolution of his will, or the delight of his eye and mind at works of beauty. Indeed an understanding of the complementary nature of conscious life and its physical interpretation appears to me a lasting element in human understanding and a proper formulation of the historic views called psycho-physical parallelism.

When the lectures were over, Oppenheimer and Kitty went first to Copenhagen to see Bohr and then to Paris, where, with security officers watching their every step, they called on the person who, of all the people in the world, Oppenheimer should *not* have been seen visiting at this time: Haakon Chevalier. Chevalier had been living in Paris for three years, working as a translator. "It was a happy reunion," Chevalier later remembered. The next day, he took Oppenheimer to meet André Malraux and listened "to an extraordinary dialogue between these two men, so different in mind and temperament, but each supreme in his field." The conversation got on to Einstein, and Oppenheimer shocked both Malraux and Chevalier by remarking: "It is very sad for us who are close to Einstein and have such enormous respect for his early contribution, to have to say that for the past twenty-five years Einstein has done no science."

Oppenheimer and Kitty returned from Europe on December 13, 1953. Waiting for Oppenheimer was an urgent message to call Strauss as soon as he could. When Oppenheimer called him the next day, Strauss told him "it might be a good idea" for them to meet in the next day or two. Having been told by the FBI that they needed more time to examine Borden's letter, however, Strauss got in touch with Oppenheimer and put off their meeting till December 21. This gave Strauss time to consult others on how to deal with Oppenheimer. At a high-level meeting at the Oval Office on December 18, involving Vice President Nixon and Allen Dulles of the CIA, it was decided to present Oppenheimer with the charges against him and offer him two possible responses: he could either resign as an AEC consultant or he could appeal against the suspension of his security clearance in front of a panel appointed by Strauss.

When Oppenheimer arrived at Strauss's office on the afternoon of December 21, he was met by both Strauss and General Kenneth Nichols, the recently appointed general manager of the AEC. Nichols had known Oppenheimer ever since the early days of the Manhattan Project and had developed an antipathy toward him almost as strong as Strauss's. After a few pleasantries about the recent sudden death of Deak Parsons, Strauss told Oppenheimer that, in the light of a presidential order of April 27, 1953, requiring the reevaluation of all individuals about whom there was "derogatory information" in their files, his security clearance had been suspended. It seems strange that Oppenheimer did not point out, upon hearing this, that his most recent reappointment as a consultant in June 1953 had occurred after this presidential order and so was presumably in accordance with its requirements, but he was evidently too shocked to think clearly. In any case he possibly did not have time to react in this way before Strauss followed up this shock with an even worse one. A letter had been drafted, Strauss told Oppenheimer, listing all the charges against him. The letter, which ran to eight pages, was then handed to Oppenheimer.

Written, but not yet signed, by General Nichols, the letter consisted of yet another summary of Oppenheimer's FBI file, running once more over the list of communist front organizations to which he had belonged in the 1930s and '40s, the number of communists among his family and friends, his opposition to the hydrogen bomb and, above all, the Chevalier Affair and Oppenheimer's delay in reporting it, all of which, the letter alleged, "raise questions as to your veracity, conduct and even your loyalty." "Accordingly," the letter continued, "your employment on Atomic Energy Commission work and your eligibility for access to restricted data are hereby suspended, effective immediately." Finally, the letter informed Oppenheimer that, if he wanted to contest these charges and the suspension of his security clearance, he had the "privilege" of appearing before an AEC personal security board. Strauss gave Oppenheimer as little leeway as possible in responding to this letter, allowing him only until the following day to decide whether or not to take up his "privilege" and refusing his request for a copy of the letter. It seems that Strauss and Nichols hoped Oppenheimer would resign, in which case the as-yet-unsigned letter could be destroyed and forgotten about.

Obviously shaken by the turn of events, Oppenheimer, after leaving Strauss's office, went to see Joe Volpe, the former AEC lawyer, the two of them being joined soon afterward by Oppenheimer's own lawyer, Herb Marks. Unknown to them, their conversation was recorded by hidden microphones installed at Strauss's request. At the end of the evening Oppenheimer took the train back to Princeton to talk it over with Kitty. Shortly after noon the next day, he received a call from Nichols, telling him he had just three more hours to reach a decision. An hour later, Oppenheimer called back to tell Nichols that he would give his decision in person the following morning.

That afternoon Oppenheimer and Kitty traveled to Washington, where, together with Marks and Volpe, they drafted a letter rejecting the idea that he should resign, on the grounds that such an action "would mean that I accept and concur in the view that I am not fit to serve this government that I have served now for some twelve years. This I cannot do." Rather than implicitly concede his guilt, he would subject himself to the ordeal of a security hearing. In the meantime, his access to restricted documents would remain suspended, as was forcibly brought home to him two days later—Christmas Eve—when representatives of the AEC arrived in Princeton with a letter telling Oppenheimer that he was "hereby directed to deliver" all remaining AEC documents in his possession. The same day, he received the letter from General Nichols that he had looked through in Strauss's office. This time it was signed.

On January 1, 1954, in accordance with the wishes of Strauss, the telephones in Oppenheimer's home and Princeton office were tapped and he himself was put under close surveillance, followed wherever he went. When the FBI agent in Newark found himself listening to conversations between Oppenheimer and his lawyers, he contacted Hoover's office expressing concern about the legality and propriety of the procedure, "in view of the fact that it might disclose attorney–client relations." As disclosing attorney–client relations was precisely the point of the surveillance (Strauss was reported to have commented to an FBI agent that "the Bureau's technical coverage on Oppenheimer at Princeton had been most helpful to the AEC in that they were aware beforehand of the moves he was contemplating"), the agent was reassured that it was all right, that such surveillance was necessary to alert the authorities to any plans Oppenheimer might have to flee the country.

In the New Year of 1954, Oppenheimer, advised by both Marks and Volpe, considered who should represent him at the hearing. Volpe thought he needed a trial lawyer, someone with experience of the cut and thrust of the courtroom. Marks, on the other hand, influenced partly by the fact that the hearing was, officially at any rate, not actually a trial, but rather an inquiry, thought Oppenheimer needed someone eminent and distinguished, instead of a tough courtroom fighter. So it was that the genteel Lloyd Garrison was chosen. Garrison lacked courtroom experience, but was from a distinguished family and was an extremely educated man. In his spare time he read philosophy and Greek literature.

"The fact that this clearance has been suspended is presently classified information," Nichols had emphasized in a letter circulated to the army, navy, air force and AEC installations. Nevertheless, news of it began to spread around Washington in early January. On January 2, Rabi, in his role as chairman of the GAC, went to see Strauss to tell him that he hoped the security board would "whitewash Oppenheimer," a suggestion that Strauss dismissed out of hand. Not long afterward Vannevar Bush told Strauss that news of Oppenheimer's suspension and forthcoming hearing was "all over town."

On January 25, Oppenheimer went to Rochester to attend the fourth in the series of conferences there on high-energy physics. The conference lasted three days and concentrated mainly on the properties of the unstable "new particles" that Oppenheimer had described in his Reith Lectures as "the greatest puzzle in today's physics." One important recent development in this field much discussed during the conference was the classification of some of those particles into two categories: hyperons, which are heavier than neutrons (an example is the Lambda hyperon, which decays into a proton and a negatively charged pi-meson), and K-particles, which are intermediate in mass between a proton and a pi-meson. What Oppenheimer had described a few years earlier as the "particle zoo" was showing no signs of becoming either less puzzling or less interesting.

Oppenheimer not only took part in the discussion of this conference, but also chaired its opening session on "Nucleon-Nucleon Scattering and Polarization." According to Jeremy Bernstein, Oppenheimer even played a "leading role" at the conference, though he adds: "I don't know how closely he had been following the physics." Those taking notes at the conference were, Bernstein says, at pains "to record Oppenheimer's often Delphic remarks." When he reread those remarks, one thing that struck Bernstein was "just how gratuitously nasty Oppenheimer could be when he thought his time was being wasted":

> My thesis adviser, the late Abraham Klein, who was then a young, very junior faculty member at Harvard, gave one of the lectures. He came to a problem and inquired if it was safe to assume that everyone was familiar with it. The notes read: "Oppenheimer remarked that it was not safe to assume that everybody was familiar with this, but it was also not safe to assume that this is any reason for discussing it."

Abraham Pais was there, too, and also reread the notes taken at the conference. What struck him was "how unusually quiet Robert had been at that time."

Neither Pais nor Bernstein knew about the suspension of Oppenheimer's clearance and his imminent security hearing, though there were several there who did, among them Edward Teller. "I'm sorry to hear about your trouble," Teller told Oppenheimer when they met between sessions. "I suppose, I hope, that you don't think that anything I did has sinister implications?" Oppenheimer replied. When Teller assured him that he did not, Oppenheimer asked him if he would speak to his new attorney, Garrison. At this point Oppenheimer knew nothing about Teller's meetings with FBI agents, and Teller knew nothing about the Chevalier Affair. When Teller met Garrison (and Marks), therefore, the issue that figured most in their conversation was the hydrogen bomb, in connection with which Teller was able to assure them that, though he and Oppenheimer disagreed, he did not think Oppenheimer was disloyal. After his meeting with Oppenheimer's lawyers, Teller later said, he left with the determination that "I would testify that Oppenheimer was a loyal citizen." Garrison, however, decided that Teller's dislike of Oppenheimer was so intense and so obvious "that I finally concluded not to call him as a witness."

By this time Strauss had chosen his own lawyer to represent the AEC at the hearing. The man in question was Roger Robb, who had a reputation as one of Washington's toughest trial lawyers. Almost immediately Robb was granted an "emergency Q clearance," which enabled him to immerse himself in Oppenheimer's FBI files, as a result of which he became convinced that "Oppenheimer was a Communist and a Russian sympathizer." Having read through the FBI material, Robb flew out to California to meet some of the scientists—Teller, Alvarez, Lawrence, Pitzer and Wendell Latimer—who were on record as having doubts about Oppenheimer's loyalty. However, the strategy he was developing would in fact focus less on Oppenheimer's alleged disloyalty, which, Robb knew, would be difficult (if not impossible) to prove, than on his "veracity," legitimate doubts about which would be very easy to demonstrate: all one had to do was to draw the hearing's attention again and again to the Chevalier Affair and to Oppenheimer's documented lies on the subject. He intended to mention the affair as early as possible at the hearing. "My theory," he later said, "was that if I could shake Oppenheimer at the beginning, he would be apt to be more communicative thereafter."

Garrison, meanwhile, was unable to study the FBI file since he did not have clearance. In January he applied for clearance on behalf of himself and his two colleagues, Herb Marks and Sam Silverman. When the AEC replied that they were willing to clear Garrison but not Marks and Silverman, Garrison responded by withdrawing his application for clearance. It was a fatal error, Garrison's justification for which reveals a fundamental misunderstanding of what he and Oppenheimer were up against. "We thought," Garrison said:

> that if we had clearance, the Personal Security Board might more readily be drawn into an examination of the technical pros and cons of proceeding with H-bomb development and with other aspects of defense related to it. They could thereby lose the main point, which is that if Dr. Oppenheimer's motives were honorable, his technical recommendations were irrelevant.

From the start, Garrison's defense of Oppenheimer took the "whole man" approach, which sought to rise above the "dredging up of all these little incidents from his past" by relying on the testimony of "men of the highest integrity and reputation," who would vouch that Oppenheimer—considered, as it were, in the round—could be entrusted with atomic secrets. If he had known what Robb's strategy was going to be, Garrison would have realized that this "whole man" approach was useless, and that the possibility of "an examination of the technical pros and cons of proceeding with H-bomb development" was the least of his worries.

For, although Borden in his letter to Hoover makes much of Oppenheimer's postwar doubts about the hydrogen bomb, and despite the fact that it was Oppenheimer's attitude to the hydrogen bomb that had aroused the suspicion and hostility of most of the people Robb would call upon to testify against Oppenheimer—Griggs, Teller, Alvarez, and so on—it was never Robb's intention to rest his case on those doubts. Indeed, concentrating on Oppenheimer's views about the hydrogen bomb might be counterproductive; it might give the impression that

Oppenheimer was being attacked for his opinions, which might arouse sympathy for him.

No, Robb's case against Oppenheimer would center squarely upon the Chevalier Affair as a cast-iron demonstration of Oppenheimer's lack of veracity. There was an obvious drawback to this approach, which was that Oppenheimer had been cleared several times *after* it had been known that he had delayed reporting the Chevalier Affair and that he had lied about it. However, between them, Strauss and Robb developed a way of overcoming this drawback, based on the claim that, since Oppenheimer had been cleared, the rules for granting and maintaining security clearance had been changed.

This is why the letter from Nichols mentions Executive Order 10450 of April 27, 1953, which, the letter claims, "requires the suspension of employment of any individual where there exists information indicating that his employment may not be clearly consistent with the interests of the national security." The issues at stake here have been discussed very illuminatingly in print by Harold Green, who was a legal officer with the AEC at the time of the suspension of Oppenheimer's clearance and who, in fact, drafted the letter that was signed by Nichols. In an article he published in the *Bulletin of the Atomic Scientists* in 1977 entitled "The Oppenheimer Case: A Study in the Abuse of Law," Green emphasizes the importance of what he describes as "the ideological struggle over the concept of security" that was being fought at the time of Oppenheimer's suspension.

The struggle was between upholders of two different concepts of security: the "Caesar's wife" concept and the "whole man" concept. The phrase "Caesar's wife" comes from the motto "Caesar's wife must be above suspicion," which dates from the time that Julius Caesar's second wife, Pompeia, was suspected of adultery. Caesar divorced her, not because he believed her to be guilty, but merely because the question of her guilt had been raised. "My wife," he famously declared, "ought not even to be under suspicion."

The "Caesar's wife" concept of security, in Green's words, held that "if there was any significant derogatory information at all that might be true, clearance should not be granted; and there was no need to waste time and money in trying to find out whether or not the information was true." The "whole man" approach, on the other hand, held that "it was unfair to those enmeshed in the security net and to the atomic energy program itself to deny security clearance merely on the basis of derogatory information without giving the individual an opportunity to set the record straight and without considering favorable information that might outweigh the blemishes, as well as the importance of the individual to the nuclear program."

Among the upholders of the "Caesar's wife" concept were J. Edgar Hoover and Lewis Strauss, but, despite this, it was the "whole man" concept that prevailed at the AEC, which is how Oppenheimer "and others with blemished backgrounds" (in Green's words) were granted clearance. Executive Order 10450, however, was, according to Green, "widely interpreted as requiring agencies to use the 'Caesar's wife' approach." The AEC, though, was an exception to this requirement, as was made explicitly clear in a letter to the AEC from the Deputy Attorney General, William P. Rogers, dated June 8, 1953, in which he reassured the AEC that, as its preexisting security program "exceeds the minimum standards of Executive Order 10450," no change was required in the AEC's approach to security. In other words, the claim that the rules had changed since Oppenheimer had previously been cleared was spurious. There was no requirement on Strauss and Nichols to apply to Oppenheimer the "Caesar's wife" concept of security that was widely believed to be embodied in Executive Order 10450.

When it came to choosing the members of the Security Board, Strauss and the lawyer acting on his behalf, William Mitchell, ignored Harold Green's advice to go for people with experience of AEC Personal Security Boards and instead selected people on the basis that their hostility to Oppenheimer could more or less be assumed. Indeed, says Green: "My knowledge that a 'hanging jury' was being chosen was one of the reasons that I asked to be relieved of any further role in the case." (The other reason was his shocked disapproval of the tactic of bugging Oppenheimer's conversations with his defense team and then making those conversations available to Robb.) The first man to be selected for the board, and the man chosen to chair it, was Gordon Gray, the politically conservative president of the University of South Carolina. The other two members were the equally conservative Thomas Morgan, chairman of the Sperry Corporation, and Ward Evans, a retired chemistry professor, who had served on AEC security panels before and had a record of repeatedly voting to deny clearance.

During the first two months of 1954, Oppenheimer, Garrison and Marks worked on their "whole man" defense, which had two main strands. The first was an autobiography written by Oppenheimer that would serve as his reply to Nichols's letter, arguing that the derogatory information listed in this letter "cannot be fairly understood except in the context of my life and my work." Second, Garrison would call a series of eminent witnesses to vouch for Oppenheimer's character and loyalty.

The list of witnesses assembled for this purpose was indeed impressive, including as it did ten present or former members of the GAC, five former AEC commissioners, two Nobel Prize–winning physicists and a third who would win it some years later, two Los Alamos security officers and the head of the Manhattan Project himself, General Groves. The list of witnesses on the other side was much less impressive, consisting of four scientists from the University of California, two air-force officers, an air-force scientist, one security officer and William Borden.

Apart from the security officer, Boris Pash, all the witnesses in the anti-Oppenheimer camp were restricted to giving testimony that related to the postwar period—concerning Oppenheimer's alleged retardation of the hydrogen-bomb project, his attempts to undermine the policy of massive retaliation, his opposition to the Livermore laboratory and so on—none of which had a very large role to play in Robb's strategy. Besides the reasons detailed above for not giving prominence to Oppenheimer's opposition to the hydrogen bomb, a new and powerful reason for not doing so was provided on March 1, 1954, when the Bravo test at Bikini Atoll seemed to provide a vivid and lethal demonstration that Oppenheimer and Conant had been right all along: a hydrogen bomb was simply *too* powerful to be considered as a weapon of war.

The device tested at Bikini, under the supervision of Los Alamos rather than the new Livermore laboratory, was a Ulam-Teller design H-bomb, using enriched lithium as its fuel. Like the Soviet device tested the previous August, this was a usable bomb, but, like the Mike blast of November 1952, its yield was measured in megatons rather than kilotons. Indeed, at fifteen megatons, its yield was more than twice what had been predicted, and to this day it remains the largest explosive ever detonated by the United States. It was this test that alerted the world in dramatic fashion to the awe-inspiring power of the H-bomb, and, in particular, to the dangers of radioactive fallout.

More than seventy miles away from Bikini at the time of the blast, a Japanese fishing boat, the *Fukuryu Maru* ("Lucky Dragon"), was trawling for tuna when its crew reported seeing "flashes of fire, as bright as the sun itself, rising to the sky." Six minutes later they heard the sound of the explosion, "like the sound of many thunders rolled into one." Then they saw a cloud rise in the sky, and about two or three hours later a fine white ash began to fall. Within a few days the entire crew of twenty-three fishermen was feeling unwell, and when they arrived back in Tokyo they were diagnosed with severe radiation sickness. In September, one of them was to die of the radiation poisoning. Already in March, six months earlier, *Life* magazine was reporting the incident under the heading "First Casualties of the H-Bomb": "The scientists had warned of the power of the hydrogen bomb, but in abstract language that did not fully register with Americans until last week when fantastic news came filtering across the Pacific." A subsequent editorial asked: "Is the strategy of retaliation as realistic as it seemed before March 1?" Clearly, this was not a good time to advance an argument based on the assumption that the H-bomb was self-evidently a good thing that made the United States safe, or to suggest that to doubt the wisdom of the policy of massive retaliation was evidence of being dangerously disloyal.

The day after the Bravo test, Garrison and Marks went to see Strauss to offer a deal that would make the security hearing unnecessary: if Strauss and Nichols would withdraw the letter of charges and restore Oppenheimer's clearance, Oppenheimer would resign his consultancy. Strauss, having rigged the process to the point where he could hardly lose, was having none of it. What they had proposed, he told Garrison and Marks, was "out of the question." Either Oppenheimer offered his resignation now, or the hearing would go ahead.

So, on March 4, Oppenheimer put the finishing touches to his long autobiographical letter to Nichols, in which he formally requested a hearing. After detailing his involvement in communist front organizations in the 1930s, his personal connections with communists, his work at Los Alamos and his postwar work as a government advisor, Oppenheimer's letter ended:

> In preparing this letter, I have reviewed two decades of my life. I have recalled instances where I acted unwisely. What I have hoped was, not that I could wholly avoid error, but that I might learn from it. What I have learned has, I think, made me more fit to serve my country.

The letter was delivered to the AEC the next day, and shortly thereafter a date for the hearing was announced: April 12, 1954.

The hearing was to last three and a half grueling weeks, during which events in Oppenheimer's past were subjected to excruciatingly intense scrutiny. Because of this, and because Oppenheimer had chosen to reply to the original charges with an autobiography, the hearings were sometimes regarded as laying bare his life. He himself, however, always reacted strongly against this notion. He said toward the end of his life: "The records printed in so many hundred pages of fine print in 1954. My big year, I've heard people say, and my life story complete in those records. But it isn't so. Almost nothing that was important to me came out there, almost nothing that meant anything to me is in those records."

He also reacted angrily to the suggestion that the hearing was a "tragedy." It was, he said, much more of a farce. He had a point. There were indeed several farcical features to the proceedings. For example, because his counsel never received the emergency clearance that had been granted to Robb, whenever—as happened frequently—Robb read from classified documents, Garrison and Marks had to leave the room. Moreover, because Robb had access to documents that Garrison had never seen, and could never see, and as he had foreknowledge of everything Garrison and Marks planned to do, whereas they had no knowledge at all of what he intended to do, the element of surprise was always on his side. There was, in addition, the farcical situation that Oppenheimer's side had prepared their defense in ignorance of the rules of the game. They thought they had to show that, considered as a whole, Oppenheimer was a loyal citizen of the United States and a valuable person to consult on atomic matters, not that he was, as Caesar's wife should have been, above suspicion.

The first day of the hearing, Monday, April 12, was taken up mainly by the reading out first of Nichols's letter to Oppenheimer and then of Oppenheimer's long, autobiographical reply, at the end of which the chairman, Gordon Gray, reminded everyone that "this proceeding is an inquiry and not in the nature of a trial." During the second day, Oppenheimer, prompted by gentle questions from Garrison, gave a detailed account of his work with the GAC and the development of his views on the hydrogen bomb. When Robb had a chance to cross-examine Oppenheimer on the third day, April 14, he revealed that *his* interests lay elsewhere. Throughout the morning he fired questions at Oppenheimer, not about the hydrogen bomb, but about his connections with communists, with Frank, Lomanitz, Bohm and Peters; then, at the end of the morning, just before lunch, he moved in for the kill. "Doctor," he began:

> on page 22 of your letter of March 4, 1954, you speak of what for convenience I will call the Eltenton-Chevalier incident. Would you please, sir, tell the board as accurately as you can, and in as much detail as you can, exactly what Chevalier said to you, and you said to Chevalier, on the occasion that you mention on page 22 of your answer?

Oppenheimer then offered the following account:

> One day, and I believe you have the time fixed better than I do, in the winter of 1942–3, Haakon Chevalier came to our home. It was, I believe, for dinner, but possibly for a drink. When I went out into the pantry, Chevalier followed me or came with me to help me.

He said, "I saw George Eltenton recently." Maybe he asked me if I remembered him. That Eltenton had told him that he had a method, he had means of getting technical information to Soviet scientists. He didn't describe the means. I thought I said, "But that is treason," but I am not sure. I said anyway something, "This is a terrible thing to do." Chevalier said or expressed complete agreement. That was the end of it. It was a very brief conversation.

After lunch, Robb, following a few more questions about Lomanitz, returned to the "Eltenton-Chevalier incident," asking Oppenheimer about his initial approach to Lieutenant Johnson in Berkeley, in which he told Johnson that Eltenton was a man to watch. When he was asked by Johnson how he knew Eltenton to be involved in suspicious activities, Oppenheimer volunteered to the hearing, "I invented a cock-and-bull story." Robb, however, refused to pick up on this straightaway; he wanted the story to unfold at *his* pace. Ignoring, for the moment, Oppenheimer's ready confession of having lied, Robb led him slowly through the order of events. The day after Oppenheimer had spoken to Johnson, Robb established, he spoke to Boris Pash:

Robb. Did you tell Pash the truth about this thing?

Oppenheimer. No.

Robb. You lied to him?

Oppenheimer. Yes.

Robb. What did you tell Pash that was not true?

Oppenheimer. That Eltenton had attempted to approach members of the project, three members of the project, through intermediaries.

Robb. What else did you tell him that wasn't true?

Oppenheimer. That is all I really remember.

Robb. That is all? Did you tell Pash that Eltenton had attempted to approach three members of the project?

Oppenheimer. Through intermediaries.

Robb. Intermediaries?

Oppenheimer. Through an intermediary.

Robb. So that we may be clear, did you discuss with or disclose to Pash the identity of Chevalier?

Oppenheimer. No.

Robb. Let us refer, then, for the time being, to Chevalier as X.

Oppenheimer. All right.

Robb. Did you tell Pash that X had approached three persons on the project?

OPPENHEIMER. I am not clear whether I said there were three Xs or
   that X approached three people.
ROBB. Didn't you say that X had approached three people?
OPPENHEIMER. Probably.
ROBB. Why did you do that, Doctor?
OPPENHEIMER. Because I was an idiot.
ROBB. Is that your only explanation, Doctor?
OPPENHEIMER. I was reluctant to mention Chevalier.
ROBB. Yes.
OPPENHEIMER. No doubt somewhat reluctant to mention myself.
ROBB. Yes. But why would you tell him that Chevalier had gone to
   three people?
OPPENHEIMER. I have no explanation for that except the one already
   offered.

To make matters worse for Oppenheimer, Robb then took him
through all the details of his conversation with Pash, highlighting
each one of his false and unnecessary elaborations on his story about
Eltenton—his mention of a contact at the Soviet consulate, of the possibility of microfilming documents, of there being two people working
at Los Alamos who had been approached, and so on—all of which Robb
got Oppenheimer to admit were not true. "Isn't it a fair statement today,
Dr. Oppenheimer," Robb summed up, "that according to your testimony now you told not one lie to Colonel Pash, but a whole fabrication
and tissue of lies?" "Right," Oppenheimer replied. From that moment
onward his "veracity" lay in ruins.

But Robb was still not finished. Turning to Oppenheimer's secret
rendezvous with Jean Tatlock in 1943, Robb had another damaging confession (previously quoted) to wring out of him:

ROBB. You spent the night with her, didn't you?
OPPENHEIMER. Yes.
ROBB. That is when you were working on a secret war project?
OPPENHEIMER. Yes.
ROBB. Did you think that consistent with good security?
OPPENHEIMER. It was, as a matter of fact. Not a word—it was not
   good practice.[69]

Though there were another three weeks of the hearing to go, the
decision was never in doubt after this merciless exposure by Robb of

---

[69] See footnote 49 on p. 372.

Oppenheimer's repeated dishonesty and of his poor judgment. On the evening after this exchange, when Robb got home, he told his wife: "I've just seen a man destroy himself on the witness stand."

Now, it did not matter how many people Garrison produced to vouch for Oppenheimer's loyalty, or how eminent they were. All Robb had to do was tell the witness about the Chevalier Affair and ask, for example, whether they would have reported the incident sooner than Oppenheimer had done, or whether they considered what Oppenheimer had said about the affair to be indicative of an honest and reliable character, or some other variation on that theme. Oppenheimer had lied, and he had lied several times, and he had admitted that he had lied several times, after which Robb's task was simply to keep reminding the hearing of these palpable facts.

The appearance of Groves on the fourth day should have provided an important boost to Oppenheimer's camp, but Robb was able to undermine all the supportive things Groves had to say about Oppenheimer with one simple question: "General, in the light of your experience with security matters and in the light of your knowledge of the file pertaining to Dr. Oppenheimer, would you clear Dr. Oppenheimer today?" To which Groves felt obliged to tell the truth, which was: "I would not clear Dr. Oppenheimer today if I were a member of the Commission."

The following day, John Lansdale, by this time a practicing lawyer no longer in the army, appeared for Oppenheimer and showed himself ready, able and willing to stand up to Robb. When Robb drew attention to the fact that the other security officers at Los Alamos, including Peer de Silva, were more suspicious of Oppenheimer than Lansdale, he tried further to maintain that their view was somehow more authoritative than Lansdale's. To this, Lansdale reacted firmly and combatively:

ROBB. He [de Silva] was certainly more of a professional than you were, wasn't he, Colonel?
LANSDALE. In what field?
ROBB. The field he was working in, security.
LANSDALE. No.
ROBB. No?
LANSDALE. No.
ROBB. He was a graduate of West Point, wasn't he?
LANSDALE. Certainly. I am a graduate of VMI [Virginia Military Institute], too. You want to fight about that?

Robb was, however, able to nullify Lansdale's support for Oppenheimer in one crucial exchange. Prompted by Garrison, Lansdale stated that, in spite of the Chevalier Affair, he still maintained his belief in Oppenheimer's general truthfulness: "I don't believe that he lied to us except about this one incident—my general impression is that his veracity is good. I don't know of any other incident." Robb's response to this was as effective as it was cunning:

> ROBB. Colonel Lansdale, as a lawyer are you familiar with the legal maxim, "*Falsus in uno, falsus in omnibus*"?
>
> LANSDALE. Yes, I am. Like all legal maxims, it is a generalization, and not of particular significance when applied to specifics.
>
> ROBB. When you are trying a jury case and the veracity of a witness is in question, do you request the court to give an instruction on that subject?
>
> LANSDALE. Oh, certainly; don't you?
>
> ROBB. Certainly, I want to know what you do.
>
> LANSDALE. The instruction usually is that the jury may, but does not have to, take that as an indication, and the judgment is to be exercised in the particular case.
>
> ROBB. And when you are trying a jury case and you examine a witness on the opposite side and you demonstrate that he has lied, don't you argue to the jury from that that they should disregard his evidence?
>
> LANSDALE. You are speaking now as to what I as an advocate do?
>
> ROBB. Yes.
>
> LANSDALE. It depends on circumstances; usually I do.
>
> ROBB. Sure. Any lawyer worth his salt would.

The following week saw a procession of pro-Oppenheimer witnesses: Gordon Dean, Hans Bethe, George Kennan, James Conant, Enrico Fermi, David Lilienthal, Isidor Rabi, Norris Bradbury, Hartley Rowe, Lee DuBridge and Vannevar Bush. By this time, however, a pattern had been established that rendered their testimony all but useless: first, they would be led by Garrison or Marks through their avowals of Oppenheimer's loyalty and truthfulness, then Robb would use the Chevalier Affair to reestablish Oppenheimer's lack of truthfulness. So established did this pattern become that, sometimes, the members of the board would raise the matter of the Chevalier Affair, as it were, on Robb's behalf. When Conant appeared, for example, it was Ward Evans who asked him: "Dr. Conant, if you had been approached by someone for security information, wouldn't you have reported it just as quickly as you could?" To which, of course, Conant had to reply: "I think I would have, yes." Perhaps feeling that Evans had not done it properly, Robb then added: "When you did report it, Doctor, you would have told the whole truth about it?" "I hope so," replied Conant. "I am sure you would," concluded Robb.

The hero of the second week was Rabi, who took the opportunity to express his feelings about the hearing. "I never hid my opinion from Mr. Strauss that I thought that this whole proceeding was a most unfortunate one," Rabi said.

> That the suspension of the clearance of Dr. Oppenheimer was a very unfortunate thing and should not have been done. In other words, there he was; he is a consultant, and if you don't want to consult the guy, you don't consult him, period. Why you have to then proceed to suspend clearance and go through all this sort of thing, he is only there when called, and that is all there was to it. So it didn't seem to me the sort of thing that called for this kind of proceeding at all against a man who had accomplished what Dr. Oppenheimer has accomplished. There is a real positive record, the way I expressed it to a friend of mine. We have an A-bomb and a whole series of it, and what more do you want, mermaids? This is just a tremendous achievement. If the end of that road is this kind of hearing, which can't help but be humiliating, I thought it was a pretty bad show. I still think so.

While the hearing was going on, it was reported and commented upon in the newspapers, often with the assumption that McCarthy had something to do with it. "McCarthy has few partisans and enjoys little prestige in the Deep South," commented *The Southeast*, "and the Oppenheimer ouster has done little, if anything, to raise his stock." During Oppenheimer's security hearing, in fact, McCarthy's "stock" sank to an all-time low, owing to his unwise decision to take on the U.S. Army. For five weeks, beginning on April 22, 1954, the entire country was gripped by the televised Army-McCarthy hearings, which marked the beginning of the end of McCarthyism.

Not that the media lost interest in the Oppenheimer case. On April 26, the first day of the third week of the Oppenheimer hearing, *Life* magazine carried a story about it, which began with the following vivid and evocative description of Oppenheimer's arrival at the hearing:

> Silently and impassively, a thin, thoughtful man wearing a porkpie hat and accompanied by a policeman and three lawyers walked with

hurried step last week through the shabby backdoor courtyard of a Washington office building.

The article was noncommittal in its sympathies, but was clear about one thing: "Whatever the truth of the charges and whatever the outcome of the inquiry, the situation which involved one of the nation's most brilliant scientific minds was in itself a national tragedy."

The third week of the hearing saw the appearance of the anti-Oppenheimer witnesses, though none of them did anything like as much damage to his case as he himself had done on the third day. Wendell Latimer, a professor of chemistry at Berkeley with a long-standing dislike of Oppenheimer, testified to Oppenheimer's "astounding" ability to influence people and his use of that ability to persuade young physicists to become pacifists and dissuade them from joining the H-bomb program. General Wilson from the air force testified to Oppenheimer's opposition to strategic bombing as being "not helpful to national defense." Kenneth Pitzer, another chemistry professor at Berkeley with a grudge against Oppenheimer, talked without any great authority or conviction about Oppenheimer's opposition to the hydrogen bomb, and David Griggs cast doubt on Oppenheimer's loyalty on the grounds of the "pattern" of his postwar activities, which seemed to Griggs to point to a desire to undermine the defense of the U.S.

The two most significant witnesses called by Robb were Luis Alvarez and Edward Teller, both of whom spoke rather cautiously. Alvarez was careful to stress that what he had to say did nothing to impugn Oppenheimer's loyalty and indeed did very little other than provide, in his own words, "corroborative testimony" to the fact that Oppenheimer was opposed to the development of the hydrogen bomb. Teller, too, stated: "I have always assumed, and I now assume that he [Oppenheimer] is loyal to the United States." When asked a slightly different question, however—namely, whether he thought Oppenheimer was a "security risk"—Teller answered:

In a great number of cases I have seen Dr. Oppenheimer act— understood that Dr. Oppenheimer acted—in a way which for me was exceedingly hard to understand. I thoroughly disagreed with him in numerous issues and his actions frankly appeared to me confused and complicated. To this extent, I feel that I would like to see the vital interests of this country in hands which I understand better, and therefore trust more. In this very limited sense, I would like to express a feeling that I would feel personally more secure if public matters would rest in other hands.

When he was asked by Gordon Gray, "Do you feel that it would endanger the common defense and security to grant clearance to Dr. Oppenheimer?" Teller replied:

> I believe, and that is merely a question of belief and there is no expertness, no real information behind it, that Dr. Oppenheimer's character is such that he would not knowingly and willingly do anything that is designed to endanger the safety of this country. To the extent, therefore, that your question is directed toward intent, I would say I do not see any reason to deny clearance. If it is a question of wisdom and judgment, as demonstrated by actions since 1945, then I would say one would be wiser not to grant clearance.

Apart from these two statements from Teller, which, though tentatively expressed, were, in the context of the hearing, extremely powerful, there was very little in the testimony from Robb's chosen witnesses that would do the Oppenheimer case much damage. Right to the end Robb scored more blows against Oppenheimer in cross-examining Garrison's witnesses than he did in examining his own. The last pro-Oppenheimer witness was John McCloy, the chairman of Chase National Bank, who had got to know Oppenheimer when they served together on a Soviet-U.S. relations study group. After McCloy had expressed his opinion that Oppenheimer was emphatically *not* a security risk, Robb developed the following variation on his reliably effective ruse of mentioning, or alluding to, the Chevalier Affair at every turn:

> ROBB. As far as you know, Mr. McCloy, do you have any employee of your bank who has been for any considerable period of time on terms of rather intimate and friendly association with thieves and safecrackers?
>
> McCLOY. No, I don't know of anyone.
>
> ROBB. I would like to ask you a few hypothetical questions, if I might, sir. Suppose you had a branch bank manager, and a friend of his came to him one day and said, "I have some friends and contacts who are thinking about coming to your bank to rob it. I would like to talk to you about maybe leaving the vault open some night so they could do it," and your branch manager rejected the suggestion. Would you expect that branch manager to report the incident?
>
> McCLOY. Yes.
>
> ROBB. If he didn't report it, would you be disturbed about it?
>
> McCLOY. Yes.

ROBB. Let us go a little bit further. Supposing the branch bank manager waited six or eight months to report it, would you be rather concerned about why he had not done it before?

McCLOY. Yes.

ROBB. Suppose when he did report it, he said this friend of mine, a good friend of mine, I am sure he was innocent, and therefore I won't tell you who he is. Would you be concerned about that? Would you urge him to tell you?

McCLOY. I would certainly urge him to tell me for the security of the bank.

ROBB. Now, supposing your branch bank manager, in telling you the story of his conversations with his friend, said, "My friend told me that these people that he knows that want to rob the bank told him that they had a pretty good plan. They had some tear gas and guns and they had a car arranged for the getaway, and had everything all fixed up," would you conclude from that it was a pretty well-defined plot?

McCLOY. Yes.

ROBB. Now, supposing some years later this branch manager told you, "Mr. McCloy, I told you that my friend and his friends had a scheme all set up as I have told you, with tear gas and guns and getaway car, but that was a lot of bunk. It just wasn't true. I told you a false story about my friend." Would you be a bit puzzled as to why he would tell you such a false story about his friend?

McCLOY. Yes; I think I would be.

ROBB. That is all.

From the chair, Gordon Gray evidently found this analogy too attractive to leave alone and was tempted to contribute his own elaboration:

GRAY. Mr. McCloy, following Mr. Robb's hypothetical question for the moment, let us go further than his assumption. Let us say that ultimately you did get from your branch manager the name of the individual who had approached him with respect to leaving the vault open, and suppose further that your branch manager was sent by you on an inspection trip of some of your foreign branches, and suppose further that you learned that while he was in London he looked up the man who had made the approach to him some years before, would this be a source of concern to you?

McCloy. Yes; I think it would. It is certainly something worthy of investigation, yes.

The last two witnesses, Boris Pash and William Borden, were the two most convinced of Oppenheimer's disloyalty. When asked whether he would consider Oppenheimer a security risk, Pash was unequivocal: "Yes, I would." Borden, meanwhile, stood by his judgment that "more probably than not" Oppenheimer was an agent of the Soviet Union, to which Gray felt obliged to point out:

> I would say to you that the board has no evidence before it that Dr. Oppenheimer volunteered espionage information to the Soviets or complied with a request for such information; that he has been functioning as an espionage agent or that he has since acted under Soviet directive.

In the light of this statement from Gray, Garrison chose not to cross-examine Borden.

The hearing ended on Thursday, May 6, with a summary statement from Garrison, in which he reiterated his "whole man" approach. "In the Commission's own view of the matter," he said:

> it is the man himself that is to be considered, commonsense to be exercised in judging the evidence, and that it is appropriate to consider in the final reckoning the fact that our long-range success in the field of atomic energy depends in large part on our ability to attract into the program men of character and vision with a wide variety of talents and viewpoints.

He conceded that Oppenheimer took a good deal of understanding: "But this man bears the closest kind of examination of what he really is, and what he stands for, and what he means to the country. It is that effort of comprehension of him that I urge upon you."

After Garrison had finished his summation the hearing was brought to a close, and the three members of the board, Gray, Morgan and Evans, were given a ten-day break before returning to Washington on May 17 to consider their findings.

In the meantime, Oppenheimer and Kitty returned to Olden Manor, where FBI microphones continued to record their every conversation. On May 7, Oppenheimer was reported to have told a friend despairingly that "he will never be through with the situation," since "all the evil of the times" was wrapped up in it. Exhausted from the hearing and nervously awaiting the result, he was described a few days later as "very depressed at the present time and has been ill-tempered with his wife."

On May 27, after considering the evidence put before it, the three-member board presented its findings to General Nichols. On the question of whether Oppenheimer's clearance should be reinstated, the board was split, with Gray and Morgan recommending that it should not, and Evans recommending that it should. The majority report, signed by Gray and Morgan, repeatedly emphasizes that none of them doubted Oppenheimer's loyalty to his country. "We have," they state, "come to a clear conclusion, which should be reassuring to the people of this country, that he is a loyal citizen."

On the other hand, they add: "We have, however, been unable to arrive at the conclusion that it would be clearly consistent with the security interests of the United States to reinstate Dr. Oppenheimer's clearance, and, therefore, do not so recommend." They give four reasons for this recommendation. The first is "that Dr. Oppenheimer's continuing conduct and associations have reflected a serious disregard for the requirements of the security system," by which they seem to mean Oppenheimer's "current associations with Dr. Chevalier," to which, they say, they attach "a high degree of significance." The second is that Oppenheimer had shown "a susceptibility to influence." What they seem to have in mind here is Oppenheimer's willingness to write letters on behalf of Lomanitz and Peters after he had been urged to do so by Ed Condon. Their third reason is the most controversial. "We find," they write, "his conduct in the hydrogen-bomb program sufficiently disturbing as to raise a doubt as to whether his future participation, if characterized by the same attitudes in a Government program relating to the national defense, would be clearly consistent with the best interests of security." What they mean by this is not entirely clear, but it seemed to many—particularly to many scientists—to amount to saying that Oppenheimer was to be judged on the basis of his beliefs, which was a very dangerous path to tread. Their fourth and final reason for denying Oppenheimer clearance is that he had been "less than candid in several instances in his testimony before this Board." In their report, Gray and Morgan do not elaborate or support this, but its basis seems to be their conviction that Oppenheimer had lied to the hearing about the Chevalier Affair.

In his minority report, Ward Evans, noting that all three members of the panel were agreed that Oppenheimer was loyal to his country, recommended the reinstatement of Oppenheimer's clearance on several grounds. First: "To deny him clearance now for what he was cleared for in 1947, when we must know he is less of a security risk now than he was then, seems to be hardly the procedure to be adopted in a free country." Second, Oppenheimer "did not hinder the development of the H-bomb and there is absolutely nothing in the testimony to show that he did." And, finally: "His witnesses are a considerable segment of the scientific backbone of our Nation and they endorse him." At the end of his report, Evans adds, in the manner of a man protesting too much: "I would like to add that this opinion was written before the *Bulletin of the Atomic Scientists* came out with its statement concerning the Oppenheimer case."

The May 1954 issue of the *Bulletin* was a special issue, largely devoted to the Oppenheimer case, in which, after printing Nichols's letter to Oppenheimer, and Oppenheimer's reply to it, the editors published a collection of statements they had received during the first week of the hearing from notable scientists. Included in the collection are statements from Samuel Allison, Harold Urey, F. W. Loomis, Linus Pauling, Julian Schwinger, Albert Einstein and Victor Weisskopf, several of whom pointed out the injustice and the danger involved in declaring a man a security risk because, when asked for his opinion, he says something the government of the day does not want to hear. The *Bulletin* also published a statement condemning the suspension of Oppenheimer's clearance by the executive committee of the Federation of American Scientists, and a petition signed by twenty-seven physicists at the University of Illinois disputing the charges brought against Oppenheimer and stating their collective wish, as people "closely associated with Dr. J. Robert Oppenheimer," to reassure the public that "there can be no reasonable doubt of his loyalty." It was very clear from this issue of the *Bulletin* that the scientists who had testified against Oppenheimer—Alvarez, Latimer, Pitzer and Teller—belonged to a very small minority, and evidently not one that Ward Evans was particularly keen to join.

On May 28, the findings of the board, including Ward's minority report, were sent by Nichols to Oppenheimer. A few days later, Garrison responded to those findings on Oppenheimer's behalf. He began by noting that the recommendation not to reinstate Oppenheimer's clearance "stands in such contrast with the Board's findings regarding Dr. Oppenheimer's loyalty and discretion as to raise doubts about the process of reasoning by which the conclusion was arrived at." Garrison also complained that, despite what Oppenheimer had said in his autobiographical letter to Nichols, the findings of the board were not "considered in the context of Dr. Oppenheimer's life as a whole."

Garrison assumed that Nichols would forward the board's findings to the AEC, together with a recommendation based upon them. In fact, in submitting the board's findings to the AEC, Nichols also submitted his own recommendations, which, while loosely based upon the recommendations of the board, differed significantly in content and in emphasis. For example, the general tone of Nichols's memo is a good deal less friendly to Oppenheimer, and, unlike both the majority and the minority reports, he does not repeatedly stress Oppenheimer's loyalty to his country, confining himself simply to the statement: "The record contains no direct evidence that Dr. Oppenheimer gave secrets to a foreign nation or that he is disloyal to the United States." Neither does Nichols endorse the majority report's suggestion that Oppenheimer's "disturbing" conduct during the hydrogen-bomb program offered a reason not to reinstate his clearance. On the contrary, Nichols is very careful to emphasize that his finding against Oppenheimer "is not based on Dr. Oppenheimer's opinions," and that "the evidence establishes no sinister motives on the part of Dr. Oppenheimer in his attitude on the hydrogen bomb, either before or after the President's decision."

In the memo, Nichols is at pains to make clear that his recommendation not to reinstate Oppenheimer's clearance is based squarely on the consideration of Oppenheimer's *veracity*. In connection with this, Nichols gives *far* more weight to the "Chevalier incident" than the board had done. It is this, above all else, Nichols's memo suggests, that establishes that Oppenheimer is not to be trusted. After all:

> if his present story is true then he admits he committed a felony in 1943. On the other hand, as Dr. Oppenheimer admitted on cross-examination, if the story Dr. Oppenheimer told Colonel Pash was true, it not only showed that Chevalier was involved in a criminal espionage conspiracy, but also reflected seriously on Dr. Oppenheimer himself.

Nichols is very clear which version of the story *he* thinks is true:

> . . . it is difficult to conclude that the detailed and circumstantial account given by Dr. Oppenheimer to Colonel Pash was false and that the story now told by Dr. Oppenheimer is an honest one. Dr. Oppenheimer's story in 1943 was most damaging to Chevalier. If Chevalier was Dr. Oppenheimer's friend and Dr. Oppenheimer, as he now says, believed Chevalier to be innocent and wanted to protect him, why then would he tell such a complicated false story to Colonel Pash? This story showed that Chevalier was not innocent, but on the contrary was deeply involved in an espionage conspiracy. By the same token, why would Dr. Oppenheimer tell a false story to Colonel Pash which showed that he himself was not blameless? Is it

reasonable to believe a man will deliberately tell a lie that seriously reflects upon himself and his friend, when he knows that the truth will show them both to be innocent?

In thus emphasizing the importance of the Chevalier Affair, Nichols was reflecting more accurately than the board members had done the case that had been presented by Robb at the hearing and also the views of Lewis Strauss. He was, moreover, closing the gap that Garrison had mentioned between the board's recommendations and its comments on Oppenheimer's loyalty and discretion. What had been murky in the panel's majority report was made abundantly clear in Nichols's memo: the reason for recommending that Oppenheimer's clearance should not be reinstated was first and foremost that he had been shown to be a liar on a matter of national security.

If Nichols thought he could bury the admiring comments about Oppenheimer's character, loyalty and service to the country that had been made in the panel's reports, he was shown to be mistaken on June 1, 1954, when Garrison leaked the text of those reports to the press. In retaliation, Strauss took a somewhat desperate step. Despite the fact that the witnesses at the hearing had been promised that their testimony would be treated in confidence, Strauss persuaded the AEC to publish the entire proceedings. On June 15, before the AEC had even announced its decision in the Oppenheimer case, the transcript, entitled *In the Matter of J. Robert Oppenheimer*, was released in book form to the press, and the following day it was available to the general public.

Two weeks later, the AEC finally announced its decision. By a vote of four to one, the commissioners voted not to reinstate Oppenheimer's clearance. The majority report, signed by Strauss, Campbell and Zuckert, followed the lines of Nichols's letter, in emphasizing that the reasons for denying clearance to Oppenheimer rested not on his opinions, or on any alleged disloyalty, but rather on his "associations" with communists and, above all, on the flaws in his character demonstrated by the "whole fabrication and tissue of lies" that he had, by his own admission, told Pash about the Chevalier incident. Commissioner Murray also voted to deny Oppenheimer clearance, but his reasons were rather different and so he wrote his own report, in which he did *not* shy away from accusing Oppenheimer of disloyalty. In an echo of the split among the panel members, the only commissioner to vote *for* the reinstatement of Oppenheimer's clearance was also the only scientist on the AEC, namely Henry DeWolf Smyth, who, in his own report, wrote that he agreed with the Gray board that Oppenheimer was "completely loyal" and that "I do not believe he is a security risk." The Chevalier incident, Smyth conceded, was "inexcusable," but "that was 11 years ago; there is no sub-sequent act even faintly similar."

The AEC announced its decision not to reinstate Oppenheimer's clearance on June 29. The following day, Oppenheimer's one-year contract as a consultant to the AEC was due to expire anyway. In effect, what had been achieved by a hearing lasting three and a half weeks, followed by several more weeks of deliberation, was that Oppenheimer's employment as an AEC consultant came to an end a day earlier than originally contracted.

19

An Open Book?

Haakon Chevalier first learned of his leading role in the Oppenheimer case on April 13, 1954, when the *New York Times* published Nichols's letter to Oppenheimer listing the charges against him, together with Oppenheimer's autobiographical reply. Chevalier found Nichols's letter "repulsive," but Oppenheimer's reply "even more distressing," because, with its talk of "intermediaries" between Eltenton and scientists working on the bomb, it seemed to paint a picture of something much more elaborate than the simple and short conversation that Chevalier remembered.

Then, on June 16, just after the AEC published the entire transcript of the hearings, Chevalier, still living in Paris, saw a headline in the *Paris-Presse* that read: "Oppie confesse: 'J'étais un idiot.'" When he bought a copy of the paper, Chevalier saw that it contained extracts from the transcript, including the exchange between Robb and Oppenheimer during which Oppenheimer admitted to having told a "tissue of lies." Reading it made Chevalier realize what, or rather who, had been the source of the story that had dogged him all those years:

> The one who had invented that highly damaging story about me was none other than my own friend, Oppenheimer, himself. It was unbelievable. It made no sense—but there it was, in black and white. More than ten years before, he had fabricated a story which had wrought havoc with my life and my career, and during all those years he had continued to give every show of an unaltered friendship. Why? What had ever led him to do this?

On June 28, *Time* magazine ran a long article on the Oppenheimer case, reporting on the board's findings, but not yet on the AEC's decision, which was announced the following day. "In the list of witnesses against J. Robert Oppenheimer," the piece said, "the most effective was J. Robert Oppenheimer himself. His testimony showed that he had lied repeatedly in the past about important security matters." "The most telling example of Oppenheimer's past capacity for untruths was drawn out in cross-examination about his relationships with his good friend Haakon Chevalier."

The rest of the article is taken up mostly with the testimony of the anti-Oppenheimer witnesses, such as Alvarez, Griggs, Latimer and Teller, and it ends with an account of Robb's cross-examination of the banker John McCloy. It concludes: "The majority of Gordon Gray's security committee wound up feeling about Oppenheimer the way McCloy felt about Roger Robb's hypothetical bank manager."

On July 7, Chevalier wrote to Oppenheimer:

Dear Robert,

I have been shattered by the revelations in the June 28th issue of *Time* Magazine.

I need not tell you what this means to me—the light it casts on the past, the implications for the present and the future.

Before making any decisions, which must in the nature of the case be irrevocable, I would like to hear directly what you have to say. And I suspend, as best I can, any final judgment. But I must hear soon.

Haakon

Oppenheimer's reply was dated July 12, and read:

Dear Haakon,

Your letter of July 7th has just come. In answer I am sending to you by airmail today a set of documents. These will tell you all that I have to tell.

These documents are public, and they are the whole of the public record. Some I made public myself: General Nichols's letter of December 23rd, my answer of March 4th, the report of the Gray Board, and the letters and arguments of counsel. The transcript was made public by the Atomic Energy Commission. There are substantial deletions. These have mostly to do with military or technical matters.

With every good wish,
Robert Oppenheimer

When Chevalier read the whole transcript, he was struck by how unfamiliar the Oppenheimer that emerged from the hearings seemed: "This was not the Oppenheimer I knew."

> The Oppenheimer I knew was brilliant, incisive, measured, resourceful, imaginative, challenging, always in command of the situation, and everything he said had the unmistakable stamp of his personality. The Oppenheimer of the *Transcript* is completely depersonalized . . . Not once in the course of the whole three-week hearing does he come out with a statement that reflects his inner self—his ideals, his purpose, his sense of destiny.

On July 27, Chevalier wrote again to Oppenheimer, "hoping—without believing—that in a burst of confidence he might reveal something that would in some measure justify the inexplicable violation of friendship." After telling Oppenheimer that the documents he had received failed to explain what he felt needed explaining, Chevalier went on:

> For the subjective observer—myself—the picture is this: I have regarded you as my very dear friend for upward of 15 years. I have loved you as I have loved no other man. I placed in you an absolute trust. I would have defended you to the death against malice or slander. Now I learn that eleven years ago, according to your own admission, you wove an elaborate fabric of lies about me of the most gravely compromising nature. During all these years you continued to show me the signs of an unaltered friendship. In 1948, after my interview with the FBI, I told you, in the garden on Eagle Hill, of my being grilled about those three scientists I was supposed to have approached. You gave me no indication that you knew of what was involved.
>
> During all these years that story, without my knowing it, has hounded me, plagued and blocked me and played untold havoc with my career and my life. With what today looks like the most consummate cynicism, you wrote me on February 24th 1950, "As you know, I have been deeply disturbed by the threat to your career which these ugly stories could constitute"—referring to stories that were as fairy tales compared to the ones you had already put into the record seven years before.
>
> . . . I do not subscribe to the naïveté theory, nor to the "idiocy" theory. I believe that that story, and the consciousness of it that you

have carried about with you for eleven years, and your awareness of
what it was doing to me, represent for you something rational and
coherent, that hangs together and makes sense, and that you can
explain and perhaps in a measure justify.

Before I finally make up my mind about the several matters
involved in all this I am asking you, as perhaps the last act of friendship, to explain what the mind conceived and to what the heart con-
sented.

It seems somehow typical of the nightmare in which Chevalier now
found himself that this deeply personal letter, crying out for an intimate,
emotional response, should have been opened and read not by Oppenheimer himself, but by his secretary, Katharine Russell, who, after making several copies of it, sent it to Lloyd Garrison, who in turn wrote to
Chevalier explaining that Oppenheimer and his family were away on
the Virgin Islands, "on a desperately needed rest." "I appreciate the fact
that it calls for a personal response by Dr. Oppenheimer," Garrison told
Chevalier, but "I am taking the liberty of referring you to a few passages
from them [the transcripts] which you may not have noticed and which
seem relevant to the subject-matter of your letter." Copies of the letter
were sent to Herb Marks, Katharine Russell and Oppenheimer himself,
to whom Garrison wrote that he hoped "that this might suffice to hold
the fort until you get back."

On August 5, Chevalier replied to Garrison, telling him: "There is
much in this whole case that is strange and baffling."

One extraordinary thing about this case is that, since I seem to
occupy such an important role in it, no one has seen fit to ask me
to contribute my two-bits' worth. It is, to me, a striking weakness
in your defense of Oppenheimer as his attorneys that you made no
attempt to use me as an asset rather than a liability, and throughout
the hearings allowed me and my name to hover somewhere back-
stage as a vague and disreputable ghost.

. . . All the passages in the record that you refer to I had read. I
have, in fact, gone through it quite thoroughly. But I am afraid neither you, nor the Board, nor the Commission, went into me quite
thoroughly enough.

On September 3, 1954, Chevalier finally had a response from
Oppenheimer himself to the letter he had sent on July 27. The response
was, however, rather disappointing. "It is not nearly as clear to me as
it appears to be to you," Oppenheimer wrote, "how much, in the past,

at present, or in the future the shadow of my cock and bull story lies over you." "In December of 1943, when I first mentioned your name I thought the story dismissed. I had supposed that for a long time it had been recognized for the fabrication that it was."

"This letter," Chevalier writes in his memoir, "seems to have been his final word." He did not reply directly to it. Rather, having decided that "I must make my side of the story public," Chevalier chose instead to write an open letter to Oppenheimer to be published in the *Nation*. He sent the piece to the magazine on September 26, but two months later it remained unpublished. The French magazine *France-Observateur* was more enthusiastic and published it on December 2 with a headline on its front cover announcing: "Un document exclusif: Robert Oppenheimer, pourquoi avez-vous menti? par Haakon Chevalier."[70] Having thus been scooped, the *Nation* declined to publish the letter.

Worried that Oppenheimer would thus read his open letter "in a truncated and perhaps distorted form," Chevalier wrote to Oppenheimer on December 13, telling him:

> I have no doubts about your intentions. But the effect of your words and acts has been incalculably disastrous (whether it is clear to you or not) both to me and to yourself. You have, I hope, found out how hard it is to untell a lie.
>   . . . This is not a trivial mistake, a casual error of judgment. It is something weighty, monstrous and calamitous borne in knowledge and conscience for years, during which time it was breeding its poisonous mischief.

"Do what we may," Chevalier told Oppenheimer, "by your unfathomable folly, you and I are linked together in a cloudy legend, which nothing, no fact, no explanation, no truth will ever unmake or unravel." He also warned Oppenheimer that he was hard at work on a novel designed to resolve the worries and problems Oppenheimer had caused him: "I hope to finish it in the spring. It is entitled *The Man Who Would Be God*."

Oppenheimer did not reply to this letter and spent the rest of his life determined to free himself from the "cloudy legend" to which Chevalier continued to feel inextricably linked. He did not speak to or about Chevalier again and, both privately and publicly, said as little as he could about the security hearing that had attached so much importance to that legend.

---

[70] "An exclusive document: Robert Oppenheimer, why did you lie? By Haakon Chevalier."

Meanwhile, the world at large continued to be fascinated by the "Oppenheimer case" and everything associated with it. *Life* magazine on September 6, 1954, carried a long profile of Edward Teller, heralded on the front cover with the words: "Dr. Teller who stood up to Oppenheimer and achieved H-Bomb for U.S." Inside the story was headed "Dr. Edward Teller's Magnificent Obsession," and portrayed Teller as the man without whom the H-bomb would never have been made. "In that event," it said, quoting Eisenhower, "Soviet power would today be on the march in every quarter of the globe." The article devoted several paragraphs to Teller's testimony against Oppenheimer, representing it as something that Teller did with a heavy heart, but felt obliged to do because of his loyalty to the U.S.

As was made clear on the first page of the article, it was based largely on a book that came out at about the same time called *The Hydrogen Bomb*, written by two Time-Life reporters called James Shepley and Clay Blair. "This book," said Gordon Dean, reviewing it for the *Bulletin of the Atomic Scientists*, "is in one sense a sort of 'Valentine' presented to Dr. Edward Teller—but it has blood stains upon it—the blood of Dr. Norris Bradbury, director of the Los Alamos weapons laboratory, the entire staff of that laboratory, Dr. Oppenheimer, and many others." What Shepley and Blair presented was the story of the hydrogen bomb as seen by Lewis Strauss and Edward Teller, a story of noble persistence triumphing—for the good of the United States and the entire Free World—over perverse, and possibly sinister, prevarication. "These two boys have done a serious disservice," thundered Dean. "Their book may very well do what the Communists would love to do—undermine the atomic energy program of this country." Isidor Rabi, meanwhile, dismissed the book as "a sophomoric science-fiction tale, to be taken seriously only by a psychiatrist."

In the October 1954 edition of *Harper's Magazine* appeared an article by Joseph and Stewart Alsop that was a kind of mirror-image of the Shepley-Blair book, presenting the Oppenheimer case as a struggle between good and evil, but this time Oppenheimer was the hero and Strauss the villain. In an echo of Emile Zola's famous article, "J'Accuse," published in 1898 in defense of the wrongfully condemned Jewish artillery officer Alfred Dreyfus, the Alsops called their essay "We Accuse!"

We accuse the Atomic Energy Commission in particular, and the American government in general, of a shocking miscarriage of justice in the case of J. Robert Oppenheimer.

We accuse Oppenheimer's chief judge, the chairman of the Atomic Energy Commission, Admiral Lewis Strauss and certain of Oppenheimer's accusers, of venting the bitterness of old disputes through the security system of this country.

And we accuse the security system itself as being subject to this kind of ugliness, and as inherently repugnant in its present standards and procedures to every high tradition of the American past.

Both the Shepley-Blair book and the Alsops' article gave rise to heated controversies that kept the Oppenheimer case in the newspapers and magazines of both the U.S. and the world beyond it for the next few years.

One person who showed no inclination whatever to take part in those controversies was Oppenheimer himself. When, immediately after the AEC announced its decision, he was asked for his reaction, he gave a studiedly bland answer that would remain his final word on the subject for many years:

> Dr. Henry D. Smyth's fair and considered statement, made with full knowledge of the facts, says what needs to be said. Without commenting on the security system which has brought all this about, I do have a further word to say. Our country is fortunate in its scientists, in their high skill, and their devotion. I know that they will work faithfully to preserve and strengthen this country. I hope that the fruit of their work will be used with humanity, with wisdom and with courage. I know that their counsel when sought will be given honestly and freely. I hope it will be heard.

To another reporter shortly afterward Oppenheimer said that he was looking forward to returning to a "cloistered life."

If Strauss had had his way, the "cloistered life" of the Institute for Advanced Study would have been closed to Oppenheimer. In July 1954, Strauss told an FBI agent that he and the Board of Trustees had decided to delay a decision about Oppenheimer's position as director of the institute until the autumn, since, if Oppenheimer were to be asked to resign straightaway, it would look like "a direct result of personal vindictiveness" on Strauss's part. When the Board met in October, however, it was clear to Strauss that there was so much support for Oppenheimer among the Trustees there was no point pushing for his resignation. He therefore switched tactics and, with a show of "magnanimity," urged the Board to reappoint Oppenheimer, which they did.

"So far as I was concerned," Freeman Dyson has written, Oppenheimer "was a better director after his public humiliation than he had been before. He spent less time in Washington and more time at the institute ... He was able to get back to doing what he liked best—reading, thinking and talking about physics." Dyson is here choosing his words carefully: Oppenheimer got back to reading, thinking and talking about physics, but not to *writing* it. He wrote a lot of popular lectures on physics during these years, but he did not return to being an active research physicist. Back in the summer of 1952, he had written to Frank: "Physics is complicated and wondersome, and much too hard for me except as a spectator; it will have to get easy again one of these days, but perhaps not soon."

As a spectator, Oppenheimer was unusually well informed, and at the institute he had some excellent people to keep him up to date with the latest research. The one who was intellectually closest to him was Abraham Pais, whose work centered on what Oppenheimer regarded as the most interesting part of the subject: particle physics. In the early 1950s, Pais had done some pioneering and important work attempting to find order in what Oppenheimer referred to as the "particle zoo." Oppenheimer was not exactly a collaborator on this work, but, for an observer, he was very close to it, even making the odd contribution here and there. For example, Pais's paper at the second Rochester Conference in January 1952 had a title provided by Oppenheimer—"An Ordering Principle for Megalomorphian Zoology"—and, when this was turned into an article for the *Physical Review*, a footnote acknowledged: "J. R. Oppenheimer, discussion remark at the Rochester Conference."

In 1954, Pais began a fruitful collaboration with Murray Gell-Mann, a brilliant young physicist who had spent a year at the institute in 1951 before accepting a position at Chicago as an instructor. Pais and Gell-Mann made an important contribution to fundamental particle theory when they introduced a new quantum number to which Gell-Mann gave the name "strangeness." Oppenheimer kept a close eye on this development, but did not contribute to it. At the end of 1954, Pais left the institute for a year to take a sabbatical at Columbia.

Freeman Dyson was still at the institute, but he and Oppenheimer never became close, either personally or intellectually. "I disappointed him by not becoming a deep thinker," Dyson has said.

> When I came to Oppenheimer asking for guidance, he said: "Follow your own destiny." I did so, and the results did not altogether please him. I followed my destiny into pure mathematics, into nuclear engineering, into space technology and astronomy, solving problems that he rightly considered remote from the mainstream of physics.

The same "difference of temperament," Dyson recalls, also appeared in their discussions about the School of Physics at the institute: "He liked to concentrate new appointments in fundamental particle physics; I liked to invite people in a wide variety of specialities."

Two people they did agree on, however, were the Chinese physicists Chen Ning Yang and Tsung-Dao Lee. Yang came to the institute in 1949, after taking his Ph.D. in Chicago under Edward Teller. In 1950, he was awarded a five-year institute membership, and when that came to an end he was made a full professor. Lee had also taken his Ph.D. at Chicago, which is where he and Yang met. In 1951, after a year at Berkeley, Lee came to the institute on a two-year membership, during which time he and Yang became close collaborators, a partnership that continued after he left the institute for Columbia in 1953. Oppenheimer did not work closely with Yang and Lee, nor was he particularly close to them personally, but he did take great pride in their achievements. By the mid-1950s, Yang, in collaboration with Lee, was the greatest physicist of which the institute could boast. As Dyson puts it, he and Oppenheimer "rejoiced together as we watched them grow over our heads and into great scientific leaders."

Just a month after Oppenheimer's reappointment as director, Ed Murrow, the television journalist who fronted the program *See It Now*, came to Princeton with his producer Fred Friendly to discuss the possibility of devoting an episode of their program to the institute. What they had in mind was a general introduction to the place where, in Murrow's words, "you find a Nobel Prize winner every time you open a door," featuring interviews with Oppenheimer, Einstein, Bohr (who happened to be visiting at the time) and whoever else they could find. As it turned out, Einstein refused to be involved, and though Bohr agreed to be interviewed, he seemed incapable of saying anything that would be intelligible to a general audience. This left Oppenheimer, who gave a mesmerizing performance, talking about his childhood, the institute, quantum physics, but *not* the security hearing, about which neither Murrow nor Oppenheimer said a single word during three hours of filming.

On their way back to New York it was clear to Murrow and Friendly that what they had recorded in Princeton was not a program about the institute ("There isn't one foot of usable film in all that stuff we did with Bohr and all the others," Murrow said to Friendly), but a first-rate interview with Oppenheimer. He needed a great deal of persuading to allow the program to go ahead on this new basis, but Murrow was so convinced of the quality of the interview, and that it could not possibly do anything but good for both Oppenheimer and the institute, that he finally gave his consent.

The program went out on January 4, 1955, and fully lived up to Murrow's expectations. It was hugely popular, offering as it did a glimpse of Oppenheimer that was many times more interesting and engaging than the saint depicted by the Alsops or the sinner condemned by Shepley and Blair. The charisma that had enchanted Born in the 1920s, Oppenheimer's graduate students in the 1930s and Groves and the Los Alamos team in the 1940s had finally been captured on film and made available for everyone to see. Key to the charm of the program was that Oppenheimer was relaxed in Murrow's company, both of them smoking heavily and each clearly trusting and admiring the other. Not that Oppenheimer's performance was entirely without artifice. Pais recalls that on the day of the filming he and Rabi "tiptoed into Robert's office and sat silently in a corner, watching the proceedings. When it was over and Murrow had left, Rabi turned to Oppenheimer and said: 'Robert, you're a ham.'"

The conversation, as broadcast, began with Oppenheimer talking about the institute and some of its members, including the mathematician Hassler Whitney and the psychologist Jean Piaget. "And Professor Einstein is still here too, isn't he?" Murrow says. "Oh, indeed he is," replies Oppenheimer with a smile. "He's one of the most lovable of men." Turning to the subject of Oppenheimer himself, Murrow asks: "Well, sir, apart from running the institute, what do you do here?" "I do two kinds of things," Oppenheimer replies:

> One is to write about what I think I know, hoping that it will be understandable in general, and one is to try to understand physics and talk and work with the physicists and sometimes . . . try to have an idea that may be helpful.

"The part I really get excited about," he continued, "is just what is called particle physics or atomic physics in its modern sense." He then goes up to his blackboard and gives a mini-lecture on physics.

Turning from physics to politics, Oppenheimer is asked about the dangers of secrecy and replies: "The trouble with secrecy isn't that it doesn't give the public a sense of participation. The trouble with secrecy is that it denies to the government itself the wisdom and resources of the whole community." In any case, he insists, "there aren't secrets about the world of nature. There are secrets about the thoughts and intentions of men. Sometimes they are secret because a man doesn't like to know what he's up to if he can avoid it."

Though there was no mention of the security hearing or of the suspension of Oppenheimer's clearance, the Murrow program achieved precisely what Lloyd Garrison had hoped to achieve at the hearing: it presented the public with the "whole man," and, in doing so, put the charges against him in perspective. The press reviews of the program were uniformly enthusiastic, most critics being captivated by, as the *New York Times* put it, Oppenheimer's "lean, almost ascetic face and his frequent poetic turn of phrase." Friendly and Murrow received 2,500 letters in response to the program, only thirty-five of which were critical of Oppenheimer, an "approval rating" of more than 98 percent.

After his appearance on *See It Now*, Oppenheimer was no longer the "controversial figure" he had been six months earlier: he was a celebrity. Wherever he went, the press followed and crowds gathered. On January 31 to February 2, Oppenheimer attended the fifth Rochester Conference, at which he chaired a session on K-mesons, his presence prompting one journalist to describe him with what Robert Marshak has called a "brilliant non sequitur": "Dr. Oppenheimer, who is the world's greatest nuclear theorist despite Federal withdrawal of his top security clearance . . ."

When Oppenheimer gave public lectures now, the audiences were huge. In April 1955, he was invited to give the Condon Lectures at Oregon State University. His subject was "The Sub-Nuclear Zoo: The Constitution of Matter," and he attracted 2,500 listeners, most of whom, as a newspaper report of the time put it, "didn't know a meson from a melon." The *Eugene Register-Guard* reported that the audience for the first of these lectures "was several hundred larger than the previous peak crowd." "Listeners sat on the floor, stood in the hallways, and filled the coffee bar and a lounge downstairs where the scientist's voice was carried by the public address system." "Not one in 50 could really understand what he was talking about," the reporter estimated. "So why did they stay?" His answer was: "The great nuclear physicist turned out to be a very appealing, human guy."

> They also saw a man so obviously in love with his work. As he warmed up to his subject and talked about protons and neutrons and the other creatures of his sub-nuclear zoo, he became quite excited. The audience, not knowing what he was talking about, became excited too.

It was on this trip out west that Oppenheimer learned (from a newspaper reporter) of the death of the only physicist whose fame and popularity exceeded his own. "For all scientists and most men," Oppenheimer said on hearing the news, "this is a day of mourning. Einstein was one of the greats of all ages."

Before returning to Princeton, Oppenheimer went to Iowa State College to give the first John Franklin Carlson Lecture. Frank Carlson, who had done his Ph.D. under Oppenheimer at Berkeley and had published a joint paper with him, had been a professor of physics at Iowa State from 1946 to 1954, when he committed suicide. Oppenheimer's memorial lecture, the text of which was published in *Physics Today*, was entitled "Electron Theory: Description and Analogy." It began with an eloquent and heartfelt tribute to Carlson:

> It is a very special sort of privilege to give this lecture in honor and in memory of Carlson who was, for many of us, both a friend and a colleague . . .
>
> Carlson was a student of mine in Berkeley. To those in this audience who are graduate students, I would recall the earnestness, the intensity, almost the terror with which he underwent the rites of initiation in a great science, and the seriousness with which he met it. In those days, he used to say, "I have only one wish, and that is to be a good physicist." I think he lived to see that wish abundantly fulfilled.

In recalling Carlson, one feels that Oppenheimer was also articulating an ideal to which he himself had aspired all his life:

> He loved the history of science; he was interested in philosophy and in literature. He was concerned and sensitive to all human problems, and yet very balanced and unfanatic, a real scholar, one of the most modest of men, a man with a great gift for teaching . . . He was loyalty itself and great friendliness, and he was very funny. He had a wonderful sense of humor which softened the sobriety, the depth, and the sense of pathos and tragedy with which he looked at human affairs. He exemplified and, with a kind of steadfastness which none of us will forget, he established that being a scientist is harmonious with and continuous with being a man.

The lecture then dealt—at a level that was no doubt somewhat beyond most of the 1,200 people crammed into the hall—with the history of electron theory, from Newton, via Heisenberg, to the new quantum electrodynamics developed by Schwinger and Feynman a few years earlier. This last Oppenheimer attempted to summarize as follows:

> And physicists then said, "Good, we will give up this attempt. We cannot calculate the mass of the electron. It would be meaningless anyway in a theory in which there are no other particles, because we

could give meaning only to its ratio to the mass of something else. We would like to calculate the charge; we would like to calculate that number one in a thousand; but we will give that up too. These things we will measure; then everything else will be given by the theory in a finite way." So they said; and this is what is called the renormalization program.

Along the way, Oppenheimer managed to fit in a description of the work that he and Carlson had done together. He also—and this was characteristic of the talks he gave in this period—hinted at an imminent breakthrough:

It is clear that we are in for one of the very difficult, probably very heroic, and at least thoroughly unpredictable revolutions in physical understanding and physical theory. One of the great times in physics lies ahead; it is certainly something that will often make us remember how much we miss the guidance and the companionship that Carlson could have given us had he lived.

Oppenheimer's sense that a fundamental breakthrough was imminent was in part based on his sense that there was something provisional about QED, that, as he put it in his Carlson lecture, "electrodynamics cannot be the whole story." Though, to a general audience, this gave the impression that Oppenheimer was at the very cutting edge of contemporary physics, to physicists it was reminiscent of Einstein's refusal to accept quantum mechanics. Oppenheimer showed no sense of being aware of this. In January 1956, he published in *Reviews of Modern Physics* a handsome appreciation of Einstein's work, which, however, having described the great advances Einstein made during "two golden decades early in this century," lingered on Einstein's increasing isolation from the mainstream of physicists during the last twenty-five years of his life and his devotion to a research program that "did not arouse the hope or indeed the active interest of many physicists."

At about the same time Oppenheimer wrote a tribute on the occasion of Bohr's seventieth birthday that was, by comparison with his tribute to Einstein, completely unequivocal in its admiration and praise.

His great discoveries, the firmness, subtlety and depth of his understanding, his philosophical courage, and his warm and broad human interests, have been an inspiriting example to generations of scientists. Just in these last years, he has taken a heroic part in furthering international cooperation in science, and in defining and upholding the ideal of an open world. If our civilizations are to have a future worthy of their great past, his example will have an enduring and ever-growing influence.

Much of Oppenheimer's time during these years was spent giving public lectures to large audiences, often to commemorate a death or an anniversary. On February 2, 1956, he gave an address to the American Institute of Physics on the occasion of its twenty-fifth anniversary. The talk, published in *Physics Today*, was entitled "Physics Tonight," and sought to give an impression of the "wonderfully diverse and varied set of enterprises" in which physicists were involved. To illustrate this diversity he discussed three examples; one each of, respectively, the physicist as discoverer, the physicist as citizen and the physicist as teacher. Predictably, under the heading of "physicist as discoverer," he discussed "what is called in the trade particle physics," drawing attention to its chaotic state in what he assumed was a transient stage of its development. "In some ways," he said, with what almost seems like nostalgia, "this field may remind us of the quantum theory of atoms as it was in the earlier years of this century; but we have not found that single key to the new physics that Planck discovered at the turn of the century, nor anything analogous to Bohr's postulates." He was, however, confident that "physics tonight" could look forward to a bright new morning:

> Surely past experience, especially in relativity and atomic mechanics, has shown that at a new level of explanation some simple notions previously taken for granted as inevitable had to be abandoned as no longer applicable.
>
> . . . Always in the past there has been an explanation of immense sweep and simplicity, and in it vast detail has been comprehended as necessary. Do we have the faith that this is inevitably true of man and nature? Do we even have the confidence that we shall have the wit to discover it? For some odd reason, the answer to both questions is yes.

Turning to the physicist as teacher, Oppenheimer's advice was a little vague, if not completely vacuous. "We must make more humane what we tell the young physicist, and must seek ways to make more robust and more detailed what we tell the man of art or letters or affairs, if we are to contribute to the integrity of our common cultural life." What he means by this, or, indeed, whether it means anything at all, seems to be open to question.

Equally opaque are his comments on the physicist as citizen, which seem designed to point out only a lack of clarity:

> Despite the "peace of mutual terror," despite "deterrence" and "retaliation," despite the growing apparent commitment to the thesis that global or total war has become "unthinkable," the full import of the new situation is surely not clear today.

The specific issues that Oppenheimer listed in "Physics Tonight" as "the special problems that at the moment seem most pressing of solution" were not ones readily comprehensible to a general audience and reflected the fact that on this occasion he was talking to fellow physicists. In Oppenheimer's words, those issues were "the relation of the τ-meson [tau-meson] and the θ-meson [theta-meson]; why the antiproton interacts with such a large cross section with nuclei; whether we can understand the scattering of pions in S states." In fact, these were exactly the issues that dominated the sixth Rochester Conference, which was held on April 3–7, 1956. It was, says Pais, "a historic meeting, for several reasons." For one thing, it was the first Rochester meeting at which Soviet scientists participated—an extraordinary gesture given that in the summer of 1956 there was no sign of a thawing in the Cold War; quite the opposite, in fact. It was also the first meeting at which the participants had a chance to discuss the issues that Oppenheimer mentioned in "Physics Tonight," issues that raised, as Oppenheimer implied, fundamental questions.

On the second day Oppenheimer gave a public address to an overflow audience on his favorite topic, the "sub-nuclear zoo," drawing particular attention to one of the puzzles he had mentioned in his *Physics Today* article, and the fundamental question that it raised. The puzzle was that two heavy mesons, the tau-meson and the theta-meson, seemed to have identical masses and identical lifetimes, yet opposite parities. The notion of "parity" can be understood in terms of a mirror-image. If you look in the mirror, left becomes right and right becomes left; or, to put it another way, spatial coordinates have been "flipped." If they are then flipped again, they go back to how they were, which is called a "rotation." A rotation has a parity of 1, a flip has a parity of −1.

Returning to tau-mesons and theta-mesons, these particles puzzled physicists because there seemed to be fairly compelling grounds for believing that they were, in fact, the same particle, and equally compelling grounds for thinking they were not. The reason for thinking they were the same particle was simply that they had exactly the same mass and exactly the same lifetime, which, if they were different particles, would be an amazing coincidence. On the other hand, they seemed to be different with respect to what happened to them when they underwent beta decay. As explained earlier, when a neutron undergoes beta decay, it emits an electron and a neutrino, and what remains is a proton. Another way of saying this is that its beta-decay products are a proton, an electron and a neutrino. The tau-meson and the theta-meson have different beta-decay products.

That a single particle can decay in two different ways would not be particularly puzzling, but what did puzzle scientists was that, if these two were the same particle, then what they thought was a fundamental law of nature—the conservation of parity—would in this case not be upheld. When a tau-meson undergoes beta decay, it produces three pions (as the "Yukawa particle" ended up being called), two positive and one negative. The theta-meson, on the other hand, decays into two pions, one positive, the other neutral. A pion has a parity of –1 (a flip), which means that a tau-meson has a parity of 1 (three flips, one for each of its pions), and the theta-meson –1 (two flips, or a rotation, so ending up the same). Assuming the law of the conservation of parity, therefore, the tau-meson and the theta-meson had to be, despite appearances, different particles.

It was in connection with this puzzle that Oppenheimer uttered two remarks that were savored by those present as being comically characteristic of him, in that they combined apparent profundity with utter unintelligibility. The first of these was: "The τ-meson will have either domestic or foreign complications. It will not be simple on both fronts." The second was: "Perhaps some oscillation between learning from the past and being surprised by the future of this tau-theta dilemma is the only way to mediate the battle." Both remarks were repeated again and again by the delegates at the conference, who delighted in their ambiguity and the fact that, as Robert Crease has said, they "hinted at a rising wave of possibly revolutionary physics without advancing the problem." In order to make sense of the experimental findings regarding the tau- and theta-mesons, the theorists had either to say that the two were—despite having the same mass and the same lifetime—different particles, or else they had to say that a principle that had been assumed to be a fundamental law of physics—the conservation of parity—was actually no such thing. On the way back from Rochester, Yang and Pais bet John Wheeler a dollar that the two were different particles. As it turned out, Yang had put himself into a win-win situation here, since he was soon to be involved in an attempt to *prove* that parity had been violated. If he succeeded, he would lose the bet and owe Wheeler a dollar; he would, however, also have made a Nobel Prize–winning contribution to physics.

Two months after the sixth Rochester Conference, Yang sent Oppenheimer an article that he and Lee had written, in which they made a bold suggestion. What they suggested was that, though parity conservation had been experimentally demonstrated with regard to *strong* interactions, such as those between nucleons, there was no such experimental data with regard to weak interactions, such as those associated with beta-decay. As the tau-meson was distinguished from the theta-meson by means of their beta-decay products, then, suggested Yang and Lee, if it turns out that the law of parity conservation does not hold in weak interactions, there would be nothing to prevent one from concluding that they were in fact the same particle. They also suggested some possible experiments that might settle the issue. When this article was published in the October 1956 issue of the *Physical Review*, the authors thanked Oppenheimer, among others, for "interesting discussions and comments." In fact, Oppenheimer's comment was to suggest—as if their proposal were not bold enough—that fundamental conceptions of space and time might have to change in order to make sense of the tau-theta puzzle.

One possible experiment suggested by Yang and Lee was to look for violations of parity in beta decay in the release of electrons from a radioactive substance such as cobalt-60. Another possible experiment was to look for violations of parity in the decays of pions and muons, other examples of weak interactions. A team of experimentalists led by Chien Shiung Wu at Columbia took up the challenge laid down by Yang and Lee, and by the end of 1956 had demonstrated beyond all doubt that they were right: the conservation of parity did not hold for weak interactions. The tau-theta puzzle had been solved: they were the same particle. Wheeler won his dollar, and Yang and Lee were awarded the 1957 Nobel Prize in physics.

In January 1957, shortly after the results came in, Yang cabled Oppenheimer, who was then in the Virgin Islands, to tell him: "Wu's experiment yielding large symmetry." Oppenheimer replied: "Walked through door. Greetings." The allusion in Oppenheimer's telegram is explained in Yang's Nobel Prize speech, in which he said:

> The situation that the physicist found himself in at that time has been likened to a man in a dark room groping for an outlet. He is aware of the fact that in some direction there must be a door which would lead him out of his predicament. But in which direction?

The excitement generated by the breakthrough of Yang and Lee was reminiscent of that which accompanied the breakthroughs of the 1920s and '30s. On January 16, 1957, the *New York Times* had it as its front-page story under the heading: "Basic concept in physics is reported upset in tests. Conservation of parity in nuclear theory challenged by scientists at Columbia and Princeton Institute." The excitement was shared by Oppenheimer, who declared: "No one today knows where this discovery will lead . . . something has been found whose meaning only the future will reveal."

In the spring of 1957, Oppenheimer—now fifty-three—gave the William James Lectures at Harvard, an annual series of talks somewhat akin in terms of prestige to the BBC's Reith Lectures. Oppenheimer's overall title was "The Hope of Order." Among those present was Jeremy Bernstein, who remembers:

> It was an occasion. At Sanders Theater, the largest lecture venue on the campus, its twelve hundred seats were filled and another eight hundred people could listen on speakers in the so-called New Lecture Hall. The lecture attracted not only the university community but people from all over Boston. Seated in front of me were two of those wonderfully elegant ancient Boston ladies with blue hair.

Bernstein was at this time coming to the end of a two-year appointment and had applied to the institute for a fellowship. He was, he recalls, "truly amazed—and absolutely thrilled—when I received a letter of acceptance . . . not long after this letter arrived, there was Oppenheimer giving a lecture at Harvard":

> Nothing that has been written about his charisma as a public lecturer has been exaggerated. It was a mixture of phrasing that was both elegant and somewhat obscure. You were not quite sure what he meant, but you were sure that it was profound and that it was your fault that you didn't see why.

After the lecture, Bernstein decided to go onto the stage to introduce himself. To begin with, Oppenheimer "looked at me with what I distinctly remember as icy hostility," but when Bernstein told him that he would be joining the institute that autumn, "his demeanor completely changed":

> It was like a sunrise. He told me who would be there—an incredible list. He ended by saying that Lee and Yang were going to be there and that they would teach us about parity . . . Then Oppenheimer said, with a broad smile, "We're going to have a ball!" I will never

forget that. It made it clear to me why he had been such a fantastic director at Los Alamos.

The lectures were never published, but the accounts of them that appeared in the *Harvard Crimson* indicate that they covered the same ground as the 1953 Reith Lectures. When interviewed by the local television station, Oppenheimer remarked: "I believe in the popularization of science. I don't think I do it terribly well. But we must know that it is as impossible as it is essential. It has those two inescapable sides, I think."

One senses that, as he spent more of his time popularizing physics, he felt himself increasingly removed from the cutting edge of the subject. When Bernstein arrived at the institute in the autumn of 1957, he was surprised to be told, immediately upon telling the secretary who he was, that Oppenheimer wanted to see him right away. As soon as he walked into Oppenheimer's office, he recalls, Oppenheimer greeted him: "What is new and firm in physics?" While Bernstein was wondering how to reply, the phone rang. "It's Kitty," Oppenheimer told him after hanging up. "She has been drinking again."

The Princeton physicist Sam Treiman remembers that every Tuesday Oppenheimer hosted a lunch in his office for a group of six or so physicists, including Yang, Pais, Dyson and Treiman himself. Oppenheimer, he recalls, "attached great importance to the lunches, often calling me a day in advance to remind." Treiman was not so convinced about the scientific value of these meetings, in which, he says, the participants "overdrank the sherry, and just rambled on about current developments in physics . . . The conversation was never highly technical. It had more to do with who's in, who's out, what are the best bet, etc."

On October 4, 1957, the Soviet Union launched *Sputnik 1*, the world's first earth-orbiting artificial satellite. The response in the United States was a frightened shock that the Soviets were, in this technology if not in others, actually *ahead*. Influenced, no doubt, by his positive experience of the Ed Murrow show, Oppenheimer agreed to be interviewed on the subject by Howard K. Smith for a CBS News program called *Where We Stand*. Much to Oppenheimer's chagrin, his interview was never aired. Oppenheimer seemed to believe that this was because he had been too controversial, though the vice president of CBS News, Sig Mickelson, told him that it was because "there was other material which was more useful to the central theme of the program than your interview." A transcript of the interview preserved in Oppenheimer's papers would seem to bear Mickelson out. For most of the time Oppenheimer was discussing very general defects in the U.S. educational system. When he was asked about the attempt to catch up with the Russians on satellite development, his response was short, bland and uninformative: "We wouldn't like to have this a Russian monopoly, we would like to be good at it."

More interesting was a talk that he gave in April 1958 to the International Press Institute in Washington under the title "The Tree of Knowledge," which was published later in the year in *Harper's Magazine*. Oppenheimer's central theme in this talk was the huge growth in the volume of scientific knowledge and its increasing specialization. "Today," he said, "it is not only that our kings do not know mathematics, but our philosophers do not know mathematics and—to go a step further—our mathematicians do not know mathematics." Expanding on what he said earlier about the impossibility of popularizing science, he told his audience that "it is almost impossible to explain what the fundamental principle of relativity is about, and this is even more true of the quantum theory":

> And as for the recent discovery—the very gay and wonderful discovery for which Dr. Yang and Dr. Lee were awarded the Nobel Prize—that nature has a preference for right-handed or left-handed screws in certain situations and is not indifferent to the handedness of the screw—to explain this is, I believe, quite beyond my capacity. And I have never heard anyone do it in a way that could be called an enrichment of culture.

Soon after this Oppenheimer left for Europe, where, as well as giving talks in Paris and Copenhagen, he attended the twelfth Solvay Congress in Brussels, which that year was on the theme of "Structure and Evolution of the Universe." Pais was also there, presenting a review of recent work on weak interactions, as was Richard Feynman, whom Pais remembers "trying to explain quantum mechanics to Queen Fabiola."

This visit to Europe was something of a watershed in the Oppenheimers' relationships with their son and daughter, who at that time were, respectively, seventeen and thirteen years old. Relations within the Oppenheimer family had been difficult ever since the children were born. For reasons both external and internal, Kitty and Robert were not ideal parents. Pat Sherr has remarked on how impatient Kitty was with Peter when he was little, adding that in her view, Kitty had "no intuitive understanding of the children." It is a view shared by Abraham Pais, who recalled: "To an outsider like me, Oppenheimer's family life looked like hell on earth. The worst of it all was that inevitably the two children had to suffer."

Relations between Peter and his parents went from bad to worse when it became clear that he had not inherited his father's academic ability. He was sensitive and intelligent, but he did not excel at school. The Oppenheimers' friends remember Kitty nagging Peter relentlessly, both about his poor academic performance and, when he began to get a little pudgy, about his weight. He responded by retreating into himself, becoming, as Serber once put it, "a shadow . . . trying not to be noticed."

Shortly before the Oppenheimers left for Europe in 1958, Peter received the bad news that his application to study at Princeton had been rejected. As a consequence, the Oppenheimers decided that, though Toni would come with them to Europe, Peter would be left behind. If the memories of Oppenheimer's secretary at the time, Verna Hobson, are correct, the decision seems to have been Kitty's rather than Robert's. "There came a time," Hobson recalled, "when Robert had to choose between Peter—of whom he was very fond—and Kitty. She made it so it had to be one or the other, and because of the compact he had made with God or with himself, he chose Kitty."

In the summer of 1958, in what looks like an effort to overcome the kind of specialization that he had identified and lamented in "The Tree of Knowledge," Oppenheimer published a long, detailed and thoughtful review of *A Study of Thinking* by Jerome Bruner. His conclusion was that, "Even the lay reader will recognize in this book some fresh and solid steps toward an understanding of characteristic traits of man's rational behavior." But: "He will also see that the psychological sciences have a very long way indeed to go." He was evidently on a mission to bridge the gaps created by specialization. On July 5, 1958, he published a piece in the *Saturday Evening Post* under the title "The Mystery of Matter," which, while attempting to explain particle physics to the general public, also tried to explain why—having argued several times that such a thing was impossible—he thought it worthwhile making the attempt. "All of us in our years of learning," he wrote:

> many if not most of us throughout our lives, need some apprentice-ship in the specialized traditions, which will make us better able to understand one another, and clearer as to the extent to which we do not. This will not be easy. To me it seems necessary for the coherence of our culture, and for our future as a free civilization.

Whether Oppenheimer was successful in explaining physicists and psychologists to each other, and both to the general public, the cumulative effect of his appearances on television, his popular articles and his public speeches was, bit by bit, to repair the damage done to his reputation by the security hearing. The tide of opinion was swinging in his favor. Joseph McCarthy died in May 1957, but the movement associated with his name had been dying for some time before that. Oppenheimer's tormentor, Lewis Strauss, too, had become an unpopular figure. In the summer of 1958, Strauss was replaced as chairman of the AEC by John McCone, who, prompted by congressional calls to reevaluate the Oppenheimer case, asked the AEC lawyer, Loren K. Olson, to take a fresh look at the files. What Olson found was "a punitive, personal abuse of the judicial system." The path was now clear for Oppenheimer to reenter public service. However, he showed no signs of wanting to go back down that path.

Meanwhile, Strauss was about to face exactly the kind of public humiliation that he had inflicted on Oppenheimer. Shortly after leaving the AEC, Strauss was chosen by Eisenhower to be his new Secretary of Commerce. First, however, he had to submit himself to questioning by the Senate Committee on Interstate and Foreign Commerce. The hearings, which began in April 1959, are described by Strauss's biographer in a way that carries a very strong echo:

> Day after weary day for the next four weeks Strauss heard himself reviled, as his attackers combed through his career for evidence against him. Committee members, other senators, scientists, even columnists accused Strauss of misconduct.

Strauss himself described the "nightmarish quality of the proceedings." "It was now clear," Strauss wrote, "that this was to be not a hearing so much as an inquisition, with the attorney for the prosecution brought in by the chief judge." Oppenheimer was too gentlemanly to point out the obvious parallels, but some of his friends were not. Bernice Brode, an old friend from the Los Alamos days, for example, attended the Strauss hearings and wrote to Oppenheimer to say that, in an "unchristianly spirit" she was enjoying Strauss's "every squirm and anguish." "It's a lovely show . . . Having a *wonderful* time—wish you were here." On June 19, 1959, the Senate voted against Strauss's appointment as Secretary of Commerce, the first cabinet nominee to be rejected since 1925. Strauss's political career was over.

In the autumn of 1959, *The Man Who Would Be God*, Chevalier's fictionalized account of his relationship with Oppenheimer, finally came out and flopped badly. It attracted almost nothing but hostile reviews in the press and aroused very little interest among the general public. Chevalier himself was too obscure, and Oppenheimer by this time too popular, for there to be much demand for an attack upon him by an embittered former friend.

How far Oppenheimer had come politically since his days as a "fellow traveler" with Chevalier was demonstrated in the summer of 1959, by his participation in a conference sponsored by the Congress for Cultural Freedom. The conference took place in Rheinfelden, on the border between Switzerland and Germany, and among the other participants were Stephen Spender, Raymond Aron, Arthur Schlesinger, Jr. and Nicolas Nabokov—just the sort of wide-ranging intellectuals who had been Oppenheimer's ideal since his days as an undergraduate at Harvard. In his talk, Oppenheimer confessed to being "profoundly in anguish over the fact that no ethical discourse of any nobility or weight has been addressed to the problem of the atomic weapons." "What are we to make," he asked, "of a civilization which has always regarded ethics as an essential part of human life . . . [but] which has not been able to talk about killing almost everybody except in prudential and game-theoretical terms?"

In October 1959, Oppenheimer published an article on "The Role of the Big Accelerators" in IBM's house magazine, *Think*, in which he provided a wonderfully clear explanation of what accelerators were and why physicists needed them in order to study the properties of fundamental particles. Protons, neutrons and electrons, he conceded, can readily be studied because they are so abundant in ordinary matter:

> But these three particles are only three of the approximately thirty whose existence has been revealed by the collision of cosmic rays with nuclear matter. What fraction they are of those that we will later come to recognize is not known. We may have the full count; we may be very, very far from it. These other particles are not to be found in a free state in ordinary matter. They have one or another or both of two properties: Some, the majority, are unstable, decaying like radioactive nuclei typically in less than a millionth of a second; even the neutron is unstable, but it lasts a convenient 1,000 seconds; or, if they are not unstable in free space, they are at once destroyed when they interact with matter. To discover these, and to study them, they must be made.

The occasion for this article was the announcement that the President's Science Advisory Committee had recommended an increase in annual expenditure for particle accelerators from $59 million to $100 million. It also recommended that, separately to this budget, the federal government foot the bill for a new electron accelerator at Stanford that would, all by itself, cost $100 million. Oppenheimer defended these recommendations, but was careful to make clear that, in his mind, the justification for the expense did not rest on any anticipated technological or practical developments. He was, he said, certain that "the same men who wish to find out more about the atomic world will enrich our technology as well as our knowledge," but:

> It is important the support for their work should probably not rest too heavily or exclusively on this argument. There is some merit in knowledge for its own sake, and some virtue in the getting of it. We can use more of both.

The real importance of accelerators was that they might allow progress to be made on "the ancient question of the constitution of matter." And perhaps even "beyond this question to a new description of happenings in space and time." Again, Oppenheimer looked forward to a big, fundamental breakthrough. "We have the sense," he wrote, "of being in the neighborhood of one of those great changes in the description of nature, of which relativity and quantum theory are two recent examples."

In his contribution to a BBC *Panorama* program on "The 1960s," which was broadcast on January 4, 1960, Oppenheimer went even further. Asked to predict what the coming decade might bring, he said:

> We may learn—I think the chance is good—something almost definitive about matter, the nature of matter and its order. This may be part of the present effort. We will learn of the birth, life, death of stars and galaxies, and about space.

But, above all, he hoped, we would learn "something about ourselves," and that "we will begin to re-knit human culture, and by the insight and the wonder of the world of nature, as science has revealed it, into relevance and meaning for the intellectual life, the spiritual life of man."

His hope of "re-knitting human culture" motivated much of what he did in his last few years, including his involvement in the Congress of Cultural Freedom, the tenth anniversary of which was celebrated in Berlin, the original home of the Congress, in the summer of 1960. Oppenheimer was delighted to give the opening speech of the anniversary conference, in which he spoke of the threats to, and hopes of, progress. The greatest threat he identified was that of nuclear annihilation: "If this next great war occurs, none of us can count on having enough living to bury our dead." Citing, as was his custom, "that beautiful poem," the Bhagavad Gita, he asked whether we could be comforted by Vishnu's words to Prince Arjuna, in which Vishnu (in the form of Krishna) attempts to allay Arjuna's anxieties about killing his fellow human beings by convincing him of the unreality of suffering and urging him to adopt an attitude of "freedom from the chains of attachment." Perhaps to the surprise of those in his audience who knew him, Oppenheimer answered negatively:

> If I cannot be comforted by Vishnu's argument to Arjuna, it is because I am too much a Jew, much too much a Christian, much too much a European, far too much an American. For I believe in the meaningfulness of human history, and of our role in it, and above all of our responsibility to it.

There *had* been progress, Oppenheimer insisted, "not merely in man's understanding, but in the conditions of man's life, in his civility, in the nobility of his institutions and his freedom," and science had played a large role in that progress. However, in the process, "we have so largely lost the ability to talk with one another," and this is why the "re-knitting" was so urgent and so important.

In September 1960, Oppenheimer and Kitty spent three weeks in Japan as a guest of the Japan Committee for Intellectual Interchange. On his arrival in Tokyo, Oppenheimer took part in what one newspaper described as a "terribly ill-planned" press conference, at which he was asked the question he had no doubt been expecting, and to which he seemed to have planned his answer: did he regret making the bomb? "I do not regret that I had something to do with the technical success of the atomic bomb," he replied. "It isn't that I don't feel bad; it is that I don't feel worse tonight than I did last night." Fearing a negative reaction and bad publicity, the Committee for Intellectual Interchange had kept Hiroshima off Oppenheimer's itinerary. They probably need not have worried; wherever Oppenheimer went, he was met with large and appreciative audiences. From the surviving typescripts and the press reports one can see that, with one glaring and interesting exception, his talks repeated the themes of the public lectures he had given elsewhere.

The exception was his participation in a discussion organized by the Society of Science and Man, a group of professors from various disciplines that met in Tokyo every month "to discuss various problems concerning the relationship between science and technology on the one hand and man and society on the other." The discussion, billed as "An Afternoon with Professor Oppenheimer," was not broadcast or published, but survives in a typed transcript that was presumably circulated among the participants, a copy of which was among Oppenheimer's private papers. His contributions to this discussion are remarkable for their tone, the courtly, evasive and elaborate style that he often used when speaking in public giving way to the blunt and abrasive directness of a man determined to speak his mind.

Some of the opinions thus expressed are surprising. C. P. Snow's famous essay, "The Two Cultures," for example, the central message of which (that our society is becoming polarized into two groups: those who understand science but not art, and those who understand art but not science) one might have expected Oppenheimer to applaud, is dismissed by him as exhibiting nothing but "triviality and childishness." Most of the other opinions he expresses are not so much surprising in themselves as for the vehemence with which they are expressed. England is "a small society because of its inherent snobbery," whose leading elite "go to the same colleges, they meet at the same clubs and they frequent each other and read the same things." English philosophers are "out of touch with science, they are out of touch with politics, they are out of touch with history. And what they are in touch with is themselves." As for advertisers, they:

> fill the air, the newspapers, the magazines, the TV screen and the very atmosphere with incredible and vulgar lies. Everybody knows this. It creates a background against which excellence withers and it is my great hope that you will be spared and will help spare your country from this pestilence.

The discussion ends with Oppenheimer's venomous telling of an anecdote about John Foster Dulles, the late U.S. Secretary of State, who had died just four months earlier. When Dulles met the Indian physicist Homi J. Bhabha, Oppenheimer said, Bhabha told Dulles that his impression of Russian science was rather favorable, to which Dulles replied: "That does not surprise me. After all they are a materialist and godless civilization, whereas we are religious and spiritual." "Well," concluded Oppenheimer, "as long as a leading politician with the destiny of the world in part in his hands can talk such blasphemous rubbish, we are not making good contact with politicians."

Oppenheimer and Kitty got back home to find the U.S. in the middle of one of the most intense and momentous presidential elections of the twentieth century, in which the Republican Vice President, Richard Nixon, faced the charismatic young-looking Democrat, John F. Kennedy.[71] The Oppenheimers got back in time to watch three of the four televised debates, in which, it is generally agreed, Kennedy outshone his

---

[71] At forty-three years old Kennedy was, in fact, only a few years younger than Nixon, who was then forty-seven.

rival. The election was held on November 8 and, by the slenderest of margins, Kennedy won.

For the first year of Kennedy's term of office, the change in administration had very little effect on Oppenheimer. As before, he gave public talks, attended to institute business and spent vacations on the island of St. John in the Virgin Islands. The Oppenheimer family had been going to the Virgin Islands in the spring, summer and winter breaks since 1954, and by 1960 they had their own beach house there. Their immediate neighbors on the island were Bob Gibney and his wife, Nancy. Bob Gibney had been editor of *The New Republic* and Nancy had worked on *Vogue*, and both were initially impressed by their new neighbors. The more they got to know the Oppenheimers, however, the less they liked them, and from about 1960 onward the two families lived in a constant state of feuding with each other.

The other islanders were friendlier; some of them found Kitty alarming, especially when she was drunk, but most of them remembered Oppenheimer himself with warmth and admiration, and all of them, except the Gibneys, were happy to accept the annual invitation to the Oppenheimers' New Year's Eve party, which would arrive without fail in September. When the children were small, they both accompanied their parents to St. John two or three times a year, but, on reaching adulthood, Peter stayed away, preferring to spend his holidays in New Mexico. Toni, on the other hand, loved everything about the island: its music, its people, its beaches and its relaxed way of life. All three—Oppenheimer, Kitty and Toni—acquired reputations as expert sailors and they would go off sailing for days at a time.

In January 1962, after spending Christmas on St. John as usual, and hosting their customary New Year's Eve beach party, the Oppenheimers left for Canada, where Robert had been invited to give the Whidden Lectures at McMaster University. The purpose of these lectures, in the words of the then-principal of University College, McMaster, "is to help students cross the barriers separating the academic departments of a modern university." The three lectures—"Space and Time," "Atom and Field" and "War and the Nations"—cover ground that was pretty well trodden by Oppenheimer by this time, but, presumably because they were aimed at students rather than at the general public, the ground was covered in greater depth and Oppenheimer was less inhibited in using mathematical expressions. In 1964, they were published as a small book with the puzzling and inaccurate title *The Flying Trapeze: Three Crises for Physicists*.

Soon after he arrived back in Princeton, Oppenheimer received a letter dated February 1 from *The Christian Century*, a nondenominational magazine, asking him to "jot down—almost on impulse" a list of up to ten books "that most shaped your attitudes in your vocation and philosophy of life." The list he sent them was as follows:

1. *Les Fleurs du mal*
2. Bhagavad Gita
3. Riemann's *Gesammelte mathematische Werke*
4. *Theaetetus*
5. *L'Éducation sentimentale*
6. *Divina Commedia*
7. Bhartrihari's Three Hundred Poems
8. "The Waste Land"
9. Faraday's notebooks
10. *Hamlet*

As an exercise in polymathic showing off, the list is peerless. In just ten titles Oppenheimer has managed to include works of drama, fiction, poetry, mathematics, physics and Hinduism, written in a total of no fewer than six languages: Sanskrit, Greek, Italian, French, German and English. Moreover, in leaving out, in most cases, the author's name, Oppenheimer is making rather large assumptions about the readers of *The Christian Century*: that they would know that *Les Fleurs du mal* is a collection of poems by Charles Baudelaire, that the *Theaetetus* is a dialogue by Plato, that *L'Éducation sentimentale* and *Divina Commedia* were works by, respectively, Flaubert and Dante, and, most obscure of all, that by "Bhartrihari's Three hundred poems" he meant the *S´atakatraya*, which are usually translated as "The Three Centuries," but which Oppenheimer's old friend Arthur Ryder translated as "Women's Eyes." The letter inviting Oppenheimer to take part in this feature had said that the lists "should inform, intrigue, and possibly inspire our readers." Well, they were probably *intrigued* at least.

On April 29, 1962, President Kennedy hosted a formal reception and dinner at the White House for forty-nine American Nobel Prize–winners plus additional guests, among whom was Oppenheimer. The company included scientists such as Linus Pauling and Glenn Seaborg (but not, significantly, Edward Teller), and writers like Robert Frost and Pearl Buck. It was, said Kennedy, "the most extraordinary collection of talent, of human knowledge, that has ever been gathered together at the White House, with the possible exception of when Thomas Jefferson dined alone." After dinner, Seaborg took Oppenheimer aside and told him that there was a good chance of reinstating his security clearance.

All Oppenheimer had to do was submit himself once more to a security-board hearing. Would he do that? The answer was swift and final: "Not on your life."

In September 1962, Oppenheimer was one of three speakers at the dedication of the Niels Bohr Library of the History of Physics at the American Institute of Physics in New York. The other two speakers were Richard Courant, professor at New York University, and George Uhlenbeck from Ann Arbor, Michigan. Less than two months later, on November 18, Bohr died at the age of seventy-seven. For the next *Year Book of the American Philosophical Society* Oppenheimer wrote a long and detailed, but emotionally restrained, biographical memoir of Bohr. Reading it, one would never imagine that he was here writing about the man he revered above all others.

Oppenheimer gave so many public talks during this time, many of them subsequently published as magazine articles, that, inevitably, their quality varied and he increasingly began to repeat himself. In the October 1962 edition of *Encounter*, the in-house magazine of the Congress for Cultural Freedom, he published an article called "Science and Culture," which seems to be little more than a rehashing of thoughts that he had published many times before. Slightly more inspired, if only for its title, was a talk he gave at the National Book Awards in New York on March 12, 1963. The title, of which he was very proud, was "The Added Cubit," an allusion to the Sermon on the Mount as given in St. Matthew, in which Jesus, in the context of exhorting his followers to "Take no thought for your life, what ye shall eat, or what ye shall drink"—that is, to trust God to provide these things—says: "Which of you by taking thought can add one cubit unto his stature?"

Before giving the lecture, Oppenheimer stopped off at Columbia and, while there, asked everyone what his title meant, and where it came from. No one knew. Jeremy Bernstein had recently joined the faculty at Columbia, and a colleague called him to tell him about Oppenheimer's triumphant exposure of the physicists' ignorance of the Bible, whereupon Bernstein, being curious, phoned his friend Robert Merton, who immediately identified the relevant passage from St. Matthew. Then, Bernstein recalls:

> I went to midtown Manhattan to the Hotel Algonquin to meet some *New Yorker* colleagues.[72] As I was passing the elevator, out walked the Oppenheimers. When he saw me he said: "Your father is a rabbi—

[72] Bernstein had by this time started writing regularly for the *New Yorker*.

you should know this." He had the wrong testament for my father, but I gave Merton's answer with no explanation. He looked at me very strangely.

It is hard to see quite why Oppenheimer was so proud of this title, but proud he was. He even ended the talk with an example of the amusement he derived from the failure of people to identify its source:

> Let me end with an anecdote. Three weeks ago a high officer of the National Book Committee asked me for a title for this talk. I did not have one then but I promised to call back shortly and give the title you have heard. He protested that my title was quite puzzling and uninformative. I said it had a history. He seemed puzzled and I quoted St. Matthew. Then he said, "From what book is that?" The National Book Committee still has a lot to do.[73]

Oppenheimer's theme in this talk is that, contrary to what Jesus says in the Sermon on the Mount, we *should* "take thought" and *not* place our trust in fate, or God, or our leaders. "By taking thought of our often grim responsibility," Oppenheimer told his audience, "by knowing something of our profound and omnipresent imperfection, we may help our children's children to a world less cruel, perhaps less unjust, less likely to end in a catastrophe beyond words. We may even find our way to put an end to the orgy, the killing and the brutality that is war."

The "imperfection" of mankind had by this time become one of Oppenheimer's favorite themes, though it is here given a new intensity. In our secularized age, he says, we have lost something that can be found in the great religions and is "a truth whose recognition seems to me essential to the very possibility of a permanently peaceful world, and to be indispensable also in our dealings with people with radically different history and culture and tradition":

> It is the knowledge of the inwardness of evil, and an awareness that in our dealings with this we are very close to the center of life. It is true of us as a people that we tend to see all devils as foreigners; it is true of us ourselves, most of us, who are not artists, that in our public life, and to a distressing extent our private life as well, we reflect and project and externalize what we cannot bear to see within us. When

---

[73] Inexplicably, when this talk was published in *Encounter*, the last line was changed to: "Readers and writers still have a lot to do," which removes the sting—and most of the humor—from it.

we are blind to the evil in ourselves, we dehumanize ourselves, and we deprive ourselves not only of our own destiny, but of any possibility of dealing with the evil in others.

This, fundamentally, is why the arts are important, since "it is almost wholly through the arts that we have a living reminder of the terror, of the nobility of what we can be, and what we are."

At the institute Oppenheimer had to deal not so much with evil as with pettiness and squabbling. Several senior members of the institute—including, most vehemently, the mathematicians Deane Montgomery and André Weil—did not like the way it was going under Oppenheimer's leadership. They thought he brought too many physicists, psychologists, poets and sociologists to the institute, and not enough mathematicians. "He was out to humiliate mathematicians," said Weil:

Oppenheimer was a wholly frustrated personality, and his amusement was to make people quarrel with each other. I've seen him do it. He loved to have people at the Institute quarrel with each other. He was frustrated essentially because he wanted to be Niels Bohr or Albert Einstein, and he knew he wasn't.

Robert Crease tells a story that illustrates something about both the bitchiness of academic life and the kind of sniping at Oppenheimer that went on during this time:

Once in the 1950s, during the oral part of the physics qualifying exam at the University of Wisconsin, a student was asked what J. Robert Oppenheimer had contributed to physics. "I don't know," the student answered—and was informed that was the correct answer.

Sniping at a more personal level went on too, with Deane Montgomery referring to the Oppenheimers' home, Olden Manor, as "Bourbon Manor."

George Kennan in his *Memoirs* writes that it was a "source of profound bewilderment and disappointment" to Oppenheimer that he was unable to bring the disciplines of mathematics and history together at the institute, that he "remained so largely alone in his ability to bridge in a single inner world those wholly disparate workings of the human intellect." Mathematicians and historians would not even sit together in the cafeteria. In place of interdisciplinary harmony there was a constant and fierce rivalry between the mathematicians and the exponents of other disciplines.

The squabbling became particularly intense whenever the question of new appointments came up, the hardest-fought and most unpleasant battle occurring in the academic year 1962–3. "The faculty meetings became so acrimonious," recalls Yang, "I was afraid to go unless I had to." Abraham Pais remembers that early in 1963 he decided to leave the institute: "It started to dawn on me that I had better move on." One reason was that he was worried about becoming complacent and wanted some fresh challenges, but a contributing factor in his decision to leave was, he wrote, that "just about then, Oppenheimer was in trouble again with the faculty because of his vacillations in regard to two new faculty appointments in mathematics, which had taken days of mediation on my part, whereafter I said to myself: No more."

The dispute began when the mathematicians started pushing for the appointment of John Milnor, a mathematician at Princeton University, as a permanent member of the institute. Oppenheimer turned the request down, whereupon the mathematicians presented two further nominations. Oppenheimer proposed postponing these appointments, but was overruled by the trustees at the mathematicians' request, whereupon Pais wrote to Oppenheimer, announcing his resignation.

In April 1963, in the middle of this dispute, it was publicly announced that Oppenheimer would be the next recipient of the AEC's Enrico Fermi Award. This was an award for outstanding achievement in the nuclear field that had been established soon after Fermi's death at the end of 1954. It was awarded posthumously to Fermi, and then in successive years to von Neumann, Lawrence, Wigner, Seaborg, Bethe and Teller. Oppenheimer had known that he had been nominated for the award since the White House dinner in April 1962, when Seaborg, who had been appointed by Kennedy as the new chairman of the AEC, took him aside and told him. Seaborg had been mainly responsible for ensuring that the award went to Oppenheimer, intending it to be a public recognition by the AEC that it had done him an injustice by its decision to strip him of his clearance and that it regarded him as someone to honor rather than to hold in suspicion. Seaborg says that, having made the decision to award the prize to Oppenheimer, he called Strauss to invite him to lunch, where he told him the news: "He looked as if I'd leaned over the table and punched him."

The decision was reported in the June edition of *Physics Today*, which reproduced the AEC's announcement and the biographical sketch of Oppenheimer that they released alongside it. The biographical sketch ended with an appendix giving details of nine of Oppenheimer's most important articles. Rather oddly, what is now regarded as his greatest scientific achievement—the paper on gravitational collapse that he wrote with Snyder—is not mentioned. The presentation ceremony, *Physics Today* reported, would take place in December 1963.

In the meantime, in the summer of 1963, Oppenheimer helped to organize an odd little conference that became the first in an annual series at Seven Springs Farm, Mount Kisco, New York. The conferences were held on the estate of Agnes Meyer, the widow of Eugene Meyer, who, before his death in 1959, had been the owner of the *Washington Post*. Participation was by invitation only and the number of invitees was restricted to fifteen, in order to "maintain intimacy of discussion." Those invited comprised a diverse collection, united only by their broad sympathy with the ideals of the Congress for Cultural Freedom. In 1963, the attendees included the Princeton scholar Julian Boyd, the Oxford philosopher Stuart Hampshire, the poet Robert Lowell, the architect Wallace K. Harrison, the psychiatrist Morris Carstairs, the physicist George Kistiakowsky, as well as Oppenheimer's friends George Kennan[74] and Nicolas Nabokov.

The event provided Oppenheimer with the opportunity to give a different kind of talk from the public lectures he had been delivering to hundreds, and sometimes thousands, of people during the previous decade. For one thing, he could, while speaking, mention the members of his audience by name, often using familiar versions of their names. Harrison was "Wally," Nabokov was "Nico," and Kistiakowsky "Kisty." His talk expounded Bohr's notion of "complementarity," in a way that he had expounded in public many, many times before, except that, in extending it beyond physics, he applied it not only to the understanding of politics and society, but also to an understanding of *oneself*. This led him into an intimate, almost confessional passage, of a kind very rarely to be found in any of his other recorded utterances, whether private or public:

> Up to now, and even more in the days of my almost infinitely prolonged adolescence, I hardly took any action, hardly did anything, or failed to do anything, whether it was a paper on physics, or a lecture, or how I read a book, how I talked to a friend, how I loved, that did not arouse in me a very great sense of revulsion and of wrong. It turned out to be impossible, I will not say to live with myself, because I think there is no problem there, but for me to live with

---

[74] After they had found themselves on the same side on many political questions during the late 1940s, Oppenheimer and Kennan had become friends. At Oppenheimer's invitation, Kennan had spent eighteen months as a scholar at the Institute for Advanced Study during the years 1950–2, and joined the faculty as a permanent member in 1956, after which the friendship between them became much closer.

anybody else, without understanding that what I saw was only one part of the truth. And in an attempt to break out and be a reasonable man, I had to realize that my own worries about what I did were valid and were important, but that they were not the whole story, that there must be a complementary way of looking at them, because other people did not see them as I did. And I needed what they saw, needed them.

Never before had Oppenheimer tried so hard to reveal his inner self, as if he were determined to, so to speak, stand naked before these like-minded souls. In his mind, he told his audience, a recurring theme of the conference had been "a recognition of and a protest against, the elements of smugness, falsity, self-satisfaction and unction in our times, our societies and our lives, against the hypocritical." In that sense, he said, the conference participants had something important in common with the Beat movement in poetry, which "is surely not without artistic portent, but which is essentially, if I know the people and what they do, a kind of brutal protest against what they feel to be false in the description of the world which their elders have given them and in which they live."

On November 21, 1963, the White House issued an announcement that the Fermi Prize would be presented by the President himself to Oppenheimer on December 2. The following day, the announcement was reported in the newspapers. That afternoon, in Dallas, Texas, President Kennedy was assassinated.

So it was that the presentation was made by President Johnson. "I know every person in the room grieves with me that the late President could not give this award as he anticipated," Johnson said. "I take great pleasure and pride that I substitute for him." He then handed Oppenheimer the citation, the gold medal and a check for $50,000. Oppenheimer's short acceptance speech concentrated on "this great enterprise of our time, testing whether men can both preserve and enlarge life, liberty and the pursuit of happiness, and live without war as the great arbiter of history":

In this enterprise, no one bears a greater responsibility than the President of the United States. I think it just possible, Mr. President, that it has taken some charity and some courage for you to make this award today. That would seem to me a good augury for all our futures.

At the reception afterward Oppenheimer was photographed shaking Edward Teller's hand, with Kitty standing beside him, looking at Teller with icy contempt. "I enjoyed what you had to say," said Teller. "I'm so very glad you came," replied Oppenheimer.

Another chance for America's scientific establishment to honor Oppenheimer presented itself the following April, on the occasion of his sixtieth birthday. It was duly taken, but in a curiously unenthusiastic way. Oppenheimer's colleagues at the institute, Dyson, Pais, Strömgren and Yang, undertook to edit a special issue of *Reviews of Modern Physics* dedicated to him. However, Robert Crease records that they had difficulty persuading people to contribute. Dyson wrote to forty leading physicists, many of whom, it seems, refused to contribute. Max Born *did* contribute, but only a short and rather halfhearted "Message," rather than a proper article. Those who did contribute included Leonard Schiff, David Hawkins, Phil Morrison, Cyril Smith, Willie Fowler, Robert Christy, Eugene Wigner, Julian Schwinger, Abraham Pais, Robert Serber and Kenneth Case. It was an impressive list, but more impressive was the list of people one would have expected to contribute, but who were not there: Isidor Rabi, Victor Weisskopf, Robert Bacher, Samuel Allison, Ed Condon, F. W. Loomis, Hans Bethe, Charles Lauritsen, and so on.

One of the most interesting articles in this Festschrift is a long and detailed study by Willie Fowler of "Massive Stars, Relativist Polytropes, and Gravitational Radiation," which is one of the first published papers to recognize the importance of Oppenheimer's work in this area. It begins by quoting from Oppenheimer's papers on the subject and remarking: "It is a tribute to Robert Oppenheimer's genius that these are the few statements about massive stars accepted as true today."

This special issue of *Reviews of Modern Physics* was printed on April 22, 1964, the very day of Oppenheimer's sixtieth birthday. According to the weekly letter that Dyson wrote home to his parents, the first copy "was rushed down from New York hot from the press," just in time for the party they had arranged for Oppenheimer at the Strömgrens' house. "Oppenheimer," Dyson wrote, "seemed to be genuinely surprised and greatly moved. It was the first time I have ever seen him at a loss for a suitable speech. He just said 'Thank you' rather incoherently and sat down."

The next day, Oppenheimer flew across the United States to Berkeley, where he delivered a lecture on the life and work of Niels Bohr to an audience of 12,500. "I am very pleased to be back home," he told the massive crowd that had come to hear him. "I lived here a long time and to those of you to whom a choice is offered, don't go away." After Berkeley, Oppenheimer gave talks at Caltech, UCLA and, finally, on May 18, at Los Alamos. Everywhere he went he lectured on Bohr, emphasizing again and again the social, political and personal importance of Bohr's notion of complementarity.

In September 1964, at the Rencontres Internationales de Genève, Oppenheimer gave a talk entitled "L'Intime et le Commun" ("The Intimate and the Open"), in which he touched again upon the themes of his 1963 Mount Kisco talk, urging that the openness espoused by Bohr should be expanded to include the private as well as the public. Referring to his security hearing, which by this time was ten years in the past, he said:

> . . . when the proceedings were published, many said that my life had become an open book. That was not really true. Most of what meant most to me never appeared in those hearings. Perhaps much was not known; certainly much was not relevant. I did have occasion then to think of what it might have been like to be an open book. I have come to the conclusion that if in fact privacy is an accidental blessing, and can be taken from you, if it is worth anyone's trouble, for a few dollars, and a few hours, it may still not be such a bad way to live.

He was speaking here, of course, as someone who for many years had lived with the awareness that his phones were being tapped, his rooms bugged and his every movement followed and monitored. One might have expected him to be especially protective of his privacy, and indeed for most of his life he was. During these last years, however, he seemed to be striving for a very personal kind of openness, an important element of which was the recognition and acceptance of the evil in oneself:

> We most of all should try to be experts in the worst about ourselves: we should not be astonished to find some evil there, that we find so very readily abroad and in all others. We should not, as Rousseau tried to, comfort ourselves that it is the responsibility and the fault of others, that we are just naturally good; nor should we let Calvin persuade us that despite our obvious duty we are without any power, however small and limited, to deal with what we find of evil in ourselves. In this knowledge, of ourselves, of our profession, of our country—our often beloved country—of our civilization itself, there is scope for what we most need: self knowledge, courage, humor, and some charity. These are the great gifts that our tradition makes to us, to prepare us for how to live tomorrow.

He chose a related theme when, on September 27, 1964, he was invited to speak at the inauguration of the University of Peace, an institution founded by the Dominican friar Father Pire, who had won the Nobel Peace Prize in 1958 for his work with refugees. What Oppenheimer emphasized on this occasion was the need to overcome pride, linking that theme to the danger of nuclear weapons in the following way:

> Today we live . . . with the arms race promising death to hundreds of millions, with massive retaliation, as it is called, and with its more sophisticated, better educated young brother, deterrence, and with cold wars. They are less inhuman than war itself, and let us not forget it, but they are not very human either. Yet by casting doubt, by recognizing the nearly ultimate evil of general war in this age, they question all war; they question our national sense of self-righteousness. They limit and often mark our pride, and our pride in our power, and in the legitimacy of violence, and our resort to it, or of hate itself as a welcome element of Man's destiny.

Hearing and reading passages like this, it was natural to imagine that Oppenheimer was here confessing and apologizing for his "sin" in having been responsible for the deaths of tens of thousands of people. But, as he said over and over again, he did not regret his work at Los Alamos, nor did he think he and his colleagues had done something unjustifiable in building the bomb. When he said that physicists had "known sin," the sin he had in mind was not murder, but pride.

One person who misunderstood Oppenheimer on this crucial point was the German playwright Heinar Kipphardt, who wrote a play based on the 1954 hearings called *In the Matter of J. Robert Oppenheimer*. The play, first performed in Germany in January 1964, took much of its dialogue from the transcript, but added to it additional material, such as Oppenheimer's postwar comment that physicists had known sin and some lines of Kipphardt's own. It was these last that were the main source of the problem. At the end of the play, Kipphardt's Oppenheimer delivers a soliloquy in which he expresses regret for what he and his colleagues had done:

> I begin to wonder whether we were not perhaps traitors to the spirit of science when we handed over the results of our research to the military . . . We have spent years of our lives in developing ever sweeter means of destruction, we have been doing the work of the military and I feel in my very bones that this was wrong . . . I will never work on war projects again. We have been doing the work of the Devil.

Oppenheimer read the play in August 1964 and was horrified by it. Though the portrayal of him was clearly intended to be sympathetic, the sympathy was, from his point of view, misplaced, since it was based on misrepresenting his views. On October 12, 1964, he wrote to Kipphardt, complaining that "You make me say things which I did not and do not believe."

> Even this September in Geneva, during a conference of the Rencontres de Genève, I was asked by the Canon van Kamp whether now, knowing the results, I would again do what I did during the war: participate in a responsible way in the making of atomic weapons. To this I answered *yes*. When a voice in the audience angrily asked "Even after Hiroshima?" I repeated my *yes*.

"It seems to me," he added, "you may well have forgotten Guernica, Dachau, Coventry, Belsen, Warsaw, Dresden, Tokyo. I have not. I think that if you find it necessary so to misread and misrepresent your principal character, you should perhaps write about someone else." He finished by warning Kipphardt of legal action "against you and the producers of your play."

Meanwhile, the play was proving popular with audiences and gaining favorable reviews, not only in Germany, but also in the U.S. Oppenheimer did not carry out his threat to sue Kipphardt, but he did express his feelings to the press. "The whole damn thing was a farce," he told the *Washington Post*, "and these people are trying to make a tragedy out of it." On November 11, 1964, he issued a press statement on the subject, which identified a problem that perhaps upset him even more than the misrepresentation of his own views. Kipphardt, he pointed out, "makes me say that Bohr disapproved of the work at Los Alamos because it would make science subservient to the military." As he had spent the last eighteen months giving lecture after lecture on Bohr in which he had said that Bohr had given everyone at Los Alamos fresh hope and a revived sense of purpose, he could not let this go uncontested. He had, he insisted, "never said such a thing"; Bohr "understood and welcomed what we were doing."

When the play was performed in Paris at the end of 1964, the French director, Jean Vilar, heeded Oppenheimer's protests, removed the lines that had offended him and created a version that was faithful to the transcript and the historical facts. The result was that critics scorned it for being too literal, Kipphardt himself complained that his play had been thus rendered toothless, and audiences stayed away.

In February 1965, Oppenheimer went one step further with regard to a proposed performance of the play at the Aldwych Theatre in London and successfully had it canceled. "I have not been for this play," Oppenheimer wrote to the London producer, John Roberts. "I have not wished to have it produced in Berlin, or in Paris, or anywhere else. I would hope that it would not be produced in England, or in this country." The lines added by Kipphardt, Oppenheimer said revealingly, "seem to me, in fact, rather 'anti-American.'" A few weeks later, Roberts received a letter from Oppenheimer's lawyers, threatening to "restrain the production of the play as an unlawful invasion of privacy." By the same means, in October 1965, a proposed production in New York was also scrapped.

Why was Oppenheimer so opposed to the play? Some have suggested that he did not want to have all the unpleasantness of the hearing revived, replayed and regurgitated; others that, having won the Fermi Prize, he wanted to get his security clearance back and therefore did not want to be represented as a man in opposition to the government. But perhaps his twin descriptions of the hearing as a "farce" and the play as "anti-American" provide the real answer: whether it came in the form of an accusation from Lewis Strauss or as admiring flattery from Heinar Kipphardt, Oppenheimer was determined to resist the idea that he was opposed to his own country, because his deep love of America was one of the strongest passions he had. Einstein captured this well when, on being told that, against his advice, Oppenheimer had submitted himself to a security hearing (Einstein had advised Oppenheimer to tell the officials they were fools and then to go home), he said: "The trouble with Oppenheimer is that he loves a woman who doesn't love him—the United States government."

Another unwelcome threat to his reputation came in the summer of 1964 in the form of a letter from Haakon Chevalier. The letter came out of the blue. Oppenheimer had had nothing to do with Chevalier since the end of 1954, and the publication in 1959 of *The Man Who Would Be God* did nothing to tempt him to resume contact or to think warmly about his old friend and comrade. Chevalier was writing to tell Oppenheimer that, after publishing his fictionalized account of their relationship, he had been urged by a number of people (including, he claimed, Niels Bohr) to write "the true story of my involvement with you" in a nonfictional way. "The reason I am writing to you," Chevalier told Oppenheimer, "is that an important part of the story concerns your and my membership in the same unit of the CP from 1938 to 1942."

> I should like to deal with this in its proper perspective, telling the facts as I remember them. As this is one of the things in your life which, in my opinion, you have least to be ashamed of, and as your

commitment, attested among other things by your "Reports to our Colleagues," which today make impressive reading, was a deep and genuine one, I consider that it would be a grave omission not to give it its due prominence.

Oppenheimer's reply, dated August 7, 1964, was firm and somewhat icy:

Dear Haakon,
   Your letter came while I was away from Princeton; hence this small delay in my answering. I am glad that you wrote to me. Your letter asks whether I would have any objections. Indeed I do. What you say of yourself I find surprising. Surely in one respect what you say of me is not true. I have never been a member of the Communist Party, and thus have never been a member of a Communist Party unit. I, of course, have always known this. I thought you did too.

The following March, Lloyd Garrison phoned Oppenheimer to discuss what to do about Chevalier's book. Notes of the conversation, presumably written by Oppenheimer, survive and record what he told Garrison: "Had letter from Chevalier, obscure, slightly blackmailing. Took it to Joe Volpe. Brief answer. No further correspondence." They decided not to try and block the book, for fear of giving it free publicity. In the event, that proved wise. The book, entitled *Oppenheimer: The Story of a Friendship*, was published in the summer of 1965. It did not state that Oppenheimer had been a member of a Communist Party cell. Nor did it sell any better or get reviewed any more favorably than *The Man Who Would Be God*.

Oppenheimer was by this time a weary man, aged beyond his years. On April 15, 1965, a few days before his sixty-first birthday, he wrote to the institute's Board of Trustees, telling them that he intended to retire, not from the faculty, but from the directorship, at the end of June 1966. Two days after his birthday, on April 24, 1965, the institute announced this decision and also that Oppenheimer's plans for his forthcoming time as a nondirectorial professor of physics would include, in Oppenheimer's words, "physics, of course, which is in a most dramatic and hopeful stage, and to seek an understanding, both historical and philosophical, of what the sciences have brought to human life." When, in May 1965, the *New York Times Magazine* ran a feature on the institute, they reported that few people mourned Oppenheimer's passing and that there was, on the contrary, "a general feeling that his resignation as director is best for him and best for the Institute."

The summer of 1965 was marked by two significant anniversaries that kept Oppenheimer in the public eye: the twentieth anniversary of the Trinity test on July 16 and the twentieth anniversary of the bombing of Hiroshima on August 6. In interviews with *Newsweek*, the *New York Herald Tribune*, the *Washington Post* and *CBS Evening News with Walter Cronkite*, Oppenheimer took the opportunity yet again to say that he did not regret working on the bomb. Asked on CBS whether he had a "bad conscience" about the bomb, he replied:

> Well, I don't want to speak for others because we're all different. I think when you play a meaningful part in bringing about the death of over 100,000 people and the injury of a comparable number, you naturally don't think of that as—with ease. I believe we had a great cause to do this. But I do not think that our consciences should be entirely easy, at stepping out of the part of studying nature, learning the truth about it, to change the course of human history. Long ago I said once that, in a crude sense which no vulgarity and no humor could quite erase, the physicist had known sin, and I didn't mean by that the deaths that were caused as a result of our work. I meant that we had known the sin of pride. We had turned to affect, in what proved to be a major way, the course of man's history. We had the pride of thinking we knew what was good for man, and I do think it had left a mark on many of those who were responsibly engaged. This is not the natural business of the scientist.

Oppenheimer gave far fewer public speeches in 1965 than in previous years and those he did give were markedly different. In place of the intimate, confessional tone of his Mount Kisco lecture and the emphasis on the personal, on acknowledging the evil in oneself, of his Geneva talk, one finds—in accordance with what he had announced as his new research topics—an interest in the history and philosophy of science. Not that his talks of this year can be regarded as a contribution to the academic disciplines of the history and philosophy of science (they are far too informal for that), but, in "Physics and Man's Understanding," given at the bicentennial celebrations of the Smithsonian Institution, and in "To Live with Ourselves," given at the 1965 U.S. Army National Junior Science and Humanities Symposium, there is certainly a more detailed, more focused concentration on the history of science than in his previous talks.

The detail is particularly evident, and particularly telling, in "To Live with Ourselves," in which Oppenheimer gives examples, taken from history and from his own life, of what scientific discovery is like, his thesis being that "the life of the scientist is, along with the life of the poet, soldier, prophet and artist, deeply relevant to man's understanding of his situation and his view of his destiny." His first detailed example is from his own life, from the time when, in 1935, he and Frank took some time off to go riding in New Mexico. There, Oppenheimer told his audience, he received a letter from Milton White (then a graduate student at Berkeley), describing some experiments he had recently performed, which demonstrated, for the first time, the existence of the nuclear forces that act between protons. "This was," Oppenheimer said, "one of the many times when the question, 'how hard is matter?' got a new, fresh answer." He then discussed Rutherford's discovery of the nucleus, Hahan and Strassman's discovery of fission, Anderson's discovery of the positron, Einstein's discovery of relativity, and others. The moral he draws from these examples is: "when the discovery has any of the qualities of the great ones, it has to reach back into a solid framework of experience and understanding and a great tradition; it has to mean something."

In "Physics and Man's Understanding" Oppenheimer posed an interesting question: why did the great scientific achievements of Copernicus, Galileo and Newton have such an impact on our culture at large, while those of Einstein, Bohr and Heisenberg had a comparatively small impact? His answer was as follows:

[The] new discoveries which liberated physics have all rested on the correction of some common view which was, in fact, demonstrably in error; they have all rested on a view which could not be reconciled with the experience of physics. The shock of discovering this error, and the glory of being free of it, have meant much to the practitioners. Five centuries ago the errors that physics and astronomy and mathematics were beginning to reveal were errors common to the thought, the doctrine, the very form and hope of European culture. When they were revealed, the thought of Europe was altered. The errors relativity and quantum theory have corrected were physicists' errors, shared a little, of course, by our colleagues in related subjects.

Oppenheimer offers as a "vivid example" of this Lee and Yang's discovery of the nonconservation of parity. "The error which this corrected was limited to a very small part of mankind." It is an interesting thesis, but it is rather underdeveloped in this paper, and, unfortunately, Oppenheimer never returned to it.

At the end of 1965, Oppenheimer gave a talk on Einstein at a UNESCO meeting in Paris that was evidently an attempt to place Einstein and his work into the historical and philosophical scheme he had outlined in the papers discussed above. That is, though he acknowledged that Einstein was a great and original thinker, he wanted to show that, in accordance with the views expressed in "To Live with Ourselves," Einstein's discoveries "meant something" only in the context of a great tradition. So Oppenheimer briefly went through Einstein's great contributions to physics, showing how they related to the traditions of: first, thermodynamics; second, Maxwell's field equations; and third, the philosophical tradition associated with the Principle of Sufficient Reason. In the last twenty-five years of Einstein's life, however, said Oppenheimer, "his tradition in a certain sense failed him":

> He did not like the elements of indeterminacy. He did not like the abandonment of continuity or of causality. These were things that he had grown up with, saved by him, and enormously enlarged; and to see them lost, even though he had put the dagger in the hand of their assassin by his own work, was very hard on him.

The talk was controversial, largely because it was misunderstood and partly because Oppenheimer chose to make the above perfectly reasonable point by talking of dispelling the "clouds of myth" that surrounded Einstein. He meant the myth that saw Einstein as an individual genius operating in isolation from the tradition of physics. He made life difficult for himself, however, by appearing to be snobbish. Einstein, he said, "was almost wholly without sophistication and wholly without worldliness. I think that in England people would have said that he did not have much 'background,' and in America that he lacked 'education.'" This was a compliment, though it did not look like one, especially as Oppenheimer seemed so determined, in other small areas, to bring Einstein down to size, pointing out, for example, that "he was not that good a violinist," and also that his famous letter to Roosevelt "had very little effect."

After giving this UNESCO talk, Oppenheimer left for St. John, where he and Kitty celebrated Christmas and New Year in the usual style. In January 1966, they returned to the States and Oppenheimer attended the annual meeting of the American Physical Society, where he gave a historical lecture on "Thirty Years of Mesons." After running through the story of the meson, from Yukawa's first prediction to Lee and Yang's discovery of nonconservation of parity, Oppenheimer concluded:

> It seems to me that we are in for a far greater novelty than the discovery of "more fundamental" particles. It is not one of the privileges, as it is assuredly not one of the virtues, of senility to make predictions. I make only one. I think that we are unlikely to live again through such a ten-year joke as mistaking the mu mesons for Yukawa's particles. I do not think that could have happened if it had not been for World War II. That too, I hope, is not so likely to recur.

Oppenheimer at this time was still not sixty-two years old, but he looked much older. "You see the old man," one physicist is said to have remarked at a party given during the conference, "he's dying." But he added: "I wouldn't cross him!"

At the beginning of February 1966, Oppenheimer was diagnosed with throat cancer and started to receive radiation treatment. He spent much of March in the hospital. At the end of the month, Dyson wrote to his parents that he was only now "finding out how lonely the Oppenheimers really are in spite of their huge numbers of 'friends.' . . . These are the last two weeks of Robert's radiation treatment, and in this time he must know whether it is life or death."

> I have been over three times to talk with Robert and Kitty. Kitty believes, perhaps rightly, that I can help Robert to keep alive by keeping alive his interest in physics. She feels desperately that he needs to be convinced that he is still needed in the community of physicists. On the other hand, I find that Robert is just so physically tired from the radiation that my instinct is to hold his hand in silence rather than burden him with particles and equations.

The radiation treatment finished in April, and by June he was able to travel. He went to Mount Kisco to attend one last meeting of the group that he had helped to set up. On June 21, the *New York Times* carried the headline "Dr. Oppenheimer Plans History of Physics After His Retirement," under which, however, was a short piece not about Oppenheimer's proposed book, but about his illness and his forthcoming retirement. It quoted Oppenheimer as saying that he would be giving his "hideously complete" archive to the Library of Congress, "if anyone cares to look at it." At the end of June, Oppenheimer ceased being director of the institute, and he and Kitty moved out of Olden Manor and into a much smaller house that had been the Yangs' home.

After a last trip to St. John, the Oppenheimers returned to their new home in the autumn of 1966. In November, Oppenheimer gave his final public lecture, entitled "A Time in Need." If the talk seemed a little lackluster and somewhat platitudinous, this was hardly surprising; it was obvious by this time that he did not have long to live. He had, he said privately, "no confidence at all of enjoying good health in the future."

The Oppenheimers spent Christmas in Princeton that year for the first time in a decade. By this time the cancer was spreading and Oppenheimer was declining rapidly. In January 1967, he attended one last meeting of the Tuesday lunch group, at which he gave Treiman an earnest piece of advice: "Sam, don't smoke." The following month, on February 15, he attended his last faculty meeting. "Poor Oppenheimer is coming close to his end," wrote Dyson to his parents.

> He insisted on coming to this faculty meeting but he can hardly speak any more. We were all very polite and told him how glad we were that he came; but really it is a torture for everybody to watch him sit there speechless and suffering. His doctors have now given him up and we can only hope for a quick end.

The effort of attending the meeting exhausted Oppenheimer, and, when he got back home, he went to bed. He stayed there for most of the following three days, getting up only to receive visitors. One of these was the journalist Louis Fischer, whose life of Lenin Oppenheimer had admired. "He looked extremely thin," Fischer wrote to a friend, "his hair was sparse and white, and his lips were dry and cracked." Conversation was difficult because Oppenheimer "mumbled so badly that I suppose I understood about one word out of five." "I have a strong impression," Fischer added, "that he knew his mind was failing and that he probably wanted to die." The next day, Francis Fergusson came, but stayed only a very short while because Oppenheimer was so frail. "I walked him into his bedroom," Fergusson said in an interview years later, "and there I left him." The following evening, at 10:40 p.m. on Saturday, February 18, 1967, Oppenheimer died in his sleep.

A week later, February 25, a memorial service was held in Alexander Hall on the Princeton campus. On a bitterly cold afternoon, 600 mourners gathered to hear brief eulogies from Hans Bethe, Henry DeWolf Smyth and George Kennan. Bethe gave a summary of Oppenheimer's contributions to science and politics, after which Smyth, who had been the only AEC member to have voted in favor of reinstating Oppenheimer's security clearance, spoke about the shame he felt on America's behalf because of the security hearing: "It was a horrible period in American history, and we paid horribly for it." The same point was made more emphatically and more eloquently by Kennan, who remarked: "The truth is that the U.S. Government never had a servant more devoted at heart than this one." He also recalled how, shortly after the 1954 hearing, he had asked Oppenheimer why he had not left the United States. "Damn it," Oppenheimer replied, "I happen to love this country." Soon after the service, Kitty took Oppenheimer's ashes to St. John and scattered them in the sea.

Kitty herself survived for just five more years, most of which she spent living with Charlotte and Robert Serber. Serber, alone among Oppenheimer's friends, was devoted to Kitty. In the summer of 1972, Kitty bought an elegant fifty-two-foot ketch, which she called *Moonraker* and in which she and Serber planned to travel around the world. After setting sail from Fort Lauderdale in Forida, their plan was to cruise for a while in the Caribbean, before going through the Panama Canal on their way to Japan via the Galápagos Islands and Tahiti. When they reached Cristóbal, at the Atlantic end of the Panama Canal, however, Kitty became very ill and was admitted to a hospital in Panama City, where she died of an embolism on October 27. Five years later, Toni Oppenheimer, who had, throughout her life, been subject to bouts of depression, committed suicide at her home on St. John. Her second marriage had recently ended in divorce. Her brother Peter lived first in Perro Caliente and then in Santa Fe, where he worked as a contractor and carpenter. He is still alive, but recoils from anything connected with his famous father.

Oppenheimer loved Kitty, Toni and Peter, but he was never able to be the reliably affectionate husband or father they needed him to be. The problems he had as a child forming close bonds with other people had remained with him throughout his life. He had wanted those close bonds very much, but had not known how to create them. Similarly, and relatedly, he did not know how to open up to other people. In the last few years of his life, as we have seen, he had tried hard to overcome this trait, to reveal his inner self and become an "open book." But the book remained closed. What he called his "hideously complete" collection of private papers is impressively massive, but in those 296 boxes of letters, drafts and manuscripts there is remarkably little that gives away anything of an intimate nature. There is an abundance of material that testifies to his many-faceted brilliance—the "bright shining splinters" that Rabi described him as being made of—but little that shows Oppenheimer sharing ordinary emotions with his fellow human beings.

This aspect of his personality was touched on by George Kennan in his contribution to the memorial service. Oppenheimer, Kennan said, was "a man who had a deep yearning for friendship, for companionship, for the warmth and richness of human communication":

> The arrogance which to many appeared to be a part of his personality masked in reality an overpowering desire to bestow and receive affection. Neither circumstances nor at times the asperities of his own temperament permitted the gratification of this need in a measure remotely approaching its intensity.

Of the three people who spoke at the service, Kennan knew Oppenheimer the best by a long way. Indeed, many of Oppenheimer's friends felt that the memorial service had been hurriedly arranged and had not served its purpose well. A chance to do it better came in April 1967, when the American Physical Society organized its own memorial service. The speakers on this occasion included many of those whom one might have expected to speak at Princeton, each one allocated an aspect of Oppenheimer's life about which they had special knowledge. Robert Serber spoke on "The Early Years," Weisskopf on "The Los Alamos Years," Pais on "The Princeton Period" and Glenn Seaborg on "Public Service and Human Contributions." When the speeches were published as a book, Rabi wrote a short but illuminating introduction, which, in trying to convey the nature of Oppenheimer's complex character, emphasized his spirituality. "In Oppenheimer," Rabi remarked, "the element of earthiness was feeble."

> Yet it was essentially this spiritual quality, this refinement as expressed in speech and manner, that was the basis of his charisma. He never expressed himself completely. He always left a feeling that there were depths of sensibility and insight not yet revealed. These may be the qualities of the born leader who seems to have reserves of uncommitted strength.

The feebleness in Oppenheimer of the "element of earthiness," the sense one has of him being almost disembodied, is connected with his enigmatic elusiveness and his inability to make ordinary close contact with the people around him. But it also, Rabi perceptively suggests, was what made him so fascinating and therefore enabled Oppenheimer to become the great man he showed himself to be.

Notes and References

In the notes below Oppenheimer is referred to as "JRO"; his archive of papers, deposited at the Library of Congress, as "JRO papers, LOC"; Smith and Weiner (1980) as "S & W"; Bird and Sherwin (2005) as "B & S"; United States Atomic Energy Commission, *In the Matter of J. Robert Oppenheimer: Transcript of Hearing before Personnel Security Board* as "ITMO"; and Oppenheimer's co-correspondents, family members, biographers and interviewers as follows:

AE	Albert Einstein
AIP	American Institute of Physics (see list of interviews on pages 789–90)
AKS	Alice Kimball Smith
CA	Carl Anderson
CW	Charles Weiner
ECK	Edwin C. Kemble
EOL	Ernest O. Lawrence
ET	Edward Teller
EUC	Ed Condon
FF	Francis Fergusson
FO	Frank Oppenheimer
GU	George Uhlenbeck
HC	Haakon Chevalier
HWS	Herbert W. Smith
IIR	Isidor Isaac Rabi
JBC	James B. Conant
JE	John Edsall
JEH	J. Edgar Hoover
JW	Jeffries Wyman

KDN   Major General Kenneth D. Nichols
LRG   Leslie R. Groves
MB   Max Born
MJS   Martin J. Sherwin
NB   Niels Bohr
PAMD   Paul Adrien Maurice Dirac
PE   Paul Ehrenfest
PH   Paul Horgan
PWB   Percy W. Bridgman
REP   Raymond E. Priestley
TSK   Thomas S. Kuhn
WP   Wolfgang Pauli

Dates are given in the British (rather than the American) style, so that, for example, 1.2.1964 means February 1, 1964, not January 2, 1964.

Preface
xii. "Oppie did his physics": Kelly (2006), 136
xiii. highly derivative: compare Pais (2006) Chapter 6 with Robert Serber's article, "Particle physics in the 1930s: a view from Berkeley," in Brown and Hoddeson (1983), 206–21

PART ONE: 1904–1926

1. "Amerika, du hast es besser": Oppenheimer's German Jewish Background
3. "a man who": Rigden (1987), 231
3. "never got to be": ibid., 229
3. "tried to act": ibid., 228
3. "you carried on": Bernstein (2004), 3
3. "I understood his problem": ibid.
3. "These are my people": Rigden (1987), 229
4. Rabi was a "Polish Jew": see Rigden (1987)
4. In New York: what follows is based on the accounts of the history of the Jewish community in New York given in Barkai (1994), Cohen (1984), Diner (1992), Gay (1965), Klingenstein (1991), Kosak (2000), Mauch & Salmons (2003), Raphael (1983), Ribalow (1965) and Sorin (1992).
5. *Haskalah*: see Barkai (1994), Cohen (1984), Diner (1992) and Pulzer (1992)
6. "Amerika, du hast es besser": see *Goethes Werke*, Weimar: Hermann Bahlau, Volume 1, 137, quoted in Cohen (1984), 17. In full, the poem reads:

> *Amerika, du hast es besser*
> *Als unser Kontinent, das alte,*
> *Hast keine verfallene Schlösser*
> *Und keine Basalte.*

Dich stört nicht im Innern,
Zu lebendiger Zeit,
Unnützes Erinnern
Und vergeblicher Streit.

Benutzt die Gegenwart mit Glück!
Und wenn nun eure Kinder dichten,
Bewahre sie ein gut Geschick
Vor Ritter-, Rauber- und Gespenstergeschichten.

An English translation, published in *Fraser's Magazine* in May 1831, reads:

America, thou hast it better
Than our ancient hemisphere;
Thou hast no falling castles,
Nor basalt, as here.
Thy children, they know not,
Their youthful prime to mar,
Vain retrospection,
Nor ineffective war.

Fortune wait on thy glorious spring!
And, when in time thy poets sing,
May some good genius guard them all
From Baron, Robber, Knight, and Ghost traditional.

See Melz (1949) and Riley (1952)

6. beginning in the 1820s: see Diner (1992)
6. "the beautiful ground": quoted in Barkai (1994), 5
7. "Third Migration": see Sorin (1992)
7. their first reaction: ibid., 50
7. "the privileges and duties": ibid., 87
7. "These uptowners": ibid., 86
8. August Schönberg: Birmingham (1967), 24–5
8. Joseph Seligman: ibid., 132
8. Joseph Seligman's children: ibid.
8. Robert Anderson: see Lawson and Lawson (1911)
8. his birth certificate: see Bernstein (2004), 12, footnote 4
8. "As appears": Percy Bridgman in a letter of recommendation to Ernest Rutherford, June 24, 1925. See S & W, 77
9. "an unsuccessful small businessman": JRO, interview with TSK, 18.11.1963. See S & W, 3
9. his son, Julius: the following account of Julius, his uncles and his siblings relies on that given in Cassidy (2005), Chapter 1
10. "Our Crowd": see Birmingham (1967)
10. "Our crowd here": Sachs (1927), 219, quoted in Birmingham (1967), 256
11. in December 1862: see Cohen (1984), 148–53
11. "how thin": Cohen (1984), 149
11. Max Lilienthal: see Barkai (1994), 122

11. On January 3, 1863: ibid.

12. "becoming more Americanized": Birmingham (1967), 116

12. "the first gentile": ibid., 118

12. "The Bank": ibid., 119: italics in the original

12. "Seligman Affair": ibid., Chapter 18

13. The comic weekly *Puck*: quoted in ibid., 145

13. "Gentile and Jew": ibid., 145–6

13. "Hebrews need not apply": ibid., 147

13. "The Jews and Coney Island": reprinted in Raphael (1983), 260–3

13. "We cannot bring": ibid., 261

13. "was to have": Birmingham (1967), 147–8

13. Felix Adler: see Neumann (1951), Radest (1969)

14. "The Judaism of the Future": see Radest (1969), 17

14. "was not given": ibid.

14. in 1876, Adler gave a talk: ibid., 27

14. "We propose": ibid., 27–8

15. "Adler's proposal": ibid., 28

15. February 1877: ibid., 45

15. "The Sunday Meeting": ibid., 46

15. "Ethical Culture seemed": ibid., 47

15. In 1874–5: Cassidy (2005), 5. Cassidy reports that Solomon alone is listed, and later (23) he says that Sigmund was still in Europe at this time. As he points out himself (page 5, footnote 11), however, Sigmund's death certificate gives his year of immigration into the United States as 1869, so I am inclined to think that the company listed in the New York City *Directory* for 1874–5 actually included both brothers.

15. they appear: see Cassidy (2005), 23. Since Sigmund had been in America since 1869, I am inclined to believe that he and Solomon were both founder members of the Society.

15. funeral service: see Birmingham (1967), 149

16. In 1887: ibid., 258

16. "our good Jews": ibid.

16. "the first recognizably": ibid.

16. Solomon and Sigmund Rothfeld: Cassidy (2005), 6

16. "Race Prejudice at Summer Resorts": reprinted in Raphael (1983), 263–70

16. "Only within": ibid., 263

16. "In seeking reasons": ibid., 265

16. *The American Jew*: parts of it are reprinted in Raphael (1983), 270–8

16. "the book that": ibid., 259

17. "their hooked noses": ibid., 271

17. "long coats": ibid.

17. "Let the Jews": ibid., 276

17. "The Jew must go!": ibid., 278

17. he is listed: Cassidy (2005), 23

18. "New York's leading Jewish banker": see Birmingham (1967), 230

18. "not a personal matter": ibid., 239

18. "His bitterness": ibid., 240

18. It moved its office: Cassidy (2005), 9

18. younger brother Emil: Cassidy (2005), 4 and 9
18. In 1900: ibid., 9
18. In 1903: ibid.
18. Ella Friedman: what follows is based on the accounts given in Cassidy (2005), 10–11, and B & S, 10–11
19. According to her son: see Thorpe (2006), 21
19. her family tree: see http://americanjewisharchives.org/pdfs/stern_p021.pdf
19. mentioned several times: see Morais (1894), 104, 105, 193, 250
19. "a gentle, exquisite": see *Life* magazine, October 10, 1949, 124
19. When a girlfriend: Goodchild (1980), 22
20. Both suggestions: see, e.g., Cassidy (2005), 11
20. "spent his free hours": B & S, 10
20. "proper gentlemen": Goodchild (1980), 10
20. "there are special occasions": Adler (1886), 85–6
21. Upon Sigmund's death: Cassidy (2005), 9
21. the men who succeeded Felix Adler: Radest (1969), 95
21. "In the old days": ibid., 136
22. "supremely enviable": Adler (1915), 165
22. "I would urge": ibid., 167: italics in the original
22. "plea to the wealthy": ibid., 172
22. "The habit": Adler (1886), 97
23. "haven't enough physical courage": Sachs (1927), 219
23. a society that set up: see Neumann (1951), 19ff.
24. "Two things fill": the famous opening sentence of the conclusion of Kant's *Critique of Practical Reason*
24. "The moral law": Adler (1886), 33, 60
24. "act only": *Groundwork of the Metaphysics of Morals*, Cambridge: Cambridge University Press (1997), 31
24. "The rule reads": Adler (1933), 147
24. "high endeavor": Adler (1886), 15
24. "Truly disinterestedness": ibid.
24. "The pursuit of the artist": ibid.
24. "the Ideal": ibid., 89

2. *Childhood*

25. "My life": *Time* magazine, November 8, 1948, 70
25. "an unctuous": ibid.
25. "Not religion as a duty": Adler (1886), 97
25. "a hearty": FF, interview with MJS, 8.6.1979, quoted B & S, 13
25. A friend later recalled: HWS, interview with CW, 1.8.1974, quoted B & S, 27
26. "a woman who": B & S, 13
26. "a general distrust": FO, interview with CW, 9.2.1973, quoted Cassidy (2005), 16
26. Lewis Frank Oppenheimer: see Bernstein (2004), 6
26. "a mournful person": PH, interview with AKS, 14.4.1976, quoted S & W, 2
26. "I think my father": JRO, interview with TSK, 18.11.1963, quoted S & W, 5
27. "Just as I do": Michelmore (1969), 4. A slightly different version of the story is given in Royal (1969), 19. Neither gives a source for the story.

27. "I repaid": Royal (1969), 16

27. he met Benjamin Oppenheimer: JRO, interview with TSK, 18.11.1963, quoted S & W, 3

28. in October 1910: Cassidy (2005), 29

28. in 1878: see Cassidy (2005), 33

28. "a broad and generous education": Friess (1981), 100

28. in 1890: see Schweber (2000), 49

28. only 10 percent: ibid.

29. "We all did": B & S, 25

29. "The school is to be": Cassidy (2005), 36

29. "To larger truths": Adler (1886), 178

29. "spiritual fetters": ibid.

29. "All over this land": ibid., 178–9

29. in 1908: see Radest (1969), 94

30. "The American ideal": see Adler (1915), 73

30. Four times a year: see Cassidy (2005), 40–1

30. fabulously wealthy Guggenheim family: see Birmingham (1967), 271–5

30. "like a gentleman": ibid., 274

31. "light complexion": ibid., 272

31. "would not have surmised": ibid., 273

31. He once remarked: see Bethe (1997), 176

31. "He was still a little boy": S & W, 7

31. "rather gauche": B & S, 22

31. "a great need": ibid.

31. "Ask me a question in Latin": ibid.

31. "so far ahead": Cassidy (2005), 44

32. mostly A– and B+: ibid., 43

32. "When I was ten": S & W, 3

32. New York Mineralogical Club: see B & S, 14–15

32. an expanded version: see Adler (1915)

32. "Many of our fellow-citizens": ibid., 58

33. "Public opinion": ibid., 58–9

33. "The German ideal": ibid., 63

33. "The national ideal": ibid., 68

33. "is that of the uncommon quality": ibid., 73

33. "only a symptom": ibid., 5

33. "If we wish": ibid.

33. "The time will come": quoted in Radest (1969), 191–2

33. "high opinion": *New York Times*, January 31, 1916, quoted in Cassidy (2005), 49

33. "Anything German": ibid., 183

34. "the duty of every high school chap": *Inklings*, June 3, 1917, quoted Cassidy (2005), 53

34. "In discussing the war": Cassidy (2005), 55

34. "There is no room." *Inklings*, June 4, 1918, ibid.

34. "he swallowed Adler": S & W, 3

34. "In Flanders' fields": see Cassidy (2005), 60

35. "From conversations": Bernstein (2004), 11

35. feelings of guilt: see the remark quoted earlier (p. 26) from Royal (1969), 16

36. "business vulgarity": Thorpe (2006), 27

36. "pronounced oedipal attitude": ibid.
36. "I often felt": Royal (1969), 22
36. The other boys: the main source for this story is Royal (1969), 21–3
37. "They, as it were": ibid., 23
37. "I don't know": ibid.
37. "We talked as we walked": ibid., 21
37. "longed to demonstrate": Eliot (1965), 178
37. "It was said"; ibid., 172
38. "no spark": ibid.
38. "From that hour": ibid., 173
38. "Lydgate's conceit": ibid., 179
38. "to some extent": Royal (1969), 22
38. "He was an intellectual snob": ibid.
38. "bright and sensitive": ibid., 21
38. "did not prepare me": *Time* magazine, November 8, 1948, 70
39. "never heard a murmur": B & S, 27
39. "the most important element": Cassidy (2005), 20
39. *The Light*: see ibid. 41
39. "some of our dough boys": ibid.
39. Hans and Ernest Courant and Robert Lazarus: for more on the Courants and Lazarus, see the 2005 "Science Issue" of the Ethical Culture School magazine, *ECF Reporter*, at: http://www.ecfs.org/files/ecfreporter_winter2005.pdf, especially pages 10–12.
40. "It is almost forty-five years": Royal (1969), 23
40. "He was so brilliant": *Time* magazine, November 8, 1948, 70
40. "A very exciting experience": ibid.
40. "We must have spent": S & W, 4
41. his headmaster: Goodchild (1980), 12
41. had to be rescued: Royal (1969), 25
41. Cherry Grove: ibid., 24
41. Francis Fergusson: for more on Fergusson, see the Introduction to Fergusson (1998)
41. "It was a blowy day": B & S, 24
42. "He is to this day": S & W, 7
43. La Glorieta: see Gish (1988), especially Chapter 2
43. Franz Huning: see Huning (1973)
44. was interviewed in the 1930s: see Janet Smith's interview with Clara Fergusson, dated September 14, 1936, at: http://lcweb2.loc.gov/wpa/20040609.html
44. Sampson Noland Ferguson: see Gish (1988), Chapter 3
45. "who at that time": S & W, 7
45. "very, very kind": ibid., 5
46. "a long prospecting trip": ibid., 7
46. he was fond of saying: see, e.g., Pharr Davis (1969), 25

3. First Love: New Mexico

47. "you can't be an outsider": Sachs (1927), 219
47. "Gilbert": ibid., 220
47. Paul Horgan: see Gish (1995)
47. Horgan would later find fame: Horgan won both the Pulitzer and Bancroft

Prizes for his two-volume study of the American Southwest, *Great River: The Rio Grande in North American History* (1954), and won the Pulitzer again in 1976 for *Lamy of Santa Fe*, a biography of John Baptist Lamy, the émigré French clergyman who was the model for Willa Cather's central character in *Death Comes for the Archbishop*. He is also well known as the author of several critically and commercially successful novels, including *The Fault of Angels* (1933), *A Distant Trumpet* (1960) and *Things as They Are* (1964).

48. "polymaths," "this pygmy triumvirate," "this great troika": S & W, 8
48. Oppenheimer startled Herbert Smith: B & S, 25
48. Smith wondered: see Cassidy (2005), 62
48. "someone disparaged the Jews": ibid.
48. "He looked at me sharply": S & W, 9
49. "The Southwest can never": Erna Fergusson (1946), 18–19
49. "Such a country": ibid., 14
49. "Maybe everyone": Horgan (1942), quoted in Gish (1995), 12
49. "He was the most intelligent man": S & W, 8
50. "exquisite manners": ibid., 9
50. He later confided: ibid., 40
50. Manuel Chaves: see Simmons (1973)
50. Amado Chaves: see Simmons (1968)
51. pursued a career as a lawyer: see Twitchell (2007), 508–12
51. "all the time": B & S, 26
51. "For the first time": S & W, 10
51. "Lake Katherine": the story that Oppenheimer named this lake after Katherine Page is mentioned many times in local literature (see, e.g., http://mtnview ranch-cowles.com/page_7.htm, which is a history of a "dude ranch" similar to the one owned by the Chaveses). I do not know of an authoritative source for this story, but neither do I see any reason to doubt it.
52. "Thank God I won": B & S, 26
52. "He had become less shy": S & W, 8

4. Harvard

53. "The summer hotel": Abbot Lawrence Lowell to William Earnest Hocking, May 19, 1922, quoted in Karabel (2005), 88
54. "WASP flight": see Karabel (2005), 86–7
54. "Hebrews": ibid., 90
54. a faculty meeting on May 23, 1922: ibid.
54. "take into account": ibid.
54. "a radical departure": ibid., 92
54. "to consider principles": ibid., 93
54. "the primary object": ibid.
55. an illuminating exchange: see Raphael (1993), 292–7
55. "and other eminent Jews": ibid., 293
55. "Students of the Jewish faith": ibid., 293–4
55. "a rapidly growing anti-Semitic feeling": ibid., 294
55. "Carrying your suggestion": ibid., 296
55. "We want": ibid., 297
55. "To be an American": Feingold (1995), 17
56. the dean's office: see Karabel (2005), 94

56. Starting in the autumn of 1922: ibid.
56. "What change": ibid.
56. "religious preference": ibid.
56. On April 7, 1923: ibid., 100
56. "far removed": ibid., 95
56. "no departure": ibid., 101
56. 25 percent: ibid., 105
56. "They are . . . going": ibid., 109
57. "not a negligible fact": Palevsky (2000), 103
57. "Shylock": S & W, 13
57. "misanthropy": ibid., 31
57. "the benign Lowell": ibid., 13
57. "Harvard has so far": ibid.
58. "I wanted not to be involved": Thorpe (2006), 30
58. "a little bit possessive": ibid., 32
58. "a sort of feeling": ibid., 33
59. Black introduced him: see ibid., 31, and Cassidy (2005), 71
59. John Edsall: for more on Edsall's life and work, see Doty (2005) and Edsall (2003)
59. *The Gad-Fly*: see Cassidy (2005), 72
59. "to sting people": Plato, *Apology*, section 30e
59. "Among the collegiate herd": Cassidy (2005), 72
59. "I don't know": ibid.
59. "asinine pomposity": S & W, 15
60. He has recalled: ibid., 33
60. "a little bit precious": Thorpe (2006), 34
60. "I was very fond of music": S & W, 33–4
60. "You're the only physicist": ibid., 34
60. "Category Phoenix": Ellanby (1952)
60. "Chain Reaction": Ellanby (1956)
60. *Races and People*: Boyd and Asimov (1955)
60. Boyd and Asimov argued: ibid., Chapter 2
61. "the closest friends": S & W, 45
61. later letters to Horgan: see, e.g., ibid., 40–41
61. Prescott Street: ibid., 12
61. doubtful that he ever met Fergusson: ibid., 44
61. "Boyd, as you charitably predicted": ibid., 57
62. "seen something of Robert": ibid., 16
62. "a little science club": ibid.
62. "get professors": ibid.
62. "an aberrant Cambridge Puritan": ibid.
63. In his first year: ibid., 14
63. "a wonderful man": ibid.
63. "quiet futility": ibid., 15
64. "is not an educational institution": Cassidy (2005), 74–5
64. he applied *twice*: see S & W, 15
64. but was rejected: ibid., 57
64. "I contend": Karabel (2005), 121
65. "bookworms": ibid.

65. "fondness of": ibid.
65. a formula: ibid.
65. "I am again": S & W, 18
66. "a disgusting and doddering syphilitic": ibid., 19
66. "I shall send you my story": ibid., 20
66. "received another inspiration": ibid., 24
66. "Here are the masterpieces": ibid., 25
66. "imitation of Katherine Mansfield": ibid., 27
66. "artificiality of emotional situation": ibid.
66. "conscious": ibid.
66. "I should not have the hardihood": ibid.
67. "nothing but admiration": ibid., 52
67. "I am overwhelmed": ibid., 55
67. "skill with people": ibid.
67. "I find it hard to swallow": ibid., 56
67. "I suppose": ibid.
68. "I find these awful people": ibid., 57
68. "the whole tone": Bernstein (2004), 16
69. "Scandal": Cather (1920), 169–98
69. "While he was still": ibid., 186–7
70. "His business associates": ibid., 187
70. "that used to belong": ibid., 191
70. "She and I are in the same boat": ibid., 198
70. a huge biography: Horgan (1976)
70. "Willa Cather's Incalculable Distance": Horgan (1988), 79–92
70. "a true artist of prose": ibid., 90
70. "Doesn't A Lost Lady remind you": S & W, 51
71. "represents civilization in the West": Randall (1960), 176
71. "The Old West": Cather (1923)
72. "scintillated more": S & W, 22
72. "Are you again": ibid., 19
72. "insanely jealous": ibid., 22
72. "But oh, beloved": ibid., 32
72. "Please": ibid., 33
73. "hear about your adventures": ibid., 67
73. "the classic confectionery": ibid.
73. remarked many years later: ibid., 68
73. "similarly satisfying": ibid., 32
73. "searched the plant": ibid.
73. "Only one wretch": ibid., 32–3
74. "The job and people": ibid., 33
74. "Paul [Horgan] has been with me": ibid., 35
74. "It was my first taste": ibid., 34
74. He recalls: ibid., 36
74. "And toward the end": ibid., 38
74. Horgan himself: ibid., 37
75. Boyd was impressed: see ibid., 34 and 37
75. Bernheim, on the other hand: ibid.

75. ". . . we would go out": ibid., 36–7
75. "salt-encrusted": ibid., 28
75. "But really, maestro": ibid., 35
75. "more elementary": Jeans (1908), v
75. "The present book": ibid.
76. "what I liked in chemistry": S & W, 45
76. "I can't emphasize strongly enough": ibid., 45–6
76. wrote to Edwin C. Kemble: ibid., 28–9
77. "partial list": ibid., 29
77. his inaugural lecture: Lewis (1914)
78. "any man": ibid., 6
78. "Mr. Oppenheimer": S & W, 29
78. "Years later": ibid.
78. "the textbook bible": Kevles (1995), 160
79. a telegram: see S & W, 39
79. a great variety of courses: see ibid., 45
80. "I'm sorry to contradict you": various versions of this story have appeared in print over the years, beginning with that in *Time* magazine, November 8, 1948, 71, and continuing with: Royal (1969), 29–30, Michelmore (1969), 13, Goodchild (1980), 16, and B & S, 34. My version combines the Royal and *Time* accounts. The various versions are all substantially the same, except that, in the Michelmore/Goodchild accounts, Oppenheimer places the temple "fifty, a hundred years earlier." Oppenheimer's view that the temple was built before 400 BC receives *some* support from modern scholarship, which dates it to 430–420 BC (see Cerchiai et al. [2004], 276).
80. Jeffries Wyman: for more on Wyman's life and work, see Alberty et al. (2003), Gill (1987) and Simoni et al. (2002)
81. "Francis was full of talk": see Thorpe (2006), 29
81. "Jeffries too": S & W, 39
81. "was a little precious": ibid.
81. as Boyd had: see ibid., 33–4, where Boyd is quoted as saying that the chief thing he and Oppenheimer did *not* have in common was a love of music; while Boyd was "very fond of music," he considered Oppenheimer to be "totally amusical."
81. "completely blind": ibid., 39
81. "found social adjustment very difficult": ibid., 61
81. "We were good friends": ibid.
81. "He wasn't a comfortable person": ibid., 44
81. "he was pretty careful": ibid., 45
82. he later said: *Time* magazine, November 8, 1948, 71
82. "I am working very hard now": S & W, 51
82. "Generously, you ask what I do": ibid., 54
82. "The whole tone": Bernstein (2004), 16—see also page 68 above
82. "We were all too much in love": S & W, 60
82. "ravishing creature": ibid., 69
83. have dinner at Locke-Ober's: Michelmore (1969), 15
83. Boyd also remembers: S & W, 60–1
83. And Bernheim recalls: ibid.
83. trips to Cape Ann: ibid., 25

83. "ramshackle cottage": ibid., 24
83. "mythological landscape": ibid., 25
83. "Even in the last stages": ibid., 60
83. "For me": ibid., 62
83. Oppenheimer discovered: ibid., 65
84. "I cannot decide": ibid., 67
84. "I am taking a course": ibid.
84. "It is almost forty years ago": ibid., 71
84. In addition: for a list of courses Oppenheimer took during his final year, see ibid., 68
84. George Birkhoff: for a brief account of Birkhoff's life and work, see Dool (2003)
84. "because he'd been working on it": S & W, 69
85. "one of the world's greatest academic anti-Semites": see Siegmund-Schultze (2009), 225
85. "He is Jewish": Thorpe (2006), 35
85. "I found Bridgman": S & W, 69
85. "a certificate": ibid., 70
85. he wrote to Francis Fergusson: ibid., 72–3
85. "frantic, bad and graded A": ibid., 70
85. two Bs: ibid., 73–4
86. "got plastered": ibid., 74

5. *Cambridge*

87. "You will tell me": S & W, 73
87. "your ability": ibid., 86
87. "sailing and recuperating": ibid., 73
87. "to see about laboratory facilities": ibid., 79
88. "The Parents": ibid., 80
88. "immense, huge, pounding rain": ibid., 81
88. "near the center": ibid., 75
88. Rutherford: for more on Rutherford's life, see Eve (1939), Birks (1962), Wilson (1983) and Campbell (1999). For a shorter summary account, see Cropper (2001), Chapter 21. For the original expression of Rutherford's planetary model of the atom, see Rutherford (1911). Popular accounts of that model are available in Bizony (2007), Part Two, Gamow (1965), "Chap. 10½," Gamow (1985), Chapter II, Gamow (1988), Chapter VII, and Gribbin (1984), Chapter 2.
88. the Cavendish Laboratory: see Crowther (1974), Larsen (1962) and Thomson (1964)
89. J. J. Thomson: see Thomson (1964a and 1964b)
89. in 1897 he discovered: see Thomson (1897)
89. Niels Bohr: for Bohr's life and work, see Moore (1967), Pais (1991) and Rozental (1967)
90. the "Rutherford-Bohr model": first put forward in Bohr (1913), reprinted in Bohr (1981). Many popularizations of this model have appeared in print over the last hundred years or so. Among the ones I have consulted are: Bizony (2007), Part Two, Gamow (1965), "Chap. 10½," Gamow (1985), Chapter II, Gamow (1988), Chapter VII, Gribbin (1984), Chapter 4, Hoffmann (1959), Chapter V, and Kumar (2009), Chapter 3. Technically more sophisticated

accounts can be found in Mills (1994), Chapter 12, and Treiman (1999), Chapter 3.

91. the "Bohr-Sommerfeld model": for an accessible account of this, see Kumar (2009), 112–15

91. "that brief excursion": FF to JRO, 25.4.1925, S & W, 73

91. "perfectly prodigious": ibid., 77

92. "excellent applicants": see JRO to PWB, 29.8.1925, ibid., 82

92. *Antarctic Adventure*: Priestley (1914)

92. *Breaking the Hindenburg Line*: Priestley (1919)

93. "should like to be admitted": JRO to REP, 30.8.1925, S & W, 82–3

93. "as soon as it seems advisable": JRO to REP, 16.9.1925, ibid., 84–5

93. "knows everyone at Oxford": JRO to HWS, 11.12.1925, ibid., 90

93. meetings at Pontigny: see Smith (2000), 100–1

94. "To be invited to Pontigny": ibid., 101

94. "rather Russian account": S & W, 86

94. "I do not think": JRO to FF, 1.11.1925, ibid.

95. "some terrible complications": JRO to FF, 15.11.1925, ibid., 88

95. "The Two Cultures": Snow (1959)

95. Sir Arthur Shipley: see the obituary in the *British Medical Journal*, October 1, 1927, 615

95. "miserable hole": JRO, interview with TSK, 18.11.1963, S & W, 89

96. "I am having a pretty bad time": JRO to FF, 1.11.1925, ibid., 87

96. a curious document: see B & S, 41 and 44–5. The document is now in the Sherwin Collection, attached to an interview with FF by AKS, dated April 21, 1976.

96. "was completely at a loss": FF in interview with MJS, 18.6.1979, quoted B & S, 41 and 47

96. "seemed more self-confident": ibid., 41

96. "first class case of depression": ibid., 44

96. "He found himself": ibid.

97. "Fortunately": ibid.

97. "tried to put them together": ibid., 45

97. "ridiculously unworthy": ibid.

97. "did a very good and chiefly rhetorical imitation": ibid.

97. "There they lay": ibid.

97. "The academic standard": JRO to FF, 1.11.1925, S & W, 87

97. Patrick Blackett: see Hore (2003), Lovell (1976) and Nye (2004)

97. "a young Oedipus": I. A. Richards, quoted in Nye (2004), 25

98. his most important contributions: see Crowther (1974), Chapter 16

98. Blackett's remarkable photographs: ibid., 214

98. Nobel Prize: Franck's acceptance speech, with the rather unenticing title "Transformations of kinetic energy of free electrons into excitation energy of atoms by impacts," can be found on the Nobelprize.org. website: at http://nobelprize.org/nobel_prizes/physics/laureates/1925/franck-lecture.html

99. Max Born: for Born's life, see Born (1978) and Greenspan (2005)

99. "handsomest, gayest, happiest pair": I. A. Richards, quoted in Nye (2004), 28

99. collection of essays: Wright (1933)

99. "The Craft of Experimental Physics": ibid., 67–96

99. "is a Jack-of-All-Trades": ibid., 67

100. "The point is": Goodchild (1980), 17

100. Rutherford himself: see Pais (1986), 367. Rutherford told the story to Paul Dirac, who then repeated it to Pais. Dirac, Pais adds, "witnessed a similar occurrence later in Göttingen."

100. "felt so miserable": JW in an interview with CW, 28.5.1975, quoted B & S, 43

100. an attempt to murder his tutor: the story of the poisoned apple has been told many times in many different versions, all of them (directly or indirectly) based on accounts given by Oppenheimer to his friends. Denise Royal, basing her account on that of an unnamed "informant" (presumably Jeffries Wyman), says that in the Christmas vacation of 1925, Oppenheimer went with Wyman to Corsica and, near the end of the holiday, turned down Wyman's suggestion that they travel to Rome to meet Fergusson and Koenig, saying, with a twinkle in his eye, that he had to get back to Cambridge because he had left a poisoned apple on Blackett's table. This, Royal says, "was Robert's whimsical way of say-ing he had some work to do for Blackett" (Royal [1969], 36).

Essentially the same story (based on the interview CW conducted with JW in 1975) is told in Smith and Weiner, though they correct some of the details, placing the Corsican holiday in the spring vacation, rather than at Christmas, and mentioning that Edsall was also included in the trip. "To this day," they say, "Edsall and Wyman are not sure about the poisoned-apple story; at the time they assumed it was an hallucination on Robert's part" (S & W, 93). "Meta-phoric interpretations," they insist, "should not be excluded" (ibid.). Goodchild repeats Smith and Weiner's version of the story, and does not even entertain the idea that there actually was a poisoned apple. It was, he thinks, either an "elaborate metaphor" or a hallucination (Goodchild [1980], 18).

Bernstein, partly because he believes that Oppenheimer "must have scarcely known Blackett," is inclined to attribute the story to "the mythmaking Oppen-heimer indulged in for most of his life, sometimes with disastrous consequences for himself and others" (Bernstein [2004], 21).

My account follows that of Bird and Sherwin, who make crucial use of the recollections of Francis Fergusson, given in an interview that Sherwin con-ducted with Fergusson in 1979. Remembering a confession that Oppenheimer had made to him at the end of 1925 (so some months before the holiday in Corsica), Fergusson told Sherwin: "He [Oppenheimer] had kind of poisoned the head steward. It seemed incredible, but that was what he said. And he had actually used cyanide or something somewhere. And fortunately the tutor dis-covered it. Of course there was hell to pay with Cambridge" (B & S, 46).

Charles Thorpe mentions Bird and Sherwin's account, but, for a reason he does not make explicit, is inclined not to believe it, thinking it "more likely" that the episode was a "fantasy" on Oppenheimer's part, born out of the jeal-ousy he felt for Blackett (see Thorpe [2006], 38).

100. "Blackett was brilliant and handsome": JE in his interview with CW, 16.7.1975, quoted in Thorpe (2006), 39

101. his interview with Martin Sherwin: conducted 18.6.1979, quoted in B & S, 46

101. His father negotiated an agreement: HWS interviewed by CW, 1.8.1974, quoted in B & S, 46

101. "I saw him standing on the corner": FF interviewed by AKS, 21.4.1976, S & W, 94

101. "He looked crazy": FF interviewed by MJS, 18.6.1979, B & S, 46

101. "said that the guy was too stupid": FF interviewed by AKS, 21.4.1976, S & W, 94

101. "I was on the point": *Time* magazine, November 8, 1948, 71

101. "My reaction was dismay": FF interviewed by MJS, 18.6.1979, B & S, 47

101. "began to get very queer": ibid.

101. Oppenheimer's behavior in Paris: ibid. In his interview with AKS, Fergusson told her that Oppenheimer had been to see a prostitute, but had been unable to "get to first base" with her: "nothing would click" (quoted in B & S, 608).

102. "one of his ambiguous moods": B & S, 47

102. "I leaned over to pick up a book": ibid., the source for which is Fergusson's "Account of the Adventures of Robert Oppenheimer in Europe" and his interview with Sherwin of 18.6.1979. The same incident is described in S & W, 91, the source for which is FF's 1976 interviews with AKS.

102. "You should have": JRO to FF, 23.1.1926, S & W, 91

102. "the awful fact of excellence": ibid., 92

102. he insisted: for an account of these negotiations, see Crowther (1974), Chapter 14

103. "thought my experiments quite good": JRO to FF, 15.11.1925, S & W, 87

103. "what happened with beams of electrons": JRO in interview with TSK, 18.11.1963, quoted ibid., 88

103. "which can give an indication": JRO to REP, 16.9.1925, ibid., 84

103. "the miseries of evaporating beryllium": JRO in interview with TSK, 18.11.1963, quoted ibid., 88

103. "The business in the laboratory": ibid.

103. "there was a tremendous inner turmoil": JE interview with CW, 16.7.1975, ibid., 92

104. "the most profound revolution": Weinberg (193), 51, quoted in Kumar (2009), 153

104. "certainly some good physicists": JRO to FF, 15.11.1925, S & W, 88

104. Kapitza Club: the account of Peter Kapitza and the club named after him is based on those given in Farmelo (2009), Kragh (1990), Mehra and Rechenberg (1982e) and Nye (2004)

104. Paul Dirac: see Farmelo (2009), Kragh (1990) and Mehra and Rechenberg (1982e)

105. "not easily understood": JRO interview with TSK, 18.11.1963, quoted S & W, 96

105. "Quantum Theory (Recent Developments)": see Dirac (1995), xvii–xviii, and Kragh (1990), 30

105. "Dirac gave us": see Kragh (1990), 30

105. "a generous-spirited man": Farmelo (2009), 53

106. a series of three short papers: see *Comptes rendus* (Paris), Volume 177 (1923), 507–10, 548–50, 630–2

106. Einstein's Nobel Prize–winning suggestion: "Über einen die Erzeugung und Verwandlung des Lichtes betreffenden heuristischen Gesichtspunkt" ['On a Heuristic Viewpoint Concerning the Production and Transformation of Light'], *Annalen der Physik*, 17 (6), 132–48

106. a series of experiments: see Compton (1923)

106. an English version of de Broglie's articles: de Broglie (1924)

107. "He has lifted a corner": Abragam (1988), 30, quoted Kumar (2008), 150
107. "brimful of talk and enthusiasm": Lovell (1975), 10, quoted Nye (2004), 46
107. Paul Dirac gave a paper: see Kragh (1990), 31
107. Werner Heisenberg: the best biography of Heisenberg I know, and the source for much of my information about him, is Cassidy (1992). I have also learned much from Cassidy (2009), Powers (1994) and Rose (1998).
109. "Quantum Theoretical Reinterpretation": see Heisenberg (1925) for the original German publication; for an English translation, see Waerden (1968), 261–76
109. "What do you think of this?": Farmelo (2009), 83
109. "The Fundamental Equations": see Dirac (1925), and Waerden (1968), 307–20
109. a paper that they wrote together in September: see Born and Jordan (1925). For an English translation, see Waerden (1968), 277–306
110. "On Quantum Mechanics II": Born, Heisenberg and Jordan (1926), Waerden (1968), 321–86
110. Dirac's second paper: Dirac (1926), Waerden (1968), 417–27
110. a paper to the Del Squared V Club: see Cassidy (2005), 98
110. "My regret": JRO to FF, 7.3.1926, S & W, 92
110. "and I remember thinking": FF interview with MJS, 18.6.1979, quoted B & S, 49
111. If he could take a break: see JRO to FF, 7.3.1926, S & W, 93
111. "Quantization as a Problem of Proper Values": Schrödinger (1926a). For a summary of Schrödinger's theory in English, see Schrödinger (1926e); for an English translation of the original article, see Schrödinger (1982), 1–12
111. "wave mechanics": or, as his 1926e summary translation has it, "undulatory" mechanics
111. three further landmark papers: Schrödinger (1926a–d)
111. "like an eager child": Planck to Schrödinger, 2.4.1926, quoted Moore (1989), 209, and Kumar (2009), 209
111. "the idea of your work": Einstein to Schrödinger, 16.4.1926, quoted Moore (1989), 209, and Kumar (2009), 209
112. "deepest form of the quantum laws": quoted in Cassidy (2009), 150
112. "passionately eager": Edsall (2003), 14
112. "intensely articulate": ibid.
113. "No, no. Dostoevsky is superior": see Michelmore (1969), 18
113. "The kind of person that I admire most": JE in interview with CW, 16.7.1975, quoted S & W, 93. See Michelmore (1969), 18, for a slightly different version of the same recollected remark.
113. a misunderstanding between Edsall and the Corsican police: Michelmore (1969), 18. Michelmore gives no source, but presumably he was told the story by Edsall.
113. "what began for me in Corsica": Pharr Davis (1969), 20
113. "a great and lasting part": ibid., 19
113. "You see, don't you": ibid.
113. "You ask whether I will tell you": ibid., 20
114. "a European girl": ibid., 19
114. "one of the great experiences": Chevalier (1965), 34
114. quoting from memory: ibid.
114. "Perhaps she would not": ibid., 35
114. "We most of all": JRO, speech at Seven Springs Farm, Mount Kisco, New

York, summer 1963. Full text in the Oppenheimer Papers, Library of Congress; extract quoted in Goodchild (1980), 278, where, however, it is mistakenly dated "summer of 1964."

115. "felt much kinder": Royal (1969), 36

115. "passing through a great emotional crisis": B & S, 50

115. "I can't bear to speak of it": ibid.

115. "Well, perhaps": ibid.

116. "On the Quantum Theory of Vibration-Rotation Bands": Oppenheimer (1926a)

117. "That was a mess": JRO in interview with TSK, 18.11.1963, quoted Pais (2006), 10

117. "we went out on the river": JRO in interview with TSK, 18.11.1963, quoted S & W, 96

117. "very warm person": GU in interview with CW, 8.1.1977, quoted S & W, 97

117. "realized then": JRO in interview with TSK, 18.11.1963, quoted S & W, 97

118. "I'm in difficulties": JRO in interview with TSK, 18.11.1963, quoted S & W, 96

118. "I forgot about beryllium": ibid.

118. "I thought it put a rather useful glare": JRO in interview with TSK, 18.11.1963, quoted B & S, 54

118. Edsall remembers: JE interview with CW, 16.7.1975, quoted S & W, 93

118. "I am indebted to Mr J.T. Edsahl": Oppenheimer (1926b), 424

118. "On the Quantum Theory of the Problem of the Two Bodies": Oppenheimer (1926b)

119. Max Born: for biographical information on Born, I have relied mainly on Born (1978) and Greenspan (2005)

119. "Zur Quantenmechanik der Stossvorgänge": Born (1926a). An English translation has appeared in Wheeler and Zurek (1983), 52–61.

119. longer, more polished and refined paper: Born (1926b). English translation in Ludwig (1968), 206–30

119. "On the Quantum Mechanics of Collisions of Atoms and Electrons": see Mehra and Rechenberg (1982e), 215, and Mehra and Rechenberg (1987), 760

119. "God does not play dice": AE to MB, 26.12.1926, Born (1971)

120. Jeremy Bernstein has speculated: see Bernstein (2005)

121. "Physical Aspects of Quantum Mechanics": Born (1927), reprinted in Born (1956), 6–13

121. "particularly interested": JRO to REP, 18.8.1926, S & W, 98

121. "had very great misgivings": JRO interview with TSK, 18.11.1963, quoted S & W, 97

PART TWO: 1926–1941

6. Göttingen

125. "conscious of his superiority": Born (1978), 229

126. "I was never very good": ibid., 234

126. "much mathematical power": Bridgman to Rutherford, 24.6.1925, quoted S&W, 77

127. "bitter, sullen . . . discontent and angry": JRO interview with TSK, 20.11.1963, quoted S & W, 103

127. one of the very first branches: see Madden and Mühlberger (2007), Chapter 7

127. Achim Gercke: ibid.

128. Charlotte Riefenstahl: the story of Oppenheimer's meeting with Riefenstahl has been retold many times, but its original telling (presumably based on an interview with Riefenstahl herself) is in Michelmore (1969), 22–3.

128. "had the typical bitterness": JRO interview with TSK, 20.11.1963, quoted S & W, 103

129. "The Americans": Born (1978), 228

129. "All right": Michelmore (1969), 21

129. "Trouble is": ibid., 20

129. "He and Born became very close friends": Edward Condon, "Autobiography Notes," Condon Papers, American Physical Society, Philadelphia, quoted Schweber (2000), 63–4

130. Karl T. Compton: see Compton (1956)

130. "when he was a member": ibid., 125

130. He is reported: Margaret Compton in interview with AKS, 3.4.1976, quoted S & W, 103–4

130. "There are about 20 American physicists": JRO to FF, 14.11.1926, S & W, 100

131. "another problem": JRO to ECK, 27.11.1926, S & W, 102

131. In Born's seminar: see Born (1978), 229, and Greenspan (2005), 144

132. "I felt as if": Elsasser (1978), 53

132. "I was a little afraid of Oppenheimer": Born (1978), 229

132. one day, Born arrived: ibid. See also Greenspan (2005), 144–5

132. "This plot worked": Born (1978), 229

133. "As far as I can learn": K.T. Compton to Augustus Trowbridge, 6.12.1926, quoted Cassidy (2005), 115

133. "I would like to point out": MB to Augustus Trowbridge, 26.12.1926, quoted ibid.

133. "Zur Quantentheorie kontinuierlicher Spektren": Oppenheimer (1927a)

133. "quite important": Pais (2006), 10

133. "unexplored territory": ibid.

133. "You ought to tackle": Dalitz and Peierls (1986), 147

133. "The Development of Quantum Mechanics": Dirac (1978), 1–20

133. "It was very easy": ibid., 7

134. "The most exciting time": JRO interview with TSK, 20.11.1963, quoted Pais (2006), 10

134. "Oppenheimer indicates": PAMD interview with TSK, 14.5.1963, quoted Pais (2006), 10. The entire interview is available online at: http://www.aip.org/history/ohilist/4575_1.html

134. "I am especially happy": Dirac (1971), 10

134. "I don't see": there are many versions of this story in print, starting with Royal (1969), 38. The version I have used is from Farmelo (2009), 121. He gives Bernstein (2004) as his source, but in fact his version is slightly different from Bernstein's, and, in my opinion, slightly better.

135. where he had been since September 1926: for an account of Dirac at Copenhagen, see Farmelo (2009), Chapter Eight

135. "quite excellent": MB to W. S. Stratton, 27.2.1927, quoted S & W, 103

135. "There are three young geniuses": Earle Kennard to R.C. Gibbs, 3.3.1927, quoted Kevles (1995), 217

135. "Great ideas": Sopka (1980), 159

135. "On the Intuitive Content": Heisenberg (1927), translated into English (under the title "The Physical Content of Quantum Kinetics and Mechanics"), Wheeler and Zurek (1983), 62–84

136. "My own feeling": JRO to GU, 12.3.1927, S & W, 106

136. two papers: Oppenheimer (1927b and 1927c)

136. "I am very glad": JRO to GU, 12.3.1927, S & W, 106

137. "From what I hear": PWB to JRO, 3.4.1927, quoted S & W, 105

137. "I'm glad that is over": Michelmore (1969), 23. A slightly different version is given in B & S, 66.

138. "Economic circumstances": B & S, 66

138. "My soul": MB to PE, 7.8.1927, quoted Greenspan (2005), 146

138. "presence destroyed": MB to PE, 7.10.1928, quoted Greenspan (2005), 153

138. "Through his manner": MB to PE, 16.7.1927, quoted Greenspan (2005), 146

138. "Zur Quantentheorie der Molekeln": Oppenheimer and Born (1927)

138. "why molecules were molecules": B & S, 65

139. "I thought this was about right": ibid.

140. "I didn't like it": ibid., 66

140. "Oppenheimer is turning out": ECK to Theodore Lyman, 9.6.1927, quoted S & W, 107

140. "In the sense": JRO, interview with TSK, 20.11.1963, quoted S & W, 98

140. "ruined my young people": MB to PE, 7.10.1928, quoted Greenspan (2005), 153

141. "Oppenheimer, who was with me": MB to PE, 16.7.1927, quoted Greenspan (2005), 146

141. "Your information": MB to PE, 7.8.1927, quoted Greenspan (2005), 146

142. "The Quantum Postulate and the Recent Development of Atomic Theory": Bohr (1928)

142. "On or about December 1910": the remark is from Woolf's essay, "Mr Bennett and Mrs Brown," see Woolf (1992), 70

143. "conference will be devoted": see Kumar (2009), 255

144. The congress ran: what follows is based on the account of the Solvay Congress given in Kumar (2009), Chapter 11, 253–80.

144. "We consider": ibid., 258

144. "towering over everybody": ibid., 275

145. "I am satisfied": ibid., 276

145. "My brother and I": FO, interview with AKS, 14.4.1976, quoted S & W, 108

145. "He's too much": Michelmore (1969), 23

145. "We were not highly regarded": IIR, interview with TSK, 8.12.1963, AIP, available at: http://www.aip.org/history/ohilist/4836.html

145. "There are no physicists in America": Raymond T. Birge to John Van Vleck, 10.3.1927, quoted Schweber (1986), 55–6

146. "We all got": quoted Goodchild (1980), 22

146. Else Uhlenbeck later recalled: interview with AKS, 20.4.1976, quoted S & W, 107

146. Charlotte stayed: see Michelmore (1969), 24–5

7. *Postdoctoral Fellow*

147. "Three Notes on the Quantum Theory of Aperiodic Effects": Oppenheimer (1928a)
147. the polarization of impact radiation: see Oppenheimer (1927d)
147. the capture of electrons by alpha particles: see Oppenheimer (1928b)
147. "very best felicitations": JRO to PAMD, 28.11.1927, S & W, 108
148. "Details of the theory": Oppenheimer (1928c), 262
148. "a thin high-strung postdoctoral fellow": Morse (1977), 87, quoted S & W, 109–10
149. "Crossing": *Hound and Horn: A Harvard Miscellany*, 1 (4), 335, June 1928, quoted S & W, 110
149. "own dry, sterile intellectuality": Royal (1969), 43
150. "very much the man": JRO to ECK, 16.2.1928, S & W, 111
150. Linus Pauling: the chief source for what follows is Hager (1995)
150. the definitive textbook: Pauling (1939)
150. "was then still stuck on crystals": JRO, interview with TSK, 18.11.1963, quoted S & W, 112
151. "tryst to Mexico": Hager (1995), 152
151. "Poems by J. Robert Oppenheimer 1928": see Cassidy (2005), 125
151. "may possibly be of use to you": JRO to FO, March 1928, S & W, 113
151. Helen Campbell: see Helen C. Allison, interview with AKS, 7.12.1976, S & W, 113
152. "many invitations": JRO to KDN, 4.3.1954, ITMO, 7
152. "I am trying to decide": JRO to FO, March 1928, S & W, 113
152. "I thought I'd like to go to Berkeley": JRO, interview with TSK, 20.11.1963, quoted S & W, 114
152. April 10, 1928: see S & W, 114
152. "like to be able to accept": JRO to Theodore Lyman, 21.4.1928, S & W, 114
152. Oppenheimer wrote again: JRO to Theodore Lyman, 7.5.1928, S & W, 115
152. "the Ramsauer fiasco": JRO to ECK, 16.2.1928, S & W, 111
152. "try to learn a little physics there": JRO to Elmer Hall, 7.3.1928, quoted Cassidy (2005), 122
152. "revealed to him": Pais (2006), 15
153. on April 26, 1928: see Cassidy (2005), 123
153. "several doctors": JRO to International Education Board, 2.8.1928, S & W, 117
153. Frank, asked many years later: S & W, 117
153. "If you are out here": JRO to FO, March 1928, S & W, 113
153. in 1928 they sold the Riverside Drive: Cassidy (2005), 123
154. "Like it?": Michelmore (1969), 27. A contemporaneous, but slightly different, version is told in Royal (1969), 44
154. Francis Fergusson visited them: see Michelmore (1969), 27
154. "It now seems certain": JRO to RFB, 25.8.1928, S & W, 118
154. "slight sinus infection": Cassidy (2005), 125
155. they had an accident: see B & S, 73, and Cole (2009), 39
155. "sipping from a bottle": FO to Denise Royal, 25.2.1967, quoted B & S, 73
155. "His way of being alive": Klein (1981), 3
155. "He was not merely": Einstein (1950), 236

156. "to distrust": Weisskopf (1972), 2–3, quoted Klein (1981), 11

156. "If you intend": PE to JRO, 5.7.1928, quoted Klein (1981), 12

156. "I thought of him": JRO, interview with TSK, 20.11.1963, quoted S & W, 121

157. "I don't think": ibid.

157. "I think that": ibid.

157. "There was not a great deal of life": ibid.

157. "I absolutely do not know": see the Ehrenfest biography at: http://www.gap -system.org/~history/Biographies/Ehrenfest.html and Pais (1991)

158. "None of us": JRO to GU, autumn 1933, S & W, 168

158. "spoiled this period": JRO, interview with TSK, 20.11.1963, quoted S & W, 121

158. "Bohr is Allah": see Enz (2002), 36

158. "a lamentable ignorance": JRO to FO, 30.12.1928, S & W, 119–21

159. "at the suggestion of Ehrenfest": JRO to IEB, 3.1.1929, S & W, 122

159. "a very ingenious physicist": PE to W.E. Tisdale (secretary of the IEB), 12.1.1929, quoted S & W, 122

159. "passionately preoccupied": see page 155 above

159. "that Bohr with his largeness and vagueness": JRO, interview with TSK, 20.11.1963, quoted S & W, 121

159. "a wise judgement": Pais (2006), 16

160. "about a physicist": PE to WP, 26.11.1928, Pauli (1979), 477, quoted Pais (2006), 16

160. Dr. W. J. Robbins: see S & W, 123

160. "The luggage": JRO to W.J. Robbins, 4.2.1929, S & W, 123

160. both Oppenheimer and Pauli were in Leipzig: that Oppenheimer was in Leipzig is confirmed by Rabi, in Rabi et al. (1969), 4. He dates his meeting Oppenheimer in Leipzig to "late in 1928," but, given that Oppenheimer was still in Leiden on January 23, 1929 (the date of his letter to the IEB, quoted on page 160), it must have been shortly after this. For confirmation that Pauli was in Leipzig at this time, see Cassidy (1992), 285.

160. Heisenberg had been at Leipzig since 1927: what follows is based on the account given in Cassidy (1992), Chapter 14

162. "Dirac equation": see Dirac (1928)

162. "On the Quantum Dynamics of Wave Fields": Heisenberg and Pauli (1929); see also Cassidy (1992), 285

163. "interests changed": see Rabi et al. (1969), 12

163. "I first met him in Leipzig": Rigden (1987), 218

163. "What we needed were the leaders": IIR, interview with TSK, 8.12.1963, quoted Rigden (1987), 63

163. "I got to know him quite well": Rigden (1987), 218

163. "The time with Ehrenfest": JRO, interview with TSK, 20.11.1963, quoted S & W, 126

164. "You know, what Mr. Einstein said is not so stupid!": see Peierls (1985), 46

164. "I do not mind": ibid., 47

164. "not even wrong": the oldest and most authoritative source for this story seems to be Peierls (1960), 186

164. "His ideas": Michelmore (1969), 28

164. "nim-nim-nim-man": ibid.

164. "Pauli once remarked": Rabi et al. (1969), 5
164. "I believe": WP to PE, 15.2.1929, Pauli (1979), 486, quoted Pais (2006), 17
165. "rather short": Peierls (1985), 44
165. "worked very hard": Rabi et al. (1969), 5
166. "Using flawless methods": WP to Sommerfeld, 16.5.1929, Pauli (1979), 500, quoted Pais (2006), 18
166. "a continuation": WP to NB, 17.7.1929, Pauli (1979), 512, quoted Pais (2006), 18
166. "Note on the Theory of the Interaction of Field and Matter": Oppenheimer (1930a)
166. "First and foremost": Dr. Robbins to JRO, 30.4.1929, quoted S & W, 127
166. "fairly certain": JRO to Robbins, 14.5.1929, S & W, 128
167. "In the spring of 1929": ITMO, 7
167. "I was particularly impressed": see Royal (1969), 45
167. "the intensity": ibid.
168. "house and six acres": JRO to FO, 6.5.1929, S & W, 126
168. "We'd get sort of drunk": see B & S, 81
168. "It made me a little envious": JRO to FO, 7.9.1929, S & W, 132

8. An American School of Theoretical Physics

169. "I didn't start to make a school": JRO, interview with TSK, 20.11.1963, quoted S & W, 131
169. "the greatest school": Bethe (1997), 184
170. Condon has given vivid accounts: see EUC, interview with CW, 17.10.1967, AIP. Text available online at: http://www.aip.org/history/ohilist/4997_1.html. This interview is the source of most of what follows regarding the history of physics at Berkeley. See also Childs (1968) and Dahl (2006).
172. Ernest Lawrence: my information about Lawrence comes mainly from Childs (1968), Pharr Davis (1969) and Heilbron and Seidel (1990)
172. "Ernest is making a mistake": Pharr Davis (1969), 12
172. lecture to the Royal Society: Rutherford (1928)
173. "I'm going to be famous": Halpern (2010), 90
173. 80,000 volts: Rhodes (1988), 148
173. "unbelievable vitality": Childs (1968), 143
173. "The more intimately": Harold F. Cherniss, interview with MJS, 23.5.1979, quoted B & S, 93
174. "His mere physical appearance": ibid.
174. "It tasted like sweepings": Pharr Davis (1969), 24
174. "We passed a hot-dog stand": ibid.
174. "I have been pretty busy": JRO to FO, 7.9.1929, S & W, 133
174. "the refractory problem": JRO to FO, 14.10.1929, S & W, 135
175. "young wives falling for Robert": Helen C. Allison, interview with AKS, 7.12.1976, quoted B & S, 92
175. "I can't think": JRO to FO, 14.10.1929, S & W, 135
175. "very rarely": JRO, interview with TSK, 20.11.1963, quoted S & W, 131
175. "I think from all I hear": ibid.
175. "I found myself": ibid., quoted Pais (2006), 20
176. "Almost immediately": Birge, Raymond T., History of the Physics Department, University of California, Berkeley, quoted Cassidy (2005), 154

176. "I'm going so slowly": quoted Royal (1969), 54, and (slightly differently) Michelmore (1969), 30

176. "Since we couldn't understand": Goodchild (1980), 25

176. "In Pasadena": JRO, interview with TSK, 20.11.1963, quoted S & W, 131

177. "I didn't know": CA, interviewed by Harriett Lyle, January 9–February 8,1979, Caltech Archives

177. "Robert, I didn't understand": ibid.

177. "We had a delightful evening": Julius Oppenheimer to FO, 11.3.1930, S & W, 137

178. "From time to time": JRO to FO, 14.10.1929

178. "a dare-devil": Helen Campbell Allison to AKS, quoted B & S, 91

178. "It is not easy": JRO to FO, 12.3.1930

179. Melba Phillips: see interview with Melba Phillips by Katherine Russell Sopka, December 5, 1977, AIP, and Neuenschwander and Watkins (2008)

179. "Relativistic Theory of the Photoelectric Effect": Oppenheimer and Hall (1931)

180. "very reliable individual": see B & S, 367

180. "the character of": see Cassidy (2005), 151

180. "physics was good": Serber (1983), 206, quoted Pais (1999), 106. It is also quoted Pais (2006), 25, but there Pais gives the wrong source, mistakenly claiming that the remark is to be found in Serber's contribution to Rabi et al. (1969).

180. "carelessness": Pais (2006), 25

180. "The error was his": ibid.

181. "fundamental barrier": Serber (1983)

181. "On the Theory of Electrons and Protons": Oppenheimer (1930b)

181. "a new kind of particle": Dirac (1931), 60

181. "are not to be considered": see Farmelo (2009), 195

182. already been used by Rutherford: see Rutherford (1920)

182. The problem that Pauli sought to solve: for good historical accounts of this problem, see Franklin (2004) and Pais (1986), 309–16.

183. Bohr, among others: see Bohr, Kramers and Slater (1924) and also Bohr (1932)

183. "desperate way out": WP to Lise Meitner and Hans Geiger, 1.12.1930, quoted Franklin (2004), 70

183. "To wit": WP, letter to physicists at Tübingen, 14.12.1930, quoted Franklin (2004), 71, and Pais (1986), 315

183. "that foolish child": WP to Max Delbrück, 6.10.1958, quoted Franklin (2004), 70, and Pais (1986), 314

184. he wrote to Frank: JRO to FO, 10.8.1931, S & W, 142–3

184. the Old Testament character: see the first book of Samuel, Chapter 4, Verse 21: "And she named the child Ichabod, saying, The glory is departed from Israel"

184. "Waring": see *The Poems of Browning Volume Two, 1841–1846*, edited by John Woolford and Daniel Karlin, Harlow: Longman (1991), 143–54

184. Summer-school participants remember: see S & W, 141

184. "I am afraid": JRO to FO, 10.8.1931, S & W, 142

184. "Mother critically ill": Royal (1969), 61

184. "He had a terribly desolate look": ibid., 62

184. a short notice: Oppenheimer and Carlson (1931). The issue of *Physical Review* in which it appeared was published on November 1, 1931. The notice is dated

October 9, 1931, which was three days after Oppenheimer would have received the telegram from his father telling him that his mother was critically ill, and three days before he arrived in New York (so quite possibly on the day he left California). For an interesting and accessible discussion of Oppenheimer's work with Carlson on cosmic rays and Pauli's "magnetic neutron," see Brown (1978).

185. "birth cries": see, e.g., *Time*, 1 July 1932

185. "published very shortly": Oppenheimer and Carlson (1931), 1788

185. "I found my mother": JRO to EOL, 12.10.1931, S & W, 144

186. "sweet message": JRO to EOL, 16.10.1931, S & W, 145

186. "I am the loneliest man": HWS, interview with CW, 1.8.1974, quoted S & W, 145

186. "I feel pretty awful": JRO to EOL, 12.10.1931, S & W, 144

186. "You must let me know": JRO to EOL, 16.10.1931, S & W, 145

187. *Time* magazine: *Time*, 1 February 1932

187. "comforting words": JRO to EOL, 3.1.1932, S & W, 147

187. "Millikan loathed Oppenheimer": Pharr Davis (1969), 50

187. "Millikan just left his name": ibid.

187. "A Hydrogen Isotope of Mass 2": Urey et al. (1932)

188. "hydrogen atom of nuclear physics": quoted Kevles (1995), 226

188. "the possible existence": Rutherford (1920), 392

188. "Possible Existence of a Neutron": Chadwick (1932a)

189. "dialogue passed into Cavendish tradition": Snow (1982), 85

189. His inspiration: what follows is based on the account of the discovery of the neutron given in Brown (1997), Chapter 6.

189. "The difficulties disappear": Chadwick (1932a)

189. "The Existence of a Neutron": Chadwick (1932b)

189. "The Impacts of Fast Electrons and Magnetic Neutrons": Oppenheimer and Carlson (1932)

189. experimental evidence for the existence of neutrons: see ibid., 764

190. "a hypothetical elementary neutral particle": ibid., 763

190. "not much greater": ibid., 764

190. "One may, however": ibid.

190. "there is no experimental evidence": ibid., 792

190. a witty pastiche: see Gamow (1985), 165–218

190. "Mrs. Ann Arbor's Speakeasy": ibid., 190

190. "and says, with pride": ibid., 213

191. "In our seminars": Pharr Davis (1969), 49

191. "sat afraid": ibid., 48

191. "I wrote the figure": ibid., 40

191. "We were busy": ibid.

192. "are setting about": ibid., 41

192. Rutherford had known: see Rutherford (1927)

192. appeared in print twice: see Gamow (1928a and 1928b)

192. an article by Edward Condon and Ronald Gurney: Gurney and Condon (1928)

192. Shortly before it was published: what follows is based on the account given in Cathcart (2004).

193. publish an account of their work: see Cockcroft and Walton (1930)

193. "What we require": quoted Cathcart (2004), 173

193. "I have just been": Joseph Boyce to John Cockcroft, 8.1.1932, quoted Weiner (1972), 40–2, and Cathcart (2004), 216–17

193. "stop messing about": Cathcart (2004), 223

194. write up their experiment for *Nature*: see Cockcroft and Walton (1932)

194. "We know": Ernest Walton to Winifred Wilson, 17.4.1932, quoted Cathcart (2004), 238

194. "The Structure of Atomic Nuclei": Rutherford (1932)

195. "SCIENCE'S GREATEST DISCOVERY": this and the other newspaper reports mentioned are quoted Cathcart (2004), 246–9

195. Bertrand Russell mentioned it: see Russell (1923), 11

195. *Wings over Europe*: see Cathcart (2004), 249–50

195. "moonshine": Rutherford, speech to the British Association for the Advancement of Science, September 11, 1933, reported in *The Times* newspaper, 12 September 1933

195. Leo Szilard: see Lanouette (1992), Chapter 10

196. "The Atom Is Giving Up Its Mighty Secrets": quoted Cathcart (2004), 253

196. "Cockcroft and Walton have disintegrated the lithium atom": quoted Pharr Davis (1969), 43. See also Cathcart (2004), 254

196. "Many of the characters": Farmelo (2009), 211

197. Anderson had started his research: the account that follows is based largely on Anderson (1961) and the interview of Anderson by Harriett Lyle, January 9– February 8, 1979, Caltech Archives.

198. "talked to Oppenheimer quite a bit": Anderson, interview by Harriett Lyle, January 9–February 8, 1979, Caltech Archives.

198. "It beggars belief": Farmelo (2009), 213

198. "Tell us, Dirac": quoted ibid., 206

198. he told Heisenberg: this account was given by Heisenberg to Oskar Klein, who then repeated it to Kuhn and Heilbron in their AIP interview with him. See Oskar Klein, interview with TSK and John L. Heilbron, Session IV, 28.2.1963. See also Farmelo (2009), 206

199. "It seems necessary": Anderson (1932), 239

199. fully worked out follow-up article: Anderson (1933)

199. "It is surprising to me": Anderson, interview by Harriett Lyle, January 9– February 8, 1979, Caltech Archives

199. "Anderson's positively charged electrons": JRO to FO, autumn 1932, S & W, 159

200. "I was quite intimate": Nye (2004), 50

200. "gone nuts": Anderson, interview by Harriett Lyle, January 9–February 8, 1979, Caltech Archives

201. "Greatest Atom Discovery": quoted Farmelo (2009), 223

202. "a little house": JRO to FO, 10.8.1931, S & W, 143

202. "is very much pleased": JRO to FO, *c.* January 1932, S & W, 151

202. "looks well": ibid.

202. "after I am gone": ibid., 152

202. "I am meeting lots of Robert's friends": ibid., 153

202. "paradise": see Brian (1996), 207

203. a millionairess: ibid., 216

204. "I have urged him": JRO to FO, 12.3.1932, S & W, 154

204. "Only if things": ibid.

204. "The theoretical physics": JRO to FO, 7.10.1933, S & W, 163

204. he responded to an appeal: JRO to Theodore von Karman, *c.* March 1934, S & W, 173

204. "Tell me": Nedelsky, interview with AKS, 7.12.1976, quoted S & W, 195

204. a serious study of ancient Hindu literature: in considering Oppenheimer's interest in Hinduism, I have learned much from Hijiya (2000).

204. "I am learning Sanskrit": JRO to FO, 10.8.1931, S & W, 143

204. "a friend half divine": Ryder (1939), xxxviii

204. "Ryder felt and thought": *Time* magazine, November 8, 1948, 75

205. he alludes very briefly: S & W, 151

205. "the Cakuntala": ibid., 159

205. a year later: JRO to FO, 7.10.1933, S & W, 165

205. "the precious Meghaduta": JRO to FO, 4.6.1934, S & W, 1880

205. "The Cloud Messenger": see Thomas Clark, *Meghaduta, the Cloud Messenger: Poem of Kalidasa* (1882), Whitefish, Montana: Kessinger (2009)

205. "Garuda": JRO to FO, 7.10.1933, S & W, 164

205. "that *delectatio contemplationis*": S & W, 151

206. the extended disquisition on the notion of discipline: JRO to FO, 12.3.1932, S & W, 155

206. "I believe": ibid., 156

206. "teachers, fathers and sons": *The Bhagavad Gita*, translated by Juan Mascaro, London: Penguin (1962), Chapter 1, Verse 34

206. "evil of destruction": ibid., 1.39

207. "Set thy heart": ibid., 2.47

207. "freedom from the chains of attachment": ibid., 13.9–13.11

207. "Any work": ibid., 14.16

207. "would have been a much better physicist": quoted Rigden (1987), 228

207. "The Jewish tradition": ibid.

207. "why men of Oppenheimer's gifts": Rabi et al. (1969), 7

209. "The work is fine": JRO to FO, autumn, 1932, S & W, 159

209. "It won't be any trouble": Nedelsky, interview with AKS, 7.12.1976, quoted S & W, 149

209. Wendell Furry: what follows draws on the information provided in Furry's interview with Charles Weiner in Copenhagen, August 9, 1971, for the AIP: http://www.aip.org/history/ohilist/24324.html

210. "The state of theoretical physics": Milton S. Plesset, interviewed by Carol Bugé, December 8, 1981, Caltech Archives

210. "On the Production of the Positive Electron": Oppenheimer and Plesset (1933)

210. "The experimental discovery": ibid., 53

211. "fundamental observation": Pais (2006), 27

211. "fast electrons and positives": Oppenheimer and Plesset (1933), 55

211. "Their final formula": Pais (2006), 27

211. "I fancy": quoted Schweber (200), 68

211. "profound thanks": Oppenheimer and Plesset (1933), 55

212. Oppenheimer wrote to Bohr: S & W, 161–2

212. "swarming": Milton S. Plesset, interviewed by Carol Bugé, December 8, 1981, Caltech Archives

212. "a lot of discussion": ibid.

212. "pudgy-faced": Farmelo (2009), 230

212. "What you have said": quoted ibid., 231
212. a four-page letter: ibid., 232
212. he wrote to Frank: JRO to FO, 7.10.1933, S & W, 162–5
212. "work with pairs": ibid., S & W, 164
212. "has definitely established": ibid., S & W, 165
213. "Lawrence's first European recognition": quoted Pharr Davis (1969), 56
213. "Lawrence left the conference": ibid., 57
213. "one of Lawrence's saddest experiences": ibid.
214. "The formalism": JRO to GU, autumn 1933, S & W, 168
214. "The Production of Positives by Nuclear Gamma Rays": Oppenheimer and Nedelsky (1933)
214. Three months later: see *Physical Review*, 45, 136 (1934)
214. "On the Theory of the Electron and the Positive": Oppenheimer and Furry (1934a)
214. "it was a common sight": Michelmore (1969), 37–8
215. the Boston meeting: see S & W, 169
215. "A short while ago": quoted Mehra and Rechenberg (2001), 915
215. "I do not know": JRO to FO, 7.1.1934, S & W, 171
215. a letter to the editor: Oppenheimer and Furry (1934b)
215. another letter: Oppenheimer and Furry (1934c)
215. "from Dirac": JRO to GU, *c*. March 1934, S & W, 175
215. "Where is the nearest post office?": Serber (1998), 36
215. "golden creative streak": Farmelo (2009), 234
215. "A refusal": quoted ibid., 235
215. "He is not interested": quoted ibid., 239
215. "Thirty-One-Year-Old Professor": see ibid., 240
215. "Forgetful Prof": the newspaper page in question is reproduced in Kelly (2006), 129
216. "Like all geniuses": quoted ibid., 128
216. "I never saw": ibid.
216. "disentangling the still existing miseries": JRO to FO, 4.6.1934, S & W, 181
216. "Garuda does ninety-five": ibid., 182
217. demonstrating his car's speed: see ibid., 183
217. "that the American part of you": JRO to GU, autumn 1934, S & W, 187
217. "I have such a feeling": ibid., 188
217. Robert Serber: most of what I say about Serber comes from Serber (1998) and the three AIP interviews listed in the Bibliography, dated 1967, 1983 and 1996.
217. "When I arrived": Rabi et al. (1969), 17
217. "The word had gotten around": Serber, interviewed by Charles Weiner and Gloria Lubkin at Columbia University, February 10, 1967, AIP
217. "naturally": Lamb, in Brown and Hoddeson (1983), 313
217. "Oppenheimer's office": ibid., 314
218. "His group": Rabi et al. (1969), 18
218. a mother hen fussing over her chickens: see Pharr Davis (1969), 79
218. The first evening: see S & W, 186
218. "was a bachelor then": Rabi et al. (1969), 18
219. "Many of his students": ibid., 19
219. Lauritsen: what follows is based largely on Holbrow (2003)
219. a short paper: Oppenheimer and Lauritsen (1934)

220. Felix Bloch: see Hofstadter (1994)

220. "a rather sturdy indigenous effort": quoted Kevles (1995), 283

220. "One of us": Felix Bloch, interviewed by Charles Weiner, Stanford University, California, August 15, 1968, AIP

220. "a fish place": ibid.

220. "These were post-depression days": Rabi et al. (1969), 19

220. "Bloch grew expansive": Serber (1998), 31

221. "There were no jobs": Melba Phillips, interviewed by Katherine Russell Sopka, December 5, 1977, AIP

221. Running through the door: see Pharr Davis (1969), 58

222. "*Click . . . click . . . click*": ibid.

222. "It was a wonderful time": ibid., 59

222. "Transmutation": quoted ibid., 63

222. Oppenheimer's joint paper with Melba Phillips: Oppenheimer and Phillips (1935)

223. "an outline": JRO to EOL, *c.* spring 1935, S & W, 193

223. "Oppenheimer's lectures": Brown and Hoddeson (1983), 313

223. "I never found nuclear physics so beautiful": quoted Pharr Davis (1969), 78

224. found love in Princeton: see Farmelo (2009), Chapter Nineteen

224. "Princeton is a madhouse": JRO to FO, 11.1.1935, S & W, 190

9. Unstable Cores

225. Frank: for biographical information on Frank Oppenheimer, the main sources are Cole (2009) and the interview with Judith R. Goodstein, November 16, 1984, Caltech Archives

225. "I remember once": Frank Oppenheimer, interview with Judith R. Goodstein, November 16, 1984, Caltech Archives

226. "To inject bigotry": Graham (2005), 199

226. "When I went to Hopkins": Frank Oppenheimer, interview with Judith R. Goodstein, November 16, 1984, Caltech Archives

226. "In Italy": ibid.

227. "How *did* he end up": Graham (2006), 5

227. "In the last months": ibid., 12

228. the McCarthy period: for a detailed account of Melba Phillips's experience of McCarthyism, see Neuenschwander and Watkins (2008), 329–38, 355–9.

228. "when I stopped": Melba Phillips, draft for a eulogy for Frank Oppenheimer, 1985, quoted Neuenschwander and Watkins (2008), 309–10

228. "We were not political in any overt way": quoted ibid., 311

228. "the grim news": ibid.

229. "We were sitting": Serber (1998), 31

229. a major event: see Nelson (1988), Chapters 4 and 5

229. When the question was put directly to him: see ITMO, 277

230. "He tried": quoted Goodchild (1980), 34

230. "My brother Frank": ITMO, 9

230. "occasionally perhaps": ibid., 101

230. "defection": Michelmore (1969), 47

230. "worked fairly well": ITMO, 101

231. "Are the Formulae for the Absorption of High Energy Radiations Valid?": Oppenheimer (1934)

231. "Such clarity": ibid., 45

231. "made it possible": ibid., 44

231. "possible to do justice": ibid., 45

232. "On the Interaction of Elementary Particles I": Yukawa (1935)

233. at the summit of Pikes Peak: for a detailed (and entertaining) account of this, see Anderson, interview with Harriett Lyle, January 9–February 8, 1979, Caltech Archives.

233. scholarly account: Anderson and Neddermeyer (1936)

234. fight with Heisenberg: what follows draws heavily on the account of the matter given in Cassidy (1992), Chapter 18.

234. a paper that he published in June 1936: Heisenberg (1936)

234. "On Multiplicative Showers": Oppenheimer and Carlson (1937)

235. "It would seem": ibid., 221

235. "another cosmic ray component": ibid., 231

235. "the presence": Anderson and Neddermeyer (1937), 884

235. a short report: see Street and Stevenson, "Penetrating Corpuscular Component of the Cosmic Radiation," *Physical Review*, 51, 1005 (1937)

235. "a very conscious purpose": Brown and Hoddeson (1983), 212

235. "the possibility": Oppenheimer and Serber (1937)

236. "The point of view": Oppenheimer, Serber et al. (1937), 1038

236. "optimistic": quoted Cassidy (1992), 376

236. "it is important": ibid., 406

236. "The Limits of Applicability": see ibid., 407

237. "According to Heisenberg's recollection": ibid., 412

237. "smouldering fury": ITMO, 8

237. "Your closeness": Alfred Stern to JRO, 14.10.1966, quoted S & W, 202

237. "It is big here": Michelmore (1969), 58

238. "what the depression was doing to my students": ITMO, 8

238. "to understand": ibid.

238. "I began": ibid.

238. "I liked": ibid.

238. "The matter": ibid., 9

239. More than 3,000 U.S. citizens: Gerassi (1986), 3. For information about U.S. volunteers in the Spanish Civil War, I have also made use of Richardson (1982).

239. when he astonished a friend: see Chevalier (1965), 16, where he quotes from a notebook entry he made dated 20.7.1937: "E. told me of Oppenheimer having last summer gone East, taking with him all three volumes of Marx's *Kapital* and reading them through cover to cover on the train." He does not say who "E." is.

240. complete works of Lenin: ibid.

240. "Beginning in late 1936": ITMO, 8

240. Jean Tatlock: my main source of information about Jean Tatlock is B & S, particularly Chapter Eight

240. "active member": JRO FBI file, quoted B & S, 104

240. "the spring of 1936": ITMO, 8

241. "on again, off again": ibid.

241. "never seemed": ibid.

241. "quite composed": quoted B & S, 114

241. "these terrible depressions": ibid.

241. he twice proposed to her: see B & S, 153
241. "No more flowers": Michelmore (1969), 49
241. "Tell him to go away": ibid.
241. "disappeared for weeks": quoted Goodchild (1980), 35
242. "had probably belonged": ITMO, 3
242. "half-jocular overstatement": ibid., 9
242. "We clipped it out": FO, interview with Judith R. Goodstein, November 16, 1984, Caltech Archives
242. "quite upset": ITMO, 186
242. "the only thing": ibid., 101
242. "The meeting": ibid., 102
243. "It's really hard to imagine": FO, interview with Judith R. Goodstein, November 16, 1984, Caltech Archives
243. "they were scared": ibid.
243. He said: ITMO, 183
243. "He made it clear": ITMO, 9, quoted back to him, ITMO, 184
243. between $100 and $300: for this and the financial details that follow, see ITMO, 184-5
244. Robert A. Brady: see Dowd (1994)
244. "had enthusiasm": ITMO, 158
244. "It was a very inappropriate thing": ibid.
244. one to Mildred Edie: S & W, 205
244. two to Brady: ibid., note 54
245. "Local 349": Chevalier (1965), 23
245. "For four years": ibid.
245. "In bursts": ibid., 23-4
245. "invariably lively": ibid., 24
245. "thousands of dollars": ibid., 25
245. "miserable thing": ITMO, 156
246. Chevalier has described privately: HC to JRO, 23.7.1964, JRO papers, LOC, Box 200
246. "We had decided": Chevalier (1965), 19
246. "story . . ." of: HC to JRO, 23.7.1964, JRO papers, LOC, Box 200
246. "I have never been a member": JRO to HC, 7.8.1964, JRO papers, LOC, Box 200
246. "I had originally planned": quoted Herken (2002), 341, note 46
246. the website: http://www.brotherhoodofthebomb.com/bhbsource/documents .html
247. in private correspondence: see Herken (2002), 31
248. When Chevalier was asked: see B & S, 138
248. "Look": ITMO, 116-17
248. "might well": ibid., 10
249. "This was the era": ibid., 8
249. "I never was a member": ibid., 10
249. "that Communists stood": ibid., 115
249. ". . . it seems clear": ibid.
249. "dialectical materialism": ibid.
249. a political tract: *Report to Our Colleagues*, February 20, 1940. A second tract with the same title, dated April 6, 1940, was also said by Chevalier to have been

written by Oppenheimer. These documents are discussed in Chevalier (1965), 35–6, Herken (2002), 50–2, and B & S, 144–6. The full text of the first of these reports is available on Herken's website at: http://www.brotherhoodofthebomb .com/bhbsource/document4.html

250. the American Communist Party: for the history of the Communist Party of the United States I have made much use of Fried (1997a) and Isserman (1993). See also Haynes (1996), Klehr et al. (1995) and Lewy (1990)

250. its internal structure was reorganized: see Isserman (1993), Chapter 1

250. "wanted to be": ibid., 9

250. "The Communists began": ibid., 3

250. "Communism Is Twentieth Century Americanism": ibid., 9

250. "A significant proportion": ibid., 10

250. "What Is Communism?": Fried (1997a), 250–4

251. "The truth is": ibid., 250–3: italics in the original

251. "the talk that I heard": ITMO, 10

251. in the summer of 1938: ibid.

252. "a land of purge and terror": ibid.

252. "It's worse than you can imagine": Michelmore (1969), 57–8

252. "These conversations": Weisskopf, interviewed by MJS, 23.3.1979, quoted B & S, 148

252. "is fine": Felix Bloch to IIR, 2.11.1938, quoted Schweber (2000), 108

252. "Alone in North America": see "In Memoriam: George Michael Volkoff," at: http://www.cap.ca/pic/Archives/56.5(2000)/volkoff-Sep too.html

253. Supernovae: helpful introductory accounts of this topic can be found in Asimov (1977), Luminet (1992) and Shipman (1976).

253. appeared in AD 1054: see Luminet (1992), 87–90, and Shipman (1976), 44–8

253. "cessation of its existence": Baade and Zwicky (1934b), 76

253. "the super-nova process": ibid., 77

254. Hans Bethe's work: Bethe (1939)

254. Subrahmanyan Chandrasekhar: Luminet (1992), 75, Shipman (1976), 39

255. "Stars and Nuclei": Cassidy (2005), 174

255. "The Source of Stellar Energy": ibid.

255. "nuclear transformations": see "Minutes of the San Diego Meeting, June 22–24, 1938," *Physical Review*, 54, 235–43 (1938)

255. "On the Stability of Stellar Neutron Cores": Oppenheimer and Serber (1938)

255. "On Massive Neutron Cores": Oppenheimer and Volkoff (1938)

255. The present estimate: see Bernstein (2004), 47

256. "I remember": quoted Thorne (1994), 195

256. "the question of what happens": Oppenheimer and Volkoff (1938), 380

256. "There would seem to be": ibid., 380–1

256. "require serious consideration": ibid., 381

257. "one of the great papers": Bernstein (2004), 48

257. "the best mathematician": Serber (1998), 48

257. "On Continued Gravitational Contraction": Oppenheimer and Snyder (1939)

257. "When all thermonuclear sources": ibid., 455

257. "The results": JRO to GU, 5.2.1939, S & W, 209

257. "The star thus": Oppenheimer and Snyder (1939), 456

258. the discovery in 1967: see Shipman (1976), 51–7

258. Wheeler tried to talk to him: see Bernstein (2004), 50

10. *Fission*

259. It began: there are many, many published accounts of the discovery of fission. Among the best and most interesting are those in: Frisch (1980), Jungk (1960), Kevles (1995), Rhodes (1988) and Sime (1996).

259. December 19, 1938: see Sime (1996), 233

260. "the emission": quoted Rhodes (1988), 248

260. "But it's impossible": Frisch, interviewed by Charles Weiner, American Institute of Physics, New York City, May 3, 1967, AIP

261. "consider it *perhaps* possible": quoted Rhodes (1988), 261

262. John Archibald Wheeler: see Wheeler (2000), Chapter 1, for a firsthand account of these events

263. "We didn't make long-distance calls": Luis Alvarez, interviewed by Charles Weiner and Barry Richman, Lawrence Radiation Laboratory, February 15, 1967, AIP

263. "I remember exactly": ibid.

263. "I played it": ibid.

264. "You must come to Berkeley": Royal (1969), 76

264. "I do not recall": Rabi et al. (1969), 49

264. "The U business": JRO to Fowler, *c.* 28.1.1939, S & W, 207–8

265. "I remember very vaguely": William A. Fowler, interviewed by Charles Weiner, Caltech, June 8, 1972, Session II

265. "I think it really not too improbable": JRO to GU, 5.2.1939, S & W, 209

265. "Oppie would write": Serber (1998), 57

266. "a scrappy little man": Michelmore (1969), 51

266. "had originally started": ibid.

266. "New York Jews": Pharr Davis (1969), 81

266. "One Jew in the department": see Serber (1998), 50

267. Peters: see the obituary in *Current Science*, 64 (8), April 25, 1993

267. "a person as crazy as you": B & S, 167

267. "On the basis of the data": ibid., 168

267. "there was on the blackboard": Rhodes (1988), 274–5

268. "Oppie gave some lectures": William A. Fowler, interviewed by Charles Weiner, Caltech, June 8, 1972, Session II

268. The theory: see Bohr and Wheeler (1939)

268. "It was an exciting time": Wheeler (2000), 21

268. "Bombs and reactors": ibid., 23

268. "Now listen": Rhodes (1988), 284

269. an initial paper: Bohr (1939)

269. "the number of neutrons": quoted Rhodes (1988), 291

269. "That night": ibid., 292

269. "Couldn't you": Laura Fermi (1961), 164

270. "It can never be done": quoted Rhodes (1988), 294

270. two papers: see Joliot et al. (1939a and 1939b)

270. "Fermi was adamant": Rhodes (1998), 296

270. German government imposed a ban: ibid.

270. On July 12, 1939: Lanouette (1994), 198. Rhodes (1988), 304, gives the date as July 16. As far as I know, there is no conclusive evidence either way. Lanouette concedes that the date "has long been in dispute" (518), but claims that his account "represents the latest assessment of the evidence" (517).

270. on August 2: Lanouette (1994), 201. Rhodes (1988), 307, says that this second visit took place "probably on Sunday, July 30."

271. "it may become possible": Einstein to Roosevelt, 2.8.1939. The letter is reproduced in full in Lanouette (1994), 205–6, and in Stoff et al. (1991), 18–19.

271. October 11, 1939: Lanouette (1994), 209, Rhodes (1988), 313. On this date they are in perfect agreement. See also Jungk (1960), 106

271. "What you are after": Jungk (1960), 107. The many retellings of this exchange seem to be based on Jungk's.

272. a very thorough review: see Turner (1940)

272. "Although less than a year": ibid., 1

272. "The more familiar": Segrè (1993), 134

273. "Lawrence was a tremendous influence": quoted Pharr Davis (1969), 84

273. "the disagreeable fact": Heilbron and Seidel (1990), 472

274. "the cyclotron man": quoted Pharr Davis (1969), 69

274. "For obvious reasons": EOL, circulated letter to scientists, 7.2.1939, quoted Hodes et al. (1985), 24

274. his next machine: see Pharr Davis (1969), 88

274. Segrè reports: see Segrè (1993), 151

275. "for the invention": see http://www.nobelprize.org/nobel_prizes/physics/laureates/1939/lawrence.html

275. When the award was presented: see Pharr Davis (1969), 88–93, and Heilbron and Seidel (1990), 485–93

275. "unforeseen difficulties": Heilbron and Seidel (1990), 482

275. "synchrocyclotron": see Pharr Davis (1969), 251

275. "Talking politics": Segrè (1993), 139

275. "You have been having a very anxious time": quoted Pharr Davis (1969), 85

275. "I still think war is going to be avoided": quoted VanDeMark (2003), 57

276. ". . . was considered a demigod": Segrè (1993), 138

276. "Oppenheimer and his group": ibid., 138–9

276. "Oppenheimer and most of his acolytes": ibid., 138

276. "great Fascist": ibid., 139

277. "a wonderful contribution": quoted Isserman (1993), 34

277. "changing opinion": ITMO, 10

277. "did not mean": ibid.

277. "It was in the fall of 1939": Chevalier (1965), 31–2

278. "I know Charlie": S & W, 211

278. "took special pride in it": for Griffiths's memoir and Oppenheimer's *Report*, see the documents collected by Gregg Herken at: http://www.brotherhoodofthebomb.com/bhbsource/documents.html

279. "Keep America Out": Isserman (1993), 43

279. "There has never been": quoted Herken (2002), 32

279. "Europe is in the throes of a war": quoted ibid., 31–2

280. "The time will come": quoted above, on page 32

280. "for some reason": Chevalier (1965), 36

281. "This is a time": quoted Schweber (2000), 108

281. "the first occasion": ibid.

282. "The Communists": Isserman (1993), 64–5

282. Isserman provides telling quotations: ibid., 65

282. "Will not Hitler": ibid., 66

283. "subject to foreign control": ibid., 68

283. "the very acceptance": ibid., 69

284. "It is time now": S & W, 213

284. "fell in love with Robert": Goodchild (1980), 39

284. At the time: for Kitty's life before she met Oppenheimer, the fullest sources are Michelmore (1969), Goodchild (1980) and, especially, B & S.

284. "an impossible marriage": quoted B & S, 161

284. She had been born: the source for most of what follows is B & S, Chapter Eleven.

285. "prince of a small principality": B & S, 155

285. "I fell in love": ibid., 156

285. "These were days of poverty": Goodchild (1980), 38

285. "Because of Joe's insistence": ibid.

285. "As time went on": ibid.

286. "She literally collapsed": B & S, 160

286. "we met a very attractive girl": Serber (1998), 51

286. "Kitty might come alone": ibid., 59

286. "looking very aristocratic": ibid., 59–60

287. "a bitch": B & S, 163

287. "Kitty was a schemer": Goodchild (1980), 39

287. "the most despicable female": Pais (1997), 242

288. Steve Nelson: the main source of information about Nelson's life is Nelson et al. (1981). Additional material is contained in B & S, which draws on an interview with Nelson, conducted by MJS, 17.6.1981. Herken (2002) contains further information drawn from FBI files.

288. Oppenheimer was the featured speaker: B & S, 162

288. "I'm going to marry": ibid.

289. Hoover had written to the Secretary: Isserman (1993), 89

289. this led the FBI to Chevalier's house: see B & S, 137

289. Asked about this meeting in 1946: ITMO, 10

289. again in 1950: ibid.

289. he remembered it in some detail: ibid., 139

289. "to acquaint the interested gentry": ibid., 140

289. "the big shot": "Synopsis of Facts," 28.3.1981, paper originating case, filed by R. E. Meyer, JRO (consulted at the Library of Congress)

289. "persons to be considered": memo from San Francisco FBI office to Hoover, 28.3.1981, JRO FBI file

289. "I may be out of job": S & W, 216

290. "It was on our way": Chevalier (1965), 41

290. "we sat up": ibid., 42

290. "even now": JRO to Edwin and Ruth Uehling, 17.5.1941, S & W, 216

290. "I think we'll go to war": ibid., 217

291. "I expect": ibid.

291. "You are going": S & W, 216

291. "theories of mesotron field": ibid., 217

292. the historian of science, Silvan Schweber: see Schweber (2008), 31, 152–3

292. "but we are all agreed": JRO to F. Wheeler Loomis, 13.5.1940, S & W, 211

292. "a good physicist": ibid., 212

292. "asked Schiff searching questions": Kelly (2006), 132

292. "On more than a few occasions": ibid., 133

292. Julian Schwinger: for Schwinger's life, see Mehra and Milton (2000) and the series of articles by Mehra, Milton and Rembiesa (Mehra et al. [1999a–e]). For an outline of his contributions to science, see Milton (2008), and for a detailed account of his work on QED, see Schweber (1994).

293. "were wondering": ibid.

294. "thought Oppenheimer was a more interesting physicist": Schweber (1994), 288

294. "Oppenheimer was *the* name": Mehra et al. (1999c), 932

294. "was overwhelming": ibid., 934

295. "I spoke to Oppenheimer": ibid., 934–5

295. "At the early stage": ibid., 934

295. "After all": ibid., 935

295. a joint letter to the editor: Oppenheimer and Schwinger (1939)

295. "Schiff was then": Mehra et al. (1999c), 935–6

296. "He wrote that letter": ibid., 936

296. "means no more": ibid., 937

296. "history might have developed differently": ibid., 938

297. "I feel Oppie": Kelly (2006), 136

297. "The Production of Soft Secondaries by Mesotrons": Oppenheimer, Serber and Snyder (1939)

297. "the problem": ibid., 75

297. "everybody at Berkeley": Mehra et al. (1999c), 941

297. "On the Spin of the Mesotron": Oppenheimer (1941)

298. "On the Interaction of Mesotrons and Nuclei": Oppenheimer and Schwinger (1941)

298. "adequate technically": Mehra et al. (1999c), 957

298. "I still did not quite know": ibid., 962

298. "very much insisted": ibid., 963

299. "became more and more superficial": ibid.

299. "could pull it off": ibid., 964

300. he published a formula: Peierls (1939)

300. "One day in February or March": Peierls (1985), 153–4

301. "Even if": ibid., 154

301. a two-part report: the report in full is printed as Appendix I in Serber (1992)

301. "What is impressive": Bernstein (2004), 69

301. "Once assembled": Serber (1992), 86

301. "I am convinced": quoted Rhodes (1988), 325

302. "electrified by the possibility": ibid., 330

302. "source of power in submarines": quoted Schweber (2008), 331, note 29

302. "MET NIELS": see Rhodes (1988), 340

302. £5 million: ibid., 343

302. "the most extraordinary experience": quoted Rhodes (1988), 357. For a detailed account of Conant's visit to Britain, see Hershberg (1993), Chapter 8.

303. "introduced the subject": Rhodes (1988), 359

303. "this was entirely": quoted Hershberg (1993), 146

303. "light a fire": Rhodes (1988), 360

303. "a very good idea": ibid., 362

303. "an energetic but dispassionate review": ibid.

303. May 17, 1941: ibid., 365
304. invited Charles Lauritsen: ibid., 368
304. "that the destructive effect": ibid., 369
304. "a major push": ibid.
304. "If Congress knew": ibid., 372
304. "amazed and distressed": ibid.
304. "I thought": ibid., 373
305. joined by Oppenheimer: see Herken (2002), 40
305. "But that's terrible": Michelmore (1969), 66

PART THREE: 1941–1945

11. *In on the Secret*

309. "gossip among nuclear physicists": Rhodes (1988), 373
309. "Oliphant's behavior": Herken (2002), 40
310. Through Cairncross, for example: see West (2004), 10–18
310. "Venona" project: see Haynes and Klehr (2000) and Romerstein and Breindel (2001)
311. "involuntary conference": Rhodes (1988), 376
311. "Ernest": ibid.
312. policy group: ibid., 378
312. "Oppenheimer has important new ideas": quoted Herken (2002), 42
312. "a great deal of confidence": ibid.
312. "reliable confidential informant": Romerstein and Breindel (2001), 264
312. "him": ibid., 265
312. Oppenheimer had contacted Folkoff: ibid.
313. "I think surely": S & W, 215
313. "All of a sudden": Martin Kamen, interview with MJS, 18.1.1979, quoted B & S, 178
313. "not without envy": ITMO, 11
313. "guarantees not the right to a belief": S & W, 219
314. The meeting opened: for the details of the meeting, see Rhodes (1988), 382–3
314. 100 pounds: ibid., 382
314. Urey told Compton: see Compton (1956), 54
315. Their paper: "Radioactive Element 93," *Physical Review*, 57, 1185–6 (1940)
315. to the disgust of James Chadwick: see Brown (1997), 206
316. made a conclusive identification of element 94: on the "secret discovery" of plutonium, see Seaborg (2001), Chapter Seven.
316. which he put at about 220 pounds: Rhodes (1988), 382
316. "some hundreds of millions of dollars": Compton (1956), 57
316. "lest the government": ibid.
316. "always been rather proud": ibid.
316. "a fission bomb": ibid., 59. See also Rhodes (1988), 386
317. "I don't want you to join it": Childs (1968), 319
318. "I had hoped": JRO to EOL, 12.11.1941, S & W, 220
318. the two had lunch the next day: Schecter and Schecter (2002), 47–8. See also Sudoplatov (1994), 174–5
318. "one of the leaders": ibid., 50

319. "learn the chemistry": Compton (1956), 77

319. "The period": ibid., 79

319. "You'll never get a chain reaction going here": ibid., 81

320. "represent, in the opinion of this office": Agent Pieper to J. Edgar Hoover, 26.1.1942, JRO FBI file

320. "follow proper procedure": Hoover to Pieper, 15.4.1942, JRO FBI file

321. "Whoever gets this first": quoted Hershberg (1993), 158

321. "Oh! . . . Oh! . . .": ibid.

321. March 9, 1942: see Rhodes (1988), 405

322. "New and compelling reasons": S & W, 223

322. "the desirability": EOL to JBC, 26.3.1942, quoted Herken (2002), 51

322. "nervously chain-smoking": Herken (2002), 54

322. "Uranium was never mentioned": Lomanitz, interview with Gregg Herken, 1996, quoted Herken (2002), 348, note 141

323. The 184-inch Calutron was switched on: see Herken (2002), 60

323. "a few weeks after Pearl Harbor": Serber (1998), 65

323. "There, alone in that rural setting": ibid.

323. he did not do until May: see Rhodes (1988), 410

324. "Breit was always frightened": Goodchild (1980), 48

324. "Breit was a terrible choice": Pharr Davis (1969), 124

324. "Compton, who had": ibid., 125

324. "I do not believe": Rhodes (1988), 410

325. On April 28, 1942: see Herken (2002), 347, note 116

325. "I went down": Serber (1998), 67–8

325. May 23, 1942: Rhodes (1988), 406

325. On June 17: ibid.

326. "I didn't take up": Serber (1998), 68

326. "provided, of course": ibid.

327. "luminaries": S & W, 227

327. "Separating isotopes": Bernstein (1981), 70

328. "tremendous stacks of graphite": ibid., 71

328. "I then": ibid.

328. by Fermi: see Teller (2001), 157

329. "heavy hydrogen": quoted Rhodes (1988), 416

329. "We had a compartment": Bernstein (1981), 72

330. According to one account: see Goodchild (1980), 51

330. "Everybody agreed": Serber (1998), 71

330. "The theory of the fission bomb": Rhodes (1988), 417

330. "a detonation wave": Serber (1998), 71

330. "everybody forgot": ibid.

331. "At one point": ibid.

331. "found something": Compton (1956), 127

331. "could not be passed": ibid., 128

331. "Oppenheimer's team": ibid.

331. "some unjustified assumptions": Rhodes (1988), 419

331. "but then": ibid., 418

332. "The conference": Serber (1998), 72

332. "As Chairman": Goodchild (1980), 52–3

332. "A spirit of spontaneity": Rhodes (1988), 419

332. "The intellectual experience": Bethe (1997), 187–8

332. "would require": Rhodes (1988), 420

333. "We have become convinced": ibid., 421

333. "nothing should stand in the way": ibid., 424

333. "the biggest sonovabitch": ibid., 426

333. "The Secretary of War": Groves (1962), 3

333. "it will win the war": ibid., 4

334. On his first day in command: Rhodes (1988), 427

334. The next day: ibid.

335. "That would be the equivalent": Groueff (1967), 34

335. "Well, actually": ibid., 39

335. Oppenheimer's first meeting with Groves: Groves (1962), 61

336. "He was always": Chevalier (1965), 21

336. "discussed at some length": Groves (1962), 61

336. "In later summer": ITMO, 12

336. "I discussed with him": ibid.

337. squeezed into a tiny compartment: see Norris (2002), 241

337. "convinced of the necessity": JRO to John H. Manley, 12.10.1942, S & W, 231

337. "I let myself": Badash et al. (1980), 24

338. "I can't tell you": ibid., 25

338. "the question of site": JRO to John H. Manley, 6.11.1942, S & W, 236

338. "It is a lovely spot": ibid.

338. "anything about the developments": ibid., 237

338. On November 16: S & W, 238

338. "This will never do": Badash et al. (1980), 15

338. "As soon as Groves saw it": ibid.

339. Gregg Herken: Herken (2002), 71

339. his formal letter: see S & W, 249

339. "neither Bush, Conant nor I": Groves (1962), 61

339. "no one": ibid.

339. "had had": ibid., 62

339. "the prestige": ibid.

339. "background": ibid., 63

339. "which was not yet,: ibid.

339. "it became apparent": ibid.

340. "had a fatal weakness": Stern (1971), 40

340. "the men we are after": JRO to LRG, 2.11.1943, JRO papers, LOC

340. "I was supposed": Badash et al. (1980), 28

340. "So I dug out some maps": ibid., 29

341. "whether, if Oppenheimer": ibid., 28

341. "I bugged Oppie": ibid., 30

341. "Oppie practically threw": ibid.

341. divided the lab into four main sections: Hawkins (1946), Chapters V, VI, VII and VIII

341. the Experimental Division: ibid., Chapter VI

342. several reasons: see Rigden (1987), 152

342. "the sound of": Anderson (1974), 44

342. "The Italian navigator": Compton (1956), 144

343. 150,000 workers: these figures are taken from Hales (1997), 163

343. "New workers": ibid., 131
343. He persuaded: ibid., 167
344. a letter he wrote to Hans and Rose Bethe: S & W, 243–6
344. "is in the great effort": ibid., 245
344. a long letter of February 25, 1943: reproduced in full as Appendix 1 in Hawkins (1946), 311–15
345. "the fatherly advisor to Oppie": Bethe, interview with Rigden (Rigden [1987], 154)
346. was caught on the FBI microphones: Goodchild (1980), 66–7, Herken (2002), 72
346. "Look, what if": B & S, 188
346. Chevalier's side of the story: see Chevalier (1965), 52–5
346. "Haakon was one hundred percent": Barbara Chevalier's diary, 14.7.1984, see the extracts published on Gregg Herken's website: http://www.brotherhoodof thebomb.com/bhbsource/documents.html
347. "means of getting technical information": ITMO, 130
347. "no chance": "synopsis of facts," 12.2.1954, JRO, FBI file, quoted B & S, 199
347. Bernard Peters had told him: see Romerstein and Breindel (2001), 270
347. "I just want to say goodbye": Nelson, interview with MJS, 17.6.1981, quoted B & S, 194
347. "I think now": B & S, 189

12. Los Alamos 1: Security

349. "Bulldozers moved in": quoted Conant (2005), 62
350. "two or three fellows": Serber (1998), 75
351. "a toy one-lane suspension bridge": ibid.
351. "Cost and construction time": Badesh (1980), 29
352. "That was my introduction": ibid., 31
352. explicitly ordered by Major General Strong: Groves (1962), 138
353. "would next be reading": interview with Pash, 15.3.1954, JRO FBI file, quoted Thorpe (2006), 208
353. "Yes I did": ITMO, 823
354. The conversation: see B & S, 188–90, Herken (2002), 96–7
354. "a little bit scared": Herken (2002), 97
355. "preferably that": ibid.
355. "very much worried": ibid., 96
355. "changed a bit": B & S, 189
355. "To my sorrow": ibid.
356. "a great deal of concern" : ITMO, 260
356. "General Groves's view": ibid.
356. on April 5, 1943: Groves (1962), 138
356. some counterintelligence: what follows is based on the accounts given in Herken (2002), 98–99, Haynes and Klehr (2000), 230–2, and Romerstein and Breindel (2001), 257–9.
357. "Jesus": Herken (2002), 98
357. "very helpful": ITMO, 262
357. "The scientists": ibid.
357. "Oppie": Serber (1998), 77–8
357. "dragooned": ibid., 78

358. "We propose": JRO to LRG, 30.4.1943, S & W, 256

358. "Do you know": Serber (1998), 79

358. "that I think": JRO to WP, 20.5.1943, S & W, 257–8

358. In his reply: WP to JRO, 19.6.1943, S & W, 259

359. "Los Alamos from Below": Feynman (1992), 107–36

359. "job lot": Edward U. Condon, interviewed by Charles Weiner in Boulder, Colorado, April 27, 1968, AIP

359. "And so": Feynman (1992), 110

359. "Please inform your wife": ibid., 117

360. "until the sergeant": ibid., 118

360. "neutral": Teller (2001), 170

360. "seemed about": ibid.

360. "had confused that strange language": ibid.

360. "major responsibility": Groves (1962), 154

360. "Condon was not a happy choice": ibid.

361. "the very heart of security": ibid., 140

361. "The thing that upsets me most": EUC to JRO, April 1943, printed in full in Groves (1962), 429–32 (quotation 429)

361. "The considerations": Groves (1962), 156

362. "The object": Serber (1992), 3

362. "After a couple of minutes": ibid., 4

363. "more exact diffusion theory": ibid., 27

363. "To improve": ibid., 32–3

363. "Several kinds of damage": ibid., 33

363. "overlooked": ibid., 34

364. who suggested it at the Berkeley conference: ibid., xxxii, 59; see also Serber (1998), 72

364. "Serber is looking into it": Serber (1992), 59

364. a major ten-day conference: Hawkins (1946), 9, Hoddeson et al. (1993), 75–8

365. produced a report on December 4: Hoddeson, 36

365. a second Lewis committee: ibid., 69

365. a planning board: ibid., 68–9

365. "be more far-sighted": ibid., 69

366. "the original concept": ibid.

366. "so that": Christman (1998), 107

366. "I was plunged": ibid., 108

366. "understanding of the interplay": Groves (1962), 160

366. "produce the nuclear guts": Christman (1998), 110

367. "pulled together": ibid., 130

367. "every month's delay": Cave Brown (1977), 342

367. "All science stopped": Feynman (1992), 108

368. "Every day": ibid., 112

368. "No, no": ibid.

368. "It had been planned": Bacher, interviewed by Finn Aaserud at the California Institute of Technology, February 13, 1986, AIP

370. resulted in the identification of Weinberg: Herken (2002), 100–11, B & S, 192

370. his request was refused: see ITMO, 13, 119

370. he was drafted into the army: Lomanitz, interviewed by Shawn Mullet, July 29, 2001, AIP

370. was quickly fired: Herken (2002), 109–10
371. a visit to his ex-lover, Jean: see B & S, 231–5
371. "She had indicated": ITMO, 154
371. "Because she was": ibid.
371. What transpired: what follows is based on the account given in B & S, 232
372. "Q. You have no reason": ITMO, 154
372. "may be connected": B & S, 233
372. a memo to Lansdale: see ITMO, 821–3
373. "Consequently": ITMO, 822
373. "My working definition": ITMO, 266
373. "Mrs. Oppenheimer": ibid.
374. "I formed the conviction": ibid.
374. "believed to be": B & S, 234
374. "because of his known interest": ibid., 234–5
375. "In accordance": Groves (1962), 63
375. Bacher told him: Bacher, interview with AKS, 16.3.1978, quoted S & W, 261
375. "I am sure": President Roosevelt to JRO, 29.6.1943, quoted S & W, 260
375. "You would be glad to know": JRO to Roosevelt, 9.7.1943, S & W, 260
376. received from General Groves: S & W, 262–3
376. on July 27: Goodchild (1980), 91
376. Three days later: ibid., and Herken (2002), 110
376. "It was really": Lomanitz, interviewed by Shawn Mullet in Hawaii, July 29, 2001, AIP
376. "Oh, there has to be a mistake": ibid.
376. "Ernest Lawrence yelled": ITMO, 268
376. "very serious mistake": JRO to Col Marshall, 31.7.1943, ITMO, 123
376. "Have requested": ibid., 133
377. Lomanitz gave an interview: Lomanitz, interviewed by Shawn Mullet in Hawaii, July 29, 2001, AIP
377. a full report: see ITMO, 275–6
377. "he had been guilty": ibid., 276
377. "he must forego": ibid.
377. "That makes me mad": ibid.
378. "[He] stated that": ibid.
378. "Oppenheimer gave": ibid.
378. "On the whole": ibid.
378. FBI agents watched: Herken (2002), 110, Sibley (2004), 145
379. "California trouble": see Herken (2002), 106
379. Oppenheimer went to see Groves: B & S, 238
379. on August 25, 1943: ITMO, 136–7, B & S, 238
380. "With the approval": ITMO, 128
380. "framed": ibid., 876
380. "I persuaded him": ibid., 880
380. "I remember": Lomanitz, interviewed by Shawn Mullet in Hawaii, July 29, 2001, AIP
380. "These two fellows": ITMO., 883
380. "if they were violating": ibid.
380. dinner in Berkeley with Robert Bacher: Herken (2002), 107
382. "cock and bull story": ITMO, 137

382. "placed a certain responsibility": ibid., 285
382. "Mr. Johnson": ibid.
382. "I was rather uncertain": ibid.
382. "That is not the particular interest I have": ibid., 286
382. "I think that is true": ibid.
383. "Could you give me": ibid., 287
383. "were always": ibid.
383. "He has probably": ibid., 288
383. "I mean": ibid., 289
384. "I have known": ibid., 290
384. "I was an idiot": ibid., 137
384. "I think it would be a mistake": ibid., 292
384. "It's a member of the faculty": ibid.
384. "They were contacted": ibid., 295
384. "And then": ibid.
385. "and we may not": ibid.
385. "have a feeling": ibid.
385. "We certainly would": ibid., 850
385. "we are going to have to spend": ibid.
385. "We will be hot under the collar": ibid., 860
385. "I think that I would be": ibid., 851
385. "I feel responsible": ibid.
385. like a bloodhound: ibid., 866
386. On August 27: B & S, 233
386. "determining the identities": ibid.
386. "the part played by J.R. Oppenheimer": ibid., 273-4
386. "The writer": ibid., 274
386. "has allowed": ibid.
387. "Until alerted": ibid., 275
387. that "Oppenheimer": ibid.
387. "This Office": ibid., 273
387. On September 3: see Herken (2002), 108-9
388. "without intent of flattery": ITMO, 871
388. "I want you to know": ibid., 885
388. "I thought I might": ibid., 871
388. "They know": ibid., 872
388. "We don't want to": ibid., 873
389. "I've thought about it": ibid., 875
389. "Who do you know": ibid.
389. "I think it possible": ibid., 876
389. "How about Haakon Chevalier?": ibid., 877
389. "we've got the case": ibid., 879
390. "Don't think": ibid., 885
390. "I know that he was in Germany": ibid., 883
390. "It is essential": ibid., 815
390. "very unsatisfactory": ibid., 277
391. "Oppenheimer's attitude": ibid.
391. "who now appears": ibid.
391. "Look": Lomanitz, interviewed by Shawn Mullet in Hawaii, July 29, 2001, AIP

392. "firm conviction": Herken (2002), 110

392. "he didn't believe": ibid.

392. Oppenheimer refused to take the call: ibid., 358, note 57

392. "will continue to be loyal": see B & S, 247

392. "tedious project": ITMO, 815

392. "suddenly": Stern (1971), 55–6

393. "God's help to us": see http://www.presidency.ucsb.edu/ws/index.php?pid=724 59&st=Thanksgiving&st1=#axzz1X2POs3fI

394. "Possible identity": ITMO, 819

395. December 12 : Stern (1971), 65

395. "advised him": B & S, 247

395. sent telegrams: see Stern (1971), 66–7

395. "other than [the] three original attempts": ibid., 67

395. "the information was": ITMO, 263

396. "Yes, but": ibid., 167

396. "When I did identify Chevalier": ITMO, 889

396. The answer seems to be: based on B & S, 514–9, Herken (2002), 270–1

397. "I remember distinctly": ITMO, 264

397. "Nothing could be clearer": ibid., 264–5

397. "finally stated": B & S, 248

398. "Are you still in this world?": HC to JRO, c. November 1943, Chevalier folder, Box 26, JRO papers, LOC

398. "I can't tell you": HC to JRO, 3.12.1943, Chevalier folder, Box 26, JRO papers, LOC

399. "His face was somber": Chevalier (1965), 58

399. "The last thing": ibid.

400. "When I got to his office": Serber (1998), 86

400. Jean's body: what follows is based on the account give in B & S, Chapter Eighteen.

400. "disgusted with everything": B & S, 250

400. claims in an unpublished manuscript: B & S, 252 and 637

400. "went on": B & S, 637

400. "De Silva is not": ibid.

401. "Conversation with J.R. Oppenheimer": ITMO, 150

401. "During the course of the conversation": ibid.

401. "I think": ibid., 121

401. His unconvincing answer: ibid., 122

402. "Just look at him": Stern (1971), 123

402. Oppenheimer was understandably skeptical: ITMO, 119

402. "engaged in earnest conversation": ibid., 150

402. ". . . just as he was preparing to leave": ibid., 149

13. Los Alamos 2: Implosion

404. the Quebec Agreement: Stoff et al. (1991), 46–7, and online at: http://avalon.law.yale.edu/wwii/q002.asp

404. the only physicist: Bethe, interview with Richard Rhodes, 5.3.1993, quoted Rhodes (1996), 259

405. invited by Rudolf Peierls: Peierls (1985), 163

405. a regular informant: see Herken (2002), 89, Rhodes (1995), 57

405. the German authorities had informed the British: see Paul Reynolds, "How atom spy slipped security net," BBC News online at: http://news.bbc.co.uk/1/hi/uk/3046255.stm

405. "bears a good personal reputation": Daphne Bosanquet, quoted ibid.

405. "As he [Fuchs] has been": ibid.

405. "He is rather safer in America": Major Garrett of MI5, quoted ibid.

406. On February 5, 1944: see West (2004), 59

406. "We were desperately afraid": Peierls (1985), 168

406. "and we have no record": ibid.

406. "were in their normal places": ibid., 169

406. "did seem to be": ibid.

407. On August 21, 1943: Rhodes (1988), 511

407. "It is not necessary": ibid., 512

407. a letter written by Heisenberg: see Jungk (1960), 100–1

407. "whether it was right": ibid., 101

407. "Do you really think": ibid.

407. "Bohr was shocked": ibid.

408. "Personally": NB to Heisenberg, undated, but c. 1957. For the full text of this and other documents relating to the Bohr–Heisenberg meeting, see http://nba.nbi.dk/papers/docs/d01tra.htm

408. "less to tell": Oppenheimer, lecture on Bohr, 1964, typescript in JRO papers, LOC

409. "and an opportunity": see Brown (1997), 242, where the letter is given in full

409. "to help resist": quoted Rozental (1967), 194

409. "I have to the best of my judgment": ibid.

409. "I shall make an effort": quoted Brown (1997), 243

409. "In view": see Rose (1998), 157

409. Jeremy Bernstein has suggested: see Bernstein (2003)

410. the Nazi atomic project: for more on this, see Bernstein (2001), Powers (1994) and Rose (1998)

410. a series of Allied attacks: see Baggott (2009), 117–19, 132–6, 215–17, Powers (1994), 195–213, and Rhodes (1988), 455–7

411. Heisenberg gave a lecture: Bernstein (2003), 256

411. Thomas Powers believes: Powers (1994), 246

412. on October 5, 1943: Baggott (2009), 213

412. They arrived in New York on December 6: Powers (1994), 240

412. "It was clearly": Bethe, interview with Jeremy Bernstein, quoted Bernstein (1981), 77

412. "would be a quite useless military weapon": JRO to LRG, 1.1.1944, from the files of Robert Serber, quoted Bernstein (2003), 249

412. "since it has been": S & W, 270

413. "Bohr at Los Alamos was marvelous": JRO, "Niels Bohr Lecture 3," 11 (1963), JRO papers, LOC

413. "was to bring about": Hawkins (1946), 28–9

413. "They didn't need my help": Rhodes (1988), 525

414. "a conservative, dour and remarkably sweet man": JRO, "Niels Bohr Lecture 3," 8 (1963), JRO papers, LOC

414. While he was in Washington: Rhodes (1988), 525

414. Bohr now believed: what follows is based on Frankfurter's summary of the views Bohr expressed to him, quoted Rhodes (1988), 526

415. "shared the hope": quoted ibid.

415. "worried him to death": ibid.

415. "this devastating weapon": quoted ibid., 528

415. "On no account": ibid.

415. "where everything": ibid., 529

415. "It was perfectly absurd": ibid., 530

415. "I did not like the man": ibid.

416. "the suggestion": ibid., 537

416. "The President and I": ibid.

416. "This was not funny": JRO, "Niels Bohr Lecture 3," 14 (1963), JRO papers, LOC

416. Colonel Pash was able to enter Rome: Powers (1994), 304

417. able to interrogate: ibid., 358

417. in November 1944: ibid., 366–73

417. "disagreeable shock": Rotblat (1985), 18

417. "You realise of course": Rotblat, interview with Powers, 20.5.1988, quoted Powers (1994), 473. The same story is told in Rotblat (1985), but without direct quotation.

417. "Until then": Rotblat (1985), 18

418. "I believe your people": Pharr Davis (1969), 181

418. "the most exclusive club": ibid., 184

418. "I found a spirit of Athens": ibid., 185

418. "By the grace of God": ibid.

419. "worked at physics": ibid., 183

419. "Oppenheimer could understand everything": ibid., 182

419. "He could understand anything": ibid.,

420. "the neutron number": Hawkins (1946), 71

420. "the time between fissions": ibid.

420. "extremely unlikely": ibid.

421. "You see": Rhodes (1988), 500

421. "dead in the water": ibid., 492

422. What Seaborg pointed out: see Rhodes (1988), 548

423. "frustrations": Christman (1998), 143

424. published a book: *Atom Bombs: The Top Secret Inside Story of Little Boy and Fat Man* by John Coster-Mullen, self-published (2006)

424. Coster-Mullen's hobby was model-making: see David Samuels, "Atomic John," *New Yorker*, December 15, 2008, http://www.newyorker.com/reporting/2008/12/15/081215fa_fact_samuels

425. Oppenheimer broke the news: see Hoddeson et al. (1993), 240

425. "Do you think": ibid.

425. "went just as white": ibid.

426. a team of just eight people: ibid., 7

426. "It seems to me": Christman (1998), 126

427. "in about the manner": Hoddeson et al. (1993), 87–8

428. "an occasional visit": ibid., 131

428. "woke everybody up": ibid.

428. "Why didn't you tell me": ibid.
428. Oppenheimer gave reasons: ibid., 134
428. "there is less danger": ibid.
429. "both Groves and Conant": ibid., 135
429. "partly": ibid., 137
429. "The situation is a mess": Christman (1998), 137
429. When he eventually joined Los Alamos: see Hoddeson et al. (1993), 139
430. Apparently, the hope was: see ibid., 419, footnote 4
430. "prime objective": JRO to LRG, 25.3.1944, quoted Herken (2002), 116
431. "At that time": Peierls (1985), 187
431. "into the technical aspects": JRO to LRG, 14.2.1944, S & W, 272
431. Teller was appointed: Hoddeson et al. (1993), 157
431. "the great and increased urgency": ibid., 160
431. "Hydrodynamics of Implosion, Super": see Hawkins (1946), 84
432. "The next morning": Teller (2001), 175
432. "I want you": ibid., 177
432. "seemed far too difficult": ibid.
432. "as physicists": ibid., 176
433. "I much prefer": ibid., 177
433. "I was a little hurt": ibid.
433. "greatest urgency": JRO to LRG, 1.5.1944, quoted White (2001), 218
433. on June 3, 1944: Hoddeson et al. (1993), 162
433. "There is an element of comfort": Peierls (1985), 200
433. major breakthrough: see Hoddeson et al. (1993), 163–9
434. "a completely untried and undeveloped method": Hawkins (1946), 91
434. "not a single experimental result": ibid., 143
434. "fascination with organizational charts": Ulam (1991), 156
435. Christy suggested: Hoddeson et al. (1993), 307–8
435. "RaLa method": ibid., 268–71
436. "They were kids": Goodchild (1980), 119
436. "We had reveille at six": ibid.
436. Greenglass had studied mechanical engineering: Schecter (2002), 175–9
437. "the inexcusable Greenglass case": ITMO, 261, 262
437. "He is certainly": ibid., 278
437. "in any way": ibid., 280
438. Theodore Hall: most of my information concerning Hall comes from Albright and Kunstel (1997)
438. When his mother asked: Albright and Kunstel (1997), 35
438. "We were turning out": ibid., 120
438. "It seemed to me": ibid., 90
439. "Now we have our bomb": Hoddeson et al. (1993), 271
439. met Harry Gold in Boston: see Albright and Kunstel (1997), 123, and Rhodes (1996), 152–5
439. he simply denied everything: Albright and Kunstel (1997), Chapters 24–5
439. "in essence": ibid., 289
440. "She didn't get along very well": Goodchild (1980), 127
440. "one of the few people": Conant (2005), 180
440. "very bewitching": ibid., 181
441. "Everybody was aware of it": ibid.

441. "I was young": ibid., 182

441. "It was known": Goodchild (1980), 128

441. "would go off on a shopping trip": ibid.

441. left Los Alamos for Pittsburgh: see B & S, 263

442. "It was all very strange": ibid., 264

442. "Of course not": ibid.

442. "X-2 Development, Engineering, Tests": see Hawkins (1946), 240

442. "Trinity Project": ibid., 241

442. "Why I chose the name": JRO to LRG, 20.10.1962, quoted S & W, 290

443. Lieutenant H. C. Bush: see Szasz (1984), 37–8

443. Groves announced: see Hoddeson et al. (1993), 312

443. "spoke very quietly": S & W, 287

444. "We have been living": ibid., 288

444. dress rehearsal: Hoddeson et al. (1993), 360–2

445. "it was recognized": Groves (1962), 264

445. Oppenheimer hosted: S & W, 291

445. The minutes of these meetings: see Stoff et al. (1991), 97–103

445. "From the psychological point of view": ibid., 100

446. "is a good radar target": ibid.

446. "obtaining the greatest psychological effect": ibid., 102

446. the minutes reveal: ibid., 105–20

446. "expressed the view": ibid., 106

446. "It might be wise": ibid., 112

446. "effect of the bombing": ibid., 117

446. "several strikes": ibid.

447. figure of 20,000: ibid., 122

447. "After much discussion": ibid., 117

447. "the ancient capital of Japan": Groves (1962), 273

447. "and had been": ibid., 274

447. "On the other hand": ibid., 275

447. "There was": ibid.

448. Robert Wilson remembers: see interview with Wilson in Palevsky (2000), Chapter 5, especially 135–7

448. "Handling of Undesirable Scientists": Stoff et al. (1991), 118

448. "stated that": ibid.

448. the political and social implications of the bomb: for Szilard's attempts to stop the U.S. from using the atom bombs, see Baggott (2009), Chapter 15, Rhodes (1988), Chapter 18, and Lanouette (1994), Chapter 18.

449. "general demeanor": Lanouette (1994), 266

449. "The atomic bomb is shit": ibid.

449. "Don't you think": ibid., 266–7

449. the Franck Report: reproduced in full in Stoff et al. (1991), 140–7

449. June 12, 1945: see Compton to Stimson, 12.6.1945, ibid., 138–9

449. "international agreement": ibid., 143

449. "the eyes": ibid., 144

450. "Nuclear bombs": ibid., 146

450. "If the United States": ibid.

450. a memo dated June 16, 1945: ibid., 149–50

450. "It is clear": ibid., 150

451. "opportunity of saving": ibid.

451. "We find ourselves": ibid.

451. "the weapon": R. Gordon Arenson, memo to George L. Harrison, 25.6.1945, ibid., 157

451. "there would be considerable advantage": see George L. Harrison, memo to Stimson, 26.6.1945, ibid., 160

451. "I understand": Lanouette (1994), 269

451. "to rule that": ibid., 175

451. "However small": ibid., 270, Teller (2001), 204–5

451. "The fact that": Teller (2001), 205

452. "made good sense to me": ibid.

452. "in a way": ibid., 206

452. "What do they know": ibid.

452. "our political leaders": ibid.

452. "Of course": Lanouette (1994), 271

452. opinion poll: see Stoff et al. (1991), 173

453. Truman made the decision: see Rhodes (1988), 651

453. "Proposed Program for Japan": Stoff et al. (1991), 168–70

453. "giving them a warning": ibid., 168

453. "Japan is not": ibid., 169

453. "we should add": ibid., 170

454. "This hour": Groves (1962), 293

454. "set the example": ibid.

454. "South 10,000": see Szasz (1984), 31

454. "Every five or ten minutes": Groves (1962), 294

455. Samuel Allison started the countdown: Szasz (1984), 82

455. "I never realized": ibid.

455. "My first impression": Groves (1962), 296

455. "These plans": ibid., 297–8

455. "We knew the world": *The Day After Trinity* (1980), directed by John H. Else, KTEH television

455. "I am all-powerful Time": *Bhagavad Gita*, Penguin Classics (1962), 92

455. the famous translation: see Arnold (1993)

456. "Death am I": Ryder (2004), 88

456. "Dr. Oppenheimer": Groves (1962), 436–7

456. "Some people": Szasz (1984), 90

456. "I think we just said": *The Day After Trinity* (1980), directed by John H. Else, KTEH television

456. "A loud cry filled the air": B & S, 309

456. "Our first feeling": Szasz (1984), 91

456. "He seemed shrunken": ibid.

456. "thrilled": ibid., 90

457. "I'll never forget his walk": Goodchild (1980), 163, B & S, 308

457. "The war is over": Norris (2002), 405

457. a betting pool: see Rhodes (1988), 656

457. "My God": Szasz (1984), 85

457. "remotely located": ibid.

457. "Operated on this morning": Stoff et al. (1991), 183

457. "Doctor Groves": Szasz (1984), 145

458. "tremendously pepped up": ibid., 146

458. "For the first time in history": Stoff et al. (1991), 188

458. "deposited its dust": ibid., 189

458. "awesome roar": ibid., 191

458. "The feeling": ibid., 192

458. "Herculean project": ibid.

458. "a nation": ibid., 195

458. "beginning to feel": ibid.

459. "They were immensely pleased": ibid., 203–4

459. "unanimous in thinking": ibid., 205

14. Los Alamos 3: Heavy with Misgiving

460. "now with our new weapon": Stoff et al. (1991), 211–12

460. "I casually mentioned": Truman (1955), 416

460. "will deliver": Groves (1962), 308

460. Potsdam Declaration: Stoff et al. (1991), 215–6

461. "The prodigious land, sea and air forces": ibid., 215

461. "would stand": ibid., 225

461. Radio Tokyo: ibid.

461. "Mokusatsu": see Alperovitz (1996), Chapter 32

461. "They're going to take this thing": Pharr Davis (1969), 240

461. "Oh God": Conant (2005), 318

461. "I just keep thinking": ibid., 323. A slightly different version of the same recollection is in B & S, 314.

462. Spaatz cabled Washington: Rhodes (1988), 696

462. "Hiroshima should be given first priority": ibid.

462. Farrell reported to Groves: ibid., 699

462. called a briefing: see Christman (1998), 1–2

462. "shorten the war": Rhodes (1988), 701

462. *Enola Gay* set off from Tinian: the account of the Hiroshima raid that follows is based on those given in Christman (1998), Gordin (2007), Rhodes (1988) and Serber (1998).

462. "Fellows": Rhodes (1988), 710

462. "We turned back": ibid.

462. "a pot": ibid., 711

463. "I was trying": ibid.

463. "I just could not understand": ibid., 717

463. a long article: see Hersey (1989)

463. "in the conviction": *New Yorker*, August 31, 1946, quoted DeGroot (2005), 109

464. "He drove the boat": Hersey (1989), 45

464. "Many of them": Rhodes (1988), 718

464. "a woman with her jaw missing": ibid., 721

464. "people with their bowels and brains coming out": ibid.

464. "dead child": DeGroot (2005), 88

464. "that Hiroshima had disappeared": Rhodes (1988), 728

465. the official estimate: ibid.

465. the best estimate: see http://www.atomicarchive.com/Docs/MED/med_chp10.shtml, from which my figures were taken

465. "Deak to Farrell": Christman (1998), 193

465. to find a cable: Groves (1962), 319
465. he went out to play tennis: ibid., 320
465. "The hours went by": ibid., 321
466. "I went to sleep": ibid., 322–3
466. It arrived in triumph: see Christman (1998), 194
466. "additional information": Groves (1962), 323
466. "felt this strike": ibid.
466. "I was eating lunch": Truman (1955), 421
466. "Sixteen hours ago": Donovan (1996), 97
467. "the achievement": ibid., 98
467. "the Japanese": Cohen (1983), 22
468. "Hahn was completely shattered": Bernstein (2001), 115
468. "I don't believe a word": ibid., 116
468. "ten tons": ibid., 117
468. "Here is the news": ibid., 357
469. "By God's mercy": ibid., 361
469. "We were unable": ibid., 121
469. "I am thankful": ibid., 122
469. "I was asked": ibid., 124
469. "You are probably": Chevalier (1965), ix
470. "had often discussed": Groves (1962), 342
470. "With the success": Rhodes (1988), 738
470. On August 8: ibid., 736
471. "after about August 3": see page 460
471. "Young man": Groves (1962), 344
471. arrived at Kokura: Rhodes (1988), 740
471. The best estimate: see http://www.atomicarchive.com/Docs/MED/med_
      chp10.shtml
472. about 70,000: Rhodes (1988), 740
472. ordered him off the plane: Serber (1998), 113
472. "The only picture": ibid., 114
472. "You have known": ibid., 112
472. "our entire organization": Groves (1962), 353
472. reported to General Marshall: Rhodes (1988), 743
473. "for by that time": Groves (1962), 346
473. "any demand": Rhodes (1988), 742
473. "the most cruel": Stoff et al. (1991), 244
473. "massacring": ibid.
473. "said the thought": ibid., 245
473. "From the moment": ibid., 247
473. "I cannot endure": Rhodes (1988), 744
474. "the enemy": ibid., 745
474. "Seldom, if ever": quoted Hunner (2004), 77
474. "Let me tell you": Serber (1998), 115
474. "Hey, Oppie": Michelmore (1969), 113
474. "There's surprisingly little excitement": Serber (1998), 114
474. "A whole damn bunch": Goodchild (1980), 169
474. "Few of us": Frisch (1980), 177

475. "nervous wreck": Herken (2002), 139
475. when Lawrence came to Los Alamos: ibid., 140
475. "There is every reason": Hunner (2004), 82
475. "revulsion": Smith (1965), 77
475. "The reasons": Conant (2005), 330
475. "He smoked constantly": ibid., 333
476. "We believe": JRO to Stimson, 17.8.1945, Stoff et al. (1991), 255, S & W, 294
476. "had an opportunity": JRO to EOL, 30.8.1945, S & W, 301
476. "felt reluctant": ibid.
476. "Could all this be printed out": Smyth (1989), ix
477. "Rather": ibid.
477. "I had the fairly clear impression": JRO to EOL, 30.8.1945, S & W, 301
477. "Secretary Byrnes": Stoff et al. (1991), 256
478. "I can understand now": Chevalier (1965), x
478. "The thing had to be done": B & S, 319
478. "You will believe": JRO to HWS, 26.8.1945, S & W, 297
478. "in an earnest": JRO to Bernheim, 27.8.1945, S & W, 297–8
478. "You will understand": JRO to Deutsch, 24.8.1945, S & W, 295
478. a long letter to Charles Lauritsen: JRO to Lauritsen, *c.* 27.8.1945, S & W, 298–300
479. "a real instrument": JRO to Marcelle Bier, 31.8.1945, S & W, 303
479. "tickling the dragon's tail": see Hoddeson et al. (1993), 346–8, and Malenfant (2005)
479. suffered an accident: see Hunner (2004), 84–5
480. "I think it's good propaganda": Stoff et al. (1991), 258
480. "I'll be delayed": Serber (1998), 114
480. "The most striking impression": ibid., 123
480. "callousness": ibid., 125
480. "The ruins": ibid., 135
480. a press conference: see Norris (2002), 439–40
481. "No one": Hunner (2004), 114–5
481. origins of this organization: I am dependent here on the information provided in Piccard (1965). It is more usual to say that ALAS was formed on August 30, 1945, but, using contemporary sources and ALAS's own archive of documents, Piccard gives a fuller and more detailed account that traces the origins back to the spring of 1945.
481. "the international control": from an anonymous note in the ALAS files, dated October 24, 1945, quoted Piccard (1965), 252
482. a document: reproduced in full ibid., Appendix A
482. "In the event": ibid., 259
482. "The development of the atomic bomb": ibid.
482. "You will probably recognize": S & W, 304
482. "Mr. Harrison points out": Piccard (1965), 260
483. "If this bill passes": Lanouette (1994), 286
484. "felt that he had": Rhodes (1996), 241
484. "I must confess": Smith (1965), 140
484. "frightening": Lanouette (1994), 287
484. "Mention to a Senator's secretary": ibid., 288

485. "It was a declaration": Wilson (1996), 353
485. "not necessarily": ibid.
485. "The scientific background": Piccard (1965), 261
485. "one of the best speeches": Conant (2005), 346
486. "It is our hope": S & W, 310
486. "The peoples of this world": ibid., 311

PART FOUR: 1945–1967

15. The Insider Scientist

489. "He'd better be careful": Conant (2005), 351
489. "The woods": ibid.
489. "There were always people": ibid., 352
489. "somewhat academic": *Hearings on Science Legislation (S. 1297 and related bills): Hearings before a subcommittee of the Committee on military affairs*, United States Senate, Seventy-Ninth Congress, first session, Washington D.C.: U.S. Government Printing Office (1945), 300
489. "a plea": ibid., 301
490. "If the so-called secret": ibid., 322
490. "no technical difficulty": ibid., 325
490. "The two": ibid., 321
490. "The Johnson bill": ibid., 308
490. "oblique attack": quoted Smith (1965), 154
490. "the coolest reception": Thorpe (2006), 176
490. "Oppie's suggestions": ibid.
490. a dinner: see Lanouette (1994), 290
491. "I never saw a man": Wallace (1973), 496–7
491. May opened proceedings at 10 a.m.: see Lanouette (1994), 290–3
491. "patient consideration": ibid., 291
492. a "masterpiece": ibid., 292
492. "He talked": ibid., 293
492. "The bill": *Hearings on Science Legislation*, 127, quoted Thorpe (2006), 172
492. "To the congressmen": Lanouette (1994), 293
492. "I think it is a matter": quoted Thorpe (2006), 173
492. "an enormous technological development": *Hearings on Science Legislation*, 300, quoted Thorpe (2006), 174
492. "a plea for leaving": ibid., 301, quoted Thorpe (2006), 174
493. "I don't want to see": B & S, 332
493. "The first thing": ibid., 331
494. "Perhaps": ibid.
494. "never": ibid.
494. "sacred trust": see Piccard (1965), 257
494. "I saw him": Pharr Davis (1969), 260
494. "Mr. President": B & S, 332
494. "I told him": ibid.
494. "cry-baby scientist": ibid.
494. "Don't worry": ibid.

495. "Years later": S & W, 315

495. "But when you": ibid., 317

495. "the almost unanimous resistance": ibid.

495. "the views suggested": ibid., 324

495. "insistent tone": ibid.

496. "say that no bombs be made": ibid., 322

496. "If some of you": ibid., 315

496. "I would like": JRO to JBC, 29.9.1945, S & W, 308

496. he wrote to William Houston: S & W, 308

497. "I did actually": ITMO, 35

497. "I was sort of reluctant": ibid.

497. seized and destroyed five cyclotrons: see Groves (1962), Chapter 27, 367–72

497. "Oppenheimer and I": Bernstein (2004), 100

498. "walked back and forth": Lilienthal (1964), 13

498. "an extraordinary personage": ibid., 14

498. "worth living a lifetime": B & S, 340

498. "All the participants": Acheson (1969), 153, quoted B & S, 340

498. "knew more": Groves (1962), 411

498. "had little or no knowledge": ibid.

498. "Everybody genuflected": Goodchild (1980), 178

499. "The way it worked": ITMO, 37

499. On February 2: see ibid.

499. "we did not feel": Groves (1962), 412

500. "It would nevertheless": for Churchill's Fulton speech in full, see http://www
     .historyguide.org/europe/churchill.html

500. "That was the day": Pharr Davis (1969), 259

500. "a workable plan": Acheson (1969), 154

501. "interpreter of military policy": Herken (2002), 166

501. "for the purpose": JEH to Clark, 26.4.1946, JRO FBI file

501. "Are you there, dear?": FBI San Francisco office to JEH, 14.5.1946, JRO FBI
     file

501. "At this point": ibid.

502. first met early in April: see Meyrowitz (1990), 263

502. "Mark my words": Pharr Davis (1969), 261

502. In another: "Atomic Explosives," Oppenheimer (1955), 3–17

502. "world government": ibid., 13

502. "renunciation": ibid.

502. "has from day to day": "Justification for continuation of technical or micro-
     phone surveillance," FBI San Francisco Office, 12.7.1946, JRO FBI file

503. "the United States' top military secret": Bern to Patterson, 3.6.1946, JRO FBI
     file

503. "would place us": Gregory C. Bern to Robert P. Patterson, Secretary of War,
     3.6.1946, JRO FBI file

503. "that the United States": Miller (1976), 244–5

503. On that advice: see Norris (2002), 483

503. "Mr. Baruch told me": ITMO, 40

503. At the meeting: B & S, 344–6

504. "Baruch Plan": see Dupuy and Hammerman (1973), 302

504. their own proposal: ibid., 308, see also Gromyko (1947)
505. "the Oppenheimers": H. B. Fletcher, FBI San Francisco Office to JEH, 11.6.1946, JRO FBI file
505. a phone conversation: H. B. Fletcher, FBI San Francisco Office to JEH, 13.6.1946, JRO FBI file
505. an unsuccessful attempt: H. B. Fletcher, FBI San Francisco Office to JEH, 18.6.1946, JRO FBI file
505. on June 26: Chevalier (1965), 61, says "early June," but Chevalier's FBI file shows June 26 as the correct date—see Herken (2002), 161
505. "in monosyllables": Chevalier (1965), 63
505. "I have here": ibid., 64
505. "dropped by my house": B & S, 357
505. "I approached no one": ibid.
506. "I cannot tell you why": B & S, 356
506. "Give it back to the Indians": Teller (2001), 219
506. "Operation Crossroads": see Weisgall (1994), from where my information about these tests primarily comes.
507. "If an atomic bomb": ibid., 98
507. "the appropriateness": ibid., 99
507. WHITE: "I also have another quotation": H. B. Fletcher, FBI San Francisco Office to JEH, 11.6.1946, JRO FBI file
508. "Naval vessels": *Bulletin of the Atomic Scientists of Chicago*, 1 (5), February 15, 1946, 12
508. just what happened: what follows is derived mainly from Weisgall (1994)
508. "Dressed in all the trappings": *The Economist*, Volume 151, 1946, 9
508. "not so much": Rhodes (1996), 262
509. "common blackmail": ibid.
509. "is in deep despair": Lilienthal (1964), 69
509. "will be construed by us": ibid., 70
509. "paced up and down": ibid.
509. "He is really": ibid., 69
509. "for the last four years": S & W, 289
510. "Cosmic Rays: Report of Recent Progress, 1936–1941": Oppenheimer (1944)
510. "The situation": Oppenheimer (1944), 31
510. "Reaction of Radiation": Oppenheimer and Bethe (1946)
511. "I think": Donald Menzel to JRO, 15.7.1946, JRO papers, LOC
511. "I would like": JRO to Donald Menzel, 8.8.1946, JRO papers, LOC
511. "There are certainly": Menzel to JRO, August 1946, JRO papers, LOC
512. "He is not greatly cultivated": B & S, 362
512. "a kind of house-rewarming": Chevalier (1965), 69
512. "had been asked": ibid.
512. "was obviously": ibid.
513. "I had to report": ibid.
513. "gave no answer": ibid., 70
513. "Opje let loose": ibid.
513. Oppenheimer himself was interviewed: see Herken (2002), 161–2
514. "Dr. Oppenheimer has requested": Pais (2006), 80
515. about whom Oppenheimer had written to Birge: S & W, 268–9
515. "in every way": ibid., 268

515. Six months later: JRO to Birge, 26.5.1944, S & W, 275–6

515. "I shall of course": S & W, 284–5

515. "Would you like to come to Berkeley?": Mehra et al. (1999e), 1137

515. "I still said no": ibid.

516. "Turn around": Pais (1997), 186

516. "Oppenheimer spoke": ibid., 221

516. "As I stood waiting": ibid., 221–2

517. "Let's walk": ibid., 222

517. "I have just": ibid., 224

517. "quite long conversations": ITMO, 327

518. "You will note": JEH to General Harry H. Vaughan, 28.2.1947, JRO FBI file

518. "Well, if anyone were to print this stuff": Stern (1971), 103

518. "visibly shaken": ibid.

518. Oppenheimer had told him: see ITMO, 27

519. On March 11: Herken (2002), 179

519. "He wanted me to be quite clear": ITMO, 41

519. to hear Oppenheimer say: ibid., 344

519. On August 11: Herken (2002), 180

520. Shelter Island Conference: my main sources of information about this conference are Pais (1986), Chapter 18, Schweber (1986b), Schweber (1994) and Schwinger (1986). A good, accessible account of the conference can be found in Baggott (2011).

520. "would be remembered": Schweber (1994), 156

520. "There have been many conferences": ibid.

521. Weisskopf's outline: ibid., 179–81

521. Oppenheimer's outline: ibid., 181–3

521. a nontechnical lecture: "Atomic Energy as a Contemporary Problem," Oppenheimer (1955), 21–41

521. "of the two or three": ibid., 30

521. "would not dare": Brown and Hoddeson (1983), 222

522. "Twenty-three": quoted Schweber (1994), 172–3

522. "it was immediately evident": ibid., 173

522. "As the conference went on": ibid.

523. "I had heard Oppenheimer speak": Pais (2006), 112

524. "unexpectedly fruitful": Schweber (1994), 174

524. "the most successful conference": ibid., 175

525. "Don't worry": ibid., 174

525. "I hardly see him any more": Chevalier (1965), 79

525. "George thinks this": ibid., 80

526. "Oppenheimer became a symbol": Kevles (1995), 377

16. The Booming Years

527. "This is an unreal place": Pais (1997), 248–9

528. Life magazine ran an article: Life, December 29, 1947, 53–9

528. "devastating projection": ibid., 53

529. "The Multiple Production": Oppenheimer, Lewis and Wouthuysen (1948)

529. "Note on the Stimulated Decay": Oppenheimer, Epstein and Finkelstein (1948)

529. small conference in Copenhagen: see Pais (1997), 233–4

529. "It was": ibid., 234
530. "did not have time": Mehra and Rechenberg (2001), 1044. See also Schweber (1994), 317
530. "The importance of Schwinger's calculation": Schweber (1994), 318
530. "Physics in the Contemporary World": Oppenheimer (1955), 81–102
530. "temporarily disastrous effect": ibid., 83
530. "demands of": ibid.
530. "It has": ibid., 83–4
530. "Almost every month": ibid., 84–5
530. "A newly vigorous": ibid., 85–6
531. "the increasing understanding": ibid., 86
531. "It is the prevailing view": ibid.
531. "In some sort of crude sense": ibid., 88
532. "God is great!": Schweber (1994), 318
532. "I have heard": ibid.
532. "As he proceeded": Pais (1997), 251
533. "The great event": Schweber (1994), 320
533. "I was not showing off": Mehra and Rechenberg (2001), 1048
533. "I heard later": ibid.
533. December 10, 1947: Schweber (1994), 176
534. "Now it does not matter": Pais (2006), 115
534. "a major tour de force": ibid.
534. "I was not invited": Dyson (1979), 55
534. "had a new theory": ibid.
534. "Dick tried to tell": ibid.
534. "the speed": Pais (2006), 115
534. "The Pocono conference": Schwinger (1986), 414
534. "got together in the hallway": Mehra and Rechenberg (2001), 1059
535. "Grateful for your letter": see Schwinger (2008), 40
535. "Just because": Schweber (1994), 198
535. "remarkable work": *Physical Review* (1948), 74, 225
535. "The reason": Schweber (1994), 201
536. "whole idea": Barton (1968), 66. On the history of *Physics Today*, see also Weiner (1973).
536. "to present": Barton (1968)
537. "Out of it all": *Engineering and Science Monthly*, July 1948, 7
537. "hard to disbelieve": Oppenheimer (1949b), 181
537. "the developments": ibid.
537. "To me that was very important": Schweber (1994), 502
538. "where love had drawn him": ibid., 452
538. "I knew": Dyson (1979), 64
538. "Yesterday": Schweber (1994), 335
538. "a marvel": Dyson (1979), 66
538. "was a cut diamond": ibid.
538. "understood Schwinger's theory": ibid.
538. "As we were droning across Nebraska": ibid., 67
539. "to teach": ibid., 68
539. "five days": Kaiser (2005), 74
539. "announcing the triumph": ibid.

540. "In the middle of the conference": Rudolf Peierls, interviewed by Charles Weiner in Seattle, Washington, August 13, 1969, AIP
540. "there is the phrase": JRO to FO, 28.9.1948, quoted B & S, 391, and (slightly more fully) Michelmore (1969), 145–6
540. "more powerful methods": Schwinger (1958), 148
540. "closed": ibid., 154
540. "The atmosphere": quoted Gleick (1994), 266
541. "unreceptive to new ideas": Dyson (1979), 73
541. "but it came as a shock": ibid.
541. "The old guard": Mehra and Rechenberg (2001), 1071
541. "I might have thought": Kragh (1990), 184
541. "Recent work by Lamb": Dirac (1951), 291
542. is on record: see Kragh (1990), 183
542. "I disagree": Schweber (1994), 522
542. "As a result": ibid.
542. "I have been observing": Dyson (1979), 73
542. "we had our fiercest public battle": ibid.
543. "about some calculations": ibid., 74
543. "*Nolo Contendere*": ibid.
543. "It's a grim prospect": Schweber (1994), 527
544. "Certainly": ibid.
544. "Well": ibid., 551
544. "I am really": Schweber (1994), 550
544. "What we don't understand": *Time* magazine, November 8, 1948, 70
544. "I woke up": ibid., 76
545. "to follow in detail": JRO to FO, 28.9.1948, quoted B & S, 391
545. "where I saw an opportunity": B & S, 393
545. "intellectual hotel": *Time* magazine, November 8, 1948, 76
545. "despairing the life": ibid.
546. "Suppose you could": *New York Times*, April 18, 1948, quoted Pais (2006), 89
546. "prim and shy": Dyson (1979), 71
547. "was dying to have conversations": Pais (2006), 87. See also Pais (1997), 236, where he is merely "eager" to have conversations with Eliot.
547. "This is a nice elevator": Pais (2006), 87
547. "felt lonely and homesick": Ackroyd (1985), 288
547. "Newspapermen": Dyson (1979), 72
547. "I invited Eliot here": ibid.
547. "One piece of news": Lee (2009), 158
548. "beautiful theory": Schweber (1994), 550
548. "Oppenheimer gave a presidential address": Dyson (1979), 74–5
548. "when I really knew": Schweber (1994), 456
548. "What about Case's Theorem?": Mehra and Rechenberg (2001), 1092. See also ibid., 455
549. "That was the moment": ibid., 456
549. "But what about Slotnick's calculation?": ibid.
549. "I had fun with that": ibid.
550. "We will start work": Pais (2006), 117
550. "We had lovely weather": Schweber (1994), 552
550. "Feynman's show": Pais (2006), 117

550. "began its rapid": ibid.

550. "a real sense": Schweber (1994), 178

551. "is *known*": Feynman (1990), 3

551. "At the present time": ibid., 7

551. "We physicists": ibid., 8

17. *Massive Retaliation*

552. "The Open Mind": Oppenheimer (1955), 45–57

552. "We need to remember": ibid., 54

552. "appear to commit us": ibid., 53

553. "they would need them": ibid., 56

553. "More & more physicists": *Time* magazine, November 8, 1948, 70

553. his appearance before HUAC: see Stern (1971), 118–22, B & S, 394–6, and ITMO, 210–16. Schweber (2000), 118–30, has an excellent account both of the hearing and of its repercussions.

554. "Mr. Chairman": B & S, 396

554. "a dangerous man and quite Red": ibid., 395

554. "violently denounced": ibid.

554. "too constitutional": Stern (1971), 120

555. "Incidents in Germany": ITMO, 211

555. "It was well known": ibid.

555. "Before we adjourn": Stern (1971), 122

555. called before the committee the very next day: ibid., 123

556. "God guided their questions": ibid., 124. See also ITMO, 213, where Oppenheimer is asked twice whether he said this. The first time he denies it, the second time he says he does not remember saying it.

556. a Rochester newspaper: the story is reproduced in full in Schweber (2000), 119–20.

556. "because of his intransigence": ibid., 123

556. "If Peters loses his job": ibid., 123–4

556. "lost a good deal of sleep": ibid., 125

556. Bethe's letter: ibid.

557. "rather dismal": ibid., 127

557. "a not very successful piece": ibid.

557. "I think mostly": Michelmore (1969), 156

557. Frank's turn: Stern (1971), 130–2, B & S, 402–5

557. front-page story: the front page in question is reproduced in Goodchild (1969), 187

557. said he had never been a Communist Party member: see ibid., 188

558. he had been to see J. W. Buchta: Cole (2009), 91

558. more than fifty physicists: ibid., 92

558. "never agreed with Frank": ibid., 93

558. "Jackie was absolutely furious": ibid., 95

558. "Come back": ibid., 85

558. "Frank Oppenheimer is no longer welcome": ibid.

558. "What is going on?": B & S, 403–4

559. simply dismissed Strauss's concerns: Stern (1971), 114, 128. See also B & S, 164, and Rhodes (1996), 311

559. "incredible mismanagement": Rhodes (1996), 359

559. "inimical to our national defense": Pais (2006), 165
560. "sat in the front row": Bernstein (2004), 108
560. The specific issue at hand: see ibid., 107
560. "No one": Stern (1971), 129
560. "Even to an observer": ibid.
560. "one eye on Oppenheimer": ibid.
560. "My own rating": ibid., 129–30
560. "Well, Joe": ibid., 130
560. "There was a look of hatred": ibid.
560. the cover of *Life* magazine: *Life*, October 10, 1949
560. "the best picture": Pais (2006), 141
561. "Equations at top of the board": *Life*, October 10, 1949, 120
561. "although he tried": ibid., 134
561. "off doing the devil's work": ibid., 121
562. "Almost every month": ibid., 122
562. "what we are forced to call": ibid., 123
562. "what is at the moment": ibid., 123–4
562. "devoted most of his investigative efforts": ibid., 132
563. "the world's foremost center": ibid., 121
563. introduced the term "lepton": see Pais (1986), 450
563. "Models and Methods in the Meson Theory": Yukawa (1949)
563. a short paragraph: Oppenheimer (1949a)
563. a short, cowritten article: Oppenheimer and Arnold (1950)
564. "Of his manifold activities": *Life*, October 10, 1949, 138
564. "the news that Russia has at last": ibid., 121
564. The evidence for the Soviet bomb: Rhodes (1996), 368–74
565. "We have evidence": see "The Russian Explosion: Mr. Truman's Announcement," *Bulletin of the Atomic Scientists*, Vol. V, No. 10, October 1949, 261
565. "What shall we do?": Goodchild (1980), 197
565. "We should now": Strauss (1962), 216–7
566. "it was highly probable": Teller (2001), 281
566. "In the present situation": ibid.
566. "Having the Super weapon": ITMO, 683
566. Teller set off: see Teller (2001), 283
566. "over my dead body": ibid.
566. Hershberg, has speculated: ibid., 875
566. "Probably Oppenheimer wanted": Hershberg (1993), 472
567. "On the technical side": JRO to JBC, 21.10.1949, JRO papers, LOC, reprinted in full in ITMO, 242–3
568. "I told Ernest": Serber (1998), 168
568. "that the United States": ibid., 169
568. "perhaps the most important one": Pais (2006), 173
568. "The clear implication": Seaborg (2001), 142
568. "I expressed my opinion": ibid.
569. "Although I deplore": ITMO, 238
569. George Kennan: ibid., 358–9
569. "I met Luis": Serber (1998), 169–70
569. "mostly psychological": Lilienthal (1964), 581, also Rhodes (1996), 397–8
570. "He said that he did not think": ITMO, 785

570. "the program": ibid.

570. "interesting talk": Herken (2002), 207

570. "decision to go ahead": Lilienthal (1964), 581

570. "one must explore it": ibid.

570. Three reports: all three are published in full as the Appendix to York (1976), 150–68.

571. "an intensification": ibid., 152

571. "seeing the same film": Lilienthal (1964), 581

571. "We believe": York (1976), 154

571. "it has generally been estimated": ibid., 155

571. "It is clear": York (1976), 155

572. "Although": ibid., 155–6

572. "weapon of genocide": ibid., 157

572. "We believe a super bomb should never be produced": ibid.

572. "Should they use": ibid.

572. "In determining": ibid.

572. "necessarily an evil thing": ibid., 158

572. "the nations of the world": ibid., 159

573. "should with considerable regret": ITMO, 395

573. "enough be declassified": York (1976), 156

573. "did not tell me": Teller (2001), 283–4

573. "Washington": ibid., 284

573. "There are also forces": ibid., 285

573. "Before I could say anything": ibid., 286

573. "into a single sovereignty": Borden (1946), 41

574. "Weisskopf vividly described to me": Bernstein (1981), 93

574. "He was disappointed": ibid., 94

574. the AEC met: see Rhodes (1996), 404

574. "came back feeling happy": ibid.

575. "You know": ibid., 405

575. "If we let Russia get the super first": Bundy (1988), 211

575. "I believe": Strauss (1962), 219

575. "would improve our defense": Rhodes (1996), 406

575. "made a lot of sense": ibid., 407

576. "What the Hell are we waiting for?": ibid.

576. "to continue its work": ibid.

576. "alerted the world": Bernstein (2004), 121

576. "I never forgave Truman": ibid.

576. Oppenheimer did not even bother: Pfau (1984), 123

576. "You don't look jubilant": Goodchild (1980), 204

576. Abraham Pais has taken: Pais (2006), 177

577. "prudential and game-theoretical terms": Pharr Davis (1968), 330. The remark comes from a talk Oppenheimer gave in 1959 to the Congress for Cultural Freedom. See Chapter 19 below, page 671

578. a series of shocking revelations: see, e.g., Rhodes (1996), Chapter 21, Sibley (2004), Chapter Five, and West (2004), Chapters VII and VIII

578. McCarthy launched the era: on McCarthyism, see Fried (1997b), Haynes (1996), Morgan (2003), Rovere (1996), Schrecker (1994) and Schrecker (1998)

578. "here in my hand": Rovere (1996), 125

578. "will make a good many men": Rhodes (1996), 412
579. senator from Colorado, Edwin Johnson: see *Bulletin of the Atomic Scientists*, VI (3), March 1950, 66
579. "Our scientists": ibid.
579. "naïve and monumental indiscretion": ibid., 67
579. "make a solemn declaration": ibid., 75
580. "There is grave danger": ibid. Cf. Schweber (2000), 160
580. "Hydrogen bombs": Schweber (2000), 161
580. "I had a long talk with Oppie": McMillan (2005), 68
580. "Back to the Laboratories!": *Bulletin of the Atomic Scientists*, VI (3), March 1950, 71–2
580. "Our scientific community": ibid., 72
580. "In my mind": Wheeler (2000), 199
581. "was a great disappointment": ibid., 199–200
581. "Let Teller and Wheeler go ahead": ibid., 200
581. ". . . the hydrogen bomb can't be done": ibid.
581. "Things have advanced": ET to JRO, 17.2.1950, JRO papers, LOC
581. "regarded as a matter": Rhodes (1996), 421
581. an article by Bethe: Bethe (1950)
581. "Whether the temperatures required": ibid., 101
582. "I still believe": Schweber (2000), 163
582. "In case of war": ibid., 164
582. "With his wonderful virtuosity": Ulam (1991), 216
582. "was not easily reconciled": ibid.
583. "seemed rather glad": ibid., 217
583. "We all agree": ITMO, 788
583. "The panel contained": ibid., 684
584. "In fact": Hewlett and Duncan (1969), 531. See also Libby (1979), 312, and Goodchild (1980), 208
584. "Luis, how could you": ITMO, 788
584. "You go back": ibid., 789
584. "Comments on the Military Value of the Atom": Oppenheimer (1951)
584. "To the first impression": ibid., 43
585. "of the specific use": ibid., 44
585. "strategic air warfare": ibid.
585. "Much of what was clear": ibid.
585. "the extreme form": ibid., 45
585. "I cannot believe": ibid., 45
585. "Project Vista": see Elliot (1986), upon which my account is based
586. "the possible tactical employment": ibid., 164
586. "study group": ibid.
586. "expressed the feeling": ibid.
586. fee of $600,000: ibid., 167
586. "All of us": ibid., 169
587. "On the other hand": Vista Report, Vol. 1, 3, quoted ibid., 170
587. "explosion": ibid., 174
587. Oppenheimer was no longer to be used: York (1976), 139
588. "We have found no great new weapons": McCray (2004), 361
588. a yield of between one and fifty kilotons: Elliot (1986), 172

588. "to send material down a tube": Rhodes (1996), 457

588. "like using a blast furnace": ibid.

589. "new and elaborate instrumentation": ibid., 460

589. "staring intensely": ibid., 463

589. "From then on": ibid., 467

589. "Edward is full of enthusiasm": ibid.

590. "The new concept": ibid., 468

590. In a series of papers: see ibid., 467–70

590. "The sequence is fission-fusion-fission": Bernstein (2004), 126

590. "On Heterocatalytic Detonations": Rhodes (1996), 467–8, also McMillan (2005), 102–3

590. 225 kilotons: Rhodes (1996), 474

590. "When I came out of the water": ibid.

591. yielded twenty-five kilotons: ibid.

591. The agenda for the meeting: ibid., 475

591. "The outcome": ITMO, 20

591. "It is my judgment": ibid., 81

591. "a sweet and lovely and beautiful job": ibid., 229

592. code-named "Mike": for a detailed account of the Mike test, see Rhodes (1996), Chapter 24.

592. "In spite of the remarkable success": *Memorial Tributes: National Academy of Engineering*, Volume 6, The National Academies Press, 1993, 73–6 (quotation, 76)

592. "Somewhat negative": Teller (2001), 327

593. "If I'd given him control": Rhodes (1996), 479

593. "makes its very existence": York (1976). The words are in the minority report written by Rabi and Fermi, but the general report makes similar points, and there is no doubt that the sentiments expressed by Rabi and Fermi were widely shared among the members of the GAC.

593. "a chunk of the atmosphere": Teller (2001), 332

593. "A lot of us were really teed-off at Edward": Rhodes (1996), 479

594. "neither necessary": Oppenheimer to Dean, 13.10.1951, JRO papers, LOC

594. "among the very best": Teller (2001), 335

594. "You have to choose": Serber (1998), 172

595. "a courteous man": Teller (2001), 333

595. "Strauss told me": ibid., 334

595. "I think it would be fair to say": ibid., 336

595. "has the reputation": Schweber (2000), 147

595. "delayed or attempted to delay": B & S, 443

596. "a lot of people believe": ibid.

596. "would do most anything": Rhodes (1996), 537

596. "I want to say": ITMO, 748

596. "We felt at the time": ibid., 746

596. "crucial interview": Teller (2001), 338

596. on June 9, 1952: Herken (2002), 254

597. When Thomas Murray visited Berkeley: Herken (2002), 249

597. gave a speech: ibid.

597. "now is doubtful": FBI San Francisco office to JEH, 5.4.1952, JRO FBI file

597. "Some of the 'boys' have their axe out": Hershberg (1993), 600. Herken (2002),

250, quotes the same diary entry, worded slightly differently. I am assuming that, of the two, Hershberg is the more accustomed to Conant's handwriting.

597. "vitriolic talk": Herken (2002), 249

598. Hoover sent transcripts of those interviews: ibid.

598. "I didn't really expect": ITMO, 752

598. "suggested that we had": ibid., 753

598. "As near as I can recall": ibid., 754

598. "and I believe": ibid.

598. "paranoid": ibid.

599. "Dr Griggs had been": ibid., 339

599. "a pillar of honesty": Libby (1979), 307

599. "strongly built": ibid.

599. "I remember": ibid., 311

600. "I don't think you fellows": Stern (1971), 190

600. "Lee DuBridge and I are through": Hershberg (1993), 601

600. "he is very much concerned": FBI San Francisco office to JEH, 5.4.1952, JRO FBI file

600. "believed it would be extremely wise": FBI report by L. Hoyt McGuire, Chicago office, 9.5.1952, JRO FBI file

600. "worked out a plan": Goodchild (1980), 213

601. "magnificent": ITMO, 96

601. "deep sense of personal regret": ibid.

601. "lasting and immensely valuable": ibid., 97

603. "technical, military, and economic questions": ITMO, 598

603. "We decided we would": ibid.

603. "ZORC": ibid., 750

603. "in order to achieve world peace": ibid., 749

604. "the background": ibid., 750

604. "GRIGGS. I should say": ibid., 763

604. announced on April 28, 1952: see *Bulletin of the Atomic Scientists*, June 1952, 133. For a detailed account of this panel, see Bernstein (1989).

605. "would not require inspection and control": Bernstein (1989), 141

605. "point of no return": ibid., 143

605. "is irrevocably committed": ibid., 143–4

606. "whose destructive and retaliatory power": quoted Wells (1981), 41

606. "The most reasonable explanation": ibid., 42

606. "man for man": *Life*, May 19, 1952, 151

606. "of means to hit": ibid.

606. "Today": ibid., 152

607. the fallout from the test: see Bernstein (1989), 143

607. on October 9: ibid., 148

607. "felt that any such idea": ibid., 148–9

607. "would certainly be pleased": Rhodes (1996), 498

608. the first Ulam-Teller hydrogen bomb: the description that follows is based on that given in Rhodes (1996), Chapter 24.

608. "You would swear": ibid., 508

608. "It's a boy": ibid., 511

608. "Some people in the Air Force": B & S, 451

609. "As we sat": Teller (2001), 352

609. "I assured him": ibid., 353

609. "had not thought": ibid.

610. "was so huge": ibid.

610. "our commitment": Bernstein (1989), 154

610. five main proposals: ibid.

610. "Atomic Weapons and American Policy": Oppenheimer (1955), 61–77

610. "became very vividly and painfully aware": ITMO, 95

611. "the bright light": Oppenheimer (1955), 61

611. "Openness": ibid., 62

611. "The rule for the atom": ibid., 63

611. "It is easy to say": ibid.

611. "It is my opinion": ibid., 65

611. "likely to be small comfort": ibid.

611. "our twenty-thousandth bomb": ibid., 66

612. "a rather rigid commitment": ibid.

612. "The prevailing view": ibid., 68

612. "We need strength": ibid., 69

612. "We do not operate well": ibid., 70

612. "It must be disturbing": ibid.

612. "I am not convinced": see "The Soviet Bombs: Mr Truman's Doubts," *Bulletin of the Atomic Scientists*, March 1953, 43–5

613. "It must be shocking": Oppenheimer (1955), 70–1

613. "problematical": *Bulletin of the Atomic Scientists*, March 1953, 43

613. "does not prove": ibid.

613. "high officer of the Air Defense Command": Oppenheimer (1955), 71

613. "We need to be clear": ibid., 77

613. "The Hidden Struggle for the H-bomb": *Fortune*, May 1953, 109, 110, 230

613. "A life and death struggle": ibid., 109

614. "no confidence": ibid.

614. "another nasty and obviously inspired article": quoted Stern (1971), 201

614. "ZORC Takes Up the Fight": *Fortune*, May 1953, 110

615. "calling in Oppenheimer": L. B. Nichols to Tolson, 11.5.1953, JRO FBI file

615. Cohn and McCarthy visited J. Edgar Hoover: JEH, memo dated 19.5.1953, JRO FBI file

615. "a great deal of preliminary spade work": ibid.

615. "The McCarthy committee": McMillan (2005), 170

615. "still concerned": D. M. Ladd to JEH, 25.5.1953, JRO FBI file

616. "could not do the job": D. M. Ladd to A. H. Belmont, 5.6.1953, JRO FBI file

616. "did not completely trust": B & S, 467

616. "was perhaps": Hewlett and Holl (1989), 53

616. "It was this contract": ibid.

616. "reluctantly agreed": D. M. Ladd to A. H. Belmont, 5.6.1953, JRO FBI file

617. "Dissenter's Return": *Time*, July 6, 1953

617. "Joe 4": see Rhodes (1996), 524–5

618. "the opposition to present U.S. policy": *Life*, September 7, 1953, 32

618. Eisenhower's statement: *Life*, October 19, 1953, 38

619. "U.S. Atom Boss Lewis Strauss": *Time*, September 21, 1953

619. NSC 162/2: the entire document is available online at: http://www.fas.org/irp/offdocs/nsc-hst/nsc-162–2.pdf

619. "primary threat": NSC 162/2, 1

619. "The capability of the USSR": ibid., 2

619. "a strong military posture": ibid., 5

18. Falsus in uno

620. given Oppenheimer's AEC security file: see B & S, 473

620. "The purpose of this letter": Pais (2006), 199

621. "In April 1942": ibid.

621. "FBI Report on Vast Spy Ring": quoted in memo from W. A. Branigan to A. H. Belmont, 18.11.1953, JRO FBI file

621. "In addition": ibid.

621. "whining, whimpering appeasement": Reeves (1997), 530

622. "He moves about": *Sunday Express*, November 15, 1953

622. "He is said": *The Observer*, November 22, 1953

622. "Something different": *The Economist*, January 1, 1955

622. "what there is new": Oppenheimer (1954), dust-jacket blurb

622. "at finding": *The Economist*, January 1, 1955

623. "For us as for all men": ibid., 98

623. "rhetorically evocative": Pais (2006), 286

623. "the story of sub-nuclear matter": Oppenheimer (1954), 32–3

624. "It seems rather unlikely": ibid., 81

624. "It was a happy reunion": Chevalier (1965), 86

624. "to an extraordinary dialogue": ibid., 88

624. "It is very sad": ibid.

625. "it might be a good idea": B & S, 481

625. "raise questions": ITMO, 6

625. "Accordingly": ibid.

626. went to see Joe Volpe: B & S, 483

626. "would mean that I accept": ITMO, 22

626. "hereby directed": Stern (1971), 236

626. "in view of the fact": Hewlett and Holl (1989), 81

626. "the Bureau's technical coverage": Goodchild (1980), 227

627. "The fact": Pais (2006), 204

627. "whitewash Oppenheimer": Goodchild (1980), 229

627. "all over town": B & S, 490

627. chaired its opening session: Bernstein (2004), 94

627. "leading role": ibid.

627. "to record": ibid.

628. "My thesis adviser": ibid., 94–5

628. "how unusually quiet": Pais (2006), 122

628. "I'm sorry to hear": *Life*, December 13, 1963, 94

628. "I suppose, I hope": Goodchild (1980), 229

628. "I would testify": Teller (2001), 374

628. "that I finally concluded": Stern (1971), 516

628. "Oppenheimer was a Communist": Goodchild (1980), 230

629. "My theory": ibid., 231

629. "We thought": ibid.

629. "dredging up": ibid., 229

630. "requires the suspension": ITMO, 3

630. "the ideological struggle": Green (1977), 14

630. "My wife": Plutarch, *Life of Caesar*, 10.6

630. "if there was any": Green (1977), 14–15

630. "it was unfair": ibid., 15

631. "and others": ibid.

631. "widely interpreted": ibid.

631. "exceeds the minimum standards": quoted ibid.

631. "My knowledge": ibid., 60

631. "cannot be fairly understood": ITMO, 7

632. "flashes of fire": *Life*, March 29, 1954, 17

632. "like the sound": ibid., 19

632. "First Casualties of the H-Bomb": ibid., 17

633. "Is the strategy of retaliation": *Life*, April 12, 1954, 38

633. "out of the question": B & S, 496

633. "In preparing this letter": ITMO, 20

633. "The records printed": Pharr Davis (1969), 19

634. more of a farce: Pais (2006), 268

634. "this proceeding": ITMO, 20

634. "Doctor": ibid., 129

634. "One day": ibid., 130

635. "I invented a cock-and-bull story": ibid., 137

635. "ROBB. Did you tell Pash the truth": ibid.

636. "Isn't it a fair statement": ibid., 149

636. "ROBB. You spent the night with her, didn't you?": ibid., 154

637. "I've just seen": Goodchild (1980), 242

637. "General": ITMO, 171

637. "I would not clear Dr. Oppenheimer": ibid.

637. "ROBB. He [de Silva] was certainly more of a professional": ibid., 272

638. "I don't believe": ibid., 280

638. "ROBB. Colonel Lansdale": ibid.

638. "Dr. Conant, if you had been approached": ibid., 393

639. "When you did report it": ibid., 394

639. "I never hid my opinion": ibid., 468

639. "McCarthy has few partisans": Pais (2006), 219

639. "Silently and impassively": *Life*, April 26, 1954, 35

640. "Whatever the truth of the charges": ibid., 38

640. "astounding": ITMO, 660

640. "not helpful to national defense": ibid., 684

640. "corroborative testimony": ibid., 802

640. "I have always assumed": ibid., 710

640. "In a great number of cases": ibid.

641. "Do you feel": ibid., 726

641. "ROBB. As far as you know": ibid., 737

642. "GRAY. Mr. McCloy": ibid., 739

643. "Yes, I would": ibid., 823

643. "I would say to you": ibid., 839

643. "In the Commission's own view": ibid., 973

643. "But this man": ibid., 990

643. "he will never be through": B & S, 538

644. "very depressed": ibid.
644. "We have": Polenberg (2002), 362
644. "We have, however": ibid.
644. "that Dr. Oppenheimer's continuing conduct": ibid.
644. "a susceptibility": ibid.
644. "We find": ibid.
644. "less than candid": ibid.
644. "To deny him clearance now": ibid., 364
645. "did not hinder": ibid., 365
645. "His witnesses": ibid.
645. "I would like to add": ibid.
645. "closely associated": *Bulletin of the Atomic Scientists*, May 1954, 191
645. "stands in such contrast": Polenberg (2002), 366
645. "considered in the context": ibid., 370
646. "The record contains no direct evidence": ibid., 372
646. "is not based": ibid., 375
646. "the evidence establishes": ibid., 376
646. "if his present story is true": ibid., 373
646. ". . . it is difficult to conclude": ibid.
647. "completely loyal": ibid., 389
648. "inexcusable": ibid., 391

19. An Open Book?

649. "repulsive": Chevalier (1965), 89
649. "Oppie confesse: 'J'étais un idiot.'": ibid., 97–8
649. "The one who had invented": ibid., 100–1
650. "In the list of witnesses": *Time*, June 28, 1954
650. "The majority": ibid.
650. "Dear Robert": Chevalier (1965), 102
650. "Dear Haakon": JRO to HC, 12.7.1954, JRO papers, LOC
651. "This was not": Chevalier (1965), 105–6
651. "hoping—without believing": ibid., 106
651. "For the subjective observer": ibid., 107
652. "on a desperately needed rest": ibid., 108
652. "I appreciate the fact": Lloyd Garrison to HC, 3.8.1954, JRO papers, LOC
652. "that this might suffice": Lloyd Garrison to JRO, 3.8.1954, JRO papers, LOC
652. "There is much": HC to Lloyd Garrison, 5.8.1954, JRO papers, LOC
652. "It is not nearly as clear": JRO to HC, 3.9.1954, JRO papers, LOC
653. "This letter": Chevalier (1965), 108
653. "I must": ibid., 109
653. "Un document exclusif": *France-Observateur*, December 2, 1954, 16–18
653. "in a truncated": Chevalier (1965), 109
653. "I have no doubts": ibid., 110
653. "Do what we may": ibid., 111
653. "I hope to finish it in the spring": ibid.
654. a long profile of Edward Teller: "Dr. Edward Teller's Magnificent Obsession," *Life*, September 6, 1954, 60–74
654. "In that event": ibid., 61
654. "This book": *Bulletin of the Atomic Scientists*, November 1954, 357

654. "These two boys": ibid., 362

654. "a sophomoric science-fiction tale": *Atomic Scientists Journal*, 4, 1954, 253

654. an article by Joseph and Stewart Alsop: "We Accuse!" *Harper's Magazine*, October 1954, 25–45

654. "We accuse": ibid.

655. "Dr Henry D. Smyth's fair and considered statement": Pais (2006), 256

655. "cloistered life": ibid., 272

655. "a direct result": Goodchild (1980), 266

655. "So far as I was concerned": Dyson (1979), 76

656. "Physics is complicated": Thorpe (2006), 254

656. "An Ordering Principle": see *Proceedings of the Second Rochester Conference*, University of Rochester Report NYO-3046, 87

656. turned into an article: see Pais, A., "Some Remarks on the *V*-Particles," *Physical Review*, 86 (5) (1952), 663–71

656. "J. R. Oppenheimer": ibid., 664

656. "strangeness": see Pais (1997), 336–8

656. "I disappointed him": Dyson (1979), 76

656. "When I came to Oppenheimer": ibid., 77

657. "difference of temperament": ibid.

657. "rejoiced together": ibid.

657. *See It Now*: for an extended account of the making of this program and of its reception, see Wolverton (2008), Chapters 1, 2 and 3.

657. "you find a Nobel Prize winner": quoted ibid., 16

657. "There isn't one foot": ibid., 20

658. "tiptoed into Robert's office": Pais (1997), 330

658. "And Professor Einstein": Wolverton (2008), 31

658. "Well, sir": ibid., 35

658. "The trouble with secrecy": ibid., 38

658. "there aren't secrets": ibid., 39

659. "lean, almost ascetic face": quoted ibid., 46

659. 2,500 letters: ibid., 51

659. "brilliant non sequitur": Marshak (1970), 94

659. "didn't know a meson": quoted in Wolverton (2008), 75

659. "was several hundred larger": *Eugene Register-Guard*, April 21, 1955, copy in JRO papers, LOC

659. "Not one in 50": ibid.

659. "For all scientists": quoted in Wolverton (2008), 61

660. "It is a very special sort of privilege": Oppenheimer (1957), 12

660. "He loved the history of science": ibid.

660. "And physicists then said": ibid., 19

661. "It is clear": ibid., 20

661. "electrodynamics cannot be": ibid., 19

661. "two golden decades": Oppenheimer (1956a), 1

661. "did not arouse the hope": ibid., 2

661. "His great discoveries": typescript dated 30.9.1955 in JRO papers, LOC

662. "wonderfully diverse": Oppenheimer (1956b), 10

662. "what is called in the trade": ibid.

662. "In some ways": ibid.

662. "Surely past experience": ibid., 12

662. "We must make more humane": ibid., 13

663. "Despite the 'peace of mutual terror'": ibid.

663. "the special problems": ibid., 10

663. "a historic meeting": Pais (1997), 351

664. "The τ-meson": Pais (1997), 351, and Pais (2006), 281

664. "Perhaps some oscillation": Marshak (1970), 95

664. "hinted at a rising wave": Pais (2006), 282

664. Yang and Pais bet John Wheeler: Pais (197), 351

665. this article was published: "Question of Parity Conservation in Weak Interactions," *Physical Review*, 104 (1), October 1956, 254–8

665. Oppenheimer's comment: see Pais (2006), 282

665. "Wu's experiment": ibid.

665. "Walked through door": ibid., 283

665. "The situation": Yang (1964), 398

666. "Basic concept in physics": quoted Pais (1997), 358

666. "No one today": Pais (2006), 283

666. "It was an occasion": Bernstein (2004), 171–2

666. "truly amazed": ibid., 174

666. "Nothing that has been written": ibid.

666. "looked at me": ibid.

666. "his demeanor": ibid., 175

667. "I believe in the popularization of science": Wolverton (2008), 91

667. "What is new": Bernstein (2004), 187

667. "attached great importance": Pais (2006), 279

667. "there was other material": Wolverton (2008), 129

668. "We wouldn't like to have this": typewritten transcript, headed "Oppenheimer interview," JRO papers, LOC

668. "Today": Oppenheimer (1958a), 55

668. "it is almost impossible": ibid., 57

668. "And as for the recent discovery": ibid.

668. "trying to explain": Pais (1997), 380

668. "no intuitive understanding": interview with MJS, 20.2.1979, quoted B & S, 263 and 413

668. "To an outsider": Pais (1997), 243

669. "a shadow": interview with MJS, 11.3.1982, quoted B & S, 565

669. "There came a time": interview with MJS, 31.7.1979, quoted B & S, 565

669. "Even the lay reader": Oppenheimer (1958b), 481

669. "All of us": Oppenheimer (1958c)

670. "a punitive, personal abuse": Wolverton (2008), 150

670. "Day after weary day": Pfau (1984), 230

670. "nightmarish quality": quoted Wolverton (2008), 160

670. "It was now clear": ibid., 161

670. "unchristianly spirit": Bernice Brode to JRO, undated, quoted Wolverton (2008), 161

671. "profoundly in anguish": Oppenheimer (1960), 22

671. "But these three particles": Oppenheimer (1959), 11

672. "the same men": ibid.

672. "the ancient question": ibid.

672. "We may learn": typed transcript of program recorded December 1959, JRO papers, LOC

672. "If this next great war occurs": Oppenheimer (1984), 118

672. "that beautiful poem": "Speech at Opening Session of Conference on Progress in Freedom," Tenth Anniversary Conference, June 1960, typescript, JRO papers, LOC. The printed version—Oppenheimer (1984), 117–20—omits these words.

673. "If I cannot be comforted": Oppenheimer (1984), 120

673. "not merely": ibid.

673. "we have so largely lost": "Speech at Opening Session of Conference on Progress in Freedom," typescript, 4. Omitted from the printed version.

673. "terribly ill-planned": Wolverton (2008), 179

673. "I do not regret": Goodchild (1980), 274

673. "to discuss various problems": Society of Science and Man, "Prospectus," July 1958, typescript in JRO papers, LOC

674. "triviality and childishness": "An Afternoon with Professor Oppenheimer," 2, JRO papers, LOC

674. "a small society": ibid., 4

674. "out of touch with science": ibid., 12

674. "fill the air": ibid., 13

674. "That does not surprise me": ibid., 20

675. the island of St. John in the Virgin Islands: a detailed account of the Oppenheimers' time in the Virgin Islands is given in B & S, Chapter 39, from which my account is taken.

675. "is to help students": Oppenheimer (1964), v

676. "jot down": Martin E. Marty to JRO, 1.2.1962, JRO papers, LOC

676. The list he sent them: copy in the JRO papers, LOC, on which a handwritten note says that it was mailed on 9.2.1962

676. "the most extraordinary collection of talent": quoted Wolverton (2008), 195

677. "Not on your life": Goodchild (1980), 275

677. one of three speakers: "Talk at the Dedication of the Niels Bohr Library of the History of Physics," 26.9.1962, 4, JRO papers, LOC

677. "Science and Culture": *Encounter*, Vol. 19, No. 4, October 1962, 3–10, reprinted in Oppenheimer (1984), 123–38

677. "I went to midtown Manhattan": Bernstein (2004), 196

678. "Let me end with an anecdote": "The Added Cubit," typescript, 6, JRO papers, LOC

678. "Readers and writers": *Encounter*, August 1963, 47

678. "By taking thought": ibid.

678. "a truth": ibid., 46

679. "it is almost wholly through the arts": ibid.

679. "He was out": Regis (1989), 152

679. "Once in the 1950s": Pais (2006), 278

679. "Bourbon Manor": Regis (1989), 151

679. "source of profound bewilderment": quoted Pais (2006), 278

680. "The faculty meetings": ibid., 277

680. "It started to dawn": Pais (1997), 385

680. "just about then": ibid.

680. "He looked": Seaborg (2001), 225

680. The decision was reported: *Physics Today*, June 1963, 21–3

681. "maintain intimacy of discussion": Agnes Meyer, letter of invitation, 27.2.1963, quoted Thorpe (2006), 274

681. "Up to now": untitled typescript of JRO's talk at Seven Springs Farm, June 1963, JRO papers, LOC—quotation on page 5

682. "a recognition of": ibid., 6

682. "is surely not": ibid.

682. "I know every person": quoted Wolverton (2008), 221

682. "this great enterprise": typescript of JRO's acceptance speech, undated, JRO papers, LOC

683. "I enjoyed what you had to say": "Brotherly Spirit," *Newsweek*, 16.12.1963, quoted Wolverton (2008), 222

683. special issue: *Reviews of Modern Physics*, 36 (2), April 1964

683. Robert Crease records: Pais (2006), 296

683. "Message": *Reviews of Modern Physics*, 36 (2), April 1964, 509

683. "Massive Stars, Relativist Polytropes, and Gravitational Radiation": ibid., 545–5

683. "It is a tribute": ibid., 545

683. "was rushed down": Dyson, letter to his parents, 25.4.1964, quoted Pais (2006), 296

683. "I am very pleased": *San Francisco Examiner*, April 24, 1964, quoted Wolverton (2008), 226

684. "L'Intime et le Commun": Oppenheimer (1984), 157–66

684. "when the proceedings were published": ibid., 165

684. "We most of all should try": ibid., 165–6

685. "Today we live": "The Fraternal Dialogue," Supplement to the bulletin *From Heart to Heart*, No. 15, November 1964, 2

685. "I begin to wonder": Heinar Kipphardt, *In the Matter of J. Robert Oppenheimer: A Play Freely Adapted, on the Basis of the Documents*, London: Methuen (1967), 106

686. "You make me say things": JRO to Heinar Kipphardt, 12.10.1964, JRO papers, LOC

686. "The whole damn thing": *Washington Post*, 13.11.1964, A18, quoted Pais (2006), 268

686. "makes me say": JRO, statement to the press, 11.11.1964, JRO papers, LOC, quoted Wolverton (2008), 237

686. When the play was performed in Paris: see Wolverton (2008), 238–9

687. "I have not been for this play": JRO to John Roberts, 22.2.1965, quoted ibid., 240–1

687. "restrain the production": ibid., 241

687. "The trouble with Oppenheimer": see Serber (1998), 183–4

687. "the true story": HC to JRO, 23.7.1964, JRO papers, LOC

688. "Dear Haakon": JRO to HC, 7.8.1964, JRO papers, LOC

688. "Had letter from Chevalier": notes of telephone conversation, 18.3.1965, JRO papers, LOC

688. "physics, of course": *New York Times*, April 25, 1965, quoted Pais (2006), 297

689. "a general feeling": *New York Times Magazine*, May 15, 1966, quoted Wolverton (2008), 271

689. "Well, I don't want to speak for others": typescript of interview with Martin Agronsky for *CBS Evening News with Walter Cronkite*, 5.8.1965, JRO papers, LOC

689. "Physics and Man's Understanding": Oppenheimer (1984), 181–9

690. "To Live with Ourselves": ibid., 169–79

690. "the life of the scientist": ibid., 170

690. "This was": ibid., 170–1

690. "when the discovery": ibid., 178

690. "[The] new discoveries which liberated physics": ibid., 185

690. "The error which this corrected": ibid.

691. a talk on Einstein: delivered at UNESCO House in Paris on December 13, 1965, published as "On Albert Einstein," *New York Review of Books*, March 17, 1966, 4–5, available online at: http://www.nybooks.com/articles/archives/1966/mar/17/on-albert-einstein/?page=1

691. "his tradition": ibid., 4

691. "clouds of myth": ibid.

691. "was almost wholly without sophistication": ibid., 5

691. "Thirty Years of Mesons": Oppenheimer (1966)

692. "It seems to me": ibid., 58

692. "You see the old man": Pais (2006), 300

692. "finding out": Dyson, letter to his parents, 30.3.1966, quoted Pais (2006), 301

692. "Dr. Oppenheimer Plans History of Physics": *New York Times*, June 21, 1966, 46, copy in JRO papers, LOC

693. "A Time in Need": Oppenheimer (1984), 191–2

693. "no confidence": Pais (2006), 303

693. "Sam, don't smoke": ibid., 304

693. "Poor Oppenheimer": Dyson to his parents, 16.2.1967, quoted Pais (2006), 304–5

693. "He looked extremely thin": B & S, 587

693. "I walked him": ibid.

693. "It was a horrible period": Pais (2006), 305

694. "The truth is": ibid., 306

694. "Damn it": ibid.

695. "a man who had": ibid.

695. "In Oppenheimer": Rabi et al. (1969), 8

Bibliography

Abragam, A., "Louis Victor Pierre Raymond de Broglie," *Biographical Memoirs of Fellows of the Royal Society*, 34, 22–4, London: Royal Society (1988)

Acheson, Dean, *Present at the Creation: My Years in the State Department*, New York: Norton (1969)

Ackroyd, Peter, *T. S. Eliot*, London: Abacus (1985)

Adam, Ian, "Character and Destiny in George Eliot's Fiction," *Nineteenth-Century Fiction*, Vol. 20, No. 2, 127–43 (Sep. 1965)

Adler, Felix, *Creed and Deed: A Series of Discourse*, New York: Putnam (1886)

—— "The Problem of Unsectarian Moral Instruction," *International Journal of Ethics*, Vol. 2, No. 1, 11–19 (Oct. 1891)

—— "The Relation of Ethical Culture to Religion and Philosophy," *International Journal of Ethics*, Vol. 4, No. 3, 335–47 (Apr. 1894)

—— "The Moral Value of Silence," *International Journal of Ethics*, Vol. 8, No. 3, 345–57 (Apr. 1898)

—— "The Parting of the Ways in the Foreign Policy of the United States," *International Journal of Ethics*, Vol. 9, No. 1, 1–12 (Oct. 1898)

—— "A Critique of Kant's Ethics," *Mind*, New Series, Vol. 11, No. 42, 162–95 (Apr. 1902)

—— "The Problem of Teleology," *International Journal of Ethics*, Vol. 14, No. 3, 265–80 (Apr. 1904)

—— "The Moral Ideal," *International Journal of Ethics*, Vol. 20, No. 4, 387–94 (Jul. 1910)

—— "The Relation of the Moral Ideal to Reality," *International Journal of Ethics*, Vol. 22, No. 1, 1–18 (Oct. 1911)

—— *The World Crisis and Its Meaning*, New York: D. Appleton & Co. (1915)

—— "The Ethical Problem," *The Philosophical Review*, Vol. 38, No. 2, 105–24 (Mar. 1929)

—— *An Ethical Philosophy of Life*, London: D. Appleton-Century (1933)

Al-Khalili, *Quantum: A Guide for the Perplexed*, London: Weidenfeld and Nicolson (2004)

Alberty, Robert A. and Cera, Enrico Di, *Jeffries Wyman 1901–1995: A Biographical*

Memoir, *National Academy of Sciences Biographical Memoirs 83*, Washington DC: National Academies Press (2003)

Albright, Joseph and Kunstel, Marcia, *Bombshell: The Secret Story of America's Unknown Spy Conspiracy*, New York: Times Books (1997)

Alperovitz, Gar, *The Decision to Use the Atomic Bomb*, New York: Vintage (1996)

Anderson, Carl D., "The Apparent Existence of Easily Deflectable Positives," *Science*, 76, 239–40 (1932)

—— "The Positive Electron," *Physical Review*, 43, 491–4 (1933)

—— "Early Work on the Positron and Muon," *American Journal of Physics*, Vol. 29, Issue 12, 825–30 (1961)

Anderson, Carl D. and Neddermeyer, Seth H., "Cloud Chamber Observations of Cosmic Rays at 4300 Meters and Near Sea Level," *Physical Review*, 50, 263–71 (1936)

—— "Note on the Nature of Cosmic Ray Particles," *Physical Review*, 51, 884–6 (1937)

Anderson, Herbert L., "'All in Our Time': Fermi, Szilard and Trinity," *Bulletin of the Atomic Scientists*, 30 (8), 40–7 (1974)

Arnold, Sir Edwin, *Bhagavadgita*, New York: Dover (1993)

Asimov, Isaac, *The Collapsing Universe*, London: Hutchinson (1977)

Baade, W. and Zwicky, F., "On Super-Novae," *Proceedings of the National Academy of Science*, 20, 254–9 (1934a)

—— "Remarks on Super-Novae and Cosmic Rays," *Physical Review*, 46, 76–7 (1934b)

Badash, Lawrence, Hirschfelder, Joseph O. and Broida, Herbert P. (eds.), *Reminiscences of Los Alamos, 1943–45*, Dordrecht: Reidel (1980)

Baggott, Jim, *Atomic. The First War of Physics and the Secret History of the Atom Bomb: 1939–49*, London: Icon Books (2009)

—— *The Quantum Story: A History in 40 Moments*, Oxford: Oxford University Press (2011)

Ball, Philip, *The Elements: A Very Short Introduction*, Oxford: Oxford University Press (2004)

Barkai, Avraham, *Branching Out: German-Jewish Immigration to the United States, 1820–1914*, New York: Holmes & Meier (1994)

Barton, Henry A., "Twenty Years of Physics Today: The Early Years," *Physics Today*, 66–8 (May 1968)

Barut, Asim O., Merwe, Alwyn van der and Odabasi, Halis (eds.), *Selected Popular Writings of E.U. Condon*, New York: Springer-Verlag (1991)

Bernstein, Barton J., "In the Matter of J. Robert Oppenheimer," *Historical Studies in the Physical Sciences*, Vol. 12, No. 2, 195–252 (1982)

—— "Crossing the Rubicon: A Missed Opportunity to Stop the H-Bomb?," *International Security*, Vol. 14, No. 2, 132–60 (1989)

Bernstein, Jeremy, *Hans Bethe: Prophet of Energy*, New York: Dutton (1981)

—— *Hitler's Uranium Club: The Secret Recordings at Farm Hall*, New York: Copernicus Books (2001)

—— "The Drawing or Why History Is Not Mathematics," *Physics in Perspective*, 5, 243–61 (2003)

—— *Oppenheimer: Portrait of an Enigma*, Chicago: Ivan R. Dee (2004)

—— "Max Born and the Quantum Theory," *American Journal of Physics*, 73 (11), 999–1008 (2005)

—— *Plutonium: A History of the World's Most Dangerous Element*, Ithaca and London: Cornell University Press (2007)

Bethe, H. A., "Energy production in stars," *Physical Review*, 55, 434–56 (1939)

—— "The Hydrogen Bomb," *Bulletin of the Atomic Scientists*, VI (4), 99–104, 125 (1950)

—— "J. Robert Oppenheimer: A Biographical Memoir," *Biographical Memoirs of the National Academy of Sciences Volume 71*, 175–219, Washington D.C.: National Academies Press (1997)

Bird, Kai and Sherwin, Martin J. [B & S], *American Prometheus: The Triumph and Tragedy of J. Robert Oppenheimer*, New York: Alfred A. Knopf (2005)

Birkhoff, George, *Aesthetic Measure*, Cambridge: Harvard University Press (1933)

Birks, J. B., *Rutherford at Manchester*, London: Heywood & Co. (1962)

Birmingham, Stephen, *"Our Crowd": The Great Jewish Families of New York*, New York: Harper & Row (1967)

Bizony, Piers, *Atom*, Cambridge: Icon Books (2007)

Blackett, P. M. S., "The Craft of Experimental Physics," in Wright (1933), 67–96

Bohr, Niels, "On the Constitution of Atoms and Molecules," *Philosophical Magazine*, 26, 1–25, 476–502, 857–75 (1913)

—— "The Quantum Postulate and the Recent Development of Atomic Theory," *Nature*, 121, 580–90 (1928)

—— "Faraday Lecture: Chemistry and the Quantum Theory of Atomic Constitution," *Journal of the Chemical Society*, 135, 349–84 (1932)

—— "Resonance in Uranium and Thorium Disintegrations and the Phenomenon of Nuclear Fission," *Physical Review*, 55, 418–19 (1939)

—— *Atomic Physics and Human Knowledge*, New York: Wiley (1958)

—— *Collected Works*, edited by L. Rosenfeld:

Volume 1. *Early Work (1905–1911)*, edited by J. Rud Nielson, Amsterdam: North Holland (1972)

Volume 2. *Work on Atomic Physics (1912–1917)*, edited by Ulrich Hoyer, Amsterdam: North Holland (1981)

Volume 3. *The Correspondence Principle*, edited by J. Rud Nielson, Amsterdam: North Holland (1976)

Volume 4. *The Periodic Table (1920–1923)*, edited by J. Rud Nielson, Amsterdam: North Holland (1977)

Volume 5. *The Emergence of Quantum Mechanics*, edited by Klaus Stolzenburg, Amsterdam: North Holland (1984)

Volume 6. *Foundations of Quantum Physics I*, edited by Jørgen Kalckar, Amsterdam: North Holland (1985)

Volume 7. *Foundations of Quantum Physics II*, edited by Jørgen Kalckar, Amsterdam: Elsevier (1996) [published out of sequence]

Volume 8. *The Penetration of Charged Particles through Matter*, edited by Jens Thorson, Amsterdam: North Holland (1987)

Volume 9. *Nuclear Physics (1929–1952)*, edited by Sir Rudolf Peierls, Amsterdam: North Holland (1986)

Bohr, Niels, Kramers, H. A., and Slater, J. C., "The Quantum Theory of Radiation," *Philosophical Magazine*, 47, 785–802 (1924)

Bohr, Niels and Wheeler, John Archibald, "The Mechanism of Nuclear Fission," *Physical Review*, 56, 426–50 (1939)

Borden, William Liscum, *There Will Be No Time*, New York: Macmillan (1946)

Born, Max, "Zur Quantenmechanik der Stoßvorgänge," *Zeitschrift für Physik*, 37 (12), 863–7 (1926a)

—— "Quantenmechanik der Stoßvorgänge," *Zeitschrift für Physik*, 38 (11–12), 803–27, (1926b)

—— "Physical Aspects of Quantum Mechanics," *Nature*, Vol. 119, 354–7 (1927)

—— *The Restless Universe*, London: Blackie & Son (1935)

—— *Physics in My Generation: A Selection of Papers*, London: Pergamon (1956)

—— *The Born-Einstein Letters*, London: Macmillan (1971)

—— *My Life: Recollections of a Nobel Laureate*, London: Taylor & Francis (1978)

—— *Atomic Physics*, New York: Dover (1989)

Born, Max, Heisenberg, Werner and Jordan, Pascual, "Zur Quantenmechanik II," *Zeitschrift für Physik*, 35, 557–615 (1926)

Born, Max and Jordan, Pascual, "Zur Quantenmechanik," *Zeitschrift für Physik*, 34, 858–88 (1925)

Boyd, William C., *Genetics and the Races of Man*, Oxford: Blackwell (1950)

Boyd, William C. and Asimov, Isaac, *Races and People*, New York: Abelard-Schuman (1955)

Brian, Denis, *Einstein: A Life*, New York: Wiley (1996)

Broglie, Louis de, "A Tentative Theory of Light Quanta," *The Philosophical Magazine*, 446–58 (1924)

Brown, Andrew, *The Neutron and the Bomb: A Biography of Sir James Chadwick*, Oxford: Oxford University Press (1997)

Brown, Laurie M., "The Idea of the Neutrino," *Physics Today*, 31, 23–8 (1978)

Brown, Laurie M. and Hoddeson, Lillian (eds.), *The Birth of Particle Physics*, Cambridge: Cambridge University Press (1983)

Brown, Stephen G., "The Curse of the 'Little Phrase': Swann and the Sorrows of the Sapphic Sublime," *College Literature*, 30.4 (Fall 2003)

Bundy, McGeorge, *Danger and Survival: Choices About the Bomb in the First Fifty Years*, New York: Random House (1988)

Campbell, J., *Rutherford: Scientist Supreme*, Christchurch: AAS Publications (1999)

Cashman, Sean Dennis, *America in the Gilded Age: From the Death of Lincoln to the Rise of Theodore Roosevelt*, New York: New York University Press (1984)

Cassidy, David C., *Uncertainty: The Life and Science of Werner Heisenberg*, New York: W.H. Freeman & Co. (1992)

—— *J. Robert Oppenheimer and the American Century*, New York: Pi Press (2005)

—— *Beyond Uncertainty: Heisenberg, Quantum Physics and the Bomb*, New York: Bellevue Literary Press (2009)

Cathcart, Brian, *The Fly in the Cathedral: How a Small Group of Cambridge Scientists Won the Race to Split the Atom*, London: Viking (2004)

Cather, Willa, *Youth and the Bright Medusa*, New York: Alfred A. Knopf (1920)

—— *A Lost Lady*, New York: Alfred A. Knopf (1923)

—— *Death Comes for the Archbishop*, New York: Alfred A. Knopf (1927)

Cave Brown, Anthony, *The Secret History of the Atomic Bomb*, New York: Dial Press (1977)

Cerchiai, Luca, Jannelli, Lorena and Longo, Fausto, *The Greek Cities of Magna Graecia and Sicily*, Los Angeles: Getty Publications (2004)

Chadwick, James, "Possible Existence of a Neutron," *Nature*, 129, 312 (1932a)

—— "The Existence of a Neutron," *Proceedings of the Royal Society of London Series A*, Vol. 136, No. 830, 692–708 (1932b)

Chevalier, Haakon, *Oppenheimer: The Story of a Friendship*, New York: George Braziller (1965)

Childs, Herbert, *An American Genius: The Life of Ernest Orlando Lawrence*, New York: Dutton (1968)

Christman, Al, *Target Hiroshima: Deak Parsons and the Creation of the Atomic Bomb*, Annapolis, Maryland: Naval Institute Press (1998)

Cockcroft, John and Walton, Ernest, "Experiments with High Velocity Positive Ions," *Proceedings of the Royal Society Series A*, Vol. 129, 477–89 (1930)

—— "Disintegration of Lithium by Swift Protons," *Nature*, Vol. 129, 649 (1932)

Cohen, Naomi W., *Encounter with Emancipation: The German Jews in the United States 1830–1914*, Philadelphia: The Jewish Publication Society of America (1984)

Cohen, S. T., *The Truth about the Neutron Bomb*, New York: Morrow (1983)

Cole, K. C., *Something Incredibly Wonderful Happens: Frank Oppenheimer and the world he made up*, Boston: Houghton Mifflin (2009)

Compton, Arthur H., "A Quantum Theory of the Scattering of X-Rays by Light Elements," *Physical Review*, 21 (5), 483–502 (1923)

—— *Atomic Quest: A Personal Narrative*, London: Oxford University Press (1956)

Conant, Jennet, *109 East Palace: Robert Oppenheimer and the Secret City of Los Alamos*, New York: Simon & Schuster (2005)

Coughlan, C. D., Dodd, J. E. and Gripaios, B. M., *The Ideas of Particle Physics: An Introduction for Scientists*, Cambridge: Cambridge University Press (2006)

Cropper, William H., *Great Physicists: The Life and Times of Leading Physicists from Galileo to Hawking*, Oxford: Oxford University Press (2001)

Crowther, James Arnold, *Molecular Physics*, Philadelphia: P. Blackiston's Son & Co. (1914, 1st edition; 1923, 3rd edition)

Crowther, J. G., *The Cavendish Laboratory: 1874–1974*, London: Macmillan (1974)

Dahl, Per F., "The Physical Tourist: Berkeley and Its Physics Heritage," *Physics in Perspective*, 8, 90–101 (2006)

Dalitz, R. H. and Peierls, Rudolf, "Paul Adrien Maurice Dirac," *Biographical Memoirs of Fellows of the Royal Society*, 32, 138–85 (1986)

DeGroot, Gerard J., *The Bomb: A History of Hell on Earth*, London: Pimlico (2005)

Diner, Hasia R., *A Time for Gathering: The Second Migration 1820–1880 (The Jewish People in America, Vol. 2)*, Baltimore: Johns Hopkins University Press (1992)

Dirac, Paul, "The Fundamental Equations of Quantum Mechanics," *Proceedings of the Royal Society Series A*, Vol. 109, No. 752, 642–53 (1925)

—— "Quantum Mechanics and a Preliminary Investigation of the Hydrogen Atom," *Proceedings of the Royal Society Series A*, Vol. 110, No. 755, 561–79 (1926)

—— "The Quantum Theory of the Electron," *Proceedings of the Royal Society Series A*, Vol. 117, No. 778, 610–24 (1928)

—— "Quantised Singularities in the Electromagnetic Field," *Proceedings of the Royal Society Series A*, Vol. 133, No. 821, 60–72 (1931)

—— "A New Classical Theory of Electrons," *Proceedings of the Royal Society Series A*, Vol. 209, No. 1098, 291–6 (1951)

—— *The Development of Quantum Theory: J. Robert Oppenheimer Memorial Prize acceptance speech*, London: Gordon and Breach (1971)

—— *Directions in Physics: Lectures delivered during a visit to Australia and New Zealand August/September 1975*, New York: Wiley (1978)

—— "The Origin of Quantum Field Theory," in Brown and Hoddeson (1983), 39–55

—— *The Collected Works of P. A. M. Dirac 1924–1948*, edited by R. H. Dalitz, Cambridge: Cambridge University Press (1995)

Donovan, Robert J., *The Words of Harry S. Truman*, New York: Newmarket Press (1996)

Dool, Huug van den, "George David Birkhoff (1884–1944): Dutch-American Mathematician Extraordinaire," *Proceedings of 14th Biennial AADAS Conference, The Dutch in Urban America*, edited by R. Swierenga, D. Sinnema and H. Krabbendam, Amsterdam: The Joint Archives of Holland, 76–93 (2003)

Doty, Paul, "John T. Edsall: 3 November 1902–12 June 2002," *Proceedings of the American Philosophical Society*, Vol. 149, No. 1, 89–92 (March 2005)

Dowd, Doug, "Against Decadence: The Work of Robert A. Brady (1901–63)," *Journal of Economic Issues*, Vol. XXVIII, No. 4, 1031–61 (1994)

Dupuy, Trevor Nevitt and Hammerman, Gary M., *A Documentary History of Arms Control and Disarmament*, Washington D.C.: T.N. Dupuy Associates (1973)

Dyson, Freeman, *Disturbing the Universe*, New York: Basic Books (1979)

Edsall, John T., "Some personal history and reflections from the life of a Biochemist," *Biophysical Chemistry*, 100, 9–28 (2003)

Edwards, Rebecca, *New Spirits: Americans in the Gilded Age 1865–1905*, Oxford: Oxford University Press (2006)

Einstein, Albert, *Out of My Later Years*, London: Thames and Hudson (1950)

Eliot, George, *Middlemarch*, Harmondsworth: Penguin, (1965)

Ellanby, Boyd [William C. Boyd], "Category Phoenix," *Galaxy Science Fiction*, Vol. 4, No. 2, 4–44 (May 1952)

—— "Chain Reaction," *Galaxy Science Fiction*, Vol.12, No. 5, 128–43 (Sep. 1956)

Elliot, David C., "Project Vista and Nuclear Weapons in Europe," *International Security*, Vol. 11, No. 1, 163–83 (1986)

Elsasser, Walter M., *Memoirs of a Physicist in the Atomic Age*, London: Adam Hilger Ltd./Science History Publications (1978)

Enz, Charles P., *No Time to Be Brief: A Scientific Biography of Wolfgang Pauli*, Oxford: Oxford University Press (2002)

Ermarth, Elizabeth, "Incarnations: George Eliot's Conception of 'Undeviating Law,'" *Nineteenth-Century Fiction*, Vol. 29, No. 3, 273–86 (Dec. 1974)

Eve, Arthur S., *Rutherford: Being the Life and Letters of the Rt. Hon. Lord Rutherford, O.M.*, Cambridge: Cambridge University Press (1939)

Farmelo, Graham, *The Strangest Man: The Hidden Life of Paul Dirac, Quantum Genius*, London: Faber (2009)

Feingold, Henry L., *A Time for Searching: Entering the Mainstream, 1920–1945*, Baltimore: Johns Hopkins University Press (1995)

Fergusson, Erna, *Our South West*, New York: Alfred A. Knopf (1946)

—— *New Mexico: A pageant of three peoples*, Albuquerque: University of New Mexico Press (1973)

—— *Dancing Gods: Indian Ceremonials of New Mexico and Arizona*, Albuquerque: University of New Mexico Press (1988)

—— *Mexican Cookbook*, Albuquerque: University of New Mexico Press (1999)

Fergusson, Francis, *The Idea of a Theater*, Princeton: Princeton University Press (1949)

—— *Sallies of the Mind*, edited by John McCormick and George Core, New Brunswick: Transaction (1998)

Fergusson, Harvey, *The Blood of the Conquerors*, New York: Alfred A. Knopf (1921)

—— *Wolf Song*, New York: Alfred A. Knopf (1927)

—— *In Those Days: An Impression of Change*, New York: Alfred A. Knopf (1929)

—— *Rio Grande*, New York: Alfred A. Knopf (1933)

—— *Home in the West: An Inquiry Into My Origins*, New York: Duell, Sloan and Pearce (1944)

—— *The Conquest of Don Pedro*, New York: William Morrow (1954)

Fergusson, Harvey Butler, *New Mexico in 1910: Letters and Addresses Relating to the Constitution*, Farmington Hills, Michigan: Gale (2010)

Fermi, Laura, *Atoms in the Family: My Life with Enrico Fermi*, Chicago: Chicago University Press (1961)

Feynman, Richard P., *QED: The Strange Theory of Light and Matter*, London: Penguin (1990)

—— *"Surely You're Joking, Mr. Feynman!" Adventures of a Curious Character as told to Ralph Leighton*, London: Vintage (1992)

Franklin, Allan, *Are There Really Neutrinos? An Evidential History*, Boulder, Colorado: Westview Press (2004)

Fried, Albert, *Communism in America: A History in Documents*, New York: Columbia University Press (1997a)

—— *McCarthyism : The Great American Red Scare: A Documentary History*, New York: Oxford University Press (1997b)

Friess, H. L., *Felix Adler and Ethical Culture: Memories and Studies*, New York: Columbia University Press (1981)

Frisch, Otto, *What Little I Remember*, Cambridge: Cambridge University Press (1980)

Gamow, George, "Zur Quantentheorie des Atomkernes," *Zeitschrift für Physik*, Vol. 51, No. 3, 204–12 (1928a)

—— "The Quantum Theory of Nuclear Disintegration," *Nature*, 122, 805–6 (1928b)

—— *Mr. Tomkins in Paperback*, Cambridge: Cambridge University Press (1965)

—— *Thirty Years that Shook Physics: The Story of Quantum Theory*, New York: Dover (1985)

—— *The Great Physicists from Galileo to Einstein*, New York: Dover (1988)

Gay, Ruth, *Jews in America*, New York: Basic Books (1965)

Gerassi, John, *The Premature Antifascists: North American Volunteers in the Spanish Civil War 1936–39: An Oral History*, New York: Praeger (1986)

Gerstle, Gary, "Theodore Roosevelt and the Divided Character of American Nationalism," *The Journal of American History*, Vol. 86, No. 3, *The Nation and Beyond: Transnational Perspectives on United States History: A Special Issue*, 1280–1307 (Dec. 1999)

Gibbs, Josiah Willard, "On the Equilibrium of Heterogeneous Substances," *Transactions of the Connecticut Academy of Arts and Sciences*, Vol. III, 198–248, 343–524 (1874–8)

Gill, Stanley, "Conversations with Jeffries Wyman," *Annual Review of Biophysics and Biophysical Chemistry*, 16, 1–23 (1987)

Ginger, Ray, *Age of Excess: The United States from 1877 to 1914*, London: Collier Macmillan (1975)

Gish, Robert, "Paul Horgan," in *A Literary History of the American West*, Fort Worth: Texas Christian University Press, 574–86 (1987)

—— *Frontier's End: The Life and Literature of Harvey Fergusson*, Lincoln: University of Nebraska Press (1988)

—— *Nueva Granada: Paul Horgan and the Southwest*, Texas: A & M University Press (1995)

—— *Beautiful Swift Fox: Erna Fergusson and the Modern Southwest*, Texas: A & M University Press (1996)

Gleick, James, *Genius: Richard Feynman and Modern Physics*, London: Abacus (1994)

Goodchild, Peter, *J. Robert Oppenheimer: "Shatterer of Worlds,"* London: BBC (1980)

—— *Edward Teller: The Real Dr. Strangelove*, London: Weidenfeld & Nicolson (2004)

Goodstein, Judith, "A Conversation with Hans Bethe," *Physics in Perspective*, I, 253–81 (1999)

Gordin, Michael D., *Five Days in August: How World War II Became a Nuclear War*, Princeton: Princeton University Press (2007)

Graham, Frank, *Al Smith American: An Informal Biography*, Whitefish, Montana: Kessinger (2005)

Graham, Loren R., *Moscow Stories*, Bloomington: Indiana University Press (2006)

Green, Harold P., "The Oppenheimer Case: A Study in the Abuse of Law," *Bulletin of the Atomic Scientists*, 33 (7), 12–16, 56–61 (Sep. 1977)

Greenspan, Nancy Thorndike, *The End of the Certain World: The Life and Science of Max Born*, London: Wiley (2005)

Gribbin, John, *In Search of Schrödinger's Cat*, London: Corgi (1984)

Gromyko, Andrei A., "Soviet Proposals for Atomic Energy Control," *Bulletin of the Atomic Scientists*, 3 (8), 219–20 (1947)

Groueff, Stephane, *Manhattan Project: The Untold Story of the Making of the Atomic Bomb*, New York: Little Brown (1967)

Groves, Leslie R., *Now It Can Be Told: The Story of the Manhattan Project*, New York: Da Capo (1962)

Gurney, Ronald W. and Condon, Edward U., "Wave Mechanics and Radioactive Disintegration," *Nature*, 122, 439 (1928)

Hager, Thomas, *Force of Nature: The Life of Linus Paul*, New York: Simon and Schuster (1995)

Hales, Peter Bacon, *Atomic Spaces: Living on the Manhattan Project*, Urbana and Chicago: University of Illinois Press (1997)

Halpern, Paul, *Collider: The Search for the World's Smallest Particles*, Hoboken, New Jersey: John Wiley (2010)

Harrington, Fred H., "The Anti-Imperialist Movement in the United States, 1898–1900," *The Mississippi Valley Historical Review*, Vol. 22, No. 2, 211–30 (Sep., 1935)

Hawkins, David, *Manhattan District History. Project Y: The Los Alamos Project*, unpublished, commissioned by the Los Alamos Scientific Laboratory for "special distribution" (1946)

Haynes, John Earl, *Red Scare or Menace? American Communism and Anticommunism in the Cold War Era*, Chicago: Ivan R. Dee (1996)

Haynes, John Earl and Klehr, Harvey, *Venona: Decoding Soviet Espionage in America*, New Haven: Yale Note Bene (2000)

Heilbron, J. L. and Seidel, Robert W., *Lawrence and His Laboratory: A History of the Lawrence Berkeley Laboratory, Volume I*, Berkeley: University of California Press (1990)

Heisenberg, Werner, "Über quantentheoretische Umdeutung kinematischer und mechanischer Beziehungen," *Zeitschrift für Physik*, 33, 879–93 (1925)

—— "Über den anschulichen Inhalt der quantentheoretischen Kinematik und Mechanik," *Zeitschrift für Physik*, 43, 172–98 (1927)

—— "Zur Theorie der 'Schauer' in der Hohenstrahlung," *Zeitschrift für Physik*, 101, 533–40 (1936)

—— *Physics and Beyond: Encounters and Conversations*, London: Allen & Unwin (1971)

Heisenberg, Werner and Pauli, Wolfgang, "Zur Quantendynamik der Wellenfelder," *Zeitschrift für Physik*, 56, 1–61 (1929)

—— "Zur Quantentheorie der Wellenfelder II," *Zeitschrift für Physik*, 59, 168–90 (1930)

Hendry, John, *The Creation of Quantum Mechanics and the Bohr–Pauli Dialogue*, Dordrecht: Reidel (1984)

Herken, Gregg, *Brotherhood of the Bomb: The Tangled Lives and Loyalties of Robert Oppenheimer, Ernest Lawrence, and Edward Teller*, New York: Henry Holt & Co. (2002)

Hersey, John, *Hiroshima*, New York: Vintage (1989)

Hershberg, James G., *James B. Conant: Harvard to Hiroshima and the Making of the Nuclear Age*, Stanford: Stanford University Press (1993)

Hewlett, Richard G. and Duncan, Francis, *Atomic Shield, 1947–1952: History of the United States Atomic Energy Commission, Volume II*, University Park: Pennsylvania State University Press (1969)

Hewlett, Richard G. and Holl, Jack M., *Atoms for Peace and War, 1953–1961: Eisenhower and the Atomic Energy Commission (History of the United States Atomic Energy Commission, Volume III)*, Berkeley: University of California Press (1989)

Hijiya, James A., "The *Gita* of Robert Oppenheimer," *Proceedings of the American Philosophical Society*, 144 (2), 123–67 (2000)

Hoddeson, Lillian et al., *Critical Assembly: A Technical History of Los Alamos during the Oppenheimer Years, 1943–1945*, Cambridge: Cambridge University Press (1993)

Hodes, Elizabeth, Tiddens, Adolph and Badash, Lawrence, "Nuclear Fission: Reaction to the Discovery in 1939," *Institute on Global Conflict and Cooperation Research Paper I*, Philadelphia: American Philosophical Association (1985)

Hoffmann, Banesh, *The Strange Story of the Quantum*, New York: Dover (1959)

Hofstadter, Robert, "Felix Bloch 1905–1983: A Biographical Memoir," *Biographical Memoirs of the National Academy of Sciences*, Washington DC: National Academies Press (1994)

Hohoff, Tay, *A Ministry to Man: The Life of John Lovejoy Elliott*, New York: Harper (1959)

Holbrow, Charles H., "In Appreciation. Charles C. Lauritsen: A Reasonable Man in an Unreasonable World," *Physics in Perspective*, 5, 419–72 (2003)

Hore, Peter (ed.), *Patrick Blackett: Sailor, Scientist, and Socialist*, London: F. Cass (2003)

Horgan, Paul, *The Fault of Angels*, New York: Harper (1933)

—— *The Common Heart*, New York: Harper & Brothers (1942)

—— *Great River: The Rio Grande in North American History*, New York: Rinehart (1954)

—— *A Distant Trumpet*, New York: Farrar, Straus and Cudahy (1960)

—— *Things as They Are*, New York: Farrar, Straus & Co. (1964)

—— *Lamy of Santa Fe*, New York: Farrar, Straus and Giroux (1976)

—— *Of America East & West: Selections from the Writings of Paul Horgan*, New York: Farrar Straus and Giroux (1985)

——— *Under the Sangre de Cristo*, Flagstaff, Arizona: Northland Publishing (1987)

——— *A Certain Climate: Essays in History, Arts, and Letters*, Middletown, Connecticut: Wesleyan University Press (1988)

Hughes, Jeff, *The Manhattan Project: Big Science and the Atom Bomb*, Cambridge: Icon Books (2002)

Huning, Franz, *Trader on the Santa Fe Trail: The Memoirs of Franz Huning*, Albuquerque, University of Albuquerque Press (1973)

Hunner, Jon, *Inventing Los Alamos: The Growth of an Atomic Community*, Norman: University of Oklahoma Press (2004)

——— *J. Robert Oppenheimer, the Cold War, and the Atomic West*, Norman: University of Oklahoma Press (2009)

Isserman, Maurice, *Which Side Were You On? The American Communist Party during the Second World War*, Urbana: University of Illinois Press (1993)

Jeans, J. H., *The Mathematical Theory of Electricity and Magnetism*, Cambridge: Cambridge University Press (1908)

——— *The Universe around Us*, Cambridge: Cambridge University Press (1929)

——— *The Mysterious Universe*, Cambridge: Cambridge University Press (1930)

——— *Physics and Philosophy*, Cambridge: Cambridge University Press (1942)

Jenkins, Philip, *A History of the United States*, Basingstoke: Palgrave (2003)

Joliot, F., von Halba, H. and Kowarski, L., "Liberation of Neutrons in the Nuclear Explosion of Uranium," *Nature*, 143, 470 (1939a)

——— "Number of Neutrons Liberated in the Nuclear Fission of Uranium," *Nature*, 143, 680 (1939b)

Jungk, Robert, *Brighter Than a Thousand Suns: A Personal History of the Atomic Scientists*, London: Penguin (1960)

Kaiser, David, *Drawing Theories Apart: The Dispersion of Feynman Diagrams in Postwar Physics*, Chicago: Chicago University Press (2005)

Karabel, Jerome, *The Chosen: The Hidden History of Admission and Exclusion at Harvard, Yale, and Princeton*, New York: Houghton Mifflin Company (2005)

Kelly, Cynthia C. (ed.), *Oppenheimer and the Manhattan Project: Insights into J. Robert Oppenheimer, "Father of the Atomic Bomb,"* Hackensack, New Jersey: World Scientific (2006)

Kevles, Daniel J., *The Physicists: The History of a Scientific Community in Modern America*, Cambridge: Harvard University Press (1995)

Klehr, Harvey, Haynes, John Earl and Firsov, Fridrikh Igorevich, *The Secret World of American Communism*, New Haven: Yale University Press (1995)

Klein, Martin J., *Paul Ehrenfest*, Amsterdam: North Holland Pub. Co. (1970)

——— "Not by Discoveries Alone: The Centennial of Paul Ehrenfest," *Physica*, 106A, 3–14 (1981)

Klingenstein, Susanne, *Jews in the American Academy 1900–1940: The Dynamics of Intellectual Assimilation*, New Haven: Yale University Press (1991)

Kosak, Hadassa, *Cultures of Opposition: Jewish Immigrant Workers, New York City, 1881–1905*, New York: State University of New York Press (2000)

Kragh, Helge, *Dirac: A Scientific Biography*, Cambridge: Cambridge University Press (1990)

——— *Quantum Generations: A History of Physics in the Twentieth Century*, Princeton: Princeton University Press (1999)

Kraus, Joe, "How the Melting Pot Stirred America: The Reception of Zangwill's

Play and Theater's Role in the American Assimilation Experience," *MELUS*, Vol. 24, No. 3, Varieties of Ethnic Criticism, 3–19 (Autumn 1999)

Kumar, Manit, *Quantum: Einstein, Bohr and the Great Debate about the Nature of Reality*, London: Icon Books (2009)

Lamb, Willis E., "The Fine Structure of Hydrogen," in Brown and Hoddeson (1983), 311–28

Lankevich, George J., *American Metropolis: A History of New York City*, New York: New York University Press (1998)

Lanouette, William, *Genius in the Shadows: A Biography of Leo Szilard*, Chicago: Chicago University Press (1994)

Larsen, Egon, *The Cavendish Laboratory: Nursery of Genius*, London: Edmund Ward (1962)

Lawton, Eliza and Lawson, Eba, *Major Robert Anderson and Fort Sumter, 1861*, New York: Knickerbocker Press (1911)

Lee, Sabine, *Sir Rudolf Peierls: Selected Private and Scientific Correspondence Volume 2*, London: World Scientific Publishing (2009)

Lee, Sabine and Brown, Gerry E., "Hans Albrecht Bethe 2 July 1906–6 March 2005," *Biographical Memoirs of Fellows of the Royal Society*, 53, 1–20 (2007)

Levine, George, "Determinism and Responsibility in the Works of George Eliot," *PMLA*, Vol. 77, No. 3, 268–79 (Jun. 1962),

Lewis, Gilbert Newton and Randall, Merle, *Thermodynamics and the Free Energy of Chemical Substances*, New York: McGraw-Hill (1923)

Lewis, William C. McC., *Physical Chemistry and Scientific Thought: An Inaugural Lecture delivered at the University of Liverpool on Friday, 16 January 1914*, Liverpool: Liverpool University Press (1914)

—— *A System of Physical Chemistry* (published in the series, *Textbooks of Physical Chemistry*, edited by Sir William Ramsay), London and New York: Longmans, Green & Co., *Volume I: Considerations Based Upon the Kinetic Theory* (1918, 2nd edition; 1920, 3rd edition), *Volume II: Thermodynamics* (1919, 2nd edition; 1920, 3rd edition), *Volume III: Quantum Theory* (1920, 2nd edition; 1921, 3rd edition)

Lewy, Günter, *The Cause that Failed: Communism in American Political Life*, New York: Oxford University Press (1990)

Libby, Leona Marshall, *The Uranium People*, New York: Crane Russak (1979)

Lilienthal, David E., *The Journals of David E. Lilienthal, Volume 2: The Atomic Energy Years, 1945–1950*, New York: Harper & Row (1964)

Lovell, Bernard, "Patrick Maynard Stuart Blackett, Baron Blackett, of Chelsea," *Biographical Memoirs of Fellows of the Royal Society*, 21, 1–115, London: Royal Society (1975), published separately as *P. M. S. Blackett: A Biographical Memoir*, London: The Royal Society (1976)

Ludwig, Gunther (ed.), *Wave Mechanics*, New York: Pergamon (1968)

Luminet, Jean-Pierre, *Black Holes*, Cambridge: Cambridge University Press (1992)

McCarthy, Patrick J., "Lydgate, 'The New, Young Surgeon' of Middlemarch," *Studies in English Literature, 1500–1900*, Vol. 10, No. 4: Nineteenth Century, 805–16 (Autumn 1970)

McCray, W. Patrick, "Project Vista, Caltech, and the dilemmas of Lee DuBridge," *Historical Studies in the Physical and Biological Sciences*, Vol. 34, No. 2, 339–70 (2004)

McMillan, Priscilla J., *The Ruin of J. Robert Oppenheimer and the Birth of the Modern Arms Race*, New York: Viking (2005)

Madden, Paul and Mühlberger, Detlef, *The Nazi Party: The Anatomy of a People's Party*, Bern: Peter Lang (2007)

Malenfant, Richard E., *Experiments with the Dragon Machine*, Los Alamos: National Laboratory (2005)

Mansell, Darrel, Jr., "George Eliot's Conception of Tragedy," *Nineteenth-Century Fiction*, Vol. 22, No. 2, 155–71 (Sep. 1967)

Marsden, E., "The Rutherford Memorial Lecture, 1954: Rutherford—His Life and Work, 1871–1937," *Proceedings of the Royal Society A*, 283–305 (1954)

Marshak, Robert E., "The Rochester Conferences: The Rise of International Cooperation in High Energy Physics," *Bulletin of the Atomic Scientists*, XXVI (6), 92–8 (1970)

Mauch, Christof and Salmons, Joseph (eds.), *German-Jewish Identities in America*, Madison: Max Kade Institute for German-American Studies (2003)

Maxwell, James Clerk, *A Treatise on Electricity and Magnetism*, Oxford: Clarendon Press (1873)

Mehra, Jagdish and Milton, Kimball A., *Climbing the Mountain: The Scientific Biography of Julian Schwinger*, Oxford: Oxford University Press (2000)

Mehra, Jagdish, Milton, Kimball A. and Rembiesa, Peter, "The Young Julian Schwinger I. A New York City Childhood," *Foundations of Physics*, Vol. 29, No. 5, 767–86 (1999a)

—— "The Young Julian Schwinger II. Julian Schwinger at Columbia University," *Foundations of Physics*, Vol. 29, No. 5, 787–817 (1999b)

—— "The Young Julian Schwinger III. Schwinger Goes to Berkeley," *Foundations of Physics*, Vol. 29, No. 6, 931–66 (1999c)

—— "The Young Julian Schwinger IV. During the Second World War," *Foundations of Physics*, Vol. 29, No. 6, 967–1010 (1999d)

—— "The Young Julian Schwinger. V. Winding Up at the Radiation Lab, Going to Harvard, and Marriage," *Foundations of Physics*, Vol. 29, No. 7, 1119–62 (1999e)

Mehra, Jagdish and Rechenberg, Helmut, *The Historical Development of Quantum Theory*:

    Volume 1, Parts 1 and 2: The Quantum Theory of Planck, Einstein, Bohr and Sommerfeld: Its Foundation and the Rise of Its Difficulties 1900–1925, Berlin: Springer (1982a and 1982b)

    Volume 2: The Discovery of Quantum Mechanics, Berlin: Springer (1982c)

    Volume 3: The Formulation of Matrix Mechanics and Its Modifications 1925–1926, Berlin: Springer (1982d)

    Volume 4, Part 1: The Fundamental Equations of Quantum Mechanics 1925–1926, and *Part 2: The Reception of the New Quantum Mechanics 1925–1926*, Berlin: Springer (1982e)

    Volume 5, Parts 1 and 2: Erwin Schrödinger and the Rise of Wave Mechanics, Berlin: Springer (1987)

    Volume 6, Part 1: The Completion of Quantum Mechanics 1926–1941, Berlin: Springer (2000)

    Volume 6, Part 2: The Completion of Quantum Mechanics 1926–1941, Berlin: Springer (2001)

Melz, Christian F., "Goethe and America," *College English*, Vol. 10, No. 8 425–31 (May 1949)

Meyrowitz, Elliott L., *Prohibition of Nuclear Weapons: The Relevance of International Law*, New York: Transnational (1990)

Michelmore, Peter, *The Swift Years: The Robert Oppenheimer Story*, New York: Dodd, Mead & Co. (1969)

Miller, Merle, *Plain Speaking: An Oral Biography of Harry S. Truman*, London: Coronet (1976)

Mills, Robert, *Space, Time and Quanta: An Introduction to Contemporary Physics*, New York: W.H. Freeman and Company (1994)

Milton, Kimball A., "In Appreciation. Julian Schwinger: From Nuclear Physics and Quantum Electrodynamics to Source Theory and Beyond," *Physics in Perspective*, 9, 70–114 (2007)

Moore, Ruth, *Niels Bohr: The Man and the Scientist*, London: Hodder & Stoughton (1967)

Moore, Walter, *Schrödinger: Life and Thought*, Cambridge: Cambridge University Press (1989)

Morais, Henry Samuel, *The Jews of Philadelphia: Their History from the Earliest Settlements to the Present Time*, Philadelphia: The Levytype Company (1894)

Morgan, H. Wayne, *Unity and Culture: The United States, 1877–1900*, London: Allen Lane (1971)

Morgan, Ted, *McCarthyism in Twentieth Century America*, New York: Random House (2003)

Morse, Philip M., *In at the Beginning: A Physicist's Life*, Cambridge: MIT Press (1977)

Nelson, Bruce, *Workers on the Waterfront: Seamen, Longshoremen, and Unionism in the 1930s*, Urbana: University of Illinois Press (1988)

Nelson, Steve, Barrett, James R. and Ruck, Rob, *Steve Nelson, American Radical*, Pittsburgh: Pittsburgh University Press (1981)

Neuenschwander, Dwight E. and Watkins, Sallie A., "In Appreciation. Professional and Personal Coherence: The Life and Work of Melba Newell Phillips," *Physics in Perspective*, 10, 295–364 (2008)

Neumann, Henry, *Spokesmen for Ethical Religion*, Boston: Beacon Press (1951)

Norris, Robert S., *Racing for the Bomb: General Leslie R. Groves, the Manhattan Project's Indispensable Man*, South Royalton, Vermont: Steerforth Press (2002)

Nye, Mary Jo, *Blackett: Physics, War, and Politics in the Twentieth Century*, Cambridge: Harvard University Press (2004)

—— "Blackett as Scientific Leader: Physics, War and Politics in the Twentieth Century," lecture given at Imperial College, London, 26 January 2005, full text at: http://www3.imperial.ac.uk/physics/about/history/blackett_nye/lecture

Oppenheimer, J. Robert, "On the Quantum Theory of Vibration-Rotation Bands," *Proceedings of the Cambridge Philosophical Society*, 23, 327–35 (1926a)

—— "On the Quantum Theory of the Problem of the Two Bodies," *Proceedings of the Cambridge Philosophical Society*, 23, 422–31 (1926b)

—— "Quantum Theory and Intensity Distribution in Continuous Spectra," *Nature*, 118, 771 (1926c)

—— "Quantentheorie des kontinuierlichen Absorptionsspektrums," *Naturwissenschaften*, 14, 1282 (1926d)

—— "Zur Quantentheorie kontinuierlicher Spektren," *Zeitschrift für Physik*, 41, 268–93 (1927a)

—— "Zur Quantenmechanik der Richtungsentartung," *Zeitschrift für Physik*, 43, 27–46 (1927b)

—— "Bermerkung zur Zerstreuung der α-Teilchen," *Zeitschrift für Physik*, 43, 413–5 (1927c)

—— "On the Quantum Theory of the Polarization of Impact Radiation," *Proceedings of the National Academy of Sciences*, 13, 800–5 (1927d)

—— "Three Notes on the Quantum Theory of Aperiodic Effects," *Physical Review*, 31, 66–81 (1928a)

—— "On the Quantum Theory of the Capture of Electrons," *Physical Review*, 31, 349–56 (1928b)

—— "On the Quantum Theory of the Ramsauer Effect," *Proceedings of the National Academy of Sciences*, 14, 261–2 (1928c)

—— "On the Quantum Theory of Field Currents," *Physical Review*, 31, 914 (1928d)

—— "On the Quantum Theory of the Autoelectric Field Currents," *Proceedings of the National Academy of Sciences*, 14, 363–5 (1928e)

—— "Über die Strahlung der freien Elektronen im Coulombfeld," *Zeitschrift für Physik*, 55, 725–37 (1929)

—— "Note on the Theory of the Interaction of Field and Matter," *Physical Review*, 35, 461–77 (1930a)

—— "On the Theory of Electrons and Protons," *Physical Review*, 35, 562–3 (1930b)

—— "Are the Formulae for the Absorption of High Energy Radiations Valid?," *Physical Review*, 47, 44–52 (1934)

—— "Cosmic Rays: Report of Recent Progress, 1936–1941," *Science in the University*, Berkeley: University of California Press, 23–38 (1944)

—— "Electron Theory: Report to the Solvay Congress for Physics at Brussels, Belgium, September 27 to October 2, 1948," in Schwinger (1958), 145–55 (1948)

—— "Discussion on the Disintegration and Nuclear Absorption of Mesons: Remarks on μ-decay," *Reviews of Modern Physics*, 21 (1), 34–5 (1949a)

—— "Concluding Remarks to Cosmic-Ray Symposium," *Reviews of Modern Physics*, 21 (1), 181–3 (1949b)

—— "Comments on the Military Value of the Atom," *Bulletin of the Atomic Scientists*, VII (2), 43–5 (1951)

—— "Atomic Weapons and American Policy," *Foreign Affairs*, 31 (4), 525–35 (July 1953), also *Bulletin of the Atomic Scientists*, IX (96), 202–5 (July 1953)

—— *Science and the Common Understanding*, New York: Simon & Schuster (1954)

—— *The Open Mind*, New York: Simon & Schuster (1955)

—— "Einstein," *Reviews of Modern Physics*, 28 (1), 1–2 (January 1956 = 1956a)

—— "Physics Tonight," *Physics Today*, 10–13 (July 1956 = 1956b)

—— "Electron Theory: Description and Analogy," *Physics Today* 12–20 (July 1957)

—— "The Tree of Knowledge," *Harper's Magazine*, 55–60 (October 1958 = 1958a)

—— "A Study of Thinking," *The Sewanee Review*, 46, 481–90 (1958b)

—— "The Mystery of Matter," *Saturday Evening Post* (5 July 1958 = 1958c)

—— "The Role of the Big Accelerators," *Think* 8–11 (October 1959)

—— "In the Keeping of Unreason," *Bulletin of the Atomic Scientists*, XVI (1), 18–22 (1960)

—— "Niels Henrik David Bohr," *Year Book of the American Philosophical Society*, 107–17 (1963)

—— *The Flying Trapeze: Three Crises for Physicists*, London: Oxford University Press (1964)

—— "Thirty Years of Mesons," *Physics Today*, 51–8 (November 1966)

—— *Uncommon Sense*, Boston: Birkhäuser (1984)

Oppenheimer, J. Robert and Arnold, W., "Internal Conversion in the Photosynthetic Mechanism of Blue Green Algae," *Journal of General Physiology*, 33, 423–5 (1950)

Oppenheimer, J. Robert and Bethe, Hans, "Reaction of Radiation on Electron Scattering and Heitler's Theory of Radiation Damping," *Physical Review*, 70, 451–8 (1946)

Oppenheimer, J. Robert and Born, Max, "Zur Quantentheorie der Molekeln," *Annalen der Physik*, 84, 457–84 (1927)

Oppenheimer, J. Robert and Carlson, J. F., "On the Range of Fast Electrons and Neutrons," *Physical Review*, 38, 1787–8 (1931)

—— "The Impacts of Fast Electrons and Magnetic Neutrons," *Physical Review*, 39, 763–92 (1932)

—— "On Multiplicative Showers," *Physical Review*, 51, 220–31 (1937)

Oppenheimer, J. Robert, Epstein, S. T. and Finkelstein, R. J., "Note on Stimulated Decay of Negative Mesons," *Physical Review*, 73, 1140–1 (1948)

Oppenheimer, J. Robert and Furry, Wendell H., "On the Theory of the Electron and the Positive," *Physical Review*, 45, 245–62 (1934a)

—— "On the Theory of the Electron and the Positive," *Physical Review*, 45, 343–4 (1934b)

—— "On the Limitations of the Theory of the Positron," *Physical Review*, 45, 903–4 (1934c)

—— "On the Spin of the Mesotron," *Physical Review*, 59, 462 (1941)

Oppenheimer, J. Robert and Hall, Harvey, "Relativistic Theory of the Photoelectric Effect," *Physical Review*, 38, 57–9 (1931)

Oppenheimer, J. Robert and Lauritsen, C. C., "On the Scattering of the Th C'' γ-Rays," *Physical Review*, 46, 80–1 (1934)

Oppenheimer, J. Robert, Lewis, H. W. and Wouthuysen, S. A., "The Multiple Production of Mesons," *Physical Review*, 73, 127–40 (1948)

Oppenheimer, J. Robert and Nedelsky, Leo, "The Production of Positives by Nuclear Gamma Rays," *Physical Review*, 44, 948–9 (1933)

Oppenheimer, J. Robert and Phillips, M., "Note on the Transmutation Function for Deuterons," *Physical Review*, 48, 500–2 (1935)

Oppenheimer, J. Robert and Plesset, Milton S., "On the Production of the Positive Electron," *Physical Review*, 44, 53–5 (1933)

Oppenheimer, J. Robert and Schwinger, J. S., "On Pair Emission in the Proton Bombardment of Fluorine," *Physical Review*, 56, 1066–7 (1939)

—— "On the Interaction of Mesotrons and Nuclei," *Physical Review*, 60, 150–2 (1941)

Oppenheimer, J. Robert and Serber, R., "Note on the Nature of Cosmic-Ray Particles," *Physical Review*, 51, 1113 (1937)

—— "On the Stability of Stellar Neutron Cores," *Physical Review*, 54, 540 (1938)

Oppenheimer, J. Robert, Serber, R., Nordheim, G. and Nordheim, L. W., "The Disintegration of High-Energy Protons," *Physical Review*, 51, 1037–45 (1937)

Oppenheimer, J. Robert, Serber, R. and Snyder, H., "The Production of Soft Secondaries by Mesotrons," *Physical Review*, 57, 75–81 (1939)

Oppenheimer, J. Robert and Snyder, H., "On Continued Gravitational Contraction," *Physical Review*, 56, 455–9 (1939)

Oppenheimer, J. Robert and Volkoff, G. M., "On Massive Neutron Cores," *Physical Review*, 55, 374–81 (1939)

Pais, Abraham, *"Subtle Is the Lord . . .": The Science and the Life of Albert Einstein*, Oxford: Oxford University Press (1982)

—— *Inward Bound: Of Matter and Forces in the Physical World*, Oxford: Clarendon (1986)

—— *Niels Bohr's Times, in Physics, Philosophy and Polity*, Oxford: Oxford University Press (1991)

—— *A Tale of Two Continents: A Physicist's Life in a Turbulent World*, Oxford: Oxford University Press (1997)

—— "In Memoriam: Robert Serber (1909–1997)," *Physics in Perspective*, 1, 105–10 (1999)

—— *The Genius of Science: A Portrait Gallery*, Oxford: Oxford University Press (2000)

—— (with supplemental material by Robert P. Crease), *J. Robert Oppenheimer: A Life*, Oxford: Oxford University Press (2006)

Palevsky, Mary, *Atomic Fragments: A Daughter's Questions*, Berkeley: University of California Press (2000)

Pauli, Wolfgang, *Scientific Correspondence with Bohr, Einstein, Heisenberg, a.O., Volume 1, 1919–1929*, Berlin: Springer (1979)

Pauling, Linus, *The Nature of the Chemical Bond*, Cornell: Cornell University Press (1939)

Peierls, Rudolf, "Critical Conditions in Neutron Multiplication," *Proceedings of the Cambridge Philosophical Society*, 35, 610–5 (1939)

—— "Wolfgang Ernst Pauli, 1900–1958," *Biographical Memoirs of Fellows of the Royal Society*, 5, 174–92 (1960)

—— *Bird of Passage: Recollections of a Physicist*, Princeton: Princeton University Press (1985)

Pfau, Tichard, *No Sacrifice Too Great: The Life of Lewis L. Strauss*, Charlottesville, University Press of Virginia (1984)

Pharr Davis, Nuel, *Lawrence and Oppenheimer*, Greenwich, Conn.: Fawcett Publications (1969)

Philip, Michel, "The Hidden Onlooker," *Yale French Studies*, No. 34, Proust, 37–42 (1965)

Piccard, Paul J., "Scientists and Public Policy: Los Alamos, August–November, 1945," *The Western Political Quarterly*, Vol. 18, No. 2, 251–62 (1965)

Pilkington, William T., "Harvey Fergusson," in *A Literary History of the American West*, Fort Worth: Texas Christian University Press, 546–58 (1987)

Polenberg, Richard (ed.), *In the Matter of J. Robert Oppenheimer: The Security Clearance Hearing*, Ithaca: Cornell University Press (2002)

Polkinghorne, John, *Quantum Theory: A Very Short Introduction*, Oxford: Oxford University Press (2002)

Powers, Thomas, *Heisenberg's War: The Secret History of the German Bomb*, London: Penguin (1994)

Priestley, Raymond E., *Antarctic Adventure: Scott's Northern Party*, London: T. Fisher Unwin (1914)

—— *Breaking the Hindenberg Line: The Story of the 46th (North Midland) Division*, London: T. Fisher Unwin (1919)

Pulzer, Peter, *Jews and the German State: The Political History of a Minority, 1848–1933*, Oxford: Blackwell (1992)

Rabi, I. I. et al., *Oppenheimer*, New York: Charles Scribner's Sons (1969)

Radest, Howard B., *Toward Common Ground: The Story of the Ethical Societies in the United States*, New York: Frederick Ungar (1969)

Randall, John Herman, *The Landscape and the Looking Glass: Willa Cather's Search for Value*, New York: Houghton Mifflin (1960)

Raphael, Marc Lee, *Jews and Judaism in the United States: A Documentary History*, New York: Behrman House (1983)

Reeves, Thomas C., *The Life and Times of Joe McCarthy*, New York: Madison Books (1997)

Regis, Ed, *Who Got Einstein's Office? Eccentricity and Genius at the Institute for Advanced Study*, London: Penguin (1989)

Rhodes, Richard, *The Making of the Atom Bomb*, London: Penguin (1988)

—— *Dark Sun: The Making of the Hydrogen Bomb*, New York: Touchstone (1996)

Ribalow, Harold U. (ed.), *Autobiographies of American Jews*, Philadelphia: The Jewish Publication Society of America (1965)

Richardson, R. Dan, *Comintern Army: The International Brigades and the Spanish Civil War*, Lexington: University Press of Kentucky (1982)

Ridley, B. K., *Time, Space and Things*, Cambridge: Cambridge University Press (1994)

Rigden, John S., *Rabi: Scientist and Citizen*, New York: Basic Books (1987)

Riley, Thomas A., "Goethe and Parker Cleaveland," *PMLA*, Vol. 67, No. 4, 350–74 (June 1952)

Robertson, Peter, *The Early Years: The Niels Bohr Institute 1921–1930*, Copenhagen: Akademisk (1979)

Romerstein, Herbert and Breindel, Eric, *The Venona Secrets: Exposing Soviet Espionage and America's Traitors*, Washington D.C.: Regnery (2001)

Roosevelt, Theodore, *The Winning of the West: An Account of the Exploration and Settlement of Our Country from the Alleghanies to the Pacific* (four volumes), New York: G.P. Putnam's Sons (1889–96)

Rose, Paul Lawrence, *Heisenberg and the Nazi Atomic Bomb Project: A Study in German Culture*, Berkeley: University of California Press (1998)

Rotblat, Joseph, "Leaving the Bomb Project," *Bulletin of the Atomic Scientists*, 41 (7), 16–19 (1985)

Rouzé, Michel, *Robert Oppenheimer: The Man and His Theories*, London: Souvenir Press (1964)

Rovere, Richard Halworth, *Senator Joe McCarthy*, Berkeley: University of California Press (1996)

Royal, Denise, *The Story of J. Robert Oppenheimer*, New York: St. Martin's Press (1969)

Rozental, Stefan (ed.), *Niels Bohr: His Life and Work as Seen by His Friends and Colleagues*, Amsterdam: North Holland (1967)

Russell, Bertrand, *The ABC of Atoms*, London: Kegan Paul (1923)

Rutherford, Ernest, "The scattering of α and ß particles by matter and the structure of the atom," *Philosophical Magazine*, 21, 669–88 (1911)

—— "Bakerian Lecture. Nuclear Constitution of Atoms," *Proceedings of the Royal Society Series A*, Vol. 97, 374–400 (1920)

—— "The Structure of the Radioactive Atom and the Origin of the Alpha Rays," *Philosophical Magazine*, 22, 580–605 (1927)

—— "Address of the President," *Proceedings of the Royal Society Series A*, Vol. 117, 300–16 (1928)

—— "The Structure of Atomic Nuclei," *Proceedings of the Royal Society Series A*, Vol. 136, 735–62 (1932)

Ryder, Arthur W., *Original Poems Together with Translations from the Sanskrit*, Berkeley: University of California Press (1939)

—— *The Bhagavad Gita 1929*, Whitefish, Montana: Kessinger (2004)

Sachs, Emanie, *Red Damask: A Study of Nurture and Nature*, New York: Harper & Brothers (1927)

Schecter, Jerold and Leona, *Sacred Secrets: How Soviet Intelligence Operations Changed American History*, Washington D.C.: Brassey's (2002)

Schrecker, Ellen, *The Age of McCarthyism: A Brief History with Documents*, Boston: Bedford (1994)

—— *Many Are the Crimes: McCarthyism in America*, Princeton: Princeton University Press (1998)

Schrödinger, Erwin, "Quantisierung als Eigenwertproblem," *Annalen der Physik*, 4 (79), 361–76, 489–527; 4 (80), 437–90; 4 (81), 109–39 (1926a, 1926b, 1926c, 1926d)

—— "An Undulatory Theory of the Mechanics of Atoms and Molecules," *Physical Review*, Vol. 28, No. 6, 1049–70 (1926e)

—— *Collected Papers on Wave Mechanics*, Providence, Rhode Island: American Mathematical Society, 3rd edition (1982)

Schweber, S. S., "The Empiricist Temper Regnant: Theoretical Physics in the United States 1920–1950," *Historical Studies in the Physical and Biological Sciences*, 17, 1, 55–98, (1986a)

—— "Shelter Island, Pocono, and Oldstone: The Emergence of American Quantum Electrodynamics after World War II," *Osiris*, 2nd Series, Vol. 2, 265–302 (1986b)

—— *QED and the Men Who Made It*, Princeton: Princeton University Press (1994)

—— *In the Shadow of the Bomb: Bethe, Oppenheimer, and the Moral Responsibility of the Scientist*, Princeton: Princeton University Press (2000)

—— *Einstein and Oppenheimer: The Meaning of Genius*, Cambridge: Harvard University Press (2008)

Schwinger, Julian (ed.), *Selected Papers on Quantum Electrodynamics*, New York: Dover (1958)

—— "Quantum Electrodynamics—An Individual View," *Journal de Physique*, Colloque C8, Supplement 12 (43), 409–23 (1982)

—— "Tomonaga Sin-Itiro: A Memorial—Two Shakers of Physics," *Lecture Notes in Physics*, 746, 27–42 (2008)

Seaborg, Glenn, *Adventures in the Atomic Age: From Watts to Washington*, New York: Farrar, Straus and Giroux (2001)

Segrè, Emilio, *Enrico Fermi: Physicist*, Chicago: Chicago University Press (1972)

—— *A Mind Always in Motion: The Autobiography of Emilio Segrè*, Berkeley: University of California Press (1993)

Serber, Robert, "Particle Physics in the 1930s: A View from Berkeley," in Brown and Hoddeson (1983), 206–21

—— *The Los Alamos Primer: The First Lectures on How to Build an Atomic Bomb*, Berkeley: University of California Press (1992)

—— *Peace and War: Reminiscences of a Life on the Frontiers of Science*, New York: Columbia University Press (1998)

Sherwin, Martin J., *A World Destroyed: The Atomic Bomb and the Grand Alliance*, New York: Vintage (1977)

Shipman, Harry L., *Black Holes, Quasars, & the Universe*, Boston: Houghton Mifflin (1976)

Sibley, Katherine A. S., *Red Spies in America: Stolen Secrets and the Dawn of the Cold War*, Lawrence: University of Kansas Press (2004)

Siegmund-Schultze, Reinhard, *Mathematicians Fleeing from Nazi Germany: Individual Fates and Global Impact*, Princeton: Princeton University Press (2009)

Sime, Ruth Lewin, *Lise Meitner: A Life in Physics*, Berkeley: University of California Press (1996)

Simmons, Marc, *Two Southwesterners: Charles Lummis and Amado Chaves*, Austin, Texas: San Marcos Press (1968)

—— *The Little Lion of the Southwest: A Life of Manuel Antonio Chaves*, Chicago: The Swallow Press (1973)

Simoni, Robert D., Hill, Robert L. and Vaughan, Martha, "Protein Chemistry and the Development of Allosterism: Jeffries Wyman," *The Journal of Biological Chemistry*, Vol. 277, No. 46, 76–8 (Nov. 15, 2002)

Smith, Alice Kimball, *A Peril and a Hope: The Scientists' Movement in America, 1945–47*, Chicago: University of Chicago Press (1965)

Smith, Alice Kimball and Weiner, Charles (eds.) [S & W], *Robert Oppenheimer: Letters and Recollections*, Stanford: Stanford University Press (1980)

Smith, G. S., *D. S. Mirsky: A Russian-English Life 1890–1939*, Oxford: Oxford University Press (2000)

Smyth, Henry DeWolf, *Atomic Energy for Military Purposes: The Office Report on the Development of the Atomic Bomb Under the Auspices of the United States Government, 1940–1945*, Stanford: Stanford University Press (1989)

Snow, C. P., *The Two Cultures and the Scientific Revolution*, Cambridge: Cambridge University Press (1959)

—— *The Physicists*, London: Macmillan (1982)

Sommerfeld, Arnold, *Atombau und Spektrallinien*, Braunschweig: Friedrich Vieweg und Sohn (1919), translated as *Atomic Structure and Spectral Lines*, New York: Dutton (1923)

Sopka, Katherine R., *Quantum Physics in America 1920–1935*, New York: Arno Press (1980)

Sorin, Gerald, *A Time for Building: The Third Migration 1880–1920*, Baltimore: Johns Hopkins University Press (1992)

Stern, Philip M., *The Oppenheimer Case: Security on Trial*, London: Rupert Hart-Davis (1971)

Stoff, Michael B., Fanton, Jonathan F. and Williams, R. Hal (eds.), *The Manhattan Project: A Documentary Introduction to the Atomic Age*, New York: McGraw–Hill (1991)

Strauss, Lewis L., *Men and Decisions*, New York: Doubleday (1962)

Sudoplatov, Pavel and Anatoli, *Special Tasks: The Memoirs of an Unwanted Witness—A Soviet Spymaster*, Boston: Little Brown (1994)

Szasz, Ferenc Morton, *The Day the Sun Rose Twice: The Story of the Trinity Site Nuclear Explosion July 16, 1945*, Albuquerque: University of New Mexico Press (1984)

Taylor, John, *Black Holes: The End of the Universe?*, London: Souvenir Press (1973)

Teller, Edward, *Memoirs: A Twentieth-Century Journey in Science and Politics*, Oxford: Perseus (2001)

Thomson, George Paget, *J. J. Thomson and the Cavendish Laboratory in His day*, London: Nelson (1964a)

—— *J. J. Thomson: Discoverer of the Electron*, London: Nelson (1964b)

Thomson, J. J., "Cathode rays," *Philosophical Magazine*, Vol. 44, 293 (1897)

Thorne, Kip, *Black Holes and Time Warps*, New York: Norton (1994)

Thorpe, Charles, *Oppenheimer: The Tragic Intellect*, London: University of Chicago Press (2006)

Tractenberg, Alan, *The Incorporation of America: Culture & Society in the Gilded Age*, New York: Hill & Wang (1982)

Treiman, Sam, *The Odd Quantum*, Princeton: Princeton University Press (1999)

Truman, Harry S., *Years of Decision*, New York: Doubleday (1955)

Turner, Louis A., "Nuclear Fission," *Reviews of Modern Physics*, 12, 1–29 (1940)

Twitchell, Ralph Emerson, *The Leading Facts of New Mexican History, Vol. II*, Santa Fe, New Mexico: Sunstone Press (2007)

Ulam, S. M., *Adventures of a Mathematician*, Berkeley: University of California Press (1991)

United States Atomic Energy Commission, *In the Matter of J. Robert Oppenheimer: Transcript of Hearing before Personnel Security Board, Washington D.C., April 12, 1954 Through May 6, 1954* [ITMO], Washington D.C.: U.S. Government Printing Office (1954)

Urey, Harold, Brickwedde, F. G., and Murphy, G. N., "A Hydrogen Isotope of Mass 2," *Physical Review*, 39, 164–5 (1932)

VanDeMark, Brian, *Pandora's Keeper: Nine Men and the Atomic Bomb*, New York: Little, Brown (2003)

Waerden, B. L. van der (ed.), *Sources of Quantum Mechanics*, New York: Dover (1968)

Wallace, Henry A., *The Price of Vision: The Diary of Henry A. Wallace, 1942–1946*, Boston: Houghton Mifflin (1973)

Weinberg, Steven, *Dreams of a Final Theory: The Search for the Fundamental Laws of Nature*, London: Hutchinson (1993)

Weiner, Charles, "1932—Moving into the New Physics," *Physics Today*, 25 (5), 40–2 (1972)

—— "Physics Today and the Spirit of the Forties," *Physics Today*, 23–8 (May 1973)

Weisgall, Jonathan M., *Operation Crossroads: The Atomic Tests at Bikini Atoll*, Washington D.C.: Naval Institute Press (1994)

Weisskopf, V. F., *Physics in the Twentieth Century: Selected Essays*, Cambridge: MIT Press (1972)

Wells, Samuel F., "The Origins of Massive Retaliation," *Political Science Quarterly*, Vol. 96, No. 1, 31–52 (1981)

West, Nigel, *Mortal Crimes. The Greatest Theft in History: Soviet Penetration of the Manhattan Project*, New York: Enigma Books (2004)

Wheeler, John Archibald, *Geons, Black Holes, and Quantum Foam: A Life in Physics*, New York: Norton (2000)

Wheeler, John Archibald and Zurek, Wajciech Hubert (eds.), *Quantum Theory and Measurement*, Princeton: Princeton University Press (1983)

White, Michael, *Rivals: Conflict as the Fuel of Science*, London: Secker & Warburg (2001)

Wilson, D., *Rutherford: Simple Genius*, London: Hodder & Stoughton (1983)

Wilson, R. R., "Hiroshima: The Scientists" Social and Political Reaction," *Proceedings, American Philosophical Society*, Vol. 140, No. 3, 350–7 (1996)

Wolverton, Mark, *A Life in Twilight: The Final Years of J. Robert Oppenheimer*, New York: St. Martin's Press (2008)

Woolf, Virginia, *A Woman's Essays. Selected Essays: Volume One*, London: Penguin, 1992

Wright, Harold (ed.), *University Studies: Cambridge 1933*, London: Nicholson and Watson (1933)

Yang, Chen Ning, "The law of parity conservation and other symmetry laws of physics," *Nobel Lectures, Physics 1942–1962*, Amsterdam: Elsevier Publishing Company (1964)

York, Herbert F., *The Advisors: Oppenheimer, Teller and the Superbomb*, San Francisco: W.H. Freeman (1976)

Yukawa, Hideki, "On the Interaction of Elementary Particles I," *Proceedings of the Physical and Mathematical Society of Japan*, 17, 48–57 (1935)

—— "Models and Methods in the Meson Theory," *Reviews of Modern Physics*, 21 (3), 474–9 (1949)

INTERVIEWS

American Institute of Physics (AIP)

Luis Alvarez, interviewed by Charles Weiner and Barry Richman, Lawrence Radiation Laboratory (Feb. 15, 1967): http://www.aip.org/history/ohilist/4483_2.html

Robert Bacher, interviewed by Finn Aaserud at the California Institute of Technology (Feb. 13, 1986): http://www.aip.org/history/ohilist/27979.html

Felix Bloch, interviewed by Charles Weiner, Stanford University, California (Aug. 15, 1968): http://www.aip.org/history/ohilist/4510.html

Edward U. Condon, interviewed by Charles Weiner in Boulder, Colorado Oct. 17, 1967, April 27, 1968 and Sep. 11, 1973): http://www.aip.org/history/ohilist/4997_1.html

William A. Fowler, interviewed by Charles Weiner, Caltech (June 8, 1972), Sessions I–V: http://www.aip.org/history/ohilist/4608_1.html

Otto Frisch, interviewed by:

1. Thomas S. Kuhn, Cavendish Laboratory (May 8, 1963): 1. http://www.aip.org/history/ohilist/4615.html

2. Charles Weiner, American Institute of Physics, New York City (May 3, 1967): http://www.aip.org/history/ohilist/4616.html

Wendell H. Furry, interviewed by Charles Weiner in Copenhagen (Aug. 9, 1971): http://www.aip.org/history/ohilist/24324.html

Oskar Klein, interviewed by Thomas S. Kuhn and John L. Heilbron in Copenhagen (Sep. 25, 1962–July 16, 1963): http://www.aip.org/history/ohilist/4709_1.html

Willis Lamb, interviewed by Dr. Joan Bromberg in Tucson, Arizona (March 7, 1985): http://www.aip.org/history/ohilist/27491_1.html

Rossi Lomanitz, interviewed by Shawn Mullet in Hawaii (July 26–Aug. 18, 2001): http://www.aip.org/history/ohilist/24703_1.html

J. Robert Oppenheimer, interviewed by Thomas S. Kuhn in Princeton (Nov. 18, 1963): not on line

Rudolf Peierls, interviewed by Charles Weiner in Seattle, Washington (Aug. 11, 12 and 13, 1969): http://www.aip.org/history/ohilist/4816_1.html

Melba Phillips, interviewed by Katherine Russell Sopka (Dec. 5, 1977): http://www.aip.org/history/ohilist/4821.html

Robert Serber, interviewed by:

1. Charles Weiner and Gloria Lubkin at Columbia University (Feb. 10, 1967): http://www.aip.org/history/ohilist/4878.html
2. Frederick Fellows at Columbia University (Dec. 19, 1983): http://www.aip.org/history/ohilist/4880.html
3. Anne Fitzpatrick in New York City (Nov. 26, 1996): http://www.aip.org/history/ohilist/25100.html

Caltech Archives

Carl Anderson, interviewed by Harriett Lyle (Jan. 9–Feb. 8, 1979): http://oral histories.library.caltech.edu/89/

William A. Fowler, interviewed by John Greenberg and Carol Bugé (May 3, 1983–May 31, 1984, Oct. 3, 1986)

Frank Oppenheimer, interviewed by Judith R. Goodstein (Nov. 16, 1984)

Milton S. Plesset, interviewed by Carol Bugé (Dec. 8, 1981)

Index